How to Use MyAccountingLab

If you have not yet had a chance to explore the benefits of the MyAccountingLab (MAL) Web site, I would encourage you to log in now and see what a valuable tool it can be. MyAccountingLab is a terrific tool for helping you grasp the accounting concepts that you are learning. So what exactly is MyAccountingLab? MyAccountingLab is a homework management tool that allows you to complete homework online.

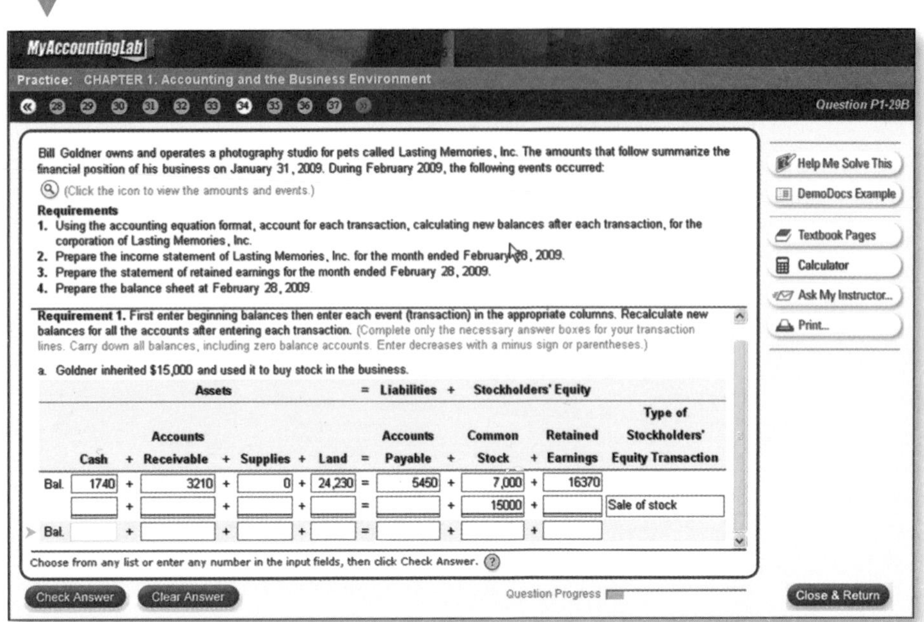

What is so great about completing the homework online, you might wonder?

Well, how about the ability to ask for and receive help *immediately* while you are working the problems? MAL allows you to click on a ***Help Me Solve This*** button at anytime while you are working the problem, and a pop-up window appears with tips to help you solve the specific part of the problem that you are working on. It is similar to having someone standing over your shoulder to help you—right in the middle of the problem—so that you can get through it and understand how to solve it.

MAL also has a button that you can click on that will open an ***online version of the textbook***—it even takes you right to the section of the textbook that explains the topic related to the problem that you are working on.

Another great feature of MAL is the ***Ask My Instructor...*** button. If your instructor allows you to e-mail questions, you are able to send an e-mail to your instructor in which you can explain what you are having difficulties with. When your instructor receives the e-mail, there will be a link that will take the instructor right to the problem you were working on in MAL.

You will also find two different types of problems in MAL, ***bookmatch*** and ***algorithmic*** problems. The bookmatch problems are the exact problems right out of your textbook (your instructor must make these available in MAL). The algorithmic problems are identical to the ones in the textbook, except they have several variables that change in the problem every time it is selected. The algorithmic problems allow you to have an unlimited number of problems you can work in order to master the material. This means that you can see how to do a problem similar to the one in the book.

The other benefit of working the problems in MAL is that each problem is broken down into different parts. MAL gives you three attempts at working each part and then it fills in the correct answer. This allows you to learn from your mistakes as you go.

Support is always available for you online at: http://www.myaccountinglab.com/support/student.html.

Homework and Tests: Quizzes & Tests Legend

Show All | Homework | Quizzes & Tests | Chapters

All Quizzes and Tests

Due	Assignment	Time Limit	Attempts	Gradebook Score
	Chapter 1A Pre-Test		0 of ∞	

Sample Tests
Sample tests can be taken for practice or to build your study plan. Sample tests do not affect your grade.

Sample Tests	Attempts	Gradebook Score
Chapter 1A Pre-Test	0 of ∞	
Chapter 1B Post-Test	0 of ∞	
Chapter 2A Pre-Test	0 of ∞	
Chapter 2B Post-Test	0 of ∞	
Chapter 3A Pre-Test	0 of ∞	
Chapter 3B Post-Test	0 of ∞	
Chapter 4A Pre-Test	0 of ∞	
Chapter 4B Post-Test	0 of ∞	
Chapter 5A Pre-Test	0 of ∞	
Chapter 5B Post-Test	0 of ∞	
Chapter 6A Pre-Test	0 of ∞	
Chapter 6B Post-Test	0 of ∞	
Chapter 7A Pre-Test	0 of ∞	

How to Maximize Your Time in MyAccountingLab

1. Read the textbook material.
2. Review the Demo Docs in your textbook and your study guide.
3. Work the algorithmic problems in MAL utilizing the ***Help Me Solve This*** hints as needed. If your instructor has not assigned any of the homework problems in MAL, you can access the algorithmic problems by clicking on the ***Study Plan*** button. Although it would be helpful to work all of the problems, you should focus on the problems that your instructor has assigned for each chapter, if any.
4. Rework any of the problems that you had difficulty understanding as many times as you need in order to achieve understanding. If you open the Study Plan, you can see which problems you had incorrect answers on.
5. Work the homework problems that were assigned by your instructor if any (either in MAL or from the textbook using paper and pencil).
6. In order to prepare for a quiz or exam using MAL, rework the algorithmic equivalent of any of the assigned homework. Additionally, if your instructor has made them available, you can access the ***Sample Tests*** in the ***Take a Test*** section. There is a sample pre-test and post-test available for every chapter in the text so you can focus on the chapters covered in your quiz or exam.

Overall, using MyAccountingLab can be a great benefit to you in this course. It provides immediate feedback while doing homework and is a great preparation for exams. We encourage you to try it and see how it can help you have a more successful course experience.

Accounting

EIGHTH EDITION

Charles T. Horngren
Stanford University
Walter T. Harrison Jr.
Baylor University
M. Suzanne Oliver
Northwest Florida State College

Pearson Education International

AVP/Executive Editor: Jodi McPherson
VP/Publisher: Natalie Anderson
Director, Product Development: Pamela Hersperger
Editorial Project Manager: Rebecca Knauer
Editorial Assistant: Rosalinda Simone
Development Editor: Karen Misler
AVP/Executive Editor, Media: Richard Keaveny
AVP/Executive Producer: Lisa Strite
Editorial Media Project Manager: Ashley Lulling
Production Media Project Manager: Lorena Cerisano
Marketing Manager: Maggie Moylan
Marketing Assistant: Justin Jacob
Senior Managing Editor, Production: Cynthia Zonneveld
Production Project Manager: Melissa Feimer
Permissions Coordinator: Charles Morris
Senior Operations Supervision: Nick Sklitsis
Senior Art Director: Jonathan Boylan
Cover Design: Jonathan Boylan
Director, Image Resource Center: Melinda Patelli
Manager, Rights and Permissions: Zina Arabia
Manager, Visual Research: Beth Brenzel
Manager, Cover Visual Research & Permissions: Karen Sanatar
Image Permission Coordinator: Jan Marc Quisumbing
Photo Researcher: Teri Stratford
Composition: GEX Publishing Services
Full-Service Project Management: GEX Publishing Services
Printer/Binder: Courier Kendallville
Typeface: 10/12 Sabon

Credits and acknowledgments borrowed from other sources and reproduced, with permission, in this textbook appear on the appropriate page within the text.

Pearson Education Ltd., London
Pearson Education Singapore, Pte. Ltd
Pearson Education, Canada, Inc.
Pearson Education–Japan
Pearson Education Australia PTY, Limited
Pearson Education North Asia Ltd., Hong Kong
Pearson Educación de Mexico, S.A. de C.V.
Pearson Education Malaysia, Pte. Ltd.
Pearson Education, Upper Saddle River, New Jersey

Prentice Hall
is an imprint of

www.pearsonhighered.com

10 9 8 7 6 5 4 3 2 1
ISBN-13: 978-0-13-609342-8
ISBN-10: 0-13-609342-6

Brief Contents

This text contains acetate inserts that were taken directly from the U.S. edition. As a result, the following pages are out of page sequence:

Pages 21–22, which contain Exhibit 1-9
Pages 71–72, which contain Exhibits 2-5 and 2-6
Pages 207–208, which contain Exhibits 4-1 through 4-6
Pages 399–400, which contain Exhibit 7-12
Pages 685–686, which contain Exhibits 13-3 through 13-7
Pages 883–884, which contain Exhibits 16A-6 through 16A-10
Pages 887–888, which contain Exhibits 16A-12 through 16A-15

Contents

This text contains acetate inserts that were taken directly from the U.S. edition. As a result pages in parenthesis are out of page sequence.

CHAPTER 8

Receivables 457

CHAPTER 9

Plant Assets and Intangibles 508

CHAPTER 10

Current Liabilities, Payroll, and Long-Term Liabilities 552

CHAPTER 13

CHAPTER 14

CHAPTER 15

CHAPTER 16

CHAPTER 17

The *Accounting, 8e,* Student Learning System: For professors whose greatest joy is hearing students say, "I get it!"

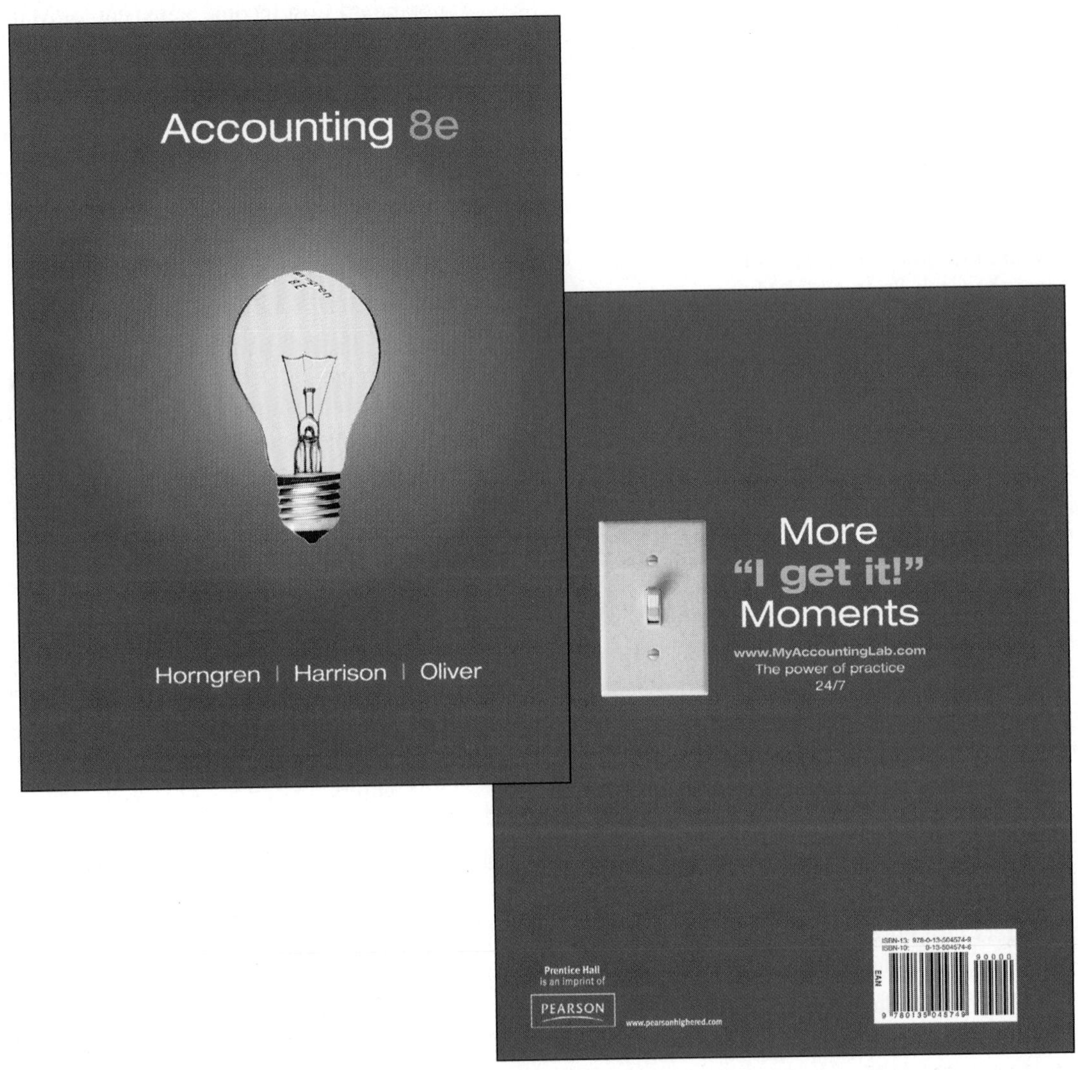

Help your students achieve "I get it!" moments when you're with them AND when you're NOT.

When you're there demonstrating how to solve a problem in class, students "get it." When you're not there, they get stuck—it's only natural.

That's where we come in, at these "they have the book, but they don't have you" moments.

The ***Accounting, 8e,* Student Learning System** will help students at those critical and challenging times by replicating the classroom experience. All components and features of the student textbook, study resources, and MyAccountingLab are designed to work together to provide students with more "I Get It!" moments, both inside AND outside of the classroom.

Students Will "Get it" Anytime, Anywhere With Horngren/Harrison/Oliver's Student Learning System!

Overview of Student Learning System

Students understand (or "get it") right after you do a problem in class. However, as soon as they leave class, their ability to do the problems and complete their homework diminishes with each passing hour. Often, this results in students struggling to complete their homework on their own. Even worse, the frustration can lead to students quitting on the material altogether and falling behind in the course. As a result, an entire class can fall behind as instructors attempt to keep everyone on the same page.

With the ***Accounting Student Learning System***, all features of the **student textbook**, **study resources** and **online homework system** are designed to work together to provide students with more "I Get It!" moments, especially outside the classroom where they struggle the most. The **consistency**, **repetition** and **strong details** throughout the entire **student learning system** allow students to achieve success inside and outside the classroom while keeping both instructors and students on track!

- **Replication of the Classroom Experience with Demo Doc Examples:**
  The Demo Doc Examples consist of entire problems, worked through step-by-step and from start to finish, narrated with the kind of comments that INSTRUCTORS would say in class. These Demo Doc Examples exist in the first four chapters of this text to support the critical accounting cycle chapters, as well as in the Study Guide as Flash animation and in print. The Flash versions are also on MyAccountingLab's online homework and are a part of the instructor package for both traditional and online courses.

- **Consistency, Repetition, and Details Throughout The Learning Process:**
  Consistency is stressed across all mediums: text, student, and instructor supplements. Students will experience consistency, repetition, and strong details throughout the chapter, the end of chapter examples, and in MyAccountingLab in both look and feel, and in the language. This minimizes confusion, ensures clarity, and allows students to focus on what's important—the accounting topics. As a result, students will develop a solid understanding throughout each step of the learning process.

- **Experiencing the Power of Practice with MyAccountingLab:**
  The online homework system combines "I get it!" moments with the power of practice. Students can work on book-match and algorithmic problems assigned by the instructor or use the "Study Plan" for self-assessment and customized study outlines.

Components of the Student Learning System

Duplicating the Classroom Experience

Demo Docs Introductory accounting students consistently tell us "When doing homework, I get stuck trying to solve problems the way they were demonstrated in class." Likewise, instructors consistently tell us, "I have so much to cover in so little time; I can't afford to go back and review homework in class." These challenges inspired us to develop Demo Docs. Demo Docs are comprehensive, worked-through problems that are available for the first four chapters of our introductory accounting text. Demo Docs will aid students when they are trying to solve exercises and problems on their own with the goal being to help students duplicate the classroom experience outside of class. Entire problems, mirroring end-of-chapter material, are presented and then solved along with annotated explanations written in a conversational style—essentially imitating what an instructor might say if standing over a student's shoulder. All Demo Docs are in the textbook in print, in the study guide in print version as well as on CD in Flash, and online in MyAccountingLab so that students can easily refer to them as needed.

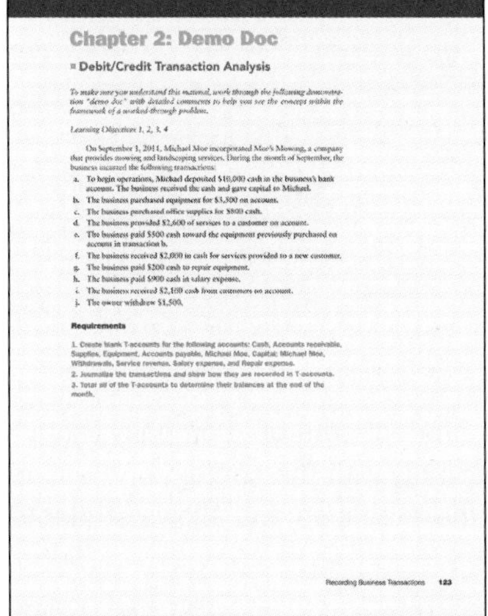

Chapter 2: Demo Doc

Debit/Credit Transaction Analysis

To make sure you understand this material, work through the following demonstration "demo doc" with detailed comments to help you see the concept within the framework of a worked-through problem.

Learning Objectives 1, 2, 3, 4

On September 1, 2011, Michael Moe incorporated Moe's Mowing, a company that provides mowing and landscaping services. During the month of September, the business incurred the following transactions:

a. To begin operations, Michael deposited $10,000 cash in the business's bank account. The business received the cash and gave capital to Michael.
b. The business purchased equipment for $3,500 on account.
c. The business purchased office supplies for $800 cash.
d. The business provided $2,600 of services to a customer on account.
e. The business paid $500 cash toward the equipment previously purchased on account in transaction b.
f. The business received $2,000 in cash for services provided to a new customer.
g. The business paid $200 cash to repair equipment.
h. The business paid $900 cash in salary expense.
i. The business received $2,100 cash from customers on account.
j. The owner withdrew $1,500.

Requirements

1. Create blank T-accounts for the following accounts: Cash, Accounts receivable, Supplies, Equipment, Accounts payable, Michael Moe, Capital; Michael Moe, Withdrawals, Service revenue, Salary expense, and Repair expense.
2. Journalize the transactions and show how they are recorded in T-accounts.
3. Total all of the T-accounts to determine their balances at the end of the month.

Recording Business Transactions 123

Consistency, Repetition, and Details in the Learning Process

The entire package matters. Consistency in terminology and problem set-ups from one medium to another—test bank to study guide to MyAccountingLab—is critical to success in the classroom. So when students ask, "Where do the numbers come from?" they can go to our text or go online and see what to do. If the material is worded one way in the text, you can count on it being worded the same way in the supplements for instructors and students.

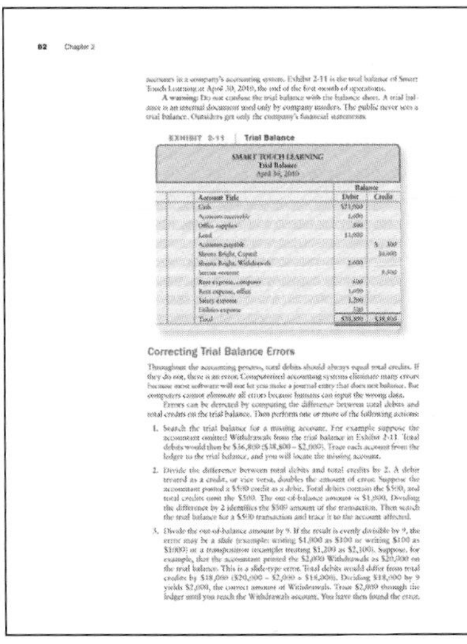

82 Chapter 2

EXHIBIT 2-11 Trial Balance

SMART TOUCH LEARNING
Trial Balance
April 30, 2010

Correcting Trial Balance Errors

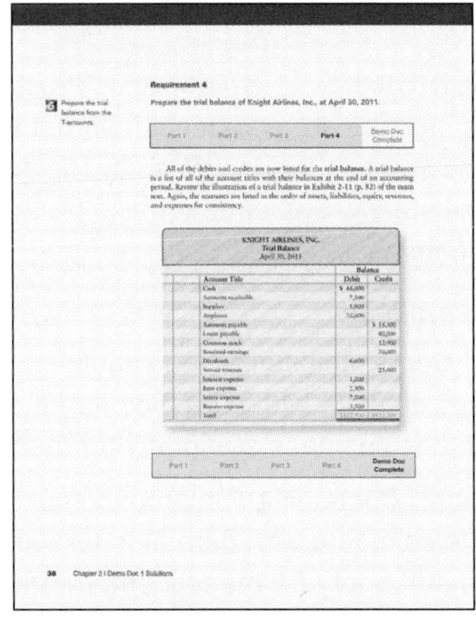

Requirement 4

Prepare the trial balance of Knight Airlines, Inc., at April 30, 2011.

KNIGHT AIRLINES, INC.
Trial Balance
April 30, 2011

30 Chapter 2 | Demo Doc 1 Solutions

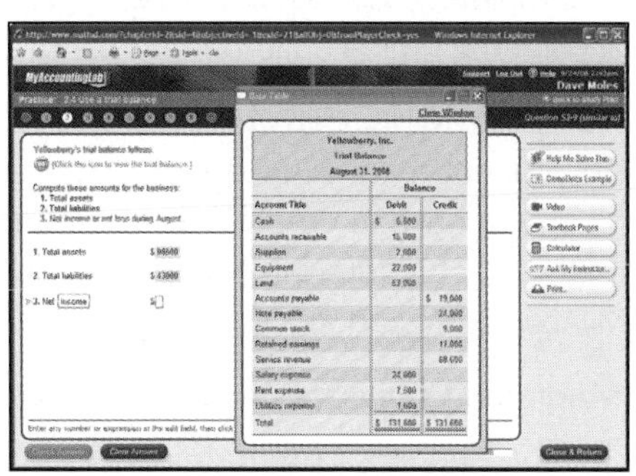

The entire student learning system reinforces consistency, repetition, and clear details in order to enhance the student learning experience. For example, in Chapter 2, Journalizing Transactions and Posting to the Ledger is addressed. For EVERY transaction, the same set of information is presented to the students in several different formats—in text, in journal entry, and in ledger accounts. These exact same formats are shown for EVERY transaction. In repeating these formats, the authors eliminate the assumption that the student understands the concept completely. As such, the chapter explains each detail for EVERY transaction to provide repetition and reinforcement of the concepts. This also allows students to quickly find, track, and correct their mistakes in the learning process.

NEW Consistent Examples Three different sets of "Company Facts" carry through all "in chapter examples." As a result, students gain a sense of familiarity with the context of these examples throughout the text. This consistency provides a level of comfort with the examples and allows students to focus on learning the accounting principles as they are presented.

NEW Continuing Exercise The unique "Continuing Exercise" takes a single company and adds transactions or questions in each chapter to the existing fact pattern. As students move throughout the text, they complete additional steps in this comprehensive exercise. Students are able to see the big picture and learn how the accounting topics build off one another. Accounting is a process and the continuing exercise allows students to put it all together.

NEW Continuing Problem For more detailed and in-depth practice, a "Continuing Problem" is also available. Like the Continuing Exercise, the Continuing Problem takes a single company and adds transactions or questions in each chapter to the existing fact pattern. As students move throughout the text, they complete additional steps in completing this comprehensive problem. Again, students are able to see the big picture and learn how the accounting topics build off one another.

NEW Unique Practice Set Within Chapters 1–8 An in-text "Practice Set" is built into Chapters 1–8 of the student text. Students do not have to purchase any additional material for their practice sets and instructors no longer have to create their own. Since the Practice Set is written by the same authors that write the student textbook, students will once again have consistency. Students will also be able to complete the Practice Set within MyAccountingLab, for automatic grading and immediate feedback.

Additional separate practice sets are also available.

- **Runners Corporation Lab Manual** Containing numerous simulated real-world examples, the Runners Corporation practice set is available complete with data files for Peachtree, QuickBooks, and PH General Ledger. Each practice set also includes business stationery for manual entry work.
- **A-1 Photography-Manual Lab Manual** Containing numerous simulated real-world examples, the A-1 Photography practice set is available complete with data files for Peachtree, QuickBooks, and PH General Ledger. Each set includes business stationery for manual entry work.

Clutter-Free Design The reviewer-inspired design is built on the premise that "Less is More." Extraneous boxes and features, as well as non-essential bells and whistles, have been removed. The authors know that excess crowds what really matters—the concepts, the problems, and the learning objectives. In addition, the equations are called out in a blue box so students can quickly locate them when studying.

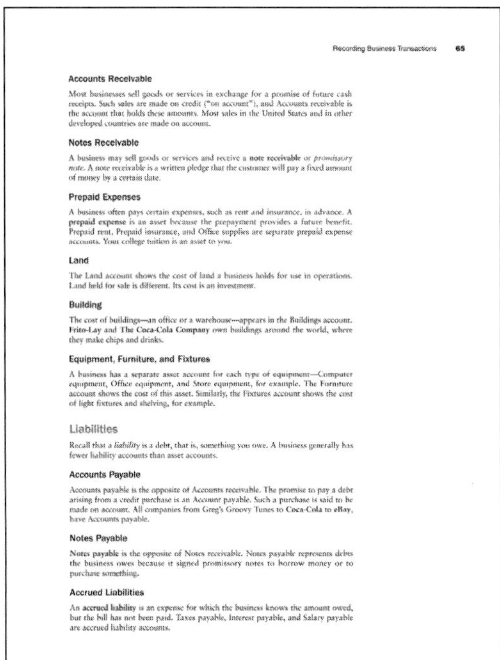

Recording Business Transactions 65

Accounts Receivable

Most businesses sell goods or services in exchange for a promise of future cash receipts. Such sales are made on credit ("on account"), and Accounts receivable is the account that holds these amounts. Most sales in the United States and in other developed countries are made on account.

Notes Receivable

A business may sell goods or services and receive a **note receivable** or *promissory note*. A note receivable is a written pledge that the customer will pay a fixed amount of money by a certain date.

Prepaid Expenses

A business often pays certain expenses, such as rent and insurance, in advance. A **prepaid expense** is an asset because the prepayment provides a future benefit. Prepaid rent, Prepaid insurance, and Office supplies are separate prepaid expense accounts. Your college tuition is an asset to you.

Land

The Land account shows the cost of land a business holds for use in operations. Land held for sale is different. Its cost is an investment.

Building

The cost of buildings—an office or a warehouse—appears in the Buildings account. **Frito-Lay** and **The Coca-Cola Company** own buildings around the world, where they make chips and drinks.

Equipment, Furniture, and Fixtures

A business has a separate asset account for each type of equipment—Computer equipment, Office equipment, and Store equipment, for example. The Furniture account shows the cost of this asset. Similarly, the Fixtures account shows the cost of light fixtures and shelving, for example.

Liabilities

Recall that a *liability* is a debt, that is, something you owe. A business generally has fewer liability accounts than asset accounts.

Accounts Payable

Accounts payable is the opposite of Accounts receivable. The promise to pay a debt arising from a credit purchase is an Account payable. Such a purchase is said to be made on account. All companies from Greg's Groovy Tunes to **Coca-Cola** to **eBay**, have Accounts payable.

Notes Payable

Notes payable is the opposite of Notes receivable. Notes payable represents debts the business owes because it signed promissory notes to borrow money or to purchase something.

Accrued Liabilities

An **accrued liability** is an expense for which the business knows the amount owed, but the bill has not been paid. Taxes payable, Interest payable, and Salary payable are accrued liability accounts.

Additional Features to Create More "I GET IT" Moments

Decision Guidelines Decision Guidelines explain why the accounting concepts addressed in the chapter are important in business. The left hand side of the table explains the decision or action being asked of the student in the simplest terms. The right-hand side of the table shows the accounting topics that will help them facilitate those decisions. In accounting, good numbers equate to good decisions, while inaccurate numbers can lead to poor decisions. The Decision Guidelines help illustrate this concept for students.

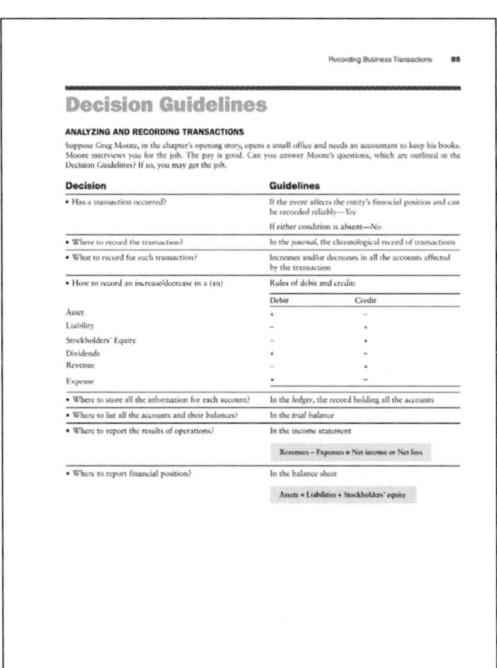

Recording Business Transactions 85

Decision Guidelines

ANALYZING AND RECORDING TRANSACTIONS

Suppose Greg Moore, in the chapter's opening story, opens a small office and needs an accountant to keep his books. Moore interviews you for the job. The pay is good. Can you answer Moore's questions, which are outlined in the Decision Guidelines? If so, you may get the job.

Decision	Guidelines	
• Has a transaction occurred?	If the event affects the entity's financial position and can be recorded reliably—*Yes* If either condition is absent—*No*	
• Where to record the transaction?	In the *journal*, the chronological record of transactions	
• What to record for each transaction?	Increases and/or decreases in all the accounts affected by the transaction	
• How to record an increase/decrease in a (an)	Rules of debit and credit:	
	Debit	Credit
Asset	+	–
Liability	–	+
Stockholders' Equity	–	+
Dividends	+	–
Revenue	–	+
Expense	+	–
• Where to store all the information for each account?	In the *ledger*, the record holding all the accounts	
• Where to list all the accounts and their balances?	In the *trial balance*	
• Where to report the results of operations?	In the income statement **Revenues – Expenses = Net income or Net loss**	
• Where to report financial position?	In the balance sheet **Assets = Liabilities + Stockholders' equity**	

NEW Success Keys/Learning Objectives

To build cohesiveness, clearly defined learning objectives are labeled throughout the chapter sections, end-of-chapter questions, and also in MyAccountingLab. After a student finishes reading a section within a chapter, he or she can turn to the back of the chapter and complete the labeled questions in order to self-assess their understanding. If the student doesn't "get it," he or she can sign on to MyAccountingLab for interactive learning resources to answer their questions and also to complete additional practice.

Every learning Objective has at least one Starter, Exercise, or Problem to teach and assess the students.

NEW Stop and Think The "Stop and Think" sections relate accounting concepts to students' everyday lives by using examples that make sense to students.

NEW Completion Time for End-of-Chapter Material All Starters, Exercises, and Problems in the textbook list the average completion time for students.

****NEW*** Table of Contents The authors slightly restructured the table of contents to respond to customers' current level of coverage in the Principles of Accounting course. Financial coverage is consolidated into 14 chapters so it can be effectively covered in one semester. The Financial chapters are also arranged to reflect the order of working through a balance sheet. In addition, the managerial chapters represent a more logical flow, including all costing chapters grouped together.

EXHIBIT 2-10 | Ledger Accounts After Posting

Category	Account	Left	Right
ASSETS	Cash	Apr 1 30,000; Apr 8 5,500; Apr 22 2,000; Apr 24 9,000; Bal 21,000	Apr 2 20,000; Apr 15 3,200; Apr 21 300; Apr 30 2,000
	Accounts receivable	Apr 10 3,000; Bal 1,000	Apr 22 2,000[†]
	Office supplies	Apr 3 500; Bal 500	
	Land	Apr 2 20,000; Bal 11,000	Apr 24 9,000
LIABILITIES	Accounts payable	Apr 21 300	Apr 3 500; Apr 30 100; Bal 300
STOCKHOLDERS' EQUITY[*]	Common stock		Apr 1 30,000; Bal 30,000
	Dividends	Apr 30 2,000; Bal 2,000	
REVENUE	Service revenue		Apr 8 5,500; Apr 10 3,000; Bal 8,500
EXPENSES	Rent expense, computer	Apr 15 600; Bal 600	
	Rent expense, office	Apr 15 1,000[†]; Bal 1,000	
	Salary expense	Apr 15 1,200; Bal 1,200	
	Utilities expense	Apr 15 400; Apr 30 100; Bal 500[†]	

[*] We add the Retained earnings account in Chapter 3, when it arises at the end of the period.
[†] These values are intentionally different than those presented in Chapter 1.

Stop & Think...

Have you ever walked along the beach and gathered sea shells? Maybe you had more than one bucket and you put all the sand dollars in one, all the hermit crabs in another, and so on. That separation is essentially what happens in posting. All we are doing is gathering transactions that affect the same account (for example, all the transactions to Cash) and putting them in the T-account. They are placed either on the left or right side of the T-account based on whether they were on the left or right side of the journal entry. Posting is merely a sorting process—no change to debits or credits occurs from transaction to posting.

Preparing the Trial Balance from the T-Accounts

A **trial balance** summarizes the ledger by listing all the accounts with their balances—assets first, followed by liabilities, and then stockholders' equity. In a manual accounting system, the trial balance provides an accuracy check by showing whether total debits equal total credits. In all types of systems, the trial balance is a useful summary of the accounts and their balances because it shows the balances on a specific date for

5 Prepare the trial balance from the T-accounts

The Power of Practice – Student Resources

NEW Five Book-Match Sets of Problems and Exercises (A, B, C, D, E)

PROBLEMS: Students will have access to A and B Problems within the text. Static Problem Sets C, D, and E can be assigned by the instructor and completed by students through MyAccountingLab.

EXERCISES: Students will have access to exercise set A within the text. Static exercise sets B, C, D, and E can be assigned by the instructor and completed by the student through MyAccountingLab.

MyAccountingLab Online Homework and Assessment MyAccountingLab is where "I get it!" moments meet the power of practice. This online homework and assessment tool supports the text and resources by providing students "I get it!" moments at their teachable moment, whether that is 1 PM or 1 AM. MyAccountingLab is packed with algorithmic problems, because practice makes perfect. It is also includes the exact same end-of-chapter material in the text that instructors can assign for homework. MyAccountingLab features the same look and feel for exercises and problems with journal entries and financial statements so that students are familiar and comfortable working with the material.

Study Guide including Flash Demo Doc CD and Working Papers Demo Docs are available in the Study Guide— both in print and on CD in Flash, so students can easily refer to them when needed. The Study Guide also includes a summary of key topics and multiple-choice and short-answer questions that students can use to test their knowledge.

Free electronic working papers are included on the accompanying CD.

Companion Web Site–www.pearsonhighered.com/horngren

The book's Web site at www.pearsonhighered.com/horngren—contains the following:

- Self-study quizzes for each chapter

- Microsoft Excel templates that students can use to complete homework assignments for each chapter (e-working papers)
- Samples of the Flash Demo Docs for students to work through the accounting cycle

The Instructors' Teaching System is for Professors whose greatest joy is hearing students say, "I GET IT!"

Overview of the Instructor Teaching System

The goal of Horngren/Harrison/Oliver, ***Accounting, 8e***, is to help students achieve "I get it!" moments when they are with the instructor AND when they are NOT.

The student learning system is there for students when instructors can't be, and the Instructor Teaching System is there to help when instructors ARE.

We have asked several instructors how we can help them successfully implement new course-delivery methods (e.g. online, hybrid), while maintaining their regular campus schedule of classes and academic responsibilities. In response, we developed a system of instruction for those who are long on commitment and expertise, but short on time and assistance.

Components of the Instructor Teaching System

Instructor's Edition Featuring Instructor Demo Docs

The primary goal of the Instructor's Edition is **ease of implementation, using any delivery method—traditional, self-paced, or online**. The Instructor's Edition offers a quick cross-reference with key additional teaching resources with everything in one place. The Instructor's Edition includes chapter summaries, teaching tips provided by reviewers, pitfalls for new students, and "best of" practices from instructors from across the world.

To effectively implement the wealth of instructors' resources available, a "Resource Roadmap" is provided to give the description and location of each resource, along with recommendations on classroom applications.

Instructor's Edition Demo Docs In the Instructor Demo Docs, we walk the students through how to solve a problem as if it were the first time they have seen it. There are no lengthy passages of text. Instead, bits of expository text are woven into the steps needed to solve the problem, in the exact sequence—for instructors to provide at the teachable "I get it!" moment. This is the point at which the student has a context within which he or she can understand the concept. We provide conversational text around each of the steps so the student stays engaged in solving the problem.

We also provide notes to the instructor for key teaching points around the Demo Docs, and "best of" practice suggestions before each Instructor Demo Doc.

The Instructor Demo Docs are written with everyday classroom realities in mind while trying to save instructor's time in prepping new examples. Additionally, algorithmic versions of these Demo Docs are provided to students in their student guide. We keep the terminology consistent with the text so there are no surprises for students as they try to work through a problem the first time.

Additional Instructor's Edition Resources

In addition to the Demo Docs, the Instructor's Edition also provides the following helpful material:

- **"First Day of Class" Student Handout:** This is a resource used to help students log onto MyAccountingLab, to teach them how to effectively use Demo Docs, and to provide tips for success in the course.
- **Chapter Summary and Outline:** Teaching Notes for Online and Hybrid Courses
- **Assignment Grid:** The assignment grid outlines all end-of-chapter exercises and problems available in Excel templates as well as General Ledger, Peachtree, or Quickbooks software.

- **10 Minute Quizzes:** Short quizzes can be used to quickly assess students' understanding of the chapter material.
- **Average Completion Time for End-of-Chapter Material:** Allows instructors to assign the appropriate amount of homework for the students. This is also noted in students' texts.

Instructor's Resource Center CD or www.pearsonhighered.com/horngren

The Instructor Resource CD and password-protected site includes the following:

- **The Instructor's Edition**
- **Solutions Manual with Interactive Excel Solutions:** The Solutions Manual contains solutions to all end-of-chapter questions, multiple-choice questions, short exercises, exercise sets, problems sets, and Internet exercises. The Solutions Manual is available through PDF and in print on demand. Solutions to select end-of-chapter exercises and problems are also available in interactive MS Excel format so that instructors can present material in dynamic, step-by-step sequences in class.
- **Solutions Transparencies:** Transparency masters of the Solutions are available on demand in an easy-to-use format for class lectures.
- **Test Bank:** The test item file includes more than 3,000 questions and is formatted for use with WebCT, Blackboard, and Course Compass. Both objective based questions and computational problems are available.
- **PowerPoints:** The PowerPoints summarize and reinforce key text materials. They capture classroom attention with original problems and solved step-by-step exercises. These walk-throughs are designed to help facilitate classroom discussion and demonstrate where the numbers come from and what they mean to the concept at hand. There are approximately 35 slides per chapter.
- **Working Papers in Excel and PDF Format**
- **Image Library**
- **Excel in Practice Templates**
- **Solution Files**

Five Book-Match Sets of Questions (A, B, C, D, E)

Problems Students will have access to A and B Problems within the text. Instructors will have access to static Problem Sets C, D, and E through MyAccountingLab. The solutions manual will also be available through MyAccountingLab.

Exercises Students will have access to exercise set A. Instructors will have access to static exercise sets B, C, D, and E that will also be available in MyAccountingLab with a complete instructors' solution manual.

MyAccountingLab Online Homework and Assessment Manager

The "I get it!" moment meets the power of practice. The power of repetition when you "get it" means learning happens. MyAccountingLab is about helping students at their teachable moments, whether it's 1 PM or 1 AM.

MyAccountingLab is an online homework and assessment tool, packed with algorithmic versions of every text problem, because practice makes perfect. It's also packed with the exact same end-of chapter material that you're used to assigning for homework. Additionally, MyAccountingLab includes the following:

1. A Demo Doc for each of the end-of-chapter exercises and problems that students can refer to as they work through the questions.
2. A Guided Solution to problems they are working on. It helps students when they're trying to solve a problem the way it was demonstrated in class.
3. A full e-book so the students can reference the book at the point of practice.
4. New topic-specific videos that walk students through difficult concepts.

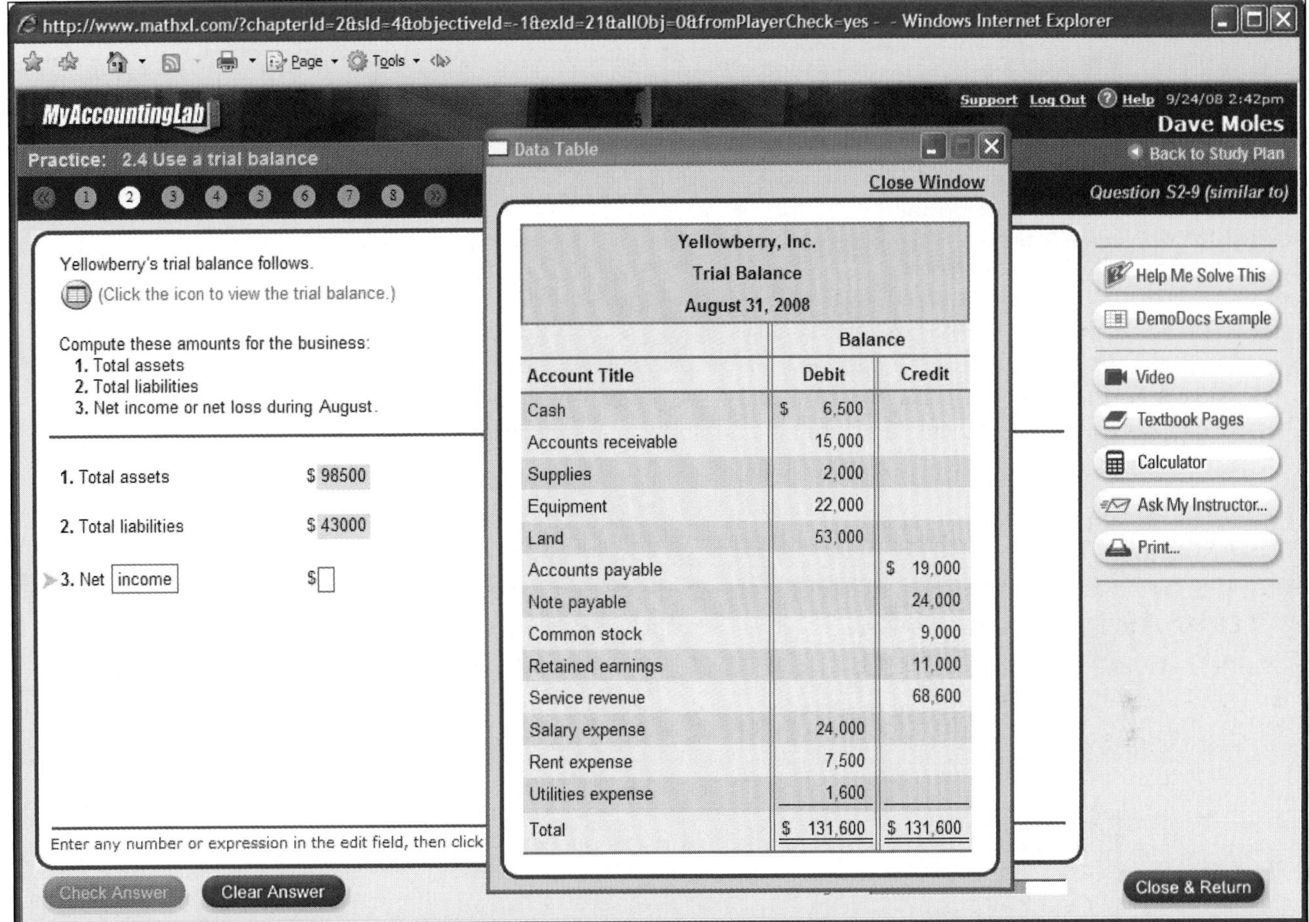

Yellowberry, Inc.
Trial Balance
August 31, 2008

Account Title	Balance Debit	Balance Credit
Cash	$ 6,500	
Accounts receivable	15,000	
Supplies	2,000	
Equipment	22,000	
Land	53,000	
Accounts payable		$ 19,000
Note payable		24,000
Common stock		9,000
Retained earnings		11,000
Service revenue		68,600
Salary expense	24,000	
Rent expense	7,500	
Utilities expense	1,600	
Total	$ 131,600	$ 131,600

Companion Web Site–www.pearsonhighered.com/horngren

The book's web site at www.pearsonhighered.com/horngren —contains the following:

- Self-study quizzes—interactive study guide for each chapter
- MS Excel templates that students can use to complete homework assignments for each chapter (e-working papers)
- Samples of the Flash Demo Docs for students to work through the accounting cycle

Online Courses with WebCT/BlackBoard/Course Compass

Pearson offers a link to MyAccountingLab through the Blackboard and WebCT Course Management Systems.

Classroom Response Systems (CRS)

CRS is an exciting new wireless polling technology that makes large and small classrooms even more interactive because it enables instructors to pose questions to their students, record results, and display those results instantly. Students can easily answer questions using compact remote-control-type transmitters. Pearson has partnerships with leading classroom response-systems providers and can show you everything you need to know about setting up and using a CRS system. Pearson will provide the classroom hardware, text-specific PowerPoint slides, software, and support. Visit www.prenhall.com/crs to learn more.

EXHIBIT 1-9 | **Financial Statements of Smart Touch Learning**

SMART TOUCH LEARNING
Income Statement
Month Ended April 30, 2010

Revenue:		
Service revenue		$8,500
Expenses:		
Salary expense	$1,200	
Rent expense, office	1,100	
Rent expense, computer	600	
Utilities expense	400	
Total expenses		3,300
Net income		$5,200

1

SMART TOUCH LEARNING
Statement of Owner's Equity
Month Ended April 30, 2010

Sheena Bright, Capital, April 1, 2010	$ 0
Add: Investments by owner	$30,000
Net income for the month	5,200
	35,200
Less: Owner withdrawals	(2,000)
Sheena Bright, Capital, April 30, 2010	$33,200

2

SMART TOUCH LEARNING
Balance Sheet
April 30, 2010

Assets		**Liabilities**	
Cash	$19,900	Accounts payable	$ 200
Accounts receivable	2,000		
Office supplies	500	**Owner's Equity**	
Land	11,000	Sheena Bright, Capital	33,200
Total assets	$33,400	Total liabilities and owner's equity	$33,400

3

SMART TOUCH LEARNING
Statement of Cash Flows*
Month Ended April 30, 2010

Cash flows from operating activities:		
Receipts:		
Collections from customers ($5,500 + $1,000)		$ 6,500
Payments:		
To suppliers ($600 + $1,100 + $400 + $300)	$ (2,400)	
To employees	(1,200)	(3,600)
Net cash provided by operating activities		2,900
Cash flows from investing activities:		
Acquisition of land	$(20,000)	
Sale of land	9,000	
Net cash used for investing activities		(11,000)
Cash flows from financing activities:		
Investments by owner	$ 30,000	
Owner withdrawals	(2,000)	
Net cash provided by financing activities		28,000
Net increase in cash		19,900
Cash balance, April 1, 2010		0
Cash balance, April 30, 2010		$19,900

*Chapter 13 shows how to prepare this statement.

Color-Coded Accounting Equation

This color-coded accounting equation is a tool you will use throughout your first accounting course. This tool is so important that we have to put it here for quick reference. You may find this helpful when preparing your homework assignments. Each financial statement is identified by a unique color. You will see these colors throughout the chapters when we present a financial statement.

1 The **income statement**, enclosed in the red box, provides the details of revenues earned and expenses incurred.

2 The revenue and expense transactions are then condensed into one number—net income—that becomes part of the **statement of retained earnings**, which appears in the yellow box.

3 Information from the statement of retained earnings flows into the **balance sheet**, shown in the blue box.

4 The **statement of cash flows**, as indicated by the green box, provides details of how a company got its cash and how it spent cash during the accounting period.

Acknowledgments

We'd like to thank the following contributors:

Florence McGovern *Bergen Community College*
Sherry Mills *New Mexico State University*
Helen Brubeck *San Jose State University*

We'd like to extend a special thank you to the following members of our advisory panel:

Jim Ellis *Bay State College, Boston*
Mary Ann Swindlehurst *Carroll Community College*
Andy Williams *Edmonds Community College*
Donnie Kristof-Nelson *Edmonds Community College*
Joan Cezair *Fayetteville State University*
David Baglia *Grove City College*
Anita Ellzey *Harford Community College*
Cheryl McKay *Monroe County Community College*
Todd Jackson *Northeastern State University*
Margaret Costello Lambert *Oakland Community College*
Al Fagan *University of Richmond*

We'd also like to thank the following supplements authors and reviewers:

Robert Lin *California State University—East Bay*
Lily Sieux *California State University—East Bay*
Allan Sheets *International Business College—Fort Wayne*
Rajeev Chopra *Las Positas College*
Shirley Glass *Macomb Community College*
Courtney Baillie *Nebraska Wesleyan University*
Roberta Wheeler *Northwest Florida State College*
Jamie McCracken *Saint Mary-of-the-Woods College*
Jennie Mitchell *Saint Mary-of-the-Woods College*
Randy Johnston *University of Colorado at Boulder*

We'd also like to thank the following reviewers:

Shi-Mu (Simon) Yang *Adelphi University*
Thomas Stolberg *Alfred State University*
Thomas Branton *Alvin Community College*
Maria Lehoczky *American Intercontinental University*
Suzanne Bradford *Angelina College*
Judy Lewis *Angelo State University*
Roy Carson Anne *Arundel Community College*
Paulette Ratliff-Miller *Arkansas State University*
Joseph Foley *Assumption College*
Jennifer Niece *Assumption College*
Bill Whitley *Athens State University*
Shelly Gardner *Augustana College*

Becky Jones *Baylor University*
Betsy Willis *Baylor University*
Michael Robinson *Baylor University*
Kay Walker-Hauser *Beaufort County Community College, Washington*
Joe Aubert *Bemidji State University*
Calvin Fink *Bethune Cookman College*
Michael Blue *Bloomsburg University*
Scott Wallace *Blue Mountain College*
Lloyd Carroll *Borough Manhattan Community College*
Ken Duffe *Brookdale Community College*
Chuck Heuser *Brookdale Community College*
Shafi Ullah *Broward Community College South*
Lois Slutsky *Broward Community College South*
Ken Koerber *Bucks County Community College*
Julie Browning *California Baptist University*
Richard Savich *California State University—San Bernardino*
David Bland *Cape Fear Community College*
Robert Porter *Cape Fear Community College*
Vickie Campbell *Cape Fear Community College*
Cynthia Thompson *Carl Sandburg College—Carthage*
Liz Ott *Casper College*
Joseph Adamo *Cazenovia College*
Julie Dailey *Central Virginia Community College*
Jeannie Folk *College of DuPage*
Lawrence Steiner *College of Marin*
Dennis Kovach *Community College Allegheny County—Allegheny*
Norma Montague *Central Carolina Community College*
Debbie Schmidt *Cerritos College*
Janet Grange *Chicago State University*
Bruce Leung *City College of San Francisco*
Pamela Legner *College of DuPage*
Bruce McMurrey *Community College of Denver*
Martin Sabo *Community College of Denver*
Jeffrey Jones *Community College of Southern Nevada*
Tom Nohl *Community College of Southern Nevada*
Christopher Kelly *Community College of Southern Nevada*
Patrick Rogan *Cosumnes River College*
Kimberly Smith *County College of Morris*

Jerold Braun *Daytona Beach Community College*
Greg Carlton *Davidson County Community College*
Irene Bembenista *Davenport University*
Thomas Szczurek *Delaware County Community College*
Charles Betts *Delaware Technical and Community College*
Patty Holmes *Des Moines Area Community College—Ankeny*
Tim Murphy *Diablo Valley College*

Phillipe Sammour *Eastern Michigan University*
Saturnino (Nino) Gonzales *El Paso Community College*
Lee Cannell *El Paso Community College*
John Eagan *Erie Community College*

Ron O'Brien *Fayetteville Technical Community College*
Patrick McNabb *Ferris State University*
John Stancil *Florida Southern College*
Lynn Clements *Florida Southern College*
Alice Sineath *Forsyth Technical Community College*
James Makofske *Fresno City College*
Marc Haskell *Fresno City College*
James Kelly *Ft. Lauderdale City College*

Christine Jonick *Gainesville State College*
Bruce Lindsey *Genesee Community College*
Constance Hylton *George Mason University*
Cody King *Georgia Southwestern State University*
Lolita Keck *Globe College*
Kay Carnes *Gonzaga University, Spokane*
Carol Pace *Grayson County College*
Rebecca Floor *Greenville Technical College*
Geoffrey Heriot *Greenville Technical College*
Jeffrey Patterson *Grove City College*
Lanny Nelms *Gwinnet Technical College*
Chris Cusatis *Gwynedd Mercy College*

Bridgette Mahan *Harold Washington College*
Tim Griffin *Hillsborough Community College*
Clair Helms *Hinds Community College*
Michelle Powell *Holmes Community College*
Greg Bischoff *Houston Community College*
Donald Bond *Houston Community College*
Marina Grau *Houston Community College*
Carolyn Fitzmorris *Hutchinson Community College*

Susan Koepke *Illinois Valley Community College*
William Alexander *Indian Hills Community College—Ottumwa*
Dale Bolduc *Intercoast College*
Thomas Carr *International College of Naples*
Lecia Berven *Iowa Lakes Community College*
Nancy Schendel *Iowa Lakes Community College*
Michelle Cannon *Ivy Tech*
Vicki White *Ivy Tech*

Chuck Smith *Iowa Western Community College*

Stephen Christian *Jackson Community College*
DeeDee Daughtry *Johnston Community College*
Richard Bedwell *Jones County Junior College*

Ken Mark *Kansas City Kansas Community College*
Ken Snow *Kaplan Education Centers*
Charles Evans *Keiser College*
Bunney Schmidt *Keiser College*
Amy Haas *Kingsborough Community College*

Jim Racic *Lakeland Community College*
Doug Clouse *Lakeland Community College*
Patrick Haggerty *Lansing Community College*
Patricia Walczak *Lansing Community College*
Humberto M. Herrera *Laredo Community College*
Christie Comunale *Long Island University*
Ariel Markelevich *Long Island University*
Randy Kidd *Longview Community College*
Kathy Heltzel *Luzerne County Community College*
Lori Major *Luzerne County Community College*

Fred Jex *Macomb Community College*
Glenn Owen *Marymount College*
Behnaz Quigley *Marymount College*
Penny Hanes *Mercyhurst College, Erie*
Peg Johnson *Metropolitan Community College*
John Miller *Metropolitan Community College*
Idalene Williams *Metropolitan Community College*
Denise Leggett *Middle Tennessee State University*
William Huffman *Missouri Southern State College*
Ted Crosby *Montgomery County Community College*
Beth Engle *Montgomery County Community College*
David Candelaria *Mount San Jacinto College*
Linda Bolduc *Mount Wachusett Community College*

Barbara Gregorio *Nassau Community College*
James Hurat *National College of Business and Technology*
Denver Riffe *National College of Business and Technology*
Asokan Anandarajan *New Jersey Institute of Technology*
Robert Schoener *New Mexico State University*
Stanley Carroll *New York City Technical College of CUNY*
Audrey Agnello *Niagara County Community College*
Catherine Chiang *North Carolina Central University*
Karen Russom *North Harris College*
Dan Bayak *Northampton Community College*
Elizabeth Lynn Locke *Northern Virginia Community College*
Roberta Wheeler *Northwest Florida State College*
Debra Prendergast *Northwestern Business College*
Nat Briscoe *Northwestern State University*
Tony Scott *Norwalk Community College*

Deborah Niemer *Oakland Community College*
John Boyd *Oklahoma City Community College*
Kathleen O'Donnell *Onondaga Community College*
J.T. Ryan *Onondaga Community College*

Toni Clegg *Palm Beach Atlantic College*
David Forsyth *Palomar College*
John Graves *PCDI*
Carla Rich *Pensacola Junior College*
Judy Grotrian *Peru State College*
Judy Daulton *Piedmont Technical College*
Cheryl Clark *Point Park University*
John Stone *Potomac State College*
Betty Habershon *Prince George's Community College*

Kathi Villani *Queensborough Community College*

William Black *Raritan Valley Community College*
Verne Ingram *Red Rocks Community College*
Paul Juriga *Richland Community College*
Patty Worsham *Riverside Community College*
Margaret Berezewski *Robert Morris College*
Phil Harder *Robert Morris College*
Shifei Chung *Rowan University of New Jersey*

Charles Fazzi *Saint Vincent College*
Lynnette Yerbuy *Salt Lake Community College*
Gloria Grayless *Sam Houston State University*
Margaret Quarles *Sam Houston State University*
Linda Serres Sweeny *Sam Houston State University*
Susan Blizzard *San Antonio College*
Hector Martinez *San Antonio College*
Audrey Voyles *San Diego Miramar College*
Margaret Black *San Jacinto College*
Merrily Hoffman *San Jacinto College*
Randall Whitmore *San Jacinto College*
Carroll Buck *San Jose State University*
Cynthia Coleman *Sandhills Community College*
Barbara Crouteau *Santa Rosa Junior College*
Pat Novak *Southeast Community College*
Susan Pallas *Southeast Community College*
Al Case *Southern Oregon University*
Gloria Worthy *Southwest Tennessee Community College*
Melody Ashenfelter *Southwestern Oklahoma State University*
Douglas Ward *Southwestern Community College*
Brandi Shay *Southwestern Community College*
John May *Southwestern Oklahoma State University*
Jeffrey Waybright *Spokane Community College*
Renee Goffinet *Spokane Community College*
Susan Anders *St. Bonaventure University*
Sue Counte *St. Louis Community College*
John Olsavsky *SUNY at Fredonia*

Peter Van Brunt *SUNY College of Technology at Delhi*

David L. Davis *Tallahassee Community College*
Kathy Crusto-Way *Tarrant County Community College*
Sally Cook *Texas Lutheran University*
Bea Chiang *The College of New Jersey*
Matt Hightower *Three Rivers Community College*

Susan Pope *University of Akron*
Joe Woods *University of Arkansas*
Allen Blay *University of California, Riverside*
Barry Mishra *University of California, Riverside*
Laura Young *University of Central Arkansas*
Jane Calvert *University of Central Oklahoma*
Bambi Hora *University of Central Oklahoma*
Joan Stone *University of Central Oklahoma*
Kathy Terrell *University of Central Oklahoma*
Harlan Etheridge *University of Louisiana*
Pam Meyer *University of Louisiana*
Sandra Scheuermann *University of Louisiana*
Tom Wilson *University of Louisiana*
Lawrence Leaman *University of Michigan*
Larry Huus *University of Minnesota*
Brian Carpenter *University of Scranton*
Ashraf Khallaf *University of Southern Indiana*
Tony Zordan *University of St. Francis*
Gene Elrod *University of Texas, Arlington*
Cheryl Prachyl *University of Texas, El Paso*
Karl Putnam *University of Texas, El Paso*
Phil Fink *University of Toledo*
Stephen Rockwell *University of Tulsa*
Chula King *University of West Florida*
Charles Baird *University of Wisconsin—Stout*

Mary Hollars *Vincennes University*
Lisa Nash *Vincennes University*
Elaine Dessouki *Virginia Wesleyan College*

Sueann Hely *West Kentucky Community and Technical College*
Darlene Pulliam *West Texas A&M University, Canyon*
Dennis Roth *West Virginia Northern Community College*
Judy Beebe *Western Oregon University*
Michelle Maggio *Westfield State College*
Kathy Pellegrino *Westfield State College*
Nora McCarthy *Wharton County Junior College*
Sally Stokes *Wilmington College*
Maggie Houston *Wright State University*

Gerald Caton *Yavapai College*
Chris Crosby *York Technical College*
Harold Gellis *York College of CUNY*

About the Authors

Charles T. Horngren is the Edmund W. Littlefield professor of accounting, emeritus, at Stanford University. A graduate of Marquette University, he received his MBA from Harvard University and his PhD from the University of Chicago. He is also the recipient of honorary doctorates from Marquette University and DePaul University.

A Certified Public Accountant, Horngren served on the Accounting Principles Board for six years, the Financial Accounting Standards Board Advisory Council for five years, and the Council of the American Institute of Certified Public Accountants for three years. For six years he served as a trustee of the Financial Accounting Foundation, which oversees the Financial Accounting Standards Board and the Government Accounting Standards Board.

Horngren is a member of the Accounting Hall of Fame.

A member of the American Accounting Association, Horngren has been its President and its Director of Research. He received its first annual Outstanding Accounting Educator Award.

The California Certified Public Accountants Foundation gave Horngren its Faculty Excellence Award and its Distinguished Professor Award. He is the first person to have received both awards.

The American Institute of Certified Public Accountants presented its first Outstanding Educator Award to Horngren.

Horngren was named Accountant of the Year, in Education, by the national professional accounting fraternity, Beta Alpha Psi.

Professor Horngren is also a member of the Institute of Management Accountants, from whom he has received its Distinguished Service Award. He was a member of the institute's Board of Regents, which administers the Certified Management Accountant examinations.

Horngren is the author of other accounting books published by Pearson Prentice Hall: *Cost Accounting: A Managerial Emphasis*, thirteenth edition, 2008 (with Srikant Datar and George Foster); *Introduction to Financial Accounting*, ninth edition, 2006 (with Gary L. Sundem and John A. Elliott); *Introduction to Management Accounting*, fourteenth edition, 2008 (with Gary L. Sundem and William Stratton); *Financial Accounting*, seventh edition, 2008 (with Walter T. Harrison, Jr.).

Horngren is the Consulting Editor for Pearson Prentice Hall's Charles T. Horngren Series in Accounting.

Walter T. Harrison, Jr. is professor emeritus of accounting at the Hankamer School of Business, Baylor University. He received his BBA degree from Baylor University, his MS from Oklahoma State University, and his PhD from Michigan State University.

Professor Harrison, recipient of numerous teaching awards from student groups as well as from university administrators, has also taught at Cleveland State Community College, Michigan State University, the University of Texas, and Stanford University.

A member of the American Accounting Association and the American Institute of Certified Public Accountants, Professor Harrison has served as Chairman of the Financial Accounting Standards Committee of the American Accounting Association, on the Teaching/Curriculum Development Award Committee, on the Program Advisory Committee for Accounting Education and Teaching, and on the Notable Contributions to Accounting Literature Committee.

Professor Harrison has lectured in several foreign countries and published articles in numerous journals, including *Journal of Accounting Research*, *Journal of Accountancy*, *Journal of Accounting and Public Policy*, *Economic Consequences of Financial Accounting Standards*, *Accounting Horizons*, *Issues in Accounting Education*, and *Journal of Law and Commerce*.

He is co-author of *Financial Accounting*, seventh edition, 2008 (with Charles T. Horngren), published by Pearson Prentice Hall. Professor Harrison has received scholarships, fellowships, and research grants or awards from PriceWaterhouse Coopers, Deloitte & Touche, the Ernst & Young Foundation, and the KPMG Foundation.

M. Suzanne Oliver is an assistant professor of accounting at Northwest Florida State College in Niceville, Florida. She received her BA in Accounting Information Systems and her Masters in Accountancy from the University of West Florida.

Professor Oliver began her career in accounting in the tax department of a regional accounting firm, specializing in benefit plan administration. She has served as a software analyst for a national software development firm (CPASoftware) and as the Oracle fixed assets analyst for Spirit Energy, formerly part of Union Oil of California (Unocal). A Certified Public Accountant, Oliver is a member of the Florida Institute of Certified Public Accountants.

Professor Oliver has taught financial accounting, managerial accounting, intermediate accounting, tax accounting, accounting software applications, payroll accounting, auditing, accounting systems, advanced accounting, managerial finance, business math, and supervision. She has also taught pension continuing education classes for CPAs and has developed and instructed online courses using MyAccountingLab, WebCT, and other proprietary software.

Professor Oliver lives in Niceville where she is a member of the First United Methodist Church with her husband Greg and son C.J.

1 Accounting and the Business Environment

Learning Objectives/Success Keys

1. Define accounting vocabulary
2. Define the users of financial information
3. Describe the accounting profession and the organizations that govern it
4. Identify the different types of business organizations
5. Delineate the distinguishing characteristics and organization of a proprietorship
6. Apply accounting concepts and principles
7. Define and use the accounting equation
8. Depict accounting for business transactions
9. Explain and prepare the financial statements
10. Use financial statements to evaluate business performance

You may dream of running your own business. Where do you begin? How much money does it take? How will you measure success or failure?

Hannah Sherman operated a lawn-service business while in college and graduated with thousands in the bank. Greg Moore started a successful music business. How did they do it? By following their dreams, treating people fairly, and having realistic expectations. It did not hurt that Moore majored in accounting. His accounting knowledge gave him a leg up on organizing the business and keeping track of important details.

We will start with a small business such as Sherman Lawn Service or Greg's Groovy Tunes. What role does accounting play for Sherman Lawn Service or Greg's Groovy Tunes?

Accounting Vocabulary: The Language of Business

1 Define accounting vocabulary

Accounting is the information system that measures business activity, processes the data into reports, and communicates the results to decision makers. Accounting is "the language of business." The better you understand the language of business, the better you can manage your own business. For example, how will you decide whether or not to borrow money? You need to consider your income and whether or not you will be able to pay back that loan. The concept of income comes straight from accounting.

A key product of accounting is a set of reports called financial statements. **Financial statements** report on a business in monetary terms. Is Sherman Lawn Service making a profit? Should Greg's Groovy Tunes expand? The financial statements help answer these questions.

Exhibit 1-1 illustrates the role of accounting in business. The process shows people making decisions.

EXHIBIT 1-1 | **How People Use Accounting Information**

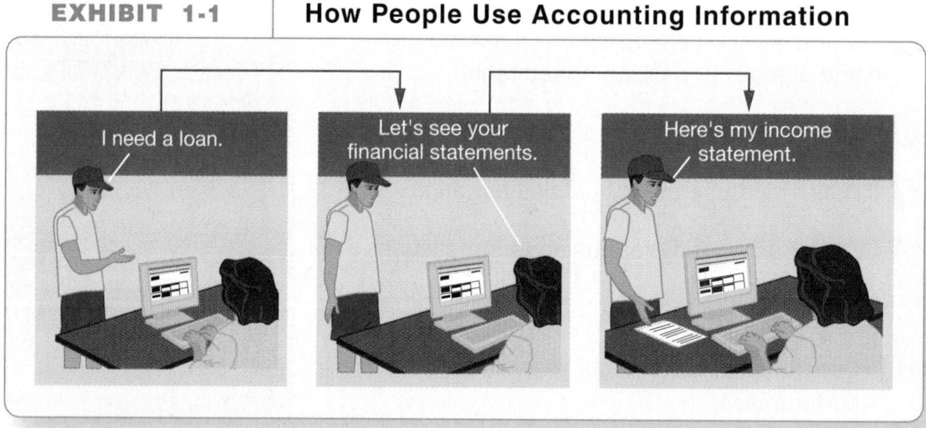

Decision Makers: The Users of Accounting Information

2 Define the users of financial information

Decision makers need information. The bigger the decision, the more information decision makers need. Here are some of the ways people use accounting information.

Individuals

You use accounting information to manage your cash, to evaluate a new job, and to decide whether or not you can afford a new computer. Hannah Sherman and Greg Moore make the same decisions that you do.

Businesses

Business owners use accounting information to set goals, to measure progress toward those goals, and to make adjustments when needed. For example, Greg Moore must decide how many microphones he will need for each music concert. Accounting helps provide this information.

Investors

Outside investors often provide the money to get a business going. To decide whether to invest, a person predicts the amount of income to be earned on the investment. The investor then analyzes the financial statements and keeps current with the company. To view the financial statements of large public companies, log on to finance.yahoo.com, finance.google.com or the SEC's EDGAR database.

Creditors

Any person or business that loans money is a **creditor**. Before lending money to Hannah Sherman, a bank evaluates Sherman's ability to make the loan payments. This requires a report on Sherman's predicted income. If you try to borrow money for a new car, the bank will review accounting data to determine your ability to make the car payments.

Taxing Authorities

Local, state, and federal governments levy taxes. Income tax is figured using accounting information. Sales tax depends upon a company's sales.

Financial Accounting and Management Accounting

Accounting can be divided into two fields—financial accounting and management accounting.

Financial accounting provides information for external decision makers, such as outside investors and lenders. These outsiders use the company's financial statements. Chapters 2–14 of this book deal primarily with financial accounting.

Management accounting focuses on information for internal decision makers, such as the company's managers. Chapters 15–23 of this book cover management accounting. Exhibit 1-2 illustrates the difference between financial accounting and management accounting.

EXHIBIT 1-2 | Financial Accounting and Management Accounting

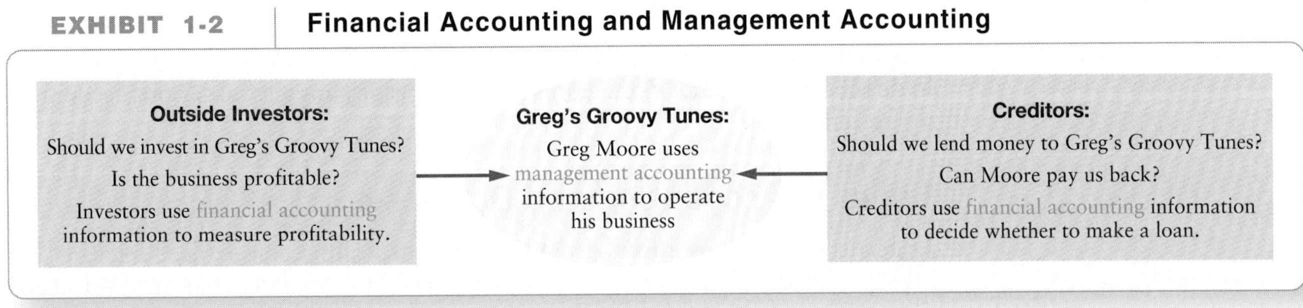

The Accounting Profession and the Organizations that Govern it

3 Describe the accounting profession and the organizations that govern it

There are several learned professions, including accounting, architecture, engineering, law, and medicine. To be certified in a profession, one must pass a qualifying exam, and professionals are paid quite well. For example, the average starting salary in 2007 for a college graduate with a bachelor's degree in accounting was almost

$44,000. A graduate with a master's degree earns about 10% more to start and **certified public accountants** earn another 10%.

Many accounting firms are organized as partnerships, and the partners are the owners. It usually takes 10 to 15 years to rise to the rank of partner. The partners of the large accounting firms earn from $150,000 to $500,000 per year. In private accounting, the top position is called the chief financial officer (CFO), and a CFO earns about as much as a partner in an accounting firm.

What do businesses such as Sherman Lawn Service, Greg's Groovy Tunes, **Wal-Mart**, and the **Coca-Cola Company** have in common? They all need accountants! That is why accounting opens so many doors upon graduation.

Accountants get to the top of organizations as often as anyone else. Why? Because the accountants must deal with everything in the company in order to record all of its activities. Accountants often have the broadest view of what is going on in the company.

As you move through this book, you will learn to account for everything that affects a business—all the income, all the expenses, all the cash, all the inventory, and all the debts. Accounting requires you to consider everything, and that is why it is so valuable to an organization. Ultimately, accounting affects everyone, which is why it is important to you.

All professions have regulations. Let us look at the organizations that govern the accounting profession.

Governing Organizations

In the United States the **Financial Accounting Standards Board (FASB)**, a private organization, formulates accounting standards. The FASB works with governmental agencies like the Securities and Exchange Commission (SEC) and with congressionally created groups like the Public Companies Accounting Oversight Board (PCAOB), and private groups like the American Institute of Certified Public Accountants (AICPA) and the Institute of Management Accountants (IMA). **Certified public accountants**, or **CPAs**, are licensed professional accountants who serve the general public. **Certified management accountants**, or **CMAs**, are licensed professionals who work for a single company.

The standards or guidelines for public information are called **generally accepted accounting principles (GAAP)**. Some of these guidelines are described later in this chapter. Exhibit 1-3 diagrams the relationships among the various accounting organizations.

Ethics in Accounting and Business

Ethical considerations affect accounting. Investors and creditors need relevant and reliable information about a company such as **Amazon.com** or **Wal-Mart**. Companies want to look good to attract investors, so there is a conflict of interest here. To provide reliable information, the SEC requires companies to have their financial statements audited by independent accountants. An **audit** is a financial examination. The independent accountants then tell whether or not the financial statements give a fair picture of the company's situation.

The vast majority of accountants do their jobs professionally and ethically, but we never hear about them. Unfortunately, only those who cheat make the headlines. In recent years we have seen more accounting scandals than at any time since the 1920s.

Enron, Corp., for example, was one of the largest companies in the United States before it began reporting misleading data. **WorldCom**, a major long-distance

EXHIBIT 1-3 | **Key Accounting Organizations**

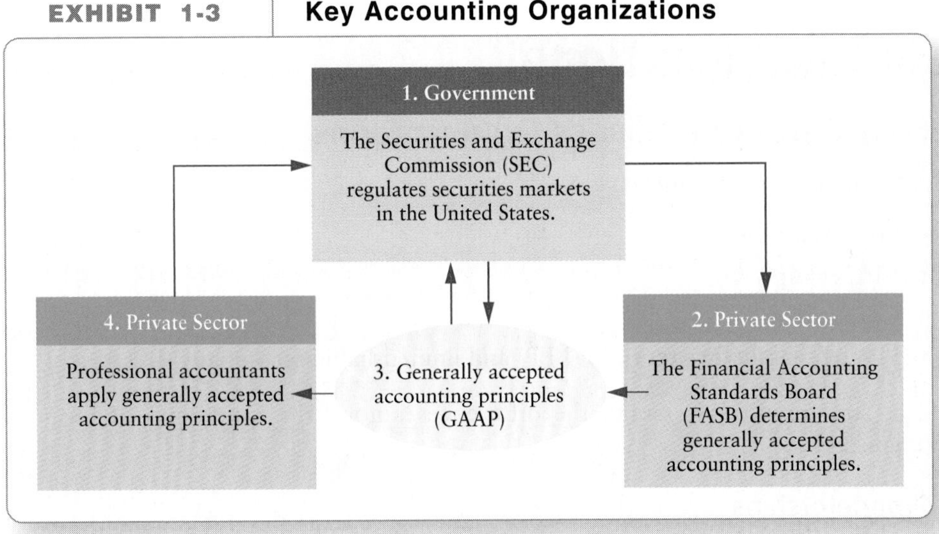

telephone provider, admitted accounting for expenses as though they were **assets** (economic resources). These and other scandals rocked the business community and hurt investor confidence. Innocent people lost their jobs, and the stock market suffered. The U.S. government took swift action. It passed the Sarbanes-Oxley Act that made it a criminal offense to falsify financial statements. It also created a new watchdog agency, the Public Companies Accounting Oversight Board, to monitor the work of independent accountants who audit public companies.

Standards of Professional Conduct

The AICPA's Code of Professional Conduct for Accountants provides guidance to CPAs in their work. Ethical standards are designed to produce relevant and reliable information for decision making. The preamble to the code states:

> "[A] certified public accountant assumes an obligation of self-discipline above and beyond the requirements of laws and regulations ... [and] an unswerving commitment to honorable behavior... ."

The opening paragraph of the Standards of Ethical Conduct of the Institute of Management Accountants (IMA) states:

> "Management accountants have an obligation to the organizations they serve, their profession, the public, and themselves to maintain the highest standards of ethical conduct."

Most companies also set standards of ethical conduct for employees. For example, Greg's Groovy Tunes must comply with copyright laws in order to serve customers ethically. **Microsoft** has a highly developed set of business conduct guidelines. A business's or an individual's reputation is often hard earned and can easily be lost. As one chief executive has stated, "Ethical practice is simply good business." Truth is always better than dishonesty—in accounting, in business, and in life.

Types of Business Organizations

4 Identify the different types of business organizations

Four Types of Business Organizations

A business can be organized as a

- Proprietorship
- Partnership
- Corporation
- Limited-liability partnership (LLP) and limited-liability company (LLC)

You should understand the differences among the four types of business organizations.

Proprietorships

A **proprietorship** has a single owner, called the proprietor, who often manages the business. Proprietorships tend to be small retail stores or professional businesses, such as attorneys and accountants. From an accounting perspective, every sole proprietorship is distinct from its owner: The accounting records of the proprietorship do *not* include the proprietor's personal records. However, from a legal perspective, the business *is* the proprietor. In this book, we start with a proprietorship.

Partnerships

A **partnership** joins two or more individuals as co-owners. Each owner is a partner. Many retail stores and professional organizations of physicians, attorneys, and accountants are partnerships. Most partnerships are small or medium-sized, but some are gigantic, with thousands of partners. For accounting purposes, the partnership is a separate organization, distinct from the partners.

Corporations

A **corporation** is a business owned by **stockholders**, or **shareholders**. These are the people who own shares of stock in the business. A business becomes a corporation when the state approves its articles of incorporation and the first stock share is issued. Unlike a proprietorship and a partnership, a corporation is a legal entity distinct from its owners. This legal distinction between corporations and traditional proprietorships and partnerships can be very important for the following reason. If a proprietorship or a partnership cannot pay its debts, lenders can take the owners' personal assets to satisfy the obligations. But if a corporation goes bankrupt, lenders *cannot* take the personal assets of the stockholders. The largest businesses in the United States and in other countries are corporations. The **Coca-Cola Company**, for example, has billions of shares of stock owned by many stockholders. An investor with no personal relationship to **Coca-Cola** can become a stockholder by buying 50, 100, 5,000, or any number of shares of **Coca-Cola** stock.

Limited-Liability Partnerships (LLPs) and Limited-Liability Companies (LLCs)

A **limited-liability partnership** is one in which a wayward partner cannot create a large liability for the other partners. Each partner is liable only for his or her own actions and those under his or her control. Similarly, a business can be organized as a **limited-liability company**. In an LLC the business, and not the members of the LLC, is liable for the company's debts. Today most proprietorships and partnerships are organized as LLCs and LLPs. The limited-liability aspect gives these organizations one of the chief advantages of a corporation. Exhibit 1-4 summarizes the differences among the four types of business organization.

EXHIBIT 1-4 | **Comparison of the Four Forms of Business Organization**

	Proprietorship	Partnership	Corporation	LLC
1. Owner(s)	Proprietorship—only one owner	Partners—two or more owners	Stockholders—generally many owners	Members
2. Life of the organization	Limited by the owner's choice, or death	Limited by the owner's choice, or death	Indefinite	Indefinite
3. Personal liability of the owner(s) for the business's debts	Proprietor is personally liable	Partners are personally liable*	Stockholders are not personally liable	Members are not personally liable

*unless it is a limited-liability partnership (LLP)

Stop & Think...

How does a company pick the best type of organization?

Deciding on the type of business organization that best meets a company's needs and objectives should be a well-thought-out decision. Often, small businesses consult other professionals, such as attorneys and accountants for advice.

Distinguishing Characteristics and Organization of a Proprietorship

5 Delineate the distinguishing characteristics and organization of a proprietorship

There are several features that distinguish a proprietorship from other types of business organizations. They are described in detail below.

Separate Entity with No Continuous Life

A **proprietorship** is a business entity that is not formally "created" by registering with a state agency. It is formed when one individual decides to create a business. Although it is not a distinct entity from a legal perspective, it is an entity that exists apart from its owner.

The ownership interest of a proprietorship is recognized in the owner's capital account. This is listed in the entity's books as NAME OF OWNER, CAPITAL. So, for example, Greg Moore's capital account in the accounting records of Greg's Groovy Tunes would be listed as Greg Moore, Capital. The life of the proprietorship business is limited by either the owner's choice or the owner's death, whichever comes first. Thus, there is no transferability of ownership in a proprietorship.

Unlimited Liability of Owner

A proprietor has unlimited liability for the business's debts. General partners in partnerships have the same liability, but stockholders in corporations have limited liability. This liability makes owning a proprietorship very unattractive due to the owner's real fear of losing all of his or her personal wealth because of a business failure.

Unification of Ownership and Management

The owners also manage the business. This unification between owners and management is definitely beneficial to the business and its sole owner because their goals are the same.

Business Taxation

Proprietorships are not separate taxable entities. The income flows directly from the business to the sole owner. The owner pays tax on the business income on his or her personal tax return. Additionally, the owner must pay self-employment tax (both the employee and employer portions, which are discussed in Chapter 10).

Government Regulation

Government regulation is an advantage for the proprietorship. There are no stockholders to notify and no articles of incorporation to follow. Decisions can easily be made by the owner/manager.

Organization of a Corporation

Creation of a corporation is different than a proprietorship. It begins when its organizers, called the incorporators, obtain a charter from the state. The charter includes the authorization for the corporation to issue a certain number of shares of stock, which represent the ownership in the corporation. The incorporators pay fees, sign the charter, and file the required documents with the state. Once the first share of stock is issued, the corporation comes into existence. The incorporators agree to a set of bylaws, which act as the constitution for governing the corporation.

The ultimate control of the corporation rests with the stockholders, who normally receive one vote for each share of stock they own. The stockholders elect the members of the board of directors, which sets policy for the corporation and appoints the officers. The board elects a chairperson, who usually is the most powerful person in the corporation. The board also designates the president, who as chief operating officer manages day-to-day operations. Most corporations also have vice presidents in charge of sales, operations, accounting and finance, and other key areas. Exhibit 1-5 shows the authority structure in a corporation.

EXHIBIT 1-5 **Structure of a Corporation**

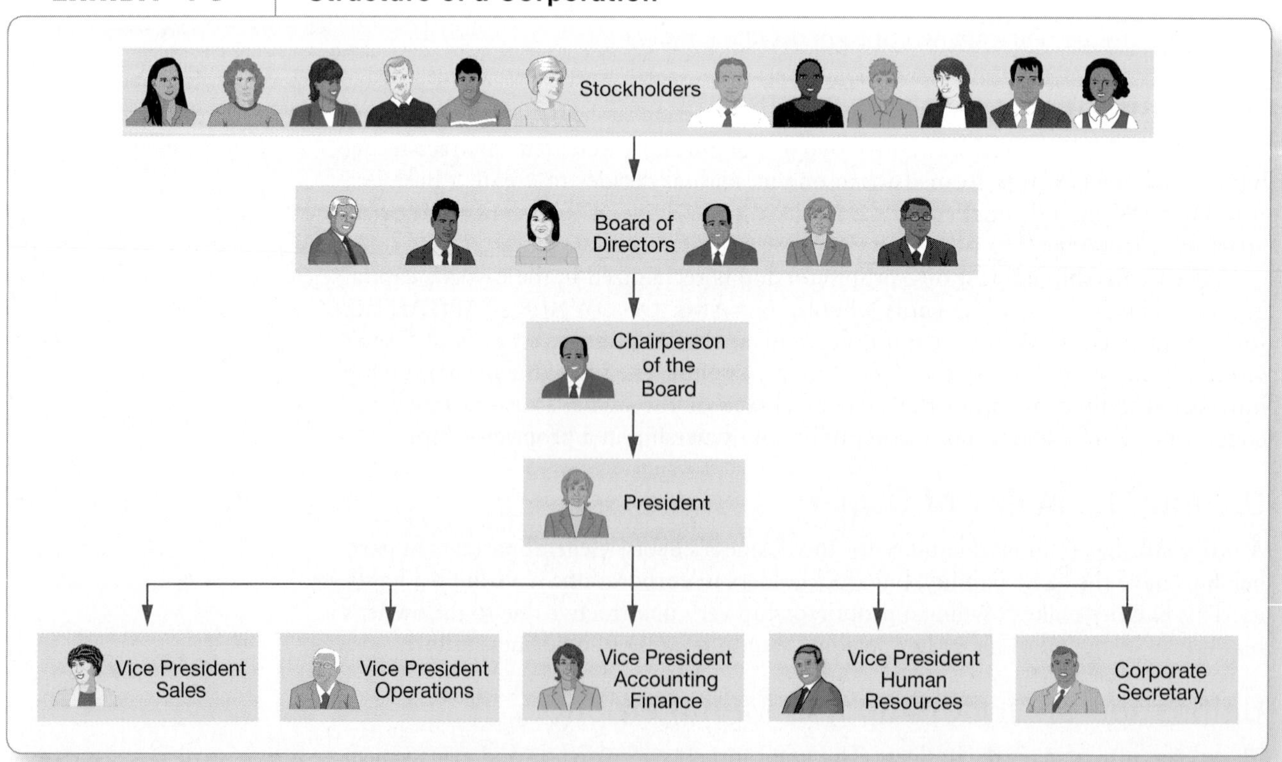

Accounting Concepts and Principles

6 Apply accounting concepts and principles

As mentioned earlier in the chapter, the guidelines that govern accounting fall under the heading GAAP, which stands for generally accepted accounting principles. GAAP rests on a conceptual framework. The primary objective of financial reporting is to provide information useful for making investment and lending decisions. To be useful, information must be relevant, reliable, and comparable. We begin the discussion of GAAP by introducing basic accounting concepts and principles.

The Entity Concept

The most basic concept in accounting is that of the **entity**. An accounting entity is an organization that stands apart as a separate economic unit. We draw boundaries around each entity to keep its affairs distinct from those of other entities.

Consider Sherman Lawn Service. Assume Hannah Sherman started the business with $500 obtained from a bank loan. Following the entity concept, Sherman would account for the $500 separately from her personal assets, such as her clothing and automobile. To mix the $500 of business cash with her personal assets would make it difficult to measure the success or failure of Sherman Lawn Service.

Consider **Toyota**, a huge organization with several divisions. **Toyota** management evaluates each division as a separate entity. If **Lexus** sales are dropping, **Toyota** can find out why. But if sales figures from all divisions of the company are combined, management cannot tell that **Lexus** sales are going down. Thus, *the entity concept applies to any economic unit that needs to be evaluated separately.*

The Reliability (Objectivity) Principle

Accounting information is based on the most reliable data available. This guideline is the **reliability principle**, also called the **objectivity principle**. Reliable data are verifiable, which means they may easily be confirmed by any independent observer. For example, a bank loan is supported by a promissory note. This is objective evidence of the loan. Without the reliability principle, accounting data might be based on whims and opinions.

Suppose Greg Moore transfers a small building to Greg's Groovy Tunes. He believes the building is worth $50,000. A real estate appraiser, however, values the building at $40,000. Which is the more reliable estimate of the building's value, Moore's estimate of $50,000 or the $40,000 professional appraisal? The $40,000 estimate is more reliable because it is supported by a professional appraisal. Greg's Groovy Tunes should record the building at $40,000.

The Cost Principle

The **cost principle** states that acquired assets and services should be recorded at their actual cost (also called *historical cost*). Even though the purchaser may believe the price is a bargain, the item is recorded at the price actually paid and not at the "expected" cost. Suppose Moore purchases recording equipment from a supplier that is going out of business. Assume that he gets a good deal and pays only $2,000 for equipment that would have cost him $3,000 elsewhere. The cost principle requires Moore to record the equipment at its actual cost of $2,000, not the $3,000 that he believes the equipment is worth.

The cost principle also holds that the accounting records should continue reporting the historical cost of an asset over its useful life. Why? Because cost is a reliable measure. Suppose Moore holds the recording equipment for six months.

During that time recording equipment prices rise, and the equipment can be sold for $3,500. Should its accounting value—the figure on the books—be the actual cost of $2,000 or the current market value of $3,500? By the cost principle, the accounting value of the equipment remains at the actual cost of $2,000.

The Going-Concern Concept

Another reason for measuring assets at historical cost is the **going-concern concept.** This concept assumes that the entity will remain in operation for the foreseeable future. Under the going-concern concept, accountants assume that the business will remain in operation long enough to use existing resources for their intended purpose.

To understand the going-concern concept better, consider the alternative—which is to go out of business. A store that is closing intends to cease future operations. In that case, the relevant measure is current market value. But going out of business is the exception rather than the rule.

The Stable Monetary Unit Concept

In the United States, we record transactions in dollars because the dollar is the medium of exchange. The value of a dollar changes over time, and a rise in the price level is called inflation. During periods of inflation, a dollar will purchase less food and less gas for your car. But accountants assume that the dollar's purchasing power is stable. This assumption is the basis of the **stable monetary unit concept.**

The Accounting Equation

7 Define and use the accounting equation

The basic tool of accounting is the **accounting equation.** It measures the resources of a business and the claims to those resources.

Assets and Liabilities

Assets are economic resources that are expected to benefit the business in the future. They are something you own that has value. Cash, merchandise inventory, furniture, and land are assets.

Claims to those assets come from two sources. **Liabilities** are debts payable to outsiders who are known as creditors. They are something you owe. For example, a creditor who has loaned money to Greg's Groovy Tunes has a claim to some of the business's assets until the business pays the debt. Many liabilities have the word *payable* in their titles. Examples include Accounts payable, Notes payable, and Salary payable.

The owners' claims to the assets of the business are called **owner's equity.** These insider claims begin when an owner, such as Greg Moore, invests assets in the business and receives capital.

The accounting equation shows how assets, liabilities, and owner's equity are related. Assets appear on the left side of the equation, and the liabilities and owner's equity appear on the right side.

Exhibit 1-6 diagrams how the two sides must always be equal (amounts are assumed for this illustration):

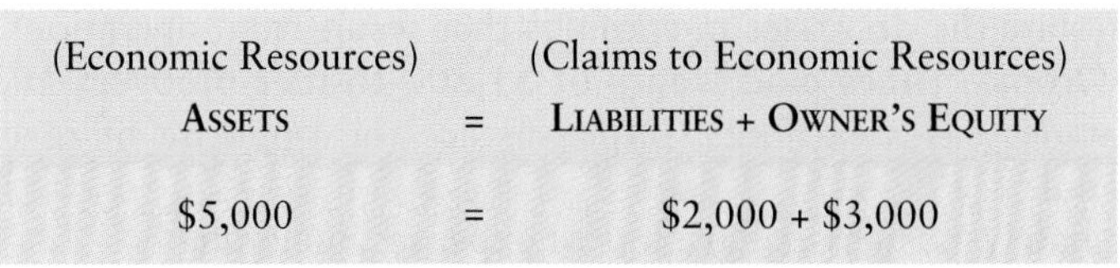

EXHIBIT 1-6 | **The Accounting Equation**

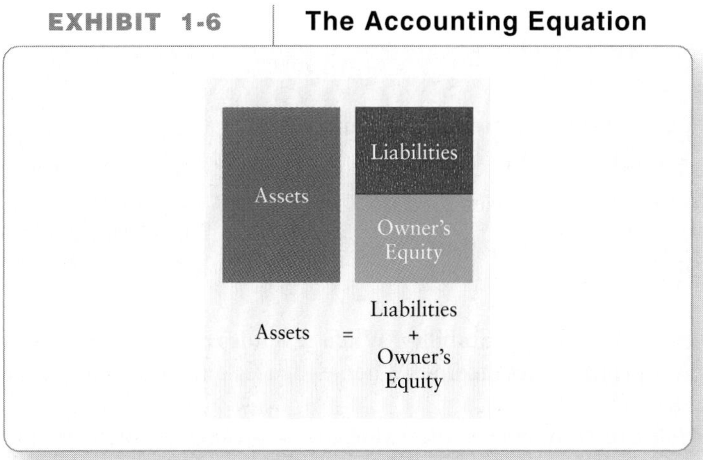

Owner's Equity

The owner's equity of a proprietorship is called capital. For a proprietorship the accounting equation can be written as

ASSETS = LIABILITIES + OWNER'S EQUITY
ASSETS = LIABILITIES + CAPITAL

- **Capital** is the amount invested in the business by its owners.
- Capital also contains the amount earned by income-producing activities and kept for use in the business. Two types of transactions that affect earnings are revenues and expenses. **Revenues** are increases in capital from delivering goods or services to customers. For example, when Moore provided music for a wedding party and earned $1,500 of revenue, the business's capital increased by $1,500.

There are relatively few types of revenue, including:

- **Sales revenue.** Greg's Groovy Tunes earns sales revenue by selling CDs to customers.
- **Service revenue.** Sherman Lawn Service earns service revenue by mowing customers' lawns.
- **Interest revenue.** Interest revenue is earned on bank deposits and on money lent out to others.
- **Dividend revenue.** Dividend revenue is earned on investments in the stock of other corporations.

Expenses are the decreases in earnings that result from operations. For example, Greg's Groovy Tunes paid wages of $1,200 to its employees and that is an expense that decreases earnings. Expenses are the opposite of revenues. They decrease capital.

Unfortunately, businesses have lots of expenses, including

- Store (or office) rent expense
- Salary expense for employees
- Advertising expense
- Utilities expense for water, electricity, and gas
- Insurance expense
- Supplies expense for supplies used up
- Interest expense on loans payable
- Property tax expense

Businesses strive for profitability. When revenues exceed expenses, the result of operations is a profit or **net income**. When expenses exceed revenues, the result is a **net loss**.

An owner can contribute more value to the business, which can increase capital. An owner may also withdraw cash (or other assets) from the business. Owner withdrawals are the fourth type of transaction that affects capital. **Withdrawals** are distributions to owners of assets (usually cash); they are not expenses. A proprietorship may or may not distribute withdrawals to the owner. Exhibit 1-7 shows the components of owner's equity (capital).

EXHIBIT 1-7 | Components of Capital

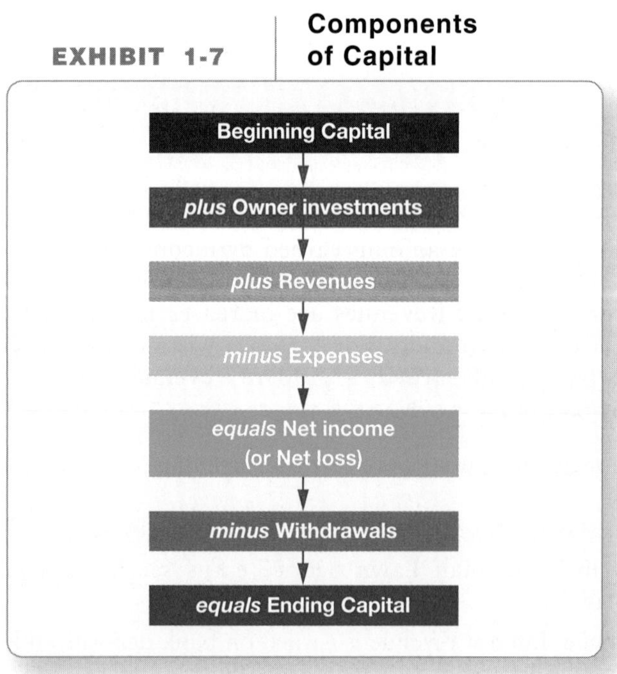

The equity of corporations is different. These types of businesses separate paid-in capital from retained earnings.

Stop & Think...

The accounting equation is important to a business, but it is also important to the individual. Consider your "personal" accounting equation. Are you content with your current net worth (equity) or do you want to increase it? Do you think your education will help you to increase your net worth?

Students enroll in education programs for many unique reasons. However, underneath all the stated reasons is a basic desire of the student to increase his or her net worth through knowledge, higher paying job skills, or other business reasons.

Accounting for Business Transactions

8 Depict accounting for business transactions

Accounting is based on actual transactions, not opinions or desires. A **transaction** is any event that affects the financial position of the business *and* can be measured reliably. Many events affect a company, including economic booms and recessions. Accountants, however, do not record the effects of those events. An accountant records only those events that have dollar amounts that can be measured reliably, such as the purchase of a building, a sale of merchandise, and the payment of rent.

What are some of your personal transactions? You may have bought a car. Your purchase was a transaction. If you are making payments on an auto loan, your payments are also transactions. You need to record all your business transactions just as Greg's Groovy Tunes does in order to manage your business affairs.

Transactions Analysis for Smart Touch Learning

To illustrate accounting for a business, let us use Smart Touch Learning, an e-learning agency organized as a proprietorship. Online customers can access and pay for training through the business's Web site. The Web site offers courses in accounting, economics, marketing, and management, in addition to software training on specific applications, like Microsoft Excel and QuickBooks. The Web site allows the agency to transact more business. Now let us account for the transactions of Smart Touch Learning.

Transaction 1: Starting the Business

Sheena Bright starts the new business as a proprietorship named Smart Touch Learning. In April 2010 the e-learning agency receives $30,000 cash from the proprietor (owner), Sheena Bright, and gives her Capital in the business. The effect of this transaction on the accounting equation of the business is

Assets		Liabilities	+	Owner's Equity (OE)	Type of OE Transaction
Cash	=			Sheena Bright, Capital	
(1) +30,000				+30,000	*Owner investment*

For each transaction, the amount on the left side of the equation must equal the amount on the right side. The first transaction increases both the assets (in this case, Cash) and the Owner's equity (Capital) of the business. To the right of the transaction, we write "Owner investment" to keep track of the source of the equity.

BE SURE TO START ON THE RIGHT TRACK—Keep in mind that we are doing the accounting for Smart Touch Learning the business. We are *not* accounting for Sheena Bright, the person.

View all transactions, and do all the accounting, from the perspective of the business—not from the viewpoint of the proprietor/owner. This same idea applies throughout accounting.

Transaction 2: Purchase of Land

The business purchases land for an office location, paying cash of $20,000. This transaction affects the accounting equation of Smart Touch Learning as follows:

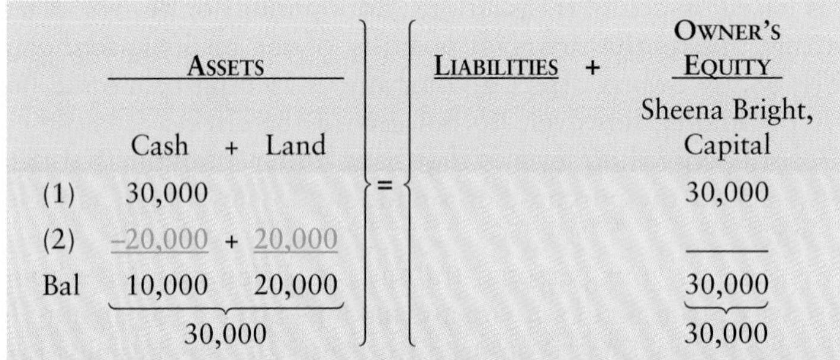

	ASSETS			LIABILITIES +	OWNER'S EQUITY
	Cash +	Land			Sheena Bright, Capital
(1)	30,000		=		30,000
(2)	−20,000 +	20,000			
Bal	10,000	20,000			30,000
	30,000				30,000

The cash purchase of land increases one asset, Land, and decreases another asset, Cash. After the transaction is completed, the business has cash of $10,000, land of $20,000, no liabilities, and owner's equity of $30,000. Note that the total balances (abbreviated Bal) on both sides of the equation must always be equal—in this case $30,000.

Transaction 3: Purchase of Office Supplies

The e-learning agency buys stationery and other office supplies that the company will use in the future, agreeing to pay $500 within 30 days. This transaction increases both the assets and the liabilities of the business, as follows:

	ASSETS				LIABILITIES +	OWNER'S EQUITY
	Cash +	Office supplies +	Land		Accounts payable +	Sheena Bright, Capital
Bal	10,000		20,000	=		30,000
(3)		+500			+500	
Bal	10,000	500	20,000		500	30,000
		30,500			30,500	

Office supplies is an asset, not an expense, because the supplies can be used in the future. The liability created by this transaction is an **Account payable.** A payable is always a liability.

Transaction 4: Earning of Service Revenue

Smart Touch Learning earns service revenue by providing training services for clients. The business earns $5,500 of revenue and collects this amount in cash. The effect on the accounting equation is an increase in Cash and an increase in Sheena Bright, Capital, as follows:

	Assets				Liabilities +	Owner's Equity	Type of OE Transaction
	Cash +	Office supplies +	Land		Accounts payable +	Sheena Bright, Capital	
Bal	10,000	500	20,000	=	500	30,000	
(4)	+5,500	—	—		—	+5,500	*Service revenue*
Bal	15,500	500	20,000		500	35,500	
	36,000				36,000		

A revenue transaction grows the business, as shown by the increases in assets and owner's equity (Sheena Bright, Capital).

Transaction 5: Earning of Service Revenue on Account

Smart Touch performs a service for clients who do not pay immediately. The business receives the clients' promise to pay $3,000 within one month. This promise is an asset, an **Account receivable**, because the agency expects to collect the cash in the future. In accounting, we say that Smart Touch performed this service *on account*. It is performing the service (doing the work), not collecting the cash, that *earns* the revenue. As in transaction 4, increasing earnings increases Sheena Bright, Capital. Smart Touch records the earning of $3,000 of revenue on account, as follows:

	Assets					Liabilities +	Owner's Equity	Type of OE Transaction
	Cash +	Accounts receivable +	Office supplies +	Land		Accounts payable +	Sheena Bright, Capital	
Bal	15,500		500	20,000	=	500	35,500	
(5)	—	+3,000	—	—		—	+3,000	*Service revenue*
Bal	15,500	3,000	500	20,000		500	38,500	
	39,000					39,000		

Transaction 6: Payment of Expenses

During the month, the business pays $3,300 in cash expenses: rent expense on a computer, $600; office rent, $1,100; employee salary, $1,200; and utilities, $400. The effects on the accounting equation are

	ASSETS					LIABILITIES +	OWNER'S EQUITY	TYPE OF OE TRANSACTION
	Cash +	Accounts receivable +	Office supplies +	Land		Accounts payable +	Sheena Bright, Capital	
Bal	15,500	3,000	500	20,000		500	38,500	
(6)	−600						−600	*Rent expense, computer*
(6)	−1,100				=		−1,100	*Rent expense, office*
(6)	−1,200						−1,200	*Salary expense*
(6)	−400						−400	*Utilities expense*
Bal	12,200	3,000	500	20,000		500	35,200	
	35,700					35,700		

Expenses have the opposite effect of revenues. Expenses shrink the business, as shown by the decreased balances of assets and owner's equity (Sheena Bright, Capital).

Each expense should be recorded separately. The expenses are listed together here for simplicity. We could record the cash payment in a single amount for the sum of the four expenses: $3,300 ($600 + $1,100 + $1,200 + $400). However the expenses are recorded, the accounting equation must balance.

Transaction 7: Payment on Account

The business pays $300 to the store from which it purchased supplies in transaction 3. In accounting, we say that the business pays $300 *on account*. The effect on the accounting equation is a decrease in Cash and a decrease in Accounts payable, as shown here:

	ASSETS					LIABILITIES +	OWNER'S EQUITY
	Cash +	Accounts receivable +	Office supplies +	Land		Accounts payable +	Sheena Bright, Capital
Bal	12,200		500	20,000	=	500	35,200
(7)	−300					−300	
Bal	11,900	3,000	500	20,000		200	35,200
	35,400					35,400	

The payment of cash on account has no effect on office supplies or expenses, as Smart Touch was paying off a liability, not an expense.

Transaction 8: Personal Transaction

Sheena Bright buys groceries at a cost of $200, paying cash from personal funds. This event is *not* a transaction of Smart Touch Learning. It has no effect on the e-learning agency and, therefore, is not recorded by the business. It is a transaction of the Sheena Bright *personal* entity, not the e-learning agency. This transaction illustrates the *entity concept*.

Transaction 9: Collection on Account

In transaction 5, the business performed services for a client on account. The business now collects $1,000 from the client. We say that Smart Touch collects the cash *on account*. The business will record an increase in the asset Cash. Should it also record an increase in service revenue? No, because the business already recorded the revenue when it earned the revenue in transaction 5. The phrase "collect cash on account" means to record an increase in Cash and a decrease in Accounts receivable. Accounts receivable is decreased because the $1,000 that the business was to collect at some point in the future is being collected today. The effect on the accounting equation is

	ASSETS					LIABILITIES +	OWNER'S EQUITY
	Cash +	Accounts receivable +	Office supplies +	Land		Accounts payable +	Sheena Bright, Capital
Bal	11,900	3,000	500	20,000	=	200	35,200
(9)	+1,000	−1,000					
Bal	12,900	2,000	500	20,000		200	35,200
	35,400					35,400	

Total assets are unchanged from the preceding total. Why? Because Smart Touch exchanged one asset (Cash) for another (Accounts receivable).

Transaction 10: Sale of Land

The business sells some land owned by the e-learning agency. The sale price of $9,000 is equal to the cost of the land. The business receives $9,000 cash, and the effect on the accounting equation follows:

	ASSETS					LIABILITIES +	OWNER'S EQUITY
	Cash +	Accounts receivable +	Office supplies +	Land		Accounts payable +	Sheena Bright, Capital
Bal	12,900	2,000	500	20,000	=	200	35,200
(10)	+9,000			−9,000			
Bal	21,900	2,000	500	11,000		200	35,200
	35,400					35,400	

Transaction 11: Owner Withdrawal

Sheena Bright withdraws $2,000 cash from the business. The effect on the accounting equation is

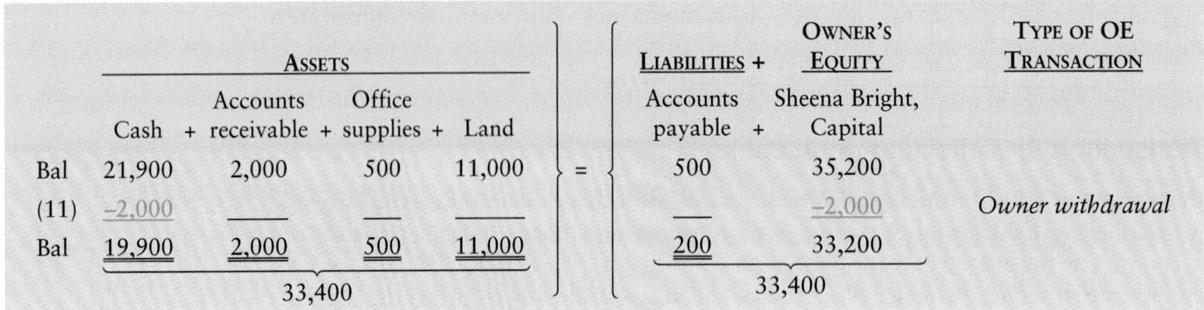

	ASSETS					LIABILITIES +	OWNER'S EQUITY	TYPE OF OE TRANSACTION
	Cash +	Accounts receivable +	Office supplies +	Land		Accounts payable +	Sheena Bright, Capital	
Bal	21,900	2,000	500	11,000	=	500	35,200	
(11)	−2,000						−2,000	*Owner withdrawal*
Bal	19,900	2,000	500	11,000		200	33,200	
	33,400					33,400		

The withdrawal decreases the business's Cash and owner's equity (Sheena Bright, Capital). *Withdrawals do not represent an expense because they are not related to the earning of revenue. Therefore, withdrawals do not affect the business's net income or net loss.* The double underlines below each column indicate a final total after the last transaction.

Preparing the Financial Statements—the User Perspective of Accounting

9 Explain and prepare the financial statements

We have now recorded Smart Touch Learning's transactions, and they are summarized in Exhibit 1-8. Note that every transaction maintains the equation

Assets = Liabilities + Owner's Equity

But a basic question remains: How will people actually use this information? The mass of data in Exhibit 1-8 will not tell a lender whether Smart Touch Learning can pay off a loan. The data in the exhibit do not tell whether the business is profitable.

To address these important questions, we need financial statements. The **financial statements** are business documents that report on a business in monetary terms. People use the financial statements to make business decisions, such as:

- Sheena Bright wants to know whether the business is profitable. Is the business earning a net income, or is it experiencing a net loss? The **income statement** answers this question by reporting the net income or net loss of the business.
- Suppose the business needs $200,000 to buy an office building. The banker will want to know how much in assets the e-learning company has and how much it already owes. The **balance sheet** answers this question by reporting the business's assets and liabilities. The banker asks what the business did with any profits earned. Did the owner take out large withdrawals, or did she keep the money in the training agency? The **statement of owner's equity** answers this question.

EXHIBIT 1-8 | **Analysis of Transactions, Smart Touch Learning**

PANEL A—Details of Transactions

1. The e-learning agency received $30,000 cash and gave capital to the owner.
2. Paid $20,000 cash for land.
3. Bought $500 of office supplies on account.
4. Received $5,500 cash from clients for service revenue earned.
5. Performed travel service for clients on account, $3,000.
6. Paid cash expenses: computer rent, $600; office rent, $1,100; employee salary, $1,200; utilities, $400.
7. Paid $300 on the account payable created in transaction 3.
8. Bright buys $200 of groceries. This is *not* a transaction of the business.
9. Collected $1,000 on the account receivable created in transaction 5.
10. Sold land for cash at its cost of $9,000.
11. Owner withdrew $2,000.

PANEL B—Analysis of Transactions

	Assets					Liabilities +	Owner's Equity	Type of Owner's Equity Transaction
	Cash +	Accounts receivable +	Office supplies +	Land		Accounts payable +	Sheena Bright, Capital	
1.	+ 30,000						+ 30,000	*Owner investment*
Bal	30,000						30,000	
2.	− 20,000			+ 20,000				
Bal	10,000			20,000			30,000	
3.			+ 500			+ 500		
Bal	10,000		500	20,000		500	30,000	
4.	+ 5,500						+ 5,500	*Service revenue*
Bal	15,500		500	20,000		500	35,500	
5.		+ 3,000					+3,000	*Service revenue*
Bal	15,500	3,000	500	20,000		500	38,500	
6.	− 600				=		− 600	*Rent expense, computer*
6.	− 1,100						− 1,100	*Rent expense, office*
6.	− 1,200						− 1,200	*Salary expense*
6.	− 400						− 400	*Utilities expense*
Bal	12,200	3,000	500	20,000		500	35,200	
7.	− 300					− 300		
Bal	11,900	3,000	500	20,000		200	35,200	
8.	Not a transaction of the business							
9.	+ 1,000	− 1,000						
Bal	12,900	2,000	500	20,000		200	35,200	
10.	+ 9,000			− 9,000				
Bal	21,900	2,000	500	11,000		200	35,200	
11.	− 2,000						− 2,000	*Owner withdrawal*
Bal	19,900	2,000	500	11,000		200	33,200	
	33,400					33,400		

- The banker wants to know if the training agency generates enough cash to pay its bills. The **statement of cash flows** answers this question by reporting cash receipts and cash payments and whether cash increased or decreased.
- Lenders also use financial statements. Smart Touch Learning may need to raise cash for an expansion. Suppose you are considering making a loan to the training agency. In making this decision, you would ask the same questions that Sheena Bright and the banker have been asking.

In summary, the main users of financial statements are

- Business owners and managers
- Lenders

Others also use the financial statements, but these user groups are paramount, and we will be referring to them throughout this book. Now let us examine the financial statements in detail.

The Financial Statements

After analyzing transactions, we want to see the overall results. Let us look now at the financial statements discussed in the preceding section. The financial statements summarize the transaction data into a form that is useful for decision making. As we discussed previously, the financial statements are the

- Income statement
- Statement of owner's equity
- Balance sheet
- Statement of cash flows

Headings

Each financial statement has a heading that provides three pieces of data:

- Name of the business (such as Smart Touch Learning)
- Name of the financial statement (income statement, balance sheet, and so on)
- Date or time period covered by the statement (April 30, 2010, for the balance sheet; month ended April 30, 2010, for the other statements)

An income statement (or a statement of owner's equity) that covers a year that ended in December 2010 is dated "Year Ended December 31, 2010." A monthly income statement (or statement of owner's equity) for September 2010 shows "Month Ended September 30, 2010." A quarterly income statement (or statement of owner's equity) for the three months ending June 30, 2010, shows "Quarter Ended June 30, 2010."

Income Statement

The income statement presents a summary of an entity's revenues and expenses for a period of time, such as a month, quarter, or year. The **income statement**, also called the **statement of earnings** or **statement of operations**, is like a video—a moving picture of operations during the period. The income statement holds one of the most important pieces of information about a business:

- **Net income** (total revenues greater than total expenses) or
- **Net loss** (total expenses greater than total revenues)

Net income is good news, and a net loss is bad news. What was the result of Smart Touch Learning's operations during April? Good news—the business earned net income of $5,200 (see the first overlay showing the top part of Exhibit 1-9). The income statement is very important!

Statement of Owner's Equity

The statement of owner's equity (shown in the second overlay of Exhibit 1-9) shows the changes in owner's equity during a time period, such as a month, quarter, or year.

The only increase in owner's equity comes from

- Net income (revenues exceed expenses)

Decreases in owner's equity result from two things:

- Withdrawals
- Net loss (expenses exceed revenues)

Balance Sheet

The balance sheet lists the entity's assets, liabilities, and owner's equity as of a specific date, usually the end of a month, quarter, or year. The balance sheet is like a snapshot of the entity. For this reason, it is also called the **statement of financial position** (see the third and fourth overlays showing the middle of Exhibit 1-9). The balance sheet is also very important!

Statement of Cash Flows

The statement of cash flows reports the cash coming in (cash receipts) and the cash going out (*cash payments*) during a period. Business activities result in a net cash inflow or a net cash outflow. The statement of cash flows reports the net increase or decrease in cash during the period and the ending cash balance. (See the final overlay of Exhibit 1-9.)

In the first part of this book, we focus on the

- Income statement
- Balance sheet
- Statement of owner's equity

The income statement and the balance sheet are more important than the statement of owner's equity. In Chapter 13 we cover the statement of cash flows in detail.

EXHIBIT 1-9 Financial Statements of Smart Touch Learning

SMART TOUCH LEARNING Income Statement Month Ended April 30, 2010		
Revenue:		
Service revenue		$8,500

Using Financial Statements to Evaluate Business Performance

Relationships Among the Financial Statements

10 Use financial statements to evaluate business performance

Exhibit 1-9 illustrates all four financial statements. The data come from the transaction analysis in Exhibit 1-8 that covers the month of April 2010. Study the exhibit carefully. Then, observe the following in Exhibit 1-9:

1. The *income statement* for the month ended April 30, 2010
   a. Reports April's revenues and expenses.
   b. Lists expenses in decreasing order of their amount, with the largest expense first.
   c. Calculates and lists total expenses.
   d. Reports *net income* of the period if total revenues exceed total expenses. If total expenses exceed total revenues, a *net loss* is reported instead.
2. The *statement of owner's equity* for the month ended April 30, 2010
   a. Opens with the capital balance at the beginning of the period (zero for a new entity).
   b. Adds *net income* directly from the income statement (see arrow 1 in Exhibit 1-9).
   c. Subtracts *owner withdrawals* (and net loss, if applicable). Parentheses indicate a subtraction.
   d. Ends with the capital balance at the end of the period.
3. The *balance sheet* at April 30, 2010
   a. Reports all *assets*, all *liabilities*, and *owner's equity* at the end of the period.
   b. Lists assets in the order of their liquidity (closeness to cash) with cash coming first because it is the most liquid asset.
   c. Reports liabilities similarly. That is, the liability that must be paid first is listed first, usually Accounts payable.
   d. Reports that total assets equal total liabilities plus total equity.
   e. Reports the ending capital balance, taken directly from the statement of owner's equity (see arrow 2).
4. The *statement of cash flows* for the month ended April 30, 2010
   a. Reports cash flows from three types of business activities (*operating*, *investing*, and *financing activities*) during the month. Each category of cash-flow activities includes both cash receipts (positive amounts), and cash payments (negative amounts denoted by parentheses).
   b. Reports a net increase (or decrease) in cash during the month and ends with the cash balance at April 30, 2010. This is the amount of cash to report on the balance sheet (see arrow 3).

Each of the statements identified in Exhibit 1-9 provides different information about the company to the users of the financial statements. The income statement provides information about profitability for a particular period for the company. Recall that expenses are listed in this statement from largest to smallest. This ordering shows users which expenses are consuming the largest part of the revenues. The statement of owner's equity informs users about how much of the earnings were reinvested in the company. Recall from Exhibit 1-9 that two main items appear in this statement that explains the change in the capital balance:

1. Net income or net loss
2. Owner withdrawals

If the owner withdrawals were larger than income for the period, this could signal concern to financial statement users. The balance sheet in Exhibit 1-9 provides valuable information to financial statement users about economic resources the company owns (assets) as well as debts the company owes (liabilities). Thus, the balance sheet presents the overall financial position of the company on a specific date. This allows decision makers to determine their opinion about the financial status of the company. The cash flow statement is covered in detail in a later chapter in the textbook. Briefly, its purpose and value to users is to explain why the net income number on the income statement does not equal the change in the cash balance for the period. As we conclude this chapter, we return to our opening question: Have you ever thought of having your own business? The Decision Guidelines feature on the next page shows how to make some of the decisions that you will face if you start a business. Decision Guidelines appear in each chapter.

Decision Guidelines

MAJOR BUSINESS DECISIONS

Suppose you open a business to take photos at parties at your school. You hire a professional photographer and line up suppliers for party favors and photo albums. Here are some factors you must consider if you expect to be profitable.

Decision	Guidelines
• How to organize the business?	If a single owner—a *proprietorship*. If two or more owners, but not incorporated— a *partnership* or *limited liability company*. If the business issues stock to stockholders—a *corporation*.
• What to account for?	Account for the business, a separate entity apart from its owner (*entity concept*). Account for transactions and events that affect the business and can be measured reliably.
• How much to record for assets and liabilities?	Actual historical amount (*cost principle*).
• How to analyze a transaction?	The accounting equation: (own) = (owe) + (net worth) Assets = Liabilities + Owner's Equity
• How to measure profits and losses?	Income statement: Revenues – Expenses = Net Income (or Net Loss)
• Did owner's equity increase or decrease?	Statement of owner's equity: Beginning Capital + Net income (or – Net loss) – Withdrawals = Ending Capital
• Where does the business stand financially?	Balance sheet (accounting equation): Assets = Liabilities + Owner's Equity

Summary Problem

Ron Smith opens an apartment-locator business near a college campus. The business will be named Campus Apartment Locators. During the first month of operations, July 2010, the business completes the following transactions:

a. Smith invests $35,000. The business receives $35,000 cash and gives capital to Smith.
b. Purchases $350 of office supplies on account.
c. Pays cash of $30,000 to acquire a lot next to the campus. Smith intends to use the land as a future building site for the business office.
d. Locates apartments for clients and receives cash of $1,900.
e. Pays $100 on the account payable he created in transaction b.
f. Pays $2,000 of personal funds for a vacation.
g. Pays cash expenses for office rent, $400, and utilities, $100.
h. Returns office supplies of $150 from transaction b.
i. Owner withdrawal of $1,200.

Requirements

1. Analyze the preceding transactions in terms of their effects on the accounting equation of Campus Apartment Locators. Use Exhibit 1-8 as a guide, but show balances only after the last transaction.
2. Prepare the income statement, statement of owner's equity, and balance sheet of the business after recording the transactions. Use Exhibit 1-9 as a guide.

Solution

Requirement 1

Analysis of transactions

	ASSETS					LIABILITIES +	OWNER'S EQUITY	TYPE OF OE TRANSACTION
	Cash	+	Office supplies	+	Land	Accounts payable +	Ron Smith, Capital	
(a)	+35,000						+35,000	*Owner investment*
(b)			+350			+350		
(c)	−30,000				+30,000			
(d)	+1,900						+1,900	*Service revenue*
(e)	−100				=	−100		
(f)	Not a transaction of the business							
(g)	−400						−400	*Rent expense*
	−100						−100	*Utilities expense*
(h)			−150			−150		
(i)	−1,200						−1,200	*Owner withdrawal*
Bal	5,100		200		30,000	100	35,200	
	35,300					35,300		

Requirement 2

Financial Statements of Campus Apartment Locators

CAMPUS APARTMENT LOCATORS **Income Statement** Month Ended July 31, 2010		
Revenue:		
Service revenue		$1,900
Expenses:		
Rent expense	$400	
Utilities expense	100	
Total expenses		500
Net income		$1,400

CAMPUS APARTMENT LOCATORS **Statement of Owner's Equity** Month Ended July 31, 2010	
Ron Smith, Capital, July 1, 2010	$ 0
Add: Owner investment	$35,000
Net income for the month	1,400
	36,400
Less: Owner withdrawals	(1,200)
Ron Smith, Capital, July 31, 2010	$35,200

CAMPUS APARTMENT LOCATORS **Balance Sheet** July 31, 2010			
Assets		**Liabilities**	
Cash	$ 5,100	Accounts payable	$ 100
Office supplies	200		
Land	30,000	**Owner's Equity**	
		Ron Smith, Capital	35,200
Total assets	$35,300	Total liabilities and owner's equity	$35,300

Review Accounting and the Business Environment

Accounting Vocabulary

Account Payable (p. 43)
A liability backed by the general reputation and credit standing of the debtor.

Account Receivable (p. 43)
A promise to receive cash from customers to whom the business has sold goods or for whom the business has performed services.

Accounting (p. 30)
The information system that measures business activities, processes that information into reports, and communicates the results to decision makers.

Accounting Equation (p. 38)
The basic tool of accounting, measuring the resources of the business and the claims to those resources: Assets = Liabilities + Owner's Equity.

Asset (p. 33)
An economic resource that is expected to be of benefit in the future.

Audit (p. 32)
An examination of a company's financial situation.

Balance Sheet (p. 46)
An entity's assets, liabilities, and owner's equity as of a specific date. Also called the **statement of financial position**.

Capital (p. 39)
Representation of ownership investment by an owner of a proprietorship.

Certified Management Accountant (CMA) (p. 32)
A licensed accountant who works for a single company.

Certified Public Accountants (CPAs) (p. 32)
Licensed accountants who serve the general public rather than one particular company.

Corporation (p. 34)
A business owned by stockholders. A corporation begins when the state approves its articles of incorporation and the first share of stock is issued. It is a legal entity, an "artificial person," in the eyes of the law.

Cost Principle (p. 37)
A principle that states that acquired assets and services should be recorded at their actual cost.

Creditor (p. 31)
Someone to whom a business owes money.

Entity (p. 37)
An organization or a section of an organization that, for accounting purposes, stands apart from other organizations and individuals as a separate economic unit.

Equity (p. 38)
The claim of a proprietorship's owner to the assets of the business. Also called **owner's equity**.

Expenses (p. 40)
Decrease in equity that occurs from using assets or increasing liabilities in the course of delivering goods or services to customers.

Financial Accounting (p. 31)
The branch of accounting that focuses on information for people outside the firm.

Financial Accounting Standards Board (FASB) (p. 32)
The private organization that determines how accounting is practiced in the United States.

Financial Statements (p. 46)
Documents that report on a business in monetary amounts, providing information to help people make informed business decisions.

Generally Accepted Accounting Principles (GAAP) (p. 32)
Accounting guidelines, formulated by the Financial Accounting Standards Board, that govern how accountants measure, process, and communicate financial information.

Going-Concern Concept (p. 38)
This concept assumes that the entity will remain in operation for the foreseeable future.

Income Statement (p. 48)
Summary of an entity's revenues, expenses, and net income or net loss for a specific period. Also called the **statement of earnings** or the **statement of operations**.

Liabilities (p. 38)
Economic obligations (debts) payable to an individual or an organization outside the business.

Limited-Liability Company (p. 34)
Company in which each member is only liable for his or her own actions or those under his or her control.

Limited-Liability Partnership (p. 34)
Company in which each partner is only liable for his or her own actions or those under his or her control.

Management Accounting (p. 31)
The branch of accounting that focuses on information for internal decision makers of a business.

Mutual Agency (p. 36)
The ability of partners in a partnership to commit other partners and the business to a contract.

Net Income (p. 40)
Excess of total revenues over total expenses. Also called **net earnings** or **net profit**.

Net Loss (p. 40)
Excess of total expenses over total revenues.

Objectivity Principle (p. 37)
Principle that asserts that data are verifiable and objective. Also called the **reliability principle**.

Owner's Equity (p. 38)
The claim of an owner to the assets of the business.

Partnership (p. 34)
A business with two or more owners that is not organized as a corporation.

Proprietorship (p. 34)
A business with a single owner.

Reliability Principle (p. 37)
Principle that asserts that data are verifiable and objective. Also called the **objectivity principle**.

Revenue (p. 39)
Amounts earned by delivering goods or services to customers. Revenues increase retained earnings.

Shareholder (p. 34)
A person who owns stock in a corporation.

Stable Monetary Unit Concept (p. 38)
The concept that says that accountants assume that the dollar's purchasing power is stable.

Statement of Cash Flows (p. 48)
Report of cash receipts and cash payments during a period.

Statement of Earnings (p. 49)
Summary of an entity's revenues, expenses, and net income or net loss for a specific period. Also called the **income statement** or the **statement of operations**.

Statement of Financial Position (p. 49)
An entity's assets, liabilities, and owner's equity as of a specific date. Also called the **balance sheet**.

Statement of Operations (p. 49)
Summary of an entity's revenues, expenses, and net income or net loss for a specific period. Also called the **income statement** or **statement of earnings**.

Statement of Owner's Equity (p. 46)
Summary of the changes in an owner's capital account during a specific period.

Stock (p. 35)
A document indicating ownership of a corporation. The holders of stock are called **stockholders** or **shareholders**.

Stockholder (p. 34)
A person who owns stock in a corporation. Also called a **shareholder**.

Stockholders' Equity (p. 40)
The claim of a corporation's owners to the assets of the business. Also called **owner's equity** or **shareholders' equity**.

Transaction (p. 41)
An event that affects the financial position of a particular entity and can be measured and recorded reliably.

Quick Check

1. Generally accepted accounting principles (GAAP) are formulated by the
   a. Securities and Exchange Commission (SEC)
   b. Institute of Management Accountants (IMA)
   c. Financial Accounting Standards Board (FASB)
   d. American Institute of Certified Public Accountants (AICPA)
2. Which type of business organization is owned by its stockholders?
   a. Corporation
   b. Partnership
   c. Proprietorship
   d. All the above are owned by stockholders
3. Which accounting concept or principle specifically states that we should record transactions at amounts that can be verified?
   a. Going-concern concept
   b. Entity concept
   c. Cost principle
   d. Reliability principle
4. **Fossil** is famous for fashion wristwatches and leather goods. At the end of a recent year, **Fossil's** total assets added up to $345 million, and owner's equity was $240 million. How much were **Fossil's** liabilities?
   a. Cannot determine from the data given
   b. $345 million
   c. $105 million
   d. $240 million

5. Assume that **Fossil** sold watches to a department store on account for $43,000. How would this transaction affect **Fossil's** accounting equation?
   a. Increase both liabilities and equity by $43,000
   b. Increase both assets and liabilities by $43,000
   c. Increase both assets and equity by $43,000
   d. No effect on the accounting equation because the effects cancel out
6. Which parts of the accounting equation does a sale on account affect?
   a. Accounts receivable and Accounts payable
   b. Accounts receivable and Capital
   c. Accounts payable and Capital
   d. Accounts payable and Cash
7. Assume that **Fossil** paid expenses totaling $40,000. How does this transaction affect **Fossil's** accounting equation?
   a. Increases assets and decreases liabilities
   b. Decreases assets and increases liabilities
   c. Decreases both assets and equity
   d. Increases both assets and equity
8. Consider the overall effects on **Fossil** of selling watches on account for $53,000 and paying expenses totaling $37,000. What is **Fossil's** net income or net loss?
   a. Net loss of $16,000
   b. Net income of $16,000
   c. Net income of $53,000
   d. Cannot determine from the data given
9. The balance sheet reports
   a. Results of operations for a specific period
   b. Financial position on a specific date
   c. Results of operations on a specific date
   d. Financial position for a specific period
10. The income statement reports
   a. Financial position on a specific date
   b. Results of operations on a specific date
   c. Results of operations for a specific period
   d. Financial position for a specific period

Answers are given after Apply Your Knowledge (p. 81).

Assess Your Progress

■ Short Exercises

S1-1 *(L. OBJ. 1)* **Explaining revenues and expenses [5 min]**
Sherman Lawn Service has been open for one year, and Hannah Sherman, the owner, wants to know whether the business earned a net income or a net loss for the year. First, she must identify the revenues earned and the expenses incurred during the year.

Requirement

1. What are *revenues* and *expenses*?

S1-2 *(L. OBJ. 2)* **Users of financial information [5 min]**
Suppose you need a bank loan in order to purchase music equipment for Greg's Groovy Tunes, which you manage. In evaluating your loan request, the banker asks about the assets and liabilities of your business. In particular, the banker wants to know the amount of the business's owner's equity.

Requirements

1. Is the banker considered an internal or external user of financial information?
2. Which financial statement would provide the best information to answer the banker's questions?

S1-3 *(L. OBJ. 3)* **Organizations that govern CPAs [5–10 min]**
Suppose you are starting a business, T-Shirts Plus, to imprint logos on T-shirts. In organizing the business and setting up its accounting records, you take your information to a CPA to prepare financial statements for the bank. You state to the CPA, "I really need to get this loan, so be sure you make my financial statements look great."

Requirement

1. Name the organization that governs the majority of the guidelines that the CPA will use to prepare financial statements for T-Shirts Plus.

S1-4 *(L. OBJ. 4)* **Types of business organizations [5–10 min]**
Claire Hunter plans on opening Claire Hunter Floral Designs. She is considering the various types of business organizations and wishes to organize her business with unlimited life and limited liability features.

Requirement

1. Which type of business organization will meet Claire's needs best?

S1-5 *(L. OBJ. 5)* **Organizing a proprietorship [5–10 min]**

You begin A-1 Cell Service by investing $2,000 of your own money in a business bank account. You receive capital for your investment. Then the business borrows $1,000 cash by signing a note payable to Summit Bank.

Requirement

1. Listed below are the steps that you must take to organize the business and run it. Place the steps in their proper order:
   a. The bank approves your loan.
   b. You deposit a personal check for $2,000 into the account for A-1 Cell Service.
   c. You contact the bank and set up a checking account for your new business called A-1 Cell Service.
   d. Representing A-1 Cell Service, you apply for a loan from the bank.

S1-6 *(L. OBJ. 6)* **Applying accounting concepts and principles [5–10 min]**

Wendy Craven is the sole proprietor of a property management company near the campus of Pensacola Junior College. The business has cash of $6,000 and furniture that cost $12,000 and has a market value of $16,000. Debts include accounts payable of $5,000. Wendy's personal home is valued at $350,000 and her personal bank account has $9,000.

Requirements

1. Consider the accounting principles discussed in the chapter and define the principle that best matches the situation:
   a. Wendy's personal assets are not recorded on the property management company's balance sheet.
   b. Wendy records furniture at its cost of $12,000, not its market value of $16,000.
   c. Wendy does not make adjustments for inflation.
   d. The account payable of $5,000 is documented by a statement from the furniture company showing the business still owes $5,000 on the furniture. Wendy's friend thinks she should only owe about $4,000. The account payable is recorded at $5,000.
2. How much equity is in the business?

S1-7 *(L. OBJ. 7)* **Using the accounting equation [5 min]**

Snail Creek Kennel earns service revenue by caring for the pets of customers. Snail Creek's main expense is the salary paid to an employee.

Requirement

1. Write the accounting equation for the transactions below:
   a. Receiving cash of $420 for service revenue earned
   b. The payment of $135 for salary expense

S1-8 *(L. OBJ. 8)* **Analyzing transactions [5 min]**

Monte Hall Gaming paid $20,000 cash to purchase land. To buy the land, the business was obligated to pay for it.

Requirement

1. Why did the business record no liability in this transaction?

S1-9 *(L. OBJ. 8)* **Analyzing transactions [5 min]**
Awesome Adventures Travel recorded revenues of $2,400 earned on account by providing travel service for clients.

Requirements

1. How much are the business's cash and total assets after the transaction?
2. Name the business's asset that was increased as a result of the transaction.

S1-10 *(L. OBJ. 8)* **Analyzing transactions [5 min]**
Brad Polson collected cash on account from a client for whom the business had provided delivery services one month earlier.

Requirements

1. Why did the business fail to record revenue when it collected the cash on account?
2. Write two accounting equations to show the effects of
   a. Receiving cash of $300 for service revenue earned
   b. Receiving cash of $300 from customer on account

S1-11 *(L. OBJ. 9)* **Preparing the balance sheet [10 min]**
Examine Exhibit 1-8. The exhibit summarizes the transactions of Smart Touch Learning for the month of April 2010. Suppose the business has completed only the first seven transactions and needs a bank loan on April 21. The vice president of the bank requires financial statements to support all loan requests.

Requirement

1. Prepare the balance sheet that the business would present to the banker *after completing the first seven transactions* on April 21, 2010. Exhibit 1-9 shows the format of the balance sheet.

S1-12 *(L. OBJ. 9)* **Preparing the income statement [10 min]**
Party Planners Extraordinaire has just completed operations for the year ended December 31, 2011. This is the third year of operations for the company. As the owner, you want to know how well the business performed during the year. To address this question, you have assembled the following data:

Insurance expense	3,000	Salary expense	44,000
Service revenue	109,000	Accounts payable	7,700
Supplies expense	900	Supplies	2,400
Rent expense	14,000	Withdrawals	40,000

Requirement

1. Prepare the income statement of Party Planners Extraordinaire for the year ended December 31, 2011.

S1-13 *(L. OBJ. 10)* **Evaluating business performance [10 min]**
Consider the facts presented in S1-12 for Party Planners Extraordinaire.

Requirement

1. Review the income statement prepared in S1-12. Evaluate the results of 2011 operations for Planners Extraordinaire. Was the year good or bad?

Exercises

E1-14 *(L. OBJ. 1, 5, 6)* **Using accounting vocabulary [10–15 min]**
Match the following accounting terms with their correct definition:

TERMS:	DEFINITIONS:
1. Accounting Equation	A. An economic resource that is expected to be of benefit in the future
2. Asset	B. An economic obligation (a debt) payable to an individual or an organization outside the business
3. Balance Sheet	C. Excess of total expenses over total revenues
4. Expense	D. Excess of total revenues over total expenses
5. Income Statement	E. The basic tool of accounting, stated as Assets = Liabilities + Equity
6. Liability	F. Decrease in equity that occurs from using assets or increasing liabilities in the course of delivering goods or services to customers
7. Net Income	G. Amounts earned by delivering goods or services to customers
8. Net Loss	H. Report of cash receipts and cash payments during a period
9. Revenue	I. Report of an entity's assets, liabilities, and equity as of a specific date
10. Statement of Cash Flows	J. Report of an entity's revenues, expenses, and net income/net loss for the period
11. Statement of Owner's Equity	K. Report that shows the changes in capital for a period of time

E1-15 *(L. OBJ. 2, 3, 4, 9)* **Users of financial information; the accounting profession, types of business organizations, and preparing the financial statements [15–20 min]**
Terry Maness publishes a travel magazine. In need of cash, the business asks Metro Bank for a loan. The bank requires borrowers to submit financial statements. With little knowledge of accounting, Terry Maness, the owner, does not know how to proceed.

Requirements

1. Explain how to prepare the balance sheet and the income statement.
2. Which organization is the self-regulating body of accountants that defines pronouncements that guide how the financial statements will be prepared?
3. Indicate why a lender would require this information.
4. What type of organization is Terry Maness?

E1-16 *(L. OBJ. 5, 6, 7)* **Characteristics of a proprietorship, accounting concepts, and using the accounting equation [5–10 min]**
Select financial information for three proprietorships follows:

	Assets	Liabilities	Owner's Equity
Nice Cuts	$?	$25,000	$43,000
Love Dry Cleaners	85,000	?	54,000
Hudson Gift and Cards	102,000	49,000	?

Requirements

1. Compute the missing amount in the accounting equation for each entity.
2. List in alphabetical order the five main characteristics of a proprietorship.
3. Which accounting concept tells us that the previous three companies will cease to exist if the owners die?

E1-17 *(L. OBJ. 7, 8)* **Using the accounting equation and analyzing business transactions [5–10 min]**
Bell Computers' balance sheet data at May 31, 2010, and June 30, 2010, follow:

	May 31, 2010	June 30, 2010
Total assets	$174,000	$208,000
Total liabilities	104,000	127,000

Requirement

1. Following are three situations about owner's investments and withdrawals from the business during June. For each situation, compute the amount of net income or net loss during June 2010.

    a. The owner invested $5,000 and made no withdrawals.
    b. The owner invested nothing and made $14,000 of withdrawals.
    c. The owner invested $15,000 and made $28,000 of withdrawals.

E1-18 *(L. OBJ. 7, 8)* **Using the accounting equation to analyze transactions [5–10 min]**
As the manager of an Aunty Pasta restaurant, you must deal with a variety of business transactions.

Requirement

1. Give an example of a transaction that has each of the following effects on the accounting equation:

    a. Increase one asset and decrease another asset.
    b. Decrease an asset and decrease owner's equity.
    c. Decrease an asset and decrease a liability.
    d. Increase an asset and increase owner's equity.
    e. Increase an asset and increase a liability.

E1-19 *(L. OBJ. 7, 8)* **Using the accounting equation to analyze transactions [10–20 min]**

Requirement

1. Indicate the effects of the following business transactions on the accounting equation of a Flickster Video store. Transaction (a) is answered as a guide.

    a. Received cash of $10,000 and the owner received capital.
    Answer: Increase asset (Cash)
    Increase owner's equity (Capital)
    b. Earned video rental revenue on account, $1,200.
    c. Purchased office furniture on account, $600.
    d. Received cash on account, $300.
    e. Paid cash on account, $200.
    f. Sold land for $12,000, which was the cost of the land.
    g. Rented videos and received cash of $600.
    h. Paid monthly office rent of $800.
    i. Paid $100 cash to purchase supplies that will be used in the future.

E1-20 *(L. OBJ. 7, 8)* **Using the accounting equation to analyze transactions [10–20 min]**

Cindy Surrette opened a medical practice. During July, the first month of operation, the business, titled Cindy Surrette, M.D., experienced the following events:

Jul 6	Surrette invested $53,000 in the business by opening a bank account in the name of Cindy Surrette, M.D. The business gave her capital.
9	Paid $35,000 cash for land.
12	Purchased medical supplies for $1,900 on account.
15	Officially opened for business.
15–31	During the rest of the month, Surrette treated patients and earned service revenue of $7,000, receiving cash.
29	Paid cash expenses: employees' salaries, $2,190; office rent, $1,000; utilities, $300.
30	Returned supplies purchased on the 12th for the cost of those supplies, $600.
31	Paid $1,500 on account.

Requirement

1. Analyze the effects of these events on the accounting equation of the medical practice of Cindy Surrette, M.D. Use a format similar to that of Exhibit 1-8, with headings for Cash, Medical supplies, Land, Accounts payable, and Cindy Surette, Capital.

E1-21 *(L. OBJ. 7, 8, 9)* **Using the accounting equation to analyze transactions and calculate net income or net loss [10–15 min]**

The analysis of the first eight transactions of Printman Copy & Print Service follows. The owner made only one investment and there were no owner withdrawals.

	Cash	+	Accounts receivable	+	Equipment	=	Accounts payable	+	Joe Printman, Capital
1	+ 23,000								+ 23,000
2			+ 3,400						+ 3,400
3					+ 12,700		+ 12,700		
4	+ 150		− 150						
5	− 500				+ 500				
6	− 7,600						− 7,600		
7	+ 900								+900
8	− 2,100								− 2,100

Requirements

1. Describe each transaction.
2. If these transactions fully describe the operations of Printman Copy & Print Service during the month, what was the amount of net income or net loss?

E1-22 *(L. OBJ. 7, 10)* **Using the accounting equation and evaluating business performance [10 min]**

Eager Beaver started 2011 with total assets of $24,000 and total liabilities of $11,000. At the end of 2011, the business's total assets stood at $34,000, and its total liabilities were $17,000.

Requirements

1. Did the owner's equity of Eager Beaver increase or decrease during 2011? By how much?
2. Identify two possible reasons for the change in owner's equity during the year.

E1-23 *(L. OBJ. 7, 9, 10)* **Using the accounting equation, preparing financial statements, and evaluating business performance [10–15 min]**
The 2011 annual report of Priority Parcel Service (PPS) reported revenue of $28 billion. Total expenses for the year were $21 billion. PPS ended the year with total assets of $37 billion, and it owed debts totaling $17 billion. At year-end 2010, the business reported total assets of $30 billion and total liabilities of $17 billion.

Requirements

1. Compute PPS's net income for 2011.
2. Did PPS's owner's equity increase or decrease during 2011? By how much?
3. How would you rate PPS's performance for 2011—good or bad? Give your reason. (Challenge)

E1-24 *(L. OBJ. 7, 9, 10)* **Using the accounting equation, preparing financial statements, and evaluating business performance [30–40 min]**
Compute the missing amount for Jones Company. You will need to work through total owner's equity.

Beginning:		**Owner's Equity:**	
Assets	$48,000	Owner investments	$ 0
Liabilities	22,000	Owner withdrawals	14,000
Ending:		**Income Statement:**	
Assets	$60,000	Revenues	$231,000
Liabilities	27,000	Expenses	?

Requirements

1. Did Jones earn a net income or suffer a net loss for the year? Compute the amount.
2. Would you consider Jones's performance for the year to be good or bad? Give your reason.

E1-25 *(L. OBJ. 8)* **Analyzing business transactions [10–15 min]**
Jake's Roasted Peanuts supplies snack foods. The business experienced the following events:

a. Jake's Roasted Peanuts gave capital after receiving cash from the sole proprietor.
b. Cash purchase of land for a building site.
c. Paid cash on accounts payable.
d. Purchased equipment; signed a note payable.
e. Performed service for a customer on account.
f. Owner withdrew cash.
g. Received cash from a customer on account receivable.
h. Borrowed money from the bank.

Requirement

1. State whether each event (1) increased, (2) decreased, or (3) had no effect on the *total assets* of the business. Identify any specific asset affected.

E1-26 *(L. OBJ. 9, 10)* **Preparing financial statements and evaluating business performance [10–20 min]**
The account balances of Tompkins Towing Service at June 30, 2012, follow:

Equipment	$13,900	Service revenue	$10,600
Supplies	400	Accounts receivable	5,400
Note payable	6,300	Accounts payable	3,300
Rent expense	500	T. Tompkins, Capital	3,700
Cash	1,600	Salary expense	2,100

Requirements

1. Prepare the balance sheet of the business at June 30, 2012.
2. What does the balance sheet report—financial position or operating results?
3. Which financial statement reports the other accounts listed for the business?

E1-27 *(L. OBJ. 9, 10)* **Preparing financial statements and evaluating business performance [10–15 min]**

The assets, liabilities, owner's equity, revenues, and expenses of Carter Design Studio have the following balances at December 31, 2010, the end of its first year of operation. During the year, the owner invested $17,000.

Note payable	$ 43,000	Office furniture	$ 48,000
Rent expense	20,000	Utilities expense	6,800
Cash	3,500	Accounts payable	3,100
Office supplies	5,000	Owner's equity	17,300
Salary expense	64,000	Service revenue	158,500
Salaries payable	2,100	Accounts receivable	9,000
Property tax expense	1,400	Supplies expense	4,500

Requirements

1. Prepare the income statement of Carter Design Studio for the year ended December 31, 2010. What is the result of operations for 2010?
2. What was the amount of the owner's withdrawals during the year?

■ Problems (Group A)

P1-28A *(L. OBJ. 1, 2, 3, 4, 5, 6)* **Accounting vocabulary, financial statement users, accounting profession, types of business organizations, business characteristics, and accounting concepts [15–20 min]**

Consider the following terms and definitions:

TERMS:	DEFINITIONS:
1. Proprietorship	A. Applies to corporations and proprietors or partners of LLPs or LLCs
2. Reliability principle	B. Holds that accounting records should continue reporting the historical cost of an asset over its useful life
3. Partnership	C. Is composed of accountants
4. Stock	D. One owner equity
5. Limited liability	E. States that data should be able to be confirmed by any independent observer
6. Limited Liability Company	F. Revenues of $55,000 and expenses of $30,000
7. Cost principle	G. Change in owners creates new entity
8. FASB	H. A corporation's unit of division of ownership
9. Net income of $25,000	I. Entity where the business, and not the proprietor, is liable for the company's debts

Requirement

1. Match the terms with their correct definitions.

P1-29A *(L. OBJ. 5, 6, 9)* **Proprietorship attributes, applying the entity concept, and preparing financial statements [20–25 min]**

Natalie Williams is a realtor. She organized her business as a proprietorship, Natalie Williams, Realtor, by investing $27,000 cash. The business gave capital to her. Consider the following facts at August 31, 2010.

a. The business owes $57,000 on a note payable for land that the business acquired for a total price of $80,000.
b. The business spent $27,000 for a Linka Banker real estate franchise, which entitles the business to represent itself as a Linka Banker office. This franchise is a business asset.
c. Williams owes $40,000 on a personal mortgage for her personal residence, which she acquired in 2010 for a total price of $130,000.
d. Williams has $6,000 in her personal bank account, and the business has $13,000 in its bank account.
e. Williams owes $3,000 on a personal charge account with Chico's.
f. The office acquired business furniture for $17,000 on August 25. Of this amount, the business owes $8,000 on account at August 31.
g. Office supplies on hand at the real estate office total $1,100.

Requirements

1. Natalie was concerned about liability exposure. Which proprietorship feature, if any, limits Natalie's personal liability?
2. Prepare the balance sheet of the real estate business of Natalie Williams, Realtor, at August 31, 2010.
3. Identify the personal items that would not be reported on the business records.

P1-30A *(L. OBJ. 6, 7, 8, 9, 10)* **Applying the entity concept, using the accounting equation for transaction analysis, preparing financial statements, and evaluating business performance [20–30 min]**
Robert Ryan practiced accounting with a partnership for five years. Recently he opened his own accounting firm, which he operates as a proprietorship. The name of the new entity is Robert Ryan, CPA. Ryan experienced the following events during the organizing phase of the new business and its first month of operations. Some of the events were personal and did not affect the business.

Feb	4	Ryan received $28,000 cash from former accounting partners.*
	5	Deposited $40,000 in a new business bank account titled Robert Ryan, CPA. The business gave capital to Ryan.
	6	Paid $500 cash for letterhead stationery for the new office.
	7	Purchased office furniture for the office. The business will pay the account payable, $9,000, within 3 months.
	10	Ryan sold personal investment in Amazing.com stock, which he had owned for several years, receiving $56,000 cash.*
	11	Ryan deposited the $56,000 cash from sale of the Amazing.com stock in his personal bank account.*
	12	A representative of a large company telephoned Ryan and told him of the company's intention to transfer its accounting business to Ryan.
	18	Finished tax hearings on behalf of a client and submitted a bill for accounting services, $13,000. Ryan expected to collect from this client within two weeks.
	25	Paid office rent, $1,800.
	28	Withdrew $10,000 for personal use.

*Personal transaction of Ryan.

Requirements

1. Analyze the effects of the events on the accounting equation of the corporation of Robert Ryan, CPA. Use a format similar to Exhibit 1-8.
2. As of February 28, compute:
   a. Total assets
   b. Total liabilities
   c. Total owner's equity
   d. Net income or net loss for February

P1-31A *(L. OBJ. 6, 7, 8, 9, 10)* **Applying the entity concept, using the accounting equation for transaction analysis, preparing financial statements, and evaluating business performance [20–30 min]**

Arlene Lavoie practiced law with a partnership for 10 years. Recently she opened her own law office, which she operates as a proprietorship. The name of the new entity is Arlene Lavoie, Attorney. Lavoie experienced the following events during the organizing phase of the new business and its first month of operation. Some of the events were personal and did not affect the law practice. Others were business transactions and should be accounted for by the business.

May 1	Sold personal investment in **eBay** stock, which she had owned for several years, receiving $30,000 cash.
2	Deposited the $30,000 cash from sales of the **eBay** stock in her personal bank account.
3	Received $155,000 cash from former law partners.
5	Deposited $105,000 cash in a new business bank account titled Arlene Lavoie, Attorney. The business gave her capital.
7	Paid $600 cash for ink cartirdges for the printer.
9	Purchased computer for the law office, agreeing to pay the account, $9,700, within 3 months.
23	Finished court hearings on behalf of a client and submitted a bill for legal services, $14,500, on account.
30	Paid utilities, $1,100.
31	Lavoie withdrew $8,000.

Requirements

1. Analyze the effects of the preceding events on the accounting equation of the corporation of Arlene Lavoie, Attorney. Use a format similar to Exhibit 1-8.
2. At May 31, compute the business's
   a. Total assets
   b. Total liabilities
   c. Total owner's equity
   d. Net income or net loss for the month
3. Evaluate Arlene Lavoie's first month of operations. Were the results good or bad?

P1-32A *(L. OBJ. 7, 8)* **Using the accounting equation for transaction analysis [20–25 min]**

Carter Roofing was recently formed as a proprietorship. The balance of each item in the company's accounting equation is shown for December 1 and for each of the following business days.

	Cash	Accounts receivable	Supplies	Land	Accounts payable	Larry Carter, Capital
Dec 1	$2,000	$7,000	$ 800	$11,000	$3,800	10,000
4	7,000	7,000	800	11,000	3,800	15,000
9	4,000	7,000	800	14,000	3,800	15,000
13	4,000	7,000	1,100	14,000	4,100	15,000
16	2,000	7,000	1,100	14,000	2,100	15,000
19	3,400	5,600	1,100	14,000	2,100	15,000
22	11,400	5,600	1,100	14,000	2,100	23,000
25	10,900	5,600	1,100	14,000	1,600	23,000
27	10,300	5,600	1,700	14,000	1,600	23,000
30	5,200	5,600	1,700	14,000	1,600	24,900

Requirement

1. A single transaction took place on each day. Briefly describe the transaction that most likely occurred on each day, beginning with December 4. Indicate which accounts were increased or decreased and by what amounts. Assume that no revenue or expense transactions occurred during the month.

P1-33A *(L. OBJ. 7, 8, 9, 10)* **Using the accounting equation for transaction analysis, preparing financial statements, and evaluating business performance [60–75 min]**

Marilyn Mansion owns and operates a public relations firm called Goth. The following amounts summarize her business on August 31, 2011:

	Assets				=	Liabilities	+	Owner's equity
Date	Cash	+ Accounts receivable	+ Supplies	+ Land	=	Accounts payable	+	Marilyn Mansion, Capital
Bal	2,500	1,500	0	13,000		4,000		13,000

During September 2011, the business completed the following transactions:

a. Owner invested cash of $10,000.
b. Performed service for a client and received cash of $1,100.
c. Paid off the beginning balance of accounts payable.
d. Purchased supplies from **OfficeMax** on account, $700.
e. Collected cash from a customer on account, $600.
f. Received cash of $1,700 from owner.
g. Consulted for a new band and billed the client for services rendered, $4,300.
h. Recorded the following business expenses for the month:
   1. Paid office rent, $1,000.
   2. Paid advertising, $300.
i. Returned supplies to **OfficeMax** for $100 cash, which was the cost of the supplies.
j. Owner withdrew $2,200.

Requirements

1. Analyze the effects of the preceding transactions on the accounting equation of Goth. Adapt the format to that of Exhibit 1-8.
2. Prepare the income statement of Goth for the month ended September 30, 2011.
3. Prepare the entity's statement of owner's equity for the month ended September 30, 2011.
4. Prepare the balance sheet at September 30, 2011.

P1-34A *(L. OBJ. 9, 10)* **Preparing financial statements and evaluating business performance [20–30 min]**

Presented here are the accounts of Town and Country Realty for the year ended December 31, 2011.

Land	$ 6,000		
Note payable	26,000	Accounts payable	13,000
Property tax expense	2,400	Accounts receivable	4,800
Withdrawals	26,000	Advertising expense	14,000
Rent expense	18,000	Building	133,900
Salary expense	68,000	Cash	8,000
Salary payable	1,400	Equipment	20,000
Service revenue	195,000	Insurance expense	2,300
Supplies	6,000	Interest expense	9,000
Heidi Gentry, Capital 12/31/2010	83,000		

Requirements

1. Prepare Town and Country Realty's income statement.
2. Prepare the statement of owner's equity.
3. Prepare the balance sheet.

4. Answer these questions about the company:
   a. Was the result of operations for the year a profit or a loss? How much?
   b. How much in total economic resources does the company have as it moves into the new year?
   c. How much does the company owe?
   d. What is the dollar amount of the owner's equity in the business at the end of the year?

P1-35A *(L. OBJ. 9, 10)* **Preparing financial statements and evaluating business performance [20–30 min]**

Picture Gallery works weddings and prom-type parties. The balance of capital was $18,000 at December 31, 2010. At December 31, 2011, the business's accounting records show these balances:

Insurance expense	$ 9,000	Accounts receivable	$ 11,000
Cash	15,000	Note payable	15,000
Accounts payable	9,000	Net income	?
Advertising expense	4,000	Salary expense	20,000
Service revenue	72,000	Equipment	70,000
Owner withdrawals	16,000	Owner investments	31,000

Requirements

1. Prepare the following financial statements for Picture Gallery for the year ended December 31, 2011:
   a. Income statement
   b. Statement of owner's equity
   c. Balance sheet

P1-36A *(L. OBJ. 9, 10)* **Preparing financial statements and evaluating business performance [20–30 min]**

The bookkeeper of Beautiful World Landscaping prepared the company's balance sheet while the accountant was ill. The balance sheet contains numerous errors. In particular, the bookkeeper knew that the balance sheet should balance, so he plugged in the owner's equity amount needed to achieve this balance. The owner's equity is incorrect. All other amounts are right, but some are out of place.

BEAUTIFUL WORLD LANDSCAPING Balance Sheet Month Ended August 31, 2007			
Assets		**Liabilities**	
Cash	$ 5,100	Accounts receivable	$ 2,400
Office supplies	700	Investments by Lori	8,000
Land	36,100	Service revenue	39,400
Salary expense	3,900	Property tax expense	1,700
Office furniture	5,900	Accounts payable	2,000
Note payable	23,300		
Rent expense	600	**Owner's Equity**	
		Lori Lindros, Capital	22,100
Total assets	$ 75,600	Total liabilities	$ 75,600

Requirements

1. Prepare a corrected balance sheet.
2. Consider the original balance sheet as presented and the corrected balance sheet you prepared for requirement 1. Did total assets, as presented in your

corrected balance sheet increase, decrease, or stay the same from the original balance sheet? Why?

Problems (Group B)

P1-37B *(L. OBJ. 1, 2, 3, 4, 5, 6)* **Accounting vocabulary, financial statement users, accounting profession, types of business organizations, business characteristics, and accounting concepts [15–20 min]**
Consider the following terms and definitions:

TERMS:	DEFINITIONS:
1. Proprietorship	A. One of the chief advantages of a corporation.
2. Reliability principle	B. Holds that accounting records should continue reporting the historical cost of an asset
3. Partnership	over its useful life
4. Stock	C. Stands for Financial Accounting Standards Board
5. Limited liability	D. For this entity, from a legal perspective, the business is the proprietor
6. Limited Liability Company	E. Also called the objectivity principle
7. Cost principle	F. Revenues of $80,000 and expenses of $105,000
8. FASB	G. Joins two or more individuals as co-owners
9. Net loss of $25,000	H. A corporation's unit of division of ownership
	I. Owners are referred to as members

Requirement

1. Match the terms with their correct definitions.

P1-38B *(L. OBJ. 5, 6, 9)* **Proprietorship attributes, applying the entity concept, and preparing financial statements [20–25 min]**
Beth Plum is a realtor. She organized her business as a proprietorship, Beth Plum, Realtor, by investing $23,000 cash. The business gave capital to her. Consider the following facts at November 30, 2010:

a. The business owes $61,000 on a note payable for land that the business acquired for a total price of $85,000.
b. The business spent $30,000 for a Cinko Banker real estate franchise, which entitles the business to represent itself as a Cinko Banker office. This franchise is a business asset.
c. Plum owes $50,000 on a personal mortgage for her personal residence, which she acquired in 2010 for a total price of $170,000.
d. Plum has $5,000 in her personal bank account, and the business has $10,000 in its bank account.
e. Plum owes $1,000 on a personal charge account with Chico's.
f. The office acquired business furniture for $15,000 on November 25. Of this amount, the business owes $1,000 on account at November 30.
g. Office supplies on hand at the real estate office total $500.

Requirements

1. Beth was concerned about liability exposure. Which proprietorship feature, if any, limits Beth's personal liability?
2. Prepare the balance sheet of the real estate business of Beth Plum, Realtor, at November 30, 2010.
3. Identify the personal items that would not be reported on the business records.

P1-39B *(L. OBJ. 6, 7, 8, 9, 10)* **Applying the entity concept, using the accounting equation for transaction analysis, preparing financial statements, and evaluating business performance [20–30 min]**

Arthur Shore practiced accounting with a partnership for five years. Recently he opened his own accounting firm, which he operates as a proprietorship. The name of the new entity is Arthur Shore, CPA. Shore experienced the following events during the organizing phase of the new business and its first month of operations. Some of the events were personal and did not affect the business.

Feb	4	Shore received $26,000 cash from former accounting partners.*
	5	Deposited $70,000 in a new business bank account titled Arthur Shore, CPA. The business gave capital to Shore.
	6	Paid $700 cash for letterhead stationery for the new office.
	7	Purchased office furniture for the office. The business will pay the account payable, $9,900, within 3 months.
	10	Shore sold personal investment in Amazing.com stock, which he had owned for several years, receiving $54,000 cash.*
	11	Shore deposited the $54,000 cash from sale of the Amazing.com stock in his personal bank account.*
	12	A representative of a large company telephoned Shore and told him of the company's intention to transfer its accounting business to Shore.
	18	Finished tax hearings on behalf of a client and submitted a bill for accounting services, $16,000. Shore expected to collect from this client within two weeks.
	25	Paid office rent, $1,000.
	28	Owner withdrew $1,000.

*Personal transaction of Arthur Shore.

Requirements

1. Analyze the effects of the events on the accounting equation of the corporation of Arthur Shore, CPA. Use a format similar to Exhibit 1-8.
2. As of February 28, compute the following:
   a. Total assets
   b. Total liabilities
   c. Total owner's equity
   d. Net income or net loss for February

P1-40B *(L. OBJ. 6, 7, 8, 9, 10)* **Applying the entity concept, using the accounting equation for transaction analysis, preparing financial statements, and evaluating business performance [20–30 min]**

Anna Judge practiced law with a partnership for 10 years. Recently she opened her own law office, which she operates as a proprietorship. The name of the new entity is Anna Judge, Attorney. Judge experienced the following events during the organizing phase of the new business and its first month of operation. Some of the events were personal and did not affect the law practice. Others were business transactions and should be accounted for by the business.

Jul	1	Sold personal investment in **eBay** stock, which she had owned for several years, receiving $34,000 cash.
	2	Deposited the $34,000 cash from sales of the **eBay** stock in her personal bank account.
	3	Received $133,000 cash from former law partners.
	5	Deposited $83,000 cash in a new business bank account titled Anna Judge, Attorney. The business gave capital to Judge.
	7	Paid $800 cash for ink cartirdges for the printer.
	9	Purchased a computer for the law office, agreeing to pay the account, $9,000, within 3 months.
	23	Finished court hearings on behalf of a client and submitted a bill for legal services, $13,000, on account.
	30	Paid utilities, $1,700.
	31	Owner withdrew $9,000.

Requirements

1. Analyze the effects of the preceding events on the accounting equation of the corporation of Anna Judge, Attorney. Use a format similar to Exhibit 1-8.
2. At July 31, compute the business's
   a. Total assets
   b. Total liabilities
   c. Total owner's equity
   d. Net income or net loss for the month
3. Evaluate Anna Judge's first month of operations. Were the results good or bad?

P1-41B *(L. OBJ. 7, 8,)* **Using the accounting equation for transaction analysis [20–25 min]**

Pelligrini Electronics was recently formed as a proprietorship. The balance of each item in the company's accounting equation is shown for November 1 and for each of the following business days:

	Cash	Accounts receivable	Supplies	Land	Accounts payable	Philip Johnson, Capital
Nov 1	$2,000	$7,000	$ 800	$11,000	$3,800	10,000
4	6,000	7,000	800	11,000	3,800	14,000
9	3,000	7,000	800	14,000	3,800	14,000
13	3,000	7,000	900	14,000	3,900	14,000
16	1,400	7,000	900	14,000	2,300	14,000
19	2,500	5,900	900	14,000	2,300	14,000
22	10,500	5,900	900	14,000	2,300	22,000
25	10,000	5,900	900	14,000	1,800	22,000
27	9,300	5,900	1,600	14,000	1,800	22,000
30	3,400	5,900	1,600	14,000	1,800	23,100

Requirement

1. A single transaction took place on each day. Briefly describe the transaction that most likely occurred on each day, beginning with November 4. Indicate which accounts were increased or decreased and by what amounts. Assume that no revenue or expense transactions occurred during the month.

P1-42B *(L. OBJ. 7, 8, 9, 10)* **Using the accounting equation for transaction analysis, preparing financial statements, and evaluating business performance [60–75 min]**

Marian Crone owns and operates a public relations firm called Dance Fever. The following amounts summarize her business on August 31, 2011:

	Assets							=	Liabilities	+	Equity
Date	Cash	+	Accounts receivable	+	Supplies	+	Land	=	Accounts payable	+	Marian Crone, Capital
Bal	2,400	+	1,800	+	0	+	14,000	=	3,000	+	15,200

During September 2011, the business completed the following transactions:

a. Owner invested cash of $15,000.
b. Performed service for a client and received cash of $1,200.
c. Paid off the beginning balance of accounts payable.
d. Purchased supplies from **OfficeMax** on account, $500.
e. Collected cash from a customer on account, $600.
f. Received cash of $2,000 from owner.
g. Consulted for a new band and billed the client for services rendered, $5,300.
h. Recorded the following business expenses for the month:
   1. Paid office rent, $1,100.
   2. Paid advertising, $500.
i. Returned supplies to **OfficeMax** for $90 cash, which was the cost of the supplies.
j. Owner withdrew $2,000.

Requirements

1. Analyze the effects of the preceding transactions on the accounting equation of Dance Fever. Adapt the format to that of Exhibit 1-8.
2. Prepare the income statement of Dance Fever for the month ended September 30, 2011.
3. Prepare the entity's statement of owner's equity for the month ended September 30, 2011.
4. Prepare the balance sheet at September 30, 2011.

P1-43B *(L. OBJ. 9, 10)* **Preparing financial statements and evaluating business performance [20–30 min]**
Presented here are the accounts of Plantscapes Décor Services for the year ended December 31, 2011.

Land	$ 9,000		
Note payable	32,000	Accounts payable	11,000
Property tax expense	2,500	Accounts receivable	4,000
Withdrawals	28,000	Advertising expense	19,000
Rent expense	11,000	Building	128,100
Salary expense	66,000	Cash	9,000
Salary payable	800	Equipment	18,000
Service revenue	189,000	Insurance expense	2,200
Supplies	6,000	Interest expense	6,000
Tom English, Capital 12/31/2010	76,000		

Requirements

1. Prepare Plantscapes Décor Services' income statement.
2. Prepare the statement of owner's equity.
3. Prepare the balance sheet.
4. Answer these questions about the company:
   a. Was the result of operations for the year a profit or a loss? How much?
   b. How much in total economic resources does the company have as it moves into the new year?
   c. How much does the company owe?
   d. What is the dollar amount of the owner's equity in the business at the end of the year?

P1-44B *(L. OBJ. 9, 10)* **Preparing financial statements and evaluating business performance [20–30 min]**

Accent Photography works weddings and prom-type parties. The balance of capital was $20,000 at December 31, 2010. At December 31, 2011, the business's accounting records show these balances:

Insurance expense	$ 8,000	Accounts receivable	$ 10,000
Cash	31,000	Note payable	12,000
Accounts payable	6,000	Owner's equity	?
Advertising expense	1,000	Salary expense	27,000
Service revenue	81,000	Equipment	60,000
Owner withdrawals	15,000	Owner investment	33,000

Requirement

1. Prepare the following financial statements for Accent Photography for the year ended December 31, 2011:
   a. Income statement
   b. Statement of owner's equity
   c. Balance sheet

P1-45B *(L. OBJ. 9, 10)* **Preparing financial statements and evaluating business performance [20–30 min]**

The bookkeeper of Lone Star Landscaping prepared the company's balance sheet while the accountant was ill. The balance sheet contains numerous errors. In particular, the bookkeeper knew that the balance sheet should balance, so he plugged in the owner's equity amount needed to achieve this balance. The owner's equity is incorrect. All other amounts are right, but some are out of place.

LONE STAR LANDSCAPING Balance Sheet Month Ended May 31, 2007			
Assets		**Liabilities**	
Cash	$ 5,500	Accounts receivable	$ 2,500
Office supplies	900	Capital	12,000
Land	35,300	Service revenue	39,300
Salary expense	2,700	Property tax expense	1,600
Office furniture	6,200	Accounts payable	2,300
Note payable	22,800		
Rent expense	400	**Owner's Equity**	
		Walt Temple, Capital	16,100
Total assets	$ 73,800	Total liabilities	$ 73,800

Requirements

1. Prepare a corrected balance sheet.
2. Consider the original balance sheet as presented and the corrected balance sheet you prepared for requirement 1.
3. Did total assets as presented in your corrected balance sheet increase, decrease, or stay the same from the original balance sheet? Why?

■ Continuing Exercise

Exercise 1-46 is the first exercise in a sequence that begins an accounting cycle. The cycle is continued in Chapter 2 and completed in Chapter 5.

E1-46 Sherman Lawn Service began operations and completed the following transactions during August:

Aug	1	Received $1,000 from owner, Hannah Sherman. Deposited this amount in bank account titled Sherman Lawn Service.
	3	Purchased on account a mower, $1,000, and weed whacker, $400. The equipment is expected to remain in service for four years.
	5	Purchased $20 of gas. Wrote check #1 from the new bank account.
	6	Performed lawn services for client on account, $200.
	8	Purchased $50 of fertilizer from the lawn store. Wrote check #2 from the new bank account.
	17	Completed landscaping job for client, received cash $500.
	31	Received $50 on account from Aug 6 sale.

Requirement

1. Analyze the effects of Sherman Lawn Service transactions on the accounting equation. Use the format of Exhibit 1-8, and include these headings: Cash, Accounts receivable, Lawn supplies, Equipment, Accounts payable, and Hannah Sherman, Capital.

In Chapter 2, we will account for these same transactions a different way—as the accounting is actually performed in practice.

■ Continuing Problem

Problem 1-47 is the first problem in a sequence that begins an accounting cycle. The cycle is continued in Chapter 2 and completed in Chapter 5.

P1-47 Haupt Consulting began operations and completed the following transactions during the first half of December:

Dec	2	Received $10,000 cash from owner Carl Haupt.
	2	Paid monthly office rent, $500.
	3	Paid cash for a Dell computer, $2,000. This equipment is expected to remain in service for five years.
	4	Purchased office furniture on account, $3,600. The furniture should last for five years.
	5	Purchased supplies on account, $300.
	9	Performed consulting service for a client on account, $1,700.
	12	Paid utility expenses, $200.
	18	Performed service for a client and received cash of $800.

Requirements

1. Analyze the effects of Haupt Consulting's transactions on the accounting equation. Use the format of Exhibit 1-8, and include these headings: Cash, Accounts receivable, Supplies, Equipment, Furniture, Accounts payable, and Carl Haupt, Capital.
2. Prepare the income statement of Haupt Consulting for the month ended December 31, 2010.
3. Prepare the statement of owner's equity for the month ended December 31, 2010.
4. Prepare the balance sheet at December 31, 2010.

In Chapter 2, we will account for these same transactions a different way—as the accounting is actually performed in practice.

■ Practice Set

Create an initial chart of accounts based on the following transactional data for the first month of operations of Crystal Clear Cleaning.

Apr 1: CJ Oliver deposited $20,000 in the business account. Also on this date, CJ transferred his truck title, worth $5,000, to the business. CJ received capital in return.

Apr 2: Wrote a check for $1,600 to Prestige Properties. In the "for" area of the check, it states "April thru July Rent."

Apr 3: Purchased business insurance policy for $1,200 for the term April 1, 2009, through March 31, 2010 and paid cash.

Apr 4: CJ went to the Cleaning Supply Company and purchased $220 of cleaning supplies on account. The invoice is due 20 days from the date of purchase.

Apr 5: Purchased on account an industrial vacuum cleaner from Save-Now costing $2,000. The invoice is payable on or before April 25.

Apr 7: Purchased a computer and printer costing a total of $1,500. A check for the same amount to the computer store was written on the same date.

Apr 9: Performed cleaning services on account for Bob's Burger House in the amount of $3,200.

Apr 10: Deposited Bob's check for $200 in the bank.

Apr 15: Wrote check payable to Ben Larrison for $300 for contract labor.

Apr 16: Received $1,200 for 1 year contract beginning April 1 for cleaning services to be provided to the Oar Restaurant. Contract begins April 1, 2009, and ends March 31, 2010.

Apr 17: Provided cleaning services for In Balance Solutions for $700. In Balance paid with a check.

Apr 18: Received water and electric bill for $200 with due date of May 4, 2009.

Apr 20: Borrowed $10,000 from bank with interest at rate of 8% per year.

Apr 21: Deposited check from Bob's Burger House for $1,000 paid on account.

Apr 25: Wrote check to Save Now for invoice #1035 in the amount of $1,500.

Apr 29: Wrote check payable to Pensacola News for $200 for advertising.

Apr 30: CJ Oliver withdrew $500.

Requirements

1. Create an initial list of accounts that Crystal Clear will need.
2. Prepare an analysis of the April activity using the format displayed in Exhibit 1-8 as a guide.

Apply Your Knowledge

■ Decision Cases

Case 1. This case follows up on the chapter-opening story about Sherman Lawn Service and Greg's Groovy Tunes. It is now the end of the first year of operations, and both owners—Hannah Sherman and Greg Moore—want to know how well they came out at the end of the year. Neither business kept complete accounting records (even though Greg Moore majored in accounting). Sherman and Moore throw together the following data at year end:

Sherman Lawn Service:	
Total assets	$12,000
Equity	8,000
Total revenues	35,000
Total expenses	22,000
Greg's Groovy Tunes:	
Total liabilities	$ 7,000
Equity	6,000
Total expenses	44,000
Net income	9,000

Working in the lawn-service business, Moore has forgotten all the accounting he learned in college. Sherman majored in environmental science, so she never learned any accounting. To gain information for evaluating their businesses, they ask you several questions. For each answer, you must show your work to convince Sherman and Moore that you know what you are talking about.

1. Which business has more assets?
2. Which business owes more to creditors?
3. In which business has the owner invested more?
4. Which business brought in more revenue?
5. Which business is more profitable?
6. Which of the foregoing questions do you think is most important for evaluating these two businesses? Why? (Challenge)
7. Which business looks better from a financial standpoint? (Challenge)

Case 2. Dave and Reba Guerrera saved all their married life to open a bed and breakfast (B&B) named Tres Amigos. Dave invested $100,000 of their own money and the company gave capital to Dave. The business then got a $100,000 bank loan for the $200,000 needed to get started. The company bought a run-down old Spanish colonial home in Tucson for $80,000. It cost another $50,000 to renovate. Dave and Reba found most of the furniture at antique shops and flea markets—total cost was $20,000. Kitchen equipment cost $10,000, and a **Dell** computer set cost $2,000.

Prior to the grand opening, the banker requests a report on the business's activities thus far. Tres Amigos' bank statement shows a cash balance of $38,000. Dave and Reba feel pretty good with that much net income in only six months. To better understand how well they are doing, they prepare the following income statement for presentation to the bank:

TRES AMIGOS BED AND BREAKFAST **Income Statement** Six Months Ended June 30, 2010	
Revenues:	
Investments by owner	$100,000
Bank loan	100,000
Total revenues	200,000
Expenses:	
Cost of the house	$ 80,000
Repairs to the house	50,000
Furniture expense	20,000
Kitchen equipment expense	10,000
Computer expense	2,000
Total expenses	162,000
Net income	38,000

1. Suppose you are the Guerreras' banker, and they have given you this income statement. Would you congratulate them on their net income? If so, explain why. If not, how would you advise them to measure the net income of the business? Does the amount of cash in the bank measure net income? Explain. (Challenge)
2. Prepare Tres Amigos' balance sheet from its data.

Ethical Issues

Ethical Issue 1. The board of directors of Xiaping Trading Company is meeting to discuss the past year's results before releasing financial statements to the public. The discussion includes this exchange:

Wai Lee, company president: "This has not been a good year! Revenue is down and expenses are way up. If we are not careful, we will report a loss for the third year in a row. I can temporarily transfer some land that I own into the company's name, and that will beef up our balance sheet. Brent, can you shave $500,000 from expenses? Then we can probably get the bank loan that we need."

Brent Ray, company chief accountant: "Wai Lee, you are asking too much. Generally accepted accounting principles are designed to keep this sort of thing from happening."

Requirements

1. What is the fundamental ethical issue in this situation? (Challenge)
2. Discuss how Wai Lee's proposals violate generally accepted accounting principles. Identify each specific concept or principle involved.

Ethical Issue 2. The tobacco companies have paid billions because of smoking-related illnesses. In particular, **Philip Morris**, a leading cigarette manufacturer, paid over $3 billion in one year.

Requirements

1. Suppose you are the chief financial officer (CFO) responsible for the financial statements of **Philip Morris**. What ethical issue would you face as you consider what to report in your company's annual report about the cash payments? What is the ethical course of action for you to take in this situation? (Challenge)
2. What are some of the negative consequences to **Philip Morris** for not telling the truth? What are some of the negative consequences to **Philip Morris** for telling the truth? (Challenge)

■ Financial Statement Case

This and similar cases in later chapters focus on the financial statement of a real company—**Amazon.com**, the Internet shopping leader. As you work each case, you will gain confidence in your ability to use the financial statements of real companies.

Refer to **Amazon.com's** financial statements in Appendix A at the end of the book.

Requirements

1. How much in cash (including cash equivalents) did **Amazon.com** have on December 31, 2007?
2. What were the company's total assets at December 31, 2007? At December 31, 2006?
3. Write the company's accounting equation at December 31, 2007, by filling in the dollar amounts:

ASSETS = LIABILITIES + EQUITY

4. Identify net sales (revenue) for the year ended December 31, 2007. How much did total revenue increase or decrease from 2006 to 2007?
5. How much net income or net loss did **Amazon** earn for 2007 and for 2006? Based on net income, was 2007 better or worse than 2006?

■ Team Projects

Project 1. You are opening Quail Creek Pet Kennel. Your purpose is to earn a profit, and you organize as a proprietorship.

1. Make a detailed list of 10 factors you must consider to establish the business.
2. Identify 10 or more transactions that your business will undertake to open and operate the kennel.
3. Prepare the Quail Creek Pet Kennel income statement, statement of owner's equity, and balance sheet at the end of the first month of operations before you have had time to pay all the business's bills. Use made-up figures and include a complete heading for each financial statement. Date the balance sheet as of January 31, 20XX.
4. Discuss how you will evaluate the success of your business and how you will decide whether to continue its operation.

Project 2. You are promoting a rock concert in your area. Your purpose is to earn a profit, and you organize Concert Enterprises as a proprietorship.

Requirements

1. Make a detailed list of 10 factors you must consider to establish the business.
2. Describe 10 of the items your business must arrange in order to promote and stage the rock concert.
3. Prepare your business's income statement, statement of owner's equity, and balance sheet on June 30, 20XX, immediately after the rock concert and before you have had time to pay all the business's bills and to collect all receivables. Use made-up amounts, and include a complete heading for each financial statement. For the income statement and the statement of owner's equity, assume the period is the three months ended June 30, 20XX.
4. Assume that you will continue to promote rock concerts if the venture is successful. If it is unsuccessful, you will terminate the business within three months after the concert. Discuss how you will evaluate the success of your venture and how you will decide whether to continue in business.

Quick Check Answers

For online homework, exercises, and problems that provide you immediate feedback, please visit www.myaccountinglab.com.

1. *c* 2. *a* 3. *d* 4. *c* 5. *c* 6. *b* 7. *c* 8. *b* 9. *b* 10. *c*

Chapter 1: Demo Doc

■ Transaction Analysis Using Accounting Equation/Financial Statement Preparation

To make sure you understand this material, work through the following demonstration "demo doc" with detailed comments to help you see the concept within the framework of a worked-through problem.

Learning Objectives 7, 8, and 9

On March 1, 2011, David Richardson opened a painting business near an historical housing district. David was the sole owner of the company, which he named DR Painting. During March 2011, DR Painting engaged in the following transactions:

a. **DR Painting received cash of $40,000 from David Richardson and gave capital to David.**
b. **The business paid $20,000 cash to acquire a truck.**
c. **The business purchased supplies costing $1,800 on account.**
d. **The business painted a house for a client and received $3,000 cash.**
e. **The business painted a house for a client for $4,000. The client agreed to pay next week.**
f. **The business paid $800 cash toward the supplies purchased in transaction c.**
g. **The business paid employee salaries of $1,000 in cash.**
h. **The owner withdrew $1,500.**
i. **The business collected $2,600 from the client in transaction e.**
j. **David paid $100 cash for personal groceries.**

Requirements

1. Analyze the preceding transactions in terms of their effects on the accounting equation of DR Painting. Use Exhibit 1-8 as a guide, but show balances only after the last transaction.

2. Prepare the income statement, statement of owner's equity, and balance sheet of the business after recording the transactions. Use Exhibit 1-9 in the text as a guide.

Demo Doc Solutions

Requirement 1

Analyze the preceding transactions in terms of their effects on the accounting equation of DR Painting. Use Exhibit 1-8 as a guide, but show balances only after the last transaction.

Part 1	Part 2	Part 3	Part 4	Demo Doc Complete

a. **DR Painting received $40,000 cash from David Richardson and gave capital to David.**

The business is receiving cash from an owner, so this is a recordable transaction for DR Painting.

The business's Cash (an asset) is increased by $40,000 and David Richardson, Capital (Owner's equity) is also increased by $40,000.

The effect of this transaction on the accounting equation is

	Assets	+ Liabilities	=	Owner's Equity	Type of Owner's Equity Transaction
	Cash	+	=	David Richardson, Capital	
a.	+40,000			+40,000	*Owner investment*
	40,000		=	40,000	

To record this in the table, we add $40,000 under Assets (Cash) and add $40,000 under Owner's Equity (David Richardson, Capital). To the right of the transaction, we write "Owner investment" to help us keep track of changes in the equity of the business. Before we move on, we should double-check to see that the left side of the equation equals the right side. It is important to remember that the equation must always balance after each transaction is recorded.

b. **The business paid $20,000 cash to acquire a truck.**

The Truck (an asset) is increased by $20,000, while Cash (an asset) decreases by $20,000.

The effect of this transaction on the accounting equation is

	Assets			Liabilities +	Owner's Equity	Type of Owner's Equity Transaction
	Cash	+ Truck			David Richardson, Capital	
a.	40,000		=		40,000	*Owner investment*
b.	−20,000	20,000				
Bal	20,000	+ 20,000	=		40,000	
		40,000	=	40,000		

Note that transactions do not have to affect both sides of the equation. However, the accounting equation *always* holds, so *both sides must always balance*. It helps to check that this is true after every transaction.

c. **The business purchased supplies costing $1,800 on account.**

The supplies are an asset that is increased by $1,800. However, the supplies were not paid for in cash, but instead *on account*. This relates to accounts payable (because it will have to be *paid* later). Because we now have *more* money that has to be paid later, it is an increase to Accounts payable (a liability) of $1,800.

The effect of this transaction on the accounting equation is

	ASSETS			=	LIABILITIES	+	OWNER'S EQUITY
	Cash	+ Supplies +	Truck	=	Accounts payable	+	David Richardson, Capital
Bal	20,000		20,000				40,000
c.		+1,800			+1,800		
Bal	20,000	1,800	20,000	=	1,800		40,000 Bal
			41,800	=	*41,800*		

Remember that the supplies will be recorded as an asset until the time that they are used by the business (the adjustment will be addressed in a later chapter). The obligation to pay the $1,800 will remain in Accounts payable until it is paid.

d. **The business painted a house for a client and received cash of $3,000.**

When the business paints houses, it is doing work, or performing services for clients, which is the way that the business makes money. By performing services, the business is earning service revenues (as opposed to *sales* revenues).

This means that there is an increase in Service revenue (which increases Capital) of $3,000. Because the clients paid in cash, there is also an increase in Cash (an asset) of $3,000.

Remember: Revenues *increase* net income, which increases Capital.

The effect of this transaction on the accounting equation is

	ASSETS			=	LIABILITIES	+	OWNER'S EQUITY	TYPE OF OWNER'S EQUITY TRANSACTION
	Cash	+ Supplies +	Truck	=	Accounts payable	+	David Richardson, Capital	
Bal	20,000	1,800	20,000	=	1,800		40,000	
d.	+3,000						+3,000	*Service revenue*
Bal	20,000	1,800	20,000	=	1,800		43,000	
			44,800	=	*44,800*			

Note that we write "Service revenue" to the right of the Capital column to record the type of transaction.

e. **The business painted a house for a client for $4,000. The client agreed to pay next month.**

This transaction is similar to transaction **d**, except that the business is not receiving the cash immediately. Does this mean that we should wait to record the revenue when the cash is received? No, DR Painting should recognize the revenue when the service is performed, regardless of whether it has received the cash.

Again, the business is performing services for clients, which means that it is earning service revenues. This results in an increase to Service revenue (Capital) of $4,000.

However, this time the client did not pay in cash but instead agreed to pay later. This is the same as charging the services *on account*. This is money that the business will *receive* in the future (when the customers eventually pay), so it is called accounts *receiv*able. Accounts receivable (an asset) is increasing by $4,000. Accounts receivable represents amounts owed to the business and decreases when a customer pays.

The effect of this transaction on the accounting equation is

	ASSETS				= LIABILITIES +	OWNER'S EQUITY	TYPE OF OWNER'S EQUITY TRANSACTION
	Cash	Accounts receivable	Supplies	Truck	Accounts payable	David Richardson, Capital	
Bal	23,000		1,800	20,000	1,800	43,000	
e.		+4,000				+4,000	*Service revenue*
Bal	23,000	4,000	1,800	20,000 =	1,800	47,000	
				48,800 =	48,800		

f. The business paid $800 cash toward the supplies purchased in transaction c.

Think of Accounts payable (a liability) as a list of companies to which the business will *pay* money at some point in the future. In this particular problem, the business owes money to the company from which it purchased supplies on account in transaction c. When the business *pays* the money in full, it can cross this company off of the list. Right now, the business is paying only *part* of the money owed.

This is a decrease to Accounts payable (a liability) of $800 and a decrease to Cash (an asset) of $800. Because the business is only paying part of the money it owes to the supply store, the balance of Accounts payable is $1,800 – $800 = $1,000.

You should note that this transaction does not affect Supplies because we are not buying more supplies. We are simply paying off a liability, not acquiring more assets or incurring a new expense.

The effect of this transaction on the accounting equation is

	ASSETS				= LIABILITIES +	OWNER'S EQUITY	TYPE OF OWNER'S EQUITY TRANSACTION
	Cash	Accounts receivable	Supplies	Truck	Accounts payable	David Richardson, Capital	
Bal	23,000	4,000	1,800	20,000	1,800	47,000	
f.	–800				–800		
Bal	22,200	4,000	1,800	20,000 =	1,000	47,000	
				48,000 =	48,000		

g. The business paid employee salaries of $1,000 cash.

The work the employees have given to the business has *already been used*. By the end of March, DR Painting has had the employees working and painting for customers for the entire month. This means that the *benefit* of the work has already been received. This means that it is a salary *expense*. So, Salary expense would increase by $1,000, which is a decrease to owner's equity.

Remember: Expenses *decrease* net income, which decreases Capital.

The salaries were paid in cash, so Cash (an asset) is also decreased by $1,000.

The effect of this transaction on the accounting equation is

	ASSETS				= LIABILITIES +	OWNER'S EQUITY	TYPE OF OWNER'S EQUITY TRANSACTION
	Cash	Accounts receivable	Office supplies	Truck	Accounts payable	David Richardson, Capital	
Bal	22,200	4,000	1,800	20,000	1,000		
g.	−1,000					−1,000	*Salary expense*
Bal	21,200	4,000	1,800	20,000 =	1,000	46,000	
				47,000 =	47,000		

h. The owner withdrew $1,500.

When the business pays cash, it is a recordable transaction. In this case, there is a decrease of $1,500 to Cash (an asset). David is an owner and is being given some of his value/ownership in cash. In other words, some of the *earnings* that were *retained* by the company are now being distributed to the owner. This results in a decrease of $1,500 to owner's equity, because Capital is decreasing.

You should note that *withdrawals are not an expense* because the cash is not used for operations. The cash withdrawn is for the owner's personal use rather than to earn revenue for the business.

The effect of this transaction on the accounting equation is

	ASSETS				= LIABILITIES +	OWNER'S EQUITY	TYPE OF OWNER'S EQUITY TRANSACTION
	Cash	Accounts receivable	Office supplies	Truck	Accounts payable	David Richardson, Capital	
Bal	21,200	4,000	1,800	20,000	1,000	46,000	
h.	−1,500					−1,500	*Owner withdrawal*
Bal	19,700	4,000	1,800	20,000 =	1,000	44,500	
				45,500 =	45,500		

i. The business collected $2,600 from the client in transaction e.

Think of Accounts receivable (an asset) as a list of clients from whom the business will *receive* money at some point in the future. Later, when the business collects (*receives*) the cash in full from any particular customer, it can cross that customer off the list.

In transaction e, DR Painting performed services for a client on account. Now, DR is receiving part of that money. This is a collection that decreases Accounts receivable (an asset) by $2,600.

Because the cash is received, this is an increase to Cash (an asset) of $2,600.

The effect of this transaction on the accounting equation is

	ASSETS				= LIABILITIES +	OWNER'S EQUITY	TYPE OF OWNER'S EQUITY TRANSACTION
	Cash	Accounts receivable	Office supplies	Truck	Accounts payable	David Richardson, Capital	
Bal	19,700	4,000	1,800	20,000	1,000	44,500	
i.	2,600	−2,600					
Bal	22,300	1,400	1,800	20,000 =	1,000	44,500	
				45,500 =	45,500		

j. David paid $100 cash for personal groceries.

David is using $100 of *his own cash* for groceries. This is a *personal* expense for David's *personal* use that does not relate to the business and therefore is not a recordable transaction for the business. This transaction has no effect on the business's accounting equation. Had David used the *business's* cash to purchase groceries, *then* the business would record the transaction.

	ASSETS				= LIABILITIES +	OWNER'S EQUITY
	Cash	+ Accounts receivable	+ Supplies +	Truck	= Accounts payable +	David Richardson, Capital
a.	+$40,000					+$40,000
b.	−$20,000			+$20,000		
c.			+$1,800		+$1,800	
d.	+$3,000					+$3,000
e.		+$4,000				+4,000
f.	−$800				−$800	
g.	−$1,000					−$1,000
h.	−$1,500					−$1,500
i.	+$2,600	−$2,600				
j.	Not a transaction of business					
Bal	$22,300	$1,400	$1,800	$20,000 =	$1,000	$44,500
				$45,500 =	$45,500	

Requirement 2

Prepare the income statement, statement of owner's equity, and balance sheet of the business after recording the transactions. Use Exhibit 1-9 in the text as a guide.

Part 1	**Part 2**	Part 3	Part 4	Demo Doc Complete

Income Statement

The income statement is the first statement that can be prepared because the other financial statements rely upon the net income number calculated on the income statement.

The income statement reports the profitability of the business. To prepare an income statement, begin with the proper heading. A proper heading includes the name of the company (DR Painting), the name of the statement (Income Statement), and the time period covered (Month Ended March 31, 2011). Notice that we are reporting income for a period of time, rather than a single date.

The income statement lists all revenues and expenses. It uses the following formula to calculate net income:

Revenues – Expenses = Net Income

First, you should list revenues. Second, list the expenses. Having trouble finding the revenues and expenses? Look in the equity column of the accounting equation. After you have listed and totaled the revenues and expenses, you subtract the total expenses from total revenues to determine net income or net loss. If you have a positive number, then you will record net income. A negative number indicates that expenses exceeded revenues, and you will record this as a net loss.

In the case of DR Painting, transactions **d** and **e** increased Service revenue (by \$3,000 and \$4,000, respectively). This means that total Service revenue for the month was \$3,000 + \$4,000 = \$7,000.

The only expenses that were incurred were in transaction **g**, which resulted in a Salary expense of \$1,000. On the income statement, these would be recorded as follows:

DR PAINTING Income Statement Month Ended March 31, 2011		
Revenue:		
Service revenue		\$7,000
Expenses:		
Salary expense	\$1,000	
Total expenses		1,000
Net income		\$6,000

Note the result is a net income of \$6,000 (\$7,000 – \$1,000 = \$6,000). You will use this amount on the statement of owner's equity.

Part 1	Part 2	**Part 3**	Part 4	Demo Doc Complete

Statement of Owner's Equity

The statement of owner's equity shows the changes in capital for a period of time. To prepare a statement of owner's equity, begin with the proper heading. A proper heading includes the name of the company (DR Painting), the name of the statement (Statement of Owner's Equity), and the time period covered (Month Ended March 31, 2011). As with the income statement, we are reporting Owner's Equity for a period of time, rather than a single date.

Net income is used on the statement of owner's equity to calculate the new balance in owner's equity. This calculation uses the following formula:

Beginning Capital
+ Net Income (or – Net Loss)
– Withdrawals
Ending Capital

Start the body of the statement of owner's equity with the capital at the beginning of the period (March 1). Then, list net income. You should notice that the amount of net income comes directly from the income statement. Following net income you will list the withdrawals paid, which reduces capital. Finally, total all amounts and compute the capital at the end of the period.

In this case, because this is a new company, the beginning capital is zero. Owner investments made during the month of $40,000 are added. Net income as reported on the income statement ($6,000) is added. In transaction **h**, the owner withdrew $1,500. These withdrawals are deducted. The statement of owner's equity follows:

DR PAINTING Statement of Owner's Equity Month Ended March 31, 2011	
David Richardson, Capital, March 1, 2011	$ 0
Add: Investments by owner	40,000
Net income for the month	6,000
Less: Withdrawals	(1,500)
David Richardson, Capital, March 31, 2011	$ 44,500

Note the result is a balance of $44,500 ($40,000 + $6,000 – $1,500 = $44,500) for Ending Capital. You will use this amount on the balance sheet.

Part 1	Part 2	Part 3	**Part 4**	Demo Doc Complete

Balance Sheet

The balance sheet reports the financial position of the business. To prepare a balance sheet, begin with the proper heading. A proper heading includes the name of the company (DR Painting), the name of the statement (Balance Sheet), and the time period covered (March 31, 2011). Unlike the income statement and statement of owner's equity, we are reporting the financial position of the company for a specific date rather than a period of time.

The balance sheet is a listing of all assets, liabilities, and equity, with the accounting equation verified at the bottom.

To prepare the body of the statement, begin by listing assets. Then you will record liabilities and owner's equity. Notice that the balance sheet is organized in the same order as the accounting equation. You should note that the amount of Capital comes directly from the ending Capital on your statement of owner's equity. You should then total both sides to make sure that they are equal. If they are not equal, then you will need to look for an error.

In this case, assets include the cash balance of $22,300, accounts receivable of $1,400, $1,800 worth of supplies, and the truck's value of $20,000, for a total of $45,500 in assets. Liabilities total $1,000, the balance of the Accounts payable account. The figures for assets and liabilities come directly from the accounting equation work sheet. From the statement of owner's equity, we have ending Capital of $44,500. This gives us a total for liabilities and equity of $1,000 + $44,500 = $45,500, confirming that assets = liabilities + equity.

DR PAINTING
Balance Sheet
March 31, 2011

Assets		**Liabilities**	
Cash	$22,300	Accounts payable	$ 1,000
Accounts receivable	1,400		
Supplies	1,800	**Owner's Equity**	
Truck	20,000	David Richardson, Capital	44,500
		Total liabilities and	
Total assets	$45,500	owner's equity	$45,500

Part 1	Part 2	Part 3	Part 4	**Demo Doc Complete**

2 Recording Business Transactions

Learning Objectives/ Success Keys

1. Explain accounts, journals, and ledgers as they relate to recording transactions and describe common accounts
2. Define debits, credits, and normal account balances. Use double entry accounting and T-accounts
3. List the steps of the transaction recording process
4. Journalize and post sample transactions to the ledger
5. Prepare the trial balance from the T-accounts

Sherman Lawn Service and Greg's Groovy Tunes are now up and running. Both businesses are buying supplies, earning revenues, collecting cash, and paying expenses. The owners, Hannah Sherman and Greg Moore, naturally want to know how they are doing.

In Chapter 1 Sherman and Moore learned about the income statement and the balance sheet—two financial statements that help them measure progress. Sherman and Moore also learned to record transactions in terms of the accounting equation. That procedure works well for a handful of transactions. But even small businesses, such as Sherman Lawn Service or Greg's Groovy Tunes, would need a huge Excel spreadsheet to record all their transactions with the accounting equation. Fortunately, there is a better way.

In this chapter we show how accounting is actually done in business. This may be the most important chapter of the whole book. After you master this material, you will have a foundation for learning accounting.

The following diagram summarizes the accounting process covered in this chapter.

The Account, the Journal, and the Ledger

1 Explain accounts, journals, and ledgers as they relate to recording transactions and describe common accounts

The basic summary device of accounting is the account. An **account** is the detailed record of all the changes that have occurred in a particular asset, liability, or owner's equity during a specified period. As we saw in Chapter 1, business transactions cause the changes.

Accountants record transactions first in a **journal**, which is the chronological record of transactions. Accountants then copy (post) the data to the book of accounts called the **ledger**. A list of all the ledger accounts and their balances is called a **trial balance**.

Take a moment to memorize these important terms. You will be using them over and over again.

- **Account**—the detailed record of the changes in a particular asset, liability, or owner's equity
- **Ledger**—the book holding all the accounts
- **Journal**—the chronological record of transactions
- **Trial balance**—the list of all the accounts with their balances

Accounts are grouped in three broad categories, according to the accounting equation:

Assets = Liabilities + Owner's equity

Assets

Assets are economic resources that will benefit the business in the future, or simply, something the business owns that has value. Most firms use the following asset accounts:

Cash

The Cash account is a record of the cash effects of transactions. Cash includes money, such as a bank balance, paper currency, coins, and checks. Cash is the most pressing need of start-up businesses, such as Sherman Lawn Service and Greg's Groovy Tunes.

Accounts Receivable

Most businesses sell goods or services in exchange for a promise of future cash receipts. Such sales are made on credit ("on account"), and Accounts receivable is the account that holds these amounts. Most sales in the United States and in other developed countries are made on account.

Notes Receivable

A business may sell goods or services and receive a **note receivable** or *promissory note.* A note receivable is a written pledge that the customer will pay a fixed amount of money by a certain date.

Prepaid Expenses

A business often pays certain expenses, such as rent and insurance, in advance. A **prepaid expense** is an asset because the prepayment provides a future benefit. Prepaid rent, Prepaid insurance, and Office supplies are separate prepaid expense accounts. Your college tuition is an asset to you.

Land

The Land account shows the cost of land a business holds for use in operations. Land held for sale is different. Its cost is an investment.

Building

The cost of buildings—an office or a warehouse—appears in the Buildings account. **Frito-Lay** and **The Coca-Cola Company** own buildings around the world, where they make chips and drinks.

Equipment, Furniture, and Fixtures

A business has a separate asset account for each type of equipment—Computer equipment, Office equipment, and Store equipment, for example. The Furniture account shows the cost of this asset. Similarly, the Fixtures account shows the cost of light fixtures and shelving, for example.

Liabilities

Recall that a *liability* is a debt, that is, something you owe. A business generally has fewer liability accounts than asset accounts.

Accounts Payable

Accounts payable is the opposite of Accounts receivable. The promise to pay a debt arising from a credit purchase is an Account payable. Such a purchase is said to be made on account. All companies from Greg's Groovy Tunes to **Coca-Cola** to **eBay**, have Accounts payable.

Notes Payable

Notes payable is the opposite of Notes receivable. Notes payable represents debts the business owes because it signed promissory notes to borrow money or to purchase something.

Accrued Liabilities

An **accrued liability** is a liability for which the business knows the amount owed, but the bill has not been paid. Taxes payable, Interest payable, and Salary payable are accrued liability accounts.

Owner's Equity

The owners' claim to the assets of the business is called *owner's equity*. A company has separate accounts for the various elements of owner's equity.

Capital

The capital account represents the net investment of the owner in the business. It holds the accumulation of owner investment, withdrawals, and net income (loss) of the business over the life of the business. In other words, capital is the net worth invested in the business by an owner.

Withdrawals

The owner may withdraw cash or other assets at any time from the company. This represents a return of his or her capital investment, as well as a distribution of earnings from the company.

Revenues

The increase in equity created by delivering goods or services to customers is called *revenue*. The ledger contains as many revenue accounts as needed. Smart Touch Learning, for example, needs a Service revenue account for amounts earned by providing e-learning services. If Smart Touch lends money to an outsider, it needs an Interest revenue account for the interest earned on the loan. If the business rents out a building to a tenant, it needs a Rent revenue account.

Expenses

Expenses use up assets or create liabilities in the course of operating a business. Expenses have the opposite effect of revenues. Expenses *decrease* equity. A business needs a separate account for each type of expense, such as Salary expense, Rent expense, Advertising expense, and Utilities expense. Businesses strive to minimize their expenses in order to maximize net income—whether that business is **General Electric**, Smart Touch Learning, or Sherman Lawn Service.

Exhibit 2-1 shows how asset, liability, and owner's equity accounts can be grouped in the ledger.

Chart of Accounts

The ledger contains the accounts grouped under these headings:

- Assets, Liabilities, and Owner's Equity
- Revenues and Expenses

Companies use a **chart of accounts** to list all their accounts along with the account numbers. Account numbers are just shorthand versions of the account names. One number equals one account name—just like your social security number is unique to you.

EXHIBIT 2-1 **The Ledger—Asset, Liability, and Owner's Equity Accounts**

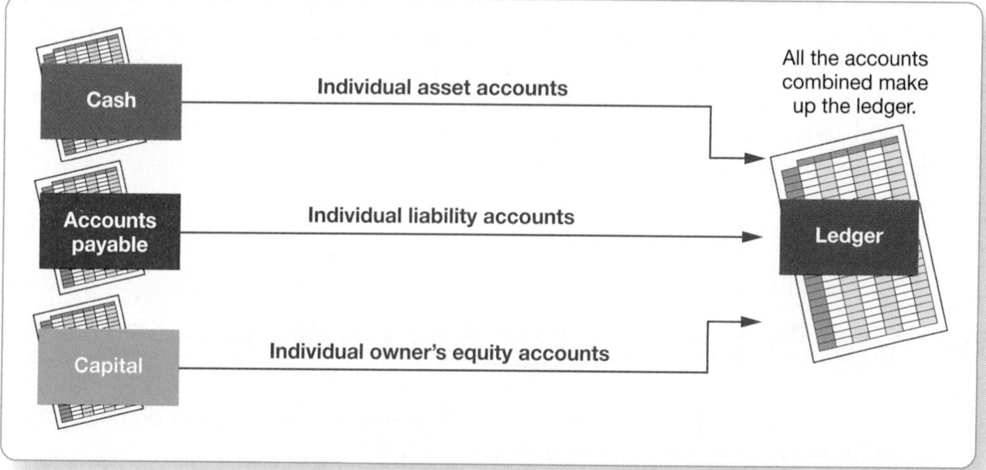

Account numbers usually have two or more digits. Assets are often numbered beginning with 1, liabilities with 2, owner's equity with 3, revenues with 4, and expenses with 5. The second and third digits in an account number indicate where the account fits within the category. For example, if Sheena Bright is using three digit account numbers, cash may be account number 101, the first asset account. Accounts receivable may be account number 111, the second asset. Accounts payable may be number 201, the first liability. When numbers are used, all accounts are numbered by this system. However, each company chooses its own account numbering system.

The chart of accounts for Smart Touch Learning appears in Exhibit 2-2. Notice the gap in account numbers between 121 and 141. Bright may need to add another asset account in the future. For example, she may start selling some type of inventory and want to use account number 131 for Inventory.

EXHIBIT 2-2 **Chart of Accounts—Smart Touch Learning**

Balance Sheet Accounts

Assets	Liabilities	Owner's Equity
101 Cash	201 Accounts payable	301 Sheena Bright, Capital
111 Accounts receivable	211 Salary payable	311 Sheena Bright, Withdrawals
121 Notes receivable	221 Interest payable	
141 Supplies	231 Notes payable	
151 Furniture		
171 Building		
191 Land		

Income Statement Accounts
(Part of Owner's Equity)

Revenues	Expenses
401 Service revenue	501 Rent expense, Computer
411 Interest revenue	502 Rent expense, Office
	505 Salary expense
	510 Depreciation expense
	520 Utilities expense
	530 Advertising expense
	540 Supplies expense

The back inside covers of this book give expanded, unnumbered charts of accounts that we hope you will find helpful throughout this course. The first chart lists the typical accounts of a *service* business, such as Smart Touch Learning. The second chart is for a *merchandising* business, which sells a product rather than a service. The third chart lists the accounts for a *manufacturing* company. You will use the manufacturing accounts in Chapters 15–23. Study the proprietorships now, and refer to the other charts of accounts as needed later. This will help you to learn the names of commonly used accounts.

Debits, Credits, and Double-Entry Accounting

2 Define debits, credits, and normal account balances. Use double entry accounting and T-accounts

As we saw in Chapter 1, accounting is based on transaction data, not on mere whim or opinion. Each business transaction has dual effects:

- The receiving side
- The giving side

For example, in the $30,000 cash receipt by Smart Touch Learning in Chapter 1, the business:

- Received cash of $30,000
- Gave $30,000 of capital

Accounting uses the double-entry system, which means that we record the dual effects of each transaction. As a result, every transaction affects at least two accounts. It would be incomplete to record only the giving side, or only the receiving side, of a transaction.

Consider a cash purchase of supplies. What are the dual effects? A cash purchase of supplies:

1. Increases supplies (you received supplies)
2. Decreases cash (you gave cash)

Similarly, a credit purchase of equipment (a purchase on account):

1. Increases equipment (you received equipment)
2. Increases accounts payable (you gave your promise to pay in the future)

The T-Account

The most widely used form of account is called the **T-account** because it takes the form of the capital letter *T*. The vertical line divides the account into its left and right sides, with the title at the top. For example, the Cash account appears as follows.

Cash	
(Left side) Debit	(Right side) Credit

The left side of the account is called the **Debit** side, and the right side is called the **Credit** side. To become comfortable using these terms, remember that:

Debit = Left	Credit = Right

The terms *debit* and *credit* are deeply entrenched in business.[1] They are abbreviated as follows:

DR = Debit	CR = Credit

Increases and Decreases in the Accounts

The account category (asset, liability, equity) governs how we record increases and decreases. For any given account, increases are recorded on one side, and decreases are recorded on the opposite side. The following T-accounts provide a summary:

Assets	
Increase = Debit	Decrease = Credit

Liabilities and Owner's Equity	
Decrease = Debit	Increase = Credit

These are the *rules of debit and credit*. In your study of accounting, forget the bank's usage of credit and debit because the bank is talking about its books. We will focus on how accounting uses these terms.

Whether an account is increased or decreased by a debit or a credit depends on the type of account. Debits are not "good" or "bad." Neither are credits. Debits are not always increases or decreases—neither are credits.

In a computerized accounting system, the computer interprets debits and credits as increases or decreases, based on the account type. For example, a computer reads a debit to Cash as an increase, because it is an asset account. The computer reads a debit to Accounts payable as a decrease, because it is a liability account.

Exhibit 2-3 shows the relationship between the accounting equation and the rules of debit and credit.

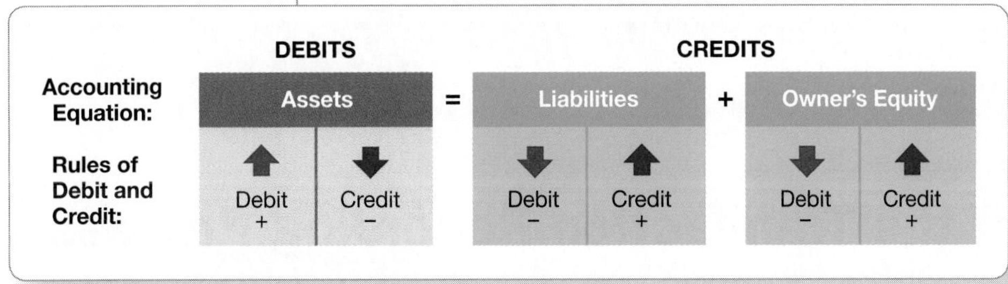

To illustrate the ideas diagrammed in Exhibit 2-3, let us look at the first transaction from Chapter 1 again. Smart Touch Learning received $30,000 cash and gave capital to Sheena Bright. Which accounts of the business are affected?

The answer: The business's assets and equity would increase by $30,000, as the T-accounts show.

ASSETS	=	LIABILITIES	+	OWNER'S EQUITY

Cash	
Debit for increase, 30,000	

Sheena Bright, Capital	
	Credit for increase, 30,000

[1]The words *debit;* and *credit* abbreviate the Latin terms *debitum* and *creditum*. Luca Pacioli, the Italian monk who wrote about accounting in the fifteenth century, popularized these terms.

The amount remaining in an account is called its *balance*. The first transaction gives Cash a $30,000 debit balance and Sheena Bright, Capital a $30,000 credit balance.

The second transaction is a $20,000 purchase of land. Exhibit 2-4 illustrates the accounting equation after Smart Touch Learning's first two transactions. After transaction 2, Cash has a $10,000 debit balance, Land has a debit balance of $20,000, and Capital has a $30,000 credit balance.

We create accounts as needed. The process of creating a new account is called *opening the account*. For transaction 1, we opened the Cash account and the Capital account. For transaction 2, we opened the Land account.

EXHIBIT 2-4 **The Accounting Equation after the First Two Transactions of Smart Touch Learning**

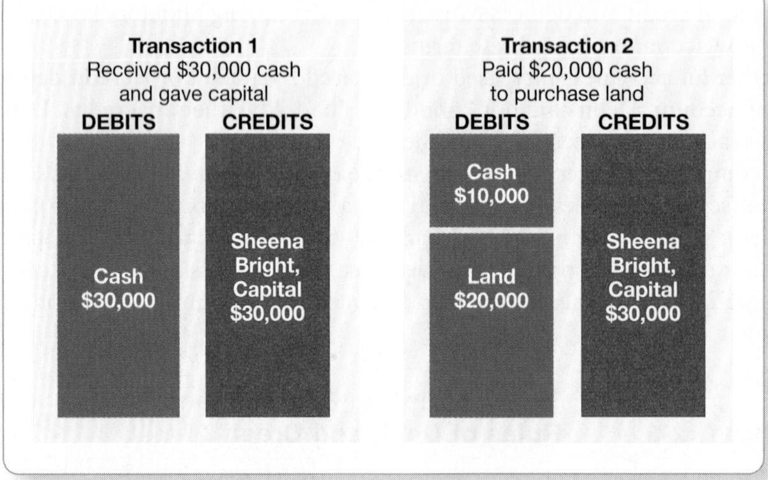

List the Steps of the Transaction Recording Process

3 List the steps of the transaction recording process

In practice, accountants record transactions in a *journal*. The journalizing process has three steps:

1. Identify each account affected and its type (asset, liability, or owner's equity).
2. Determine whether each account is increased or decreased. Use the rules of debit and credit.
3. Record the transaction in the journal, including a brief explanation. The debit side of the entry is entered first. Total debits should always equal total credits. This step is also called "making the journal entry" or "journalizing the transaction."

These steps are the same whether done by computer or manually.

Let us journalize the first transaction of Smart Touch Learning—the receipt of $30,000 cash and investment of capital.

STEP 1: The accounts affected by the receipt of cash and issuance of stock are *Cash* and *Sheena Bright, Capital*. Cash is Capital.

STEP 2: Both accounts increase by $30,000. Assets increase with debits. Therefore, we debit Cash because it is an asset. Equity increases in the business because of the owner investment. To increase equity, we credit. Therefore, we credit Capital.

STEP 3: The journal entry is

Journal Page 1

Date	Accounts and Explanation	Debit	Credit
Apr 1[a]	Cash[b] (A+)	30,000[b]	
	Sheena Bright, Capital[c] (Q+)		30,000[c]
	Owner investment.[d]		

Footnotes a, b, c, and d are explained as follows. The journal entry includes four parts:

a. Date of the transaction

b. Title of the account debited, along with the dollar amount

c. Title of the account credited, along with the dollar amount

d. Brief explanation of the transaction

Dollar signs are omitted because it is understood that the amounts are in dollars.

The journal entry presents the full story for each transaction. To help reinforce your learning of the account types and how they increase or decrease, we will indicate after each account in the journal what type of account it is and whether it is increasing or decreasing. For example, Assets increasing will be shown as (A+), Capital (Equity) increasing will be shown as (Q+), and so on. Exhibit 2-5 shows how Journal Page 1 looks after the business has recorded the first transaction.

EXHIBIT 2-5 | The Journal Page

Journal Page 1

Date	Accounts and Explanation	Debit	Credit
Apr 1	Cash (A+)	30,000	
	Sheena Bright, Capital (Q+)		30,000
	Owner investment.		

Posting (Copying Information) from the Journal to the Ledger

Journalizing a transaction records the data only in the journal—but not in the ledger. The data must also be copied to the ledger. The process of copying from the journal to the ledger is called **posting**. We *post* from the journal to the ledger.

Debits in the journal are posted as debits in the ledger and credits as credits—no exceptions. The first transaction of Smart Touch Learning is posted to the ledger in Exhibit 2-6.

EXHIBIT 2-6 **Making a Journal Entry and Posting to the Ledger**

Journal Entry:

		Accounts and Explanation	Debit	Credit
	Apr 1	Cash (A+)	30,000	

Expanding the Rules of Debit and Credit: Revenues and Expenses

As we have noted, *revenues* are increases in equity that result from providing goods or services for customers. *Expenses* are decreases in equity that result from using up assets or increasing liabilities in the course of operations. Therefore, we must expand the accounting equation. There are several elements of owner's equity.

Exhibit 2-7 shows revenues and expenses under owner's equity because they directly affect equity.

EXHIBIT 2-7 **The Accounting Equation Includes Revenues and Expenses**

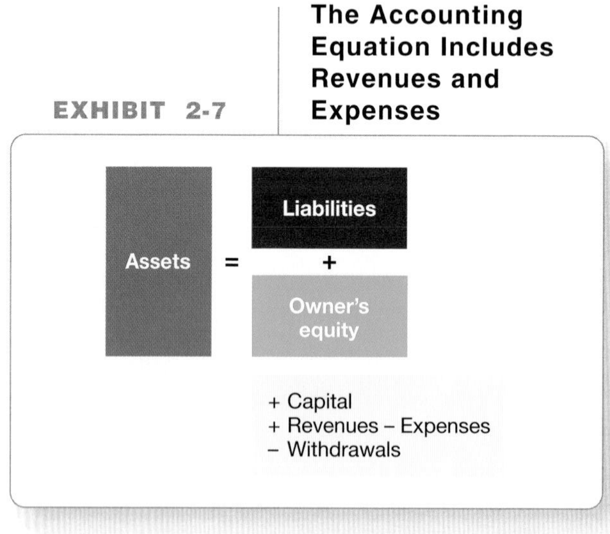

We can now express the rules of debit and credit in final form as shown in Exhibit 2-8. Note that the accounting equation now includes revenues and expenses.

EXHIBIT 2-8 **Final Rules of Debit and Credit**

Assets		=	Liabilities		+	Owner's equity										
Assets		=	Liabilities		+	Capital		+	Revenues		−	Expenses		−	Withdrawals	
DR	CR		DR	CR		DR	CR		DR	CR		DR	CR		DR	CR
+	−		−	+		−	+		−	+		+	−		+	−

The Normal Balance of An Account

An account's **normal balance** appears on the side—debit or credit—where we record an *increase*. For example, assets normally have a debit balance, so assets are *debit-balance accounts*. Liabilities and equity accounts normally have the opposite balance, so they are *credit-balance accounts*. Expenses and Withdrawals are equity accounts that have debit balances—unlike the other equity accounts. They have debit balances because they decrease equity. Revenues increase equity, so a revenue's normal balance is a credit.

As we have seen, Owner's equity includes:

Capital—a credit-balance account

Withdrawals—a debit-balance account

A debit account may occasionally have a credit balance. That indicates a negative amount of the item. For example, Cash will have a credit balance if the business overdraws its bank account. Also, the liability Accounts payable—a credit balance account—will have a debit balance if the entity overpays its account. In other cases, an odd balance indicates an error. For example, a credit balance in Office supplies, Furniture, or Buildings is an error because negative amounts of these assets make no sense.

Stop & Think...

The terms debit and credit really just mean left and right. A way to remember what normal account balance a particular account has is to associate the accounts with the accounting equation. Assets are on the LEFT so they have a normal Debit balance. Liabilities are on the RIGHT so they have a normal Credit balance, and so on. So think of debit as left and credit as right when remembering normal balance of accounts.

Now let us put your new learning into practice. Let us account for the early transactions of Smart Touch Learning.

Exhibit 2-9 summarizes the flow of data through the accounting system. In the pages that follow, we record Smart Touch Learning's early transactions. Keep in mind that we are accounting for the e-learning business. We are *not* accounting for Sheena Bright's personal transactions because of the entity concept we learned in Chapter 1.

EXHIBIT 2-9 **Flow of Accounting Data from the Journal to the Ledger**

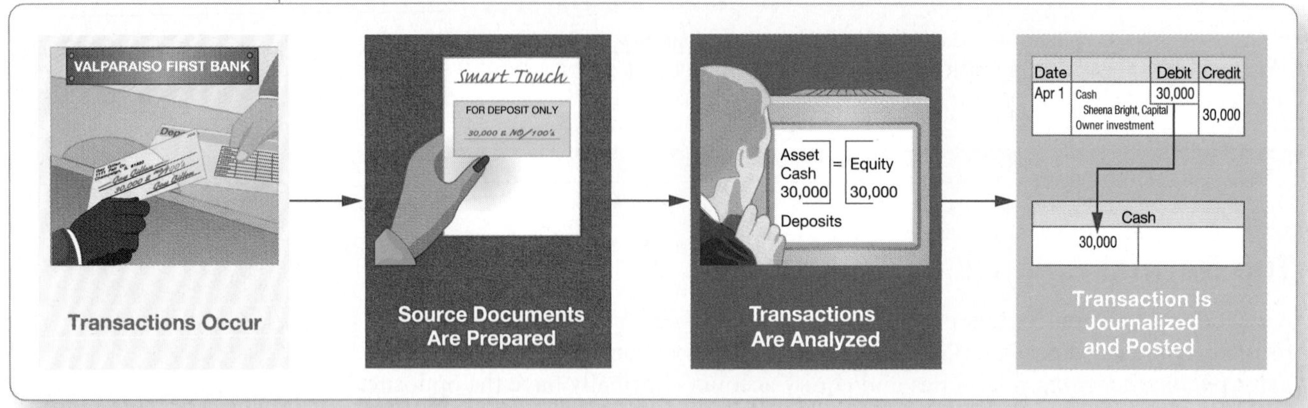

Source Documents—The Origin of the Steps

Accounting data come from source documents, as shown in the second segment of Exhibit 2-9. In that exhibit, Smart Touch Learning received $30,000 and gave capital to Sheena Bright. The *bank deposit ticket* is the document that shows the amount of cash received by the business. Based on these documents, Bright can see how to record this transaction in the journal.

When the business buys supplies on account, the vendor sends Smart Touch an invoice requesting payment. The *purchase invoice* is the source document that tells the business to pay the vendor. The invoice shows what Smart Touch purchased and how much it cost—telling the business how to record the transaction.

Smart Touch may pay the account payable with a *bank check*, another source document. The check and the purchase invoice give the business the information it needs to record the cash payment accurately.

When Smart Touch provides education services for a client, the business faxes a sales invoice to the client. Smart Touch's *sales invoice* is the source document that tells the business how much revenue to record.

There are many different types of source documents in business. In the transactions that follow, we illustrate some of the more common types of documents that Smart Touch Learning uses in its business.

Journalizing Transactions and Posting to the Ledger

Practice Journalizing with Specific Examples

4 Journalize and post sample transactions to the ledger

Transaction 1

Smart Touch Learning received $30,000 cash on April 1 from Sheena Bright and gave her capital in the business. The business deposited the money in its bank account, as proved by the following deposit ticket:

DEPOSIT TICKET

Smart Touch Learning
281 Wave Ave
Niceville, FL 32578

DATE April 1, 2010

VALPARAISO FIRST BANK
John Sims Pkwy
Valparaiso, FL

1:1 2 2000661:1400"03857

CASH	CURRENCY		
	COIN		
LIST CHECKS SEPARATELY		30,000	00
TOTAL FROM OTHER SIDE			
TOTAL		30,000	00
LESS CASH RECEIVED			
NET DEPOSIT		30,000	00

The business increased cash, which is an asset, so we debit Cash. The business also increased owner's equity, so we credit Sheena Bright, Capital.

Journal Entry

Date	Accounts and Explanation	Debit	Credit
Apr 1	Cash (A+)	30,000	
	Sheena Bright, Capital (Q+)		30,000
	Owner investment.		

Ledger Accounts

Cash			
Apr 1	30,000		

Sheena Bright, Capital			
		Apr 1	30,000

Transaction 2

On April 2, Smart Touch paid $20,000 cash for land. The purchase decreased cash. Therefore, we credit Cash. The asset, land, increased, so we debit the Land account.

Journal Entry

Date	Accounts and Explanation	Debit	Credit
Apr 2	Land (A+)	20,000	
	Cash (A–)		20,000
	Paid cash for land.		

Ledger Accounts

Cash			
Apr 1	30,000	Apr 2	20,000

Land			
Apr 2	20,000		

Transaction 3

Smart Touch purchased $500 of office supplies on account on April 3, as shown on this purchase invoice.

INVOICE (purchase)

WHOLESALE OFFICE SUPPLY
500 HENDERSON ROAD
DESTIN, FL 32540

Date: April 3, 2010
Terms: 30 days
Sold to: **Smart Touch Learning**
281 Wave Ave
Niceville, FL 32578

Quantity	Item	Price	Total
38	Laser paper	$10	$380.00
8	Desk calendars	15	120.00
	Total amount due:		**$500.00**

The supplies will benefit Smart Touch in future periods, so they are an asset to the company until they are used. (We will talk about accounting for using the supplies in Chapter 3.)

The asset office supplies increased, so we debit Office supplies. The liability accounts payable increased, so we credit Accounts payable.

Journal Entry

Date	Accounts and Explanation	Debit	Credit
Apr 3	Office supplies (A+)	500	
	Accounts payable (L+)		500
	Purchased supplies on account.		

Ledger Accounts

Office supplies		Accounts payable	
Apr 3 500			Apr 3 500

Transaction 4

On April 8, Smart Touch collected cash of $5,500 for service revenue that the business earned by providing e-learning services for clients. The source document is Smart Touch's sales invoice on the following page.

INVOICE (sale)

Smart Touch Learning
281 Wave Ave.
Niceville, FL 32578

Date: April 8, 2010
Sold to: **Allied Energy**
325 Brooks Street

Invoice No: **15**
Service: 1000 DVD0503

PAID

Total amount due: $5,500

All accounts are due and payable within 30 days.

The asset cash increased, so we debit Cash. Revenue increased, so we credit Service revenue.

Journal Entry

Date	Accounts and Explanation	Debit	Credit
Apr 8	Cash (A+)	5,500	
	Service revenue (R+)		5,500
	Performed service and received cash.		

Ledger Accounts

Cash

Debit		Credit	
Apr 1	30,000	Apr 2	20,000
Apr 8	5,500		

Service revenue

Debit		Credit	
		Apr 8	5,500

In Chapter 1 we listed service revenue and expenses under Capital. Here we record the revenues and the expenses directly in their own accounts. There is no contradiction because revenues and expenses affect Capital, as we will see in Chapter 4.

Transaction 5

On April 10, Smart Touch performed service for clients and let them pay later. The business earned $3,000 of service revenue on account.

This transaction increased Accounts receivable, so we debit this asset. Service revenue is increased with a credit.

Journal Entry

Date	Accounts and Explanation	Debit	Credit
Apr 10	Accounts receivable (A+)	3,000	
	Service revenue (R+)		3,000
	Performed service on account.		

Ledger Accounts

Accounts receivable

Debit		Credit	
Apr 10	3,000		

Service revenue

Debit		Credit	
		Apr 8	5,500
		Apr 10	3,000

Notice the differences and the similarities between transactions 4 and 5. In both transactions, Service revenue was increased because in both cases the company had earned revenue. However, in transaction 4, the company was paid at the time of service. In transaction 5, on the other hand, the company will receive cash later (Accounts receivable). This is key, because the amount of earnings is not determined by when the company receives cash. Earnings (Revenue) are recorded when the company does work, or earns revenue.

Transaction 6

Smart Touch paid the following cash expenses on April 15: Rent expense on a computer, $600; Office rent, $1,000; Salary expense, $1,200; Utilities expense, $400. We need to debit each expense account to record its increase and credit Cash for the total decrease.

Journal Entry

	Date	Accounts	Debit	Credit
	Apr 15	Rent expense, computer (E+)	600	
		Rent expense, office (E+)	1,000	
		Salary expense (E+)	1,200	
		Utilities expense (E+)	400	
		Cash (A–)		3,200
		Paid cash expenses.		

Note: In practice, the business would record these expenses in four separate journal entries. Here we show them together to illustrate a **compound journal entry**.

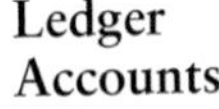

Ledger Accounts

Cash

	Debit		Credit
Apr 1	30,000	Apr 2	20,000
Apr 8	5,500	Apr 15	3,200

Rent expense, computer

	Debit		Credit
Apr 15	600		

Rent expense, office

	Debit		Credit
Apr 15	1,000		

Salary expense

	Debit		Credit
Apr 15	1,200		

Utilities expense

	Debit		Credit
Apr 15	400		

Transaction 7

On April 21, Smart Touch paid $300 on the account payable created in transaction 3. The paid check is Smart Touch's source document, or proof, for this transaction.

Smart Touch Learning
281 Wave Ave.
Niceville, FL 32578

6283

Date 4-21-10 88-894/1119 02

Pay to the Order of Wholesale Office Supply $ 300.00

Three hundred and no/100 Dollars

VALPARAISO FIRST BANK
Box 1739 Terminal Annex
Valparaiso, FL

For Payment on account Sheena Bright

⑆:122000661⑆:1400⑈03857

The payment decreased cash, so we credit Cash. The payment decreased Accounts payable, so we debit that liability.

Journal Entry

Date	Accounts and Explanation	Debit	Credit
Apr 21	Accounts payable (L–)	300	
	Cash (A–)		300
	Paid cash on account.		

Ledger Accounts

Cash			
Apr 1	30,000	Apr 2	20,000
Apr 8	5,500	Apr 15	3,200
		Apr 21	300

Accounts payable			
Apr 21	300	Apr 3	500

Transaction 8

Sheena Bright remodeled her home with personal funds. This is not a transaction of the business, so there is no entry on the business's books (based on the entity concept).

Transaction 9

On April 22, Smart Touch collected $2,000 cash from the client in transaction 5. Cash is increased, so we debit Cash. Accounts receivable is decreased, so we credit Accounts receivable.

Journal Entry

Date	Accounts and Explanation	Debit	Credit
Apr 22	Cash (A+)	2,000	
	Accounts receivable (A–)		2,000
	Received cash on account.		

Note: This transaction has no effect on revenue; the related revenue was recorded in transaction 5.

Ledger Accounts

Cash			
Apr 1	30,000	Apr 2	20,000
Apr 8	5,500	Apr 15	3,200
Apr 22	2,000	Apr 21	300

Accounts receivable			
Apr 10	3,000	Apr 22	2,000

Transaction 10

On April 24, Smart Touch sold a parcel of land owned by the business. The sale price, $9,000, equaled the cost. Cash increased, so we debit Cash. Land decreased, so we credit Land.

Journal Entry

Date	Accounts and Explanation	Debit	Credit
Apr 24	Cash (A+)	9,000	
	Land (A–)		9,000
	Sold land at cost.		

Ledger Accounts

Cash			
Apr 1	30,000	Apr 2	20,000
Apr 8	5,500	Apr 15	3,200
Apr 22	2,000	Apr 21	300
Apr 24	9,000		

Land			
Apr 2	20,000	Apr 24	9,000

Transaction 11

On April 30, Smart Touch received a telephone bill for $100 and will pay this expense next month. There is no cash payment now. The Utilities expense increased, so we debit this expense. The liability accounts payable increased, so we credit Accounts payable.

Journal Entry

Date	Accounts and Explanation	Debit	Credit
Apr 30	Utilities expense (E+)	100	
	Accounts payable (L+)		100
	Received utility bill.		

Ledger Accounts

Accounts payable

Apr 21	300	Apr 3	500
		Apr 30	100

Utilities expense

Apr 15	400		
Apr 30	100		

Transaction 12

Also on April 30, Sheena Bright withdrew $2,000. Withdrawals decrease the entity's cash, so we credit Cash. The withdrawal also decreased total owner's equity. Decreases in equity that result from withdrawals are debited to the Withdrawals account, so we debit that account.

Journal Entry

Date	Accounts and Explanation	Debit	Credit
Apr 30	Sheena Bright, Withdrawals (W+)	2,000	
	Cash (A–)		2,000
	Owner withdrawal.		

Ledger Accounts

Cash

Apr 1	30,000	Apr 2	20,000
Apr 8	5,500	Apr 15	3,200
Apr 22	2,000	Apr 21	300
Apr 24	9,000	Apr 30	2,000

Sheena Bright, Withdrawals (W+)

Apr 30	2,000		

Each journal entry posted to the ledger is keyed by date or by transaction number. In this way, any transaction can be traced back and forth between the journal and the ledger. This helps locate any information you may need.

The Ledger Accounts After Posting

We next show the accounts of Smart Touch Learning after posting. The accounts are grouped under their headings in Exhibit 2-10.

Each account has a balance. An account balance is the difference between the account's total debits and its total credits. For example, the $21,000 balance in the Cash account is the difference between:

- Total debits, $46,500 ($30,000 + $5,500 + $2,000 + $9,000)
- Total credits, $25,500 ($20,000 + $3,200 + $300 + $2,000)

We set a balance apart from the transaction amounts by a horizontal line. The final figure, below the horizontal line, is denoted as the balance (Bal).

EXHIBIT 2-10 | **Ledger Accounts After Posting**

ASSETS

Cash			
Apr 1	30,000	Apr 2	20,000
Apr 8	5,500	Apr 15	3,200
Apr 22	2,000	Apr 21	300
Apr 24	9,000	Apr 30	2,000
Bal	21,000		

Accounts receivable			
Apr 10	3,000	Apr 22	2,000*
Bal	1,000		

Office supplies			
Apr 3	500		
Bal	500		

Land			
Apr 2	20,000	Apr 24	9,000
Bal	11,000		

LIABILITIES

Accounts payable			
Apr 21	300	Apr 3	500
		Apr 30	100
		Bal	300

OWNER'S EQUITY*

Sheena Bright, Capital			
		Apr 1	30,000
		Bal	30,000

Sheena Bright, Withdrawals			
Apr 30	2,000		
Bal	2,000		

REVENUE

Service revenue			
		Apr 8	5,500
		Apr 10	3,000
		Bal	8,500

EXPENSES

Rent expense, computer			
Apr 15	600		
Bal	600		

Rent expense, office			
Apr 15	1,000*		
Bal	1,000		

Salary expense			
Apr 15	1,200		
Bal	1,200		

Utilities expense			
Apr 15	400		
Apr 30	100		
Bal	500*		

*These values are intentionally different than those presented in Chapter 1.

Stop & Think...

Have you ever walked along the beach and gathered sea shells? Maybe you had more than one bucket and you put all the sand dollars in one, all the hermit crabs in another, and so on. That separation is essentially what happens in posting. All we are doing is gathering transactions that affect the same account (for example, all the transactions to Cash) and putting them in the T-account. They are placed either on the left or right side of the T-account based on whether they were on the left or right side of the journal entry. Posting is merely a sorting process—no change to debits or credits occurs from transaction to posting.

Preparing the Trial Balance from the T-Accounts

5 Prepare the trial balance from the T-accounts

A **trial balance** summarizes the ledger by listing all the accounts with their balances—assets first, followed by liabilities, and then owner's equity. In a manual accounting system, the trial balance provides an accuracy check by showing whether total debits equal total credits. In all types of systems, the trial balance is a useful summary of the accounts and their balances because it shows the balances on a specific date for all accounts in a company's accounting system. Exhibit 2-11 is the trial balance of Smart Touch Learning at April 30, 2010, the end of the first month of operations.

A warning: Do not confuse the trial balance with the balance sheet. A trial balance is an internal document used only by company insiders. The public never sees a trial balance. Outsiders get only the company's financial statements.

EXHIBIT 2-11 | Trial Balance

SMART TOUCH LEARNING
Trial Balance
April 30, 2010

Account Title	Balance Debit	Balance Credit
Cash	$21,000	
Accounts receivable	1,000	
Office supplies	500	
Land	11,000	
Accounts payable		$ 300
Sheena Bright, Capital		30,000
Sheena Bright, Withdrawals	2,000	
Service revenue		8,500
Rent expense, computer	600	
Rent expense, office	1,000	
Salary expense	1,200	
Utilities expense	500	
Total	$38,800	$38,800

Correcting Trial Balance Errors

Throughout the accounting process, total debits should always equal total credits. If they do not, there is an error. Computerized accounting systems eliminate many errors because most software will not let you make a journal entry that does not balance. But computers cannot *eliminate* all errors because humans can input the wrong data.

Errors can be detected by computing the difference between total debits and total credits on the trial balance. Then perform one or more of the following actions:

1. Search the trial balance for a missing account. For example, suppose the accountant omitted Withdrawals from the trial balance in Exhibit 2-11. Total debits would then be $36,800 ($38,800 – $2,000). Trace each account from the ledger to the trial balance, and you will locate the missing account.

2. Divide the difference between total debits and total credits by 2. A debit treated as a credit, or vice versa, doubles the amount of error. Suppose the accountant posted a $500 credit as a debit. Total debits contain the $500, and total credits omit the $500. The out-of-balance amount is $1,000. Dividing the difference by 2 identifies the $500 amount of the transaction. Then search the trial balance for a $500 transaction and trace it to the account affected.

3. Divide the out-of-balance amount by 9. If the result is evenly divisible by 9, the error may be a *slide* (example: writing $1,000 as $100 or writing $100 as $1000) or a *transposition* (example: treating $1,200 as $2,100). Suppose, for example, that the accountant printed the $2,000 Withdrawals as $20,000 on the trial balance. This is a slide-type error. Total debits would differ from total credits by $18,000 ($20,000 – $2,000 = $18,000). Dividing $18,000 by 9 yields $2,000, the correct amount of withdrawals. Trace $2,000 through the ledger until you reach the Withdrawals account. You have then found the error.

Details of Journals and Ledgers

In practice, the journal and the ledger provide details to create a "trail" through the records. Suppose a supplier bills us twice for an item that we purchased. To show we have already paid the bill, we must prove our payment. That requires us to use the journal and the ledger.

Details in the Journal

Exhibit 2-12 illustrates a transaction and then shows the journal with these details:

- The *transaction date*, April 1, 2010
- The *accounts* debited and credited, along with their dollar amounts
- The *posting reference*, abbreviated Post. Ref.

EXHIBIT 2-12 | Details of Journalizing and Posting

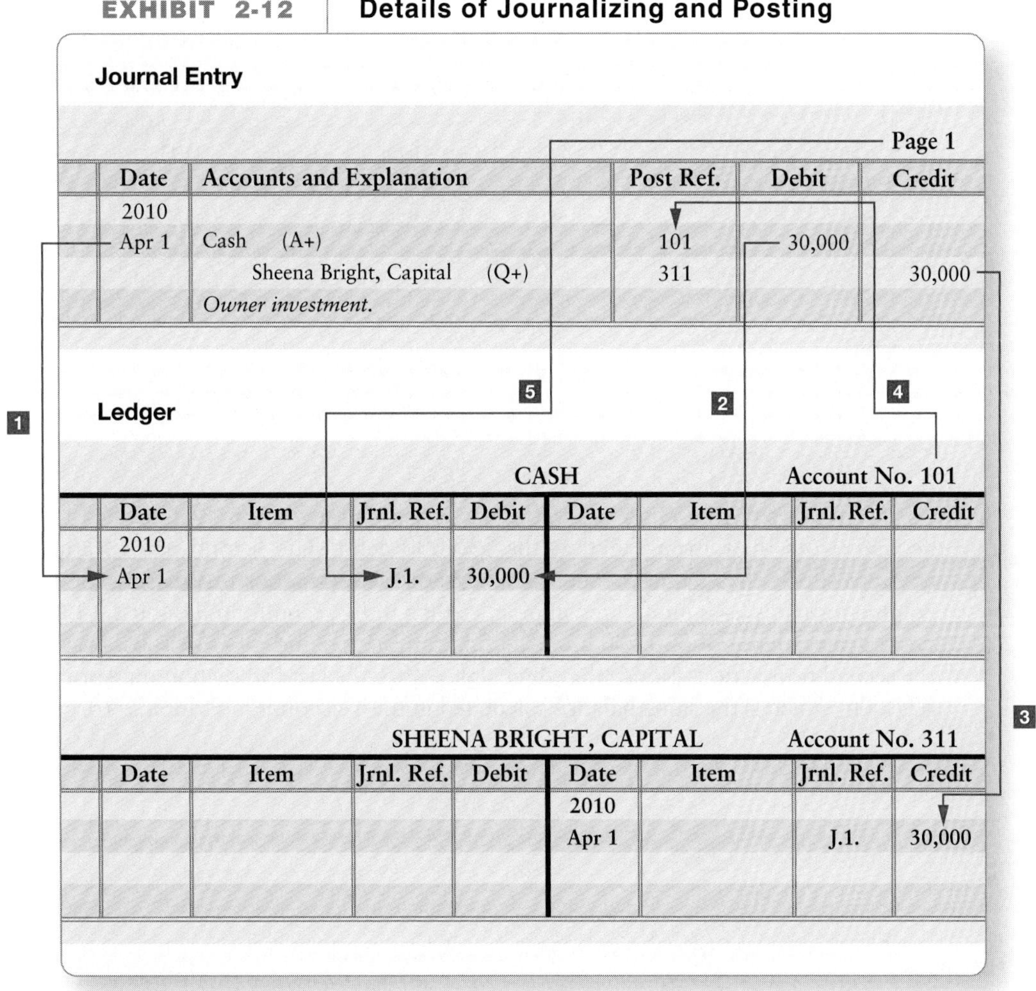

Details in the Ledger

Posting means copying information from the journal to the ledger. But how do we handle the details? Exhibit 2-12 illustrates the steps, denoted by arrows:

Arrow 1—Post the transaction **date** from the journal to the ledger.

Arrow 2—Post the debit, $30,000, from the journal as a debit to the Cash account in the ledger.

Arrow 3—Likewise, post the credit, $30,000, from the journal to the Capital account in the ledger. Now the ledger accounts have correct amounts.

Arrow 4—Post the account numbers (**101** and **311**) from the ledger back to the journal. This step shows that the debit and the credit have both been posted to the ledger. **Post. Ref.** is the abbreviation for Posting Reference.

Arrow 5—Post the page number from the journal to the ledger. **Jrnl. Ref.** means Journal Reference, and **J.1** refers to Journal Page **1**. This step shows where the data came from, in this case Journal Page 1.

The Four-Column Account: An Alternative to the T-Account

The ledger accounts illustrated thus far appear as T-accounts, with the debit on the left and the credit on the right. The T-account clearly separates debits from credits and is used for teaching, where there is not much detail. Another account format has four amount columns, as illustrated in Exhibit 2-13.

EXHIBIT 2-13 | Account in Four-Column Format

CASH					Account No. 101	
					Balance	
Date	Item	Jrnl. Ref.	Debit	Credit	Debit	Credit
2010						
Apr 1		J.1	30,000		30,000	
Apr 2		J.1		20,000	10,000	
Apr 8		J.1	5,500		15,500	
Apr 15		J.1		3,200	12,300	
Apr 21		J.1		300	12,000	
Apr 22		J.1	2,000		14,000	
Apr 24		J.1	9,000		23,000	
Apr 30		J.1		2,000	21,000	

The first pair of Debit/Credit columns is for transaction amounts posted to the account from the journal, such as the $30,000 debit. The second pair of amount columns shows the balance of the account as of each date. For this reason, the four-column format is used more often in practice than the T-account. In Exhibit 2-13, Cash has a debit balance of $30,000 after the first transaction and a $10,000 balance after the second transaction. Notice that the balance after the last transaction on April 30 is $21,000, which is the same balance calculated in the T-account in Exhibit 2-10.

Decision Guidelines

ANALYZING AND RECORDING TRANSACTIONS

Suppose Greg Moore, in the chapter's opening story, opens a small office and needs an accountant to keep his books. Moore interviews you for the job. The pay is good. Can you answer Moore's questions, which are outlined in the Decision Guidelines? If so, you may get the job.

Decision	Guidelines	
• Has a transaction occurred?	If the event affects the entity's financial position and can be recorded reliably—*Yes* If either condition is absent—*No*	
• Where to record the transaction?	In the *journal*, the chronological record of transactions	
• What to record for each transaction?	Increases and/or decreases in all the accounts affected by the transaction	
• How to record an increase/decrease in a (an)	Rules of debit and credit:	
	Debit	Credit
Asset	+	–
Liability	–	+
Capital	–	+
Withdrawal	+	–
Revenue	–	+
Expense	+	–
• Where to store all the information for each account?	In the *ledger*, the record holding all the accounts	
• Where to list all the accounts and their balances?	In the *trial balance*	
• Where to report the results of operations?	In the income statement **Revenues – Expenses = Net income or Net loss**	
• Where to report financial position?	In the balance sheet **Assets = Liabilities + Owner's equity**	

Summary Problem

The trial balance of Harper Service Center on March 1, 2009, lists the entity's assets, liabilities, and equity on that date.

Account Title	Balance Debit	Balance Credit
Cash	$26,000	
Accounts receivable	4,500	
Accounts payable		$ 2,000
Marc Harper, Capital		28,500
Total	$30,500	$30,500

During March, the business engaged in the following transactions:

a. Borrowed $45,000 from the bank and signed a note payable in the name of the business.
b. Paid cash of $40,000 to acquire land.
c. Performed service for a customer and received cash of $5,000.
d. Purchased supplies on credit, $300.
e. Performed customer service and earned revenue on account, $2,600.
f. Paid $1,200 on account.
g. Paid the following cash expenses: salaries, $3,000; rent, $1,500; and interest, $400.
h. Received $3,100 on account.
i. Received a $200 utility bill that will be paid next week.
j. Owner withdrew $1,800.

Requirements

1. Open the following accounts, with the balances indicated, in the ledger of Harper Service Center. Use the T-account format.
   - **Assets**—Cash, $26,000; Accounts receivable, $4,500; Supplies, no balance; Land, no balance
   - **Liabilities**—Accounts payable, $2,000; Note payable, no balance
   - **Owners equity**—Marc Harper, Capital, $28,500; Withdrawals, $0
   - **Revenues**—Service revenue, no balance
   - **Expenses**—(none have balances) Salary expense, Rent expense, Utilities expense, Interest expense
2. Journalize each transaction. Key journal entries by transaction letter.
3. Post to the ledger.
4. Prepare the trial balance of Harper Service Center at March 31, 2009.

Solution

Requirement 1

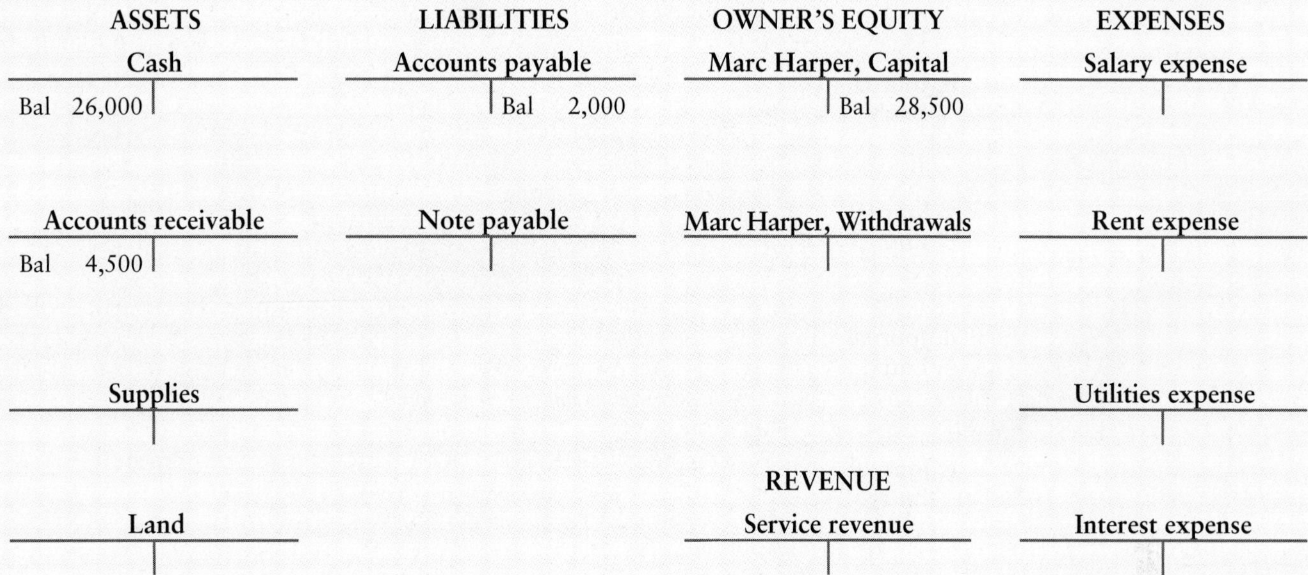

Requirement 2

		Account	Debit	Credit
a. Journal Entry		Cash (A+)	45,000	
		Note payable (L+)		45,000
		Borrowed cash on note payable.		
b. Journal Entry		Land (A+)	40,000	
		Cash (A–)		40,000
		Purchased land.		
c. Journal Entry		Cash (A+)	5,000	
		Service revenue (R+)		5,000
		Performed service and received cash.		
d. Journal Entry		Supplies (A+)	300	
		Accounts payable (L+)		300
		Purchased supplies on account.		
e. Journal Entry		Accounts receivable (A+)	2,600	
		Service revenue (R+)		2,600
		Performed service on account.		
f. Journal Entry		Accounts payable (L–)	1,200	
		Cash (A–)		1,200
		Paid on account.		
g. Journal Entry		Salary expense (E+)	3,000	
		Rent expense (E+)	1,500	
		Interest expense (E+)	400	
		Cash (A–)		4,900
		Paid expenses.		
h. Journal Entry		Cash (A+)	3,100	
		Accounts receivable (A–)		3,100
		Received cash on account.		
i. Journal Entry		Utilities expense (E+)	200	
		Accounts payable (L+)		200
		Received utility bill.		
j. Journal Entry		Marc Harper, Withdrawals (W+)	1,800	
		Cash (A–)		1,800
		Owner withdrawal.		

Requirement 3

ASSETS

Cash			
Bal	26,000	(b)	40,000
(a)	45,000	(f)	1,200
(c)	5,000	(g)	4,900
(h)	3,100	(j)	1,800
Bal	31,200		

Accounts receivable			
Bal	4,500	(h)	3,100
(e)	2,600		
Bal	4,000		

Supplies			
(d)	300		
Bal	300		

Land			
(b)	40,000		
Bal	40,000		

LIABILITIES

Accounts payable			
(f)	1,200	Bal	2,000
		(d)	300
		(i)	200
		Bal	1,300

Note payable			
		(a)	45,000
		Bal	45,000

OWNER'S EQUITY

Marc Harper, Capital			
		Bal	28,500

Marc Harper, Withdrawals			
(j)	1,800		
Bal	1,800		

REVENUE

Service revenue			
		(c)	5,000
		(e)	2,600
		Bal	7,600

EXPENSES

Salary expense			
(g)	3,000		
Bal	3,000		

Rent expense			
(g)	1,500		
Bal	1,500		

Interest expense			
(g)	400		
Bal	400		

Utilities expense			
(i)	200		
Bal	200		

Requirement 4

HARPER SERVICE CENTER
Trial Balance
March 31, 2009

	Balance	
Account Title	Debit	Credit
Cash	$31,200	
Accounts receivable	4,000	
Supplies	300	
Land	40,000	
Accounts payable		$ 1,300
Note payable		45,000
Marc Harper, Capital		28,500
Marc Harper, Withdrawals	1,800	
Service revenue		7,600
Salary expense	3,000	
Rent expense	1,500	
Interest expense	400	
Utilities expense	200	
Total	$82,400	$82,400

Review Recording Business Transactions

Accounting Vocabulary

Account (p. 92)
The detailed record of the changes in a particular asset, liability, or owner's equity during a period. The basic summary device of accounting.

Accrued liability (p. 93)
A liability for which the business knows the amount owed but the bill has not been paid.

Chart of Accounts (p. 94)
A list of all the accounts with their account numbers.

Compound journal entry (p. 106)
Same as a journal entry, except this entry is characterized by having multiple debits and/or multiple credits. The total debits still equal the total credits in the compound journal.

Credit (p. 96)
The right side of an account.

Debit (p. 96)
The left side of an account.

Journal (p. 92)
The chronological accounting record of an entity's transactions.

Ledger (p. 92)
The record holding all the accounts.

Normal Balance (p. 101)
The balance that appears on the side of an account—debit or credit—where we record increases.

Notes Payable (p. 93)
Represents debts the business owes because it signed promissory notes to borrow money or to purchase something.

Note Receivable (p. 93)
A written promise for future collection of cash.

Posting (p. 99)
Copying amounts from the journal to the ledger.

Prepaid expenses (p. 93)
Expenses paid in advance of their use.

T-account (p. 96)
Summary device that is shaped like a capital "T" with debits posted on the left side of the vertical line and credits on the right side of the vertical line.

Trial Balance (p. 92)
A list of all the accounts with their balances.

Quick Check

1. Which sequence correctly summarizes the accounting process?
   a. Post to the accounts, journalize transactions, prepare a trial balance
   b. Journalize transactions, prepare a trial balance, post to the accounts
   c. Journalize transactions, post to the accounts, prepare a trial balance
   d. Prepare a trial balance, journalize transactions, post to the accounts
2. The left side of an account is used to record:
   a. Increases
   b. Debits
   c. Credits
   d. Debit or credit, depending on the type of account
3. Suppose Frazier has receivables of $63,000, furniture totaling $198,000, and cash of $45,000. The business has a $108,000 note payable and owes $84,000 on account. How much is Frazier's owner's equity?
   a. $114,000
   b. $192,000
   c. $24,000
   d. $306,000
4. Your business purchased supplies of $1,000 on account. The journal entry to record this transaction is:

a.

Supplies	1,000	
Accounts receivable		1,000

b.

Accounts payable	1,000	
Supplies		1,000

c.

Inventory	1,000	
Accounts payable		1,000

d.

Supplies	1,000	
Accounts payable		1,000

5. Which journal entry records your payment for the supplies purchase described in Quick Check question 4?

a.

Accounts payable	1,000	
Cash		1,000

b.

Cash	1,000	
Accounts payable		1,000

c.

Accounts payable	1,000	
Accounts receivable		1,000

d.

Supplies	1,000	
Cash		1,000

6. Posting a $1,000 purchase of supplies on account appears as follows:

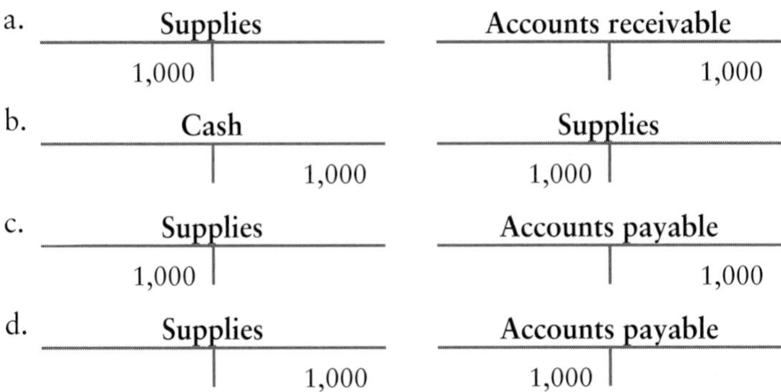

7. You paid $500 for supplies and purchased additional supplies on account for $700. Later you paid $400 of the accounts payable. What is the balance in your Supplies account?
   a. $1,200
   b. $1,600
   c. $500
   d. $800

8. Quick Copies recorded a cash collection on account by debiting Cash and crediting Accounts payable. What will the trial balance show for this error?
   a. Too much for expenses
   b. Too much for liabilities
   c. The trial balance will not balance
   d. Too much for cash

9. Michael Daigle, Attorney, began the year with total assets of $122,000, liabilities of $71,000, and owner's equity of $51,000. During the year the business earned revenue of $109,000 and paid expenses of $36,000. The owner also withdrew $68,000. How much is the business's equity at year-end?
   a. $56,000
   b. $104,000
   c. $160,000
   d. $124,000

10. Wayne Robichaud, Attorney, began the year with total assets of $127,000, liabilities of $78,000, and owner's equity of $49,000. During the year the business earned revenue of $107,000 and paid expenses of $37,000. The owner also withdrew $67,000. How would Wayne Robichaud record expenses paid of $37,000?

a.

Expenses	37,000	
Accounts payable		37,000

b.

Accounts payable	37,000	
Cash		37,000

c.

Cash	37,000	
Expenses		37,000

d.

Expenses	37,000	
Cash		37,000

Answers are given after Apply Your Knowledge (p. 150).

Assess Your Progress

■ Short Exercises

S2-1 *(L. OBJ. 1)* **Using accounting vocabulary [5 min]**
Tighten your grip by filling in the blanks to review some key accounting definitions.

Rita Bowden is describing the accounting process for a friend who is a philosophy major. Rita states, "The basic summary device in accounting is the _______.The left side is called the _______ side, and the right side is called the _______ side. We record transactions first in a _______. Then we post (copy the data) to the _______. It is helpful to list all the accounts with their balances on a _______."

S2-2 *(L. OBJ. 1)* **Using accounting vocabulary [10 min]**
Accounting has its own vocabulary and basic relationships.

Requirement

1. Match the accounting terms on the left with the corresponding definitions on the right. (Challenge)

_______	1. Equity	A. Record of transactions
_______	2. Debit	B. An asset
_______	3. Expense	C. Left side of an account
_______	4. Net income	D. Side of an account where increases are recorded
_______	5. Ledger	E. Copying data from the journal to the ledger
_______	6. Posting	F. Using up assets in the course of operating a business
_______	7. Normal balance	G. Always a liability
_______	8. Payable	H. Revenues – Expenses = _______
_______	9. Journal	I. Book of accounts
_______	10. Receivable	J. Assets – Liabilities = _______

S2-3 *(L. OBJ. 1, 2)* **Explaining accounts and the rules of debit and credit [5 min]**
Allison Franklin is tutoring Blaine McCormick, who is taking introductory accounting. Allison explains to Blaine that *debits* are used to record increases in accounts and *credits* record decreases. Blaine is confused and seeks your advice.

Requirements

1. When are debits increases? When are debits decreases?
2. When are credits increases? When are credits decreases?

S2-4 *(L. OBJ. 2)* **Normal account balances [5 min]**
Accounting records include three basic types of accounts: assets, liabilities, and owner's equity. In turn, owner's equity holds the following types: capital, withdrawals, revenues, and expenses.

Requirement

1. Identify which types of the accounts have a normal debit balance and which types have a normal credit balance.

S2-5 *(L. OBJ. 3)* **Journalizing transactions [10 min]**
Otis Carpenter opened a medical practice in Alexandria, Virginia.

Sep 1	The business received $33,000 cash and gave capital to the owner.
2	Purchased medical supplies on account $7,000.
2	Paid monthly office rent of $3,700.
3	Recorded $10,000 revenue for service rendered to patients on account.

Requirement

1. Record the preceding transactions in the journal of Otis Carpenter, M.D. Include an explanation with each entry.

S2-6 *(L. OBJ. 3)* **Journalizing transactions [10 min]**
Lakeview Sales Consultants completed the following transactions during the latter part of March:

Mar 22	Performed service for customers on account, $4,000.
30	Received cash on account from customers, $3,000.
31	Received a utility bill, $130, which will be paid during April.
31	Paid monthly salary to salesman, $2,300.
31	Paid advertising expense of $400.

Requirement

1. Journalize the transactions of Lakeview Sales Consultants. Include an explanation with each journal entry.

S2-7 *(L. OBJ. 3, 4)* **Journalizing transactions and posting to T-accounts [10–15 min]**
Nancy Carpenter Optical Dispensary purchased supplies on account for $1,200. Two weeks later, the business paid half on account.

Requirements

1. Journalize the two transactions for Nancy Carpenter Optical Dispensary. Include an explanation for each entry.
2. Open the Accounts payable T-account and post to Accounts payable. Compute the balance, and denote it as *Bal.*

S2-8 *(L. OBJ. 3, 4)* **Journalizing transactions and posting [10–15 min]**
Jonathan Law Firm performed legal services for a client who could not pay immediately. The business expected to collect the $9,000 the following month. Later, the business received $5,400 cash from the client.

Requirements

1. Record the two transactions for Jonathan Law Firm. Include an explanation for each transaction.
2. Open these T-accounts: Cash; Accounts receivable; Service revenue. Post to all three accounts. Compute each T-account's balance, and denote as *Bal.*
3. Answer these questions based on your analysis:
   a. How much did the business earn? Which account shows this amount?
   b. How much in total assets did the business acquire as a result of the two transactions? Identify each asset and show its amount.

S2-9 *(L. OBJ. 4, 5)* **Posting, balancing T-accounts, and preparing a trial balance [10–15 min]**
Use the September transaction data for Otis Carpenter, M.D., given in Short Exercise 2-5.

Requirements

1. Open the following T-accounts: Cash, Accounts receivable, Medical supplies, Accounts payable, Otis Carpenter, Capital, Service revenue, and Rent expense.
2. After making the journal entries in Short Exercise 2-5, post to the T-accounts. No dates or posting references are required. Compute the balance of each account, and denote it as *Bal.*
3. Prepare the trial balance, complete with a proper heading, at September 3, 2010.

S2-10 *(L. OBJ. 5)* **Preparing a trial balance [10 min]**
Redwing Floor Coverings reported the following summarized data at December 31, 2009. Accounts appear in no particular order.

Revenues	$32,000	Other liabilities	$17,000
Equipment	43,000	Cash	6,000
Accounts payable	1,000	Expenses	26,000
Shelly Royce, Capital	25,000		

Requirement

1. Prepare the trial balance of Redwing Floor Coverings at December 31, 2009.

S2-11 *(L. OBJ. 5)* **Correcting a trial balance [10 min]**
Georgia Lapp Travel Design prepared its trial balance. Suppose Lapp made an error: She erroneously listed capital of $30,100 as a debit rather than a credit.

GEORGIA LAPP TRAVEL DESIGN		
Trial Balance		
April 30, 2010		
	Balance	
Account Title	Debit	Credit
Cash	$ 16,000	
Accounts receivable	1,000	
Office supplies	500	
Land	16,000	
Accounts payable		$ 200
Georgia Lapp, Capital	30,100	
Georgia Lapp, Withdrawals	2,000	
Service revenue		8,500
Rent expense, computer	800	
Rent expense, office	900	
Salary expense	1,200	
Utilities expense	400	
Total		

Requirement

1. Compute the incorrect trial balance totals for debits and credits. Then show how to correct this error.

S2-12 *(L. OBJ. 5)* **Correcting a trial balance [10 min]**
Review Kelly Long Travel Design's trial balance. Assume that Long accidentally listed withdrawals as $100 instead of the correct amount of $1,000.

KELLY LONG TRAVEL DESIGN		
Trial Balance		
January 31, 2011		
	Balance	
Account Title	Debit	Credit
Cash	$ 19,000	
Accounts receivable	1,000	
Office supplies	500	
Land	13,000	
Accounts payable		$ 400
Kelly Long, Capital		29,000
Kelly Long, Withdrawals	100	
Service revenue		8,400
Rent expense, computer	800	
Rent expense, office	1,100	
Salary expense	1,100	
Utilities expense	300	
Total		

Requirement

1. Compute the incorrect trial balance totals for debits and credits. Then show how to correct this error, which is called a *slide*.

■ Exercises

E2-13 *(L. OBJ. 1)* **Using accounting vocabulary [10 min]**
Review basic accounting definitions by completing the following crossword puzzle.

Down:
1. Right side of an account
4. The basic summary device of accounting
6. Book of accounts
7. An economic resource
8. Record of transactions
9. Normal balance of a revenue

Across:
2. Records a decrease in a liability
3. List of accounts with their balances
5. Another word for liability

E2-14 *(L. OBJ. 1)* **Using accounting vocabulary [10–15 min]**
Sharpen your use of accounting terms by working this crossword puzzle.

Down:
1. Records a decrease in a liability
4. Bottom line of an income statement
7. Revenue – net income = ________

Across:
2. Amount collectible from a customer
3. Statement of financial position
5. Copy data from the journal to the ledger
6. Records a decrease in an asset

E2-15 *(L. OBJ. 1, 2)* **Using debits and credits with the accounting equation [10–15 min]**
Link Back to Chapter 1 (Accounting Equation). Jane's Cream Soda makes specialty soft drinks. At the end of 2010, Jane's had total assets of $300,000 and liabilities totaling $220,000.

Requirements

1. Write the company's accounting equation, and label each amount as a debit or a credit.
2. The business's total revenues for 2010 were $460,000, and total expenses for the year were $380,000. How much was the business's net income (or net loss) for 2010? Write the equation to compute the company's net income, and indicate which element is a debit and which is a credit. Does net income represent a net debit or a net credit?

E2-16 *(L. OBJ. 2, 3)* **Analyzing and journalizing transactions [10–15 min]**
The following transactions occurred for Advanced Engineering:

Sep	2	Paid utilities expense of $300.
	5	Purchased equipment on account, $2,000.
	10	Performed service for a client on account, $1,800.
	12	Borrowed $10,000 cash, signing a note payable.
	19	Sold for $36,000 land that had cost this same amount.
	21	Purchased supplies for $600 and paid cash.
	27	Paid the liability from Sept. 5.

Requirement

1. Record the transactions in the journal.

E2-17 *(L. OBJ. 2, 3, 4, 5)* **Describing transactions, posting to T-accounts, and preparing a trial balance [20–30 min]**
The journal of Bell Technology Solutions includes the following entries for August, 2010:

Aug	1	The business received cash of $86,000 and gave capital to the owner
	2	Purchased supplies of $700 on account
	4	Paid $58,000 cash for a building
	6	Performed service for customers and received cash, $2,700
	9	Paid $100 on accounts payable
	17	Performed service for customers on account, $2,100
	23	Received $1,300 cash from a customer on account
	31	Paid the following expenses: salary, $1,200; rent, $500

Requirements

1. Describe each transaction.
2. Set up T-accounts using the following account numbers: Cash, 110; Accounts receivable, 120; Supplies, 130; Accounts payable, 210; Lulu Bell, Capital, 310; Service revenue, 410; Rent expense, 510; Salary expense, 520.
3. Post to the accounts. Write dates and journal references in the accounts. Compute the balance of each account after posting.
4. Prepare the trial balance of Bell Technology Solutions at August 31, 2010.

E2-18 *(L. OBJ. 2, 3, 4, 5)* **Analyzing accounting errors [20–30 min]**
Bridget Battle has trouble keeping her debits and credits equal. During a recent month, Bridget made the following accounting errors:

a. In preparing the trial balance, Bridget omitted a $5,000 note payable.
b. Bridget posted a $1,000 utility expense as $100. The credit to Cash was correct.
c. In recording a $200 payment on account, Bridget debited Supplies instead of Accounts payable.
d. In journalizing a receipt of cash for service revenue, Bridget debited Cash for $50 instead of the correct amount of $500. The credit was correct.
e. Bridget recorded a $340 purchase of supplies on account by debiting Supplies and crediting Accounts payable for $430.

Requirements

1. For each of these errors, state whether total debits equal total credits on the trial balance.
2. Identify each account that has an incorrect balance, and indicate the amount and direction of the error (such as "Accounts receivable $500 too high").

E2-19 *(L. OBJ. 2, 4, 5)* **Applying the rules of debit and credit, posting, and preparing a trial balance [15–25 min]**
Refer to the transactions of Advanced Engineering in Exercise 2-16.

Requirements

1. Open the following T-accounts with their September 1 balances: Cash, debit balance $3,000; Accounts receivable $0; Equipment $0; Land, debit balance $36,000; Supplies $0; Accounts payable $0; Notes payable $0; Al Nyquist, Capital, credit balance $39,000; Service revenue $0; Utilities expense $0.
2. Post the transactions of Exercise 2-16 to the T-accounts. Use the dates as posting references. Start with September 2.
3. Compute the September 30, 2010, balance for each account, and prove that total debits equal total credits by preparing a trial balance.

E2-20 *(L. OBJ. 2, 3, 4, 5)* **Journalizing transactions, posting, and preparing a trial balance [10 min]**
In October, 2011, the first five transactions of Fine's Maid Service have been posted to the accounts as follows:

Cash	
(1) $57,000	(3) 31,000
(4) 42,000	(5) 4,900

Supplies	
(2) 600	

Equipment	
(5) 4,900	

Building	
(3) 31,000	

Accounts payable	
	(2) 600

Note payable	
	(4) 42,000

Mrs. Clean, Capital	
	(1) $57,000

Requirements

1. Prepare the journal entries that served as the sources for the five transactions. Include an explanation for each entry as illustrated in Chapter 2.
2. Prepare the trial balance of Fine's Maid Service at October 31, 2011.

E2-21 *(L. OBJ. 3)* **Using actual business documents [10 min]**
Suppose your name is Grant Scheffer, and Advanced Automotive repaired your car. You settled the bill as noted on the following invoice. To you this is a purchase invoice. To Advanced Automotive, it is a sales invoice.

ADVANCED AUTOMOTIVE
4605 VALLEY DRIVE
WACO, TX 76719
(254) 728-7241

Repair Order #0020879
Date: 5/9/2011
Page: 1
Center: 1

Customer:	Grant Scheffer	**Vehicle:**	2005 MERB E320 WAGON
Address:	4000 Ranch Road	**License:**	JFG682
City:	WACO, TX 76726	**VIN:**	WDBEA92E1SF3
Phone 1:	(254) 752-0273	**Engine:**	3.06 CYL **Trans:** AUTO
Phone 2:	(254) 710-6009	**Mileage:**	105654

Op	Tech / Quan	Description / Part Number	Part Description	Reason for Replacement	Labor	Parts	Subtotal / Price:
		Recommendation		Recommendation			Recommendation

PAID
MAY 09 2011
BY: check

I hereby authorize the repair work to be done along with the necessary parts and materials and hereby grant you and/or your employees permission to operate the vehicle herin described on streets, highways or elsewhere, at your discretion, for the purpose of testing and/or inspection. An express mechanics lien is hereby acknowledged on the above vehicle to secure the amount of repairs thereto. I understand that dealer/owner is not responsible for delay or other consequence due to the unavailability of parts shipments beyond their control. Not responsible for damage or articles left in car in case of fire, theft or any other cause beyond our control.
WARRANTY IS 12 MONTHS OR 12,000 MILES, WHICH EVER COMES FIRST

x Grant Scheffer

Labor:	$192.00
Parts:	$260.90
Sublet:	$0.00
Other fees:	$0.00
Shop Supplies:	$9.60
Subtotal:	$462.50
Sales Tax:	$21.52
Paid By:	
Total:	$484.02
Pay Ref:	
Paid:	$0.00
Due:	$484.02

Requirements

1. Journalize your repair expense transaction.
2. Journalize Advanced Automotive's service revenue transaction.

E2-22 *(L. OBJ. 3, 4, 5)* **Recording transactions, using four-column ledger accounts, and preparing a trial balance [20–25 min]**
The following transactions occurred during the month for Mona Wade, CPA:

a. Wade opened an accounting firm by investing $16,500 cash and office furniture valued at $5,300. The business gave $21,800 of capital to Wade.
b. Paid monthly rent of $1,400.
c. Purchased office supplies on account, $700.
d. Paid employee's salary, $1,600.
e. Paid $400 of the account payable created in transaction (c).
f. Performed accounting service on account, $5,800.
g. Owner withdrew $6,800.

Requirements

1. Open the following four-column accounts of Mona Wade, CPA, Cash; Accounts receivable; Office supplies; Office furniture; Accounts payable; Mona Wade, Capital; Mona Wade, Withdrawals; Service revenue; Salary expense; Rent expense.
2. Journalize the transactions and then post to the four-column accounts. Use the letters to identify the transactions. Keep a running balance in each account.
3. Prepare the trial balance, at December 31, 2011.

E2-23 *(L. OBJ. 4)* **Journalizing transactions [10–20 min]**
Granger Technology Solutions completed the following transactions during January 2011, its first month of operations:

Jan	1	Received cash of $46,000 and gave capital to the owner.
	2	Purchased supplies of $600 on account.
	4	Paid $42,000 cash for a building.
	6	Performed service for customers and received cash, $5,800.
	9	Paid $400 on accounts payable.
	17	Performed service for customers on account, $1,900.
	23	Received $1,300 cash from a customer on account.
	31	Paid the following expenses: salary, $2,400; rent, $1,000.

Requirement

1. Record the preceding transactions in the journal of Granger Technology Solutions. Include an explanation for each entry, as illustrated in the chapter. Use the following accounts: Cash; Accounts receivable; Supplies; Building; Accounts payable; Gib Granger, Capital; Service revenue; Salary expense; Rent expense.

E2-24 *(L. OBJ. 4, 5)* **Posting to the ledger and preparing a trial balance [15–20 min]**
Refer to Exercise 2-23 for the transactions of Granger Technology Solutions.

Requirements

1. After journalizing the transactions of Exercise 2-23, post to the ledger using the T-account format. Date the ending balance of each account Jan. 31.
2. Prepare the trial balance of Granger Technology Solutions at January 31, 2011.

E2-25 *(L. OBJ. 5)* **Preparing a trial balance [10 min]**
The accounts of Valentine Moving Company follow with their normal balances at April 30, 2010. The accounts are listed in no particular order.

Shug Valentine, Capital	$ 59,500	Trucks	$ 122,000
Insurance expense	700	Fuel expense	2,000
Accounts payable	4,000	Shug Valentine, Withdrawals	5,600
Service revenue	77,000	Utilities expense	400
Building	44,000	Accounts receivable	10,300
Supplies expense	300	Note payable	56,000
Cash	6,000	Supplies	200
Salary expense	5,000		

Requirement

1. Prepare Valentine's trial balance at April 30, 2010.

E2-26 *(L. OBJ. 5)* **Correcting errors in a trial balance [15–20 min]**
The following trial balance of Jeana Jones Tutoring Service at August 31, 2011, does not balance:

JEANA JONES TUTORING SERVICE Trial Balance August 31, 2011		
Account	**Debit**	**Credit**
Cash	$ 3,100	
Accounts receivable	1,900	
Supplies	700	
Computer equipment	26,100	
Accounts payable		$ 11,400
Jeana Jones, Capital		11,900
Service revenue		9,600
Salary expense	1,600	
Rent expense	900	
Utilities expense	500	
Total	$ 34,800	$ 32,900

Investigation of the accounting records reveals that the bookkeeper:

a. Recorded a $400 cash revenue transaction by debiting Accounts receivable. The credit entry was correct.
b. Posted a $2,000 credit to Accounts payable as $200.
c. Did not record utilities expense or the related account payable in the amount of $500.
d. Understated owner's investment by $100.

Requirement

1. Prepare the corrected trial balance at August 31, 2011, complete with a heading; journal entries are not required.

Problems (Group A)

P2-27A *(L. OBJ. 2, 3, 4, 5)* **Analyzing and journalizing transactions, posting, and preparing a trial balance [40–50 min]**
Party Time Amusements Company owns movie theaters. Party Time engaged in the following business transactions in 2012:

Nov	1	Darrell Palusky invested $350,000 personal cash in the business by depositing that amount in a bank account titled Party Time Amusements. The business gave capital to Palusky.
	2	Paid $320,000 cash to purchase a theater building.
	5	Borrowed $220,000 from the bank. Palusky signed a note payable to the bank in the name of Party Time.
	10	Purchased theater supplies on account, $1,000.
	15	Paid $600 on account.
	15	Paid property tax expense on theater building, $1,400.
	16	Paid employees' salaries $2,900, and rent on equipment $1,300. Make a single compound entry.
	28	Palusky withdrew $8,000.
	30	Received $20,000 cash from service revenue and deposited that amount in the bank.

Party Time Amusements uses the following accounts: Cash; Supplies; Building; Accounts payable; Notes payable; Darrell Palusky, Capital; Darrell Palusky, Withdrawals; Service revenue; Salary expense; Rent expense; Property tax expense.

Requirements

1. Journalize each transaction of Party Time as shown for November 1. Explanations are not required.

Nov 1	Cash	350,000	
	Darrell Palusky, Capital		350,000

2. Post the transactions to the T-accounts, using transaction dates as posting references in the ledger accounts. Label the balance of each account *Bal*, as shown in the chapter.

P2-28A *(L. OBJ. 2, 3, 4, 5)* **Analyzing and journalizing transactions, posting, and preparing a trial balance [45–60 min]**

William White practices medicine under the business title William White, M.D. During January, the medical practice completed the following transactions:

Jan 1	White deposited $74,000 cash in the business bank account. The business gave capital to White.
5	Paid monthly rent on medical equipment, $600.
9	Paid $24,000 cash to purchase land for an office site.
10	Purchased supplies on account, $1,500.
19	Borrowed $18,000 from the bank for business use. White signed a note payable to the bank in the name of the business.
22	Paid $1,200 on account.
31	Revenues earned during the month included $6,400 cash and $4,300 on account.
31	Paid employees' salaries $2,600, office rent $1,700, and utilities $350. Make a single compound entry.
31	White withdrew $9,000 for personal use.

The business uses the following accounts: Cash; Accounts receivable; Supplies; Land; Accounts payable; Notes payable; William White, Capital; William White, Withdrawals; Service revenue; Salary expense; Rent expense; Utilities expense.

Requirements

1. Journalize each transaction, as shown for January 1. Explanations are not required.

Jan 1	Cash	74,000	
	William White, Capital		74,000

2. Post the transactions to the T-accounts, using transaction dates as posting references in the ledger accounts. Label the balance of each account *Bal*, as shown in the chapter.
3. Prepare the trial balance of William White, M.D., at January 31, 2010.

P2-29A *(L. OBJ. 2, 3, 4, 5)* **Journalizing transactions, posting to T-accounts, and preparing a trial balance [45–60 min]**
Donna White started her practice as a design consultant on January 1, 2010. During the first month of operations, the business completed the following transactions:

Jan	1	Received $35,000 cash and gave capital to White.
	4	Purchased supplies, $300, and furniture, $2,200, on account.
	6	Performed services for a law firm and received $2,000 cash.
	7	Paid $23,000 cash to acquire land for a future office site.
	10	Performed service for a hotel and received its promise to pay the $900 within one week.
	14	Paid for the furniture purchased January 4 on account.
	15	Paid secretary's bi-monthly salary, $590.
	17	Received cash on account, $700.
	20	Prepared a design for a school on account, $700.
	28	Received $2,400 cash for consulting with Plummer & Gorden.
	31	Paid secretary's bi-monthly salary, $590.
	31	Paid rent expense, $490.
	31	White withdrew $2,300 for personal use.

Requirements

1. Open the following T-accounts: Cash; Accounts receivable; Supplies; Furniture; Land; Accounts payable, Donna White, Capital; Donna White, Withdrawals; Service revenue; Salary expense; Rent expense.
2. Record each transaction in the journal, using the account titles given. Key each transaction by date. Explanations are not required.
3. Post the transactions to the T-accounts, using transaction dates as posting references in the ledger accounts. Label the balance of each account *Bal*, as shown in the chapter.
4. Prepare the trial balance of Donna White, Designer, at January 31, 2010.

P2-30A *(L. OBJ. 2, 3, 4, 5)* **Journalizing transactions, posting to accounts in four-column format, and preparing a trial balance [45–60 min]**
Vince Smith opened a law office on March 2, 2010. During the first month of operations, the business completed the following transactions:

Dec	2	Smith deposited $42,000 cash in the business bank account Vince Smith, Attorney.
	3	Purchased supplies, $400, and furniture, $1,900, on account.
	4	Performed legal service for a client and received cash, $1,900.
	7	Paid cash to acquire land for a future office site, $26,000.
	11	Prepared legal documents for a client on account, $800.
	15	Paid secretary's bi-monthly salary, $550.
	16	Paid for the supplies purchased March 3 on account.
	18	Received $2,300 cash for helping a client sell real estate.
	19	Defended a client in court and billed the client for $700.
	29	Received cash on account, $600.
	31	Paid secretary's bi-monthly salary, $550.
	31	Paid rent expense, $910.
	31	Smith withdrew $2,100 for personal use.

Requirements

1. Open the following T-accounts: Cash; Accounts receivable; Supplies; Furniture; Land; Accounts payable; Vince Smith, Capital; Vince Smith, Withdrawals; Service revenue; Salary expense; Rent expense.

2. Record each transaction in the journal, using the account titles given. Key each transaction by date. Explanations are not required.
3. Post the transactions to T-accounts, using transaction dates as posting references in the ledger. Label the balance of each account *Bal*, as shown in the chapter.
4. Prepare the trial balance of Vince Smith, Attorney, at March 31, 2010.

P2-31A *(L. OBJ. 2, 3, 4, 5)* **Journalizing transactions, posting to accounts in four-column format, and preparing a trial balance [45–60 min]**

The trial balance of Seth Knoll, CPA, is dated November 30, 2011:

SETH KNOLL, CPA Trial Balance November 30, 2011			
Account No.	**Account**	**Debit**	**Credit**
11	Cash	$ 3,000	
12	Accounts receivable	8,700	
13	Supplies	700	
14	Land	16,000	
21	Accounts payable		$ 4,200
31	Seth Knoll, Capital		24,200
32	Seth Knoll, Withdrawals		
41	Service revenue		
51	Salary expense		
52	Rent expense		
	Total	$ 28,400	$ 28,400

During December, Knoll or his business completed the following transactions:

Dec	4	Collected $5,000 cash from a client on account.
	8	Performed tax services for a client on account, $4,500.
	13	Paid business debt on account, $2,300.
	18	Purchased office supplies on account, $800.
	20	Knoll withdrew $1,900.
	21	Knoll paid for a deck for his private residence, using personal funds, $9,000.
	22	Received $2,200 cash for consulting work just completed.
	28	Paid office rent, $400.
	28	Paid employee salary, $1,200.

Requirements

1. Record the December transactions in the journal. Include an explanation for each entry.
2. Post the transactions to four-column accounts in the ledger, using dates, account numbers, journal references, and posting references. Open the ledger accounts listed in the trial balance, together with their balances at November 30.
3. Prepare the trial balance Seth Knoll, CPA, at December 31, 2011.

P2-32A *(L. OBJ. 2, 3, 4, 5)* **Journalizing transactions, posting to T-accounts, and preparing a trial balance [45–60 min]**

The trial balance of Shelley Summers, Registered Dietician, at December 31, 2010, follows.

SHELLEY SUMMERS, REGISTERED DIETICIAN Trial Balance December 31, 2010			
Account No.	Account	Debit	Credit
11	Cash	$ 4,000	
12	Accounts receivable	8,300	
13	Supplies	800	
14	Equipment	16,000	
21	Accounts payable		$ 5,500
31	Shelley Summers, Capital		23,600
32	Shelley Summers, Withdrawals		
41	Service revenue		
51	Salary expense		
52	Rent expense		
	Total	$ 29,100	$ 29,100

During January, Summers or her business completed the following transactions:

Jan	4	Collected $5,000 cash from a client on account.
	7	Performed a nutritional analysis for a hospital on account, $6,400.
	12	Summers used personal funds to pay for the renovation of her private residence, $53,000.
	16	Purchased supplies on account, $600.
	19	Summers withdrew $2,200.
	20	Paid business debt on account, $2,600.
	24	Received $2,400 cash for consulting with Pelican Foods.
	31	Paid rent, $700.
	31	Paid employee salary, $1,500.

Requirements

1. Record the January transactions in the business's journal. Include an explanation for each entry.
2. Post the transactions to four-column accounts in the ledger, using dates, account numbers, journal references, and posting references.
3. Prepare the trial balance of Shelley Summers, Registered Dietician, at January 31, 2011.

P2-33A *(L. OBJ. 2, 3, 4, 5)* **Recording transactions, using four-column accounts, posting, and preparing a trial balance [45–60 min]**

Mike Smith started an environmental consulting company and during the first month of operations (December 2012) the business completed the following transactions:

a. Smith began the business with an investment of $49,000 cash and a building at $22,000. The business issued $71,000 of capital to Smith.
b. Purchased office supplies on account, $2,300.
c. Paid $16,000 for office furniture.
d. Paid employee's salary, $1,900.
e. Performed consulting services on account, $3,300.
f. Paid $500 of the account payable created in transaction (b).
g. Received a $500 bill for advertising expense that will be paid in the near future.
h. Performed consulting service for cash, $900.
i. Received cash on account, $1,600.
j. Paid the following cash expenses:
   (1) Rent on equipment, $1,000.
   (2) Utilities, $800.
k. Smith withdrew $3,000.

Requirements

1. Open the following four-column accounts: Cash; Accounts receivable; Office supplies; Office furniture; Building; Accounts payable; Mike Smith, Capital; Mike Smith, Withdrawals; Service revenue; Salary expense; Rent expense; Advertising expense; Utilities expense.
2. Record each transaction in the journal. Use the letters to identify the transactions.
3. Post to the accounts and keep a running balance for each account.
4. Prepare the trial balance of Smith Environmental Consulting Company at December 31, 2012.

P2-34A *(L. OBJ. 2, 3, 4, 5)* **Recording transactions, using four-column accounts, posting, and preparing a trial balance [45–60 min]**

Val Vaughn started Vaughn Carpet Installers, and during the first month of operations (December 2011) the business completed the following selected transactions:

a. Vaughn began the business with an investment of $43,000 cash and an automobile worth $26,000. The business issued $69,000 of capital to Vaughn.
b. Paid $36,000 for equipment.
c. Purchased supplies on account, $400.
d. Paid employee's salary, $1,600.
e. Received $1,100 for a carpet installation job.
f. Received a $500 bill for advertising expense that will be paid in the near future.
g. Paid the account payable created in transaction (c).
h. Installed carpet for a hotel on account, $1,700.
i. Received cash on account, $1,700.
j. Paid the following cash expenses:
   (1) Rent, $1,100.
   (2) Insurance, $900.
k. Vaughn withdrew $2,000.

Requirements

1. Open the following four-column accounts: Cash; Accounts receivable; Supplies; Equipment; Automobile; Accounts payable; Val Vaughn, Capital; Val Vaughn, Withdrawals; Service revenue; Salary expense; Rent expense; Advertising expense; and Insurance expense.
2. Record the transactions in the journal. Use the letters to identify the transactions.
3. Post to the accounts and keep a running balance for each account.
4. Prepare the trial balance of Vaughn Carpet Installers at December 31, 2011.

P2-35A *(L. OBJ. 2, 5)* **Correcting errors in a trial balance [15–25 min]**
The trial balance of Kind Care Child Care does not balance.

KIND CARE CHILD CARE Trial Balance April 30, 2012		
Account	**Debit**	**Credit**
Cash	$ 6,600	
Accounts receivable	8,000	
Supplies	600	
Equipment	89,000	
Accounts payable		$ 55,000
Ron Lazer, Capital		50,700
Ron Lazer, Withdrawals	2,300	
Service revenue		4,500
Salary expense	4,100	
Rent expense	800	
Total	$ 111,400	$ 110,200

The following errors are detected:

a. Cash is understated by $2,000.
b. A $1,000 debit to Accounts receivable was posted as a credit.
c. A $1,400 purchase of supplies on account was neither journalized nor posted.
d. Equipment's cost is $84,300 not $89,000
e. Salary expense is overstated by $500.

Requirement

1. Prepare the corrected trial balance at April 30, 2012. Journal entries are not required.

P2-36A *(L. OBJ. 2, 5)* **Correcting errors in a trial balance [15–25 min]**
The trial balance for Gold Rush Exploration Company does not balance.

GOLD RUSH EXPLORATION COMPANY Trial Balance October 31, 2012		
Account	Debit	Credit
Cash	$ 6,200	
Accounts receivable	1,000	
Supplies	700	
Exploration equipment	22,400	
Computers	46,000	
Accounts payable		$ 2,500
Note payable		18,400
Ozzy Faulk, Capital		50,800
Ozzy Faulk, Withdrawals	8,000	
Service revenue		4,200
Salary expense	1,200	
Rent expense	500	
Advertising expense	700	
Utilities expense	100	
Total	$ 86,800	$ 75,900

The following errors were detected:

a. The cash balance is overstated by $2,000.
b. Rent expense of $390 was erroneously posted as a credit rather than a debit.
c. A $6,600 credit to Service revenue was not posted.
d. A $200 debit to Accounts receivable was posted as $20.
e. The balance of Utilities expense is understated by $10.
f. A $200 purchase of supplies on account was neither journalized nor posted.
g. Exploration equipment should be $19,130.

Requirement

1. Prepare the corrected trial balance at October 31, 2012. Journal entries are not required.

P2-37A *(L. OBJ. 5)* **Preparing financial statements from the trial balance [20–30 min]**
Link Back to Chapter 1 (Income Statement, Statement of Owner's Equity, Balance Sheet). Refer to Problem 2-27A. After completing the ledger in Problem 2-27A, prepare the following financial statements for Party Time Amusements Company:

Requirements

1. Income statement for the month ended November 30, 2012.
2. Statement of Owner's Equity for the month ended November 30, 2012. The beginning balance of Capital was $0.
3. Balance sheet at November 30, 2012.

P2-38A *(L. OBJ. 5)* **Preparing financial statements from the trial balance [20–30 min]** *Link Back to Chapter 1 (Income Statement, Statement of Owner's Equity, Balance Sheet)*. Refer to Problem 2-28A. After completing the trial balance in Problem 2-28A, prepare the following financial statements for William White. M.D.:

Requirements

1. Income statement for the month ended January 31, 2010.
2. Statement of Owner's Equity for the month ended January 31, 2010. The beginning balance of Capital was $0.
3. Balance sheet at January 31, 2010.

P2-39A *(L. OBJ. 5)* **Preparing financial statements from the trial balance [20–30 min]** *Link Back to Chapter 1 (Income Statement, Statement of Owner's Equity, Balance Sheet)*. Refer to Problem 2-29A. After completing the trial balance in Problem 2-29A, prepare the following financial statements for Donna White, Designer:

Requirements

1. Income statement for the month ended January 31, 2010.
2. Statement of Owner's Equity for the month ended January 31, 2010. The beginning balance of Capital was $0.
3. Balance sheet at January 31, 2010.

P2-40A *(L. OBJ. 5)* **Preparing financial statements from the trial balance [20–30 min]** *Link Back to Chapter 1 (Income Statement, Statement of Owner's Equity, Balance Sheet)*. Refer to Problem 2-30A. After completing the trial balance in Problem 2-30A, prepare the following financial statements for Vince Smith, Attorney:

Requirements

1. Income statement for the month ended March 31, 2010.
2. Statement of Owner's Equity for the month ended March 31, 2010. The beginning balance of Capital was $0.
3. Balance sheet at March 31, 2010.

P2-41A *(L. OBJ. 5)* **Preparing financial statements from the trial balance [20–30 min]** *Link Back to Chapter 1 (Income Statement, Statement of Owner's Equity, Balance Sheet)*. Refer to Problem 2-31A. After completing the trial balance in Problem 2-31A, prepare the following financial statements for Seth Knoll, CPA, at December 31, 2011:

Requirements

1. Income statement for the month ended December 31, 2011.
2. Statement of Owner's Equity for the month ended December 31, 2011.
3. Balance sheet at December 31, 2011.

P2-42A *(L. OBJ. 5)* **Preparing financial statements from the trial balance [20–30 min]** *Link Back to Chapter 1 (Income Statement, Statement of Owner's Equity, Balance Sheet)*. Refer to Problem 2-32A. After completing the trial balance in Problem 2-32A, prepare the following financial statements for Shelley Summers, Registered Dietician:

Requirements

1. Income statement for the month ended January 31, 2011.
2. Statement of Owner's Equity for the month ended January 31, 2011.
3. Balance sheet at January 31, 2011.

P2-43A *(L. OBJ. 5)* **Preparing financial statements from the trial balance [20–30 min]** *Link Back to Chapter 1 (Income Statement, Statement of Owner's Equity, Balance Sheet)*. Refer to Problem 2-33A. After completing the trial balance in Problem 2-33A, prepare the following financial statements for Smith Environmental Consulting Company:

Requirements

1. Income statement for the month ended December 31, 2012.
2. Statement of Owner's Equity for the month ended December 31, 2012. The beginning balance of Capital was $0.
3. Balance sheet at December 31, 2012.

P2-44A *(L. OBJ. 5)* **Preparing financial statements from the trial balance [20–30 min]** *Link Back to Chapter 1 (Income Statement, Statement of Owner's Equity, Balance Sheet)*. Refer to Problem 2-34A. After completing the trial balance in Problem 2-34A, prepare the following financial statements for Vaughn Carpet Installers:

Requirements

1. Income statement for the month ended December 31, 2011.
2. Statement of Owner's Equity for the month ended December 31, 2011.
3. Balance sheet at December 31, 2011.

■ Problems (Group B)

P2-45B *(L. OBJ. 2, 3, 4, 5)* **Analyzing and journalizing transactions, posting, and preparing a trial balance [40–50 min]**
Big Screen Amusements Company owns movie theaters. Big Screen engaged in the following business transactions in 2012:

Aug	1	Don Cougliato invested $390,000 personal cash in the business by depositing that amount in a bank account titled Big Screen Amusements. The business gave capital to Cougliato.
	2	Paid $300,000 cash to purchase a theater building.
	5	Borrowed $210,000 from the bank. Cougliato signed a note payable to the bank in the name of Big Screen.
	10	Purchased theater supplies on account, $1,100.
	15	Paid $800 on account.
	15	Paid property tax expense on theater building, $1,400.
	16	Paid employees' salaries $2,300, and rent on equipment $1,700. Make a single compound entry.
	28	Owner withdrew $10,000.
	31	Received $22,000 cash from service revenue and deposited that amount in the bank.

Big Screen Amusements uses the following accounts: Cash; Supplies; Building; Accounts payable; Notes payable; Don Cougliato, Capital; Don Cougliato, Withdrawals; Service revenue; Salary expense; Rent expense; Property tax expense.

Requirements

1. Journalize each transaction of Big Screen as shown for August 1. Explanations are not required.

Aug 1	Cash	390,000	
	Don Cougliato, Capital		390,000

2. Post the transactions to the T-accounts, using transaction dates as posting references in the ledger accounts. Label the balance of each account *Bal*, as shown in the chapter.

P2-46B *(L. OBJ. 2, 3, 4, 5)* **Analyzing and journalizing transactions, posting, and preparing a trial balance [45–60 min]**

Warren Smith practices medicine under the business title Warren Smith, M.D. During April, the medical practice completed the following transactions:

Apr	1	Smith deposited $78,000 cash in the business bank account. The business gave capital to Smith.
	5	Paid monthly rent on medical equipment, $780.
	9	Paid $18,000 cash to purchase land for an office site.
	10	Purchased supplies on account, $1,200.
	19	Borrowed $20,000 from the bank for business use. Smith signed a note payable to the bank in the name of the business.
	22	Paid $800 on account.
	30	Revenues earned during the month included $5,900 cash and $4,900 on account.
	30	Paid employees' salaries $2,000, office rent $1,800, and utilities $420. Make a single compound entry.
	30	Owner withdrew $9,000.

The business uses the following accounts: Cash; Accounts receivable; Supplies; Land; Accounts payable; Notes payable; Warren Smith, Capital; Warren Smith, Withdrawals; Service revenue; Salary expense; Rent expense; Utilities expense.

Requirements

1. Journalize each transaction, as shown for April 1. Explanations are not required.

Apr 1	Cash	78,000	
	Warren Smith, Capital		78,000

2. Post the transactions to the T-accounts, using transaction dates as posting references in the ledger accounts. Label the balance of each account *Bal*, as shown in the chapter.
3. Prepare the trial balance of Warren Smith, M.D., at April 30, 2010.

P2-47B *(L. OBJ. 2, 3, 4, 5)* **Journalizing transactions, posting to T-accounts, and preparing a trial balance [45–60 min]**

Ann Duxbury started her practice as a design consultant on March 1, 2010. During the first month of operations, the business completed the following transactions:

Mar	1	Received $37,000 cash and gave the owner capital.
	4	Purchased supplies, $700, and furniture, $2,100, on account.
	6	Performed services for a law firm and received $1,700 cash.
	7	Paid $26,000 cash to acquire land for a future office site.
	10	Performed service for a hotel and received its promise to pay the $1,100 within one week.
	14	Paid for the furniture purchased March 4 on account.
	15	Paid secretary's bi-monthly salary, $460.
	17	Received cash on account, $800.
	20	Prepared a design for a school on account, $800.
	28	Received $2,000 cash for consulting with Plummer & Gorden.
	31	Paid secretary's bi-monthly salary, $460.
	31	Paid rent expense, $890.
	31	Owner withdrew $2,500.

Requirements

1. Open the following T-accounts: Cash; Accounts receivable; Supplies; Furniture; Land; Accounts payable; Ann Duxbury, Capital; Ann Duxbury, Withdrawals; Service revenue; Salary expense; Rent expense.
2. Record each transaction in the journal, using the account titles given. Key each transaction by date. Explanations are not required.
3. Post the transactions to the T-accounts, using transaction dates as posting references in the ledger accounts. Label the balance of each account *Bal*, as shown in the chapter.
4. Prepare the trial balance of Ann Duxbury, Designer, at March 31, 2010.

P2-48B *(L. OBJ. 2, 3, 4, 5)* **Journalizing transactions, posting to accounts in four-column format, and preparing a trial balance [45–60 min]**

Timothy Muse opened a law office on October 2, 2010. During the first month of operations, the business completed the following transactions:

Oct	2	Muse deposited $34,000 cash in the business bank account Timothy Muse, Attorney, and the business gave Muse capital.
	3	Purchased supplies, $700, and furniture, $2,100, on account.
	4	Performed legal service for a client and received cash, $1,700.
	7	Paid cash to acquire land for a future office site, $22,000.
	11	Prepared legal documents for a client on account, $700.
	15	Paid secretary's bi-monthly salary, $520.
	16	Paid for the supplies purchased October 3 on account.
	18	Received $1,600 cash for helping a client sell real estate.
	19	Defended a client in court and billed the client for $800.
	29	Received cash on account, $800.
	31	Paid secretary's bi-monthly salary, $520.
	31	Paid rent expense, $630.
	31	Owner withdrew $2,400.

Requirements

1. Open the following T-accounts: Cash; Accounts receivable; Supplies; Furniture; Land; Accounts payable; Timothy Muse, Capital; Timothy Muse, Withdrawals; Service revenue; Salary expense; Rent expense.
2. Record each transaction in the journal, using the account titles given. Key each transaction by date. Explanations are not required.
3. Post the transactions to T-accounts, using transaction dates as posting references in the ledger. Label the balance of each account *Bal*, as shown in the chapter.
4. Prepare the trial balance of Timothy Muse, Attorney, at October 31, 2010.

P2-49B *(L. OBJ. 2, 3, 4, 5)* **Journalizing transactions, posting to accounts in four-column format, and preparing a trial balance [45–60 min]**
The trial balance of John Hilton, CPA, is dated September 30, 2011:

JOHN HILTON, CPA Trial Balance September 30, 2011			
Account No.	Account	Debit	Credit
11	Cash	$ 4,000	
12	Accounts receivable	8,000	
13	Supplies	700	
14	Land	17,000	
21	Accounts payable		$ 6,300
31	John Hilton, Capital		23,400
32	John Hilton, Withdrawals		
41	Service revenue		
51	Salary expense		
52	Rent expense		
	Total	$29,700	$29,700

During October, Hilton or his business completed the following transactions:

Oct	4	Collected $6,000 cash from a client on account.
	8	Performed tax services for a client on account, $4,800.
	13	Paid business debt on account, $2,200.
	18	Purchased office supplies on account, $900.
	20	Hilton withdrew $2,300.
	21	Hilton paid for a deck for his private residence, using personal funds, $10,000.
	22	Received $2,400 cash for consulting work just completed.
	28	Paid office rent, $500.
	28	Paid employee salary, $1,400.

Requirements

1. Record the October transactions in the journal. Include an explanation for each entry.
2. Post the transactions to four-column accounts in the ledger, using dates, account numbers, journal references, and posting references. Open the ledger accounts listed in the trial balance, together with their balances at September 30.
3. Prepare the trial balance of John Hilton, CPA, at October 31, 2011.

P2-50B *(L. OBJ. 2, 3, 4, 5)* **Journalizing transactions, posting to T-accounts, and preparing a trial balance [45–60 min]**
The trial balance of Sharon Silver, Registered Dietician, at September 30, 2011, follows:

SHARON SILVER, REGISTERED DIETICIAN Trial Balance September 30, 2011			
Account No.	Account	Debit	Credit
11	Cash	$ 7,000	
12	Accounts receivable	6,800	
13	Supplies	800	
14	Equipment	15,000	
21	Accounts payable		$ 5,000
31	Sharon Silver, Capital		24,600
32	Sharon Silver, Withdrawals		
41	Service revenue		
51	Salary expense		
52	Rent expense		
	Total	$29,600	$29,600

During October, Silver or her business completed the following transactions:

Oct	4	Collected $6,000 cash from a client on account.
	7	Performed a nutritional analysis for a hospital on account, $4,200.
	12	Silver used personal funds to pay for the renovation of private residence, $57,000.
	16	Purchased supplies on account, $700.
	19	Owner withdrew $1,900.
	20	Paid business debt on account, $2,400.
	24	Received $2,300 cash for consulting with Pelican Foods.
	31	Paid rent, $600.
	31	Paid employee salary, $1,900.

Requirements

1. Record the October transactions in the business's journal. Include an explanation for each entry.
2. Post the transactions to four-column accounts in the ledger, using dates, account numbers, journal references, and posting references.
3. Prepare the trial balance of Sharon Silver, Registered Dietician, at October 31, 2011.

P2-51B *(L. OBJ. 2, 3, 4, 5)* **Recording transactions, using four-column accounts, posting, and preparing a trial balance [45–60 min]**
Fran Stein started an environmental consulting company and during the first month of operations (February 2012) the business completed the following transactions:

a. Stein began the business with an investment of $42,000 cash and a building at $25,000. The business gave $67,000 of capital to Stein.
b. Purchased office supplies on account, $2,200.
c. Paid $19,000 for office furniture.
d. Paid employee's salary, $2,000.
e. Performed consulting services on account, $3,100.
f. Paid $700 of the account payable created in transaction (b).
g. Received a $600 bill for advertising expense that will be paid in the near future.
h. Performed consulting service for customers and received cash, $800.
i. Received cash on account, $1,300.
j. Paid the following cash expenses:
   (1) Rent on equipment, $900.
   (2) Utilities, $800.
k. Owner withdrew $2,900.

Requirements

1. Open the following four-column accounts: Cash; Accounts receivable; Office supplies; Office furniture; Building; Accounts payable; Fran Stein, Capital; Fran Stein, Withdrawals; Service revenue; Salary expense; Rent expense; Advertising expense; Utilities expense.
2. Record each transaction in the journal. Use the letters to identify the transactions.
3. Post to the accounts and keep a running balance for each account.
4. Prepare the trial balance of Stein Environmental Consulting Company at February 29, 2012.

P2-52B *(L. OBJ. 2, 3, 4, 5)* **Recording transactions, using four-column accounts, posting, and preparing a trial balance [45–60 min]**
Vann Stubbs started Stubbs Carpet Installers and during the first month of operations (December 2011) the business completed the following selected transactions:

a. Stubbs began the business with an investment of $40,000 cash and an automobile worth $20,000. The business gave Stubbs capital worth $60,000.
b. Paid $35,000 for equipment.
c. Purchased supplies on account, $600.
d. Paid employee's salary, $1,800.
e. Received $900 for a carpet installation job.
f. Received a $300 bill for advertising expense that will be paid in the near future.
g. Paid the account payable created in transaction (c).
h. Installed carpet for a hotel on account, $3,000.
i. Received cash on account, $1,100.
j. Paid the following cash expenses:
   (1) Rent, $1,200.
   (2) Insurance, $500.
k. Owner withdrew $2,200.

Requirements

1. Open the following four-column accounts: Cash; Accounts receivable; Supplies; Equipment; Automobile; Accounts payable; Vann Stubbs, Capital; Vann Stubbs, Withdrawals; Service revenue; Salary expense; Rent expense; Advertising expense; Insurance expense.
2. Record the transactions in the journal. Use the letters to identify the transactions.
3. Post to the accounts and keep a running balance for each account.
4. Prepare the trial balance of Stubbs Carpet Installers at December 31, 2011.

P2-53B *(L. OBJ. 2, 5)* **Correcting errors in a trial balance [15–25 min]**
The trial balance of URNO 1 Child Care does not balance.

URNO 1 CHILD CARE Trial Balance March 31, 2012		
Account	**Debit**	**Credit**
Cash	$ 6,100	
Accounts receivable	8,000	
Supplies	800	
Equipment	89,000	
Accounts payable		$ 56,000
Peg Johnson, Capital		50,000
Peg Johnson, Withdrawals	2,200	
Service revenue		4,200
Salary expense	3,600	
Rent expense	700	
Total	$ 110,400	$ 110,200

The following errors are detected:

a. Cash is understated by $5,000.
b. A $3,000 debit to Accounts receivable was posted as a credit.
c. A $1,000 purchase of supplies on account was neither journalized nor posted.
d. Equipment's cost is $78,200 not $89,000.
e. Salary expense is overstated by $400.

Requirement

1. Prepare the corrected trial balance at March 31, 2012. Journal entries are not required.

P2-54B *(L. OBJ. 2, 5)* **Correcting errors in a trial balance [15–25 min]**
The trial balance for Silver Shovels Exploration Company does not balance.

SILVER SHOVELS EXPLORATION COMPANY Trial Balance September 30, 2012		
Account	**Debit**	**Credit**
Cash	$ 6,500	
Accounts receivable	3,000	
Supplies	800	
Exploration equipment	22,700	
Computers	45,000	
Accounts payable		$ 2,200
Note payable		18,100
Philip Fink, Capital		50,900
Philip Fink, Withdrawals	1,000	
Service revenue		4,000
Salary expense	1,700	
Rent expense	400	
Advertising expense	700	
Utilities expense	300	
Total	$ 82,100	$ 75,200

The following errors were detected:

a. The cash balance is overstated by $3,000.
b. Rent expense of $390 was erroneously posted as a credit rather than a debit.
c. A $6,200 credit to Service revenue was not posted.
d. A $300 debit to Accounts receivable was posted as $30.
e. The balance of Utilities expense is understated by $40.
f. A $200 purchase of supplies on account was neither journalized nor posted.
g. Exploration equipment should be $23,910.

Requirement

1. Prepare the corrected trial balance at September 30, 2012. Journal entries are not required.

P2-55B *(L. OBJ. 5)* **Preparing financial statements from the trial balance [20–30 min]** *Link Back to Chapter 1 (Income Statement, Statement of Owner's Equity, Balance Sheet).* Refer to Problem 2-45B. After completing the ledger in Problem 2-45B, prepare the following financial statements for Big Screen Amusements Company:

Requirements

1. Income statement for the month ended August 31, 2012.
2. Statement of Owner's Equity for the month ended August 31, 2012. The beginning balance of Capital was $0.
3. Balance sheet at August 31, 2012.

P2-56B *(L. OBJ. 5)* **Preparing financial statements from the trial balance [20–30 min]** *Link Back to Chapter 1 (Income Statement, Statement of Owner's Equity, Balance Sheet).* Refer to Problem 2-46B. After completing the trial balance in Problem 2-46B, prepare the following financial statements for Warren Smith, M.D.:

Requirements

1. Income statement for the month ended April 30, 2010.
2. Statement of Owner's Equity for the month ended April 30, 2010. The beginning balance of Capital was $0.
3. Balance sheet at April 30, 2010.

P2-57B *(L. OBJ. 5)* **Preparing preparing financial statements from the trial balance [20–30 min]** *Link Back to Chapter 1 (Income Statement, Statement of Owner's Equity, Balance Sheet).* Refer to Problem 2-47B. After completing the trial balance in Problem 2-47B, prepare the following financial statements for Ann Duxbury, Designer:

Requirements

1. Income statement for the month ended March 31, 2010.
2. Statement of Owner's Equity for the month ended March 31, 2010. The beginning balance of Capital was $0.
3. Balance sheet at March 31, 2010.

P2-58B *(L. OBJ. 5)* **Preparing financial statements from the trial balance [20–30 min]** *Link Back to Chapter 1 (Income Statement, Statement of Owner's Equity, Balance Sheet).* Refer to Problem 2-48B. After completing the trial balance in Problem 2-48B, prepare the following financial statements for Timothy Muse, Attorney:

Requirements

1. Income statement for the month ended October 31, 2010.
2. Statement of Owner's Equity for the month ended October 31, 2010. The beginning balance of Capital was $0.
3. Balance sheet at October 31, 2010.

P2-59B *(L. OBJ. 5)* **Preparing financial statements from the trial balance [20–30 min]** *Link Back to Chapter 1 (Income Statement, Statement of Owner's Equity, Balance Sheet).* Refer to Problem 2-49B. After completing the trial balance in Problem 2-49B, prepare the following financial statements for John Hilton, CPA:

Requirements

1. Income statement for the month ended October 31, 2011.
2. Statement of Owner's Equity for the month ended October 31, 2011. The beginning balance of Capital was $0.
3. Balance sheet at October 31, 2011.

P2-60B *(L. OBJ. 5)* **Preparing financial statements from the trial balance [20–30 min]** *Link Back to Chapter 1 (Income Statement, Statement of Owner's Equity, Balance Sheet).* Refer to Problem 2-50B. After completing the trial balance in Problem 2-50B, prepare the following financial statements for Sharon Silver, Registered Dietician:

Requirements

1. Income statement for the month ended October 31, 2011.
2. Statement of Owner's Equity for the month ended October 31, 2011. The beginning balance of Capital was 0.
3. Balance sheet at October 31, 2011.

P2-61B *(L. OBJ. 5)* **Preparing financial statements from the trial balance [20–30 min]** *Link Back to Chapter 1 (Income Statement, Statement of Owner's Equity, Balance Sheet).* Refer to Problem 2-51B. After completing the trial balance in Problem 2-51B, prepare the following financial statements for Stein Environmental Consulting Company:

Requirements

1. Income statement for the month ended February 29, 2012.
2. Statement of Owner's Equity for the month ended February 29, 2012. The beginning balance of Capital was $0.
3. Balance sheet at February 29, 2012.

P2-62B *(L. OBJ. 5)* **Preparing financial statements from the trial balance [20–30 min]** *Link Back to Chapter 1 (Income Statement, Statement of Owner's Equity, Balance Sheet).* Refer to Problem 2-52B. After completing the trial balance in Problem 2-52B, prepare the following financial statements for Stubbs Carpet Installers:

Requirements

1. Income statement for the month ended December 31, 2011.
2. Statement of Owner's Equity for the month ended December 31, 2011.
3. Balance sheet at December 31, 2011.

Continuing Exercise

Exercise 2-63 continues with the consulting business of Sherman Lawn Service begun in Exercise 1-46. Here you will account for Sherman Lawn Service's transactions as it is actually done in practice.

E2-63 Sherman Lawn Service completed the following transactions during August:

Aug	1	Received $1,000 from owner, Hannah Sherman. Opened bank account titled Sherman Lawn Service.
	3	Purchased on account a mower, $1,000, and weed whacker, $400. The equipment is expected to remain in service for four years.
	5	Purchased $20 of gas. Wrote check #1 from the new bank account.
	6	Performed lawn services for client on account, $200.
	8	Purchased $50 of fertilizer from the lawn store. Wrote check #2 from the new bank account.
	17	Completed landscaping job for client, received cash $500.
	31	Received $50 on account from Aug 6 sale.

Requirements

1. Open T-accounts in the ledger: Cash; Accounts receivable; Lawn supplies; Equipment; Accounts payable; Hannah Sherman, Capital; Service revenue; Fuel expense.
2. Journalize the transactions. Explanations are not required.
3. Post to the T-accounts. Key all items by date, and denote an account balance as *Bal.* Formal posting references are not required.
4. Prepare a trial balance at August 31, 2009.

■ Continuing Problem

Problem 2-64 continues with the consulting business of Carl Haupt, begun in Problem 1-47. Here you will account for Haupt Consulting's transactions as it is actually done in practice.

P2-64 Haupt Consulting completed the following transactions during the first half of December, 2010:

Dec	2	Received $10,000 cash from owner Carl Haupt.
	2	Paid monthly office rent, $500.
	3	Paid cash for a **Dell** computer, $2,000. This equipment is expected to remain in service for five years.
	4	Purchased office furniture on account, $3,600. The furniture should last for five years.
	5	Purchased supplies on account, $300.
	9	Performed consulting service for a client on account, $1,700.
	12	Paid utility expenses, $200.
	18	Performed service for a client and received cash of $800.

Requirements

1. Open T-accounts in the ledger: Cash; Accounts receivable; Supplies; Equipment; Furniture; Accounts payable; Carl Haupt, Capital; Carl Haupt Withdrawals; Service revenue; Rent expense; Utilities expense.
2. Journalize the transactions. Explanations are not required.
3. Post to the T-accounts. Key all items by date, and denote an account balance as *Bal.* Formal posting references are not required.
4. Prepare a trial balance at December 18. In the Continuing Problem of Chapter 3, we will add transactions for the remainder of December and prepare a trial balance at December 31.

Practice Set

Use the chart of accounts you created in Chapter 1 (and add accounts where necessary). All of the first month's activity for Crystal Clear Cleaning is as follows.

Apr	1	CJ Oliver deposited $20,000 in the business account. Also on this date, CJ transferred his truck title, worth $5,000, to the business. CJ received capital.
	2	Wrote a check for $1,600 to Prestige Properties. In the "for" area of the check, it states "April thru July Rent."
	3	Purchased business insurance policy for $1,200 for the term April 1, 2009, through March 31, 2010, and paid cash.
	4	CJ went to the Cleaning Supply Company and purchased $220 of cleaning supplies on account. The invoice is due 20 days from the date of purchase.
	5	Purchased on account an industrial vacuum cleaner from Save-Now costing $2,000. The invoice is payable on or before April 25.
	7	Purchased a computer and printer costing a total of $1,500. A check for the same amount to the computer store was written on the same date.
	9	Performed cleaning services on account for Bob's Burger House in the amount of $3,200.
	10	Deposited Bob's check for $200 in the bank.
	15	Wrote check payable to Ben Larrison for $300 for contract labor.
	16	Received $1,200 for 1 year contract beginning April 1 for cleaning services to be provided to the Oar Restaurant. Contract begins April 1, 2009, and ends March 31, 2010.
	17	Provided cleaning services for In Balance Solutions for $700. In Balance paid with a check.
	18	Received water and electric bill for $200 with due date of May 4, 2009.
	20	Borrowed $10,000 from bank with interest at rate of 8% per year.
	21	Deposited check from Bob's Burger House for $1,000, with the notation: on account.
	25	Wrote check to Save Now for invoice #1035 in the amount of $1,500.
	29	Wrote check payable to **Pensacola News** for $200 for advertising.
	30	CJ Oliver withdrew $500.

Requirements

1. Journalize transactions as required from the activity data.
2. Post journal entries to T-accounts and calculate account balances.
3. Prepare Trial Balance for April 30.

Apply Your Knowledge

Decision Cases

Case 1. You have been requested by a friend named Dean McChesney to advise him on the effects that certain transactions will have on his business. Time is short, so you cannot journalize the transactions. Instead, you must analyze the transactions without a journal. McChesney will continue the business only if he can expect to earn monthly net income of $6,000. The business completed the following transactions during June:

a. McChesney deposited $10,000 cash in a business bank account to start the company. The company gave capital to McChesney.

b. Paid $300 cash for supplies.

c. Incurred advertising expense on account, $700.

d. Paid the following cash expenses: secretary's salary, $1,400; office rent, $1,100.

e. Earned service revenue on account, $8,800.

f. Collected cash from customers on account, $1,200.

Requirements

1. Open the following T-accounts: Cash; Accounts receivable; Supplies; Accounts payable; Dean McChesney, Capital; Service revenue; Salary expense; Rent expense; Advertising expense.

2. Post the transactions directly to the accounts without using a journal. Key each transaction by letter. Follow the format illustrated here for the first transaction.

Cash		Dan McChesney, Capital	
(a) 10,000			(a) 10,000

3. Prepare a trial balance at June 30, 2009. List the largest expense first, the next largest second, and so on. The business name is A-Plus Travel Planners.

4. Compute the amount of net income or net loss for this first month of operations. Would you recommend that McChesney continue in business?

Case 2. Answer the following questions. Consider each question separately. (Challenge)

Requirements

1. Explain the advantages of double-entry bookkeeping over single-entry bookkeeping to a friend who is opening a used book store.

2. When you deposit money in your bank account, the bank credits your account. Is the bank misusing the word *credit* in this context? Why does the bank use the term *credit* to refer to your deposit, instead of *debit*?

Ethical Issue

Better Days Ahead, a charitable organization, has a standing agreement with First National Bank. The agreement allows Better Days Ahead to overdraw its cash balance at the bank when donations are running low. In the past, Better Days Ahead managed funds wisely, and rarely used this privilege. Jacob Henson has recently become the manager of Better Days. To expand operations, Henson acquired office equipment and spent large amounts on fundraising. During Henson's tenure, Better Days Ahead has maintained a negative bank balance of approximately $10,000.

Requirement

1. What is the ethical issue in this situation? State why you approve or disapprove of Henson's management of Better Days Ahead's funds.

Financial Statement Case

This problem helps you develop skill in recording transactions by using a company's actual account titles. Refer to the **Amazon.com** financial statements in Appendix A. Assume that **Amazon.com** completed the following selected transactions during December 2007:

Dec	1	Earned sales revenue and collected cash, $60,000.
	9	Borrowed $200,000 by signing a note payable.
	12	Purchased equipment on account, $10,000.
	22	Paid half the account payable from December 12.
	28	Paid electricity bill for $3,000 (this is an administrative expense)
	31	Paid $100,000 of the note payable, plus interest expense of $1,000.

Requirement

1. Journalize these transactions, using the following account titles taken from the **Amazon.com** financial statements: Cash, Equipment, Accounts payable, Note payable, Sales revenue, Administrative expense, and Interest expense. Explanations are not required.

■ Team Project

Contact a local business and arrange with the owner to learn what accounts the business uses.

Requirements

1. Obtain a copy of the business's chart of accounts.
2. Prepare the company's financial statements for the most recent month, quarter, or year. You may use either made-up account balances or balances supplied by the owner.

If the business has a large number of accounts within a category, combine related accounts and report a single amount on the financial statements. For example, the company may have several cash accounts. Combine all cash amounts and report a single Cash amount on the balance sheet.

You will probably encounter numerous accounts that you have not yet learned. Deal with these as best you can. The chart of accounts given in the inside covers of this book will be helpful.

Keep in mind that the financial statements report the balances of the accounts listed in the company's chart of accounts. Therefore, the financial statements must be consistent with the chart of accounts.

Quick Check Answers

1. *c* 2. *b* 3. *a* 4. *d* 5. *a* 6. *c* 7. *a* 8. *b* 9. *a* 10. *d*

For online homework, exercises, and problems that provide you immediate feedback, please visit www.myaccountinglab.com.

Chapter 2: Demo Doc

■ Debit/Credit Transaction Analysis

To make sure you understand this material, work through the following demonstration "demo doc" with detailed comments to help you see the concept within the framework of a worked-through problem.

Learning Objectives 1, 2, 3, 4

On September 1, 2011, Michael Moe started Moe's Mowing, a company that provides mowing and landscaping services. During the month of September, the business incurred the following transactions:

a. **To begin operations, Michael deposited $10,000 cash in the business's bank account. The business received the cash and gave capital to Michael.**

b. **The business purchased equipment for $3,500 on account.**

c. **The business purchased office supplies for $800 cash.**

d. **The business provided $2,600 of services to a customer on account.**

e. **The business paid $500 cash toward the equipment previously purchased on account in transaction b.**

f. **The business received $2,000 in cash for services provided to a new customer.**

g. **The business paid $200 cash to repair equipment.**

h. **The business paid $900 cash in salary expense.**

i. **The business received $2,100 cash from customers on account.**

j. **The owner withdrew $1,500.**

Requirements

1. Create blank T-accounts for the following accounts: Cash; Accounts receivable; Supplies; Equipment; Accounts payable; Michael Moe, Capital; Michael Moe, Withdrawals; Service revenue; Salary expense; Repair expense.
2. Journalize the transactions and show how they are recorded in T-accounts.
3. Total all of the T-accounts to determine their balances at the end of the month.

Demo Doc Solutions

Requirement 1

Create blank T-accounts for the following accounts: Cash; Accounts receivable; Supplies; Equipment; Accounts payable; Michael Moe, Capital; Michael Moe, Withdrawals; Service revenue; Salary expense; Repair expense.

Part 1	Part 2	Part 3	Demo Doc Complete

Opening a T-account means drawing a blank account that looks like a capital "T" and putting the account title across the top. T-accounts give you a diagram of the additions and subtractions made to the accounts. For easy reference, they are usually organized into assets, liabilities, owner's equity, revenue, and expenses (in that order).

ASSETS = LIABILITIES + OWNER'S EQUITY

Cash

Supplies

Accounts payable

Michael Moe, Capital

Michael Moe, Withdrawals

Service revenue

Accounts receivable

Equipment

Salary expense

Repair expense

Requirement 2

Journalize the transactions and show how they are recorded in T-accounts.

Part 1	**Part 2**	Part 3	Demo Doc Complete

a. To begin operations, Michael deposited $10,000 cash in the business's bank account. The business received the cash and gave capital to Michael.

First, we must determine which accounts are affected.

The business received $10,000 cash from its sole owner (Michael Moe). In exchange, the business gave capital to Michael. So, the accounts involved are Cash and Michael Moe, Capital.

The next step is to determine what type of accounts these are. Cash is an asset and Michael Moe, Capital is part of equity.

Next, we must determine if these accounts increased or decreased. From *the business's* point of view, Cash (an asset) has increased. Michael Moe, Capital (equity) has also increased.

Now we must determine if these accounts should be debited or credited. According to the rules of debit and credit, an increase in assets is a debit, while an increase in equity is a credit.

So, Cash (an asset) increases, which is a debit. Michael Moe, Capital (equity) also increases, which is a credit.

The journal entry would be as follows:

a.		Cash (A+)	10,000	
		Michael Moe, Capital (Q+)		10,000
		Owner investment.		

Note that the total dollar amounts of debits will equal the total dollar amounts of credits.

Remember to use the transaction letters as references. This will help as we post this entry to the T-accounts.

Each T-account has two sides for recording debits and credits. To record the transaction to the T-account, simply transfer the amount of the debit(s) to the correct account(s) as a debit (left-side) entry, and transfer the amount of the credit(s) to the correct account(s) as a credit (right-side) entry.

For this transaction, there is a debit of $10,000 to cash. This means that $10,000 is entered on the left side of the Cash T-account. There is also a credit of $10,000 to Michael Moe, Capital. This means that $10,000 is entered on the right side of the Michael Moe, Capital account.

Cash	
a. 10,000	

Michael Moe, Capital	
	a. 10,000

b. The business purchased equipment for $3,500 on account.

The business received equipment in exchange for a promise to pay for the cost ($3,500) at a future date. So the accounts involved in the transaction are Equipment and Accounts payable.

Equipment is an asset and Accounts payable is a liability.

The asset Equipment has increased. The liability Accounts payable has also increased.

Looking at Exhibit 2-8, an increase in assets (in this case, the increase in Equipment) is a debit, while an increase in liabilities (in this case, Accounts payable) is a credit.

The journal entry would be as follows:

b.	Equipment (A+)	3,500	
	Accounts payable (L+)		3,500
	Purchase of equipment on account.		

$3,500 is entered on the debit (left) side of the Equipment T-account. $3,500 is entered on the credit (right) side of the Accounts payable account.

Equipment			Accounts payable	
b.	3,500		b.	3,500

c. **The business purchased office supplies for $800 cash.**

The business purchased supplies in exchange for cash ($800). So the accounts involved in the transaction are Supplies and Cash.

Supplies and Cash are both assets.

Supplies (an asset) has increased. Cash (an asset) has decreased.

Looking at Exhibit 2-8, an increase in assets is a debit, while a decrease in assets is a credit.

So the increase to Supplies (an asset) is a debit, while the decrease to Cash (an asset) is a credit.

The journal entry would be as follows:

c.	Supplies (A+)	800	
	Cash (A–)		800
	Purchase of supplies for cash.		

$800 is entered on the debit (left) side of the Supplies T-account. $800 is entered on the credit (right) side of the Cash account.

Cash				Supplies	
a.	10,000	c.	800	c.	800

Notice the $10,000 already on the debit side of the Cash account. This is from transaction a.

d. **The business provided $2,600 of services to a customer on account.**

The business received promises from customers to send cash ($2,600) next month in exchange for services rendered. So the accounts involved in the transaction are Accounts receivable and Service revenue.

Accounts receivable is an asset and Service revenue is revenue.

Accounts receivable (an asset) has increased. Service revenue (revenue) has also increased.

Looking at Exhibit 2-8, an increase in assets is a debit, while an increase in revenue is a credit.

So the increase to Accounts receivable (an asset) is a debit, while the increase to Service revenue (revenue) is a credit.

The journal entry is as follows:

d.	Accounts receivable (A+)	2,600	
	Service revenue (R+)		2,600
	Provided services on account.		

$2,600 is entered on the debit (left) side of the Accounts receivable T-account. $2,600 is entered on the credit (right) side of the Service revenue account.

Accounts receivable			
d.	2,600		

Service revenue			
		d.	2,600

e. **The business paid $500 cash toward the equipment previously purchased on account in transaction b.**

The business paid *some* of the money that was owed on the purchase of equipment in transaction b. The accounts involved in the transaction are Accounts payable and Cash.

Accounts payable is a liability that has decreased. Cash is an asset that has also decreased.

Remember, the Accounts payable account is a list of creditors to whom the business will have to make payments in the future (a liability). When the business makes these payments to the creditors, the amount of this account decreases, because the business now owes less (in this case, it reduces from $3,500—in transaction **b**—to $3,000).

Looking at Exhibit 2-8, a decrease in liabilities is a debit, while a decrease in assets is a credit.

So Accounts payable (a liability) decreases, which is a debit. Cash (an asset) decreases, which is a credit.

e.	Accounts payable (L–)	500	
	Cash (A–)		500
	Partial payment on Accounts payable.		

$500 is entered on the debit (left) side of the Accounts payable T-account. $500 is entered on the credit (right) side of the Cash account.

Cash			
a.	10,000		
		c.	800
		e.	500

Accounts payable			
		b.	3,500
e.	500		

Again notice the amounts already in the T-accounts from previous transactions. We can tell which transaction caused each amount to appear by looking at the reference letter next to each number.

f. The business received $2,000 in cash for services provided to a new customer.

The business received cash, $2,000, in exchange for mowing and landscaping services rendered to clients. The accounts involved in the transaction are Cash and Service revenue.

Cash is an asset that has increased and Service revenue is revenue, which has also increased.

Looking at Exhibit 2-8, an increase in assets is a debit, while an increase in revenue is a credit.

f.	Cash (A+)	2,000	
	Service revenue (R+)		2,000
	Provided services for cash.		

So the increase to Cash (an asset) is a debit. The increase to Service revenue (revenue) is a credit.

$2,000 is entered on the debit (left) side of the Cash T-account. $2,000 is entered on the credit (right) side of the Service revenue account.

Cash

	Debit		Credit
a.	10,000		
		c.	800
		e.	500
f.	2,000		

Service revenue

	Debit		Credit
		d.	2,600
		f.	2,000

Notice how we keep adding onto the T-accounts. The values from previous transactions are already in place.

g. The business paid $200 cash to repair equipment.

The business paid $200 cash to repair equipment. Because the benefit of the repairs has already been used, the repairs are recorded as Repair expense. Because the repairs were paid in cash, the Cash account is also involved.

Repair expense is an expense that has increased and Cash is an asset that has decreased.

Looking at Exhibit 2-8, an increase in expenses is a debit, while a decrease in an asset is a credit.

So Repair expense (an expense) increases, which is debit. Cash (an asset) decreases, which is a credit.

g.	Repair expense (E+)	200	
	Cash (A–)		200
	Payment for repairs.		

$200 is entered on the debit (left) side of the Repair expense T-account. $200 is entered on the credit (right) side of the Cash account.

Cash

	Debit		Credit
a.	10,000		
		c.	800
		e.	500
f.	2,000		
		g.	200

Repair expense

	Debit		Credit
g.	200		

h. The business paid $900 cash for salary expense.

The business paid employees $900 in cash. Because the benefit of the employees' work has already been used, their salaries are recorded as Salary expense. Because the salaries were paid in cash, the Cash account is also involved.

Salary expense is an expense that has increased and Cash is an asset that has decreased.

Looking at Exhibit 2-8, an increase in expenses is a debit, while a decrease in an asset is a credit.

In this case, Salary expense (an expense) increases, which is a debit. Cash (an asset) decreases, which is a credit.

h.	Salary expense (E+)	900	
	Cash (A–)		900
	Payment of salary using cash.		

$900 is entered on the debit (left) side of the Salary expense T-account. $900 is entered on the credit (right) side of the Cash account.

Cash

	Debit		Credit
a.	10,000		
		c.	800
		e.	500
f.	2,000		
		g.	200
		h.	900

Salary expense

	Debit	Credit
h.	900	

i. The business received $2,100 cash from customers on account.

The business received payments ($2,100) from customers for services previously provided in transaction d. The accounts involved in this transaction are Cash and Accounts receivable.

Cash and Accounts receivable are both assets.

The asset Cash has increased, and the asset Accounts receivable has decreased.

Remember, Accounts receivable is a list of customers from whom the business will receive money. When the business receives these payments from its customers, the amount of this account decreases, because the business now has less to receive in the future (in this case, it reduces from $2,600—in transaction d—to $500).

Looking at Exhibit 2-8, an increase in assets is a debit, while a decrease in assets is a credit.

So Cash (an asset) increases, which is a debit. Accounts receivable (an asset) decreases, which is a credit.

i.	Cash (A+)	2,100	
	Accounts receivable (A–)		2,100
	Receipt of payment from customer.		

$2,100 is entered on the debit (left) side of the Cash T-account. $2,100 is entered on the credit (right) side of the Accounts receivable account.

Cash

	Debit		Credit
a.	10,000		
		c.	800
		e.	500
f.	2,000		
		g.	200
		h.	900
i.	2,100		

Accounts receivable

	Debit		Credit
d.	2,600	i.	2,100

j. The owner withdrew $1,500.

Michael Moe (the owner) withdrew cash from the business. This caused Michael's ownership interest (equity) to decrease. The accounts involved in this transaction are Withdrawals and Cash.

Withdrawals have increased and Cash is an asset that has decreased.

Looking at Exhibit 2-8, an increase in withdrawals is a debit, while a decrease in an asset is a credit.

Remember that Withdrawals are a negative element of owner's equity. Therefore, when Withdrawals increase, owner's equity decreases. So in this case, Withdrawals decrease equity with a debit. Cash (an asset) decreases with a credit.

			Debit	Credit
j.		Michael Moe, Withdrawals (W+)	1,500	
		Cash (A–)		1,500
		Owner withdrawals.		

$1,500 is entered on the debit (left) side of the Withdrawals T-account. $1,500 is entered on the credit (right) side of the Cash account.

Cash

	Debit		Credit
a.	10,000		
		c.	800
		e.	500
f.	2.000		
		g.	200
		h.	900
i.	2,100		
		j.	1,500

Michael Moe, Withdrawals

	Debit		Credit
j.	1,500		

Now we will summarize all of the journal entries during the month:

Ref.	Accounts and Explanation	Debit	Credit
a.	Cash	10,000	
	Michael Moe, Capital		10,000
	Owner investment.		
b.	Equipment	3,500	
	Accounts payable		3,500
	Purchase of equipment on account.		
c.	Supplies	800	
	Cash		800
	Purchase of supplies for cash.		
d.	Accounts receivable	2,600	
	Service revenue		2,600
	Provided services on credit.		
e.	Accounts payable	500	
	Cash		500
	Partial payment on account.		
f.	Cash	2,000	
	Service revenue		2,000
	Provided services for cash.		
g.	Repair expense	200	
	Cash		200
	Payment for repairs.		
h.	Salary expense	900	
	Cash		900
	Payment of salary.		
i.	Cash	2,100	
	Accounts receivable		2,100
	Receipt of cash on account.		
j.	Michael Moe, Withdrawals	1,500	
	Cash		1,500
	Owner withdrawals.		

Requirement 3

Total all of the T-accounts to determine their balances at the end of the month.

Part 1	Part 2	**Part 3**	Demo Doc Complete

To compute the balance in a T-account (total the T-account), add up the numbers on the debit/left side of the account and (separately) the credit/right side of the account. The difference between the total debits and total credits is the account's balance, which is placed on the side of the larger number (that is, the side with a balance). This gives the balance in the T-account (the net total of both sides combined).

For example, for the Cash account, the numbers on the left side total $10,000 + $2,000 + $2,100 = $14,100. The credit/right side = $800 + $500 + $200 + $900 + $1,500 = $3,900. The difference is $14,100 – $3,900 = $10,200. We put the $10,200 on the debit side because that was the side of the bigger number of $14,100. This is called a debit balance.

An easy way to think of totaling T-accounts is:

> Beginning balance in T-account
> + Increases to T-account
> – Decreases to T-account
> T-account balance (total)

T-accounts after posting all transactions and totaling each account:

ASSETS = LIABILITIES + OWNER'S EQUITY

Cash

	Debit		Credit
a.	10,000		
		c.	800
		e.	500
f.	2,000		
		g.	200
		h.	900
i.	2,100		
		j.	1,500
Bal	10,200		

Accounts receivable

	Debit		Credit
d.	2,600		
		i.	2,100
Bal	500		

Supplies

	Debit		Credit
c.	800		
Bal	800		

Equipment

	Debit		Credit
b.	3,500		
Bal	3,500		

Accounts payable

	Debit		Credit
		b.	3,500
e.	500		
		Bal	3,000

Michael Moe, Capital

	Debit		Credit
		a.	10,000
		Bal	10,000

Michael Moe, Withdrawals

	Debit		Credit
j.	1,500		
Bal	1,500		

Service revenue

	Debit		Credit
		d.	2,600
		f.	2,000
		Bal	4,600

Salary expense

	Debit		Credit
h.	900		
Bal	900		

Repair expense

	Debit		Credit
g.	200		
Bal	200		

Part 1 | Part 2 | Part 3 | **Demo Doc Complete**

3 The Adjusting Process

Learning Objectives/Success Keys

1. Differentiate between accrual and cash-basis accounting
2. Define and apply the accounting period concept, revenue, and matching principles
3. Explain why adjusting entries are needed
4. Journalize and post adjusting entries
5. Explain the purpose of and prepare an adjusted trial balance
6. Prepare the financial statements from the adjusted trial balance

Chapter 1 introduced you to the accounting equation and the financial statements. Chapter 2 brought T-accounts, debits, credits, and the trial balance. You are now ready for the next step in the accounting cycle.

Sherman Lawn Service and Greg's Groovy Tunes have well-oiled accounting systems. At the end of each period, Hannah Sherman and Greg Moore need to measure their

- Operating performance
- Financial position

Chapter 3 continues the accounting cycle by showing how to update the accounts at the end of the period. The process is called *adjusting the books* and it requires special journal entries called *adjusting entries.*

Study this material carefully. It applies to small businesses like Greg's Groovy Tunes and Smart Touch Learning and to giant companies such as **eBay** and **ExxonMobil.** It also applies to the business you may operate someday.

Accountants have concepts and principles to guide their work. Chief among these are the following:

- Accrual accounting versus cash-basis accounting
- The accounting period

- The revenue principle
- The matching principle

In this chapter, we apply these principles to Smart Touch Learning for the month of April. **ExxonMobil, eBay,** and all other companies follow the same principles.

Accrual Accounting Versus Cash-Basis Accounting

1 Differentiate between accrual and cash-basis accounting

There are two ways to do accounting:

- **Accrual accounting** records the effect of each transaction as it occurs—that is, revenues are recorded when earned and expenses are recorded when incurred. Most businesses use the accrual basis as covered in this book.
- **Cash-basis accounting** records only cash receipts and cash payments. It ignores receivables, payables, and depreciation. Only very small businesses use the cash basis of accounting.

Suppose Smart Touch Learning purchased $200 of office supplies on account on May 15, 2010, and paid the account in full on June 3, 2010. On the accrual basis, the business records this transaction as follows:

May 15	Office supplies (A+)	200	
	Accounts payable (L+)		200
	Purchased supplies on account.		
Jun 3	Accounts payable (L–)	200	
	Cash (A–)		200
	Paid on account.		

In contrast, cash-basis accounting ignores this transaction on May 15 because the business paid no cash. The cash basis records only cash receipts and cash payments. *In the cash basis,*

- Cash receipts are treated as revenues.
- Cash payments are treated as expenses.

Under the cash basis, Smart Touch Learning would record each cash payment as an expense. So for our office supplies example, the company would recognize the cash basis expense on June 3, 2010, because that is the date that cash was paid. This is faulty accounting because the business acquired supplies, which are assets.

Now let us see how differently the accrual basis and the cash basis account for a revenue. Suppose Smart Touch Learning performed service and earned revenue on May 20, 2010, but did not collect cash until June 5, 2010. Under the accrual basis, the business records $1,000 of revenue on account on May 20 as follows:

May 20	Accounts receivable (A+)	1,000	
	Service revenue (R+)		1,000
	Earned revenue on account.		
Jun 5	Cash (A+)	1,000	
	Accounts receivable (A–)		1,000
	Received on account.		

Under the cash basis, the business would record no revenue until the cash receipt, which in this case would be on June 5. As a result, cash-basis accounting never reports accounts receivable from customers. In this case, cash-basis accounting actually shows the revenue in the wrong accounting period (June). Revenue should be recorded when it is earned (May), and that is how the accrual basis operates.

Exhibit 3-1 illustrates the difference between the accrual basis and the cash basis for a florist. Keep in mind that the accrual basis is the correct way to do accounting.

EXHIBIT 3-1 Accrual Accounting Versus Cash-Basis Accounting

Stop & Think...

Most of us think in terms of cash. Did our bank balance go up or down? This is in essence what the cash basis measures—changes in the cash balance. But consider your job. When do you actually earn your salary— when you go to work or when you get paid? When you go to work you earn. That is when you accrue revenue under the accrual basis—not when you get paid by your employer.

Other Accounting Principles

The Accounting Period

2 Define and apply the accounting period concept, revenue, and matching principles

Smart Touch Learning will know with 100% certainty how well it has operated only if the company sells the assets, pays the liabilities, and gives any leftover cash to the owner. This process of going out of business is called **liquidation**. For obvious reasons, it is not practical to measure income this way. Because businesses need periodic reports on their affairs, accountants slice time into small segments and prepare financial statements for specific periods, such as a month, quarter, or year.

The basic accounting period is one year, and all businesses prepare annual financial statements. For most companies, the annual accounting period runs the calendar year from January 1 through December 31. Other companies use a *fiscal year*, which ends on a date other than December 31. The year-end date is usually the low point in business activity for the year. Retailers are a notable example. For instance, **Wal-Mart**, **JCPenney**, and most other retailers use a fiscal year that ends on January 31 because their low point comes about a month after Christmas.

Companies also prepare financial statements for *interim* periods, such as monthly, quarterly, and semiannually. Most of our discussions are based on an annual accounting period, but everything can be applied to interim periods as well.

The Revenue Principle

The **revenue principle** tells accountants

- *When* to record revenue—that is, when to make a journal entry for a revenue
- The *amount* of revenue to record

"Recording" something in accounting means making an entry in the journal. That is where the process starts.

When to Record Revenue

The revenue principle says to record revenue when it has been earned—but not before. Revenue has been earned when the business has delivered a good or service to the customer. The company has done everything required by the sale agreement—that is, the earnings process is complete.

Exhibit 3-2 shows two situations that provide guidance on when to record revenue for Smart Touch Learning. The first situation illustrates when *not* to record revenue—because the client merely states his plan. Situation 2 illustrates when revenue *should* be recorded—after the e-learning agency has performed a service for the client.

EXHIBIT 3-2 | **Recording Revenue: The Revenue Principle**

Situation 1
No transaction: Do Not Record Revenue

Situation 2
The client has taken the course: Record Revenue

The Amount of Revenue to Record

Record revenue for the actual value of the item or service transferred to the customer. Suppose that in order to obtain a new client, Sheena Bright performs e-learning services for the cut-rate price of $100. Ordinarily, the business would have charged $200 for this service. How much revenue should the business record? The answer is $100 because that was the value of this particular transaction. Sheena Bright did not charge $200, so that is not the amount of revenue. Smart Touch charged only $100, so it records $100 of revenue.

The Matching Principle

The **matching principle** guides accounting for expenses. Recall that expenses—such as salaries, rent, utilities, and advertising—are assets used up and liabilities incurred in order to earn revenue. The matching principle

1. Measures all the expenses incurred during the period
2. Matches the expenses against the revenues of the period

To match expenses against revenues means to subtract expenses incurred during one month from revenues earned during that same month. The goal is to compute net income or net loss. Exhibit 3-3 illustrates the matching principle.

EXHIBIT 3-3 | Recording Expenses: The Matching Principle

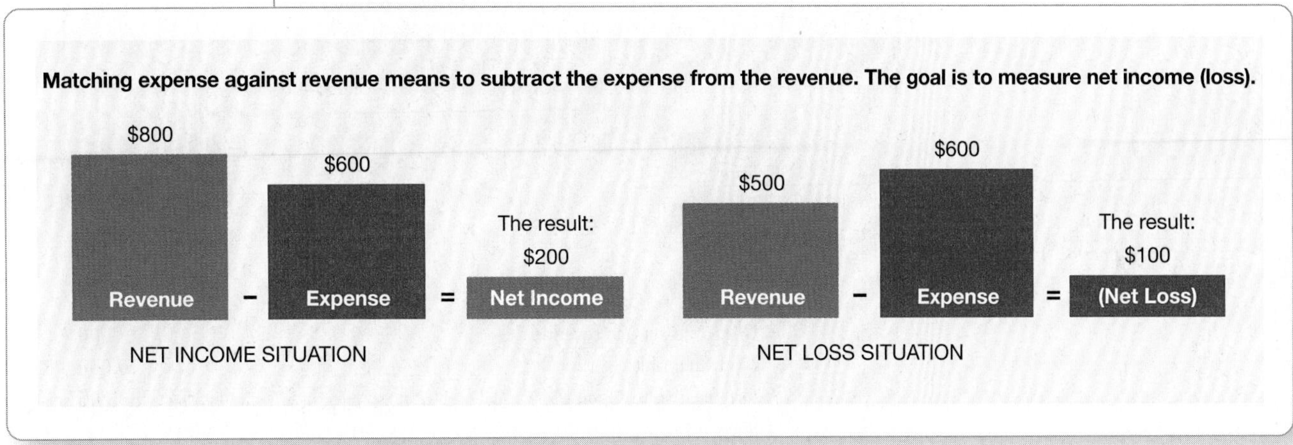

There is a natural link between some expenses and revenues. For example, Smart Touch Learning pays a commission to the employee who sells the e-learning agency's services. Other expenses are not so easy to link to sales. For example, Smart Touch Learning's monthly rent expense occurs regardless of the revenues earned that month. The matching principle tells us to identify those expenses with a particular period, such as a month or a year. The business will record rent expense each month based on the rental agreement. Smart Touch also pays a monthly salary to its employee.

How does Smart Touch Learning bring its accounts up to date for the financial statements? To address this question, accountants use the time-period concept.

The Time-Period Concept

Owners need periodic reports on their businesses. The **time-period concept** ensures that information is reported often. To measure income, companies update their accounts at the end of each period.

Let us look at Smart Touch Learning for an example of an expense accrual. On May 31, the business recorded salary expense of $900 that it owed the employee at the end of the month. Smart Touch's accrual entry was

May 31	Salary expense (E+)	900	
	Salary payable (L+)		900
	Accrued salary expense.		

This entry assigns the salary expense to May because that was the month when the employee worked for the company. Without this entry, May's expenses would be understated, and net income would be overstated. The accrual entry also records the liability owed at May 31. Without this entry, total liabilities would be understated. The remainder of the chapter shows how to adjust the accounts and bring the books up to date.

Why We Adjust the Accounts

3 Explain why adjusting entries are needed

At the end of the period, the accountant prepares the financial statements. The end-of-period process begins with the trial balance. Exhibit 3-4 is the trial balance of Smart Touch Learning at May 31, 2010.

EXHIBIT 3-4 Unadjusted Trial Balance

SMART TOUCH LEARNING Unadjusted Trial Balance May 31, 2010		
Cash	$ 4,800	
Accounts receivable	2,200	
Supplies	700	
Prepaid rent	3,000	
Furniture	18,000	
Building	48,000	
Accounts payable		$18,200
Unearned service revenue		600
Notes payable		20,000
Sheena Bright, Capital		33,200
Sheena Bright, Withdrawals	1,000	
Service revenue		7,000
Salary expense	900	
Utilities expense	400	
Total	$79,000	$79,000

This *unadjusted trial balance* lists the revenues and expenses of the e-learning agency for May. But these amounts are incomplete because they omit various revenue and expense transactions. That is why the trial balance is *unadjusted.* Usually, however, we refer to it simply as the trial balance, without the label "unadjusted."

Accrual accounting requires adjusting entries at the end of the period. We must have correct balances for the financial statements. To see why, consider the Supplies account in Exhibit 3-4.

Smart Touch Learning uses supplies during the month. This reduces the supplies on hand and creates an expense. It is a waste of time to record supplies expense every time supplies are used. But by the end of the month, some of the $700 of Supplies on the unadjusted trial balance (Exhibit 3-4) have probably been used. So how does Sheena Bright account for the supplies expense? She must adjust the accounts at May 31.

Adjusting entries assign revenues to the period when they are earned and expenses to the period when they are incurred. Adjusting entries also update the asset and liability accounts. Adjustments are needed to properly measure two things:

1. Net income (loss) on the income statement and
2. Assets and liabilities on the balance sheet.

This end-of-period process is called *making the adjustments* or *adjusting the books*. Remember the following three facts about adjusting entries:

1. Adjusting entries never involve cash.
2. Adjusting entries either
   a. Increase revenue earned (Revenue credit) or
   b. Increase an expense (Expense debit)
3. The word "accrued" means you must journalize whatever amount you are being told about. (This will be explained further in an example later in the chapter.)

Two Categories of Adjusting Entries

4 Journalize and post adjusting entries

The two basic categories of adjustments are *prepaids* and *accruals*. In a *prepaid* adjustment, the cash payment occurs before an expense is recorded. *Accrual* adjustments are the opposite. An accrual records an expense before the cash payment.

Adjusting entries fall into five types:

1. Prepaid expenses
2. Depreciation
3. Accrued expenses
4. Accrued revenues
5. Unearned revenues

The focus of this chapter is on learning how to account for these five types of adjusting entries.

Prepaid Expenses

Prepaid expenses are advance payments of expenses. For example, **McDonald's**, the restaurant chain, makes prepayments for rent, insurance, and supplies. Prepaid expenses are assets, rather than expenses. When the prepayment is used up, the used portion of the asset becomes an expense via an adjusting journal entry.

Prepaid Rent

Landlords require tenants to pay rent in advance. This prepayment creates an asset for the renter. Suppose Smart Touch Learning prepays three months' office rent on May 1, 2010. If the lease specifies a monthly rental of $1,000, the entry to record the payment is

May 1	Prepaid rent ($1,000 × 3) (A+)	3,000	
	Cash (A–)		3,000
	Paid rent in advance.		

After posting, Prepaid rent has a $3,000 debit balance.

ASSETS

Prepaid rent	
May 1 3,000	

The trial balance at May 31, 2010, lists Prepaid rent with a debit balance of $3,000 (Exhibit 3-4). Throughout May, Prepaid rent maintains this balance. But $3,000 is *not* the amount of Prepaid rent for the balance sheet at May 31. Why?

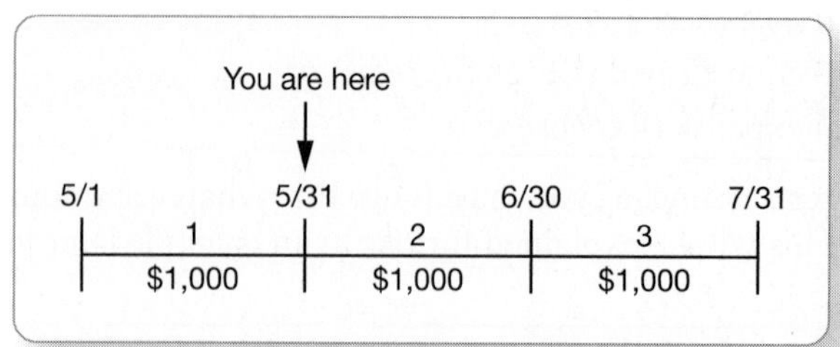

At May 31, Prepaid rent should be decreased for the amount that has been used up. The used-up portion is one month of the three months prepaid, or one-third of the prepayment. Recall that an asset that has expired is an *expense*. The adjusting entry transfers $1,000 ($3,000 × 1/3) from the Prepaid rent to Rent expense. The adjusting entry is

a.	May 31	Rent expense ($3,000 × 1/3) (E+)	1,000	
		Prepaid rent (A–)		1,000
		To record rent expense.		

After posting, Prepaid rent and Rent expense show correct ending balances:

ASSETS

Prepaid rent

May 1	3,000	May 31	1,000
Bal	2,000		

EXPENSES

Rent expense

May 31	1,000	
Bal	1,000	

Correct asset amount:		Total accounted for:		Correct expense amount:
$2,000	→	$3,000	←	$1,000

The Prepaid rent is an example of an asset that was overstated prior to posting the adjusting entry. Notice that the ending balance in Prepaid rent is now $2,000. Prepaid rent is an asset account. For Smart Touch, it should contain only two more months of rent on May 31 (for June and July). $1,000 rent per month times two months equals the $2,000 Prepaid rent balance.

The same analysis applies to the prepayment of three months of insurance. The only difference is in the account titles. Prepaid insurance would be used instead of Prepaid rent and Insurance expense would be used instead of Rent expense. In a computerized system, the adjusting entry can be programmed to recur automatically each accounting period.

Appendix 3A shows an alternative treatment of prepaid expenses. The end result on the financial statements is the same as illustrated here.

Supplies

Supplies are accounted for as prepaid expenses. On May 2, Sheena Bright paid $500 for office supplies.

	May 2	Supplies (A+)	500	
		Cash (A–)		500
		Paid cash for supplies.		

The May 31 trial balance, therefore, still lists Supplies with a $700 debit balance, as shown in Exhibit 3-4. But Bright's May 31 balance sheet should *not* report supplies of $700. Why not?

During May, the e-learning agency used supplies to conduct business. The cost of the supplies used becomes *supplies expense*. To measure supplies expense, Bright counts the supplies on hand at the end of May. This is the amount of the asset still owned by the business. Assume that supplies costing $600 remain at May 31. Use the supplies T-account to determine the value of the supplies that were used:

ASSETS

Supplies

May 2	500		
May 15	200	Supplies Used	???
Bal	600		

EXPENSES

Supplies expense

	???	
Bal	???	

So, we can solve for the supplies used as

Beginning Supplies – Supplies Used = Ending Supplies
$700 (500 + 200) – Supplies Used = $600
Supplies Used = $100

The May 31 adjusting entry updates Supplies and records Supplies expense for May as follows:

b.	May 31	Supplies expense ($700 – $600) (E+)	100	
		Supplies (A–)		100
		To record supplies expense.		

After posting, Supplies and Supplies expense hold correct ending balances:

ASSETS

Supplies

May 2	500		
May 15	200	May 31	100
Bal	600		

EXPENSES

Supplies expense

May 31	100	
Bal	100	

The Supplies account then enters June with a $600 balance, and the adjustment process is repeated each month. Supplies is another example of an asset that was overstated at $700 on the trial balance prior to posting the adjusting entry. That entry then reflected the correct balance of Supplies on May 31 of $600.

Depreciation

Plant assets are long-lived tangible assets used in the operation of a business. Examples include land, buildings, equipment, and furniture. As a business uses the assets, their value and usefulness decline. The decline in usefulness of a plant asset is an expense, and accountants systematically spread the asset's cost over its useful life. The allocation of a plant asset's cost to expense is called **depreciation**. Land is the exception. We record no depreciation for land, as its value typically does not decline with use.

Similarity to Prepaid Expenses

The concept of accounting for plant assets is the same as for a prepaid expense. The major difference is the length of time it takes for the asset to be used up. Prepaid expenses usually expire within a year, while plant assets remain useful for several years. Let us review an example for Smart Touch Learning. On May 3 Smart Touch Learning purchased furniture for $18,000 and made the following journal entry:

May 3	Furniture (A+)	18,000	
	Cash (A–)		18,000
	Purchased furniture.		

After posting, the Furniture account has an $18,000 balance:

ASSETS	
Furniture	
May 3 18,000	

Sheena Bright believes the furniture will remain useful for five years and then be worthless. One way to compute depreciation is to divide the cost of the asset ($18,000) by its expected useful life (five years). So, the depreciation for each month is $300 ($18,000/5 years = $3,600/12 months = $300 per month). Depreciation expense for May is recorded by the following entry:

c.	May 31	Depreciation expense—furniture (E+)	300	
		Accumulated depreciation—furniture (CA+)		300
		To record depreciation on furniture.		

The Accumulated Depreciation Account

Accumulated depreciation, rather than Furniture, is credited because it is helpful to keep the original cost in the Furniture account. Managers can then refer to the Furniture account to see how much the asset actually cost them. This information may help decide how much to pay for new furniture. The Accumulated depreciation account holds the sum of all the depreciation recorded for the asset and that total increases over time.

Accumulated depreciation is a contra asset, which means that it is an asset account with a normal credit balance. A **contra account** has two main characteristics:

- A contra account is paired with and follows its related account.
- A contra account's normal balance (debit or credit) is the opposite of the balance of the related account.

For example, Accumulated depreciation is the contra account that follows Furniture. Furniture has a debit balance, so Accumulated depreciation, a contra asset, has a credit balance.

A business may have a separate Accumulated depreciation account for each depreciable asset. If Smart Touch Learning has both a building and a furniture account, it may have two accounts: Accumulated depreciation—building, and Accumulated depreciation—furniture. However, small companies often have only one Accumulated depreciation account for all their assets.

After posting the depreciation, the accounts appear as follows:

ASSETS

NORMAL ASSET

Furniture		
May 3	18,000	
Bal	18,000	

CONTRA ASSET

Accumulated depreciation—furniture		
	May 31	300
	Bal	300

EXPENSES

Depreciation expense—furniture		
May 31	300	
Bal	300	

Book Value

The balance sheet reports both Furniture and Accumulated depreciation. Because it is a contra account, Accumulated depreciation is subtracted from Furniture. The resulting net amount (cost minus accumulated depreciation) of a plant asset is called its **book value.** For Smart Touch Learning's Furniture, the book value is

Book value of plant assets:	
Furniture	$18,000
Less: Accumulated depreciation	(300)
Book value of the furniture	$17,700

The book value represents costs (life) invested in the asset that the business has not yet used (expensed).

Suppose the e-learning agency also owns a building that cost $48,000, with monthly depreciation of $200. The following entry would record depreciation for May:

d.	May 31	Depreciation expense—building (E+)	200	
		Accumulated depreciation—building (CA+)		200
		To record depreciation on building.		

The May 31 balance sheet would report plant assets as shown in Exhibit 3-5.

EXHIBIT 3-5 **Plant Assets on the Balance Sheet of Smart Touch Learning (May 31)**

Plant Assets		
Furniture	$18,000	
Less: Accumulated depreciation	(300)	$17,700
Building	$48,000	
Less: Accumulated depreciation	(200)	47,800
Plant assets, net		$65,500

Accrued Expenses

Businesses often incur expenses before paying for them. The term **accrued expense** refers to an expense of this type. Consider an employee's salary. The salary expense grows as the employee works, so the expense is said to *accrue*. Another accrued expense is interest expense on a note payable. Interest accrues as time passes on the note. An accrued expense always creates a liability.

Companies do not make weekly journal entries to accrue expenses. Instead they wait until the end of the period. They make an adjusting entry to bring each expense (and the related liability) up to date for the financial statements.

Remember that prepaids and accruals are opposites.

- A *prepaid expense* is paid first and expensed later.
- An *accrued expense* is expensed first and paid later.

Now let us see how to account for accrued expenses.

Accruing Salary Expense

Suppose Smart Touch pays its employee a monthly salary of $1,800, half on the 15th and half on the first day of the next month. Here is a calendar for May and June with the two paydays circled:

May 2010						
Sunday	Monday	Tuesday	Wednesday	Thursday	Friday	Saturday
Apr 25	26	27	28	29	30	May 1
2	3	4	5	6	7	8
9	10	11	12	13	14	(15)
16	17	18	19	20	21	22
23	24	25	26	27	28	29
30	31	(Jun 1)	2	3	4	5

During May, Sheena Bright paid the first half-month salary on Saturday, May 15, and made this entry:

May 15	Salary expense (E+)	900	
	Cash (A–)		900
	To pay salary.		

After posting, Salary expense shows the following balance:

EXPENSES

Salary expense		
May 15	900	

The trial balance at May 31 (Exhibit 3-4) includes Salary expense, with a debit balance of $900. This is Smart Touch's salary expense for the first half of May. The second payment of $900 will occur on June 1, so the business must accrue salary expense for the second half of May. At May 31, Smart Touch makes the following adjusting entry:

e.	May 31	Salary expense (E+)	900	
		Salary payable (L+)		900
		To accrue salary expense.		

After posting, both Salary expense and Salary payable are up to date:

EXPENSES

Salary expense		
May 15	900	
May 31	900	
Bal	1,800	

LIABILITIES

Salary payable		
	May 31	900
	Bal	900

Salary expense holds a full month's salary, and Salary payable shows the liability owed at May 31. This is an example of a liability that was understated before the adjusting entry was made.

Accruing Interest Expense

Borrowing money creates a liability for a Note payable. If, on May 1, 2010, Smart Touch borrows $20,000 from the bank after signing a one-year note payable, the entry to record the note on May 1, 2010, is

May 1	Cash (A+)	20,000	
	Note payable (L+)		20,000
	Borrowed money.		

Interest on this note is payable one year later, on May 1, 2011. On May 31, 2010, the company must make an adjusting entry to record the interest expense that has accrued for the month of May. Assume one month's interest expense on this note is $100. Your May 31 adjusting entry to accrue interest expense is

f.	May 31	Interest expense (E+)	100	
		Interest payable (L+)		100
		To accrue interest expense.		

This is another example of a liability that was understated before the adjusting entry was made. After posting, Interest expense and Interest payable have the following balances:

EXPENSES

Interest expense			
May 31	100		
Bal	100		

LIABILITIES

Interest payable			
		May 31	100
		Bal	100

Accrued Revenues

As we have just seen, expenses can occur before a company makes a cash payment for them, which creates an accrued expense. Similarly, businesses can earn revenue before they receive the cash. This calls for an **accrued revenue**, which is a revenue that has been earned but not yet collected in cash.

Assume that Smart Touch Learning is hired on May 15 to perform e-learning services for the **University of West Florida.** Under this agreement, Smart Touch will earn $800 monthly. During May, Smart Touch will earn half a month's fee, $400, for work May 16 through May 31. On May 31, Smart Touch makes the following adjusting entry to accrue the revenue earned during May 16 through 31:

g.	May 31	Accounts receivable ($800 × 1/2) (A+)	400	
		Service revenue (R+)		400
		To accrue service revenue.		

The unadjusted trial balance in Exhibit 3-4 shows that Accounts receivable has an unadjusted balance of $2,200. Service revenue's unadjusted balance is $7,000 from the regular May activity. (Detailed entries for May transactions are not shown. Only adjusting entries are shown.) The adjustment updates both accounts.

ASSETS

Accounts receivable			
	2,200		
May 31	400		
Bal	2,600		

REVENUES

Service revenue			
			7,000
		May 31	400
		Bal	7,400

Without the adjustment, Smart Touch's financial statements would understate both an asset, Accounts receivable, and a revenue, Service revenue.

Now we turn to the final category of adjusting entries.

Unearned Revenues

Some businesses collect cash from customers in advance of performing work. Receiving cash before earning it creates a liability to perform work in the future called **unearned revenue.** The company owes a product or a service to the customer, or it owes the customer his or her money back. Only after completing the job will the business *earn* the revenue. Because of this delay, unearned revenue is also called **deferred revenue.**

Suppose, for example, a law firm engages Smart Touch Learning to provide ethics e-learning services, agreeing to pay $600 monthly, beginning immediately.

Sheena Bright collects the first amount on May 21. Smart Touch records the cash receipt and a liability as follows:

	Date	Accounts and Explanation	Debit	Credit
	May 21	Cash (A+)	600	
		Unearned service revenue (L+)		600
		Collected revenue in advance.		

Now the liability account, Unearned service revenue, shows that Smart Touch owes $600.

LIABILITIES

Unearned service revenue			
		May 21	600

Unearned service revenue is a liability because the company owes a service to a client in the future.

The May 31 trial balance (Exhibit 3-4) lists Unearned service revenue with a $600 credit balance. During the last 10 days of the month—May 21 through May 31—Smart Touch will *earn* approximately one-third (10 days divided by 30 days) of the $600, or $200. Therefore, Smart Touch makes the following adjusting entry to record earning $200 of revenue:

	Date	Accounts and Explanation	Debit	Credit
h.	May 31	Unearned service revenue ($600 × 1/3) (L–)	200	
		Service revenue (R+)		200
		To record service revenue that was collected in advance.		

This adjusting entry shifts $200 from liability to revenue. Service revenue increases by $200, and Unearned service revenue decreases by $200. Now both accounts are up-to-date at May 31:

LIABILITIES

Unearned service revenue			
May 31	200	May 21	600
		Bal	400

REVENUES

Service revenue			
			7,000
		May 31	400
		May 31	200
		Bal	7,600

This is an example of a liability that was overstated prior to posting the adjusting journal entry. Remember this key point:

> An unearned revenue is a liability, not a revenue.

An unearned revenue to one company is a prepaid expense to the company that paid in advance. Consider the law firm in the preceding example. The law firm had prepaid e-learning expense—an asset. Smart Touch Learning had unearned service revenue—a liability.

Exhibit 3-6 summarizes the timing of prepaid and accrual adjustments. Study the exhibit from left to right, and then move down. Appendix 3A shows an alternative treatment for unearned revenues.

EXHIBIT 3-6 | **Prepaid and Accrual Adjustments**

PREPAIDS—Cash transaction comes *first*.

Prepaid Expenses

Entry	Debit	Credit
Pay expense in advance and record an asset.		
Prepaid rent (A+)	XXX	
Cash (A–)		XXX

Entry	Debit	Credit
Record the expense later.		
Rent expense (E+)	XXX	
Prepaid rent (A–)		XXX

Unearned Revenues

Entry	Debit	Credit
Receive cash in advance and record a liability.		
Cash (A+)	XXX	
Unearned service revenue (L+)		XXX

Entry	Debit	Credit
Record the revenue later.		
Unearned service revenue (L–)	XXX	
Service revenue (R+)		XXX

ACCRUALS—Cash transaction comes *later*.

Accrued Expenses

Entry	Debit	Credit
Accrue an expense first.		
Salary expense (E+)	XXX	
Salary payable (L+)		XXX

Entry	Debit	Credit
Pay the liability later.		
Salary payable (L–)	XXX	
Cash (A–)		XXX

Accrued Revenues

Entry	Debit	Credit
Accrue a revenue first.		
Interest receivable (A+)	XXX	
Interest revenue (R+)		XXX

Entry	Debit	Credit
Collect cash later.		
Cash (A+)	XXX	
Interest receivable (A–)		XXX

Source: The authors thank Darrel Davis and Alfonso Oddo for suggesting this exhibit.

Summary of the Adjusting Process

The adjusting process has two purposes:

1. To measure net income or net loss on the *income statement*. Every adjustment affects a *revenue* or an *expense*.
2. To update the *balance sheet*. Every adjustment affects an *asset* or a *liability*.

Exhibit 3-7 summarizes the effects of the various adjusting entries.

EXHIBIT 3-7 Summary of Adjusting Entries

Category of Adjusting Entry	Debit	Credit
Prepaid expense	Expense	Asset
Depreciation	Expense	Contra asset
Accrued expense	Expense	Liability
Accrued revenue	Asset	Revenue
Unearned revenue	Liability	Revenue

Source: Adapted from material provided by Beverly Terry.

Exhibit 3-8 on the following page summarizes the adjusting entries of Smart Touch Learning at May 31.

The adjustments are keyed by letter.

- Panel A gives the data for each adjustment.
- Panel B shows the adjusting entries.
- Panel C gives the accounts after posting.

Stop & Think...

Look at the eight adjusting entries in Exhibit 3-8. Notice that only the last two adjusting entries, (g) and (h), increased revenues. On the other hand, six of the eight adjusting entries increased expenses. So, when in doubt about an adjustment, most likely it will be an adjusting entry that increases (debits) an expense account.

EXHIBIT 3-8 Journalizing and Posting the Adjusting Entries of Smart Touch Learning

PANEL A—Information for Adjustments at May 31, 2010

a. Prepaid rent expired, $1,000.
b. Supplies expense, $100.
c. Depreciation on furniture, $300.
d. Depreciation on building, $200.
e. Accrued salary expense, $900.
f. Accrued interest on note, $100.
g. Accrued service revenue, $400.
h. Service revenue that was collected in advance and now has been earned, $200.

PANEL B—Adjusting Entries

a.		Rent expense (E+)	1,000	
		Prepaid rent (A–)		1,000
		To record rent expense.		
b.		Supplies expense (E+)	100	
		Supplies (A–)		100
		To record supplies used.		
c.		Depreciation expense—furniture (E+)	300	
		Accumulated depreciation—furniture (CA+)		300
		To record depreciation on furniture.		
d.		Depreciation expense—building (E+)	200	
		Accumulated depreciation—building (CA+)		200
		To record depreciation on building.		
e.		Salary expense (E+)	900	
		Salary payable (L+)		900
		To accrue salary expense.		
f.		Interest expense (E+)	100	
		Interest payable (L+)		100
		To accrue interest expense.		
g.		Accounts receivable (A+)	400	
		Service revenue (R+)		400
		To accrue service revenue.		
h.		Unearned service revenue (L–)	200	
		Service revenue (R+)		200
		To record revenue that was collected in advance.		

EXHIBIT 3-8 | Continued

PANEL C—Ledger Accounts

Assets

Cash

	Debit		Credit
Bal	4,800		

Accounts receivable

	Debit		Credit
	2,200		
(g)	400		
Bal	2,600		

Supplies

	Debit		Credit
	700	(b)	100
Bal	600		

Prepaid rent

	Debit		Credit
	3,000	(a)	1,000
Bal	2,000		

Furniture

	Debit		Credit
Bal	18,000		

Accumulated depreciation—furniture

	Debit		Credit
		(c)	300
		Bal	300

Building

	Debit		Credit
Bal	48,000		

Accumulated depreciation—building

	Debit		Credit
		(d)	200

Liabilities

Accounts payable

	Debit		Credit
		Bal	18,200

Salary payable

	Debit		Credit
		(e)	900
		Bal	900

Unearned service revenue

	Debit		Credit
(h)	200		600
		Bal	400

Interest payable

	Debit		Credit
		(f)	100

Notes payable

	Debit		Credit
		Bal	20,000

Owner's Equity

Sheena Bright, Capital

	Debit		Credit
		Bal	33,200

Sheena Bright, Withdrawals

	Debit		Credit
Bal	1,000		

Revenue

Service revenue

	Debit		Credit
			7,000
		(g)	400
		(h)	200
		Bal	7,600

Expenses

Rent expense

	Debit		Credit
(a)	1,000		
Bal	1,000		

Salary expense

	Debit		Credit
	900		
(e)	900		
Bal	1,800		

Supplies expense

	Debit		Credit
(b)	100		
Bal	100		

Depreciation expense—furniture

	Debit		Credit
(c)	300		
Bal	300		

Utilities expense

	Debit		Credit
Bal	400		

Depreciation expense—building

	Debit		Credit
(d)	200		

Interest expense

	Debit		Credit
(f)	100		

The Adjusted Trial Balance

5 Explain the purpose of and prepare an adjusted trial balance

This chapter began with the *unadjusted* trial balance (Exhibit 3-4). After the adjustments, the accounts appear as shown in Exhibit 3-8, Panel C. A useful step in preparing the financial statements is to list the accounts, along with their adjusted balances, on an **adjusted trial balance**. Exhibit 3-9 shows how to prepare the adjusted trial balance.

EXHIBIT 3-9 Preparation of Adjusted Trial Balance

SMART TOUCH LEARNING
Preparation of Adjusted Trial Balance
May 31, 2010

	Trial Balance		Adjustments		Adjusted Trial Balance		
	Debit	Credit	Debit	Credit	Debit	Credit	
Cash	4,800				4,800		
Accounts receivable	2,200		(g) 400		2,600		
Supplies	700			(b) 100	600		
Prepaid rent	3,000			(a) 1,000	2,000		
Furniture	18,000				18,000		
Building	48,000				48,000		
Accumulated depreciation—furniture				(c) 300		300	
Accumulated depreciation—building				(d) 200		200	Balance Sheet *(Exhibit 3-12)*
Accounts payable		18,200				18,200	
Salary payable				(e) 900		900	
Interest payable				(f) 100		100	
Unearned service revenue		600	(h) 200			400	
Notes payable		20,000				20,000	
Sheena Bright, Capital		33,200				33,200	Statement of Owner's Equity *(Exhibit 3-11)*
Sheena Bright, Withdrawals	1,000				1,000		
Service revenue		7,000		(g) 400		7,600	
				(h) 200			
Rent expense			(a) 1,000		1,000		
Salary expense	900		(e) 900		1,800		
Supplies expense			(b) 100		100		Income Statement *(Exhibit 3-10)*
Depreciation expense—furniture			(c) 300		300		
Depreciation expense—building			(d) 200		200		
Interest expense			(f) 100		100		
Utilities expense	400				400		
	79,000	79,000	3,200	3,200	80,900	80,900	

Exhibit 3-9 is a *work sheet*. We will continue this work sheet in Chapter 4. For now, simply note how clear this format is. The Account Titles and the Trial Balance are copied directly from the trial balance in Exhibit 3-4. The two Adjustments columns show the adjusting journal entries from Exhibit 3-8.

The Adjusted Trial Balance columns give the adjusted account balances. Each amount in these columns is computed by combining the trial balance amounts plus or minus the adjustments. For example, Accounts receivable starts with a debit balance of $2,200. Adding the $400 debit from adjustment (g) gives Accounts receivable an adjusted balance of $2,600. Supplies begins with a debit balance of $700. After the $100 credit adjustment, Supplies has a $600 balance. More than one entry may affect a single account. Service revenue, for example, has two adjustments, (g) and (h), and both increased the Service revenue balance.

The Financial Statements

6 Prepare the financial statements from the adjusted trial balance

The May financial statements of Smart Touch Learning can be prepared from the adjusted trial balance in Exhibit 3-9. In the right margin, we see how the accounts are distributed to the financial statements. As always,

- the income statement (Exhibit 3-10) reports revenues and expenses.
- the statement of owner's equity (Exhibit 3-11) shows why the owner's capital changed during the period.
- the balance sheet (Exhibit 3-12) reports assets, liabilities, and owner's equity.

Preparing the Statements

The financial statements should be prepared in the following order:

1. Income statement—to determine net income or net loss
2. Statement of owner's equity—which needs net income or net loss from the income statement to compute ending capital
3. Balance sheet—which needs the amount of ending capital to achieve its balancing feature

All financial statements include the following elements:

Heading

- Name of the entity—such as Smart Touch Learning
- Title of the statement—income statement, statement of owner's equity, or balance sheet
- Date, or period, covered by the statement—May 31, 2010, or Month Ended May 30, 2010

Body of the statement

The income statement should list expenses in descending order by amount, as shown in Exhibit 3-10.

Relationships Among the Financial Statements

The arrows in Exhibits 3-10, 3-11, and 3-12 on the following page show how the financial statements relate to each other.

1. Net income from the income statement increases capital. A net loss decreases capital.
2. Ending capital from the statement of owner's equity goes to the balance sheet and makes total liabilities plus owner's equity equal total assets, satisfying the accounting equation.

To solidify your understanding of these relationships, trace net income from the income statement to the statement of owner's equity. Then trace ending capital to the balance sheet.

EXHIBIT 3-10 | **Preparing the Income Statement from the Adjusted Trial Balance**

SMART TOUCH LEARNING
Income Statement
Month Ended May 31, 2010

Revenue:		
Service revenue		$7,600
Expenses:		
Salary expense	$1,800	
Rent expense	1,000	
Utilities expense	400	
Depreciation expense—furniture	300	
Depreciation expense—building	200	
Interest expense	100	
Supplies expense	100	
Total expenses		3,900
Net income		$3,700

EXHIBIT 3-11 | **Preparing the Statement of Owner's Equity from the Adjusted Trial Balance**

SMART TOUCH LEARNING
Statement of Owner's Equity
Month Ended May 31, 2010

Sheena Bright, Capital, May 1, 2010	$33,200
Add: Net income	3,700
	36,900
Less: Owner withdrawals	(1,000)
Sheena Bright, Capital, May 31, 2010	$35,900

EXHIBIT 3-12 | **Preparing the Balance Sheet from the Adjusted Trial Balance**

SMART TOUCH LEARNING
Balance Sheet
May 31, 2010

Assets			**Liabilities**	
Cash		$ 4,800	Accounts payable	$18,200
Accounts receivable		2,600	Salary payable	900
Supplies		600	Interest payable	100
Prepaid rent		2,000	Unearned service revenue	400
Furniture	$18,000		Notes payable	20,000
Less: Accumulated depreciation—furniture	-300	17,700	Total liabilities	39,600
Building	48,000			
Less: Accumulated depreciation—building	-200	47,800	**Owner's Equity**	
			Sheena Bright, Capital	35,900
Total assets		$75,500	Total liabilities and owner's equity	$75,500

Ethical Issues in Accrual Accounting

Like all areas of business, accounting poses ethical challenges. Accountants must be honest in their work. Only with complete and accurate information can people make wise decisions. Let us look at an example.

Smart Touch Learning has done well as a business and wishes to open another office. Assume the company needs to borrow $30,000.

Suppose the e-learning agency understated expenses in order to inflate net income on the income statement. A banker could be tricked into lending the company money. Then if the business could not pay the loan, the bank would lose—all because the banker relied on incorrect accounting information.

Accrual accounting provides opportunities for unethical behavior. For example, a dishonest businessperson could easily overlook depreciation expense at the end of the year. Failing to record depreciation would overstate net income and paint a more favorable picture of the company's financial position. It is important for accountants to prepare accurate and complete financial statements because other people rely on the data for their decisions.

Decision Guidelines

THE ACCOUNTING PROCESS

Take the role of Hannah Sherman who owns Sherman Lawn Service. Assume it is now the end of the first year, and Sherman wants to know where the business stands financially. The Decision Guidelines give a map of the accounting process to help Sherman manage the business.

Decision	Guidelines
• Which basis of accounting better measures business income?	*Accrual basis*, because it provides more complete reports of operating performance and financial position
• How to measure revenues?	Revenue principle—Record revenues only after they are earned
• How to measure expenses?	Matching principle—Subtract expenses from revenues in order to measure net income
• Where to start with the measurement of income at the end of the period?	Unadjusted trial balance, usually referred to simply as the *trial balance*
• How to update the accounts for the financial statements?	*Adjusting entries* at the end of the period
• What are the categories of adjusting entries?	Prepaid expenses; Accrued revenues; Depreciation of plant assets; Unearned revenues; Accrued expenses
• How do the adjusting entries differ from other journal entries?	1. Adjusting entries are made only at the end of the period. 2. Adjusting entries never affect cash. 3. All adjusting entries debit or credit • At least one *income statement* account (a revenue or an expense), and • At least one *balance sheet* account (an asset or a liability)
• Where are the accounts with their adjusted balances summarized?	*Adjusted trial balance*, which aids preparation of the financial statements

Summary Problem

The trial balance of Super Employment Services pertains to December 31, 2011, the end of Super's annual accounting period. Data needed for the adjusting entries include the following:

a. **Supplies on hand at year-end, $200.**
b. **Depreciation on furniture, $2,000.**
c. **Depreciation on building, $1,000.**
d. **Salaries owed but not yet paid, $500.**
e. **Accrued service revenue, $1,300.**
f. **$3,000 of the unearned service revenue has been earned.**

Requirements

1. Open the ledger accounts with their unadjusted balances as shown for Accounts receivable:

Accounts receivable	
5,000	

2. Journalize Super's adjusting entries at December 31, 2011. Key entries by letter, as in Exhibit 3-8.
3. Post the adjusting entries.
4. Write the trial balance on a work sheet, enter the adjusting entries, and prepare an adjusted trial balance, as shown in Exhibit 3-9.
5. Prepare the income statement, the statement of owner's equity, and the balance sheet. Draw arrows linking the three financial statements.

SUPER EMPLOYMENT SERVICES
Trial Balance
December 31, 2011

	Balance	
Account Title	Debit	Credit
Cash	$ 6,000	
Accounts receivable	5,000	
Supplies	1,000	
Furniture	10,000	
Accumulated depreciation—furniture		$ 4,000
Building	50,000	
Accumulated depreciation—building		30,000
Accounts payable		2,000
Salary payable		
Unearned service revenue		8,000
Dan Mudge, Capital		12,000
Dan Mudge, Withdrawals	25,000	
Service revenue		60,000
Salary expense	16,000	
Supplies expense		
Depreciation expense—furniture		
Depreciation expense—building		
Advertising expense	3,000	
Total	$116,000	$116,000

Solution

Requirements 1 and 3

ASSETS

Cash	
Bal 6,000	

Accounts receivable	
5,000	
(e) 1,300	
Bal 6,300	

Supplies	
1,000	(a) 800
Bal 200	

Furniture	
Bal 10,000	

Accumulated depreciation—furniture	
	4,000
	(b) 2,000
	Bal 6,000

Building	
Bal 50,000	

Accumulated depreciation—building	
	30,000
	(c) 1,000
	Bal 31,000

LIABILITIES

Accounts payable	
	Bal 2,000

Salary payable	
	(d) 500
	Bal 500

Unearned service revenue	
(f) 3,000	8,000
	Bal 5,000

OWNER'S EQUITY

Dan Mudge, Capital	
	Bal 12,000

Dan Mudge, Withdrawals	
Bal 25,000	

REVENUE

Service revenue	
	60,000
	(e) 1,300
	(f) 3,000
	Bal 64,300

EXPENSES

Salary expense	
16,000	
(d) 500	
Bal 16,500	

Supplies expense	
(a) 800	
Bal 800	

Depreciation expense—furniture	
(b) 2,000	
Bal 2,000	

Depreciation expense—building	
(c) 1,000	
Bal 1,000	

Advertising expense	
Bal 3,000	

Requirement 2

	2011			
a.	Dec 31	Supplies expense ($1,000 – $200) (E+)	800	
		Supplies (A–)		800
		To record supplies used.		
b.	31	Depreciation expense—furniture (E+)	2,000	
		Accumulated depreciation—furniture (CA+)		2,000
		To record depreciation expense on furniture.		
c.	31	Depreciation expense—building (E+)	1,000	
		Accumulated depreciation—building (CA+)		1,000
		To record depreciation expense on building.		
d.	31	Salary expense (E+)	500	
		Salary payable (L+)		500
		To accrue salary expense.		
e.	31	Accounts receivable (A+)	1,300	
		Service revenue (R+)		1,300
		To accrue service revenue.		
f.	31	Unearned service revenue (L–)	3,000	
		Service revenue (R+)		3,000
		To record service revenue that was collected in advance.		

Requirement 4

SUPER EMPLOYMENT SERVICES Preparation of Adjusted Trial Balance December 31, 2011						
	Trial Balance		Adjustments		Adjusted Trial Balance	
Account Title	Debit	Credit	Debit	Credit	Debit	Credit
Cash	6,000				6,000	
Accounts receivable	5,000		(e) 1,300		6,300	
Supplies	1,000			(a) 800	200	
Furniture	10,000				10,000	
Accumulated depreciation—furniture		4,000		(b) 2,000		6,000
Building	50,000				50,000	
Accumulated depreciation—building		30,000		(c) 1,000		31,000
Accounts payable		2,000				2,000
Salary payable				(d) 500		500
Unearned service revenue		8,000	(f) 3,000			5,000
Dan Mudge, Capital		12,000				12,000
Dan Mudge, Withdrawals	25,000				25,000	
Service revenue		60,000		(e) 1,300		
				(f) 3,000		64,300
Salary expense	16,000		(d) 500		16,500	
Supplies expense			(a) 800		800	
Depreciation expense—furniture			(b) 2,000		2,000	
Depreciation expense—building			(c) 1,000		1,000	
Advertising expense	3,000				3,000	
Total	116,000	116,000	8,600	8,600	120,800	120,800

Requirement 5

SUPER EMPLOYMENT SERVICES **Income Statement** Year Ended December 31, 2011		
Revenue:		
Service revenue		$64,300
Expenses:		
Salary expense	$16,500	
Advertising expense	3,000	
Depreciation expense—furniture	2,000	
Depreciation expense—building	1,000	
Supplies expense	800	
Total expenses		23,300
Net income		$41,000

SUPER EMPLOYMENT SERVICES **Statement of Owner's Equity** Year Ended December 31, 2011	
Dan Mudge, Capital, January 1, 2011	$ 12,000
Add: Net income	41,000
	53,000
Less: Owner withdrawals	(25,000)
Dan Mudge, Capital, December 31, 2011	$ 28,000

SUPER EMPLOYMENT SERVICES **Balance Sheet** December 31, 2011				
Assets			**Liabilities**	
Cash		$ 6,000	Accounts payable	$ 2,000
Accounts receivable		6,300	Salary payable	500
Supplies		200	Unearned service revenue	5,000
Furniture	$10,000		Total liabilities	7,500
Less: Accumulated depreciation—furniture	(6,000)	4,000		
Building	50,000			
Less: Accumulated depreciation—building	(31,000)	19,000	**Owner's Equity**	
			Dan Mudge, Capital	28,000
Total assets		$35,500	Total liabilities and owner's equity	$35,500

Review The Adjusting Process

Accounting Vocabulary

Accrual Accounting (p. 162)
Accounting that records the impact of a business event as it occurs regardless of whether the transaction affected cash.

Accrued Expense (p. 172)
An expense that the business has incurred but not yet paid.

Accrued Revenue (p. 174)
A revenue that has been earned but not yet collected in cash.

Accumulated Depreciation (p. 170)
The sum of all depreciation expense recorded to date for an asset.

Adjusted Trial Balance (p. 180)
A list of all the accounts with their adjusted balances.

Adjusting Entries (p. 166)
Entries made at the end of the period to assign revenues to the period in which they are earned and expenses to the period in which they are incurred. Adjusting entries help measure the period's income and bring the related asset and liability accounts to correct balances for the financial statements.

Book Value (of a plant asset) (p. 171)
The asset's cost minus accumulated depreciation.

Cash-Basis Accounting (p. 162)
Accounting that records transactions only when cash is received or paid.

Contra Account (p. 170)
An account that always has a companion account and whose normal balance is opposite that of the companion account.

Deferred Revenue (p. 174)
A liability created when a business collects cash from customers in advance of doing work. Also called **unearned revenue**.

Depreciation (p. 170)
The allocation of a plant asset's cost to expense over its useful life.

Liquidation (p. 163)
The process of going out of business by selling all the assets, paying all the liabilities, and giving any leftover cash to the owner.

Matching Principle (p. 165)
Guide to accounting for expenses. Identify all expenses incurred during the period, measure the expenses, and match them against the revenues earned during that same time period.

Plant Assets (p. 170)
Long-lived tangible assets—such as land, buildings, and equipment—used in the operation of a business.

Revenue Principle (p. 164)
The basis for recording revenues; tells accountants when to record revenue and the amount of revenue to record.

Time-Period Concept (p. 165)
Ensures that information is reported at regular intervals.

Unearned Revenue (p. 174)
A liability created when a business collects cash from customers in advance of doing work. Also called **deferred revenue**.

Quick Check

1. What are the distinctive features of accrual accounting and cash-basis accounting?
   a. Cash-basis accounting records all transactions.
   b. Accrual accounting is superior because it provides more information.
   c. Accrual accounting records only receivables, payables, and depreciation.
   d. All the above are true.
2. The revenue principle says
   a. Measure revenues and expenses in order to compute net income
   b. Divide time into annual periods to measure revenue properly
   c. Record revenue only after you have earned it
   d. Record revenue after you receive cash
3. Adjusting the accounts is the process of
   a. Recording transactions as they occur during the period
   b. Zeroing out account balances to prepare for the next period
   c. Subtracting expenses from revenues to measure net income
   d. Updating the accounts at the end of the period

4. Which types of adjusting entries are natural opposites?
   a. Expenses and revenues
   b. Net income and net loss
   c. Prepaids and depreciation
   d. Prepaids and accruals
5. Assume that the weekly payroll of Off the Runway Boutique is $390. December 31, end of the year, falls on Monday, and Off the Runway will pay its employee on Friday for the full week. What adjusting entry will Off the Runway make on Monday, December 31? (Use five days as a full work week.)

a.

Salary payable	390	
Salary expense		390

b.

Salary expense	78	
Salary payable		78

c.

Salary expense	312	
Cash		312

   d. No adjustment is needed because the company will pay the payroll on Friday.
6. Hercules Workout World gains a client who prepays $630 for a package of six physical training sessions. Hercules Workout World collects the $630 in advance and will provide the training later. After two training sessions, what should Hercules Workout World report on its income statement?
   a. Unearned service revenue of $210
   b. Service revenue of $210
   c. Cash of $420
   d. Service revenue of $630
7. Assume you prepay Hercules Workout World for a package of six physical training sessions. Which type of account should you have in your records?
   a. Prepaid expense
   b. Accrued expense
   c. Accrued revenue
   d. Unearned revenue
8. Unearned revenue is always a(an)
   a. Asset
   b. Liability
   c. Revenue
   d. Owner's equity because you collected the cash in advance
9. The adjusted trial balance shows
   a. Amounts ready for the financial statements
   b. Amounts that may be out of balance
   c. Assets, liabilities, and owner's equity only
   d. Revenues and expenses only

10. Accounting data flow from the
    a. Balance sheet to the income statement
    b. Statement of owner's equity to the balance sheet
    c. Income statement to the statement of owner's equity
    d. Both b and c are correct

Answers are given after Apply Your Knowledge (p. 217).

Assess Your Progress

■ Short Exercises

S3-1 *(L.OBJ. 1)* **Comparing accrual and cash basis accounting [5 min]**
Suppose you work summers house-sitting for people while they are away on vacation. Most of your customers pay you immediately after you finish a job. A few ask you to send them a bill. It is now June 30 and you have collected $600 from cash-paying customers. Your remaining customers owe you $1,400.

Requirements

1. How much service revenue would you have under the
   a. cash basis?
   b. accrual basis?
2. Which method of accounting provides more information about your house-sitting business?

S3-2 *(L.OBJ. 1)* **Comparing accrual and cash basis accounting [5 min]**
The Michelle Cook Law Firm uses a client database. Suppose Michelle Cook paid $5,000 for a computer.

Requirements

1. Describe how the business should account for the $5,000 expenditure under
   a. the cash basis.
   b. the accrual basis.
2. State why the accrual basis is more realistic for this situation.

S3-3 *(L.OBJ. 2)* **Applying the revenue principle [5 min]**
Arizona Magazine sells annual subscriptions for the 12 monthly magazines mailed out each year. The company collects cash in advance and then mails out the magazines to subscribers each month.

Requirement

1. Apply the revenue principle to determine
   a. when *Arizona Magazine* should record revenue for this situation.
   b. the amount of revenue *Arizona Magazine* should record for the magazines mailed out January through March.

S3-4 *(L.OBJ. 2)* **Applying the matching principle [5 min]**
Suppose on January 1 you prepaid apartment rent of $4,200 for the full year.

Requirement

1. At September 30, what are your two account balances for this situation?

S3-5 *(L.OBJ. 3)* **Identifying types of adjusting entries [5 min]**
On April 1 your company prepaid six months of rent, $4,800.

Requirement

1. What type of adjusting entry is this?

Note: Short Exercise 3-6 should be used only after completing Short Exercise 3-5.

S3-6 *(L.OBJ. 4)* **Journalizing adjusting entries [5 min]**
Consider the facts presented in Short Exercise 3-5.

Requirements

1. Prepare the journal entry for the April 1 payment.
2. Prepare the adjusting entry required at April 30.
3. Post to the two accounts involved and show their balances at April 30.

S3-7 *(L.OBJ. 4)* **Posting adjusting entries [5 min]**
On December 1 your company paid cash of $51,300 for computers that are expected to remain useful for four years. At the end of four years, the value of the computers is expected to be zero, so depreciation is $12,825 per year.

Requirements

1. Post the purchase of December 1 and the depreciation on December 31 to T-accounts for the following accounts: Computer equipment, Accumulated depreciation-Computer equipment, and Depreciation expense-Computer equipment. Show their balances at December 31. (Assume that the journal entries have been completed.)
2. What is the computer equipment's book value on December 31?

S3-8 *(L.OBJ. 4)* **Accruing interest expense and posting to T-accounts [10 min]**
Harris Travel borrowed $48,000 on September 1, 2011, by signing a one-year note payable to Street One Bank. Harris interest expense for the remainder of the fiscal year (September through November) is $888.

Requirements

1. Make the adjusting entry to accrue interest expense at November 30, 2011. Date the entry and include its explanation.
2. Post to the T-accounts of the two accounts affected by the adjustment.

S3-9 *(L.OBJ. 4)* **Accounting for unearned revenues [5–10 min]**
Modern Magazine collects cash from subscribers in advance and then mails the magazines to subscribers over a one-year period.

Requirements

1. Journalize the entry to record the original receipt of $100,000 cash.
2. Journalize the adjusting entry that *Modern Magazine* makes to record the earning of $5,000 of subscription revenue that was collected in advance. Include an explanation for the entry.

S3-10 *(L.OBJ. 5)* **Preparing an adjusted trial balance [10 min]**
A Cut Above Hair Stylists has begun the preparation of its adjusted trial balance as follows:

A CUT ABOVE HAIR STYLISTS Preparation of Adjusted Trial Balance December 31, 2010						
	Trial Balance		Adjustments		Adjusted Trial Balance	
Account	Debit	Credit	Debit	Credit	Debit	Credit
Cash	600					
Supplies	800					
Equipment	16,200					
Accumulated depreciation		1,100				
Accounts payable		500				
Interest payable						
Note payable		2,900				
Tim Adams, Capital		5,300				
Service revenue		13,000				
Rent expense	4,800					
Supplies expense						
Depreciation expense						
Interest expense	400					
Total	22,800	22,800				

Year-end data includes the following:

a. Supplies on hand, $200
b. Depreciation, $1,100
c. Accrued interest expense, $400

Requirement

1. Complete A Cut Above's adjusted trial balance. Key each adjustment by letter.

Note: Short Exercise 3-11 and 3-12 should be used only after completing Short Exercise 3-10.

S3-11 *(L.OBJ. 6)* **Preparing an income statement [10–15 min]**
Refer to the data in Short Exercise 3-10.

Requirement

1. Compute A Cut Above's net income for the year ended December 31, 2010.

S3-12 *(L.OBJ. 6)* **Preparing a balance sheet [5 min]**
Refer to the data in Short Exercise 3-10.

Requirement

1. Compute A Cut Above's total assets at December 31, 2010.

Exercises

E3-13 *(L.OBJ. 1, 2)* **Comparing accrual and cash basis accounting, and applying the revenue principle [5–10 min]**

Captured Moments is a photography business that shoots videos at college parties. The freshman class pays $110 in advance on January 3 just to guarantee your services for its party to be held February 2. The sophomore class promises a minimum of $300 for filming its formal dance, and actually pays cash of $440 on January 28 at the party.

Requirements

1. Answer the following questions about the correct way to account for revenue under the accrual basis.
   a. Considering the $110 paid by the freshman class, on what date was revenue earned? Did the earnings occur on the same date cash was received?
   b. Considering the $440 paid by the sophomore class, on what date was revenue earned? Did the earnings occur on the same date cash was received?

E3-14 *(L.OBJ. 1, 4, 6)* **Comparing accrual and cash basis accounting, preparing adjusting entries, and preparing income statements [15-25 min]**

Cuisine Catering completed the following selected transactions during June, 2012:

Jun	1	Prepaid rent for three months, $1,800
	5	Paid electricity expenses, $500
	9	Received cash for meals served to customers, $2,500
	14	Paid cash for kitchen equipment, $3,000
	23	Served a banquet on account, $3,500
	30	Made the adjusting entry for rent (from June 1)
	30	Accrued salary expense, $1,400

Requirements

1. Prepare journal entries for each transaction.
2. Using the journal entries as a guide, show whether each transaction would be handled as a revenue or an expense using both the accrual and cash basis by completing the following table:

	Amount of Revenue (Expense) for June	
Date	Cash Basis Amount of Revenue (Expense)	Accrual-Basis Amount of Revenue (Expense)

3. After completing the table, calculate the amount of net income or net loss for Cuisine Catering under the accrual and cash basis for June.
4. Considering your results from requirement 3, which method gives the best picture of the true earnings of Cuisine Catering? Why?

E3-15 *(L.OBJ. 2)* **Accrual accounting concepts and principles [5–10 min]**

Identify the accounting concept or principle (there may be more than one) that gives the most direction on how to account for each of the following situations:

a. The owner of a business desires *monthly* financial statements to measure the progress of the entity on an ongoing basis.
b. Expenses of the period total $5,500. This amount should be subtracted from revenue to compute the period's net income.
c. Expenses of $1,200 must be accrued in order to measure net income properly.
d. A customer states her intention to switch health clubs. The health club records no revenue.

E3-16 *(L.OBJ. 2, 4)* **Applying accounting principles and preparing journal entries for prepaid rent [10–15 min]**

Consider the facts presented in the following table for Island View:

	Situation			
	A	B	C	D
Beginning Prepaid rent	$ 1,100	$ 600	$ 400	$ 500
Payments for Prepaid rent during the year	700	?	1,400	?
Total amount to account for	1,800	1,500	?	?
Subtract: Ending Prepaid rent	(500)	(600)	?	(400)
Rent expense	$?	$ 900	$1,500	$ 900

Requirements

1. Complete the table by filling in the missing values.
2. Prepare the four journal entries for each situation. Label the journal entries by letter.

E3-17 *(L.OBJ. 3, 4)* **Categorizing and journalizing adjusting entries [10–15 min]**

Consider the following independent situations at December 31, 2009.

a. On November 1, a business collected $6,600 rent in advance, debiting Cash and crediting Unearned rent revenue. The tenant was paying one year's rent in advance. At December 31, the business must account for the amount of rent it has earned.
b. Salary expense is $1,800 per day—Monday through Friday—and the business pays employees each Friday. This year December 31 falls on a Tuesday.
c. The unadjusted balance of the Supplies account is $3,300. Supplies on hand total $1,200.
d. Equipment depreciation was $500.
e. On June 1, when business prepaid $6,000 for a two-year insurance policy, business debited Prepaid insurance and credited Cash.

Requirements

1. For each item, indicate which category of adjustment is described.
2. Journalize the adjusting entry needed on December 31 for each situation. Use the letters to label the journal entries.

E3-18 *(L.OBJ. 4)* **Recording adjustments in T-accounts and calculating ending balances [10–20 min]**

The accounting records of Erin Foley Architect include the following selected, unadjusted balances at March 31: Accounts receivable, $1,500; Supplies, $700; Salary payable, $0; Unearned service revenue, $900; Service revenue, $5,000; Salary expense, $1,100; Supplies expense, $0. The data developed for the March 31 adjusting entries are

a. Service revenue accrued, $800
b. Unearned service revenue that has been earned, $300
c. Supplies on hand, $500
d. Salary owed to employee, $400

Requirement

1. Open a T-account for each account and record the adjustments directly in the T-accounts, keying each adjustment by letter. Show each account's adjusted balance. Journal entries are not required.

E3-19 *(L.OBJ. 4, 5)* **Preparing adjusting entries and preparing an adjusted trial balance [10–15 min]**

Shining Image Company, the cleaning service, started the preparation of its adjusted trial balance as follows:

SHINING IMAGE COMPANY Preparation of Adjusted Trial Balance December 31, 2010		
	Trial Balance	
Account	Debit	Credit
Cash	1,100	
Supplies	2,000	
Prepaid insurance	600	
Equipment	30,000	
Accumulated depreciation		2,000
Accounts payable		1,700
Salary payable		
Unearned service revenue		400
Roberta Defuniak, Capital		15,600
Roberta Defuniak, Withdrawals	1,000	
Service revenue		22,000
Salary expense	7,000	
Supplies expense		
Depreciation expense		
Insurance expense		
Total	41,700	41,700

During the twelve months ended December 31, 2010, Shining Image did the following:

a. Used supplies of $1,100
b. Used up prepaid insurance of $590
c. Used up $510 of the equipment through depreciation
d. Accrued salary expense of $270 that Shining Image has not paid yet
e. Earned $370 of the unearned service revenue

Requirement

1. Complete the adjusted trial balance. Key each adjustment by letter.

Note: Exercise 3-20 should be used only in conjunction with Exercise 3-19.

E3-20 *(L.OBJ. 4, 5)* **Using an adjusted trial balance to prepare adjusting journal entries [10 min]**

Refer to the data in Exercise 3-19.

Requirement

1. Journalize the five adjustments, all dated December 31, 2010. Explanations are not required.

E3-21 *(L.OBJ. 4, 5)* **Using the adjusted trial balance to determine the adjusting journal entries [10–15 min]**

The adjusted trial balance of Best Jobs Employment Service follows but is incomplete.

BEST JOBS EMPLOYMENT SERVICE Adjusted Trial Balance April 30, 2008				
	Trial Balance		Adjusted Trial Balance	
Account	Debit	Credit	Debit	Credit
Cash	600		600	
Accounts receivable	4,600		5,800	
Supplies	1,000		900	
Equipment	32,000		32,000	
Accumulated depreciation		14,200		15,600
Salary payable				1,000
Landrum, Capital		24,500		24,500
Landrum, Withdrawals	5,200		5,200	
Service revenue		9,200		10,400
Salary expense	3,200		4,200	
Rent expense	1,300		1,300	
Depreciation expense			1,400	
Supplies expense			100	
Total	47,900	47,900	51,500	51,500

Requirements

1. Calculate and enter the adjustment amounts directly in the missing Adjustments columns.
2. Prepare each adjusting journal entry calculated in requirement 1. Date the entries and include explanations.

E3-22 *(L.OBJ. 4, 6)* **Journalizing adjusting entries and analyzing their effect on the income statement [5–10 min]**

The following data at January 31, 2011 is given for BPM.

a. Depreciation, $100
b. Prepaid rent expired, $400
c. Interest expense accrued, $900
d. Employee salaries owed for Monday through Thursday of a five-day workweek; weekly payroll, $14,000
e. Unearned service revenue earned, $800

Requirements

1. Journalize the adjusting entries needed on January 31, 2011.
2. Suppose the adjustments made in requirement 1 were not made. Compute the overall overstatement or understatement of net income as a result of the omission of these adjustments. (Challenge)

E3-23 *(L.OBJ. 4, 6)* **Using adjusting journal entries and computing financial statement amounts [10–20 min]**

The adjusted trial balances of Erie International at March 31, 2012, and March 31, 2011, include the following amounts:

	2012	2011
Supplies	$ 2,100	$ 1,300
Salary payable	2,300	4,400
Unearned service revenue	12,000	16,300

Analysis of the accounts at March 31, 2012, reveals the following transactions for the fiscal year ending in 2012:

Cash payments for supplies	$ 5,900
Cash payments for salaries	47,400
Cash receipts in advance for service revenue	80,800

Requirement

1. Compute the amount of Supplies expense, Salary expense, and Service revenue to report on the Erie International income statement for 2012.

Note: Exercise 3-24 should be used only in conjunction with Exercise 3-19.

E3-24 *(L.OBJ. 5, 6)* **Using an adjusted trial balance to prepare financial statements [10 min]**

Refer to the data in Exercise 3-19.

Requirements

1. Compute Shining Image Company's net income for the period ended December 31, 2010.
2. Compute Shining Image Company's total assets at December 31, 2010.

Note: Exercise 3-25 should be used only after completing Exercise 3-21.

E3-25 *(L.OBJ. 6)* **Preparing the financial statements [20 min]**

Refer to the adjusted trial balance in Exercise 3-21 for the month ended April 30, 2010.

Requirements

1. Prepare the income statement.
2. Prepare the statement of owner's equity.
3. Prepare the balance sheet.

E3-26 *(L.OBJ. 6)* **Preparing the income statement [15 min]**
The accountant for Beth Reilly, CPA, has posted adjusting entries (a) through (e) to the accounts at December 31, 2011. Selected balance sheet accounts and all the revenues and expenses of the entity follow in T-account form.

Accounts receivable

Debit	Credit
23,200	
(e) 1,100	

Supplies

Debit	Credit
1,100	(a) 600

Acc. depr.—equipment

Debit	Credit
	4,900
	(b) 1,800

Acc. depr.—building

Debit	Credit
	29,800
	(c) 4,800

Salary payable

Debit	Credit
	(d) 600

Service revenue

Debit	Credit
	105,800
	(e) 1,100

Salary expense

Debit	Credit
28,000	
(d) 600	

Supplies expense

Debit	Credit
(a) 600	

Depreciation expense—equip.

Debit	Credit
(b) 1,800	

Depreciation expense—bldg

Debit	Credit
(c) 4,800	

Requirements

1. Prepare the income statement of Beth Reilly, CPA, for the year ended December 31, 2011.
2. Were 2011 operations successful?

E3-27 *(L.OBJ. 6)* **Preparing the statement of owner s equity [10-15 min]**
Mountain Fresh Interiors began the year with capital of $18,000. On July 12, Mountain Fresh received owner investment of $12,000 cash. The income statement for the year ended December 31, 2011, reported net income of $64,000. During this fiscal year, T. English withdrew $5,000 each month.

Requirement

1. Prepare Mountain Fresh Interiors' statement of owner's equity for the year ended December 31, 2011.

Problems (Group A)

P3-28A *(L.OBJ. 1, 4, 6)* **Comparing accrual and cash basis accounting, preparing adjusting entries, and preparing income statements [15–25 min]**
Fischer's Golf School, completed the following transactions during July, 2012:

Jul	1	Prepaid insurance for July through September, $1,200
	4	Performed services (gave golf lessons) on account, $2,300
	5	Purchased equipment on account, $1,400
	8	Paid property tax expense, $300
	11	Purchased office equipment for cash, $1,700
	19	Performed services and received cash, $800
	24	Collected $500 on account
	26	Paid account payable from July 5
	29	Paid salary expense, $1,000
	31	Recorded adjusting entry for July insurance expense (see July 1)
	31	Debited unearned revenue and credited revenue in an adjusting entry, $800

Requirements

1. Prepare journal entries for each transaction.
2. Using the journal entries as a guide, show whether each transaction would be handled as a revenue or an expense, using both the accrual and cash basis, by completing the following table.

Amount of Revenue (Expense) for July			
Date		Cash – Basis Amount of Revenue (Expense)	Accrual – Basis Amount of Revenue (Expense)
Jul	1		

3. After completing the table, calculate the amount of net income or net loss for the company under the accrual and cash basis for July.
4. Considering your results from requirement 3, which method gives the best picture of the true earnings of Fischer's Golf School? Why?

P3-29A *(L.OBJ. 4)* **Journalizing adjusting entries [15–25 min]**
Littleton Landscaping has the following independent cases at the end of the year on December 31, 2011.

a. Each Friday, Littleton pays employees for the current week's work. The amount of the weekly payroll is $5,500 for a five-day workweek. This year December 31 falls on a Thursday.

b. Details of Prepaid insurance are shown in the account:

Prepaid insurance	
Jan 1 $3,000	

Littleton prepays a full year's insurance each year on January 1. Record insurance expense for the year ended December 31.

c. The beginning balance of Supplies was $4,200. During the year, Littleton purchased supplies for $5,300, and at December 31 the supplies on hand total $2,200.

d. Littleton designed a landscape plan, and the client paid Littleton $10,000 at the start of the project. Littleton recorded this amount as Unearned service revenue. The job will take several months to complete, and Littleton estimates that the company has earned 70% of the total revenue during the current year.

e. Depreciation for the current year includes Equipment, $3,600; and Trucks, $1,400. Make a compound entry.

Requirement

1. Journalize the adjusting entry needed on December 31, 2011, for each of the previous items affecting Littleton Landscaping.

P3-30A *(L.OBJ. 4)* **Analyzing and journalizing adjustments [15–20 min]**
Movie Magic Production Company's unadjusted and adjusted trial balances at December 31, 2012, follow.

MOVIE MAGIC PRODUCTION COMPANY
Adjusted Trial Balance
December 31, 2012

	Trial Balance		Adjusted Trial Balance	
Account	Debit	Credit	Debit	Credit
Cash	$ 3,200		$ 3,200	
Accounts receivable	5,900		6,800	
Supplies	1,900		600	
Prepaid insurance	2,600		1,200	
Equipment	21,600		21,600	
Accumulated depreciation		$ 8,200		$ 11,900
Accounts payable		4,400		4,400
Salary payable				500
J. Bhattacharya, Capital		14,400		14,400
J. Bhattacharya, Withdrawals	29,600		29,600	
Service revenue		69,400		70,300
Depreciation expense			3,700	
Supplies expense			1,300	
Utilities expense	5,000		5,000	
Salary expense	26,600		27,100	
Insurance expense			1,400	
Total	$ 96,400	$ 96,400	$ 101,500	$ 101,500

Requirement

1. Journalize the adjusting entries that account for the differences between the two trial balances.

P3-31A *(L.OBJ. 4, 5)* **Journalizing and posting adjustments to the T-accounts and preparing an adjusted trial balance [45-60 min]**

The trial balance of Dynaclean Air Purification System at December 31, 2011, and the data needed for the month-end adjustments follow.

DYNACLEAN AIR PURIFICATION SYSTEM Trial Balance December 31, 2011		
Account	Debit	Credit
Cash	$ 7,600	
Accounts receivable	19,300	
Prepaid rent	2,700	
Supplies	1,200	
Equipment	19,600	
Accumulated depreciation		$ 3,900
Accounts payable		3,400
Salary payable		
Unearned service revenue		2,900
D. Mutt, Capital		38,900
D. Mutt, Withdrawals	9,500	
Service revenue		15,500
Salary expense	3,100	
Rent expense		
Depreciation expense		
Advertising expense	1,600	
Supplies expense		
Total	$ 64,600	$ 64,600

Adjustment data at December 31:

a. Unearned service revenue still unearned, $1,300
b. Prepaid rent still in force, $400
c. Supplies used during the month, $400
d. Depreciation for the month, $500
e. Accrued advertising expense, $800. (Credit Accounts payable.)
f. Accrued salary expense, $1,000

Requirements

1. Journalize the adjusting entries.
2. The unadjusted balances have been entered for you in the general ledger accounts. Post the adjusting entries to the ledger accounts.
3. Prepare the adjusted trial balance.
4. How will Dynaclean Air Purification System use the adjusted trial balance?

P3-32A *(L.OBJ. 4, 5, 6)* **Preparing and posting adjusting journal entries; preparing an adjusted trial balance and financial statements [45–60 min]**

The trial balance of Arlington Common Breakfast Nook at December 31, 2010, and the data needed for the month-end adjustments follow.

ARLINGTON COMMON BREAKFAST NOOK Trial Balance December 31, 2010		
Account	**Debit**	**Credit**
Cash	$ 12,200	
Accounts receivable	14,100	
Prepaid insurance	3,100	
Supplies	800	
Building	423,000	
Accumulated depreciation		$309,500
Accounts payable		1,900
Salary payable		
Unearned service revenue		2,300
W. Temple, Capital		127,000
W. Temple, Withdrawals	2,900	
Service revenue		18,300
Salary expense	2,100	
Insurance expense		
Depreciation expense		
Advertising expense	800	
Supplies expense		
Total	$459,000	$459,000

Adjustment data at December 31:

a. Prepaid insurance still in force, $500
b. Supplies used during the month, $600
c. Depreciation for the month, $1,800
d. Accrued salary expense, $700
e. Unearned service revenue still unearned, $1,500

Requirements

1. Journalize the adjusting entries.
2. The unadjusted balances have been entered for you in the general ledger accounts. Post the adjusting entries to the ledger accounts.
3. Prepare the adjusted trial balance.
4. Prepare the income statement, statement of owner's equity, and balance sheet for the business for the month ended December 31, 2010.

P3-33A *(L.OBJ. 5, 6)* **Prepare an adjusted trial balance and financial statements. [45–60 min]**

Consider the unadjusted trial balance of In Style Limo Service Company at March 31, 2012, and the related month-end adjustment data.

IN STYLE LIMO SERVICE COMPANY Trial Balance March 31, 2012		
	Trial Balance	
Account	Debit	Credit
Cash	6,300	
Accounts receivable	1,000	
Prepaid rent	3,000	
Supplies	1,200	
Automobile	72,000	
Accumulated depreciation		4,000
Accounts payable		3,700
Salary payable		
W. Jackson, Capital		72,400
W. Jackson, Withdrawals	3,700	
Service revenue		9,400
Salary expense	1,700	
Rent expense		
Fuel expense	600	
Depreciation expense		
Supplies expense		
Total	89,500	89,500

Adjustment data at March 31, 2012:

a. Accrued service revenue at March 31, $1,600
b. One-fifth of the prepaid rent expired during the month
c. Supplies on hand at March 31, $1,100
d. Depreciation on automobile for the month, $1,200
e. Accrued salary expense at March 31 for one day only. The five-day weekly payroll is $1,400.

Requirements

1. Write the trial balance on a work sheet, using Exhibit 3-9 as an example, and prepare the adjusted trial balance of In Style Limo Service Company at March 31, 2012. Key each adjusting entry by letter.
2. Prepare the income statement and the statement of owner's equity for the month ended March 31, 2012, and the balance sheet at that date.

P3-34A *(L.OBJ. 6)* **Preparing financial statements from an adjusted trial balance. [20–30 min]**

The adjusted trial balance of A Plus Events Piano Tuning Service at fiscal year end January 31, 2011, follows.

A PLUS EVENTS PIANO TUNING SERVICE Adjusted Trial Balance January 31, 2011		
	Balance	
Account Title	Debit	Credit
Cash	$ 12,400	
Accounts receivable	10,300	
Supplies	1,800	
Equipment	25,200	
Accumulated depreciation		12,600
Accounts payable		3,600
Unearned service revenue		4,500
Salary payable		700
Note payable		14,000
E. John, Capital		8,900
E. John, Withdrawals	37,000	
Service revenue		66,000
Depreciation expense	5,800	
Salary expense	9,000	
Utilities expense	4,200	
Insurance expense	3,100	
Supplies expense	1,500	
Total	$110,300	$110,300

Requirements

1. Prepare A Plus Events 2011 income statement.
2. Prepare the statement of owner's equity for the year.
3. Prepare the year-end balance sheet.
4. Which financial statement reports A Plus's results of operations? Were the 2011 operations successful? Cite specifics from the financial statements to support your evaluation.
5. Which statement reports the company's financial position? Does A Plus's financial position look strong or weak? Give the reason for your evaluation.

Problems (Group B)

P3-35B *(L.OBJ. 1, 4, 6)* **Comparing accrual and cash basis accounting, preparing adjusting entries, and preparing income statements [15–25 min]**

Warren's Golf School completed the following transactions during August, 2012:

Aug	1	Prepaid insurance for August through October, $900
	4	Performed services (gave golf lessons) on account, $2,600
	5	Purchased equipment on account, $1,900
	8	Paid property tax expense, $300
	11	Purchased office equipment for cash, $1,200
	19	Performed services and received cash, $1,300
	24	Collected $600 on account
	26	Paid account payable from August 5
	29	Paid salary expense, $1,300
	31	Recorded adjusting entry for August insurance expense (see August 1)
	31	Debited unearned revenue and credited revenue in an adjusting entry, $700

Requirements

1. Prepare journal entries for each transaction.
2. Using the journal entries as a guide, show whether each transaction would be handled as a revenue or an expense, using both the accrual and cash basis, by completing the following table:

Amount of Revenue (Expense) for August		
Date	Cash – Basis Amount of Revenue (Expense)	Accrual – Basis Amount of Revenue (Expense)
Aug 1		

3. After completing the table, calculate the amount of net income or net loss for the company under the accrual and cash basis for August.
4. Considering your results from requirement 3, which method gives the best picture of the true earnings of Warren's Golf School? Why?

P3-36B *(L.OBJ. 4)* **Journalizing adjusting entries [15–25 min]**

Loco Landscaping has the following independent cases at the end of the year on December 31, 2011.

a. Each Friday, Loco pays employees for the current week's work. The amount of the weekly payroll is $6,000 for a five-day workweek. This year December 31 falls on a Monday.

b. Details of Prepaid insurance are shown in the account:

Prepaid insurance	
Jan 1 $4,500	

Loco prepays a full year's insurance each year on January 1. Record insurance expense for the year ended December 31.

c. The beginning balance of Supplies was $3,800. During the year, Loco purchased supplies for $5,300, and at December 31 the supplies on hand total $2,100.

d. Loco designed a landscape plan, and the client paid Loco $5,000 at the start of the project. Loco recorded this amount as Unearned service revenue. The job will take several months to complete, and Loco estimates that the company has earned 60% of the total revenue during the current year.

e. Depreciation for the current year includes Equipment, $3,600; and Trucks, $1,500. Make a compound entry.

Requirement

1. Journalize the adjusting entry needed on December 31, 2011, for each of the previous items affecting Loco Landscaping.

P3-37B *(L.OBJ. 4)* **Analyzing and journalizing adjustments [15–20 min]**
Milky Way Theater Production Company's unadjusted and adjusted trial balances at December 31, 2012, follow.

MILKY WAY THEATER PRODUCTION COMPANY Adjusted Trial Balance December 31, 2012				
	Trial Balance		Adjusted Trial Balance	
Account	Debit	Credit	Debit	Credit
Cash	$ 3,200		$ 3,200	
Accounts receivable	6,100		7,000	
Supplies	1,700		300	
Prepaid insurance	2,600		1,400	
Equipment	21,600		21,600	
Accumulated depreciation		$ 8,200		$ 12,000
Accounts payable		4,400		4,400
Salary payable				400
S. Seth, Capital		14,400		14,400
S. Seth, Withdrawals	29,600		29,600	
Service revenue		69,400		70,300
Depreciation expense			3,800	
Supplies expense			1,400	
Utilities expense	5,000		5,000	
Salary expense	26,600		27,000	
Insurance expense			1,200	
Total	$ 96,400	$ 96,400	$ 101,500	$ 101,500

Requirement

1. Journalize the adjusting entries that account for the differences between the two trial balances.

P3-38B *(L.OBJ. 4, 5)* **Journalizing and posting adjustments to the T-accounts, and preparing an adjusted trial balance [45–60 min]**
The trial balance of Cambridge Air Purification System at December 31, 2011, and the data needed for the month-end adjustments follow.

CAMBRIDGE AIR PURIFICATION SYSTEM Trial Balance December 31, 2011		
Account	**Debit**	**Credit**
Cash	$ 7,400	
Accounts receivable	19,400	
Prepaid rent	2,900	
Supplies	1,600	
Equipment	19,500	
Accumulated depreciation		$ 3,900
Accounts payable		3,600
Salary payable		
Unearned service revenue		2,900
S. Biggs, Capital		38,800
S. Biggs, Withdrawals	9,500	
Service revenue		15,900
Salary expense	3,500	
Rent expense		
Depreciation expense		
Advertising expense	1,300	
Supplies expense		
Total	$ 65,100	$ 65,100

Adjustment data at December 31:

a. Unearned service revenue still unearned, $1,700
b. Prepaid rent still in force, $600
c. Supplies used during the month, $600
d. Depreciation for the month, $400
e. Accrued advertising expense, $800. (Credit Accounts payable.)
f. Accrued salary expense, $1,200

Requirements

1. Journalize the adjusting entries.
2. The unadjusted balances have been entered for you in the general ledger accounts. Post the adjusting entries to the ledger accounts.
3. Prepare the adjusted trial balance.
4. How will Cambridge Air Purification System use the adjusted trial balance?

P3-39B *(L.OBJ. 4, 5, 6)* **Preparing and posting adjusting journal entries; preparing an adjusted trial balance and financial statements. [45–60 min]**
The trial balance of North End Pub at December 31, 2010, and the data needed for the month-end adjustments follow.

NORTH END PUB Trial Balance December 31, 2010		
Account	**Debit**	**Credit**
Cash	$ 12,200	
Accounts receivable	14,100	
Prepaid insurance	3,100	
Supplies	800	
Building	443,000	
Accumulated depreciation		$315,800
Accounts payable		1,900
Salary payable		
Unearned service revenue		2,300
G. Sessions, Capital		139,000
G. Sessions, Withdrawals	2,900	
Service revenue		20,000
Salary expense	2,100	
Insurance expense		
Depreciation expense		
Advertising expense	800	
Supplies expense		
Total	$479,000	$479,000

Adjustment data at December 31:

a. Prepaid insurance still in force, $800
b. Supplies used during the month, $400
c. Depreciation for the month, $1,500
d. Accrued salary expense, $500
e. Unearned service revenue still unearned, $1,200

Requirements

1. Journalize the adjusting entries.
2. The unadjusted balances have been entered for you in the general ledger accounts. Post the adjusting entries to the ledger accounts.
3. Prepare the adjusted trial balance.
4. Prepare the income statement, statement of owner's equity, and balance sheet for the business for the month ended December 31, 2010.

P3-40B *(L.OBJ. 5, 6)* **Prepare an adjusted trial balance and financial statements [45–60 min]**

Consider the unadjusted trial balance of Hummer Limo Service Company at October 31, 2012, and the related month-end adjustment data.

HUMMER LIMO SERVICE COMPANY Trial Balance October 31, 2012		
	Trial Balance	
Account	Debit	Credit
Cash	6,700	
Accounts receivable	1,300	
Prepaid rent	3,500	
Supplies	1,000	
Automobile	75,000	
Accumulated depreciation		4,000
Accounts payable		3,500
Salary payable		
D. Andre, Capital		76,800
D. Andre, Withdrawals	4,300	
Service revenue		9,700
Salary expense	1,900	
Rent expense		
Fuel expense	300	
Depreciation expense		
Supplies expense		
Total	94,000	94,000

Adjustment data at October 31, 2012:

a. Accrued service revenue at October 31, $1,900

b. One-fifth of the prepaid rent expired during the month

c. Supplies on hand at October 31, $800

d. Depreciation on automobile for the month, $1,200

e. Accrued salary expense at October 31 for one day only. The five-day weekly payroll is $1,900.

Requirements

1. Write the trial balance on a work sheet, using Exhibit 3-9 as an example, and prepare the adjusted trial balance of Hummer Limo Service Company at October 31, 2012. Key each adjusting entry by letter.
2. Prepare the income statement and the statement of owner's equity for the month ended October 31, 2012, and the balance sheet at that date.

P3-41B *(L.OBJ. 6)* **Preparing financial statements from an adjusted trial balance [20–30 min]**

The adjusted trial balance of Event World Piano Tuning Service at fiscal year end August 31, 2011, follows.

EVENT WORLD PIANO TUNING SERVICE Adjusted Trial Balance August 31, 2011		
	Balance	
Account Title	Debit	Credit
Cash	$ 12,600	
Accounts receivable	10,300	
Supplies	1,300	
Equipment	25,900	
Accumulated depreciation		12,500
Accounts payable		3,800
Unearned service revenue		4,500
Salary payable		800
Note payable		14,000
S. Bach, Capital		5,600
S. Bach, Withdrawals	35,000	
Service revenue		68,000
Depreciation expense	5,400	
Salary expense	9,600	
Utilities expense	3,800	
Insurance expense	3,600	
Supplies expense	1,700	
Total	$109,200	$109,200

Requirements

1. Prepare Event World Piano Tuning Service's 2011 income statement.
2. Prepare the statement of owner's equity for the year.
3. Prepare the year-end balance sheet.
4. Which financial statement reports Event World Piano Tuning Service's results of operations? Were 2011 operations successful? Cite specifics from the financial statements to support your evaluation.
5. Which statement reports the company's financial position? Does Event World Piano Tuning Service's financial position look strong or weak? Give the reason for your evaluation.

■ Continuing Exercise

E3-42 This exercise continues the Sherman Lawn Service situation from Exercise 2-63 of Chapter 2. Start from the trial balance and the posted T-accounts that Sherman Lawn Service prepared at August 31, 2009.

Requirements

1. Open these additional T-accounts: Accumulated depreciation—equipment; Depreciation expense—equipment; Supplies expense.

2. Hannah determines there are $20 in Lawn Supplies left at August 31, 2009. Journalize any required adjusting journal entries.
3. Post to the T-accounts, keying all items by date.
4. Prepare the adjusted trial balance, as illustrated in Exhibit 3-9.

Continuing Problem

P3-43 This problem continues the Haupt Consulting situation from Problem 2-64 of Chapter 2. Start from the trial balance and the posted T-accounts that Haupt Consulting prepared at December 18, as follows:

HAUPT CONSULTING
Trial Balance
December 18, 2010

Account Title	Balance	
	Debit	Credit
Cash	$ 8,100	
Accounts receivable	1,700	
Supplies	300	
Equipment	2,000	
Accumulated depreciation—equipment		
Furniture	3,600	
Accumulated depreciation—furniture		
Accounts payable		$ 3,900
Salary payable		
Unearned service revenue		
Carl Haupt, Capital		10,000
Carl Haupt, Withdrawals		
Service revenue		2,500
Rent expense	500	
Utilities expense	200	
Salary expense		
Depreciation expense—equipment		
Depreciation expense—furniture		
Supplies expense		
Total	$16,400	$16,400

Later in December, the business completed these transactions, as follows:

Dec 21	Received $900 in advance for client service to be performed evenly over the next 30 days.
21	Hired a secretary to be paid $1,500 on the 20th day of each month. The secretary begins work immediately.
26	Paid $300 on account.
28	Collected $600 on account.
30	Owner withdrew $1,600.

Requirements

1. Open these additional T-accounts: Accumulated depreciation—equipment; Accumulated depreciation—furniture; Salary payable; Unearned service revenue; Depreciation expense—equipment; Depreciation expense—furniture; Supplies expense.
2. Journalize the transactions of December 21–30.
3. Post to the T-accounts, keying all items by date.
4. Prepare a trial balance at December 31. Also set up columns for the adjustments and for the adjusted trial balance, as illustrated in Exhibit 3-9.
5. At December 31, the business gathers the following information for the adjusting entries:

   a. Accrued service revenue, $400
   b. Earned $300 of the service revenue collected in advance on December 21
   c. Supplies on hand, $100
   d. Depreciation expense—equipment, $33; furniture, $60
   e. Accrued $700 expense for secretary's salary

   On your work sheet make these adjustments directly in the adjustments columns, and complete the adjusted trial balance at December 31. Throughout the book, to avoid rounding errors, we base adjusting entries on 30-day months and 360-day years.
6. Journalize and post the adjusting entries. In the T-accounts denote each adjusting amount as *Adj* and an account balance as *Bal.*
7. Prepare the income statement and the statement of owner's equity of Haupt Consulting for the month ended December 31, 2010, and prepare the balance sheet at that date.

Practice Set

Using the Trial balance prepared in Chapter 2 consider the following adjustment data gathered by CJ:

a. CJ prepared an inventory of supplies and found there were $70 of supplies in the cabinet on April 30
b. One month's combined depreciation on all assets was estimated to be $300

Requirements

1. Using the data provided from the trial balance, the previous adjustment information, and the information from Chapter 2, prepare all required adjusting journal entries for April.
2. Prepare an adjusted trial balance as of April 30 for Crystal Clear Cleaning.

Apply Your Knowledge

Decision Cases

Case 1. Lee Nicholas has been the owner and has operated World.com Advertising since its beginning 10 years ago. The company has prospered. Recently, Nicholas mentioned that he would sell the business for the right price.

Assume that you are interested in buying World.com Advertising. You obtain the most recent monthly trial balance, which follows. Revenues and expenses vary little from month to month, and January is a typical month. Your investigation reveals that the trial balance does *not* include monthly revenues of $3,800 and expenses of $1,100. Also, if you were to buy World.com Advertising, you would hire a manager so you could devote your time to other duties. Assume that this person would require a monthly salary of $5,000.

WORLD.COM ADVERTISING Trial Balance January 31, 2012		
	Balance	
Account Title	Debit	Credit
Cash	$ 9,700	
Accounts receivable	14,100	
Prepaid expenses	2,600	
Building	221,300	
Accumulated depreciation		$ 68,600
Accounts payable		13,000
Salary payable		
Unearned service revenue		56,700
Lee Nicholas, Capital		110,400
Lee Nicholas, Withdrawals	9,000	
Service revenue		12,300
Rent expense		
Salary expense	3,400	
Utilities expense	900	
Depreciation expense		
Supplies expense		
Total	$261,000	$261,000

Requirements

1. Assume that the most you would pay for the business is 20 times the monthly net income *you could expect to earn* from it. Compute this possible price.
2. Nicholas states that the least he will take for the business is an amount equal to the business's owner's equity balance on January 31. Compute this amount.
3. Under these conditions, how much should you offer Nicholas? Give your reason. (Challenge)

Case 2. One year ago, Tyler Stasney founded Swift Classified Ads. Stasney remembers that you took an accounting course while in college and comes to you for advice. He wishes to know how much net income his business earned during the past year in order to decide whether to keep the company going. His accounting records consist of the T-accounts from his ledger, which were prepared by an accountant who moved to another city. The ledger at December 31 follows. The accounts have *not* been adjusted.

Stasney indicates that at year-end, customers owe him $1,600 for accrued service revenue. These revenues have not been recorded. During the year, Stasney collected $4,000 service revenue in advance from customers, but he earned only $900 of that amount. Rent expense for the year was $2,400, and he used up $1,700 of the supplies. Stasney determines that depreciation on his equipment was $5,000 for the year. At December 31, he owes his employee $1,200 accrued salary.

Cash	
Dec 31 5,800	

Accounts receivable	
Dec 31 12,000	

Prepaid rent	
Jan 2 2,800	

Supplies	
Jan 2 2,600	

Equipment	
Jan 2 36,000	

Accumulated depreciation	

Accounts payable	
	Dec 31 21,500

Unearned service revenue	
	Dec 31 4,000

Salary payable	

T. Stasney, Capital	
	Dec 31 20,000

Depreciation expense	

T. Stasney, Withdrawals	
Dec 31 28,000	

Service revenue	
	Dec 31 59,500

Salary expense	
Dec 31 17,000	

Rent expense	

Utilities expense	
Dec 31 800	

Supplies expense	

Requirement

1. Help Stasney compute his net income for the year. Advise him whether to continue operating Swift Classified Ads.

Ethical Issue

The net income of Steinbach & Sons, a department store, decreased sharply during 2011. Mort Steinbach, manager of the store, anticipates the need for a bank loan in 2012. Late in 2011, Steinbach instructs the store's accountant to record a $2,000 sale of furniture to the Steinbach family, even though the goods will not be shipped from the manufacturer until January 2012. Steinbach also tells the accountant *not* to make the following December 31, 2011, adjusting entries:

Salaries owed to employees	$900
Prepaid insurance that has expired	400

Requirements

1. Compute the overall effects of these transactions on the store's reported income for 2011.
2. Why is Steinbach taking this action? Is his action ethical? Give your reason, identifying the parties helped and the parties harmed by Steinbach's action. (Challenge)
3. As a personal friend, what advice would you give the accountant? (Challenge)

Financial Statement Case

Amazon.com—like all other businesses—makes adjusting entries prior to year-end in order to measure assets, liabilities, revenues, and expenses properly. Examine **Amazon's** balance sheet and Note 3. Pay particular attention to Accumulated depreciation.

1. Open T-accounts for the following accounts with the balances shown on the annual reports at December 31, 2006 (amounts in millions, as in the **Amazon.com** financial statements):

Accumulated Depreciation	$ 367
Accounts Payable	1,816
Other Assets	139

2. Assume that during 2007 **Amazon.com** completed the following transactions (amounts in billions). Journalize each transaction (explanations are not required).

a.	Recorded depreciation expense, $113
b.	Paid the December 31, 2006, balance of accounts payable
c.	Purchased inventory on account, $2,795
d.	Purchased other assets for cash of $157

3. Post to the three T-accounts. Then the balance of each account should agree with the corresponding amount reported in **Amazon's** December 31, 2007, balance sheet. Check to make sure they do agree with **Amazon's** actual balances. You can find Accumulated depreciation in Note 3.

Team Project

It's Just Lunch is a nationwide service company that arranges lunch dates for clients. **It's Just Lunch** collects cash up front for a package of dates. Suppose your group is opening an **It's Just Lunch** office in your area. You must make some important decisions—where to locate, how to advertise, and so on—and you must also make some accounting decisions. For example, what will be the end of your business's accounting year? How often will you need financial statements to evaluate operating performance and financial position? Will you use the cash basis or the accrual basis? When will you account for the revenue that the business earns? How will you account for the expenses?

Requirements

Write a report (or prepare an oral presentation, as directed by your professor) to address the following considerations:

1. Will you use the cash basis or the accrual basis of accounting? Give a complete explanation of your reasoning.
2. How often do you want financial statements? Why? Discuss how you will use each financial statement.
3. What kind of revenue will you earn? When will you record it as revenue? How will you decide when to record the revenue?
4. Prepare a made-up income statement for **It's Just Lunch** for the year ended December 31, 2012. List all the business's expenses, starting with the most important (largest dollar amount) and working through to the least important (smallest dollar amount). Merely list the accounts. Dollar amounts are not required.

Quick Check Answers

1. *b* 2. *c* 3. *d* 4. *d* 5. *b* 6. *b* 7. *a* 8. *b* 9. *a* 10. *d*

For online homework, exercises, and problems that provide you immediate feedback, please visit www.myaccountinglab.com.

Alternative Treatment of Prepaid Expenses and Unearned Revenues

Chapters 1–3 illustrate the most popular way to account for prepaid expenses and unearned revenues. This appendix illustrates an alternative approach.

Prepaid Expenses

Prepaid expenses are advance payments of expenses such as Prepaid insurance, Prepaid rent, and Prepaid advertising. Supplies are also accounted for as prepaid expenses.

When a business prepays an expense—rent, for example—it can debit an *asset* account (Prepaid rent), as illustrated earlier in the chapter.

Aug 1	Prepaid rent (A+)	XXX	
	Cash (A–)		XXX

Alternatively, it can debit an *expense* account to record this cash payment:

Aug 1	Rent expense (E+)	XXX	
	Cash (A–)		XXX

Either way, the business must adjust the accounts at the end of the period to report the correct amounts of the expense and the asset.

Prepaid Expense Recorded Initially as an Expense

Prepaying an expense creates an asset. However, the asset may be so short-lived that it will expire in the current accounting period—within one year or less. Thus, the accountant may decide to debit the prepayment to an expense account at the time of payment. A $6,000 cash payment for rent (one year, in advance) on August 1 may be debited to Rent expense:

2010			
Aug 1	Rent expense (E+)	6,000	
	Cash (A–)		6,000

At December 31, only five months' prepayment has expired (for August through December), leaving seven months' rent still prepaid. In this case, the accountant must transfer 7/12 of the original prepayment of $6,000, or $3,500, to the asset account Prepaid rent. At December 31, 2010, the business still has the benefit of the prepayment for January through July of 2011. The adjusting entry at December 31 is

2010	**Adjusting Entries**		
Dec 31	Prepaid rent ($6,000 × 7/12) (A+)	3,500	
	Rent expense (E+)		3,500

After posting, the two accounts appear as follows:

Prepaid rent

2010			
Dec 31 Adjusting	3,500		
Dec 31 Balance	3,500		

Rent expense

2010		2010	
Aug 1 Payment	6,000	Dec 31 Adjusting	3,500
Dec 31 Balance	2,500		

The balance sheet at the end of 2010 reports Prepaid rent of $3,500, and the income statement for 2010 reports Rent expense of $2,500, regardless of whether the business initially debits the prepayment to an asset account or to an expense account.

Unearned (Deferred) Revenues

Unearned (deferred) revenues arise when a business collects cash before earning the revenue. Unearned revenues are liabilities because the business that receives cash owes the other party goods or services to be delivered later.

Unearned (Deferred) Revenue Recorded Initially as a Revenue

Receipt of cash in advance creates a liability, as discussed in the chapter. Another way to account for the receipt of cash is to credit a *revenue account* when it receives the cash. If the business then earns all the revenue within the same period, no adjusting entry is needed at the end. However, if the business earns only part of the revenue that period, it must make an adjusting entry.

Suppose on October 1, 2010, a law firm records as service revenue the receipt of $9,000 cash for service revenue to be earned over nine months. The cash receipt entry is

2010			
Oct 1	Cash (A+)	9,000	
	Service revenue (R+)		9,000

At December 31, 2010, the attorney has earned only 3/9 of the $9,000, or $3,000, for the months of October, November, and December. Accordingly, the law firm makes an adjusting entry to transfer the unearned portion (6/9 of $9,000, or $6,000) from the revenue account to a liability, as follows:

2010			
Dec 31	Service revenue ($9,000 × 6/9) (R–)	6,000	
	Unearned service revenue (L+)		6,000

The adjusting entry transfers the unearned portion to the liability account because the law firm still owes legal service to the client for six months, January through June of 2011. After posting, the total amount ($9,000) is properly divided between the liability account ($6,000) and the revenue account ($3,000), as follows:

Unearned service revenue

		2010	
		Dec 31 Adjusting	6,000
		Dec 31 Balance	6,000

Service revenue

2010		2010	
Dec 31 Adjusting	6,000	Oct 1 Receipt	9,000
		Dec 31 Balance	3,000

The attorney's 2010 income statement reports service revenue of $3,000, and the balance sheet reports the unearned revenue of $6,000 as a liability. The result is the same whether the business initially credits a liability account or a revenue account.

Appendix 3A Assignments

■ Exercises

E3A-1 *(L.OBJ. 4)* **Preparing adjusting entries [10–15 min]**
At the beginning of the year, supplies of $1,300 were on hand. During the year, Dubuque Air Conditioning Service paid $4,700 for more supplies. At the end of the year, Dubuque has $500 of supplies on hand.

Requirements

1. Assume that Dubuque records supplies by initially debiting an asset account. Therefore, place the beginning balance in the Supplies T-account, and record the preceding entries directly in the accounts without using a journal.
2. Assume that Dubuque records supplies by initially debiting an *expense* account. Therefore, place the beginning balance in the Supplies expense T-account, and record the preceding entries directly in the accounts without using a journal.
3. Compare the ending account balances under both approaches. Are they the same?

E3A-2 *(L.OBJ. 4)* **Preparing adjusting entries [15–25 min]**
At the beginning of the year, Mode Advertising owed customers $2,500 for unearned service revenue collected in advance. During the year, Mode received advance cash receipts of $6,800. At year-end, the liability for unearned revenue is $3,800.

Requirements

1. Assume that Mode records unearned revenues by initially crediting a *liability* account. Enter the beginning balance in Unearned service revenue T-account. Journalize the cash collection and adjusting entries, and post their dollar amounts in the T-accounts. As references in the T-accounts, denote a cash receipt by *CR*, and an adjustment by *Adj*.
2. Assume that Mode records unearned revenues by initially crediting a *revenue* account. Enter the beginning balance in Service revenue T-account. Journalize the cash collection and adjusting entries, and post their dollar amounts in the T-accounts. As references in the T-accounts, denote a cash receipt by *CR*, and an adjustment by *Adj*.
3. Compare the ending balances in the two accounts.

■ Problems (Group A)

P3A-3A *(L.OBJ. 4)* **Preparing adjusting entries [25–35 min]**
Fast Pages Pack'n Mail completed the following transactions during 2010:

Nov 1	Paid $3,900 store rent covering the three–month period ending January 31, 2011
Dec 1	Collected $4,400 cash in advance from customers. The service revenue will be earned $1,100 monthly over the four–month period ending March 31, 2011

Requirements

1. Journalize these entries by debiting an asset account for Prepaid rent and by crediting a liability account for Unearned service revenue. Explanations are unnecessary.
2. Journalize the related adjustments at December 31, 2010.

3. Post the entries to the T-accounts, and show their balances at December 31, 2010. Posting references are unnecessary.
4. Repeat requirements 1–3. This time, debit Rent expense for the rent payment and credit Service revenue for the collection of revenue in advance.
5. Compare the account balances in requirements 3 and 4. They should be equal.

Problems (Group B)

P3A-4B *(L.OBJ. 4)* **Preparing adjusting entries [25–35 min]**
Quick Pages Pack'n Mail completed the following transactions during 2010:

Nov 1	Paid $2,400 store rent covering the three–month period ending January 31, 2011
Dec 1	Collected $5,600 cash in advance from customers. The service revenue will be earned $1,400 monthly over the four–month period ending March 31, 2011

Requirements

1. Journalize these entries by debiting an asset account for Prepaid rent and by crediting a liability account for Unearned service revenue. Explanations are unnecessary.
2. Journalize the related adjustments at December 31, 2010.
3. Post the entries to the T-accounts, and show their balances at December 31, 2010. Posting references are unnecessary.
4. Repeat requirements 1–3. This time, debit Rent expense for the rent payment and credit Service revenue for the collection of revenue in advance.
5. Compare the account balances in requirements 3 and 4. They should be equal.

Chapter 3: Demo Doc

■ Preparation of Adjusting Entries, Adjusted Trial Balance, and Financial Statements

Demo Doc: To make sure you understand this material, work through the following demonstration "demo doc" with detailed comments to help you see the concept within the framework of a worked-through problem.

Learning Objectives 3–6

Cloud Break Consulting has the following information at June 30, 2011:

CLOUD BREAK CONSULTING
Unadjusted Trial Balance
June 30, 2011

Account Title	Balance Debit	Balance Credit
Cash	$131,000	
Accounts receivable	104,000	
Supplies	4,000	
Prepaid rent	27,000	
Land	45,000	
Building	300,000	
Accumulated depreciation—building		$155,000
Accounts payable		159,000
Unearned service revenue		40,000
Michael Moe, Capital		102,000
Michael Moe, Withdrawals	7,000	
Service revenue		450,000
Salary expense	255,000	
Rent expense	25,000	
Miscellaneous expense	8,000	
Total	$906,000	$906,000

Cloud Break must make adjusting entries for the following items:

a. **Supplies on hand at year-end, $1,000.**

b. **Nine months of rent ($27,000) were paid in advance on April 1, 2011. No rent expense has been recorded since that date.**

c. **Depreciation expense has not been recorded on the building for the 2011 fiscal year. Depreciation is $12,000 per year on the building.**

d. **Employees work Monday through Friday. The weekly payroll is $5,000 and is paid every Friday. June 30, 2011, is a Thursday.**

e. **Service revenue of $15,000 must be accrued.**

f. **Cloud Break received $40,000 in advance for consulting services to be provided evenly from January 1, 2011, through August 31, 2011. None of the revenue from this client has been recorded.**

Requirements

1. Open the ledger T-accounts with their unadjusted balances.
2. Journalize Cloud Break's adjusting entries at June 30, 2011, and post the entries to the T-accounts.
3. Total all of the T-accounts in the ledger.
4. Write the trial balance on a work sheet, enter the adjusting entries, and prepare an adjusted trial balance.
5. Prepare the income statement, the statement of owner's equity, and the balance sheet. Draw arrows linking the three financial statements.

Demo Doc Solution

Requirement 1

Open the ledger T-accounts with their unadjusted balances.

Part 1	Part 2	Part 3	Part 4	Part 5	Demo Doc Complete

Remember from Chapter 2 that opening a T-account means drawing a blank account that looks like a capital "T" and putting the account title across the top. To help find the accounts later, they are usually organized into assets, liabilities, owner's equity, revenue, and expenses (in that order). If the account has a starting balance, it *must* be put in on the correct side.

Remember that debits are always on the left side of the T-account and credits are always on the right side. This is true for *every* account.

The correct side to enter each account's starting balance is the side of *increase* in the account. This is because we expect all accounts to have a *positive* balance (that is, more increases than decreases).

For assets, an increase is a debit, so we would expect all assets to have a debit balance. For liabilities and owner's equity, an increase is a credit, so we would expect all of these accounts to have a credit balance. By the same reasoning, we expect revenues to have credit balances, and expenses and withdrawals to have debit balances.

The unadjusted balances to be posted into the T-accounts are simply the amounts from the starting trial balance.

ASSETS

Cash	
Bal 131,000	

Accounts receivable	
Bal 104,000	

Supplies	
Bal 4,000	

Prepaid rent	
Bal 27,000	

Land	
Bal 45,000	

Building	
Bal 300,000	

Accumulated depreciation—building	
	Bal 155,000

LIABILITIES

Accounts payable	
	Bal 159,000

Unearned service revenue	
	Bal 40,000

OWNER'S EQUITY

Michael Moe, Capital	
	Bal 102,000

Michael Moe, Withdrawals	
Bal 7,000	

REVENUE

Service revenue	
	Bal 450,000

EXPENSES

Salary expense	
Bal 255,000	

Rent expense	
Bal 25,000	

Miscellaneous expense	
Bal 8,000	

Requirement 2

Journalize Cloud Break's adjusting entries at June 30, 2011, and post the entries to the T-accounts.

Part 1	**Part 2**	Part 3	Part 4	Part 5	Demo Doc Complete

a. **Supplies on hand at year-end, $1,000.**

On June 30, 2010, the unadjusted balance in supplies was $4,000. However, a count shows that only $1,000 of supplies actually remains on hand. The supplies that are no longer there have been used. When assets/benefits are used, an expense is created.

Cloud Break will need to make an adjusting journal entry to reflect the correct amount of supplies on the balance sheet.

Looking at the Supplies T-account:

Supplies			
Bal	4,000		X
Bal	1,000		

The supplies have decreased because they have been used up. The amount of the decrease is **X**.

X = $4,000 – $1,000 = $3,000

Three thousand dollars of Supplies expense must be recorded to show the value of supplies that have been used.

a.	Jun 30	Supplies expense ($4,000 – $1,000) (E+)	3,000	
		Supplies (A–)		3,000
		To record supplies expense.		

After posting, Supplies and Supplies expense hold correct ending balances:

ASSETS

Supplies			
Bal	4,000	a.	3,000
Bal	1,000		

EXPENSES

Supplies expense			
a.	3,000		
Bal	3,000		

b. **Nine months of rent ($27,000) were paid in advance on April 1, 2011. No rent expense has been recorded since that date.**

When something is prepaid, such as is common with rent or insurance, it is a *future* benefit (an asset) because the business is now entitled to receive goods or services for the terms of the prepayment. Once those goods or services are received (in this case, once Cloud Break has occupied the building being rented), this becomes a *past* benefit, and therefore an expense.

Cloud Break prepaid $27,000 for nine months of rent on April 1. This means that Cloud Break pays $27,000/9 = $3,000 a month for rent. At June 30, Prepaid rent is adjusted for the amount of the asset that has been used up. Because Cloud Break has occupied the building being rented for three months, three months of the prepayment have been used. The amount of rent used is 3 × $3,000 = $9,000. Because that portion of the past benefit (asset) has expired, it becomes an expense (in this case, the adjustment transfers $9,000 from Prepaid rent to Rent expense).

This means that Rent expense must be increased (a debit) and Prepaid rent (an asset) must be decreased (a credit).

b.	Jun 30	Rent expense (E+)	9,000	
		Prepaid rent (A–)		9,000
		To record rent expense.		

ASSETS

Prepaid rent

Bal	27,000		
		b.	9,000
Bal	18,000		

EXPENSES

Rent expense

Bal	25,000		
b.	9,000		
Bal	34,000		

c. **Depreciation expense has not been recorded on the building for the 2011 fiscal year. Depreciation is $12,000 per year on the building.**

The cost principle compels us to keep the original cost of a plant asset in that asset account. Because there is $300,000 in the building account, we know that this is the original cost of the building. We are told in the question that depreciation expense per year is $12,000.

We will record depreciation of $12,000 in the adjusting journal entry.

The journal entry to record depreciation expense is *always* the same. It is only the *number* (dollar amount) in the entry that changes. There is always an increase to Depreciation expense (a debit) and an increase to the contra-asset account of Accumulated depreciation (a credit).

c.	Jun 30	Depreciation expense—building (E+)	12,000	
		Accumulated depreciation—building (CA+)		12,000
		To record depreciation on building.		

ASSETS

NORMAL ASSET

Building

Bal	300,000		
Bal	300,000		

CONTRA ASSET

Accumulated depreciation—building

		Bal	155,000
		c.	12,000
		Bal	167,000

EXPENSES

Depreciation expense—building

c.	12,000		
Bal	12,000		

The book value of the building is its original cost (the amount in the Building T-account) minus the accumulated depreciation on the building.

Book value of plant assets:	
Building	$ 300,000
Less: Accumulated depreciation	(167,000)
Book value of the building	$ 133,000

d. Employees work Monday through Friday. The weekly payroll is $5,000 and is paid every Friday. June 30, 2011, is a Thursday.

Salary is an accrued expense. That is, it is a liability that incurs from an *expense* that has not been paid yet. Most employers pay their employees *after* the work has been done, so the work is a past benefit. So this expense (Salary expense, in this case) grows until payday.

Cloud Break's employees are paid $5,000 for five days of work. That means they earn $5,000/5 = $1,000 per day. By the end of the day on Thursday, June 30, they have earned $1,000/day × 4 days = $4,000 of salary.

If the salaries have not been paid, then they are pay*able* (or in other words, they are *owed*) and must be recorded as some kind of payable account. You might be tempted to use accounts payable, but this account is usually reserved for *bills* received. But employees do not typically bill employers for their paychecks, they simply expect to be paid. The appropriate payable account for salaries is Salary payable.

There is an increase to the Salary expense (a debit) and an increase to the liability Salary payable (a credit) of $4,000.

d.	Jun 30	Salary expense (E+)	4,000	
		Salary payable (L+)		4,000
		To accrue salary expense.		

EXPENSES — Salary expense

	Debit	Credit
Bal	255,000	
d.	4,000	
Bal	259,000	

LIABILITIES — Salary payable

Debit		Credit
	d.	4,000
	Bal	4,000

e. Service revenue of $15,000 must be accrued.

Accrued revenue is another way of saying "Accounts receivable" (or receipt in the future). When *accrued* revenue is recorded, it means that Accounts receivable is also recorded (that is, customers received goods or services from the business, but the business has not yet received the cash). The business is entitled to these receivables because the revenue has been earned.

Service revenue must be increased by $15,000 (a credit) and the Accounts receivable asset must be increased by $15,000 (a debit).

e.	Jun 30	Accounts receivable (A+)	15,000	
		Service revenue (R+)		15,000
		To accrue service revenue.		

ASSETS — Accounts receivable

	Debit	Credit
	104,000	
e.	15,000	
Bal	119,000	

REVENUES — Service revenue

Debit		Credit
		450,000
	e.	15,000
	Bal	465,000

f. Cloud Break received $40,000 in advance for consulting services to be provided evenly from January 1, 2011, through August 31, 2011. None of the revenue from this client has been recorded.

Cloud Break received cash in advance for work it had not yet performed for the client. By accepting the cash, Cloud Break also accepted the obligation to perform that work (or provide a refund if it did not). In accounting, an obligation is a liability. We call this liability "Unearned revenue" because it *will* be revenue (after the work is performed) but it is not revenue *yet*.

The $40,000 paid in advance is still in the unearned revenue account. However, some of the revenue has been earned as of June 30. Six months of the earnings period have passed (January 1 through June 30), so six months worth of the revenue has been earned.

The entire revenue earnings period is eight months (January 1 through August 31), so the revenue earned per month is $40,000/8 = $5,000. The six months of revenue that have been earned are 6 × $5,000 = $30,000.

So Unearned service revenue, a liability, must be decreased by $30,000 (a debit). Because that portion of the revenue is now earned, it can be recorded as Service revenue. Therefore, Service revenue is increased by $30,000 (a credit).

f.	Jun 30	Unearned service revenue (L–)	30,000	
		Service revenue (R+)		30,000
		To record the earning of service revenue that was collected in advance.		

Essentially, the $30,000 has been shifted from "unearned revenue" to "earned" revenue.

LIABILITIES

Unearned service revenue

	Debit		Credit
		Bal	40,000
f.	30,000		
		Bal	10,000

REVENUES

Service revenue

Debit		Credit
	Bal	450,000
	e.	15,000
	f.	30,000
	Bal	495,000

Now we will summarize all of the adjusting journal entries:

Ref.	Date	Accounts and Explanation	Debit	Credit
	2011			
a.	Jun 30	Supplies expense ($4,000 – $1,000) (E+)	3,000	
		Supplies (A–)		3,000
		To record supplies used.		
b.	30	Rent expense (E+)	9,000	
		Prepaid rent (A–)		9,000
		To record rent expense.		
c.	30	Depreciation expense—building (E+)	12,000	
		Accumulated depreciation—building (CA+)		12,000
		To record depreciation expense on building.		
d.	30	Salary expense (E+)	4,000	
		Salary payable (L+)		4,000
		To accrue salary expense.		
e.	30	Accounts receivable (A+)	15,000	
		Service revenue (R+)		15,000
		To accrue service revenue.		
f.	30	Unearned service revenue (L–)	30,000	
		Service revenue (R+)		30,000
		To record the earning of service revenue that was collected in advance.		

Requirement 3

Total all of the T-accounts in the ledger.

Part 1	Part 2	**Part 3**	Part 4	Part 5	Demo Doc Complete

After posting all of these entries and totaling all of the T-accounts, we have the following:

ASSETS

Cash	
Bal 131,000	

Accounts receivable	
Bal 104,000	
e. 15,000	
Bal 119,000	

Supplies	
Bal 4,000	a. 3,000
Bal 1,000	

Prepaid rent	
Bal 27,000	
	b. 9,000
Bal 18,000	

Land	
Bal 45,000	

Building	
Bal 300,000	

Accumulated depreciation—building	
	155,000
	c. 12,000
	Bal 167,000

LIABILITIES

Accounts payable	
	Bal 159,000

Salary payable	
	d. 4,000
	Bal 4,000

Unearned service revenue	
f. 30,000	40,000
	Bal 10,000

OWNER'S EQUITY

Michael Moe, Capital	
	Bal 102,000

Michael Moe, Withdrawals	
Bal 7,000	

REVENUE

Service revenue	
	450,000
	e. 15,000
	f. 30,000
	Bal 495,000

EXPENSES

Salary expense	
255,000	
d. 4,000	
Bal 259,000	

Supplies expense	
a. 3,000	
Bal 3,000	

Rent expense	
25,000	
b. 9,000	
Bal 34,000	

Depreciation expense—building	
c. 12,000	
Bal 12,000	

Miscellaneous expense	
Bal 8,000	

Requirement 4

Write the trial balance on a work sheet, enter the adjusting entries, and prepare an adjusted trial balance.

Part 1	Part 2	Part 3	**Part 4**	Part 5	Demo Doc Complete

First, we must copy the account titles and trial balance amounts directly from the trial balance (shown at the beginning of the question) into the Trial Balance section (columns). Place the amounts in the correct debit or credit column.

Next, we must record the adjusting journal entries in the correct debit or credit columns of the Adjustments section (columns) of the work sheet. Each entry should include a letter identifying the adjusting entry recorded.

Now calculate the new balances for each account by adding the debits and credits across. These should be the same balances that you calculated for the T-account in Requirement 3. Place these amounts into the Adjusted Trial Balance columns to give the adjusted account balances.

CLOUD BREAK CONSULTING
Preparation of Adjusted Trial Balance
June 30, 2011

	Trial Balance		Adjustments		Adjusted Trial Balance	
Account Title	**Debit**	**Credit**	**Debit**	**Credit**	**Debit**	**Credit**
Cash	131,000				131,000	
Accounts receivable	104,000		(e)15,000		119,000	
Supplies	4,000			(a) 3,000	1,000	
Prepaid rent	27,000			(b) 9,000	18,000	
Land	45,000				45,000	
Building	300,000				300,000	
Accumulated depreciation—building		155,000		(c) 12,000		167,000
Accounts payable		159,000				159,000
Salary payable				(d) 4,000		4,000
Unearned service revenue		40,000	(f) 30,000			10,000
Michael Moe, Capital		102,000				102,000
Michael Moe, Withdrawals	7,000				7,000	
Service revenue		450,000		(e) 15,000		
				(f) 30,000		495,000
Salary expense	255,000		(d) 4,000		259,000	
Supplies expense			(a) 3,000		3,000	
Rent expense	25,000		(b) 9,000		34,000	
Depreciation expense—building			(c)12,000		12,000	
Miscellaneous expense	8,000				8,000	
Totals	906,000	906,000	73,000	73,000	937,000	937,000

You should be sure that the debit and credit columns equal before moving on to the next section.

Requirement 5

Prepare the income statement, the statement of owner's equity, and the balance sheet. Draw arrows linking the three financial statements.

Part 1	Part 2	Part 3	Part 4	**Part 5**	Demo Doc Complete

CLOUD BREAK CONSULTING
Income Statement
Year Ended June 30, 2011

Revenue:		
Service revenue		$495,000
Expenses:		
Salary expense	$259,000	
Rent expense	34,000	
Depreciation expense—building	12,000	
Supplies expense	3,000	
Miscellaneous expense*	8,000	
Total expenses		316,000
Net income		$179,000

*Miscellaneous expense is always listed last, even if it is larger than other expenses.

CLOUD BREAK CONSULTING
Statement of Owner's Equity
Year Ended June 30, 2011

Michael Moe, Capital, July 1, 2010	$102,000
Add: Net income	179,000
	281,000
Less: Owner withdrawals	(7,000)
Michael Moe, Capital, June 30, 2011	$274,000

CLOUD BREAK CONSULTING
Balance Sheet
June 30, 2011

Assets			**Liabilities**	
Cash		$131,000	Accounts payable	$159,000
Accounts receivable		119,000	Salary payable	4,000
Supplies		1,000	Unearned service revenue	10,000
Prepaid rent		18,000	Total liabilities	173,000
Land		45,000		
Building	$300,000		**Owner's Equity**	
Less: Accumulated			Michael Moe, Capital	274,000
depreciation	(167,000)	133,000	Total liabilities and	
Total assets		$447,000	owner's equity	$447,000

Part 1	Part 2	Part 3	Part 4	Part 5	**Demo Doc Complete**

■ Relationships Among the Financial Statements

The arrows in these statements show how the financial statements relate to each other. Follow the arrow that takes the ending balance of Capital to the balance sheet.

1. Net income from the income statement is reported as an increase to Capital on the statement of owner's equity. A net loss is recorded as a decrease to Capital.

2. Ending Capital from the statement of owner's equity is transferred to the balance sheet. The ending Capital is the final balancing amount for the balance sheet.

4 Completing the Accounting Cycle

Learning Objectives/ Success Keys

1. Prepare an accounting work sheet
2. Use the work sheet to prepare financial statements
3. Close the revenue, expense, and withdrawal accounts
4. Prepare the postclosing trial balance
5. Classify assets and liabilities as current or long-term
6. Use the current ratio and the debt ratio to evaluate a company

What do football, baseball, basketball, soccer, and accounting have in common? They all start the first period with a score of zero.

Hannah Sherman and Greg Moore have operated Sherman Lawn Service and Greg's Groovy Tunes, respectively, for a year. They took in revenue, incurred expenses, and earned net income during year 1. It is time to look ahead to the next period.

Should Sherman Lawn Service start year 2 with the net income that the business earned last year? No, Sherman must start from zero in order to measure its business performance in year 2. That requires Sherman to set her accounting scoreboard back to zero.

This process of getting back to zero is called closing the books, and it is the last step in the accounting cycle. The **accounting cycle** is the process by which companies produce their financial statements.

Chapter 4 completes the accounting cycle by showing how to close the books. It begins with the *adjusted trial balance*, which you learned about in Chapter 3. Here we learn how to prepare a more complete version of an adjusted trial balance document called the accounting work sheet. Work sheets help by summarizing lots of data in one place.

The accounting cycle starts with the beginning asset, liability, and owner's equity account balances left over from the preceding period. Exhibit 4-1 outlines the complete accounting cycle of Smart Touch Learning and every other business. Start with item 1 and move clockwise.

EXHIBIT 4-1 The Accounting Cycle

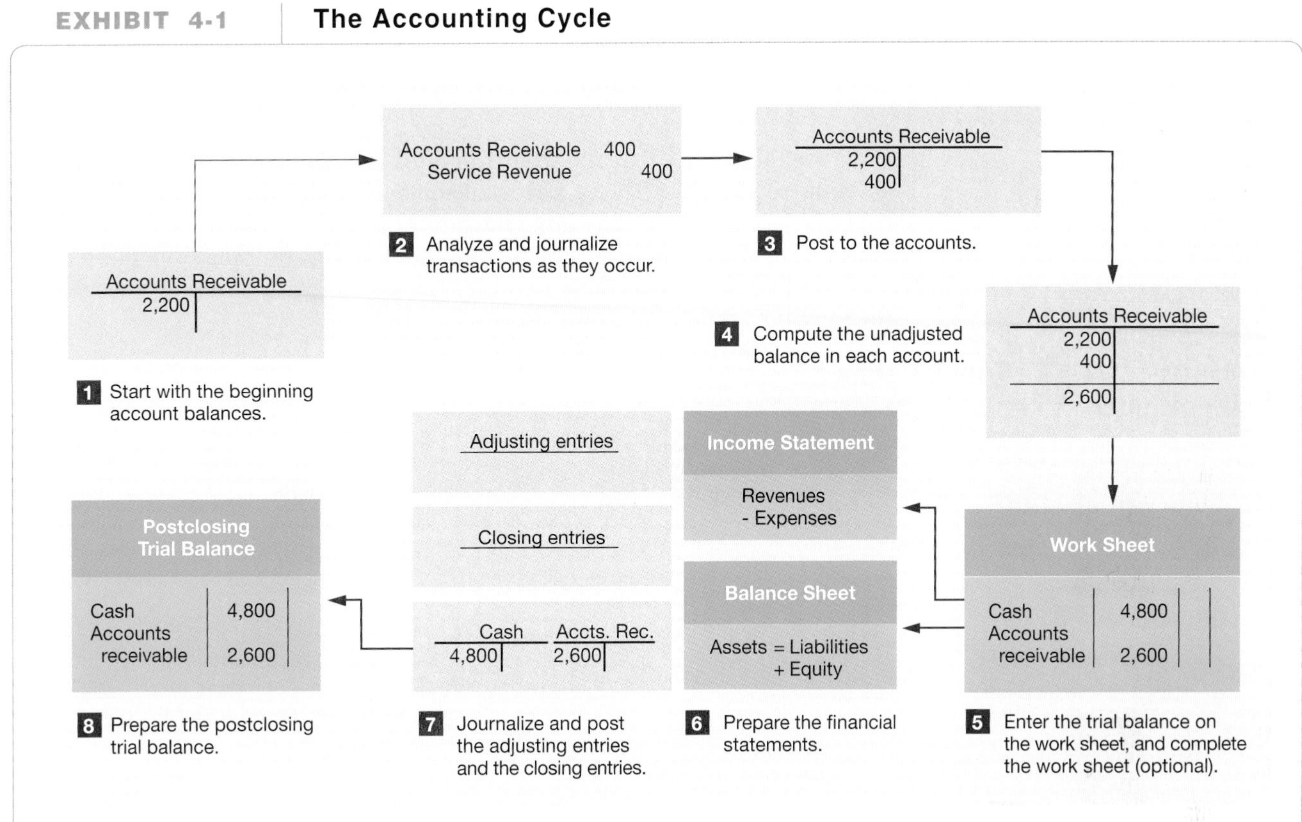

Accounting takes place at two different times:

- During the period—Journalizing transactions
  Posting to the accounts
- End of the period—Adjusting the accounts
  Closing the accounts
  Preparing the financial statements

The end-of-period work also readies the accounts for the next period. In Chapters 3 and 4, we cover the end-of-period accounting for service businesses such as Sherman Lawn Service and Smart Touch Learning. Chapter 5 shows how a merchandising entity such as **Wal-Mart** or **Sports Academy** adjusts and closes its books.

The Work Sheet

1 Prepare an accounting work sheet

Accountants often use a **work sheet**—a document with several columns—to summarize data for the financial statements. The work sheet is not a journal, a ledger, or a financial statement. It is merely a summary device that helps identify the accounts that need adjustment. An Excel spreadsheet works well for an accounting work sheet. Note that the work sheet is an internal document. It is not meant to be given to outsiders.

Exhibits 4-2 though 4-6 illustrate the development of a typical work sheet for Smart Touch Learning. The heading at the top displays the

- Name of the business (Smart Touch Learning)
- Title of the document (Accounting Work Sheet)
- Period covered by the work sheet (May 31, 2010)

A step-by-step description of the work sheet follows, with all amounts given in Exhibits 4-2 though 4-6. Simply turn the acetate pages to follow from exhibit to exhibit.

1. **Enter the account titles and their unadjusted balances in the Trial Balance columns of the work sheet, and total the amounts.** The data come from the ledger accounts before any adjustments. Accounts are listed in proper order (Cash first, Accounts receivable second, and so on). Total debits must equal total credits. Note that these two columns of the work sheet are the same as the formal trial balance from Chapter 3. (See Exhibit 4-2.)

EXHIBIT 4-2 Trial Balance

SMART TOUCH LEARNING
Accounting Work Sheet
May 31, 2010

	Trial Balance		Adjustments		Adj. Trial Balance		Income Statement		Balance Sheet	
	Debit	Credit	Debit	Credit	Debit	Credit	Debit	Credit	Debit	Credit
Cash	4,800									
Accounts receivable	2,200									
Supplies	700									
Prepaid rent	3,000									
Furniture	18,000									
Building	48,000									
Accumulated depreciation—furniture										
Accumulated depreciation—building										
Accounts payable		18,200								
Salary payable										
Interest payable										
Unearned service revenue		600								
Notes payable		20,000								
Sheena Bright, Capital		33,200								
Sheena Bright, Withdrawals	1,000									
Service revenue		7,000								
Rent expense										
Salary expense	900									
Supplies expense										
Depreciation expense—furniture										
Depreciation expense—building										
Interest expense										
Utilities expense	400									
	79,000	79,000								

2. **Enter the adjusting entries in the Adjustments columns, and total the amounts.** Exhibit 4-3 includes the May adjusting entries that we made in Chapter 3. The adjusting entries, letters a–h from Exhibit 3-9, are posted into the adjustments column of the work sheet.

3. **Compute each account's adjusted balance by combining the trial balance and adjustment figures. Enter each account's adjusted amount in the Adjusted Trial Balance columns.** Exhibit 4-4 shows the work sheet with the adjusted trial balance completed. For example, Cash is up-to-date, so it receives no adjustment. Accounts receivable's adjusted balance of $2,600 is computed by adding the unadjusted amount of $2,200 to the $400 adjustment. For Supplies we subtract the $100 credit adjustment from the unadjusted debit balance of $700. Note that an account may receive more than one adjustment. For example, Service revenue has two adjustments. The adjusted balance of $7,600 is computed by taking the unadjusted balance of $7,000 and adding the adjusted credits of $400 and $200 to arrive at the $7,600 adjusted balance. As on the trial balance, total debits must equal total credits on the adjusted trial balance. Notice how the three completed column sets of Exhibit 4-4 look exactly like Exhibit 3-9.

4. **Draw an imaginary line above the first revenue account (in this case, Service revenue). Every account above that line (assets, liabilities, and equity accounts) is copied from the Adjusted Trial Balance to the Balance Sheet columns. Every account below the line (revenues and expenses) is copied from the Adjusted Trial Balance to the Income Statement columns.** Each account's balance should appear in only one column, as shown in Exhibit 4-5.
   First, total the *income statement columns*, as follows:

Income Statement

- Debits (Dr.) → Total expenses = $3,900
- Credits (Cr.) → Total revenues = $7,600

} Difference = $3,700, a net income because total credits (revenues) exceed total debits (expenses)

Then total the *balance sheet* columns:

Balance Sheet

- Debits (Dr.) → Total assets and withdrawals = $77,000
- Credits (Cr.) → Total liabilities, owner's equity, and accumulated depreciation = $73,300

} Difference = $3,700, a net income because total debits are greater

5. **On the income statement, compute net income or net loss as total revenues minus total expenses. Enter net income(loss) as the balancing amount on the income statement. Also enter net income(loss) as the balancing amount on the balance sheet. Then total the financial statement columns.** Exhibit 4-6 presents the completed work sheet.

Revenue (total **credits** on the income statement)	$ 7,600
Less: Expenses (total **debits** on the income statement)	(3,900)
Net income	$ 3,700

Net Income

Net income of $3,700 is entered as the balancing amount in the debit column of the income statement. This brings total debits up to total credits on the income statement. Net income is also entered as the balancing amount in the credit column of the balance sheet. Net income brings the balance sheet into balance. Note that the difference in these columns is the same (net income).

Net Loss

If expenses exceed revenues, the result is a net loss. In that event, print Net loss on the work sheet next to the result. The net loss amount should be entered in the *credit* column of the income statement (to balance out) and in the *debit* column of the balance sheet (to balance out). After completion, total debits should equal total credits in both the Income Statement columns and in the Balance Sheet columns.

Now practice what you have learned by working Summary Problem 1.

Summary Problem 1

The trial balance of Super Employment Services at December 31, 2011, follows.

SUPER EMPLOYMENT SERVICES Trial Balance December 31, 2011	Balance	
Account Title	Debit	Credit
Cash	$ 6,000	
Accounts receivable	5,000	
Supplies	1,000	
Furniture	10,000	
Accumulated depreciation—furniture		$ 4,000
Building	50,000	
Accumulated depreciation—building		30,000
Accounts payable		2,000
Salary payable		
Unearned service revenue		8,000
Dan Mudge, Capital		12,000
Dan Mudge, Withdrawals	25,000	
Service revenue		60,000
Salary expense	16,000	
Supplies expense		
Depreciation expense—furniture		
Depreciation expense—building		
Advertising expense	3,000	
Total	$116,000	$116,000

Data needed for the adjusting entries include:

a. Supplies on hand at year-end, $200.
b. Depreciation on furniture, $2,000.
c. Depreciation on building, $1,000.
d. Salaries owed but not yet paid, $500.
e. Accrued service revenue, $1,300.
f. $3,000 of the unearned service revenue was earned during 2011.

Requirements

Prepare the accounting work sheet of Super Employment Services for the year ended December 31, 2011. Key each adjusting entry by the letter corresponding to the data given.

Solution

SUPER EMPLOYMENT SERVICES
Work Sheet
Year Ended December 31, 2011

	Trial Balance		Adjustments		Adjusted Trial Balance		Income Statement		Balance Sheet	
Account Title	Dr.	Cr.	Dr.	Cr.	Dr.	Cr.	Dr.	Cr.	Dr.	Cr.
Cash	6,000				6,000				6,000	
Accounts receivable	5,000		(e) 1,300		6,300				6,300	
Supplies	1,000			(a) 800	200				200	
Furniture	10,000				10,000				10,000	
Accumulated depreciation—furniture		4,000		(b) 2,000		6,000				6,000
Building	50,000				50,000				50,000	
Accumulated depreciation—building		30,000		(c) 1,000		31,000				31,000
Accounts payable		2,000				2,000				2,000
Salary payable				(d) 500		500				500
Unearned service revenue		8,000	(f) 3,000			5,000				5,000
Dan Mudge, Capital		12,000				12,000				12,000
Dan Mudge, Withdrawals	25,000				25,000				25,000	
Service revenue		60,000		(e) 1,300						
				(f) 3,000		64,300		64,300		
Salary expense	16,000		(d) 500		16,500		16,500			
Supplies expense			(a) 800		800		800			
Depreciation expense—furniture			(b) 2,000		2,000		2,000			
Depreciation expense—building			(c) 1,000		1,000		1,000			
Advertising expense	3,000				3,000		3,000			
	116,000	116,000	8,600	8,600	120,800	120,800	23,300	64,300	97,500	56,500
						Net income	41,000			41,000
							64,300	64,300	97,500	97,500

Completing the Accounting Cycle

The work sheet helps accountants prepare the financial statements, make the adjusting entries, and close the accounts. First, let us prepare the financial statements. We return to the running example of Smart Touch Learning whose financial statements are given in Exhibit 4-7 on the following page. Notice that these are identical to the financial statements prepared in Chapter 3 (Exhibits 3-11 though 3-13).

2 Use the work sheet to prepare financial statements

Preparing the Financial Statements from a Work Sheet

The work sheet shows the amount of net income or net loss for the period, but it is an internal document. We still must prepare the financial statements for external decision makers. Exhibit 4-7 shows the May financial statements for Smart Touch Learning (based on data from the work sheet in Exhibit 4-6). We can prepare the business's financial statements immediately after completing the work sheet.

Stop & Think...

Look at the formal financial statements in Exhibit 4-7 and the work sheet financial statement columns in Exhibit 4-6. The income number is the same on both sheets so why do we need to do both a work sheet and a formal document, such as an Income Statement? The answer is the decision makers. The work sheet is going to be used mainly by internal decision makers. The formal financial statements, on the other hand, may be used by external decision makers.

Recording the Adjusting Entries from a Work Sheet

Adjusting the accounts requires journalizing entries and posting to the accounts. We learned how to prepare adjusting journal entries in Chapter 3. The adjustments that are journalized after they are entered on the work sheet are *exactly* the same adjusting journal entries. Panel A of Exhibit 4-8 on page 243 repeats Sheena Bright's adjusting entries that we journalized in Chapter 3. Panel B shows the revenue and the expense accounts after all adjustments have been posted. Only the revenue and expense accounts are presented here to focus on the closing process.

EXHIBIT 4-7 **Financial Statements**

SMART TOUCH LEARNING
Income Statement
Month Ended May 31, 2010

Revenue:		
Service revenue		$7,600
Expenses:		
Salary expense	$1,800	
Rent expense	1,000	
Utilities expense	400	
Depreciation expense—furniture	300	
Depreciation expense—building	200	
Interest expense	100	
Supplies expense	100	
Total expenses		3,900
Net income		$3,700

SMART TOUCH LEARNING
Statement of Owner's Equity
Month Ended May 31, 2010

Sheena Bright, Capital, May 1, 2010	$33,200
Add: Net income	3,700
	36,900
Less: Owner withdrawals	(1,000)
Sheena Bright, Capital, May 31, 2010	$35,900

SMART TOUCH LEARNING
Balance Sheet
May 31, 2010

Assets			**Liabilities**	
Cash		$ 4,800	Accounts payable	$18,200
Accounts receivable		2,600	Salary payable	900
Supplies		600	Interest payable	100
Prepaid rent		2,000	Unearned service revenue	400
Furniture	18,000		Notes payable	20,000
Less: Accumulated depreciation—furniture	–300	17,700	Total liabilities	39,600
Building	48,000			
Less: Accumulated depreciation—building	–200	47,800	**Owner's Equity**	
			Sheena Bright, Capital	35,900
			Total owner's equity	35,900
Total assets		$75,500	Total liabilities and owner's equity	$75,500

EXHIBIT 4-8 Journalizing and Posting the Adjusting Entries of Smart Touch Learning

PANEL A—Adjusting Entries

a.		Rent expense (E+)	1,000	
		Prepaid rent (A–)		1,000
		To record rent expense.		
b.		Supplies expense (E+)	100	
		Supplies (A–)		100
		To record supplies used.		
c.		Depreciation expense—furniture (E+)	300	
		Accumulated depreciation—furniture (CA+)		300
		To record depreciation on furniture.		
d.		Depreciation expense—building (E+)	200	
		Accumulated depreciation—building (CA+)		200
		To record depreciation on building.		
e.		Salary expense (E+)	900	
		Salary payable (L+)		900
		To accrue salary expense.		
f.		Interest expense (E+)	100	
		Interest payable (L+)		100
		To accrue interest expense.		
g.		Accounts receivable (A+)	400	
		Service revenue (R+)		400
		To accrue service revenue.		
h.		Unearned service revenue (L–)	200	
		Service revenue (R+)		200
		To record revenue that was collected in advance.		

PANEL B—Ledger Accounts

Revenue

Service revenue

			7,000
		(g)	400
		(h)	200
		Bal	7,600

Expenses

Rent expense

(a)	1,000	
Bal	1,000	

Salary expense

	900	
(e)	900	
Bal	1,800	

Supplies expense

(b)	100	
Bal	100	

Depreciation expense—furniture

(c)	300	
Bal	300	

Utilities expense

Bal	400	

Depreciation expense—building

(d)	200	

Interest expense

(f)	100	

Accountants can use the work sheet to prepare monthly statements (as in Exhibit 4-7) without journalizing and posting the adjusting entries. Many companies journalize and post the adjusting entries only at the end of the year.

Now we are ready to move to the last step—closing the accounts.

Closing the Accounts

3 Close the revenue, expense, and withdrawal accounts

Closing the accounts occurs at the end of the period. Closing consists of journalizing and posting the closing entries in order to get the accounts ready for the next period. The closing process zeroes out all the revenues and all the expenses in order to measure each period's net income separately from all other periods.

Stop & Think...

Have you ever closed an account at a bank? How much was left in your account when you closed it? You needed to take all the money out, right? Well that is the same theory behind the closing journal entries—after closing, we leave a zero balance in all revenue, expense, and withdrawal accounts.

Recall that the income statement reports net income for a specific period. For example, the business's net income for 2010 relates exclusively to 2010. At December 31, 2010, Smart Touch closes its revenue and expense accounts for the year. For this reason, revenues and expenses are called **temporary accounts**. For example, Smart Touch's balance of Service revenue at May 31, 2010, is $7,600. This balance relates exclusively to May and must be zeroed out before Smart Touch records revenue for June. Similarly, the various expense account balances are for May only and must also be zeroed out at the end of the month.

The Withdrawals account is also temporary and must be closed at the end of the period because it measures the withdrawals for only that one period. All temporary accounts (withdrawals, revenues, and expenses) are closed (zeroed).

By contrast, the **permanent accounts**—the assets, liabilities, and capital—are not closed at the end of the period because their balances are not used to measure income. Another way to remember which accounts are permanent is to recall that all accounts on the balance sheet are permanent accounts because they are part of the accounting equation.

Closing entries transfer the revenue, expense, and withdrawals balances to the Capital account.

As an intermediate step the revenues and the expenses may be transferred first to an account titled **Income Summary**. Income summary *summarizes* the net income (or net loss) for the period by collecting the sum of all the expenses (a debit) and the sum of all the revenues (a credit). The Income summary account is like a temporary "holding tank" that shows the amount of net income or net loss of the current period. Its balance—net income or net loss—is then transferred (closed) to Capital (the final account in the closing process). Exhibit 4-9 summarizes the closing process.

EXHIBIT 4-9 | The Closing Process

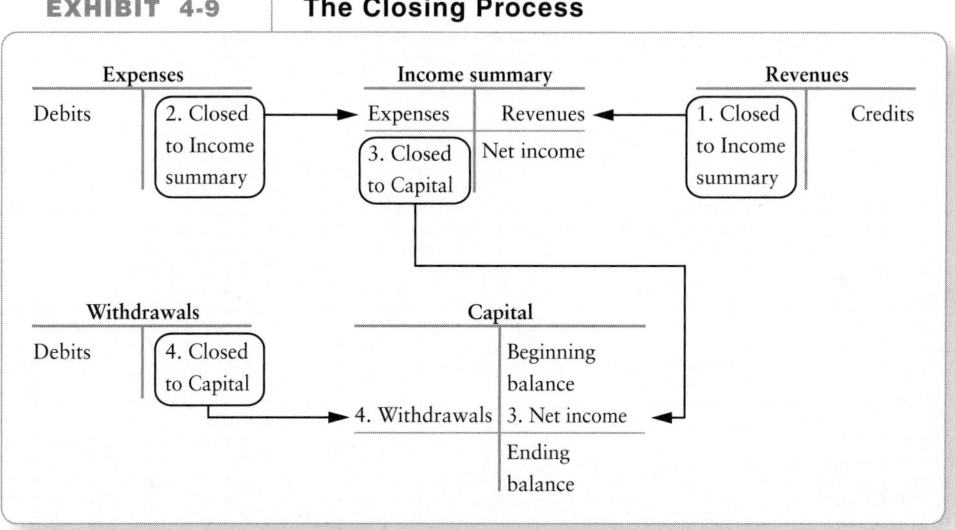

Closing Temporary Accounts

As we stated previously, all temporary accounts are closed (zeroed out) during the closing process. The four steps in closing the books follow (and are illustrated in Exhibit 4-10).

Step 1: Make the revenue accounts equal zero via the Income summary account. This closing entry transfers total revenues to the *credit* side of the Income summary.

Step 2: Make expense accounts equal zero via the Income summary account. This closing entry transfers total expenses to the *debit* side of the Income summary.

Step 3: The Income summary account now holds the net income or net loss of the period. The Income summary T-account is presented next to illustrate:

Income summary			
Closing Entry 2	Expenses	Closing Entry 1	Revenues
Expenses > Revenues	Net Loss	Revenues > Expenses	Net Income

In step 3, make the Income summary account equal zero via the Capital account. This closing entry transfers net income (or net loss) to Capital.

Step 4: Make the withdrawals account equal zero via the Capital account. This entry transfers the withdrawals to the *debit* side of Capital.

These steps are best illustrated with an example. Suppose Smart Touch Learning closes its books at the end of May. Exhibit 4-10 on the following page shows the complete closing process for Smart Touch's training agency. Panel A gives the closing entries, and Panel B shows the accounts after posting. After the closing entries, Capital ends with a balance of $35,900. Trace this balance to the statement of owner's equity and then to the balance sheet in Exhibit 4-7.

EXHIBIT 4-10 Journalizing and Posting the Closing Entries

PANEL A—Journalizing:

Closing Entries

	Date	Accounts	Debit	Credit
1	May 31	Service revenue (R–)	7,600	
		Income summary		7,600
2	31	Income summary	3,900	
		Rent expense (E–)		1,000
		Salary expense (E–)		1,800
		Supplies expense (E–)		100
		Depreciation expense—furniture (E–)		300
		Utilities expense (E–)		400
		Depreciation expense—building (E–)		200
		Interest expense (E–)		100
3	31	Income summary ($7,600 – $3,900)	3,700	
		Sheena Bright, Capital (Q+)		3,700
4	31	Sheena Bright, Capital (Q–)	1,000	
		Sheena Bright, Withdrawals (W–)		1,000

PANEL B—Posting:

Rent expense

Adj	1,000		
Bal	1,000	Clo 2	1,000

Salary expense

	900		
Adj	900		
Bal	1,800	Clo 2	1,800

Supplies expense

Adj	100		
Bal	100	Clo 2	100

Depreciation expense—furniture

Adj	300		
Bal	300	Clo 2	300

Interest expense

Adj	100		
Bal	100	Clo 2	100

Depreciation expense—building

Adj	200		
Bal	200	Clo 2	200

Utilities expense

Adj	400		
Bal	400	Clo 2	400

2

Income summary

Clo 2	3,900	Clo 1	7,600
Clo 3	3,700	Bal	3,700

1

Service revenue

			7,000
		Adj	400
		Adj	200
Clo 1	7,600	Bal	7,600

Sheena Bright, Withdrawals

Bal	1,000	Clo 4	1,000

4

Sheena Bright, Capital

Clo 4	1,000		33,200
		Clo 3	3,700
		Bal	35,900

3

Adj = Amount posted from an adjusting entry
Clo = Amount posted from a closing entry
Bal = Balance

Postclosing Trial Balance

The accounting cycle can end with a **postclosing trial balance** (Exhibit 4-11). This optional step lists the accounts and their adjusted balances after closing.

4 Prepare the postclosing trial balance

EXHIBIT 4-11 | **Postclosing Trial Balance**

SMART TOUCH LEARNING
Postclosing Trial Balance
May 31, 2010

	Debit	Credit
Cash	$ 4,800	
Accounts receivable	2,600	
Supplies	600	
Prepaid rent	2,000	
Furniture	18,000	
Building	48,000	
Accumulated depreciation—furniture		$ 300
Accumulated depreciation—building		200
Accounts payable		18,200
Salary payable		900
Interest payable		100
Unearned service revenue		400
Notes payable		20,000
Sheena Bright, Capital		35,900
	$ 76,000	$ 76,000

Only assets, liabilities, and capital accounts appear on the postclosing trial balance. No temporary accounts—revenues, expenses, or withdrawals—are included because they have been closed. The ledger is now up-to-date and ready for the next period. In summary, the postclosing trial balance contains the same accounts that the balance sheet contains—assets, liabilities, and capital.

Reversing entries are special journal entries that originate from certain adjustments at the end of the period. Reversing entries may ease the accounting of the next period. They are optional, and are covered in Appendix 4A at the end of this chapter.

Classifying Assets and Liabilities

Assets and liabilities are classified as either *current* or *long-term* to show their relative liquidity. **Liquidity** measures how quickly and easily an account can be converted to cash, because cash is the most liquid asset. Accounts receivable are relatively liquid because receivables are collected quickly. Supplies are less liquid, and furniture and buildings are even less so because of their long lives. A classified balance sheet lists assets in the order of their liquidity.

5 Classify assets and liabilities as current or long-term

Assets

Current Assets

Current assets will be converted to cash, sold, or used up during the next 12 months, or within the business's operating cycle if the cycle is longer than a year. The **operating cycle** is the time span when

1. Cash is used to acquire goods and services.
2. These goods and services are sold to customers.
3. The business collects cash from customers.

For most businesses the operating cycle is a few months. Cash, Accounts receivable, Supplies, and Prepaid expenses are current assets. Merchandising entities such as **Lowes** and **Coca-Cola** have another current asset: inventory. Inventory shows the cost of the goods the company holds for sale to customers.

Long-Term Assets

Long-term assets are all the assets that will not be converted to cash with the business's operating cycle. One category of long-term assets is plant assets (also called fixed assets or property, plant, and equipment). Land, Buildings, Furniture, and Equipment are plant assets. Of these, Smart Touch Learning has Furniture and a Building.

Other categories of long-term assets include Long-Term Investments and Other Assets (a catchall category). We will discuss these categories in later chapters.

Liabilities

Owners need to know when they must pay each liability. The balance sheet lists liabilities in the order in which they must be paid. Balance sheets report two liability categories: *current liabilities* and *long-term liabilities*.

Current Liabilities

Current liabilities must be paid either with cash or with goods and services within one year, or within the entity's operating cycle if the cycle is longer than a year. Accounts payable, Notes payable due within one year, Salary payable, Interest payable, and Unearned revenue are all current liabilities.

Long-Term Liabilities

All liabilities that do not need to be paid with the entity's operating cycle are classified as **long-term liabilities.** Many notes payable are long-term, for example, a mortgage on a building.

The Classified Balance Sheet

Thus far we have presented the *unclassified* balance sheet of Smart Touch Learning. We are now ready for the balance sheet that is actually used in practice—called a **classified balance sheet.** Exhibit 4-12 presents Smart Touch Learning's classified balance sheet using the data from Exhibit 4-7.

Smart Touch Learning classifies each asset and each liability as either current or long-term. Notice that the Total assets of $75,500 is the same as the Total assets on the unclassified balance sheet in Exhibit 4-7.

EXHIBIT 4-12 | **Classified Balance Sheet in Account Form**

SMART TOUCH LEARNING
Balance Sheet
May 31, 2010

Assets				**Liabilities**	
Current assets:				Current liabilities:	
Cash		$ 4,800		Accounts payable	$18,200
Accounts receivable		2,600		Salary payable	900
Supplies		600		Interest payable	100
Prepaid rent		2,000		Unearned service revenue	400
Total current assets			$10,000	Total current liabilities	19,600
Plant assets:				Long-term liabilities	
Furniture	$18,000			Notes payable	20,000
Less: Accumulated depreciation—furniture	-300	17,700		Total liabilities	39,600
Building	48,000				
Less: Accumulated depreciation—building	-200	47,800		**Owner's Equity**	
Total plant assets			65,500	Sheena Bright, Capital	35,900
Total assets			$75,500	Total liabilities and owner's equity	$75,500

Balance Sheet Forms

Smart Touch Learning's balance sheet in Exhibit 4-12 lists the assets at the left and the liabilities and the equity at the right in an arrangement known as the *account form.* The balance sheet of Smart Touch Learning in Exhibit 4-13 lists the assets at the top and the liabilities and owner's equity below in an arrangement known as the *report form.* Although either form is acceptable, the report form is more popular.

EXHIBIT 4-13 Classified Balance Sheet in Report Form

SMART TOUCH LEARNING Balance Sheet May 31, 2010			
Assets			
Current assets:			
Cash		$ 4,800	
Accounts receivable		2,600	
Supplies		600	
Prepaid rent		2,000	
Total current assets			$10,000
Plant assets:			
Furniture	$18,000		
Less: Accumulated depreciation—furniture	-300	17,700	
Building	48,000		
Less: Accumulated depreciation—building	-200	47,800	
Total plant assets			65,500
Total assets			$75,500
Liabilities			
Current liabilities:			
Accounts payable			$18,200
Salary payable			900
Interest payable			100
Unearned service revenue			400
Total current liabilities			19,600
Long-term liabilities			
Notes payable			20,000
Total liabilities			39,600
Owner's Equity			
Sheena Bright, Capital			35,900
Total liabilities and owner's equity			$75,500

Accounting Ratios

6 Use the current ratio and the debt ratio to evaluate a company

Accounting is designed to provide information for decision making by business owners, managers, and lenders. A bank considering lending money to the business must predict whether it can repay the loan. If Smart Touch Learning already has a lot of debt, repayment is less certain than if it does not owe much money. To measure the business's financial position, decision makers use ratios that they compute from the company's financial statements. Two of the most widely used decision aids in business are the current ratio and the debt ratio.

Current Ratio

The **current ratio** measures a company's ability to pay its current liabilities. This ratio is computed as follows:

$$\text{Current ratio} = \frac{\text{Total current assets}}{\text{Total current liabilities}}$$

A company prefers to have a high current ratio because that means it has plenty of current assets to pay its current liabilities. A current ratio that has increased from the prior period indicates improvement in a company's ability to pay its current debts. A current ratio that has decreased from the prior period signals deterioration in the company's ability to pay its current liabilities.

A Rule of Thumb A strong current ratio is 1.50, which indicates that the company has $1.50 in current assets for every $1.00 in current liabilities. A current ratio of 1.00 is considered low and somewhat risky.

Debt Ratio

A second decision aid is the **debt ratio**, which measures an organization's overall ability to pay its debts. The debt ratio is computed as follows:

$$\text{Debt ratio} = \frac{\text{Total liabilities}}{\text{Total assets}}$$

The debt ratio indicates the proportion of a company's assets that are financed with debt. A *low* debt ratio is safer than a high debt ratio. Why? Because a company with low liabilities usually has low required payments and is less likely to get into financial difficulty.

A Rule of Thumb A debt ratio below 0.60, or 60%, is considered safe for most businesses, as it indicates that the company owes only $0.60 for every $1.00 in total assets. A debt ratio above 0.80, or 80%, borders on high risk.

Now study the Decision Guidelines feature, which summarizes what you have learned in this chapter.

Decision Guidelines

COMPLETING THE ACCOUNTING CYCLE

Suppose you own Sherman Lawn Service, Greg's Groovy Tunes, or Smart Touch Learning. How can you measure the success of your business? The Decision Guidelines describe the accounting process you will use to provide the information for any accounting decisions you need to make.

Decision	Guidelines
• What document summarizes the effects of all the entity's transactions and adjustments throughout the period?	Accountant's *work sheet* with columns for • Trial balance • Adjustments • Adjusted trial balance • Income statement • Balance sheet
• What is the last *major* step in the accounting cycle?	*Closing entries for the temporary accounts:* • Revenues } Income statement accounts • Expenses } Income statement accounts • Withdrawals
• Why close out the revenues, expenses, and withdrawal accounts?	Because these *temporary accounts* have balances that relate only to one accounting period and *do not* carry over to the next period
• Which accounts do *not* get closed out?	*Permanent (balance sheet) accounts:* • Assets • Liabilities • Capital The balances of these accounts do carry over to the next period.
• How do businesses classify their assets and liabilities for reporting on the balance sheet?	*Current* (within one year, or the entity's operating cycle if longer than a year), or *Long-term* (not current)
• How do Hannah Sherman, Greg Moore, and Sheena Bright evaluate their companies?	There are many ways, such as the company's net income (or net loss) on the income statement and the trend of net income from year to year. Another way to evaluate a company is based on the company's *financial ratios*. Two key ratios are the current ratio and the debt ratio: $\text{Current ratio} = \frac{\text{Total current assets}}{\text{Total current liabilities}}$ The *current ratio* measures the ability to pay current liabilities with current assets. $\text{Debt ratio} = \frac{\text{Total liabilities}}{\text{Total assets}}$ The *debt ratio* measures the overall ability to pay liabilities. The debt ratio shows the proportion of the entity's assets that are financed with debt.

Summary Problem 2

Refer to the data in Problem 1 (Super Employment Services).

Requirements

1. Journalize and post the adjusting entries. (Before posting to the accounts, enter into each account its balance as shown in the trial balance. For example, enter the $5,000 balance in the Accounts receivable account before posting its adjusting entry.) Key adjusting entries by *letter*, as shown in the work sheet solution to Summary Problem 1. You can take the adjusting entries straight from the work sheet in the chapter.
2. Journalize and post the closing entries. (Each account should carry its balance as shown in the adjusted trial balance.) To distinguish closing entries from adjusting entries, key the closing entries by *number*. Draw arrows to illustrate the flow of data, as shown in Exhibit 4-10. Indicate the balance of the Capital account after the closing entries are posted.
3. Prepare the income statement for the year ended December 31, 2011.
4. Prepare the statement of owner's equity for the year ended December 31, 2011. Draw an arrow linking the income statement to the statement of owner's equity.
5. Prepare the classified balance sheet at December 31, 2011. Use the report form. All liabilities are current. Draw an arrow linking the statement of owner's equity to the balance sheet.

Solution

Requirement 1

		Adjusting Entries		
a.	Dec 31	Supplies expense (E+)	800	
		Supplies (A–)		800
b.	31	Depreciation expense—furniture (E+)	2,000	
		Accumulated depreciation—furniture (CA+)		2,000
c.	31	Depreciation expense—building (E+)	1,000	
		Accumulated depreciation—building (CA+)		1,000
d.	31	Salary expense (E+)	500	
		Salary payable (L+)		500
e.	31	Accounts receivable (A+)	1,300	
		Service revenue (R+)		1,300
f.	31	Unearned service revenue (L–)	3,000	
		Service revenue (R+)		3,000

Accounts receivable

Debit	Credit
5,000	
(e) 1,300	
Bal 6,300	

Supplies

Debit	Credit
1,000	(a) 800
Bal 200	

Accumulated depreciation—furniture

Debit	Credit
	4,000
	(b) 2,000
	Bal 6,000

Accumulated depreciation—building

Debit	Credit
	30,000
	(c) 1,000
	Bal 31,000

Salary payable

Debit	Credit
	(d) 500
	Bal 500

Unearned service revenue

Debit	Credit
(f) 3,000	8,000
	Bal 5,000

Service revenue

Debit	Credit
	60,000
	(e) 1,300
	(f) 3,000
	Bal 64,300

Salary expense

Debit	Credit
16,000	
(d) 500	
Bal 16,500	

Supplies expense

Debit	Credit
(a) 800	
Bal 800	

Depreciation expense—furniture

Debit	Credit
(b) 2,000	
Bal 2,000	

Depreciation expense—building

Debit	Credit
(c) 1,000	
Bal 1,000	

Requirement 2

		Closing Entries		
1.	Dec 31	Service revenue (R–)	64,300	
		Income summary		64,300
2.	31	Income summary	23,300	
		Salary expense (E–)		16,500
		Supplies expense (E–)		800
		Depreciation expense—furniture (E–)		2,000
		Depreciation expense—building (E–)		1,000
		Advertising expense (E–)		3,000
3.	31	Income summary ($64,300 – $23,300)	41,000	
		Dan Mudge, Capital (Q+)		41,000
4.	31	Dan Mudge, Capital (Q–)	25,000	
		Dan Mudge, Withdrawals (W–)		25,000

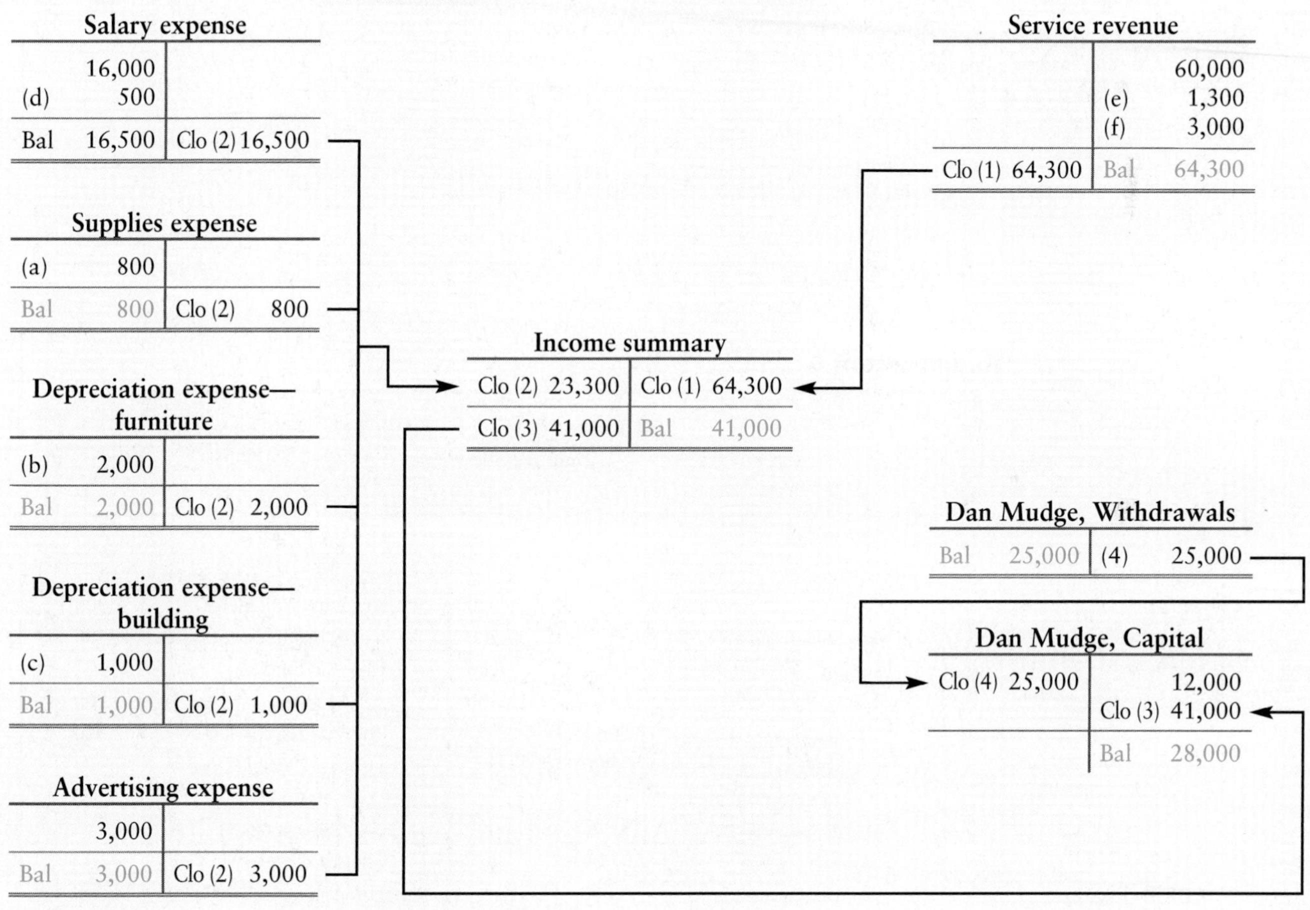

Requirement 3

SUPER EMPLOYMENT SERVICES **Income Statement** Year Ended December 31, 2011		
Revenue:		
Service revenue		$64,300
Expenses:		
Salary expense	$16,500	
Advertising expense	3,000	
Depreciation expense—furniture	2,000	
Depreciation expense—building	1,000	
Supplies expense	800	
Total expenses		23,300
Net income		$41,000

Requirement 4

SUPER EMPLOYMENT SERVICES **Statement of Owner's Equity** Year Ended December 31, 2011	
Dan Mudge, Capital, January 1, 2011	$ 12,000
Add: Net income	41,000
	53,000
Less: Owner withdrawals	(25,000)
Dan Mudge, Capital, December 31, 2011	$ 28,000

Requirement 5

SUPER EMPLOYMENT SERVICES
Balance Sheet
December 31, 2011

Assets			**Liabilities**	
Current assets:			Current liabilities:	
Cash		$ 6,000	Accounts payable	$ 2,000
Accounts receivable		6,300	Salary payable	500
Supplies		200	Unearned service	
Total current assets		12,500	revenue	5,000
Long-term assets:			Total current liabilities	7,500
Furniture	$10,000			
Less: Accumulated				
depreciation	(6,000)	4,000		
Building	$50,000		**Owner's Equity**	
Less: Accumulated			Dan Mudge, Capital	28,000
depreciation	(31,000)	19,000	Total liabilities and	
Total assets		$35,500	owner's equity	$35,500

Review Completing the Accounting Cycle

Accounting Vocabulary

Accounting Cycle (p. 234)
Process by which companies produce their financial statements for a specific period.

Classified Balance Sheet (p. 249)
A balance sheet that classifies each asset and each liability as either current or long-term.

Closing the Accounts (p. 244)
Step in the accounting cycle at the end of the period. Closing the accounts consists of journalizing and posting the closing entries to set the balances of the revenue, expense, and withdrawal accounts to zero for the next period.

Closing Entries (p. 244)
Entries that transfer the revenue, expense, and withdrawal balances to the capital account.

Current Assets (p. 248)
Assets that are expected to be converted to cash, sold, or consumed during the next 12 months, or within the business's normal operating cycle if the cycle is longer than a year.

Current Liabilities (p. 248)
Debts due to be paid with cash or with goods and services within one year, or within the entity's operating cycle if the cycle is longer than a year.

Current Ratio (p. 251)
Current assets divided by current liabilities. This ratio measures the company's ability to pay current liabilities from current assets.

Debt Ratio (p. 251)
Total liabilities divided by total assets. This ratio reveals the proportion of a company's assets that it has financed with debt.

Income Summary (p. 244)
A temporary "holding tank" account into which revenues and expenses are transferred prior to their final transfer to the owner's capital account.

Liquidity (p. 247)
Measure of how quickly an item can be converted to cash.

Long-Term Assets (p. 248)
Any assets that will NOT be converted to cash or used up within the business's operating cycle, or one year, whichever is greater.

Long-Term Liabilities (p. 248)
Liabilities that are not current.

Operating Cycle (p. 248)
Time span during which cash is paid for goods and services, which are then sold to customers from whom the business collects cash.

Permanent Accounts (p. 244)
Accounts that are *not* closed at the end of the period—the asset, liability, and capital accounts.

Postclosing Trial Balance (p. 247)
List of the accounts and their balances at the end of the period after journalizing and posting the closing entries. This last step of the accounting cycle ensures that the ledger is in balance to start the next accounting period. It should include only balance sheet accounts.

Reversing Entries (p. 247)
Special journal entries that ease the burden of accounting for transactions in the next period.

Temporary Accounts (p. 244)
The revenue and expense accounts that relate to a particular accounting period and are closed at the end of that period.

Work Sheet (p. 235)
A columnar document designed to help move data from the trial balance to their financial statements.

Quick Check

1. Consider the steps in the accounting cycle in Exhibit 4-1. Which part of the accounting cycle provides information to help a business decide whether to expand its operations?
   a. Postclosing trial balance
   b. Financial statements
   c. Adjusting entries
   d. Closing entries

2. Which columns of the accounting work sheet show unadjusted amounts?
   a. Trial Balance
   b. Balance Sheet
   c. Income Statement
   d. Adjustments
3. Which columns of the work sheet show net income?
   a. Trial Balance
   b. Income Statement
   c. Adjustments
   d. Both B and C
4. Which situation indicates a net loss on the income statement?
   a. Total credits exceed total debits
   b. Total debits equal total credits
   c. Total debits exceed total credits
   d. None of the above
5. Supplies has an $8,000 unadjusted balance on your trial balance. At year-end you count supplies of $3,000. What adjustment will appear on your work sheet?

a.

Supplies	5,000	
Supplies expense		5,000

b.

Supplies expense	5,000	
Supplies		5,000

c.

Supplies expense	3,000	
Supplies		3,000

   d. No adjustment is needed because the Supplies account already has a correct balance.
6. Which of the following accounts is *not* closed?
   a. Withdrawals
   b. Accumulated depreciation
   c. Service revenue
   d. Depreciation expense
7. What do closing entries accomplish?
   a. Bring the capital account to its correct ending balance
   b. Zero out the revenue, expense, and withdrawals
   c. Transfer revenues, expenses, and withdrawals to capital
   d. All of the above

8. Which of the following is *not* a closing entry?

a.

Capital	XXX	
Withdrawals		XXX

b.

Income summary	XXX	
Rent expense		XXX

c.

Service revenue	XXX	
Income summary		XXX

d.

Salary payable	XXX	
Income summary		XXX

9. Assets and liabilities are listed on the balance sheet in order of their:
   a. Liquidity
   b. Purchase date
   c. Balance
   d. Adjustments

10. Carrier Travel has cash of $200, receivables of $800, and supplies of $500. Carrier owes $400 on accounts payable and salary payable of $100. Carrier's current ratio is:
   a. 0.54
   b. 3.00
   c. 0.33
   d. 1.67

Answers are given after Apply Your Knowledge (p. 283).

Assess Your Progress

■ Short Exercises

S4-1 *(L.OBJ. 1)* **Explaining work sheet items [10 min]**
Link Back to Chapter 3 (Adjusting Entries). Explain why the following accounts are being adjusted in the following entries:

a. Prepaid rent
b. Unearned service revenue
c. Supplies
d. Salary payable
e. Accumulated depreciation

Journal Entry

Date		Accounts and Explanations	Debit	Credit
Apr	30	Rent expense	1,000	
		Prepaid rent		1,000
	30	Unearned service revenue	200	
		Service revenue		200
	30	Supplies expense	100	
		Supplies		100
	30	Salary expense	900	
		Salary payable		900
	30	Depreciation expense—furniture	300	
		Accumulated depreciation—furniture		300

S4-2 *(L.OBJ. 1)* **Explaining work sheet items [10–15 min]**
Link Back to Chapters 2 and 3 (Definitions of Accounts). Explain what the following terms mean:

a. Accounts receivable
b. Supplies
c. Prepaid rent
d. Furniture
e. Accumulated depreciation
f. Accounts payable
g. Unearned service revenue
h. Service revenue
i. Rent expense

S4-3 *(L.OBJ. 2)* **Using the work sheet [5–10 min]**
Answer the following questions:

1. What type of normal balance does the Capital account have—debit or credit?
2. Which Income Statement account has the same type of balance as the Capital account?
3. Which type of Income Statement account has the opposite type of balance as the Capital account?
4. What do we call the difference between total debits and total credits on the Income Statement? Into what account is the difference figure closed at the end of the period?

S4-4 *(L.OBJ. 3)* **Journalizing closing entries [10–15 min]**
It is December 31 and time for you to close the books.

Requirement

1. Journalize the closing entries for Brett Kauffman Enterprises:

   a. Withdrawals, $9,000
   b. Service revenue, $24,300
   c. Make a single closing entry for all the expenses: Salary, $6,600; Rent, $3,600; Advertising, $3,300
   d. Income summary

S4-5 *(L.OBJ. 3)* **Posting closing entries [5 min]**
It is December 31 and time for your business to close the books. The following balances appear on the books of Cedrick Owens Enterprises.

a. Withdrawals, $11,000
b. Service revenue, $25,200
c. Expense account balances: Salary, $7,500; Rent, $3,000; Advertising, $2,200

Requirements

1. Set up each T-account and insert its adjusted balance as given (denote as *Bal*) at December 31. Also set up a T-account for Capital, $20,300, and for Income summary.
2. Post the closing entries to the accounts, denoting posted amounts as *Clo*.
3. Compute the ending balance of Capital.

S4-6 *(L.OBJ. 3)* **Making closing entries [5 min]**
Lipsky Insurance Agency reported the following items at September 30, 2011:

Sales and marketing expense	$1,600	Cash	$1,000
Other assets	500	Service revenue	4,200
Depreciation expense	700	Accounts payable	300
Long-term liabilities	400	Accounts receivable	1,200

Requirement

1. Journalize Lipsky's closing entries, as needed for these accounts.

S4-7 *(L.OBJ. 3)* **Posting closing entries [5 min]**
Kaminsky Insurance Agency reported the following items at June 30:

Sales and marketing expense	$2,400	Cash	$1,000
Other assets	500	Service revenue	5,600
Depreciation expense	700	Accounts payable	300
Long-term liabilities	400	Accounts receivable	1,200

Requirement

1. Prepare T-accounts for Kaminsky Insurance Agency. Insert the account balances prior to closing. Post the closing entries to these accounts, and show each account's ending balance after closing. Also show the Income summary T-account. Denote a balance as *Bal* and a closing entry amount as *Clo*.

S4-8 *(L.OBJ. 4)* **Preparing a postclosing trial balance [10 min]**
After closing its accounts at February 28, 2010, Watts Electric Company had the following account balances:

Long-term liabilities	$ 700	Equipment	$ 4,000
Other assets	1,000	Cash	400
Accounts receivable	1,800	Service revenue	0
Total expenses	0	H. Watts, Capital	2,900
Accounts payable	900	Supplies	100
Unearned service revenue	1,300	Accumulated depreciation	1,500

Requirement

1. Prepare Watts' postclosing trial balance at February 28, 2010.

S4-9 *(L.OBJ. 5)* **Classifying assets and liabilities as current or long-term [5 min]**
Ink Jet Printing reported the following (amounts in thousands):

Buildings	$4,000	Service revenue	$1,300
Accounts payable	400	Cash	200
Total expenses	1,050	Receivables	500
Accumulated depreciation	2,800	Interest expense	90
Accrued liabilities (such as Salary payable)	300	Equipment	800
Prepaid expenses	100		

Requirements

1. Identify the assets (including contra assets) and liabilities.
2. Classify each asset and each liability as current or long-term.

S4-10 *(L.OBJ. 5)* **Classifying assets and liabilities as current or long-term [10 min]**
Link Back to Chapter 3 (Book Value). Examine Ink Jet Printing's account balances in Short Exercise 4-9.

Requirement

1. Identify or compute the following amounts for Ink Jet Printing:
   a. Total current assets
   b. Book value of plant assets
   c. Total current liabilities
   d. Total long-term liabilities

S4-11 *(L.OBJ. 6)* **Computing the current and the debt ratio [10–15 min]**
Granite State Telephone and Telegram has these account balances at December 31, 2011:

Note payable, long-term	$ 12,200	Accounts payable	$ 4,400
Prepaid rent	2,100	Accounts receivable	6,100
Salary payable	2,000	Cash	2,500
Service revenue	33,300	Depreciation expense	4,000
Supplies	1,200	Equipment	12,000

Requirements

1. Compute Granite State Telephone and Telegram's current ratio and debt ratio.
2. How much in *current* assets does Granite State Telephone and Telegram have for every dollar of *current* liabilities that it owes?

■ Exercises

E4-12 *(L.OBJ. 1, 2)* **Preparing a work sheet and using it to prepare an income statement [30–40 min]**

Data for the unadjusted trial balance of Summer's Here Tanning Salon at May 31, 2011, follow.

Cash	$ 3,100	Service revenue	$ 93,400
Equipment	66,200	Salary expense	42,900
Accumulated depreciation	21,400	Depreciation expense	
Accounts payable	6,600	Supplies expense	
Supplies	1,500	L. Nabors, Capital	(7,700)

Adjusting data for 2011 are:

a. Accrued service revenue, $3,100
b. Supplies used in operations, $1,000
c. Accrued salary expense, $900
d. Depreciation expense, $3,900

Leo Nabors, the owner, has received an offer to sell the company. He needs to know the net income for the year covered by these data.

Requirements

1. Complete the work sheet for Summer's Here Tanning Salon.
2. How much was the net income/net loss for May?

E4-13 *(L.OBJ. 1, 2)* **Preparing a work sheet and using it to calculate net income [20–30 min]**

The trial balance of Data Link at September 30 follows:

DATA LINK Trial Balance September 30, 2011		
	Trial Balance	
Account	Debit	Credit
Cash	3,700	
Accounts receivable	3,500	
Prepaid rent	1,700	
Supplies	3,600	
Equipment	32,400	
Accumulated depreciation		1,700
Accounts payable		5,400
Salary payable		
D. D'artagnon, Capital		34,400
D. D'artagnon, Withdrawals	2,200	
Service revenue		8,400
Depreciation expense		
Salary expense	2,300	
Rent expense		
Utilities expense	500	
Supplies expense		
Total	49,900	49,900

Additional information at September 30, 2011:

a. Accrued service revenue, $400
b. Depreciation, $700
c. Accrued salary expense, $500
d. Prepaid rent expired, $500
e. Supplies used, $300

Requirements

1. Complete Data Link's work sheet for the month ended September 30, 2011.
2. How much was net income for September?

Note: *Exercise 4-14 should be used only after completing E4-13.*

E4-14 *(L.OBJ. 2, 3)* **Journalizing adjusting and closing entries [15–20 min]**
Use your answer from E4-13.

Requirement

1. Journalize Data Link's adjusting and closing entries at September 30, 2011.

Note: *Exercise 4-15 should be used only after completing E4-13 and E4-14.*

E4-15 *(L.OBJ. 2, 3)* **Using the work sheet, and posting adjusting and closing entries [20–30 min]**
Consider the entries prepared in Exercise 4-14.

Requirements

1. Set up T-accounts for those accounts affected by the adjusting and closing entries in Exercise 4-14.
2. Post the adjusting and closing entries to the accounts; denote adjustment amounts by *Adj*, closing amounts by *Clo*, and balances by *Bal*. Double underline the accounts with zero balances after you close them, and show the ending balance in each account.

E4-16 *(L.OBJ. 2, 3)* **Preparing adjusting and closing entries [20 min]**
Link Back to Chapter 3 (Adjusting Entries). Emerson St. Paul Book Shop's accounting records include the following account balances:

December 31,	2010	2011
Prepaid Rent	$ 500	$ 1,500
Unearned Service Revenue	1,000	600

During 2011, the business recorded the following:

a. Prepaid annual rent of $7,000
b. Made the year-end adjustment to record rent expense of $6,000 for the year
c. Collected $4,100 cash in advance for service revenue to be earned later
d. Made the year-end adjustment to record the earning of $4,500 service revenue that had been collected in advance

Requirements

1. Set up T-accounts for Prepaid rent, Rent expense, Unearned service revenue, and Service revenue. Insert beginning and ending balances for Prepaid rent and Unearned service revenue.
2. Journalize the previous adjusting entries a–d, and post to the accounts. Explanations are not required.
3. What is the balance in Service revenue after adjusting?
4. What is the balance in Rent expense after adjusting?

E4-17 *(L.OBJ. 2, 3)* **Using a partial work sheet and preparing closing entries [15–25 min]**

The adjusted trial balance from the September work sheet of Paul Sign Company follows:

PAUL SIGN COMPANY
Work Sheet
September 30, 2011

Account	Adjusted Trial Balance	
	Debit	Credit
Cash	15,100	
Supplies	1,600	
Prepaid rent	1,500	
Equipment	46,000	
Accumulated depreciation		6,300
Accounts payable		4,700
Salary payable		100
Unearned service revenue		4,900
Note payable, long-term		4,300
P. Paul, Capital		33,500
P. Paul, Withdrawals	1,200	
Service revenue		18,000
Salary expense	3,400	
Rent expense	1,400	
Depreciation expense	300	
Supplies expense	400	
Utilities expense	900	
Total	71,800	71,800

Requirements

1. Journalize Paul's closing entries at September 30.
2. How much net income or net loss did Paul earn for September? How can you tell?

E4-18 *(L.OBJ. 3)* **Preparing a statement of owner's equity [5–10 min]**

Selected accounts of Victor St. Paul Book Shop follow:

V. Victor, Capital

Clo	30,000	Jan 1	171,000
		Clo	139,000
		Bal	280,000

V. Victor, Withdrawals

Mar 31	7,000		
Jun 30	6,000		
Sep 30	7,000		
Dec 31	10,000		
Bal	30,000	Clo	30,000

Income summary

Clo	85,000	Clo	224,000
Clo	139,000	Bal	139,000

Requirement

1. Prepare the company's statement of owner's equity for the year ended December 31, 2011.

E4-19 *(L.OBJ. 3)* **Identifying and journalizing closing entries [15 min]**
Ms. Marcia Marigold recorded the following transactions and year-end adjustments during 2010:

Journal Entry		
Accounts and Explanations	Debit	Credit
Prepaid rent	7,000	
Cash		7,000
Prepaid the annual rent.		
Rent expense	6,100	
Prepaid rent		6,100
Adjustment to record rent expense for the year.		
Cash	4,300	
Unearned service revenue		4,300
Collected cash in advance of service revenue to be earned.		
Unearned service revenue	4,900	
Service revenue		4,900
Adjustment to record revenue earned that has been collected in advance.		

Requirements

1. Assuming that there were no other service revenue and rent expense transactions during 2010, journalize Marcia's closing entries at the end of 2010 for the two accounts.
2. Open T-accounts for Service revenue and Rent expense. Post the closing entries to these accounts. What are their balances after closing?

E4-20 *(L.OBJ. 3)* **Identifying and journalizing closing entries [10–15 min]**
The accountant for Oceanside Photography has posted adjusting entries (a)–(e) to the following selected accounts at December 31, 2010.

Accounts receivable			
	41,000		
(a)	2,900		

Supplies			
	4,000	(b)	2,500

Accumulated depr.—furniture			
			5,000
		(c)	900

Accumulated depr.—building			
			33,000
		(d)	5,500

Salary payable			
		(e)	600

C. Pipeline, Capital			
			46,000

C. Pipeline, Withdrawals			
	59,000		

Service revenue			
			108,000
		(a)	2,900

Salary expense			
	25,500		
(e)	600		

Supplies expense			
(b)	2,500		

Depreciation expense—furniture			
(c)	900		

Depreciation expense—building			
(d)	5,500		

Requirements

1. Journalize Oceanside Photography's closing entries at December 31, 2010.
2. Determine Oceanside Photography's ending Capital balance at December 31, 2010.

E4-21 *(L.OBJ. 4)* **Preparing a postclosing trial balance [10–15 min]**
Review your answers from Exercises 4-14 and 4-15.

Requirement

1. Prepare the postclosing trial balance of Data Link at September 30, 2011.

E4-22 *(L.OBJ. 5, 6)* **Preparing a classified balance sheet, and calculating the current and debt ratios [15–20 min]**
The adjusted trial balance and the income statement amounts from the December work sheet of Carroll Pet Shop Company follow:

CARROLL PET SHOP COMPANY Work Sheet December 31, 2011		
	Adjusted Trial Balance	
Account	Debit	Credit
Cash	15,200	
Supplies	1,900	
Prepaid rent	1,400	
Equipment	53,000	
Accumulated depreciation		6,900
Accounts payable		4,300
Salary payable		100
Unearned service revenue		4,900
Long-term note payable		6,000
K. Carroll, Capital		37,900
K. Carroll, Withdrawals	1,000	
Service revenue		18,500
Salary expense	3,100	
Rent expense	1,400	
Depreciation expense	400	
Supplies expense	300	
Utilities expense	900	
Total	78,600	78,600

Requirements

1. Prepare the classified balance sheet of Carroll Pet Shop Company at December 31, 2011. Use the report form. You must compute the ending balance of Capital.
2. Compute Carroll's current ratio and debt ratio at December 31, 2011. One year ago, the current ratio was 1.81 and the debt ratio was 0.35. Indicate whether Carroll's ability to pay current and total debts has improved, deteriorated, or remained the same during the current year.

Problems (Group A)

P4-23A *(L.OBJ. 1, 2)* **Preparing a work sheet and the financial statements [40–50 min]**
The trial balance work sheet and adjustment data of Kara's Motors at June 30, 2010, follow:

KARA'S MOTORS Trial Balance June 30, 2010		
	Trial Balance	
Account	Debit	Credit
Cash	4,300	
Accounts receivable	27,500	
Supplies	500	
Prepaid insurance	1,400	
Equipment	53,800	
Accumulated depreciation		35,800
Accounts payable		13,300
Wages payable		
Unearned service revenue		8,400
Kara Cole, Capital		20,300
Kara Cole, Withdrawals	3,700	
Service revenue		16,400
Depreciation expense		
Wage expense	1,700	
Insurance expense		
Utilities expense	1,300	
Supplies expense		
Total	94,200	94,200

Additional data at June 30, 2010:

a. Depreciation on equipment, $700
b. Accrued wage expense, $700
c. Supplies on hand, $400
d. Prepaid insurance expired during June, $600
e. Unearned service revenue earned during June, $4,500
f. Accrued service revenue, $1,000

Requirements

1. Complete Kara's work sheet for June. Key adjusting entries by letter.
2. Prepare the income statement, the statement of owner's equity, and the classified balance sheet in account form for the month ended June 30, 2010.

P4-24A *(L.OBJ. 1, 2, 3)* **Preparing a work sheet, financial statements, and closing entries [50–60 min]**

The trial balance of Silk Investment Advisers at December 31, 2011, follows:

SILK INVESTMENT ADVISERS Trial Balance December 31, 2011		
	Trial Balance	
Account	Debit	Credit
Cash	31,000	
Accounts receivable	43,000	
Supplies	6,000	
Equipment	24,000	
Accumulated depreciation		16,000
Accounts payable		13,000
Salary payable		
Unearned service revenue		3,000
Note payable, long-term		41,000
S. Thread, Capital		28,000
S. Thread, Withdrawals	51,000	
Service revenue		100,000
Salary expense	30,000	
Supplies expense		
Depreciation expense		
Interest expense	6,000	
Rent expense	7,000	
Insurance expense	3,000	
Total	201,000	201,000

Adjustment data at December 31, 2011:

a. Unearned service revenue earned during the year, $200
b. Supplies on hand, $4,000
c. Depreciation for the year, $7,000
d. Accrued salary expense, $3,000
e. Accrued service revenue, $8,000

Requirements

1. Enter the account data in the Trial Balance columns of a work sheet, and complete the work sheet. Key each adjusting entry by the letter corresponding to the data given. Leave a blank line under Service revenue.
2. Prepare the income statement, the statement of owner's equity, and the classified balance sheet in account format.
3. Prepare closing journal entries from the work sheet.
4. Did the company have a good or a bad year during 2011? Give the reason for your answer. (Challenge)

P4-25A *(L.OBJ. 1, 2, 3, 4, 5, 6)* **Completing the accounting cycle [120–150 min]**
The trial balance of Coyote Anvils at January 31, 2011, and the data for the month-end adjustments follow:

COYOTE ANVILS Trial Balance January 31, 2011		
	Trial Balance	
Account	Debit	Credit
Cash	5,200	
Accounts receivable	15,100	
Prepaid rent	2,400	
Supplies	1,000	
Equipment	31,500	
Accumulated depreciation		3,700
Accounts payable		6,200
Salary payable		
Unearned service revenue		5,600
W.E. Coyote, Capital		30,800
W.E. Coyote, Withdrawals	5,000	
Service revenue		17,400
Salary expense	3,500	
Rent expense		
Depreciation expense		
Supplies expense		
Total	63,700	63,700

Adjustment data:

a. Unearned service revenue still unearned at January 31, $400
b. Prepaid rent still in force at January 31, $1,000
c. Supplies used during the month, $500
d. Depreciation for the month, $300
e. Accrued salary expense at January 31, $400

Requirements

1. Prepare adjusting journal entries.
2. Enter the trial balance on a work sheet and complete the work sheet of Coyote Anvils for the month ended January 31, 2011.
3. Prepare the income statement, the statement of owner's equity, and the classified balance sheet in report form.
4. Using the work sheet data that you prepare, post the adjusting entries and journalize and post the closing entries to T-accounts. Use dates and show the ending balance of each account.
5. Prepare a postclosing trial balance.
6. Calculate the current and debt ratio for the company.

P4-26A *(L.OBJ. 1, 2, 3, 4, 5, 6)* **Completing the accounting cycle [120–150 min]**
The trial balance of Speedy G Internet at May 31, 2011, follows:

SPEEDY G INTERNET Trial Balance May 31, 2011		
	Trial Balance	
Account	Debit	Credit
Cash	4,200	
Accounts receivable	15,000	
Prepaid rent	2,200	
Supplies	1,000	
Equipment	31,500	
Accumulated depreciation		4,000
Accounts payable		6,100
Salary payable		
Unearned service revenue		4,000
S. Buggy, Capital		26,600
S. Buggy, Withdrawals	3,600	
Service revenue		19,000
Salary expense	2,200	
Rent expense		
Depreciation expense		
Supplies expense		
Total	59,700	59,700

Adjusting data at May 31:

a. Unearned service revenue still unearned, $1,000
b. Prepaid rent still in force, $1,900
c. Supplies used during the month, $700
d. Depreciation for the month, $500
e. Accrued salary expense, $800

Requirements

1. Journalize adjusting journal entries.
2. Enter the trial balance on a work sheet and complete the work sheet of Speedy G Internet.
3. Prepare the income statement, statement of owner's equity, and classified balance sheet in report form.
4. Using the work sheet data that you prepared, journalize the closing entries and post the adjusting and closing entries to T-accounts. Use dates and show the ending balance of each account.
5. Prepare a postclosing trial balance.
6. Calculate the current and debt ratios for the company.

P4-27A *(L.OBJ. 2, 3)* **Journalizing adjusting and closing entries [45–60 min]**
The *unadjusted* trial balance and adjustment data of Jones Real Estate Appraisal Company at June 30, 2011, follow:

JONES REAL ESTATE APPRAISAL COMPANY Unadjusted Trial Balance June 30, 2011		
Account Title	Debit	Credit
Cash	$ 4,100	
Accounts receivable	3,900	
Supplies	4,000	
Prepaid insurance	1,700	
Building	73,800	
Accumulated depreciation		$ 18,100
Land	14,500	
Accounts payable		19,300
Interest payable		8,300
Salary payable		600
J. Jones, Capital		32,900
J. Jones, Withdrawals	26,500	
Service revenue		99,000
Salary expense	33,700	
Depreciation expense	0	
Insurance expense	5,500	
Utilities expense	3,600	
Supplies expense	6,900	
Total	$ 178,200	$ 178,200

Adjustment data at June 30, 2011:

a. Prepaid insurance expired, $500
b. Accrued service revenue, $1,500
c. Accrued salary expense, $1,200
d. Depreciation for the year, $8,300
e. Supplies used during the year, $700

Requirements

1. Open T-accounts for Capital and all the accounts that follow on the trial balance. Insert their unadjusted balances. Also open a T-account for Income summary, which has a zero balance.
2. Journalize the adjusting entries and post to the accounts that you opened. Show the balance of each revenue account and each expense account.
3. Journalize the closing entries and post to the accounts that you opened. Draw double underlines under each account balance that you close to zero.
4. Compute the ending balance of Capital.

P4-28A *(L.OBJ. 2, 3)* **Journalizing adjusting and closing entries [20–30 min]**
The accountant for John Lipnik, M.D., encountered the following situations while adjusting and closing the books at December 31. Consider each situation independently.

Requirements

1. The accountant failed to make the following adjusting entries at December 31:

    a. Accrued salary expense, $1,400
    b. Supplies expense, $400
    c. Accrued interest expense on a note payable, $800
    d. Depreciation of equipment, $700
    e. Earned service revenue that had been collected in advance, $1,800

    What is the overall effect of the adjustments to net income?
2. Journalize each omitted adjusting entry identified.
3. Assume Withdrawals were $5,000 for the year. Prepare the entry to close the Withdrawals account.

P4-29A *(L.OBJ. 5, 6)* **Preparing a classified balance sheet in report form. Use the current and debt ratios to evaluate a company [30–40 min]**
Selected accounts of Backyard Irrigation System at December 31, 2011, follow:

Insurance expense	$ 700	Accounts payable	$33,200
Note payable, long-term	2,800	Accounts receivable	42,500
Other assets	2,100	Accumulated depreciation—building	48,900
Building	54,500	Accumulated depreciation—	
Prepaid insurance	5,100	equipment	6,600
Salary expense	16,400	Cash	11,000
Salary payable	4,000	Interest payable	500
Service revenue	70,400	A. Nyquist, Capital, Dec. 31, 2012	43,400
Supplies	3,400	Equipment	22,500
Unearned service revenue	1,700		

Requirements

1. Prepare the company's classified balance sheet in report form at December 31, 2011.
2. Compute the company's current ratio and debt ratio at December 31, 2011. At December 31, 2010, the current ratio was 1.82 and the debt ratio was 0.41. Did its ability to pay debts improve or deteriorate, or did it remain the same during 2011?

■ Problems (Group B)

P4-30B *(L.OBJ. 1, 2)* **Preparing a work sheet and the financial statements [40–50 min]** The trial balance work sheet and adjustment data of Kate's Motors at June 30, 2010, follow:

KATE'S MOTORS Trial Balance June 30, 2010		
	Trial Balance	
Account	Debit	Credit
Cash	4,700	
Accounts receivable	27,300	
Supplies	600	
Prepaid insurance	1,400	
Equipment	54,300	
Accumulated depreciation		35,800
Accounts payable		13,200
Wages payable		
Unearned service revenue		8,900
K. Koon, Capital		20,500
K. Koon, Withdrawals	3,800	
Service revenue		16,900
Depreciation expense		
Wage expense	2,100	
Insurance expense		
Utilities expense	1,100	
Supplies expense		
Total	95,300	95,300

Additional data at June 30, 2010:

a. Depreciation on equipment, $1,300
b. Accrued wage expense, $400
c. Supplies on hand, $400
d. Prepaid insurance expired during June, $300
e. Unearned service revenue earned during June, $4,600
f. Accrued service revenue, $600

Requirements

1. Complete Kate's work sheet for June. Key adjusting entries by letter.
2. Prepare the income statement, the statement of owner's equity, and the classified balance sheet in account form for the month ended June 30, 2010.

P4-31B *(L.OBJ. 1, 2, 3)* **Preparing a work sheet, financial statements, and closing entries [50–60 min]**

The trial balance of Lynch Investment Advisers at December 31, 2011, follows:

LYNCH INVESTMENT ADVISERS Trial Balance December 31, 2011		
	Trial Balance	
Account	Debit	Credit
Cash	26,000	
Accounts receivable	47,000	
Supplies	6,000	
Equipment	22,000	
Accumulated depreciation		13,000
Accounts payable		15,000
Salary payable		
Unearned service revenue		2,000
Note payable, long-term		44,000
M. Lynch, Capital		30,000
M. Lynch, Withdrawals	55,000	
Service revenue		99,000
Salary expense	33,000	
Supplies expense		
Depreciation expense		
Interest expense	5,000	
Rent expense	4,000	
Insurance expense	5,000	
Total	203,000	203,000

Adjustment data at December 31, 2011:

a. Unearned service revenue earned during the year, $900
b. Supplies on hand, $4,000
c. Depreciation for the year, $6,000
d. Accrued salary expense, $5,000
e. Accrued service revenue, $8,000

Requirements

1. Enter the account data in the Trial Balance columns of a work sheet, and complete the work sheet. Key each adjusting entry by the letter corresponding to the data given. Leave a blank line under Service revenue.
2. Prepare the income statement, the statement of owner's equity, and the classified balance sheet in account format.
3. Prepare closing journal entries from the work sheet.
4. Did the company have a good or a bad year during 2011? Give the reason for your answer. (Challenge)

P4-32B *(L.OBJ. 1, 2, 3, 4, 5, 6)* **Completing the accounting cycle [120–150 min]**
The trial balance of Wolfe Anvils at July 31, 2011, and the data for the month-end adjustments follow:

WOLFE ANVILS Trial Balance July 31, 2011		
	Trial Balance	
Account	Debit	Credit
Cash	5,300	
Accounts receivable	14,600	
Prepaid rent	2,200	
Supplies	800	
Equipment	31,800	
Accumulated depreciation		4,600
Accounts payable		6,600
Salary payable		
Unearned service revenue		5,600
B.B.W., Capital		25,700
B.B.W., Withdrawals	3,300	
Service revenue		17,800
Salary expense	2,300	
Rent expense		
Depreciation expense		
Supplies expense		
Total	60,300	60,300

Adjustment data:

a. Unearned service revenue still unearned at July 31, $600
b. Prepaid rent still in force at July 31, $1,800
c. Supplies used during the month, $700
d. Depreciation for the month, $500
e. Accrued salary expense at July 31, $200

Requirements

1. Prepare adjusting journal entries.
2. Enter the trial balance on a work sheet and complete the work sheet of Wolfe Anvils for the month ended July 31, 2011.
3. Prepare the income statement, the statement of owner's equity, and the classified balance sheet in report form.
4. Using the work sheet data that you prepare, journalize and post the adjusting and closing entries to T-accounts. Use dates and show the ending balance of each account.
5. Prepare a postclosing trial balance.
6. Calculate the current and debt ratio for the company.

P4-33B *(L.OBJ. 1, 2, 3, 4, 5, 6)* **Completing the accounting cycle [120–150 min]**
The trial balance of Racer Internet at May 31, 2011, follows:

RACER INTERNET Trial Balance May 31, 2011		
	Trial Balance	
Account	Debit	Credit
Cash	4,800	
Accounts receivable	15,300	
Prepaid rent	2,100	
Supplies	1,600	
Equipment	31,500	
Accumulated depreciation		4,000
Accounts payable		6,600
Salary payable		
Unearned service revenue		4,700
J.R. Dale, Capital		29,900
J.R. Dale, Withdrawals	3,900	
Service revenue		17,700
Salary expense	3,400	
Rent expense		
Depreciation expense		
Supplies expense		
Total	62,600	62,600

Adjusting data at May 31:

a. Unearned service revenue still unearned at May 31, $700
b. Prepaid rent still in force at May 31, $1,600
c. Supplies used during the month, $900
d. Depreciation for the month, $600
e. Accrued salary expense at May 31, $800

Requirements

1. Journalize adjusting journal entries.
2. Enter the trial balance on a work sheet and complete the work sheet for Racer Internet.
3. Prepare the income statement, statement of owner's equity, and classified balance sheet in report form.
4. Using the work sheet data that you prepared, journalize the closing entries and post the adjusting and closing entries to T-accounts. Use dates and show the ending balance of each account.
5. Prepare a postclosing trial balance.
6. Calculate the current and debt ratios for the company.

P4-34B *(L.OBJ. 2, 3)* **Journalizing adjusting and closing entries [45–60 min]**
The *unadjusted* trial balance and adjustment data of Myers Real Estate Appraisal Company at June 30, 2011, follow:

MYERS REAL ESTATE APPRAISAL COMPANY Unadjusted Trial Balance June 30, 2011		
Account Title	**Debit**	**Credit**
Cash	$ 4,000	
Accounts receivable	3,500	
Supplies	3,200	
Prepaid insurance	2,400	
Building	75,000	
Accumulated depreciation		$ 18,900
Land	14,000	
Accounts payable		19,500
Interest payable		8,900
Salary payable		600
K. Burns, Capital		31,700
K. Burns, Withdrawals	27,400	
Service revenue		97,900
Salary expense	32,200	
Depreciation expense	0	
Insurance expense	5,300	
Utilities expense	4,000	
Supplies expense	6,500	
Total	$ 177,500	$ 177,500

Adjustment data at June 30, 2011:

a. Prepaid insurance expired, $500
b. Accrued service revenue, $1,700
c. Accrued salary expense, $600
d. Depreciation for the year, $7,000
e. Supplies used during the year, $1,000

Requirements

1. Open T-accounts for Capital and all the accounts that follow on the trial balance. Insert their unadjusted balances. Also open a T-account for Income summary, which has a zero balance.
2. Journalize the adjusting entries and post to the accounts that you opened. Show the balance of each revenue account and each expense account.
3. Journalize the closing entries and post to the accounts that you opened. Draw double underlines under each account balance that you close to zero.
4. Compute the ending balance of Capital.

P4-35B *(L.OBJ. 2, 3)* **Journalizing adjusting and closing entries [20–30 min]**
The accountant for Daniel Ferguson, M.D., encountered the following situations while adjusting and closing the books at December 31. Consider each situation independently.

Requirements

1. The accountant failed to make the following adjusting entries at December 31: Compute the overall net income effect of these omissions.

   a. Accrued salary expense, $1,800
   b. Supplies expense, $600
   c. Accrued interest expense on a note payable, $800
   d. Depreciation of equipment, $900
   e. Earned service revenue that had been collected in advance, $2,400

2. Journalize each omitted adjusting entry identified.
3. What is the overall effect of the adjustments to net income?
4. Assume Withdrawals were $6,000 for the year. Prepare the entry to close the Withdrawals account.

P4-36B *(L. OBJ. 5, 6)* **Preparing a classified balance sheet in report form, and using the current and debt ratios to evaluate a company [30–40 min]**
Selected accounts of Blossom Irrigation Systems at December 31, 2011, follow:

Insurance expense	$ 500	Accounts payable	$34,000
Note payable, long-term	4,000	Accounts receivable	38,900
Other assets	1,900	Accumulated depreciation—building	44,900
Building	55,000	D. Bloomer, Capital	43,300
Prepaid insurance	4,600	Accumulated depreciation—	
Salary expense	16,400	equipment	7,800
Salary payable	4,100	Cash	11,000
Service revenue	72,900	Interest payable	600
Supplies	3,500	Equipment	25,400
Unearned service revenue	1,600		

Requirements

1. Prepare the company's classified balance sheet in report form at December 31, 2011.
2. Compute the company's current ratio and debt ratio at December 31, 2011. At December 31, 2010, the current ratio was 1.65 and the debt ratio was 0.43. Did its ability to pay debts improve or deteriorate, or did it remain the same during 2011?

■ Continuing Exercise

E4-37 This exercise continues the Sherman Lawn Service situation from Exercise 3-42 of Chapter 3. Start from the posted T-accounts and the adjusted trial balance for Sherman Lawn Service prepared for the company at August 31:

Requirements

1. Complete the accounting work sheet at August 31.
2. Journalize and post the closing entries at August 31. Denote each closing amount as *Clo* and an account balance as *Bal.*

■ Continuing Problem

P4-38 This problem continues the Haupt Consulting situation from Problem 3-43 of Chapter 3. Start from the posted T-accounts and the *adjusted* trial balance that Haupt Consulting prepared for the company at December 31:

HAUPT CONSULTING Adjusted Trial Balance December 31, 2010		
	Balance	
Account Title	Debit	Credit
Cash	$ 7,700	
Accounts receivable	1,500	
Supplies	100	
Equipment	2,000	
Accumulated depreciation—equipment		$ 33
Furniture	3,600	
Accumulated depreciation—furniture		60
Accounts payable		3,600
Salary payable		700
Unearned service revenue		600
Carl Haupt, Capital		10,000
Carl Haupt, Withdrawals	1,600	
Service revenue		3,200
Rent expense	500	
Utilities expense	300	
Salary expense	700	
Depreciation expense—equipment	33	
Depreciation expense—furniture	60	
Supplies expense	200	
Total	$18,193	$18,193

Requirements

1. Complete the accounting work sheet at December 31.
2. Journalize and post the closing entries at December 31. Denote each closing amount as *Clo* and an account balance as *Bal.*
3. Prepare a classified balance sheet at December 31.

■ Practice Set

Refer to the Practice Set data provided in Chapters 1, 2, and 3.

Requirements

1. Prepare an accounting work sheet.
2. Prepare an income statement, statement of owner's equity, and balance sheet using the report format.
3. Prepare closing entries for the month.
4. Prepare a postclosing trial balance.

Apply Your Knowledge

■ Decision Case

Decision Case 1 One year ago, Ralph Collins founded Collins Consignment Sales Company, and the business has prospered. Collins comes to you for advice. He wishes to know how much net income the business earned during the past year. The accounting records consist of the T-accounts in the ledger, which were prepared by an accountant who has moved. The accounts at December 31 follow:

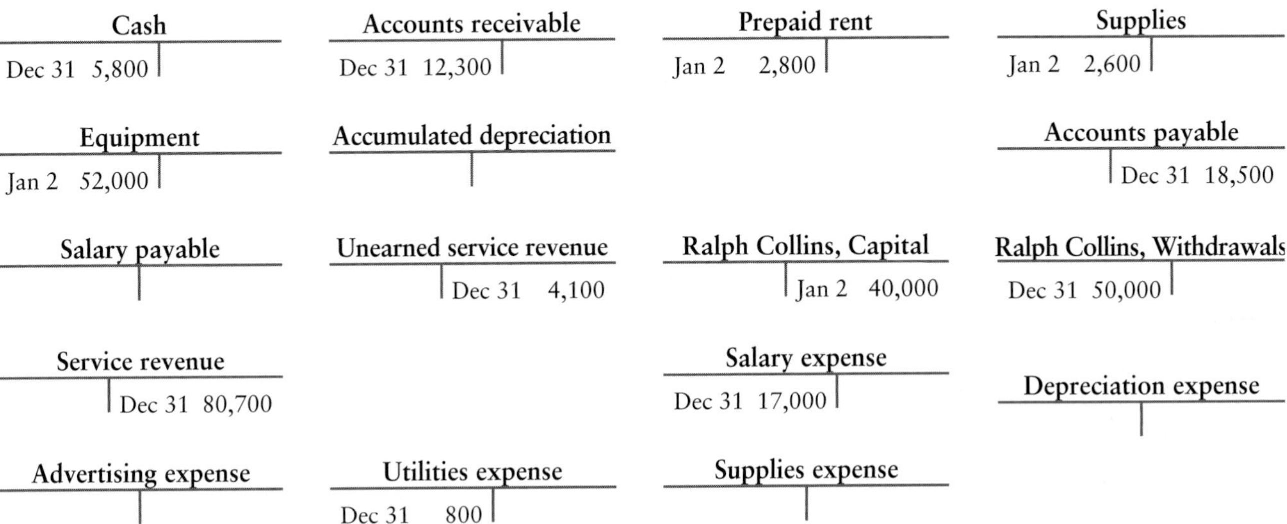

Collins indicates that, at year-end, customers owe him $1,000 accrued service revenue, which he expects to collect early next year. These revenues have not been recorded. During the year, he collected $4,100 service revenue in advance from customers, but the business has earned only $800 of that amount. Advertising expense for the year was $2,400, and he used up $2,100 of the supplies. Collins estimates that depreciation on equipment was $7,000 for the year. At December 31, he owes his employee $1,200 accrued salary. The owner made no investments during the year.

Collins expresses concern that withdrawals during the year might have exceeded the business's net income. To get a loan to expand the business, Collins must show the bank that the business's owner's equity has grown from its original $40,000 balance. Has it? You and Collins agree that you will meet again in one week.

Requirement

1. Prepare the financial statement that helps answer Collins's question. Can he expect to get the loan? Give your reason(s).

■ Ethical Issue

Link Back to Chapter 3 (Revenue Principle). Grant Film Productions wishes to expand and has borrowed $100,000. As a condition for making this loan, the bank requires that the store maintain a current ratio of at least 1.50.

Business has been good but not great. Expansion costs have brought the current ratio down to 1.40 at December 15. Rita Grant, owner of the business, is considering what might happen if she reports a current ratio of 1.40 to the bank. One course of action for Grant is to record in

December $10,000 of revenue that the business will earn in January of next year. The contract for this job has been signed.

Requirements

1. Journalize the revenue transaction, and indicate how recording this revenue in December would affect the current ratio.
2. Discuss whether it is ethical to record the revenue transaction in December. Identify the accounting principle relevant to this situation, and give the reasons underlying your conclusion.

■ Financial Statement Case

This case, based on the balance sheet of **Amazon.com** in Appendix A at the end of the book, will familiarize you with some of the assets and liabilities of that company. Use the **Amazon.com** balance sheet to answer the following questions.

Requirements

1. Which balance sheet format does **Amazon.com** use?
2. Name the company's largest current asset and largest current liability at December 31, 2007.
3. Compute **Amazon's** current ratios at December 31, 2007 and 2006. Did the current ratio improve, worsen, or hold steady during 2007?
4. Under what category does **Amazon** report furniture, fixtures, and equipment?
5. What was the cost of the company's fixed assets at December 31, 2007? What was the amount of accumulated depreciation? What was the book value of the fixed assets? See Note 3 for the data.

■ Team Project

Kathy Wintz formed a lawn service business as a summer job. To start the business on May 1, she deposited $1,000 in a new bank account in the name of the business. The $1,000 consisted of a $600 loan from Bank One and $400 of her own money. Wintz invested $400 of capital in the business. Wintz rented lawn equipment, purchased supplies, and hired other students to mow and trim customers' lawns.

At the end of each month, Wintz mailed bills to the customers. On August 31, she was ready to dissolve the business and return to college. Because she was so busy, she kept few records other than the checkbook and a list of receivables from customers.

At August 31, the business's checkbook shows a balance of $2,000, and customers still owe $750. During the summer, the business collected $5,500 from customers. The business checkbook lists payments for supplies totaling $400, and it still has gasoline, weed eater cord, and other supplies that cost a total of $50. The business paid employees $1,800 and still owes them $300 for the final week of the summer.

Wintz rented some equipment from Ludwig's Machine Shop. On May 1, the business signed a six-month lease on mowers and paid $600 for the full lease period. Ludwig's will refund the unused portion of the prepayment if the equipment is in good shape. In order to get the refund, Wintz has kept the mowers in excellent condition. In fact, the business had to pay $300 to repair a mower.

To transport employees and equipment to jobs, Wintz used a trailer that the business bought for $300. The business estimates that the summer's work used up one-third of the trailer's service potential. The business checkbook lists a payment of $500 for cash withdrawals during the summer. The business paid the loan back during August.

Requirements

1. Prepare the income statement and the statement of owner's equity of Wintz Lawn Service for the four months May through August.
2. Prepare the classified balance sheet of Wintz Lawn Service at August 31.
3. Was Wintz's summer work successful? Give the reason for your answer.

Quick Check Answers

1.*b* 2. *a* 3. b 4. *c* 5. *b* 6. *b* 7. *d* 8.*d* 9.*a* 10.*b*

For online homework, exercises, and problems that provide you immediate feedback, please visit www.myaccountinglab.com.

Appendix 4A

Reversing Entries: An Optional Step

Reversing entries are special journal entries that ease the burden of accounting for transactions in a later period. Reversing entries are the exact opposites of certain adjusting entries at the end of the prior period. Reversing entries are used most often in conjunction with accrual-type adjustments, such as accrued salary expense and accrued service revenue. *Generally accepted accounting principles do not require reversing entries. They are used only for convenience and to save time.*

Accounting for Accrued Expenses

To see how reversing entries work, return to Smart Touch Learning's unadjusted trial balance at May 31 (Exhibit 4-2). Salary expense has a debit balance of $900 for salaries paid during May. At May 31, the business still owes its employees an additional $900 for the last half of the month, so the business makes the following adjusting entry:

Adjusting Entries			
May 31	Salary expense (E+)	900	
	Salary payable (L+)		900

After posting, the accounts are updated at May 31:[1]

Salary payable

	May 31 Adj 900
	May 31 Bal 900

Salary expense

Paid during May 15 CP 900	
May 31 Adj 900	
May 31 Bal 1,800	

After the adjusting entry,

- The May income statement reports Salary expense of $1,800.
- The May 31 balance sheet reports Salary payable of $900.

The $1,800 debit balance of Salary expense is closed at May 31, 2011, with the following closing entry:

Closing Entries			
May 31	Income summary	1,800	
	Salary expense (E–)		1,800

[1]Entry explanations used throughout this discussion are
Adj = Adjusting entry
Bal = Balance
Clo = Closing entry
CP = Cash payment entry—a credit to Cash
CR = Cash receipt entry—a debit to Cash
Rev = Reversing entry

After posting the closing entries, Salary expense has a zero balance as follows:

Salary expense			
Paid during			
May 15 CP	900		
May 31 Adj	900		
May 31 Bal	1,800	May 31 Clo	1,800

Zero balance

Assume for this illustration that on June 1, the next payday, Smart Touch Learning will pay the $900 of salary payable left over from May 31. Smart Touch's next payroll payment will be $900.

Accounting Without a Reversing Entry

On June 1, the next payday, Smart Touch pays the payroll of $900 and makes the following journal entry:

Date	Accounts	Debit	Credit
Jun 1	Salary payable (L–)	900	
	Cash (A–)		900

This method of recording the cash payment is correct. However, it wastes time because Sheena Bright must refer back to the May 31 adjustments. Otherwise, she does not know the amount of the debit to Salary payable (in this example, $900). Searching May's adjusting entries wastes time and money. To save time, accountants can use reversing entries.

Making a Reversing Entry

A **reversing entry** switches the debit and the credit of a previous adjusting entry. *A reversing entry, then, is the exact opposite of a prior adjusting entry.* The reversing entry is dated the first day of the new period.

To illustrate reversing entries, recall that on May 31, Smart Touch made the following adjusting entry to accrue Salary payable:

Adjusting Entries			
May 31	Salary expense (E+)	900	
	Salary payable (L+)		900

The reversing entry just reverses the debit and the credit of the adjustment:

Reversing Entries			
Jun 1	Salary payable (L–)	900	
	Salary expense (E–)		900

Observe that the reversing entry is dated the first day of the new period. It is the exact opposite of the May 31 adjusting entry. Ordinarily, the accountant who makes the adjusting entry also prepares the reversing entry at the same time. Smart Touch dates the reversing entry as of June 1 so that it affects only the new period. Note how the accounts appear after Smart Touch posts the reversing entry:

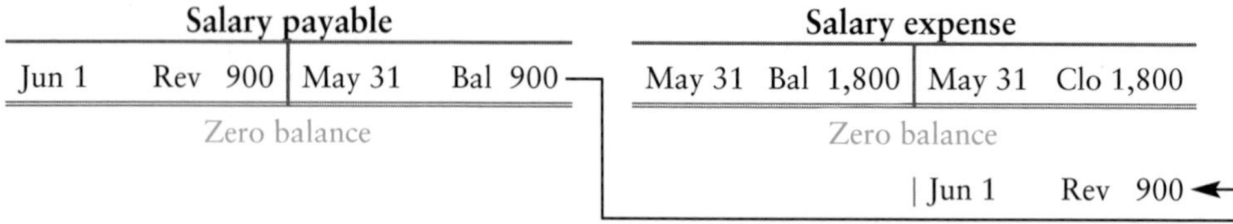

The arrow shows the transfer of the $900 credit balance from Salary payable to Salary expense. This credit balance in Salary expense does not mean that the entity has negative salary expense, as you might think. Instead, the odd credit balance in the Salary expense account is merely a temporary result of the reversing entry. The credit balance is eliminated on June 1, when Smart Touch pays the payroll and debits Salary expense:

Jun 1	Salary expense (E+)	900	
	Cash (A–)		900

This cash payment entry is posted as follows:

Salary expense					
Jun 1	CP	900	Jun 1	Rev	900
Jun 1	Bal	0			

Now Salary expense has its correct debit balance of $0, which is the amount of salary expense incurred in June as of the first. The $900 cash payment also pays the liability for Salary payable so that Salary payable has a zero balance, which is correct.

Appendix 4A Assignments

■Problem (Group A)

P4A-1A Journalizing reversing entries [20 min]
Refer to the data in Problem 4-25A.

Requirements

1. Open accounts for Salary payable and Salary expense. Insert their unadjusted balances at January 31, 2011.
2. Journalize adjusting entry (e) and the closing entry for Salary expense at January 31. Post to the accounts.
3. On February 5, Coyote Anvils paid the next payroll amount of $900. This payment included the accrued amount at January 31, plus $400 for the first few days of February. Journalize this cash payment, and post to the accounts. Show the balance in each account.

4. Using a reversing entry, repeat requirements 1–3. Compare the balances of Salary payable and Salary expense after using a reversing entry with those balances computed without the reversing entry (as they appear in your answer to requirement 3).

■ Problem (Group B)

P4A-2B Journalizing reversing entries [20 min]
Refer to the data in Problem 4-32B.

Requirements

1. Open accounts for Salary payable and Salary expense. Insert their unadjusted balances at July 31, 2011.
2. Journalize adjusting entry (e) and the closing entry for Salary expense at July 31. Post to the accounts.
3. On August 5, Wolfe Anvils paid the next payroll amount of $600. This payment included the accrued amount at July 31, plus $400 for the first few days of August. Journalize this cash payment, and post to the accounts. Show the balance in each account.
4. Using a reversing entry, repeat requirements 1–3. Compare the balances of Salary payable and Salary expense after using a reversing entry with those balances computed without the reversing entry (as they appear in your answer to requirement 3).

Comprehensive Problem for Chapters 1–4

Journalizing, Posting, Work Sheet, Adjusting, Closing the Financial Statements

Dwyer Delivery Service completed the following transactions during its first month of operations for January 2011:

a. **Dwyer Delivery Service began operations by receiving $5,000 cash and a truck valued at $10,000. The business gave owner's equity to aquire these assets.**

b. **Paid $200 cash for supplies.**

c. **Prepaid insurance, $600.**

d. **Performed delivery services for a customer and received $700 cash.**

e. **Completed a large delivery job, billed the customer $2,000, and received a promise to collect the $2,000 within one week.**

f. **Paid employee salary, $800.**

g. **Received $900 cash for performing delivery services.**

h. **Collected $500 in advance for delivery service to be performed later.**

i. **Collected $2,000 cash from a customer on account.**

j. **Purchased fuel for the truck, paying $100 with a company credit card. Credit Accounts payable.**

k. **Performed delivery services on account, $800.**

l. **Paid office rent, $500. This rent is not paid in advance.**

m. **Paid $100 on account.**

n. **Owner withdrew $1,900.**

Requirements

1. Record each transaction in the journal. Key each transaction by its letter. Explanations are not required.
2. Post the transactions that you recorded in requirement 1 in the T-accounts.

Cash	Service revenue
Accounts receivable	Salary expense
Supplies	Depreciation expense
Prepaid insurance	Insurance expense
Delivery truck	Fuel expense
Accumulated depreciation	Rent expense
Accounts payable	Supplies expense
Salary payable	
Unearned service revenue	
David Dwyer, Capital	
David Dwyer, Withdrawals	
Income summary	

3. Enter the trial balance in the work sheet for the month ended January 31, 2011. Complete the work sheet using the adjustment data given at January 31.
   a. Accrued salary expense, $800.
   b. Depreciation expense, $50.
   c. Prepaid insurance expired, $150.
   d. Supplies on hand, $100.
   e. Unearned service revenue earned during January, $400.
4. Prepare Dwyer Delivery Service's income statement and statement of owner's equity for the month ended January 31, 2011, and the classified balance sheet on that date. On the income statement list expenses in decreasing order by amount—that is, the largest expense first, the smallest expense last.
5. Journalize and post the adjusting entries beginning with o.
6. Journalize and post the closing entries.
7. Prepare a post-closing trial balance at January 31, 2011.

Chapter 4: Demo Doc

■ Accounting Work Sheets and Closing Entries

To make sure you understand this material, work through the following demonstration "demo doc" with detailed comments to help you see the concept within the framework of a worked-through problem.

Learning Objectives 1–3

This question continues on from the Cloud Break Consulting Demo Doc in Chapter 3.

Use the data from the adjusted trial balance of Cloud Break Consulting at June 30, 2011:

CLOUD BREAK CONSULTING **Adjusted Trial Balance** June 30, 2011		
Account Title	**Debit**	**Credit**
Cash	$131,000	
Accounts receivable	119,000	
Supplies	1,000	
Prepaid rent expense	18,000	
Land	45,000	
Building	300,000	
Accumulated depreciation—building		$167,000
Accounts payable		159,000
Salary payable		4,000
Unearned service revenue		10,000
Michael Moe, Capital		102,000
Michael Moe, Withdrawals	7,000	
Service revenue		495,000
Salary expense	259,000	
Supplies expense	3,000	
Rent expense	34,000	
Depreciation expense—building	12,000	
Miscellaneous expense	8,000	
Totals	$937,000	$937,000

Requirements

1. Prepare Cloud Break's accounting work sheet showing the adjusted trial balance, the income statement accounts, and the balance sheet accounts.

2. Journalize and post Cloud Break's closing entries.

Chapter 4: Demo Doc Solution

Requirement 1

Prepare Cloud Break's accounting work sheet showing the adjusted trial balance, the income statement accounts, and the balance sheet accounts.

Part 1	Part 2	Part 3	Part 4	Part 5	Demo Doc Complete

The accounting work sheet is very similar to the adjusted trial balance; however, the work sheet has additional debit and credit columns for the income statement and balance sheet.

CLOUD BREAK CONSULTING
Work Sheet
June 30, 2011

	Adjusted Trial Balance		Income Statement		Balance Sheet	
Account Title	Debit	Credit	Debit	Credit	Debit	Credit
Cash	131,000					
Accounts receivable	119,000					
Supplies	1,000					
Prepaid rent	18,000					
Land	45,000					
Building	300,000					
Accumulated depreciation—building		167,000				
Accounts payable		159,000				
Salary payable		4,000				
Unearned service revenue		10,000				
Michael Moe, Capital		102,000				
Michael Moe, Withdrawals	7,000					
Service revenue		495,000				
Salary expense	259,000					
Supplies expense	3,000					
Rent expense	34,000					
Depreciation expense—building	12,000					
Miscellaneous expense	8,000					
	937,000	937,000				

The accounts that belong on the income statement are put into the income statement columns and all other accounts are put into the balance sheet columns.

The income statement lists revenues and expenses. So Cloud Break's revenues (service revenues) and expenses (salary expense, supplies expense, rent expense, depreciation expense, and miscellaneous expense) are copied over to the income statement columns.

CLOUD BREAK CONSULTING
Work Sheet
June 30, 2011

	Adjusted Trial Balance		Income Statement		Balance Sheet	
Account Title	Debit	Credit	Debit	Credit	Debit	Credit
Cash	131,000					
Accounts receivable	119,000					
Supplies	1,000					
Prepaid rent	18,000					
Land	45,000					
Building	300,000					
Accumulated depreciation—building		167,000				
Accounts payable		159,000				
Salary payable		4,000				
Unearned service revenue		10,000				
Michael Moe, Capital		102,000				
Michael Moe, Withdrawals	7,000					
Service revenue		495,000		495,000		
Salary expense	259,000		259,000			
Supplies expense	3,000		3,000			
Rent expense	34,000		34,000			
Depreciation expense—building	12,000		12,000			
Miscellaneous expense	8,000		8,000			
	937,000	937,000	316,000	495,000		
Net income			179,000			
			495,000	495,000		

Net income is calculated by subtracting the expenses from the revenues, \$495,000 – \$316,000 = \$179,000. Notice that this is the same as net income from the income statement prepared in the Chapter 3 Demo Doc.

The other accounts (assets, liabilities, and equity) are now copied over to the balance sheet columns.

CLOUD BREAK CONSULTING
Work Sheet
June 30, 2011

Account Title	Adjusted Trial Balance Debit	Adjusted Trial Balance Credit	Income Statement Debit	Income Statement Credit	Balance Sheet Debit	Balance Sheet Credit
Cash	131,000				131,000	
Accounts receivable	119,000				119,000	
Supplies	1,000				1,000	
Prepaid rent	18,000				18,000	
Land	45,000				45,000	
Building	300,000				300,000	
Accumulated depreciation—building		167,000				167,000
Accounts payable		159,000				159,000
Salary payable		4,000				4,000
Unearned service revenue		10,000				10,000
Michael Moe, Capital		102,000				102,000
Michael Moe, Withdrawals	7,000				7,000	
Service revenue		495,000		495,000		
Salary expense	259,000		259,000			
Supplies expense	3,000		3,000			
Rent expense	34,000		34,000			
Depreciation expense—building	12,000		12,000			
Miscellaneous expense	8,000		8,000			
	937,000	937,000	316,000	495,000	621,000	442,000
Net income			179,000			179,000
			495,000	495,000	621,000	621,000

Net income is added to the credit side of the balance sheet to make total credits equal total debits. This is because net income increases Capital (and therefore equity) as seen in requirement 2 of this Demo Doc (where the closing entries are journalized).

Requirement 2

Journalize and post Cloud Break's closing entries.

Part 1	**Part 2**	Part 3	Part 4	Part 5	Demo Doc Complete

We prepare closing entries to (1) clear out the revenue, expense, and withdrawals accounts to a zero balance in order to get them ready for the next period—that is, they must begin the next period empty so that we can evaluate each period's earnings separately from other periods. We also need to (2) update the Michael Moe, Capital account by transferring all revenues, expenses, and withdrawals into it.

The Capital balance is calculated each year using the following formula:

Beginning Capital
+ Net income (or – Net loss)
– Withdrawals
Ending Capital

You can see this in the Capital T-account as well:

Capital	
	Beginning capital
	Net income
Withdrawals	
	Ending capital

This formula is the key to preparing the closing entries. We will use this formula, but we will do it *inside* the Capital T-account.

From the adjusted trial balance, we know that beginning Capital is $102,000. The first component of the formula is already in the T-account.

The next component is net income, which is *not* yet in the Capital account. There is no T-account with net income in it, but we can *create* one.

We will create a new T-account called *Income summary*. We will place in the Income summary account all the components of net income and come out with the net income number at the bottom. Remember:

Revenues – Expenses = Net income

This means that we need to get all of the revenues and expenses into the Income summary account.

Let us look at the Service revenue T-account:

Service revenue	
	Bal 495,000

In order to clear out all the income statement accounts so that they are empty to begin the next year, the first step is to debit each revenue account for the amount of its credit balance. Service revenue has a *credit* balance of $495,000, so to bring that to zero, we need to *debit* Service revenue for $495,000.

This means that we have part of our first closing entry:

1.		Service revenue (R–)	495,000	
		???		495,000

What is the credit side of this entry? The reason we were looking at Service revenue to begin with was to help calculate net income using the Income summary account. So the other side of the entry must go to the Income summary:

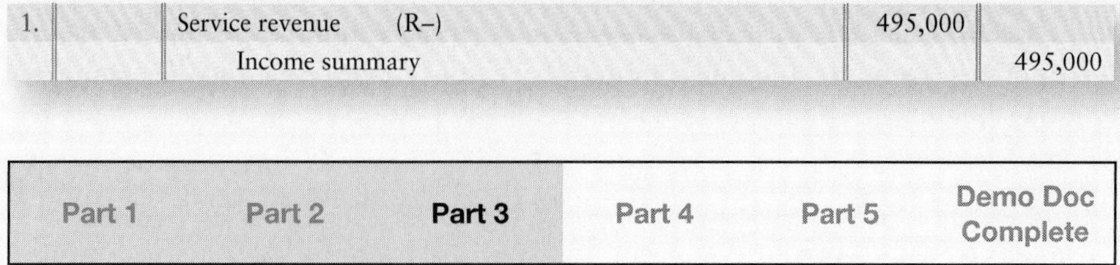

1.	Service revenue (R–)	495,000	
	Income summary		495,000

Part 1	Part 2	**Part 3**	Part 4	Part 5	Demo Doc Complete

The second step is to *credit* each expense account for the amount of its *debit* balance to bring each expense account to zero. In this case, we have five different expenses:

Salary expense

Bal	259,000	

Supplies expense

Bal	3,000	

Rent expense

Bal	34,000	

Depreciation expense—building

Bal	12,000	

Miscellaneous expense

Bal	8,000	

The sum of all the expenses will go to the debit side of the Income summary account:

2.	Income summary	316,000	
	Salary expense (E–)		259,000
	Supplies expense (E–)		3,000
	Rent expense (E–)		34,000
	Depreciation expense—building (E–)		12,000
	Miscellaneous expense (E–)		8,000

Part 1	Part 2	Part 3	**Part 4**	Part 5	Demo Doc Complete

Now let us look at the Income summary account:

Income summary

		1.	495,000
2.	316,000		
		Bal	179,000

Remember that the credit of $495,000 is from the first closing entry prepared at the beginning of this requirement.

The purpose of creating the Income summary was to get the net income number into a single account. Notice that the Income summary balance is the same net income number that appears on the income statement and in the accounting work sheet in requirement 1.

Income summary now has a *credit* balance of $179,000. The third step in the closing process is to transfer net income to the Capital account. To remove net income from the Income summary, we must *debit* the Income summary for $179,000:

3.	Income summary	179,000	
	???		179,000

What is the credit side of this entry? It is Michael Moe, Capital. The reason we created the (temporary) Income summary account was to help calculate the profit or loss for the Capital account. So the credit side of the entry must go to Capital:

3.	Income summary	179,000	
	Michael Moe, Capital (Q+)		179,000

This entry adds the net income to Capital. Notice that it also brings the Income summary account to a zero balance.

Part 1	Part 2	Part 3	Part 4	**Part 5**	Demo Doc Complete

The last component of the Capital formula is withdrawals. There is already a Withdrawal account:

Michael Moe, Withdrawals	
Bal 7,000	

The final step in the closing process is to transfer Michael Moe, Withdrawals to the debit side of the Michael Moe, Capital account. The Michael Moe, Withdrawals account has a *debit* balance of $7,000, so to bring that to zero, we need to *credit* Michael Moe, Withdrawals by $7,000. The balancing debit will go to Michael Moe, Capital:

4.	Michael Moe, Capital (Q–)	7,000	
	Michael Moe, Withdrawals (W–)		7,000

This entry subtracts withdrawals from the capital account.

Capital now holds the following data:

Michael Moe, Capital

			102,000	Beginning capital
		3.	179,000	Net income
4.	7,000			
		Bal	274,000	Ending capital

The formula to update Capital has now been re-created inside the Capital T-account.

The following accounts are included in the closing process:

Service revenue

			495,000
1.	495,000		
		Bal	0

Income summary

		1.	495,000
2.	316,000		
		Bal	179,000
3.	179,000		
		Bal	0

Salary expense

	259,000		
		2.	259,000
Bal	0		

Michael Moe, Withdrawals

	7,000		
		4.	7,000
Bal	0		

Supplies expense

	3,000		
		2.	3,000
Bal	0		

Michael Moe, Capital

			102,000
		3.	179,000
4.	7,000		
		Bal	274,000

Rent expense

	34,000		
		2.	34,000
Bal	0		

Depreciation expense—building

	12,000		
		2.	12,000
Bal	0		

Miscellaneous expense

	8,000		
		2.	8,000
Bal	0		

Notice that all the temporary accounts (the revenues, the expenses, withdrawals, and Income summary) now have a zero balance.

Part 1 | Part 2 | Part 3 | Part 4 | Part 5 | **Demo Doc Complete**

5 Merchandising Operations

Learning Objectives/ Success Keys

1. Describe and illustrate merchandising operations and the two types of inventory systems
2. Account for the purchase of inventory using a perpetual system
3. Account for the sale of inventory using a perpetual system
4. Adjust and close the accounts of a merchandising business
5. Prepare a merchandiser's financial statements
6. Use gross profit percentage and inventory turnover to evaluate a business

Chapters 1–4 began with Sherman Lawn Service and Greg's Groovy Tunes. Sherman Lawn Service and Greg's Groovy Tunes are similar. Both are sole proprietorships and they follow similar accounting procedures.

Greg Moore's music business differs from the lawn service of Hannah Sherman in one important way. Sherman provides a service for customers, whereas Moore sells both services and products—event music services and CDs. Businesses that sell a product are called **merchandisers** because they sell merchandise, or goods, to customers.

In Chapters 1–4, we accounted for service companies, such as Sherman Lawn Service and Smart Touch Learning. That enabled us to focus on basic accounting:

- Recording transactions
- Adjusting and closing the books
- Preparing the financial statements

These aspects of accounting are the same for service and merchandising entities.

Merchandisers have an additional asset—merchandise inventory—that service companies do not need. (We usually drop the term *merchandise* and refer simply to *inventory*.) **Inventory** is defined as the merchandise that a company holds for sale to customers. For example, Greg's Groovy Tunes must hold some CD inventory in order to operate. **Wal-Mart** carries food inventory in addition to clothing, housewares, and school supplies. A **Hummer** dealer holds inventories of automobiles and auto parts.

Chapter 5 introduces accounting for merchandisers. In this chapter we show how to account for the purchase and sale of inventory. Smart Touch Learning has decided to discontinue its service business and, instead, plans to sell tutorial CDs that it will purchase from various vendors. We will continue to feature Smart Touch Learning. However, with its change in business strategy, it is now considered to be a merchandiser. By continuing the same company with a different business strategy in the examples, we will give you a basis for comparison between service and merchandising businesses.

As a starting point, let us compare service entities, with which you are familiar, to merchandising companies. Exhibit 5-1 on the following page shows how a service entity (on the left) differs from a merchandiser (on the right).

EXHIBIT 5-1 | **Financial Statements of a Service Company and a Merchandiser**

SERVICE CO.* Balance Sheet June 30, 2010		MERCHANDISING CO.** Balance Sheet June 30, 2010	
Assets		**Assets**	
Current assets:		Current assets:	
Cash	$X	Cash	$X
Short-term investments	X	Short-term investments	X
Accounts receivable, net	X	Accounts receivable, net	X
Prepaid expenses	X	Inventory	X
		Prepaid expenses	X

*Such as Sherman Lawn Service

**Such as Greg's Groovy Tunes

SERVICE CO. Income Statement Year Ended June 30, 2010		MERCHANDISING CO. Income Statement Year Ended June 30, 2010	
Service revenue	$XXX	Sales revenue	$X,XXX
Expenses:		Cost of goods sold	X
Salary expense	X	Gross profit	XXX
Depreciation expense	X	Operating expenses:	
Rent expense	X	Salary expense	X
Net income	$ X	Depreciation expense	X
		Rent expense	X
		Net income	$ X

What Are Merchandising Operations?

1 Describe and illustrate merchandising operations and the two types of inventory systems

Merchandising consists of buying and selling products rather than services. Merchandisers have some new balance sheet and income statement items.

Balance Sheet:

- Inventory, an asset

Income Statement:

- Sales revenue (often abbreviated as Sales)
- Cost of goods sold, an expense

These items are highlighted in Exhibit 5-1 for Merchandising Co. Let us examine the operating cycle of a merchandising business.

The Operating Cycle of a Merchandising Business

The operating cycle of a merchandiser (see Exhibit 5-2):

1. It begins when the company purchases inventory from a **vendor**.
2. The company then sells the inventory to a **customer**.
3. Finally, the company collects cash from customers.

EXHIBIT 5-2 | **Operating Cycle of a Merchandiser**

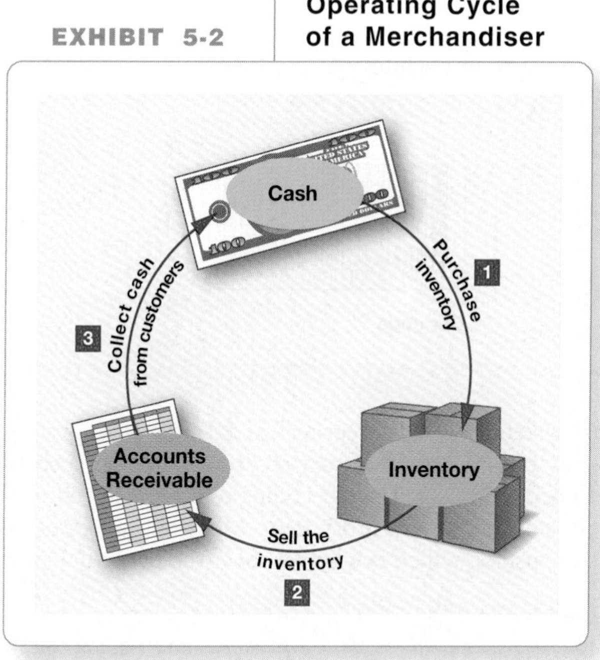

Now let us see how companies account for their inventory. We begin with journal entries. Then we post to the ledger accounts and, finally, prepare the financial statements.

Inventory Systems: Perpetual and Periodic

There are two main types of inventory accounting systems:

- Perpetual system
- Periodic system

The **perpetual inventory system** keeps a running record of inventory and cost of goods sold—that is, the inventory is perpetually (constantly) updated. This system achieves better control over the inventory. Even in a perpetual system, the business must count inventory at least once a year. The physical count captures inventory transactions that are not captured by the electronic system (such as misplaced, stolen, or damaged inventory). The count establishes the correct amount of ending inventory for the financial statements and also serves as a check on the perpetual records.

The **periodic inventory system** is normally used for relatively inexpensive goods. A convenience store without optical-scanning cash registers does not keep a running record of every loaf of bread and every key chain that it sells. Instead, the business counts its inventory periodically to determine the quantities on hand. Restaurants and small retail stores also use the periodic system. Appendix 5B covers the periodic system, which is becoming less and less popular with the use of computers.

Perpetual Inventory Systems

A modern perpetual inventory system records the following:

- Units purchased
- Units sold
- The quantity of inventory on hand

Inventory and purchasing systems are integrated with accounts receivable and sales. For example, **Target's** computers use bar codes to keep up-to-the-minute records and show the current inventory at any time.

Bar code

In a perpetual system, the "cash register" at a **Target** store is a computer terminal that records sales and updates inventory records. Bar codes such as the one illustrated here are scanned by a laser. The bar coding represents inventory and cost data that keep track of each unique inventory item. Most businesses use bar codes and computerized cash registers, which is why we cover the perpetual system.

Accounting for Inventory in the Perpetual System

2 Account for the purchase of inventory using a perpetual system

The cycle of a merchandising entity begins with the purchase of inventory. In this section, we trace the steps that Smart Touch Learning takes to account for inventory. Smart Touch plans to sell CDs and DVDs that it purchases from **RCA**.

1. **RCA** ships the CD and DVD inventory to Smart Touch and sends an invoice the same day. The **invoice** is the seller's (**RCA's**) request for payment from the buyer (Smart Touch). An invoice is also called a *bill*. Exhibit 5-3 is the purchase invoice that Smart Touch receives from **RCA**.
2. After the inventory is received, Smart Touch pays **RCA**.

Purchase of Inventory

Here we use the actual invoice in Exhibit 5-3 to illustrate the purchasing process. Suppose Smart Touch receives the goods on June 3, 2011. Smart Touch records this purchase on account as follows:

Date	Accounts	Debit	Credit
Jun 3	Inventory (A+)	700	
	Accounts payable (L+)		700
	Purchased inventory on account.		

The Inventory account, an asset, is used only for goods purchased that Smart Touch intends to resell to customers. Supplies, equipment, and other assets are recorded in their own accounts. Recall that Inventory is an asset until it is sold.

Purchase Discounts

Many businesses offer customers a discount for early payment. This is called a **Purchase discount**. RCA's **credit terms** of "3%/15, NET 30 DAYS" mean that Smart Touch may deduct 3% from the total bill if the customer pays within 15 days of the invoice date. Otherwise, the full amount—NET—is due in 30 days. These credit terms can also be expressed as "3/15, n/30."

EXHIBIT 5-3 | **Purchase Invoice**

1

RCA®

RCA SOUTHWEST BRANCH
P.O. BOX 101010
HOUSTON, TX 77212

3

Invoice	
Date	Number
6/1/11	410

2

Shipped To: SMART TOUCH LEARNING
281 WAVE AVE
NICEVILLE, FL 32578

4

Credit Terms
3% 15, NET 30 DAYS

	Description		Quantity Shipped	Unit Price	Total
	Boxes—DVD		100	$ 6.00	$600.00
	Windows CDs—Case		1	100.00	100.00
				6 Pd.	6/15/11

Due Date & Due Amount			
06/15/11			
$679 00			

7

Sub Total	$700.00
Ship. or Handl. Chg.	–
Tax (3%)	–
Total(s)	$700.00

5

Explanations:

1 The seller is RCA.

2 The purchaser is Smart Touch Learning.

3 The invoice date is needed to determine whether the purchaser gets a discount for prompt payment (see 4).

4 Credit terms: If Smart Touch pays within 15 days of the invoice date, it may deduct a 3% discount. Otherwise, the full amount—NET—is due in 30 days.

5 Total invoice amount is $700.

6 Smart Touch's payment date. How much did Smart Touch pay? (See 7.)

7 Payment occurred 14 days after the invoice date—within the discount period—so Smart Touch paid $679 ($700 – 3% discount).

Terms of "n/30" mean that no discount is offered and payment is due 30 days after the invoice date. Terms of *eom* mean that payment is due at the end of the current month.

If Smart Touch pays within the discount period, the cash payment entry would be

Jun 15	Accounts payable (L–)	700	
	Cash ($700 × 0.97) (A–)		679
	Inventory ($700 × 0.03) (A–)		21
	Paid within discount period.		

The discount is credited to Inventory because the discount for early payment decreases the actual cost paid for Inventory, as shown in the T-account:

Inventory			
Jun 3	700	Jun 15	21
Bal	679		

Notice that the balance in the Inventory account, $679, is exactly what was paid for the Inventory on June 15, 2011.

But if Smart Touch pays this invoice after the discount period, Smart Touch must pay the full $700. In that case, the payment entry is

Date	Accounts and Explanation	Debit	Credit
Jun 24	Accounts payable (L–)	700	
	Cash (A–)		700
	Paid after discount period.		

Purchase Returns and Allowances

Businesses allow customers to return merchandise that is defective, damaged, or otherwise unsuitable. This is called a **purchase return**. Alternately, the seller may deduct an allowance from the amount the buyer owes. **Purchase allowances** are granted to the purchaser as an incentive to keep goods that are not "as ordered." Together, **purchase returns and allowances** decrease the buyer's cost of the inventory.

Assume that Smart Touch has not yet paid for the original invoice of June 3. Suppose a case of Windows CDs purchased on that invoice (Exhibit 5-3) was damaged in shipment. Smart Touch returns the goods (CDs, in this case) to **RCA** and records the purchase return as follows:

Date	Accounts and Explanation	Debit	Credit
Jun 4	Accounts payable (L–)	100	
	Inventory (A–)		100
	Returned inventory to seller.		

The exact same entry is made for an allowance granted. The only difference between a return and an allowance is that, in the case of the allowance, Smart Touch keeps the Inventory. See Exhibit 5-4 for a copy of the allowance granted.

Transportation Costs

Someone must pay the transportation cost of shipping inventory from seller to buyer. The purchase agreement specifies FOB terms (**free on board**) to determine when title to the good transfers to the purchaser and who usually pays the freight. Exhibit 5-5 shows that:

- **FOB shipping point** means buyer takes ownership (title) to the goods at the shipping point. The buyer also pays the freight.
- **FOB destination** means the buyer takes ownership (title) at the delivery destination point. In that case, the seller usually pays the freight.

Freight costs are either freight in or freight out.

- **Freight in** is the transportation cost to ship goods IN the warehouse; thus, it is freight on *purchased goods*.
- **Freight out** is the transportation cost to ship goods OUT of the warehouse; thus, it is freight on *goods sold*.

EXHIBIT 5-4 | Purchase Allowance

1

RCA SOUTHWEST BRANCH
P.O. BOX 101010
HOUSTON, TX 77212

3

Credit memo	
Date	Number
6/4/11	410C

2

Shipped To: SMART TOUCH LEARNING
281 WAVE AVE.
NICEVILLE, FL 32578

4

Credit Terms
3% 15, NET 30 DAYS

	Description		Quantity Shipped	Unit Price	Total
	Windows CD Case		<1>	$100.00	($100.00)

Due Date & Due Amount

Sub Total	($100.00)
Ship. or Handl. Chg.	–
Tax (3%)	–
Total(s)	($100.00)

5

Explanations:

1 The seller is RCA.

2 The purchaser is Smart Touch Learning.

3 The date the allowance was granted.

4 Credit terms are repeated here.

5 Total allowance is $100.

EXHIBIT 5-5 | FOB Terms Determine Who Pays the Freight

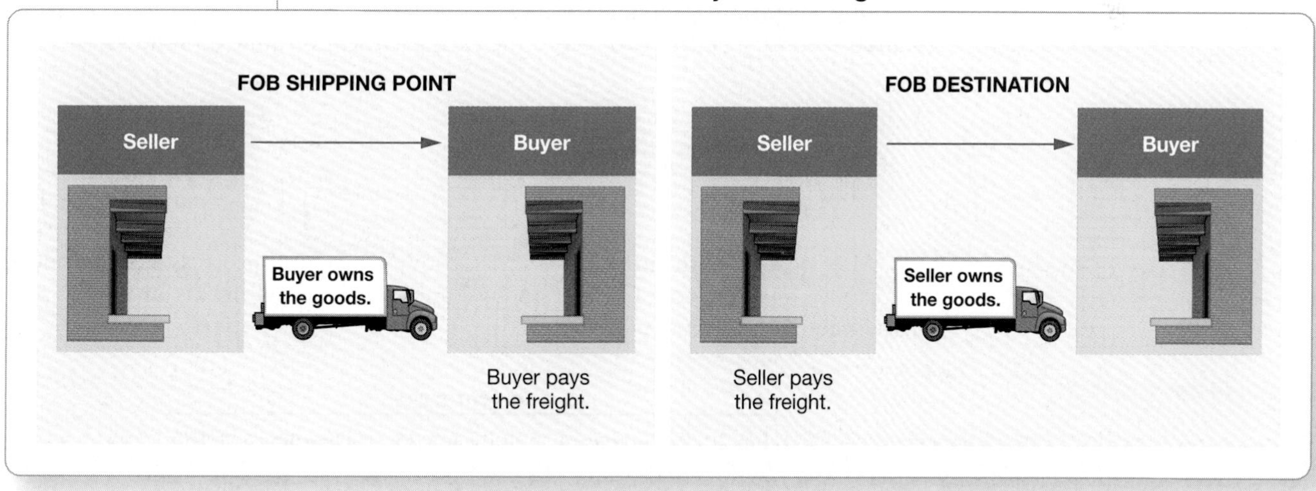

Freight In FOB shipping point is most common. The buyer owns the goods while they are in transit, so the buyer pays the freight. Because paying the freight is a cost that must be paid to acquire the Inventory, Freight in becomes part of the cost of inventory. As a result, freight in costs are debited to the Inventory account. Suppose Smart Touch pays a $60 freight charge and makes the following entry:

Jun 3	Inventory (A+)	60	
	Cash (A–)		60
	Paid a freight bill.		

The freight charge increases the net cost of the inventory to $660, as follows:

Inventory

Jun 3	Purchase	700	Jun 4	Return	100
Jun 3	Freight in	60			
Bal	Net cost	660			

Discounts are computed only on the account payable to the seller, in this case $600. Discounts are not computed on the transportation costs, because there is no discount on freight.

Under FOB shipping point, the seller sometimes prepays the transportation cost as a convenience and lists this cost on the invoice. Assume, for example, Greg's Groovy Tunes makes a $5,000 purchase of goods, coupled with a related freight charge of $400, on June 20 on terms of 3/5, n/30. The purchase would be recorded as follows:

Jun 20	Inventory ($5,000 + $400) (A+)	5,400	
	Accounts payable (L+)		5,400
	Purchased inventory on account, including freight.		

If Greg's Groovy Tunes pays within the discount period, the discount will be computed only on the $5,000 merchandise cost, not on the total invoice of $5,400. The $400 freight is not eligible for the discount. So, the 3% discount would be $150 ($5,000 × 0.03). The entry to record the early payment on June 25 follows:

Jun 25	Accounts payable (L–)	5,400	
	Inventory ($5,000 × 3%) (A–)		150
	Cash (A–)		5,250

After posting both entries to Greg's Groovy Tunes' Inventory T-account below, you can see that the cost Greg's Groovy Tunes has invested in this Inventory purchase is equal to the cost paid of $5,250.

Inventory

Jun 20	Purchase	5,400	Jun 25	Discount	150
Bal	Net cost	5,250			

Freight Out As noted above, a freight out expense is one in which the seller pays freight charges to ship goods to customers. Freight out is a delivery expense to the seller. Delivery expense is an operating expense and is debited to the Delivery expense account.

Summary of Purchase Returns and Allowances, Discounts, and Transportation Costs

Suppose Smart Touch buys $35,000 of Inventory, takes a 2% early payment discount, and returns $700 of the goods. Smart Touch also pays $2,100 of freight in. The following summary shows Smart Touch's net cost of this inventory. All amounts are assumed for this illustration.

Purchases of inventory								Net cost of inventory
Inventory	−	Purchase returns and allowances	−	Purchase discounts*	+	Freight in	=	Inventory
$35,000	−	$700	−	$686	+	$2,100	=	$35,714

Inventory

Purchases of inventory	35,000	Purchase returns & allow.	700
Freight in	2,100	Purchase discount	686*
Balance	35,714		

*Purchase discount of $686 = [Purchases $35,000 − Purchase Returns $700) × .02 discount]

Stop & Think...

The Inventory account in the perpetual system is really a "catch-all" account. It captures the net amount invested in goods available to sell. The debits to the account represent either a physical increase in the amount of goods on hand (purchases), an increase in the cost per unit (as in Freight in) or both. Conversely, the credits to the Inventory account represent either a physical decrease in the amount of goods on hand (goods sold or returned) or a decrease in the cost per unit (an allowance granted or a discount for early payment).

Sale of Inventory

3 Account for the sale of inventory using a perpetual system

After a company buys inventory, the next step is to sell the goods. We shift now to the selling side and follow Smart Touch Learning through a sequence of selling transactions.

The amount a business earns from selling merchandise inventory is called **Sales revenue** (often abbreviated as **Sales**). A sale also creates an expense, Cost of goods sold, as the seller gives up the asset Inventory. **Cost of goods sold** is the cost of inventory that has been sold to customers. Cost of goods sold (often abbreviated as **Cost of sales**) is the merchandiser's major expense.

After making a sale on account, Smart Touch may experience any of the following:

- *A sales return:* The customer may return goods to Smart Touch.
- *A sales allowance:* Smart Touch may grant a sales allowance to entice the customer to accept non-standard goods. This allowance will reduce the cash to be collected from the customer.
- *A sales discount:* If the customer pays within the discount period—under terms such as 2/10, n/30—Smart Touch collects the discounted amount.
- *Freight out:* Smart Touch may have to pay delivery expense to transport the goods to the buyer.

Let us begin with a cash sale.

Cash Sale

Sales of retailers, such as Smart Touch and Greg's Groovy Tunes, are often for cash. Suppose Smart Touch made a $3,000 cash sale on June 9, 2011, to a customer and issued the sales invoice in Exhibit 5-6.

EXHIBIT 5-6 | Sales Invoice

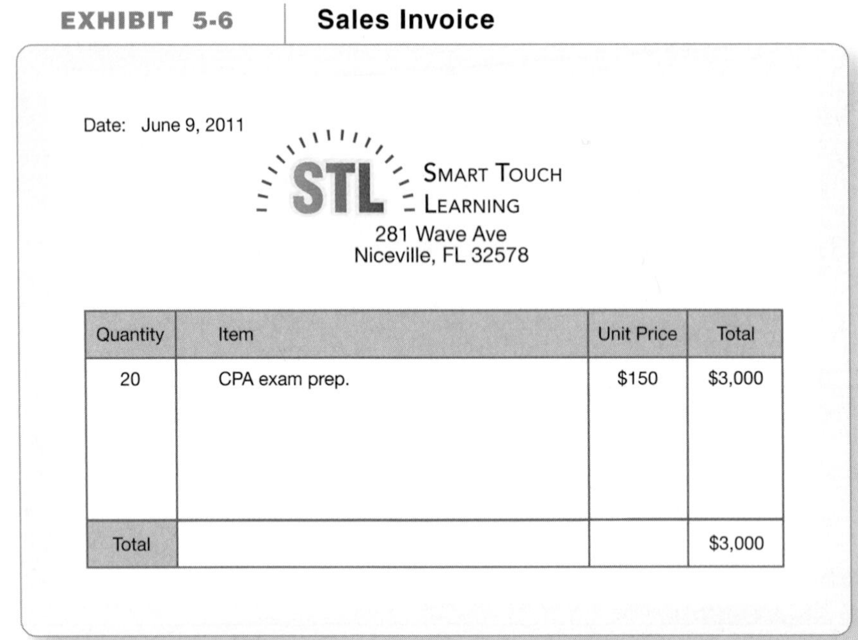

Date: June 9, 2011

STL SMART TOUCH LEARNING
281 Wave Ave
Niceville, FL 32578

Quantity	Item	Unit Price	Total
20	CPA exam prep.	$150	$3,000
Total			$3,000

Cash sales of $3,000 are recorded by debiting Cash and crediting Sales revenue as follows:

Jun 9	Cash (A+)	3,000	
	Sales revenue (R+)		3,000
	Cash sale.		

Smart Touch sold goods. Therefore a second journal entry must also be made to decrease the Inventory balance. Suppose these goods cost Smart Touch $1,900. The second journal entry will transfer the $1,900 to Cost of the goods sold from the Inventory account, as follows:

Jun 9	Cost of Goods Sold (E+)	1,900	
	Inventory (A–)		1,900
	Recorded the cost of goods sold.		

The Cost of goods sold account keeps a current balance throughout the period. In this example, Cost of goods sold is $1,900 (the cost to Smart Touch) rather than $3,000, the selling price (retail) of the goods. *Cost of goods sold is always based on the entity's cost, not the selling price.*

Inventory			
Bal	35,714	Cost of sales	1,900

↔

Cost of goods sold			
Jun 9	1,900		

The computer automatically records the Cost of goods sold entry. The cashier scans the bar code on the product and the computer performs this task.

Sale on Account

Most sales in the United States are made on account (on credit). Now, let us assume that Smart Touch made a $5,000 sale on account on terms of n/10 (no discount offered) for goods that cost $2,900. The entries to record the sale and cost of goods sold follow:

Jun 11	Accounts receivable (A+)	5,000	
	Sales revenue (R+)		5,000
	Sale on account.		

Jun 11	Cost of goods sold (E+)	2,900	
	Inventory (A–)		2,900
	Recorded the cost of goods sold.		

When Smart Touch receives the cash, it records the cash receipt on account as follows:

Jun 19	Cash (A+)	5,000	
	Accounts Receivable (A–)		5,000
	Collection on account.		

Sales Discounts and Sales Returns and Allowances

We saw that purchase returns and allowances and purchase discounts decrease the cost of inventory purchases. In the same way, **sales returns and allowances** and **sales discounts** decrease the net amount of revenue earned on sales. Sales returns and allowances and Sales discounts are contra accounts to Sales revenue. Recall that a contra account has the opposite normal balance of its companion account. So, Sales returns and allowances and Sales discounts both have normal debit balances.

Sales revenue − Sales returns and allowances − Sales discounts = Net sales revenue[1]

Companies maintain separate accounts for Sales discounts and Sales returns and allowances so they can track these items separately. **Net Sales revenue** is calculated as: Net Sales revenue = Sales revenue – Sales returns and allowances – Sales discounts.

Now let us examine a sequence of Greg's Groovy Tunes sale transactions. Assume Greg's Groovy Tunes is selling to Smart Touch. On July 7, 2011, Greg's Groovy Tunes sells CDs for $7,200 on credit terms of 2/10, n/30. These goods cost

[1]Often abbreviated as Net sales.

Greg's Groovy Tunes $4,700. Greg's Groovy Tunes' entries to record this credit sale and the related cost of goods sold follow:

Jul 7	Accounts receivable (A+)	7,200	
	Sales revenue (R+)		7,200
	Sale on account.		
7	Cost of goods sold (E+)	4,700	
	Inventory (A–)		4,700
	Recorded cost of goods sold.		

Sales Returns Assume that on July 12, 2011, the customer returns $600 of the goods. Greg's Groovy Tunes, the seller, records the sales return as follows:

Jul 12	Sales returns and allowances (CR+)	600	
	Accounts receivable (A–)		600
	Received returned goods.		

Accounts receivable decreases because Greg's Groovy Tunes will not collect cash for the returned goods.

Greg's Groovy Tunes receives the returned merchandise and updates its inventory records. Greg's Groovy Tunes must also decrease Cost of goods sold as follows (the returned goods cost $400):

Jul 12	Inventory (A+)	400	
	Cost of goods sold (E–)		400
	Placed goods back in inventory.		

Sales Allowances Suppose on July 15 Greg's Groovy Tunes grants a $100 sales allowance for goods damaged in transit. A sales allowance is recorded as follows:

Jul 15	Sales returns and allowances (CR+)	100	
	Accounts receivable (A–)		100
	Granted a sales allowance for damaged goods.		

There is no inventory entry for a sales allowance because the seller receives no returned goods from the customer.

After these entries are posted, Accounts receivable has a $6,500 debit balance, as follows:

Accounts receivable

Jul 7	Sale	7,200	Jul 12	Return	600
			15	Allowance	100
Bal		6,500			

Sales Discounts On July 17, the last day of the discount period, Greg's Groovy Tunes collects this receivable. Assuming no freight is included in the invoice, the business's cash receipt is \$6,370 [\$6,500 – (\$6,500 × 0.02)], and the collection entry is

Jul 17	Cash (A+)	6,370	
	Sales discounts (\$6,500 × 0.02) (CR+)	130	
	Accounts receivable (A–)		6,500
	Cash collection within the discount period.		

Now, Greg's Groovy Tunes' Accounts receivable balance is zero:

Accounts receivable					
Jul 7	Sale	7,200	Jul 12	Return	600
			15	Allowance	100
			17	Collection	6,500
Bal		–0–			

Sales Revenue, Cost of Goods Sold, and Gross Profit

Net sales, cost of goods sold, and gross profit are key elements of profitability. Net sales revenue minus Cost of goods sold is called **Gross profit,** or **Gross margin.** You could also think of gross profit as the mark-up on the inventory.

Net sales – Cost of goods sold = Gross profit

Gross profit, along with net income, is a measure of business success. A sufficiently high gross profit is vital to a merchandiser.

The following example will clarify the nature of gross profit. Suppose Greg's Groovy Tunes' cost to purchase a CD is \$15 and it sells the same CD for \$20. Greg's Groovy Tunes' gross profit for each CD is \$5, computed as follows:

Sales revenue earned by selling one CD	\$ 20
Less: Cost of goods sold for the CD (what the CD cost)	(15)
Gross profit on the sale of one CD	\$ 5

The gross profit reported on Greg's Groovy Tunes' income statement is the sum of the gross profits on the CDs and all the other products the company sold during the year.

Let us put into practice what you have learned in the first half of this chapter.

Summary Problem 1

Suppose Heat Miser Air Conditioner Company engaged in the following transactions during June of the current year:

Jun	3	Purchased inventory on credit terms of 1/10 net eom (end of month), $1,600.
	9	Returned 40% of the inventory purchased on June 3. It was defective.
	12	Sold goods for cash, $920 (cost, $550).
	15	Purchased goods for $5,000. Credit terms were 3/15, net 30.
	16	Paid a $260 freight bill on goods purchased.
	18	Sold inventory for $2,000 on credit terms of 2/10, n/30 (cost, $1,180).
	22	Received returned goods from the customer of the June 18 sale, $800 (cost, $480).
	24	Borrowed money from the bank to take advantage of the discount offered on the June 15 purchase. Signed a note payable to the bank for the net amount, $4,850.
	24	Paid supplier for goods purchased on June 15, less the discount.
	28	Received cash in full settlement of the account from the customer who purchased inventory on June 18, less the return on June 22, and less the discount.
	29	Paid the amount owed on account from the purchase of June 3, less the June 9 return.

Requirements

1. Journalize the preceding transactions. Explanations are not required.
2. Set up T-accounts and post the journal entries to show the ending balances in the Inventory and the Cost of goods sold accounts only.
3. Assume that the note payable signed on June 24 requires the payment of $90 interest expense. Was borrowing funds to take the cash discount a wise or unwise decision? What was the net savings or cost of the decision?

Solution

Requirement 1

Date	Accounts	Debit	Credit
Jun 3	Inventory (A+)	1,600	
	Accounts payable (L+)		1,600
9	Accounts payable ($1,600 × 0.40) (L–)	640	
	Inventory (A–)		640
12	Cash (A+)	920	
	Sales revenue (R+)		920
12	Cost of goods sold (E+)	550	
	Inventory (A–)		550
15	Inventory (A+)	5,000	
	Accounts payable (L+)		5,000
16	Inventory (A+)	260	
	Cash (A–)		260
18	Accounts receivable (A+)	2,000	
	Sales revenue (R+)		2,000
18	Cost of goods sold (E+)	1,180	
	Inventory (A–)		1,180
22	Sales returns and allowances (CR+)	800	
	Accounts receivable (A–)		800
22	Inventory (A+)	480	
	Cost of goods sold (E–)		480
24	Cash (A+)	4,850	
	Note payable (L+)		4,850
24	Accounts payable (L–)	5,000	
	Inventory ($5,000 × 0.03) (A–)		150
	Cash ($5,000 × 0.97) (A–)		4,850
28	Cash [($2,000 – $800) × 0.98] (A+)	1,176	
	Sales discounts [($2,000 – $800) × 0.02) (CR+)	24	
	Accounts receivable ($2,000 – $800) (A–)		1,200
29	Accounts payable ($1,600 – $640) (L–)	960	
	Cash (A–)		960

Requirement 2

Inventory

	Debit		Credit
Jun 3	1,600	Jun 9	640
15	5,000	12	550
16	260	18	1,180
22	480	24	150
Bal	4,820		

Cost of goods sold

	Debit		Credit
Jun 12	550	Jun 22	480
18	1,180		
Bal	1,250		

Requirement 3

Heat Miser's decision to borrow funds was wise because the discount received ($150) exceeded the interest paid ($90). Thus, Heat Miser Air Conditioner Company was $60 better off.

Adjusting and Closing the Accounts of a Merchandiser

4 Adjust and close the accounts of a merchandising business

A merchandiser adjusts and closes accounts the same way a service entity does. If a work sheet is used, the trial balance is entered, and the work sheet is completed to determine net income or net loss.

Adjusting Inventory Based on a Physical Count

The inventory account should stay current at all times in a perpetual inventory system. However, the actual amount of inventory on hand may differ from what the books show. Theft, damage, and errors occur. For this reason, businesses take a physical count of inventory *at least* once a year. The most common time to count inventory is at the end of the year. The business then adjusts the Inventory account based on the physical count.

Greg's Groovy Tunes' Inventory account shows an unadjusted balance of $40,500.

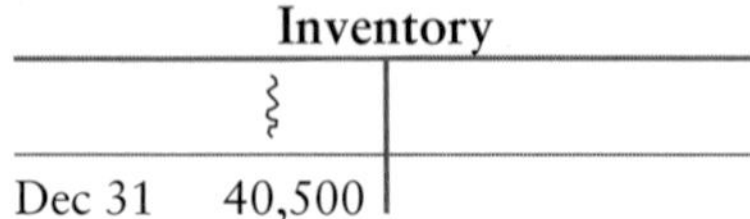

With no shrinkage—due to theft or error—the business should have inventory costing $40,500. But on December 31, Smart Touch counts the inventory on hand, and the total cost comes to only $40,200.

Inventory balance before adjustment	–	Actual inventory on hand	=	Adjusting entry to inventory
$40,500	–	$40,200	=	Credit of $300

Smart Touch records this adjusting entry for inventory shrinkage:

Date	Accounts and Explanation	Debit	Credit
Dec 31	Cost of goods sold (E+)	300	
	Inventory ($40,500 – $40,200) (A–)		300
	Adjustment for inventory shrinkage.		

This entry brings Inventory to its correct balance.

Inventory			
Dec 31 Bal	40,500	Dec 31 Adj	300
Dec 31 Adj Bal	40,200		

Other adjustments, plus a complete merchandising work sheet, are covered in Appendix 5A at the end of this chapter.

Stop & Think...

Consider the amount of goods a company has available for sale. At the end of the period, the total spent for those items can only appear in two accounts: Inventory (asset) or Cost of goods sold (expense). So what happens to the goods that are missing or damaged? This is considered a cost of doing business and those values are "buried" in the Cost of goods sold amount, rather than shown in a separate account in the ledger.

Closing the Accounts of a Merchandiser

Exhibit 5-7 presents Greg's Groovy Tunes' closing entries for December, which are similar to those in Chapter 4, except for the new accounts (highlighted in color). *All amounts are assumed* for this illustration.

EXHIBIT 5-7 Closing Entries for a Merchandiser—Amounts Assumed

Journal

Closing Entries

	Date	Accounts	Debit	Credit
1.	Dec 31	Sales revenue (R–)	169,300	
		Income summary		169,300
2.	31	Income summary	116,200	
		Sales discounts (CR–)		1,400
		Sales returns and allowances (CR–)		2,000
		Cost of goods sold (E–)		90,800
		Wage expense (E–)		10,200
		Rent expense (E–)		8,400
		Depreciation expense (E–)		600
		Insurance expense (E–)		1,000
		Supplies expense (E–)		500
		Interest expense (E–)		1,300
3.	31	Income summary ($169,300 – $116,200)	53,100	
		Greg Moore, Capital (Q+)		53,100
4.	31	Greg Moore, Capital (Q–)	54,100	
		Greg Moore, Withdrawals (W–)		54,100

Income summary

Clo 2	116,200	Clo 1	169,300
Clo 3	53,100	Bal	53,100

Greg Moore, Capital

Clo 4	54,100	Bal	25,900
		Clo 3	53,100
		Bal	24,900

Greg Moore, Withdrawals

Bal	54,100	Clo 4	54,100

The four step closing process for a merchandising company follows:

STEP 1: Make the revenue accounts equal zero via the Income summary account. This closing entry transfers total revenues to the *credit* side of Income summary, $169,300.

STEP 2: Make expense accounts and contra revenues equal zero via the Income summary account. This closing entry transfers total expenses and contra revenues (debit balance accounts) to the *debit* side of the Income summary, $116,200.

STEP 3: The Income summary account now holds the net income or net loss of the period. See the following Income summary T-account to illustrate.

Income summary

Closing entry 2	Expenses	Closing entry 1	Revenues
	Net loss if Debit balance		Net income if Credit balance

In step 3, make the Income summary account equal zero via the Capital account. This closing entry transfers net income (or net loss) to Capital.

STEP 4: Make the Withdrawals account equal zero via the Capital account. This entry transfers the withdrawals to the *debit* side of Capital.

Preparing a Merchandiser's Financial Statements

5 Prepare a merchandiser's financial statements

Exhibit 5-8 shows Greg's Groovy Tunes' financial statements for 2011.

Income Statement The income statement begins with Sales, Cost of goods sold, and Gross profit. Then come the **operating expenses**, which are those expenses (other than Cost of goods sold) that occur in the entity's major line of business.

Many companies report operating expenses in two categories:

- **Selling expenses** are expenses related to marketing the company's products—sales salaries, sales commissions, advertising, depreciation, store rent, utilities on store buildings, property taxes on store buildings, and delivery expense.
- **General expenses** include expenses *not* related to marketing the company's products—office expenses, such as the salaries of the executives and office employees; depreciation; rent, other than on stores (for example, rent on the administrative office); utilities, other than on stores (for example, utilities on the administrative office); and property taxes on the administrative office building.

Gross profit minus Operating expenses equals **Operating income** or **Income from operations.** Operating income measures the results of the entity's major ongoing activities (normal operations).

The last section of Greg's Groovy Tunes' income statement is **Other revenue and expense.** This category reports revenues and expenses that fall outside Greg's Groovy Tunes' main operations. Examples include interest revenue, interest expense, and gains and losses on the sale of plant assets. These examples have nothing to do with Greg's Groovy Tunes' "normal" business of selling CDs. As a result, they are classified as "other" items.

The bottom line of the income statement is net income:

Net income = Total revenues and gains – Total expenses and losses

EXHIBIT 5-8 | **Financial Statements—Amounts Assumed**

GREG'S GROOVY TUNES
Income Statement
Year Ended December 31, 2011

Sales revenue		$169,300
Less: Sales returns and allowances	$(2,000)	
Sales discounts	(1,400)	(3,400)
Net sales revenue		165,900
Cost of goods sold		90,800
Gross profit		75,100
Operating expenses:		
Wage expense	$10,200	
Rent expense	8,400	
Insurance expense	1,000	
Depreciation expense	600	
Supplies expense	500	20,700
Operating income		54,400
Other revenue and (expense):		
Interest expense		(1,300)
Net income		$ 53,100

GREG'S GROOVY TUNES
Statement of Owner's Equity
Year Ended December 31, 2011

Greg Moore, Capital, Dec. 31, 2011	$ 25,900
Add: Net income	53,100
	79,000
Less: Owner withdrawals	(54,100)
Greg Moore, Capital, Dec. 31, 2011	$ 24,900

GREG'S GROOVY TUNES
Balance Sheet
December 31, 2011

Assets			**Liabilities**	
Current Assets:			Current Liabilities:	
Cash		$ 2,800	Accounts payable	$39,500
Accounts receivable		4,600	Unearned sales revenue	700
Inventory		40,200	Wages payable	400
Prepaid insurance		200	Total current liabilities	40,600
Supplies		100	Long-term Liabilities:	
Total current assets		47,900	Note payable	12,600
Plant Assets:			Total liabilities	53,200
Furniture	$33,200			
Less: Accumulated			**Owner's Equity**	
depreciation	(3,000)	30,200	Greg Moore, Capital	24,900
			Total liabilities and	
Total assets		$78,100	owner's equity	$78,100

We often hear the term *bottom line* to refer to a final result. The bottom line is net income on the income statement.

Statement of Owner's Equity A merchandiser's statement of owner's equity looks exactly like that of a service business.

Balance Sheet For a merchandiser, the balance sheet is the same as for a service business, except merchandisers have an additional current asset, Inventory. Service businesses have no inventory.

Income Statement Formats: Multi-Step and Single-Step

As we saw in Chapter 4, the balance sheet appears in two formats:

- The report format (assets at top, owner's equity at bottom)
- The account format (assets at left, liabilities, and owner's equity at right)

There are also two formats for the income statement:

- The multi-step format
- The single-step format

The multi-step format is more popular.

Multi-Step Income Statement

A **multi-step income statement** lists several important subtotals. In addition to net income (the bottom line), it also reports subtotals for gross profit and income from operations. The income statements presented thus far in this chapter have been multi-step. Greg's Groovy Tunes' multi-step income statement appears in Exhibit 5-8.

Single-Step Income Statement

The **single-step income statement** is the income statement format you first learned about in Chapter 1. It groups all revenues together and all expenses together without drawing other subtotals. Many companies use this format. The single-step format clearly distinguishes revenues from expenses and works well for service entities because they have no gross profit to report. Exhibit 5-9 on page 291 shows a single-step income statement for Greg's Groovy Tunes.

Two Ratios for Decision Making

6 Use gross profit percentage and inventory turnover to evaluate a business

Inventory is the most important asset for a merchandiser. Merchandisers use several ratios to evaluate their operations, among them the gross profit percentage and the rate of inventory turnover.

The Gross Profit Percentage

Gross profit (gross margin) is net sales minus the cost of goods sold. Merchandisers strive to increase the **gross profit percentage**, which is computed as follows:

For Greg's Groovy Tunes
(Values from Exhibit 5-8)

$$\text{Gross profit percentage} = \frac{\text{Gross profit}}{\text{Net sales revenue}}$$

$$= \frac{\$75{,}100}{\$165{,}900} = 0.453 = 45.3\%$$

EXHIBIT 5-9 | **Single-Step Income Statement**

GREG'S GROOVY TUNES Income Statement Year Ended December 31, 2011		
Revenues:		
Sales revenue		$169,300
Less: Sales returns and allowances	$ 2,000	
Less: Sales discounts	(1,400)	(3,400)
Net sales revenue		165,900
Expenses:		
Cost of goods sold	$90,800	
Wage expense	10,200	
Rent expense	8,400	
Interest expense	1,300	
Insurance expense	1,000	
Depreciation expense	600	
Supplies expenses	500	
Total expenses		113,800
Net income		$ 53,100

The gross profit percentage (also called the **gross margin percentage**) is one of the most carefully watched measures of profitability. A small increase may signal an important rise in income. Conversely, a small decrease may signal trouble.

The Rate of Inventory Turnover

Owners and managers strive to sell inventory quickly because the inventory generates no profit until it is sold. Further, fast selling inventory is less likely to become obsolete (worthless). The faster the inventory sells, the larger the income. **Inventory turnover** measures how rapidly inventory is sold. It is computed as follows:

For Greg's Groovy Tunes
(Values from Exhibit 5-8)

$$\text{Inventory turnover} = \frac{\text{Cost of goods sold}}{\text{Average inventory}} = \frac{\text{Cost of goods sold}}{(\text{Beginning inventory}^{*} + \text{Ending inventory})/2}$$

$$= \frac{\$90{,}800}{(\$38{,}600^{*} + \$40{,}200)/2} = 2.3 \text{ times per year}$$

*Ending inventory from the preceding period. Amount assumed for this illustration.

A high turnover rate is desirable, and an increase in the turnover rate usually means higher profits.

Decision Guidelines

MERCHANDISING OPERATIONS AND THE ACCOUNTING CYCLE

Smart Touch Learning and Sherman Lawn Service are two very different companies. How do these two businesses differ? How are they similar? The Decision Guidelines answer these questions.

Decision	Guidelines
• How do merchandisers differ from service entities?	• Merchandisers, such as Smart Touch Learning, buy and sell *merchandise inventory*. • Service entities, such as Sherman Lawn Service, perform a *service*.
• How do a merchandiser's financial statements differ from the statements of a service business?	
Balance Sheet:	
Merchandiser has *Inventory*, an asset.	Service business has *no* inventory.
Income Statement:	
Merchandiser	*Service Business*

Merchandiser

Sales revenue	$XXX
– Cost of goods sold	(X)
= Gross profit	XX
– Operating expenses	(X)
= Net income	$ X

Service Business

Service revenue	$XX
– Operating expenses	(X)
= Net income	$ X

Decision	Guidelines
Statements of Owner's Equity:	No difference
• Which type of inventory system to use?	• At all times the *perpetual system* shows the amount of *inventory* on hand (the asset) and the cost of goods sold (the expense). • *Periodic system* shows the correct balances of inventory and cost of goods sold only after a count of the inventory, which occurs at least once each year.
• How to format the merchandiser's income statement?	**Single-Step Format**

Revenues:	Sales revenue	$ XXX
	Other revenues	X
	Total revenues	$XXXX
Expenses:	Cost of goods sold	(X)
	Operating expenses	(X)
	Other expenses	(X)
	Total expenses	XXX
	Net income	$ X

Decision	Guidelines
	Multi-Step Format

Sales revenue	$XXX
– Cost of goods sold	(X)
= Gross profit	XX
– Operating expenses	(X)
= Operating income	X
+ Other revenues	X
– Other expenses	(X)
= Net income	$ X

Decision	Guidelines
• How to evaluate merchandising operations?	Two key ratios

$$\text{Inventory} - \text{Purchase Returns and Allowances} - \text{Purchase Discounts} = \text{Net inventory}$$

$$\text{Inventory turnover}^{*} = \frac{\text{Cost of goods sold}}{\text{Average inventory}}$$

*In most cases—the higher, the better.

Summary Problem 2

The adjusted trial balance of King Cornelius Company follows:

KING CORNELIUS COMPANY Adjusted Trial Balance December 31, 2011		
Cash	$ 5,600	
Accounts receivable	37,100	
Inventory	25,800	
Supplies	1,300	
Prepaid rent	1,000	
Furniture	26,500	
Accumulated depreciation		$ 23,800
Accounts payable		6,300
Salary payable		2,000
Interest payable		600
Unearned sales revenue		2,400
Note payable, long-term		35,000
Cornelius, Capital		22,200
Cornelius, Withdrawals	48,000	
Sales revenue		244,000
Interest revenue		2,000
Sales discounts	10,000	
Sales returns and allowances	8,000	
Cost of goods sold	81,000	
Salary expense	72,700	
Rent expense	7,700	
Depreciation expense	2,700	
Utilities expense	5,800	
Supplies expense	2,200	
Interest expense	2,900	
Total	$338,300	$338,300

Requirements

1. Journalize the closing entries at December 31. Post to the Income summary account as an accuracy check on net income. Recall that the credit balance closed out of Income summary should equal net income computed on the income statement. Also post to Capital, whose balance should agree with the amount reported on the balance sheet.
2. Prepare the company's single-step income statement, statement of owner's equity, and balance sheet in account form. Draw arrows linking the statements.
3. Compute the inventory turnover for 2011. Inventory at December 31, 2010, was $21,000. Turnover for 2010 was 3.0 times. Would you expect King Cornelius Company to be more profitable or less profitable in 2011 than in 2010? Why?

Requirement 1

	Closing Entries			
	2011			
1	Dec 31	Sales revenue (R–)	244,000	
		Interest revenue (R–)	2,000	
		Income summary		246,000
2	31	Income summary	193,000	
		Sales discounts (CR–)		10,000
		Sales returns and allowances (CR–)		8,000
		Cost of goods sold (E–)		81,000
		Salary expense (E–)		72,700
		Rent expense (E–)		7,700
		Depreciation expense (E–)		2,700
		Utilities expense (E–)		5,800
		Supplies expense (E–)		2,200
		Interest expense (E–)		2,900
3	31	Income summary ($246,000 – $193,000)	53,000	
		Cornelius, Capital (Q+)		53,000
4	31	Cornelius, Capital (Q–)	48,000	
		Cornelius, Withdrawals (W–)		48,000

Income summary

Clo 2	193,000	Clo 1	246,000
Clo 3	53,000	Bal	53,000

Cornelius, Capital

			22,200
Clo 4	48,000	Clo 3	53,000
		Bal	27,200

Requirement 2

KING CORNELIUS COMPANY Income Statement Year Ended December 31, 2011		
Revenues:		
Sales revenue		$244,000
Less: Sales discounts	$ (10,000)	
Sales returns and allowances	(8,000)	(18,000)
Net sales revenue		226,000
Interest revenue		2,000
Total revenue		228,000
Expenses:		
Cost of goods sold	$81,000	
Salary expense	72,700	
Rent expense	7,700	
Utilities expense	5,800	
Interest expense	2,900	
Depreciation expense	2,700	
Supplies expense	2,200	
Total expenses		175,000
Net income		$ 53,000

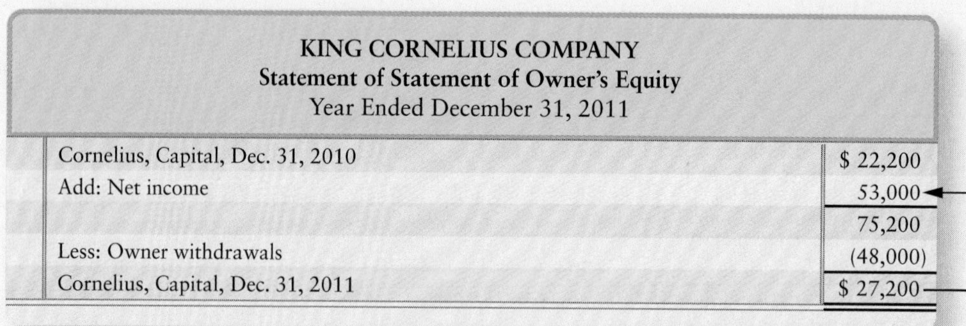

KING CORNELIUS COMPANY
Statement of Statement of Owner's Equity
Year Ended December 31, 2011

Cornelius, Capital, Dec. 31, 2010	$ 22,200
Add: Net income	53,000
	75,200
Less: Owner withdrawals	(48,000)
Cornelius, Capital, Dec. 31, 2011	$ 27,200

KING CORNELIUS COMPANY
Balance Sheet
December 31, 2011

Assets			**Liabilities**	
Current:			Current:	
Cash		$ 5,600	Accounts payable	$ 6,300
Accounts receivable		37,100	Salary payable	2,000
Inventory		25,800	Interest payable	600
Supplies		1,300	Unearned sales revenue	2,400
Prepaid rent		1,000	Total current liabilities	11,300
Total current assets		70,800	Long-term:	
Plant:			Note payable	35,000
Furniture	$26,500		Total liabilities	46,300
Less: Accumulated depreciation	(23,800)	2,700	**Owner's Equity**	
			Cornelius, Capital	27,200
Total assets		$73,500	Total liabilities and owner's equity	$73,500

Requirement 3

$$\text{Inventory turnover} = \frac{\text{Cost of goods sold}}{\text{Average inventory}}$$

$$= \frac{\$81{,}000}{(\$21{,}000 + \$25{,}800)/2} = 3.5 \text{ times}$$

The increase in the rate of inventory turnover from 3.0 to 3.5 suggests higher profits.

Review Merchandising Operations

Accounting Vocabulary

Cost of Goods Sold (p. 307)
The cost of the inventory that the business has sold to customers. Also called **cost of sales**.

Cost of Sales (p. 307)
The cost of the inventory that the business has sold to customers. Also called **cost of goods sold**.

Credit Terms (p. 302)
The terms of purchase or sale as stated on the invoice. A common example is 2/10, n/30.

Customer (p. 300)
The individual or business that buys goods from a seller.

Free On Board (FOB) (p. 304)
The purchase agreement specifies FOB terms to indicate who pays the freight. FOB terms also determine when title to the good transfers to the purchaser.

FOB Destination (p. 304)
Situation in which the buyer takes ownership (title) at the delivery destination point and the seller pays the freight.

FOB Shipping Point (p. 304)
Situation in which the buyer takes ownership (title) to the goods at the shipping point and the buyer pays the freight.

Freight In (p. 304)
The transportation cost to ship goods IN the warehouse; therefore, it is freight on purchased goods.

Freight Out (p. 304)
The transportation cost to ship goods OUT of the warehouse; therefore, it is freight on goods sold to a customer.

Gross Margin (p. 311)
Excess of net sales revenue over cost of goods sold. Also called **gross profit**.

Gross Margin Percentage (p. 319)
Gross profit divided by net sales revenue. A measure of profitability. Also called **gross profit percentage**.

Gross Profit (p. 311)
Excess of net sales revenue over cost of goods sold. Also called **gross margin**.

Gross Profit Percentage (p. 318)
Gross profit divided by net sales revenue. A measure of profitability. Also called **gross margin percentage**.

Income from Operations (p. 316)
Gross profit minus operating expenses plus any other operating revenues. Also called **operating income**.

Inventory (p. 299)
All the goods that the company owns and expects to sell to customers in the normal course of operations.

Inventory Turnover (p. 319)
Ratio of cost of goods sold divided by average inventory. Measures the number of times a company sells its average level of inventory during a year.

Invoice (p. 302)
A seller s request for cash from the purchaser.

Merchandisers (p. 298)
Businesses that sell merchandise or goods to customers.

Merchandising (p. 300)
Consists of buying and selling products rather than services.

Multi-Step Income Statement (p. 318)
Format that contains subtotals to highlight significant relationships. In addition to net income, it reports gross profit and operating income.

Net Purchases (p. 352)
Purchases less purchase discounts and purchase returns and allowances.

Net Sales Revenue (p. 309)
Sales revenue less sales discounts and sales returns and allowances.

Operating Expenses (p. 316)
Expenses, other than cost of goods sold, that are incurred in the entity's major line of business. Examples include rent, depreciation, salaries, wages, utilities, and supplies expense.

Operating Income (p. 316)
Gross profit minus operating expenses plus any other operating revenues. Also called **income from operations**.

Other Revenue and Expense (p. 316)
Revenue or expense that is outside the normal day-to-day operations of a business, such as a gain or loss on the sale of plant assets.

Periodic Inventory System (p. 301)
A system in which the business does not keep a continuous record of inventory on hand. At the end of the period, the business takes a physical count of on-hand inventory and uses this information to prepare the financial statements.

Perpetual Inventory System (p. 301)
The accounting inventory system in which the business keeps a constant/running record of inventory and cost of goods sold.

Purchase Allowances (p. 304)
An amount granted to the purchaser as an incentive to keep goods that are not "as ordered."

Purchase Discount (p. 302)
A discount that businesses offer to customers as an incentive for early payment.

Purchase Returns (p. 304)
A situation in which businesses allow customers to return merchandise that is defective, damaged, or otherwise unsuitable.

Sales (p. 307)
The amount that a merchandiser earns from selling its inventory. Short name for **Sales revenue**.

Sales Discount (p. 309)
Reduction in the amount of cash received from a customer for early payment. Offered by the seller as an incentive for the customer to pay early. A contra account to Sales revenue.

Sales Returns and Allowances (p. 309)
Decreases in the seller's receivable from a customer's return of merchandise or from granting the customer an allowance from the amount owed to the seller. A contra account to Sales revenue.

Sales Revenue (p. 307)
The amount that a merchandiser earns from selling its inventory. Also called **Sales**.

Selling Expenses (p. 318)
Expenses related to marketing and selling the company's products.

Single-Step Income Statement (p. 318)
Format that groups all revenues together and then lists and deducts all expenses together without drawing any subtotals.

Vendor (p. 300)
The individual or business from whom a company purchases goods. The merchandising company purchases mainly inventory from vendors.

Quick Check

1. Which account does a merchandiser use that a service company does not use?
   a. Cost of goods sold
   b. Inventory
   c. Sales revenue
   d. All of the above

2. The two main inventory accounting systems are the
   a. Perpetual and periodic
   b. Purchase and sale
   c. Returns and allowances
   d. Cash and accrual

3. The journal entry for the purchase of inventory on account is

a.

Accounts payable	XXX	
Inventory		XXX

b.

Inventory	XXX	
Cash		XXX

c.

Inventory	XXX	
Accounts payable		XXX

d.

Inventory	XXX	
Accounts receivable		XXX

4. Downtown Market purchased inventory for $4,400 and also paid a $370 freight bill. Downtown Market returned 30% of the goods to the seller and later took a 1% purchase discount. What is Downtown Market's final cost of the inventory that it kept?
   a. $3,306
   b. $1,307
   c. $3,419
   d. $3,049

5. Suppose Old Oak Winery had sales of $270,000 and sales returns of $41,000. Cost of goods sold was $169,000. How much gross profit did Old Oak Winery report?
   a. $101,000
   b. $60,000
   c. $229,000
   d. $45,000

6. Suppose Greg's Groovy Tunes' Inventory account showed a balance of $10,000 before the year-end adjustments. The physical count of goods on hand totaled $9,700. To adjust the accounts, Greg Moore would make the following entry:

a.

Accounts payable	300	
Inventory		300

b.

Cost of goods sold	300	
Inventory		300

c.

Inventory	300	
Cost of goods sold		300

d.

Inventory	300	
Accounts receivable		300

7. Which account in question 6 would Greg Moore close at the end of the year?
   a. Accounts receivable
   b. Inventory
   c. Cost of goods sold
   d. Accounts payable

8. The final closing entry for a proprietorship is

a.

Income summary	XXX	
Expenses		XXX

b.

Sales revenue	XXX	
Income summary		XXX

c.

Withdrawals	XXX	
Capital		XXX

d.

Capital	XXX	
Withdrawals		XXX

9. Which subtotals appear on a multi-step income statement but do not appear on a single-step income statement?
   a. Gross profit and Income from operations
   b. Operating expenses and Net income
   c. Cost of goods sold and Net income
   d. Net sales and Cost of goods sold

10. Assume Old Oak Winery made net Sales of $74,000, and Cost of goods sold totaled $40,000. Average inventory was $19,000. What was Old Oak Winery's gross profit percentage for this period?
    a. 54%
    b. 2.1 times
    c. 46%
    d. 20%

Answers are given after Apply Your Knowledge (page 346).

Assess Your Progress

■ Short Exercises

S5-1 *(L. OBJ. 1)* **Comparing periodic and perpetual inventory systems [10 min]**
You may have shopped at a Ronny's store. Suppose Ronny's purchased T-shirts on account for $18,130. Credit terms are 3/15, n/45. Ronny's paid within the discount period.

Requirements

1. If Ronny's uses a periodic inventory system, when will the purchase of inventory be recorded as an expense—when it is purchased or when it is sold?
2. If Ronny's uses the perpetual inventory system, when will the purchase of inventory be recorded as an expense—when it is purchased or when it is sold?

S5-2 *(L. OBJ. 2)* **Analyzing purchase transactions—perpetual inventory [5–10 min]**
Suppose The Funhouse buys $105,900 worth of PegaBlock toys on credit terms of 2/10, n/45. Some of the goods are damaged in shipment, so Funhouse returns $10,540 of the merchandise to PegaBlock.

Requirement

1. How much must The Funhouse pay PegaBlock:
   a. After the discount period?
   b. Within the discount period?

Note: Short Exercise 5-3 should be used only after completing Short Exercise 5-2.

S5-3 *(L. OBJ. 2)* **Journalizing purchase transactions—perpetual inventory [10 min]**
Refer to the Funhouse facts in Short Exercise 5-2.

Requirements

1. Journalize the following transactions. Explanations are not required.
   a. Purchase of the goods on July 8, 2011.
   b. Return of the damaged goods on July 12, 2011.
   c. Payment on July 15, 2011.
2. In the final analysis, how much did the inventory cost Funhouse?

S5-4 *(L. OBJ. 2)* **Journalizing purchase transactions—perpetual inventory [5–10 min]**
Suppose a BullsEye store purchases $60,000 of women's sportswear on account from Muddy John on July 1, 2011. Credit terms are 2/10, net 45. BullsEye pays electronically, and Muddy John receives the money on July 10, 2011.

Requirements

1. Journalize BullsEye's transactions for July 1, 2011, and July 10, 2011.
2. What was BullsEye's net cost of this inventory?

Note: Short Exercise 5-5 covers this same situation for the seller.

S5-5 *(L. OBJ. 3)* **Journalizing sales transactions—perpetual inventory [10 min]**
Consider the facts in the Short Exercise 5-4 as they apply to the seller, Muddy John. Muddy John sells $60,000 of women's sportswear to a BullsEye store under credit terms of 2/10, net 45. The goods cost Muddy John $32,000.

Requirement

1. Journalize Muddy John's transactions for July 1, 2011, and July 10, 2011.

Note: Short Exercise 5-4 covers the same situation for the buyer.

S5-6 *(L. OBJ. 3)* **Journalizing sales transactions—perpetual inventory [10 min]**
Suppose Southam.com sells 2,000 books on account for $19 each (cost of these books is $22,800) on October 10, 2010. One hundred of these books (cost $1,140) were damaged in shipment, so Southam.com later received the damaged goods as sales returns on October 13, 2010. Then the customer paid the balance on October 22, 2010. Credit terms offered to the customer were 2/20, net 45.

Requirement

1. Journalize Southam.com's October, 2010 transactions.

Note: Short Exercises 5-7 should be used only after completing Short Exercise 5-6.

S5-7 *(L. OBJ. 3)* **Calculating net sales and gross profit—perpetual inventory [5 min]**
Use the data in Short Exercise 5-6 for Southam.com.

Requirements

1. Calculate net sales revenue for October, 2010.
2. Calculate gross profit for October, 2010.

S5-8 *(L. OBJ. 4)* **Adjusting inventory for shrinkage [5 min]**
Josh's Furniture's Inventory account at year-end appeared as follows:

Inventory		
Unadjusted balance	68,000	

The physical count of inventory came up with a total of $66,700.

Requirement

1. Journalize the adjusting entry.

S5-9 *(L. OBJ. 4)* **Journalizing closing entries—perpetual inventory [5–10 min]**
Hart RV Center's accounting records include the following accounts at December 31, 2010:

Cost of goods sold	$387,000	Accumulated depreciation	$ 38,000
Accounts payable	19,000	Cash	44,000
Rent expense	22,000	Sales revenue	699,000
Building	114,000	Depreciation expense	14,000
Hart, Capital	203,000	Hart, Withdrawals	63,000
Inventory	256,000	Sales discounts	8,000

Requirement

1. Journalize the required closing entries for Hart RV Center for December 31, 2010.

S5-10 *(L. OBJ. 5)* **Preparing a merchandiser's income statement [5–10 min]**
Texas Communications reported the following figures in its financial statements (amounts in thousands):

Cash	$ 3,600	Cost of goods sold	$ 21,000
Total operating expenses	3,300	Equipment, net	3,900
Accounts payable	4,000	Accrued liabilities	1,800
Total owner's equity	4,100	Net sales revenue	29,000
Long–term notes payable	600	Accounts receivable	2,600
Inventory	400		

Requirement

1. Prepare the business's multi-step income statement for the year ended May 31, 2011.

Note: Short Exercise 5-11 should be used only after completing Short Exercise 5-10.

S5-11 *(L. OBJ. 5)* **Preparing a merchandiser's balance sheet [10 min]**
Review the data in Short Exercise 5-10.

Requirement

1. Prepare Texas Communications' classified balance sheet at May 31, 2011. Use the report format.

Note: Short Exercise 5-12 should be used only after completing Short Exercises 5-10 and 5-11.

S5-12 *(L. OBJ. 6)* **Computing the gross profit percentage and the rate of inventory turnover [10 min]**
Refer to the Texas Communications data in Short Exercises 5-10 and 5-11.

Requirement

1. Calculate the gross profit percentage and rate of inventory turnover for 2011. One year earlier, at May 31, 2010, Texas' inventory balance was $325.

Exercises

E5-13 *(L. OBJ. 1)* **Describing periodic and perpetual inventory systems [10–15 min]**
The following characteristics are related to either periodic inventory or perpetual inventory systems.

A. Purchases of inventory are journalized to an asset account at the time of purchase
B. Purchases of inventory are journalized to an expense account at the time of purchase
C. Inventory records are constantly updated
D. Sales made require a second entry to be journalized to record cost of goods sold
E. Bar code scanners that record sales transactions are most often associated with this inventory system
F. A physical count of goods on hand at year end is required

Requirement

1. Identify each characteristic as one of the following:
   a. Periodic inventory
   b. Perpetual inventory
   c. Both periodic and perpetual inventory
   d. Neither periodic nor perpetual inventory

E5-14 *(L. OBJ. 2)* **Journalizing purchase transactions from an invoice—perpetual inventory [10–15 min]**

As the proprietor of Discount Tire Co., you received the following invoice from a supplier:

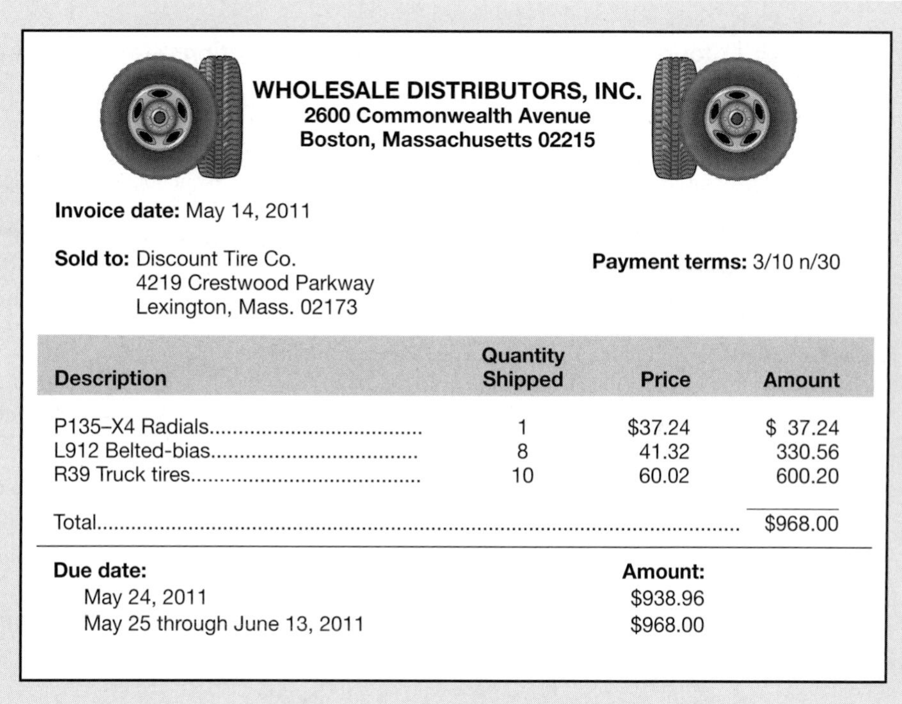

WHOLESALE DISTRIBUTORS, INC.
2600 Commonwealth Avenue
Boston, Massachusetts 02215

Invoice date: May 14, 2011

Sold to: Discount Tire Co.
4219 Crestwood Parkway
Lexington, Mass. 02173

Payment terms: 3/10 n/30

Description	Quantity Shipped	Price	Amount
P135–X4 Radials	1	$37.24	$ 37.24
L912 Belted-bias	8	41.32	330.56
R39 Truck tires	10	60.02	600.20
Total			$968.00

Due date:	Amount:
May 24, 2011	$938.96
May 25 through June 13, 2011	$968.00

Requirements

1. Journalize the transaction required on May 14, 2011.
2. Journalize the return on May 19, 2011, of the P135–X4 Radial, which was ordered by mistake.
3. Journalize the payment on May 22, 2011, to Wholesale Distributors, Inc.

E5-15 *(L. OBJ. 2)* **Journalizing purchase transactions—perpetual system [10–15 min]**

On April 30, 2012, Daigle Jewelers purchased inventory of $5,700 on account from Hart Diamonds, a jewelry importer. Terms were 3/15, net 45. The same day Daigle paid freight charges of $500. Upon receiving the goods, Daigle checked the order and found $1,200 of unsuitable merchandise, which was returned to Hart on May 4. Then, on May 14, Daigle paid the invoice.

Requirement

1. Journalize all necessary transactions for Daigle Jewelers. Explanations are not required.

E5-16 *(L. OBJ. 2, 3)* **Computing inventory and cost of goods sold amounts [10–15 min]**
Consider the following incomplete table of merchandiser's profit data:

Sales	Sales Discounts	Net Sales	Cost of Goods Sold	Gross Profit
$ 93,300	$ 1,510	$ 91,790	$ 60,300	(a)
97,400	(b)	92,470	(c)	$ 32,270
65,800	1,810	(d)	46,000	(e)
(f)	2,540	(g)	71,800	39,760

Requirement

1. Calculate the missing table values to complete the table.

E5-17 *(L. OBJ. 2, 3)* **Journalizing purchase and sales transactions—perpetual system [15–20 min]**
The following transactions occurred during February, 2012, for Angel Garden Gifts:

Feb 3	Purchased $3,000 of inventory on account under terms of 2/10, n/eom (end of month) and FOB shipping point.
7	Returned $500 of defective merchandise purchased on February 3.
9	Paid freight bill of $90 on February 3 purchase.
10	Sold inventory on account for $4,600. Payment terms were 2/15 n/30. These goods cost the company $2,500.
12	Paid amount owed on credit purchase of February 3, less the return and the discount.
16	Granted a sales allowance of $300 on the February 10 sale.
23	Received cash from February 10 customer in full settlement of her debt, less the allowance and the discount.

Requirement

1. Journalize the February transactions for Angel Garden Gifts. No explanations are required.

E5-18 *(L. OBJ. 3)* **Journalizing sales transactions—perpetual system [10–15 min]**
Refer to the facts presented in Exercise 5-15.

Requirement

1. Journalize the transactions of the seller, Hart Diamonds. Hart's cost of goods sold was 55% of the sales price. Explanations are not required.

E5-19 *(L. OBJ. 4)* **Journalizing adjusting and closing entries, and computing gross profit [10–15 min]**
Todd McKinney Magic Show's accounts at June 30, 2012, included the following unadjusted balances:

Inventory	$ 5,700
Cost of goods sold	40,500
Sales revenue	86,200
Sales discounts	700
Sales returns and allowances	2,100

The physical count of inventory on hand on June 30, 2012, was $5,500.

Requirements

1. Journalize the adjustment for inventory shrinkage.
2. Journalize the closing entries for June, 2012.
3. Compute the gross profit.

E5-20 *(L. OBJ. 4)* **Making closing entries [15–20 min]**
Brown Sheet Metal's accounting records carried the following selected accounts at May 31, 2012:

Inventory	5,600	Selling expense	7,100
Interest revenue	40	Sales revenue	38,000
Accounts payable	2,000	Interest expense	30
Cost of goods sold	26,800	Accounts receivable	400
Other expense	1,800	General and administrative expense	200
Brown, Withdrawals	600	Brown, Capital	8,720

Requirements

1. Journalize the closing entries at May 31, 2012.
2. Set up T-accounts for Income summary and Brown, Capital. Post the closing entries to the T-accounts and calculate their ending balances.

E5-21 *(L. OBJ. 4)* **Journalizing closing entries [10–15 min]**
The trial balance and adjustments columns of the work sheet of Long Pond Business Systems Co. at January 31, 2011, follow:

LONG POND BUSINESS SYSTEMS CO.
Work Sheet
Month Ended January 31, 2011

	Trial Balance		Adjustments	
Account	Debit	Credit	Debit	Credit
Cash	2,100			
Accounts receivable	8,500		(a) 1,500	
Inventory	36,100			(b) 4,200
Supplies	13,000			(c) 7,900
Equipment	42,400			
Accumulated depreciation		11,200		(d) 2,000
Accounts payable		9,300		
Salary payable				(e) 1,200
Note payable, long-term		7,500		
Long, Capital		33,900		
Long, Withdrawals	45,000			
Sales revenue		233,000		(a) 1,500
Sales discounts	2,000			
Cost of goods sold	111,600		(b) 4,200	
Selling expense	21,000		(c) 5,300	
			(e) 1,200	
General expense	10,500		(c) 2,600	
			(d) 2,000	
Interest expense	2,700			
Total	294,900	294,900	16,800	16,800

Requirements

1. Compute the adjusted balance for each account that must be closed.
2. Journalize the required closing entries at January 31, 2011.
3. How much was Long Pond's net income or net loss?

E5-22 *(L. OBJ. 4, 5)* **Preparing a merchandiser's multi-step income statement to evaluate the business [10–15 min]**
Selected amounts from the accounting records of Long Pond Business Systems Co., for the fiscal year ended January 31, 2011, follow:

Journal Entry				
Date		Accounts	Debit	Credit
Jan	31	Sales revenue	234,500	
		Income summary		234,500
Jan	31	Income summary	163,100	
		Sales discounts		2,000
		Cost of goods sold		115,800
		Selling expense		27,500
		General expense		15,100
		Interest expense		2,700
Jan	31	Income summary	71,400	
		Long, Capital		71,400
Jan	31	Long, Capital	43,000	
		Long, Withdrawals		43,000

Requirement

1. Prepare the company's *multi-step* income statement.

E5-23 *(L. OBJ. 5)* **Preparing a multi-step income statement [10–15 min]**
Review the data in Exercise 5-21.

Requirements

1. Compute the rate of inventory turnover for the fiscal year ended January 31, 2011 assuming $22,000 in average inventory.
2. The inventory turnover rate for the fiscal year ending January 31, 2010 was 3.8 times. Did the inventory turnover rate improve or deteriorate from 2010 to 2011?

E5-24 *(L. OBJ. 5, 6)* **Preparing a single-step income statement. Calculate the gross profit percentage to evaluate the business [10–15 min]**
Review the data given in Exercise 5-22.

Requirements

1. Prepare Long Pond's *single-step* income statement for 2011.
2. Calculate the gross profit percentage.
3. The gross profit percentage for the fiscal year ending January 31, 2010 was 62%. Did the gross profit percentage improve or deteriorate during the fiscal year ending January 31, 2011?

E5-25 *(L. OBJ. 6)* **Calculating gross profit percentage and inventory turnover to evaluate a business [10 min]**
Heat Miser Sunlamps earned sales revenue of $61 million in 2012. Cost of goods sold was $37 million, and net income reached $10 million, the company's highest ever. Total current assets included inventory of $5 million at December 31, 2012. Inventory was $7 million on December 31, 2011.

Requirement

1. Compute the company's gross profit percentage and rate of inventory turnover for 2012.

■ Problems (Group A)

P5-26A *(L. OBJ. 1, 2, 3)* **Journalizing purchase and sale transaction—perpetual inventory [10–15 min]**

Consider the following transactions that occurred in October, 2012 for No Deal:

Oct 1	Purchased $3,500 of inventory from B&B, terms 1/10, n.20
Oct 3	Sold $1,000 of goods to A Frames, terms 2/10, n/e.o.m. *(Cost $670)
Oct 5	A Frames returned $200 of goods (Cost $130)
Oct 11	Paid B&B
Oct 13	Received payment from A Frames

Requirements

1. What type of inventory system is No Deal using—periodic or perpetual?
2. Which transaction date helped you decide?
3. Journalize October transactions for No Deal. No explanations are required.

P5-27A *(L. OBJ. 2, 3)* **Journalizing purchase and sale transactions—perpetual inventory [20–25 min]**

Consider the following transactions that occurred in February, 2012 for Diamonds

Feb 3	Purchased inventory on terms 1/15, n/e.o.m., $3,000
Feb 4	Purchased inventory for cash of $1,500
Feb 6	Returned $300 of inventory from Feb 4 purchase
Feb 8	Sold goods on terms of 2/15, n/35 of $5,000 that cost $2,400
Feb 10	Paid for goods purchased Feb 3
Feb 12	Received goods from Feb 8 sale of $1,000 that cost $450
Feb 23	Received payment from Feb 8 customer
Feb 25	Sold goods to Barnes for $900 that cost $350. Terms of n/30 were offered. As a courtesy to Barnes, $150 of freight was added to the invoice for which cash was paid directly to UPS by Diamonds
Feb 29	Received payment from Barnes

Requirement

1. Journalize February transactions for Diamonds. No explanations are required.

P5-28A *(L. OBJ. 2, 3)* **Journalizing purchase and sale transactions—perpetual system [15–20 min]**

The following transactions occurred between Nolan Pharmaceuticals and C & C, the pharmacy chain, during January of the current year:

Jan 6 C & C purchased $7,000 of merchandise from Nolan on credit terms of 3/10, n/30, FOB shipping point. Separately, C & C paid a $75 bill for freight in. These goods cost Nolan $2,100.

10 C & C returned $1,750 of the merchandise purchased on January 6. Nolan accounted for the sales return and placed the goods back in inventory (Nolan's cost, $700).

15 C & C paid $3,500 of the invoice amount owed to Nolan for the January 6 purchase, less the discount.

27 C & C paid the remaining amount owed to Nolan for the January 6 purchase.

Requirements

1. Journalize these transactions on the books of C & C.
2. Journalize these transactions on the books of Nolan Pharmaceuticals.

P5-29A *(L. OBJ. 2, 3)* **Journalizing purchase and sale transactions—perpetual inventory [20–25 min]**

Trixie's Amusements completed the following transactions during May, 2012:

May	1	Purchased supplies for cash, $740
	4	Purchased inventory on credit terms of 3/10 net eom, $3,600
	8	Returned half the inventory purchased on May 4. It was not the inventory ordered.
	10	Sold goods for cash, $1,000 (cost, $500)
	13	Sold inventory on credit terms of 2/15, n/45, $10,100 (cost, $5,500)
	14	Paid the amount owed on account from May 4, less the return (May 8) and the discount
	17	Received defective inventory as a sales return from the May 13 sale, $800. Trixie's cost of the inventory received was $650.
	18	Purchased inventory of $3,900 on account. Payment terms were 2/10 net 30.
	26	Paid the net amount owed for the May 18 purchase
	28	Received cash in full settlement of the account from the customer who purchased inventory on May 13, less the return and the discount
	29	Purchased inventory for cash, $10,000, plus freight charges of $200

Requirement

1. Journalize the transactions on the books of Trixie's Amusements.

P5-30A *(L. OBJ. 4, 5)* **Preparing financial statements and preparing closing entries [35–45 min]**

Aria Publishers Company's selected accounts as of November 30, 2012, follow:

Selling expenses	$ 18,400	Inventory	$ 42,000
Furniture	36,800	Cash	36,500
Sales returns and allowances	3,100	Note payable	19,900
Salary payable	1,200	Accumulated depreciation	22,800
Aria, Capital	23,500	Cost of goods sold	46,000
Sales revenue	113,400	Sales discounts	2,200
Accounts payable	13,600	General expenses	9,400

Requirements

1. Prepare the multi-step income statement, statement of owner's equity, and balance sheet for the first year of operations.
2. Prepare closing entries for the first year of operations.

P5-31A *(L. OBJ. 4, 5, 6)* **Making closing entries, preparing financial statements, and computing gross profit percentage and inventory turnover [20–30 min]**

The adjusted trial balance of Gamut Music Company at February 29, 2012, follows:

GAMUT MUSIC COMPANY Adjusted Trial Balance February 29, 2012		
Account	**Debit**	**Credit**
Cash	$ 4,000	
Accounts receivable	38,300	
Inventory	17,000	
Supplies	700	
Furniture	39,800	
Accumulated depreciation		$ 9,000
Accounts payable		13,600
Salary payable		600
Unearned sales revenue		6,700
Note payable, long-term		12,000
Gamut, Capital		37,700
Gamut, Withdrawals	40,000	
Sales revenue		187,000
Sales returns	8,000	
Cost of goods sold	83,000	
Selling expense	19,400	
General expense	15,000	
Interest expense	1,400	
Total	$ 266,600	$ 266,600

Requirements

1. Journalize Gamut's closing entries.
2. Prepare Gamut's single-step income statement for the year.
3. Compute the gross profit percentage and the rate of inventory turnover for 2012. Inventory on hand one year ago, at February 28, 2011, was $12,800.
4. For the year ended February 28, 2011, Gamut's gross profit percentage was 50%, and inventory turnover was 4.9 times. Did the results for the year ended February 29, 2012 suggest improvement or deterioration in profitability over last year?

P5-32A *(L. OBJ. 5)* **Preparing a multi-step income statement and a classified balance sheet [30–40 min]**

← *Link Back to Chapter 4 (Classified Balance Sheet).* The accounts of Thompson Electronics Company are listed along with their balances before closing for the month ended July 31, 2012.

Interest revenue	$ 300	Accounts payable	$ 16,700
Inventory	45,300	Accounts receivable	33,700
Note payable, long-term	41,000	Accumulated depreciation	37,500
Salary payable	2,400	Thompson, Capital, June 30	52,700
Sales discounts	2,500	Thompson, Withdrawals	18,000
Sales returns and allowances	8,400	Cash	7,800
Sales revenue	296,700	Cost of goods sold	161,500
Selling expense	37,800	Equipment	124,800
Supplies	6,000	General expenses	16,000
Unearned sales revenue	13,300	Interest payable	1,200

Requirements

1. Prepare Thompson Electronics' *multi-step* income statement.
2. Prepare Thompson Electronics' statement of owner's equity.
3. Prepare Thompson Electronics' classified balance sheet in *report form.*

P5-33A *(L. OBJ. 5, 6)* **Preparing a multi-step income statement and calculating gross profit percentage [15–25 min]**
The records of B-1 Steak Company list the following selected accounts for the quarter ended November 30, 2011:

Interest revenue	$ 300	Accounts payable	$ 16,900
Inventory	45,500	Accounts receivable	33,000
Note payable, long-term	44,000	Accumulated depreciation	37,700
Salary payable	3,300	Nabanita, Capital, Aug 31	52,100
Sales discounts	2,200	Nabanita, Withdrawals	20,000
Sales returns and allowances	7,900	Cash	8,300
Sales revenue	296,300	Cost of goods sold	162,300
Selling expense	38,400	Equipment	126,300
Supplies	5,800	General expenses	16,100
Unearned sales revenue	13,900	Interest payable	1,300

Requirements

1. Prepare a multi-step income statement.
2. M. Nolen, manager of the company, strives to earn gross profit percentage of at least 50% and net income percentage of 20%. Did B-1 achieve these goals? Show your calculations.

Problems (Group B)

P5-34B *(L. OBJ. 1, 2, 3)* **Journalizing purchase and sale transactions—perpetual inventory [10–15 min]**
Consider the following transactions that occurred in March, 2012 for Howy:

Mar 1	Purchased $4,000 of inventory from P&G, terms 1/10, n/20
Mar 3	Sold $4,000 of goods to Four Eyes, Inc., terms 2/10, n/e.o.m. *(Cost $2,440)
Mar 5	Four Eyes, Inc., returned $100 of goods (Cost $25)
Mar 11	Paid P&G
Mar 13	Received payment from Four Eyes, Inc.

Requirements

1. What type of inventory system is Howy using—periodic or perpetual?
2. Which transaction date helped you decide?
3. Journalize March transactions for Howy. No explanations are required.

P5-35B *(L. OBJ. 2, 3)* **Journalizing purchase and sale transactions—perpetual inventory [20–25 min]**

Consider the following transactions that occurred in April, 2012 for Opals:

Apr 3	Purchased inventory on terms 1/10, n/e.o.m. $7,000
Apr 4	Purchased inventory for cash of $1,800
Apr 6	Returned $700 of inventory from Apr 4 purchase
Apr 8	Sold goods on terms of 2/15, n/35 of $6,000 that cost $2,940
Apr 10	Paid for goods purchased on Apr 3
Apr 12	Received goods from Apr 8 sale of $500 that cost $220
Apr 23	Received payment from Apr 8 customer
Apr 25	Sold goods to Harrisons for $1,200 that cost $450. Terms of n/30 were offered. As a courtesy to Harrisons, $125 of freight was added to the invoice for which cash was paid directly to UPS by Opals.
Apr 29	Received payment from Harrisons

Requirement

1. Journalize April transactions for Opals. No explanations are required.

P5-36B *(L. OBJ. 2, 3)* **Journalizing purchase and sale transactions—perpetual system [15–20 min]**

The following transactions occurred between Acre Pharmaceuticals and E & S, the pharmacy chain, during October of the current year:

Oct 6	E & S purchased $12,000 of merchandise from Acre on credit terms of 3/10, n/30, FOB shipping point. Separately, E & S paid a $75 bill for freight in. These goods cost Acre $3,600.
10	E & S returned $3,000 of the merchandise purchased on October 6. Acre accounted for the sales return and placed the goods back in inventory (Acre's cost, $1,200).
15	E & S paid $6,000 of the invoice amount owed to Acre for the October 6 purchase, less the discount.
27	E & S paid the remaining amount owed to Acre for the October 6 purchase.

Requirements

1. Journalize these transactions on the books of E & S.
2. Journalize these transactions on the books of Acre Pharmaceuticals.

P5-37B *(L. OBJ. 2, 3)* **Journalizing purchase and sale transactions—perpetual inventory [20–25 min]**

Trisha's Amusements completed the following transactions during November, 2012:

Nov 1	Purchased supplies for cash, $730
4	Purchased inventory on credit terms of 3/10 net eom, $2,800
8	Returned half the inventory purchased on November 4. It was not the inventory ordered.
10	Sold goods for cash, $1,500 (cost, $1,000)
13	Sold inventory on credit terms of 2/15, n/45, $9,900 (cost, $5,300)
14	Paid the amount owed on account from November 4, less the return (November 8) and the discount
17	Received defective inventory as a sales return from the November 13 sale, $500. Trisha's cost of the inventory received was $350.
18	Purchased inventory of $3,400 on account. Payment terms were 2/10 net 30.
26	Paid the net amount owed for the November 18 purchase
28	Received cash in full settlement of the account from the customer who purchased inventory on November 13, less the return and the discount
29	Purchased inventory for cash, $10,000, plus freight charges of $200

Requirement

1. Journalize the transactions on the books of Trisha's Amusements.

P5-38B *(L. OBJ. 4, 5)* **Preparing financial statements and preparing closing entries [35–45 min]**

Allen Publishers Company's selected accounts as of September 30, 2012, follow:

Selling expenses	$ 18,700	Inventory	$ 41,000
Furniture	37,500	Cash	36,400
Sales returns and allowances	3,400	Note payable	21,700
Salary payable	1,400	Accumulated depreciation	23,600
Allen, Capital	23,000	Cost of goods sold	48,000
Sales revenue	113,600	Sales discounts	2,200
Accounts payable	13,100	General expenses	9,200

Requirements

1. Prepare the multi-step income statement, statement of owner's equity, and balance sheet for its first year of operations.
2. Prepare closing entries for the year.

P5-39B *(L. OBJ. 4, 5, 6)* **Making closing entries, preparing financial statements, and computing gross profit percentage and inventory turnover [20–30 min]**

The adjusted trial balance of Big Brother's Music Company at January 31, 2012, follows:

BIG BROTHER'S MUSIC COMPANY
Adjusted Trial Balance
January 31, 2012

Account	Debit	Credit
Cash	$ 3,800	
Accounts receivable	38,200	
Inventory	17,400	
Supplies	300	
Furniture	40,000	
Accumulated depreciation		$ 8,100
Accounts payable		13,300
Salary payable		900
Unearned sales revenue		6,500
Note payable, long-term		17,000
McPherson, Capital		40,400
McPherson, Withdrawals	43,000	
Sales revenue		180,000
Sales returns	5,000	
Cost of goods sold	81,500	
Selling expense	18,900	
General expense	17,000	
Interest expense	1,100	
Total	$ 266,200	$ 266,200

Requirements

1. Journalize Big Brother's closing entries.
2. Prepare Big Brother's single-step income statement for the year.
3. Compute the gross profit percentage and the rate of inventory turnover for the fiscal year ending January 31, 2012. Inventory on hand one year ago, at January 31, 2011, was $12,200.

4. For the year ended January 31, 2011, Big Brother's gross profit percentage was 50%, and inventory turnover was 4.9 times. Did the results for the year ended January 31, 2012 suggest improvement or deterioration in profitability over last year?

P5-40B *(L. OBJ. 5)* **Preparing a multi-step income statement and a classified balance sheet [30–40 min]**

← *Link Back to Chapter 4 (Classified Balance Sheet).* The accounts of White Electronics Company are listed along with their balances before closing for the month ended July 31, 2012.

Interest revenue	$ 700	Accounts payable	$ 17,000
Inventory	45,200	Accounts receivable	33,300
Note payable, long-term	48,000	Accumulated depreciation	37,700
Salary payable	2,500	White, Capital, June 30	51,600
Sales discounts	2,400	White, Withdrawals	20,000
Sales returns and allowances	8,000	Cash	8,200
Sales revenue	296,900	Cost of goods sold	161,500
Selling expense	37,900	Equipment	129,800
Supplies	5,600	General expense	16,800
Unearned sales revenue	13,000	Interest payable	1,300

Requirements

1. Prepare White Electronics' *multi-step* income statement.
2. Prepare White Electronics' statement of owner's equity.
3. Prepare White Electronics' classified balance sheet in *report form.*

P5-41B *(L. OBJ. 5, 6)* **Preparing a multi-step income statement and calculating gross profit percentage [15–25 min]**

The records of Number 1 Steak Company list the following selected accounts for the quarter ended June 30, 2011:

Interest revenue	$ 700	Accounts payable	$ 16,200
Inventory	45,600	Accounts receivable	33,600
Note payable, long-term	45,000	Accumulated depreciation	38,100
Salary payable	2,500	Nylund, Capital, April 1	54,500
Sales discounts	2,700	Nylund, Withdrawals	19,000
Sales returns and allowances	7,800	Cash	7,600
Sales revenue	296,900	Cost of goods sold	162,000
Selling expense	37,600	Equipment	131,000
Supplies	6,300	General expenses	16,100
Unearned sales revenue	13,900	Interest payable	1,500

Requirements

1. Prepare a multi-step income statement.
2. M. Elwell, manager of the company, strives to earn gross profit percentage of at least 50% and net income percentage of 20%. Did Number 1 achieve these goals? Show your calculations.

Continuing Exercise

E5-42 This exercise continues the Sherman Lawn Service situation from Exercise 4-37 of Chapter 4. Sherman Lawn Service has also begun selling plants that it purchases from a wholesaler. During September, Sherman Lawn Service completed the following transactions:

Sep 2	Completed lawn service and received cash of $500
5	Purchased 100 plants on account for inventory, $250, plus freight in of $10
15	Sold 40 plants on account, $400 (cost $104)
17	Consulted with a client on landscaping design for a fee of $150 on account
20	Purchased 100 plants on account for inventory, $300
21	Paid on account, $100
25	Sold 100 plants for cash, $700 (cost $276)
30	Recorded the following adjusting entries: Depreciation $29 Physical count of plant inventory, 50 plants (cost $150)

Requirements

1. Open the following selected T-accounts in the ledger: Cash; Accounts receivable; Lawn supplies; Plant inventory; Equipment; Accumulated depreciation-equipment; Accounts payable; Salary payable; Hannah Sherman, Capital; Hannah Sherman, Withdrawals; Income summary; Service revenue; Sales revenue; Cost of goods sold; Salary expense; Rent expense; Utilities expense; Depreciation expense-equipment; Supplies expense.
2. Journalize and post the September transactions. Key all items by date. Compute each account balance, and denote the balance as *Bal.*
3. Journalize and post the closing entries. Denote each closing amount as *Clo*. After posting all closing entries, prove the equality of debits and credits in the ledger.
4. Prepare the September income statement of Sherman Lawn Service. Use the single-step format.

Continuing Problem

P5-43 This problem continues the Haupt Consulting situation from Problem 4-38 of Chapter 4. Haupt performs systems consulting. Haupt has also begun selling accounting software. During January, Haupt Consulting completed the following transactions:

Jan 2	Completed a consulting engagement and received cash of $7,200
2	Prepaid three months office rent, $1,500
7	Purchased 100 units software inventory on account, $1,900, plus freight in, $100
16	Paid employee salary, $1,400
18	Sold 70 software units on account, $3,100
19	Consulted with a client for a fee of $900 on account
21	Paid on account, $2,000
22	Purchased 200 units software inventory on account, $4,600
24	Paid utilities, $300
28	Sold 100 units software for cash, $4,000
31	Recorded the following adjusting entries: Accrued salary expense, $1,400 Depreciation, $200 Expiration of prepaid rent, $500 Physical count of inventory, 120 units, $2,760

Requirements

1. Open the following selected T-accounts in the ledger: Cash; Accounts receivable; Software inventory; Prepaid rent; Accumulated depreciation; Accounts payable; Salary payable; C. Haupt, Capital; C. Haupt, Withdrawals; Income summary; Service revenue; Sales revenue; Cost of goods sold; Salary expense; Rent expense; Utilities expense; Depreciation expense.
2. Journalize and post the January transactions. Key all items by date. Compute each account balance, and denote the balance as *Bal.*
3. Journalize and post the closing entries. Denote each closing amount as *Clo.* After posting all closing entries, prove the equality of debits and credits in the ledger.
4. Prepare the January income statement of Haupt Consulting. Use the single-step format.

Practice Set

This problem continues the Crystal Clear Cleaning practice set begun in Chapter 1 and continued through Chapters 2, 3, and 4.

P5-44 Crystal Clear Cleaning has decided that, in addition to providing cleaning services, it will sell cleaning products. During May, Crystal Clear Cleaning completed the following transactions:

May	2	Purchased 800 units of inventory for $4,000 from Sparkle Co. on terms, 2/10, n/20
	5	Purchased 300 units of inventory from Borax on terms 3/5, n/30. The total invoice was for $2,100, which included a $100 freight charge.
	7	Returned 300 units of inventory to Sparkle from the May 2 purchase (cost $1,500)
	9	Paid Borax
	11	Sold 280 units of goods to Merry Maids for $2,500 on terms 1/10, n/30. Crystal's cost of the goods was $1,400.
	12	Paid Sparkle
	15	Received 56 units with a retail price of $500 of goods back from customer Merry Maids. The goods cost Crystal $280.
	21	Received payment from Merry Maids, settling the amount due in full
	28	Sold 81 units of goods to Hillary, Inc., for cash of $600 (cost $400)
	29	Paid cash for Utilities of $350
	30	Paid cash for Sales commission expense of $700
	31	Recorded the following adjusting entries: Physical count of Inventory on May 31 showed, 206 units of goods on hand, $1,400 Depreciation, $300 Accrued salary expense of $300 Prepared all other adjustments necessary for May

Requirements

1. Add any needed accounts to Crystal's existing chart of accounts.
2. Journalize and post the May transactions. Key all items by date. Compute each account balance, and denote the balance as *Bal.*
3. Journalize and post the adjusting entries. Denote each adjusting amount as *Adj.* After posting all adjusting entries, prove the equality of debits and credits in the ledger.
4. Prepare the May multi-step income statement, statement of owner's equity, and balance sheet for the company.
5. Journalize the May closing entries for the company.

Apply Your Knowledge

■ Decision Cases

Case 1. ← *Link Back to Chapter 4 (Classified Balance Sheet, Current Ratio, and Debt Ratio).* Jan Lorange manages Poppa Rollo's Pizza, which has prospered during its second year of operation. In order to help her decide whether to open another pizzeria, Lorange has prepared the current income statement of the business. Lorange read in an industry trade journal that a successful two-year-old pizzeria meets the following criteria:

a. Gross profit percentage is at least 60%

b. Net income is at least $90,000

Lorange believes the business meets both criteria. She intends to go ahead with the expansion plan and asks your advice on preparing the income statement in accordance with generally accepted accounting principles. When you point out that the statement includes errors, Lorange assures you that all amounts are correct. But some items are listed in the wrong place.

Requirement

1. Prepare a multi-step income statement and make a recommendation about whether Lorange should undertake the expansion.

POPPA ROLLO'S PIZZA Income Statement Year Ended December 31, 2011	
Sales revenue	$195,000
Gain on sale of land	24,600
Total revenue	219,600
Cost of goods sold	85,200
Gross profit	134,400
Operating expenses:	
Salary expense	35,600
Interest expense	6,000
Depreciation expense	4,800
Utilities expense	3,700
Total operating expense	50,100
Income from operations	84,300
Other revenue:	
Sales returns	10,700
Net income	$ 95,000

Case 2. Bill Hildebrand and Melissa Nordhaus opened Party-Time T-Shirts to sell T-shirts for parties at their college. The company completed the first year of operations, and the owners are generally pleased with operating results, as shown by the following income statement:

PARTY-TIME T-SHIRTS Income Statement Year Ended December 31, 2011	
Net sales revenue	$350,000
Cost of goods sold	210,000
Gross margin	140,000
Operating expenses:	
Selling expense	40,000
General expense	25,000
Net income	$ 75,000

Hildebrand and Nordhaus are considering how to expand the business. They each propose a way to increase profits to $100,000 during 2012.

a. Hildebrand believes they should advertise more heavily. He believes additional advertising costing $20,000 will increase net sales by 30% and leave general expense unchanged.

b. Nordhaus proposes selling higher-margin merchandise, such as party dresses. An importer can supply a minimum of 1,000 dresses for $40 each; Party-Time can mark these dresses up 100% and sell them for $80. Nordhaus realizes they will have to advertise the new merchandise, and this advertising will cost $5,000. Party-Time can expect to sell only 80% of these dresses during the coming year.

Requirement

1. Help Hildebrand and Nordhaus determine which plan to pursue. Prepare a single-step income statement for 2012 to show the expected net income under each plan.

Ethical Issue

Dobbs Wholesale Antiques makes all sales under terms of FOB shipping point. The company usually receives orders for sales approximately one week before shipping inventory to customers. For orders received late in December, Kathy Dobbs, the owner, decides when to ship the goods. If profits are already at an acceptable level, Dobbs delays shipment until January. If profits for the current year are lagging behind expectations, Dobbs ships the goods during December.

Requirements

1. Under Dobbs FOB policy, when should the company record a sale?
2. Do you approve or disapprove of Dobbs' manner of deciding when to ship goods to customers and record the sales revenue? If you approve, give your reason. If you disapprove, identify a better way to decide when to ship goods. (There is no accounting rule against Dobbs' practice.)

Financial Statement Case

This case uses both the income statement (statement of operations) and the balance sheet of **Amazon.com** in Appendix A at the end of the book. It will help you understand the closing process of a business.

Requirement

1. Journalize **Amazon.com's** closing entries for the revenues and expenses of 2007. Show all amounts in millions as in the **Amazon** financial statements. You may be unfamiliar with certain revenues and expenses, but treat each item on the income statement as either a revenue or an expense. For example, Net sales is the first revenue, and Interest income is also a revenue. The last revenue is Cumulative Effect of Change in Accounting Principle. A loss is like an expense. In your closing entries ignore all subtotals such as Gross Profit, Total Operating Expenses, and Net Loss.

■ Team Project

With a small team of classmates, visit one or more merchandising businesses in your area. Interview a responsible official of the company to learn about its inventory policies and accounting system. Obtain answers to the following questions, write a report, and be prepared to make a presentation to the class if your instructor so directs.

Requirements

1. What merchandise inventory does the business sell?
2. From whom does the business buy its inventory? Is the relationship with the supplier new or longstanding?
3. What are the FOB terms on inventory purchases? Who pays the freight, the buyer or the seller? Is freight a significant amount? What percentage of total inventory cost is the freight?
4. What are the credit terms on inventory purchases—2/10, n/30, or other? Does the business pay early to get purchase discounts? If so, why? If not, why not?
5. How does the business actually pay its suppliers? Does it mail a check or pay electronically? What is the actual payment procedure?
6. Which type of inventory accounting system does the business use—perpetual or periodic? Is this system computerized?
7. How often does the business take a physical count of its inventory? When during the year is the count taken? Describe the count procedures followed by the company.
8. Does the manager use the gross profit percentage and the rate of inventory turnover to evaluate the business? If not, show the manager how to use these ratios in decision making.
9. Ask any other questions your group considers appropriate.

Quick Check Answers

1. *d* 2. *a* 3. *c* 4. *c* 5. *b* 6. *b* 7. *c* 8. *d* 9. *a* 10. *c*

For online homework, exercises, and problems that provide you immediate feedback, please visit www.myaccountinglab.com.

Work Sheet for a Merchandising Business

The work sheet of a merchandiser is similar to the work sheet for a service business. The main new account is the Inventory account, which must be adjusted based on a physical count, as discussed in the chapter. Also, the merchandiser's work sheet carries the other new merchandising accounts (Sales revenue, Cost of goods sold, and so on). Work sheet procedures are the same as for a service business. The sum of the trial balance amounts, plus or minus the adjustments, equals the adjusted trial balance amounts. Then move the revenues and the expenses to the income statement and the assets, liabilities, and equity amounts to the balance sheet.

Exhibit 5A-1 is the work sheet of Smart Touch Learning for the year ended December 31, 2011.

EXHIBIT 5A-1 **Accounting Work Sheet for a Merchandising Business**

SMART TOUCH LEARNING
Accounting Work Sheet
Year Ended December 31, 2011

	Trial Balance		Adjustments		Adjusted Trial Balance		Income Statement		Balance Sheet	
Account Title	Debit	Credit	Debit	Credit	Debit	Credit	Debit	Credit	Debit	Credit
Cash	2,800				2,800				2,800	
Accounts receivable	4,600				4,600				4,600	
Inventory	40,500			(a) 300	40,200				40,200	
Supplies	600			(e) 500	100				100	
Prepaid insurance	1,200			(c) 1,000	200				200	
Furniture	33,200				33,200				33,200	
Accumulated depreciation		2,400		(d) 600		3,000				3,000
Accounts payable		39,500				39,500				39,500
Unearned sales revenue		2,000	(b) 1,300			700				700
Wages payable				(f) 400		400				400
Note payable, long-term		12,600				12,600				12,600
Sheena Bright, Capital		25,900				25,900				25,900
Sheena Bright, Withdrawals	54,100				54,100				54,100	
Sales revenue		168,000		(b) 1,300		169,300		169,300		
Sales discounts	1,400				1,400		1,400			
Sales returns and allowances	2,000				2,000		2,000			
Cost of goods sold	90,500		(a) 300		90,800		90,800			
Wage expense	9,800		(f) 400		10,200		10,200			
Rent expense	8,400				8,400		8,400			
Depreciation expense			(d) 600		600		600			
Insurance expense			(c) 1,000		1,000		1,000			
Supplies expense			(e) 500		500		500			
Interest expense	1,300				1,300		1,300			
	250,400	250,400	4,100	4,100	251,400	251,400	116,200	169,300	135,200	82,100
Net income							53,100			53,100
							169,300	169,300	135,200	135,200

Adjustment data at December 31, 2011:

a. Actual inventory on hand, based on the physical count, $40,200. The unadjusted Inventory balance is $40,500, so we must adjust Inventory and Cost of goods sold by $300.
b. Unearned sales revenue that has been earned, $1,300
c. Prepaid insurance expired, $1,000
d. Depreciation, $600
e. Supplies on hand, $100
f. Accrued wages payable, $400

A work sheet will aid the preparation of the closing entries (Exhibit 5-7) and the financial statements (Exhibit 5-8). However, the work sheet is optional.

Appendix 5A Assignments

Exercises

E5A-1 Preparing the work sheet and journalizing closing entries [10–15 min]
The trial balance and adjustments columns of the work sheet of Long Pond Business Systems Co. at January 31, 2011, follow:

LONG POND BUSINESS SYSTEMS CO.
Work Sheet
Year Ended January 31, 2011

	Trial Balance		Adjustments	
Account	Debit	Credit	Debit	Credit
Cash	2,100			
Accounts receivable	8,500		(a) 1,500	
Inventory	36,100			(b) 4,200
Supplies	13,000			(c) 7,900
Equipment	42,400			
Accumulated depreciation		11,200		(d) 2,000
Accounts payable		9,300		
Salary payable				(e) 1,200
Note payable, long-term		7,500		
Long, Capital		33,900		
Long, Withdrawals	45,000			
Sales revenue		233,000		(a) 1,500
Sales discounts	2,000			
Cost of goods sold	111,600		(b) 4,200	
Selling expense	21,000		(c) 5,300	
			(e) 1,200	
General expense	10,500		(c) 2,600	
			(d) 2,000	
Interest expense	2,700			
Total	294,900	294,900	16,800	16,800

Requirement

1. Complete the accounting work sheet for Long Pond Business Systems Co. Prepare the multi-step income statement, statement of owner's equity, and balance sheet for the year.

Problem (Group A)

P5A-2A Preparing a merchandiser's work sheet, preparing financial statements, and preparing closing entries [35–45 min]

Chattahoochee Coolers' trial balance as of December 31, 2012, follows:

CHATTAHOOCHEE COOLERS Trial Balance December 31, 2012		
	Unadjusted	
Account	Debit	Credit
Cash	2,400	
Accounts receivable	10,400	
Inventory	71,200	
Prepaid rent	3,600	
Equipment	24,100	
Accumulated depreciation		7,200
Accounts payable		9,000
Salary payable		0
Note payable, long-term		20,100
Robert, Capital		56,000
Robert, Withdrawals	36,400	
Sales revenue		192,500
Cost of goods sold	66,000	
Salary expense	46,400	
Rent expense	14,500	
Utilities expense	6,700	
Depreciation expense	0	
Interest expense	3,100	
Total	284,800	284,800

Adjustment data at December 31, 2012:

a. Prepaid rent expired, $2,300
b. Depreciation, $4,000
c. Accrued salaries, $1,000
d. Inventory on hand, $67,900

Requirements

1. Complete the accounting work sheet for the year ended December 31, 2012. Key adjusting entries by letter.
2. Prepare the multi-step income statement, statement of owner's equity, and balance sheet for the year.
3. Prepare closing entries for the year.

■ Problem (Group B)

P5A-3B Preparing a merchandiser's work sheet, preparing financial statements, and preparing closing entries [35–45 min]

Niagra Coolers' trial balance as of December 31, 2012, follows:

NIAGARA COOLERS Trial Balance December 31, 2012		
	Unadjusted	
Account	Debit	Credit
Cash	2,900	
Accounts receivable	10,200	
Inventory	71,800	
Prepaid rent	3,800	
Equipment	23,500	
Accumulated depreciation		7,300
Accounts payable		9,100
Salary payable		0
Note payable, long-term		20,200
C. Hunt, Capital		55,800
C. Hunt, Withdrawals	36,400	
Sales revenue		191,000
Cost of goods sold	64,000	
Salary expense	46,700	
Rent expense	14,300	
Utilities expense	6,600	
Depreciation expense	0	
Interest expense	3,200	
Total	283,400	283,400

Adjustment data at December 31, 2012:

a. Prepaid rent expired, $2,000
b. Depreciation, $4,500
c. Accrued salaries, $1,400
d. Inventory on hand, $68,800

Requirements

1. Complete the accounting work sheet for the year ended December 31, 2012. Key adjusting entries by letter.
2. Prepare the multi-step income statement, statement of owner's equity, and balance sheet for the year.
3. Prepare closing entries for the year.

Accounting for Merchandise in a Periodic Inventory System

Some smaller businesses find it too expensive to invest in a perpetual inventory system. These businesses use a periodic system.

Recording the Purchase of Inventory

All inventory systems use the Inventory account. But in a periodic system, purchases, purchase discounts, purchase returns and allowances, and transportation costs are recorded in separate accounts. Let us account for Smart Touch Learning's purchase of the RCA goods in Exhibit 5B-1.

EXHIBIT 5B-1 | **Purchase Invoice**

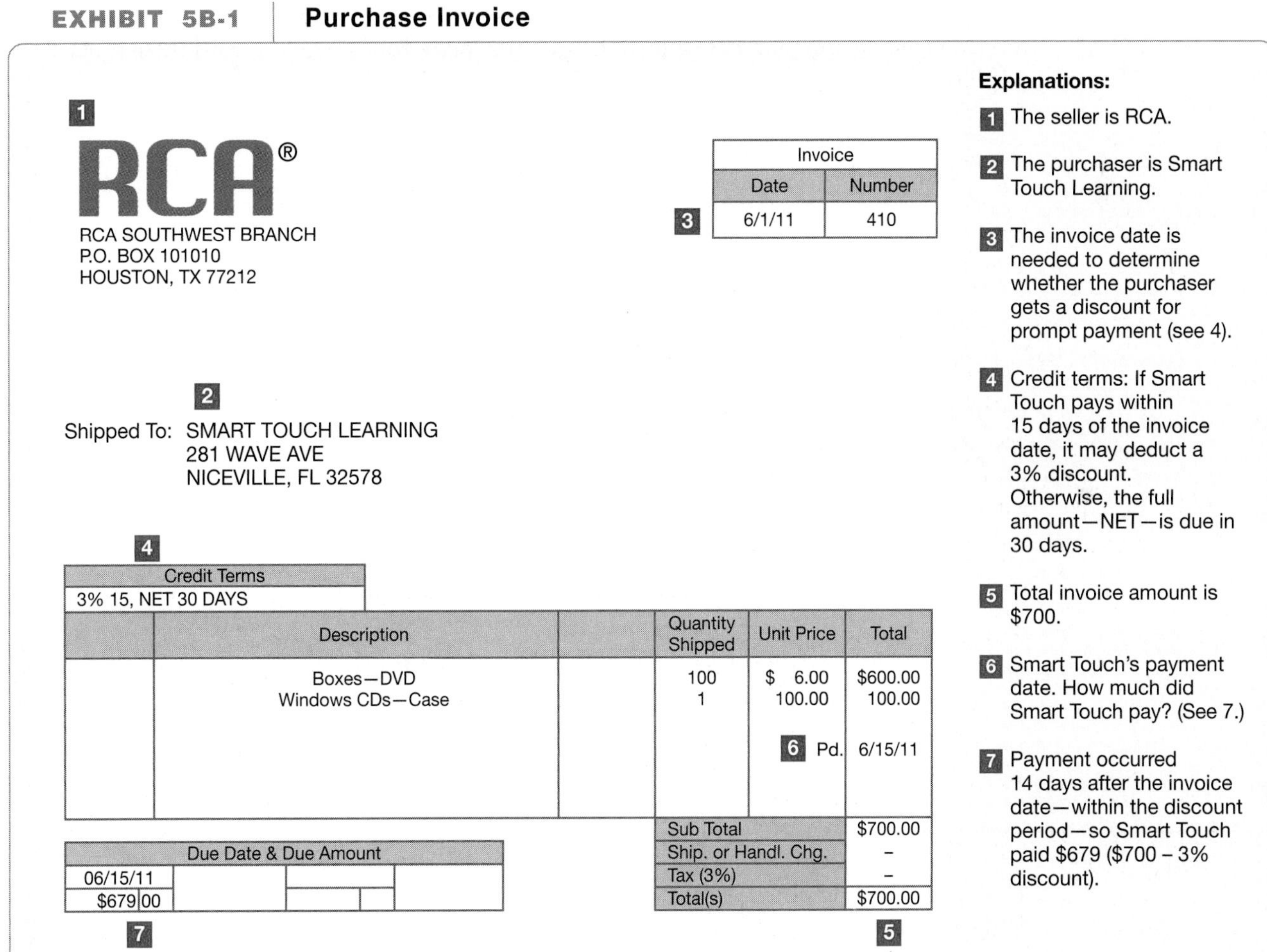

1 RCA®

RCA SOUTHWEST BRANCH
P.O. BOX 101010
HOUSTON, TX 77212

3

Invoice	
Date	Number
6/1/11	410

2
Shipped To: SMART TOUCH LEARNING
281 WAVE AVE
NICEVILLE, FL 32578

4

Credit Terms
3% 15, NET 30 DAYS

	Description		Quantity Shipped	Unit Price	Total
	Boxes—DVD		100	$ 6.00	$600.00
	Windows CDs—Case		1	100.00	100.00
				6 Pd.	6/15/11

Due Date & Due Amount			
06/15/11			
$679 00			

7

Sub Total	$700.00
Ship. or Handl. Chg.	–
Tax (3%)	–
Total(s)	$700.00

5

Explanations:

1 The seller is RCA.

2 The purchaser is Smart Touch Learning.

3 The invoice date is needed to determine whether the purchaser gets a discount for prompt payment (see 4).

4 Credit terms: If Smart Touch pays within 15 days of the invoice date, it may deduct a 3% discount. Otherwise, the full amount—NET—is due in 30 days.

5 Total invoice amount is $700.

6 Smart Touch's payment date. How much did Smart Touch pay? (See 7.)

7 Payment occurred 14 days after the invoice date—within the discount period—so Smart Touch paid $679 ($700 – 3% discount).

Recording Purchases and Purchase Discounts

The following entries record the purchase and payment on account within the discount period. Smart Touch received the goods on June 3 and paid within the discount period.

Date	Accounts and Explanation	Debit	Credit
Jun 3	Purchases (E+)	700	
	Accounts payable (L+)		700
	Purchased inventory on account.		
Jun 15	Accounts payable (L–)	700	
	Cash ($700 × 0.97) (A–)		679
	Purchase discounts ($700 × 0.03) (CE+)		21
	Paid within discount period.		

Recording Purchase Returns and Allowances

Suppose that, prior to payment, Smart Touch returned to **RCA** goods costing $100 and also received from **RCA** a purchase allowance of $10. Smart Touch would record these transactions as follows:

Date	Accounts and Explanation	Debit	Credit
Jun 4	Accounts payable (L–)	100	
	Purchase returns and allowances (CE+)		100
	Returned inventory to seller.		
4	Accounts payable (L–)	10	
	Purchase returns and allowances (CE+)		10
	Received a purchase allowance.		

During the period, the business records the cost of all inventory bought in the Purchases account. The balance of Purchases is a *gross* amount because it does not include subtractions for discounts, returns, or allowances. **Net purchases** is the remainder after subtracting the contra accounts from Purchases:

Purchases (*debit*)
– Purchase discounts (*credit*)
– Purchase returns and allowances (*credit*)
= Net purchases (a *debit* subtotal, not a separate account)

Recording Transportation Costs

Under the periodic system, costs to transport purchased inventory from seller to buyer are debited to a separate Freight in account, as shown for a $60 freight bill:

Date	Accounts and Explanation	Debit	Credit
Jun 3	Freight in (E+)	60	
	Cash (A–)		60
	Paid a freight bill.		

Recording the Sale of Inventory

Recording sales is streamlined in the periodic system. With no running record of inventory to maintain, we can record a $3,000 sale as follows:

Date	Accounts		Debit	Credit
Jun 9	Accounts receivable	(A+)	3,000	
	Sales revenue	(R+)		3,000
	Sale on account.			

There is no accompanying entry to Inventory and Cost of goods sold in the periodic system.

Accounting for sales discounts and sales returns and allowances is the same as in a perpetual inventory system, except that there are no entries to Inventory or Cost of goods sold.

Cost of goods sold (also called *cost of sales*) is the largest single expense of most businesses that sell merchandise, such as Smart Touch and **Gap, Inc.** It is the cost of the inventory the business has sold to customers. In a periodic system, cost of goods sold must be computed as shown in Exhibit 5B-2.

Cost of Goods Sold in a Periodic Inventory System

The amount of cost of goods sold is the same regardless of the inventory system—perpetual or periodic. As we have seen under the perpetual system, cost of goods sold is simply the sum of the amounts posted to that account.

Cost of goods sold is computed differently under the periodic system. At the end of each period the company combines a number of accounts to compute cost of goods sold for the period. Exhibit 5B-2 shows how to make the computation.

EXHIBIT 5B-2 **Measuring Cost of Goods Sold in the Periodic Inventory System**

Beginning Inventory + Net Purchases and Freight In

= Cost of Goods Available

− Ending Inventory = Cost of Goods Sold

Here is Greg's Groovy Tunes' computation of cost of goods sold for 2011:

Cost of goods sold:		
Beginning inventory		$ 38,600
Purchases	$91,400	
Less: Purchase discounts	(3,000)	
Purchase returns and allowances	(1,200)	
Net purchases		87,200
Freight in		5,200
Cost of goods available		131,000
Less: Ending inventory		(40,200)
Cost of goods sold		$ 90,800

Cost of goods sold is reported as the first expense on the merchandiser's income statement.

Exhibit 5B-3 summarizes this appendix by showing Greg's Groovy Tunes' net sales revenue, cost of goods sold, and gross profit on the income statement for the periodic system. (All amounts are assumed.)

Exhibit 5B-4 on page 355 is intended to provide a side by side comparison of periodic and perpetual inventory journal entries for the same company's transactions.

Appendix 5B Assignments

Short Exercises

S5B-1 *(L. OBJ. 5)* **Computing cost of goods sold in a periodic inventory system [5 min]**
T Wholesale Company began the year with inventory of $8,000. During the year, T purchased $90,000 of goods and returned $6,000 due to damage. T also paid freight charges of $1,000 on inventory purchases. At year-end T's adjusted inventory balance stood at $11,000. T uses the periodic inventory system.

Requirement

1. Compute T's cost of goods sold for the year.

Exercises

E5B-2 *(L. OBJ.5)* **Journalizing periodic transactions [10–15 min]**
On September 30, Stanley & Weaver Jewelers purchased inventory of $8,600 on account from Onyx Jewels, a jewelry importer. Terms were 3/15, net 45. On receiving the goods, Stanley & Weaver checked the order and found $700 of unsuitable merchandise. Therefore, Stanley & Weaver returned $700 of merchandise to Onyx on October 4.

On October 14, Stanley & Weaver paid the net amount owed from September 30, less the return.

Requirement

1. Journalize indicated transactions of Onyx Jewels. Use the periodic inventory system. Explanations are not required.

E5B-3 *(L. OBJ.5)* **Journalizing periodic transactions [10–15 min]**
Refer to the business situation in Exercise 5B-2.

Requirement

1. Journalize the transactions of Stanley & Weaver Jewelers. Use the periodic inventory system. Explanations are not required.

EXHIBIT 5B-3 Partial Income Statement Periodic Inventory System

GREG'S GROOVY TUNES Income Statement Year Ended December 31, 2011			
Sales revenue			$169,300
Less: Sales returns and allowances			(2,000)
Sales discounts			(1,400)
Net sales revenue			$165,900
Cost of goods sold:			
Beginning inventory		38,600	
Purchases	$91,400		
Less: Purchase discounts	(3,000)		
Purchase returns and allowances	(1,200)		
Net purchases		87,200	
Freight in		5,200	
Cost of goods available		131,000	
Less: Ending inventory		(40,200)	
Cost of goods sold			90,800
Gross profit			$ 75,100

EXHIBIT 5B-4 Perpetual vs. Periodic Inventory

PERPETUAL INVENTORY / **PERIODIC INVENTORY**

Jan 1: Purchase of Inventory for $500 (Terms: 1/10, n/15)

Perpetual	DR	CR	Periodic	DR	CR
Inventory	500		Purchases	500	
Accounts payable		500	Accounts payable		500

Jan 4: Purchaser returns $100 of inventory because it is not the size ordered

Perpetual	DR	CR	Periodic	DR	CR
Accounts payable	100		Accounts payable	100	
Inventory		100	Purchase returns & allowances		100

Jan 10: Purchaser pays balance taking advantage of terms

Perpetual	DR	CR	Periodic	DR	CR
Accounts payable	400		Accounts payable	400	
Inventory (400 × 1%)		4	Purchase discounts		4
Cash		396	Cash		396

Jan 12: Purchaser pays freight bill of $15 to UPS for shipping of Jan 1 purchase

Perpetual	DR	CR	Periodic	DR	CR
Inventory	15		Freight in	15	
Cash		15	Cash		15

Note that the net COST of all goods acquired is the same.

1) Perpetual: Inventory (500DR – 100CR – 4CR + 15DR = 411)
2) Periodic: Purchases 500DR – Purchase Returns 100CR – Purchase Discounts 4CR + Freight In 15DR = 411

E5B-4 *(L. OBJ. 6)* **Cost of goods sold in a periodic system [10–15 min]**
Foxtrot Electric, Co., uses the periodic inventory system. Foxtrot reported the following selected amounts at December 31, 2011:

Inventory, December 31, 2010	$ 19,000	Freight in	$ 6,000
Inventory, December 31, 2011	24,000	Sales revenue	169,000
Purchases (of inventory)	82,000	Sales discounts	5,000
Purchase discounts	4,000	Sales returns	13,000
Purchase returns	8,000	Owner's equity	47,000

Requirement

1. Compute Foxtrot's:
   a. Net sales revenue
   b. Cost of goods sold
   c. Gross profit

Problem (Group A)

P5B-5A *(L. OBJ.5)* **Journalizing periodic transactions [10–15 min]**
Assume that the following transactions occurred between Cambridge Medical Supply and a Drops drug store during September of the current year.

Sep	6	Drops purchased $5,900 of merchandise from Cambridge Medical Supply on credit terms of 2/10, n/30, FOB shipping point. Separately, Drops paid freight in of $250.
	10	Drops returned $1,100 of the merchandise to Cambridge
	15	Drops paid $2,950 of the invoice amount owed to Cambridge for the September 6 purchase, less the discount
	27	Drops paid the remaining amount owed to Cambridge for the September 6 purchase

Requirement

1. Journalize these transactions, first on the books of the Drops drug store and second on the books of Cambridge Medical Supply. Use the periodic inventory system.

Problem (Group B)

P5B-6B *(L. OBJ.5)* **Journalizing periodic transactions [10–15 min]**
Assume that the following transactions occurred between Boston Medical Supply and a Rite-Help drug store during April of the current year.

Apr	6	Rite-Help purchased $6,000 of merchandise from Boston Medical Supply on credit terms of 2/10, n/30, FOB shipping point. Separately, Rite-Help paid freight in of $250
	10	Rite-Help returned $800 of the merchandise to Boston
	15	Rite-Help paid $3,000 of the invoice amount owed to Boston for the April 6 purchase, less the discount
	27	Rite-Help paid the remaining amount owed to Boston for the April 6 purchase

Requirement

1. Journalize these transactions, first on the books of the Rite-Help drug store and second on the books of Boston Medical Supply. Use the periodic inventory system.

Comprehensive Problem for Chapters 1–5

Completing a Merchandiser's Accounting Cycle

The end-of-month trial balance of St. James Technology at January 31, 2011, follows:

ST. JAMES TECHNOLOGY Trial Balance January 31, 2011		
Cash	$ 16,430	
Accounts receivable	19,090	
Inventory	65,400	
Supplies	2,700	
Building	188,170	
Accumulated depreciation—building		$ 36,000
Furniture	45,600	
Accumulated depreciation—furniture		5,800
Accounts payable		28,300
Salary payable		
Unearned sales revenue		6,560
Note payable, long-term		87,000
James, Capital		144,980
James, Withdrawals	9,200	
Sales revenue		187,970
Sales discounts	7,300	
Sales returns and allowances	8,140	
Cost of goods sold	103,000	
Selling expense	21,520	
General expense	10,060	
Total	$496,610	$496,610

Additional data at January 31, 2011:

---

a. Supplies consumed during the month, $1,500. Half is selling expense, and the other half is general expense.

b. Depreciation for the month: building, $4,000; furniture, $4,800. One-fourth of depreciation is selling expense, and three-fourths is general expense.

c. Unearned sales revenue earned during January, $4,580.

d. Accrued salaries, a general expense, $1,150.

e. Inventory on hand, $63,720. St. James uses the perpetual inventory system.

Requirements

1. Using four-column accounts, open the accounts listed on the trial balance, inserting their unadjusted balances. Date the balances of the following accounts January 1: Supplies; Building; Accumulated depreciation—building; Furniture; Accumulated depreciation—furniture; Unearned sales revenue; James, Capital. Date the balance of James, Withdrawals, January 31. Also open the Income summary account.
2. Enter the trial balance on an accounting work sheet, and complete the work sheet for the month ended January 31, 2011. St. James Technology groups all operating expenses under two accounts, Selling expense and General expense. Leave two blank lines under Selling expense and three blank lines under General expense.
3. Prepare the company's *multi-step* income statement and statement of owner's equity for the month ended January 31, 2011. Also prepare the balance sheet at that date in *report* form.
4. Journalize the adjusting and closing entries at January 31.
5. Post the adjusting and closing entries, using dates.

6 Merchandise Inventory

Learning Objectives/Success Keys

1. Define accounting principles related to inventory
2. Define inventory costing methods
3. Account for perpetual inventory by the three most common costing methods
4. Compare the effects of the three most common costing methods
5. Apply the lower-of-cost-or-market rule to inventory
6. Measure the effects of inventory errors
7. Estimate ending inventory by the gross profit method

Chapter 5 introduced the accounting for merchandise inventory. It showed how Smart Touch Learning, an e-learning company, recorded the purchase and sale of its inventory. **Amazon.com**, **Wal-Mart**, and **Rocky Mountain Sportswear** are other merchandising companies. The current chapter completes the accounting for merchandise inventory.

Smart Touch Learning may select from several different methods to account for its inventory. Inventory is the first area in which you must pick the accounting method you will use. In this chapter we use Smart Touch Learning to illustrate the different inventory accounting methods.

First let us review how merchandise inventory affects a company. Exhibit 6-1 gives a partial balance sheet and income statement for Smart Touch Learning. Inventories, cost of goods sold, and gross profit are highlighted. These amounts (I, C, and P) are left blank to indicate that throughout the chapter we will be computing them using various inventory accounting methods.

The remainder of the chapter explores how to compute these amounts in Exhibit 6-1:

- Ending inventory (I) on the balance sheet
- Cost of goods sold (C) and gross profit (P) on the income statement

EXHIBIT 6-1 **Merchandising Sections of the Financial Statements**

SMART TOUCH LEARNING
Balance Sheet (partial)
July 31, 2011

Assets	
Current assets:	
Cash	$ 6,000
Short-term investments	3,000
Accounts receivable	12,000
Inventories	I
Prepaid expenses	4,000

SMART TOUCH LEARNING
Income Statement (partial)
Year Ended July 31, 2011

		(Millions)
Net sales		$80,000
Cost of goods sold		C
Gross profit		G

We turn now to the accounting principles affecting inventories.

Accounting Principles and Inventories

1 Define accounting principles related to inventory

Several accounting principles affect inventories. Among them are consistency, disclosure, materiality, and accounting conservatism.

Consistency Principle

The **consistency principle** states that businesses should use the same accounting methods from period to period. Consistency helps investors compare a company's financial statements from one period to the next.

Suppose you are analyzing a company's net income over a two-year period. The company switched to a different inventory method from the method they had been using. Its net income increased dramatically but only as a result of the change in inventory method. If you did not know about the change, you might believe that the company's income really increased. Therefore, companies must report any changes in the accounting methods they use. Investors need this information to make wise decisions about the company.

Disclosure Principle

The **disclosure principle** holds that a company should report enough information for outsiders to make wise decisions about the company. In short, the company should report *relevant*, *reliable*, and *comparable* information about itself. This means disclosing the method being used to account for inventories. Suppose a banker is comparing two companies—one using inventory method A, and the other using inventory method B. The B company reports higher net income, but only because of the inventory method it selected. Without knowledge of these accounting methods, the banker could lend money to the wrong business.

Materiality Concept

The **materiality concept** states that a company must perform strictly proper accounting *only* for significant items. Information is significant—or, in accounting terms, *material*—when it would cause someone to change a decision. The materiality concept frees accountants from having to report every last item in strict accordance with GAAP.

Accounting Conservatism

Conservatism in accounting means exercising caution in reporting items in the financial statements. Conservatism says,

- "Anticipate no gains, but provide for all probable losses."
- "If in doubt, record an asset at the lowest reasonable amount and a liability at the highest reasonable amount."
- "When there's a question, record an expense rather than an asset."

The goal of conservatism is to report realistic figures.

Inventory Costing Methods

2 Define inventory costing methods

As we saw in Chapter 5,

Ending inventory = Number of units *on hand* × Unit cost

Cost of goods sold = Number of units *sold* × Unit cost

Companies determine the number of units from perpetual inventory records backed up by a physical count. The cost of each unit of inventory is,

Cost per unit = Purchase price – Purchase discounts + Freight-in

Exhibit 6-2 gives the inventory data for DVD0503 (Basic Excel Training DVD) for Smart Touch Learning.

EXHIBIT 6-2 **Perpetual Inventory Record—Quantities Only**

Item: DVD0503

Date	Quantity Purchased	Quantity Sold	Cost	Quantity on Hand
Jul 1			40	1
5	6		45	7
15		4	80	3
26	7		50	10
31		8	80	2
Totals	13	12	N/A	2

In this illustration, Smart Touch began July with 1 DVD0503 in inventory. Smart Touch had 2 DVD0503 at the end of July. Assume that Smart Touch's unit cost of each DVD0503 is $40. In this case,

Ending inventory	=	Number of units *on hand* (Exhibit 6-2)		Unit cost		
		2	×	$40	=	$80

Cost of goods sold	=	Number of units *sold* (Exhibit 6-2)		Unit cost		
		12	×	$40	=	$480

Measuring inventory cost is easy when prices do not change. But unit cost does change often. A DVD0503 that cost Smart Touch $40 in July may cost $45 in August. Suppose Smart Touch sells 10,000 DVD0503's in July and August. How many of the DVD0503's that were sold cost $40? How many cost $45? To compute ending inventory and cost of goods sold, Smart Touch must assign a specific unit cost to each item. The four costing methods GAAP allows are

1. Specific unit cost
2. Average cost
3. First-in, first-out (FIFO) cost
4. Last-in, first-out (LIFO) cost

A company may use any of these methods to account for its inventory.

The **specific-unit-cost method** is also called the **specific-identification method.** This method uses the specific cost of each unit of inventory. This costing method is best for businesses that sell unique, easily identified inventory items, such as automobiles (identified by the vehicle identification number [VIN]), jewels (a specific diamond ring), and real estate (identified by address). For instance, a **Chevrolet** dealer may have two **Monte Carlo** vehicles with *exactly* the same colors, interior, and options package. Assume one of the **Monte Carlo's** was purchased by the dealership on January 5 for $16,000 and the other was purchased on March 8 for

$19,000. The dealer would determine the cost of each of the identical vehicles sold based on the vehicle identification number. If the dealer sells the model whose VIN is on the March 8 invoice, cost of goods sold is $19,000. Suppose the other **Monte Carlo** is the only unit left in inventory at the end of the period. In that case, ending inventory would be $16,000—the cost of the January 5 vehicle.

Amazon.com uses the specific-unit-cost method to account for its inventory. But very few other companies use this method, so let us shift our focus to the more popular inventory costing methods.

Exhibit 6-3 illustrates the inventory prices from Exhibit 6-2.

EXHIBIT 6-3 | **Cost Flows for Three Inventory Methods**

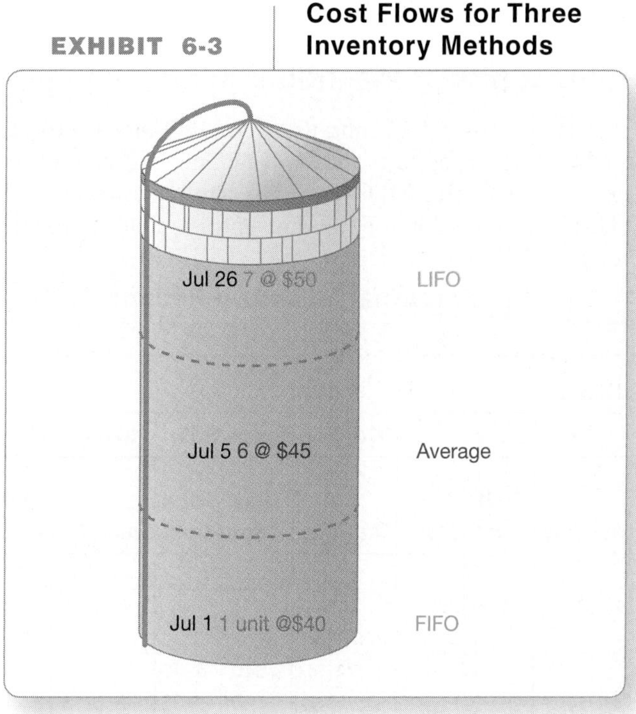

- Under the **FIFO (First-In, First-Out) method**, the cost of goods sold is based on the oldest purchases—that is the First In is the First Out of the warehouse (sold). In Exhibit 6-3, this is illustrated by the Cost of goods sold coming from the *bottom* of the container. FIFO costing is consistent with the physical movement of inventory (for most companies). That is, they sell their oldest inventory first.
- LIFO is the opposite of FIFO. Under the **LIFO (Last-In, First-Out) method**, ending inventory comes from the oldest costs (first purchases) of the period. The cost of goods sold is based on the most recent purchases (new costs)—that is the Last In is the First Out of the warehouse (sold). This is illustrated by the Cost of goods sold coming from the *top* of the container.
- Under the **average-cost method**, the business computes a new average cost per unit after each purchase. Ending inventory and cost of goods sold are then based on the same average cost per unit. This is illustrated by the cost of goods sold coming from the *middle* of the container.

Now let us see how Smart Touch would compute inventory amounts under FIFO, LIFO, and average costing for all of July. We use the transaction data from Exhibit 6-2 for all the illustrations.

In the body of the chapter, we show inventory costing in a perpetual system. Appendix 6A shows inventory costing in a periodic system.

Inventory Accounting in a Perpetual System

3 Account for perpetual inventory by the three most common costing methods

The different inventory costing methods produce different amounts for

- Ending inventory
- Cost of goods sold
- Gross profit

Let us begin with the FIFO method.

First-In, First-Out (FIFO) Method

Let us assume that Smart Touch Learning uses the FIFO method to account for its inventory. Under FIFO, the first costs incurred by Smart Touch are the first costs assigned to cost of goods sold. FIFO leaves in ending inventory the last—the newest—costs. This is illustrated in the FIFO inventory record in Exhibit 6-4.

EXHIBIT 6-4 | **Perpetual Inventory Record: FIFO**

DVD0503

	Purchases			Cost of Goods Sold			Inventory on Hand		
Date	Quantity	Unit Cost	Total Cost	Quantity	Unit Cost	Total Cost	Quantity	Unit Cost	Total Cost
Jul 1							1	$40	$40
5	6	$45	$270				1	40	40
							6	45	270
15				1	$40	$ 40			
				3	45	135	3	45	135
26	7	50	350				3	45	135
							7	50	350
31				3	45	135			
				5	50	250	2	50	100
31	13		$620	12		$560	2		$100

Smart Touch began July with 1 DVD0503 that cost $40. After the July 5 purchase, the inventory on hand consists of 7 units.

7 units on hand	1 @ $40	= $ 40
	6 @ $45	= 270
	Inventory on hand	= $310

On July 15, Smart Touch sold 4 units. Under FIFO, the first unit sold has the oldest cost ($40 per unit). The next 3 units sold cost $45 each. That leaves 3 units in inventory on July 15 at $45 each. The remainder of the inventory record follows the same pattern. Consider the sale on July 31 of 8 units. The oldest cost is from July 5 (3 units @ $45). The next oldest cost is from the July 26 purchase at $50 each (5 units @ $50). This leaves 2 units in inventory on July 31 at $50 each.

The FIFO monthly summary at July 31 is

- Cost of goods sold: 12 units that cost a total of $560
- Ending inventory: 2 units that cost a total of $100

Smart Touch measures cost of goods sold and inventory in this manner to prepare its financial statements.

Journal Entries Under FIFO

The journal entries under FIFO follow the data in Exhibit 6-4. For example, on July 5, Smart Touch purchased $270 of inventory and made the first journal entry. On July 15, Smart Touch sold 4 DVD0503 for the sale price of $80 each. Smart Touch recorded the sale, $320, and the cost of goods sold, $175 (figured in Exhibit 6-4 as 1 @ $40 + 3 @ $45). The remaining journal entries (July 26 and 31) follow the inventory data in Exhibit 6-4.

The amounts unique to FIFO are highlighted for emphasis. All other amounts are the same for all three inventory methods.

FIFO Journal Entries (All purchases and sales on account) The sales price of a DVD0503 is $80			
Jul 5	Inventory (6 × $45) (A+)	270	
	Accounts payable (L+)		270
	Purchased inventory on account.		
15	Accounts receivable (4 × $80) (A+)	320	
	Sales revenue (R+)		320
	Sale on account.		
15	Cost of goods sold (1 @ $40 + 3 @ $45) (E+)	175	
	Inventory (A–)		175
	Cost of goods sold.		
26	Inventory (7 × $50) (A+)	350	
	Accounts payable (L+)		350
	Purchased inventory on account.		
31	Accounts receivable (8 × $80) (A+)	640	
	Sales revenue (R+)		640
	Sale on account.		
31	Cost of goods sold (3 @ $45 + 5 @ $50) (E+)	385	
	Inventory (A–)		385
	Cost of goods sold.		

Last-In, First-Out (LIFO) Method

Exhibit 6-5 gives a perpetual inventory record for the LIFO method.

EXHIBIT 6-5 | **Perpetual Inventory Record: LIFO**

DVD0503

	Purchases			Cost of Goods Sold			Inventory on Hand		
Date	Quantity	Unit Cost	Total Cost	Quantity	Unit Cost	Total Cost	Quantity	Unit Cost	Total Cost
Jul 1							1	$40	$40
5	6	$45	$270				1	40	40
							6	45	270
15				4	$45	$180	1	40	40
							2	45	90
26	7	50	350				1	40	40
							2	45	90
							7	50	350
31				7	50	350			
				1	45	45	1	40	40
							1	45	45
31	13		$620	12		$575	2		$85

Again, Smart Touch had 1 DVD0503 at the beginning. After the purchase on July 5, Smart Touch holds 7 units of inventory (1 @ $40 plus 6 @ $45). On July 15, Smart Touch sells 4 units. Under LIFO, the cost of goods sold always comes from the newest purchase. That leaves three DVD0503's in inventory on July 15.

3 units on hand	1 @ $40	= $ 40
	2 @ $45	= 90
	Inventory on hand	= $130

The purchase of 7 units on July 26 adds a new $50 layer to inventory. Now inventory holds 10 units.

10 units on hand	1 @ $40	= $ 40
	2 @ $45	= 90
	7 @ $50	= 350
	Inventory on hand	= $480

Then the sale of 8 units on July 31 peels back units in LIFO order. The LIFO monthly summary at July 31 is

- Cost of goods sold: 12 units that cost a total of $575
- Ending inventory: 2 units that cost a total of $85

Under LIFO, Smart Touch could measure cost of goods sold and inventory in this manner to prepare its financial statements.

Journal Entries Under LIFO

The journal entries under LIFO follow the data in Exhibit 6-5. On July 5, Smart Touch purchased inventory of $270. The July 15 sale brought in sales revenue (4 units @ $80 = $320) and cost of goods sold ($180). The July 26 and 31 entries also come from the data in Exhibit 6-5. Amounts unique to LIFO are shown in color.

	LIFO Journal Entries (All purchases and sales on account) The sales price of a DVD0503 is $80		
Jul 5	Inventory (6 × $45) (A+)	270	
	Accounts payable (L+)		270
	Purchased inventory on account.		
15	Accounts receivable (4 × $80) (A+)	320	
	Sales revenue (R+)		320
	Sale on account.		
15	Cost of goods sold (4 @ $45) (E+)	180	
	Inventory (A−)		180
	Cost of goods sold.		
26	Inventory (7 × $50) (A+)	350	
	Accounts payable (L+)		350
	Purchased inventory on account.		
31	Accounts receivable (8 × $80) (A+)	640	
	Sales revenue (R+)		640
	Sale on account.		
31	Cost of goods sold (7 @ $50 + 1 @ $45) (E+)	395	
	Inventory (A−)		395
	Cost of goods sold.		

Average Cost Method

Suppose Smart Touch uses the average-cost method to account for its inventory of DVD0503. Exhibit 6-6 shows a perpetual inventory record for the average-cost method. We round average unit cost to the nearest cent and total cost to the nearest dollar.

EXHIBIT 6-6 **Perpetual Inventory Record: Average Cost**

DVD0503

	Purchases			Cost of Goods Sold			Inventory on Hand		
Date	Quantity	Unit Cost	Total Cost	Quantity	Unit Cost	Total Cost	Quantity	Unit Cost	Total Cost
Jul 1							1	$40.00	$ 40
5	6	$45	$270				7	44.29	310
15				4	$44.29	$177	3	44.29	133
26	7	50	350				10	48.30	483
31				8	48.30	386	2	48.30	97
31	13		$620	12		$563	2		$ 97

As noted previously, after each purchase, Smart Touch computes a new average cost per unit. For example, on July 5, the new average unit cost is

	Total cost of inventory on hand		Number of units on hand		Average cost per unit
Jul 5	$40 + $270 = $310	÷	7 units	=	$44.29

The goods sold on July 15 are then costed out at $44.29 per unit. On July 26 when the next purchase is made, the new average unit cost is

	Total cost of inventory on hand		Number of units on hand		Average cost per unit
Jul 26	(3 @ $44.29) + (7 @ $50)	÷	3 + 7	=	?
	133 + 350 or $483	÷	10	=	$48.30

The average-cost summary at July 31 is

- Cost of goods sold: 12 units that cost a total of $563
- Ending inventory: 2 units that cost a total of $97

Under the average-cost method, Smart Touch could use these amounts to prepare its financial statements.

Journal Entries Under Average Costing

The journal entries under average costing follow the data in Exhibit 6-6. On July 5, Smart Touch purchased $270 of inventory and made the first journal entry. On July 15, Smart Touch sold 4 DVD0503's for $80 each. Smart Touch recorded the sale ($320) and the cost of goods sold ($177). The remaining journal entries (July 26 and 31) follow the data in Exhibit 6-6. Amounts unique to the average cost method are highlighted.

Average Cost Journal Entries (All purchases and sales on account) **The sales price of a DVD0503 is $80**			
Jul 5	Inventory (6 × $45) (A+)	270	
	Accounts payable (L+)		270
	Purchased inventory on account.		
15	Accounts receivable (4 × $80) (A+)	320	
	Sales revenue (R+)		320
	Sale on account.		
15	Cost of goods sold (4 @ $44.29) (E+)	177	
	Inventory (A–)		177
	Cost of goods sold.		
26	Inventory (7 × $50) (A+)	350	
	Accounts payable (L+)		350
	Purchased inventory on account.		
31	Accounts receivable (8 × $80) (A+)	640	
	Sales revenue (R+)		640
	Sale on account.		
31	Cost of goods sold (8 @ $48.30) (E+)	386	
	Inventory (A–)		386
	Cost of goods sold.		

Comparing FIFO, LIFO, and Average Cost

4 Compare the effects of the three most common costing methods

Exhibit 6-7 shows that FIFO is the most popular inventory costing method, LIFO is the next most popular, and average cost ranks third.

EXHIBIT 6-7 **Use of the Various Inventory Methods**

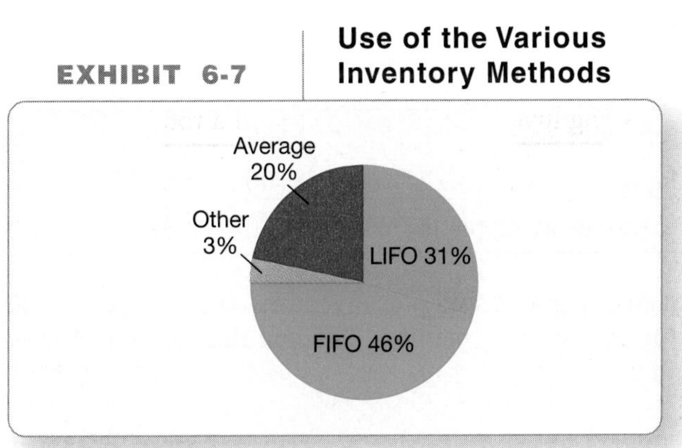

What leads Smart Touch Learning to select the FIFO method, **General Electric** to use LIFO, and **Fossil** (the watch company) to use average cost? The different methods have different benefits.

Exhibit 6-8 summarizes the results for the three inventory methods for Smart Touch. It shows sales revenue, cost of goods sold, and gross profit for FIFO, LIFO, and average cost.

EXHIBIT 6-8 **Comparative Results for FIFO, LIFO, and Average Cost**

	FIFO	LIFO	Average
Sales revenue	$960	$960	$960
– Cost of goods sold (From Exh 6-4, 6-5, & 6-6)	560	575	563
= Gross profit	$400	$385	$397

Exhibit 6-8 shows that FIFO produces the lowest cost of goods sold and the highest gross profit. Net income is also the highest under FIFO when inventory costs are rising. Many companies prefer high income in order to attract investors and borrow on good terms. FIFO offers this benefit, in a period of rising prices.

LIFO results in the highest cost of goods sold and the lowest gross profit. That lets companies pay the lowest income taxes when inventory costs are rising. Low tax payments conserve cash and that is the main benefit of LIFO. The downside of LIFO is that the company reports low net income.

The average-cost method generates amounts that fall between the extremes of FIFO and LIFO. Companies that seek a "middle-ground" solution, therefore, use the average-cost method for inventory. Consider again the purchases made by Smart Touch during July. Smart Touch had total inventory in July as follows:

Jul 1	1 @ $40	$ 40
Jul 5	6 @ $45	$270
Jul 26	7 @ $50	$350
Total cost of July inventory available for sale		$660

Only one of two things can happen to the DVDs— either they remain in the warehouse (Inventory) or they are sold (Cost of goods sold). Consider the results from each of the costing methods for July for Smart Touch.

Jul 2011	FIFO	LIFO	Average
Cost of goods sold	$560	$575	$563
+ Ending Inventory	$100	$ 85	$ 97
= Cost of goods available for sale	$660	$660	$660

The sum of cost of goods sold plus inventory equals the **cost of goods available for sale**, $660 for each costing method. Finding this figure is a good way to spot check your results.

Summary Problem 1

Fossil specializes in designer watches and leather goods. Assume **Fossil** began June holding 10 wristwatches that cost $50 each. During June, **Fossil** bought and sold inventory as follows:

Jun 3	Sold 8 units for $100 each
16	Purchased 10 units @ $55 each
23	Sold 8 units for $100 each

Requirements

1. Prepare a perpetual inventory record for **Fossil** under:
   - FIFO
   - LIFO
   - Average Cost

   Round unit cost to the nearest cent and all other amounts to the nearest dollar.
2. Journalize all of **Fossil's** inventory transactions for June under all three costing methods.
3. Show the computation of gross profit for each method.
4. Which method maximizes net income? Which method minimizes income taxes?

Solution

1. Perpetual inventory records:

FIFO

Wristwatches

	Purchases			Cost of Goods Sold			Inventory on Hand		
Date	Quantity	Unit Cost	Total Cost	Quantity	Unit Cost	Total Cost	Quantity	Unit Cost	Total Cost
Jun 1							10	$50	$500
3				8	$50	$400	2	50	100
16	10	$55	$550				2	50	100
							10	55	550
23				2	50	100			
				6	55	330	4	55	220
30				16		$830	4		$220

LIFO

Wristwatches									
	Purchases			Cost of Goods Sold			Inventory on Hand		
Date	Quantity	Unit Cost	Total Cost	Quantity	Unit Cost	Total Cost	Quantity	Unit Cost	Total Cost
Jun 1							10	$50	$500
3				8	$50	$400	2	50	100
16	10	$55	$550				2	50	100
							10	55	550
23				8	55	440	2	50	100
							2	55	110
30				16		$840	4		$210

AVERAGE COST

Wristwatches									
	Purchases			Cost of Goods Sold			Inventory on Hand		
Date	Quantity	Unit Cost	Total Cost	Quantity	Unit Cost	Total Cost	Quantity	Unit Cost	Total Cost
Jun 1							10	$50.00	$500
3				8	$50.00	$400	2	50.00	100
16	10	$55	$550				12	54.17	650
23				8	54.17	433	4	54.17	217
30				16		$833	4		217

2. Journal Entries:

		FIFO		LIFO		Average	
Jun 3	Accounts receivable (A+)	800		800		800	
	Sales revenue (R+)		800		800		800
3	Cost of goods sold (E+)	400		400		400	
	Inventory (A–)		400		400		400
16	Inventory (A+)	550		550		550	
	Accounts payable (L+)		550		550		550
23	Accounts receivable (A+)	800		800		800	
	Sales revenue (R+)		800		800		800
23	Cost of goods sold (E+)	430		440		433	
	Inventory (A–)		430		440		433

3. Gross Profit:

	FIFO	LIFO	Average
Sales revenue ($800 + $800)	$1,600	$1,600	$1,600
– Cost of goods sold ($400 + $430)	830		
($400 + $440)		840	
($400 + $433)			833
= Gross profit	$ 770	$ 760	$ 767

4. FIFO maximizes net income.
   LIFO minimizes income taxes.

Lower-of-Cost-or-Market Rule

5 Apply the lower-of-cost-or-market rule to inventory

In addition to the FIFO, LIFO, and average costing methods, accountants face other inventory issues, such as the **lower-of-cost-or-market rule** (abbreviated as **LCM**). LCM shows accounting conservatism in action and requires that inventory be reported in the financial statements at whichever is lower—

- the historical cost of the inventory, or
- the market value of the inventory.

For inventories, market value generally means the current replacement cost (that is, the cost to replace the inventory on hand). If the replacement cost of inventory is less than its historical cost, the business must write down the inventory value. On the balance sheet the business reports ending inventory at its LCM value.

Suppose Smart Touch Learning paid $3,000 for a CD01 inventory. By July 31, the inventory can now be replaced for $2,200, and the decline in value appears permanent. Market value is below cost, and the entry to write down the inventory to LCM is as follows:

		Cost of goods sold (cost, $3,000 – market, $2,200) (E+)	800	
		Inventory (A–)		800
		To write inventory down to market value		

In this case, Smart Touch Learning's balance sheet would report this inventory as follows:

Balance Sheet	
Current assets:	
Inventory, at market	
(which is lower than FIFO cost)	$2,200

Companies often disclose LCM in notes to their financial statements, as shown here for Smart Touch Learning:

NOTE 2: STATEMENT OF SIGNIFICANT ACCOUNTING POLICIES

Inventories. Inventories are carried at the *lower of cost or market.* Cost is determined using the first-in, first-out method.

Effects of Inventory Errors

6 Measure the effects of inventory errors

Businesses count their inventory at the end of the period. For the financial statements to be accurate, it is important to get a correct count of ending inventory. This can be difficult for a company with widespread operations.

An error in ending inventory creates a whole string of errors. To illustrate, suppose Smart Touch Learning accidentally counted $5,000 more ending inventory than it actually had. In that case, ending inventory would be overstated by $5,000 on the balance sheet. The following shows how an overstatement of ending inventory affects cost of goods sold, gross profit, and net income:

	Ending Inventory Overstated $5,000
Sales revenue	Correct
Cost of goods sold:	
Beginning inventory	Correct
Net purchases	Correct
Cost of goods available	Correct
Ending inventory	ERROR: Overstated $5,000
Cost of goods sold	Understated $5,000
Gross profit	Overstated $5,000
Operating expenses	Correct
Net income	Overstated $5,000

Understating the ending inventory—reporting the inventory too low—has the opposite effect. If Smart Touch understated the Inventory by $1,200, the effect would be as shown here:

	Ending Inventory Understated $1,200
Sales revenue	Correct
Cost of goods sold:	
Beginning inventory	Correct
Net purchases	Correct
Cost of goods available	Correct
Ending inventory	ERROR: Understated $1,200
Cost of goods sold	Overstated $1,200
Gross profit	Understated $1,200
Operating expenses	Correct
Net income	Understated $1,200

Recall that one period's ending inventory becomes the next period's beginning inventory. As a result, an error in ending inventory carries over into the next period. Exhibit 6-9 on page 376 illustrates the effect of an inventory error, assuming all other items on the income statement are unchanged for the 3 periods. Period 1's ending inventory is overstated by $5,000; period 1's ending inventory should be $10,000. The error carries over to period 2. Period 3 is correct. In fact, both Period 1 and Period 2 should look like Period 3.

EXHIBIT 6-9 Inventory Errors: An Example

SAMPLE COMPANY
Income Statement
For the years ended Period 1, 2 and 3

	Period 1 *Ending* Inventory Overstated by $5,000		Period 2 *Beginning* Inventory Overstated by $5,000		Period 3 Correct	
Sales revenue		$100,000		$100,000		$100,000
Cost of goods sold:						
Beginning inventory	$10,000		$ 15,000		$ 10,000	
Net purchases	50,000		50,000		50,000	
Cost of goods available	60,000		65,000		60,000	
Ending inventory	(15,000)		(10,000)		(10,000)	
Cost of goods sold		45,000		55,000		50,000
Gross profit		$ 55,000		$ 45,000		$ 50,000

The correct gross profit is $50,000 for each period. $100,000

Source: The authors thank Carl High for this example.

Ending inventory is *subtracted* to compute cost of goods sold in one period and the same amount is *added* as beginning inventory in the next period. Therefore, an inventory error cancels out after two periods. The overstatement of cost of goods sold in Period 2 counterbalances the understatement for Period 1. Thus, total gross profit for the two periods combined is correct. These effects are summarized in Exhibit 6-10.

EXHIBIT 6-10 Effects of Inventory Errors

SAMPLE COMPANY
Income Statement
For the years ended Period 1 and 2

	Period 1		Period 2	
	Cost of Goods Sold	Gross Profit and Net Income	Cost of Goods Sold	Gross Profit and Net Income
Period 1 Ending inventory *overstated*	Understated	Overstated	Overstated	Understated
Period 1 Ending inventory *understated*	Overstated	Understated	Understated	Overstated

Estimating Ending Inventory

Estimate ending inventory by the gross profit method

Often a business must *estimate* the value of its ending inventory. The **gross profit method** provides a way to estimate inventory as follows:

Beginning inventory
+ Net purchases
= Cost of goods available
– Ending inventory
= Cost of goods sold

Rearranging *ending inventory* and *cost of goods sold* helps to estimate ending inventory:

Beginning inventory
+ Net purchases
= Cost of goods available
– Cost of goods sold (Sales – Gross profit = COGS)
= Ending inventory

Suppose Smart Touch Learning suffers a hurricane loss and must estimate the value of the inventory destroyed. To collect insurance, the company must estimate the cost of the inventory destroyed. Using its normal *gross profit percent* (that is, gross profit divided by net sales revenue), Smart Touch can estimate cost of goods sold. Then it needs to subtract cost of goods sold from goods available to estimate ending inventory. Exhibit 6-11 illustrates the gross profit method (amounts assumed for this illustration):

EXHIBIT 6-11 **Gross Profit Method of Estimating Inventory (amounts assumed)**

Beginning inventory		$ 14,000
Net purchases		66,000
Cost of goods available		80,000
Estimated cost of goods sold:		
Sales revenue	$100,000	
Less: Estimated gross profit of 40%	(40,000)	
Estimated cost of goods sold		(60,000)
Estimated cost of *ending inventory*		$ 20,000

Ethical Issues

No area of accounting has a deeper ethical dimension than inventory. Companies whose profits are lagging can be tempted to "cook the books." An increase in reported income will make the business look more successful than it really is.

There are two main schemes for cooking the books. The easiest way is to overstate ending inventory. In Exhibit 6-10, we saw how an inventory error affects net income.

The second way to cook the books involves sales. **Datapoint Corporation** and **MiniScribe**, both computer-related companies, were charged with creating fictitious sales to boost reported profits. By increasing sales without having a corresponding cost of goods sold, the profits were overstated.

Datapoint is alleged to have hired drivers to transport its inventory around the city so that the goods could not be counted. **Datapoint's** plan seemed to create the impression that the inventory must have been sold. The scheme broke down when the trucks returned the goods to **Datapoint**. The sales returns were much too high to be realistic, and the sales proved to be phony.

MiniScribe is alleged to have cooked its books by shipping boxes of bricks labeled as computer parts. The scheme boomeranged when **MiniScribe** had to record the sales returns. In virtually every area, accounting imposes a discipline that brings out the facts sooner or later.

Decision Guidelines

GUIDELINES FOR INVENTORY MANAGEMENT

Assume you are starting a business to sell school supplies to your college friends. You will need to stock jump drives, notebooks, and other inventory items. To manage the business, you will also need some accounting records. Here are some of the decisions you will face.

Decision	Guidelines	System or Method
• Which inventory system to use?	• Expensive merchandise	Perpetual system
	• Cannot control inventory by visual inspection	Perpetual system
	• Can control inventory by visual inspection	Periodic system
• Which costing method to use?	• Unique and/or high dollar inventory items	Specific unit cost
	• The most current cost of ending inventory	FIFO
	• Maximizes reported income when costs are rising	FIFO
	• The most current measure of cost of goods sold and net income	LIFO
	• Minimizes income tax when costs are rising	LIFO
	• Middle-of-the-road approach for income tax and net income	Average-cost method
• How to estimate the cost of ending inventory?	• The cost-of-goods-sold model provides the framework	Gross profit method

Summary Problem 2

Suppose Greg's Groovy Tunes has the following inventory records for July 2011:

Date	Item	Quantity	Unit Cost	Sale Price
Jul 1	Beginning inventory	100 units	$ 8	
10	Purchase..............................	60 units	9	
15	Sale	70 units		$20
21	Purchase..............................	100 units	10	
30	Sale	90 units		25

Operating expense for July was $1,900.

Requirement

1. Prepare the July income statement in multi-step format. Show amounts for FIFO, LIFO, and average cost. Label the bottom line "Operating income." (Round the average cost per unit to three decimal places and all other figures to whole-dollar amounts.) Show your computations, and use the cost-of-goods-sold model in the chapter to compute cost of goods sold.

Solution

GREG'S GROOVY TUNES
Income Statement for Computer Parts
Month Ended July 31, 2011

	FIFO		LIFO		Average Cost	
Sales revenue		$3,650		$3,650		$3,650
Cost of goods sold:						
Beginning inventory	$ 800		$ 800		$ 800	
Net purchases	1,540		1,540		1,540	
Cost of goods available	2,340		2,340		2,340	
Ending inventory	(1,000)		(800)		(923)	
Cost of goods sold		1,340		1,540		1,417
Gross profit		2,310		2,110		2,233
Operating expenses		1,900		1,900		1,900
Operating income		$ 410		$ 210		$ 333

Computations

Sales revenue:	(70 × $20) + (90 × $25)	= $3,650
Beginning inventory:	100 × $8	= $800
Purchases:	(60 × $9) + (100 × $10)	= $1,540
Ending inventory:		
FIFO	100* × $10	= $1,000
LIFO	100 × $8	= $800
Average cost:	100 × $9.23	= $923

*Number of units in ending inventory = 100 + 60 − 70 + 100 − 90 =100

Review *Merchandise Inventory*

Accounting Vocabulary

Average-Cost Method (p. 363)
Inventory costing method based on the average cost of inventory during the period. Average cost is determined by dividing the cost of goods available for sale by the number of units available.

Conservatism (p. 361)
Reporting the least favorable figures in the financial statements.

Consistency Principle (p. 360)
A business should use the same accounting methods and procedures from period to period.

Cost of Goods Available for Sale (p. 370)
The total cost spent on inventory that was available to be sold during a period.

Disclosure Principle (p. 361)
A business's financial statements must report enough information for outsiders to make knowledgeable decisions about the company.

First-In, First-Out (FIFO) Inventory Costing Method (p. 363)
Inventory costing method: The first costs into inventory are the first costs out to cost of goods sold. Ending inventory is based on the costs of the most recent purchases.

Gross Profit Method (p. 376)
A way to estimate inventory on the basis of the cost-of-goods-sold model: Beginning inventory + Net purchases = Cost of goods available for sale. Cost of goods available for sale – Cost of goods sold = Ending inventory.

Last-In, First-Out (LIFO) Inventory Costing Method (p. 363)
Inventory costing method: The last costs into inventory are the first costs out to cost of goods sold. The method leaves the oldest costs—those of beginning inventory and the earliest purchases of the period—in ending inventory.

Lower-of-Cost-or-Market (LCM) Rule (p. 374)
Rule that an asset should be reported in the financial statements at whichever is lower—its historical cost or its market value.

Materiality Concept (p. 361)
A company must perform strictly proper accounting only for items that are significant to the business's financial situations.

Specific-Identification Method (p. 362)
Inventory costing method based on the specific cost of particular units of inventory. Also called the **specific-unit-cost method**.

Specific-Unit-Cost Method (p. 362)
Inventory costing method based on the specific cost of particular units of inventory. Also called the **specific-identification method**.

Quick Check

1. T. J. Brown made sales of $9,400 and ended June with inventories totaling $500. Cost of goods sold was $5,400. Total operating expenses were $3,000. How much net income did Brown earn for the month?
   a. $6,400
   b. $500
   c. $1,000
   d. $4,000
2. Which inventory costing method assigns to ending inventory the newest—the most recent—costs incurred during the period?
   a. First-in, first-out (FIFO)
   b. Average cost
   c. Specific unit cost
   d. Last-in, first-out (LIFO)

3. Assume ShoeFanatic.com began September with 8 units of inventory that cost a total of $144. During September, ShoeFanatic purchased and sold goods as follows:

Sep 8	Purchase	24 units @ $19
14	Sale	20 units @ $38
22	Purchase	16 units @ $21
27	Sale	24 units @ $38

Under the FIFO inventory method, how much is ShoeFanatic's cost of goods sold for the sale on September 14?

a. $600

b. $390

c. $372

d. $760

4. Under the FIFO method, ShoeFanatic.com's journal entry (entries) on September 14 is (are):

a.

Accounts receivable	372	
Inventory		372

b.

Cost of goods sold	372	
Inventory		372

c.

Accounts receivable	760	
Sales revenue		760

d. Both b and c are correct.

5. After the purchase on September 22, what is ShoeFanatic's cost of the inventory on hand? ShoeFanatic.com uses FIFO.

a. $936

b. $864

c. $564

d. $608

6. Which inventory costing method results in the lowest net income during a period of rising inventory costs?

a. Average cost

b. Specific unit cost

c. First-in, first-out (FIFO)

d. Last-in, first-out (LIFO)

7. Suppose ShoeFanatic.com used the average-cost method and the perpetual inventory system. Use the ShoeFanatic data in question 3 to compute the average unit cost of the company's inventory on hand at September 8. Round unit cost to the nearest cent.

a. $56.10

b. $18.75

c. $44.00

d. Cannot be determined from the data given

8. Which of the following is most closely linked to accounting conservatism?
   a. Lower-of-cost-or-market rule
   b. Materiality concept
   c. Disclosure principle
   d. Consistency principle
9. At December 31, 2011, McAdam Company overstated ending inventory by $40,000. How does this error affect cost of goods sold and net income for 2011?
   a. Understates costs of goods sold and overstates net income
   b. Overstates cost of goods sold and understates net income
   c. Leaves both cost of goods sold and net income correct because the errors cancel each other
   d. Overstates both cost of goods sold and net income
10. Suppose Colorado Sportswear suffered a hurricane loss and needs to estimate the cost of the goods destroyed. Beginning inventory was $106,000, net purchases totaled $636,000, and sales came to $1,060,000. Colorado's normal gross profit percentage is 53%. Use the gross profit method to estimate the cost of the inventory lost in the hurricane.
    a. $498,200
    b. $243,800
    c. $742,000
    d. $561,800

Answers are given after Apply Your Knowledge. (p. 398).

Assess Your Progress

Short Exercises

S6-1 *(L.OBJ. 1)* **Inventory accounting principles [5 min]**
Shepherd Cycles used the FIFO inventory method in 2010. Shepherd Cycles plans to continue using the FIFO method in future years.

Requirement

1. Which inventory principle is most relevant to Shepherd's decision?

S6-2 *(L.OBJ. 2)* **Inventory methods [5 min]**
Shepherd Cycles does not expect prices to change dramatically and wants to use a method that averages price changes.

Requirements

1. Which inventory method would best meet Shepherd's goal?
2. What if Shepherd wanted to expense out the newer purchases of goods instead? Which inventory would best meet that need?

S6-3 *(L.OBJ. 3)* **Perpetual inventory record—FIFO [10 min]**
Innovation Cycles uses the FIFO inventory method. Innovation started March with 10 bicycles that cost $60 each. On March 16, Innovation bought 20 bicycles at $70 each. On March 31, Innovation sold 25 bicycles.

Requirement

1. Prepare Innovation's perpetual inventory record.

S6-4 *(L.OBJ. 3)* **Perpetual inventory record—LIFO [10 min]**
Review the facts on Innovation Cycles in Short Exercise 6-3.

Requirement

1. Prepare a perpetual inventory record for the LIFO method.

S6-5 *(L.OBJ. 3)* **Perpetual inventory record—average cost [10 min]**
Review the facts on Innovation Cycles in Short Exercise 6-3.

Requirement

1. Prepare a perpetual inventory record for the average-cost method. Round average cost per unit to the nearest cent and all other amounts to the nearest dollar.

S6-6 *(L.OBJ. 3)* **Journalizing inventory transactions—FIFO [5–10 min]**
Use the Innovation Cycles data in Short Exercise 6-3 to journalize

Requirements

1. The March 16 purchase of inventory on account.
2. The March 31 sale of inventory on account. Innovation sold each bicycle for $120.
3. Cost of goods sold under FIFO on March 31.

S6-7 *(L.OBJ. 3)* **Journalizing inventory transactions—LIFO [5–10 min]**
Use the Innovation Cycles data in Short Exercise 6-4 to journalize

Requirements

1. The March 16 purchase of inventory on account.
2. The March 31 sale of inventory on account. Innovation sold each bicycle for $120.
3. The Cost of goods sold under LIFO on March 31.

S6-8 *(L.OBJ. 3)* **Journalizing inventory transactions—average cost [5–10 min]**
Use the Innovation Cycles data in Short Exercise 6-5 to journalize

Requirements

1. The March 16 purchase of inventory on account.
2. The March 31 sale of inventory on account. Innovation sold each bicycle for $120.
3. The Cost of goods sold under average cost on March 31.

S6-9 *(L.OBJ. 4)* **Comparing Cost of goods sold under FIFO, LIFO, and average cost [5–10 min]**
Refer to Short Exercises 6-3 through 6-8. After completing those exercises, answer the following questions:

Requirements

1. Which method of inventory accounting produced the lowest cost of goods sold?
2. Which method of inventory accounting produced the highest cost of goods sold?
3. If prices had been declining instead of rising, which inventory method would have produced the highest cost of goods sold?

S6-10 *(L.OBJ. 5)* **Applying the lower-of-cost-or-market rule [5–10 min]**
Assume that a Queen Burger restaurant has the following perpetual inventory record for hamburger patties:

Hamburger Patties			
Date	Purchases	Cost of Goods Sold	Inventory on Hand
Apr 9	$ 550		$ 550
22		$ 250	300
30	160		460

Requirements

1. At April 30, the accountant for the restaurant determines that the current replacement cost of the ending inventory is $515. Make any adjusting entry needed to apply the lower-of-cost-or-market rule. Inventory would be reported on the balance sheet at what value on April 30?
2. Inventory would be reported on the balance sheet at what value if Queen uses the average-cost method?

S6-11 *(L.OBJ. 6)* **Effect of an inventory error—one year only [5 min]**
Boston Cycles' inventory data for the year ended December 31, 2011, follow:

Sales revenue		$ 46,000
Cost of goods sold:		
Beginning inventory	$5,400	
Net purchases	26,700	
Cost of goods available	32,100	
Less: Ending inventory	(3,600)	
Cost of goods sold		28,500
Gross profit		$ 17,500

Assume that the ending inventory was accidentally overstated by $2,200.

Requirement

1. What are the correct amounts for cost of goods sold and gross profit?

S6-12 *(L.OBJ. 6)* **Next year's effect of an inventory error [5–10 min]**
Refer back to the Boston Cycles' inventory data in Short Exercise 6-11.

Requirement

1. How would the inventory error affect Boston Cycles' cost of goods sold and gross profit for the year ended December 31, 2012, if the error is not corrected in 2011?

S6-13 *(L.OBJ. 7)* **Estimating ending inventory by the gross profit method [10 min]**
Electronic Company began the year with inventory of $55,800 and purchased $277,000 of goods during the year. Sales for the year are $476,000, and Electronic's gross profit percentage is 45% of sales.

Requirement

1. Compute the estimated cost of ending inventory by the gross profit method.

■ Exercises

E6-14 *(L.OBJ. 1, 2)* **Accounting principles related to inventory and inventory costing methods defined [15–20 min]**

Review inventory accounting definitions and principles.

Requirement

1. Complete the preceding crossword puzzle using the following clues:

Down:

1. Treats the oldest inventory purchases as the first units sold.
3. Identifies exactly which inventory item was sold. Usually used for higher cost inventory. (2 words)
6. Principle whose foundation is to exercise caution in reporting financial statement items.
7. Business should use the same accounting methods from period to period.

Across:

2. Requires that a company report enough information for outsiders to make decisions.
4. Calculates an average cost based on the purchases made and the units acquired. (2 words)
5. Treats the most recent/newest purchases as the first units sold.
8. Principle that states significant items must conform to GAAP.

E6-15 *(L.OBJ. 3)* **Measuring and journalizing inventory and cost of goods sold in a perpetual system—FIFO [20–25 min]**

Putter's Paradise carries an inventory of putters and other golf clubs. Putter's Paradise uses the FIFO method and a perpetual inventory system. The sales price of each putter is $135. Company records indicate the following for a particular line of Putter's Paradise putters:

Date	Item	Quantity	Unit Cost
Sep 1	Balance	5	$61
6	Sale	3	
8	Purchase	10	66
17	Sale	4	
30	Sale	2	

Requirements

1. Prepare a perpetual inventory record for the putters. Then determine the amounts Putter's Paradise should report for ending inventory and cost of goods sold using the FIFO method.
2. Journalize Putter's Paradise inventory transactions using the FIFO method.

E6-16 *(L.OBJ. 3)* **Measuring ending inventory and cost of goods sold in a perpetual system—LIFO [20–25 min]**

Refer to the Putter's Paradise inventory data in Exercise 6-15. Assume that Putter's Paradise uses the perpetual LIFO cost method.

Requirements

1. Prepare Putter's Paradise perpetual inventory record for the putters on the LIFO basis. Then identify the cost of ending inventory and cost of goods sold for the month.
2. Journalize Putter's Paradise inventory transactions using the perpetual LIFO method.

E6-17 *(L.OBJ. 3)* **Measuring ending inventory and cost of goods sold in a perpetual system-average cost [20–25 min]**

Refer to the Putter's Paradise inventory data in Exercise 6-15. Assume that Putter's Paradise uses the average-cost method.

Requirements

1. Prepare Putter's Paradise perpetual inventory record for the putters on the average-cost basis. Round average cost per unit to the nearest cent and all other amounts to the nearest dollar. Then identify the cost of ending inventory and cost of goods sold for the month.
2. Journalize Putter's Paradise inventory transactions using the perpetual average cost method.

E6-18 *(L.OBJ. 3)* **Journalizing perpetual inventory transactions-cost of sales given [10–15 min]**

Accounting records for Rich's Shopping Bags yield the following data for the year ended July 31, 2011:

Inventory, July 31, 2010	$ 7,000
Purchases of inventory (on account)	49,000
Sales of inventory – 76% on account; 24% for cash (cost $40,000) ...	78,000
Inventory, July 31, 2011	?

Requirements

1. Journalize the inventory transactions for the company using the data given.
2. Report ending inventory on the balance sheet, and sales, cost of goods sold, and gross profit on the income statement.

E6-19 *(L.OBJ. 4)* **Comparing amounts for ending inventory—perpetual inventory—FIFO and LIFO [5–10 min]**

Assume that an RK Toys store bought and sold a line of dolls during December as follows:

Beginning inventory	14	units @	$ 10
Sale	8	units	
Purchase	15	units @	$ 15
Sale	13	units	

RK Toys uses the perpetual inventory system.

Requirements

1. Compute the cost of ending inventory under FIFO.
2. Compute the cost of ending inventory under LIFO.
3. Which method results in a higher cost of ending inventory?

E6-20 *(L.OBJ. 4)* **Comparing cost of goods sold in a perpetual system—FIFO and LIFO [15–20 min]**
Review the data in Exercise 6-19.

Requirements

1. Compute the cost of goods sold under FIFO.
2. Compute the cost of goods sold under LIFO.
3. Which method results in the higher cost of goods sold?

E6-21 *(L.OBJ. 4)* **Comparing cost of goods sold in a perpetual system—FIFO, LIFO, and average-cost amounts [15–20 min]**
Assume that an RB Tire Store completed the following perpetual inventory transactions for a line of tires:

Beginning inventory	22	tires @	$ 58
Purchase	9	tires @	$ 75
Sale	17	tires @	$ 110

Requirements

1. Compute cost of goods sold and gross profit under FIFO.
2. Compute cost of goods sold and gross profit using LIFO.
3. Compute cost of goods sold and gross profit using average cost. (Round average cost per unit to the nearest cent and all other amounts to the nearest dollar.)
4. Which method results in the largest gross profit and why?

E6-22 *(L.OBJ. 5)* **Applying the lower-of-cost-or-market rule to inventories [5 min]**
Rapid Resources, which uses the FIFO method, has the following account balances at December 31, 2012, prior to releasing the financial statements for the year:

Inventory

	Debit	Credit
Beg Bal	10,000	
End Bal	14,000	

Cost of goods sold

	Debit	Credit
Bal	68,000	

Sales revenue

Debit		Credit
	Bal	119,000

Rapid has determined that the replacement cost (current market value) of the December 31, 2012, ending inventory is $12,500.

Requirements

1. Prepare any adjusting journal entry required from the information given.
2. What value would Rapid report on the balance sheet at December 31, 2012, for inventory?

E6-23 *(L.OBJ. 5)* **Applying the lower-of-cost-or-market rule to inventories [5 min]**
Natural Foods reports inventory at the lower of average cost or market. Prior to releasing its December 2012 financial statements, Natural's *preliminary* income statement, before the year-end adjustments, appears as follows:

NATURAL FOODS Income Statement (partial) For the year ended December 31, 2012	
Sales revenue	$ 120,000
Cost of goods sold	49,000
Gross profit	71,000

Natural has determined that the replacement cost of ending inventory is $20,000. Cost is $21,000.

Requirements

1. Journalize the adjusting entry for inventory, if any is required.
2. Prepare a revised income statement to show how Natural Foods should report sales, cost of goods sold, and gross profit.

E6-24 *(L.OBJ. 6)* **Measuring the effect of an inventory error [10–15 min]**
Hudson River Bakery reported sales revenue of $29,000 and cost of goods sold of $11,000.

Requirement

1. Compute Hudson River's correct gross profit if the company made either of the following independent accounting errors. Show your work.
   a. Ending inventory is overstated by $3,000.
   b. Ending inventory is understated by $3,000.

E6-25 *(L.OBJ. 6)* **Correcting an inventory error—two years [15–20 min]**
Earth Foods Grocery reported the following comparative income statement for the years ended June 30, 2012 and 2011:

EARTH FOODS GROCERY Income Statements Years Ended June 30, 2012 and 2011				
	2012		2011	
Sales revenue		$ 142,000		$ 121,000
Cost of goods sold:				
Beginning inventory	$15,000		$10,000	
Net purchases	73,000		66,000	
Cost of goods available	88,000		76,000	
Ending inventory	(19,500)		(15,000)	
Cost of goods sold		68,500		61,000
Gross profit		73,500		60,000
Operating expenses		26,000		24,000
Net income		$ 47,500		$ 36,000

During 2012, Earth Foods discovered that ending 2011 inventory, as previously reported, was overstated by $3,500.

Requirements

1. Prepare the corrected comparative income statement for the two-year period, complete with a heading for the statement.
2. What was the effect of the error on net income for the two years combined? Explain your answer.

E6-26 *(L.OBJ. 7)* **Estimating ending inventory by the gross profit method [10–15 min]**
All Makes Auto Parts holds inventory all over the world. Assume that the records for one auto part show the following:

Beginning inventory	$ 170,000
Net purchases	870,000
Net sales	1,080,000
Gross profit rate	40%

Suppose this inventory, stored in the United States, was lost in a fire.

Requirement

1. Estimate the amount of the loss to All Makes Auto Parts. Use the gross profit method.

E6-27 *(L.OBJ. 7)* **Estimating ending inventory by the gross profit method [10–15 min]**
New Life Landscaping and Nursery began December with inventory of $47,000. During December, New Life made net purchases of $30,300 and had net sales of $63,000. For the past several years, New Life's gross profit has been 35% of sales.

Requirement

1. Use the gross profit method to estimate the cost of the ending inventory for December.

■ Problems (Group A)

P6-28A *(L.OBJ. 1, 5)* **Accounting principles for inventory and applying the lower-of-cost-or-market rule [15–20 min]**
Some of L and M Electronics' merchandise is gathering dust. It is now December 31, 2012, and the current replacement cost of the ending inventory is $25,000 below the business's cost of the goods, which was $105,000. Before any adjustments at the end of the period, the company's Cost of goods sold account has a balance of $405,000.

Requirements

1. Journalize any required entries.
2. At what amount should the company report for Inventory on the balance sheet?
3. At what amount should the company report for Cost of goods sold?
4. Which accounting principle or concept is most relevant to this situation?

P6-29A *(L.OBJ. 2, 3, 4)* **Accounting for inventory using the perpetual system—LIFO; journalizing inventory transactions [30–40 min]**

Vitamin World began January with an inventory of 90 crates of vitamins that cost a total of $3,600. During the month, Vitamin World purchased and sold merchandise on account as follows:

Purchase 1	120 crates	@ $ 45
Sale 1	170 crates	@ $ 80
Purchase 2	120 crates	@ $ 50
Sale 2	130 crates	@ $ 90

Vitamin World uses the LIFO method.

Cash payments on account totaled $5,100. Operating expenses for the month were $2,400, with two-thirds paid in cash, and the rest accrued as Accounts payable.

Requirements

1. Which inventory method most likely mimics the physical flow of Vitamin World's inventory?
2. Prepare a perpetual inventory record, using LIFO cost, for this merchandise.
3. Journalize all transactions using LIFO.

P6-30A *(L.OBJ. 3, 4)* **Accounting for results on income for inventory using the LIFO cost method [20–30 min]**

Refer to the Vitamin World situation in Problem 6-29A.

Requirement

1. Using the results from the LIFO costing method calculations in Problem 6-29A, prepare a multi-step income statement for Vitamin World for the month ended January 31, 2011.

P6-31A *(L.OBJ. 3, 4)* **Accounting for inventory using the perpetual system—FIFO, LIFO, and average cost; comparing FIFO, LIFO, and average cost [20–25 min]**

Fancy Iron Industries began October with 54 units of iron inventory that cost $39 each. During October, the company completed the following inventory transactions:

	Units	Unit Cost	Unit Sale Price
Oct 3 Sale	44		$70
8 Purchase.................	84	$44	
21 Sale	74		$74
30 Purchase.................	14	$48	

Requirements

1. Prepare a perpetual inventory record for the inventory using FIFO.
2. Prepare a perpetual inventory record for the inventory using LIFO.
3. Prepare a perpetual inventory record for the inventory using average cost.
4. Determine the company's cost of goods sold for October using FIFO, LIFO, and average cost.
5. Compute gross profit for October using FIFO, LIFO, and average cost.

P6-32A *(L.OBJ. 5)* **Applying the lower-of-cost-or-market rule to inventories [5 min]**

Rocky Bayou Golf Clubs, which uses the FIFO method, has the following account balances at October 31, 2012, prior to releasing the financial statements for the year:

Inventory		Cost of goods sold		Sales revenue	
Bal 14,000		Bal 70,000			Bal 110,000

Rocky Bayou has determined that the replacement cost (current market value) of the October 31, 2012, ending inventory is $13,000.

Requirements

1. Prepare any adjusting journal entry required from the information given.
2. What value would Rocky Bayou report on the balance sheet at October 31, 2012, for inventory?

P6-33A *(L.OBJ. 6)* **Correcting inventory errors over a three-year period [15–20 min]**
Antique Carpets' books show the following data (in thousands). In early 2013, auditors found that the ending inventory for 2010 was understated by $8 thousand and that the ending inventory for 2012 was overstated by $9 thousand. The ending inventory at December 31, 2011, was correct.

(Thousands)	2012		2011		2010	
Net sales revenue		$ 206		$ 160		$ 175
Cost of goods sold:						
Beginning inventory	$ 19		$ 23		$ 43	
Net purchases	138		95		81	
Cost of goods available	157		118		124	
Ending inventory	(30)		(19)		(23)	
Cost of goods sold		127		99		101
Gross profit		79		61		74
Operating expenses		52		37		34
Net income		$ 27		$ 24		$ 40

Requirements

1. Prepare corrected income statements for the three years.
2. State whether each year's net income—before your corrections—is understated or overstated and indicate the amount of the understatement or overstatement.

P6-34A *(L.OBJ. 7)* **Estimating ending inventory by the gross profit method and preparing the income statement [25–30 min]**
Gala Costumes estimates its inventory by the gross profit method. The gross profit has averaged 28% of net sales. The company's inventory records reveal the following data (amounts in thousands):

Inventory, December 1	$ 295
Transactions during December:	
Purchases	7,639
Purchase discounts	177
Purchase returns	39
Sales	8,623
Sales returns	21

Requirements

1. Estimate the December 31 inventory, using the gross profit method.
2. Prepare the December income statement through gross profit for Gala Costumes.

Problems (Group B)

P6-35B *(L.OBJ. 1, 5)* **Accounting principles for inventory and applying the lower-of-cost-or-market rule [15–20 min]**
Some of J and B Electronics' merchandise is gathering dust. It is now December 31, 2012, and the current replacement cost of the ending inventory is $15,000 below the business's cost of the goods, which was $90,000. Before any adjustments at the end of the period, the company's Cost of goods sold account has a balance of $400,000.

Requirements

1. Journalize any required entries.
2. What amount should the company report for Inventory on the balance sheet?
3. What amount should the company report for Cost of goods sold?
4. Which accounting principle or concept is most relevant to this situation?

P6-36B *(L.OBJ. 2, 3, 4)* **Accounting for inventory using the perpetual system—LIFO and journalizing inventory transactions [30–40 min]**
Fit World began January with an inventory of 60 crates of vitamins that cost a total of $3,000. During the month, Fit World purchased and sold merchandise on account as follows:

Purchase 1	140 crates	@ $ 55
Sale 1	180 crates	@ $ 100
Purchase 2	150 crates	@ $ 60
Sale 2	160 crates	@ $ 110

Fit World uses the LIFO method.
Cash payments on account totaled $5,000. Operating expenses for the month were $2,400, with two-thirds paid in cash and the rest accrued as Accounts payable.

Requirements

1. Which inventory method most likely mimics the physical flow of Fit World's inventory?
2. Prepare a perpetual inventory record, using LIFO cost, for this merchandise.
3. Journalize all transactions using LIFO.

P6-37B *(L.OBJ. 3, 4)* **Accounting for results on income for inventory using the LIFO cost method [20–30 min]**
Refer to the Fit World situation in Problem 6-36B.

Requirement

1. Using the results from the LIFO costing method calculations in Problem 6-36B, prepare a multi-step income statement for Fit World for the month ended January 31, 2011.

P6-38B *(L.OBJ. 3, 4)* **Accounting for inventory using the perpetual system—FIFO, LIFO, and average cost; comparing FIFO, LIFO, and average cost [20–25 min]**
Decorative Steel began October with 47 units of iron inventory that cost $35 each. During October, Decorative Steel completed the following inventory transactions:

	Units	Unit Cost	Unit Sale Price
Oct 3 Sale	37		$66
8 Purchase	77	$41	
21 Sale	67		$70
30 Purchase	7	$45	

Requirements

1. Prepare a perpetual inventory record for the inventory using FIFO.
2. Prepare a perpetual inventory record for the inventory using LIFO.
3. Prepare a perpetual inventory record for the inventory using average cost.
4. Determine the company's cost of goods sold for October using FIFO, LIFO, and average cost.
5. Compute gross profit for October using FIFO, LIFO, and average cost.

P6-39B *(L.OBJ. 5)* **Applying the lower-of-cost-or-market rule to inventories [5 min]**
Callowater Golf Clubs, which uses the FIFO method, has the following account balances at May 31, 2012, prior to releasing the financial statements for the year:

Inventory		Cost of goods sold		Sales revenue	
Bal 14,000		Bal 67,000			Bal 120,000

Callowater has determined that the replacement cost (current market value) of the May 31, 2012, ending inventory is $12,000.

Requirements

1. Prepare any adjusting journal entry required from the information given.
2. What value would Callowater report on the balance sheet at May 31, 2012, for inventory?

P6-40B *(L.OBJ. 6)* **Correcting inventory errors over a three-year period [15–20 min]**
Harmony Carpets' books show the following data (in thousands). In early 2013, auditors found that the ending inventory for 2010 was understated by $9 thousand and that the ending inventory for 2012 was overstated by $9 thousand. The ending inventory at December 31, 2011, was correct.

(Thousands)	2012		2011		2010	
Net sales revenue		$ 218		$ 170		$ 179
Cost of goods sold:						
Beginning inventory	$ 16		$ 21		$ 38	
Net purchases	137		102		93	
Cost of goods available	153		123		131	
Ending inventory	(28)		(16)		(21)	
Cost of goods sold		125		107		110
Gross profit		93		63		69
Operating expenses		68		36		31
Net income		$ 25		$ 27		$ 38

Requirements

1. Prepare corrected income statements for the three years.
2. State whether each year's net income—before your corrections—is understated or overstated and indicate the amount of the understatement or overstatement.

P6-41B *(L.OBJ. 7)* **Estimating ending inventory by the gross profit method and preparing the income statement [25–30 min]**
Elite Costumes estimates its inventory by the gross profit method. The gross profit has averaged 33% of net sales. The company's inventory records reveal the following data (amounts in thousands):

Inventory, May 1	$ 274
Transactions during May:	
Purchases	7,799
Purchase discounts	175
Purchase returns	19
Sales	8,877
Sales returns	38

Requirements

1. Estimate the May 31 inventory, using the gross profit method.
2. Prepare the May income statement through gross profit for Elite Costumes.

Continuing Exercise

E6-42 This exercise continues the Sherman Lawn Service situation from Exercise 5-42 in Chapter 5. Consider the September transactions for Sherman Lawn Service that were presented in Chapter 5. (Cost data has been removed from the sale transactions.)

Sep 2	Completed lawn service and received cash of $500
5	Purchased 100 plants on account for inventory, $250, plus freight in of $10
15	Sold 40 plants on account, $400
17	Consulted with a client on landscaping design for a fee of $150 on account
20	Purchased 100 plants on account for inventory, $300
21	Paid on account, $100
25	Sold 100 plants for cash, $700
30	Recorded the following adjusting entries: Depreciation, $29 Physical count of plant inventory, 50 plants

Requirements

1. Prepare perpetual inventory records for September for Sherman using the FIFO method. (Note: You must figure cost on the 15th, 25th, and 30th.)
2. Journalize and post the September transactions using the perpetual inventory record created in requirement 1. Key all items by date. Compute each account balance, and denote the balance as *Bal.*
3. Journalize and post the adjusting entries. Denote each adjusting amount as *Adj.* After posting all adjusting entries, prove the equality of debits and credits in the ledger.

Continuing Problem

P6-43 This problem continues the Haupt Consulting Company situation from Problem 5-43 in Chapter 5. Consider the January transactions for Haupt Consulting Company that were presented in Chapter 5. (Cost data has been removed from the sale transactions.)

Jan	2	Completed a consulting engagement and received cash of $7,200
	2	Prepaid three months' office rent, $1,500
	7	Purchased 100 units software inventory on account, $1,900, plus freight in, $100
	16	Paid employee salary, $1,400
	18	Sold 70 software units on account, $3,100
	19	Consulted with a client for a fee of $900 on account
	21	Paid on account, $2,000
	22	Purchased 200 units software inventory on account, $4,600
	24	Paid utilities, $300
	28	Sold 100 units of software for cash, $4,000
	31	Recorded the following adjusting entries: Accrued salary expense, $1,400 Depreciation, $200 Expiration of prepaid rent, $500 Physical count of inventory, 120 units

Requirements

1. Prepare perpetual inventory records for January for Haupt using the LIFO perpetual method. (Note: You must figure cost on the 18th, 22nd, 28th, and 31st.)
2. Journalize and post the January transactions using the perpetual inventory record created in requirement 1. Key all items by date. Compute each account balance, and denote the balance as *Bal.*
3. Journalize and post the adjusting entries. Denote each adjusting amount as *Adj.* After posting all adjusting entries, prove the equality of debits and credits in the ledger.

Practice Set

This problem continues the Crystal Clear Cleaning problem begun in Chapter 1 and continued through Chapter 5.

P6-44 Consider the May transactions for Crystal Clear Cleaning that were presented in Chapter 5. (Cost data has been removed from the sale transactions.)

May	2	Purchased 800 units of inventory, $4,000, from Sparkle Co. on terms, 2/10, n/20
	5	Purchased 300 units of inventory from Borax on terms 3/5, n/30. The total invoice was for $2,100, which included a $100 freight charge.
	7	Returned 300 units of inventory to Sparkle from the May 2 purchase
	9	Paid Borax
	11	Sold 280 units of goods to Merry Maids for $2,500 on terms 1/10, n/30
	12	Paid Sparkle
	15	Received 56 units with a retail price of $500 of goods back from customer Merry Maids
	21	Received payment from Merry Maids, settling the amount due in full
	28	Sold 81 units of goods to Hillary for cash of $600
	29	Paid cash for Utilities of $350
	30	Paid cash for Sales commission expense of $700
	31	Recorded these adjusting entries: Physical count of Inventory on May 31 revealed 206 units of goods on hand Depreciation, $300 Accrued salary expense of $300 Prepared all other adjustments necessary for May

Requirements

1. Prepare perpetual inventory records for May for Crystal Clear using the FIFO method. (Note: You must figure cost on the 11th and 28th.)
2. Journalize and post the May transactions using the perpetual inventory record created in requirement 1. Key all items by date. Compute each account balance, and denote the balance as *Bal.*
3. Journalize and post the adjusting entries. Denote each adjusting amount as *Adj.* After posting all adjusting entries, prove the equality of debits and credits in the ledger.

Apply Your Knowledge

■ Decision Cases

Case 1. Assume you are opening a **Bed Bath & Beyond** store. To finance the business, you need a $500,000 loan, and your banker requires a set of forecasted financial statements. Assume you are preparing the statements and must make some decisions about how to do the accounting for the business.

Requirements

Answer the following questions (refer back to Chapter 5 if necessary):

1. Which type of inventory system will you use? Give your reason.
2. Show how to compute net purchases and net sales. How will you treat the cost of transportation-in?
3. How often do you plan to do a physical count of inventory on hand? What will the physical count accomplish?
4. Inventory costs are rising. Which inventory costing method will you use in order to
   a. maximize net income?
   b. pay the least amount of income tax?

Case 2. Suppose you manage Campbell Appliance. The store's summarized financial statements for 2012, the most recent year, follow:

CAMPBELL APPLIANCE **Income Statement** Year Ended December 31, 2012	
	(Thousands)
Sales	$800
Cost of goods sold	660
Gross profit	140
Operating expenses	100
Net income	$ 40

CAMPBELL APPLIANCE Balance Sheet December 31, 2012			
(Thousands)	Assets	Liabilities and Equity	
Cash	$ 30	Accounts payable	$ 35
Inventories	75	Note payable	280
Land and buildings, net	360	Total liabilities	315
		Owner's equity	150
Total assets	$465	Total liabilities and equity	$465

Assume that you need to double net income. To accomplish your goal, it will be very difficult to raise the prices you charge because there is a **Best Buy** nearby. Also, you have little control over your cost of goods sold because the appliance manufacturers set the price you must pay.

Requirement

1. Identify several strategies for doubling net income. (Challenge)

■ Ethical Issue

During 2012, Crop-Paper-Scissors, a craft store, changed to the LIFO method of accounting for inventory. Suppose that during 2013, Crop-Paper-Scissors switches back to the FIFO method and the following year switches back to LIFO again.

Requirements

1. What would you think of a company's ethics if it changed accounting methods every year?
2. What accounting principle would changing methods every year violate?
3. Who can be harmed when a company changes its accounting methods too often? How?

■ Financial Statement Case

The notes are an important part of a company's financial statements, giving valuable details that would clutter the tabular data presented in the statements. This case will help you learn to use a company's inventory notes. Refer to the **Amazon.com** financial statements and related notes in Appendix A at the end of the book, and answer the following questions:

Requirements

1. How much was the **Amazon.com** merchandise inventory at December 31, 2007? At December 31, 2006?
2. Which cost method does **Amazon** use for inventories? How does **Amazon** value its inventories? See Note 1.
3. By rearranging the cost-of-goods-sold formula, you can compute purchases, which are not reported in the **Amazon** statements. How much were **Amazon's** inventory purchases during 2007?

■ Team Project

Link Back to Chapter 5 (Gross Profit Percentage and Inventory Turnover). Obtain the annual reports of as many companies as you have team members—one company per team member. Most companies post their financial statements on their Web sites.

Requirements

1. Identify the inventory method used by each company.
2. Compute each company's gross profit percentage and rate of inventory turnover for the most recent two years.
3. For the industries of the companies you are analyzing, obtain the industry averages for gross profit percentage and inventory turnover from Robert Morris Associates, *Annual Statement Studies*; Dun and Bradstreet, *Industry Norms and Key Business Ratios;* or Leo Troy, *Almanac of Business and Industrial Financial Ratios*.
4. How well does each of your companies compare to the average for its industry? What insight about your companies can you glean from these ratios?

Quick Check Answers

1. *c* 2. *a* 3. *c* 4. *d* 5. *c* 6. *d* 7. *b* 8. *a* 9. a 10. *b*

For online homework, exercises, and problems that provide you immediate feedback, please visit www.myaccountinglab.com.

Accounting for Inventory in a Periodic System

We described the periodic inventory system briefly in Chapter 5. Accounting is simpler in a periodic system because the company keeps no daily running record of inventory on hand. The only way to determine the ending inventory and cost of goods sold in a periodic system is to count the goods—usually at the end of the year. The periodic system works well for a small business in which the inventory can be controlled by visual inspection—that is, the inventory usually is not large in size or dollar amount.

This appendix illustrates how the periodic system works. The accounting in a periodic system is similar to a perpetual system, except:

1. The periodic system uses four additional accounts:
   - **Purchases**—this account holds the cost of inventory as it is purchased. Purchases carries a debit balance and is an expense account.
   - **Purchase Discounts**—this contra account carries a credit balance. Discounts for early payment of purchases are recorded here.
   - **Purchase Returns and Allowances**—this contra account carries a credit balance. Items purchased but returned to the vendor are recorded in this account. Allowances granted by a vendor are also recorded in this account.
   - **Freight-in**—this account holds the transportation cost paid on inventory purchases. It carries a debit balance and is an expense account.

   In the perpetual system, all these costs go into the Inventory account.
2. The end-of-period entries are more extensive in the periodic system because we must close out the beginning inventory balance and set up the cost of the ending inventory. This Appendix illustrates the closing process for the periodic system.
3. Cost of goods sold in a periodic system is computed by the following formula (using assumed amounts for this illustration):

Beginning inventory (ending inventory from the preceding period)	$ 5,000
Net purchases (often abbreviated as Purchases)	20,000*
Cost of goods available	25,000
Less: Ending inventory (on hand at the end of the current period)	(7,000)
Cost of goods sold	$18,000

* Net purchases is determined as follows (all amounts assumed):

Purchases	$21,000
Less: Purchase discounts	(2,000)
Purchase returns and allowances	(5,000)
Add: Freight-in	6,000
Net purchases	$20,000

Inventory Costing in the Periodic System

The various costing methods (FIFO, LIFO, and average) in a periodic inventory system follow the pattern illustrated earlier for the perpetual system. To show how the periodic system works, we use the same Smart Touch Learning data that we used for the perpetual system, as follows:

SMART TOUCH LEARNING DVD0503

		Number of Units	Unit Cost
Jul 1	Beginning inventory	1	$40
5	Purchase	6	45
26	Purchase	7	50
30	Ending inventory	2	?

We use these data to illustrate

- FIFO
- LIFO
- Average cost

For all three methods cost of goods available is always the sum of beginning inventory plus net purchases:

Beginning inventory (1 unit @ $40)	$ 40
Net purchases (6 units @ $45) + (7 units @ $50)	620
Cost of goods available (14 units)	$660

The different methods—FIFO, LIFO, and average cost—compute different amounts for ending inventory and cost of goods sold. In other words, the $660 invested in cost of goods available for sale will be either on the balance sheet in Inventory, or expensed on the income statement, Cost of goods sold.

First-In, First-Out (FIFO) Method

Under FIFO, the ending inventory comes from the newest—the most recent—purchases, which cost $50 per unit. FIFO is illustrated in the box that follows on the next page. Notice that the FIFO periodic Cost of goods sold is $560, exactly the same amount as we got using the FIFO perpetual system. Periodic and Perpetual are *always* the same for FIFO because FIFO sells oldest inventory acquisitions first. Therefore, it does not matter when FIFO is calculated; the first purchase will always be the same whether we calculate cost of goods sold on the sale date (Perpetual) or at the end of the period (Periodic).

Last-In, First-Out (LIFO) Method

Under LIFO, the ending inventory comes from the oldest cost of the period—in this case the beginning inventory that cost $40 per unit, plus the first purchase at $45. LIFO is also illustrated in the box that follows on the next page.

Average-Cost Method

In the average-cost method, we compute a single average cost per unit for the entire period:

Cost of goods available	÷	Number of units available	=	Average cost per unit
$660	÷	14 units	=	$47.14

Then apply this average cost to compute ending inventory and cost of goods sold, as shown in the far right column:

	FIFO	LIFO	Average
Cost of goods available	$660	$660	$660
Less: Ending inventory			
FIFO (2 units @ $50)	(100)		
LIFO (1 unit @ $40			
1 unit @ $45)		(85)	
Average (2 units @ $47.14)			(94)
Cost of goods sold	$560	$575	$566

Comparing the Perpetual and Periodic Inventory Systems

Exhibit 6A-1 on the following page provides a side-by-side comparison of the perpetual and the periodic inventory systems. It gives the

- Journal entries
- Ledger accounts
- Reporting in the financial statements

EXHIBIT 6A-1 **Comparing the Perpetual and Periodic Inventory Systems (all amounts assumed for this illustration)**

JOURNAL ENTRIES

Perpetual System			Periodic System		
Inventory	$570,000		Purchases	$570,000	
Accounts payable		570,000	Accounts payable		$570,000
Purchased on account.			*Purchased inventory on account.*		
Accounts payable	20,000		Accounts payable	20,000	
Inventory		20,000	Purchase returns and allowances		20,000
Returned damaged goods to seller.			*Returned damaged goods to seller.*		
Accounts receivable	900,000		Accounts receivable	900,000	
Sales revenue		900,000	Sales revenue		900,000
Sale on account.			*Sale on account.*		
Cost of goods sold	530,000		No entry for cost of goods sold.		
Inventory		530,000			
Cost of goods sold.					

CLOSING ENTRIES

End of the Period			End of the Period		
			1. Cost of goods sold	$100,000	
			Inventory (beginning)		$100,000
			Transfer beginning inventory to cost of goods sold.		
			2. Inventory (ending)	120,000	
			Cost of goods sold		120,000
			Record ending inventory based on a physical count.		
			3. Cost of goods sold	550,000	
			Purchase returns and allowances	20,000	
			Purchases		570,000
			Transfer net purchases to cost of goods sold.		
1. Income Summary	530,000		4. Income summary	530,000	
Cost of goods sold		530,000	Cost of goods sold		530,000
Close cost of goods sold.			*Close cost of goods sold.* ($100,000 – $120,000 + $550,000 = $530,000)		

EXHIBIT 6A-1 Continued

LEDGER ACCOUNTS

Perpetual System

Inventory

Debit	Credit
100,000*	20,000
570,000	530,000
120,000	

Cost of goods sold

Debit	Credit
530,000	530,000

Periodic System

Inventory

Debit	Credit
100,000*	100,000
120,000	

Cost of goods sold

Debit	Credit
100,000	120,000
550,000	530,000

*Beginning inventory was $100,000.

REPORTING IN THE FINANCIAL STATEMENTS

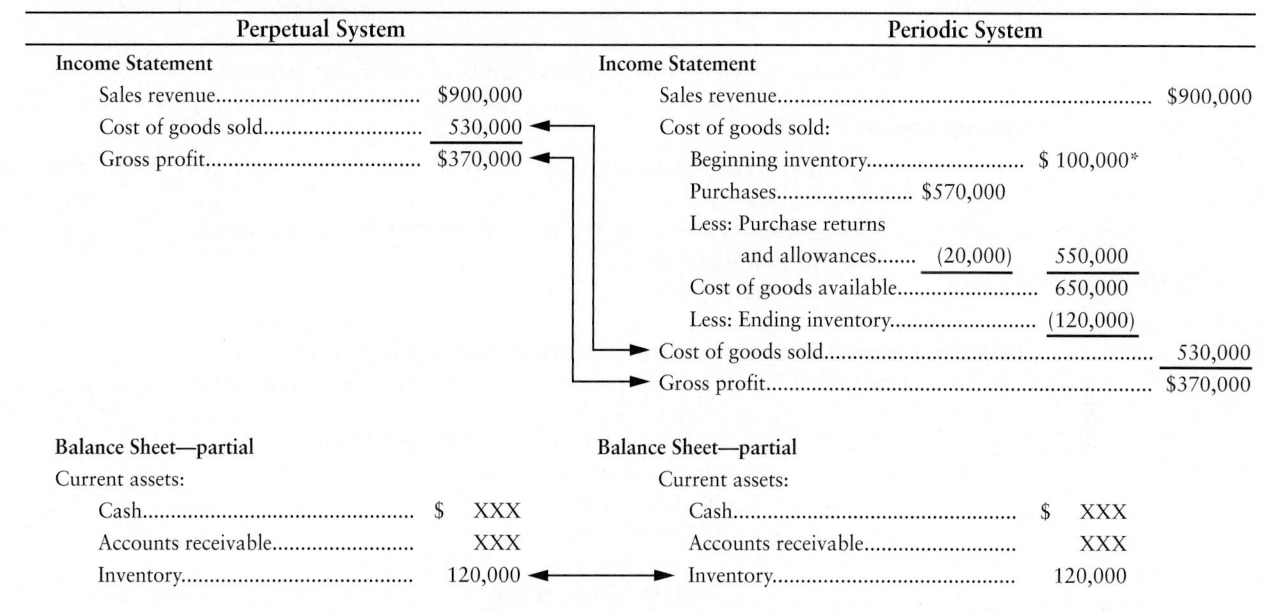

Perpetual System

Income Statement

Sales revenue	$900,000
Cost of goods sold	530,000
Gross profit	$370,000

Balance Sheet—partial

Current assets:	
Cash	$ XXX
Accounts receivable	XXX
Inventory	120,000

Periodic System

Income Statement

Sales revenue			$900,000
Cost of goods sold:			
Beginning inventory		$ 100,000*	
Purchases	$570,000		
Less: Purchase returns and allowances	(20,000)	550,000	
Cost of goods available		650,000	
Less: Ending inventory		(120,000)	
Cost of goods sold			530,000
Gross profit			$370,000

Balance Sheet—partial

Current assets:	
Cash	$ XXX
Accounts receivable	XXX
Inventory	120,000

Appendix 6A Assignments

Exercises

E6A-1 Computing periodic inventory amounts [10–15 min]

The periodic inventory records of Cambridge Prosthetics indicate the following at October 31:

Oct 1	Beginning inventory . . .	7 units @ $59
8	Purchase	2 units @ $59
15	Purchase	13 units @ $69
26	Purchase	4 units @ $79

At October 31 Cambridge counts 5 units of inventory on hand.

Requirement

1. Compute ending inventory and cost of goods sold, using each of the following methods:
   a. Average cost (round average unit cost to the nearest cent)
   b. First-in, first-out
   c. Last-in, first-out

E6A-2 Journalizing periodic inventory transactions [10–15 min]

Flexon Prosthetics uses the periodic inventory system and had the following transactions.

a. Purchase of inventory on account, $2,040
b. Sale of inventory for $2,900
c. Closing entries:
   (1) Beginning inventory, $510
   (2) Ending inventory at FIFO cost, $650
   (3) Purchases, $2,040
   (4) Cost of goods sold at FIFO cost, $1,900

Requirement

1. Journalize the transactions for the company.

E6A-3 Computing periodic inventory amounts [10–15 min]

Consider the data of the following companies:

Company	Net sales	Beginning Inventory	Net Purchases	Ending Inventory	Cost of goods sold	Gross Profit
Ash	$ 100,000	$ 21,000	$ 62,000	$ 18,000	(a)	$ 35,000
Elm	(b)	28,000	90,000	(c)	95,000	41,000
Fir	94,000	(d)	56,000	20,000	64,000	(e)
Oak	84,000	8,000	(f)	6,000	(g)	50,000

Requirements

1. Supply the missing amounts in the table above.
2. Prepare the income statement for Ash Company, which uses the periodic inventory system. Include a complete heading and show the full computation of cost of goods sold. Ash's operating expenses for the year were $10,000.

■ Problem (Group A)

P6A-4A Computing periodic inventory amounts [15–20 min]

A Futuristic Electronic Center began December with 91 units of inventory that cost $73 each. During December, the store made the following purchases:

Dec	3	22	@	$78
	12	47	@	$80
	18	77	@	$83

Futuristic uses the periodic inventory system, and the physical count at December 31 indicates that 115 units of inventory are on hand.

Requirements

1. Determine the ending inventory and cost-of-goods-sold amounts for the December financial statements under the average cost, FIFO, and LIFO methods.
2. Sales revenue for December totaled $24,000. Compute Futuristic's gross profit for December under each method.
3. Which method will result in the lowest income taxes for Futuristic? Why? Which method will result in the highest net income for Futuristic? Why?

■ Problem (Group B)

P6A-5B Computing periodic inventory amounts [15–20 min]

A 25th Century Electronic Center began December with 94 units of inventory that cost $72 each. During December, the store made the following purchases:

Dec	3	20	@	$77
	12	52	@	$79
	18	79	@	$82

25th Century uses the periodic inventory system, and the physical count at December 31 indicates that 112 units of inventory are on hand.

Requirements

1. Determine the ending inventory and cost-of-goods-sold amounts for the December financial statements under the average cost, FIFO, and LIFO methods.
2. Sales revenue for December totaled $23,000. Compute 25th Century's gross profit for December under each method.
3. Which method will result in the lowest income taxes for 25th Century? Why? Which method will result in the highest net income for 25th Century? Why?

7 Internal Control and Cash

Learning Objectives/ Success Keys

1. Define internal control
2. Explain the Sarbanes-Oxley Act
3. List and describe the components of internal control and control procedures
4. Explain control procedures unique to e-commerce
5. Demonstrate the use of a bank account as a control device
6. Prepare a bank reconciliation and journalize the related entries
7. Apply internal controls to cash receipts
8. Apply internal controls to cash payments
9. Explain and journalize petty cash transactions
10. Describe ethical business issues related to accounting

In the preceding chapter, Smart Touch Learning sold training DVDs. The training DVDs were a big hit, so Smart Touch plans to expand the business. Sheena Bright's brother, Andrew, wants to get in on the action and has agreed to join Smart Touch Learning as the marketing director. He can sell the training materials around neighboring colleges and also help develop an online marketing plan for new DVDs. In addition, he received an A in Accounting 101, so Sheena will let him do the accounting.

With boxes of DVDs crammed into every corner, Smart Touch's current office space is getting quickly outgrown. Sheena will need to rent warehouse space or possibly buy another building. Expansion will bring a new set of challenges:

- How will Sheena safeguard Smart Touch's assets?
- How will she ensure that her brother follows policies that are best for the business?

This chapter presents a framework for dealing with these issues. It also shows how to account for cash, the most liquid of all assets.

Internal Control

1 Define internal control

A key responsibility of a business manager is to control operations. Owners set goals, hire managers to lead the way, and hire employees to carry out the business plan. **Internal control** is the organizational plan and all the related measures designed to

1. **Safeguard assets.** A company must protect its assets; otherwise it is throwing away resources. If you fail to safeguard your cash, the most liquid of assets, it will quickly slip away.
2. **Encourage employees to follow company policy.** Everyone in an organization needs to work toward the same goals. With Sheena's brother, Andrew, operating part of Smart Touch Learning it is important for the business to identify policies to help meet the company's goals. These policies are also important for the company so that all customers are treated similarly, and so that results can be measured effectively.
3. **Promote operational efficiency.** Businesses cannot afford to waste resources. Sheena and Andrew work hard to make sales for Smart Touch and do not want to waste any of the benefits. If Smart Touch can buy a particular training DVD for $3, why pay $4? Reduce expenses and increase business profits.
4. **Ensure accurate, reliable accounting records.** Good records are essential. Without reliable records, managers cannot tell which part of the business is profitable and which part needs improvement. Smart Touch could be losing money on every DVD sold and not realize it—unless it keeps good records for the cost of its products.

Stop & Think...

Internal controls do not only apply to "big business." We do things every day that mirror the four internal control measures defined above. Consider your car, for example. You always lock the doors and you buy gas at the station with the lowest price per gallon. How do these personal acts relate to an internal control plan? Locking the door is an example of safeguarding assets. Finding the lowest price per gallon for gas is an example of operational efficiency.

So really, how critical are internal controls? They are so important that the U.S. Congress passed a law that requires **public companies**—those that sell their stock to the general public—to maintain a system of internal controls.

The Sarbanes-Oxley Act (SOX)

2 Explain the Sarbanes-Oxley Act

The **Enron** and **WorldCom** accounting scandals rocked the United States. **Enron** overstated profits and went out of business almost overnight. **WorldCom** (now part of **Verizon**) reported expenses as assets and overstated both profits and assets. Significantly, the same accounting firm, **Arthur Andersen**, had audited both companies' financial statements. **Arthur Andersen** voluntarily closed its doors in 2002, after nearly 90 years in public accounting.

As the scandals unfolded, many people asked, "How could this happen? Where were the auditors?" To address public concern, Congress passed the **Sarbanes-Oxley Act**, abbreviated as SOX. SOX revamped corporate governance in the United States and affected the accounting profession. Here are some of the SOX provisions:

1. Public companies must issue an internal control report, and an outside auditor must evaluate the client's internal controls.
2. A new body, the Public Company Accounting Oversight Board, oversees the work of auditors of public companies.
3. Accounting firms may not audit a public client and also provide certain consulting services for the same client.
4. Stiff penalties await violators—25 years in prison for securities fraud and 20 years for an executive making false sworn statements.

In 2005, the former chief executive of **WorldCom** was convicted of securities fraud and sentenced to 25 years in prison. The top executives of **Enron** were also sent to prison. You can see that internal controls and related matters can have serious consequences.

Exhibit 7-1 diagrams the shield that internal controls provide for an organization. Protected by the wall, people do business securely. How does a business achieve good internal control? The next section identifies the components of internal control.

EXHIBIT 7-1 | The Shield of Internal Control

The Components of Internal Control

3 List and describe the components of internal control and control procedures

A business can achieve its internal control objectives by applying five components. (TIP: You can remember the five components by using the acronym MICER.)

- Monitoring of controls
- Information system

- Control procedures
- control Environment
- Risk assessment

Monitoring of Controls

Companies hire auditors to monitor their controls. **Internal auditors** are employees of the business who ensure that the company's employees are following company policies and that operations are running efficiently. These internal auditors also determine whether the company is following legal requirements that monitor internal controls to safeguard assets. **External auditors** are outside accountants who are completely independent of the business. They evaluate the controls to ensure that the financial statements are presented fairly in accordance with the generally accepted accounting principles (GAAP) and they may suggest improvements to help the business.

Information System

As we have seen, the information system is critical. The decision makers need accurate information to keep track of assets and measure profits and losses.

Control Procedures

These are the procedures designed to ensure that the business's goals are achieved. The next section discusses internal control procedures.

Control Environment

The control environment is the "tone at the top" of the business. It starts with the owner or CEO and the top managers. They must behave honorably to set a good example for company employees. Each must demonstrate the importance of internal controls if he or she expects the employees to take the controls seriously. Former executives of **Enron** and **WorldCom** failed to establish a good control environment and are in prison as a result.

Risk Assessment

A company must identify its risks. For example, **Kraft Foods** faces the risk that its food products may harm people, **American Airlines**, planes may crash, **Sony** faces copyright infringement risks, and all companies face the risk of bankruptcy. Companies facing difficulties are tempted to falsify the financial statements to make themselves look better than they really are.

Internal Control Procedures

Whether the business is Smart Touch Learning, **Microsoft**, or a **BP** gas station, all companies need the following internal control procedures:

Competent, Reliable, and Ethical Personnel

Employees should be competent, reliable, and ethical. Paying good salaries will attract high-quality employees. Employees should also be trained to do the job and their work should be adequately supervised.

Assignment of Responsibilities

In a business with good internal controls, no important duty is overlooked. Each employee has certain responsibilities. At Smart Touch, Sheena Bright is the president. Suppose she writes the checks in order to control cash payments. She lets Andrew, her brother, do the accounting. In a large company the person in charge of writing checks is called the **treasurer**. The chief accounting officer is called the **controller**. Clearly assigned responsibilities create job accountability, thus ensuring that all important tasks get done.

Separation of Duties

Smart management divides responsibility between two or more people. **Separation of duties** limits fraud and promotes the accuracy of the accounting records. Separation of duties can be divided into two parts:

1. **Separate operations from accounting.** Accounting should be completely separate from the operating departments, such as production and sales. What would happen if sales personnel recorded the company's revenue? Sales figures could be inflated, and then, top managers would not know how much the company actually sold. This is why you should separate accounting and sales duties.

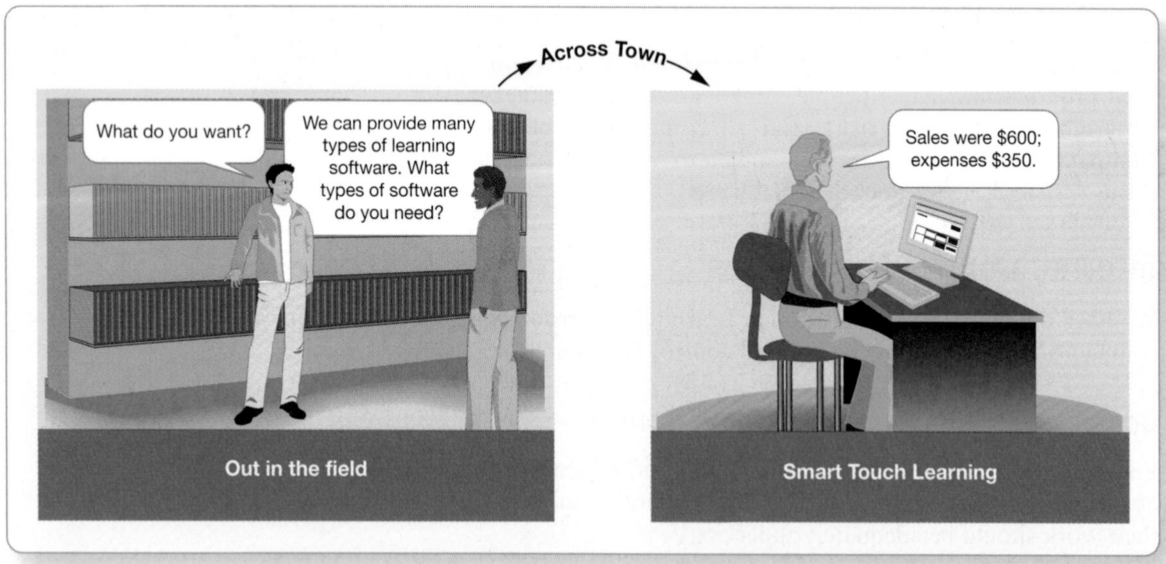

2. **Separate the custody of assets from accounting.** Accountants must not handle cash, and cashiers must not have access to the accounting records. If one employee has both duties, that person could steal cash and conceal the theft in the accounting records. The treasurer of a company handles cash, and the controller accounts for that cash. Neither person has both responsibilities.

Audits

To assess their accounting records, most companies perform audits. An audit is an examination of the company's financial statements and accounting system. To evaluate the accounting system, auditors must examine the internal controls.

Documents

Documents provide the details of business transactions. Documents include invoices and fax orders. Documents should be pre-numbered to prevent theft and inefficiency. A gap in the numbered sequence draws attention.

For example, for Sherman Lawn Service, a key document is the customer invoice. The manager can compare the total sales on the invoices with the amount of cash received and deposited by Hannah Sherman.

Electronic Devices

Accounting systems are relying less on paper documents and more on electronic documents and digital storage devices. For example, retailers such as **Target** and **Macy's** control inventory by attaching an electronic sensor to merchandise. The cashier removes the sensor. If a customer tries to leave the store with the sensor attached, an alarm sounds. According to Checkpoint Systems, these devices reduce theft by as much as 50%.

Other Controls

The types of other controls are as endless as the types of businesses that exist. The key to controls is that the cost of the control should not exceed the benefit (savings) from implementing that control. Some examples of other common controls are

- Fireproof vaults to store important documents;
- Burglar alarms, fire alarms, and security cameras;
- Loss-prevention specialists train company employees to spot suspicious activity.

As another control, fidelity bonds are purchased for employees who handle cash. The bond is an insurance policy that reimburses the company for any losses due to employee theft. Mandatory vacations and job rotation improve internal control. These controls also improve morale by giving employees a broad view of the business.

Internal Controls for E-Commerce

4 Explain control procedures unique to e-commerce

E-commerce creates its own unique types of risks. Hackers may gain access to confidential information, such as account numbers and passwords, or may introduce computer viruses, Trojans, or Phishing expeditions.

Stolen Account Numbers or Passwords

Suppose you buy CDs from Greg's Groovy Tunes' online store. To make the purchase, you must create an online account with a password for the Web site. When you submit your purchase, your credit card number must travel through the Internet, potentially exposing it, your account, and password information. Additionally, wireless networks (Wi-Fi) are creating new security hazards.

For example, on December 6, 2007, the University of Michigan-Flint reported that several of its servers were "breached," potentially exposing confidential student information, which in turn could lead to ID theft.

Computer Viruses and Trojans

A **computer virus** is a malicious program that (a) enters program code without consent and (b) performs destructive actions. A **Trojan** hides inside a legitimate program and works like a virus. Both can destroy or alter data, make bogus calculations, and infect files. Most firms have found a virus at some point in time in their system.

Suppose that an individual plants a virus into your school's computer that changes all the grades for students for a semester. This type of virus or Trojan could undermine not only a grade, but a school's reputation, to say the least.

Phishing Expeditions

Thieves phish by creating bogus Web sites, such as AOL4Free.com. The neat-sounding Web site attracts lots of visitors, and the thieves obtain account numbers and passwords from unsuspecting people who use the bogus site. They then use the data for illicit purposes.

Security Measures

To address the risks posed by e-commerce, companies have devised a number of security measures, including encryption and firewalls. The server holding confidential information may not be secure. One technique for protecting customer data is encryption. **Encryption** rearranges messages by a mathematical process. The encrypted message cannot be read by those who do not know the code. An accounting example uses check-sum digits for account numbers. Each account number has its last digit equal to the sum of the previous digits. For example, consider customer number 2237, where 2 + 2 + 3 = 7. Any account number that fails this test triggers an error message.

Another technique for protecting data is firewalls. **Firewalls** limit access into a local network. Members can access the network but nonmembers cannot. Usually several firewalls are built into the system. Think of a fortress with multiple walls protecting the king's chamber in the center. At the point of entry, passwords, PINs (personal identification numbers), and signatures are used. More sophisticated firewalls are used deeper in the network. Start with Firewall 3, and work toward the center.

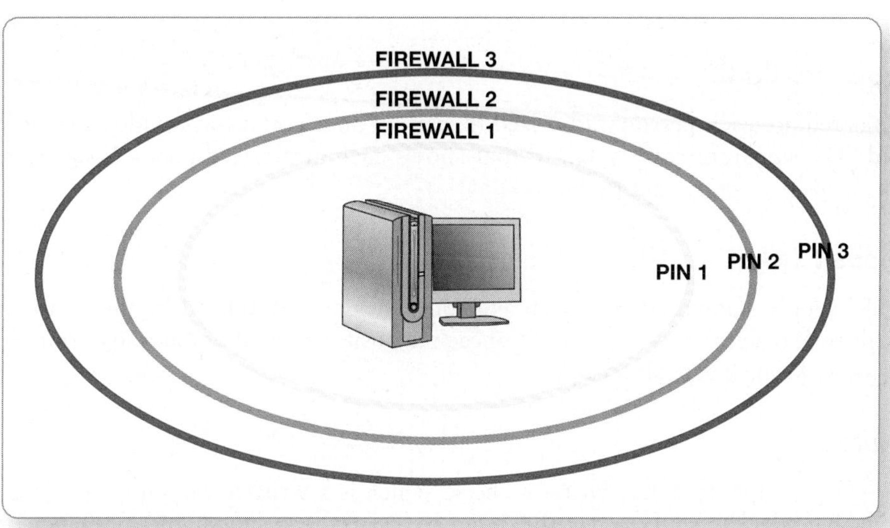

The Limitations of Internal Control—Costs and Benefits

Unfortunately, most internal controls can be overcome. **Collusion**—two or more people working together—can beat internal controls. For example, consider the following scenario with Galaxy Theater. Ralph and Lana can design a scheme in which Ralph, the ticket seller, sells tickets and pockets the cash from 10 customers. Lana, the ticket taker, admits 10 customers without taking their tickets. Ralph and Lana split the cash. Collusion has occurred to circumvent controls. To prevent this situation, the manager must take additional steps, such as matching the number of people in the theater against the number of ticket stubs retained. But that takes time away from other duties. It is difficult and costly to plan controls to prevent collusion.

The stricter the internal control system, the more it costs. A complex system of internal control can strangle the business with red tape. How tight should the controls be? Internal controls must always be judged in light of their costs versus their benefits. Following is an example of a good cost/benefit relationship: A security guard at a **Wal-Mart** store costs about $28,000 a year. On average, each guard prevents about $50,000 of theft. The net savings to **Wal-Mart** is $22,000. An example of a bad cost/benefit relationship would be paying the same security guard $28,000 a year to guard a $1,000 cash drawer. The net cost exceeds the benefit by $27,000.

The Bank Account as a Control Device

5 Demonstrate the use of a bank account as a control device

Cash is the most liquid asset because it is the medium of exchange. Cash is easy to conceal and relatively easy to steal. As a result, most businesses create specific controls for cash.

Keeping cash in a **bank account** helps control cash because banks have established practices for safeguarding customers' money. The documents used to control a bank account include the following:

- Signature card
- Deposit ticket
- Check
- Bank statement
- Bank reconciliation

Signature Card

Banks require each person authorized to sign on an account to provide a **signature card**. The signature card is a card that shows each authorized person's signature. This helps protect against forgery.

Deposit Ticket

Banks supply standard forms such as **deposit tickets**. Completed by the customer, the deposit ticket shows the amount of each deposit. As proof of the transaction, the customer keeps a deposit receipt.

Check

To pay cash, the depositor writes a **check**, which is a written, pre-numbered document that tells the bank to pay the designated party a specified amount. There are three parties to a check:

- The **maker**, who signs the check
- The **payee**, to whom the check is paid
- The bank, on which the check is drawn

Exhibit 7-2 shows a check drawn by Smart Touch Learning, the maker. The check has two parts, the check itself and the **remittance advice** below. This optional attachment tells the payee the reason for the payment.

Bank Statement

Banks send monthly statements to customers. A **bank statement** reports what the bank did with the customer's cash. The statement shows the account's beginning and ending balances, cash receipts, and payments. Included with the statement are physical or scanned copies of the maker's **canceled checks** (or the actual paid checks). Exhibit 7-3 is the April, 2010, bank statement of Smart Touch Learning.

Electronic funds transfer

Electronic funds transfer (**EFT**) moves cash by electronic communication. It is cheaper to pay without having to mail a check, so many people pay their mortgage, rent, and insurance by EFT.

EXHIBIT 7-2 | **Check with Remittance Advice**

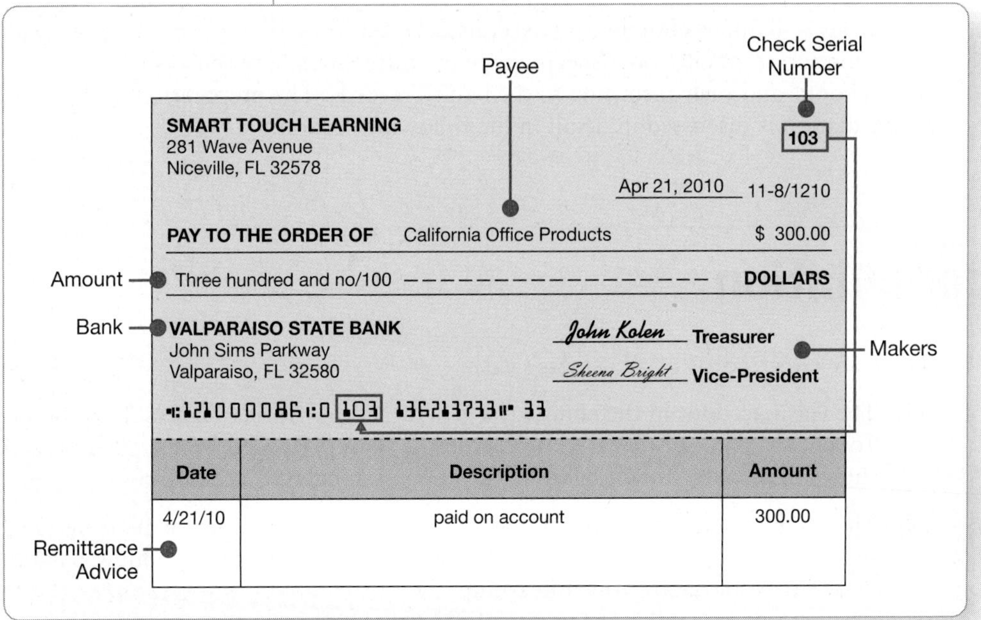

EXHIBIT 7-3 | **Bank Statement**

BANK STATEMENT

VALPARAISO STATE BANK
JOHN SIMS PARKWAY, VALPARAISO, FL 32580

Smart Touch Learning
281 Wave Avenue
Niceville, FL 32578

CHECKING ACCOUNT 136–213733
APRIL 30, 2010

BEGINNING BALANCE	TOTAL DEPOSITS	TOTAL WITHDRAWALS	SERVICE CHARGES	ENDING BALANCE
0	43,130	29,040	20	14,070

TRANSACTIONS

DEPOSITS	DATE	AMOUNT
Deposit	04/01	30,000
Deposit	04/10	5,500
Deposit	04/22	2,000
EFT—Collection from customer	04/27	100
Deposit	04/28	5,500
Interest	04/30	30

CHARGES	DATE	AMOUNT
Service Charge	04/30	20

CHECKS

Number	Amount	Number	Amount	Number	Amount
102	3,200	103	300		
101	20,000				

OTHER DEDUCTIONS	DATE	AMOUNT
	04/11	5,500
EFT—Water Works	04/20	40

Bank Reconciliation

Preparing a bank reconciliation is considered a control over cash. The **bank reconciliation** reconciles on a specific date the differences between cash on the company's books and cash according to the bank's records. The preparation of the bank reconciliation is discussed in detail in the following section.

The Bank Reconciliation

6 Prepare a bank reconciliation and journalize the related entries

There are two records of a business's cash:

1. The Cash account in the company's general ledger. April's T-account for Smart Touch, originally presented in Chapter 2, is reproduced below. Exhibit 7-4 shows that Smart Touch Learning's ending cash balance is $21,000.
2. The bank statement, which shows the cash receipts and payments transacted through the bank. In Exhibit 7-3, however, the bank shows an ending balance of $14,070 for Smart Touch Learning.

EXHIBIT 7-4 Smart Touch's Cash T-account

Cash			
Apr 1	30,000	Apr 2	20,000
Apr 8	5,500	Apr 15	3,200
Apr 22	2,000	Apr 21	300
Apr 24	9,000	Apr 30	2,000
Bal Apr 30	21,000		

The books and the bank statement usually show different cash balances. Differences arise because of a time lag in recording transactions, called **timing difference.** Three examples of timing differences follow:

- When you write a check, you immediately deduct it in your checkbook. But the bank does not subtract the check from your account until it pays the check a few days later.
- Likewise, you immediately add the cash receipt for all your deposits. But it may take a day or two for the bank to add deposits to your balance.
- Your EFT payments and cash receipts are often recorded by the bank before you learn of them.

To ensure accurate cash records, you need to update your checkbook either online or after you receive your bank statement. The result of this updating process creates a bank reconciliation that you must prepare. The bank reconciliation explains all differences between your cash records and your bank's records of your balance. The person who prepares the bank reconciliation should have no other cash duties. This means that the reconciler should not be a person who has access to cash or has duties requiring journalizing cash transactions. Otherwise, he or she could steal cash and manipulate the reconciliation to conceal the theft.

Preparing the Bank Reconciliation

Here are the items that appear on a bank reconciliation. They all cause differences between the bank balance and the book balance. (We call your checkbook record the "Books.")

Bank Side of the Reconciliation

The bank side contains items not yet recorded by the bank or errors made by the bank. These items include the following:

1. **Deposits in transit** (outstanding deposits). These deposits have been recorded and have already been added to the book balance, but the bank has not yet recorded them. These are shown as "Add deposits in transit" on the bank side because when the bank does record these deposits, it will increase the bank balance.
2. **Outstanding checks.** These checks have been recorded and have already been deducted from the book balance, but the bank has not yet paid (deducted) them. They are shown as "Subtract outstanding checks" on the bank side because when the bank does record the checks, it will decrease the bank balance.
3. **Bank errors.** Bank errors are posting errors made by the bank that either incorrectly increase or decrease the bank balance. Correct all bank errors on the Bank side of the reconciliation by reversing the effect of the errors.

Book Side of the Reconciliation

The book side contains items not yet recorded by the company on the internal books, but that are recorded by the bank. Items to show on the *Book* side include the following:

1. **Bank collections.** Bank collections are cash receipts that the bank has received and recorded for your account but that you have not recorded yet on the company's books. An example of a bank collection would be if a business has its customers pay directly to its bank. This is called a **lock-box system.** This system helps to reduce theft. Another example is a bank's collecting of a note receivable for you. Any increase to the bank balance that appears on the bank statement will show as "Add bank collections" on the book side of the reconciliation because it represents cash receipts not yet recorded by the company.
2. **Electronic funds transfers.** The bank may receive or pay cash on your behalf. An EFT may be a cash receipt or a cash payment. These will either show up as "Add EFT" for receipts not yet added to the company's books or "Subtract EFT" for payments not yet deducted on the company's books.
3. **Service charge.** This cash payment is the bank's fee for processing your transactions. This will show as "Subtract service charges" on the book side of the reconciliation because it represents cash payments not yet recorded in the company's cash balance.
4. **Interest revenue on your checking account.** You earn interest if you keep enough cash in your account. The bank statement tells you of this cash receipt. This will show as "Add interest revenue" on the book side of the reconciliation because it represents cash receipts not yet added in the company's cash balance.
5. **Nonsufficient funds (NSF) checks.** These are your earlier cash receipts that have turned out to be worthless. NSF checks (sometimes called *hot checks* or *bad checks*) are treated as cash payments on your bank reconciliation. Subtract NSF checks.

6. **The cost of printed checks.** This cash payment is handled like a service charge. Subtract this cost.

7. **Book errors.** Book errors are errors made on the books of the company that either incorrectly increase or decrease the cash balance in the company's general ledger. Correct all book errors on the Book side of the reconciliation.

Bank Reconciliation Illustrated

The bank statement in Exhibit 7-3 shows that the April 30 bank balance of Smart Touch Learning is $14,070 (upper-right corner). However, the company's Cash account has a balance of $21,000, as shown in Exhibit 7-4. This situation calls for a bank reconciliation. Exhibit 7-5, Panel A, lists the reconciling items for your easy reference, and Panel B shows the completed reconciliation.

EXHIBIT 7-5 Bank Reconciliation

PANEL A—Reconciling Items

Bank side:

1. Deposit in transit, Apr 24, $9,000.
2. Outstanding check no. 104, $2,000.

Book side:

3. EFT receipt from customer, $100.
4. Interest revenue earned on bank balance, $30.
5. Bank service charge, $20.
6. EFT payment of water bill, $40.

PANEL B—Bank Reconciliation

SMART TOUCH LEARNING
Bank Reconciliation
April 30, 2010

Bank Reconciliation			BOOKS		
Balance, Apr 30		$14,070	Balance, Apr 30		$21,000
ADD:			ADD:		
1. Deposit in transit		9,000	3. EFT receipt from customer		100
		23,070	4. Interest revenue earned on bank balance		30
					21,130
LESS:			LESS:		
2. Outstanding checks			5. Service charge	$20	
No. 104	$2,000	(2,000)	6. EFT payment of water bill	40	–60
Adjusted bank balance		$21,070	Adjusted bank balance		$21,070

These amounts should agree.

SUMMARY OF THE VARIOUS RECONCILING ITEMS:

BANK BALANCE—ALWAYS

- *Add* deposits in transit.
- *Subtract* outstanding checks.
- *Add* or *subtract* corrections of bank errors.

BOOK BALANCE—ALWAYS

- *Add* bank collections, interest revenue, and EFT receipts.
- *Subtract* service charges, NSF checks, and EFT payments.
- *Add* or *subtract* corrections of book errors.

Stop & Think...

Although we all have our own personal methods for balancing our check book, some are more formal than others. The bank reconciliation in Exhibit 7-5 is mirrored on the back page of each statement you receive from the bank every month. Take a look at your most recent statement and see how similar parts of it look to the one in Exhibit 7-3.

Journalizing Transactions from the Reconciliation

The bank reconciliation is an accountant's tool separate from the journals and ledgers. It does *not* account for transactions in the journal. To get the transactions into the accounts, we must make journal entries and post to the ledger. All items on the Book side of the bank reconciliation require journal entries. We make no entries on the Bank side, because we do not have access to the bank's general ledger.

The bank reconciliation in Exhibit 7-5 requires Smart Touch Learning to make journal entries to bring the Cash account up-to-date. Numbers in the journal entries in Exhibit 7-6 correspond to the reconciling items listed in Exhibit 7-5, Panel A, and to the Book side of the reconciliation in Panel B.

EXHIBIT 7-6 | Adjusting entries from Bank Reconciliation

	2010			
3	Apr 30	Cash (A+)	100	
		Accounts receivable (A–)		100
		To record account receivable collected by bank.		
4	30	Cash (A+)	30	
		Interest revenue (R+)		30
		To record interest earned on bank balance.		
5	30	Miscellaneous expense (or Bank service charge expense) (E+)	20	
		Cash (A–)		20
		To record bank service charges incurred.		
6	30	Utilities expense (E+)	40	
		Cash (A–)		40
		To record payment of water bill by EFT.		

After posting the entries from Exhibit 7-6, the cash T-account will then appear as follows:

Cash

Apr 1	30,000	Apr 2	20,000
Apr 8	5,500	Apr 15	3,200
Apr 22	2,000	Apr 21	300
Apr 24	9,000	Apr 30	2,000
Bal Apr 30 before bank recon.	21,000		
AJE 3	100	AJE 5	20
AJE 4	30	AJE 6	40
Bal Apr 30 after posting bank reconciliation entries	21,070		

Stop & Think...

How do we "journalize" transactions from our personal bank reconciliation? For most of us, the answer is we write it down in our checkbook ledger. That is our personal "journal" of bank transactions.

Online Banking

Online banking allows you to pay bills and view your bank account electronically—you do not have to wait until the end of the month to get a bank statement. With online banking you can reconcile transactions at any time and keep your account current whenever you wish. Exhibit 7-7 shows a page from the account history of Toni Anderson's bank account.

EXHIBIT 7-7 **Online Banking—Account History (like a Bank Statement)**

Account History for Toni Anderson Checking # 5401-632-9
as of Close of Business 07/27/2017

Account Details
Current Balance $4,136.08

Date ↓	Description	Withdrawals	Deposits	Balance
	Current Balance			**$4,136.08**
07/27/17	DEPOSIT		1,170.35	
07/26/17	28 DAYS-INTEREST		2.26	
07/25/17	Check #6131 View Image	443.83		
07/24/17	Check #6130 View Image	401.52		
07/23/17	EFT PYMT CINGULAR	61.15		
07/22/17	EFT PYMT CITICARD PAYMENT	3,172.85		
07/20/17	Check #6127 View Image	550.00		
07/19/17	Check #6122 View Image	50.00		
07/16/17	Check #6116 View Image	2,056.75		
07/15/17	Check #6123 View Image	830.00		
07/13/17	Check #6124 View Image	150.00		
07/11/17	ATM 4900 SANGER AVE	200.00		
07/09/17	Check #6119 View Image	30.00		
07/05/17	Check #6125 View Image	2,500.00		
07/04/17	ATM 4900 SANGER AVE	100.00		
07/01/17	DEPOSIT		9,026.37	

FDIC EQUAL HOUSING LENDER E-Mail

The account history—like a bank statement—lists deposits, checks, EFT payments, ATM withdrawals, and interest earned on your bank balance. But depending on the particular bank, the account history does not always show your beginning balance, so you cannot work from your beginning balance to your ending balance.

More and more banks today make it much easier to do the reconciliations. They not only have running daily balances available on the history, but they also have radio buttons and/or checkboxes to reconcile to the checkbook online. In addition, banks promote a paperless approach to the reconciliation process and also offer transaction downloads to Excel and other financial software packages so that the paper statements are becoming obsolete.

The authors wish to thank Ron Burris, GEX Publishing Services, for his contributions to this section.

Summary Problem 1

The cash account of Baylor Associates at February 28, 2011, follows.

Cash			
Feb 1	Bal 3,995	Feb 3	400
6	800	12	3,100
15	1,800	19	1,100
23	1,100	25	500
28	2,400	27	900
Feb 28	Bal 4,095		

Baylor Associates received the following bank statement on February 28, 2011 (negative amounts are in parentheses):

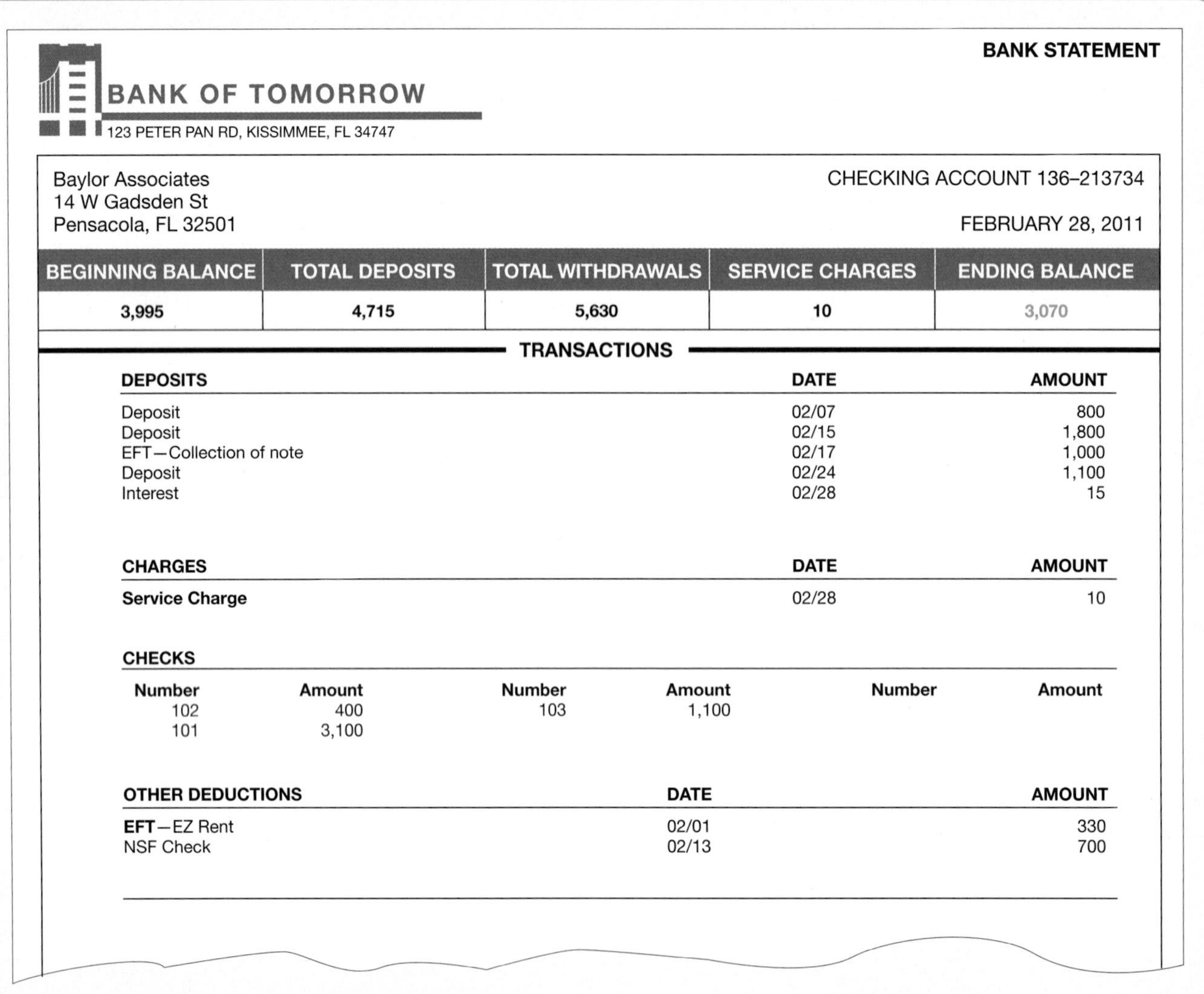

BANK STATEMENT

BANK OF TOMORROW
123 PETER PAN RD, KISSIMMEE, FL 34747

Baylor Associates
14 W Gadsden St
Pensacola, FL 32501

CHECKING ACCOUNT 136–213734

FEBRUARY 28, 2011

BEGINNING BALANCE	TOTAL DEPOSITS	TOTAL WITHDRAWALS	SERVICE CHARGES	ENDING BALANCE
3,995	4,715	5,630	10	3,070

TRANSACTIONS

DEPOSITS	DATE	AMOUNT
Deposit	02/07	800
Deposit	02/15	1,800
EFT—Collection of note	02/17	1,000
Deposit	02/24	1,100
Interest	02/28	15

CHARGES	DATE	AMOUNT
Service Charge	02/28	10

CHECKS

Number	Amount	Number	Amount	Number	Amount
102	400	103	1,100		
101	3,100				

OTHER DEDUCTIONS	DATE	AMOUNT
EFT—EZ Rent	02/01	330
NSF Check	02/13	700

Additional data:
Baylor deposits all cash receipts in the bank and makes all payments by check.

Requirements

1. Prepare the bank reconciliation of Baylor Associates at February 28, 2011.
2. Journalize the entries based on the bank reconciliation.

Solution

Requirement 1

BAYLOR ASSOCIATES Bank Reconciliation February 28, 2011		
Bank:		
Balance, February 28, 2011		$ 3,070
Add: Deposit of February 28 in transit		2,400
		5,470
Less: Outstanding checks issued on February 25 ($500) and February 27 ($900)		(1,400)
Adjusted bank balance, February 28, 2011		$ 4,070
Books:		
Balance, February 28, 2011		$ 4,095
Add: Bank collection of note receivable		1,000
Interest revenue earned on bank balance		15
		5,110
Less: Service charge	$ 10	
NSF check	700	
EFT—Rent expense	330	(1,040)
Adjusted book balance, February 28, 2011		$ 4,070

Requirement 2

Feb 28	Cash (A+)	1,000	
	Note receivable (A–)		1,000
	Note receivable collected by bank.		
28	Cash (A+)	15	
	Interest revenue (R+)		15
	Interest earned on bank balance.		
28	Miscellaneous expense (E+)	10	
	Cash (A–)		10
	Bank service charge.		
28	Accounts receivable—M. E. Crown (A+)	700	
	Cash (A–)		700
	NSF check returned by bank.		
28	Rent expense (E+)	330	
	Cash (A–)		330
	Monthly rent expense.		

Internal Control over Cash Receipts

7 Apply internal controls to cash receipts

All cash receipts should be deposited for safekeeping in the bank—quickly. Companies receive cash over the counter and through the mail. Each source of cash has its own security measures.

Cash Receipts over the Counter

Exhibit 7-8 illustrates a cash receipt over the counter in a store. The point-of-sale terminal (cash register) provides control over the cash receipts. Consider a **Target** store. For each transaction, **Target** issues a receipt to ensure that each sale is recorded. The cash drawer opens when the clerk enters a transaction, and the machine (cash register) records it. At the end of the day, a manager proves the cash by comparing the cash in the drawer against the machine's record of sales. This step helps prevent theft by the clerk.

EXHIBIT 7-8 | **Cash Receipts over the Counter**

At the end of the day—or several times a day if business is brisk—the cashier deposits the cash in the bank. The machine tape then goes to the accounting department to record the journal entry to record cash receipts and sales revenue. These measures, coupled with oversight by a manager, discourage theft.

Cash Receipts by Mail

Many companies receive cash by mail. Exhibit 7-9 shows how companies control cash received by mail. All incoming mail is opened by a mailroom employee. The mailroom then sends all customer checks to the treasurer, who has the cashier deposit the money in the bank. The remittance advices go to the accounting department for journal entries to Cash and customer accounts. As a final control, the controller compares the following records for the day:

- Bank deposit amount from the treasurer
- Debit to Cash from the accounting department

The debit to Cash should equal the amount deposited in the bank. All cash receipts are safe in the bank, and the company books are up-to-date.

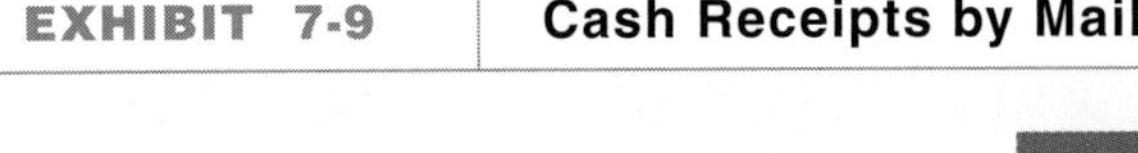

EXHIBIT 7-9 | Cash Receipts by Mail

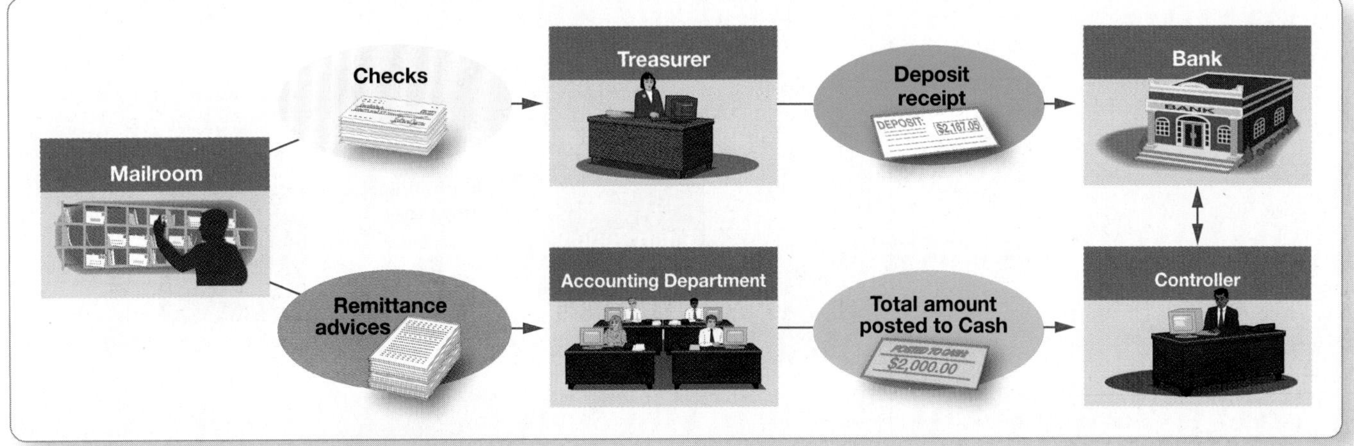

Many companies use a lock-box system, as discussed earlier in the chapter. Customers send their checks directly to the company's bank account. Internal control is tight because company personnel never touch incoming cash. The lock-box system puts business cash to work immediately.

Internal Control over Cash Payments

8 Apply internal controls to cash payments

Companies make most payments by check. They also pay small amounts from a petty cash fund, which is discussed later in this section. Let us begin with cash payments by check.

Controls over Payment by Check

As we have seen, you need a good separation of duties between operations and writing checks for cash payments. Payment by check is an important internal control, for the following reasons:

- The check provides a record of the payment.
- The check must be signed by an authorized official.
- Before signing the check, the official reviews the invoice or other evidence supporting the payment.

Controls over Purchase and Payment

To illustrate the internal control over cash payments by check, suppose Smart Touch Learning buys its inventory from **Sony**. The purchasing and payment process follows these steps, as shown in Exhibit 7-10.

Start with the box for Smart Touch Learning on the left side.

STEP **1**: Smart Touch faxes a *purchase order* to **Sony**. Smart Touch says, "Please send us 1,000 DVD-Rs."

STEP **2**: **Sony** ships the goods and faxes an *invoice* back to Smart Touch. **Sony** sends the goods.

STEP **3**: Smart Touch receives the *inventory* and prepares a *receiving report*. Smart Touch got its DVD-Rs.

STEP **4**: After approving all documents, Smart Touch sends a *check* to **Sony**. Smart Touch says, "Okay, we'll pay you."

EXHIBIT 7-10 | Cash Payments by Check

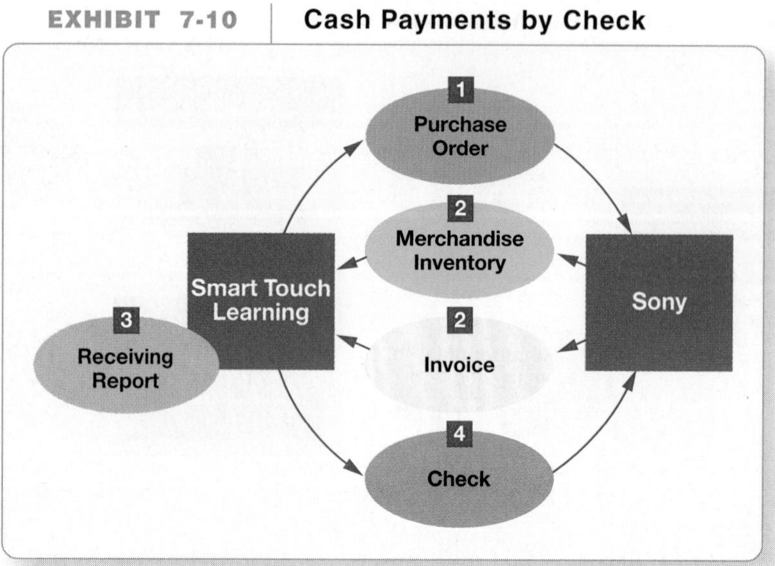

For good internal control, the purchasing agent should neither receive the goods nor approve the payment. If these duties are not separated, a purchasing agent can buy goods and have them shipped to his or her home. Or a purchasing agent can spend too much on purchases, approve the payment, and split the excess with the supplier.

Exhibit 7-11 shows Smart Touch's payment packet of documents. Before signing the check, the controller or the treasurer should examine the packet to prove that all the documents agree. Only then does the company know that

1. it received the goods ordered.
2. it is paying only for the goods received.

EXHIBIT 7-11 | Payment Packet

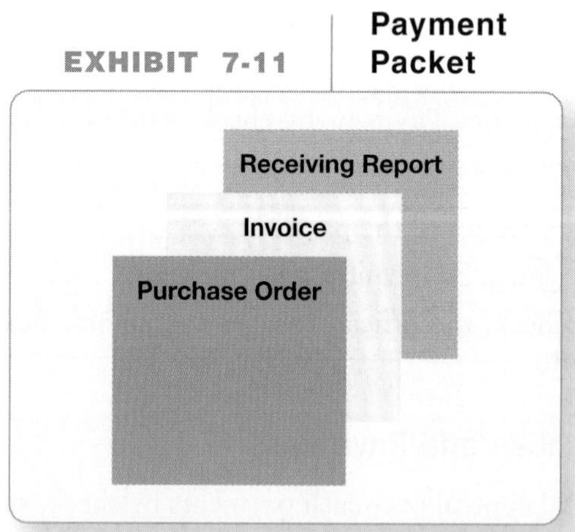

After payment, the check signer punches a hole through the payment packet. Dishonest people have been known to run a bill through twice for payment. This hole confirms that the bill has been paid.

The Voucher System

Many companies use the voucher system for internal control over cash payments. A **voucher** is a document authorizing a cash payment.

The voucher system uses (1) vouchers, (2) a voucher register (similar to a purchases journal discussed in a later chapter), and (3) a check register (similar to a cash payments journal, also discussed in a later chapter). All expenditures must be approved before payment. This approval takes the form of a voucher.

Exhibit 7-12 illustrates a voucher of Smart Touch Learning. To enhance internal control, Smart Touch could add this voucher to the payment packet illustrated in Exhibit 7-11.

EXHIBIT 7-12 Voucher

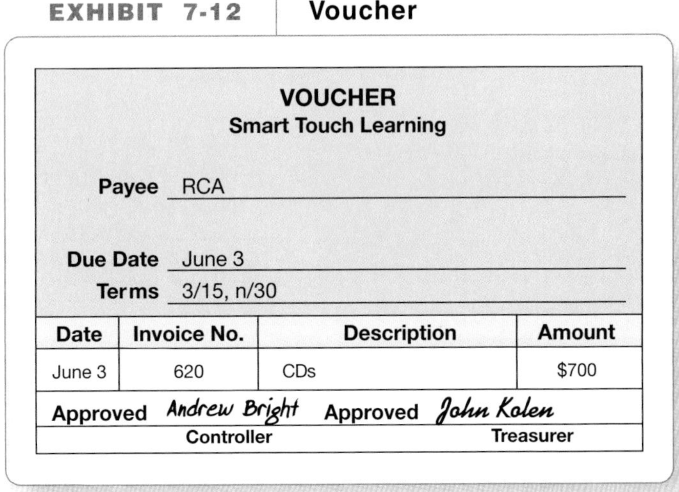

VOUCHER
Smart Touch Learning

Payee RCA

Due Date June 3
Terms 3/15, n/30

Date	Invoice No.	Description	Amount
June 3	620	CDs	$700

Approved *Andrew Bright* Controller Approved *John Kolen* Treasurer

Streamlined Procedures

Technology is streamlining payment procedures. **Evaluated Receipts Settlement (ERS)** compresses the approval process into a single step: Compare the receiving report to the purchase order. If those documents match, then Smart Touch got the DVD-Rs it ordered. In that case Smart Touch pays **Sony**, the vendor.

An even more streamlined process bypasses paper documents altogether. In **Electronic Data Interchange (EDI)**, **Wal-Mart's** computers communicate directly with the computers of suppliers like **Hanes** textiles and **Hershey Foods**. When **Wal-Mart's** inventory of **Hershey** candy reaches a low level, the computer creates and sends an electronic purchase order to **Hershey**. **Hershey** ships the candy and invoices to **Wal-Mart**. **Wal-Mart** manager approves the invoice and then an electronic fund transfer (EFT) sends **Wal-Mart's** payment to **Hershey**. These streamlined EDI procedures are used for both cash payments and cash receipts in many companies.

Controlling Small Cash Payments

It is not cost-effective to write a check for a taxi fare or the delivery of a package across town. To meet these needs and to streamline record keeping for small cash transactions, companies keep cash on hand to pay small amounts. This fund is

The Petty Cash Fund

9 Explain and journalize petty cash transactions

We have already established that cash is the most liquid of assets. Petty cash is more liquid than cash in the bank because none of the bank controls are in place. Therefore, petty cash needs controls such as the following:

- Designate a **custodian of the petty cash fund.** The custodian is the individual assigned responsibility for the petty cash fund.
- Designate a specific amount of cash to be kept in the petty cash fund.

- Support all petty cash fund payments with a **petty cash ticket**. The petty cash ticket serves as an authorization voucher and explanation.

Setting Up the Petty Cash Fund

The petty cash fund is opened when you write a check for the designated amount. Make the check payable to Petty cash. On August 1, 2010, Smart Touch creates a petty cash fund of $200. The custodian cashes a $200 check and places the money in the fund. The journal entry is

Aug 1	Petty cash (A+)	200	
	Cash in bank (A–)		200
	To open the petty cash fund.		

For each petty cash payment, the custodian prepares a petty cash ticket like the one in Exhibit 7-13 on the following page.

Signatures (or initials) identify the recipient of the cash and the fund custodian. The custodian keeps the petty cash tickets in the fund box. The sum of the cash plus the total of the petty cash tickets should equal the fund balance, $200, at all times.

Maintaining the Petty cash account at its designated balance is the nature of an **imprest system**. The imprest system requires that, at any point in time, the petty cash box contains cash and receipts that total the amount of the imprest balance. This clearly identifies the amount of cash for which the custodian is responsible, and that is the system's main internal control feature. Payments deplete the fund, so periodically it must be replenished.

Replenishing the Petty Cash Fund

On August 31 the petty cash fund holds

- $118 in petty cash, and
- $80 in petty cash tickets (1 ticket for $60 for office supplies and 1 ticket for $20 for a delivery).

You can see that $2 is missing:

Fund balance	$200
Cash on hand	$118
Petty cash tickets	80
Total accounted for	$198
Amount of cash missing	$ 2

To replenish the petty cash fund, you need to bring the cash on hand up to $200. The company writes a check, payable to Petty cash, for $82 ($200 imprest balance – $118 petty cash on hand). The fund custodian cashes this check and puts $82 back in the fund. Now the fund holds $200 cash as it should.

The petty cash tickets tell you what to debit and the check amount tells you what to credit, as shown in this incomplete entry to replenish the fund:

2010			
Aug 31	Office supplies (A+)	60	
	Delivery expense (E+)	20	
	Cash (A–)		82

EXHIBIT 7-13 | Petty Cash Ticket

PETTY CASH TICKET

Date Aug 25, 2010

Amount $60

For Letterhead invoices

Debit Office Supplies

Received by *Lewis Wright* Fund Custodian MAR

Missing petty cash funds are either debited (or credited) to a new account, Cash short & over. In this case, $2 was missing, so we debit Cash short & over for the missing petty cash. Another way to look at this is that we needed another $2 debit to make the journal entry balance.

At times the sum of cash in the petty cash fund plus the tickets may exceed the fund balance. Consider the previous example. Assume the petty cash ticket #2 for delivery was for $30, instead of $20. We know the amount of the petty cash tickets and the amount of the check to replenish the funds. Consider the following partial journal entry:

2010			
Aug 31	Office supplies (A+)	60	
	Delivery expenses (E+)	30	
	Cash (A–)		82

We know the total debits are $90 ($60 + $30). We know that the check to replenish the fund was still $82 (credit to cash). For this situation, we need $8 credit to make the journal entry balance. That situation creates a gain, which is credited to Cash short & over, as follows (using assumed amounts):

2010			
Aug 31	Office supplies (A+)	60	
	Delivery expenses (E+)	30	
	Cash short & over		8
	Cash (A–)		82

Over time the Cash short & over account should net out to a zero balance.

The Petty cash account keeps its $200 balance at all times. Petty cash is debited only when the fund is started (see the August 1 entry) or when its amount is changed. If the business raises the fund amount from $200 to $250, this would require a check to be cashed for $50 and the debit would be to Petty cash.

Stop & Think...

We are all custodians of a petty cash fund—the cash in our wallets. Sometimes we are good trackers of our petty cash, keeping receipts and tracking where the cash goes. Sometimes we are not, as in "Gee, I just got $50 from the ATM and now I have only $5—where did my money go?" Sometimes we increase our petty cash imprest balance ("I need to get out an extra $200 for my trip to Raleigh."). Sometimes we decrease our petty cash imprest balance ("I am going to put $30 of the $60 in my wallet back in the bank so I don't spend it.").

Ethics and Accounting

10 Describe ethical business issues related to accounting

Roger Smith, the former chairman of **General Motors**, said, "Ethical practice is [...] good business." Smith knows that unethical behavior does not work. Sooner or later it comes back to haunt you. Moreover, ethical behavior wins out in the long run because it is the right thing to do. **Ethics** in business is really analyzing right from wrong.

Corporate and Professional Codes of Ethics

Most companies have a code of ethics to encourage employees to behave ethically. But codes of ethics are not enough by themselves. Owners and managers must set a high ethical tone, as we saw in the earlier section in this chapter on Control Environment. The owner or CEO must make it clear that the company will not tolerate unethical conduct.

As professionals, accountants are expected to maintain higher standards than society in general. Their ability to do business depends entirely on their reputation. Most independent accountants are members of the American Institute of Certified Public Accountants and must abide by the *AICPA Code of Professional Conduct*. Accountants who are members of the Institute of Management Accountants are bound by the *Standards of Ethical Conduct for Management Accountants*.

Ethical Issues in Accounting

In many situations, the ethical choice is obvious. For example, stealing cash is both unethical and illegal. In other cases, the choices are more difficult. But in every instance, ethical judgments boil down to a personal decision: What should I do in a given situation? Let us consider two ethical issues in accounting.

Situation 1

Grant Jacobs is preparing the income tax return of a client who has earned more income than expected. On January 2, the client pays for advertising and asks Jacobs to backdate the expense to the preceding year. Backdating the deduction would lower the client's immediate tax payments. After all, there is a difference of only two days between December 31 and January 2. This client is important to Jacobs. What should he do?

> Jacobs should refuse the request because the transaction took place in January of the new year.

If Jacobs backdated the transaction in the accounting records, what control device could prove that he behaved unethically? An IRS audit could prove that the expense occurred in January rather than in December. Falsifying IRS documents is both unethical and illegal and is subject to severe preparer penalties.

Situation 2

Chris Morris' software company owes $40,000 to **Bank of America**. The loan agreement requires Morris' company to maintain a current ratio (current assets divided by current liabilities) of 1.50 or higher. At present, the company's current ratio is 1.40. At this level, Morris is in violation of her loan agreement. She can increase the current ratio to 1.53 by paying off some current liabilities right before year-end. Is it ethical to do so?

Yes, because paying the bills early is a real business transaction.

Morris should be aware that paying off the liabilities is only a delaying tactic. It will hold off the bank for now, but the current ratio must remain above 1.50 in order to keep from violating the agreement in the future.

Dudley Dorite, CPA, the lead auditor of Nimron, thinks Nimron may be understating the liabilities on its balance sheet. Nimron's transactions are very complex, and outsiders may never figure this out. Dorite asks his firm's standards committee how he should handle the situation. The committee replies, "Require Nimron to report all its liabilities." Nimron is Dorite's most important client, and Nimron is pressuring him to certify the liabilities. Dorite can rationalize that Nimron's reported amounts are okay. What should he do? To make his decision, Dorite consults the framework outlined in the following Decision Guidelines feature.

Decision Guidelines

FRAMEWORK FOR MAKING ETHICAL JUDGMENTS

Weighing tough ethical judgments requires a decision framework. Answering these four questions will guide you through tough decisions. Let us apply them to Dorite's situation.

Decision	Guidelines
• What is the ethical issue?	1. *Identify the ethical issue.* Dorite's ethical dilemma is to decide what he should do with the information he has uncovered.
• What are Dorite's options?	2. *Specify the alternatives.* For Dorite, the alternatives include (a) go along with Nimron's liabilities as reported or (b) force Nimron to report higher amounts of liabilities.
• What are the possible consequences?	3. *Assess the possible outcomes.* a. If Dorite certifies Nimron's present level of liabilities—and if no one ever objects—Dorite will keep this valuable client. But if Nimron's actual liabilities turn out to be higher than reported, Nimron investors may lose money and take Dorite to court. That would damage his reputation as an auditor and hurt his firm. b. If Dorite follows his company policy, he must force Nimron to increase its reported liabilities. That will anger the company, and Nimron may fire Dorite as its auditor. In that case, Dorite will save his reputation, but it will cost him some business in the short run.
• What should he do?	4. *Make the decision.* In the end Dorite went along with Nimron and certified the company's liabilities. He went directly against his firm's policies and GAAP. Nimron later admitted understating its liabilities, Dorite had to retract his audit opinion, and Dorite's firm collapsed quickly. Dorite should have followed company policy. Rarely is one person smarter than a team of experts. Furthermore, it is never worthwhile to act unethically, as Dorite did.

Summary Problem 2

Misler Company established a $300 petty cash fund on January 2, 2012. Karen Misler (KM) is the fund custodian. At the end of the month, the petty cash fund contains the following:

a. Cash: $163
b. Petty cash tickets, as follows:

No.	Amount	Issued to	Signed by	Account Debited
44	$14	B. Jarvis	B. Jarvis and KM	Office supplies
45	39	S. Bell	S. Bell	Delivery expense
47	43	R. Tate	R. Tate and KM	—
48	33	L. Blair	L. Blair and KM	Travel expense

Requirements

1. Identify three internal control weaknesses revealed in the given data.
2. Journalize the following transactions:
   a. Establishment of the petty cash fund on January 2, 2012.
   b. Replenishment of the fund on January 31, 2012. Assume that petty cash ticket no. 47 was issued for the purchase of office supplies.
3. What is the balance in the Petty cash account immediately before replenishment? Immediately after replenishment?

Solution

Requirement 1

The three internal control weaknesses are

1. Petty cash ticket no. 46 is missing. There is no indication of what happened to this ticket. The company should investigate.
2. The petty cash custodian (KM) did not sign petty cash ticket no. 45. This omission may have been an oversight on her part. However, it raises the question of whether she authorized the payment. Both the fund custodian and the recipient of cash should sign the petty cash ticket.
3. Petty cash ticket no. 47 does not indicate which account to debit on the actual ticket. If Tate could not remember where the $43 went, then Misler will not know what account should be debited.

Requirement 2

Petty cash journal entries:

a. Entry to establish the petty cash fund:
b. Entry to replenish the fund:

Jan 12	Petty cash (A+)	300	
	Cash in bank (A–)		300

Jan 31	Office supplies ($14 + $43) (A+)	57	
	Delivery expense (E+)	39	
	Travel expense (E+)	33	
	Cash short & over (E+)	8	
	Cash in bank (A–)		137

Requirement 3

The balance in Petty cash is *always* its specified balance, in this case $300.

Review Internal Control and Cash

Accounting Vocabulary

Bank Account (p. 414)
Helps control cash because banks have established practices for safeguarding customers' money.

Bank Collections (p. 417)
Collection of money by the bank on behalf of a depositor.

Bank Errors (p. 417)
Posting errors made by the bank that either incorrectly increase or decrease the bank balance.

Bank Reconciliation (p. 416)
Document explaining the reasons for the difference between a depositor's cash records and the depositor's cash balance in its bank account.

Bank Statement (p. 414)
Document the bank uses to report what it did with the depositor's cash. Shows the bank account beginning and ending balance and lists the month's cash transactions conducted through the bank.

Book Errors (p. 418)
Posting errors made in the company's general ledger that either incorrectly increase or decrease the book balance.

Canceled Checks (p. 414)
Physical or scanned copies of the maker's paid checks.

Check (p. 414)
Document that instructs a bank to pay the designated person or business a specified amount of money.

Collusion (p. 413)
Two or more people working together to circumvent internal controls and defraud a company.

Computer Virus (p. 412)
A malicious program that (a) reproduces itself, (b) enters program code without consent, and (c) performs destructive actions.

Controller (p. 410)
The chief accounting officer of a company.

Custodian of the Petty Cash Fund (p. 427)
The individual assigned responsibility for the petty cash fund.

Deposits in Transit (p. 417)
A deposit recorded by the company but not yet by its bank.

Deposit Tickets (p. 414)
Completed by the customer, shows the amount of each deposit.

Electronic Data Interchange (EDI) (p. 427)
Streamlined process that bypasses paper documents altogether. Computers of customers communicate directly with the computers of suppliers to automate routine business transactions.

Electronic Funds Transfer (EFT) (p. 414)
System that transfers cash by electronic communication rather than by paper documents.

Encryption (p. 413)
Rearranging plain-text messages by a mathematical process, the primary method of achieving confidentiality in e-commerce.

Ethics (p. 430)
Analyzing right from wrong.

Evaluated Receipts Settlement (p. 427)
Compresses the approval process into a single step: Compare the receiving report to the purchase order.

External Auditors (p. 409)
Outside accountants completely independent of the business who monitor the controls to ensure that the financial statements are presented fairly in accordance with GAAP.

Firewalls (p. 413)
Devices that enable members of a local network to access the Internet, while keeping nonmembers out of the network.

Imprest System (p. 428)
A way to account for petty cash by maintaining a constant balance in the petty cash account, supported by the fund (cash plus payment tickets) totaling the same amount.

Internal Auditors (p. 409)
Employees of the business who ensure that the company's employees are following company policies, meeting legal requirements, and that operations are running efficiently.

Internal Control (p. 407)
Organizational plan and all the related measures adopted by an entity to safeguard assets, encourage employees to follow company policy, promote operational efficiency, and ensure accurate and reliable accounting records.

Lock-Box System (p. 417)
A system in which customers pay their accounts directly to a business's bank.

Maker (p. 414)
A system in which customers pay their accounts directly to a business's bank.

Nonsufficient Funds (NSF) Check (p. 417)
A "hot" check; one for which the maker's bank account has insufficient money to pay the check.

Outstanding Checks (p. 417)
A check issued by the company and recorded on its books but not yet paid by its bank.

Payee (p. 414)
On a check, the person to whom the check is paid.

Petty Cash (p. 427)
Fund containing a small amount of cash that is used to pay for minor expenditures.

Petty Cash Ticket (p. 428)
Supports all petty cash fund payments. The petty cash ticket serves as an authorization voucher and explanation of the expenditure.

Public Companies (p. 407)
Companies that sell their stock to the general public.

Remittance Advice (p. 414)
An optional attachment to a check that tells the payee the reason for the payment.

Sarbanes-Oxley Act (p. 408)
An act passed by Congress, abbreviated as SOX. SOX revamped corporate governance in the United States and affected the accounting profession.

Separation of Duties (p. 410)
Dividing responsibility between two or more people.

Service Charge (p. 417)
A cash payment that is the bank's fee for processing your transactions.

Signature Card (p. 414)
A card that shows each authorized person's signature for a bank account.

Timing Difference (p. 416)
Differences that arise between the balance on the bank statement and the balance on the books because of a time lag in recording transactions.

Treasurer (p. 410)
In a large company, the person in charge of writing checks.

Trojan (p. 412)
A malicious computer program that hides inside a legitimate program and works like a virus.

Voucher (p. 426)
Instrument authorizing a cash payment.

Quick Check

1. Which of the following is *not* part of the definition of internal control?
   a. Promote operational efficiency
   b. Safeguard assets
   c. Encourage employees to follow company policy
   d. Separation of duties
2. Internal auditors focus on ______; external auditors are more concerned with ______. Fill in the blanks.
   a. cash receipts; cash payments
   b. documents; records
   c. operations; financial statements
   d. e-commerce; fraud
3. Darice Goodrich receives cash from customers. Her other assigned job is to post the collections to customer accounts receivable. Her company has weak
   a. Ethics
   b. Assignment of responsibilities
   c. Computer controls
   d. Separation of duties
4. Encryption
   a. Rearranges messages by a special process
   b. Avoids the need for separation of duties
   c. Creates firewalls to protect data
   d. Cannot be broken by hackers
5. The document that explains all differences between the company's cash records and the bank's figures is called a(n):
   a. Bank reconciliation
   b. Electronic fund transfer
   c. Bank statement
   d. Bank collection

6. What items appear on the Book side of a bank reconciliation?
   a. Outstanding checks
   b. Deposits in transit
   c. Both a and b
   d. None of the above
7. What items appear on the Bank side of a bank reconciliation?
   a. Outstanding checks
   b. Deposits in transit
   c. Both a and b
   d. None of the above
8. Navarro Company's Cash account shows an ending balance of $850. The bank statement shows a $26 service charge and an NSF check for $190. A $300 deposit is in transit, and outstanding checks total $470. What is Navarro's adjusted cash balance?
   a. $686
   b. $634
   c. $680
   d. $464
9. After performing a bank reconciliation, we need to journalize
   a. All items on the Bank side of the reconciliation
   b. All items on the Book side of the reconciliation
   c. All items on the reconciliation
   d. No items from the reconciliation because the cash transactions need no adjustments
10. Separation of duties is important for internal control of
   a. Cash payments
   b. Cash receipts
   c. Neither of the above
   d. Both a and b

Answers are given after Apply Your Knowledge (p. 456)

Assess Your Progress

■ Short Exercises

S7-1 *(L. OBJ. 1)* **Definition of internal control [5 min]**
Internal controls are designed to safeguard assets, encourage employees to follow company policies, promote operational efficiency, and ensure accurate accounting records.

Requirements

1. Which objective is most important?
2. Which must the internal controls accomplish for the business to survive? Give your reason.

S7-2 *(L. OBJ. 2)* **Sarbanes-Oxley Act [5 min]**
The Sarbanes-Oxley Act affects public companies.

Requirement

1. How does the Sarbanes-Oxley Act relate to internal controls? Be specific.

S7-3 *(L. OBJ. 3)* **Characteristics of internal control [5–10 min]**
Separation of duties is a key internal control.

Requirement

1. Explain in your own words why separation of duties is often described as the cornerstone of internal control for safeguarding assets. Describe what can happen if the same person has custody of an asset and also accounts for the asset.

S7-4 *(L. OBJ. 4)* **Pitfalls of e-commerce [5 min]**
There are many characteristics identified in the chapter as pitfalls of e-commerce.

Requirement

1. List the 5 characteristics identified in the chapter as pitfalls of e-commerce.

S7-5 *(L. OBJ. 5)* **Bank account controls [5–10 min]**
Answer the following questions about the controls in bank accounts:

Requirements

1. Which bank control protects against forgery?
2. Which bank control reports what the bank did with the customer's cash each period?
3. Which bank control confirms the amount of money put into the bank?

S7-6 *(L. OBJ. 6)* **Preparing a bank reconciliation [10 min]**
The Cash account of Safe and Secure Security Systems reported a balance of $2,490 at May 31, 2011. There were outstanding checks totaling $500 and a May 31 deposit in transit of $300. The bank statement, which came from Tri Cities Bank, listed the May 31 balance of $3,360. Included in the bank balance was a collection of $680 on account from Ryan Saar, a Safe and Secure customer who pays the bank directly. The bank statement also shows a $20 service charge and $10 of interest revenue that Safe and Secure earned on its bank balance.

Requirement

1. Prepare Safe and Secure's bank reconciliation at May 31.

Note: Short Exercise 7-7 should be used only after completing Short Exercise 7-6.

S7-7 *(L. OBJ. 6)* **Recording transactions from a bank reconciliation [5 min]**
Review your results from preparing Safe and Secure Security Systems' bank reconciliation in Short Exercise 7-6.

Requirement

1. Journalize the company's transactions that arise from the bank reconciliation. Include an explanation with each entry.

S7-8 *(L. OBJ. 7)* **Control over cash receipts [5 mins]**
Diedre Chevis sells furniture for DuBois Furniture Company. Chevis is having financial problems and takes $500 that she received from a customer. She rang up the sale through the cash register.

Requirement

1. What will alert Betsy DuBois, the controller, that something is wrong?

S7-9 *(L. OBJ. 7)* **Control over cash receipts by mail [5–10 min]**
Review the internal controls over cash receipts by mail presented in the chapter.

Requirement

1. Exactly what is accomplished by the final step in the process, performed by the controller?

S7-10 *(L. OBJ. 8)* **Internal control over cash payments by check [5 min]**
A purchasing agent for Westgate Wireless receives the goods that he purchases and also approves payment for the goods.

Requirements

1. How could this purchasing agent cheat his company?
2. How could Westgate avoid this internal control weakness?

S7-11 *(L. OBJ. 9)* **Petty cash [10 min]**
The following petty cash transactions of Lexite Laminated Surfaces occurred in August:

Aug	1	Established a petty cash fund with a $300 balance.
	31	The petty cash fund has $29 in cash and $284 in petty cash tickets that were issued to pay for Office supplies ($104) and Entertainment expense ($180). Replenished the fund with $271 of cash and recorded the expenses.

Requirement

1. Prepare journal entries without explanations.

S7-12 *(L.OBJ. 10)* **Making an ethical judgment [5 min]**
Gwen O'Malley, an accountant for Ireland Limited, discovers that her supervisor, Blarney Stone, made several errors last year. Overall, the errors overstated the company's net income by 20%. It is not clear whether the errors were deliberate or accidental.

Requirement

1. What should O'Malley do?

Exercises

E7-13 *(L. OBJ. 1, 2, 3)* **Sarbanes-Oxley; Identifying internal control strengths and weaknesses [10–15 min]**
The following situations suggest a strength or a weakness in internal control.

a. Top managers delegate all internal control procedures to the accounting department.
b. The accounting department orders merchandise and approves invoices for payment.
c. Cash received over the counter is controlled by the sales clerk, who rings up the sale and places the cash in the register. The sales clerk matches the total recorded by the register to each day's cash sales.
d. The officer who signs checks need not examine the payment packet because he is confident the amounts are correct.

Requirements

1. Define internal control.
2. The system of internal control must be tested by external auditors. What law or rule requires this testing?
3. Identify each item as either a strength or a weakness in internal control and give the reason for your answer.

E7-14 *(L. OBJ. 3)* **Identifying internal controls [10 min]**
Consider the following situations.

a. While reviewing the records of Discount Pharmacy, you find that the same employee orders merchandise and approves invoices for payment.
b. Business is slow at Fun City Amusement Park on Tuesday, Wednesday, and Thursday nights. To reduce expenses, the owner decides not to use a ticket taker on those nights. The ticket seller (cashier) is told to keep the tickets as a record of the number sold.
c. The same trusted employee has served as cashier for 10 years.
d. When business is brisk, Stop-n-Go deposits cash in the bank several times during the day. The manager at one store wants to reduce the time employees spend delivering cash to the bank, so he starts a new policy. Cash will build up over weekends, and the total will be deposited on Monday.
e. Grocery stores such as Grocer's Market and Comfort Foods purchase most merchandise from a few suppliers. At another grocery store, the manager decides to reduce paperwork. He eliminates the requirement that the receiving department prepare a receiving report listing the goods actually received from the supplier.

Requirement

1. Consider each situation separately. Identify the missing internal control procedure from these characteristics:
   - Assignment of responsibilities
   - Separation of duties
   - Audits
   - Electronic controls
   - Other controls (specify)

E7-15 *(L. OBJ. 4)* **E-commerce control procedures [10–15 min]**
The following situations suggest a strength or a weakness in e-commerce internal controls.

a. Cybersales sells merchandise over the internet. Customers input their credit card information for payment.
b. Cybersales maintains employee information on the company intranet. Employees can retrieve information about annual leave, payroll deposits, and benefits from any computer using their login information.
c. Cybersales maintains trend information about its customers, products, and pricing on the company's intranet.
d. Tax identification numbers for all vendors are maintained in Cybersales' database.

Requirement

1. Identify the control that will best protect the company.

E7-16 *(L. OBJ. 5)* **Using a bank reconciliation as a control device [10 min]**
Lori Root owns Root's Boot City. She fears that a trusted employee has been stealing from the company. This employee receives cash from customers and also prepares the monthly bank reconciliation. To check up on the employee, Root prepares her own bank reconciliation, as shown on the following page. This reconciliation is both complete and accurate.

ROOT'S BOOT CITY			
Bank Reconciliation			
June 30, 2011			
Bank		**Books**	
Balance, June 30	$ 1,550	Balance, June 30	$ 1,100
Add: Deposit in transit	400	Add: Bank collection	840
		Interest revenue	10
Less: Outstanding checks	(1,090)	Less: Service charge	(25)
Adjusted bank balance	$ 860	Adjusted book balance	$ 1,925

Requirements

1. How is the preparation of a bank reconciliation considered to be a control device?
2. Which side of the reconciliation shows the true cash balance?
3. What is Root's true cash balance?
4. Does it appear that the employee has stolen from the company?
5. If so, how much? Explain your answer.

E7-17 *(L.OBJ. 6)* **Classifying bank reconciliation items [5 min]**
The following items could appear on a bank reconciliation:

a. Outstanding checks
b. Deposits in transit
c. NSF check
d. Bank collection of our note receivable
e. Interest earned on bank balance
f. Service charge
g. Book error: We credited Cash for $200. The correct amount was $2,000.
h. Bank error: The bank decreased our account for a check written by another customer.

Requirement

1. Classify each item as (1) an addition to the book balance, (2) a subtraction from the book balance, (3) an addition to the bank balance, or (4) a subtraction from the bank balance.

E7-18 *(L.OBJ. 6)* **Preparing a bank reconciliation [10–20 min]**
D. J. Hill's checkbook lists the following:

Date	Check No.	Item	Check	Deposit	Balance
5/1					$ 535
4	622	Art Cafe	$ 20		515
9		Dividends received		$ 110	625
13	623	General Tire Co.	40		585
14	624	QuickMobil	60		525
18	625	Cash	70		455
26	626	Woodway Baptist Church	95		360
28	627	Bent Tree Apartments	275		85
31		Paycheck		1,205	1,290

Hill's May bank statement shows the following:

Balance				$ 535
Add: Deposits				110
Debit Checks:	No.	Amount		
	622	$ 20		
	623	40		
	624	100 *		
	625	70		(230)
Other charges:				
Printed checks			$ 25	
Service charge			15	(40)
Balance				$ 375

*This is the correct amount for check number 624.

Requirements

1. Prepare Hill's bank reconciliation at May 31, 2012.
2. How much cash does Hill actually have on May 31, 2012?

E7-19 *(L. OBJ. 6)* **Preparing a bank reconciliation [20–25 min]**
Fred Root operates four bowling alleys. He just received the February 28 bank statement from City National Bank, and the statement shows an ending balance of $890. Listed on the statement are an EFT rent collection of $420, a service charge of $15, NSF checks totaling $75, and a $25 charge for printed checks. In reviewing his cash records, Root identified outstanding checks totaling $475 and a deposit in transit of $1,765. During February, he recorded a $270 check by debiting Salary expense and crediting Cash for $27. His Cash account shows a February 28 balance of $2,118.

Requirements

1. Prepare the bank reconciliation at February 28.
2. Journalize any transactions required from the bank reconciliation.

E7-20 *(L. OBJ. 7)* **Evaluating internal control over cash receipts [10 min]**
When you check out at a **Target** store, the cash register displays the amount of the sale. It also shows the cash received and any change returned to you. Suppose the register also produces a customer receipt but keeps no internal record of the transactions. At the end of the day, the clerk counts the cash in the register and gives it to the cashier for deposit in the company bank account.

Requirements

1. Identify the internal control weakness over cash receipts.
2. What could you do to correct the weakness?

E7-21 *(L. OBJ. 8)* **Evaluating internal control over cash payments [10 min]**
Codie's Custom Cars purchases high performance auto parts from a Michigan vendor. Hal Rodman, the accountant for Codie's, verifies receipt of merchandise and then, prepares, signs, and mails the check to the vendor.

Requirements

1. Identify the internal control weakness over cash payments.
2. What could you do to correct the weakness?

E7-22 *(L. OBJ. 9)* **Accounting for petty cash [10–15 min]**
Louise's Dance Studio created a $200 imprest petty cash fund. During the month, the fund custodian authorized and signed petty cash tickets as follows:

Petty Cash Ticket No.	Item	Account Debited	Amount
1	Delivery of programs to customers	Delivery expense	$ 15
2	Mail package	Postage expense	10
3	Newsletter	Supplies expense	30
4	Key to closet	Miscellaneous expense	45
5	Computer jumpdrive	Supplies expense	75

Requirement

1. Make the general journal entries to
   a. create the petty cash fund and
   b. record its replenishment. Cash in the fund totals $15, so $10 is missing. Include explanations.

E7-23 *(L. OBJ. 9)* **Control over petty cash [10 min]**
Steppin' Out Night Club maintains an imprest petty cash fund of $150, which is under the control of Brenda Montague. At December 31, the fund holds $14 cash and petty cash tickets for office supplies, $111, and delivery expense, $30.

Requirements

1. Explain how an *imprest* petty cash system works.
2. Journalize establishment of the petty cash fund on December 1 and replenishment of the fund on December 31.
3. Prepare a T-account for Petty cash, and post to the account. What is Petty cash's balance at all times?

E7-24 *(L. OBJ. 10)* **Evaluating the ethics of conduct by government legislators [15–20 min]**
Members of the U.S. House of Representatives wrote a quarter million dollars of checks on the House bank without having the cash in their accounts. In effect, these representatives were borrowing money from each other on an interest-free, no-service-charge basis. The House closed its bank after these events were featured on FOX, CNN, ABC, and NBC.

Requirement

1. Suppose you are a new congressional representative from your state. Apply the ethical judgment framework outlined in the Decision Guidelines to decide whether you would intentionally write NSF checks through the House bank.

■ Problems (Group A)

P7-25A *(L. OBJ. 1, 2, 3, 4)* **Internal control, components, procedures and laws [20–25 min]**

TERMS:	DEFINITIONS:
1. Internal control	A. What internal and external auditors do
2. Control procedures	B. Part of internal control that ensures resources are not wasted
3. Firewalls	C. Law that requires testing internal control systems
4. Encryption	D. Provides the details of business transactions
5. Control environment	E. Limits access to a local network
6. Information system	F. Control procedure that divides responsibility between two or more people
7. Separation of duties	G. Identification and evaluation of threats to the business
8. Monitoring of controls	H. May be internal and external
9. Documents	I. Component of internal control that helps ensure decision makers receive accurate data
10. Audits	J. The organizational plan and all the related measures that safeguard assets, encourage employees to follow company policy, promote operational efficiency, and insure accurate reliable accounting data
11. Operational efficiency	
12. Risk assessment	
13. Sarbanes-Oxley Act	K. Component of internal control that helps ensure business goals are achieved
	L. Rearranges data by a mathematical process
	M. The "tone at the top"

Requirement

1. Match the terms with their definitions.

P7-26A *(L. OBJ. 3, 5, 7, 8)* **Correcting internal control weakness [10–20 min]**
Each of the following situations has an internal control weakness.

a. Rite-Way Applications sells accounting software. Recently, development of a new program stopped while the programmers redesigned Rite-Way's accounting system. Rite-Way's accountants could have performed this task.

b. Betty Grable has been your trusted employee for 30 years. She performs all cash-handling and accounting duties. Ms. Grable just purchased a new Lexus and a new home in an expensive suburb. As owner of the company, you wonder how she can afford these luxuries because you pay her only $35,000 a year and she has no source of outside income.

c. Sanchez Hardwoods, a private company, falsified sales and inventory figures in order to get an important loan. The loan went through, but Sanchez later went bankrupt and could not repay the bank.

d. The office supply company where Champs Sporting Goods purchases sales receipts recently notified Champs that its documents were not prenumbered. Alex Champ, the owner, replied that he never uses receipt numbers.

e. Discount stores such as Tallon make most of their sales for cash, with the remainder in credit-card sales. To reduce expenses, one store manager ceases purchasing fidelity bonds on the cashiers.

f. Bob's Burger House keeps all cash received from sales in a safe because Bob thinks banks are not "safe."

Requirements

1. Identify the missing internal control characteristics in each situation.
2. Identify the possible problem caused by each control weakness.
3. Propose a solution to each internal control problem.

P7-27A *(L. OBJ. 6)* **Preparing a bank reconciliation and journal entries [20–25 min]**
The April cash records of Donald Insurance follow:

Cash Receipts		Cash Payments	
Date	Cash Debit	Check No.	Cash Credit
Apr 4	$ 4,160	1416	$ 890
9	530	1417	140
14	520	1418	670
17	2,170	1419	1,290
30	1,860	1420	1,450
		1421	800
		1422	660

Donald Insurance's Cash account shows a balance of $17,040 at April 30. On April 30, Donald Insurance received the following bank statement:

Bank Statement for April			
Beginning balance			$ 13,700
Deposits and other Credits:			
Apr 1	EFT	500	
5		4,160	
10		530	
15		520	
18		2,170	
22	BC	1,600	9,480
Checks and other Debits:			
Apr 8	NSF	$ 900	
11 (check no. 1416)		890	
19	EFT	200	
22 (check no. 1417)		140	
29 (check no. 1418)		670	
30 (check no. 1419)		1,920	
30	SC	30	4,750
Ending balance			$ 18,430

Explanations: BC–bank collection; EFT–electronic funds transfer; NSF–nonsufficient funds checks; SC–service charge

Additional data for the bank reconciliation:

a. The EFT credit was a receipt of rent. The EFT debit was an insurance payment.
b. The NSF check was received from a customer.
c. The $1,600 bank collection was for a note receivable.
d. The correct amount of check 1419 for rent expense is $1,920. Donald's controller mistakenly recorded the check for $1,290.

Requirements

1. Prepare the bank reconciliation of Donald Insurance at April 30, 2011.
2. Journalize any required entries from the bank reconciliation.

P7-28A *(L. OBJ. 6)* **Preparing a bank reconciliation and journal entries [20 min]**
The May 31 bank statement of Wood's Healthcare has just arrived from Federal Bank. To prepare the bank reconciliation, you gather the following data.
Data list:

a. The May 31 bank balance is $4,860.
b. The bank statement includes two charges for NSF checks from customers. One is for $380 (#1), and the other for $100(#2).
c. The following Wood checks are outstanding at May 31

Check No.	Amount
237	$ 60
288	180
291	570
294	600
295	60
296	130

d. Wood collects from a few customers by EFT. The May bank statement lists a $1,100 EFT deposit for a collection on account.
e. The bank statement includes two special deposits that Wood hasn't recorded yet: $870, for dividend revenue, and $10, the interest revenue Wood earned on its bank balance during May.
f. The bank statement lists a $40 subtraction for the bank service charge.
g. On May 31, the Wood treasurer deposited $300, but this deposit does not appear on the bank statement.
h. The bank statement includes a $900 deduction for a check drawn by Multi-State Freight Company. Wood notified the bank of this bank error.
i. Wood's Cash account shows a balance of $3,000 on May 31.

Requirements

1. Prepare the bank reconciliation for Wood's Healthcare at May 31, 2012.
2. Journalize any required entries from the bank reconciliation. Include an explanation for each entry.

P7-29A *(L. OBJ. 7)* **Identifying internal control weakness in cash receipts [10–15 min]**
Pendley Productions makes all sales on credit. Cash receipts arrive by mail. Larry Padgitt in the mailroom opens envelopes and separates the checks from the accompanying remittance advices. Padgitt forwards the checks to another employee, who makes the daily bank deposit but has no access to the accounting records. Padgitt sends the remittance advices, which show cash received, to the accounting department for entry in the accounts. Padgitt's only other duty is to grant sales allowances to customers. (A *sales allowance* decreases the amount receivable.) When Padgitt receives a customer check for $350 less a $20 allowance, he records the sales allowance and forwards the document to the accounting department.

Requirements

1. Identify the internal control weakness in this situation.
2. Who should record sales allowances?

P7-30A *(L. OBJ. 9)* **Accounting for petty cash transactions [20–30 min]**
On November 1, Fab Salad Dressings creates a petty cash fund with an imprest balance of $400. During November, Sunny Lewis, the fund custodian, signs the following petty cash tickets:

Petty Cash Ticket Number	Item	Amount
101	Office supplies	$ 20
102	Cab fare for executive	15
103	Delivery of package across town	25
104	Dinner money for city manager to entertain the mayor	30
105	Inventory	70

On November 30, prior to replenishment, the fund contains these tickets plus cash of $245. The accounts affected by petty cash payments are Office supplies expense, Travel expense, Delivery expense, Entertainment expense, and Inventory.

Requirements

1. Explain the characteristics and the internal control features of an imprest fund.
2. On November 30, how much cash should the petty cash fund hold before it is replenished?
3. Journalize all required entries to create the fund and replenish it. Include explanations.
4. Make the December 1 entry to increase the fund balance to $450. Include an explanation, and briefly describe what the custodian does.

P7-31A *(L. OBJ. 9)* **Accounting for petty cash transactions [20–30 min]**
Suppose that on April 1, Party Gyrations, a disc jockey service, creates a petty cash fund with an imprest balance of $250. During April, Michael Martell, fund custodian, signs the following petty cash tickets:

Petty Cash Ticket Number	Item	Amount
1	Postage for package received	$ 15
2	Decorations and refreshments for office party	20
3	Two boxes of stationery	25
4	Printer cartridges	35
5	Dinner money for sales manager entertaining a customer	70

On April 30, prior to replenishment, the fund contains these tickets plus cash of $80. The accounts affected by petty cash payments are Office supplies expense, Entertainment expense, and Postage expense.

Requirements

1. On April 30, how much cash should this petty cash fund hold before it is replenished?
2. Journalize all required entries to (a) create the fund and (b) replenish it. Include explanations.
3. Make the entry on May 1 to increase the fund balance to $350. Include an explanation.

P7-32A *(L.OBJ. 10)* **Making an ethical judgment [15–30 min]**

Federal Credit Bank has a loan receivable from Hawthorne Construction Company. Hawthorne is late making payments to the bank, and Robert Wheeler, a Federal Credit Bank vice president, is helping Hawthorne restructure its debt. Wheeler learns that Hawthorne is depending on landing a $1,000,000 contract from Starstruck Theater, another Federal Credit Bank client. Wheeler also serves as Starstruck's loan officer at the bank. In this capacity, he is aware that Starstruck is considering declaring bankruptcy. Wheeler has been a great help to Hawthorne, and Hawthorne's owner is counting on him to carry the company through this difficult restructuring. To help the bank collect on this large loan, Wheeler has a strong motivation to help Hawthorne survive.

Requirements

1. Identify the ethical issue that Wheeler is facing. Specify the two main alternatives available to Wheeler.
2. Identify the possible consequences of Wheeler identifying Starstruck's financial position to Hawthorne Construction Company.
3. Identify the correct ethical decision Wheeler must make based on the two alternatives identified in requirement 2.

Problems (Group B)

P7-33B *(L. OBJ. 1, 2, 3, 4)* **Internal control, components, procedures and laws [20–25 min]**

TERMS:	DEFINITIONS:
1. Internal control	A. Companies often hire auditors to perform this task.
2. Control procedures	B. Businesses tend to promote this in order to reduce the amount of wasted resources.
3. Firewalls	C. Law passed by congress to address public concerns following the Enron and WorldCom scandals.
4. Encryption	D. Can be in paper or electronic form.
5. Control environment	E. Limits access to a local network.
6. Information system	F. Control procedure that divides responsibility between two or more people.
7. Separation of duties	G. Identification and evaluation of threats to the business.
8. Monitoring controls	H. May be internal and external.
9. Documents	I. Without a sufficient one of these, information cannot properly be gathered and summarized.
10. Audit	J. The organizational plan and all related measures that promote operational efficiency.
11. Operational efficiency	K. Component of internal control that helps ensure business goals are achieved.
12. Risk assessment	L. Rearranges data by a mathematical process.
13. Sarbanes–Oxley Act	M. Former executives of Enron and WorldCom failed to establish a good one of these.

Requirement

1. Match the terms with their definitions.

P7-34B *(L.OBJ. 3, 5, 7, 8)* **Correcting internal control weakness [10–20 min]**
Each of the following situations has an internal control weakness:

a. Techno Dot Applications sells purchasing software. Recently, development of a new program stopped while the programmers redesigned Techno Dot's accounting system. Techno Dot's accountants could have performed this task.

b. Norma McCann has been your trusted employee for 25 years. She performs all cash collections and bad debt writeoffs. Ms. McCann just purchased a new Lexus and a new home in an expensive suburb. As owner of the company, you wonder how she can afford these luxuries because you pay her only $30,000 a year and she has no source of outside income.

c. Sanchez Hardwoods, a private company, falsified sales and operating expense figures in order to get an important loan. The loan went through, but Sanchez later went bankrupt and could not repay the bank.

d. The office supply company where Home Hardware Goods purchases purchase orders recently notified Home Hardware Goods that its documents were not prenumbered. Henry Dickson, the owner, replied that he never uses the purchase order numbers.

e. Discount stores such as Tallon make most of their sales for cash, with the remainder in credit-card sales. To reduce expenses, Sally Sandspur, the store manager, ceases requiring employees to take their vacations.

f. Sheila's Sea Shells keeps all cash received from sales in a petty cash box for all the business expenses.

Requirements

1. Identify the missing internal control characteristics in each situation.
2. Identify the possible problem caused by each control weakness.
3. Propose a solution to each internal control problem.

P7-35B *(L.OBJ. 6)* **Preparing a bank reconciliation and journal entries [20–25 min]**
The July cash records of Dickson Insurance follow:

Cash Receipts		Cash Payments	
Date	Cash Debit	Check No.	Cash Credit
Jul 4	$ 4,160	1416	$ 860
9	530	1417	120
14	540	1418	650
17	2,130	1419	1,590
31	1,840	1420	1,440
		1421	1,100
		1422	620

Dickson Insurance's Cash account shows a balance of $16,520 at July 31. On July 31, Dickson Insurance received the following bank statement:

Bank Statement for July				
Beginning balance				$ 13,700
Deposits and other Credits:				
Jul	1	EFT	200	
	5		4,160	
	10		530	
	15		540	
	18		2,130	
	22	BC	1,400	8,960
Checks and other Debits:				
Jul	8	NSF	$ 500	
	11 (check no. 1416)		860	
	19	EFT	300	
	22 (check no. 1417)		120	
	29 (check no. 1418)		650	
	31 (check no. 1419)		1,950	
	31	SC	10	4,390
Ending balance				$ 18,270

Explanations: BC–bank collection; EFT–electronic funds transfer; NSF–nonsufficient funds checks; SC–service charge

Additional data for the bank reconciliation:

a. The EFT deposit was a receipt of rent. The EFT debit was an insurance payment.
b. The NSF check was received from a customer.
c. The $1,400 bank collection was for a note receivable.
d. The correct amount of check 1419 for rent expense is $1,950. Dickson's controller mistakenly recorded the check for $1,590.

Requirements

1. Prepare the bank reconciliation of Dickson Insurance at July 31, 2011.
2. Journalize any required entries from the bank reconciliation.

P7-36B *(L.OBJ. 6)* **Preparing a bank reconciliation and journal entries [20 min]**
The August 31 bank statement of Watson's Healthcare has just arrived from Union Bank. To prepare the bank reconciliation, you gather the data on the following page.

Data list:

a. The August 31 bank balance is $4,660.
b. The bank statement includes two charges for NSF checks from customers. One is for $360 (#1), and the other for $160 (#2).
c. The following Watson checks are outstanding at August 31:

Check No.	Amount
237	$ 80
288	180
291	550
294	630
295	30
296	120

d. Watson collects from a few customers by EFT. The August bank statement lists a $1,100 EFT deposit for a collection on account.
e. The bank statement includes two special deposits that Watson hasn't recorded yet: $950, for dividend revenue, and $40, the interest revenue Watson earned on its bank balance during August.
f. The bank statement lists a $60 subtraction for the bank service charge.
g. On August 31, the Watson treasurer deposited $340, but this deposit does not appear on the bank statement.
h. The bank statement includes a $500 deduction for a check drawn by Multi-State Freight Company. Watson notified the bank of this bank error.
i. Watson's Cash account shows a balance of $2,400 on August 31.

Requirements

1. Prepare the bank reconciliation for Watson's Healthcare at August 31, 2012.
2. Journalize any required entries from the bank reconciliation. Include an explanation for each entry.

P7-37B *(L.OBJ. 7)* **Identifying internal control weakness in cash receipts [10–15 min]**
Two Brother Productions makes all sales on credit. Cash receipts arrive by mail. Nathan Spieler in the mailroom opens envelopes and separates the checks from the accompanying remittance advices. Spieler forwards the checks to another employee, who makes the daily bank deposit, but has no access to the accounting records. Spieler sends the remittance advices, which show cash received, to the accounting department for entry in the accounts. Spieler's only other duty is to grant sales allowances to customers. (A *sales allowance* decreases the amount receivable.) When Spieler receives a customer check for $575 less a $70 sales allowance, he records the sales allowance and forwards the document to the accounting department.

Requirements

1. Identify the internal control weakness in this situation.
2. Who should record sales allowances?

P7-38B *(L.OBJ. 9)* **Accounting for petty cash transactions [20–30 min]**
On April 1, Rockin' Salad Dressings creates a petty cash fund with an imprest balance of $500. During April, Melody Tau, the fund custodian, signs the following petty cash tickets:

Petty Cash Ticket Number	Item	Amount
101	Office supplies	$ 15
102	Cab fare for executive	10
103	Delivery of package across town	20
104	Dinner money for city manager to entertain the mayor	30
105	Inventory	60

On April 30, prior to replenishment, the fund contains these tickets plus cash of $370. The accounts affected by petty cash payments are Office supplies expense, Travel expense, Delivery expense, Entertainment expense, and Inventory.

Requirements

1. Explain the characteristics and the internal control features of an imprest fund.
2. On April 30, how much cash should the petty cash fund hold before it is replenished?
3. Journalize all required entries to create the fund and replenish it. Include explanations.
4. Make the May 1 entry to increase the fund balance to $550. Include an explanation, and briefly describe what the custodian does.

P7-39B *(L.OBJ. 9)* **Accounting for petty cash transactions [20–30 min]**

Suppose that on June 1, Cool Gyrations, a disc jockey service, creates a petty cash fund with an imprest balance of $500. During June, Jackson Demers, fund custodian, signs the following petty cash tickets:

Petty Cash Ticket Number	Item	Amount
1	Postage for package received	$ 25
2	Decorations and refreshments for office party	15
3	Two boxes of stationery	30
4	Printer cartridges	20
5	Dinner money for sales manager entertaining a customer	80

On June 30, prior to replenishment, the fund contains these tickets plus cash of $325. The accounts affected by petty cash payments are Office supplies expense, Entertainment expense, and Postage expense.

Requirements

1. On June 30, how much cash should this petty cash fund hold before it is replenished?
2. Journalize all required entries to (a) create the fund and (b) replenish it. Include explanations.
3. Make the entry on July 1 to increase the fund balance to $575. Include an explanation.

P7-40B *(L.OBJ. 10)* **Making an ethical judgment [15–30 min]**

North Bank has a loan receivable from Westminster Publishing Company. Westminster is late making payments to the bank, and Richard Connelly, a North Bank vice president, is helping Westminster restructure its debt. Connelly learns that Westminster is depending on landing a $1,750,000 contract from Aubrey Theater, another North Bank client. Connelly also serves as Aubrey's loan officer at the bank. In this capacity, he is aware that Aubrey is considering declaring bankruptcy. Connelly has been a great help to Westminster, and Westminster's owner is counting on him to carry the company through this difficult restructuring. To help the bank collect on this large loan, Connelly has a strong motivation to help Westminster survive.

Requirements

1. Identify the ethical issue that Connelly is facing. Specify the two main alternatives available to Connelly.
2. Identify the possible consequences of Connelly identifying Aubrey's financial position to Westminster Publishing Company.
3. Identify the correct ethical decision Connelly must make based on the two alternatives identified in requirement 2.

■ Continuing Exercise

E7-41 This exercise continues the Sherman Lawn Service situation from Exercise 6-42 of Chapter 6. During October, Sherman Lawn Service decided that it needed a petty cash fund. Sherman started the fund by cashing a check from her business bank account for $150. At the end of October, Sherman had $73 in the petty cash fund. She also had three receipts, as shown below:

a. Receipt for $48 from the lawn supply store for Lawn Supplies
b. Receipt for $10 from the gas station for fuel
c. Receipt for $15 for lunch with a potential client

Requirements

1. Journalize the entry to establish the Petty cash fund.
2. Journalize any entries to replenish the fund at the end of October. Add any new accounts to the chart for Sherman that may be necessary.

■ Continuing Problem

P7-42 This problem continues the Haupt Consulting Company situation from Problem 6-43 of Chapter 6. Haupt performs systems consulting. Haupt's February Cash from its general ledger appears below:

Cash

Jan 31 Bal	10,000	ck207	4,000	Feb 1
Feb 6	2,500	ck208	795	Feb 14
Feb 13	3,000	ck209	1,415	Feb 14
Feb 20	4,800	ck210	190	Feb 28
Feb 27	3,600	ck211	400	Feb 28
Feb 28 Unadj Bal	17,100			

Haupt's bank statement dated February 28 follows:

Bank Statement for February		
Beginning Balance, January 31		10,500
Deposits and other Credits:		
Feb 1	750	
Feb 8	2,500	
Feb 14	3,000	
Feb 20 EFT Hot Houses-a customer	500	
Feb 22	4,800	
Feb 28 interest credit	7	11,557
Checks and other Debits:		
Feb 2 EFT to Cheap Checks	17	
Feb 2 ck#206	1,250	
Feb 17 ck#207	4,000	
Feb 18 ck#209	1,415	
Feb 28 EFT to Internet Service	125	
Feb 28 ck#208	795	
Bank Service Charge	13	7,615
Ending Balance, February 28, 2009		14,442

Requirements

1. Prepare the February bank reconciliation.
2. Journalize and post any transactions required from the bank reconciliation. Key all items by date. Compute each account balance, and denote the balance as *Bal.*

■ Practice Set

This problem continues the Crystal Clear Cleaning problem begun in Chapter 1 and continued through Chapters 2–6.

P7-43 Consider the April 2009 transactions for Crystal Clear Cleaning that were presented in Chapter 2. The bank statement dated April 30, 2009, for Crystal Clear follows.

Bank Statement for April, 2009		
Beginning Balance, March 31, 2009		0
Deposits and other Credits:		
Apr 2	20,000	
Apr 10	200	
Apr 18	1,900	
Apr 21	10,000	
Apr 29 EFT Bob's Burger House	500	
Apr 30 interest credit	7	32,607
Checks and other Debits:		
Apr 2 EFT to Checks Plus	26	
Apr 5 ck#101	1,600	
Apr 9 ck#103	1,500	
Apr 9 ck#102	1,200	
Apr 26 ck#105	1,500	
Apr 28 EFT to Gulf Power	125	
Apr 28 ck#106	200	
Bank Service Charge	10	6,161
Ending Balance, April 30, 2009		26,446

Requirements

1. Prepare bank reconciliation.
2. Journalize any required entries from the bank reconciliation.

Apply Your Knowledge

■ Decision Cases

Case 1. Go to sarbox.org, the Web site for the Sarbanes-Oxley Act.

Requirement

1. Surf around for information on internal control, write a report of your findings, and present it to your class (if required by your instructor).

Case 2. This case is based on an actual situation. Centennial Construction Company, headquartered in Dallas, built a Rodeway Motel 35 miles north of Dallas. The construction foreman, whose name was Slim Chance, hired the 40 workers needed to complete the project. Slim had the construction workers fill out the necessary tax forms, and he sent their documents to the home office.

Work on the motel began on April 1 and ended September 1. Each week, Slim filled out a time card of hours worked by each employee during the week. Slim faxed the time sheets to the home office, which prepared the payroll checks on Friday morning. Slim drove to the home office on Friday, picked up the payroll checks, and returned to the construction site. At 5 PM on Friday, Slim distributed payroll checks to the workers.

Requirements

1. Describe in detail the main internal control weakness in this situation. Specify what negative result(s) could occur because of the internal control weakness.
2. Describe what you would do to correct the internal control weakness.

Case 3. San Diego Harbor Tours has poor internal control over cash. Ben Johnson, the owner, suspects the cashier of stealing. Here are some details of company cash at September 30.

a. **The Cash account in the ledger shows a balance of $6,450.**

b. **The September 30 bank statement shows a balance of $4,300. The bank statement lists a $200 bank collection, a $10 service charge, and a $40 NSF check.**

c. **At September 30, the following checks are outstanding:**

Amount
$100
300
600
200

d. **There is a $3,000 deposit in transit at September 30.**

e. **The cashier handles all incoming cash and makes bank deposits. He also writes checks and reconciles the monthly bank statement.**

Johnson asks you to determine whether the cashier has stolen cash from the business and, if so, how much.

Requirements

1. Perform your own bank reconciliation using the format illustrated in the chapter. There are no bank or book errors.
2. Explain how Johnson can improve his internal controls.

■ Ethical Issue

Mel O'Conner owns rental properties in Michigan. Each property has a manager who collects rent, arranges for repairs, and runs advertisements in the local newspaper. The property managers transfer cash to O'Conner monthly and prepare their own bank reconciliations. The manager in Lansing has been stealing from the company. To cover the theft, he understates the amount of the outstanding checks on the monthly bank reconciliation. As a result, each monthly bank reconciliation appears to balance. However, the balance sheet reports more cash than O'Conner actually has in the bank. In negotiating the sale of the Lansing property, O'Conner is showing the balance sheet to prospective investors.

Requirements

1. Identify two parties other than O'Conner who can be harmed by this theft. In what ways can they be harmed?
2. Discuss the role accounting plays in this situation.

■ Financial Statement Case

Study the audit opinion (labeled Report of Ernst & Young LLP) of **Amazon.com** and the **Amazon** financial statements given in Appendix A at the end of this book. Answer the following questions about the company.

Requirements

1. What is the name of **Amazon.com**'s outside auditing firm (independent registered public accounting firm)? What office of this firm signed the audit report? How long after the **Amazon** year-end did the auditors issue their opinion?
2. Who bears primary responsibility for the financial statements? How can you tell?
3. Does it appear that the **Amazon** internal controls are adequate? How can you tell?
4. What standard of auditing did the outside auditors use in examining the **Amazon** financial statements? By what accounting standards were the statements evaluated?
5. By how much did **Amazon**'s cash balance (including cash equivalents) change during 2007? What were the beginning and ending cash balances?

■ Team Project

You are promoting a rock concert in your area. Each member of your team will invest $10,000 of his or her hard-earned money in this venture. It is April 1, and the concert is scheduled for June 30. Your promotional activities begin immediately, and ticket sales start on May 1. You expect to sell all the business's assets, pay all the liabilities, and distribute all remaining cash to the group members by July 31.

Requirement

1. Write an internal control manual that will help safeguard the assets of the business. The starting point of the manual is to assign responsibilities among the group members. Authorize individuals, including group members and any outsiders that you need to hire, to perform specific jobs. Separate duties among the group and any employees.

Quick Check Answers

1. *d* 2. *c* 3. *d* 4. *a* 5. *a* 6. *d* 7. *c* 8. *b* 9. *b* 10. *d*

For online homework, exercises, and problems that provide you immediate feedback, please visit www.myaccountinglab.com.

8 Receivables

Learning Objectives/Success Keys

1. Define and explain common types of receivables
2. Design internal controls for receivables
3. Use the allowance method to account for uncollectibles
4. Understand the direct write-off method for uncollectibles
5. Report receivables on the balance sheet
6. Journalize credit-card, bankcard, and debit-card sales
7. Account for notes receivable
8. Use the acid-test ratio and days' sales in receivables to evaluate a company

Smart Touch Learning is doing well—so well in fact that Sheena's alma mater, The University of West Florida, has ordered 50 Microsoft Outlook training DVDs. The dean will give a DVD to all new faculty members. This is quite a vote of confidence, and the free publicity may bring in more business. But there is a hitch.

The college cannot pay Sheena immediately. It usually takes around 30 days to clear the paperwork and cut a check. Can Smart Touch wait 30 days to get the money?

Most businesses face this situation. There are both advantages and disadvantages to extending credit to customers. In the case of the college, the pluses outweigh the minuses, so Smart Touch will let them pay later.

The main advantage of selling on credit (selling on account) is expanding the business's customer base, which is a way to increase sales. The disadvantages are that Smart Touch has to wait to receive cash and some customers may never pay, which means that Smart Touch may never collect some of the receivables.

This chapter focuses on accounting for receivables.

Receivables: An Introduction

1 Define and explain common types of receivables

You have a **receivable** when you sell goods or services to another party on credit. The receivable is the seller's claim for the amount of the transaction. You also have a receivable when you loan money to another party. So a receivable is really the right to *receive* cash in the future from a current transaction. It is something the business owns; therefore, it is an asset. *Each* receivable transaction involves two parties:

- The **creditor**, who gets a receivable (an asset)
- The **debtor**, who takes on an obligation/payable (a liability)

Types of Receivables

The two major types of receivables follow:

- Accounts receivable
- Notes receivable

Accounts receivable, also called **trade receivables**, are amounts to be collected from customers from sales made on credit. Accounts receivable serves as a control account, because it summarizes the total of all customer receivables. A **control account** is an account in the general ledger that summarizes related **subsidiary** accounts. Companies also keep a ledger of each receivable from each customer. This customer ledger, called a **subsidiary ledger**, contains the details by individual customer that are summarized in the control account. This is illustrated as follows:

GENERAL LEDGER			ACCOUNTS RECEIVABLE SUBSIDIARY LEDGER		
Accounts receivable			Brown		
Bal	15,000		Bal	5,000	
			Dell		
			Bal	10,000	

Total for Accounts receivable subsidiary ledger 15,000

The control account, Accounts receivable, shows a balance of $15,000. The individual customer accounts in the subsidiary ledger (Brown $5,000 + Dell $10,000) add up to a total of $15,000.

Notes receivable are usually longer in term than accounts receivable. *Notes receivable* represent the right to receive a certain amount of cash in the future from a customer or other party. Notes usually include a charge for interest. The debtor of a note promises to pay the creditor a definite sum at a future date—called the **maturity date**. A written document known as a **promissory note** serves as the evidence of the indebtedness and is signed by both the creditor and the debtor. Notes receivable due within one year or less are current assets. Notes due beyond one year are long-term.

Other receivables make up a miscellaneous category that includes any other type of cash that is receivable in the future. Common examples include loans to employees and interest receivable. These other receivables may be either long-term or current assets, depending on if they are due within one year or less.

Internal Control over Collection of Receivables

2 Design internal controls for receivables

Businesses that sell on credit receive cash by mail, so internal control over collections is important. As we discussed in the previous chapter, a critical element of internal control is the separation of cash-handling and cash-accounting duties.

Most companies have a credit department to evaluate customers' credit applications. The extension of credit requires a balancing act. The company does not want to lose sales to good customers, but it also wants to avoid receivables that will never be collected.

For good internal control over cash collections from receivables, the credit department should have no access to cash. Additionally, those who handle cash should not be in a position to grant credit to customers. For example, if a credit department employee also handles cash, the company would have no separation of duties. The employee could pocket money received from a customer. He or she could then label the customer's account as uncollectible, and the company would write off the account receivable, as discussed in the next section. The company would stop billing that customer, and the employee would have covered his or her theft. For this reason, separation of duties is important.

The Decision Guidelines feature identifies the main issues in controlling and managing receivables. These guidelines serve as a framework for the remainder of the chapter.

Decision Guidelines

CONTROLLING AND MANAGING RECEIVABLES

Sherman Lawn Service, Greg's Groovy Tunes, Smart Touch Learning, and all other companies that sell on credit face the same accounting challenges.

The main issues in controlling and managing receivables, plus a plan of action, are as follows:

Issue	Action
• Extend credit only to customers who are most likely to pay.	Run a credit check on prospective customers.
• Separate cash-handling, credit, and accounting duties to prevent potential theft by employees of cash collected from customers.	Design the internal control system to separate duties.
• Pursue collection from customers to maximize cash flow.	Keep a close eye on collections from customers.

Accounting for Uncollectibles (Bad Debts)

As we discussed earlier, selling on credit (on account) creates an account receivable. The creation of this account receivable is really the first step in the process. However, if the company sells only for cash, it has no accounts receivable and, therefore, no bad debts from unreceived customer accounts. Let us assume, for example, that Greg's Groovy Tunes sells $5,000 in services to customer Brown and also sells $10,000 of inventory to Customer **Dell** on August 8, 2011. The revenue is recorded as follows:

	2011			
1a	Aug 8	Accounts receivable (A+)	5,000	
		Service revenue (R+)		5,000
		Performed service on account.		

1a	Aug 8	Accounts receivable (A+)	10,000	
		Service revenue (R+)		10,000
		Sold goods on account.		

The business collects cash from both customers on August 29, $4,000 from Brown and $8,000 from **Dell**. Collecting cash is the second step in the process and Greg's makes the following entry:

2	Aug 29	Cash (A+)	12,000	
		Accounts receivable (A–)		12,000
		Collected cash on account.		

Selling on credit brings both a benefit and a cost.

- **The benefit:** Increase revenues and profits by making sales to a wider range of customers.
- **The cost:** Some customers do not pay, and that creates an expense called **uncollectible-account expense, doubtful-account expense,** or **bad-debt expense.** All three account names mean the same thing—a customer did not pay his or her account balance.

There are two methods of accounting for uncollectible receivables:

- the allowance method,
- or, in certain limited cases, the direct write-off method.

We begin with the allowance method because it is the method preferred by GAAP.

The Allowance Method

3 Use the allowance method to account for uncollectibles

Most companies use the allowance method to measure bad debts. The **allowance method** is based on the matching principle; thus, the key concept is to record uncollectible-accounts expense in the same period as the sales revenue. The offset to the expense is to a contra account called **Allowance for uncollectible accounts** or the

Allowance for doubtful accounts. The business does not wait to see which customers will not pay. Instead, it records a bad debt expense based on estimates developed from past experience and uses the allowance for uncollectible accounts to house the pool of "unknown" bad debtors.

Estimating Uncollectibles

So, how are uncollectible receivables estimated? Companies use their past experience as well as considering the economy, the industry they operate in, and other variables. In short, they make an educated guess, called an estimate. There are two basic ways to estimate uncollectibles:

- Percent-of-sales
- Aging-of-accounts-receivable

Both approaches are part of the allowance method, and both normally require a journal entry.

Percent-of-Sales Method

The **percent-of-sales method** computes uncollectible-account expense as a percentage of net credit sales. This method is also called the **income-statement approach** because it focuses on the amount of expense. Let us go back to our Greg's Groovy Tunes receivables for August. The accounts have the following balances:

Accounts receivable	
3,000	

Allowance for uncollectible accounts	
	0

Interpretation: Accounts receivable reports the amount that customers owe you. If you were to collect from all customers, you would receive $3,000. Allowance for uncollectible accounts should report the amount of the receivables that you *never* expect to collect. At this point, Greg's Groovy Tunes thinks all receivables are collectible ($0 balance in Allowance).

How the Percent-of-Sales Method Works

Based on prior experience, Greg's uncollectible-account expense is normally 2% of net credit sales, which totaled $15,000 for August. The journal entry records the following at August 31, 2011:

	Date	Accounts	Debit	Credit
	2011			
1b	Aug 31	Uncollectible account expense ($15,000 × 0.02) (E+)	300	
		Allowance for uncollectible accounts (CA+)		300
		Recorded expense for the year.		

After posting, the accounts are ready for the balance sheet.

Accounts receivable	
3,000	

Allowance for uncollectible accounts		
		0
	Aug 31	300
	End Bal	300

Net Accounts receivable, $2,700

Now the allowance for uncollectible accounts is realistic. The balance sheet will report accounts receivable at the net amount of $2,700 on August 31, 2011. The income statement will report uncollectible-account expense for August of $300.

Aging-of-Accounts-Receivable Method

The other approach for estimating uncollectible receivables is the **aging-of-accounts method.** This method is also called the **balance-sheet approach** because it focuses on the actual age of the accounts receivable and determines a target allowance balance from that age. Assume it is December 31, 2011, and Greg's Groovy Tunes has recorded the remainder of the year's activity in the accounts such that the accounts now have the following balances *before the year-end adjustments:*

Accounts receivable	
2,800	

Allowance for uncollectible accounts	
	150

In the aging approach, you group individual accounts (Broxson, Andrews, etc.) according to how long they have been outstanding. The computer can sort customer accounts by age. Exhibit 8-1 shows how Greg's Groovy Tunes groups its accounts receivable. This is called an aging schedule.

EXHIBIT 8-1 **Aging the Accounts Receivable of Greg's Groovy Tunes**

	Age of Account				
Customer Name	1–30 Days	31–60 Days	61–90 Days	Over 90 Days	Total Balance
Broxson	$ 500				$ 500
Phi Chi Fraternity	1,300				1,300
Andrews		80			80
Jones		120			120
Other accounts	60		340	$400	800
Totals	$1,860	$200	$340	$400	$2,800
Estimated percentage uncollectible	× 1%	× 2%	× 5%	× 90%	
Allowance for Uncollectible Accounts balance	+ $ 19	+ $ 4	+ $ 17	+ $360	= $ 400

Interpretation: Customers owe you $2,800, but you expect not to collect $400 of this amount. These amounts appear in the lower right corner of the aging schedule in Exhibit 8-1. Notice that the percentage uncollectible increases as a customer account gets older.

Stop & Think...

Have you ever loaned money to a friend? If so, you have had a receivable. The longer time goes on from when you loaned that friend money, the less likely you are to receive your cash back. This is the premise of the aging method in Exhibit 8-1. Another way to say this is that the older accounts have a HIGHER percentage of uncollectibility.

How the Aging Method Works

The aging method tells you what the credit balance of the allowance account needs to be—the target allowance balance—$400 in this case. So, place the target balance into the Allowance T-account as follows:

Accounts receivable			Allowance for uncollectible accounts	
2,800				150
				$400 Target Balance

Then consider the account information:

$150 Credit balance plus/minus adjustment = $400 Credit Target Balance

The Allowance account needs $250 more in Credit. To adjust the allowance, make the following entry at year end:

	Date	Accounts	Debit	Credit
	2011			
4	Dec 31	Uncollectible account expense (E+)	250	
		Allowance for uncollectible accounts ($400 – $150) (CA+)		250
		Adjusted the allowance account.		

After posting, the accounts are up-to-date and ready for the balance sheet.

Accounts receivable			Allowance for uncollectible accounts	
2,800				150
			Adj	250
			End Bal	400

Net Accounts receivable, $2,400

Report accounts receivable at net realizable value of $2,400 because that is the amount Greg's Groovy Tunes expects to collect in cash in the future. **Net realizable value** is the net value that the company expects to collect of its receivables.

Using Percent-of-Sales and Aging Methods Together

In practice, companies use the percent-of-sales and the aging-of-accounts methods together.

- For *interim statements* (monthly or quarterly), companies use the percent-of-sales method because it is easier.
- At the end of the year, companies use the aging method to ensure that Accounts receivable is reported at *net realizable value*.
- Using the two methods together provides good measures of both the expense and the asset. Exhibit 8-2 summarizes and compares the two methods.

EXHIBIT 8-2 | **Comparing the Percent-of-Sales and Aging Methods**

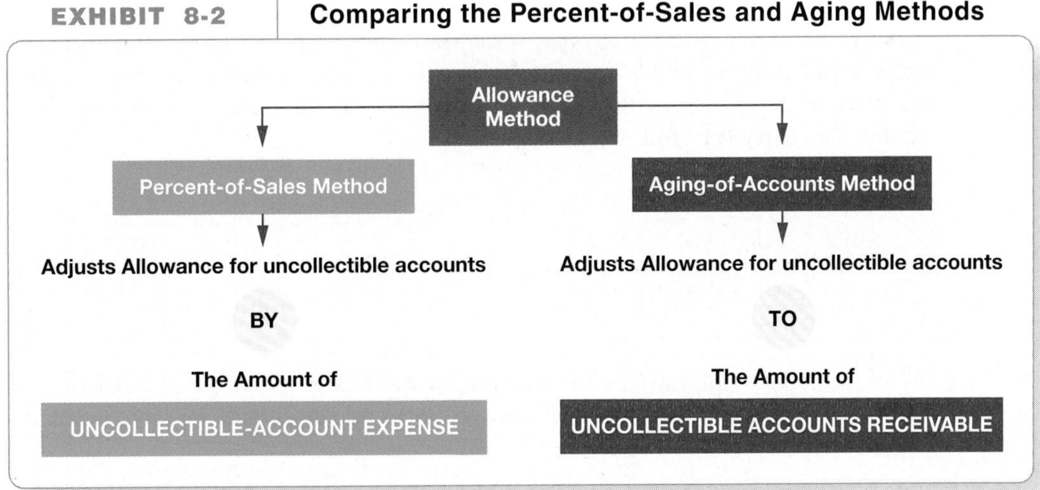

Identifying and Writing Off Uncollectible Accounts

Early in 2012, Greg's Groovy Tunes collects most of its accounts receivable and records the cash receipts as follows (amount assumed):

	2012			
2	Jan 5	Cash (A+)	2,000	
		Accounts receivable (A–)		2,000
		Collected on account.		

Suppose that, after repeated attempts, Greg's accountant finally decides on January 10, 2012, that the company cannot collect a total of $200 from customers Andrews and Jones. At the time these bad debts are identified, the entry is made to write off the receivables from these customers, as follows:

	2012			
3	Jan 10	Allowance for uncollectible accounts (CA–)	200	
		Accounts receivable—Andrews (A–)		80
		Accounts receivable—Jones (A–)		120
		Wrote off uncollectible accounts.		

Recovery of Accounts Previously Written Off—Allowance Method

When an account receivable is written off as uncollectible, the receivable does not die: The customer still owes the money. However, the company stops pursuing collection and writes off the account as uncollectible. Some companies turn delinquent receivables over to an attorney or other collection agency to recover some of the cash for them.

Recall that Greg's Groovy Tunes wrote off the $80 receivable from customer Andrews on January 10, 2012. It is now March 4, 2012, and Greg's unexpectedly receives $80 from Andrews. To account for this recovery, the company must reverse the effect of the earlier write-off to the allowance account and record the cash collection. The entry is as follows:

	2012			
5	Mar 4	Cash (A+)	80	
		Allowance for uncollectible accounts (CA+)		80

Exhibit 8-3 summarizes the entries we have covered using the Allowance method of accounting for uncollectible accounts and the entries we have made for Greg's Groovy Tunes:

EXHIBIT 8-3 | **Greg's Groovy Tunes—Allowance Method**

PANEL A—Transactions

1a) Make sales on Account
1b) Establish a pool for future potential uncollectibility (2%)
2) Collect cash on account
3) Identify a bad debt
4) Adjust allowance account to reflect adjustments to the estimate
5) Recover previously written off account

PANEL B—Journal Entries

1a	Aug 8, 2011	Accounts receivable (A+)	5,000	
		Service revenue (R+)		5,000
		Accounts receivable (A+)	10,000	
		Service revenue (R+)		10,000
1b	Aug 31, 2011	Uncollectible-account expense (E+)	300	
		Allowance for uncollectible accounts (CA+)		300
		(15,000 credit sales × 2%)		
2	Aug 20, 2011	Cash (A+)	12,000	
		Accounts receivable (A–)		12,000
3	Jan 20, 2012	Allowance for uncollectible accounts (CA–)	200	
		Accounts receivable—Andrews (A–)		80
		Accounts receivable—Jones (A–)		120
4	Dec 31, 2011	Uncollectible-account expense (E+)	250	
		Allowance for uncollectible accounts (CA+)		250
5	Mar 4, 2012	Cash (A+)	80	
		Allowance for uncollectible accounts (CA+)		80

The Direct Write-Off Method

There is another way to account for uncollectible receivables that is primarily used by small, non-public companies. It is called the **direct write-off method.** Under the direct write-off method, you do not use the Allowance for uncollectible accounts to record the expense based on an estimate. Instead, you wait until you determine that you will never collect from a specific customer. Then you write off the customer's account receivable by debiting Uncollectible-account expense and crediting the customer's Account receivable. For example, let us reconsider Greg's Groovy Tunes' identified bad debts from January 10, 2012. The entry under the direct write-off method would be as follows:

4 Understand the direct write-off method for uncollectibles

	2012			
3	Jan 10	Uncollectible account expense (E+)	200	
		Accounts receivable—Andrews (A–)		80
		Accounts receivable—Jones (A–)		120
		Wrote off a bad account.		

The direct write-off method is defective for two reasons:

1. It does not set up an allowance for uncollectible account. As a result, the direct write-off method always reports accounts receivables at their full amount. Thus, assets are overstated on the balance sheet.
2. It does not match Uncollectible-account expense against revenue very well. In this example, Greg's Groovy Tunes made the sales to Andrews and Jones in 2011 and journalized Sales revenue on August 31 of that year. However, Greg's wrote off the bad debts by recording the Uncollectible-account expense on January 10, 2012, a different year. As a result, Greg's Groovy Tunes *overstates* net income in 2011 and *understates* net income in 2012.

The direct write-off method is acceptable only when uncollectible receivables are very low. It works for retailers such as **Wal-Mart, McDonald's,** and **Gap** because those companies carry almost no receivables.

Recovery of Accounts Previously Written Off—Direct Write-Off Method

As with the allowance method, under the direct write-off method account receivable that is written off as uncollectible does not die: The customer still owes the money. However, the accounting between the two methods differs slightly. Recall that Greg's Groovy Tunes wrote off the $80 receivable from customer Andrews on January 10, 2012. It is now March 4, 2012, and the company unexpectedly receives $80 from Andrews. To account for this recovery, the company must reverse the effect of the earlier write-off to the Uncollectible-account expense account and record the cash collection. The entry is as follows:

Mar 4	Cash (A+)	80	
	Uncollectible account expense (E–)		80
	Collect Andrews' account receivable.		

Exhibit 8-4 summarizes the entries that would be made using the Direct write-off method of accounting for uncollectible accounts and the entries we have made for Greg's Groovy Tunes:

EXHIBIT 8-4 | **Greg's Groovy Tunes—Direct Write-off Method**

PANEL A—Transactions

1a) Make sales on Account
1b) N/A
2) Collect cash on account
3) Identify a bad debt
4) N/A
5) Recover previously written off account

PANEL B—Journal Entries

	Date	Accounts	Debit	Credit
1a	Aug 8, 2011	Accounts receivable (A+)	5,000	
		Service revenue (R+)		5,000
		Accounts receivable (A+)	10,000	
		Service revenue (R+)		10,000
1b	Aug 31, 2011	no entry		
2	Aug 20, 2011	Cash (A+)	12,000	
		Accounts receivable (A–)		12,000
3	Jan 20, 2012	Uncollectible-account expense (E+)	200	
		Accounts receivable—Andrews (A–)		80
		Accounts receivable—Jones (A–)		120
4	Dec 31, 2011	no entry		
5	Mar 4, 2012	Cash (A+)	80	
		Uncollectible-account expense (E+)		80

Compare Exhibit 8-4, using the direct write-off method previously mentioned, and Exhibit 8-3, using the allowance method. The entries that differ between the two methods are highlighted in blue.

Reporting Receivables on the Balance Sheet

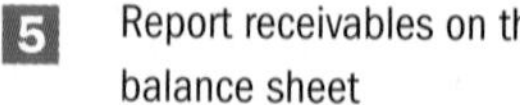
5 Report receivables on the balance sheet

Accounts receivable appear in the current assets section of the Balance Sheet. There are two ways to show Accounts receivable on that financial statement. For example, Greg's Groovy Tunes could report its accounts receivable from the data presented earlier in the chapter as shown here:

Greg's Groovy Tunes BALANCE SHEET (PARTIAL): January 12, 2012	
Accounts receivable	$2,800
Less: Allowance for uncollectible accounts	(400)
Accounts receivable, net	$2,400

Greg's Groovy Tunes BALANCE SHEET (PARTIAL): January 12, 2012	
Accounts receivable, net of allowance for doubtful accounts of $400	$2,400

Most companies use the second approach, but either is acceptable. The key is to show Accounts receivable at their net realizable value.

Credit-Card, Bankcard, and Debit-Card Sales

Credit-Card Sales

6 Journalize credit-card, bankcard, and debit-card sales

Credit-card sales are common in retailing. Customers present credit cards like **American Express** or **Discover® Card** to pay for purchases. The credit-card company pays the seller and then bills the customer.

Customer settles bill of $50 by paying with his credit card

Seller collects $48 from credit card company

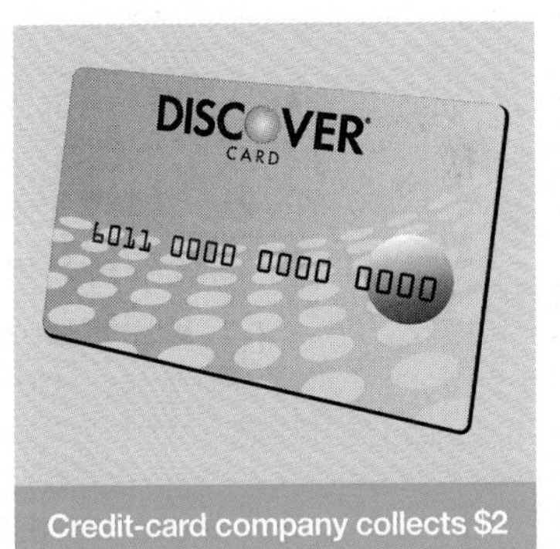

Credit-card company collects $2

Source: © Logo Courtesy of Discover Card.

Credit cards offer the convenience of buying without having to pay cash immediately. A **Discover** Cardmember receives a monthly statement from **Discover® Card**, detailing each transaction. The card holder can then write just one check to cover many purchases.

Retailers also benefit. They do not have to check each customer's credit rating. The credit-card company has already done so. Retailers do not have to keep accounts receivable records or pursue collection from customers.

The benefits do not come free. The seller receives less than 100% of the face value of the sale. The credit-card company takes a fee of 1% to 5% on the sale.

Suppose you and your family have dinner at a **Good Eats** restaurant. You pay the bill—$50—with a **Discover® Card.**

Good Eats' entry to record the $50 sale, subject to the credit-card company's 4% discount, is:

	Accounts receivable—Discover® (A+)	48	
	Credit-card discount expense ($50 × 0.04) (E+)	2	
	Sales revenue (R+)		50
	Recorded credit-card sales.		

On collection of the cash, **Good Eats** records the following:

	Cash (A+)	48	
	Accounts receivable—Discover® (A–)		48
	Collected from Discover®.		

Bankcard Sales

Most banks issue their own cards, known as **bankcards,** which operate much like credit cards. **VISA** and **MasterCard** are the two main bankcards. When a company makes a sale and accepts a **VISA** card as payment, the company receives cash at the point of sale. The cash received is less than the full amount of the sale because the bank deducts its fee (the 1% to 5% mentioned earlier). Suppose your family paid the $50 **Good Eats** bill mentioned earlier with a **VISA** card. The restaurant accepts the payment with the **VISA** card, and the bank that issued the card charges a 2% fee. **Good Eats** would record the bankcard sale as follows:

	Cash (A+)	49	
	Bankcard discount expense ($50 × 0.02) (E+)	1	
	Sales revenue (R+)		50
	Recorded a bankcard sale.		

Debit-Card Sales

Debit cards are fundamentally different from credit cards and bankcards. Using a debit card is like paying with cash, except that you do not have to carry cash or write a check at **Target** (or another retailer). The buyer swipes the card through a special terminal to pay for purchases, and the buyer's bank balance is automatically decreased. **Target's** Cash account is increased immediately. **Target** does not have to deposit a check and wonder if it will bounce. With a debit card there is no third party, such as **VISA** or **MasterCard,** so there is no Bankcard discount expense or Credit-card discount expense.

Summary Problem 1

Monarch Map Company's balance sheet at December 31, 2011, reported the following:

Accounts receivable	$60,000
Allowance for uncollectible accounts	2,000

Requirements

1. How much of the receivable did Monarch expect to collect? Stated differently, what was the net realizable value of these receivables?
2. Journalize, without explanations, 2012 entries for Monarch:
   a. Total sales for the first three quarters of the year were $80,000; 3% of sales were estimated to be uncollectible. Monarch received cash payments on account during 2012 of $74,300.
   b. Accounts receivable identified to be uncollectible totaled $2,700.
   c. December 31, 2012, aging of receivables indicates that $2,200 of the receivables is uncollectible (target balance).

   Prepare a T-account for Allowance for uncollectible accounts, as follows:

   Allowance for uncollectible accounts

		Dec 31, 2011 Bal	2,000
2012 Write-offs	?	2012 Expense	?
		Bal before Adj	
		Dec 31, 2012 Adj	?
		Dec 31, 2012 Bal	2,200

   Post all three transactions to the allowance account.
3. Calculate and report Monarch's receivables and related allowance on the December 31, 2012, balance sheet. What is the net realizable value of receivables at December 31, 2012? How much is the uncollectible-account expense for 2012?

Solution

Requirement 1

Net realizable value of receivables ($60,000 – $2,000)...........	$58,000

Requirement 2

a.		Accounts receivable (A+)	80,000	
		Service revenue (R+)		80,000
		Cash (A+)	74,300	
		Accounts receivable (A–)		74,300
		Uncollectible-account expense (80,000 × 3%) (E+)	2,400	
		Allowance for uncollectible accounts (CA+)		2,400
b.		Allowance for uncollectible accounts (CA–)	2,700	
		Accounts receivable (A–)		2,700
c.		Uncollectible-account expense ($2,200 – $1,700) (E+)	500	
		Allowance for uncollectible accounts (CA+)		500

Allowance for uncollectible accounts

		Dec 31, 2011 Bal	2,000
2012 Write-offs	2,700	2012 Expense	2,400
		Bal before Adj	1,700
		Dec 31, 2012 Adj	500
		Dec 31, 2012 Bal	2,200

Requirement 3

Accounts receivable	$63,000
Less: Allowance for uncollectible accounts	(2,200)
Accounts receivable, net	$60,800
Uncollectible-account expense for 2012 ($2,400 + $500)	$ 2,900

Notes Receivable

7 Account for notes receivable

Notes receivable are more formal than accounts receivable. The debtor signs a promissory note as evidence of the transaction. Before launching into the accounting, let us define the special terms used for notes receivable.

- **Promissory note:** A written promise to pay a specified amount of money at a particular future date.
- **Maker of the note (debtor):** The entity that signs the note and promises to pay the required amount; the maker of the note is the *debtor.*
- **Payee of the note (creditor)** : The entity to whom the maker promises future payment; the payee of the note is the *creditor.*
- **Principal:** The amount loaned out by the payee and borrowed by the maker of the note.
- **Interest:** The revenue to the payee for loaning money. Interest is expense to the debtor and income to the creditor.
- **Interest period:** The period of time during which interest is computed. It extends from the original date of the note to the maturity date. Also called the **note term.**
- **Interest rate:** The percentage rate of interest specified by the note. Interest rates are almost always stated for a period of one year. A 9% note means that the amount of interest for *one year* is 9% of the note's principal.
- **Maturity date:** As stated earlier, this is the date when final payment of the note is due. Also called the **due date.**
- **Maturity value:** The sum of the principal plus interest due at maturity.

Exhibit 8-5 illustrates a promissory note. Study it carefully.

EXHIBIT 8-5 | **A Promissory Note**

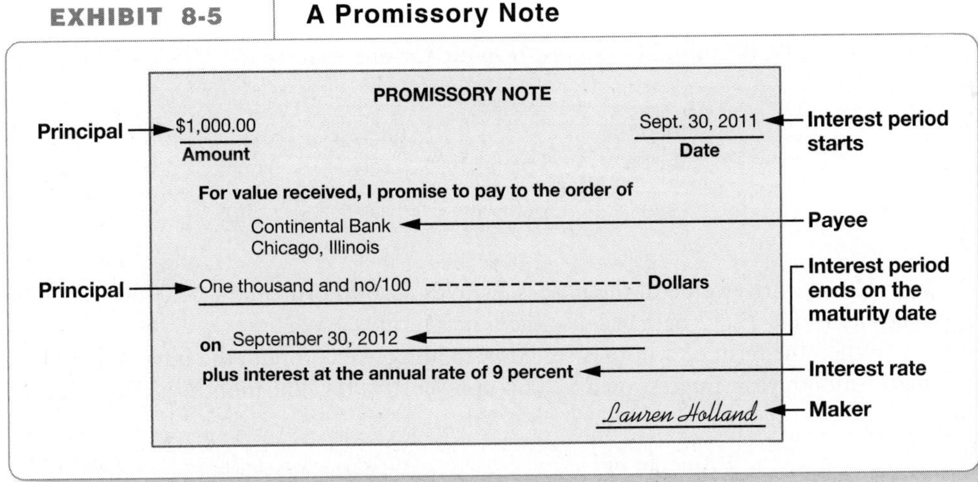
PROMISSORY NOTE
$1,000.00
Amount
Sept. 30, 2011
Date
For value received, I promise to pay to the order of
Continental Bank
Chicago, Illinois
One thousand and no/100 ---------------- Dollars
on September 30, 2012
plus interest at the annual rate of 9 percent
Lauren Holland

Identifying Maturity Date

Some notes specify the maturity date. For example, September 30, 2012, is the maturity date of the note shown in Exhibit 8-5. Other notes state the period of the note in days or months. When the period is given in months, the note's maturity date falls on the same day of the month as the date the note was issued. For example, a six-month note dated February 16, 2011, would mature on August 16, 2011.

When the period is given in days, the maturity date is determined by counting the actual days from the date of issue. A 180-day note dated February 16, 2011, matures on August 15, 2011, as shown here:

Month	Number of Days	Cumulative Total
Feb 2011	28 – 16 = 12	12
Mar 2011	31	43
Apr 2011	30	73
May 2011	31	104
Jun 2011	30	134
Jul 2011	31	165
Aug 2011	15	180

In counting the days remaining for a note, remember to

- count the maturity date.
- omit the date the note was issued.

Computing Interest on a Note

The formula for computing the interest is as follows:

Amount of interest	=	Principal	×	Interest rate	×	Time

In the formula, **time period** represents the portion of a year that interest has accrued on the note. It may be expressed as a fraction of a year in months (x/12) or a fraction of a year in days (x/360 or x/365). Using the data in Exhibit 8-5, Continental Bank computes interest revenue for one year as:

Amount of interest	=	Principal	×	Interest rate	×	Time
$90		$1,000		0.09		12/12

The maturity value of the note is $1,090 ($1,000 principal + $90 interest). The time element is 12/12 or 1 because the note's term is 1 year.

When the term of a note is stated in months, we compute the interest based on the 12-month year. Interest on a $2,000 note at 10% for nine months is computed as:

Amount of interest	=	Principal	×	Interest rate	×	Time
$150		$2,000		0.10		9/12

When the interest period is stated in days, we sometimes compute interest based on a 360-day year rather than on a 365-day year.[1] The interest on a $5,000 note at 12% for 60 days can be computed as:

[1] A 360-day year eliminates some rounding.

Amount of interest	=	Principal	×	Interest rate	×	Time
$100		$5,000		0.12		60/360

Keep in mind that interest rates are stated as an annual rate. Therefore, the time in the interest formula should also be expressed in terms of a fraction of the year.

Accruing Interest Revenue

A note receivable may be outstanding at the end of an accounting period. The interest revenue earned on the note up to year-end is part of that year's earnings. Recall that interest revenue is earned over time, not just when cash is received. Because of the matching principle, we want to record the earnings from the note in the year in which they were earned.

Let us continue with the Continental Bank note receivable from Exhibit 8-5. Continental Bank's accounting period ends December 31.

- How much of the total interest revenue does Continental Bank earn in 2011 (from September 30 through December 31)?

$1,000 × .09 × 3/12 = $22.50

Continental Bank makes the following adjusting entry at December 31, 2011:

2011			
Dec 31	Interest receivable ($1,000 × 0.09 × 3/12) (A+)	22.50	
	Interest revenue (R+)		22.50
	Accrued interest revenue.		

- How much interest revenue does Continental Bank earn in 2012 (for January 1 through September 30)?

$1,000 × .09 × 9/12 = $67.50

On the note's maturity date, Continental Bank makes the following entry:

2012			
Sep 30	Cash [$1,000 + ($1,000 × 0.09)]	1,090	
	Note Receivable—L. Holland		1,000
	Interest Receivable ($1,000 × 0.09 × 3/12)		22.50
	Interest Revenue ($1,000 × 0.09 × 9/12)		67.50
	Collected note receivable plus interest.		

Earlier we determined that total interest on the note was $90 ($1,000 × .09 × 12/12). These entries assign the correct amount of interest to each year:

- $22.50 for 2011 + $67.50 for 2012 = $90 total interest

Stop & Think...

Why do we calculate interest on notes if it does not have to be paid yet? Think about any debts you may have. Does the interest continue to accrue until the point you pay off the debt? Yes, it does. The same is true for businesses. So, we accrue interest on the notes because the customers owe the interest to the company as soon as time expires on the note.

Consider the loan agreement shown in Exhibit 8-5. Lauren Holland signs the note, and Continental Bank gives Holland $1,000 cash. At maturity, Holland pays the bank $1,090 ($1,000 principal plus $90 interest). The bank's entries are as follows:

Loan Out Money

	Continental Bank's General Journal		
2011			
Sep 30	Notes receivable—L. Holland (A+)	1,000	
	Cash (A–)		1,000
Dec 31	Interest receivable ($1,000 × .09 × 3/12) (A+)	22.50	
	Interest revenue (R+)		22.50
2012			
Sep 30	Cash [$1,000 + ($1,000 × .09 × 12/12)] (A+)	1,090	
	Notes receivable—L. Holland (A–)		1,000
	Interest receivable (A–)		22.50
	Interest revenue ($1,000 × .09 × 9/12) (R+)		67.50

Some companies sell merchandise in exchange for notes receivable. Assume that on July 1, 2011, **General Electric** sells household appliances for $2,000 to Dorman Builders. Dorman signs a 9 month promissory note at 10% annual interest. **General Electric's** entries to record the sale, interest accrual, and collection from Dorman are as follows:

Sell on a Note Receivable

	General Electric's General Journal		
2011			
Jul 1	Notes receivable—Dorman Builders (A+)	2,000	
	Sales revenue (R+)		2,000
Dec 31	Interest receivable ($2,000 × .10 × 6/12) (A+)	100	
	Interest revenue (R+)		100
2012			
Mar 31	Cash [$2,000 + ($2,000 × .10 × 9/12)] (A+)	2,150	
	Notes receivable—Dorman Builders (A–)		2,000
	Interest receivable (A–)		100
	Interest revenue ($2,000 × .10 × 3/12) (R+)		50

A company may accept a note receivable from a trade customer who fails to pay an account receivable. The customer signs a promissory note and gives it to the creditor. Suppose Sports Club cannot pay Blanding Services. Blanding may accept a 60 day, $5,000 note receivable, with 12% interest, from Sports Club on November 20, 2011. Blanding's entries are as follows:

Converting Accounts receivable to Notes receivable

		Blanding Services' General Journal		
	2011			
	Nov 20	Notes receivable—Sports Club (A+)	5,000	
		Accounts receivable—Sports Club (A–)		5,000
	Dec 31	Interest receivable ($5,000 × .12 × 42/360) (A+)	70	
		Interest revenue (R+)		70
	2012			
	Jan 18	Cash [$5,000 + ($5,000 × .12 × 60/360)] (A+)	5,100	
		Notes receivable—Sports Club (A–)		5,000
		Interest receivable (A–)		70
		Interest revenue ($5,000 × .12 × 18/360) (R+)		30

A company holding a note may need cash before the note matures. A procedure for selling the note to receive cash immediately, called discounting a note receivable, appears in Appendix 8A.

Dishonored Notes Receivable

If the maker of a note does not pay at maturity, the maker **dishonors** (**defaults on**) the note. Because the note has expired, it is no longer in force. But the debtor still owes the payee. The payee can transfer the note receivable amount to Accounts receivable. Suppose Rubinstein Jewelers has a 6-month, 10% note receivable for $1,200 from Mark Adair that was signed on March 3, 2011, and Adair defaults. Rubinstein Jewelers will record the default on September 3, 2011, as follows:

2011			
Sep 3	Accounts receivable—M. Adair	1,260	
	Note receivable—M. Adair		1,200
	Interest revenue ($1,200 × 0.10 × 6/12)		60
	Recorded a dishonored note receivable.		

Rubinstein will then bill Adair for the account receivable.

Computers and Receivables

Accounting for receivables by a company like **Mars** requires thousands of postings for credit sales and cash collections. Manual accounting cannot keep up. However, Accounts receivable can be computerized. At **Mars** the order entry, shipping, and billing departments work together, as shown in Exhibit 8-6.

EXHIBIT 8-6 | **Order Entry, Shipping, and Billing Working Together at Mars**

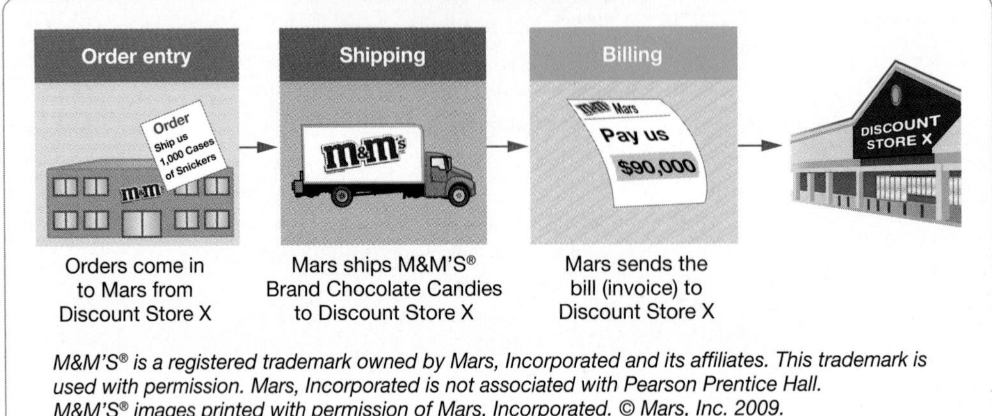

M&M'S® is a registered trademark owned by Mars, Incorporated and its affiliates. This trademark is used with permission. Mars, Incorporated is not associated with Pearson Prentice Hall. M&M'S® images printed with permission of Mars, Incorporated. © Mars, Inc. 2009.

Using Accounting Information for Decision Making

8 Use the acid-test ratio and days' sales in receivables to evaluate a company

As discussed earlier in the text, the balance sheet lists assets in order of liquidity (closeness to cash).

The partial balance sheet of Greg's Groovy Tunes provides an example in Exhibit 8-7. Focus on the current assets at December 31, 2012.

Balance-sheet data become more useful by showing the relationships among assets, liabilities, and revenues. Let us examine two important ratios.

EXHIBIT 8-7 | **Greg's Groovy Tunes Balance Sheet**

GREG'S GROOVY TUNES
Balance Sheet—Partial
December 31, 2012 and 2011

Assets	December 31, 2012	2011
Current assets:		
Cash	$ 800	$ 400
Short-term investments	1,500	300
Accounts receivable, net of allowance for doubtful accounts of $400 in 2012 and $300 in 2011	2,400	2,600
Inventory	800	600
Total current assets	5,500	3,900
Liabilities		
Current liabilities:		
Total current liabilities	$4,400	$2,900

Acid-Test (or Quick) Ratio

In Chapter 4, we discussed the current ratio, which measures ability to pay current liabilities with current assets. A more stringent measure of ability to pay current liabilities is the **acid-test ratio** (or **quick ratio**). The acid-test ratio reveals whether the entity could pay all its current liabilities if they were to become due immediately.

For Greg's Groovy Tunes (Exhibit 8-7)

$$\text{Acid-test ratio} = \frac{\text{Cash} + \text{Short-term investments} + \text{Net current receivables}}{\text{Total current liabilities}}$$

$$= \frac{\$800 + \$1{,}500 + \$2{,}400}{\$4{,}400} = 1.07$$

The higher the acid-test ratio, the more able the business is to pay its current liabilities. Greg's acid-test ratio of 1.07 means that the business has \$1.07 of quick assets to pay each \$1 of current liabilities. This is a strong position.

What is an acceptable acid-test ratio? That depends on the industry. **Wal-Mart** operates smoothly with an acid-test ratio of less than 0.20. Several things make this possible: **Wal-Mart** collects cash rapidly and has almost no receivables. The acid-test ratios for most department stores are about 0.80, while travel agencies average 1.10. In general, an acid-test ratio of 1.00 is considered safe.

Days' Sales in Receivables

After making a credit sale, the next step is to collect the receivable. **Days' sales in receivables**, also called the **collection period**, indicates how many days it takes to collect the average level of receivables. The shorter the collection period, the more quickly the organization can use its cash. The longer the collection period, the less cash is available for operations. Days' sales in receivables can be computed in two steps, as follows:[2]*

For Greg's Groovy Tunes (Exhibit 8-7)

1. $$\text{One day's sales} = \frac{\text{Net sales (or Total revenues)}}{365 \text{ days}}$$

$$= \frac{\$22{,}600^*}{365} = \$62 \text{ per day}$$

2. $$\text{Days' sales in average accounts receivable} = \frac{\text{Average net accounts receivable}}{\text{One day's sales}}$$

$$= \frac{\left(\text{Beginning net receivables} + \text{Ending net receivables}\right)/2}{\text{One day's sales}}$$

$$= \frac{(\$2{,}400 + \$2{,}600)/2}{\$62} = 40 \text{ days}$$

*From Greg's 2012 income statement, which is not reproduced here.

[2]Days' sales in average receivables can also be computed in this one step:

$$\text{Days' sales in average receivables} = \frac{\text{Average net receivables}}{\text{Net sales}} \times 365$$

On average, it takes Greg's Groovy Tunes 40 days to collect its accounts receivable. The length of the collection period depends on the credit terms of the sale. For example, sales on net 30 terms should be collected within approximately 30 days. When there is a discount, such as 2/10, net 30, the collection period may be shorter. Credit terms of net 45 result in a longer collection period.

Investors and creditors do not evaluate a company on the basis of one or two ratios. Instead, they analyze all the information available. Then they stand back and ask, "What is our overall impression of this company?" We present all the financial ratios in Chapter 14. By the time you get to that point of your study, you will have an overall view of the company.

Decision Guidelines

ACCOUNTING FOR RECEIVABLES

The Decision Guidelines feature summarizes some key decisions for receivables.

Accounting for receivables is the same for Greg's Groovy Tunes as for a large company like **Mars**. Suppose you decide that Greg's will sell on account, as most other companies do. How should you account for your receivables? These guidelines show the way.

Decision	Guidelines
ACCOUNTS RECEIVABLE	
• How much of our receivables will we collect?	Less than the full amount of the receivables because we cannot collect from some customers.

• How to report receivables at their net realizable value?	• Use the *allowance method* to account for uncollectible receivables. Set up the Allowance for uncollectible accounts.
	• Estimate uncollectibles by the
	  • *Percent-of-sales method (income-statement approach).*
	  • *Aging-of-accounts method (balance sheet approach).*
	• Write off uncollectible receivables as they prove uncollectible.
	• **Net accounts receivable = Accounts receivable – Allowance for uncollectible accounts**

• Is there a simpler way to account for uncollectible receivables?	Yes, but it is unacceptable for most companies. The *direct write-off-method* uses no Allowance for the uncollectible account. It simply debits Uncollectible-accounts expense and credits a customer's Accounts receivable to write it off when it has proved uncollectible. This method is acceptable only when uncollectibles are insignificant.
NOTES RECEIVABLE	
• What two other accounts are related to notes receivable?	Notes receivable are related to • Interest revenue. • Interest receivable (Interest revenue earned but not yet collected).
• How to compute the interest on a note receivable?	**Amount of interest = Principal × Interest rate × Time**
• How can you use receivables to evaluate a company's financial position?	$$\text{Acid-test ratio} = \frac{\text{Cash + Short-term investments + Net current receivables}}{\text{Total current liabilities}}$$ $$\text{Days' Sales in average receivables} = \frac{\text{Average net accounts receivable}}{\text{One day's sales}}$$
• How to report receivables on the balance sheet?	Accounts (or Notes) receivable $XXX Less: Allowance for uncollectible accounts (X) Accounts (or notes) receivable, net $ XX

Summary Problem 2

Suppose First Fidelity Bank engaged in the following transactions:

2010	
Apr 1	Loaned out $8,000 to Bland Co. Received a six-month, 10% note
Oct 1	Collected the Bland note at maturity
Dec 1	Loaned $6,000 to Flores on a 180-day, 12% note
Dec 31	Accrued interest revenue on the Flores note
2011	
May 30	Collected the Flores note at maturity

First Fidelity's accounting period ends on December 31.

Requirements

Explanations are not needed. Use a 360-day year to compute interest.

1. Record the 2010 transactions on April 1 through December 1 on First Fidelity's books.
2. Make the adjusting entry needed on December 31, 2010.
3. Record the May 30, 2011, collection of the Flores note.

Solution

Requirement 1

2010			
Apr 1	Note receivable—Bland Co. (A+)	8,000	
	Cash (A–)		8,000
Oct 1	Cash ($8,000 + $400) (A+)	8,400	
	Note receivable—Bland Co. (A–)		8,000
	Interest revenue ($8,000 × 0.10 × 6/12) (R+)		400

Requirement 2

2010			
Dec 1	Note receivable—Flores (A+)	6,000	
	Cash (A–)		6,000
31	Interest receivable (A+)	60	
	Interest revenue ($6,000 × 0.12 × 30/360) (R+)		60

Requirement 3

2011			
May 30	Cash [$6,000 + ($6,000 × 0.12 × 180/360) (A+)	6,360	
	Note receivable—Flores (A–)		6,000
	Interest receivable (A–)		60
	Interest revenue ($6,000 × 0.12 × 150/360) (R–)		300

Review Receivables

Accounting Vocabulary

Acid-Test Ratio (p. 479)
Ratio of the sum of cash plus short-term investments plus net current receivables, to total current liabilities. Tells whether the entity could pay all its current liabilities if they came due immediately. Also called the **quick ratio**.

Aging-of-Accounts Method (p. 463)
A way to estimate bad debts by analyzing individual accounts receivable according to the length of time they have been receivable from the customer. Also called the **balance-sheet approach**.

Allowance for Doubtful Accounts (p. 462)
A contra account, related to accounts receivable, that holds the estimated amount of collection losses. Also called **allowance for uncollectible accounts**.

Allowance for Uncollectible Accounts (p. 461)
A contra account, related to accounts receivable, that holds the estimated amount of collection losses. Also called **allowance for doubtful accounts**.

Allowance Method (p. 461)
A method of recording collection losses on the basis of estimates instead of waiting to see which customers the company will not collect from.

Bad-Debt Expense (p. 461)
Cost to the seller of extending credit. Arises from the failure to collect from credit customers. Also called **doubtful-account expense** or **uncollectible-account expense**.

Balance-Sheet Approach (p. 463)
A way to estimate bad debts by analyzing individual accounts receivable according to the length of time they have been receivable from the customer. Also called the **aging-of-accounts method**.

Bankcards (p. 470)
Issued by banks, with an operation much like a credit card. VISA and MasterCard are the two main bankcards.

Collection Period (p. 479)
Ratio of average net accounts receivable to one day s sales. Tells how many days' sales it takes to collect the average level of receivables. Also called the **days' sales in receivables**.

Control Account (p. 458)
An account in the general ledger that summarizes related subsidiary accounts.

Days' Sales in Receivables (p. 479)
Ratio of average net accounts receivable to one day's sales. Tells how many days' sales it takes to collect the average level of receivables. Also called the **collection period**.

Debtor (p. 458)
The party to a credit transaction who makes a purchase and has a payable.

Default on a Note (p. 477)
Failure of a note's maker to pay a note receivable at maturity. Also called **dishonor of a note**.

Direct Write-Off Method (p. 467)
A method of accounting for uncollectible receivables, in which the company waits until the credit department decides that a customer's account receivable is uncollectible and then debits Uncollectible-account expense and credits the customer's Account receivable.

Discounting a Note Receivable (p. 505)
Selling a note receivable before its maturity date.

Dishonor of a Note (p. 477)
Failure of a note's maker to pay a note receivable at maturity. Also called **default on a note**.

Doubtful-Account Expense (p. 461)
Cost to the seller of extending credit. Arises from the failure to collect from credit customers. Also called **uncollectible-account expense** or **bad-debt expense**.

Due Date (p. 473)
The date when final payment of the note is due. Also called the **maturity date**.

Income-Statement Approach (p. 462)
A method of estimating uncollectible receivables that calculates uncollectible-account expense. Also called the **percent-of-sales method**.

Interest (p. 473)
The revenue to the payee for loaning money; the expense to the debtor.

Interest Period (p. 473)
The period of time during which interest is computed. It extends from the original date of the note to the maturity date. Also called the **note term**, or simply **time period.**

Interest Rate (p. 473)
The percentage rate of interest specified by the note. Interest rates are almost always stated for a period of one year.

Maturity Date (p. 459)
The date when final payment of the note is due. Also called the **due date**.

Maturity Value (p. 473)
The sum of the principal plus interest due at maturity.

Net Realizable Value (p. 464)
Net value that a company expects to collect of its receivables.

Note Term (p. 473)
The period of time during which interest is computed. It extends from the original date of the note to the maturity date. Also called the **interest period**.

Percent-of-Sales Method (p. 462)
A method of estimating uncollectible receivables that calculates uncollectible-account expense. Also called the **income-statement approach**.

Principal (p. 473)
The amount loaned out by the payee and borrowed by the maker of the note.

Promissory Note (p. 459)
A written promise to pay a specified amount of money at a particular future date.

Quick Ratio (p. 479)
Ratio of the sum of cash plus short-term investments plus net current receivables, to total current liabilities. Tells whether the entity could pay all its current liabilities if they came due immediately. Also called the **acid-test ratio**.

Receivable (p. 458)
Monetary claim against a business or an individual.

Subsidiary Ledger (p. 458)
Contains the details by individual customer that are summarized in the control account.

Time Period (p. 474)
The period of time during which interest is computed. It extends from the original date of the note to the maturity date. Also called the **note term** or **interest period**.

Trade Receivables (p. 458)
Amounts to be collected from customers from sales made on credit. Also called **Accounts receivable**.

Uncollectible-Account Expense (p. 461)
Cost to the seller of extending credit. Arises from the failure to collect from credit customers. Also called **doubtful-account expense** or **bad-debt expense**.

■ Quick Check

1. With good internal controls, the person who handles cash can also,
   a. issue credits to customers for sales returns.
   b. account for cash payments.
   c. account for cash receipts from customers.
   d. None of the above
2. "Bad debts" are the same as
   a. Uncollectible accounts
   b. Doubtful accounts.
   c. Neither of the above
   d. Both a. and b.
3. Which method of estimating uncollectible receivables focuses on Uncollectible-account expense for the income statement?
   a. Net-realizable-value approach
   b. Aging-of-accounts approach
   c. Percent-of-sales approach
   d. All of the above
4. Your company uses the allowance method to account for uncollectible receivables. At the beginning of the year, Allowance for uncollectible accounts had a credit balance of $1,400. During the year you recorded Uncollectible-account expense of $3,400 and wrote off bad receivables of $1,900. What is your year-end balance in Allowance for uncollectible accounts?
   a. $100
   b. $3,300
   c. $500
   d. $2,900
5. Your ending balance of Accounts receivable is $20,500. Use the data in the preceding question to compute the net realizable value of Accounts receivable at year-end.
   a. $17,600
   b. $3,300
   c. $20,500
   d. $100

6. What is wrong with the direct write-off method of accounting for uncollectibles?
   a. The direct write-off method does not set up an allowance for uncollectibles.
   b. The direct write-off method overstates assets on the balance sheet.
   c. The direct write-off method does not match expenses against revenue very well.
   d. All of the above
7. At December 31, you have a $9,900 note receivable from a customer. Interest of 7% has accrued for 7 months on the note. What will your financial statements report for this situation?
   a. Nothing, because you have not received the cash yet.
   b. The Balance sheet will report the note receivable of $9,900 and interest receivable of $404.
   c. The Income statement will report a note receivable of $9,900.
   d. The Balance sheet will report the note receivable of $9,900.
8. Return to the data in the preceding question. What will the income statement report for this situation?
   a. Nothing, because you have not received the cash yet
   b. Interest revenue of $404
   c. Note receivable of $9,900
   d. Both b. and c.
9. At year-end, your company has cash of $11,800, receivables of $47,700, inventory of $36,200, and prepaid expenses totaling $4,800. Liabilities of $62,800 must be paid next year. What is your acid-test ratio?
   a. 0.76
   b. 1.52
   c. 0.95
   d. Cannot be determined from the data given
10. Return to the data in the preceding question. A year ago receivables stood at $66,900, and sales for the current year totaled $706,600. How many days did it take you to collect your average level of receivables?
   a. 35
   b. 49
   c. 30
   d. 29

Answers are given after Apply Your Knowledge (p. 504).

Assess Your Progress

■ Short Exercises

S8-1 *(L.OBJ. 1)* **Different types of receivables [5 min]**
Consider accounts receivable and notes receivable.

Requirement

1. What is the difference between accounts receivable and notes receivable?

S8-2 *(L.OBJ. 2)* **Internal control over the collection of receivables [5 min]**
Consider internal control over receivables collections.

Requirement

1. What job must be withheld from a company's credit department in order to safeguard its cash? If the credit department does perform this job, what can a credit department employee do to hurt the company?

S8-3 *(L.OBJ. 3)* **Applying the allowance method (percentage of sales) to account for uncollectibles [5 min]**
During its first year of operations, World Class Sport Shoes earned revenue of $388,000 on account. Industry experience suggests that bad debts will amount to 4% of revenues. At December 31, 2012, accounts receivable total $35,000. The company uses the allowance method to account for uncollectibles.

Requirements

1. Journalize World Class' sales and uncollectible-account expense using the percent-of-sales method.
2. Show how to report accounts receivable on the balance sheet at December 31, 2012. Use the long reporting format illustrated in the chapter.

S8-4 *(L.OBJ. 3)* **Applying the allowance method (percentage of sales) to account for uncollectibles [5–10 min]**
The Accounts receivable balance for Turning Leaves Furniture Restoration at December 31, 2010, was $15,000. During 2011, Turning Leaves completed the following transactions:

a. Sales revenue on account, $422,000 (ignore cost of goods sold)
b. Collections on account, $422,000
c. Write-offs of uncollectibles, $6,000
d. Uncollectible-account expense, 3% of sales revenue

Requirement

1. Journalize Turning's 2011 transactions.

S8-5 *(L.OBJ. 3)* **Applying the allowance method (aging of accounts) to account for uncollectibles [10 min]**
Spring Garden Flowers had the following balances at December 31, 2011, before the year-end adjustments:

Accounts receivable		Allowance for uncollectible accounts	
77,000			1,700

The aging of accounts receivable yields the following data:

	Age of Accounts receivable		
	0–60 Days	Over 60 Days	Total Receivables
Accounts receivable . . .	$71,000	$6,000	$77,000
Percent uncollectible . . .	× 1%	× 20%	

Requirements

1. Journalize Spring's entry to adjust the allowance account to its correct balance at December 31, 2011.
2. Prepare a T-account to compute the ending balance of Allowance for uncollectible accounts.

S8-6 *(L.OBJ. 4)* **Applying the direct write-off method to account for uncollectibles [10 min]**
Sheena Stone is an attorney in Los Angeles. Stone uses the direct write-off method to account for uncollectible receivables.

At November 30, 2010, Stone's accounts receivable totaled $21,000. During December, she earned revenue of $24,000 on account and collected $23,000 on account. She also wrote off uncollectible receivables of $1,440 on December 31, 2010.

Requirements

1. Use the direct write-off method to journalize Stone's write-off of the uncollectible receivables.
2. What is Stone's balance of Accounts receivable at December 31, 2010? Does Stone expect to collect the total amount?

S8-7 *(L.OBJ. 4)* **Collecting a receivable previously written off—direct write-off method [5–10 min]**
Foley's Furniture Repair had trouble collecting its account receivable from Steve Stone. On July 19, 2012, Foley's finally wrote off Stone's $900 account receivable. Foley's turned the account over to an attorney, who hounded Stone for the rest of the year. On December 31, Stone sent a $900 check to Foley's Furniture Repair with a note that said, "Here's your money. Please call off your bloodhound!"

Requirement

1. Journalize the entries required for Foley's Furniture Repair.

S8-8 *(L.OBJ. 5)* **Reporting receivables and other accounts in the financial statements [10–15 min]**
Lakeland Medical Center included the following items in its financial statements:

Allowance for doubtful accounts	$ 110	Service revenue	$ 14,600
Cash	1,400	Other assets	350
Accounts receivable	2,330	Cost of services sold and other expenses	12,700
Accounts payable	1,110	Notes payable	3,280

Requirements

1. How much net income did Lakeland earn for the month?
2. Show two ways Lakeland can report receivables on its classified balance sheet.

S8-9 *(L.OBJ. 6)* **Recording credit-card and bankcard sales [5 min]**
Restaurants do a large volume of business by credit cards and bankcards. Suppose Salad Company restaurant had these transactions on January 28, 2011:

National Express credit–card sales	$ 10,200
ValueCard bankcard sales	8,000

Suppose National Express charges merchants 2.00% and ValueCard charges 1.50%

Requirement

1. Journalize these sale transactions for the restaurant.

S8-10 *(L.OBJ. 7)* **Computing interest amounts on notes receivable [10 min]**
A table of notes receivable for 2012 follows:

	Principal	Interest Rate	Interest Period During 2012
Note 1	$ 40,000	13%	10 months
Note 2	6,000	8%	75 days
Note 3	20,000	11%	90 days
Note 4	90,000	9%	5 months

Requirement

1. For each of the notes receivable, compute the amount of interest revenue earned during 2012. Use a 360-day year, and round to the nearest dollar.

S8-11 *(L.OBJ. 7)* **Accounting for a note receivable [5–10 min]**
Lantana Bank & Trust Company lent $90,000 to Sylvia Peters on a 30-day, 11% note.

Requirement

1. Journalize the following transactions for the bank (explanations are not required):

   a. Lending the money on May 6.
   b. Collecting the principal and interest at maturity. Specify the date. For the computation of interest, use a 360-day year.

S8-12 *(L.OBJ. 8)* **Using the acid-test ratio and days' sales in receivables to evaluate a company [10–15 min]**
West Highland Clothiers reported the following items at August 31, 2012 (amounts in thousands, with last year's—2011—amounts also given as needed):

Accounts payable	$ 380	Accounts receivable, net:	
Cash	250	August 31, 2012	$ 220
Inventories		August 31, 2011	110
August 31, 2012	260	Cost of goods sold	1,160
August 31, 2011	220	Short-term investments	170
Net sales revenue	2,555	Other current assets	50
Long-term assets	360	Other current liabilities	160
Long-term liabilities	80		

Requirement

1. Compute West Highland's (a) acid-test ratio and (b) days' sales in average receivables for 2012. Evaluate each ratio value as strong or weak. West Highland sells on terms of net 30.

Exercises

E8-13 *(L.OBJ. 1)* **Common receivables terms [10–15 min]**

TERMS:	DEFINITIONS:
1. Account receivable	A. Transaction results in a liability for this party
2. Promissory note	B. Transaction results in a receivable for this party
3. Borrower	C. The debtor promises to pay the creditor a definite sum at a future date usually with
4. Note receivable	interest
5. Maturity date	D. Amounts to be collected from customers from sales made on credit
6. Creditor	E. Serves as evidence of the indebtedness and includes the terms of the debt
	F. The date a note is due to be paid in full

Requirement

1. Match the terms with their correct definition.

E8-14 *(L.OBJ. 2)* **Identifying and correcting internal control weakness [10 min]**
Suppose Big Trucks Dealership is opening a regional office in St. Louis. Lesa Carter, the office manager, is designing the internal control system. Carter proposes the following procedures for credit checks on new customers, sales on account, cash collections, and write-offs of uncollectible receivables:

- The credit department runs a credit check on all customers who apply for credit. When an account proves uncollectible, the credit department authorizes the write-off of the account receivable.
- Cash receipts come into the credit department, which separates the cash received from the customer remittance slips. The credit department lists all cash receipts by customer name and amount of cash received.
- The cash goes to the treasurer for deposit in the bank. The remittance slips go to the accounting department for posting to customer accounts.
- The controller compares the daily deposit slip to the total amount posted to customer accounts. Both amounts must agree.

Requirement

1. Identify the internal control weakness in this situation, and propose a way to correct it.

E8-15 *(L.OBJ. 3, 5)* **Accounting for uncollectible accounts using the allowance method and reporting receivables on the balance sheet [15-30 min]**
At December 31, 2012, the Accounts receivable balance of Solar Energy Manufacturing is $170,000. The Allowance for doubtful accounts has a $10,100 credit balance. Solar Energy Manufacturing prepares the following aging schedule for its accounts receivable:

	Age of Accounts			
Accounts receivable	1–30 Days	31–60 Days	61–90 Days	Over 90 Days
$170,000	$70,000	$50,000	$30,000	$20,000
Estimated percent uncollectible	0.6 %	3.0 %	9.0 %	40.0 %

Requirements

1. Journalize the year-end adjusting entry for doubtful accounts on the basis of the aging schedule. Show the T-account for the Allowance for uncollectible accounts at December 31, 2012.
2. Show how Solar Energy Manufacturing will report Accounts receivable on its December 31, 2012, balance sheet.

E8-16 *(L.OBJ. 3, 5)* **Accounting for uncollectible accounts using the allowance method and reporting receivables on the balance sheet [15–20 min]**
At September 30, 2011, Eagle Mountain Flagpoles had Accounts receivable of $33,000 and Allowance for uncollectible accounts had a credit balance of $4,000. During October 2011, Eagle Mountain Flagpoles recorded the following:

- Sales of $186,000 ($161,000 on account; $25,000 for cash)
- Collections on account, $127,000
- Uncollectible-account expense, estimated as 2% of credit sales
- Write-offs of uncollectible receivables, $2,200

Requirements

1. Journalize sales, collections, uncollectible-account expense using the allowance method (percent-of-sales method), and write-offs of uncollectibles during October 2011.
2. Prepare T-accounts to show the ending balances in Accounts receivable and Allowance for uncollectible accounts. Compute *net* accounts receivable at October 31. How much does Eagle Mountain expect to collect?
3. Show how Eagle Mountain Flagpoles will report Accounts receivable on its October 31, 2011, balance sheet.

E8-17 *(L.OBJ. 4, 5)* **Accounting for uncollectible accounts using the direct write-off method and reporting receivables on the balance sheet [10–15 min]**
Refer to the facts presented in Exercise 8-16.

Requirements

1. Journalize sales, collections, uncollectible-account expense using the direct write-off method, and write-offs of uncollectibles during October 2011.
2. Show how Accounts receivable would be reported for Eagle Mountain Flagpoles on its October 31, 2011, balance sheet under the direct write-off method.

E8-18 *(L.OBJ. 4, 5)* **Journalizing transactions using the direct-write off system and reporting receivables on the balance sheet [10–20 min]**
Top Performance Cell Phones sold $18,000 of merchandise to Andrew Trucking Company on account. Andrew fell on hard times and paid only $4,000 of the account receivable. After repeated attempts to collect, Top Performance finally wrote off its accounts receivable from Andrew. Six months later Top Performance received Andrew's check for $14,000 with a note apologizing for the late payment.

Requirements

1. Journalize for Top Performance:

   a. Sale on account, $18,000. (Ignore cost of goods sold.)
   b. Collection of $4,000 on account
   c. Write-off of the remaining portion of Andrew's account receivable. Top Performance uses the allowance method for uncollectibles.
   d. Reinstatement of Andrew's account receivable
   e. Collection in full from Andrew, $14,000

2. Show how Top Performance would report receivables on its balance sheet after all entries have been posted.

E8-19 *(L.OBJ. 6, 7)* **Journalizing bankcard sales, note receivable transactions, and accruing interest [10–15 min]**
Speedy Running Shoes reports the following:

2011	
Jan 3	Recorded Estate bankcard sales of $104,000, less a 2% discount
Oct 1	Loaned $24,000 to Jean Porter, an executive with the company, on a one-year, 10% note
Dec 31	Accrued interest revenue on the Porter note
2012	
Oct 1	Collected the maturity value of the Porter note

Requirement

1. Journalize all entries required for Speedy Running Shoes.

E8-20 *(L.OBJ. 7)* **Computing note receivable amounts [15–25 min]**
On April 30, 2011, Statewide Bank loaned $80,000 to Kelsey Sperry on a one-year, 11% note.

Requirements

1. Journalize all entries related to the note for 2011 and 2012.
2. Which party has a
   a. Note receivable?
   b. Note payable?
   c. Interest revenue?
   d. Interest expense?
3. How much in total would Sperry pay the bank if she pays off the note early on November 30, 2011?

E8-21 *(L.OBJ. 7)* **Journalizing note receivable transactions [10–15 min]**
The following selected transactions occurred during 2012 for Mediterranean Importers. The company ends its accounting year on June 30, 2012:

Apr 1	Loaned $20,000 cash to Bud Shyne on a one-year, 9% note
Jun 6	Sold goods to Green Pro, receiving a 90-day, 10% note for $11,000
30	Made a single entry to accrue interest revenue on both notes

Requirement

1. Journalize all required entries from April 1 through June 30, 2012. Use a 360-day year for interest computations.

E8-22 *(L.OBJ. 7)* **Journalizing note receivable transactions [10 min]**
Beautiful Steam Cleaning performs service on account. When a customer account becomes four months old, Beautiful converts the account to a note receivable. During 2012, the company completed the following transactions:

Jun 28	Performed service on account for Parkview Club, $24,000
Nov 1	Received a $24,000, 60-day, 12% note from Parkview Club in satisfaction of its past-due account receivable
Dec 31	Collected the Parkview Club note at maturity

Requirement

1. Record the transactions in Beautiful's journal.

E8-23 *(L.OBJ. 8)* **Evaluating ratio data [15–20 min]**
Abanaki Carpets reported the following amounts in its 2011 financial statements. The 2010 figures are given for comparison.

	2011		2010	
Current assets:				
Cash		$ 6,000		$ 12,000
Short-term investments		22,000		11,000
Accounts receivable	$ 61,000		$ 74,000	
Less: Allowance for uncollectibles	(7,000)	54,000	(6,000)	68,000
Inventory		194,000		190,000
Prepaid insurance		3,000		3,000
Total current assets		$ 279,000		$ 284,000
Total current liabilities		$ 107,000		$ 109,000
Net sales		$ 730,000		$ 733,000

Requirements

1. Calculate Abanaki's acid-test ratio for 2011. Determine whether Abanaki's acid-test ratio improved or deteriorated from 2010 to 2011. How does Abanaki's acid-test ratio compare with the industry average of 0.80?
2. Calculate the days' sales in receivables for 2011. How do the results compare with Abanaki's credit terms of net 30?

E8-24 *(L.OBJ. 8)* **Collection period for receivables [10–15 min]**
Modern Media Sign Company sells on account. Recently, Modern reported the following figures:

	2012	2011
Net sales	$ 571,000	$ 601,000
Receivables at end of year	38,500	49,100

Requirements

1. Compute Modern's average collection period on receivables during 2012.
2. Suppose Modern's normal credit terms for a sale on account are "2/10 net 30." How well does Modern's collection period compare to the company's credit terms? Is this good or bad for Modern?

Problems (Group A)

P8-25A *(L.OBJ. 1, 2)* **Explaining common types of receivables and designing internal controls for receivables [20–30 min]**
Mail Plus performs mailing services on account, so virtually all cash receipts arrive in the mail. Gina Star, the owner, has just returned from a meeting with new ideas for the business. Among other things, Star plans to institute stronger internal controls over cash receipts from customers.

Requirements

1. What types of receivables are most likely to be collected by Mail Plus?
2. List the following procedures in the correct order.

   a. Another person, such as the owner or the manager, compares the amount of the bank deposit to the total of the customer credits posted by the accountant. This gives some assurance that the day's cash receipts went into the bank and that the same amount was posted to customer accounts.
   b. The person who handles cash should not prepare the bank reconciliation.
   c. An employee with no access to the accounting records deposits the cash in the bank immediately.
   d. The remittance slips go to the accountant, who uses them for posting credits to the customer accounts.
   e. Someone other than the accountant opens the mail. This person separates customer checks from the accompanying remittance slips.

P8-26A *(L.OBJ. 3, 4, 5)* **Accounting for uncollectible accounts using the allowance and direct write-off methods and reporting receivables on the balance sheet [20–30 min]**

On May 31, 2011, Lilly Floral Supply had a $145,000 debit balance in Accounts receivable and a $5,800 credit balance in Allowance for uncollectible accounts. During June, Lilly made

- Sales on account, $530,000
- Collections on account, $573,000
- Write-offs of uncollectible receivables, $5,000

Requirements

1. Journalize all June entries using the *allowance* method. Uncollectible-account expense was estimated at 2% of credit sales. Show all June activity in Accounts receivable, Allowance for uncollectible accounts, and Uncollectible-account expense (post to these T-accounts).
2. Using the same facts, assume instead that Lilly used the direct write-off method to account for uncollectible receivables. Journalize all June entries using the *direct write-off* method. Post to Accounts receivable and Uncollectible-account expense and show their balances at June 30, 2011.
3. What amount of uncollectible-account expense would Lilly report on its June income statement under each of the two methods? Which amount better matches expense with revenue? Give your reason.
4. What amount of *net* accounts receivable would Lilly report on its June 30, 2011, balance sheet under each of the two methods? Which amount is more realistic? Give your reason.

P8-27A *(L.OBJ. 3, 5)* **Accounting for uncollectible accounts using the allowance method, and reporting receivables on the balance sheet [25–35 min]**

At September 30, 2011, the accounts of South Terrance Medical Center (STMC) include the following:

Accounts receivable	$ 146,000
Allowance for uncollectible accounts (credit balance) ...	3,300

During the last quarter of 2011, STMC completed the following selected transactions:

Dec 28	Wrote off accounts receivable as uncollectible: Black Co., $1,700; Jim Waters, $1,000; and Moon, $400
Dec 31	Recorded uncollectible-account expense based on the aging of accounts receivable, as follows:

	Age of Accounts			
Accounts receivable	1–30 Days	31–60 Days	61–90 Days	Over 90 Days
$166,000	$100,000	$ 40,000	$ 16,000	$ 10,000
Estimated percent uncollectible	0.1%	1%	10%	30%

Requirements

1. Journalize the transactions.
2. Open the Allowance for uncollectible accounts T-account, and post entries affecting that account. Keep a running balance.
3. Show how South Terrance Medical Center should report accounts receivable on its December 31, 2011, balance sheet. Use the three line reporting format.

P8-28A *(L.OBJ. 3, 5)* **Accounting for uncollectible accounts using the allowance method (percentage of sales), and reporting receivables on the balance sheet [20–30 min]**

Beta Watches completed the following selected transactions during 2010 and 2011:

2010	
Dec 31	Estimated that uncollectible-account expense for the year was 1% of credit sales of $440,000 and recorded that amount as expense. Use the allowance method.
Dec 31	Made the closing entry for uncollectible-account expense
2011	
Jan 17	Sold inventory to Manny Vasquez, $500, on account. Ignore cost of goods sold.
Jun 29	Wrote off Manny Vasquez's account as uncollectible after repeated efforts to collect from him
Aug 6	Received $500 from Manny Vasquez, along with a letter apologizing for being so late. Reinstated Vasquez' account in full and recorded the cash receipt.
Dec 31	Made a compound entry to write off the following accounts as uncollectible: Brian Kemper, $1,700; Mary Martin, $1,400; and Richard Renik, $200.
Dec 31	Estimated that uncollectible-account expense for the year was 1% on credit sales of $480,000 and recorded the expense
Dec 31	Made the closing entry for uncollectible-account expense

Requirements

1. Open T-accounts for Allowance for uncollectible accounts and Uncollectible-account expense. Keep running balances, assuming all accounts begin with a zero balance.
2. Record the transactions in the general journal, and post to the two T-accounts.
3. The December 31, 2011, balance of Accounts receivable is $133,000. Show how Accounts receivable would be reported on the balance sheet at that date. Use the three line format of reporting the net accounts receivable.

P8-29A *(L.OBJ. 3, 6, 7)* **Accounting for uncollectible accounts (aging of accounts method), bankcard sales, notes receivable, and accrued interest revenue [20–30 min]**

Quality Recliner Chairs completed the following selected transactions:

2010	
Jul 1	Sold inventory to Good – Mart, receiving a $41,000, 9-month, 7% note. Ignore cost of goods sold.
Dec 31	Made an adjusting entry to accrue interest on the Good – Mart note
31	Made an adjusting entry to record uncollectible-account expense based on an aging of accounts receivable. The aging schedule shows that $14,100 of accounts receivable will not be collected. Prior to this adjustment, the credit balance in Allowance for uncollectible accounts is $10,500.
2011	
Apr 1	Collected the maturity value of the Good – Mart note
Jun 23	Sold merchandise to Allure receiving a 60-day, 12% note for $8,000. Ignore cost of goods sold.
Aug 22	Allure dishonored its note (failed to pay) at maturity; we converted the maturity value of the note to an account receivable.
Nov 16	Loaned $20,000 cash to Crosby, receiving a 90-day, 9% note
Dec 5	Collected in full on account from Allure
31	Accrued the interest on the Crosby note

Requirement

1. Record the transactions in the journal of Quality Recliner Chairs. Explanations are not required.

P8-30A *(L.OBJ. 7)* **Accounting for notes receivable and accruing interest [35–45 min]**
Cathy Realty loaned money and received the following notes during 2010.

Note	Date	Principal Amount	Interest Rate	Term
(1)	Jun 1	$ 18,000	10%	1 year
(2)	Sep 30	15,000	11%	3 months
(3)	Oct 19	7,000	9%	60 days

Requirements

For each note, compute interest using a 360-day year. Explanations are not required.

1. Determine the due date and maturity value of each note.
2. Journalize the entry to record the inception of the three notes and also journalize a single adjusting entry at October 31, 2010, the fiscal year end, to record accrued interest revenue on all three notes.
3. Journalize the collection of principal and interest at maturity of all three notes.

P8-31A *(L.OBJ. 7)* **Accounting for notes receivable, dishonored notes, and accrued interest revenue [20–30 min]**
Consider the following transactions for AM Publishing.

2011	
Dec 6	Received a $5,000, 60-day, 9% note on account from Hey There Music
31	Made an adjusting entry to accrue interest on the Hey There Music note
31	Made a closing entry for interest revenue
2012	
Feb 4	Collected the maturity value of the Hey There Music note
Jul 1	Loaned $15,000 cash to Pop Music, receiving a 6-month, 8% note
Oct 2	Received a $2,000, 60-day, 8% note for a sale to Union Music. Ignore cost of goods sold.
Dec 1	Union Music dishonored their note at maturity; wrote off the note as uncollectible, debiting Allowance for uncollectible notes.
30	Collected the maturity value of the Pop Music note

Requirement

1. Journalize all transactions for AM Publishing. Round all amounts to the nearest dollar.

P8-32A *(L.OBJ. 8)* **Using ratio data to evaluate a company's financial position [20–30 min]**
The comparative financial statements of True Beauty Cosmetic Supply for 2012, 2011, and 2010 include the data shown here:

	(In thousands)		
	2012	2011	2010
Balance sheet—partial			
Current assets:			
Cash	$ 80	$ 60	$ 50
Short–term investments	130	165	105
Receivables, net	260	270	230
Inventories	365	325	305
Prepaid expenses	55	20	45
Total current assets	$ 890	$ 840	$ 735
Total current liabilities	$ 570	$ 640	$ 660
Income statement—partial			
Sales revenue	$5,870	$5,150	$4,230

Requirements

1. Compute these ratios for 2012 and 2011:
   a. Current ratio
   b. Acid-test ratio
   c. Days' sales in receivables
2. Considering each ratio individually, which ratios improved from 2011 to 2012 and which ratios deteriorated? Is the trend favorable or unfavorable for the company?

■ Problems (Group B)

P8-33B *(L.OBJ. 1, 2)* **Explaining common types of receivables and designing internal controls for receivables [20–30 min]**

The Computer Geeks perform technical consulting services on account, so virtually all cash receipts arrive by mail and are then mailed immediately to the bank. Average daily cash receipts are $28,000. Corrin Strumble, the owner, has just returned from a meeting with new ideas for the business. Among other things, Strumble plans to institute stronger internal controls over cash receipts from customers.

Requirements

1. What types of receivables are most likely to be collected by The Computer Geeks?
2. List the procedures described below in the correct order.

    a. Another person, such as the owner or the manager, compares the amount of the bank deposit to the total of the customer credits posted by the accountant. This gives some assurance that the day's cash receipts went into the bank and that the same amount was posted to customer accounts.

    b. The person who handles cash should not prepare the bank reconciliation.

    c. An employee with no access to the accounting records deposits the cash in the bank immediately.

    d. The remittance slips go to the accountant, who uses them for posting credits to the customer accounts.

    e. Someone other than the accountant opens the mail. This person separates customer checks from the accompanying remittance slips.

P8-34B *(L.OBJ. 3, 4, 5)* **Accounting for uncollectible accounts using the allowance and direct write-off methods and reporting receivables on the balance sheet [20–30 min]**

On May 31, 2011, Rosebud Floral Supply had a $140,000 debit balance in Accounts receivable and a $5,600 credit balance in Allowance for uncollectible accounts. During June, Rosebud made

- Sales on account, $580,000
- Collections on account, $613,000
- Write-offs of uncollectible receivables, $8,000

Requirements

1. Journalize all June entries using the *allowance* method. Uncollectible-account expense was estimated at 2% of credit sales. Show all June activity in Accounts receivable, Allowance for uncollectible accounts, and Uncollectible-account expense (post to these T-accounts).
2. Using the same facts, assume instead that Rosebud used the direct write-off method to account for uncollectible receivables. Journalize all June entries using the *direct write-off* method. Post to Accounts receivable and Uncollectible-account expense and show their balances at June 30, 2011.
3. What amount of uncollectible-account expense would Rosebud report on its June income statement under each of the two methods? Which amount better matches expense with revenue? Give your reason.
4. What amount of *net* accounts receivable would Rosebud report on its June 30, 2011, balance sheet under each of the two methods? Which amount is more realistic? Give your reason.

P8-35B *(L.OBJ. 3, 5)* **Accounting for uncollectible accounts using the allowance method, and reporting receivables on the balance sheet [25–35 min]**
At September 30, 2011, the accounts of East Terrance Medical Center (ETMC) include the following:

Accounts receivable	$ 144,000
Allowance for uncollectible accounts (credit balance) ...	3,100

During the last quarter of 2011, ETMC completed the following selected transactions:

Dec 28	Wrote off accounts receivable as uncollectible: Green Co., $1,500; Jacob Weiss, $900; and Star, $400.
Dec 31	Recorded uncollectible-account expense based on the aging of accounts receivable, as follows:

	Age of Accounts			
Accounts receivable	1–30 Days	31–60 Days	61–90 Days	Over 90 Days
$164,000	$100,000	$ 40,000	$ 15,000	$ 9,000
Estimated percent uncollectible	0.1%	1%	10%	30%

Requirements

1. Journalize the transactions.
2. Open the Allowance for uncollectible accounts T-account, and post entries affecting that account. Keep a running balance.
3. Show how East Terrance Medical Center should report accounts receivable on its December 31, 2011, balance sheet. Use the three line reporting format.

P8-36B *(L.OBJ. 3, 5)* **Accounting for uncollectible accounts using the allowance method (percentage of sales), and reporting receivables on the balance sheet [20–30 min]**
Dialex Watches completed the following selected transactions during 2010 and 2011:

2010	
Dec 31	Estimated that uncollectible-account expense for the year was 1% of credit sales of $430,000 and recorded that amount as expense. Use the allowance method.
Dec 31	Made the closing entry for uncollectible-account expense
2011	
Jan 17	Sold inventory to Marty Viller, $700, on account. Ignore cost of goods sold.
Jun 29	Wrote off Marty Viller's account as uncollectible after repeated efforts to collect from him
Aug 6	Received $700 from Marty Viller, along with a letter apologizing for being so late. Reinstated Viller's account in full and recorded the cash receipt.
Dec 31	Made a compound entry to write off the following accounts as uncollectible: Bob Keffer, $1,700; Maggie Marquet, $1,200; and Ronald Richter, $400.
Dec 31	Estimated that uncollectible-account expense for the year was 1% on credit sales of $500,000 and recorded the expense
Dec 31	Made the closing entry for uncollectible-account expense

Requirements

1. Open T-accounts for Allowance for uncollectible accounts and Uncollectible-account expense. Keep running balances, assuming all accounts begin with a zero balance.
2. Record the transactions in the general journal, and post to the two T-accounts.
3. The December 31, 2011, balance of Accounts receivable is $132,000. Show how Accounts receivable would be reported on the balance sheet at that date. Use the three line format of reporting the net accounts receivable.

P8-37B *(L.OBJ. 3, 6, 7)* **Accounting for uncollectible accounts (aging of accounts method), bankcard sales, notes receivable, and accrued interest revenue [20–30 min]**

Resting Recliner Chairs completed the following selected transactions:

2010	
Jul 1	Sold inventory to Green – Mart, receiving a $41,000, 9-month, 12% note. Ignore cost of goods sold.
Dec 31	Made an adjusting entry to accrue interest on the Green – Mart note
31	Made an adjusting entry to record uncollectible account expense based on an aging of account receivable. The aging schedule shows that $14,900 of accounts receivable will not be collected. Prior to this adjustment, the credit balance in Allowance for uncollectible accounts is $11,800.
2011	
Apr 1	Collected the maturity value of the Green – Mart note
Jun 23	Sold merchandise to Aglow, receiving a 60-day, 9% note for $11,000. Ignore cost of goods sold.
Aug 22	Aglow dishonored its note (failed to pay) at maturity; we converted the maturity value of the note to an account receivable.
Nov 16	Loaned $19,000 cash to Crane, receiving a 90-day, 8% note
Dec 5	Collected in full on account from Aglow
31	Accrued the interest on the Crane note

Requirement

1. Record the transactions in the journal of Resting Recliner Chairs. Explanations are not required.

P8-38B *(L.OBJ. 7)* **Accounting for notes receivable and accruing interest [35–45 min]**

Kelly Realty loaned money and received the following notes during 2010:

Note	Date	Principal Amount	Interest Rate	Term
(1)	Jun 1	$ 16,000	13%	1 year
(2)	Sep 30	14,000	8%	3 months
(3)	Oct 19	11,000	9%	60 days

Requirements

For each note, compute interest using a 360-day year. Explanations are not required.

1. Determine the due date and maturity value of each note.

2. Journalize the entry to record the inception of the note and also journalize a single adjusting entry at October 31, 2010, the fiscal year end, to record accrued interest revenue on all three notes.
3. Journalize the collection of principal and interest at maturity of all three notes.

P8-39B *(L.OBJ. 7)* **Accounting for notes receivable, dishonored notes, and accrued interest revenue [20–30 min]**

Consider the following transactions for TLC Company.

2010	
Dec 21	Received a $6,500, 60-day, 11% note on account from GG Publishing
31	Made an adjusting entry to accrue interest on the GG Publishing note
31	Made a closing entry for interest revenue
2011	
Feb 19	Collected the maturity value of the GG Publishing note
Jul 1	Loaned $13,000 cash to Love Joy Music, receiving a 6-month, 10% note
Oct 2	Received a $2,600, 60-day, 10% note for a sale to Union Music. Ignore cost of goods sold.
Dec 1	Union Music dishonored their note at maturity; wrote off the note as uncollectible, debiting Allowance for uncollectible notes.
30	Collected the maturity value of the Love Joy Music note

Requirement

1. Journalize all transactions for TLC Company. Round all amounts to the nearest dollar.

P8-40B *(L.OBJ. 8)* **Using ratio data to evaluate a company's financial position [20–30 min]**

The comparative financial statements of True Beauty Cosmetic Supply for 2012, 2011, and 2010 include the data that follow:

	(In thousands)		
	2012	2011	2010
Balance sheet—partial			
Current assets:			
Cash	$ 70	$ 60	$ 50
Short-term investments	150	160	105
Receivables, net	290	260	250
Inventories	360	330	310
Prepaid expenses	70	10	40
Total current assets	$ 940	$ 820	$ 755
Total current liabilities	$ 570	$ 600	$ 670
Income statement—partial			
Sales revenue	$5,880	$5,140	$4,230

Requirements

1. Compute these ratios for 2012 and 2011:
   a. Current ratio
   b. Acid-test ratio
   c. Days' sales in receivables
2. Considering each ratio individually, which ratios improved from 2011 to 2012 and which ratios deteriorated? Is the trend favorable or unfavorable for the company?

Continuing Exercise

E8-41 This exercise continues the Sherman Lawn Service situation from Exercise 7-41 of Chapter 7. Sherman reviewed the receivables list from the September transactions (from Chapter 6). Sherman identified that Daniel was not going to pay his receivable from September 15. Sherman uses the direct write-off method to account for uncollectible accounts.

Requirement

1. Journalize the entry to record Daniel's uncollectible account.

Continuing Problem

P8-42 This problem continues the Haupt Consulting situation from Problem 7-42 of Chapter 7. Haupt reviewed the receivables list from the January transactions (from Chapter 6). Haupt identified that Gene was not going to pay his receivable from January 28. Haupt uses the allowance method for receivables, estimating uncollectibles to be 3% of credit sales.

Requirements

1. Journalize the entry to record and establish the allowance using the percentage method for February credit sales.
2. Journalize the entry to record the identification of Gene's bad debt.

Practice Set

This problem continues the Crystal Clear Cleaning problem begun in Chapter 1 and continued through Chapters 2–7.

P8-43 Consider the following June transactions for Crystal Clear Cleaning:

1	Sold goods to Amanda's A-list for $5,000 on terms, 2/10, n/20. Cost of goods sold was $2,200.
3	Crystal Clear decides to adopt the allowance method. Uncollectible account expense is estimated at 1% of credit sales.
10	Borrowed money Vanguard Bank, $10,000, 10% for 180 days
12	Wrote off outstanding receivable from Amanda's A list as uncollectible
15	Sold goods to Brighton for $2,000 on terms 2/10, n/30. Cost of goods sold was $800.
15	Recorded uncollectible account expense estimate for Brighton sale
28	Sold goods to Hillary for cash of $600 (cost $200)
28	Collected from Amanda's A list $3,000 of receivable previously written off. Reinstated the remaining balance of Amanda's receivable.
29	Paid cash for Utilities of $350.
30	Created an aging schedule for Crystal Clear for accounts receivable. Crystal determined that accounts 1-20 days old were 1% uncollectible and accounts Over 20 days old were 10% uncollectible. She prepared an aging schedule and adjusted the Allowance for uncollectible accounts to the aging schedule.
30	Crystal prepared all other adjusting entries necessary for June

Requirement

1. Prepare all required journal entries and post them to Crystal Clear's ledger.

Apply Your Knowledge

■ Decision Cases

Case 1. Weddings on Demand sells on account and manages its own receivables. Average experience for the past three years has been as follows:

	Total
Sales	$350,000
Cost of goods sold	210,000
Bad-debt expense	4,000
Other expenses	61,000

Aledia Sanchez, the owner, is considering whether to accept bankcards (**VISA, MasterCard**) from customers because some are slow to pay. Typically, accepting bankcards increases total sales and cost of goods sold by 10%. But **VISA** and **MasterCard** charge a fee of approximately 2% of bankcard sales. If Sanchez switches to bankcards, she will no longer have bad-debt expense. She can also save $5,000 on other expenses. After the switchover to bankcards, Sanchez expects credit card sales of $200,000.

Requirement

1. Should Sanchez start accepting bankcards? Show the computations of net income under her present arrangement and under the bankcard plan. (Challenge)

Case 2. Pauline's Pottery has always used the direct write-off method to account for uncollectibles. The company's revenues, bad-debt write offs, and year-end receivables for the most recent year follow:

Year	Revenues	Write-Offs	Receivables at Year-End
2011	$150,000	$3,900	$14,000

The business is applying for a bank loan, and the loan officer requires figures based on the allowance method of accounting for bad debts. In the past, bad debts have run about 4% of revenues.

Requirements

Pauline must give the banker the following information:

1. How much more or less would net income be for 2011 if Pauline's Pottery were to use the allowance method for bad debts?
2. How much of the receivables balance at the end of 2011 does Pauline's Pottery actually expect to collect?
3. Compute these amounts, and then explain for Pauline's Pottery why net income is more or less using the allowance method versus the direct write-off method for uncollectibles.

Ethical Issue

E-Z Loan, Co., makes loans to high-risk borrowers. E-Z borrows from its bank and then lends money to people with bad credit. The bank requires E-Z Loan to submit quarterly financial statements in order to keep its line of credit. E-Z's main asset is Notes receivable. Therefore, Uncollectible-note expense and Allowance for uncollectible notes are important accounts.

Slade McMurphy, the owner of E-Z Loan, wants net income to increase in a smooth pattern, rather than increase in some periods and decrease in others. To report smoothly increasing net income, McMurphy underestimates Uncollectible-note expense in some periods. In other periods, McMurphy overestimates the expense. He reasons that over time the income overstatements roughly offset the income understatements.

Requirement

1. Is McMurphy's practice of smoothing income ethical? Why or why not?

Financial Statement Case

Use **Amazon.com's** balance sheet and the Note 1 data on "Allowance for doubtful accounts" in Appendix A at the end of this book.

Requirements

1. Do accounts receivable appear to be an important asset for **Amazon.com**? What about **Amazon's** business affects the importance of accounts receivable?
2. Assume that all of "Accounts receivable, Net, and Other Current Assets" is accounts receivable. Further assume that gross receivables at December 31, 2007, were $317 million. Answer the following questions based on these data, plus what is reported on the balance sheet.
   a. How much did customers owe **Amazon.com** at December 31, 2007?
   b. How much did **Amazon.com** expect to collect from customers after December 31, 2007?
   c. Of the total receivable amount at December 31, 2007, how much did **Amazon.com** expect *not* to collect?
3. Compute **Amazon.com's** acid-test ratio at the end of 2007. Marketable securities are short-term investments. Assume that other current assets are zero. If all the current liabilities came due immediately, could **Amazon** pay them?

Team Project

Notes Receivable of the Bank. Bob Davidson and Sheila Thornton worked for several years as sales representatives for **Xerox Corporation**. During this time, they became close friends as they acquired expertise with the company's full range of copier equipment. Now they see an opportunity to put their experience to work and fulfill lifelong desires to establish their own business. Rolltide College, located in their city, is expanding, and there is no copy center within five miles of the campus. Business in the area is booming, and the population in this section of the city is growing.

Davidson and Thornton want to open a copy center, similar to a **FedEx Kinko's**, near the campus. A small shopping center across the street from the college has a vacancy that would fit their needs. Davidson and Thornton each have $20,000 to invest in the business, and they forecast the need for $30,000 to renovate the store. **Xerox Corporation** will lease two large copiers to them at a total monthly rental of $4,000. With enough cash to see them through the first six months of operation, they are confident they can make the business succeed. The two work very well together, and both have excellent credit ratings. Davidson and Thornton must borrow $80,000 to start the business, advertise its opening, and keep it running for its first six months.

Assume the role of Davidson and Thornton, the partners who will own Rolltide Copy Center.

Requirements

1. As a group, visit a copy center to familiarize yourselves with its operations. If possible, interview the manager or another employee. Then write a loan request that Davidson and Thornton will submit to a bank with the intent of borrowing $80,000 to be paid back over three years. The loan will be a personal loan to the partnership of Davidson and Thornton, not to Rolltide Copy Center. The request should specify all the details of Davidson and Thornton's plan that will motivate the bank to grant the loan. Include a budgeted income statement for the first six months of the copy center's operation.
2. As a group, interview a loan officer in a bank. Have the loan officer evaluate your loan request. Write a report, or make a presentation to your class—as directed by your instructor—to reveal the loan officer's decision.

Quick Check Answers

1. *d* 2. *d* 3. *c* 4. *d* 5. *a* 6. *d* 7. *b* 8. *b* 9. *c* 10. *c*

For online homework, exercises, and problems that provide you immediate feedback, please visit www.myaccountinglab.com.

Appendix 8A

Discounting a Note Receivable

A payee of a note receivable may need cash before the maturity date of the note. When this occurs, the payee may sell the note, a practice called **discounting a note receivable.** The price to be received for the note is determined by present-value concepts. But the transaction between the seller and the buyer of the note can take any form agreeable to the two parties. Here we illustrate one procedure used for discounting short-term notes receivable. To receive cash immediately, the seller accepts a lower price than the note's maturity value.

To illustrate discounting a note receivable, recall that earlier in the chapter, Blanding Services loaned $1,000 to L. Holland on September 30, 2011. Blanding took a note receivable from Holland. The maturity date of the 1 year 9% Holland note is September 30, 2012. Suppose Blanding discounts the Holland note at First City Bank on November 30, 2011, when the note is 2 months old. The bank applies a 12% annual interest rate to determine the discounted value of the note. The bank will use a discount rate that is higher than the note's interest rate in order to earn some interest on the transaction. The discounted value, called the *proceeds*, is the amount Blanding receives from the bank. The proceeds can be computed in five steps, as shown in Exhibit 8A-1.

EXHIBIT 8A-1 | Discounting (Selling) a Note Receivable

Step	Computation		
1. Compute the original amount of interest on the note receivable.	$1,000 × .09 × 12/12	=	$ 90
2. Maturity value of the note = Principal + Interest	$1,000 + $90	=	$1,090
3. Determine the period (number of days, months, or years) the *bank* will hold the note (the discount period).	Dec 1, 2011 to Sep 30, 2012	=	10 months
4. Compute the bank's discount on the note. This is the bank's interest revenue from holding the note.	$1,090 × 0.12 × 10/12	=	$ 109
5. Seller's proceeds from discounting the note receivable = Maturity value of the note − Bank's discount on the note.	$1,090 − $109	=	$ 981

The authors thank Doug Hamilton for suggesting this exhibit.

Blanding's entry to record discounting (selling) the note on November 30, 2011, is:

2011			
Nov 30	Cash (A+)	981	
	Interest expense (E+)	19	
	Note receivable—L. Holland (A−)		1,000
	Discounted a note receivable.		

When the proceeds from discounting a note receivable are less than the principal amount of the note, the payee records a debit to Interest expense for the amount of the difference. When the proceeds from discounting the note are more than the note principal, the payee records a credit to Interest revenue. For example, assume Blanding discounts the note receivable for cash proceeds of $1,020. The entry to record this discounting transaction is:

2011			
Nov 30	Cash (A+)	1,020	
	Note receivable—L. Holland (A–)		1,000
	Interest revenue (R+)		20
	Discounted a note receivable.		

Appendix 8A Assignments

Exercise

E8A-1 **Journalizing notes receivable transactions [10–15 min]**
Big Tex Toys sells on account. When a customer account becomes three months old, Big Tex converts the account to a note receivable and immediately discounts the note to a bank. During 2012, Big Tex completed the following transactions:

Aug 29	Sold goods on account to V. Miner, $4,000
Dec 1	Received a $4,000, 60-day, 8% note from Miner in satisfaction of his past-due account receivable
Dec 1	Sold the Miner note by discounting it to a bank for $3,700

Requirement

1. Record the transactions in Big Tex's journal.

Problem (Group A)

P8A-2 **Journalizing notes receivable transactions [15–20 min]**
A company received the following notes during 2012. The notes were discounted on the dates and at the rates indicated:

Note	Date	Principal Amount	Interest Rate	Term	Date Discounted	Discount Rate
(1)	Aug 1	$ 9,000	12%	120 days	Oct 15	15%
(2)	Jun 19	8,000	10%	90 days	Jun 20	12%
(3)	Aug 15	6,000	6%	6 months	Sep 15	8%

Requirements

Identify each note by number, compute interest using a 360-day year, and round all interest amounts to the nearest dollar. Explanations are not required.

1. Determine the due date and maturity value of each note.
2. Determine the discount and proceeds from the sale (discounting) of each note.
3. Journalize the discounting of notes (1) and (2).

Problem (Group B)

P8A-3 Journalizing notes receivable transactions [15–20 min]

A company received the following notes during 2012. The notes were discounted on the dates and at the rates indicated:

Note	Date	Principal Amount	Interest Rate	Term	Date Discounted	Discount Rate
(1)	Sep 1	$ 10,000	11%	120 days	Nov 2	14%
(2)	Jun 19	12,000	7%	90 days	Jun 20	9%
(3)	Aug 15	5,000	9%	6 months	Sep 15	11%

Requirements

Identify each note by number, compute interest using a 360-day year, and round all interest amounts to the nearest dollar. Explanations are not required.

1. Determine the due date and maturity value of each note.
2. Determine the discount and proceeds from the sale (discounting) of each note.
3. Journalize the discounting of notes (1) and (2).

9 Plant Assets and Intangibles

Learning Objectives/ Success Keys

1. Measure the cost of a plant asset
2. Account for depreciation
3. Record the disposal of an asset by sale or trade
4. Account for natural resources
5. Account for intangible assets
6. Describe ethical issues related to plant assets

Your business, Smart Touch Learning, is at a crossroads. So far, you have hired outsiders to create the CDs and DVDs that you sell. By letting three manufacturers compete against each other, you have been able to hold costs down. But two of the manufacturers have gone out of business and the only one remaining has increased fees. What can you do?

One option is to purchase CD/DVD burning equipment and create the training CDs and DVDs yourself. You will have to pay $30,000 for the equipment, but the cost savings should help you recoup your outlay within a year. Plus, you will not have to wait for the manufacturers. Sheena Bright decides to purchase the equipment.

Equipment is one type of plant asset. Other types include land, buildings, computers, and furniture. Often plant assets are referred to as Property, Plant, and Equipment. Plant assets have some special characteristics. For example, you hold them for use in the business—not to sell as inventory. Also,

- plant assets are relatively expensive.
- the full cost invested in plant assets can be a challenge to determine, because of the difficulty of tracking installation, shipping, and other costs related to the asset.
- plant assets usually last several years and, as a result, should be allocated over the years they are expected to be used.
- plant assets may be sold or traded in. Accounting for the disposal of a plant asset is important because the disposal may create a gain or loss that must be reported on the income statement.

As you can see, plant assets pose some accounting challenges. This chapter addresses these issues and shows how to account for the following:

1. **Real or tangible assets.** This includes assets whose physical characteristics define their utility or usefulness, such as buildings, desks, and equipment.
2. **Intangible assets.** This includes assets whose value is not derived from their physicality. For example, software programs on a CD are intangible assets. The "physical" CD is not the value—the knowledge/programs on the CD really represent the asset.
3. **Natural resources assets.** This includes assets that come from the ground and can ultimately be used up. For example, oil, diamonds, and coal are all natural resource assets.

Chapter 9 concludes our coverage of assets, except for investments. After completing this chapter, you should understand the various assets of a business and how to account for them.

Plant assets have their own terminology. Exhibit 9-1 shows which expense applies to each category of plant asset.

EXHIBIT 9-1 | **Plant Assets and Their Related Expenses**

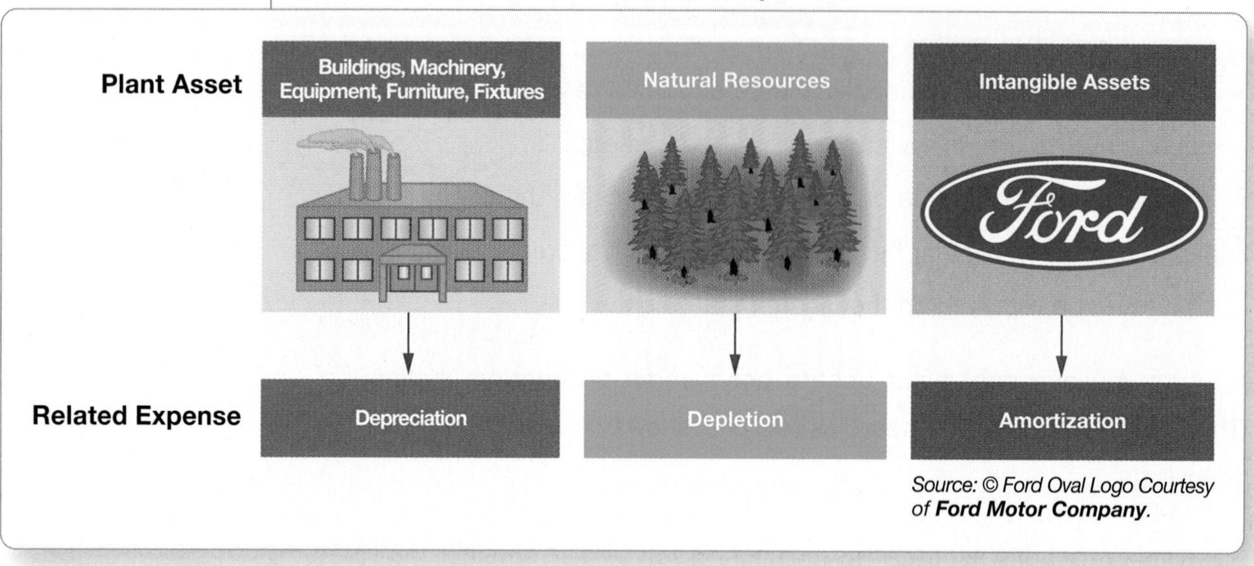

*Source: © Ford Oval Logo Courtesy of **Ford Motor Company**.*

Measuring the Cost of a Plant Asset

1 Measure the cost of a plant asset

The *cost principle* says to carry an asset at its historical cost—the amount paid for the asset. The rule for measuring cost is as follows:

Cost of an asset = Sum of all the costs incurred to bring the asset to its intended purpose, net of all discounts

The *cost of a plant asset* is its purchase price plus taxes, purchase commissions, and all other amounts paid to ready the asset for its intended use. In Chapter 6, we applied this principle to inventory. These costs vary, so let us discuss each asset individually.

Land and Land Improvements

The cost of land is not depreciated. It includes the following costs paid by the purchaser:

- Purchase price
- Brokerage commission
- Survey and legal fees
- Property taxes in arrears
- Taxes assessed to transfer the ownership (title) on the land
- Cost of clearing the land and removing unwanted buildings

The cost of land does *not* include the following costs:

- Fencing
- Paving

- Sprinkler systems
- Lighting
- Signs

These separate plant assets—called **land improvements**—are subject to depreciation.

Suppose Smart Touch Learning needs property and purchases land for $50,000 with a note payable for the same amount. Smart Touch also pays cash as follows: $4,000 in property taxes in arrears, $2,000 in transfer taxes, $5,000 to remove an old building, and a $1,000 survey fee. What is the company's cost of this land? Exhibit 9-2 shows all the costs incurred to bring the land to its intended use:

EXHIBIT 9-2 | Measuring the Cost of Land

Purchase price of land		$50,000
Add related costs:		
Back property taxes	$4,000	
Transfer taxes	2,000	
Removal of building	5,000	
Survey fee	1,000	
Total related costs		12,000
Total cost of land		$62,000

The entry to record the purchase of the land on August 1, 2010, follows:

2010			
Aug 1	Land (A+)	62,000	
	Note payable (L+)		50,000
	Cash (A–)		12,000

We would say that Smart Touch *capitalized* the cost of the land at $62,000. **Capitalized** means that an asset account was debited (increased) for an asset. So, for our land example, Smart Touch debited the Land account for $62,000, the capitalized cost of the asset.

Suppose Smart Touch then pays $20,000 for fences, paving, lighting, and signs on August 15, 2010. The following entry records the cost of these land improvements:

2010			
Aug 15	Land improvements (A+)	20,000	
	Cash (A–)		20,000

Land and Land Improvements are two entirely separate assets. Recall that land is not depreciated. However, the cost of land improvements *is* depreciated over that asset's useful life.

Buildings

The cost of a building includes

- Architectural fees
- Building permits
- Contractor charges
- Payments for material, labor, and overhead

The time to complete a building can be months, even years. If the company constructs its own assets, the cost of the building may include the cost of interest on borrowed money. If it purchases an existing building, its cost includes the purchase price, plus the cost to repair and renovate the building for its intended use.

Machinery and Equipment

The cost of machinery and equipment includes its

- Purchase price (less any discounts)
- Transportation charges
- Insurance while in transit
- Sales and other taxes
- Purchase commission
- Installation costs
- Cost of testing the asset before it is used

After the asset is up and running, the company no longer debits insurance, taxes, and maintenance costs to the Equipment account. From that point on, insurance, taxes, repairs, and maintenance costs are recorded as expenses.

There are many different kinds of equipment. Smart Touch Learning has CD/DVD burning equipment. **American Airlines** has airplanes, and **Kinko's** has copiers. Most businesses have computer equipment.

Furniture and Fixtures

Furniture and fixtures include desks, chairs, file cabinets, display racks, shelving, and so forth. The cost of furniture and fixtures includes the basic cost of each asset (less any discounts), plus all other costs to ready the asset for its intended use. For example, for a desk, this may include the costs to ship the desk to the business and the cost paid to a handyman to assemble the desk.

A Lump-Sum (Basket) Purchase of Assets

A company may pay a single price for several assets as a group—a "basket purchase." For example, Smart Touch Learning may pay one price for land and a building. For accounting, the company must identify the cost of each asset, as shown in the following diagram. The total cost (100%) is divided among the assets according to their relative sales values. This is called the **relative-sales-value method.**

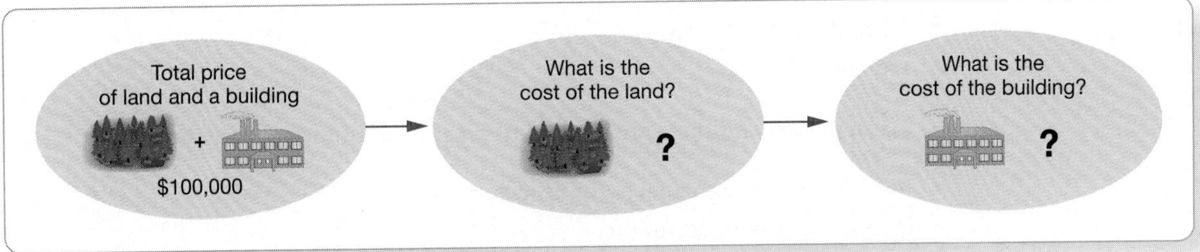

Suppose Smart Touch paid a combined purchase price of $100,000 on August 1 for the land and building. An appraisal performed a month before the purchase indicates that the land's market (sales) value is $30,000 and the building's market (sales) value is $90,000. It is clear that Smart Touch got a good deal, paying less than fair market value, which is $120,000 for the combined assets. But how will Smart Touch allocate the $100,000 paid for both assets?

First, figure the ratio of each asset's market value to the total for both assets combined. The total appraised value is $120,000.

Land M.V.	+	Building M.V.	=	Total Market Value
$30,000	+	$90,000	=	$120,000

The land makes up 25% of the total market value, and the building 75%, as follows:

Asset	Market (Sales) Value	Percentage of Total Value	×	Total Purchase Price	=	Cost of Each Asset
Land	$ 30,000	$30,000/$120,000 = 25%	×	$100,000	=	$ 25,000
Building	90,000	$90,000/$120,000 = 75%	×	100,000	=	75,000
Total	$120,000	100%				$100,000

For Smart Touch's accounting, the land cost $25,000 and the building cost $75,000. Suppose Smart Touch paid with a 100% notes payable. The entry to record the purchase of the land and building is as follows:

2010			
Aug 1	Land (A+)	25,000	
	Building (A+)	75,000	
	Notes payable (L+)		100,000

Capital Expenditures

Accountants divide spending made on plant assets into two categories:

- Capital expenditures
- Expenses

Capital expenditures are debited to an asset account because they

- increase the asset's capacity or efficiency, or
- extend the asset's useful life.

Examples of capital expenditures include the purchase price plus all the other costs to bring an asset to its intended use, as discussed in the preceding sections. Also, an **extraordinary repair** is a capital expenditure because it extends the asset's capacity or useful life. An example of an extraordinary repair would be rebuilding the engine on a five-year-old truck. This extraordinary repair would extend the asset's life past the normal expected life. As a result, its cost would be debited to the asset account for the truck.

Expenses incurred to maintain the asset in working order, such as repair or maintenance expense, are *not* debited to an asset account. Examples include the costs of maintaining equipment, such as repairing the air conditioner on a truck, changing the oil filter, and replacing its tires. These **ordinary repairs** are debited to Repair and maintenance expense. Exhibit 9-3 shows some (a) capital expenditures and (b) expenses for a delivery truck.

EXHIBIT 9-3 **Delivery Truck Expenditures—Capital Expenditure or Expense?**

CAPITAL EXPENDITURE: Debit an Asset Account	EXPENSE: Debit Repair and maintenance expense
Extraordinary repairs:	*Ordinary repairs:*
Major engine or transmission overhaul	Repair of transmission or engine
Modification for new use	Oil change, lubrication, and so on
Addition to storage capacity	Replacement of tires or windshield
	Paint job

Treating a capital expenditure as an expense, or vice versa, creates an accounting error. Suppose Greg's Groovy Tunes replaces the engine in the truck. This would be an extraordinary repair because it increases the truck's life. If the company expenses the cost by debiting Repair and maintenance expense, rather than capitalizing it (debiting the asset), the company would be making an accounting error. This error

- Overstates Repair and maintenance expenses
- Understates net income
- Understates Capital
- Understates the Equipment account on the balance sheet

Incorrectly capitalizing an expense creates the opposite error. Assume a minor repair, such as replacing the water pump on the truck, was incorrectly debited to the Asset account. The error would result in expenses being understated and net income being overstated. Additionally, the balance sheet would overstate the truck assets by the amount of the repair bill.

Depreciation

2 Account for depreciation

As we learned in an earlier chapter, *depreciation* is the allocation of a plant asset's cost to expense over its useful life. Depreciation matches the expense against the revenue generated from using the asset to measure net income. Exhibit 9-4 illustrates this matching of revenues and depreciation expense for a $40,000 truck (numbers assumed).

EXHIBIT 9-4 | **Depreciation and the Matching of Expense with Revenue**

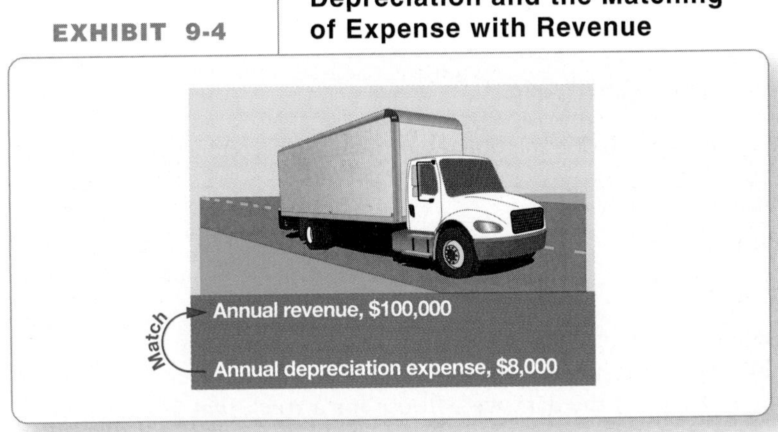

Causes of Depreciation

All assets, except land, wear out as they are used. Greg's delivery truck can only go so many miles before it is worn out. As the truck is driven, this use is part of what causes depreciation. Additionally, physical factors, like age and weather, can cause depreciation of assets.

Some assets, such as computers and software, may become *obsolete* before they wear out. An asset is **obsolete** when a newer asset can perform the job more efficiently. As a result, an asset's useful life may be shorter than its physical life. In all cases, the asset's cost is depreciated over its useful life. Now that we have discussed causes of depreciation, let us contrast with what depreciation is *not.*

1. *Depreciation is not a process of valuation.* Businesses do not record depreciation based on changes in the asset's market (sales) value. Depreciation is recapturing the cost invested in the asset.
2. *Depreciation does not mean that the business sets aside cash to replace an asset when it is used up.* Depreciation has nothing to do with cash.

Measuring Depreciation

Depreciation of a plant asset is based on three factors:

1. Cost
2. Estimated useful life
3. Estimated residual value

Cost is known and, as mentioned earlier in this chapter, includes all items spent for the asset to perform its intended function. The other two factors are estimates.

Estimated useful life is the length of the service period expected from the asset. Useful life may be expressed in years, units, output, or miles. For each asset, the goal is to define the estimated useful life with the measure (years, units, etc.) that best mimics the asset's decline or use. For example, a building's life is stated in years, a truck's in the number of miles it can drive, and a **Xerox** copier's in the number of copies it can make.

Estimated residual value—also called **salvage value**—is the asset's expected cash value at the end of its useful life. A delivery truck's useful life may be 100,000 miles. When the truck has driven that distance, the company will sell or scrap it. The expected cash receipt at the end of the truck's life is the truck's estimated residual value. Estimated residual value is *not* depreciated because you expect to receive this amount at the end. Cost minus residual value is called **depreciable cost.**

Depreciable cost = Cost – Estimated residual value

Depreciation Methods

There are many depreciation methods, but three are used most commonly:

- Straight-line
- Units-of-production
- Declining-balance

These methods work differently in *how* they derive the yearly depreciation amount, but they all result in the same total depreciation over the total life of the asset. Exhibit 9-5 gives the data we will use for a truck that Greg's Groovy Tunes purchases and places in service on January 1, 2011.

EXHIBIT 9-5 Data for Recording Depreciation on a Truck

Data Item	Amount
Cost of truck	$41,000
Less: Estimated residual value	(1,000)
Depreciable cost	$40,000
Estimated useful life	
Years	5 years
Units	100,000 mi.

Straight-Line Method

The **straight-line (SL) method** allocates an equal amount of depreciation to each year. Greg's Groovy Tunes might want to use this method for the truck if it thinks time is the best indicator of the truck's depreciation. The equation for SL depreciation, applied to the Greg's Groovy Tunes' truck, is as follows:

$$\text{Straight-line depreciation} = (\text{Cost} - \text{Residual value}) \times \frac{1}{\text{life}} \times \frac{\#}{12}$$

$$= (41{,}000 - 1{,}000) \times \frac{1}{5} \times \frac{12}{12}$$

$$= \$8{,}000 \text{ per year}$$

represents the number of months used in a year

Since the asset was placed in service on the first day of the year, the entry to record each year's depreciation is as follows:

	Account	Debit	Credit
	Depreciation expense (A+)	8,000	
	Accumulated depreciation (CA+)		8,000

A straight-line depreciation schedule for this truck is shown in Exhibit 9-6.

EXHIBIT 9-6 **Straight-Line Depreciation for a Truck**

		Depreciation for the Year							
Date	Asset Cost	Depreciation Rate		Depreciable Cost		Depreciation Expense	Accumulated Depreciation	Book Value	
1-1-2011	$41,000							$41,000	
12-31-2011		0.20*	×	$40,000	=	$8,000	$ 8,000	33,000	
12-31-2012		0.20	×	40,000	=	8,000	16,000	25,000	
12-31-2013		0.20	×	40,000	=	8,000	24,000	17,000	
12-31-2014		0.20	×	40,000	=	8,000	32,000	9,000	
12-31-2015		0.20	×	40,000	=	8,000	40,000	1,000	← Residual value

*1/5 year = 0.20 per year

The final column shows the asset's *book value*, which is cost less accumulated depreciation.

As an asset is used, accumulated depreciation increases and book value decreases. See the Accumulated depreciation and Book value columns in Exhibit 9-6. At the end, the asset is said to be **fully depreciated.** An asset's final book value is called its residual value ($1,000 in this example).

Units-of-Production (UOP) Method

The **units-of-production (UOP) method** allocates a fixed amount of depreciation to each unit of output. As we noted above, a unit of output can be miles, units, hours, or output, depending on which unit type best defines the asset's use.

$$\text{Units-of-production depreciation per unit of output} = (\text{Cost} - \text{Residual value}) \times \frac{1}{\text{life in units}}$$

$$= (41{,}000 - 1{,}000) \times \frac{1}{100{,}000}$$

$$= \$.40 \text{ per mile}$$

The truck in our example is estimated to be driven 20,000 miles the first year, 30,000 the second, 25,000 the third, 15,000 the fourth, and 10,000 during the fifth (for a total of 100,000 miles). The UOP depreciation each period varies with the number of units (miles, in the case of the truck) the asset produces.

Units-of-Production for Greg's Groovy Tunes' truck is illustrated in Exhibit 9-7. Greg's Groovy Tunes might want to use UOP depreciation for the truck if it thinks miles is the best measure of the truck's depreciation.

EXHIBIT 9-7 | **Units-of-Production Depreciation for a Truck**

		Depreciation for the Year							
Date	Asset Cost	Depreciation Per Unit		Number of Units		Depreciation Expense	Accumulated Depreciation	Book Value	
1-1-2011	$41,000							$41,000	
12-31-2011		$0.40	×	20,000	=	$ 8,000	$ 8,000	33,000	
12-31-2012		0.40	×	30,000	=	12,000	20,000	21,000	
12-31-2013		0.40	×	25,000	=	10,000	30,000	11,000	
12-31-2014		0.40	×	15,000	=	6,000	36,000	5,000	
12-31-2015		0.40	×	10,000	=	4,000	40,000	1,000	← Residual value

Double-Declining-Balance Method

The main accelerated method of depreciation is the **double-declining-balance (DDB)**. An **accelerated depreciation method** writes off more depreciation near the start of an asset's life than straight-line does. Greg's Groovy Tunes might want to use this method for its tax return preparation so it could recover more depreciation in the earlier years of the truck's use and pay less taxes. The DDB method multiplies decreasing book value by a constant percentage that is twice the straight-line rate. DDB amounts can be computed using the following formula:

Double-Declining Balance depreciation = (Cost – Accumulated depreciation) × 2/life × #/12

For the first year of the truck, the calculation would be as shown:

DDB, year 1 = (41,000 – 0) × 2/5 × 12/12 or $16,400

In year 2, the amount of depreciation would decline because the asset has accumulated some depreciation (the $16,400 for the first year). For the second year of the truck, therefore, the calculation would be as shown:

DDB, year 2 = (41,000 – 16,400) × 2/5 × 12/12 or $9,840

Note that **residual value is not included in the formula. Residual value is ignored until the last year.**

Final-year depreciation is calculated as the amount needed to bring the asset to its residual value. In the case of the truck, Residual value was given at $1,000. In the DDB schedule Exhibit 9-8 notice that, after year 4 (12/31/2014), the truck's book value is $5,314. By definition, the truck is to last five years, which ends on 12/31/2015. Also by definition, at the end of the asset's life, its value should equal the residual value. Therefore, in the final-year, depreciation is book value, $5,314, less the $1,000 residual value, or $4,314 in depreciation expense.

EXHIBIT 9-8 | **Double-Declining-Balance Depreciation for a Truck**

		Depreciation for the Year							
Date	Asset Cost	DDB Rate		Book Value		Depreciation Expense	Accumulated Depreciation	Book Value	
1-1-2011	$41,000							$41,000	
12-31-2011		0.40	×	$41,000	=	$16,400	$16,400	24,600	
12-31-2012		0.40	×	24,600	=	9,840	26,240	14,760	
12-31-2013		0.40	×	14,760	=	5,904	32,144	8,856	
12-31-2014		0.40	×	8,856	=	3,542	35,686	5,314	
12-31-2015					=	4,314*	40,000	1,000	← Residual value

*Last-year depreciation is the "plug figure" needed to reduce book value to the residual amount ($5,314 – $1,000 = $4,314).

SWITCHOVER TO STRAIGHT-LINE Some companies change to the straight-line method during the next-to-last year of the asset's life to "level-off" end-of-life depreciation. Let us use this plan to compute annual depreciation for 2014 and 2015. In Exhibit 9-8, at the end of 2013,

Book value = $8,856
Depreciable cost = $7,856 ($8,856 – $1,000)
Straight-line depreciation for 2014 and 2015 = $3,928 ($7,856 ÷ 2 years remaining)

Comparing Depreciation Methods

Let us compare the depreciation methods. Annual amounts vary, but total accumulated depreciation is $40,000 for all three methods.

AMOUNT OF DEPRECIATION PER YEAR

			Accelerated Method
Year	Straight-Line	Units-of-Production	Double-Declining-Balance (no switch to Straight-line)
1	$ 8,000	$ 8,000	$16,400
2	8,000	12,000	9,840
3	8,000	10,000	5,904
4	8,000	6,000	3,542
5	8,000	4,000	4,314
Total Accumulated Depreciation	$40,000	$40,000	$40,000

Deciding which method is best depends on the asset. A business should match an asset's expense against the revenue that the asset produces. The following are some guidelines:

Straight-Line

For an asset that generates revenue evenly over time, the straight-line method follows the matching principle. Each period shows an equal amount of depreciation. For example, the straight-line method would be good for depreciating a building.

Units-of-Production

The UOP method works best for an asset that depreciates due to wear and tear, rather than obsolescence. More use causes greater depreciation. For example, UOP would be good for depleting natural resources, like oil or coal. UOP is also good for vehicles (miles) and machinery (machine hours).

Double-Declining-Balance

The accelerated method (DDB) works best for assets that produce more revenue in their early years. Higher depreciation in the early years is matched against the greater revenue. For example, DDB would be good for depreciating computers.

Comparisons

Exhibit 9-9 graphs annual depreciation for the three methods.

EXHIBIT 9-9 | Depreciation Patterns for the Various Methods

Straight-Line
9,000
8,000
7,000
6,000
5,000
4,000
3,000
2,000
1,000
0
2011 2012 2013 2014 2015

Units-of-Production
14,000
12,000
10,000
8,000
6,000
4,000
2,000
0
2011 2012 2013 2014 2015

Double-Declining Balance
18,000
16,000
14,000
12,000
10,000
8,000
6,000
4,000
2,000
0
2011 2012 2013 2014 2015

Exhibit 9-10 shows the three methods in one graph for additional comparison.

EXHIBIT 9-10 | Annual Depreciation by Method

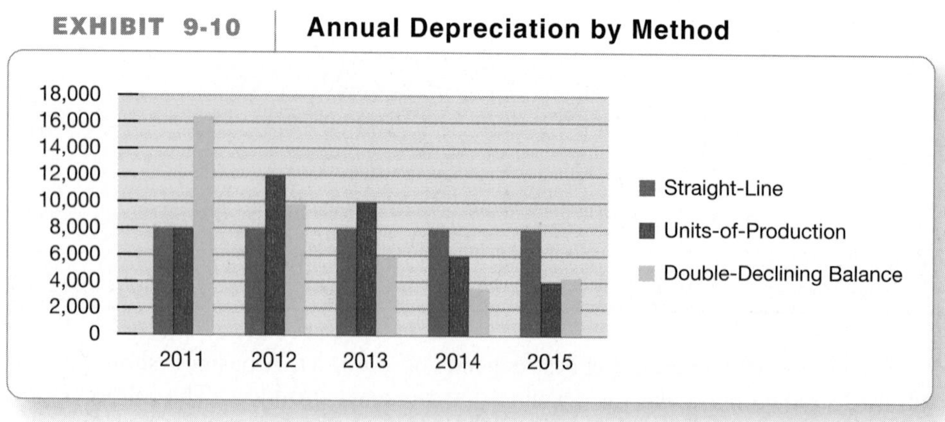

Stop & Think...

Let us personalize depreciation. Think about your car. What best mirrors its decline in value? Is it the age of the car, or is it how many miles you drive per year? How many miles you drive would probably be the best measure. That is how companies should pick depreciation methods—they should figure out what is the best measure of the asset's decline and then pick a depreciation method that mirrors that decline.

Other Issues in Accounting for Plant Assets

Changing the Useful Life of a Depreciable Asset

Estimating the useful life of a plant asset poses a challenge. As the asset is used, the business may change its estimated useful life. For example, Greg's Groovy Tunes may find that its truck lasts eight years instead of five. This is a change in estimate. Accounting changes like this are common because they are estimates and, as a result, are not based on perfect foresight. When a company makes an accounting change, generally accepted accounting principles require the business to report the nature, reason, and effect of the accounting change.

For a change in either estimated asset life or residual value, the asset's remaining depreciable book value is spread over the asset's remaining life. Suppose Greg's Groovy Tunes used the truck purchased on January 1, 2011, for two full years. Under the straight-line method, accumulated depreciation would be $16,000. (Refer to Exhibit 9-6.)

Straight-line depreciation for 2 years = ($41,000 – $1,000) × 1/5 × 12/12
= $8,000 per year × 2 years
= $16,000

Remaining depreciable book value (cost *less* accumulated depreciation *less* residual value) is $24,000 ($41,000 – $16,000 – $1,000). Suppose Greg's Groovy Tunes believes the truck will remain useful for six more years (for a total of eight years). At the start of 2013, the company would re-compute depreciation as follows:

Remaining Depreciable Book Value	÷	(New) Estimated Useful Life Remaining	=	(New) Annual Depreciation, 2013–2018
$24,000	÷	6 years	=	$4,000

In years 2013–2018, the yearly depreciation entry based on the new useful life would be as follows:

Dec 31	Depreciation expense—truck (E+)	4,000	
	Accumulated depreciation—truck (CA+)		4,000

Revised straight-line depreciation is computed very much like straight-line depreciation, except the accumulated depreciation taken to date is accounted for in the following formula:

$$\text{Revised SL depreciation} = (\text{Cost} - \text{Accumulated depreciation} - \text{New residual value}) \times \frac{1}{\text{new remaining life}} \times \frac{\#}{12}$$

Using Fully-Depreciated Assets

As explained earlier in the chapter, a fully-depreciated asset is one that has reached the end of its *estimated* useful life. No more depreciation is recorded for the asset. If the asset is no longer useful, it is disposed of. If the asset is still useful, the company may continue using it. The asset account and its accumulated depreciation remain on the books, but no additional depreciation is recorded. In short, the asset never goes below residual value.

Summary Problem 1

Latté On Demand purchased a coffee drink machine on January 1, 2011, for \$44,000. Expected useful life is 10 years or 100,000 drinks. In 2010, 3,000 drinks were sold and in 2011, 14,000 drinks were sold. Residual value is \$4,000. Under three depreciation methods, annual depreciation and total accumulated depreciation at the end of 2011 and 2012 are as follows:

	Method A		Method B		Method C	
Year	Annual Depreciation Expense	Accumulated Depreciation	Annual Depreciation Expense	Accumulated Depreciation	Annual Depreciation Expense	Accumulated Depreciation
2011	\$1,200	\$1,200	\$8,800	\$ 8,800	\$4,000	\$4,000
2012	5,600	6,800	7,040	15,840	4,000	8,000

Requirements

1. Identify the depreciation method used in each instance, and show the equation and computation for each method. (Round to the nearest dollar.)
2. Assume use of the same method through 2013. Compute depreciation expense, accumulated depreciation, and asset book value for 2011–2013 under each method, assuming 12,000 units of production in 2013.

Solution

Requirement 1

Method A: Units-of-Production

$$\text{Depreciation per unit} = \frac{\$44{,}000 - \$4{,}000}{100{,}000 \text{ units}} = \$0.40/\text{drink}$$

2011: $\$0.40 \times 3{,}000$ units = \$1,200
2012: $\$0.40 \times 14{,}000$ units = \$5,600

Method B: Double-Declining-Balance

$$\text{Rate} = \frac{1}{10 \text{ years}} \times 2 = 20\%$$

2011: $0.20 \times \$44{,}000 = \$8{,}800$
2012: $0.20 \times (\$44{,}000 - \$8{,}800) = \$7{,}040$

Method C: Straight-Line

Depreciable cost = \$44,000 – \$4,000 = \$40,000
Each year: \$40,000/10 years = \$4,000

Requirement 2

Year	Annual Depreciation Expense	Accumulated Depreciation	Book Value
Start			$44,000
2011	$1,200	$ 1,200	42,800
2012	5,600	6,800	37,200
2013	4,800	11,600	32,400

Year	Annual Depreciation Expense	Accumulated Depreciation	Book Value
Start			$44,000
2011	$8,800	$ 8,800	35,200
2012	7,040	15,400	28,160
2013	5,632	21,472	22,528

Year	Annual Depreciation Expense	Accumulated Depreciation	Book Value
Start			$44,000
2011	$4,000	$ 4,000	40,000
2012	4,000	8,000	36,000
2013	4,000	12,000	32,000

Units-of-production	$0.40 × 12,000 units = $4,800
Double-declining-balance	0.20 × $28,160 = $5,632
Straight-line	$40,000/10 years = $4,000

Disposing of a Plant Asset

3 Record the disposal of an asset by sale or trade

Eventually, an asset wears out or becomes obsolete. The owner then has two choices:

- Trade the asset for non-like property. This choice includes selling or scrapping the asset, or trading for an asset that is not similar in functionality. Examples include selling a **Ford** truck for cash, scrapping a **Toyota** truck for no cash, or trading a truck for a copier machine. All are non-like property exchanges and a gain or loss on the transaction must be recognized by the company.
- Trade the asset for another asset that has similar functionality. This is called a **like-kind exchange.** No gain or loss is recognized on like-kind exchanges. An example of a like-kind asset exchange would be trading a **Ford** truck for a **Chevy** truck.

Regardless of the type of exchange (like or non-like kind property), the four steps for journalizing disposals or trades are similar and are as follows:

1. Bring the depreciation up to date.
2. Remove the old, disposed of asset from the books.
   a. Make the Asset account equal zero by crediting the asset for its original cost.
   b. Make the Accumulated depreciation account for the asset equal zero by debiting it for all the depreciation taken to date on the asset.
3. Record the value of any cash (or other accounts) paid (or received) for the asset. For example, if cash is given, credit Cash. If cash is received, debit Cash. If a notes payable was signed, credit Notes payable.
4. Finally, determine the difference between the total debits and total credits made in the journal entry.
   a. If the asset was traded for a like-kind asset, the net difference in debits and credits will be recorded as a debit to the new asset account.
   b. If the asset was traded in a non-like kind manner, then the net difference will represent gain or loss on the disposal (or sale) of the disposed asset. Record the gain or loss to the Income Statement as follows:
      - If the total debits > total credits—a credit entry will be made to make the journal entry balance. The credit represents a Gain on sale (or disposal) of an asset.
      - If the total debits < total credits—a debit entry will be made to make the journal entry balance. The debit represents a Loss on sale (or disposal) of an asset.
      - If total debits = total credits—there is no Gain or Loss on sale (or disposal) of the asset.

To apply this, let us consider the truck that Greg's Groovy Tunes purchased on January 1, 2011. Assume the business recorded depreciation using the straight-line method through December 31, 2012. According to Exhibit 9-6 presented earlier in the chapter, Greg's Groovy Tunes' historical cost of the truck was $41,000, and $16,000 has been recorded in total accumulated depreciation through 12/31/2012.

Before we consider any transactions, the T-accounts would appear as follows:

Truck	
41,000	

Accumulated depreciation—truck	
	16,000

To illustrate accounting for disposal of an asset, let us consider the five options that Greg's Groovy Tunes has to dispose of the truck. All options are assumed to take place on March 31, 2013. Exhibit 9-11 illustrates all five options.

1. Situation A – The truck is in an accident and is totaled. The truck is completely worthless and must be scrapped for $0. There are no insurance proceeds from the accident.
2. Situation B – Greg's Groovy Tunes sells the truck to Bob's Burger House for $10,000 cash.
3. Situation C – Greg's Groovy Tunes sells the truck to Harry's Hot Dogs. Harry's gives Greg's $20,000 cash and a piece of equipment worth $5,000 for the truck.
4. Situation D – Greg's Groovy Tunes trades the old truck in for a new **Toyota** truck. The suggested retail price of the **Toyota** truck is $32,000.
5. Situation E – Greg's Groovy Tunes trades the old truck and $3,000 in cash for a new **Toyota** truck. The MSRP of the **Toyota** truck is $32,000.

EXHIBIT 9-11 **Five Options to Dispose of the Truck**

Situation A—Scrap the Truck

Step	Date	Accounts	Debit	Credit
Step 1	2013	Depreciation expense (E+)	2,000	
	Mar 31	Accumulated depreciation (CA+)		2,000
		[(41,000 Cost – 1,000 Residual Value) × 1/5yr × 3/12		
Step 2		Accumulated depreciation (16,000 + 2,000) (CA–)	18,000	
		???	???	???
		Truck (A–)		41,000
		(incomplete entry)		
Step 3—no change to Step 2 entry				
Step 4—complete Step 2 entry				
		Accumulated depreciation (16,000 + 2,000) (CA–)	18,000	
		Loss on disposal of truck (E+)	23,000	
		Truck (A–)		41,000

Situation B—Sell the Truck for $10,000

Step	Date	Accounts	Debit	Credit
Step 1	2013	Depreciation expense (E+)	2,000	
	Mar 31	Accumulated depreciation (CA+)		2,000
		[(41,000 Cost – 1,000 Residual Value) × 1/5yr × 3/12		
Step 2		Accumulated depreciation (16,000 + 2,000) (CA–)	18,000	
		???	???	???
		Truck (A–)		41,000
		(incomplete entry)		
Step 3—change Step 2 entry to record cash received				
		Cash (A+)	10,000	
		Accumulated depreciation (16,000 + 2,000) (CA–)	18,000	
		???	???	???
		Truck (A–)		41,000
Step 4—complete Step 2 entry				
		Cash (A+)	10,000	
		Accumulated depreciation (16,000 + 2,000) (CA–)	18,000	
		Loss on sale of truck (E+)	13,000	
		Truck (A–)		41,000

would give $146 billion for **Time Warner's** net tangible assets of only $9 billion. Why so much for so little? Because **Time Warner's** intangible assets were worth billions. Intangibles can account for most of a company's market value, so companies must value their intangibles, just as they value inventory and equipment.

A **patent** is an intangible asset that is a federal government grant conveying an exclusive 20-year right to produce and sell an invention. The invention may be a product or a process—for example, the Dolby noise-reduction process. The acquisition cost of a patent is debited to the Patents account. The intangible is expensed through **amortization**, the systematic reduction of the asset's carrying value on the books. Amortization applies to intangibles exactly as depreciation applies to equipment and depletion to oil and timber.

Amortization is computed over the asset's estimated useful life—usually by the straight-line method. Obsolescence is the most common reason an intangible's useful life gets shortened from its expected length. Amortization expense for an intangible asset can be credited directly to the asset instead of using an accumulated amortization account. The residual value of most intangibles is zero.

Some intangibles have indefinite lives. For them, the company records no systematic amortization each period. Instead, it accounts for any decrease in the value of the intangible as goodwill (to be discussed later in the chapter).

Specific Intangibles

As noted earlier, patents, copyrights, and trademarks are intangible assets. Accounting for their purchase and their decline in value for each is the same. We will illustrate the accounting by using a patent.

Patents

Like any other asset, a patent may be purchased. Suppose Greg's Groovy Tunes pays $200,000 to acquire a patent on January 1, 2011. Greg's Groovy Tunes believes this patent's useful life is only five years, because it is likely a new, more efficient process will be developed within that time. Amortization expense is $40,000 per year ($200,000/5 years). Acquisition and amortization entries for this patent are as follows:

2011			
Jan 1	Patents (A+)	200,000	
	Cash (A–)		200,000
	To acquire a patent.		
Dec 31	Amortization expense—patents ($200,000/5) (E+)	40,000	
	Patents (A–)		40,000
	To amortize the cost of a patent.		

At the end of the first year, Greg's Groovy Tunes will report this patent at $160,000 ($200,000 minus first-year amortization of $40,000), the next year at $120,000, and so forth. Each year for five years the value of the patent will be reduced until the end of its five year life, at which point its net book value will be $0.

Copyrights

A **copyright** is the exclusive right to reproduce and sell a book, musical composition, film, or other work of art or intellectual property. Copyrights also protect computer software programs, such as **Microsoft Windows**™ and the **Excel** spreadsheet. Issued by the federal government, a copyright extends 70 years beyond the author's life.

A company may pay a large sum to purchase an existing copyright. For example, the publisher **Simon & Schuster** may pay $1 million for the copyright on a popular novel because it thinks it will be able to make profit from selling the novel. Most copyrights have short useful lives.

Trademarks, Brand Names

Trademarks and **brand names** (also known as **trade names**) are assets that represent distinctive products or services, such as the **NIKE** "swoosh" or the **NASCAR** number 3 for Dale Earnhardt. Legally protected slogans include **Chevrolet's** "Like a Rock" and **Avis** Rent A Car's "We try harder." The cost of a trademark or trade name is amortized over its useful life.

Franchises, Licenses

Franchises and **licenses** are privileges granted by a private business or a government to sell goods or services under specified conditions. The **Dallas Cowboys** football organization is a franchise granted by the **National Football League. McDonald's** restaurants and **Holiday Inns** are well-known business franchises. The acquisition cost of a franchise or license is amortized over its useful life.

Goodwill

Goodwill in accounting has a different meaning from the everyday phrase "goodwill among men." In accounting, **goodwill** is the excess of the cost to purchase another company over the market value of its net assets (assets minus liabilities).

Suppose **Wal-Mart** acquired **Monterrey Company** in Mexico on January 1, 2011. The sum of the market values of **Monterrey's** assets was $9 million and its liabilities totaled $1 million, so **Monterrey's** net assets totaled $8 million. Suppose **Wal-Mart** paid $10 million to purchase **Monterrey Company**. In this case, **Wal-Mart** paid $2 million above the value of **Monterrey's** net assets. Therefore, that $2 million is considered goodwill and is computed as follows:

Purchase price to acquire Monterrey Company..........		$10 million
Market value of Monterrey Company's assets...........	$9 million	
Less: Monterrey Company's liabilities.......................	(1 million)	
Market value of Monterrey Company's net assets......		8 million
Excess, called *goodwill*..		$ 2 million

Wal-Mart's entry to record the purchase of **Monterrey**, including the goodwill that **Wal-Mart** purchased, would be as follows:

2011			
Jan 1	Assets (Cash, Receivables, Inventories, Plant assets,		
	all at market value) (A+)	9,000,000	
	Goodwill (A–)	2,000,000	
	Liabilities (L+)		1,000,000
	Cash (A–)		10,000,000
	Purchased Monterrey Company.		

Goodwill has some special features:

1. Goodwill is recorded only by an acquiring company when it purchases another company. An outstanding reputation may create goodwill, but that company never records goodwill for its own business.
2. According to generally accepted accounting principles (GAAP), goodwill is *not* amortized. Instead, the acquiring company measures the current value of its goodwill each year. If the goodwill has increased in value, there is nothing to record. But if goodwill's value has decreased, then the company records a loss and writes the goodwill down. For example, suppose **Wal-Mart's** goodwill—which we talked about with its purchase of **Monterrey**—is worth only \$1,500,000 on December 31, 2011. In that case, **Wal-Mart** would make the following entry:

2011			
Dec 31	Loss on goodwill (E+)	500,000	
	Goodwill (\$2,000,000 – \$1,500,000) (A–)		500,000
	Recorded loss on goodwill.		

Wal-Mart would then report this goodwill at its reduced current value of \$1,500,000.

Accounting for Research and Development Costs

Research and development (R&D) costs are the lifeblood of companies such as **Procter & Gamble, General Electric, Intel,** and **Boeing.** In general, companies do not report R&D assets on their balance sheets because GAAP requires companies to expense R&D costs as they are incurred.

Ethical Issues

6 Describe ethical issues related to plant assets

The main ethical issue in accounting for plant assets is whether to capitalize or expense a cost. In this area, company opinions vary greatly. On the one hand, companies want to save on taxes. This motivates them to expense all costs and decrease taxable income. On the other hand, they want to look as good as possible to investors, with high net income and huge assets.

In most cases, a cost that is capitalized or expensed for tax purposes must be treated the same way in the financial statements. What, then, is the ethical path? Accountants should follow the general guidelines for capitalizing a cost:

Capitalize all costs that provide a future benefit.
Expense all other costs.

Many companies have gotten into trouble by capitalizing costs that were really expenses. They made their financial statements look better than the facts warranted. **WorldCom** committed this type of accounting fraud, and its former top executives are now in prison as a result. There are very few cases of companies getting into trouble by following the general guidelines, or even by erring on the side of accounting conservatism. Following the guidelines works.

Decision Guidelines

ACCOUNTING FOR PLANT ASSETS AND RELATED EXPENSES

The Decision Guidelines summarize key decisions a company makes in accounting for plant assets. Suppose you buy a **Starbucks** or a **Curves International** franchise and invest in related equipment. You have some decisions to make about how to account for the franchise and the equipment. The Decision Guidelines will help you maximize your cash flow and properly account for the business.

Decision	Guidelines
• Capitalize or expense a cost?	General rule: Capitalize all costs that provide *future benefit.* Expense all costs that provide *no future benefit.*
• Capitalize or expense:	
• Cost associated with a new asset?	Capitalize all costs that bring the asset to its intended use.
• Cost associated with an existing asset?	Capitalize only those costs that add to the asset's usefulness or extend its useful life. Expense all other costs as repairs or maintenance.
• Which depreciation method to use:	
• For financial reporting?	Use the method that best matches depreciation expense against the revenues produced by the asset.

Summary Problem 2

The following figures appear in the Answers to Summary Problem 1, Requirement 2.

	Method B: Double-Declining-Balance			Method C: Straight-Line		
Year	Annual Depreciation Expense	Accumulated Depreciation	Book Value	Annual Depreciation Expense	Accumulated Depreciation	Book Value
Start			$44,000			$44,000
2011	$8,800	$ 8,800	35,200	$4,000	$ 4,000	40,000
2012	7,040	15,840	28,160	4,000	8,000	36,000
2013	5,632	21,472	22,528	4,000	12,000	32,000

Latté on Demand purchased equipment on January 1, 2011. Management has depreciated the equipment by using the double-declining-balance method. On July 1, 2013, the company sold the equipment for $27,000 cash.

Requirement

1. Record Latté on Demand's depreciation for 2013 and the sale of the equipment on July 1, 2013.

Solution

Requirement 1

To record depreciation to date of sale and the sale of the Latté on Demand equipment:

Date	Accounts	Debit	Credit
2013			
Jul 1	Depreciation expense ($5,632 × 6/12) (E+)	2,816	
	Accumulated depreciation (CA+)		2,816
	To update depreciation.		
Jul 1	Cash (A+)	27,000	
	Accumulated depreciation ($15,840 + $2,816) (CA−)	18,656	
	Equipment (A−)		44,000
	Gain on sale of equipment (R+)		1,656
	To record the sale of equipment.		

Review Plant Assets and Intangibles

Accounting Vocabulary

Accelerated Depreciation Method (p. 518)
A depreciation method that writes off more of the assets cost near the start of its useful life than the straight-line method does.

Amortization (p. 531)
Systematic reduction of the asset's carrying value on the books. Expense that applies to intangibles in the same way depreciation applies to plant assets and depletion to natural resources.

Brand Names (p. 532)
Assets that represent distinctive identifications of a product or service.

Capital Expenditures (p. 514)
Expenditures that increase the capacity or efficiency of an asset or extend its useful life. Capital expenditures are debited to an asset account.

Capitalized (p. 511)
An asset account that was debited (increased) for an asset.

Copyright (p. 531)
Exclusive right to reproduce and sell a book, musical composition, film, other work of art, or computer program. Issued by the federal government, copyrights extend 70 years beyond the author's life.

Depletion Expense (p. 530)
Portion of a natural resource's cost used up in a particular period. Computed in the same way as units-of-production depreciation.

Depreciable Cost (p. 516)
The cost of a plant asset minus its estimated residual value.

Double-Declining-Balance (DDB) Method (p. 518)
An accelerated depreciation method that computes annual depreciation by multiplying the asset's decreasing book value by a constant percent that is two times the straight-line rate.

Estimated Residual Value (p. 516)
Expected cash value of an asset at the end of its useful life. Also called **salvage value**.

Estimated Useful Life (p. 515)
Length of the service period expected from an asset. May be expressed in years, units of output, miles, or another measure.

Extraordinary Repair (p. 514)
Repair work that generates a capital expenditure.

Franchises (p. 532)
Privileges granted by a private business or a government to sell a product or service under specified conditions.

Fully-Depreciated Asset (p. 517)
An asset that has reached the end of its estimated useful life. No more depreciation is recorded for the asset.

Goodwill (p. 532)
Excess of the cost of an acquired company over the sum of the market values of its net assets (assets minus liabilities).

Intangible Assets (p. 509)
Assets with no physical form. Valuable because of the special rights they carry. Examples are patents and copyrights.

Land Improvements (p. 511)
Depreciable improvements to land, such as fencing, sprinklers, paving, signs, and lighting.

Licenses (p. 532)
Privileges granted by a private business or a government to sell a product or service under specified conditions.

Like-Kind Exchange (p. 525)
Trading an asset for another asset that has similar functionality. No gain or loss is recognized on like-kind exchanges.

Natural Resources (p. 530)
Plant assets that come from the earth. Natural resources are like inventories in the ground (oil) or on top of the ground (timber).

Obsolete (p. 515)
A newer asset can perform the job more efficiently than the old.

Ordinary Repairs (p. 514)
Repair work that is debited to an expense account.

Patent (p. 531)
An intangible asset that is a federal government grant conveying an exclusive 20-year right to produce and sell a process or formula.

Real assets (p. 509)
Assets with physical form. Examples include: truck, building.

Relative-Sales-Value Method (p. 513)
Method of allocating the total cost (100%) of multiple assets purchased at one time. Total cost is divided among the assets according to their relative sales values.

Salvage Value (p. 516)
Expected cash value of an asset at the end of its useful life. Also called **residual value**.

Straight-Line (SL) Depreciation Method (p. 516)
Depreciation method in which an equal amount of depreciation expense is assigned to each year of asset use.

Tangible assets (p. 509)
Assets with physical form. Examples include: truck, building.

Trademarks (p. 532)
Assets that represent distinctive identifications of a product or service.

Trade Names (p. 532)
Assets that represent distinctive identifications of a product or service.

Units-of-Production (UOP) Depreciation Method (p. 517)
Depreciation method by which a fixed amount of depreciation is assigned to each unit of output produced by an asset.

Quick Check

1. Which cost is *not* recorded as part of the cost of a building?
   a. Annual building maintenance
   b. Real estate commission paid to buy the building
   c. Earthmoving for the building's foundation
   d. Construction materials and labor
2. British Tran bought four used Unlimited Airline airplanes. Each plane was worth $39 million, but the owner sold the combination for $144 million. How much is British Tran's cost of each plane?
   a. $39 million
   b. $156 million
   c. $36 million
   d. $144 million
3. How should you record a capital expenditure?
   a. Debit a liability
   b. Debit capital
   c. Debit an asset
   d. Debit an expense
4. Which method almost always produces the most depreciation in the first year?
   a. Units-of-production
   b. Straight-line
   c. Double-declining-balance
   d. All produce the same total depreciation
5. An Unlimited Airlines jet costs $42 million and is expected to fly 370 million miles during its 8-year life. Residual value is expected to be zero because the plane was used when acquired. If the plane travels 39 million miles the first year, how much depreciation should Unlimited Airlines record under the units-of-production method?
   a. $4.43 million
   b. $8.81 million
   c. $5.25 million
   d. Cannot be determined from the data given
6. Which depreciation method would you generally prefer to use for income tax purposes? Why?
   a. Units-of-production because it best tracks the asset's use
   b. Straight-line because it is simplest
   c. Double-declining-balance because it gives the fastest tax deductions for depreciation
   d. Double-declining-balance because it gives the most total depreciation over the asset's life

7. A copy machine costs $43,000 when new and has accumulated depreciation of $28,000. Suppose Johnson Printing junks this machine, receiving nothing. What is the result of the disposal transaction?
   a. No gain or loss
   b. Loss of $28,000
   c. Gain of $15,000
   d. Loss of $15,000
8. Suppose Johnson Printing in the preceding question sold the machine for $15,000. What is the result of this disposal transaction?
   a. Loss of $5,000
   b. Gain of $36,000
   c. Gain of $5,000
   d. No gain or loss
9. Which method is used to compute depletion?
   a. Depletion method
   b. Double-declining-balance method
   c. Units-of-production method
   d. Straight-line method
10. Which intangible asset is recorded only as part of the acquisition of another company?
   a. Franchise
   b. Patent
   c. Copyright
   d. Goodwill

Answers are given after Apply Your Knowledge (p. 551).

Assess Your Progress

■ Short Exercises

S9-1 *(L. OBJ. 1)* **Measuring plant asset cost [5 min]**
This chapter lists the costs included for the acquisition of land. First is the purchase price, which is obviously included in the cost of the land. The reasons for including the other costs are not so obvious. For example, removing a building looks more like an expense.

Requirements

1. State why the costs listed in the chapter are included as part of the cost of the land.
2. After the land is ready for use, will these costs be capitalized or expensed?

S9-2 *(L. OBJ. 1)* **Lump-sum asset purchase [10 min]**
Advanced Automotive pays $140,000 for a group purchase of land, building, and equipment. At the time of your acquisition, the land has a market value of $75,000, the building $60,000, and the equipment $15,000.

Requirement

1. Journalize the lump-sum purchase of the 3 assets for a total cost of $140,000. You sign a note payable for this amount.

S9-3 *(L. OBJ. 2)* **Computing first-year depreciation and book value [10 min]**
At the beginning of the year, Logan Services purchased a used airplane for $65,000,000. Logan Services expects the plane to remain useful for 4 years (6 million miles) and to have a residual value of $5,000,000. The company expects the plane to be flown 1.3 million miles the first year.

Requirements

1. Compute Logan Services' *first-year* depreciation on the plane using the following methods:
   a. Straight-line
   b. Units-of-production
   c. Double-declining-balance
2. Show the airplane's book value at the end of the first year under the straight-line method.

S9-4 *(L. OBJ. 2)* **Computing second-year depreciation and accumulated depreciation [10–15 min]**
At the beginning of 2011, Texas Aero purchased a used airplane at a cost of $59,000,000. Texas Aero expects the plane to remain useful for 5 years (6 million miles) and to have a residual value of $5,000,000. Texas Aero expects the plane to be flown 1.4 million miles the first year and 1.3 million miles the second year.

Requirements

1. Compute *second-year (2012)* depreciation on the plane using the following methods:
   a. Straight-line
   b. Units-of-production
   c. Double-declining-balance
2. Calculate the balance in Accumulated depreciation at the end of the second-year using the Straight-line method of depreciation.

S9-5 *(L. OBJ. 2)* **Selecting the best depreciation method for tax purposes [10 min]**
This exercise uses the Logan Services data from Short Exercise 9-3. Logan Services is deciding which depreciation method to use for income tax purposes.

Requirements

1. Which depreciation method offers the tax advantage for the first year? Describe the nature of the tax advantage.
2. How much extra depreciation will Logan Services get to deduct for the first year as compared with the straight-line method?

S9-6 *(L.OBJ. 2)* **Partial year depreciation [5–10 min]**
On February 28, 2011, Solar Energy Consulting purchased a **Xerox** copy machine for $23,100. Solar Energy Consulting expects the machine to last for 3 years and to have a residual value of $1,500.

Requirement

1. Compute depreciation on the machine for the year ended December 31, 2011, using the straight-line method.

S9-7 *(L.OBJ. 2)* **Change in the estimated life of an asset [10 min]**
Assume that Smith's Auto Sales paid $50,000 for equipment with a 10-year life and zero expected residual value. After using the equipment for 4 years, the company determines that the asset will remain useful for only 3 more years.

Requirements

1. Record depreciation on the equipment for year 5 by the straight-line method.
2. What is accumulated depreciation at the end of year 5?

S9-8 *(L.OBJ. 3)* **Sale of asset at gain or loss [10 min]**
ABC Catering Service purchased equipment on January 1, 2010, for $58,500. ABC Catering Service expected the equipment to last for 6 years and to have a residual value of $4,500. Suppose ABC Catering Service sold the equipment for $43,000 on December 31, 2012, after using the equipment for three full years. Assume depreciation for 2012 has been recorded.

Requirement

1. Journalize the sale of the equipment, assuming straight-line depreciation was used.

S9-9 *(L.OBJ. 3)* **Like-kind exchange [5–10 min]**
Micron Precision purchased a computer for $3,100, debiting Computer equipment. During 2010 and 2011, Micron Precision recorded total depreciation of $2,200 on the computer. On January 1, 2012, Micron Precision traded in the computer for a new one, paying $2,900 cash.

Requirement

1. Journalize Micron Precision's exchange of computers.

S9-10 *(L.OBJ. 4)* **Accounting for depletion of natural resources [5–10 min]**
Arabia Petroleum holds huge reserves of oil and gas assets. Assume that at the end of 2010, Arabia Petroleum's cost of oil and gas reserves totaled $84 billion, representing 7 billion barrels of oil and gas.

Requirements

1. Which depreciation method does Arabia Petroleum use to compute depletion?
2. Suppose Arabia Petroleum removed 0.7 billion barrels of oil during 2011. Journalize depletion expense for 2011.

S9-11 *(L.OBJ. 5)* **Accounting for goodwill [10 min]**
When one media company buys another, goodwill is often the most costly asset. Decca Publishing paid $240,000 to acquire *Tri Town Daily*, a weekly advertising paper. At the time of the acquisition, *Tri Town Daily's* balance sheet reported total assets of $160,000 and liabilities of $80,000. The fair market value of *Tri Town Daily's* assets was $120,000.

Requirements

1. How much goodwill did Decca Publishing purchase as part of the acquisition of *Tri Town Daily*?
2. Journalize Decca Publishing's acquisition of *Tri Town Daily*.

S9-12 *(L.OBJ.6)* **Ethics-capitalizing vs. expensing assets [5 min]**
Lexington Precision Tools repaired one of its **Boeing** 737 aircrafts at a cost of $100,000. Lexington Precision Tools erroneously capitalized this cost as part of the cost of the plane.

Requirements

1. How will this accounting error affect Lexington Precision Tools' net income? Ignore depreciation.
2. Should the company correct the error or can it ignore the error to report more favorable earnings results?

■ Exercises

E9-13 *(L.OBJ. 1)* **Determining the cost of assets [5–10 min]**
Ayer Furniture Co. purchased land, paying $95,000 cash plus a $270,000 note payable. In addition, Ayer paid delinquent property tax of $2,000, title insurance costing $2,500, and $3,000 to level the land and remove an unwanted building. The company then constructed an office building at a cost of $550,000. It also paid $52,000 for a fence around the property, $17,000 for a sign near the entrance, and $4,000 for special lighting of the grounds.

Requirements

1. Determine the cost of the land, land improvements, and building.
2. Which of these assets will Ayer depreciate?

E9-14 *(L.OBJ. 1)* **Lump-sum purchase of assets [10–15 min]**
Maplewood Properties bought three lots in a subdivision for a lump-sum price. An independent appraiser valued the lots as follows:

Lot	Appraised Value
1	$ 90,000
2	60,000
3	100,000

Maplewood paid $240,000 in cash.

Requirement

1. Record the purchase in the journal, identifying each lot's cost in a separate Land account. Round decimals to three places, and use your computed percentages throughout.

E9-15 *(L.OBJ. 1)* **Distinguishing capital expenditures from expenses [5–10 min]**
Consider the following expenditures:

a. Purchase price
b. Ordinary recurring repairs to keep the machinery in good working order
c. Lubrication before machinery is placed in service
d. Periodic lubrication after machinery is placed in service
e. Major overhaul to extend useful life by three years
f. Sales tax paid on the purchase price
g. Transportation and insurance while machinery is in transit from seller to buyer
h. Installation
i. Training of personnel for initial operation of the machinery
j. Income tax paid on income earned from the sale of products manufactured by the machinery

Requirement

1. Classify each of the expenditures as a capital expenditure or an expense related to machinery.

E9-16 *(L.OBJ. 2)* **Explaining the concept of depreciation [10–15 min]**
Ron Zander just slept through the class in which Professor Chen explained the concept of depreciation. Because the next test is scheduled for Friday, Zander telephones Sven Svensen to get his notes from the lecture. Svensen's notes are concise: "Depreciation—Sounds like Greek to me." Zander next tries Lisa Lake, who says she thinks depreciation is what happens when an asset wears out. Jason Gerbing is confident that depreciation is the process of creating a cash fund to replace an asset at the end of its useful life.

Requirement

1. Explain the concept of depreciation for Zander. Evaluate the explanations of Lake and Gerbing. Be specific.

E9-17 *(L.OBJ. 2)* **Computing depreciation—three methods [10–15 min]**
Mama's Fried Chicken bought equipment on January 2, 2010, for $15,000. The equipment was expected to remain in service 4 years and to perform 3,000 fry jobs. At the end of the equipment's useful life, Mama's estimates that its residual value will be $3,000. The equipment performed 300 jobs the first year, 900 the second year, 1,200 the third, and 600 the fourth year.

Requirements

1. Prepare a schedule of *depreciation expense* per year for the equipment under the three depreciation methods. After two years under double-declining-balance depreciation, the company switched to the straight-line method. Show your computations. *Note: 3 depreciation schedules must be prepared.*
2. Which method tracks the wear and tear on the equipment most closely?

E9-18 *(L.OBJ. 2)* **Selecting the best depreciation method for tax purposes [15–20 min]**
Tumble Gymnastics Center paid $120,000 for fitness equipment that is expected to have a 10-year life. The expected residual value is $40,000.

Requirement

1. Select the appropriate depreciation method for income tax purposes. Then determine the extra amount of depreciation that Tumble can deduct by using the selected method, versus straight-line, during the first two years of the equipment's life.

E9-19 *(L.OBJ. 2)* **Changing an asset's useful life [10–15 min]**
A-1 Computer Consultants purchased a building for $510,000 and depreciated it on a straight-line basis over a 40-year period. The estimated residual value is $100,000. After using the building for 15 years, A-1 realized that wear and tear on the building would wear it out before 40 years. Starting with the 16th year A-1 began depreciating the building over a revised total life of 25 years.

Requirement

1. Journalize depreciation on the building for years 15 and 16.

E9-20 *(L.OBJ. 2, 3)* **Partial year depreciation and sale of an asset [10–15 min]**
On January 2, 2011, Ditto Clothing Consignments purchased showroom fixtures for $16,000 cash, expecting the fixtures to remain in service for five years. Ditto has depreciated the fixtures on a double-declining-balance basis, with zero residual value. On August 31, 2012, Ditto sold the fixtures for $7,600 cash.

Requirement

1. Record both depreciation for 2012 and sale of the fixtures on August 31, 2012.

E9-21 *(L.OBJ. 3)* **Trade in asset—two situations [10–15 min]**
Peace Bank recently traded in office fixtures. Here are the facts:
Old fixtures:

- Cost, $99,000
- Accumulated depreciation, $73,000

New fixtures:

- Cash paid, $105,000, plus the old fixtures

Requirements

1. Record Peace Bank's trade-in of old fixtures for new ones.
2. Now let us change one fact and see a different outcome. Peace Bank feels compelled to do business with Crescent Furniture, a bank customer, even though the bank can get the fixtures elsewhere at a better price. Peace Bank is aware that the new fixtures' market value is only $123,000. Now record the trade-in.

E9-22 *(L.OBJ. 3)* **Measuring asset cost, UOP depreciation, and asset trade [10–15 min]**
Travel Trucking Company uses the units-of-production (UOP) depreciation method because UOP best measures wear and tear on the trucks. Consider these facts about one **Mack** truck in the company's fleet.

When acquired in 2010, the rig cost $380,000 and was expected to remain in service for 10 years or 1,000,000 miles. Estimated residual value was $100,000. The truck was driven 79,000 miles in 2010, 119,000 miles in 2011, and 159,000 miles in 2012. After 38,000 miles in 2013, the company traded in the **Mack** truck for a less-expensive **Freightliner**. Travel also paid cash of $27,000.

Requirement

1. Determine Travel's cost of the new truck. Journal entries are not required.

E9-23 *(L.OBJ. 4)* **Natural resource depletion [10–15 min]**
Cannon Mountain Mining paid $488,500 for the right to extract mineral assets from a 400,000-ton deposit. In addition to the purchase price, Cannon also paid a $500 filing fee, a $1,000 license fee to the state of Nevada, and $90,000 for a geological survey of the property. Because Cannon purchased the rights to the minerals only, it expects the asset to have zero residual value. During the first year, Cannon removed 20,000 tons of the minerals.

Requirement

1. Make journal entries to record (a) purchase of the minerals (debit Mineral Asset), (b) payment of fees and other costs, and (c) depletion for the first year.

E9-24 *(L.OBJ. 5)* **Acquisition of Patent, Amortization, and Change in useful life [10–15 min]**
Maynard Printers (MP) manufactures printers. Assume that MP recently paid $400,000 for a patent on a new laser printer. Although it gives legal protection for 20 years, the patent is expected to provide a competitive advantage for only 10 years.

Requirements

1. Assuming the straight-line method of amortization, make journal entries to record (a) the purchase of the patent and (b) amortization for year 1.
2. After using the patent for five years, MP learns at an industry trade show that another company is designing a more efficient printer. On the basis of this new information, MP decides, starting with year 6, to amortize the remaining cost of the patent over two remaining years, giving the patent a total useful life of seven years. Record amortization for year 6.

E9-25 *(L.OBJ. 5)* **Measuring and recording goodwill [10–15 min]**
Pilgrim has acquired several other companies. Assume that Pilgrim purchased Kate, Co., for $9 million cash. The book value of Kate's assets is $15 million (market value, $18 million), and it has liabilities of $13 million.

Requirements

1. Compute the cost of the goodwill purchased by Pilgrim.
2. Record the purchase of Kate by Pilgrim.

E9-26 *(L.OBJ. 6)* **Ethics [10–15 min]**
Reader.com uses automated shipping equipment. Assume that early in year 1, Reader purchased equipment at a cost of $500,000. Management expects the equipment to remain in service 5 years, with zero residual value. Reader uses straight-line depreciation. Reader's CEO informs the controller to expense the entire cost of the equipment at the time of purchase because Reader's profits are too high.

Requirements

1. Compute the overstatement or understatement in the following items immediately after purchasing the equipment:
   a. Equipment
   b. Net income
2. Is there an ethics violation? What should the controller do?

Problems (Group A)

P9-27A *(L.OBJ. 1, 2)* **Capitalized asset cost and Partial year depreciation [20–25 min]**
Airport Parking, near an airport, incurred the following costs to acquire land, make land improvements, and construct and furnish a small building:

a. Purchase price of 3 acres of land	$ 82,000
b. Delinquent real estate taxes on the land to be paid by Airport Parking	6,300
c. Additional dirt and earthmoving	8,700
d. Title insurance on the land acquisition	3,300
e. Fence around the boundary of the property	9,800
f. Building permit for the building	700
g. Architect's fee for the design of the building	23,100
h. Signs near the front of the property	9,300
i. Materials used to construct the building	218,000
j. Labor to construct the building	167,000
k. Interest cost on construction loan for the building	9,100
l. Parking lots on the property	28,800
m. Lights for the parking lots	11,400
n. Salary of construction supervisor (75% to building; 25% to parking lot and concrete walks)	70,000
o. Furniture	11,100
p. Transportation of furniture from seller to the building	2,600
q. Landscaping (shrubs)	6,200

Airport Parking depreciates land improvements over 15 years, buildings over 30 years, and furniture over 12 years, all on a straight-line basis with zero residual value.

Requirements

1. Set up columns for Land, Land Improvements, Building, and Furniture. Show how to account for each cost by listing the cost under the correct account. Determine the total cost of each asset.
2. All construction was complete and the assets were placed in service on May 1. Record partial-year depreciation for the year ended December 31.

P9-28A *(L.OBJ. 1, 2)* **Capitalized asset cost and first year depreciation, and identifying depreciation results that meet management objectives [30–40 min]**

On January 9, 2010, Swifty Delivery Service purchased a truck at a cost of $67,000. Before placing the truck in service, Swifty spent $2,200 painting it, $500 replacing tires, and $5,000 overhauling the engine. The truck should remain in service for 6 years and have a residual value of $14,700. The truck's annual mileage is expected to be 15,000 miles in each of the first 4 years and 10,000 miles in each of the next 2 years—80,000 miles in total. In deciding which depreciation method to use, Jerry Speers, the general manager, requests a depreciation schedule for each of the depreciation methods (straight-line, units-of-production, and double-declining-balance).

Requirements

1. Prepare a depreciation schedule for each depreciation method, showing asset cost, depreciation expense, accumulated depreciation, and asset book value.
2. Swifty prepares financial statements using the depreciation method that reports the highest net income in the early years of asset use. For income-tax purposes, the company uses the depreciation method that minimizes income taxes in the early years. Consider the first year that Swifty uses the truck. Identify the depreciation methods that meet the general manager's objectives, assuming the income tax authorities permit the use of any of the methods.

P9-29A *(L.OBJ. 2, 3)* **Lump sum asset purchases and partial year depreciation [20–25 min]**

Whitney Plumb Associates surveys American eating habits. The company's accounts include Land, Buildings, Office equipment, and Communication equipment, with a separate accumulated depreciation account for each asset. During 2011, Whitney Plumb completed the following transactions:

Jan 1	Traded in old office equipment with book value of $26,000 (cost of $126,000 and accumulated depreciation of $100,000) for new equipment. Plumb also paid $82,000 in cash.
Apr 1	Acquired land and communication equipment in a group purchase. Total cost was $410,000 paid in cash. An independent appraisal valued the land at $322,875 and the communication equipment at $107,625.
Sep 1	Sold a building that cost $565,000 (accumulated depreciation of $265,000 through December 31 of the preceding year). Plumb received $350,000 cash from the sale of the building. Depreciation is computed on a straight-line basis. The building has a 40-year useful life and a residual value of $45,000.
Dec 31	Recorded depreciation as follows: Communication equipment is depreciated by the straight-line method over a 5-year life with zero residual value. Office equipment is depreciated double-declining-balance over 6 years with $4,000 residual value.

Requirement

1. Record the transactions in the journal of Whitney Plumb Associates. The company ends its accounting year on December 31.

P9-30A *(L.OBJ. 4)* **Natural resource accounting [15–20 min]**
Donahue Oil Company has an account titled Oil and Gas Properties. Donahue paid $6,400,000 for oil reserves holding an estimated 500,000 barrels of oil. Assume the company paid $590,000 for additional geological tests of the property and $400,000 to prepare for drilling. During the first year, Donahue removed 70,000 barrels of oil, which it sold on account for $31 per barrel. Operating expenses totaled $840,000, all paid in cash.

Requirement

1. Record all of Donahue's transactions, including depletion for the first year.

P9-31A *(L.OBJ. 5)* **Accounting for intangibles [20–25 min]**
Central States Telecom provides communication services in Iowa, Nebraska, the Dakotas, and Montana. Central States purchased goodwill as part of the acquisition of Sheldon Wireless Company, which had the following figures:

Book value of assets	$	800,000
Market value of assets		1,200,000
Liabilities		510,000

Requirements

1. Journalize the entry to record Central States' purchase of Sheldon Wireless for $480,000 cash plus a $720,000 note payable.
2. What special asset does Central States' acquisition of Sheldon Wireless identify? How should Central States Telecom account for this asset after acquiring Sheldon Wireless? Explain in detail.

P9-32A *(L.OBJ. 6)* **Ethics [10–20 min]**
On May 31, 2010, Deliver It, the overnight shipper, had total assets of $24 billion and total liabilities of $17 billion. Included among the assets were property, plant, and equipment with a cost of $19 billion and accumulated depreciation of $11 billion. During the year ended May 31, 2010, Deliver It earned total revenues of $32 billion and had total expenses of $27 billion, of which 5 billion was depreciation expenses. The CFO and the Controller are concerned that the results of 2010 will make investors unhappy. Additionally, both hold stock options to purchase shares at a reduced price, so they would like to see the market price continue to grow. They decide to "extend" the life of assets so that depreciation will be reduced to three billion for 2010.

Requirements

1. What is the change to net income due to their decision?
2. What appears to be their motivation for the change in asset lives? Is this ethical? Explain.

■ Problems (Group B)

P9-33B *(L.OBJ. 1, 2)* **Capitalized asset cost and Partial year depreciation [20–25 min]**
Park and Fly Parking, near an airport, incurred the following costs to acquire land, make land improvements, and construct and furnish a small building:

a. Purchase price of 3 acres of land	$ 86,000
b. Delinquent real estate taxes on the land to be paid by Park and Fly	5,700
c. Additional dirt and earthmoving	8,400
d. Title insurance on the land acquisition	3,400
e. Fence around the boundary of the property	9,300
f. Building permit for the building	1,200
g. Architect's fee for the design of the building	23,200
h. Signs near the front of the property	9,200
i. Materials used to construct the building	217,000
j. Labor to construct the building	169,000
k. Interest cost on construction loan for the building	9,100
l. Parking lots on the property	29,500
m. Lights for the parking lots	10,400
n. Salary of construction supervisor (80% to building; 20% to parking lot and concrete walks)	60,000
o. Furniture	11,900
p. Transportation of furniture from seller to the building	2,700
q. Landscaping (shrubs)	6,400

Park and Fly Airport Parking depreciates land improvements over 15 years, buildings over 30 years, and furniture over 8 years, all on a straight-line basis with zero residual value.

Requirements

1. Set up columns for Land, Land Improvements, Building, and Furniture. Show how to account for each cost by listing the cost under the correct account. Determine the total cost of each asset.
2. All construction was complete and the assets were placed in service on September 1. Record partial-year depreciation for the year ended December 31.

P9-34B *(L.OBJ. 1, 2)* **Capitalized asset cost and first year depreciation, and identifying depreciation results that meet management objectives [30–40 min]**

On January 4, 2010, Swifty Delivery Service purchased a truck at a cost of $62,000. Before placing the truck in service, Swifty spent $2,200 painting it, $300 replacing tires, and $5,500 overhauling the engine. The truck should remain in service for 6 years and have a residual value of $14,700. The truck's annual mileage is expected to be 15,000 miles in each of the first 4 years and 12,120 miles in each of the next 2 years—84,240 miles in total. In deciding which depreciation method to use, Mike Magnuson, the general manager, requests a depreciation schedule for each of the depreciation methods (straight-line, units-of-production, and double-declining-balance).

Requirements

1. Prepare a depreciation schedule for each depreciation method, showing asset cost, depreciation expense, accumulated depreciation, and asset book value.
2. Swifty prepares financial statements using the depreciation method that reports the highest net income in the early years of asset use. For income-tax purposes, the company uses the depreciation method that minimizes income taxes in the early years. Consider the first year that Swifty uses the truck. Identify the depreciation methods that meet the general manager's objectives, assuming the income tax authorities permit the use of any of the methods.

P9-35B *(L.OBJ. 2, 3)* **Lump sum asset purchases and partial year depreciation [20–25 min]**

Guilda Bell Associates surveys American eating habits. The company's accounts include Land, Buildings, Office equipment, and Communication equipment, with a separate accumulated depreciation account for each asset. During 2011, Bell completed the following transactions:

Jan 1	Traded in old office equipment with book value of $38,000 (cost of $130,000 and accumulated depreciation of $92,000) for new equipment. Bell also paid $82,000 in cash.
Apr 1	Acquired land and communication equipment in a group purchase. Total cost was $450,000 paid in cash. An independent appraisal valued the land at $354,375 and the communication equipment at $118,125.
Sep 1	Sold a building that cost $580,000 (accumulated depreciation of $280,000 through December 31 of the preceding year). Bell received $360,000 cash from the sale of the building. Depreciation is computed on a straight-line basis. The building has a 40-year useful life and a residual value of $40,000.
Dec 31	Recorded depreciation as follows: Communication equipment is depreciated by the straight-line method over a 5-year life with zero residual value. Office equipment is depreciated using the double-declining-balance over 6 years with $3,000 residual value.

Requirement

1. Record the transactions in the journal of Guilda Bell Associates. Bell ends its accounting year on December 31.

P9-36B *(L.OBJ. 4)* **Natural resource accounting [15–20 min]**

Chapman Oil Company has an account titled Oil and Gas Properties. Chapman paid $6,600,000 for oil reserves holding an estimated 500,000 barrels of oil. Assume the company paid $590,000 for additional geological tests of the property and $430,000 to prepare for drilling. During the first year, Chapman removed 72,000 barrels of oil, which it sold on account for $34 per barrel. Operating expenses totaled $870,000, all paid in cash.

Requirement

1. Record all of Chapman's transactions, including depletion for the first year.

P9-37B *(L.OBJ. 5)* **Accounting for intangibles [20–25 min]**

Midtown Telecom provides communication services in Iowa, Nebraska, the Dakotas, and Montana. Midtown purchased goodwill as part of the acquisition of Surety Wireless Company, which had the following figures:

Book value of assets	$ 850,000
Market value of assets	1,200,000
Liabilities	560,000

Requirements

1. Journalize the entry to record Midtown's purchase of Surety Wireless for $440,000 cash plus a $660,000 note payable.
2. What special asset does Midtown's acquisition of Surety Wireless identify? How should Midtown Telecom account for this asset after acquiring Surety Wireless? Explain in detail.

P9-38B *(L.OBJ. 6)* **Ethics [10–20 min]**

On May 31, 2010, Ship It, the overnight shipper, had total assets of $25 billion and total liabilities of $16 billion. Included among the assets were property, plant, and equipment with a cost of $17 billion and accumulated depreciation of $10 billion. During the year ended May 31, 2010, Ship It earned total revenues of $24 billion and had total expenses of $20 billion, of which 4 billion was depreciation expenses. The CFO and the Controller are concerned that the results of 2010 will make investors unhappy. Additionally, both hold stock options to purchase shares at a reduced price, so they would like to see the market price continue to grow. They decide to "extend" the life of assets so that depreciation will be reduced to 1 billion for 2010.

Requirements

1. What is the change to net income due to their decision?
2. What appears to be their motivation for the change in asset lives? Is this ethical? Explain.

Continuing Exercise

E9-39 This exercise continues the Sherman Lawn Service situation from Exercise 8-41 of Chapter 8. Refer to the Chapter 2 data for Exercise 2-63. In Chapter 2, we learned that Sherman Lawn Service had purchased a lawn mower and weed whacker on August 3 and that they were expected to last four years.

Requirements

1. Calculate the amount of depreciation for each asset for the year ended December 31, 2009, assuming both assets are using straight-line depreciation.
2. Record the entry for the partial year's depreciation. Date it December 31, 2009.

Continuing Problem

P9-40 This problem continues the Haupt Consulting situation from Problem 8-42 of Chapter 8. Refer to Problem 2-64 of Chapter 2. In Chapter 2, we learned that Haupt Consulting had purchased a **Dell** computer and office furniture on December 3 and 4, respectively, and that they were expected to last five years.

Requirements

1. Calculate the amount of depreciation for each asset for the year ended December 31, 2010, assuming both assets are using double-declining-balance depreciation.
2. Record the entry for the one month's depreciation. Date it December 31, 2010.

Apply Your Knowledge

Decision Cases

Suppose you are considering investing in two businesses, Shelly's Seashell Enterprises and Jeremy Feigenbaum Systems. The two companies are virtually identical, and both began operations at the beginning of the current year. During the year, each company purchased inventory as follows:

Jan	4	10,000 units at $4 =	$ 40,000
Apr	6	5,000 units at 5 =	25,000
Aug	9	7,000 units at 6 =	42,000
Nov	27	10,000 units at 7 =	70,000
Totals		32,000	$177,000

During the first year, both companies sold 25,000 units of inventory.

In early January, both companies purchased equipment costing $143,000, with a 10-year estimated useful life and a $20,000 residual value. Shelly uses the inventory and depreciation methods that maximize reported income (FIFO and straight-line). By contrast, Feigenbaum uses the inventory and depreciation methods that minimize income taxes (LIFO and double-declining-balance). Both companies' trial balances at December 31 included the following:

Sales revenue	$270,000
Operating expenses	80,700

Requirements

1. Prepare both companies' income statements.
2. Write an investment letter to address the following questions for your clients: Which company appears to be more profitable? Which company has more cash to invest in new projects? Which company would you prefer to invest in? Why?

Ethical Issue

Western Bank & Trust purchased land and a building for the lump sum of $3 million. To get the maximum tax deduction, Western allocated 90% of the purchase price to the building and only 10% to the land. A more realistic allocation would have been 70% to the building and 30% to the land.

Requirements

1. Explain the tax advantage of allocating too much to the building and too little to the land.
2. Was Western's allocation ethical? If so, state why. If not, why not? Identify who was harmed.

■ Financial Statement Case

Refer to the **Amazon.com** financial statements, including Notes 1 and 3, in Appendix A at the end of this book. Answer the following questions.

Requirements

1. Which depreciation method does **Amazon.com** use for reporting in the financial statements? What type of depreciation method does the company probably use for income tax purposes? Why is this method preferable for tax purposes?
2. Depreciation expense is embedded in the operating expense amounts listed on the income statement. Note 3 gives the amount of depreciation expense. What was the amount of depreciation for 2007? Record **Amazon's** depreciation expense for 2007.
3. The statement of cash flows reports the purchases of fixed assets. How much were **Amazon's** fixed asset purchases during 2007? Journalize the company's cash purchase of fixed assets.

■ Team Project

Visit a local business.

Requirements

1. List all its plant assets.
2. If possible, interview the manager. Gain as much information as you can about the business's plant assets. For example, try to determine the assets' costs, the depreciation method the company is using, and the estimated useful life of each asset category. If an interview is impossible, then develop your own estimates of the assets' costs, useful lives, and book values, assuming an appropriate depreciation method.
3. Determine whether the business has any intangible assets. If so, list them and learn as much as possible about their nature, cost, and estimated useful lives.
4. Write a detailed report of your findings and be prepared to present it to the class.

Quick Check Answers

1. *a* 2. *c* 3. *c* 4. *c* 5. *a* 6. *c* 7. *d* 8. *d* 9. *c* 10. *d*

For online homework, exercises, and problems that provide you immediate feedback, please visit www.myaccountinglab.com.

10 Current Liabilities, Payroll, and Long-Term Liabilities

Learning Objectives/ Success Keys

1. Account for current liabilities of known amount
2. Account for current liabilities that must be estimated
3. Calculate payroll and payroll tax amounts
4. Journalize basic payroll transactions
5. Describe bonds payable
6. Measure interest expense on bonds using the straight-line amortization method
7. Report liabilities on the balance sheet
8. Compare issuing bonds to issuing stocks

Most companies have several types of liabilities. In this chapter you will learn more about accounts payable, payroll, and other current liabilities. Recall that *current liabilities* are obligations due within one year or within the company's operating cycle if it is longer than a year. Obligations due beyond that period are *long-term liabilities*. You will see how companies account for product **warranties**, which are product guarantees. Further, we will cover a special type of long-term liability, bonds payable. Lastly, we will summarize the chapter by showing how Smart Touch's liabilities appear on the Balance Sheet.

Current Liabilities of Known Amount

The amounts of most liabilities are known. Let us begin with current liabilities of a known amount.

1 Account for current liabilities of known amount

Accounts Payable

Amounts owed for products or services purchased on account are *accounts payable*. Since these are due on average in 30 days, they are current liabilities. We have seen many accounts payable illustrations in preceding chapters. Consider the Balance Sheet for May 31, 2010, prepared in Chapter 4 for Smart Touch Learning and reproduced as follows:

EXHIBIT 10-1 **Classified Balance Sheet in Account Form (Reproduced from Exhibit 4-12)**

SMART TOUCH LEARNING
Balance Sheet
May 31, 2010

Assets				Liabilities	
Current assets:				Current liabilities:	
Cash		$ 4,800		Accounts payable	$18,200
Accounts receivable		2,600		Salary payable	900
Supplies		600		Interest payable	100
Prepaid rent		2,000		Unearned service revenue	400
Total current assets			$10,000	Total current liabilities	19,600
Plant assets:				Long-term liabilities	
Furniture	$18,000			Notes payable	20,000
Less: Accumulated depreciation—furniture	−300	17,700		Total liabilities	39,600
Building	48,000				
Less: Accumulated depreciation—building	−200	47,800		**Owner's Equity**	
Total plant assets			65,500	Sheena Bright, Capital	35,900
Total assets			$75,500	Total liabilities and owner's equity	$75,500

Notice that the balance on May 31, 2010, for Accounts payable is $18,200. As we learned in Chapter 5, one of Smart Touch's common transactions is the credit purchase of inventory. With accounts payable and inventory systems integrated, Smart Touch records the purchase of inventory on account. A reproduction of the Chapter 5 entry that Smart Touch made on June 3 to purchase $700 of inventory on account follows:

Jun 3	Inventory (A+)	700	
	Accounts payable (L+)		700
	Purchase on account.		

Then, when Smart Touch paid the liability and took advantage of the purchase discount on June 15, the entry was as follows:

Jun 15	Accounts payable (L−)	700	
	Cash (A−)		679
	Inventory (A−)		21
	Paid on account within discount period.		

Short-Term Notes Payable

Short-term notes payable are a common form of financing. Short-term notes payable are promissory notes that must be paid within one year. Consider how the entry on June 3 would change if Smart Touch had purchased the inventory with a 10%, one year note payable. The modified June 3 purchase entry follows:

2010				
Jun 3	Inventory (A+)	700		
	Note payable, short-term (L+)		700	A*
	Purchased inventory on a one-year, 10% note.			

At year-end it is necessary to accrue interest expense for the 7 months from June to December as follows:

2010				
Dec 31	Interest expense ($700 × 0.10 × 7/12) (E+)	41		
	Interest payable (L+)		41	B
	Accrued interest expense at year-end.			

The interest accrual at December 31, 2010, allocated $41 of the interest on this note to 2010. During 2011, the interest on this note for the 5 remaining months is $29, as shown in the following entry for the payment of the note in 2011:

2011			
Jun 3	Note payable, short-term (L–)	700	
	Interest payable (L–)	41	
	Interest expense ($700 × 0.10 × 5/12) (E+)	29	
	Cash (A–)		770
	Paid note and interest at maturity.		

Sales Tax Payable

Most states assess sales tax on retail sales. Retailers collect the sales tax in addition to the price of the item sold. Sales tax payable is a current liability because the retailer must pay the state in less than a year. Let us apply this to Smart Touch Learning.

Suppose December's taxable sales for Smart Touch Learning totaled $10,000. Smart Touch collected an additional 6% sales tax, which would equal $600 ($10,000 × 0.06). Smart Touch would record that month's sales as follows:

2010				
Dec 31	Cash ($10,000 × 1.06) (A+)	10,600		
	Sales revenue (R+)		10,000	
	Sales tax payable ($10,000 × 0.06) (L+)		600	C
	To record cash sales and the related sales tax.			

As noted above, Sales tax payable is a current liability. Notice how it shows as an obligation (credit balance) in the Sales tax payable T-account, just after the sale.

*The red colored boxes throughout the chapter reference Exhibit 10-9

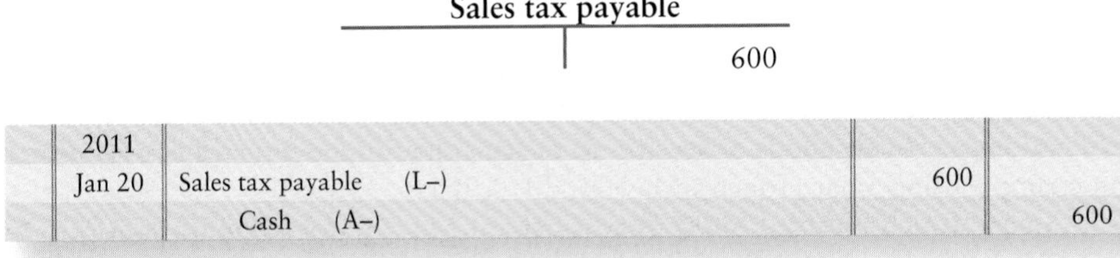

Sales tax payable	
	600

2011			
Jan 20	Sales tax payable (L–)	600	
	Cash (A–)		600

Companies forward the sales tax to the state at regular intervals. They normally submit it monthly, but they could file it at other intervals, depending on the state and the amount of the tax. To pay the tax, the company debits Sales tax payable and credits Cash.

Current Portion of Long-Term Notes Payable

Most long-term notes payable are paid in installments. The **current portion of notes payable** (also called **current maturity**) is the principal amount that will be paid within one year—a current liability. The remaining portion is long-term. Let us consider the $20,000 notes payable that Smart Touch Learning signed in May, 2010 (refer to Exhibit 10-1). If the note will be paid over four years with payments of $5,000 plus interest due each May 1, what portion of the note is current? The portion that must be paid within one year, $5,000, is current. At the inception of the note, the company recorded the entire note as long term. An adjusting entry to the account for the $5,000 principal that is current will need to be made at year-end.

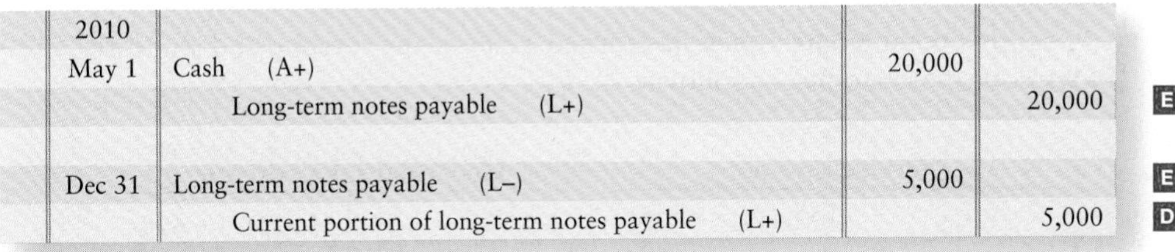

2010				
May 1	Cash (A+)	20,000		
	Long-term notes payable (L+)		20,000	E
Dec 31	Long-term notes payable (L–)	5,000		E
	Current portion of long-term notes payable (L+)		5,000	D

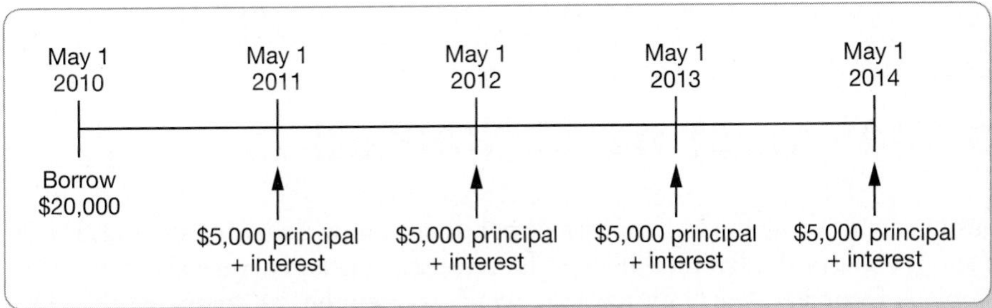

Notice that the reclassification entry on December 31 does not change the total amount of debt. It only reclassifies $5,000 of the total debt from long-term to current.

Accrued Expenses (Accrued Liabilities)

In Chapter 3, we learned that an accrued expense is any expense that has been incurred but has not yet been paid. That is why accrued expenses are also called accrued liabilities. Accrued expenses typically occur with the passage of time, such as interest on a note payable.

Refer to Exhibit 10-1, Smart Touch Learning's May 31, 2010, Balance Sheet. Like most other companies, Smart Touch has accrued liabilities for salaries payable and interest payable.

Unearned Revenues

Unearned revenue is also called *deferred revenue*. Unearned revenue arises when a business has received cash in advance of performing work and, therefore, has an obligation to provide goods or services to the customer in the future. Let us consider an example using Smart Touch's May 31, 2010, Balance Sheet.

Smart Touch received $600 in advance on May 21 for a month's work. On May 31, because it received cash before earning the revenue, Smart Touch has a liability to perform 20 more days of work for the client. The liability is called Unearned service revenue. The entry made by Smart Touch on May 21, 2010, follows:

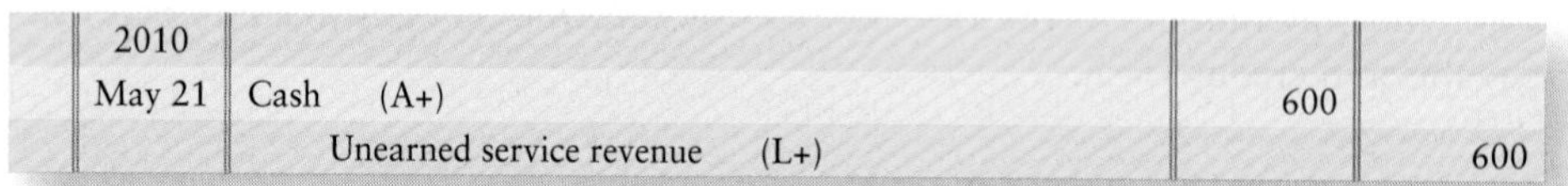

2010			
May 21	Cash (A+)	600	
	Unearned service revenue (L+)		600

During May, Smart Touch delivered one-third of the work and earned $200 ($600 × 1/3) of the revenue. The May 31, 2010, adjusting entry made by Smart Touch decreased the liability, and increased the revenue, as follows:

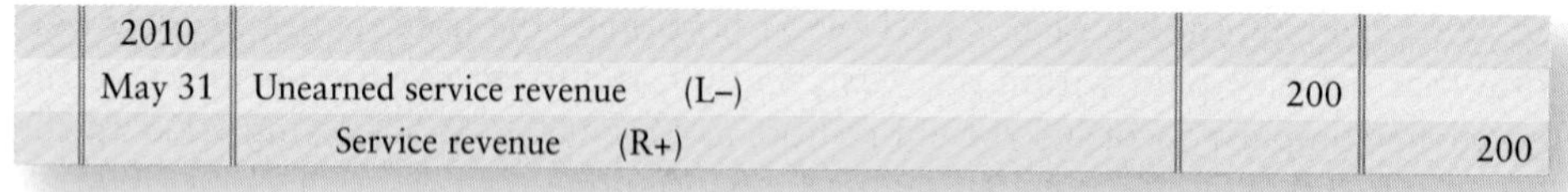

2010			
May 31	Unearned service revenue (L–)	200	
	Service revenue (R+)		200

At this point Smart Touch has earned $200 of the revenue and still owes $400 of work to the customer, as follows:

Service revenue			
		May 31	200

Unearned sales revenue			
May 31	200	May 21	600
		Bal	400

F

Current Liabilities that must be Estimated

2 Account for current liabilities that must be estimated

A business may know that a liability exists, but not know the exact amount. It cannot simply ignore the liability. It must be reported on the balance sheet. A prime example is Estimated warranty payable, which is common for companies like **Dell** and **Sony**.

Estimated Warranty Payable

Many companies guarantee their products against defects under *warranty* agreements. Both ninety-day and one-year warranties are common.

The matching principle says to record the *Warranty expense* in the same period that we record the revenue related to that warranty. The expense, therefore, is incurred when you make a sale, not when you pay the warranty claims. At the time of the sale, the company does not know the exact amount of warranty expense, but the business can estimate it.

Assume that Smart Touch Learning made sales of $50,000 subject to product warranties on June 10, 2010. Smart Touch estimates that 3% of its products may require warranty repairs. The company would record the sales and the warranty expense in the same period, as follows:

Jun 10	Accounts receivable (A+)	50,000	
	Sales revenue (R+)		50,000
	Sales on account.		
Jun 10	Warranty expense ($50,000 × 0.03) (E+)	1,500	
	Estimated warranty payable (L+)		1,500
	To accrue warranty payable.		

Assume that Smart Touch's customers make claims that must be honored through the warranty offered by the company. The warranty payments total $800 and are made on June 27, 2010. Smart Touch repairs the defective goods and makes the following journal entry:

2010			
Jun 27	Estimated warranty payable (L–)	800	
	Cash (A–)		800
	To pay warranty claims.		

Smart Touch's expense on the income statement is $1,500, the estimated amount, not the $800 actually paid. After paying for these warranties, Smart Touch's liability account has a credit balance of $700. This $700 balance represents warranty claims Smart Touch expects to pay in the future based on its estimates; therefore, the $700 is a liability to Smart Touch.

Estimated warranty payable

Debit	Credit
800	1,500
	Bal 700

G

Contingent Liabilities

A **contingent liability** is a potential, rather than an actual liability, because it depends on a *future* event. For example, suppose Smart Touch is sued because of alleged patent infringement on one of its learning DVDs. Smart Touch, therefore, faces a contingent liability, which may or may not become actual. If the outcome of this lawsuit is unfavorable, it could hurt Smart Touch. Therefore, it would be unethical to withhold knowledge of the lawsuit from investors and creditors.

Another contingent liability arises when you *cosign a note payable* for another entity. An example of this would occur if Greg's Groovy Tunes were to cosign Smart Touch's note payable. The company co-signing (Greg's Groovy Tunes) has a contingent liability until the note comes due and is paid by the other entity (Smart Touch). If the other company (Smart Touch) pays off the note, the contingent liability vanishes (for Greg's Groovy Tunes). If not, the co-signing company (Greg's Groovy Tunes) must pay the debt for the other entity (Smart Touch).

As shown in Exhibit 10-2, the accounting profession divides contingent liabilities into three categories—remote, reasonably possible, and probable—based on the likelihood of an actual loss.

EXHIBIT 10-2 | Contingent Liabilities: Three Categories

Likelihood of an Actual Loss	How to Report the Contingency
Remote	Ignore. *Example:* A frivolous lawsuit.
Reasonably possible	Describe the situation in a note to the financial statements. *Example:* The company is the defendant in a significant lawsuit and the outcome is unknown.
Probable, and the amount of the loss can be estimated	Record an expense and an actual liability, based on estimated amounts. *Example:* Warranty expense, as illustrated in the preceding section.

Stop & Think...

Do you ever guess how much money it will take to fill the gas tank in your car? If you do, you are making an informal sort of accounting estimate. Estimations can be formal or informal, but we all make accounting estimates. The key to why we estimate is so that we can measure income properly. In the case of estimating your fuel bill, it might be just so you are sure you have enough cash on hand to pay it. Journalizing an estimate, such as for the fuel bill, is an example of an accrued liability.

Stop and review what you have learned by studying the Decision Guidelines.

Decision Guidelines

ACCOUNTING FOR CURRENT LIABILITIES

Suppose you are in charge of accounting for your student service club. The club decides to borrow $1,000 for a **Habitat for Humanity** project. The bank requires your club's balance sheet. These Decision Guidelines will help you report current liabilities accurately.

Decision	Guidelines
• What are the two main issues in accounting for current liabilities?	• *Recording* the liability in the journal • *Reporting* the liability on the balance sheet
• What are the two basic categories of current liabilities?	• Current liabilities of *known amount:* Accounts payable; Accrued expenses (accrued liabilities) Short-term notes payable; Salary, wages, commission, and bonus payable Sales tax payable; Unearned revenues Current portion of long-term notes payable • Current liabilities that *must be estimated*: Estimated warranty payable

Summary Problem 1

Answer each question independently.

Requirements

1. A **Wendys** restaurant made cash sales of $4,000 subject to a 5% sales tax. Record the sales and the related sales tax. Also record **Wendy's** payment of the tax to the state of South Carolina.
2. At December 31, 2011, Chastains' Hair Salons reported a 6% long-term note payable as follows:

Current Liabilities	
Portion of long-term note payable due within one year................	$ 10,000
Interest payable ($210,000 × 0.06 × 6/12)..................................	6,300
Long-Term Liabilities	
Long-term note payable	$200,000

   Chastains' Hair Salons pays interest on June 30 each year.

   Show how Chastains' Hair Salons would report its liabilities on the year-end balance sheet one year later—December 31, 2012. The current maturity of the long-term note payable is $10,000 each year until the liability is paid off.
3. How does a contingent liability differ from an actual liability?

Solution

Requirement 1

	Accounts	Debit	Credit
	Cash ($4,000 × 1.05) (A+)	4,200	
	Sales revenue (R+)		4,000
	Sales tax payable ($4,000 × 0.05) (L+)		200
	To record cash sales and sales tax.		
	Sales tax payable (L–)	200	
	Cash (A–)		200
	To pay sales tax.		

Requirement 2

Chastains' Hair Salons' balance sheet at December 31, 2012, is as follows:

Current Liabilities	
Portion of long-term note payable due within one year................	$ 10,000
Interest payable ($200,000 × 0.06 × 6/12)..................................	6,000
Long-Term Liabilities	
Long-term note payable	$190,000

Requirement 3

A contingent liability is a *potential* liability. The contingency may or may not become an actual liability.

Accounting for Payroll

3 Calculate payroll and payroll tax amounts

Payroll, also called **employee compensation**, also creates accrued expenses. For service organizations—such as CPA firms and travel agencies—payroll is *the* major expense. Labor cost is so important that most businesses develop a special payroll system. There are numerous ways to label an employee's pay:

- *Salary* is pay stated at an annual, monthly, or weekly rate, such as $48,000 per year, $4,000 per month, or $1,000 per week.
- *Wages* are pay amounts stated at an hourly rate, such as $10 per hour.
- *Commission* is pay stated as a percentage of a sale amount, such as a 5% commission on a sale. A realtor who earns 5% commission, for example, earns $5,000 on a $100,000 sale of real estate.
- *Bonus* is pay over and above base salary (wage or commission). A bonus is usually paid for exceptional performance—in a single amount after year-end.
- *Benefits* are extra compensation—items that are not paid directly to the employee. Benefits cover health, life, and disability insurance. The employer pays the insurance company, which then provides coverage for the employee. Another type of benefit, retirement, sets aside money for the employee for his or her future retirement.

Businesses pay employees at a base rate for a set period—called *straight time.* For additional hours—*overtime*—the employee may get a higher pay rate, depending on the job classification and wage and hour laws.

Assume Ryan Oliver was hired as an accountant for Smart Touch Learning. His pay is as follows:

- Ryan earns a salary of $600 per week for straight time (40 hours), so his hourly pay rate is $15 ($600/40).
- The company pays *time-and-a-half* for overtime. That rate is 150% (1.5 times) the straight-time pay rate. Thus, Ryan earns $22.50 per hour of overtime ($15.00 × 1.5 = $22.50).
- For working 42 hours during a week, he earns gross pay of $645, computed as follows:

Straight-time pay for 40 hours	$600
Overtime pay for 2 overtime hours: 2 × $22.50	45
Gross pay	$645

Gross Pay and Net (Take-Home) Pay

Two pay amounts are important for accounting purposes:

- **Gross pay** is the total amount of salary, wages, commission, and bonus earned by the employee during a pay period. Gross pay is the amount before taxes or any other deductions. Gross pay is an expense to the employer. In the preceding example, Ryan Oliver's gross pay was $645.
- **Net pay**, also called **take-home pay**, is the amount the employee gets to keep. Take-home pay equals gross pay minus all deductions. The employer writes a paycheck to each employee for his or her take-home pay.

Payroll Withholding Deductions

The federal government and most states require employers to deduct taxes from employee paychecks. Insurance companies and investment companies may also get some of the employee's pay. Amounts withheld from paychecks are called *withholding deductions*. Payroll withholding deductions are the difference between gross pay and take-home pay. These deductions are withheld from paychecks and sent directly to the government, to insurance companies, or to other entities. Payroll deductions fall into two categories:

- *Required deductions*, such as employee federal and state income tax and Social Security tax. Employees pay their income tax and Social Security tax through payroll deductions.
- *Optional deductions*, including insurance premiums, retirement plan contributions, charitable contributions, and other amounts that are withheld at the employee's request.

After being withheld, payroll deductions become the liability of the employer, who then pays the outside party—taxes to the government and contributions to charitable organizations, for example.

Required Withholding for Employee Income Tax

United States law requires companies to withhold income tax from employee paychecks. The income tax deducted from gross pay is called **withheld income tax.** The amount withheld depends on the employee's gross pay and on the number of *withholding allowances* he or she claims.

An employee files Form W-4 with his or her employer to indicate the number of allowances claimed for income-tax withholding. Each allowance lowers the amount of tax withheld:

- An unmarried taxpayer usually claims one allowance.
- A childless married couple usually claims two allowances.
- A married couple with one child usually claims three allowances, and so on.

Exhibit 10-3 shows a W-4 for Ryan Oliver, who claims married with three allowances (line 5).

Required Withholding for Employee Social Security (FICA) Tax

The **Federal Insurance Contributions Act (FICA)**, also known as the Social Security Act, created the Social Security Tax. The Social Security program provides retirement, disability, and medical benefits. The law requires employers to withhold **Social Security (FICA) tax** from employees' paychecks. The FICA tax has two components:

1. Old age, survivors, and disability insurance (OASDI)
2. Health insurance (Medicare)

The amount of tax withheld varies from year to year because the taxable wage base changes each year. For 2008, the OASDI tax applies to the first $102,000 of employee earnings in a year. The taxable amount of earnings is adjusted annually. The OASDI tax rate is 6.2%. Therefore, the maximum OASDI tax that an employee paid in 2008 was $6,324 ($102,000 × 0.062).

The Medicare portion of the FICA tax applies to all employee earnings—that means that there is no maximum tax. This tax rate is 1.45%. Therefore, an employee pays a combined FICA tax rate of 7.65% (6.2% + 1.45%) of the first $102,000 of annual earnings, plus 1.45% of earnings above $102,000.

EXHIBIT 10-3 | **W4 for Ryan Oliver**

Form **W-4**
Department of the Treasury
Internal Revenue Service

Employee's Withholding Allowance Certificate

▶ **Whether you are entitled to claim a certain number of allowances or exemption from withholding is subject to review by the IRS. Your employer may be required to send a copy of this form to the IRS.**

OMB No. 1545-0074
2008

1 Type or print your first name and middle initial.	Last name	2 Your social security number
Ryan G.	Oliver	123 : 45 : 6789

Home address (number and street or rural route)	3 ☐ Single ☑ Married ☐ Married, but withhold at higher Single rate. **Note.** If married, but legally separated, or spouse is a nonresident alien, check the "Single" box.
305 Lost Key Drive	
City or town, state, and ZIP code	4 **If your last name differs from that shown on your social security card, check here. You must call 1-800-772-1213 for a replacement card.** ▶ ☐
Pensacola, FL 32526	

5 Total number of allowances you are claiming (from line **H** above **or** from the applicable worksheet on page 2) — **5** 3

6 Additional amount, if any, you want withheld from each paycheck . . . . — **6** $

7 I claim exemption from withholding for 2008, and I certify that I meet **both** of the following conditions for exemption.
- Last year I had a right to a refund of **all** federal income tax withheld because I had **no** tax liability **and**
- This year I expect a refund of **all** federal income tax withheld because I expect to have **no** tax liability.

If you meet both conditions, write "Exempt" here . . . . ▶ **7**

Under penalties of perjury, I declare that I have examined this certificate and to the best of my knowledge and belief, it is true, correct, and complete.

Employee's signature
(Form is not valid unless you sign it.) ▶ Ryan G. Oliver — **Date** ▶

8 Employer's name and address (Employer: Complete lines 8 and 10 only if sending to the IRS.)	9 Office code (optional)	10 Employer identification number (EIN)
Smart Touch Learning; 281 Wave Ave; Niceville, FL 32578		20 : 1234567

For Privacy Act and Paperwork Reduction Act Notice, see page 2. Cat. No. 10220Q Form **W-4** (2008)

To make your calculations easier to compute, let us assume that the 2010 FICA tax is 7.65%. The wage limit for social security (6.2%) is only on the first $102,000 of employee earnings each year. For Medicare, there is no wage limit. (Use these numbers when you complete this chapter's assignments.)

Assume that James Kolen, another employee of Smart Touch, earned $95,000 prior to December. Kolen's salary for December is $10,000.

- How much of Kolen's December salary is subject to FICA tax? Only $7,000 is subject to social security tax—from $95,000 up to the $102,000 maximum. All $10,000 is subject to Medicare tax.
- How much FICA tax will be withheld from Kolen's December paycheck? The computation follows:

	OASDI (Social Security)	HI (Medicare)
Employee earnings subject to the tax in one year	$102,000	No max
Employee earnings prior to the current month	– 95,000	
Current pay subject to OASDI portion of FICA tax	$ 7,000	$ 10,000
FICA tax rate	× 0.062	× 0.0145
FICA tax to be withheld from the current paycheck	$ 434	$ 145
Total OASDI & HI tax (434 + 145)	$ 579	

Optional Withholding Deductions

As a convenience to employees, some companies withhold payroll deductions and then pay designated organizations according to employee instructions. Insurance premiums, retirement savings, union dues, and gifts to charities are examples.

The following table summarizes James Kolen's final pay period of the year (amounts assumed):

Gross pay		$10,000
Withholding deductions:		
Employee income tax (20%)	$2,000	
Employee FICA tax	579	
Employee co-pay for health insurance	180	
Employee contribution to United Way	20	
Total withholdings		2,779
Net (take-home) pay		$ 7,221

Employer Payroll Taxes

In addition to income tax and FICA tax, which are withheld from employee paychecks, *employers* must pay at least three payroll taxes. These taxes do *not* come out of employee paychecks.

1. Employer **(FICA) tax**
2. State **unemployment compensation tax**
3. Federal **unemployment compensation tax**

Employer FICA Tax

In addition to the FICA tax withheld from the employee's paycheck, the employer must pay an equal amount into the program. The Social Security system is funded by equal contributions from employer and employee.

State and Federal Unemployment Compensation Taxes

State and federal **unemployment compensation taxes** finance workers' compensation for people laid off from work. In recent years, employers have paid a combined tax of 6.2% on the first $7,000 of each employee's annual earnings for unemployment tax. The proportion paid to the state *depends* on the individual state, but for many it is 5.4% to the state, plus 0.8% to the federal government. For this payroll tax the employer uses two liability accounts:

- Federal Unemployment Tax Payable (FUTA)
- State Unemployment Tax Payable (SUTA)

Exhibit 10-4 shows a typical distribution of payroll costs for Sheena Bright, who earns a weekly salary from Smart Touch of $1,000. All amounts are assumed.

EXHIBIT 10-4 | **Typical Breakdown of Payroll Costs for One Employee**

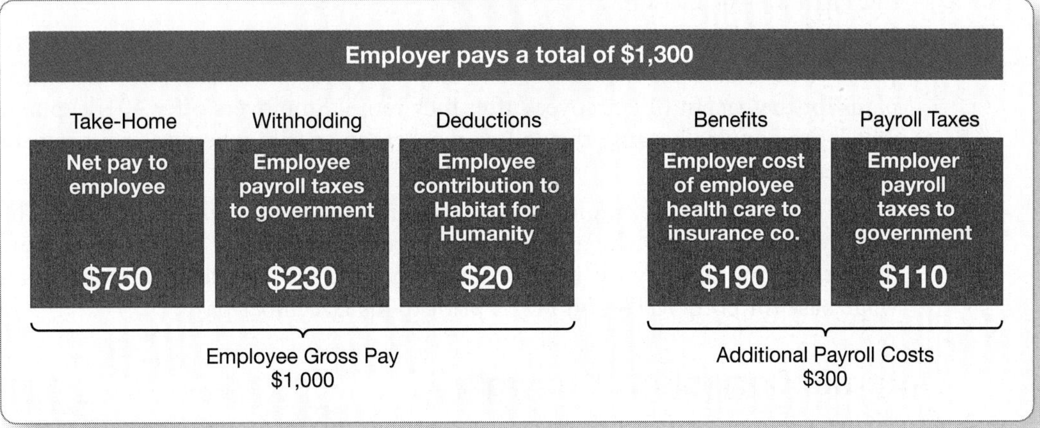

Journalizing Payroll Transactions

Exhibit 10-5 summarizes an employer's entries for a monthly payroll of $10,000. All amounts are assumed, based on James Kolen's December salary.

4 Journalize basic payroll transactions

EXHIBIT 10-5 | **Payroll Accounting by the Employer—James Kolen's pay**

2010				
Dec 31	A. Salary Expense			
	Salary expense (or Wage expense or Commission expense) (E+)	10,000		
	Employee income tax payable (L+)		2,000	H
	FICA tax payable (L+)		579	I
	Payable to health insurance (L+)		180	J
	Payable to United Way (L+)		20	K
	Salary payable (take-home pay) (L+)		7,221	L
	To record salary expense.			
Dec 31	B. Benefits Expense			
	Health insurance expense (E+)	800		
	Life insurance expense (E+)	200		
	Retirement plan expense (E+)	500		
	Employee benefits payable (L+)		1,500	M
	To record employee benefits payable by the employer.			
Dec 31	C. Payroll Tax Expense			
	Payroll tax expense (E+)**	579		
	FICA tax payable (L+)		579	I
	To record employer's payroll taxes.			

**No FUTA or SUTA tax is due because James is over the maximum wage base.

- Entry A records salary expense. Gross salary is $10,000, and net (take-home) pay is $7,221. There is a payable to United Way of $20 because employees specify this charitable deduction.
- Entry B records *benefits* paid by the employer. This company pays for part of James' health and life insurance. The employer also pays cash into retirement plans for the benefit of employees after they retire. Employers offer 401(k) plans, which are popular because they allow workers to specify where their retirement funds are invested.
- Entry C records the employer's *payroll tax expense*, which includes the employer's $579 in matching FICA tax. There are no state or federal unemployment taxes on this payroll because James had already reached the maximum wage base for both SUTA and FUTA prior to his December pay.

Internal Control over Payroll

There are two main controls for payroll:

- Controls for efficiency
- Controls to safeguard payroll disbursements

Controls for Efficiency

Reconciling the bank account can be time-consuming because there may be many outstanding paychecks. To limit the outstanding checks, a company may use two payroll bank accounts. It pays the payroll from one account one month and from the other account the next month. This way the company can reconcile each account every other month, and that decreases accounting expense.

Payroll transactions are ideal for computer processing. The payroll data are stored in a file, and the computer makes the calculations, prints paychecks, and updates all records electronically.

Controls to Safeguard Payroll Disbursements

The owner of a small business can monitor his or her payroll by personal contact with employees. Large companies cannot. A particular risk is that a paycheck may be written to a fictitious person and cashed by a dishonest employee. To guard against this, large businesses adopt strict internal controls for payrolls.

Hiring and firing employees should be separated from accounting and from passing out paychecks. Photo IDs ensure that only actual employees are paid. Employees clock in at the start and clock out at the end of the workday to prove their attendance and hours worked.

As we saw in Chapter 7, the foundation of internal control is the separation of duties. This is why companies have separate departments for the following payroll functions:

- The Human Resources Department hires and fires workers.
- The Payroll Department maintains employee earnings records.
- The Accounting Department records all transactions.
- The Treasurer (or bursar) distributes paychecks to employees.

Now let us summarize the accounting for payroll by examining the Decision Guidelines.

Decision Guidelines

ACCOUNTING FOR PAYROLL

What decisions must Smart Touch Learning (or any another company) make to account for payroll?

Decision	Guidelines
• What records will Smart Touch keep in its payroll system to determine how much income tax to withhold from an employee's pay?	Employee's Withholding Allowance Certificate, Form W-4
• How does Smart Touch determine an employee's take-home pay?	*Gross pay* (Total amount earned by the employee) – *Payroll withholding deductions*: a. Withheld income tax b. Withheld FICA tax—equal amount also paid by employer c. Optional withholding deductions (insurance, retirement, charitable contributions, union dues) = *Net (take-home) pay*
• What is Smart Touch's total payroll expense?	Total payroll expense = Gross pay + *Employer paid benefits* a. Insurance (health, life, and disability) b. Retirement benefits + *Employer payroll taxes* a. Employer FICA tax—equal amount also paid by employee b. Employer state and federal unemployment taxes
• Where will Smart Touch report payroll costs?	• Payroll expenses on the income statement • Payroll liabilities on the balance sheet

Summary Problem 2

Rags-to-Riches, a clothing resale store, employs one salesperson, Dee Hunter. Hunter's straight-time salary is $400 per week, with time-and-a-half pay for hours above 40. Rags-to-Riches withholds income tax (10%) and FICA tax (7.65%) from Hunter's pay. Rags-to-Riches also pays payroll taxes for FICA (7.65%) and state and federal unemployment (5.4% and 0.8%, respectively). In addition, Rags-to-Riches contributes 6% of Hunter's gross pay into her retirement plan.

During the week ended December 26, Hunter worked 50 hours. Prior to this week, she had earned $2,000.

Requirements

(Round all amounts to the nearest dollar.)

1. Compute Hunter's gross pay and net pay for the week.
2. Record the payroll entries that Rags-to-Riches would make for:
   a. Hunter's gross pay, including overtime
   b. Expense for employee benefits
   c. Employer payroll taxes
   d. Payment of net pay to Hunter
   e. Payment for employee benefits
   f. Payment of all payroll taxes
3. How much was Rags-to-Riches' total payroll expense for the week?

Solution

Requirement 1

Gross pay:	Straight-time pay for 40 hours		$400
	Overtime pay:		
	Rate per hour ($400/40 × 1.5)	$15	
	Hours (50 – 40)	10	150
	Gross pay		$550
Net pay:	Gross pay		$550
	Less: Withheld income tax ($550 × 0.10)	$55	
	Withheld FICA tax ($550 × 0.0765)	42	97
	Net pay		$453

Requirement 2

a.	Sales salary expense (E+)	550	
	Employee income tax payable (L+)		55
	FICA tax payable (L+)		42
	Salary payable (L+)		453
b.	Retirement-Plan expense ($550 × 0.06) (E+)	33	
	Employee benefits payable (L+)		33
c.	Payroll tax expense (E+)	76	
	FICA tax payable ($550 × 0.0765) (L+)		42
	State unemployment tax payable ($550 × 0.054) (L+)		30
	Federal unemployment tax payable ($550 × 0.008) (L+)		4
d.	Salary payable (L–)	453	
	Cash (A–)		453
e.	Employee benefits payable (L–)	33	
	Cash (A–)		33
f.	Employee income tax payable (L–)	55	
	FICA Tax Payable (42 × 2) (L–)	84	
	State unemployment tax payable (L–)	30	
	Federal unemployment tax payable (L–)	4	
	Cash (A–)		118

Requirement 3

Rags-to-Riches incurred *total payroll expense* of $659 (gross pay of $550 + payroll taxes of $76 + benefits of $33). See entries (**a**) through (**c**).

Bonds: An Introduction

5 Describe bonds payable

Large companies such as **Blockbuster** and **Google** need large amounts of money to finance operations. They may borrow long-term from banks or issue bonds payable to the public to raise the money. **Bonds payable** are groups of long-term notes payable issued to multiple lenders, called bondholders. By issuing bonds payable, **Blockbuster** can borrow millions of dollars from thousands of investors, rather than depending on a loan from one single bank or lender. Each investor can buy a specified amount of **Blockbuster** bonds.

Each bondholder gets a bond certificate that shows the name of the company that borrowed the money, exactly like a note payable. The certificate states the *principal*, which is the amount the company has borrowed. The bond's principal amount is also called *maturity value*, or *par value*. The company must then pay each bondholder the principal amount at a specific future date, called the *maturity date*. Earlier in the chapter, we saw how to account for short-term notes payable. There are many similarities between the accounting for short-term notes payable and long-term notes payable.

People buy bonds to earn interest. The bond certificate states the interest rate that the company will pay and the dates the interest is due, generally semi-annually (twice a year). Exhibit 10-6, shows a bond certificate issued by Smart Touch Learning.

Review the following bond fundamentals in Exhibit 10-6.

- **Principal amount** (also called *maturity value*, or **par value**) The amount the borrower must pay back to the bondholders on the maturity date.
- **Maturity date** The date on which the borrower must pay the principal amount to the bondholders.
- **Stated interest rate** The annual rate of interest that the borrower pays the bondholders.

Types of Bonds

There are various types of bonds, including the following:

- **Term bonds** all mature at the same specified time. For example, $100,000 of term bonds may all mature five years from today.
- **Serial bonds** mature in installments at regular intervals. For example, a $500,000, five-year serial bond may mature in $100,000 annual installments over a five-year period.
- **Secured bonds** give the bondholder the right to take specified assets of the issuer if the issuer fails to pay principal or interest. A **mortgage** on a house is an example of a secured bond.
- **Debentures** are unsecured bonds that are not backed by assets. They are backed only by the good will of the bond issuer.

Bond Prices

A bond can be issued at any price agreed upon by the issuer and the bondholders. There are three basic categories of bond prices. A bond can be issued at,

- **Par value**; Example: A $1,000 bond issued for $1,000. A bond issued at par has no discount or premium. Also called bond maturity value.
- **Discount (or Bond Discount)**, a price below maturity (par) value. Example: A $1,000 bond issued for $980. The discount is $20 ($1,000 – $980).
- **Premium (or Bond Premium)**, a price above maturity (par) value. Example: A $1,000 bond issued for $1,015. The premium is $15 ($1,015 – $1,000).

EXHIBIT 10-6 | **Bond Certificate**

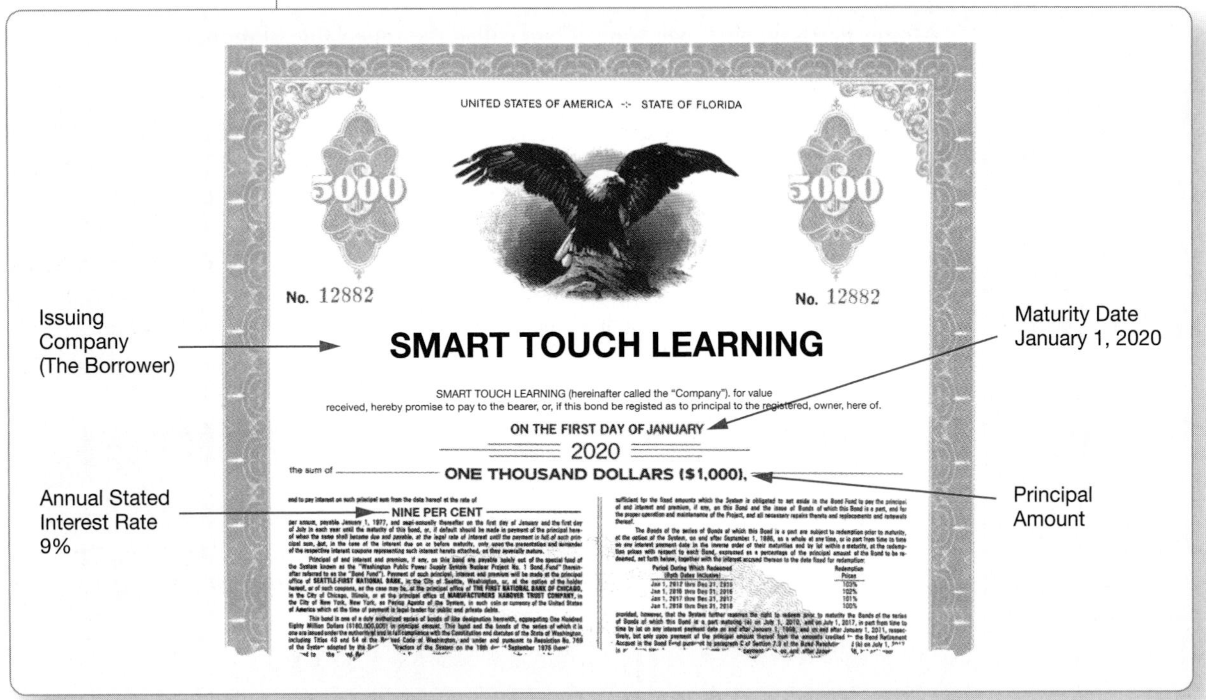

The issue price of a bond does not affect the required payment at maturity. In all of the preceding cases the company must pay the maturity value of the bonds when they mature.

As a bond approaches maturity, its market price moves toward maturity value. On the maturity date, the market value of a bond exactly equals the maturity value because the company pays that amount to retire the bond.

After a bond is issued, investors may buy and sell it through the bond market just as they buy and sell stocks through the stock market. The most famous bond market is the New York Exchange, which lists several thousand bonds.

Bond prices are quoted as a percentage of maturity value. For example,

- A $1,000 bond quoted at 100 is bought or sold for 100% of maturity value, ($1,000 × 1.00).
- A $1,000 bond quoted at 101.5 has a price of $1,015 ($1,000 × 1.015).
- A $1,000 bond quoted at 88.375 has a price of $883.75 ($1,000 × .88375).

The issue price of a bond determines the amount of cash the company receives when it issues the bond. In all cases, the company must pay the bond's maturity value to retire it at maturity.

Exhibit 10-7 shows example price information for the bonds of Smart Touch Learning. On this particular day, 12 of Smart Touch's 9% bonds maturing in 2020 (indicated by 20) were traded. The bonds' highest price on this day was $795 ($1,000 × 0.795). The lowest price of the day was $784.50 ($1,000 × 0.7845). The closing price (last sale of the day) was $795.

EXHIBIT 10-7 | **Bond Price Information for Smart Touch Learning (SMT)**

Bonds	Volume	High	Low	Close
SMT 9% of 20	12	79.5	78.45	79.5

Present Value

Money earns income over time, a fact called the **time value of money**. Appendix 10A covers the time value of money in detail.

Let us see how the time value of money affects bond prices. Assume that a $1,000 bond reaches maturity three years from now and carries no interest. Would you pay $1,000 to purchase this bond? No, because paying $1,000 today to receive $1,000 later yields no income on your investment. How much would you pay today in order to receive $1,000 in three years? The answer is some amount less than $1,000. Suppose $750 is a fair price. By investing $750 now to receive $1,000 later, you will earn $250 over the three years. The diagram that follows illustrates the relationship between a bond's price (present value) and its maturity amount (future value).

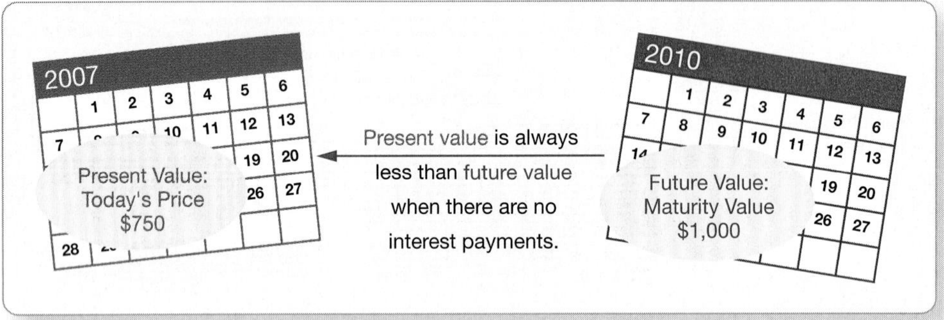

The amount that a person would invest *at the present time* is called the **present value.** The present value is the bond's market price. In our example, $750 is the present value (bond price), and the $1,000 maturity value to be received in three years is the future amount. We show how to compute present value in Appendix 10A.

Bond Interest Rates

Bonds are sold at their market price, which is the present value of the interest payments the bondholder will receive while holding the bond plus the bond principal paid at the end of the bond's life. Two interest rates work together to set the price of a bond:

- The **stated interest rate** determines the amount of cash interest the borrower pays each year. The stated interest rate is printed on the bond and *does not change* from year to year. For example, Smart Touch Learning's 9% bonds payable have a stated interest rate of 9% (See Exhibit 10-6). Therefore, Smart Touch Learning pays $90 of interest annually on each $1,000 bond. The dollar amount of interest paid is not affected by the issue or selling price of the bond.
- The **market interest rate** (also known as the **effective interest rate**) is the rate that investors demand to earn for loaning their money. The market interest rate *varies* daily. A company may issue bonds with a stated interest rate that differs from the market interest rate, due to the time gap between the decision of what the stated rate should be and the actual issuance of the bonds.

Smart Touch Learning may issue its 9% bonds when the market rate has risen to 10%. Will the Smart Touch bonds attract investors in this market? No, because investors can earn 10% on other bonds. Therefore, investors will purchase Smart Touch bonds only at a price *less* than maturity value. The difference between the lower price and the bonds' maturity value is a *discount* that will allow the investor to earn 10%, even though Smart Touch's interest checks will be paid at 9%. The difference between what is paid for the bond (less than $1,000) and the bond principal of $1,000 is the interest rate difference between 9% and 10% over the life of the bond.

On the other hand, if the market interest rate is 8%, Smart Touch's 9% bonds will be so attractive that investors will pay more than maturity value for them because investors will receive more in interest payments. The difference between the higher price and maturity value is a *premium*. Exhibit 10-8 shows how the stated interest rate and the market interest rate work together to determine the price of a bond.

EXHIBIT 10-8 **Interaction of the Stated Interest Rate and the Market Interest Rate to Determine the Price of a Bond**

Example: Bond with a Stated Interest Rate of 9%

Bond's Stated Interest Rate		Market Interest Rate		Issue Price of Bonds Payable
9%	=	9%	→	Maturity value of the bond
9%	<	10%	→	Discount (price below maturity value)
9%	>	8%	→	Premium (price above maturity value)

Accounting for Bonds Payable - Straight Line Method

6 Measure interest expense on bonds using the straight-line amortization method

The basic journal entry to record the issuance of bonds payable debits Cash and credits Bonds payable. As noted previously, a company may issue bonds, a long-term liability, for three different bond prices:

- At *maturity (par)* value
- At a *discount*
- At a *premium*

We begin with the simplest case—issuing bonds payable at maturity (par) value.

Issuing Bonds Payable at Maturity (Par) Value

Smart Touch Learning has $100,000 of 9% bonds payable that mature in five years. Smart Touch issues these bonds at maturity (par) value on January 1, 2010. The issuance entry is as follows:

2010			
Jan 1	Cash (A+)	100,000	
	Bonds payable (L+)		100,000
	Issued bonds.		

Smart Touch, the borrower, makes this one-time journal entry to record the receipt of cash and issuance of bonds payable. Interest payments occur each June 30 and December 31. Smart Touch's first semiannual interest payment is journalized as follows:

2010			
Jun 30	Interest expense ($100,000 × 0.09 × 6/12) (E+)	4,500	
	Cash (A–)		4,500
	Paid semiannual interest.		

Each semiannual interest payment follows this same pattern.

At maturity, Smart Touch will record payment of the bonds as follows:

2014			
Dec 31	Bonds payable (L–)	100,000	
	Cash (A–)		100,000
	Paid off bonds at maturity.		

Now let us see how to issue bonds payable at a discount. This is one of the most common situations.

Issuing Bonds Payable at a Discount

We know that market conditions may force a company such as Smart Touch Learning to accept a discount price for its bonds. Suppose Smart Touch issues $100,000 of its 9%, five-year bonds when the market interest rate is 10%. The market price of the bonds drops to 98.149, which means 98.149% of par value. Smart Touch receives $98,149 ($100,000 × 0.98149) at issuance and makes the following journal entry:

2010			
Jan 1	Cash ($100,000 × 0.98149) (A+)	98,149	
	Discount on bonds payable (CL+)	1,851	
	Bonds payable (L+)		100,000
	Issued bonds at a discount.		

After posting, the bond accounts have the following balances:

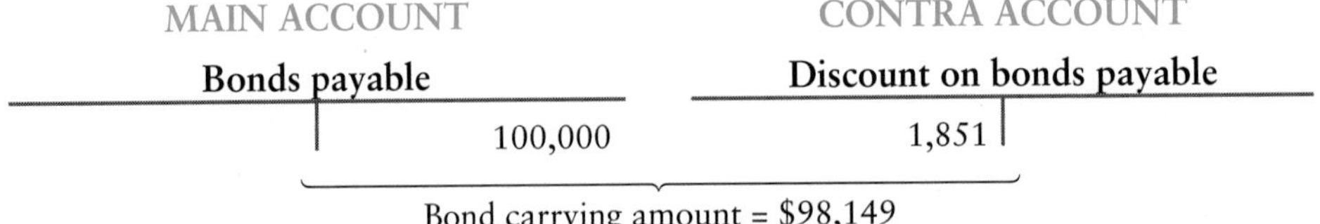

Discount on bonds payable is a contra account to Bonds payable. Bonds payable *minus* the discount gives the **carrying amount of the bonds.** Smart Touch would report these bonds payable as follows immediately after issuance.

Long-term liabilities:		
Bonds payable	$100,000	
Less: Discount on bonds payable.....	(1,851)	$98,149

Interest Expense on Bonds Payable with a Discount

In this case, we see that a bond's stated interest rate may differ from the market interest rate. The market rate was 10% when Smart Touch issued its 9% bonds. This 1% interest-rate difference created the $1,851 discount on the bonds. Smart Touch needed to offer this discount because investors were willing to pay only $98,149 for a $100,000, 9% bond when they could earn 10% on other bonds.

Smart Touch borrowed $98,149 but still must pay $100,000 when the bonds mature five years later. What happens to the $1,851 discount? The discount is additional interest expense to Smart Touch. The discount raises Smart Touch's true interest expense on the bonds to the market interest rate of 10%. The discount becomes interest expense for Smart Touch through a process called *amortization*, the gradual reduction of an item over time.

Straight-Line Amortization of Bond Discount

We can amortize a bond discount by dividing it into equal amounts for each interest period. This method is called *straight-line amortization* and it works very much like the straight-line depreciation method we discussed in the Plant Assets chapter. In our example, the initial discount is $1,851, and there are 10 semiannual interest periods during the bonds' five-year life.

Therefore, 1/5 years × 6/12 of the year or 1/10 of the $1,851 bond discount ($185) is amortized each interest period. Smart Touch's first semiannual interest entry is as follows:

2010			
Jun 30	Interest expense (E+)	4,685	
	Cash ($100,000 × 0.09 × 6/12) (A–)		4,500
	Discount on bonds payable ($1,851 × 1/5 yrs × 6/12)		185
	Paid interest and amortized discount.		

Interest expense of $4,685 for each six-month period is the sum of

- the stated interest ($4,500, which is paid in cash),
- *plus* the amortization of discount, $185.

Discount on bonds payable has a debit balance. Therefore we credit the Discount account to amortize (reduce) its balance. Ten amortization entries will decrease the Discount to zero (with rounding). Then the carrying amount of the bonds payable will be $100,000 at maturity—$100,000 in Bonds payable minus $0 in Discount on bonds payable.

Finally, the entry to pay off the bonds at maturity is as follows:

2014			
Dec 31	Bonds payable (L–)	100,000	
	Cash (A–)		100,000
	Paid off bonds at maturity.		

Decision Guidelines

LONG-TERM LIABILITIES—PART A

Smart Touch Learning has borrowed some money by issuing bonds payable. What type of bonds did Smart Touch issue? How much cash must Smart Touch pay each interest period? How much cash must Smart Touch pay at maturity? The Decision Guidelines address these and other questions.

Decision	Guidelines
• When will you pay off the bonds? • At maturity?	Types of bonds: • Term bonds

• Are the bonds secured?
  • Yes
  • No
	
	• Mortgage (secured) bonds
	• Debenture (unsecured) bonds

• How are bond prices
  • Quoted?
  • Determined?
	
	• As a percentage of maturity value (Example: A \$500,000 bond priced at \$510,000 would be quoted at 102 (\$510,000 / \$500,000 = 1.02))
	• Present value of the future principal amount to pay *plus* present value of the future interest payments (see Appendix 10A)

• What are the two interest rates used for bonds?	• The *stated interest rate* determines the amount of cash interest the borrower pays. This interest rate does *not* change. • The *market interest rate* is the rate that investors demand to earn for loaning their money. This interest rate determines the bonds' market price and varies daily.

• What causes a bond to be priced at
  • Maturity (par) value?
  • A discount?
  • A premium?
	
	• The *stated* interest rate on the bond *equals* the *market* interest rate.
	• The *stated* interest rate on the bond is *less than* the *market* interest rate.
	• The *stated* interest rate on the bond is *greater than* the *market* interest rate.

• How to report bonds payable on the balance sheet?	Maturity (par) value { – Discount on bonds payable or + Premium on bonds payable }

• What is the relationship between interest expense and interest payments when bonds are issued at
  • Maturity (par) value?
  • A discount?
  • A premium?
	
	• Interest expense *equals* the interest payment.
	• Interest expense is *greater than* the interest payment.
	• Interest expense is *less than* the interest payment.

Issuing Bonds Payable at a Premium

The issuance of bonds payable at a premium is rare because companies do not like to pay a stated interest rate that is higher than the market rate.

To illustrate a bond premium, let us change the Smart Touch Learning example. Assume that the market interest rate is 8% when Smart Touch issues its 9%, five-year bonds. These 9% bonds are attractive in an 8% market, and investors will pay a premium to acquire them. Assume the bonds are priced at 104 (104% of maturity value). In that case, Smart Touch receives $104,000 cash upon issuance. Smart Touch's entry to borrow money and issue these bonds is as follows:

2010			
Jan 1	Cash ($100,000 × 1.04) (A+)	104,000	
	Bonds payable (L+)		100,000
	Premium on bonds payable (CL+)		4,000
	Issued bonds at a premium.		

After posting, the bond accounts have the following balances:

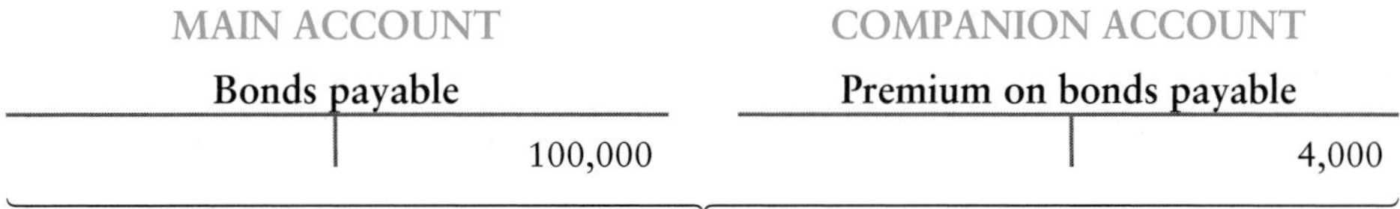

Bond carrying amount $104,000

Bonds payable and the Premium account each carries a credit balance. The Premium is a companion account to Bonds payable. Therefore, we add the Premium on bonds payable to the bonds payable to determine the bond carrying amount. Smart Touch Learning would report these bonds payable as follows immediately after issuance:

Long-term liabilities:		
Bonds payable	$100,000	
Add: Premium on bonds payable.....	4,000	$104,000

Interest Expense on Bonds Payable with a Premium

The 1% difference between the bonds' 9% stated interest rate and the 8% market rate creates the $4,000 premium ($104,000 – $100,000 face). Smart Touch borrows $104,000 but must pay back only $100,000 at maturity. The premium is like a saving of interest expense to Smart Touch. The premium cuts Smart Touch's cost of borrowing and reduces interest expense to 8%, the market rate. The amortization of bond premium decreases interest expense over the life of the bonds.

Straight-Line Amortization of Bond Premium

In our example, the beginning premium is $4,000, and there are 10 semiannual interest periods during the bonds' five-year life. Therefore, 1/5 years × 6/12 months or 1/10 of the $4,000 ($400) of bond premium is amortized each interest period. Smart Touch's first semiannual interest entry is:

2010			
Jun 30	Interest expense (E+)	4,100	
	Premium on bonds payable ($4,000 × 1/5 yrs × 6/12) (CL–)	400	
	Cash ($100,000 × 0.09 × 6/12) (A–)		4,500
	Paid interest and amortized premium.		

Interest expense of $4,100 is:

- the stated interest ($4,500, which is paid in cash),
- *minus* the amortization of the premium of $400.

At June 30, 2010, immediately after amortizing the bond premium, the bonds have the following carrying amount:

$103,600 [$100,000 + ($4,000 – $400)]

At December 31, 2010, the bonds' carrying amount will be as follows:

$103,200 [$100,000 + ($4,000 – $400 – $400)]

At maturity on December 31, 2014, the bond premium will have been fully amortized (it will have a zero balance), and the bonds' carrying amount will be $100,000 (the amount in the Bonds payable account).

Stop & Think...

If companies could change the rate on the bonds to equal market it would be easier, would it not? Then there would be no need for discounts or premiums. That sounds great but, in reality, the market is constantly changing and reacting to many things that ultimately affect the required rate of return for investors (market interest rate). The discount or premium still allows the company to raise capital, just a different amount of capital than the principal amount of the bonds. Remember that the discount or premium is really just the value today or the interest difference.

Adjusting Entries for Bonds Payable

Companies may issue bonds payable when they need cash. The interest payments seldom occur on December 31, so interest expense must be accrued at year end. The accrual entry should also amortize any bond discount or premium.

Suppose Smart Touch Learning issued $100,000 of 8%, 10-year bonds at a $2,000 discount on October 1, 2010. The interest payments occur on March 31 and September 30 each year. On December 31, Smart Touch accrues interest and amortizes bond discount for three months (October, November, and December) as follows:

2010			
Dec 31	Interest expense (E+)	2,050	
	Interest payable ($100,000 × 0.08 × 3/12) (L+)		2,000
	Discount on bonds payable ($2,000 × 1/10 × 3/12) (CL–)		50
	Accrued interest and amortized discount.		

Interest payable is credited for three months (October, November, and December). Discount on bonds payable must also be amortized for these three months.

The next semiannual interest payment occurs on March 31, 2011, and Smart Touch makes the following journal entry:

2011			
Mar 31	Interest payable (from Dec. 31) (L–)	2,000	
	Interest expense (E+)	2,050	
	Cash ($100,000 × 0.08 × 6/12) (A–)		4,000
	Discount on bonds payable ($2,000 × 1/10 × 3/12) (CL–)		50
	Paid interest and amortized discount.		

Amortization of a bond premium is similar except that Premium on bonds payable is debited.

Issuing Bonds Payable Between Interest Dates

In most of the examples we have seen thus far, Smart Touch Learning issued bonds payable on an interest date, such as January 1. Companies can also issue bonds between interest dates. If they do so, however, they must account for the accrued interest.

Let us assume that Smart Touch Learning has $100,000 of 8% bonds payable that are dated January 1. That means the interest starts accruing on January 1.

Suppose Smart Touch issues these bonds on April 1 when the market rate of interest is also 8% (no discount or premium). How should we account for the interest for January, February, and March? At issuance on April 1, Smart Touch collects three months' accrued interest from the bondholder and records the issuance of bonds payable as follows:

2010			
Apr 1	Cash (A+)	102,000	
	Bonds payable (L+)		100,000
	Interest payable ($100,000 × 0.08 × 3/12) (L+)		2,000
	Issued bonds three months after the inception date of the bonds.		

Companies cannot split up interest payments. They pay in either six-month or annual amounts as stated on the bond certificate.

On the next interest date, Smart Touch will pay six months' interest to whoever owns the bonds at that time. But Smart Touch will have interest expense only for the three months the bonds have been outstanding (April, May, and June). To allocate interest expense to the correct months, Smart Touch makes the following entry on June 30 for the customary six-month interest payment:

2010			
Jun 30	Interest payable (from April 1) (L–)	2,000	
	Interest expense (for April, May, June) (E+)	2,000	
	Cash ($100,000 × 0.08 × 6/12) (A–)		4,000
	Paid interest.		

Reporting Liabilities on the Balance Sheet

7 Report liabilities on the balance sheet

At the end of each period, a company reports all of its current and long-term liabilities on the balance sheet. As we have seen throughout, there are two categories of liabilities, current and long-term. Smart Touch Learning's liabilities portion of its Balance Sheet from data within the chapter is shown in Exhibit 10-9. The red blocked letters correspond to the matching letters on several figures within the chapter to help you visualize where the numbers on the balance sheet came from.

EXHIBIT 10-9 **Liabilities Portion of Balance Sheet**

SMART TOUCH LEARNING Balance Sheet—partial		
Liabilities		
Current liabilities:		
Accounts payable	17,000	*Value assumed
Employee income tax payable	2,000	H
FICA tax payable	1,158	I
Payable to health insurance	180	J
Payable to United Way	20	K
Salary payable	7,221	L
Employee benefits payable	1,500	M
Interest payable	41	B
Sales tax payable	600	C
Unearned service revenue	400	F
Estimated warranty payable	700	G
Short-term notes payable	700	A
Current portion long-term notes payable	5,000	D
Total current liabilities	36,520	
Long-term liabilities:		
Long-term notes payable	15,000	E
Bonds payable, net discount of $1,851	98,149	N
Total long-term liabilities	113,149	
Total liabilities	149,669	

The balance sheet presentation of bonds payable used the discount bond example within the chapter. The presentation of bonds payable issued at a premium is shown in the Premium section of this chapter.

Issuing Bonds Versus Stock

8 Compare issuing bonds to issuing stocks

Borrowing by issuing bonds payable carries a risk: The company may be unable to pay off the bonds. Why then do companies borrow so heavily? Because debt is a cheaper source of money than stock. Companies face the following decision: How shall we finance a new project—with bonds or with stock?

Suppose Smart Touch Learning has net income of $300,000 and 100,000 shares of common stock outstanding before they begin a new project. Smart Touch needs $500,000 for the project and the company is considering two plans:

- Plan 1 is to borrow $500,000 at 10% (issue $500,000 of 10% bonds payable).
- Plan 2 is to issue 50,000 shares of common stock for $500,000.

Smart Touch management believes the new cash can be used to earn income of $200,000 before interest and taxes.

Exhibit 10-10 shows the advantage of borrowing.

EXHIBIT 10-10 Earnings-per-Share Advantage of Borrowing Versus Issuing Stock

	Plan 1 Issue $500,000 of 10% Bonds Payable		Plan 2 Issue $500,000 of Common Stock	
Net income before new project		$300,000		$300,000
Expected income on the new project before interest and income tax expenses	$200,000		$200,000	
Less: Interest expense ($500,000 × 0.10)	(50,000)		0	
Project income before income tax	150,000		200,000	
Less: Income tax expense (40%)	(60,000)		(80,000)	
Project net income		90,000		120,000
Net income with new project		$390,000		$420,000
Earnings per share with new project:				
Plan 1 ($390,000/100,000 shares)		$3.90		
Plan 2 ($420,000/150,000 shares)				$2.80

The earnings per one share of stock is higher if Smart Touch issues bonds. If all goes well, the company can earn more on the new project ($90,000) than the interest it pays on the bonds ($50,000). Earning more income on borrowed money than the related interest expense is called using **leverage**. It is widely used to increase earnings per share of common stock. Notice that, even though income is higher under Plan 2, the earnings per share is lower. Why? Because the earnings must be shared among 50,000 more stockholders.

Borrowing can increase the earnings per share, but borrowing has its disadvantages. Debts must be paid during bad years as well as good years. Interest expense may be high enough to eliminate net income and can even lead to bankruptcy. This happens to lots of overly ambitious companies.

Ethical Issues in Reporting Liabilities

Accounting for liabilities poses an ethical challenge. Businesses like to show high levels of net income because that makes them look successful. As a result, owners and managers may be tempted to overlook some expenses and liabilities at the end of the accounting period. For example, a company can fail to accrue warranty expense. This will cause total expenses to be understated and net income to be overstated.

Contingent liabilities also pose an ethical challenge. Because contingencies are not real liabilities, they are easier to overlook. But a contingency can turn into a real liability and can significantly change the company's financial position. Successful people do not play games with their accounting. Falsifying financial statements can land a person in prison.

Now let us wrap up the chapter with some Decision Guidelines.

Decision Guidelines

LONG-TERM LIABILITIES—PART B

Suppose Greg's Groovy Tunes needs $50 million to purchase manufacturing facilities and equipment. Greg's Groovy Tunes issues bonds payable to finance the purchase and now must account for the bonds payable. The Decision Guidelines outline some of the issues Greg's Groovy Tunes must decide.

Decision	Guidelines
• What happens to the bonds' carrying amount when bonds payable are issued at	
• Maturity (par) value?	• Carrying amount *stays* at maturity (par) value
• A premium?	• Carrying amount *decreases* gradually to maturity value
• A discount?	• Carrying amount *increases* gradually to maturity value
• How to account for the retirement of bonds payable?	**At maturity date:** Bonds payable .... Maturity value Cash .... Maturity value **Before maturity date** (assume a discount on the bonds and a gain on retirement): Bonds payable .... Maturity value Discount on bonds payable .... Balance Cash .... Amount Paid Gain on retirement of bonds payable... Excess
• What are the advantages of financing operations with	
• Stock?	• Creates no liability or interest expense. Less risky to the issuing company.
• Bonds (or notes) payable?	• Results in higher earnings per share—under normal conditions.

Summary Problem 3

West Virginia Power Company has 8% 10-year bonds payable that mature on June 30, 2020. The bonds are issued on June 30, 2010, and West Virginia Power pays interest each June 30 and December 31.

Requirements

1. Will the bonds be issued at par, at a premium, or at a discount if the market interest rate on the date of issuance is 7%? If the market interest rate is 9%?
2. West Virginia Power issued $100,000 of the bonds at 94.
   a. Record issuance of the bonds on June 30, 2010.
   b. Record the payment of interest and amortization of the discount on December 31, 2010. Use the straight-line amortization method.
   c. Compute the bonds' carrying amount at December 31, 2010.
   d. Record the payment of interest and amortization of discount on June 30, 2011.

Solution

Requirement 1

Market Interest Rate	Bond Price for an 8% Bond
7%	Premium
9%	Discount

Requirement 2

	2010			
a.	Jun 30	Cash ($100,000 × 0.94) (A+)	94,000	
		Discount on bonds payable (CL+)	6,000	
		Bonds payable (L+)		100,000
		Issued bonds at a discount.		
b.	Dec 31	Interest expense (E+)	4,300	
		Cash ($100,000 × 0.08 × 6/12) (A–)		4,000
		Discount on bonds payable ($6,000 × 1/10 yrs. × 6/12) (CL–)		300
		Paid interest and amortized discount.		
c.		Bond carrying amount at Dec. 31, 2010:		
		$94,300 [$100,000 – ($6,000 – $300)]		
	2011			
d.	Jun 30	Interest expense (E+)	4,300	
		Cash ($100,000 × 0.08 × 6/12) (A–)		4,000
		Discount on bonds payable ($6,000 × 1/10 yrs. × 6/12) (CL–)		300
		Paid interest and amortized discount.		

Review Current Liabilities, Payroll, and Long-Term Liabilities

Accounting Vocabulary

Bond Discount (p. 570)
Excess of a bond's maturity value over its issue price. Also called a **discount (on a bond)**.

Bond Premium (p. 570)
Excess of a bond's issue price over its maturity value. Also called a **premium**.

Bonds Payable (p. 570)
Groups of notes payable issued to multiple lenders called bondholders.

Callable Bonds (p. 617)
Bonds that the issuer may call or pay off at a specified price whenever the issuer wants.

Carrying Amount of Bonds (p. 574)
Bonds payable *minus* the discount or *plus* the premium.

Contingent Liability (p. 557)
A potential liability that depends on some future event.

Convertible Bonds (p. 618)
Bonds that may be converted into the common stock of the issuing company at the option of the investor.

Current Maturity (p. 555)
Amount of the principal that is payable within one year. Also called **current portion of notes payable**.

Current Portion of Notes Payable (p. 555)
Amount of the principal that is payable within one year. Also called **current maturity**.

Debentures (p. 570)
Unsecured bonds backed only by the good faith of the borrower.

Discount (on a bond) (p. 570)
Excess of a bond's maturity value over its issue price. Also called a **bond discount**.

Effective Interest Method (p. 609)
Method of amortizing bond premium or discount that uses the present-value concepts covered in Appendix A.

Effective Interest Rate (p. 572)
Interest rate that investors demand in order to loan their money. Also called the **market interest rate**.

Employee Compensation (p. 561)
A major expense. Also called **payroll**.

Federal Insurance Contributions Act (FICA) Tax (p. 562)
Federal Insurance Contributions Act (FICA) tax, which is withheld from employees' pay and matched by the employer. Also called **Social Security tax**.

Gross Pay (p. 561)
Total amount of salary, wages, commissions, or any other employee compensation before taxes and other deductions.

Leverage (p. 581)
Earning more income on borrowed money than the related interest expense, thereby increasing the earnings for the owners of the business.

Market Interest Rate (p. 572)
Interest rate that investors demand in order to loan their money. Also called the **effective interest rate**.

Mortgage (p. 570)
Borrower's promise to transfer the legal title to certain assets to the lender if the debt is not paid on schedule.

Net (Take-Home) Pay (p. 561)
Gross pay minus all deductions. The amount of compensation that the employee actually takes home.

Par Value (p. 570)
The amount a borrower must pay back to the bondholders on the maturity date. Also called principal amount or maturity value.

Payroll (p. 561)
A major expense. Also called **employee compensation**.

Premium (p. 570)
Excess of a bond's issue price over its maturity value. Also called **bond premium**.

Present Value (p. 572)
Amount a person would invest now to receive a greater amount in the future.

Secured Bonds (p. 570)
Bonds that give bondholders the right to take specified assets of the issuer if the issuer fails to pay principal or interest.

Serial Bonds (p. 570)
Mature in installments at regular intervals.

Short-Term Note Payable (p. 554)
Promissory note payable due within one year; a common form of financing.

Social Security (FICA) Tax (p. 562)
Federal Insurance Contributions Act (FICA) tax, which is withheld from employees' pay and matched by the employer. Also called **FICA tax**.

Stated Interest Rate (p. 572)
Interest rate that determines the amount of cash interest the borrower pays and the investor receives each year.

Term Bonds (p. 570)
Bonds that all mature at the same time.

Time Value of Money (p. 572)
Recognition that money earns income over time.

Unemployment Compensation Tax (p. 564)
Payroll tax paid by employers to the government, which uses the money to pay unemployment benefits to people who are out of work.

Warranties (p. 552)
Product guarantees.

Withheld Income Tax (p. 562)
Income tax deducted from employees' gross pay.

Quick Check

1. Known liabilities of uncertain amounts are
   a. Ignored (Record them when paid.)
   b. Reported on the balance sheet
   c. Contingent liabilities
   d. Reported only in the notes to the financial statements

2. On January 1, 2011, you borrowed $14,000 on a five-year, 9% note payable. At December 31, 2012, you should *record*:
   a. Note receivable of $14,000
   b. Cash payment of $14,000
   c. Interest payable of $1,260
   d. Nothing (the note is already on the books)

3. Your company sells $110,000 of goods and you collect sales tax of 6%. What current liability does the sale create?
   a. Sales tax payable of $6,600
   b. Sales revenue of $116,600
   c. Unearned revenue of $6,600
   d. None; you collected cash up front

4. **Burnham Electric** (**BE**) owed Estimated warranty payable of $1,500 at the end of 2011. During 2012, **BE** made sales of $100,000 and expects product warranties to cost the company 6% of the sales. During 2012, **BE** paid $2,700 for warranties. What is **BE's** Estimated warranty payable at the end of 2012?
   a. $2,700
   b. $4,800
   c. $4,200
   d. $4,500

5. At December 31, your company owes employees for three days of the five-day workweek. The total payroll for the week is $7,000. What journal entry should you make at December 31, ignoring payroll taxes?
   a. Nothing because you will pay the employees on Friday.
   b.

Salary expense	7,000	
Salary payable		7,000

   c.

Salary payable	4,200	
Salary expense		4,200

   d.

Salary expense	4,200	
Salary payable		4,200

6. A $400,000 bond priced at 105.5 can be bought or sold for
   a. $400,000 + interest.
   b. $422,000.
   c. $22,000.
   d. $42,200.

7. Which interest rate on a bond determines the amount of the semiannual interest payment?
   a. Stated rate
   b. Market rate
   c. Semiannual rate
   d. Effective rate
8. Lafferty Corporation's bonds payable carry a stated interest rate of 7%, and the market rate of interest is 8%. The price of the Lafferty bonds will be at
   a. Par value.
   b. Premium.
   c. Maturity value.
   d. Discount.
9. Jade Larson Antiques issued its 12%, 10-year bonds payable at a price of $770,000 (maturity value is $800,000). The company uses the straight-line amortization method for the bonds. Interest expense for each year is
   a. $92,400.
   b. $96,000.
   c. $99,000.
   d. $80,000.
10. Sydney Park Fitness Gym has $500,000 of 10-year bonds payable outstanding. These bonds had a discount of $45,000 at issuance, which was five years ago. The company uses the straight-line amortization method. The carrying amount of these bonds payable is
    a. $500,000.
    b. $477,500.
    c. $455,000.
    d. $545,000.

Answers are given after Apply Your Knowledge (p. 603).

Assess Your Progress

Short Exercises

S10-1 *(L.OBJ. 1)* **Accounting for a note payable [10 min]**
On August 31, 2010, Gordon Co. purchased $7,000 of inventory on a one-year, 12% note payable.

Requirements

1. Journalize the company's accrual of interest expense on February 28, 2011, their fiscal year-end.
2. Journalize the company's payment of the note plus interest on August 31, 2011.

S10-2 *(L.OBJ. 2)* **Accounting for warranty expense and warranty payable [10 min]**
Catskills Corporation guarantees its snowmobiles for three years. Company experience indicates that warranty costs will add up to 5% of sales.

Assume that the Catskills dealer in Colorado Springs made sales totaling $519,000 during 2011. The company received cash for 20% of the sales and notes receivable for the remainder. Warranty payments totaled $19,000 during 2011.

Requirements

1. Record the sales, warranty expense, and warranty payments for the company.
2. Post to the Estimated warranty payable T-account. At the end of 2011, how much in Estimated warranty payable does the company owe?

S10-3 *(L.OBJ. 2)* **Interpreting an actual company's contingent liabilities [5–10 min]**
Farley Motors, a motorcycle manufacturer, included the following note (adapted) in its annual report:

> Notes to Consolidated Financial Statements
>
> *7 Commitments and Contingencies (Adapted)*
>
> The Company self-insures its product liability losses in the United States up to $3 million. Catastrophic coverage is maintained for individual claims in excess of $3 million up to $25 million.

Requirements

1. Why are these *contingent* (versus real) liabilities?
2. How can a contingent liability become a real liability for Farley Motors? What are the limits to the company's product liabilities in the United States?

S10-4 *(L.OBJ. 3)* **Computing an employee's total pay [10 min]**
Gina Tarver is paid $720 for a 40-hour workweek and time-and-a-half for hours above 40.

Requirements

1. Compute Tarver's gross pay for working 52 hours during the first week of February.
2. Tarver is single, and her income tax withholding is 20% of total pay. Tarver's only payroll deductions are payroll taxes. Compute Tarver's net (take-home) pay for the week. Use an 8% FICA tax rate, and carry amounts to the nearest cent.

Note: Short Exercise 10-5 should be used only after completing Short Exercise 10-4.

S10-5 *(L.OBJ. 3)* **Computing the payroll expense of an employer [10 min]**
Return to the Gina Tarver payroll situation in Short Exercise 10-4. Tarver's employer, College of St. Mary, pays all the standard payroll taxes plus benefits for employee retirement plan (4% of total pay), health insurance ($105 per employee per month), and disability insurance ($11 per employee per month).

Requirement

1. Compute College of St. Mary's total expense of employing Gina Tarver for the 52 hours that she worked during the first week of February. Carry amounts to the nearest cent.

S10-6 *(L.OBJ. 3)* **Computing payroll amounts late in the year [10 min]**
Suppose you work for DePetro-Carr, the accounting firm, all year and earn a monthly salary of $6,800. There is no overtime pay. Your withheld income taxes consume 25% of gross pay. In addition to payroll taxes, you elect to contribute 6% monthly to your retirement plan. DePetro-Carr also deducts $110 monthly for your co-pay of the health insurance premium.

Requirement

1. Compute your net pay for November. Use an 8% FICA tax rate.

Note: Short Exercise 10-7 should be used only after completing Short Exercises 10-4 and 10-5.

S10-7 *(L.OBJ. 4)* **Journalizing payroll [10 min]**
Consult your solutions for Short Exercises 10-4 and 10-5.

Requirements

1. Journalize salary expense for College of St. Mary related to the employment of Gina Tarver.
2. Journalize benefits expense for College of St. Mary related to the employment of Gina Tarver.
3. Journalize employer payroll taxes for College of St. Mary related to the employment of Gina Tarver.

S10-8 *(L.OBJ. 5)* **Determining bond prices [5 min]**
Bond prices depend on market rate of interest, stated rate of interest, and time.

Requirement

1. Determine whether the following bonds payable will be issued at maturity value, at a premium, or at a discount:

   a. The market interest rate is 7%. Denver Co. issues bonds payable with a stated rate of 6 1/2%.
   b. Houston issued 7% bonds payable when the market rate was 6 3/4%.
   c. Cincinnati Company issued 8% bonds when the market interest rate was 8%.
   d. Miami Company issued bonds payable that pay stated interest of 7%. At issuance, the market interest rate was 8 1/4%.

S10-9 *(L.OBJ. 5)* **Pricing bonds [5 min]**
Bond prices depend on market rate of interest, stated rate of interest, and time.

Requirement

1. Compute the price of the following 6% bonds of City Telecom.

   a. $300,000 issued at 75.75
   b. $300,000 issued at 105.25
   c. $300,000 issued at 94.50
   d. $300,000 issued at 104.75

Note: Short Exercise 10-10 should be used only after completing Short Exercise 10-9.

S10-10 *(L.OBJ. 5)* **Maturity value of a bond [5 min]**
Consider the prices you calculated in Short Exercise 10-9.

Requirement

1. Which bond will City Telecom have to pay the most to retire the bond at maturity? Explain your answer.

S10-11 *(L.OBJ. 6)* **Journalizing bond transactions [10 min]**
Deer Company issued a $80,000, 7%, seven-year bond payable.

Requirement

1. Journalize the following transactions for Deer and include an explanation for each entry:

   a. Issuance of the bond payable at par on January 1, 2010
   b. Payment of semiannual cash interest on July 1, 2010
   c. Payment of the bond payable at maturity. (Give the date.)

S10-12 *(L.OBJ. 6)* **Determining bond amounts [5 min]**
Starlight Drive-Ins borrowed money by issuing $3,000,000 of 7% bonds payable at 98.5.

Requirements

1. How much cash did Starlight receive when it issued the bonds payable?
2. How much must Starlight pay back at maturity?
3. How much cash interest will Starlight pay each six months?

S10-13 *(L.OBJ. 6)* **Determining bond interest rates [5 min]**
A 5%, 10-year bond was issued at a price of 94.

Requirement

1. Was the market interest rate at the date of issuance closest to 4%, 5%, or 6%? Explain.

S10-14 *(L.OBJ. 6)* **Journalizing bond transactions [10 min]**
Oliver issued a $80,000, 7%, 10-year bond payable at a price of 95 on January 1, 2010.

Requirements

1. Journalize the issuance of the bond payable on January 1, 2010.
2. Journalize payment of semiannual interest and amortization of bond discount or premium on July 1, 2010, using the straight-line method to amortize bond discount or premium.

S10-15 *(L.OBJ. 6)* **Journalizing bond transactions [10 min]**
Weatherbee Mutual Insurance Company issued a $40,000, 8%, 10-year bond payable at a price of 109 on January 1, 2011.

Requirements

1. Journalize the issuance of the bond payable on January 1, 2011.
2. Journalize payment of semiannual interest and amortization of bond discount or premium on July 1, 2011, using the straight-line method to amortize bond discount or premium.

S10-16 *(L.OBJ. 6)* **Journalizing bond transactions [10 min]**
Truestar Communication issued $90,000 of 9%, 10-year bonds payable on August 1, 2012, at par value. Truestar's accounting year ends on December 31.

Requirements

1. Journalize the issuance of the bonds on August 1, 2012.
2. Journalize the accrual of interest expense on December 31, 2012.
3. Journalize payment of the first semiannual interest amount on February 1, 2013.

S10-17 *(L.OBJ. 6)* **Journalizing bond transactions—issuance between interest payment dates [10 min]**
Seacoast Realty issued $325,000 of 9%, 10-year bonds payable at par value on May 1, 2010, four months after the bond's original issue date of January 1, 2010.

Requirements

1. Journalize issuance of the bonds payable on May 1, 2010.
2. Journalize the payment of the first semiannual interest amount on July 1, 2010.

S10-18 *(L.OBJ.7)* **Preparing the liabilities section of the Balance Sheet [5 min]**
Grand Suites Hotels includes the following selected accounts in its general ledger at December 31, 2011:

Note payable, long-term	$ 100,000	Accounts payable	$ 38,000
Bonds payable	425,000	Discount on bonds payable	12,750
Interest payable (due next year)	1,100	Salary payable	3,000
Estimated warranty payable	1,500	Sales tax payable	700

Requirement

1. Prepare the liabilities section of Grand Suites' balance sheet at December 31, 2011, to show how the company would report these items. Report a total for current liabilities.

S10-19 *(L.OBJ. 8)* **Compare issuing bonds to issuing stock [10–15 min]**
Speegleville Marina needs to raise $1 million to expand. Speegleville's president is considering two plans:

- Plan A: Issue $2,000,000 of 8% bonds payable to borrow the money
- Plan B: Issue 100,000 shares of common stock at $20 per share

Before any new financing, the company expects to earn net income of $500,000, and the company already has 100,000 shares of common stock outstanding. Speegleville believes the expansion will increase income before interest and income tax by $200,000. The income tax rate is 40%.

Requirement

1. Prepare an analysis similar to Exhibit 10-10 to determine which plan is likely to result in higher earnings per share. Which financing plan would you recommend?

Exercises

E10-20 *(L.OBJ. 1)* **Recording sales tax [5–15 min]**
Consider the following transactions of Johnson Software:

Jul 31	Recorded cash sales of $210,000, plus sales tax of 8% collected for the state of Texas.
Aug 6	Sent July sales tax to the state.

Requirement

1. Journalize the transactions for the company.

E10-21 *(L.OBJ. 1)* **Recording note payable transactions [5–10 min]**
Consider the following note payable transactions of Crandell Video Productions.

2011	
Mar 1	Purchased equipment costing $16,000 by issuing a one-year, 9% note payable.
Dec 31	Accrued interest on the note payable.
2012	
Mar 1	Paid the note payable at maturity.

Requirement

1. Journalize the transactions for the company.

E10-22 *(L.OBJ. 1)* **Recording and reporting current liabilities [10–15 min]**
Worldwide Publishing completed the following transactions during 2011:

Oct 1	Sold a six-month subscription, collecting cash of $200, plus sales tax of 5%.
Nov 15	Remitted (paid) the sales tax to the state of Tennessee.
Dec 31	Made the necessary adjustment at year-end to record the amount of subscription revenue earned during the year.

Requirement

1. Journalize the transactions (explanations are not required).

E10-23 *(L.OBJ. 1)* **Journalizing current liabilities [15 min]**
Ed O'Connor Associates reported short-term notes payable and salary payable as follows:

	2012	2011
Current liabilities (partial)		
Short–term notes payable	$ 16,700	$ 15,500
Salary payable	3,800	3,200

During 2012, O'Connor paid off both current liabilities that were left over from 2011. During 2012, O'Connor borrowed money on short-term notes payable and accrued salary expense during 2012.

Requirement

1. Journalize all four of these transactions for O'Connor during 2012.

E10-24 *(L.OBJ. 2)* **Accounting for warranty expense and warranty payable [5–15 min]**
The accounting records of Earthtone Ceramics included the following at December 31, 2011:

Estimated warranty payable	
	Beginning balance 3,000

In the past, Earthtone's warranty expense has been 5% of sales. During 2012, Earthtone made sales of $115,000 and paid $4,000 to satisfy warranty claims.

Requirements

1. Journalize Earthtone's warranty expense and warranty payments during 2012. Explanations are not required.
2. What balance of Estimated warranty payable will Earthtone report on its balance sheet at December 31, 2012?

E10-25 *(L.OBJ. 3, 4)* **Computing and recording gross and net pay [10–15 min]**
Herman Simms manages a Dairy House drive-in. His straight-time pay is $14 per hour, with time-and-a-half for hours in excess of 40 per week. Simms' payroll deductions include withheld income tax of 9%, FICA tax of 8%, and a weekly deduction of $10 for a charitable contribution to United Fund. Simms worked 62 hours during the week.

Requirements

1. Compute Simms' gross pay and net pay for the week. Carry amounts to the nearest cent.
2. Journalize Dairy House's wage expense—including payroll deductions—for Simms' work. An explanation is not required.

E10-26 *(L.OBJ. 4)* **Recording a payroll [10–15 min]**

Juan's Mexican Restaurants incurred salary expense of $62,000 for 2009. The payroll expense includes employer FICA tax of 8%, in addition to state unemployment tax of 5.4% and federal unemployment tax of 0.8%. Of the total salaries, $19,000 is subject to unemployment tax. Also, the company provides the following benefits for employees: health insurance (cost to the company, $2,040), life insurance (cost to the company, $380), and retirement benefits (cost to the company, 5% of salary expense).

Requirement

1. Record Juan's expenses for employee benefits and for payroll taxes. Explanations are not required.

E10-27 *(L.OBJ. 5)* **Determining bond prices [5–10 min]**

Havens is planning to issue long-term bonds payable to borrow for a major expansion. The chief executive, Richie Havens, asks your advice on some related matters.

Requirement

1. Answer the following questions:

   a. At what type of bond price will Havens have total interest expense equal to the cash interest payments?
   b. Under which type of bond price will Havens' total interest expense be greater than the cash interest payments?
   c. The stated interest rate on the bonds is 7%, and the market interest rate is 8%. What type of bond price can Havens expect for the bonds?
   d. Havens could raise the stated interest rate on the bonds to 9% (market rate is 8%). In that case, what type of price can Havens expect for the bonds?

E10-28 *(L.OBJ. 6)* **Journalizing bond issuance and interest payments [10 min]**

On January 1, Durkin Limited issues 9%, 20-year bonds payable with a maturity value of $70,000. The bonds sell at 97 and pay interest on January 1 and July 1. Durkin amortizes bond discount by the straight-line method.

Requirements

1. Journalize the issuance of the bonds on January 1.
2. Journalize the semiannual interest payment and amortization of bond discount on July 1.

E10-29 *(L.OBJ. 6)* **Journalizing bond transactions [15–20 min]**

Jefferson issued $80,000 of 10-year, 8% bonds payable on January 1, 2010. Jefferson pays interest each January 1 and July 1 and amortizes discount or premium by the straight-line method. The company can issue its bonds payable under various conditions.

Requirements

1. Journalize Jefferson's issuance of the bonds and first semiannual interest payment assuming the bonds were issued at par value. Explanations are not required.
2. Journalize Jefferson's issuance of the bonds and first semiannual interest payment assuming the bonds were issued at a price of 93. Explanations are not required.
3. Journalize Jefferson's issuance of the bonds and first semiannual interest payment assuming the bonds were issued at a price of 105. Explanations are not required.
4. Which bond price results in the most interest expense for Jefferson? Explain in detail.

E10-30 *(L.OBJ. 6)* **Journalizing bond transactions—year end interest accrual [10 min]**
Fredrickson Homebuilders issued $220,000 of 7%, 10-year bonds at par on October 31, 2011. Fredrickson pays semiannual interest on April 30 and October 31.

Requirements

1. Journalize the issuance of the bonds payable on October 31, 2011.
2. Journalize the accrual of interest on December 31, 2011.
3. Journalize the payment of semiannual interest on April 30, 2012.

E10-31 *(L.OBJ. 7)* **Reporting current and long-term liabilities [5–15 min]**
Orthopedic Dispensary borrowed $600,000 on January 2, 2011, by issuing a 15% note payable that must be paid in three equal annual installments plus interest for the year. The first payment of principal and interest comes due January 2, 2012.

Requirement

1. Insert the appropriate amounts to show how Orthopedic Dispensary should report its current and long-term liabilities.

	December 31		
	2011	2012	2013
Current liabilities:			
Current portion of note payable	$______	$______	$______
Interest payable	______	______	______
Long–term liabilities:			
Long-term note payable	______	______	______

E10-32 *(L.OBJ. 7)* **Reporting liabilities [10 min]**
At December 31, MediPoint Precision Instruments owes $52,000 on accounts payable, plus salary payable of $11,000, and income tax payable of $9,000. MediPoint also has $260,000 of bonds payable that require payment of a $20,000 installment next year and the remainder in later years. The bonds payable require an annual interest payment of $7,000, and MediPoint still owes this interest for the current year.

Requirement

1. Report MediPoint's liabilities on its classified balance sheet. List the current liabilities in descending order (largest first, and so on), and show the total of current liabilities.

E10-33 *(L.OBJ. 8)* **Analyzing alternative plans to raise money [15–20 min]**
SG Electronics is considering two plans for raising $3,000,000 to expand operations. Plan A is to issue 6% bonds payable, and plan B is to issue 100,000 shares of common stock. Before any new financing, SG has net income of $300,000 and 200,000 shares of common stock outstanding. Management believes the company can use the new funds to earn additional income of $500,000 before interest and taxes. The income tax rate is 40%.

Requirement

1. Analyze SG Electronics' situation to determine which plan will result in higher earnings per share. Use Exhibit 10-10 as a guide.

■ Problems (Group A)

P10-34A *(L.OBJ. 1, 2)* **Journalizing liability transactions [30–40 min]**
The following transactions of Brewton Pharmacies occurred during 2010 and 2011:

2010	
Jan 9	Purchased computer equipment at a cost of $10,000, signing a six-month, 8% note payable for that amount
29	Recorded the week's sales of $67,000, three-fourths on credit, and one-fourth for cash. Sales amounts are subject to a 6% state sales tax.
Feb 5	Sent the last week's sales tax to the state
28	Borrowed $210,000 on a four-year, 9% note payable that calls for $50,000 annual installment payments plus interest. Record the short-term and long-term portions of the note payable in two separate accounts.
Jul 9	Paid the six-month, 8% note, plus interest, at maturity
Aug 31	Purchased inventory for $6,000, signing a six-month, 10% note payable
Dec 31	Accrued warranty expense, which is estimated at 3% of sales of $601,000
31	Accrued interest on all outstanding notes payable. Make a separate interest accrual for each note payable.
2011	
Feb 28	Paid the first installment and interest for one year on the four-year note payable
28	Paid off the 10% note plus interest at maturity

Requirement

1. Journalize the transactions in Brewton's general journal. Explanations are not required.

P10-35A *(L.OBJ. 1, 3, 7)* **Journalizing, posting, and reporting liabilities [35–45 min]**
The general ledger of Seal-N-Ship at June 30, the end of the company's fiscal year, includes the following account balances before adjusting entries.

Accounts payable	$ 110,000
Current portion of notes payable	______
Interest payable	______
Salary payable	______
Employee payroll taxes payable	______
Employer payroll taxes payable	______
Unearned rent revenue	6,300
Long–term note payable	200,000

The additional data needed to develop the adjusting entries at June 30 are as follows:

a. The long-term debt is payable in annual installments of $40,000, with the next installment due on July 31. On that date, Seal – N – Ship will also pay one year's interest at 9%. Interest was last paid on July 31 of the preceding year. Make the adjusting entry to shift the current installment of the long-term note payable to a current liability. Also accrue interest expense at year end.
b. Gross salaries for the last payroll of the fiscal year were $4,600. Of this amount, employee payroll taxes payable were $960, and salary payable was $3,640.
c. Employer payroll taxes payable were $870.
d. On February 1, the company collected one year's rent of $6,300 in advance.

Requirements

1. Using four-column format, open the listed accounts, inserting the unadjusted June 30 balances.
2. Journalize and post the June 30 adjusting entries to the accounts that you opened. Key adjusting entries by letter.
3. Prepare the liabilities section of the balance sheet at June 30, 2012. Show total current liabilities and total liabilities.

P10-36A *(L.OBJ. 3, 4)* **Computing and journalizing payroll amounts [25–35 min]**

Logan White is general manager of Moonwalk Tanning Salons. During 2010, White worked for the company all year at a $6,100 monthly salary. He also earned a year-end bonus equal to 5% of his salary.

White's federal income tax withheld during 2010 was $810 per month, plus $932 on his bonus check. State income tax withheld came to $80 per month, plus $70 on the bonus. The FICA tax withheld was 8% of the first $90,000 in annual earnings. White authorized the following payroll deductions: United Fund contribution of 1% of total earnings and life insurance of $20 per month.

Moonwalk incurred payroll tax expense on White for FICA tax of 8% of the first $90,000 in annual earnings. The company also paid state unemployment tax of 5.4% and federal unemployment tax of 0.8% on the first $7,000 in annual earnings. In addition, Moonwalk provides White with health insurance at a cost of $110 per month. During 2010, Moonwalk paid $2,000 into White's retirement plan.

Requirements

1. Compute White's gross pay, payroll deductions, and net pay for the full year 2010. Round all amounts to the nearest dollar.
2. Compute Moonwalk's total 2010 payroll expense for White.
3. Make the journal entry to record Moonwalk's expense for White's total earnings for the year, his payroll deductions, and net pay. Debit Salary expense and Bonus expense as appropriate. Credit liability accounts for the payroll deductions and Cash for net pay. An explanation is not required.

P10-37A *(L.OBJ. 5, 6)* **Analyzing and journalizing bond transactions [30–40 min]**

On March 1, 2011, Professors Credit Union (PCU) issued 6%, 20-year bonds payable with maturity value of $900,000. The bonds pay interest on February 28 and August 31. PCU amortizes bond premium and discount by the straight-line method.

Requirements

1. If the market interest rate is 5% when PCU issues its bonds, will the bonds be priced at maturity (par) value, at a premium, or at a discount? Explain.
2. If the market interest rate is 7% when PCU issues its bonds, will the bonds be priced at par, at a premium, or at a discount? Explain.
3. The issue price of the bonds is 97. Journalize the following bond transactions:

   a. Issuance of the bonds on March 1, 2011
   b. Payment of interest and amortization of discount on August 31, 2011
   c. Accrual of interest and amortization of discount on December 31, 2011
   d. Payment of interest and amortization of discount on February 28, 2012

P10-38A *(L.OBJ. 5, 6, 7)* **Analyzing, journalizing, and reporting bond transactions [30 min]**
Captain Johnny Whizbang Hamburgers issued 4%, 10-year bonds payable at 85 on December 31, 2010. At December 31, 2012, Captain Johnny reported the bonds payable as follows:

Long–Term Debt:		
Bonds payable . . .	$ 300,000	
Less: Discount . . .	(36,000)	$ 264,000

Captain Johnny uses the straight-line amortization method and pays semiannual interest each June 30 and December 31.

Requirements

1. Answer the following questions about Captain Johnny Whizbang's bonds payable:

   a. What is the maturity value of the bonds?
   b. What is the carrying amount of the bonds at December 31, 2012?
   c. What is the annual cash interest payment on the bonds?
   d. How much interest expense should the company record each year?

2. Record the June 30, 2013, semiannual interest payment and amortization of discount.
3. What will be the carrying amount of the bonds at December 31, 2013?

P10-39A *(L.OBJ. 5, 6, 7)* **Journalizing and reporting bond transactions [20–25 min]**
The board of directors of Epsilon Health Spa authorizes the issuance of $450,000 of 8%, 10-year bonds payable. The semiannual interest dates are May 31 and November 30. The bonds are issued on July 31, 2010, at par plus accrued interest.

Requirements

1. Journalize the following transactions:

   a. Issuance of the bonds on July 31, 2010
   b. Payment of interest on November 30, 2010
   c. Accrual of interest on December 31, 2010
   d. Payment of interest on May 31, 2011

2. Report interest payable and bonds payable as they would appear on the Epsilon balance sheet at December 31, 2010.

P10-40A *(L.OBJ. 7)* **Report liabilities on the balance sheet [10–15 min]**
The accounting records of Path Leader Wireless include the following:

Accounts payable	$ 75,000	Salary payable	$ 7,000
Mortgage note payable, long–term	77,000	Bonds payable, current installment	20,000
Interest payable	17,000	Premium on all bonds payable	
Bonds payable, long–term	159,000	(all long–term)	8,000
Equity	155,000	Unearned service revenue	3,300

Requirement

1. Report these liabilities on the Path Leader Wireless balance sheet, including headings and totals for current liabilities and long-term liabilities.

P10-41A *(L.OBJ. 8)* **Analyzing alternative plans to raise money [15–20 min]**
Corny's Corndogs is considering two plans for raising $3,000,000 to expand operations. Plan A is to issue 7% bonds payable, and plan B is to issue 200,000 shares of common stock. Before any new financing, Corny has net income of $400,000 and 100,000 shares of common stock outstanding. Management believes the company can use the new funds to earn additional income of $700,000 before interest and taxes. The income tax rate is 35%.

Requirement

1. Analyze Corny's situation to determine which plan will result in higher earnings per share. Use Exhibit 10-10 as a guide.

Problems (Group B)

P10-42B *(L.OBJ. 1, 2)* **Journalizing liability transactions [30–40 min]**
The following transactions of Chicago Pharmacies occurred during 2010 and 2011:

2010	
Jan 9	Purchased computer equipment at a cost of $9,000, signing a six-month, 8% note payable for that amount
29	Recorded the week's sales of $61,000, three-fourths on credit, and one-fourth for cash. Sales amounts are subject to a 6% state sales tax.
Feb 5	Sent the last week's sales tax to the state
28	Borrowed $208,000 on a 4-year, 9% note payable that calls for $52,000 annual installment payments plus interest. Record the short-term and long-term portions of the note payable in two separate accounts.
Jul 9	Paid the six-month, 8% note, plus interest, at maturity
Aug 31	Purchased inventory for $12,000, signing a six-month, 10% note payable
Dec 31	Accrued warranty expense, which is estimated at 3% of sales of $609,000
31	Accrued interest on all outstanding notes payable. Make a separate interest accrual for each note payable.
2011	
Feb 28	Paid the first installment and interest for one year on the four-year note payable
28	Paid off the 10% note plus interest at maturity

Requirement

1. Journalize the transactions in Chicago's general journal. Explanations are not required.

P10-43B *(L.OBJ. 1, 3, 7)* **Journalizing, posting, and reporting liabilities [35–45 min]**
The general ledger of Quick Ship at June 30, the end of the company's fiscal year, includes the following account balances before adjusting entries.

Accounts payable	$ 117,000
Current portion of notes payable	______
Interest payable	______
Salary payable	______
Employee payroll taxes payable	______
Employer payroll taxes payable	______
Unearned rent revenue	6,000
Long–term note payable	200,000

The additional data needed to develop the adjusting entries at June 30 are as follows:

a. The long-term debt is payable in annual installments of $40,000, with the next installment due on July 31. On that date, Quick Ship will also pay one year's interest at 9%. Interest was last paid on July 31 of the preceding year. Make the adjusting entry to shift the current installment of the long-term note payable to a current liability. Also accrue interest expense at year end.
b. Gross salaries for the last payroll of the fiscal year were $4,200. Of this amount, employee payroll taxes payable were $920, and salary payable was $3,280.
c. Employer payroll taxes payable were $870.
d. On February 1, the company collected one year's rent of $6,000 in advance.

Requirements

1. Using four-column format, open the listed accounts, inserting the unadjusted June 30 balances.
2. Journalize and post the June 30 adjusting entries to the accounts that you opened. Key adjusting entries by letter.
3. Prepare the liabilities section of the balance sheet at June 30, 2012. Show total current liabilities and total liabilities.

P10-44B *(L.OBJ. 3, 4)* **Computing and journalizing payroll amounts [25–35 min]**
Lee Werner is general manager of United Tanning Salons. During 2010, Werner worked for the company all year at a $6,300 monthly salary. He also earned a year-end bonus equal to 10% of his salary.

Werner's federal income tax withheld during 2010 was $840 per month, plus $925 on his bonus check. State income tax withheld came to $90 per month, plus $50 on the bonus. The FICA tax withheld was 8% of the first $90,000 in annual earnings. Werner authorized the following payroll deductions: United Fund contribution of 1% of total earnings, and life insurance of $30 per month.

United incurred payroll tax expense on Werner for FICA tax of 8% of the first $90,000 in annual earnings. The company also paid state unemployment tax of 5.4% and federal unemployment tax of 0.8% on the first $7,000 in annual earnings. In addition, United provides Werner with health insurance at a cost of $150 per month. During 2010, United paid $5,000 into Werner's retirement plan.

Requirements

1. Compute Werner's gross pay, payroll deductions, and net pay for the full year 2010. Round all amounts to the nearest dollar.
2. Compute United's total 2010 payroll expense for Werner.
3. Make the journal entry to record United's expense for Werner's total earnings for the year, his payroll deductions, and net pay. Debit Salary expense and Bonus expense as appropriate. Credit liability accounts for the payroll deductions and Cash for net pay. An explanation is not required.

P10-45B *(L.OBJ. 5, 6)* **Analyzing and journalizing bond transactions [30–40 min]**
On March 1, 2011, Technicians Credit Union (TCU) issued 8%, 20-year bonds payable with maturity value of $700,000. The bonds pay interest on February 28 and August 31. TCU amortizes bond premium and discount by the straight-line method.

Requirements

1. If the market interest rate is 6% when TCU issues its bonds, will the bonds be priced at maturity (par) value, at a premium, or at a discount? Explain.

2. If the market interest rate is 9% when TCU issues its bonds, will the bonds be priced at par, at a premium, or at a discount? Explain.
3. The issue price of the bonds is 98. Journalize the following bond transactions:

   a. Issuance of the bonds on March 1, 2011
   b. Payment of interest and amortization of discount on August 31, 2011
   c. Accrual of interest and amortization of discount on December 31, 2011
   d. Payment of interest and amortization of discount on February 29, 2012

P10-46B *(L.OBJ. 5, 6, 7)* **Analyzing, journalizing, and reporting bond transactions [30 min]**
Captain Billy Whirlywhirl Hamburgers issued 7%, 10-year bonds payable at 70 on December 31, 2010. At December 31, 2012, Captain Billy reported the bonds payable as follows:

Long–term debt:		
Bonds payable . . .	$ 300,000	
Less: Discount . . .	(72,000)	$ 228,000

Captain Billy Whirlywhirl uses the straight-line amortization method and pays semi-annual interest each June 30 and December 31.

Requirements

1. Answer the following questions about Captain Billy Whirlywhirl's bonds payable:

   a. What is the maturity value of the bonds?
   b. What is the carrying amount of the bonds at December 31, 2012?
   c. What is Captain Billy Whirlywhirl's annual cash interest payment on the bonds?
   d. How much interest expense should Captain Billy Whirlywhirl record each year?

2. Record the June 30, 2013, semiannual interest payment and amortization of discount.
3. What will be the carrying amount of the bonds at December 31, 2013?

P10-47B *(L.OBJ. 5, 6, 7)* **Journalizing and reporting bond transactions [20–25 min]**
The board of directors of Zeta Health Spa authorizes the issuance of $500,000 of 8%, 10-year bonds payable. The semiannual interest dates are May 31 and November 30. The bonds are issued on July 31, 2010, at par plus accrued interest.

Requirements

1. Journalize the following transactions:

   a. Issuance of the bonds on July 31, 2010
   b. Payment of interest on November 30, 2010
   c. Accrual of interest on December 31, 2010
   d. Payment of interest on May 31, 2011

2. Report interest payable and bonds payable as they would appear on the Zeta balance sheet at December 31, 2010.

P10-48B *(L.OBJ. 7)* **Reporting liabilities on the balance sheet [10–15 min]**
The accounting records of Placeless Wireless include the following:

Accounts payable	$ 69,000	Salary payable	$ 11,000
Mortgage note payable, long-term	74,000	Bonds payable, current installment	30,000
Interest payable	15,000	Premium on all bonds payable	
Bonds payable, long-term	160,000	(all long-term)	16,000
Equity	180,000	Unearned service revenue	2,900

Requirement

1. Report these liabilities on the Placeless Wireless balance sheet, including headings and totals for current liabilities and long-term liabilities.

P10-49B *(L.OBJ. 8)* **Analyzing alternative plans to raise money [15–20 min]**
Walter's Surf Shop is considering two plans for raising $2,500,000 to expand operations. Plan A is to issue 6% bonds payable, and plan B is to issue 100,000 shares of common stock. Before any new financing, Walter's has net income of $350,000 and 25,000 shares of common stock outstanding. Management believes the company can use the new funds to earn additional income of $950,000 before interest and taxes. The income tax rate is 33%.

Requirement

1. Analyze Walter's situation to determine which plan will result in higher earnings per share. Use Exhibit 10-10 as a guide.

■ Continuing Exercise

E10-50 This exercise continues the Sherman Lawn Service situation from Exercise 9-30 of Chapter 9. Refer to the Chapter 2 data for Exercise 2-63. Sherman Lawn Service is considering hiring its first "real" employee. The employee will earn $600 weekly and will have $60 in federal income tax and $25 for health insurance withheld, in addition to FICA, each week. Assume the employee will pay no state or other taxes. The employer must pay FICA tax, Federal unemployment tax of .8% of the first $7,000 in pay, and State unemployment tax of 2.7% of the first $7,000 in pay.

Requirements

1. Calculate the amount of the employee's weekly net pay.
2. Journalize the entries to accrue the weekly payroll on October 31, to record the employer's payroll taxes associated with the payroll on the same date, and to pay the payroll on November 4, 2009.

■ Continuing Problem

P10-51 This problem continues the Haupt Consulting situation from Problem 9-31 of Chapter 9. Refer to Problem 2-64 of Chapter 2. Haupt Consulting is considering raising capital for a planned business expansion to a new market. Haupt believes the company will need $500,000 and plans to raise the capital by issuing 6%, 10 year bonds on March 1. The bonds pay interest semiannually on March 1 and September 1. On March 1, the market rate of interest required by similar bonds by investors is 8%.

Requirements

1. Will Haupt's bond's issue at par, a premium, or a discount?
2. Calculate and record the cash received on the bond issue date.

3. Journalize the first interest payment on September 1 and amortize the premium or discount using the effective interest method.
4. Journalize the entry required, if any, on December 31 related to the bonds.

Apply Your Knowledge

Decision Cases

Case 1. Golden Bear Construction Co. operates throughout California. The owner, Gaylan Beavers, employs 15 work crews. Construction supervisors report directly to Beavers, and the supervisors are trusted employees. The home office staff consists of an accountant and an office manager.

Because employee turnover is high in the construction industry, supervisors hire and fire their own crews. Supervisors notify the office of all personnel changes. Also, supervisors forward to the office the employee W-4 forms. Each Thursday, the supervisors submit weekly time sheets for their crews, and the accountant prepares the payroll. At noon on Friday, the supervisors come to the office to get paychecks for distribution to the workers at 5 PM.

The company accountant prepares the payroll, including the paychecks. Beavers signs all paychecks. To verify that each construction worker is a bona fide employee, the accountant matches the employee's endorsement signature on the back of the canceled paycheck with the signature on that employee's W-4 form.

Requirements

1. Identify one way that a supervisor can defraud Golden Bear Construction under the present system.
2. Discuss a control feature that the company can use to *safeguard* against the fraud you identified in Requirement 1.

Case 2. Sell-Soft Company is the defendant in numerous lawsuits claiming unfair trade practices. Sell-Soft has strong incentives not to disclose these contingent liabilities. However, GAAP requires that companies report their contingent liabilities.

Requirements

1. Why would a company prefer *not* to disclose its contingent liabilities?
2. Describe how a bank could be harmed if a company seeking a loan did not disclose its contingent liabilities.
3. What ethical tightrope must companies walk when they report contingent liabilities?

Case 3. The following questions are not related.

Requirements

1. Duncan Brooks Co. needs to borrow $500,000 to open new stores. Brooks can borrow $500,000 by issuing 5%, 10-year bonds at a price of 96. How much will Brooks actually be borrowing under this arrangement? How much must Brooks pay back at maturity? How will Brooks account for the difference between the amount borrowed and the amount paid back?
2. Brooks prefers to borrow for longer periods when interest rates are low and for shorter periods when interest rates are high. Why is this a good business strategy? (Challenge)

Case 4. Business is going well for Email Designers. The board of directors of this family-owned company believes that Email Designers could earn an additional $1,000,000 income before interest and taxes by expanding into new markets. However, the $4,000,000 the business needs for growth cannot be raised within the family. The directors, who strongly wish to retain family control of the company, must issue securities to outsiders. They are considering two financing plans.

Plan A is to borrow at 6%. Plan B is to issue 100,000 shares of common stock. Email Designers currently has net income of $1,200,000 and 400,000 shares of common stock outstanding. The company's income tax rate is 40%.

Requirements

1. Prepare an analysis similar to Exhibit 10-10 to determine which plan will result in the highest earnings per share of common stock.
2. Recommend one plan to the board of directors. Give your reasons.

Ethical Issue

Bombadier Industries manufactures aircraft-related electronic devices. Bombadier borrows heavily to finance operations. Often Bombadier is profitable because it can earn operating income much higher than its interest expense. However, when the business cycle has turned down, the company's debt burden has pushed the company to the brink of bankruptcy. Operating income is sometimes less than interest expense.

Requirement

1. Is it unethical for managers to saddle a company with a high level of debt? Or is it just risky? Who can get hurt when a company takes on too much debt? Discuss.

Financial Statement Case

Details about a company's liabilities appear in a number of places in the annual report. Use **Amazon.com's** financial statements, including Notes 1 and 4, to answer the following questions. **Amazon's** financial statements are in Appendix A at the end of this book.

Requirements

1. Give the breakdown of **Amazon.com's** current liabilities at December 31, 2007. Give the January 2008 entry to record the payment of accrued expenses and other current liabilities that **Amazon** owed at December 31, 2007.
2. At December 31, 2007, how much did **Amazon** owe customers for unearned revenue that **Amazon** had collected in advance? Which account on the balance sheet reports this liability?
3. How much was **Amazon's** long-term debt at December 31, 2007? Of this amount, how much was due within one year? How much was payable beyond one year in the future?
4. Journalize in a single entry **Amazon's** interest expense for 2007. **Amazon** paid cash of $67 million for interest.
5. Refer to Note 4 and compute the annual interest on **Amazon's** 4.75% convertible subordinated notes. Round to the nearest thousand.

Team Projects

Project 1. In recent years, the airline industry has dominated headlines. Consumers are shopping **Priceline.com** and other Internet sites for the lowest rates. The airlines have also lured customers with frequent-flyer programs, which award free flights to passengers who accumulate specified miles of travel. Unredeemed frequent-flyer mileage represents a liability that airlines must report on their balance sheets, usually as Air Traffic Liability.

Southwest Airlines, a profitable, no-frills carrier based in Dallas, has been rated near the top of the industry. **Southwest** controls costs by flying to smaller, less-expensive airports; using only one model of aircraft; serving no meals; increasing staff efficiency; and having a shorter turnaround time on the ground between flights. The fact that most of the cities served by Southwest have predictable weather maximizes its on-time arrival record.

Requirements

With a partner or group, lead your class in a discussion of the following questions, or write a report as directed by your instructor.

1. Frequent-flyer programs have grown into significant obligations for airlines. Why should a liability be recorded for those programs? Discuss how you might calculate the amount of this liability. Can you think of other industries that offer incentives that create a similar liability?
2. One of **Southwest Airlines'** strategies for success is shortening stops at airport gates between flights. The company's chairman has stated, "What [you] produce is lower fares for the customers because you generate more revenue from the same fixed cost in that airplane." Look up **fixed cost** in the Glindex of this book. What are some of the "fixed costs" of an airline? How can better utilization of assets improve a company's profits?

Project 2. Each member of the team should select a large corporation and go to its Web site. Surf around until you find the company's balance sheet. Often the appropriate tab is labeled as

- Investor Relations
- About the Company
- Financial Reports
- 10-K Report

From the company's balance sheet scroll down until you find the liabilities.

Requirements

1. List all the company's liabilities—both current and long-term—along with each amount.
2. Read the company's notes to the financial statements and include any details that help you identify the amount of a liability.
3. Compute the company's current ratio and debt ratio.
4. Bring your findings to your team meeting, compare your results with those of your team members, and prepare either a written report or an oral report, as directed by your instructor.

Quick Check Answers

1. *b* 2. *c* 3. *a* 4. *b* 5. *d* 6. *b* 7. *a* 8. *d* 9. *c* 10. *b*

For online homework, exercises, and problems that provide you immediate feedback, please visit www.myaccountinglab.com.

Appendix 10A

The Time Value of Money: Present Value of a Bond and Effective-Interest Amortization

The term *time value of money* refers to the fact that money earns interest over time. Interest is the cost of using money. To borrowers, interest is the expense of using someone else's money. To lenders, interest is the revenue earned from lending. In this appendix, we focus on the borrower, who owes money on the bonds payable.

Present Value

Often a person knows a future amount, such as the maturity value of a bond, and needs to know the bond's present value. The present value of the bond measures its price and tells an investor how much to pay for the bond.

Present Value of $1

Suppose an investment promises you $5,000 at the *end* of one year. How much would you pay *now* to acquire this investment? You would be willing to pay the present value of the $5,000 future amount.

Present value depends on three factors:

1. The amount to be received in the future
2. The time span between your investment and your future receipt
3. The interest rate

Computing a present value is called *discounting* because the present value is *always less* than the future value.

In our example, the future receipt is $5,000. The investment period is one year. Assume that you require an annual interest rate of 10% on your investment. You can compute the present value of $5,000 at 10% for one year, as follows:

$$\frac{\text{Future value}}{(1 + \text{Interest rate})} = \frac{\$5{,}000}{1.10} = \$4{,}545$$

So, the present value of $5,000 to be received one year from now is $4,545.

The following diagram demonstrates the relationship between present value and future value.

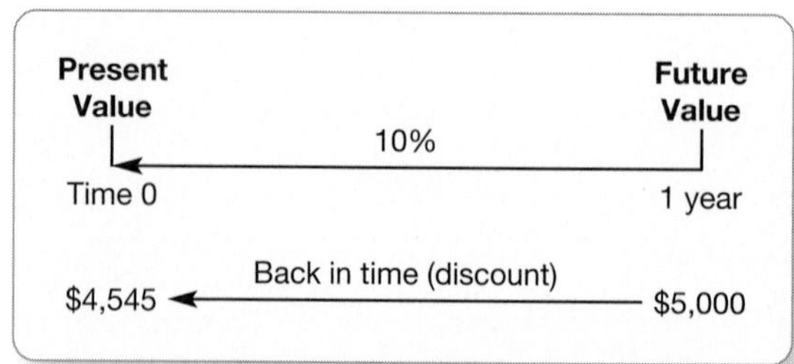

If the $5,000 is to be received two years from now, the calculation is as follows:

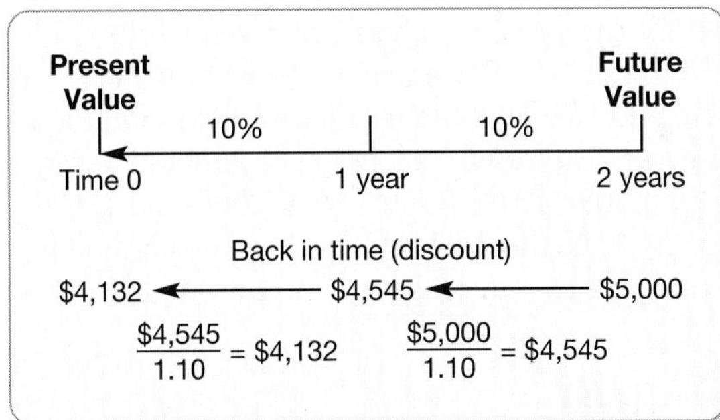

So, the present value of $5,000 to be received two years from now is $4,132.

Present-Value Tables

We have shown how to compute a present value. But that computation is burdensome for an investment that spans many years. Present-value tables ease our work. Let us reexamine our examples of present value by using Exhibit 10A-1, Present Value of $1. (Also presented in Exhibit B.)

EXHIBIT 10A-1 **Present Value of $1**

Present Value of $1

Period	4%	5%	6%	7%	8%	10%	12%	14%	16%
1	0.962	0.952	0.943	0.935	0.926	0.909	0.893	0.877	0.862
2	0.925	0.907	0.890	0.873	0.857	0.826	0.797	0.769	0.743
3	0.889	0.864	0.840	0.816	0.794	0.751	0.712	0.675	0.641
4	0.855	0.823	0.792	0.763	0.735	0.683	0.636	0.592	0.552
5	0.822	0.784	0.747	0.713	0.681	0.621	0.567	0.519	0.476
6	0.790	0.746	0.705	0.666	0.630	0.564	0.507	0.456	0.410
7	0.760	0.711	0.665	0.623	0.583	0.513	0.452	0.400	0.354
8	0.731	0.677	0.627	0.582	0.540	0.467	0.404	0.351	0.305
9	0.703	0.645	0.592	0.544	0.500	0.424	0.361	0.308	0.263
10	0.676	0.614	0.558	0.508	0.463	0.386	0.322	0.270	0.227
11	0.650	0.585	0.527	0.475	0.429	0.350	0.287	0.237	0.195
12	0.625	0.557	0.497	0.444	0.397	0.319	0.257	0.208	0.168
13	0.601	0.530	0.469	0.415	0.368	0.290	0.229	0.182	0.145
14	0.577	0.505	0.442	0.388	0.340	0.263	0.205	0.160	0.125
15	0.555	0.481	0.417	0.362	0.315	0.239	0.183	0.140	0.108
16	0.534	0.458	0.394	0.339	0.292	0.218	0.163	0.123	0.093
17	0.513	0.436	0.371	0.317	0.270	0.198	0.146	0.108	0.080
18	0.494	0.416	0.350	0.296	0.250	0.180	0.130	0.095	0.069
19	0.475	0.396	0.331	0.277	0.232	0.164	0.116	0.083	0.060
20	0.456	0.377	0.312	0.258	0.215	0.149	0.104	0.073	0.051

For the 10% investment for one year, we find the junction in the 10% column and across from 1 in the Period column. The figure 0.909 is computed as follows: 1/1.10 = 0.909. This work has been done for us and all the present values are given in the table. The heading in Exhibit 10A-1 states Present Value of $1. To figure present value for $5,000, we multiply $5,000 by 0.909. The result is $4,545, which matches the result we obtained earlier.

For the two-year investment, we read down the 10% column and across the Period 2 row. We multiply 0.826 (computed as 0.909/1.10 = 0.826) by $5,000 and get $4,130, which confirms our earlier computation of $4,132 (the difference is due to rounding in the present-value table). Using the table, we can compute the present value of any single future amount.

Present Value of an Annuity

Let us return to the investment example that provided a single future receipt ($5,000 at the end of two years). Annuity investments provide multiple receipts of an equal amount at equal time intervals.

Consider an investment that promises *annual* cash receipts of $10,000 to be received at the end of each of three years. Assume that you demand a 12% return on your investment. What is the investment's present value? The present value determines how much you would pay today to acquire the investment. The investment spans three periods, and you would pay the sum of three present values. The computation follows:

Year	Annual Cash Receipt	×	Present Value of $1 at 12% (Exhibit 10A-1)	=	Present Value of Annual Cash Receipt
1	$10,000	×	0.893	=	$ 8,930
2	10,000	×	0.797	=	7,970
3	10,000	×	0.712	=	7,120
	Total present value of investment			=	$24,020

The present value of this annuity is $24,020. By paying $24,020 today, you will receive $10,000 at the end of each of the three years while earning 12% on your investment.

The example illustrates repetitive computations of the three future amounts using the Present Value of $1 table. One way to ease the computational burden is to add the three present values of $1 (0.893 + 0.797 + 0.712) and multiply their sum (2.402) by the annual cash receipt ($10,000) to obtain the present value of the annuity ($10,000 × 2.402 = $24,020).

An easier approach is to use a present value of an annuity table. Exhibit 10A-2 shows the present value of $1 to be received at the end of each period for a given number of periods.

The present value of a three-period annuity at 12% is 2.402 (the junction of the Period 3 row and the 12% column). So, $10,000 received annually at the end of each of three years, discounted at 12%, is $24,020 ($10,000 × 2.402), which is the present value.

EXHIBIT 10A-2 | **Present Value of Annuity of $1**

Present Value of Annuity of $1

Period	4%	5%	6%	7%	8%	10%	12%	14%	16%
1	0.962	0.952	0.943	0.935	0.926	0.909	0.893	0.877	0.862
2	1.886	1.859	1.833	1.808	1.783	1.736	1.690	1.647	1.605
3	2.775	2.723	2.673	2.624	2.577	2.487	2.402	2.322	2.246
4	3.630	3.546	3.465	3.387	3.312	3.170	3.037	2.914	2.798
5	4.452	4.329	4.212	4.100	3.993	3.791	3.605	3.433	3.274
6	5.242	5.076	4.917	4.767	4.623	4.355	4.111	3.889	3.685
7	6.002	5.786	5.582	5.389	5.206	4.868	4.564	4.288	4.039
8	6.733	6.463	6.210	5.971	5.747	5.335	4.968	4.639	4.344
9	7.435	7.108	6.802	6.515	6.247	5.759	5.328	4.946	4.607
10	8.111	7.722	7.360	7.024	6.710	6.145	5.650	5.216	4.833
11	8.760	8.306	7.887	7.499	7.139	6.495	5.938	5.453	5.029
12	9.385	8.863	8.384	7.943	7.536	6.814	6.194	5.660	5.197
13	9.986	9.394	8.853	8.358	7.904	7.103	6.424	5.842	5.342
14	10.563	9.899	9.295	8.745	8.244	7.367	6.628	6.002	5.468
15	11.118	10.380	9.712	9.108	8.559	7.606	6.811	6.142	5.575
16	11.652	10.838	10.106	9.447	8.851	7.824	6.974	6.265	5.669
17	12.166	11.274	10.477	9.763	9.122	8.022	7.120	6.373	5.749
18	12.659	11.690	10.828	10.059	9.372	8.201	7.250	6.467	5.818
19	13.134	12.085	11.158	10.336	9.604	8.365	7.366	6.550	5.877
20	13.590	12.462	11.470	10.594	9.818	8.514	7.469	6.623	5.929

Present Value of Bonds Payable

The present value of a bond—its market price—is the sum of

- the present value of the principal amount to be received at maturity—a single amount (present value of $1),
- *plus* the present value of the future stated interest amounts—an annuity because it occurs in equal amounts over equal time periods (present value of annuity of $1).

Discount Price

Let us compute the present value of the 9%, five-year bonds of Smart Touch Learning. The maturity value of the bonds is $100,000 and they pay (9% × 6/12) or 4½% stated interest semiannually. At issuance, the annual market interest rate is 10% (5% semiannually). Therefore, the market interest rate for each of the 10 semiannual periods is 5%. We use 5% to compute the present value (PV) of the maturity and the present value (PV) of the stated interest. The market price of these bonds is $96,149, computed as follows:

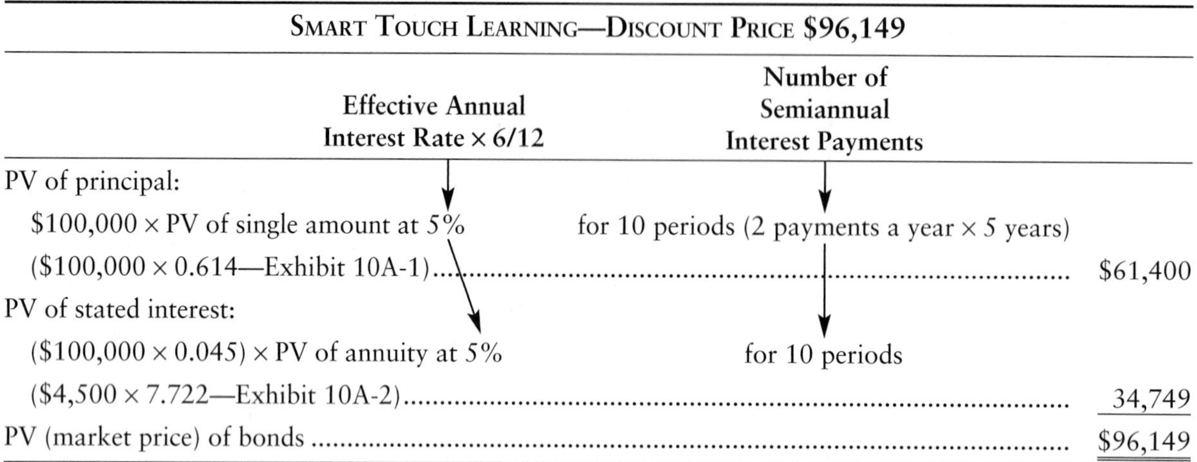

SMART TOUCH LEARNING—DISCOUNT PRICE $96,149

	Effective Annual Interest Rate × 6/12	Number of Semiannual Interest Payments	
PV of principal:			
$100,000 × PV of single amount at 5%		for 10 periods (2 payments a year × 5 years)	
($100,000 × 0.614—Exhibit 10A-1)			$61,400
PV of stated interest:			
($100,000 × 0.045) × PV of annuity at 5%		for 10 periods	
($4,500 × 7.722—Exhibit 10A-2)			34,749
PV (market price) of bonds			$96,149

The market price of the Smart Touch bonds shows a discount because the stated interest rate on the bonds (9%) is less than the market interest rate (10%). We discuss these bonds in more detail in the next section of this appendix.

Premium Price

Let us consider a premium price for the Smart Touch bonds. Now suppose the market interest rate is 8% at issuance (4% for each of the 10 semiannual periods). We would compute the market price of these bonds as follows:

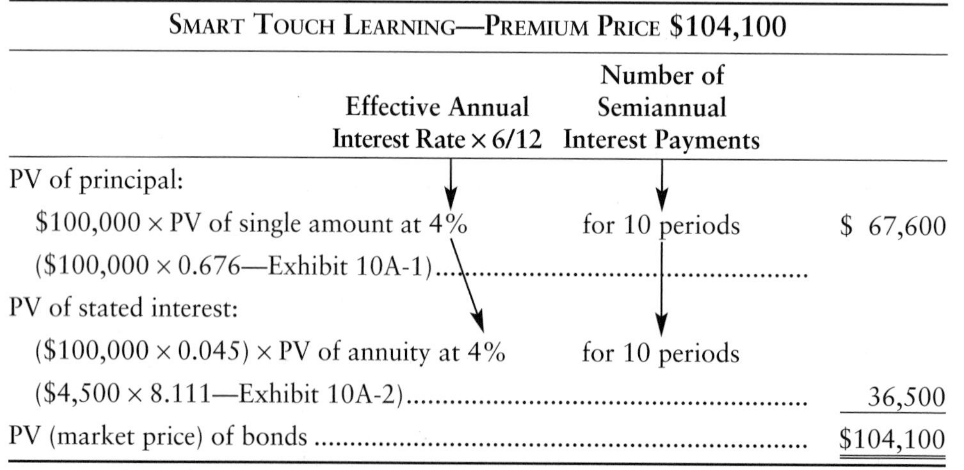

SMART TOUCH LEARNING—PREMIUM PRICE $104,100

	Effective Annual Interest Rate × 6/12	Number of Semiannual Interest Payments	
PV of principal:			
$100,000 × PV of single amount at 4%		for 10 periods	$ 67,600
($100,000 × 0.676—Exhibit 10A-1)			
PV of stated interest:			
($100,000 × 0.045) × PV of annuity at 4%		for 10 periods	
($4,500 × 8.111—Exhibit 10A-2)			36,500
PV (market price) of bonds			$104,100

The market price of the Smart Touch bonds shows a premium because the stated interest rate on the bonds (9%) is higher than the market interest rate (8%). We discuss accounting for these bonds in the next section.

Effective-Interest Method of Amortization

We began this chapter with straight-line amortization to introduce the concept of amortizing bonds. A more precise way of amortizing bonds is used in practice, and it is called the **effective-interest method**. That method uses the present-value concepts covered in this appendix to amortize bond premium or discount.

Generally accepted accounting principles require that interest expense be measured using the *effective-interest method* unless the straight-line amounts are similar. In that case, either method is permitted. Total interest expense over the life of the bonds is the same under both methods. Let us look at how the effective-interest method works.

Effective-Interest Amortization for a Bond Discount

Assume that Smart Touch Learning issues $100,000 of 9% bonds at a time when the market rate of interest is 10%. These bonds mature in five years and pay interest semiannually, so there are 10 semiannual interest payments. As we just saw, the issue price of the bonds is $96,149, and the discount on these bonds is $3,851 ($100,000 – $96,149). Exhibit 10A-3 shows how to measure interest expense by the effective-interest method. (You will need an amortization table to account for bonds by the effective-interest method.)

The *accounts* debited and credited under the effective-interest method and the straight-line method are the same. Only the *amounts* differ.

Exhibit 10A-3 on page 610 gives the amounts for all the bond transactions of Smart Touch Learning. Let us begin with issuance of the bonds payable on January 1, 2010, and the first interest payment on June 30. Entries follow, using amounts from the respective lines of Exhibit 10A-3.

EXHIBIT 10A-3 | **Effective-Interest Amortization of a Bond Discount**

PANEL A—Bond Data

Maturity value—$100,000

Stated interest rate—9%

Interest paid—semiannually, $4,500 ($100,000 × .09 × 6/12)

Market interest rate at time of issue—10% annually

Issue price—$96,149 on January 1, 2010

PANEL B—Amortization Table

	A	B	C	D	E
End of Semiannual Interest Period	Interest *Payment* (9% × 6/12)	Interest *Expense* (10% × 6/12) × Bond Carrying Value	Discount Amortization (B – A)	Discount Balance (D – C)	Bond Carrying Amount ($100,000 – D)
Jan 1, 2010				$3,851	$ 96,149
Jun 30	$4,500	$4,807	$307	3,544	96,456
Dec 31, 2010	4,500	4,823	323	3,221	96,779
Jun 30, 2011	4,500	4,839	339	2,882	97,118
Dec 31	4,500	4,856	356	2,526	97,474
Jun 30, 2012	4,500	4,874	374	2,152	97,848
Dec 31	4,500	4,892	392	1,760	98,240
Jun 30, 2013	4,500	4,912	412	1,348	98,652
Dec 31	4,500	4,933	433	915	99,085
Jun 30, 2014	4,500	4,954	454	461	99,539
Dec 31	4,500	4,961*	461	0	100,000

*Adjusted for effect of rounding.

Notes

- *Column A* The interest payments are constant.
- *Column B* The interest expense each period is the preceding bond carrying amount multiplied by the market interest rate.
- *Column C* The excess of interest expense (B) over interest payment (A) is the discount amortization.
- *Column D* The discount decreases by the amount of amortization for the period (C).
- *Column E* The bonds' carrying amount increases from $96,149 at issuance to $100,000 at maturity.

2010			
Jan 1	Cash (column E) (A+)	96,149	
	Discount on bonds payable (column D) (CL+)	3,851	
	Bonds payable (maturity value) (L+)		100,000
	Issued bonds at a discount.		

2010			
Jun 30	Interest expense (column B) (E+)	4,807	
	Discount on bonds payable (column C) (CL–)		307
	Cash (column A) (A–)		4,500
	Paid interest and amortized discount.		

Effective-Interest Amortization of a Bond Premium

Smart Touch Learning may issue its bonds payable at a premium. Assume that Smart Touch issues $100,000 of five-year, 9% bonds when the market interest rate is 8%. The bonds' issue price is $104,100, and the premium is $4,100.

Exhibit 10A-4 provides the data for all the bond transactions of Smart Touch Learning.

EXHIBIT 10A-4 Effective-Interest Amortization of a Bond Premium

PANEL A—Bond Data

Maturity value—$100,000

Stated interest rate—9%

Interest paid—semiannually, $4,500 ($100,000 × .09 × 6/12)

Market interest rate at time of issue—8% annually, 4% semiannually

Issue price—$104,100 on January 1, 2010

PANEL B—Amortization Table

	A	B	C	D	E
End of Semiannual Interest Period	Interest *Payment* (9% × 6/12 of maturity value)	Interest *Expense* (8% × 6/12 of preceding bond carrying amount)	Premium Amortization (B – A)	Premium Balance (D – C)	Bond Carrying Amount ($100,000 + D)
Jan 1, 2010				$4,100	$104,100
Jun 30	$4,500	$4,164	$336	3,764	103,764
Dec 31	4,500	4,151	349	3,415	103,415
Jun 30, 2011	4,500	4,137	363	3,052	103,052
Dec 31	4,500	4,122	378	2,674	102,674
Jun 30, 2012	4,500	4,107	393	2,281	102,281
Dec 31	4,500	4,091	409	1,872	101,872
Jun 30, 2013	4,500	4,075	425	1,447	101,447
Dec 31	4,500	4,058	442	1,005	101,005
Jun 30, 2014	4,500	4,040	460	545	100,545
Dec 31	4,500	3,955*	545	0	100,000

*Adjusted for effect of rounding.

Notes
- *Column A* The interest payments are constant.
- *Column B* The interest expense each period is the preceding bond carrying amount multiplied by the market interest rate.
- *Column C* The excess of interest payment (A) over interest expense (B) is the premium amortization.
- *Column D* The premium balance decreases by the amount of amortization for the period.
- *Column E* The bonds' carrying amount decreases from $104,100 at issuance to $100,000 at maturity.

Let us begin with issuance of the bonds on January 1, 2010, and the first interest payment on June 30. These entries follow:

2010			
Jan 1	Cash (column E) (A+)	104,100	
	Bonds payable (maturity value) (L+)		100,000
	Premium on bonds payable (column D) (CL+)		4,100
	Issued bonds at a premium.		

2010			
Jun 30	Interest expense (column B) (E+)	4,164	
	Premium on bonds payable (column C) (CL–)	336	
	Cash (column A) (A–)		4,500
	Paid interest and amortized premium.		

Appendix 10A Assignments

Problems (Group A)

P10A-1A Calculating present value [15–25 min]
Lexo Company needs new manufacturing equipment. Two companies can provide similar equipment but under different payment plans:

Plan A: LG offers to let Lexo pay $45,000 each year for five years. The payments include interest at 10% per year.

Plan B: Northernhouse will let Lexo make a single payment of $450,000 at the end of five years. This payment includes both principal and interest at 10%.

Requirements

1. Calculate the present value of Plan A.
2. Calculate the present value of Plan B.
3. Lexo will purchase the equipment that costs the least, as measured by present value. Which equipment should Lexo select? Why? (Challenge)

P10A-2A Calculating the value of bonds when stated rate and market rate are different [40–50 min]
Interest rates determine the present value of future amounts.

Requirements

1. Determine the present value of 10-year bonds payable with maturity value of $88,000 and stated interest rate of 12%, paid semiannually. The market rate of interest is 12% at issuance.
2. Same bonds payable as in requirement 1, but the market interest rate is 14%.
3. Same bonds payable as in requirement 1, but the market interest rate is 10%.

Note: Problem 10A-2A must be completed before attempting Problem 10A-3A.

P10A-3A Journalizing bond transactions [20–30 min]
Consider your answers from requirements 1–3 of Problem 10A-2A.

Requirement

1. Journalize issuance of the bond and the first semiannual interest payment under each of the 3 assumptions in Problem 10A-2A. The company amortizes bond premium and discount by the effective-interest method. Explanations are not required.

P10A-4A Calculating and recording bonds when stated rate and market rate are different [15–20 min]
VEX Company issued $500,000 of 14%, 10-year bonds payable at a price of 90.226 on March 31, 2010. The market interest rate at the date of issuance was 16%, and the bonds pay interest semiannually.

Requirements

1. How much cash did the company receive upon issuance of the bonds payable?

2. Prepare an effective-interest amortization table for the bond discount through the first two interest payments. Use Exhibit 10A-3 as a guide, and round amounts to the nearest dollar.
3. Journalize the issuance of the bonds on March 31, 2010, and on September 30, 2010, payment of the first semiannual interest amount and amortization of the bond discount. Explanations are not required.

P10A-5A Calculating and recording bonds when stated rate and market rate are different [15–20 min]

Ben Norton Co. issued $100,000 of 5%, 10-year bonds payable at a price of 108.178 on May 31, 2010. The market interest rate at the date of issuance was 4%, and the bonds pay interest semiannually.

Requirements

1. How much cash did the company receive upon issuance of the bonds payable?
2. Prepare an effective-interest amortization table for the bond premium, through the first two interest payments. Use Exhibit 10A-4 as a guide, and round amounts to the nearest dollar.
3. Journalize the issuance of the bonds on May 31, 2010, and, on November 30, 2010, payment of the first semiannual interest amount and amortization of the bond premium. Explanations are not required.

P10A-6A Calculating and recording bonds when stated rate and market rate are different [20–25 min]

Calming Company is authorized to issue 7%, 10-year bonds payable. On January 2, 2011, when the market interest rate is 8%, the company issues $300,000 of the bonds and receives cash of $279,495. Calming amortizes bond discount by the effective-interest method. Interest dates are January 2 and July 2.

Requirements

1. Prepare an amortization table for the first two semiannual interest periods. Follow the format of Exhibit 10A-3.
2. Journalize the issuance of the bonds payable and the first semiannual interest payment on July 2.

P10A-7A Calculating and recording bonds when stated rate and market rate are different [15–20 min]

On January 1, 2011, Snitzel Company issued $100,000 of 11.375%, five-year bonds payable when the market interest rate was 12%. Snitzel pays interest annually at year-end. The issue price of the bonds was $97,747.

Requirement

1. Create a spreasheet model to measure interest and bond discount amortization based on the table.

1	A	B	C	D	E	F
2						Bond
3		Interest	Interest	Discount	Discount	Carrying
4	Date	Payment	Expense	Amortization	Balance	Amount
5	1-1-11				$ ☐	$97,747
6	12-31-11	$ ☐	$ ☐	$ ☐	↓	☐
7	12-31-12	↓	↓	↓	↓	↓
8	12-31-13	↓	↓	↓	↓	↓
9	12-31-14	↓	↓	↓	↓	↓
10	12-31-15	↓	↓	↓	↓	↓
		100,000*.11,375	+F5*.12	+C6–B6	100,000–F5	+F5+D6

P10A-8A Calculating and recording bonds when stated rate and market rate are different [30–40 min]

On December 31, 2010, when the market interest rate is 8%, Timmony Realty Co. issues $200,000 of 5.25%, 10-year bonds payable. The bonds pay interest semiannually.

Requirements

1. Determine the present value of the bonds at issuance.
2. Assume that the bonds are issued at the price computed in requirement 1. Prepare an effective-interest method amortization table for the first two semiannual interestinstallments.
3. Using the amortization table prepared in requirement 2, journalize issuance of the bonds and the first two interest payments.

■ Problems (Group B)

P10A-9B Calculating present value [15–25 min]

Axel needs new manufacturing equipment. Two companies can provide similar equipment but under different payment plans:

Plan A: MRE offers to let Axel pay $55,000 each year for five years. The payments include interest at 12% per year.

Plan B: Westernhome will let Axel make a single payment of $425,000 at the end of five years. This payment includes both principal and interest at 12%.

Requirements

1. Calculate the present value of Plan A.
2. Calculate the present value of Plan B.
3. Axel will purchase the equipment that costs the least, as measured by present value. Which equipment should Axel select? Why? (Challenge)

P10A-10B Calculating the value of bonds when stated rate and market rate are different [40–50 min]

Interest rates determine the present value of future amounts.

Requirements

1. Determine the present value of ten-year bonds payable with maturity value of $84,000 and stated interest rate of 14%, paid semiannually. The market rate of interest is 14% at issuance.
2. Same bonds payable as in requirement 1, but the market interest rate is 16%.
3. Same bonds payable as in requirement 1, but the market interest rate is 8%.

Note: Problem 10A-10B must be completed before attempting Problem 10A-11B.

P10A-11B Journalizing bond transactions [20–30 min]

Consider your answers from requirements 1–3 of Problem 10A-10B.

Requirement

1. Journalize issuance of the bond and the first semiannual interest payment under each of the 3 assumptions in Problem 10A-10B. The company amortizes bond premium and discount by the effective-interest method. Explanations are not required.

P10A-12B Calculating and recording bonds when stated rate and market rate are different [15–20 min]

TVX issued $700,000 of 9%, 10-year bonds payable at a price of 93.779 on March 31, 2010. The market interest rate at the date of issuance was 10%, and the bonds pay interest semiannually.

Requirements

1. How much cash did the company receive upon issuance of the bonds payable?
2. Prepare an effective-interest amortization table for the bond discount, through the first two interest payments. Use Exhibit 10A-3 as a guide, and round amounts to the nearest dollar.
3. Journalize the issuance of the bonds on March 31, 2010, and on September 30, 2010, payment of the first semiannual interest amount and amortization of the bond discount. Explanations are not required.

P10A-13B Calculating and recording bonds when stated rate and market rate are different [15–20 min]

Jon Spelman Co. issued $200,000 of 9%, 10-year bonds payable at a price of 106.755 on May 31, 2010. The market interest rate at the date of issuance was 8%, and the bonds pay interest semiannually.

Requirements

1. How much cash did the company receive upon issuance of the bonds payable?
2. Prepare an effective-interest amortization table for the bond premium, through the first two interest payments. Use Exhibit 10A-4 as a guide, and round amounts to the nearest dollar.
3. Journalize the issuance of the bonds on May 31, 2010, and, on November 30, 2010, payment of the first semiannual interest amount and amortization of the bond premium. Explanations are not required.

P10A-14B Calculating and recording bonds when stated rate and market rate are different [20–25 min]

Tranquility is authorized to issue 5%, 10-year bonds payable. On January 2, 2011, when the market interest rate is 6%, the company issues $300,000 of the bonds and receives cash of $277,785. Tranquility amortizes bond discount by the effective-interest method. Interest dates are January 2 and July 2.

Requirements

1. Prepare an amortization table for the first two semiannual interest periods. Follow the format of Exhibit 10A-3.
2. Journalize the issuance of the bonds payable and the first semiannual interest payment on July 2.

P10A-15B Calculating and recording bonds when stated rate and market rate are different [15–20 min]

On January 1, 2011, Federag issued $200,000 of 14.375%, five-year bonds payable when the market interest rate was 16%. Federag pays interest annually at year-end. The issue price of the bonds was $189,328.

Requirement

1. Create a spreadsheet model to measure interest and bond discount amortization based on the following table:

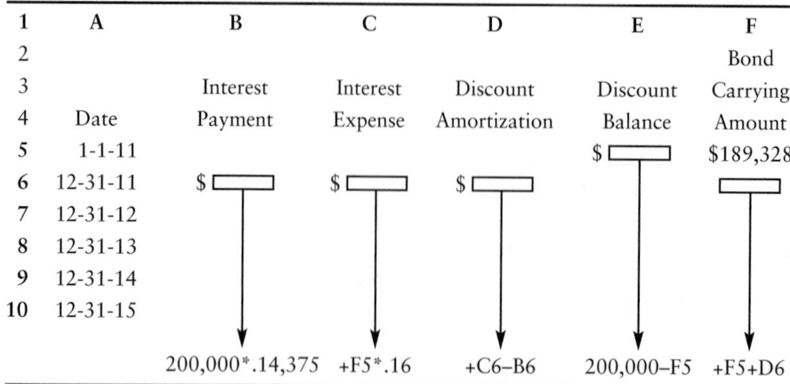

1	A	B	C	D	E	F
2						Bond
3		Interest	Interest	Discount	Discount	Carrying
4	Date	Payment	Expense	Amortization	Balance	Amount
5	1-1-11				$	$189,328
6	12-31-11	$	$	$		
7	12-31-12					
8	12-31-13					
9	12-31-14					
10	12-31-15					
		200,000*.14,375	+F5*.16	+C6–B6	200,000–F5	+F5+D6

P10A-16B Calculating and recording bonds when stated rate and market rate are different [30–40 min]

On December 31, 2010, when the market interest rate is 10%, Kennedy Realty Co. issues $600,000 of 7.25%, 10-year bonds payable. The bonds pay interest semiannually.

Requirements

1. Determine the present value of the bonds at issuance.
2. Assume that the bonds are issued at the price computed in requirement 1. Prepare an effective-interest method amortization table for the first two semi-annual interest installments.
3. Using the amortization table prepared in requirement 2, journalize issuance of the bonds and the first two interest payments.

Retiring and Converting Bonds Payable

Retirement of Bonds Payable

Normally, companies wait until maturity to pay off, or *retire*, their bonds payable. The basic retirement entry debits Bonds payable and credits Cash, as we saw earlier. But companies sometimes retire their bonds prior to maturity. The main reason for retiring bonds early is to relieve the pressure of paying the interest payments.

Some bonds are **callable**, which means the company may *call*, or pay off, the bonds at a specified price. The call price is usually 100 or a few percentage points above par value, perhaps 101 or 102 to provide an incentive to the bond holder. Callable bonds give the issuer the flexibility to pay off the bonds whenever it is beneficial. An alternative to calling the bonds is to purchase them in the open market at their current market price. Whether the bonds are called or purchased in the open market, the journal entry is the same.

Suppose on June 30, 2010, Smart Touch Learning has $100,000 of bonds payable outstanding with a remaining discount balance of $1,666 (the original discount of $1,851 ($100,000-$98,149) less the amortization of $185).

Lower interest rates have convinced management to pay off these bonds now. These bonds are callable at 100. If the market price of the bonds is 95, should Smart Touch call the bonds at 100 or purchase them in the open market at 95? The market price is lower than the call price, so Smart Touch should buy the bonds on the open market at their market price. Retiring the bonds on June 30, 2010, at 95 results in a gain of $3,334, computed as follows:

Maturity value of bonds being retired	$100,000
Less: Discount	(1,666)
Carrying amount of bonds payable	98,334
Market price ($100,000 × 0.95) paid to retire the bonds	95,000
Gain on retirement of bonds payable	$ 3,334

The following entry records retirement of the bonds, immediately after an interest date:

Date	Accounts	Debit	Credit
2010			
Jun 30	Bonds payable (L–)	100,000	
	Discount on bonds payable (CL–)		1,666
	Cash ($100,000 × 0.95) (A–)		95,000
	Gain on retirement of bonds payable (R+)		3,334
	Retired bonds payable.		

After posting, the bond accounts have zero balances.

Bonds payable

Debit	Credit
Retirement 100,000	Prior balance 100,000
	0

Discount on bonds payable

Debit	Credit
Jan 1 1,851	Jun 30 Amort. 185
	Retirement 1,666
0	

The journal entry removes the bonds from the books and records a gain on retirement. Any existing premium would be removed with a debit. If Smart Touch retired only half of these bonds, it would remove only half the discount or premium.

When retiring bonds before maturity, follow these steps:

1. Record partial-period amortization of discount or premium if the retirement date does not fall on an interest payment date.
2. Write off the portion of Discount or Premium that relates to the bonds being retired.
3. Credit a gain or debit a loss on retirement.

Convertible Bonds Payable

Convertible bonds are popular both with investors and with companies needing to borrow money. **Convertible bonds** may be converted into common stock at the option of the investor. Although we cover stock issuance in detail in Chapter 11, we have presented this topic in Chapter 10 with the other bond topics. These bonds combine the benefits of interest and principal on the bonds with the opportunity for a gain on the stock. The conversion feature is so attractive that investors accept a lower interest rate than on non-convertible bonds. For example, **Amazon.com**'s convertible bonds payable carry an interest rate of only 4 3/4%. The low interest benefits **Amazon.com**.

The issuance of convertible bonds payable is recorded like any other debt: Debit Cash and credit Convertible bonds payable. Then, if the market price of **Amazon**'s stock rises above the value of the bonds, the bondholders will convert the bonds into stock. The corporation then debits the bond accounts and credits the stock. The carrying amount of the bonds becomes the book value of the newly issued stock. The transaction is treated similar to a like-kind exchange, therefore, there is no gain or loss.

Assume that, instead of retiring the bonds, Smart Touch Learning's bondholders convert $100,000 of bonds payable into 20,000 shares (assumed number of shares) of Smart Touch Learning's $.50 par common stock. The carrying amount of the bonds on June 30, 2010, is $98,334. Therefore, there is a bond discount of $1,666. To record the conversion, Smart Touch would make the following journal entry:

2010			
Jun 30	Bonds payable (L–)	100,000	
	Discount on bonds payable (CL–)		1,666
	Common stock (20,000 × $0.50) (Q+)		10,000
	Paid-in capital in excess of par (100,000 – 1,666 – 10,000) (Q+)		88,334
	Recorded conversion of bonds payable.		

The entry zeroes out the Bonds payable account and its related Discount exactly as in the bond retirement example. This journal entry transfers the carrying amount of the bonds ($98,334) to stockholders' equity, as follows:

Common stock		Paid-in capital in excess of par	
	10,000		88,334

Total new stockholders' equity = $98,334

Stop & Think...

Why would anyone want to buy a convertible bond? Why not just buy the stock? Most often people buy convertible bonds from start-up companies. These companies have a need to raise capital, but they do not have a track record of good credit. The convertible feature allows the start-up company to pay smaller interest payments than they would without the conversion attribute.

Appendix 10B Assignments

■ Short Exercises

S10B-1 Retiring bonds payable [10 min]
On January 1, 2011, Petullo, Inc., issued $300,000 of 8%, five-year bonds payable at 105. Petullo has extra cash and wishes to retire the bonds payable on January 1, 2012, immediately after making the second semiannual interest payment. To retire the bonds, Petullo pays the market price of 95.

Requirements

1. What is Petullo's carrying amount of the bonds payable on the retirement date?
2. How much cash must Petullo pay to retire the bonds payable?
3. Compute Petullo's gain or loss on the retirement of the bonds payable.

S10B-2 Converting bonds payable [5–10 min]
Manchester, Corp., has $1,900,000 of convertible bonds payable outstanding, with a bond premium of $38,000 also on the books. The bondholders have notified Manchester that they wish to convert the bonds into stock. Specifically, the bonds may be converted into 400,000 shares of Manchester's $1 par common stock.

Requirements

1. What is Manchester's carrying amount of its convertible bonds payable prior to the conversion?
2. Journalize Manchester's conversion of the bonds payable into common stock. No explanation is required.

■ Exercises

E10B-3 Retiring bonds payable [15–20 min]
Quantum Transportation issued $600,000 of 8% bonds payable at 94 on October 1, 2010. These bonds are callable at 100 and mature on October 1, 2018. Quantum pays interest each April 1 and October 1. On October 1, 2015, when the bonds' market price is 99, Quantum retires the bonds in the most economical way available.

Requirement

1. Record the payment of the interest and amortization of bond discount at October 1, 2015, and the retirement of the bonds on that date. Quantum uses the straight-line amortization method.

E10B-4 Converting bonds payable [15–20 min]
Westview Magazine, Inc., issued $600,000 of 15-year, 9% convertible bonds payable on July 31, 2010, at a price of 95. Each $1,000 maturity amount of the bonds is convertible into 50 shares of $2 par stock. On July 31, 2013, bondholders converted the bonds into common stock.

Requirements

1. What would cause the bondholders to convert their bonds into common stock?

2. Without making journal entries, compute the carrying amount of the bonds payable at July 31, 2013. The company uses the straight-line method to amortize bond discount.
3. Assume all amortization has been recorded properly. Journalize the conversion transaction at July 31, 2013. No explanation is required.

E10B-5 Retiring and converting bonds payable [10–15 min]

Superpower Industries reported the following at September 30:

Long–term liabilities:		
Convertible bonds payable	$ 270,000	
Less: Discount on bonds payable . .	(16,200)	$ 253,800

Requirements

1. Journalize retirement of half of the bonds on October 1 at the call price of 104.
2. Journalize conversion of the remainder of the bonds into 19,000 shares of Superpower Industries $1 par common stock on October 1. What would cause the bondholders to convert their bonds into stock?

Comprehensive Problem for Chapters 7–10

Comparing Two Businesses

Suppose you created a software package, sold the business, and now are ready to invest in a resort property. Several locations look promising: Monterrey, California; Durango, Colorado; and Mackinac Island, Michigan. Each place has its appeal, but Durango wins out. Two small resorts are available in Durango. The property owners provide the following data:

GOLD RUSH RESORTS & MOUNTAIN HIDEAWAY Balance Sheets December 31, 2010		
	Gold Rush Resorts	Mountain Hideaway
Cash	$ 31,000	$ 63,000
Accounts receivable	20,000	18,000
Inventory	64,000	70,000
Land	270,000	669,000
Buildings	1,200,000	1,500,000
Accumulated depreciation—buildings	(20,000)	(100,000)
Furniture	750,000	900,000
Accumulated depreciation—furniture	(75,000)	(180,000)
Total assets	$2,240,000	$2,940,000
Total liabilities	$1,300,000	$1,000,000
Owner's equity	940,000	1,940,000
Total liabilities and owner's equity	$2,240,000	$2,940,000

Income statements for the last year report net income of $500,000 for Gold Rush Resorts and $400,000 for Mountain Hideaway.

Inventories Gold Rush Resorts uses the FIFO inventory method, and Mountain Hideaway uses LIFO. If Gold Rush had used LIFO, its ending inventory would have been $7,000 lower.

Plant Assets Gold Rush Resorts uses the straight-line depreciation method and an estimated useful life of 40 years for buildings and 10 years for furniture. Estimated residual values are $400,000 for buildings and $0 for furniture. Gold Rush's buildings are one-year old. Annual depreciation expense for the buildings is $20,000 and $75,000 per year on the furniture.

Mountain Hideaway uses the double-declining-balance method and depreciates buildings over 30 years. The furniture, also one-year old, is being depreciated over 10 years. First year depreciation expense for the buildings is $100,000 and $180,000 for the furniture.

Accounts Receivable Gold Rush Resorts uses the direct write-off method for uncollectible receivables. Mountain Hideaway uses the allowance method. The Gold Rush owner estimates that $2,000 of the company's receivables are doubtful. Mountain Hideaway receivables are already reported at net realizable value.

Requirements

1. To compare the two resorts, convert Gold Rush Resorts' net income to the accounting methods and the estimated useful lives used by Mountain Hideaway.
2. Compare the two resorts' net incomes after you have revised Gold Rush's figures. Which resort looked better at the outset? Which looks better when they are placed on equal footing?

11 Corporations: Paid-In Capital and the Balance Sheet

Learning Objectives/ Success Keys

1. Identify the distinguishing characteristics of a corporation
2. Describe the two sources of stockholders' equity and the classes of stock
3. Journalize the issuance of stock and prepare the stockholders' equity section of a corporation balance sheet
4. Illustrate Retained earnings transactions
5. Account for cash dividends
6. Use different stock values in decision making
7. Evaluate return on assets and return on stockholders' equity
8. Account for the income tax of a corporation

It is 6 AM and the Smart Touch Learning team has pulled an all-nighter putting together a big order. In her sleep deprived state, Sheena Bright, President of Smart Touch, decides that the company needs to raise capital for expansion. How will the company do it? The same way other large companies like **Google**, or **IHOP** do—issue stock.

We reviewed corporation basics in Chapter 1. Now, let us review corporations with Smart Touch Learning as the focus company.

Corporations: An Overview

1 Identify the distinguishing characteristics of a corporation

Corporations dominate business activity in the United States. Proprietorships and partnerships are more numerous, but corporations do much more business and are larger. Most well-known companies, such as **Intel** and **NIKE**, are corporations. Their full names include *Corporation* or *Incorporated* (abbreviated *Corp.* and *Inc.*) to show that they are corporations—for example, **Intel Corporation** and **NIKE, Inc.** What makes the corporate form of organization so attractive? Several things. There are several features that distinguish a corporation from other types of business organizations. They are described in detail in the following sections.

Separate Legal Entity

A corporation is a business entity formed under state law. The state grants a **charter,** which is the document that gives the state's permission to form a corporation. This is called **authorization** because the state "authorizes" or approves the establishment of the corporate entity. A corporation is a distinct entity from a legal perspective. It is an entity that exists apart from its owners, the stockholders, or shareholders. The corporation has many of the rights that a person has. For example, a corporation may buy, own, and sell property; enter into contracts; sue, and be sued. Assets and liabilities in the business belong to the corporation and not to the individual stockholders. The ownership interest of a corporation is divided into shares of stock. A person becomes a stockholder by purchasing the stock of the corporation. The corporate charter specifies how much stock the corporation is authorized to issue (sell) to the public.

Continuous Life and Transferability of Ownership

Corporations have continuous lives regardless of changes in the ownership of their stock. Stockholders may transfer stock as they wish by selling or trading the stock to another person, giving the stock away, bequeathing it in a will, or disposing of the stock in any other way. The transfer of the stock has no effect on the continuity of the corporation. Proprietorships and partnerships, on the other hand, terminate when their ownership changes for any reason.

No Mutual Agency

Mutual agency of the owners is not present in a corporation as it is in a partnership. This means that the stockholder of a corporation cannot commit the corporation to a contract unless that stockholder is acting as an officer in the business.

Limited Liability of Stockholders

A stockholder has limited liability for the corporation's debts. Unlike proprietors and partners, a stockholder has no personal obligation for corporation liabilities. The most that a stockholder can lose is the amount he or she originally paid for the stock. On the other hand, proprietors and partners are personally liable for the debts of their businesses.

The combination of limited liability and no mutual agency means that persons can invest unlimited amounts in a corporation without fear of losing all their personal wealth because of a business failure. This feature enables a corporation to raise more money than proprietorships and partnerships.

Separation of Ownership and Management

Stockholders own the business, but a board of directors—elected by the stockholders—appoints corporate officers to manage the business. Thus, stockholders do not have to manage the business or disrupt their personal affairs.

This separation between stockholders (owners of the corporation) and management may create problems. Corporate officers may decide to run the business for their own benefit rather than to benefit the company. Stockholders may find it difficult to lodge an effective protest against management because of the distance between them and the top managers.

Corporate Taxation

Corporations are separate taxable entities. They pay a variety of taxes not borne by proprietorships or partnerships. Depending on the state in which the organization incorporated and the state or states in which the corporation operates, the taxes could include some or all of the following:

- Annual franchise tax levied by the state. The franchise tax is paid to keep the corporation charter in force and enables the corporation to continue in business.
- Federal and state income taxes. Corporate earnings are subject to double taxation. First, corporations pay their own income tax on corporate income. Then, the stockholders pay personal income tax on the cash dividends that they receive from corporations. This is different from proprietorships and partnerships, which pay no business income tax. Instead, the tax falls solely on the individual owners.

Government Regulation

Government regulation is a disadvantage for corporations and it can be expensive for a business. Because stockholders have only limited liability for corporation debts, outsiders doing business with the corporation can look no further than the corporation itself for any claims that may arise against the business. To protect persons who loan money to a corporation or who invest in its stock, states monitor the affairs of corporations. Exhibit 11-1 summarizes the advantages and disadvantages of a corporation.

EXHIBIT 11-1 Advantages and Disadvantages of a Corporation

Advantages	Disadvantages
1. Corporations can raise more money than a proprietorship or partnership.	1. Ownership and management are separated.
2. A corporation has a continuous life.	2. Double taxation.
3. The transfer of corporate ownership is easy.	3. Government regulation is expensive.
4. There is no mutual agency among the stockholders.	
5. Stockholders have limited liability.	

Organization of a Corporation

Creation of a corporation begins when its organizers, called the incorporators, obtain a charter from the state. The charter includes the authorization for the corporation to issue a certain number of shares of stock, which represent the ownership in the corporation. The incorporators pay fees, sign the charter, and file the required documents with the state. Once the first share of stock is issued, the corporation comes into existence. The incorporators agree to a set of bylaws, which act as the constitution for governing the corporation. The ultimate control of the corporation rests with the stockholders, who normally receive one vote for each share of stock they own. The stockholders elect the members of the board of directors, which sets policy for the corporation and appoints the officers. The board elects a chairperson, who usually is the most powerful person in the corporation. The board also designates the president who, as chief operating officer, manages day-to-day operations. Most corporations also have vice-presidents in charge of sales, operations, accounting and finance, and other key areas.

Capital Stock

The state authorizes in the bylaws of a corporation how many shares of a stock class the corporation may issue. This is called **authorization of stock.** A corporation issues **stock certificates** to the stockholders when they buy the stock. The stock certificate represents the individual's ownership of the corporation's capital, so it is called **capital stock.** The basic unit of stock is a **share.** A corporation may issue a stock certificate for any number of shares. Exhibit 11-2 shows a stock certificate for 288 shares of Smart Touch Learning common stock owned by Courtney Edwards. The certificate shows the following:

- Company name
- Stockholder name
- Number of shares owned by the stockholder

Stock that is held by the stockholders is said to be **outstanding stock.** The outstanding stock of a corporation represents 100% of its ownership.

EXHIBIT 11-2 | Stock Certificate

Stockholders' Equity Basics

2 Describe the two sources of stockholders' equity and the classes of stock

A corporation's owners' equity is called stockholders' equity. State laws require corporations to report their sources of capital because some of the capital must be maintained by the company. The two basic sources of corporate equity are as follows:

- **Paid-in capital** (also called **contributed capital**) represents amounts received from the stockholders. **Common stock** is the main source of paid-in capital. This is *externally* generated capital and results from transactions with outsiders.

- **Retained earnings** is capital earned by profitable operations. This is *internally* generated capital and results from internal corporate decisions and earnings.

Exhibit 11-3 outlines a summarized version of the stockholders' equity of Smart Touch Learning, before the first share of stock is issued:

EXHIBIT 11-3 | **Stockholders' Equity of Smart Touch Learning**

Stockholders' Equity	
Paid-in capital:	
Common stock	$0
Retained earnings	0
Total stockholders' equity	$0

Stop & Think...

Consider your checking account as a sort of "capital" for yourself. You have cash, or "capital," paid in from outside sources, like financial aid or family contributions. You also have capital that you have saved for use while in school. The financial aid and family contributions are like paid-in capital to a corporation as they are outside sources of funds. The money you have saved is like retained earnings because you have retained it for your use while in school.

Stockholders' Rights

A stockholder has four basic rights, unless a right is withheld by contract:

1. **Vote.** Stockholders participate in management by voting on corporate matters. This is the only way in which a stockholder can help to manage the corporation. Normally, each share of common stock carries one vote.
2. **Dividends.** Dividends are distributions to stockholders of assets (usually cash). Stockholders receive a proportionate part of any dividend. Each share of stock receives an equal dividend so, for example, a shareholder who owns 1% of the total shares in the company receives 1% of any dividend.
3. **Liquidation.** Stockholders receive their proportionate share of any assets remaining after the corporation pays its debts and liquidates (goes out of business).
4. **Preemption.** Stockholders can maintain their proportionate ownership in the corporation. Suppose you own 5% of a corporation's stock. If the corporation issues 100,000 new shares of stock, it must offer you the opportunity to buy 5% (5,000) of the new shares. This right, however, is usually withheld by contract for most corporations.

Classes of Stock

Corporations can issue different classes of stock. The stock of a corporation may be either

- common or preferred.
- par or no-par.

Common Stock and Preferred Stock

Every corporation issues **common stock**, which represents the basic ownership of the corporation. The real "owners" of the corporation are the common stockholders. Some companies issue Class A common stock, which carries the right to vote. They may also issue Class B common stock, which may be non-voting. There must be at least one voting "class" of stock. However, there is no limit as to the number or types of classes of stock that a corporation may issue. Each class of stock has a separate account in the company's ledger.

Preferred stock gives its owners certain advantages over common. Most notably, preferred stockholders receive dividends before the common stockholders. They also receive assets before common stockholders if the corporation liquidates. Corporations pay a fixed dividend on preferred stock, which is printed on the face of the preferred stock certificate. Investors usually buy preferred stock to earn those fixed dividends. With these advantages, preferred stockholders take less investment risk than common stockholders.

Owners of preferred stock also have the four basic stockholder rights, unless a right is withheld. The right to vote, however, is usually withheld from preferred stock. Companies may issue different series of preferred stock (Series A and Series B, for example). Each series is recorded in a separate account. Preferred stock is rarer than you might think. A recent survey of 600 corporations revealed that only 16% had some preferred stock outstanding (Exhibit 11-4).

EXHIBIT 11-4 | **Preferred Stock**

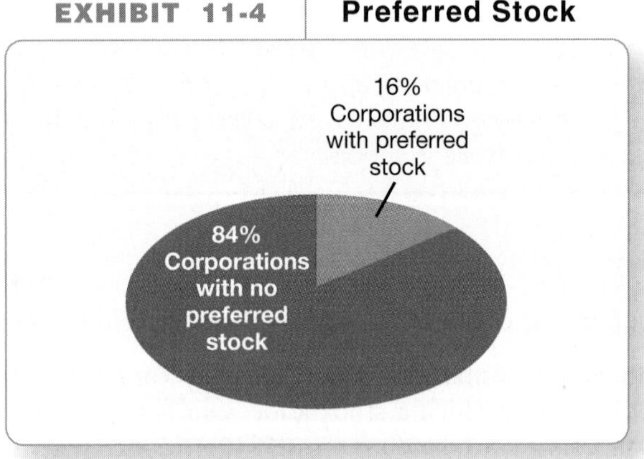

Par Value, Stated Value, and No-Par Stock

Stock may carry a par value or it may be no-par stock. **Par value** is an arbitrary amount assigned by a company to a share of its stock. Most companies set par value low to avoid legal difficulties from issuing their stock below par. Companies maintain a minimum amount of stockholders' equity for the protection of creditors, and this minimum represents the corporation's legal capital.

The par value of **IHOP**'s common stock is $0.01 (1 cent) per share. **Deere & Co.**, which makes John Deere tractors, and **Whirlpool**, the appliance company, have common stock with a par value of $1 per share. Par value of preferred stock can be higher—$25 or $100. Par value is arbitrary and is assigned when the organizers file the corporate charter with the state. There is no real "reason" for why par values vary. It is a choice made by the organizers of the corporation. Smart Touch Learning's common stock has $1 par value.

No-par stock does not have par value. **Pfizer**, the pharmaceutical company, has preferred stock with no par value. But some no-par stock has a **stated value**, an arbitrary amount similar to par-value. Usually the state the company incorporates in will determine whether a stock may be par or stated value stock. As far as accounting for it goes, par is treated the same as stated value. Let us review some stock issuance examples to further illustrate this idea.

Issuing Stock

3 Journalize the issuance of stock and prepare the stockholders' equity section of a corporation balance sheet

Corporations such as **Intel** and **Nike** need huge quantities of money. They cannot finance all their operations through borrowing, so they raise capital by issuing stock. A company can sell its stock directly to stockholders or it can use the services of an **underwriter**, such as the brokerage firms **Merrill Lynch** and **Morgan Stanley**. An underwriter usually agrees to buy all the stock it cannot sell to its clients.

The price that the corporation receives from issuing stock is called the **issue price.** Usually, the issue price exceeds par value because par value is normally set quite low. In the following sections, we use Smart Touch Learning to show how to account for the issuance of stock.

Issuing Common Stock

The *Wall Street Journal* is the most popular medium for advertising stock. The ads are called *tombstones*. Exhibit 11-5 demonstrates what Smart Touch Learning's tombstone would look like.

EXHIBIT 11-5 Announcement of Public Offering of Smart Touch Learning Stock

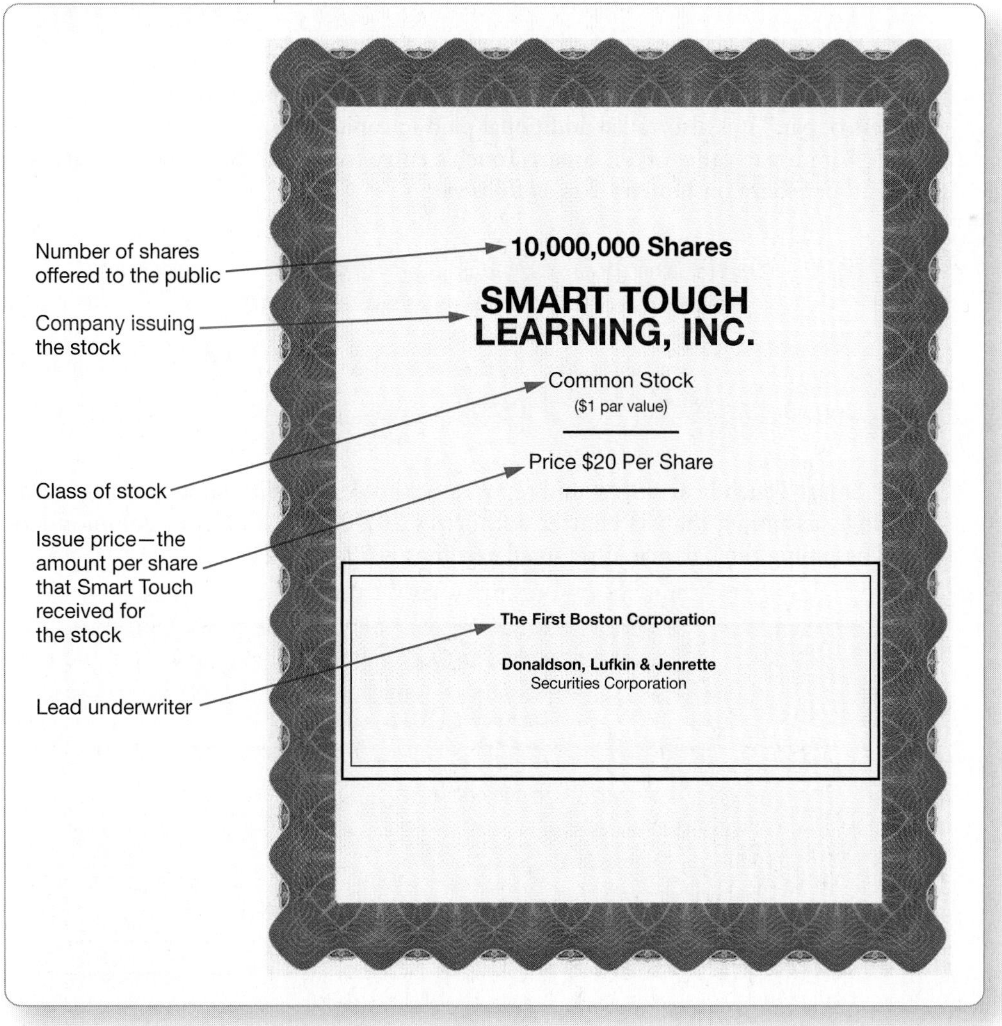

Smart Touch's tombstone shows that the company hoped to raise approximately \$200 million of capital (10,000,000 shares × \$20 per share).

Issuing Common Stock at Par

Suppose Smart Touch's common stock carried a par value of \$1 per share. The stock issuance entry of one million shares at par value on January 1 would be as follows:

Date	Accounts and Explanation	Debit	Credit
Jan 1	Cash (1,000,000 × \$1) (A+)	1,000,000	
	Common stock (Q+)		1,000,000
	Issued common stock at par.		

Issuing Common Stock at a Premium

As stated above, most corporations set par value low and issue common stock for a price above par. The amount above par is called a **premium.** Assume Smart Touch's stock sells an additional one million shares for \$20 a share on January 2. The \$19 difference between the issue price (\$20) and par value (\$1) is a premium.

A premium on the sale of stock is not a gain, income, or profit for the corporation because the company is dealing with its own stock. This situation illustrates one of the fundamentals of accounting:

A company can have no profit or loss when buying or selling its own stocks.

So, the premium is another type of paid-in capital account called "Paid-in capital in excess of par." It is also called **additional paid-in capital.**

With a par value of \$1, Smart Touch's entry to record the issuance of its stock at \$20 per share on January 2 is as follows:

Date	Accounts and Explanation	Debit	Credit
Jan 2	Cash (1,000,000 shares × \$20 issue price) (A+)	20,000,000	
	Common stock (1,000,000 shares × \$1 par value) (Q+)		1,000,000
	Paid-in capital in excess of par— common [1,000,000 shares × (\$20 – \$1)] (Q+)		19,000,000
	Issued common stock at a premium.		

Smart Touch Learning would report stockholders' equity on its balance sheet as follows, assuming that its charter authorizes 20,000,000 shares of common stock and assuming the balance of retained earnings is \$9,000,000.

SMART TOUCH LEARNING, INC. **Stockholders' Equity** January 2, 2011	
Paid-in capital:	
Common stock; \$1 par; 20,000,000 shares authorized; 2,000,000 shares issued	\$ 2,000,000
Paid-in capital in excess of par	19,000,000
Total paid-in capital	21,000,000
Retained earnings	9,000,000
Total stockholders' equity	\$30,000,000

The balance of the Common stock account is calculated as follows:

Common stock balance	=	Number of shares issued	×	Par value per share
$2,000,000	=	2,000,000	×	$1

Paid-in capital in excess of par is the total amount received from issuing the common stock minus its par value. For Smart Touch, we find this amount in the January 2 sale, as follows:

Paid-in capital in excess of par—common	
	$19,000,000

Altogether, total paid-in capital is the sum of the following:

Total paid-in capital	=	Common stock	+	Paid-in capital in excess of par
$21,000,000	=	$2,000,000	+	$19,000,000

Issuing No-Par Stock

When a company issues no-par stock, it debits the asset received and credits the stock account. For no-par stock there can be no paid-in capital in excess of par, because there is no par to be in excess of.

Assume that, instead of $1 par value, Smart Touch Learning's common stock were no-par. How would that change the recording of the issuance of 1,000,000 shares for $1 on January 1 and 1,000,000 shares for $20 on January 2? The stock-issuance entries would be as follows:

Jan 1	Cash (1,000,000 × $1) (A+)	1,000,000	
	Common stock (Q+)		1,000,000
Jan 2	Cash (1,000,000 × $20) (A+)	20,000,000	
	Common stock (Q+)		20,000,000
	Issued no-par common stock.		

Regardless of the stock's price, Cash is debited and Common stock is credited for the cash received. So, although the total equity of $21,000,000 remains the same, the Common stock account differs between par ($2,000,000) and no-par ($21,000,000) stock.

Let us consider how the stockholders' equity section of the balance sheet would change:

SMART TOUCH LEARNING, INC. Stockholders' Equity January 2, 2011	
Paid-in capital:	
Common stock; no par; 20,000,000 shares authorized,	
2,000,000 shares issued	$21,000,000
Retained earnings	9,000,000
Total stockholders' equity	$30,000,000

Issuing No-Par Stock with a Stated Value

Accounting for no-par stock with a stated value is almost identical to accounting for par-value stock. The only difference is that no-par stock with a stated value uses an account titled Paid-in capital in excess of *stated* value to record amounts received above the stated value.

Issuing Stock for Assets Other Than Cash

A corporation may issue stock for assets other than cash. It records the assets received at their current market value and credits the stock accounts accordingly. The assets' prior book value is irrelevant. Now let us reconsider the January 2 entry for Smart Touch. Assume that, instead of cash, Smart Touch received a building worth $20,000,000 in exchange for the 1,000,000 shares of its $1 par common stock on January 2. How would the entry change?

Jan 2	Building (A+)	20,000,000	
	Common stock (1,000,000 × $1) (Q+)		1,000,000
	Paid-in capital in excess of par—		
	common (20,000,000 – 1,000,000) (E+)		19,000,000
	Issued common stock in exchange for a building.		

As you can see, the only change is in the asset received, the building.

Issuing Preferred Stock

Accounting for preferred stock follows the pattern illustrated for issuing common stock. Let us assume that Smart Touch decides to issue 1,000 shares of its $50 par, 6% preferred stock on January 3 at par value. The issuance entry would be as follows:

Jan 3	Cash (A+)	50,000	
	Preferred stock (1,000 shares × $50 par) (Q+)		50,000
	Issued preferred stock.		

Most preferred stock is issued at par value. Therefore, Paid-in capital in excess of par is rare for preferred stock. Assume, however, that Smart Touch issues another 1,000 shares of preferred stock on January 4 for $55. The issuance entry would be as follows:

Jan 4	Cash (1,000 shares × $55 issue price) (A+)	55,000	
	Preferred stock (1,000 shares × $50 par) (Q+)		50,000
	Paid-in capital in excess of par—		
	preferred (55,000 – 50,000) (E+)		5,000

Ethical Considerations

Issuance of stock for *cash* poses no ethical challenge because the value of the asset received is clearly understood. Issuing stock for assets other than cash can pose a challenge. The company issuing the stock wants to look successful—record a large amount for the asset received and the stock issued. Why? Because large asset and equity amounts make the business look prosperous. The desire to look good can motivate a company to record an unjustifiably high amount for the assets.

A company is supposed to record an asset received at its current market value. But one person's evaluation of a building can differ from another's. One person may appraise the building at a market value of $4 million. Another may honestly believe the building is worth only $3 million. A company receiving the building in exchange for its stock must decide whether to record the building at $3 million, $4 million, or some other amount.

The ethical course of action is to record the asset at its current market value, as determined by independent appraisers. Corporations are rarely found guilty of *understating* their assets, but companies have been sued for *overstating* their assets.

Review of Accounting for Paid-In Capital

Let us review the first half of this chapter by showing the stockholders' equity section of Smart Touch Learning's balance sheet in Exhibit 11-6, assuming both stocks were par value.

EXHIBIT 11-6 **Part of Smart Touch Learning's Balance Sheet**

SMART TOUCH LEARNING, INC. Stockholders' Equity January 4, 2011	
Paid-in capital:	
Preferred stock, 6%, $50 par; 2,000 shares authorized, 2,000 shares issued	$ 100,000
Paid-in capital in excess of par—preferred	5,000
Common stock, $1 par, 10,000,000 shares authorize, 2,000,000 shares issued	2,000,000
Paid-in capital in excess of par—common	19,000,000
Total paid-in capital	21,105,000
Retained earnings	9,000,000
Total stockholders' equity	$30,105,000

Observe the order of the equity accounts:

- Preferred stock
- Paid-in capital in excess of par (belongs to the preferred stockholders)
- Common stock at par value
- Paid-in capital in excess of par (belongs to the common stockholders)
- Retained earnings (after the paid-in capital accounts)

The Decision Guidelines will solidify your understanding of stockholders' equity.

Decision Guidelines

THE STOCKHOLDERS' EQUITY OF A CORPORATION

Suppose you are interested in investing in stock. The following guidelines are relevant to your decision.

Decision	Guidelines
• What are the two main segments of stockholders' equity?	• Paid-in capital • Retained earnings
• Which is more permanent, paid-in capital or retained earnings?	Paid-in capital is more permanent because corporations can use retained earnings for dividends, which decreases the size of the company's equity.

• How are paid-in capital and retained earnings
  • Similar?
  • Different?
	• Both represent stockholders' equity (ownership) of the corporation.
	• Paid-in capital and retained earnings come from different sources:
	a. *Paid-in capital* comes from the stockholders (outside the company).
	b. *Retained earnings* comes from profitable operations (inside the company).

• What are the main categories of paid-in capital?	• Preferred stock, plus paid-in capital in excess of par, preferred • Common stock, plus paid-in capital in excess of par, common

Summary Problem 1

1. Is each of the following statements true or false?
   a. A stockholder may bind the corporation to a contract.
   b. The policy-making body in a corporation is called the board of directors.
   c. The owner of 100 shares of preferred stock has greater voting rights than the owner of 100 shares of common stock.
   d. Par-value stock is more valuable than no-par stock.
   e. Issuance of 1,000 shares of $5 par-value stock at $12 increases paid-in capital by $7,000.
   f. The issuance of no-par stock with a stated value is fundamentally different from issuing par-value stock.
   g. A corporation issues its preferred stock in exchange for land and a building with a combined market value of $200,000. This transaction increases the corporation's stockholders' equity by $200,000 regardless of the assets' prior book value.

2. Delphian Corporation has two classes of common stock. The company's balance sheet includes the following:

DELPHIAN CORPORATION Stockholders' Equity December 31, 2010	
Paid-in capital:	
Class A common stock, voting, $1 par value,	
authorized and issued 1,200,000 shares	$ 1,200,000
Additional paid-in capital—Class A common	2,000,000
Class B common stock, nonvoting, no par value,	
authorized and issued 11,000,000 shares	55,000,000
	58,200,000
Retained earnings	800,000,000
Total stockholders' equity	$858,200,000

Requirements

a. Journalize the issuance of the Class A common stock.
b. Journalize the issuance of the Class B common stock.
c. What is the total paid-in capital of the company?
d. What was the average issue price of each share of Class B common stock?

Solution

1. Answers to true/false statements:

   a. False
   b. True
   c. False
   d. False
   e. False
   f. False
   g. True

2.

a.		Cash (A+)	3,200,000	
		Common stock—Class A (Q+)		1,200,000
		Additional paid-in capital (Q+)		2,000,000
		To record issuance of Class A common stock.		
b.		Cash (A+)	55,000,000	
		Common stock—Class B (Q+)		55,000,000
		To record issuance of Class B common stock.		
c.		Total paid-in capital is $58,200,000 ($1,200,000 + $2,000,000 + $55,000,000).		
d.		Average issue price = $5 ($55,000,000/11,000,000 shares)		

Retained Earnings

4 Illustrate Retained earnings transactions

Recall that corporations close their revenues and expenses into Income summary. Then, they close net income to Retained earnings. Let us assume Smart Touch Learning's revenues were $500,000 and expenses totaled $400,000 for December. The closing entries would be as follows:

①	Dec 31	Sales revenue (R–)	500,000	
		Income summary		500,000
		To close sales revenue.		
②	31	Income summary	400,000	
		Expenses (detailed) (E–)		400,000
		To close expenses.		

Now, the Income summary holds revenues, expenses, and net income.

Income summary

② Expenses	400,000	① Revenues	500,000
		Balance (net income)	100,000

Finally, the Income summary's balance is closed to Retained earnings.

③	Dec 31	Income summary	100,000	
		Retained earnings (Q+)		100,000
		To close net income to Retained earnings.		

This closing entry completes the closing process. The Income summary is zeroed out, and Retained earnings now holds net income, as follows:

Income summary

② Expenses	400,000	① Revenues	500,000
③ Closing	100,000		
			0

Retained earnings

		③ Closing (net income)	100,000

If Smart Touch's expenses had been $560,000 instead of $400,000, the company would have had a $60,000 net *loss* instead, and Income summary would have a debit balance, as follows:

Income summary

Expenses	560,000	Revenues	500,000
Net loss	60,000		

To close this $60,000 loss, the final closing entry credits Income summary and debits Retained earnings as follows:

	Dec 31	Retained earnings (Q–)	60,000	
		Income summary		60,000
		To close net loss to Retained earnings.		

The accounts now have their final balances.

Income summary			
② Expenses	560,000	① Revenues	500,000
		③ Closing	60,000
			0

Retained earnings		
③ Closing (net loss)	60,000	

A Retained Earnings Deficit

A loss may cause a debit balance in Retained earnings. This condition—called a Retained earnings **deficit**—is reported as a negative amount in stockholders' equity. Reconsider the stockholders' equity presented for Smart Touch:

Smart Touch Learning's Balance Sheet—Retained Earnings Deficit Stockholders' Equity	
Paid-in capital:	
Preferred stock, 6%, $50 par, 2,000 shares authorized, 2,000 shares issued	$ 100,000
Paid-in capital in excess of par—preferred	5,000
Common stock, $1 par, 10,000,000 shares authorize, 2,000,000 shares issued	2,000,000
Paid-in capital in excess of par—common	19,000,000
Total paid-in capital	21,105,000
Retained earnings	(60,000)
Total stockholders' equity	$21,045,000

Now let us look at how to account for dividends.

Accounting for Cash Dividends

5 Account for cash dividends

A profitable corporation may distribute cash to the stockholders in the form of *dividends*. Dividends cause a decrease in both assets and equity (Retained earnings). Most states prohibit using paid-in capital for dividends. Accountants, therefore, use the term **legal capital** to refer to the portion of stockholders' equity that cannot be used for dividends. Corporations declare cash dividends from Retained earnings and then pay with cash.

Dividend Dates

A corporation declares a dividend before paying it. Three dividend dates are relevant:

1. **Declaration date.** On the declaration date—say, May 1—the board of directors announces the intention to pay the dividend. The declaration of a cash dividend creates an obligation (liability) for the corporation.
2. **Date of record.** Those stockholders holding the stock at the end of business on the date of record—a week or two after declaration, say, May 15—will receive the dividend check.

3. **Payment date.** Payment of the dividend usually follows the record date by a week or two—say, May 30. "The check's in the mail."

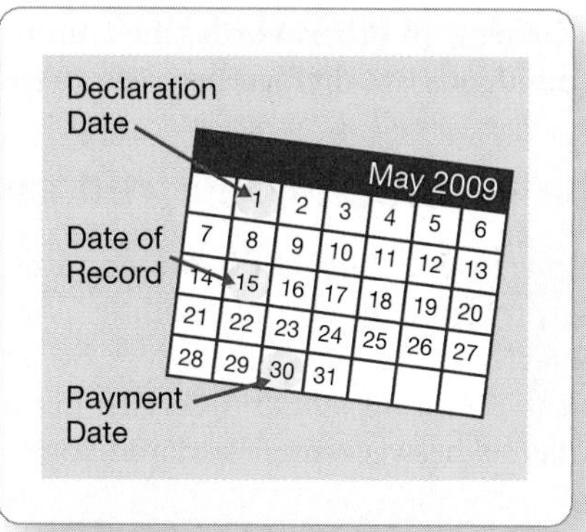

Declaring and Paying Dividends

The cash dividend rate on *preferred stock* is often expressed as a percentage of the preferred-stock par value, such as 6%. But sometimes cash dividends on preferred stock are expressed as a flat dollar amount per share, such as $2 per share. Therefore, preferred dividends are computed two ways, depending on how the preferred-stock cash-dividend rate is expressed. Let us look at the two ways to compute preferred dividends, using Smart Touch Learning's 2,000 outstanding shares of 6%, $50 par preferred stock. (Smart Touch's flat rate instead of 6% could be stated as $3 per share.)

1. Outstanding shares × par value × preferred dividend rate% = preferrred dividend

   2,000 shares × $50 par × 6% = $6,000

2. Outstanding shares × flat dividend rate = preferrred dividend

   2,000 shares × $3 per share = $6,000

Cash dividends on *common stock* are computed the second way, because those cash dividends are not expressed as a percentage.

To account for the declaration of a cash dividend we debit Retained earnings and credit Dividends payable on the date of declaration. For Smart Touch's preferred dividend, the entry is as follows: [1]

May 1	Retained earnings (Q–)	6,000	
	Dividends payable (L+)		6,000
	Declared a cash dividend.		

To pay the dividend on the payment date, debit Dividends payable and credit Cash.

May 30	Dividends payable (L–)	6,000	
	Cash (A–)		6,000
	Paid the cash dividend.		

[1]Some accountants debit a Dividends account, which is closed to Retained earnings. But most businesses debit Retained earnings directly, as shown here.

Dividends payable is a current liability. When a company has issued both preferred and common stock, the preferred stockholders get their dividends first. The common stockholders receive dividends only if the total dividend is large enough to satisfy the preferred requirement. In other words, the common stockholders get the leftovers. Let us see how dividends are divided between preferred and common.

Dividing Dividends Between Preferred and Common

Smart Touch has common stock, 2,000,000 outstanding, $1 par shares, plus 2,000 shares of $50, 6% preferred stock outstanding. We calculated earlier that Smart Touch's annual preferred dividend was $6,000. So, total declared dividends must exceed $6,000 for the common stockholders to get anything. Exhibit 11-7 shows the division of dividends between preferred and common for two situations.

EXHIBIT 11-7 | Dividing a Dividend Between Preferred Stock and Common Stock

Case A: Total dividend of $5,000:	
Preferred dividend (the full $5,000 goes to preferred because the annual preferred dividend is $6,000)	$ 5,000
Common dividend (none because the total dividend did not cover the preferred dividend for the year)	0
Total dividend	$ 5,000
Case B: Total dividend of $50,000:	
Preferred dividend (2,000 shares × $50 par × 6%)	$ 6,000
Common dividend ($50,000 – $6,000)	44,000
Total dividend	$50,000

If Smart Touch's dividend is large enough to cover the preferred dividend (Case B), the preferred stockholders get their regular dividend, and the common stockholders get the remainder ($44,000). But if the year's dividend falls below the annual preferred amount (Case A), the preferred stockholders will receive the entire dividend, and the common stockholders get nothing that year.

Dividends on Cumulative and Noncumulative Preferred

Preferred stock can be either

- cumulative or
- noncumulative.

Most preferred stock is cumulative. As a result, preferred is assumed to be cumulative unless it is specifically designated as noncumulative. Let us see how this plays out.

A corporation may fail to pay the preferred dividend if, for example, it does not have cash to fund the dividend. This is called *passing the dividend*, and the dividends are said to be in **arrears**. **Cumulative preferred stock** shareholders must receive all dividends in arrears before the common stockholders get any dividend.

The preferred stock of Smart Touch Learning is cumulative. How do we know this? Because it is not labeled as noncumulative.

Suppose Smart Touch passed the 2009 preferred dividend of $6,000. Before paying any common dividend in 2010, Smart Touch must first pay preferred dividends of $6,000 for 2009 and $6,000 for 2010, a total of $12,000. In 2010, Smart Touch declares a $50,000 dividend. How much of this dividend goes to preferred? How much goes to common? The allocation of this $50,000 dividend is as follows:

	Total dividend		$50,000
	Preferred gets		
	2009: 2,000 shares × $50 par × 6%	$6,000	
	2010: 2,000 shares × $50 par × 6%	6,000	
	Total to preferred		12,000
	Common gets the remainder		$38,000

Smart Touch's entry to record the declaration of this dividend on September 6, 2010 is as follows:

2010			
Sep 6	Retained earnings (Q–)	50,000	
	Dividends payable, preferred (L+)		12,000
	Dividends payable, common (L+)		38,000
	Declared a cash dividend.		

If the preferred stock is *noncumulative*, the corporation need not pay any dividends in arrears. Suppose Smart Touch's preferred stock was noncumulative and the company passed the 2009 dividend. The preferred stockholders would lose the 2009 dividend of $6,000 forever. Then, before paying any common dividends in 2010, Smart Touch would have to pay only the 2010 preferred dividend of $6,000, which would leave $44,000 for the common stockholders.

Dividends in arrears are *not* a liability. A liability for dividends arises only after the board of directors declares the dividend. But a corporation reports cumulative preferred dividends in arrears in notes to the financial statements. This shows the common stockholders how big the declared dividend will need to be for them to get any dividends.

Stop & Think...

Think about a big holiday dinner, such as Thanksgiving, when a lot of people are there and you usually have a lot of food. Do you have that one family member who always seems to be in the dinner line first? That person is like the preferred stockholders in a corporation—they always are the first class of stockholders in line to get whatever is being "served" by the corporation, whether it is dividends or liquidation. Common stockholders are like the leftovers the day after a holiday. Sometimes the leftovers are really good and there are a lot of them, and sometimes there is nothing left.

Different Values of Stock

There are several different stock values in addition to par value. Market value, book value, and liquidation value are all used for decision making.

6 Use different stock values in decision making

Market Value

Market value, or *market price*, is the price for which a person can buy or sell a share of stock. The corporation's net income and general economic conditions affect market value. The Internet and most newspapers report stock prices. Log on to any company's Web site to track its stock price, which usually changes daily. *In almost all cases, stockholders are more concerned about the market value of a stock than about any other value.*

Liquidation Value

Liquidation value is the amount that is guaranteed to the preferred shareholders in the event a company liquidates. If a liquidation value exists, it will be printed on the face of the preferred stock certificate. Note that this value only has meaning if the corporation liquidates.

Book Value

Book value per share of stock is the amount of stockholders' equity on the company's books for each share of its stock.

If the company has both preferred and common outstanding, owners of preferred stock have first claim to the equity—just like they have first claim to the dividends. Therefore, we subtract preferred equity from total equity to compute book value per share of common. The preferred equity is as follows:

Book value attributred to preferred stock + Any dividends that are in arrears

1. Book value attributed to preferred stock is either
   a. the number of outstanding preferred shares × liquidation value per share, OR
   b. the book value of preferred equity (Preferred stock), PLUS
2. any dividends that are in arrears.

The common stockholders, once again, get whatever is leftover in stockholders' equity. Exhibit 11-8 gives a form for calculating book value per share for each class of stock.

EXHIBIT 11-8 **Calculating Book Value per Share**

Book Value (BV) attributed to Preferred stock (P/S):	
1) Liquidation value × outstanding shares, OR 2) Preferred stock	A
Dividends in Arrears on outstanding preferred shares	B
Total BV attributed to P/S	A + B
Outstanding preferred shares	C
Book Value per share on Preferred stock	(A + B)/C
Book Value attributed to Common stock (C/S)	
Total Stockholders' equity	D
Less Book Value attributed to P/S (figured above)	(A + B)
Total BV attributed to C/S (leftovers)	D – (A + B)
Outstanding common shares	E
Book Value per share on Common stock	{D – (A + B)}/E

To illustrate, let us apply the calculation to Smart Touch Learning's Stockholders' Equity presented earlier in Exhibit 11-6, assuming that preferred dividends are in arrears for one year. The results are presented in Exhibit 11-9.

EXHIBIT 11-9 | **Calculating Book Value per Share for Smart Touch Learning**

Book Value (BV) attributed to Preferred stock (P/S):		
~~1) Liquidation value × outstanding shares, OR~~ 2) Preferred stock ($100,000)	$	100,000
Dividends in Arrears on outstanding preferred shares (2,000 shares × $50 par × 6% × 1 year) =	$	6,000
Total BV attributed to P/S ($100,000 + $6,000)	$	106,000
Outstanding preferred shares		2,000
Book Value per share on Preferred stock	$	53.00
Book Value attributed to Common stock (C/S)		
Total Stockholders' equity (from Exhibit 11-6)	$30,105,000	
Less Book Value attributed to P/S (figured above)	$	106,000
Total BV attributed to C/S (leftovers)	$29,999,000	
Outstanding common shares		2,000,000
Book Value per share on Common stock (result rounded to nearest penny)	$	15.00

Book value may figure into the price to pay for a closely-held company, whose stock is not publicly traded. In addition, a company may buy out a stockholder by paying the book value of the person's stock. Book value may also be considered in takeover bids for companies, especially if the book value is much greater than the market value per share.

Some investors compare the book value of a stock with its market value. The idea is that a stock selling below book value is a good buy. But the book value/market value relationship is far from clear. Other investors believe that a stock selling below book value means the company must be having problems.

Evaluating Operations

Investors are constantly comparing companies' profits. To compare companies, we need some standard profitability measures. Two important ratios to use for comparison are return on assets and return on common stockholders' equity.

7 Evaluate return on assets and return on stockholders' equity

Rate of Return on Total Assets

The **rate of return on total assets,** or simply **return on assets,** measures a company's success in using assets to earn income. Two groups invest money to finance a corporation:

- Stockholders
- Creditors

Net income and interest expense are the returns to these two groups. The stockholders earn the corporation's net income, and the creditors get its interest expense.

The sum of net income plus interest expense is the numerator of the return-on-assets ratio. The denominator is average total assets. Net income and interest expense are taken from the income statement. Average total assets comes from the beginning and ending balance sheets.

Let us assume Smart Touch has the following data for 2010:

Net income	\$33 million
Interest expense	\$22 million
Total assets, 12/31/2010	\$843 million
Total assets, 12/31/2009	\$822 million
Preferred dividends	\$6 million

Return on assets is computed as follows:

$$\text{Rate of Return on Total Assets} = \frac{\text{Net Income + Interest Expense}}{\text{Average Total Assets}}$$

$$= \frac{\$33 + \$22}{(\$843 + \$822)\,/\,2} = \frac{\$55}{\$832.5} = 0.066$$

What is a good rate of return on total assets? There is no single answer because rates of return vary widely by industry. In most industries, a 10% return on assets is considered good. Smart Touch's 6.6% return on assets would not be considered good if the industry average is 10%.

Rate of Return on Common Stockholders' Equity

Rate of return on common stockholders' equity, often shortened to **return on equity**, shows the relationship between net income available to the common stockholders and their average common equity. The numerator is net income minus preferred dividends. Preferred dividends are subtracted because the preferred stockholders have first claim to any dividends. The denominator is *average common stockholders' equity*—total equity minus preferred equity. Let us return to Smart Touch's data for 2010. Let us assume Smart Touch's Common Equity was \$280 million in 2009 and \$300 million in 2010. Smart Touch's rate of return on common stockholders' equity for 2010 is computed as follows (amounts in millions):

$$\text{Rate of Return on Common Stockholders' Equity} = \frac{\text{Net Income − Preferred Dividends}}{\text{Average Common Stockholders' Equity}}$$

$$= \frac{\$33 - \$6}{(\$280 + \$300)\,/\,2} = \frac{\$27}{\$290} = 0.093$$

Smart Touch's rates of return carry both bad news and good news.

- The bad news is that these rates of return are low. Most companies strive for return on equity of 15% or higher. Smart Touch's 9.3% is disappointing.
- The good news is that return on equity exceeds return on assets. That means Smart Touch is earning more for its stockholders than it is paying for interest expense, and that is a healthy sign.

If return on assets ever exceeds return on equity, the company is in trouble. Why? Because the company's interest expense is greater than its return on equity. In that case, no investor would buy the company's stock. Return on assets should always be significantly lower than return on equity.

Accounting for Income Taxes by Corporations

8 Account for the income tax of a corporation

Corporations pay income tax just as individuals do, but not at the same rates. At this writing, the federal tax rate on most corporate income is 35%. Most states also levy a corporate income tax, so most corporations pay a combined federal and state income tax rate of approximately 40%.

To account for income tax, a corporation measures two income tax amounts:

- Income tax expense
- Income tax payable

In general, income tax expense and income tax payable can be computed as follows: [2]

Income tax *expense*	=	Income before tax from the income statement	×	Income tax rate

Income tax *payable*	=	Taxable income from the tax return filed with the IRS	×	Income tax rate

The income statement and the income tax return are entirely separate documents. You have been studying the income statement throughout this course, but the tax return is new. It reports taxes to the Internal Revenue Service (IRS).

For most companies, income tax expense and income tax payable differ. The most important difference occurs when a corporation uses straight-line depreciation for the income statement and accelerated depreciation for the tax return (to save tax dollars).

Continuing with the Smart Touch illustration, Smart Touch's 2010 figures are as follows:

- Income before income tax of $33 million (This comes from the income statement, which is not presented here.)
- Taxable income of $20 million (This comes from the tax return, which is not presented here.)

Smart Touch will record income tax for 2010 as follows (dollar amounts in millions and assume an income tax rate of 40%):

2010			
Dec 31	Income tax expense ($33 mill × 0.40) (E+)	13,200,000	
	Income tax payable (20 mill × 0.40) (L+)		8,000,000
	Deferred tax liability (L+)		5,200,000
	Recorded income tax for the year.		

Smart Touch will pay the $8 million of Income tax payable to the IRS and the applicable states within a few months. The difference between Income tax expense and Income tax payable is the Deferred tax liability of $5,200,000. The Deferred tax liability account is long-term, so Smart Touch will pay this debt over a number of years.

[2] The authors thank Jean Marie Hudson for suggesting this presentation.

Decision Guidelines

DIVIDENDS, STOCK VALUES, EVALUATING OPERATIONS, AND CORPORATE INCOME TAX

Suppose you are considering buying some **IHOP** stock. You are naturally interested in how well the company is doing. Does **IHOP** pay dividends? What are **IHOP's** stock values? What are the rates of return on **IHOP's** assets and equity? The Decision Guidelines will help you evaluate the company.

Decision	Guidelines
Dividends • Whether to declare a cash dividend?	• Must have enough Retained earnings to declare the dividend. • Must have enough cash to pay the dividend.
• What happens with a dividend?	• The **IHOP** board of directors declares the dividend. Then the dividend becomes a liability for **IHOP**. • The date of record determines who will receive the dividend. • Payment of the dividend occurs later.
• Who receives the dividend?	• Preferred stockholders get their dividends first. Preferred dividends have a specified rate. • Common stockholders receive the remainder.
Stock Values • How much to pay for a stock?	Its market value
• How is book value used in decision making?	Can measure the value of a stock that is not traded on a stock exchange
Evaluating Operations • How to evaluate the operations of a corporation?	Two measures: • Rate of return on total assets (return on assets) • Rate of return on common equity (return on equity) For a healthy company, return on equity should exceed return on assets by a wide margin.
Accounting for Income Tax • What are the three main tax accounts?	• Income tax expense • Income tax payable, a current liability • Deferred tax liability, usually long-term
• How to measure	
• Income tax expense?	Income before income tax (from the income statement) × Income tax rate
• Income tax payable?	Taxable income (from the income tax return filed with the Internal Revenue Service) × Income tax rate
• Deferred tax liability?	Difference between income tax expense and income tax payable

Summary Problem 2

Use the following accounts and related balances to prepare the classified balance sheet of Fiesta, Inc., at September 30, 2011. Use the account format of the balance sheet. Compute the book value per share of Fiesta's common stock. $5,000 of preferred dividends are in arrears, and Fiesta has not declared the current-year dividend.

Common stock, $1 par, 50,000 shares authorized, 20,000 shares issued	$20,000	Long-term note payable	$ 70,000
Salary payable	3,000	Inventory	85,000
Cash	15,000	Property, plant, and equipment, net	205,000
Accounts payable	20,000	Accounts receivable, net	25,000
Retained earnings	80,000	Preferred stock, $2.50, no-par, 10,000 shares authorized, 2,000 shares issued	50,000
Paid-in capital in excess of par—common	75,000	Income tax payable	12,000

Solution

FIESTA, INC.
Balance Sheet
September 30, 2011

Assets		Liabilities		
Current:		Current:		
Cash	$ 15,000	Accounts payable		$ 20,000
Accounts receivable, net	25,000	Salary payable		3,000
Inventory	85,000	Income tax payable		12,000
Total current assets	125,000	Total current liabilities		35,000
Property, plant, and equipment, net	205,000	Long-term note payable		70,000
		Total liabilities		105,000
		Stockholders' Equity		
		Preferred stock, $2.50, no-par, 10,000 shares authorized, 2,000 shares issued	$ 50,000	
		Common stock, $1 par, 50,000 shares authorized, 20,000 shares issued	20,000	
		Paid-in capital in excess of par—common	75,000	
		Total paid-in capital	145,000	
		Retained earnings	80,000	
		Total stockholders' equity		225,000
Total assets	$330,000	Total liabilities and stockholders' equity		$330,000

Book Value (BV) attributed to Preferred stock (P/S):

1) Liquidation value × outstanding shares, OR 2) Preferred stock	$ 50,000
Dividends in Arrears on outstanding preferred shares	5,000
Total BV attributed to P/S	$ 55,000
Outstanding preferred shares	2,000
Book Value per share on Preferred stock	$ 27.50

Book Value attributed to Common stock (C/S)

Total Stockholders' equity	$225,000
Less Book Value attributed to P/S (figured above)	55,000
Total BV attributed to C/S (leftovers)	$170,000
Outstanding common shares	20,000
Book Value per share on Common stock	$ 8.50

Review Corporations: Paid-In Capital and the Balance Sheet

■ Accounting Vocabulary

Additional Paid-In Capital (p. 630)
The paid-in capital in excess of par, common plus other accounts combined for reporting on the balance sheet. Also called **Paid-in capital in excess of par** or **contributed capital**.

Arrears (p. 640)
A preferred stock is in arrears if the cumulative dividend has not been paid for the year.

Authorization (p. 624)
The acceptance by the state of the Corporate by-laws.

Authorization of Stock (p. 626)
Provision in a corporate charter that gives the state s permission for the corporation to issue—that is, to sell—a certain number of shares of stock.

Book Value per share of Stock (p. 642)
Amount of owners' equity on the company's books for each share of its stock.

Capital Stock (p. 626)
Represents the individual's ownership of the corporation's capital.

Charter (p. 624)
Document that gives the state's permission to form a corporation.

Common Stock (p. 626)
Represents the basic ownership of every corporation.

Contributed Capital (p. 626)
The amount invested in the corporation by its owners, the stockholders.

Cumulative Preferred Stock (p. 640)
Preferred stock whose owners must receive all dividends in arrears before the corporation pays dividends to the common stockholders.

Deficit (p. 638)
Debit balance in the Retained Earnings account.

Dividends (p. 627)
Distributions by a corporation to its stockholders.

Issue Price (p. 629)
The price the stock initially sells for the first time it is sold.

Legal Capital (p. 638)
The portion of stockholders' equity that cannot be used for dividends.

Liquidation Value (p. 642)
The amount guaranteed to the preferred shareholders in the event a company liquidates.

Market Value (p. 641)
Price for which a person could buy or sell a share of stock.

Outstanding Stock (p. 626)
Stock in the hands of stockholders.

Paid-In Capital (p. 626)
The amount invested in the corporation by its owners, the stockholders. Also called **contributed capital**.

Par Value (p. 628)
Arbitrary amount assigned to a share of stock.

Preferred Stock (p. 628)
Stock that gives its owners certain advantages over common stockholders, such as the right to receive dividends before the common stockholders and the right to receive assets before the common stockholders if the corporation liquidates.

Premium (p. 630)
The amount above par at which a stock is issued.

Rate of Return on Common Stockholders' Equity (p. 644)
Net income minus preferred dividends, divided by average common stockholders' equity. A measure of profitability. Also called **return on equity**.

Rate of Return on Total Assets (p. 643)
The sum of net income plus interest expense divided by average total assets. Measures the success a company has in using its assets to earn income for those financing the business. Also called **return on assets**.

Retained Earnings (p. 627)
The amount earned by income-producing activities and kept (retained) for use in the business.

Return on Assets (p. 643)
The sum of net income plus interest expense divided by average total assets. Measures the success a company has in using its assets to earn income for those financing the business. Also called **rate of return on total assets**.

Return on Equity (p. 644)
Net income minus preferred dividends, divided by average common stockholders' equity. A measure of profitability. Also called **rate of return on common stockholders' equity**.

Share (p. 626)
Portions into which the owners' equity of a corporation is divided. Also called a **stock certificate** or **stock**.

Stated Value (p. 628)
An arbitrary amount that accountants treat as though it were par value.

Stock (p. 626)
A document indicating ownership of a corporation. The holders of stock are called **stockholders** or **shareholders**.

Stock Certificate (p. 626)
Shares into which the owners' equity of a corporation is divided. Also called **stock**.

Underwriter (p. 629)
A firm, such as **Morgan Keegan**, that usually agrees to buy all the stock a company wants to issue if the firm cannot sell to the stock to its clients.

Quick Check

1. Which characteristic of a corporation is most attractive?
   a. Limited liability
   b. Mutual agency
   c. Double taxation
   d. All of the above
2. Which corporate characteristic is a disadvantage?
   a. Mutual agency
   b. Double taxation
   c. Limited liability
   d. None of the above
3. The two basic sources of corporate capital are
   a. Paid-in capital and Retained earnings.
   b. Assets and equity.
   c. Retained earnings and Dividends.
   d. Preferred and common.
4. Which class of stockholders takes the greater investment risk?
   a. Common
   b. Preferred
   c. Neither; bondholders take the most risk
   d. Both preferred and common take equal risk
5. Suppose Home Décor Imports issued 100,000 shares of $0.05 par common stock at $1 per share. Which journal entry correctly records the issuance of this stock?

a.

Cash	100,000	
Common stock		5,000
Paid-in capital in excess of par		95,000

b.

Common stock	100,000	
Cash		100,000

c.

Common stock	100,000	
Cash		5,000
Paid-in capital in excess of par		95,000

d.

Cash	100,000	
Common stock		100,000

6. Suppose Happy Sweets Bakery issues common stock to purchase a building. Happy Sweets Bakery should record the building at
   a. the par value of the stock given.
   b. its book value.
   c. its market value.
   d. a value assigned by the board of directors.

7. Conner Health Foods has 20,000 shares of $4 par common stock outstanding, which was issued at $10 per share. Conner also has Retained earnings of $83,000. How much is Conner's total stockholders' equity?
   a. $80,000
   b. $283,000
   c. $200,000
   d. $120,000
8. Chewning Corporation has 10,000 shares of 6%, $5 par preferred stock, and 52,000 shares of common stock outstanding. Chewning declared no dividends in 2010. In 2011, Chewning declares a total dividend of $51,000. How much of the dividends go to the common stockholders?
   a. $45,000
   b. $48,000
   c. $51,000
   d. None; it all goes to preferred
9. Dale Corporation has the following data:

Net income	$ 25,000	Average total assets	$ 330,000
Interest expense	8,100	Average common equity	94,000
Preferred dividends	11,600		

   Dale's return on assets is
   a. 14%.
   b. 5%.
   c. 10%.
   d. 8%.
10. A corporation's income tax payable is computed as,
   a. Taxable income × Income tax rate.
   b. Net income × Income tax rate.
   c. Income before tax × Income tax rate.
   d. Return on equity × Income tax rate.

Answers are given after Apply Your Knowledge (p. 668).

Assess Your Progress

Short Exercises

S11-1 *(L.OBJ. 1)* **Corporation characteristics [5 min]**
Due to the recent hamburger meat recalls, Bob's Burger House is considering incorporating.

Requirement

1. Which advantage of incorporating will help protect Bob's personal assets in the event the restaurant is sued?

S11-2 *(L.OBJ. 2)* **Sources of stockholders' equity [5 min]**
Stockholders' equity may arise from several sources.

Requirements

1. Identify the two primary sources of stockholders' equity.
2. Which source would be considered to be "internally" generated?

S11-3 *(L.OBJ. 3)* **Issuing stock [5 min]**
Maine Corporation has two classes of stock: Common, $3 par; Preferred, $30 par.

Requirement

1. Journalize Maine's issuance of
   a. 1,000 shares of common stock for $9 per share.
   b. 1,000 shares of preferred stock for a total of $30,000.

S11-4 *(L.OBJ. 3)* **Effect of a stock issuance [5 min]**
WESIT issued common stock and received $32,000,000. The par value of the WESIT stock was only $32,000.

Requirement

1. Is the excess amount of $31,968,000 a profit to WESIT? Does the excess affect net income? If not, what was it?

S11-5 *(L.OBJ. 3)* **Issuing stock and interpreting stockholders' equity [5–10 min]**
Rainbowpages.com issued stock during 2010 and reported the following on its balance sheet at December 31, 2010:

Common stock, $ 0.50 par value	
Authorized: 10,000 shares	
Issued: 8,000 shares	$ 4,000
Paid-in capital in excess of par	3,950
Retained earnings	25,000

Requirement

1. Journalize the company's issuance of the stock for cash.

S11-6 *(L.OBJ. 3)* **Preparing the stockholders' equity section of the balance sheet [5 min]**
Valleyview Corporation reported the following accounts:

Cost of goods sold	$ 59,000	Accounts payable	$ 7,000
Paid–in capital in excess of par	16,800	Retained earnings	17,000
Common stock, $ 2 par value,		Unearned revenue	5,000
40,000 shares issued	80,000	Total assets	?
Cash	24,000	Long–term note payable	7,600

Requirement

1. Prepare the stockholders' equity section of the Valleyview's balance sheet.

S11-7 *(L.OBJ. 4)* **Closing entries [5–10 min]**
The data for Tamara's Tax Service, Inc., for the year ended December 31, 2010, follow:

Cost of goods sold	$ 58,500	Sales revenue	100,000
Dividends	10,000	Operating expenses	45,000
Interest revenue	1,200		

Requirement

1. Journalize the required closing entries for the year.

S11-8 *(L.OBJ. 4, 5)* **Accounting for cash dividends [10 min]**
Greentea Company earned net income of $800,000 during the year ended December 31, 2010. On December 15, Greentea declared the annual cash dividend on its 2% preferred stock (par value, $110,000) and a $1.00 per share cash dividend on its common stock (65,000 shares). Greentea then paid the dividends on January 4, 2011.

Requirement

1. Journalize for Greentea:
   a. Declaring the cash dividends on December 15, 2010.
   b. Paying the cash dividends on January 4, 2011.

S11-9 *(L.OBJ. 5)* **Dividing cash dividends between preferred and common stock [5–10 min]**
Platinum Trust has the following stockholders' equity:

Paid–in capital:	
Preferred stock, 6 %, $10 par, 8,000 shares authorized, 6,500 shares issued	$ 65,000
Common stock, $0.10 par, 1,400,000 shares authorized and issued	140,000
Paid–in capital in excess of par–common	350,000
Total paid–in capital	555,000
Retained earnings	275,000
Total stockholders' equity	$ 830,000

Requirements

1. Is Platinum's preferred stock cumulative or noncumulative? How can you tell?
2. Platinum declares cash dividends of $15,000 for 2010. How much of the dividends goes to preferred? How much goes to common?
3. Platinum passed the preferred dividend in 2011 and 2012. In 2013 the company declares cash dividends of $25,000. How much of the dividend goes to preferred? How much goes to common?

S11-10 *(L.OBJ. 6)* **Book value per share of common stock [5–10 min]**
Golden Trust has the following stockholders' equity:

Paid–in capital:	
Preferred stock, 7 %, $13 par, 5,000 shares authorized, 3,500 shares issued	$ 45,500
Common stock, $0.30 par, 1,400,000 shares authorized and issued	420,000
Paid–in capital in excess of par–common	325,000
Total paid–in capital	790,500
Retained earnings	260,000
Total stockholders' equity	$ 1,050,500

Golden has not declared preferred dividends for five years (including the current year).

Requirement

1. Compute the book value per share of Golden's preferred and common stock.

S11-11 *(L.OBJ. 7)* **Computing return on assets and return on equity [5–10 min]**
Boga's 2011 financial statements reported the following items—with 2010 figures given for comparison (adapted, in millions):

BOGA Balance Sheet		
	2011	2010
Total assets	$ 31,328	$ 27,352
Total liabilities	15,390	13,252
Total stockholders' equity (all common)	15,938	14,100
Total liabilities and equity	$ 31,328	$ 27,352

BOGA Income Statement	
Net sales	$ 21,962
Cost of goods sold	7,639
Gross profit	14,323
Selling, administrative, and general expenses	8,147
Interest expense	198
All other expenses	1,133
Net Income	$ 4,845

Requirement

1. Compute Boga's rate of return on total assets and rate of return on common stockholders' equity for 2011. Do these rates of return look high or low?

S11-12 *(L.OBJ. 8)* **Accounting for income tax [5–10 min]**
Foxey Flowers had income before income tax of $85,000 and taxable income of $75,000 for 2010, the company's first year of operations. The income tax rate is 35%.

Requirements

1. Make the entry to record Foxey's income taxes for 2010.
2. Show what Foxey Flowers will report on its 2010 income statement, starting with income before income tax.

Exercises

E11-13 *(L.OBJ. 1)* **Advantages and disadvantages of a corporation [5–10 min]**
Following is a list of advantages and disadvantages of the corporate form of business.

1. Ownership and management are separated
2. Has continuous life
3. Transfer of ownership is easy
4. Stockholders' liability is limited
5. Double taxation
6. Can raise more money than a partnership or proprietorship
7. Government regulation is expensive

Requirement

1. Identify each quality as either an advantage or a disadvantage.

E11-14 *(L.OBJ. 2)* **Paid-in capital for a corporation [10 min]**
Alexa Corporation recently organized. The company issued common stock to an inventor in exchange for a patent with a market value of $53,000. In addition, Alexa received cash both for 5,000 shares of its $20 par preferred stock at par value and for 6,500 shares of its no-par common stock at $25 per share.

Requirement

1. Without making journal entries, determine the total *paid-in capital* created by these transactions.

E11-15 *(L.OBJ. 3)* **Issuing stock [10–15 min]**
Sarah Systems completed the following stock issuance transactions:

Oct 19	Issued 1,300 shares of $1 par common stock for cash of $12.00 per share
Nov 3	Sold 200 shares of $2.00, no–par preferred stock for $10,000 cash
11	Received equipment with market value of $18,000. Issued 6,000 shares of the $1 par common stock in exchange

Requirements

1. Journalize the transactions. Explanations are not required.
2. How much paid-in capital did these transactions generate for Sarah Systems?

E11-16 *(L.OBJ. 3)* **Recording issuance of no-par stock [5–10 min]**
Pates, Corp., issued 2,000 shares of no-par common stock for $6 per share.

Requirements

1. Record issuance of the stock if the stock
   a. Is true no-par stock and
   b. has stated value of $1 per share.
2. Which type of stock results in more total paid-in capital?

E11-17 *(L.OBJ. 3)* **Issuing stock to finance the purchase of assets [10 min]**
This exercise shows the similarity and the difference between two ways for Able, Inc., to acquire plant assets.

Case A - *Issue stock and buy the assets in separate transactions:*
Able, Inc., issued 12,000 shares of its $15 par common stock for cash of $800,000. In a separate transaction, Able purchased a building for $550,000 and equipment for $250,000. Journalize the two transactions.

Case B - *Issue stock to acquire the assets:*
Able issued 12,000 shares of its $15 par common stock to acquire a building valued at $550,000 and equipment worth $250,000. Journalize this single transaction.

Requirements

1. Compare the balances in all accounts after making both sets of entries.
2. Are the account balances similar or different?

E11-18 *(L.OBJ. 3)* **Issuing stock and preparing the stockholders' equity section of the balance sheet [15–20 min]**
The charter for WPAC-TV authorizes the company to issue 100,000 shares of $3, no-par preferred stock and 500,000 shares of common stock with $1 par value. During its start-up phase, WPAC completed the following transactions:

Aug	6	Issued 500 shares of common stock to the promoters who organized the corporation, receiving cash of $15,000
	12	Issued 700 shares of preferred stock for cash of $27,000
	14	Issued 1,600 shares of common stock in exchange for land valued at $17,000
	31	Closed net income of $35,000 into Retained earnings

Requirements

1. Record the transactions in the general journal.
2. Prepare the stockholders' equity section of the WPAC-TV balance sheet at August 31, 2010.

E11-19 *(L.OBJ. 3)* **Stockholders' equity section of the balance sheet [10–15 min]**
The charter of Cherry Blossom Capital Corporation authorizes the issuance of 1,000 shares of preferred stock and 1,000 shares of common stock. During a two-month period, Cherry Blossom completed these stock-issuance transactions:

Nov 23	Issued 210 shares of $2 par common stock for cash of $14.00 per share
Dec 12	Received inventory valued at $27,000 and equipment with a market value of $19,000 for 350 shares of the $2 par common stock
17	Issued 1,000 shares of 6%, $10 par preferred stock for $10 per share

Requirement

1. Prepare the stockholders' equity section of the Cherry Blossom balance sheet for the transactions given in this exercise. Retained Earnings has a balance of $72,000.

E11-20 *(L.OBJ. 4)* **Stockholders' equity section of a balance sheet [10–15 min]**
Bretton Publishing Company has the following selected account balances at June 30, 2010.

Inventory	$ 113,000	Common stock, no par with $1.00	
Machinery and equipment	107,000	stated value, 1,000 shares	
Dividends	5,000	authorized and issued	1,000
Depreciation expense	10,000	Accumulated depreciation	64,000
Rent expense	25,000	Salary expense	80,000
Utilities expense	8,000	Retained earnings, June 30, 2009	120,000
Cost of goods sold	82,000	Sales revenue	230,000

Requirements

1. Journalize all required closing entries for the year.
2. Calculate the balance in Retained earnings at June 30, 2010. Use a T-account to show your calculations.

E11-21 *(L.OBJ. 5)* **Dividing dividends between preferred and common stock [10–15 min]**
Western Communications has the following stockholders' equity:

WESTERN COMMUNICATIONS Stockholders' Equity	
Paid–in Capital:	
Preferred stock, 4%, $10 par, 100,000 shares authorized	
24,000 shares issued and outstanding	$ 240,000
Common stock, $0.50 par, 500,000 shares authorized	
380,000 shares issued and outstanding	190,000
Paid–in capital in excess of par—common	640,000
Total paid–in capital	1,070,000
Retained earnings	160,000
Total stockholders' equity	$1,230,000

Requirements

1. First, determine whether preferred stock is cumulative or noncumulative.
2. Compute the amount of dividends to preferred and to common for 2010 and 2011 if total dividends are $7,600 in 2010 and $48,000 in 2011.

E11-22 *(L.OBJ. 5)* **Computing dividends on preferred and common stock [15–20 min]**
The following elements of stockholders' equity are adapted from the balance sheet of Smitts Marketing, Corp.

SMITTS MARKETING, CORP. Stockholders' Equity	
Preferred stock, 8% cumulative, $2 par,	
80,000 shares authorized, issued and outstanding	$ 160,000
Common stock, $0.10 par, 10,000,000 shares authorized,	
9,250,000 shares, issued and outstanding	925,000

Smitts paid no preferred dividends in 2008.

Requirement

1. Compute the dividends to preferred and common for 2009 if total dividends are $150,000.

E11-23 *(L.OBJ. 6)* **Book value per share of common stock [0–15 min]**
The balance sheet of Matt Taft Wireless, Inc., reported the following:

Preferred stock, 4%, $30 par, 1,000 shares issued	
and outstanding	$ 30,000
Common stock, no–par value, 10,000 shares authorized;	
5,300 shares issued	220,000
Total stockholders' equity	$ 250,000

Assume that Taft has paid preferred dividends for the current year and all prior years (no divdends in arrears).

Requirement

1. Compute the book value per share of the common stock.

E11-24 *(L.OBJ. 6)* **Book value per share of common stock, and preferred dividends in arrears [10–15 min]**

The balance sheet of Mitt Trull, Inc., reported the following:

Preferred stock, 8%, $40 par, 1,600 shares issued and outstanding	$ 64,000
Common stock, no–par value, 10,000 shares authorized; 5,600 shares issued	224,000
Total stockholders' equity	$ 288,000

Requirement

1. Compute the book value per share of Trull's preferred and common stock if three years' preferred dividends (including dividends for the current year) are in arrears.

E11-25 *(L.OBJ.7)* **Evaluating profitability [10–15 min]**

La Salle Exploration Company reported these figures for 2011 and 2010:

	2011	2010
Income Statement—partial:		
Interest expense	12,100,000	17,100,000
Net Income	17,600,000	19,300,000

	2011	2010
Balance Sheet—partial:		
Total assets	$ 326,000,000	$ 316,000,000
Preferred stock, $2, no–par, 100,000 issued and outstanding	2,000,000	2,000,000
Common stockholders' equity	180,000,000	$ 172,000,000
Total stockholders' equity	182,000,000	174,000,000

Requirements

1. Compute rate of return on total assets and rate of return on common stockholders' equity for 2011.
2. Do these rates of return suggest strength or weakness? Give your reason.

E11-26 *(L.OBJ. 8)* **Accounting for corporate income tax [10–15 min]**

The income statement of Terri's Cards, Inc., reported income before income tax of $450 million (rounded) during a recent year. Assume Terri's taxable income for the year was $343 million. The company's income tax rate was close to 37.0%.

Requirements

1. Journalize Terri's entry to record income tax for the year.
2. Show how Terri's would report income tax expense on its income statement and income tax liabilities on its balance sheet. Complete the income statement, starting with income before tax. For the balance sheet, assume all beginning balances were zero.

Problems (Group A)

P11-27A *(L.OBJ. 1, 3)* **Organizing a corporation, and issuing stock [10–20 min]**

Drake and John are opening an mp3 player store. There are no competing mp3 player stores in the area. Their fundamental decision is how to organize the business. They anticipate profits of $200,000 the first year, with the ability to sell franchises in the future. Although they have enough to start the business now as a partnership, cash flow will be an issue as they grow. They feel the corporate form of operation will be best for the long term. They seek your advice.

Requirements

1. What is the main advantage they gain by selecting a corporate form of business now?
2. Would you recommend they initially issue preferred or common stock. Why?
3. If they decide to issue $1 par common stock and anticipate an initial market price of $50 per share, how many shares will they need to issue to raise $2,000,000?

P11-28A *(L.OBJ. 2, 3, 5)* **Sources of equity, Stock issuance, and Dividends [15–20 min]**

Tree Comfort Specialists, Inc., reported the following stockholders' equity on its balance sheet at June 30, 2011:

TREE COMFORT SPECIALISTS, INC. Stockholders' Equity June 30, 2011	
Paid-in Capital:	
Preferred stock, 7%, $5 par, 600,000 shares authorized, 220,000 shares issued	$ 1,100,000
Common stock, par value $1 per share, 9,000,000 shares authorized, 1,340,000 shares issued and outstanding	1,340,000
Additional paid-in capital—common	2,900,000
Total paid-in capital	5,340,000
Retained earnings	12,000,000
Total stockholders' equity	$ 17,340,000

Requirements

1. Identify the different issues of stock that Tree has outstanding.
2. What is the par value per share of Tree's preferred stock?
3. Make two summary journal entries to record issuance of all the Tree stock for cash. Explanations are not required.
4. No preferred dividends are in arrears. Journalize the declaration of a $400,000 dividend at June 30, 2011. Use separate Dividends payable accounts for Preferred and Common. An explanation is not required.

P11-29A *(L.OBJ. 2, 6)* **Analyzing the stockholders' equity section of the balance sheet [15–20 min]**

The balance sheet of Ballcraft, Inc., reported the following:

Preferred stock, $6 par, 6%, 5,000 shares authorized and issued	$ 30,000
Common stock, $4.00 par value, 45,000 shares authorized; 10,000 shares issued	40,000
Additional paid–in capital–common	219,000
Total paid–in capital	289,000
Retained earnings	90,000
Total stockholders' equity	$ 379,000

Preferred dividends are in arrears for two years, including the current year. On the balance sheet date, the market value of the Ballcraft common stock was $31 per share.

Requirements

1. Is the preferred stock cumulative or noncumulative? How can you tell?
2. What is the total paid-in capital of the company?
3. What was the total market value of the common stock?
4. Compute the book value per share of the common stock.

P11-30A *(L.OBJ. 3)* **Journalizing corporate transactions and preparing the stockholders' equity section of the balance sheet [20–25 min]**

C-Mobile Wireless needed additional capital to expand, so the business incorporated. The charter from the state of Georgia authorizes C-Mobile to issue 60,000 shares of 10%, $150-par preferred stock, and 140,000 shares of no-par common stock. C-Mobile completed the following transactions:

Dec 2	Issued 21,000 shares of common stock for equipment with a market value of $140,000
6	Issued 500 shares of preferred stock to acquire a patent with a market value of $75,000
9	Issued 10,000 shares of common stock for cash of $60,000

Requirements

1. Record the transactions in the general journal.
2. Prepare the stockholders' equity section of the C-Mobile Wireless balance sheet at December 31. The ending balance of Retained Earnings is $90,000.

P11-31A *(L.OBJ. 3)* **Issuing stock and preparing the stockholders' equity section of the balance sheet [15–20 min]**

Lockridge-Priest, Inc., was organized in 2009. At December 31, 2009, the Lockridge-Priest balance sheet reported the following stockholders' equity:

LOCKRIDGE-PRIEST, INC. Stockholders' Equity December 31, 2009	
Paid–in Capital:	
Preferred stock, 5%, $45 par, 140,000 shares authorized, none issued	$ 0
Common stock, $2 par, 525,000 shares authorized, 62,000 shares issued and outstanding	124,000
Paid–in capital in excess of par – common	42,000
Total paid–in capital	$ 166,000
Retained earnings	28,000
Total stockholders' equity	$ 194,000

Requirements

1. During 2010, the company completed the following selected transactions. Journalize each transaction. Explanations are not required.
   a. Issued for cash 1,400 shares of preferred stock at par value.
   b. Issued for cash 2,300 shares of common stock at a price of $3 per share.
   c. Net income for the year was $79,000, and the company declared no dividends. Make the closing entry for net income.
2. Prepare the stockholders' equity section of the Lockridge-Priest balance sheet at December 31, 2010.

P11-32A *(L.OBJ. 3, 4)* **Stockholders' equity section of the balance sheet [20–25 min]**

The following summaries for Maryland Service, Inc., and Grayhound, Co., provide the information needed to prepare the stockholders' equity section of each company's balance sheet. The two companies are independent.

* *Maryland Service, Inc.*: Maryland is authorized to issue 40,000 shares of $1 par common stock. All the stock was issued at $15 per share. The company incurred net losses of $42,000 in 2008 and $14,000 in 2009. It earned net income of $32,000 in 2010 and $176,000 in 2011. The company declared no dividends during the four-year period.
* *Grayhound, Co.*: Grayhound's charter authorizes the issuance of 60,000 shares of 7%, $15 par preferred stock and 500,000 shares of no-par common stock. Grayhound issued 1,500 shares of the preferred stock at $15 per share. It issued 160,000 shares of the common stock for $320,000. The company's retained earnings balance at the beginning of 2011 was $70,000. Net income for 2011 was $93,000, and the company declared the specified preferred dividend for 2011. Preferred dividends for 2010 were in arrears.

Requirement

1. For each company, prepare the stockholders' equity section of its balance sheet at December 31, 2011. Show the computation of all amounts. Entries are not required.

P11-33A *(L.OBJ. 5)* **Computing dividends on preferred and common stock [15–20 min]**

Hip Skincare has 5,000 shares of 5%, $15 par value preferred stock and 80,000 shares of $2.25 par common stock outstanding. During a three-year period, Hip declared and paid cash dividends as follows: 2010, $2,000; 2011, $15,000; and 2012, $20,000.

Requirements

1. Compute the total dividends to preferred and to common for each of the three years if
   a. preferred is noncumulative.
   b. preferred is cumulative.

2. For requirement l.b., journalize the declaration of the 2011 dividends on December 22, 2011, and payment on January 14, 2012. Use separate Dividends payable accounts for Preferred and Common.

P11-34A *(L.OBJ. 7)* **Preparing a corporate balance sheet and measuring profitability [40–50 min]**

The following accounts and December 31, 2010, balances of Florida Optical Corporation are arranged in no particular order.

Retained earnings	$ 120,000	Common stock, $5 par	
Inventory	101,000	100,000 shares authorized,	
Property, plant, and equipment, net	282,000	22,000 shares issued	$ 110,000
Prepaid expenses	12,000	Dividends payable	3,000
Goodwill	62,000	Paid–in capital in excess of par–common	160,000
Accrued liabilities payable	19,000	Accounts payable	34,000
Long–term note payable	105,000	Preferred stock, 4%, $10 par,	
Accounts receivable, net	102,000	25,000 shares authorized,	
Cash	42,000	5,000 shares issued	50,000

Total assets, Dec 31, 2009	$ 505,000
Common equity, Dec 31, 2009	306,000
Net income, 2010	43,000
Interest expense, 2010	3,600

Requirements

1. Prepare the company's classified balance sheet in account format at December 31, 2010.
2. Compute Florida Optical's rate of return on total assets and rate of return on common stockholders' equity for the year ended December 31, 2010.
3. Do these rates of return suggest strength or weakness? Give your reasoning.

P11-35A *(L.OBJ. 8)* **Computing and recording a corporation's income tax [15–20 min]**

The accounting records of Restore Redwood Corporation provide income statement data for 2011.

Total revenue	$ 910,000
Total expenses	700,000
Income before tax	$ 210,000

Total expenses include depreciation of $56,000 computed on the straight-line method. In calculating taxable income on the tax return, Restore Redwood uses the modified accelerated cost recovery system (MACRS). MACRS depreciation was $81,000 for 2011. The corporate income tax rate is 40%.

Requirements

1. Compute taxable income for the year. For this computation, substitute MACRS depreciation in place of straight-line depreciation.
2. Journalize the corporation's income tax for 2011.
3. Show how to report the two income tax liabilities on Restore's classified balance sheet.

■ Problems (Group B)

P11-36B *(L.OBJ. 1, 3)* **Organizing a corporation and issuing stock [10–20 min]**
Josh and Aaron are opening a couture clothing boutique. There are no competing couture clothing boutiques in the area. Their fundamental decision is how to organize the business. They anticipate profits of $450,000 the first year, with the ability to sell franchises in the future. Although they have enough to start the business now as a partnership, cash flow will be an issue as they grow. They feel the corporate form of operation will be best for the long term. They seek your advice.

Requirements

1. What is the main advantage they gain by selecting a corporate form of business now?
2. Would you recommend they initially issue preferred or common stock? Why?
3. If they decide to issue $5 par common stock and anticipate an initial market price of $100 per share, how many shares will they need to issue to raise $3,500,000?

P11-37B *(L.OBJ. 2, 3, 5)* **Sources of equity, Stock issuance, and Dividends [15–20 min]**
Travel Comfort Specialists, Inc., reported the following stockholders' equity on its balance sheet at June 30, 2011.

TRAVEL COMFORT SPECIALISTS, INC. Stockholders' Equity June 30, 2011	
Paid–in Capital:	
Preferred stock, 7%, $50 par, 725,000 shares authorized, 220,000 shares issued	$ 1,100,000
Common stock, par value $1 per share, 5,000,000 shares authorized, 1,320,000 shares issued and outstanding	1,320,000
Additional paid–in capital—common	2,400,000
Total paid–in capital	4,820,000
Retained earnings	12,400,000
Total stockholders' equity	$ 17,220,000

Requirements

1. Identify the different issues of stock that Travel has outstanding.
2. What is the par value per share of Travel's preferred stock?
3. Make two summary journal entries to record issuance of all the Travel stock for cash. Explanations are not required.
4. No preferred dividends are in arrears. Journalize the declaration of an $800,000 dividend at June 30, 2011. Use separate Dividends Payable accounts for Preferred and Common. An explanation is not required.

P11-38B *(L.OBJ. 2, 6)* **Analyzing the stockholders' equity section of the balance sheet [15–20 min]**

The balance sheet of Beachcraft, Inc., reported the following:

Preferred stock, $5 par, 7%,	
3,000 shares authorized and issued	$ 15,000
Common stock, $1.00 value, 44,000 shares authorized;	
13,000 shares issued	13,000
Additional paid–in capital–common	218,000
Total paid–in capital	246,000
Retained earnings	70,000
Total stockholders' equity	$ 316,000

Preferred dividends are in arrears for two years, including the current year. On the balance sheet date, the market value of the Beachcraft common stock was $28 per share.

Requirements

1. Is the preferred stock cumulative or noncumulative? How can you tell?
2. What is the total paid-in capital of the company?
3. What was the total market value of the common stock?
4. Compute the book value per share of the common stock.

P11-39B *(L.OBJ. 3)* **Journalizing corporate transactions and preparing the stockholders' equity section of the balance sheet [20–25 min]**

A – Cell Wireless needed additional capital to expand, so the business incorporated. The charter from the state of Georgia authorizes A – Cell to issue 40,000 shares of 8%, $50-par preferred stock and 130,000 shares of no-par common stock. A – Cell completed the following transactions:

Dec 2	Issued 19,000 shares of common stock for equipment with a market value of $100,000
6	Issued 1,000 shares of preferred stock to acquire a patent with a market value of $50,000
9	Issued 11,000 shares of common stock for cash of $44,000

Requirements

1. Record the transactions in the general journal.
2. Prepare the stockholders' equity section of the A – Cell Wireless balance sheet at December 31. The ending balance of Retained Earnings is $92,000.

P11-40B *(L.OBJ. 3)* **Issuing stock and preparing the stockholders' equity section of the balance sheet [15–20 min]**

Lavallee-Priest, Inc., was organized in 2009. At December 31, 2009, the Lavallee-Priest balance sheet reported the following stockholders' equity:

LAVALLEE-PRIEST, INC. Stockholders' Equity December 31, 2009	
Paid–in Capital:	
Preferred stock, 8%, $50 par, 100,000 shares authorized, none issued	$ 0
Common stock, $1 par, 530,000 shares authorized, 61,000 shares issued and outstanding	61,000
Paid–in capital in excess of par – common	42,000
Total paid–in capital	$ 103,000
Retained earnings	25,000
Total stockholders' equity	$ 128,000

Requirements

1. During 2010, the company completed the following selected transactions. Journalize each transaction. Explanations are not required.
   a. Issued for cash 1,200 shares of preferred stock at par value.
   b. Issued for cash 2,300 shares of common stock at a price of $4 per share.
   c. Net income for the year was $79,000, and the company declared no dividends. Make the closing entry for net income.
2. Prepare the stockholders' equity section of the Lavallee-Priest balance sheet at December 31, 2010.

P11-41B *(L.OBJ. 3, 4)* **Stockholders' equity section of the balance sheet [20–25 min]**

The following summaries for Montgomery Service, Inc., and Gendron, Co., provide the information needed to prepare the stockholders' equity section of each company's balance sheet. The two companies are independent.

* *Montgomery Service, Inc.*: Montgomery is authorized to issue 41,000 shares of $1 par common stock. All the stock was issued at $13 per share. The company incurred net losses of $45,000 in 2008 and $14,000 in 2009. It earned net income of $29,000 in 2010 and $180,000 in 2011. The company declared no dividends during the four-year period.
* *Gendron, Co.*: Gendron's charter authorizes the issuance of 70,000 shares of 7%, $13 par preferred stock and 540,000 shares of no-par common stock. Gendron issued 1,100 shares of the preferred stock at $13 per share. It issued 110,000 shares of the common stock for $220,000. The company's retained earnings balance at the beginning of 2011 was $70,000. Net income for 2011 was $90,000, and the company declared the specified preferred dividend for 2011. Preferred dividends for 2010 were in arrears.

Requirement

1. For each company, prepare the stockholders' equity section of its balance sheet at December 31, 2011. Show the computation of all amounts. Entries are not required.

P11-42B *(L.OBJ. 5)* **Computing dividends on preferred and common stock [15–20 min]**

Fashionista Skincare has 5,000 shares of 4%, $20 par value preferred stock, and 110,000 shares of $2.50 par common stock outstanding. During a three-year period, Fashionista declared and paid cash dividends as follows: 2010, $2,000; 2011, $10,000; and 2012, $18,000.

12 Corporations: Effects on Retained Earnings and the Income Statement

Learning Objectives/ Success Keys

1. Account for stock dividends
2. Account for stock splits
3. Account for treasury stock
4. Report restrictions on retained earnings
5. Complete a corporate income statement including earnings per share

Smart Touch Learning, Inc., is considering options to reward its stockholders without using up the corporation's cash. Additionally, Smart Touch wants to provide employee bonuses that are not going to use cash. How can Smart Touch accomplish these objectives? It can do so by creatively using its own stocks.

This chapter takes corporate equity a few steps further, as follows:

Chapter 11 Covered	Chapter 12 Covers
Paid-in capital	Stock dividends
Issuing stock	Stock splits
Retained earnings	Buying back a corporation's stock (treasury stock)
Cash dividends	
Corporate balance sheet	Corporate income statement

Chapter 12 completes our discussion of corporate equity. It begins with *stock dividends* and *stock splits*—terms you have probably heard. Let us see what these terms mean.

Stock Dividends

1 Account for stock dividends

We have seen that the owners equity of a corporation is called *stockholders' equity* or *shareholders' equity*. Paid-in capital and Retained earnings make up stockholders' equity. We studied paid-in capital and retained earnings in Chapter 11. Now let us focus on stock dividends.

A **stock dividend** is a distribution of a corporation's own stock to its shareholders. Unlike cash dividends, stock dividends do not give any assets to the shareholders. Stock dividends

- affect *only* stockholders' equity accounts (including Retained earnings and Common stock).
- have *no* effect on total stockholders' equity.
- have *no* effect on assets or liabilities.

As Exhibit 12-1 shows, a stock dividend decreases Retained earnings and increases Common stock, as it is a transfer *from* Retained earnings *to* Common stock. Total equity is unchanged.

EXHIBIT 12-1 | Effects of a Stock Dividend

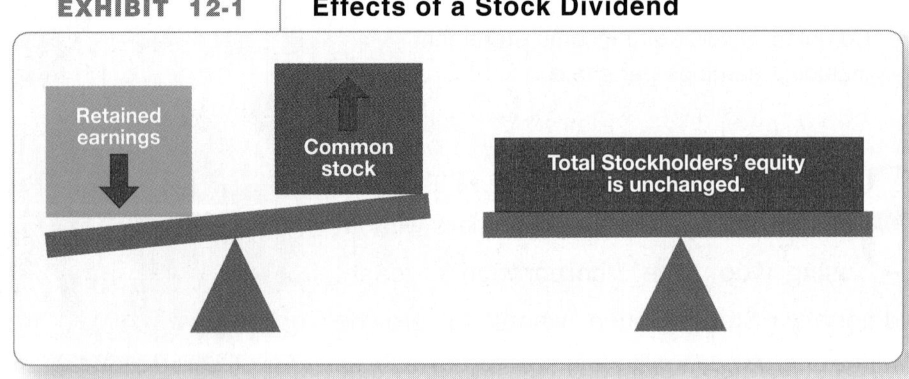

The corporation distributes stock dividends to stockholders in proportion to the number of shares the stockholders already own. Suppose you own 1,000 shares of Smart Touch Learning's common stock. If Smart Touch distributes a 10% stock dividend, you would receive 100 (1,000 × 0.10) additional shares. You would now own 1,100 shares of the stock. All other Smart Touch stockholders also receive additional shares equal to 10% of their holdings; so you are all in the same relative position after the dividend as you were before.

Why Issue Stock Dividends?

A company issues stock dividends for several reasons:

1. **To continue dividends but conserve cash.** A company may wish to continue dividends to keep stockholders happy, but needs to keep its cash for operations. A stock dividend is a way to do so without using corporate cash.
2. **To reduce the market price of its stock.** A stock dividend may cause the company's stock price to fall because of the increased supply of the stock. Suppose that a share of Smart Touch Learning's stock was traded at $50 recently. Doubling the shares

outstanding by issuing a stock dividend would likely drop Smart Touch's stock market price to $25 per share. The objective behind a stock dividend is to make the stock less expensive and, therefore, more available and attractive to investors.

3. **To reward investors.** Investors often feel like they have received something of value when they get a stock dividend.

Recording Stock Dividends

As with a cash dividend, there are three dates for a stock dividend:

- Declaration date
- Record date
- Distribution (payment) date

The board of directors announces the stock dividend on the declaration date. The date of record and the distribution date then follow.

The declaration of a stock dividend does *not* create a liability because the corporation is not obligated to pay assets. (Recall that a liability is a claim on *assets*.) With a stock dividend, the corporation has declared its intention to distribute its stock. Assume that Smart Touch has the following stockholders' equity prior to a stock dividend:

SMART TOUCH LEARNING, INC. **Stockholders' Equity** January 4, 2011	
Paid-in capital:	
Preferred stock, 6%, $50 par, 2,000 shares authorized, 2,000 shares issued	$ 100,000
Paid-in capital in excess of par—preferred	5,000
Common stock, $1 par, 10,000,000 shares authorized, 2,000,000 shares issued	2,000,000
Paid-in capital in excess of par—common	19,000,000
Total paid-in capital	21,105,000
Retained earnings	9,000,000
Total stockholders' equity	$30,105,000

The entry to record a stock dividend depends on the size of that dividend. Generally accepted accounting principles (GAAP) distinguish between

- a **small stock dividend** (less than 20% to 25% of issued stock), and
- a **large stock dividend** (25% or more of issued stock).

Stock dividends between 20% and 25% are rare.

SMALL STOCK DIVIDENDS—LESS THAN 20% TO 25% Small stock dividends are accounted for at their market value. Here is how the various accounts are affected:

- Retained earnings is debited for the market value of the dividend shares.
- Common stock is credited for the dividend stock's par value.
- Paid-in capital in excess of par is credited for the remainder.

Assume, for example, that Smart Touch Learning distributes a 5% stock dividend when the market value of Smart Touch common stock is $50 per share. Exhibit 12-2 illustrates the accounting for this 5% stock dividend.[1]

EXHIBIT 12-2 | Accounting for a Small Stock Dividend—5%

Feb 1	Retained earnings (2,000,000 shares × 0.05 × $50 market value) (Q–)	5,000,000	
	Common stock (2,000,000 shares × 0.05 × $1 par) (Q+)		100,000
	Paid-in capital in excess of par—common (Q+)		4,900,000

Remember that a stock dividend does not affect assets, liabilities, or *total* stockholders' equity. A stock dividend merely rearranges the balances in the equity accounts, leaving total equity unchanged. Exhibit 12-3 shows what Smart Touch's stockholders' equity looks like after the 5% stock dividend.

EXHIBIT 12-3 | Smart Touch Learning, Inc.'s, Stockholders' Equity After 5% Stock Dividend

SMART TOUCH LEARNING, INC. Stockholders' Equity February 1, 2011	
Paid-in capital:	
Preferred stock, 6%, $50 par, 2,000 shares authorized, 2,000 shares issued	$ 100,000
Paid-in capital in excess of par—preferred	5,000
Common stock, $1 par, 10,000,000 shares authorized, 2,100,000 shares issued	2,100,000
Paid-in capital in excess of par—common	23,900,000
Total paid-in capital	26,105,000
Retained earnings	4,000,000
Total stockholders' equity	$30,105,000

Note that total stockholders' equity stays at $30,105,000.

LARGE STOCK DIVIDENDS—25% OR MORE Large stock dividends are rare, but when they are declared, they are accounted for at par value, instead of market value. Par value is used because the larger number of shares will reduce market value, making it an invalid measurement of the dividend value. Assume, for example, that Smart Touch Learning then distributes a second 50% stock dividend when the market value of Smart Touch common stock is $50 per share. The entry to record the large stock dividend is as follows:

	50% Stock Dividend		
Feb 2	Retained earnings (2,100,000 shares × 50% × $1par) (Q–)	1,050,000	
	Common stock (Q+)		1,050,000

[1]A stock dividend can be recorded with two journal entries—for (1) the declaration and (2) the stock distribution. But most companies record stock dividends with a single entry on the date of distribution, as we illustrate here.

The effect on the stockholders' equity after the 50% stock dividend is illustrated in Exhibit 12-4:

EXHIBIT 12-4 **Smart Touch Learning, Inc.'s, Stockholders' Equity After 50% Stock Dividend**

SMART TOUCH LEARNING, INC. Stockholders' Equity February 2, 2011	
Paid-in capital:	
Preferred stock, 6%, $50 par, 2,000 shares authorized, 2,000 shares issued	$ 100,000
Paid-in capital in excess of par—preferred	5,000
Common stock, $1 par, 10,000,000 shares authorized, 3,150,000 shares issued	3,150,000
Paid-in capital in excess of par—common	23,900,000
Total paid-in capital	27,155,000
Retained earnings	2,950,000
Total stockholders' equity	$30,105,000

Notice that the large dividend also does not change total stockholders' equity of $30,105,000.

Stop & Think...

Have you ever been to one of those bulk stores where you can buy, say 100 rolls of toilet paper at a cheaper price per roll than if you bought 4 rolls at your grocery store? Why do you think that it is cheaper? The answer is the volume. (Of course, packaging and marketing come into play, too.) The volume principle applies when we are valuing small stock dividends at market value and large stock dividends (those that are 25% or more) at par value. The key is that, when the stock dividend is so large, it "waters down" the market price so much that it is no longer a valid measure, much like the bulk toilet paper purchase. Therefore, par value is used to account for large stock dividends.

Stock Splits

2 Account for stock splits

A **stock split** is fundamentally different from a stock dividend. A stock split increases the number of authorized, issued, and outstanding shares of stock. A stock split also decreases par value per share, whereas stock dividends do not affect par value or the number of authorized shares. For example, if Smart Touch splits its common stock 2 for 1, the number of outstanding shares is doubled and par value per share is cut in half. A stock split also decreases the market price of the stock.

The market price of a share of Smart Touch Learning common stock has been approximately $50. Assume that Smart Touch wishes to decrease the market price to approximately $25. The company can make the market price drop to around $25 by affecting a 2-for-1 split of its common stock. A 2-for-1 stock split means that Smart Touch will have twice as many shares of stock outstanding after the split as it did before, and each share's par value is cut in half. Let us consider Smart Touch's balance sheet from Exhibit 12-4. It shows 3,150,000 shares outstanding of $1 par common stock before the split. Exhibit 12-5 on page 674 shows the before and after of how a 2-for-1 split affects Smart Touch's equity.

EXHIBIT 12-5 Smart Touch Learning, Inc.'s, Stockholders' Equity Before & After 2-for-1 Common Stock Split

SMART TOUCH LEARNING, INC. Stockholders' Equity—Before February 2, 2011		SMART TOUCH LEARNING, INC. Stockholders' Equity—After February 3, 2011	
Paid-in capital:		Paid-in capital:	
Preferred stock, 6%, $50 par; 2,000 shares authorized, 2,000 shares issued	$ 100,000	Preferred stock, 6%, $50 par; 2,000 shares authorized, 2,000 shares issued	$ 100,000
Paid-in capital in excess of par—preferred	5,000	Paid-in capital in excess of par—preferred	5,000
Common stock, $1 par, 10,000,000 shares authorized, 3,150,000 shares issued	3,150,000	Common stock, $.50 par, 20,000,000 shares authorized, 6,300,000 shares issued	3,150,000
Paid-in capital in excess of par—common	23,900,000	Paid-in capital in excess of par—common	23,900,000
Total paid-in capital	27,155,000	Total paid-in capital	27,155,000
Retained earnings	2,950,000	Retained earnings	2,950,000
Total stockholders' equity	$30,105,000	Total stockholders' equity	$30,105,000

Study the exhibit and you will see that a 2-for-1 stock split does the following:

- Cuts par value per share in half
- Doubles the shares of stock authorized and issued
- Leaves all account balances and total equity unchanged

Because the stock split does not affect any account balances, no formal journal entry is needed. Instead, the split is recorded in a **memorandum entry**, a journal entry that "notes" a significant event, but which has no debit or credit amount. The following is an example of a memorandum entry:

Date	Description	Debit	Credit
Feb 3	Split the common stock 2 for 1		
	OLD: 10,000,000 shares authorized; 3,150,000 shares issued, $1 par		
	NEW: 20,000,000 shares authorized; 6,300,000 shares issued, $.50 par		

After the split, the stockholders' equity section will appear as in Exhibit 12-6.

EXHIBIT 12-6 Smart Touch Learning, Inc.'s, Stockholders' Equity AFTER 2-for-1 Common Stock Split

SMART TOUCH LEARNING, INC. Stockholders' Equity February 3, 2011	
Paid-in capital:	
Preferred stock, 6%, $50 par, 2,000 shares authorized, 2,000 shares issued	$ 100,000
Paid-in capital in excess of par—preferred	5,000
Common stock, $.50 par, 20,000,000 shares authorized, 6,300,000 shares issued	3,150,000
Paid-in capital in excess of par—common	23,900,000
Total paid-in capital	27,155,000
Retained earnings	2,950,000
Total stockholders' equity	$30,105,000

Stop & Think...

Take a dollar out of your pocket. If you were to take that dollar to the bank and exchange it for four quarters, what amount of money would you have? You would still have a dollar. Getting change for a dollar is just like a stock split. You have more pieces of paper (stock), but your value and ownership percentage in the company remain the same.

Stock Dividends and Stock Splits Compared

Stock dividends and stock splits have some similarities and some differences. Exhibit 12-7 summarizes their effects on stockholders' equity. For completeness, it also covers cash dividends.

EXHIBIT 12-7 | **Effects of Dividends and Stock Splits on the Following Accounts**

Event	Common Stock	Paid-In Capital in Excess of Par	Retained Earnings	Total Stockholders' Equity
Cash dividend	No effect	No effect	Decrease	Decrease
Stock dividend	Increase	Increase	Decrease	No effect
Stock split	No effect	No effect	No effect	No effect

Treasury Stock

A company's own stock that it has previously issued and later reacquired is called **treasury stock.**[2] In effect, the corporation holds the stock in its treasury. A corporation, such as Smart Touch, may purchase treasury stock for several reasons:

3 Account for treasury stock

1. Management wants to increase net assets by buying low and selling high.
2. Management wants to support the company's stock price.
3. Management wants to avoid a takeover by an outside party.
4. Management wants to reward valued employees with stock.

Treasury stock transactions are common among corporations. A recent survey of 600 companies showed that 66% held treasury stock.

Treasury Stock Basics

Here are the basics of accounting for treasury stock:

- The Treasury stock account has a debit balance, which is the opposite of the other equity accounts. Therefore, *Treasury stock is contra equity.*
- Treasury stock is recorded at cost, without reference to par value.

[2]We illustrate the *cost* method of accounting for treasury stock because it is used most widely. Intermediate accounting courses also cover an alternative method.

- The Treasury stock account is reported beneath Retained earnings on the balance sheet as a reduction to total stockholders' equity.

Treasury stock decreases the company's stock that is outstanding—held by outsiders (the stockholders). We compute outstanding stock as follows:

Outstanding stock = Issued stock – Treasury stock

Outstanding shares are important because only outstanding shares have voting rights and receive cash dividends. Treasury stock does not carry a vote, and it gets no dividends. Now let us illustrate how to account for treasury stock, continuing with Smart Touch Learning.

Purchase of Treasury Stock

After the stock split, discussed earlier in the chapter, Smart Touch Learning had the stockholders' equity before purchasing treasury stock shown in Exhibit 12-6.

Assume that on March 31, Smart Touch purchased 1,000 shares of treasury stock-common, paying $5 per share. To record the purchase, debit Treasury stock and credit Cash as follows:

Mar 31	Treasury stock (1,000 × $5) (CQ+)	5,000	
	Cash (A–)		5,000
	Purchased treasury stock.		

Treasury stock	
5,000	

Sale of Treasury Stock

Companies buy their treasury stock with a view toward reselling it. A company may sell treasury stock at, above, or below its cost.

Sale at Cost

If treasury stock is sold for cost—the same price the corporation paid for it—then there is no difference between cost and sale price to journalize. Let us assume Smart Touch sells 100 of the treasury shares on April 1 for $5 each. The entry follows:

Apr 1	Cash (A+) 100 shares × $5 mkt (A+)	500	
	Treasury stock (CE–) 100 shares × $5 cost (CQ–)		500

Sale Above Cost

If treasury stock is sold for more than cost, the difference is credited to a new account, Paid-in capital from treasury stock transactions. This excess is additional paid-in capital because it came from the company's stockholders. It has no effect on net income. Suppose Smart Touch resold 200 of its treasury shares for $6 per share on April 2 (recall that cost was $5). The entry to sell treasury stock for a price above cost is as follows:

Apr 2	Cash (A+) 200 shares × $6 mkt (A+)	1,200	
	Paid-in capital from treasury stock transactions (Q+)		200
	Treasury stock 200 shares × $5 cost (CQ–)		1,000

Paid-in capital from treasury stock transactions is reported with the other paid-in capital accounts on the balance sheet, beneath Common stock and Paid-in capital in excess of par.

Sale Below Cost

The resale price of treasury stock can be less than cost. The shortfall is debited first to Paid-in capital from treasury stock transactions. If this account's balance is too small, then debit Retained earnings for the remaining amount. To illustrate, let us assume Smart Touch Learning had two additional treasury stock sales. First, on April 3, Smart Touch sold 200 treasury shares for $4.30 each. The entry to record the sale is as follows:

Apr 3	Cash (A+) 200 shares × $4.30 mkt (A+)	860	
	Paid-in capital from treasury stock transactions (Q–)	140	
	Treasury stock 200 shares × $5 cost (CQ–)		1,000

The total loss on the sale of the treasury shares is $140. Smart Touch had previous gains of $200 from the April 2 sale of treasury stock, so there was enough Paid-in capital from treasury stock transactions to cover the loss.

Now what happens if Smart Touch sells an additional 200 treasury shares for $4.50 each on April 4?

Apr 4	Cash (A+) 200 shares × $4.50 mkt (A+)	900	
	Paid-in capital from treasury stock transactions (Q–)	60	
	Retained earnings (1,000 – 900 – 60) (Q–)	40	
	Treasury stock 200 shares × $5 cost (CQ–)		1,000

The total loss on the sale is $100 [($5 cost per share minus $4.50 sales price per share) × 200 shares]. Only $60 remains in the Paid-in capital from the treasury stock transactions account to absorb the loss. The remainder, 100 – 60 or $40 in loss, is debited to Retained earnings.

So, what is left in stockholders' equity for Smart Touch after the treasury stock transactions? First, let us post the treasury stock activity to the affected accounts:

Treasury stock

Mar 31	5,000		
		Apr 1	500
		Apr 2	1,000
		Apr 3	1,000
		Apr 4	1,000
	1,500		

Paid-in capital from treasury stock transactions

		Apr 2	200
Apr 3	140		
Apr 4	60		
			0

Retained earnings

			2,950,000
Apr 4	40		
			2,949,960

Now, we can show the revised stockholders' equity for Smart Touch as in Exhibit 12-8:

EXHIBIT 12-8 | **Smart Touch Learning, Inc.'s, Stockholders' Equity After Treasury Stock Transactions**

SMART TOUCH LEARNING, INC. Stockholders' Equity April 4, 2011	
Paid-in capital:	
Preferred stock, 6%, $50 par, 2,000 shares authorized, 2,000 shares issued	$ 100,000
Paid-in capital in excess of par—preferred	5,000
Common stock, $.50 par, 20,000,000 shares authorized, 6,300,000 shares issued	3,150,000
Paid-in capital in excess of par—common	23,900,000
Total paid-in capital	27,155,000
Retained earnings	2,949,960
Less: treasury stock at cost (300 shares @ $5)	(1,500)
Total stockholders' equity	$30,103,460

Retirement of Stock

Not all companies purchase their stock to hold it in the treasury. A corporation may retire its stock by canceling the stock certificates. Retired stock cannot be reissued.

Retirements of preferred stock are common as companies seek to avoid paying the preferred dividends. To purchase stock for retirement, debit the stock account—for example, Preferred stock—and credit Cash. That removes the retired stock from the company's books.

Restrictions on Retained Earnings

4 Report restrictions on retained earnings

Dividends and treasury stock purchases require a cash payment. These outlays leave fewer resources to pay liabilities. A bank may agree to loan $50,000 only if Smart Touch Learning maintains a minimum level of equity by limiting both its payment of dividends and its purchases of treasury stock.

Limits on Dividends and Treasury Stock Purchases

To ensure that a corporation maintains a minimum level of equity, lenders may restrict the amount of treasury stock a corporation may purchase. The restriction often focuses on the balance of retained earnings. Companies usually report their retained earnings restrictions in notes to the financial statements. The following disclosure by Smart Touch Learning is typical:

> **Note F—Long-Term Debt** The Smart Touch Learning Company's loan agreements with Bank X restrict cash dividends and treasury stock purchases. Under the most restrictive of these provisions, retained earnings of $1,000,000 were unrestricted at December 31, 2010.

With this restriction, the maximum dividend that Smart Touch can pay is $1,000,000.

Appropriations of Retained Earnings

Appropriations of Retained Earnings are Retained earnings restrictions recorded by formal journal entries. A corporation may *appropriate*—that is, segregate in a separate account—a portion of Retained earnings for a specific use. For example, the board of directors may appropriate part of Retained earnings for expansion. Appropriated Retained earnings can be reported as shown in the bottom box of Exhibit 12-9 for an example company.

EXHIBIT 12-9 **Formats for Reporting Stockholders' Equity—Example Company**

SAMPLE COMPANY A
Stockholders' Equity
December 31, 2009

Teaching Format		Real-World Format	
Stockholders' equity		Stockholders' equity	
Paid-in capital:			
Preferred stock, 8%, $10 par,		Preferred stock, 8%, $10 par,	
30,000 shares authorized and issued	$ 300,000	30,0000 shares authorized and issued	$ 300,000
Common stock, $1 par,		Common stock, $1 par,	
100,000 shares authorized,		100,000 shares authorized, 60,000 shares issued	60,000
60,000 shares issued	60,000	Additional paid-in capital	2,170,000
Paid-in capital in excess of par—common	2,150,000	Retained earnings (Note 7)	1,500,000
Paid-in capital from treasury stock transactions	20,000	Less: Treasury stock, common	
Total paid-in capital	2,530,000	(1,000 shares at cost)	(30,000)
Retained earnings appropriated		Total stockholders' equity	$4,000,000
for contingencies	500,000		
Retained earnings—unappropriated	1,000,000	*Note 7—Restriction on retained earnings.*	
Total retained earnings	1,500,000	At December 31, 2009, $500,000 of retained	
Subtotal	4,030,000	earnings is restricted for contingencies.	
Less: Treasury stock, common		Accordingly, dividends are limited to a	
(1,000 shares at cost)	(30,000)	maximum of $1,000,000.	
Total stockholders' equity	$4,000,000		

Variations in Reporting Stockholders' Equity

Companies can report their stockholders' equity in ways that differ from our examples. They assume that investors understand the details. One of the most important skills you will learn in this course is how to read the financial statements of real companies. In Exhibit 12-9, we present a side-by-side comparison of our teaching format and the format you are likely to encounter. Note the following points in the real-world format:

1. The heading Paid-in capital does not appear. It is commonly understood that Preferred stock, Common stock, and Additional paid-in capital are elements of paid-in capital.

2. For presentation in the financial statements, all additional paid-in capital accounts are combined and reported as a single amount labeled Additional paid-in capital. It follows Common stock in the real-world format.

Retained earnings appropriations are rare. Most companies report retained earnings restrictions in the notes to the financial statements, as shown for Smart Touch Learning on the previous page and in the real-world format of Exhibit 12-9.

Review the first half of the chapter by studying the Decision Guidelines.

Decision Guidelines

ACCOUNTING FOR DIVIDENDS, AND TREASURY STOCK

Retained earnings, dividends, and treasury stock can affect a corporation's equity. The Decision Guidelines will help you understand their effects.

Decision	Guidelines		
How to record:			
• Distribution of a small stock dividend (less than 20% to 25%)?	Retained earnings	Market value	
	Common stock		Par value
	Paid-in capital in excess of par		Excess
• Stock split?	Memorandum only: Split the common stock 2-for-1. Called in the outstanding $1 par common stock and distributed two shares of $.50 par for each old share outstanding.		

What are the effects of stock dividends and stock splits on	Effects of Stock	
	Dividend	**Split**
• Number of shares issued?	Increase	Increase
• Shares outstanding?	Increase	Increase
• Par value per share?	No effect	Decrease
• Total assets, total liabilities, and total equity?	No effect	No effect
• Common Stock?	Increase	No effect
• Retained Earnings?	Decrease	No effect

How to record:

Decision		Account	Debit	Credit
1. Purchase of treasury stock	1.	Treasury stock (CQ+)	Cost	
		Cash (A–)		Cost
2. Sale of treasury stock: at cost (Amount received = Cost)	2.	Cash (A+)	Amount Received	
		Treasury stock (CQ–)		Cost
3. Sale of stock: above cost	3.	Cash (A+)	Amount Received	
		Paid-in capital from treasury stock transactions (Q+)		Amount Received—Cost
		Treasury stock (CQ–)		Cost
4. Sale of treasury stock: below cost	4.	Cash (A+)	Amount Received	
		Paid-in capital from treasury stock transactions (Q+)	Up to Balance of Account	
		Retained earnings (Q–)	Excess	
		Treasury stock (CQ–)		Cost

What are the effects of the purchase and sale of treasury stock on	**Effects of Purchase**	**Effects of Sale**
• Total assets?	Decrease total assets by full amount of payment	Increase total assets by full amount of cash receipt
• Total stockholders' equity?	Decrease total equity by full amount of payment	Increase total equity by full amount of cash receipt

Summary Problem 1

Simplicity Graphics, creator of magazine designs, reported shareholders' equity as follows:

SIMPLICITY GRAPHICS Shareholders' Equity	
Preferred stock, $10.00 par value	
Authorized—10,000 shares; Issued—None	$ —
Common Stock, $1 par value	
Authorized 30,000 shares; Issued 15,000 shares	15,000
Capital in excess of par value	45,000
Retained earnings	90,000
Total paid-in capital	150,000
Less: Treasury stock, at cost (2,000 common shares)	(16,000)
Total stockholders' equity	$134,000

Requirements

1. What was the average issue price per share of the common stock?
2. Journalize the issuance of 1,000 shares of common stock at $4 per share. Use Simplicity's account titles.
3. How many shares of Simplicity's common stock are outstanding?
4. How many shares of common stock would be outstanding after Simplicity split its common stock 3 for 1?
5. Using Simplicity account titles, journalize the distribution of a 10% stock dividend when the market price of Simplicity common stock is $5 per share. Simplicity distributes the common stock dividend on the shares outstanding, which were computed in requirement 3.
6. Journalize the following treasury stock transactions, which occur in the order given:
   a. Simplicity purchases 500 shares of treasury stock at $8 per share.
   b. Simplicity sells 100 shares of treasury stock for $9 per share.
   c. Simplicity sells 200 shares of treasury stock for $6 per share.

Solution

1		Average issue price of common stock was \$4 per share [(15,000 + \$45,000)/15,000 shares] = \$4 per share		
2		Cash (1,000 × \$4) (A+)	4,000	
		Common stock (1,000 × \$1) (Q+)		1,000
		Paid-in capital in excess of par—common (Q+)		3,000
		Issued common stock.		
3		Shares outstanding = 14,000 (16,000 shares issued minus 2,000 shares of treasury stock)		
4		Shares outstanding after a 3-for-1 stock split = 48,000 (16,000 issued shares × 3)		
5		Retained earnings (14,000 × .10 × \$5) (Q–)	7,000	
		Common stock (14,000 × .10 × \$1) (Q+)		1,400
		Paid-in capital in excess of par—common (Q+)		5,600
		Distributed a 10% common stock dividend.		
6	a.	Treasury stock (500 × \$8) (CQ–)	4,000	
		Cash (A–)		4,000
		Purchased treasury stock.		
	b.	Cash (100 × \$9) (A+)	900	
		Treasury stock (100 × \$8)		800
		Paid-in capital from treasury stock transactions (Q+)		100
		Sold treasury stock.		
	c.	Cash (200 × \$6) (A+)	1,200	
		Paid-in capital from treasury stock transactions (Q–)	100	
		Retained earnings (Q–)	300	
		Treasury stock (200 × \$8) (CQ–)		1,600
		Sold treasury stock.		

The Corporate Income Statement

5 Complete a corporate income statement including earnings per share

The stockholders' equity of a corporation is more complex than the capital of a proprietorship or a partnership. Also, a corporation's income statement includes some unique items that do not often apply to a smaller business. Most of the income statements you will see belong to corporations. Why not proprietorships or partnerships? Because they are privately held; proprietorships and partnerships do not have to publish their financial statements. But public corporations do have to publish their financial statements, so we turn now to the corporate income statement.

Suppose you are considering investing in the stock of **IHOP**, **NIKE**, or **Intel**. You would examine these companies' income statements. Of particular interest is the amount of net income they can expect to earn year after year. To understand net income, let us examine Exhibit 12-10, the income statement of Greg's Groovy Tunes. New items are in color for emphasis.

EXHIBIT 12-10 **Income Statement in Multi-Step Format**

GREG'S GROOVY TUNES, INC.
Income Statement
Year Ended December 31, 2010

Continuing Operations	Net sales revenue	$500,000
	Cost of goods sold	240,000
	Gross profit	260,000
	Operating expenses (detailed)	181,000
	Operating income	79,000
	Other gains (losses):	
	Gain on sale of machinery	11,000
	Income from continuing operations before income tax	90,000
	Income tax expense	36,000
	Income from continuing operations	54,000
Special Items	Discontinued operations, income of $35,000, less income tax of $14,000	21,000
	Income before extraordinary item	75,000
	Extraordinary flood loss, $20,000, less income tax saving of $8,000	(12,000)
	Net income	$ 63,000
Earnings Per Share	Earnings per share of common stock (20,000 shares outstanding):	
	Income from continuing operations	$2.70
	Income from discontinued operations	1.05
	Income before extraordinary item	3.75
	Extraordinary loss	(0.60)
	Net income	$3.15

Continuing Operations

In Exhibit 12-10, the topmost section reports continuing operations. This part of the business should continue from period to period. Income from continuing operations, therefore, helps investors make predictions about future earnings. We may use

EXHIBIT 13-1 | Timing of the Financial Statements

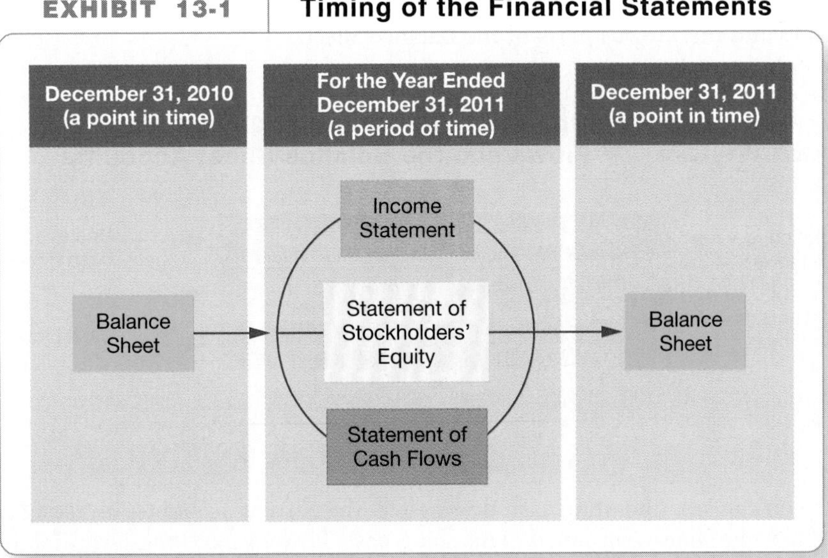

Operating, Investing, and Financing Activities

2 Distinguish among operating, investing, and financing cash flows

There are three basic types of cash-flow activities and the Statement of Cash Flows has a section for each:

- Operating activities
- Investing activities
- Financing activities

Let us see what each section reports.

Operating Activities

- Is the most important category of cash flows because it reflects the day-to-day operations that determine the future of an organization
- Create revenues, expenses, gains, and losses
- Affect net income on the Income Statement
- Affect current assets and current liabilities on the Balance Sheet

Investing Activities

- Increase and decrease long-term assets, such as computers, software, land, buildings, and equipment
- Include purchases and sales of these assets, plus loans receivable from others and collections of those loans

Financing Activities

- Increase and decrease long-term liabilities and equity
- Include issuing stock, paying dividends, and buying and selling treasury stock
- Include borrowing money and paying off loans

Exhibit 13-2 shows the relationship between operating, investing, and financing cash flows and the various parts of the Balance Sheet.

EXHIBIT 13-2 **Operating, Investing, and Financing Cash Flows and the Balance-Sheet Accounts**

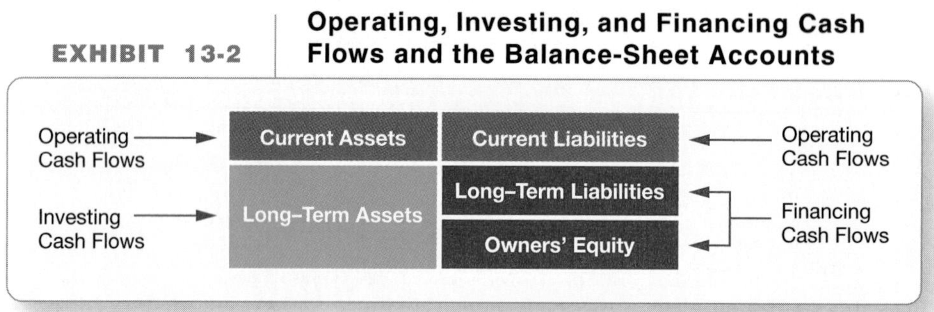

As you can see, operating cash flows affect the current accounts. Investing cash flows affect the long-term assets. Financing cash flows affect long-term liabilities and equity.

Two Formats for Operating Activities

There are two ways to format operating activities on the Statement of Cash Flows:

- The **indirect method** starts with net income and adjusts it to net cash provided by operating activities.
- The **direct method** restates the Income Statement in terms of cash. The direct method shows all the cash receipts and all the cash payments from operating activities.

The indirect and direct methods:

- use different computations but produce the same amount of cash flow from operations.
- have no effect on investing activities or financing activities.

Let us begin with the indirect method because most companies use it. To focus on the direct method, go to Appendix 13A.

Preparing the Statement of Cash Flows by the Indirect Method

3 Prepare the Statement of Cash Flows by the indirect method

To prepare the Statement of Cash Flows, you need the Income Statement and both the beginning and the ending Balance Sheets. Consider Smart Touch Learning's financial statements on page 715. To prepare the Statement of Cash Flows by the indirect method follow Steps 1–4:

STEP 1: Lay out the statement format as shown in Exhibit 13-3. Steps 2–4 will complete the Statement of Cash Flows.

EXHIBIT 13-3 | **Format of the Statement of Cash Flows: Indirect Method**

SMART TOUCH LEARNING, INC. Statement of Cash Flows Year Ended December 31, 2011		
Cash flows from operating activities:		
Net income		
Adjustments to reconcile net income to net cash provided by operating activities:		
+ Depreciation / amortization expense		
+ Loss on sale of long-term assets		
– Gain on sale of long-term assets		
– Increases in current assets other than cash		
+ Decreases in current assets other than cash		
+ Increases in current liabilities		
– Decreases in current liabilities		
Net cash provided by operating activities		
± Cash flows from investing activities:		
+ Cash receipts from sales of long-term assets (investments, land, building, equipment, and so on)		
– Purchases of long-term assets		
Net cash provided by (used for) investing activities		
± Cash flows from financing activities:		
+ Cash receipts from issuance of stock		
+ Sale of treasury stock		
– Purchase of treasury stock		
+ Cash receipts from issuance of notes or bonds payable (borrowing)		
– Payment of notes or bonds payable		
– Payment of dividends		
Net cash provided by (used for) financing activities		
= Net increase (decrease) in cash during the year		
+ Cash at December 31, 2010		
= Cash at December 31, 2011		

STEP 2: Compute the change in cash from the comparative Balance Sheet. The change in cash is the "key reconciling figure" for the Statement of Cash Flows. Exhibit 13-8 is the comparative Balance Sheet of Smart Touch Learning, where the top line shows that cash decreased by $20,000 during 2011.

STEP 3: Take net income, depreciation, and any gains or losses from the Income Statement. Exhibit 13-9 gives the 2011 Income Statement of Smart Touch Learning, with the relevant items highlighted.

STEP 4: Complete the Statement of Cash Flows, using data from the Income Statement and the Balance Sheet. The statement is complete only after you have explained all the year-to-year changes in all the accounts on the Balance Sheet.

Let us apply these steps to show the operating activities of Smart Touch Learning. Exhibit 13-4 gives the operating activities section of the Statement of Cash Flows. All items are highlighted for emphasis. That makes it easy to trace the data from one statement to the other.

EXHIBIT 13-4 | Operating Activities

	SMART TOUCH LEARNING, INC. Statement of Cash Flows Year Ended December 31, 2011		
	Cash flows from operating activities:		*(Thousands)*
A	Net income		$ 40
	Adjustments to reconcile net income to net cash provided by operating activities:		
B	Depreciation	$ 20	
C	Gain on sale of plant assets	(10)	
D	Increase in accounts receivable	(17)	
D	Decrease in inventory	2	
D	Increase in accounts payable	40	
D	Decrease in accrued liabilities	(5)	30
	Net cash provided by operating activities		70

Cash Flows from Operating Activities

Operating cash flows begin with net income, taken from the Income Statement.

A Net Income

The Statement of Cash Flows—indirect method—begins with net income because revenues and expenses, which affect net income, produce cash receipts and cash payments. Revenues bring in cash receipts, and expenses must be paid. But net income is accrual based and the cash flows (cash basis net income) do not always equal the accrual basis revenues and expenses. For example, sales *on account* are revenues that increase net income, but the company has not yet collected cash from those sales. Accrued expenses decrease your net income, but you have not paid cash *if the expenses are accrued*.

To go from net income to cash flow from operations, we must make some adjustments to net income on the Statement of Cash Flows. These additions and subtractions follow net income and are labeled *Adjustments to reconcile net income to net cash provided by operating activities*.

this information to predict that Greg's Groovy Tunes, Inc., will earn approximately $54,000 next year.

The continuing operations of Greg's Groovy Tunes include two items that need explanation:

- Greg's Groovy Tunes had a gain on the sale of machinery, which is outside the company's core business of selling music products. This is why the gain is reported in the "other" category—separately from Greg's sales revenue, cost of goods sold, and gross profit.
- Income tax expense ($36,000) is subtracted to arrive at income from continuing operations. Greg's Groovy Tunes' income tax rate is 40% ($90,000 × 0.40 = $36,000).

Special Items

After continuing operations, an income statement may include two distinctly different gains and losses:

- Discontinued operations
- Extraordinary gains and losses

Discontinued Operations

Most corporations engage in several lines of business. For example, **IHOP** is best known for its restaurants. But at one time **IHOP** owned **Golden Oaks Retirement Homes, United Rent-Alls**, and even a business college. **General Motors** is best known for its automobiles, but it also has a financing company (**GMAC**) and insurance foreign subsidiary company (**GMLAAM** and **GMAP**).

Each identifiable division of a company is called a **segment of the business. GMAC** is the financing segment of **General Motors.** A company may sell a segment of its business. For example, **IHOP** sold its retirement homes, **United Rent-Alls**, and its business college. These were discontinued operations for **IHOP.**

Financial analysts are always keeping tabs on companies they follow. They predict companies' net income, and most analysts do not include discontinued operations because the discontinued segments will not be around in the future. The income statement reports information on the segments that have been sold under the heading Discontinued operations. In our example, income from discontinued operations ($35,000) is taxed at 40% and is reported as shown in Exhibit 12-10. A loss on discontinued operations is reported similarly, but with a subtraction for the income tax *savings* on the loss (the tax savings reduces the loss).

Gains and losses on the sale of plant assets are *not* reported as discontinued operations. Instead, they are reported as "Other gains (losses)" up among continuing operations, because companies dispose of old plant assets and equipment all the time.

Extraordinary Gains and Losses (Extraordinary Items)

Extraordinary gains and losses, also called **extraordinary items**, are both unusual and infrequent. Losses from natural disasters (floods, earthquakes, and tornadoes) and the taking of company assets by a foreign government (expropriation) are extraordinary items. They are reported separate from normal operations because of their infrequent nature.

Extraordinary items are reported along with their income tax effect. During 2010, Greg's Groovy Tunes lost $20,000 of inventory in a flood. This flood loss reduced both Greg's Groovy Tunes' income and its income tax. The tax effect decreases the net amount of Greg's Groovy Tunes' loss the same way income tax reduces net income. An extraordinary loss can be reported along with its tax effect, as follows:

Extraordinary flood loss....................................	$(20,000)
Less: Income tax saving....................................	8,000
Extraordinary flood loss, net of tax....................	$(12,000)

Trace this item to the income statement in Exhibit 12-10. An extraordinary gain is reported the same as a loss—net of the income tax effect.

The following items do *not* qualify as extraordinary:

- Gains and losses on the sale of plant assets
- Losses due to lawsuits
- Losses due to employee labor strikes

These gains and losses fall outside the business's central operations, so they are reported on the income statement as other gains and losses. One example for Greg's Groovy Tunes is the gain on sale of machinery reported up in the Other gains (losses) section of Exhibit 12-10.

Earnings per Share

The final segment of a corporate income statement reports the company's earnings per share, abbreviated as EPS. EPS is the most widely used of all business statistics. **Earnings per share (EPS)** reports the amount of net income for each share of the company's *outstanding common stock*. Recall that,

Outstanding stock = Issued stock – Treasury stock

For example, Greg's Groovy Tunes has issued 25,000 shares of its common stock and holds 5,000 shares as treasury stock. Greg's Groovy Tunes, therefore, has 20,000 shares of common stock outstanding, and so we use 20,000 shares to compute EPS.

EPS is a key measure of success in business. EPS is computed as follows:

$$\text{Earnings per share} = \frac{\text{Net income} - \text{Preferred dividends}}{\text{Average number of common shares outstanding}}$$

Corporations report a separate EPS figure for each element of income. Greg's Groovy Tunes' EPS calculations follow:

Earnings per share of common stock (no preferred stock)	
(20,000 shares outstanding):	
Income from continuing operations ($54,000/20,000)..................	$ 2.70
Income from discontinued operations ($21,000/20,000)	1.05
Income before extraordinary item ($75,000/20,000)	3.75
Extraordinary loss ($12,000/20,000)..	(0.60)
Net income ($63,000/20,000)	$ 3.15

The final section of Exhibit 12-10 reports the EPS figures for Greg's Groovy Tunes.

Effect of Preferred Dividends on Earnings per Share

Preferred dividends also affect EPS. Remember that EPS is earnings per share of *common* stock. Remember also that dividends on preferred stock are paid first. Therefore, preferred dividends must be subtracted from income to compute EPS.

Suppose Greg's Groovy Tunes had 10,000 shares of preferred stock outstanding, each share paying a $1.00 dividend. The annual preferred dividend would be $10,000 (10,000 shares × $1.00). The $10,000 is subtracted from each of the income subtotals (lines 1, 3, and 5), resulting in the following EPS computations for Greg's Groovy Tunes:

	Earnings per share of common stock (20,000 common shares outstanding & 10,000 preferred shares outstanding):	
1	Income from continuing operations ($54,000 – $10,000)/20,000.....	$ 2.20
2	Income from discontinued operations ($21,000/20,000)	1.05
3	Income before extraordinary item ($75,000 – $10,000)/20,000	3.25
4	Extraordinary loss ($12,000/20,000)...	(0.60)
5	Net income ($63,000 – $10,000)/20,000..	$ 2.65

Basic and Diluted Earnings per Share

Some corporations must report two sets of EPS figures, as follows:

- EPS based on outstanding common shares (*basic* EPS).
- EPS based on outstanding common shares plus the additional shares of common stock that would arise if convertible preferred stock (or other dilutive items) were exchanged for common shares (*diluted* EPS). Diluted EPS is always lower than basic EPS.

Statement of Retained Earnings

The statement of retained earnings reports how the company moved from its beginning balance of Retained earnings to its ending balance during the period. This statement is not altogether new.

Exhibit 12-11 shows the statement of retained earnings of Greg's Groovy Tunes for 2010.

EXHIBIT 12-11 | Statement of Retained Earnings

GREG'S GROOVY TUNES, INC. **Statement of Retained Earnings** Year Ended December 31, 2010	
Retained earnings, December 31, 2009	$130,000
Add: Net income for 2010	63,000
	193,000
Less: Dividends for 2010	(53,000)
Retained earnings, December 31, 2010	$140,000

Corporate dividends appear where withdrawals would appear if we were talking about sole proprietorships or partnerships. Greg's Groovy Tunes' net income comes from the income statement in Exhibit 12-10. All other data are assumed.

Combined Statement of Income and Retained Earnings

Companies can report income and retained earnings on a single statement. Exhibit 12-12 illustrates how Greg's Groovy Tunes would combine its income statement and its statement of retained earnings.

EXHIBIT 12-12 | Combined Statement of Income and Retained Earnings

GREG'S GROOVY TUNES, INC.
Combined Statement of Income and Retained Earnings
Year Ended December 31, 2010

Income Statement	Sales revenue	$500,000
	Cost of goods sold	240,000
	Gross profit	260,000
	Expenses (listed individually)	197,000
Statement of retained earnings	Net income for 2010	$ 63,000
	Retained earnings, December 31, 2009	130,000
		193,000
	Dividends for 2010	(53,000)
	Retained earnings, December 31, 2010	$140,000

Prior-Period Adjustments

A company may make an accounting error. After the books are closed, Retained earnings holds the error, and its balance is wrong until corrected. Corrections to Retained earnings for errors of an earlier period are called **prior-period adjustments.** The prior-period adjustment either increases or decreases the beginning balance of Retained earnings and appears on that statement.

In recent years there have been more prior-period adjustments than in the 20 previous years combined. Many companies have restated their net income to correct accounting errors. To illustrate, assume Greg's Groovy Tunes recorded $30,000 of income tax expense for 2009. The correct amount of income tax was $40,000. This error

- understated income tax expense by $10,000, and
- overstated net income by $10,000.

In 2010 Greg's paid the extra $10,000 in taxes for the prior year. Greg's prior-period adjustment decreased Retained earnings as shown in Exhibit 12-13 (all amounts are assumed):

EXHIBIT 12-13 | Error Correction

GREG'S GROOVY TUNES, INC. Statement of Retained Earnings Year Ended December 31, 2010	
Retained earnings, December 31, 2009, as originally reported	$140,000
Prior-period adjustment—To correct error in 2009	(10,000)
Retained earnings, December 31, 2009, as adjusted	130,000
Net income for 2010	63,000
	193,000
Dividends for 2010	(53,000)
Retained earnings, December 31, 2010	$140,000

Reporting Comprehensive Income

As we have seen, all companies report net income or net loss on the income statement. However, there is another income figure. **Comprehensive income** is the company's change in total stockholders' equity from all sources other than its owners. Comprehensive income includes net income plus some specific gains and losses, as follows:

- Unrealized gains or losses on certain investments
- Foreign-currency translation adjustments

These items do not enter into the determination of net income but instead are reported as other comprehensive income. Let us assume, for example, that Greg's had unrealized gains of $1,000 from investments in 2010. Comprehensive income for 2010 for Greg's would be as shown in Exhibit 12-14.

EXHIBIT 12-14 | Reporting Comprehensive Income

GREG'S GROOVY TUNES, INC. Statement of Income and Comprehensive Income Year Ended December 31, 2010	
Revenues	$500,000
Expenses (summarized)	437,000
Net income	63,000
Other comprehensive income:	
Unrealized gain on investments	1,000
Comprehensive income	$ 64,000

Earnings per share apply only to net income and its components, as discussed earlier. Earnings per share are *not* reported for other comprehensive income.

Decision Guidelines

ANALYZING A CORPORATE INCOME STATEMENT

Three years out of college, you have saved $5,000 and are ready to start investing. Where do you start? You might begin by analyzing the income statements of **IHOP**, **NIKE**, and **Intel**. These Decision Guidelines will help you analyze a corporate income statement.

Decision	Guidelines	
• What are the main sections of the income statement? See Exhibit 12-10 for an example.	Continuing operations	• Continuing operations, including other gains and losses and less income tax expense
	Special items	• Discontinued operations—gain or loss—less the income tax effect • Extraordinary gain or loss, less the income tax effect • Net income (or net loss) • Other comprehensive income (Exhibit 12-14)
• What earnings-per-share (EPS) figures must a corporation report?	Earnings per share	• Earnings per share—applies only to net income (or net loss), not to other comprehensive income
	Separate EPS figures for:	• Income from continuing operations • Discontinued operations • Income before extraordinary item • Extraordinary gain or loss • Net income (or net loss)
• How to compute EPS for net income?	$\text{EPS} = \dfrac{\text{Net income} - \text{Preferred dividends}}{\text{Average number of common shares outstanding}}$	

Summary Problem 2

The following information was taken from the ledger of Calenergy Corporation at December 31, 2011.

Common stock, no-par, 45,000 shares issued	$180,000	Discontinued operations, income	$20,000
Sales revenue	620,000	Prior-period adjustment—credit to Retained Earnings	5,000
Extraordinary gain	26,000	Gain on sale of plant assets	21,000
Loss due to lawsuit	11,000	Income tax expense (saving):	
General expenses	62,000	Continuing operations	32,000
Preferred stock 8%	50,000	Discontinued operations	8,000
Selling expenses	108,000	Extraordinary gain	10,000
Retained earnings, beginning, as originally reported	103,000	Treasury stock, common (5,000 shares)	25,000
Dividends	14,000		
Cost of goods sold	380,000		

Requirement

1. Prepare a single-step income statement and a statement of retained earnings for Calenergy Corporation for the year ended December 31, 2011. Include the EPS presentation and show your computations. Calenergy had no changes in its stock accounts during the year.

Solution

CALENERGY CORPORATION Income Statement Year Ended December 31, 2011		
Revenue and gains:		
Sales revenue		$620,000
Gain on sale of plant assets		21,000
Total revenues and gains		641,000
Expenses and losses:		
Cost of goods sold	$380,000	
Selling expenses	108,000	
General expenses	62,000	
Loss due to lawsuit	11,000	
Income tax expense	32,000	
Total expenses and losses		593,000
Income from continuing operations		48,000
Discontinued operations, income of $20,000, less income tax of $8,000		12,000
Income before extraordinary item		60,000
Extraordinary gain, $26,000, less income tax, $10,000		16,000
Net income		$ 76,000
Earnings per share:		
Income from continuing operations [($48,000 – $4,000) / 40,000 shares]		$1.10
Income from discontinued operations ($12,000 / $40,000 shares)		0.30
Income before extraordinary item [($60,000 – $4,000) / 40,000 shares]		1.40
Extraordinary gain ($16,000 / 40,000 shares)		0.40
Net income [($76,000 – $4,000) / 40,000 shares]		$1.80

$$\text{EPS} = \frac{\text{Income} - \text{Preferred dividends}}{\text{Average common shares outstanding}}$$

CALENERGY CORPORATION Statement of Retained Earnings Year Ended December 31, 2011	
Retained earnings balance, beginning, as originally reported	$103,000
Prior-period adjustment—credit	5,000
Retained earnings balance, beginning, as adjusted	108,000
Net income	76,000
	184,000
Dividends	(14,000)
Retained earnings balance, ending	$170,000

Review Corporations: Effects on Retained Earnings and the Income Statement

Accounting Vocabulary

Appropriation of Retained Earnings (p. 679)
Restriction of a portion of retained earnings that is recorded by a formal journal entry.

Comprehensive Income (p. 689)
Company's change in total stockholders' equity from all sources other than the owners.

Earnings per Share (EPS) (p. 686)
Amount of a company's net income for each share of its outstanding stock.

Extraordinary Gains and Losses (p. 685)
A gain or loss that is both unusual for the company and infrequent. Also called **extraordinary items**.

Extraordinary Item (p. 685)
A gain or loss that is both unusual for the company and infrequent. Also called **extraordinary gain and loss**.

Large Stock Dividend (p. 671)
A stock dividend of 25% or more of the issued stock.

Memorandum Entry (p. 674)
A journal entry that "notes" a significant event, but has no debit or credit amount.

Prior-Period Adjustment (p. 688)
A correction to retained earnings for an error of an earlier period.

Segment of the Business (p. 685)
One of various separate divisions of a company.

Small Stock Dividend (p. 671)
A stock dividend of less than 20–25% of the issued stock.

Stock Dividend (p. 670)
A distribution by a corporation of its own stock to its shareholders.

Stock Split (p. 673)
An increase in the number of outstanding shares of stock coupled with a proportionate reduction in the value of the stock.

Treasury Stock (p. 675)
A corporation's own stock that it has issued and later reacquired.

Quick Check

1. A stock dividend
   a. increases Retained earnings.
   b. decreases Common stock.
   c. has no effect on total equity.
   d. All of the above
2. In a small stock dividend,
   a. Retained earnings is debited for the market value of the shares issued.
   b. Net income is always decreased.
   c. Paid-in capital in excess of par is debited for the difference between the debits to Retained earnings and to Common stock.
   d. Common stock is debited for the par value of the shares issued.
3. Stock splits
   a. decrease par value per share.
   b. increase the number of shares of stock issued.
   c. Both a and b
   d. None of the above
4. A company's own stock that it has issued and repurchased is called
   a. outstanding stock.
   b. issued stock.
   c. treasury stock.
   d. dividend stock.

5. Assume that a company paid $10 per share to purchase 1,000 of its $1 par common as treasury stock. The purchase of treasury stock
   a. increased total equity by $10,000.
   b. decreased total equity by $1,000.
   c. decreased total equity by $10,000.
   d. increased total equity by $1,000.
6. Assume that the bank requires XO, Co., to maintain at least $100,000 in Retained earnings. The $100,000 would be shown as
   a. a long-term liability.
   b. a restriction to Retained earnings.
   c. a current liability.
   d. a ratio of the $100,000 restriction divided by total Retained earnings.
7. Greg's Groovy Tunes in Exhibit 12-10 is most likely to earn net income of $x next year. How much is $x?
   a. $90,000
   b. $54,000
   c. $63,000
   d. $79,000
8. Which of the following events would be an extraordinary loss?
   a. Loss on discontinued operations
   b. Loss due to an earthquake
   c. Loss on the sale of equipment
   d. All of the above are extraordinary items.
9. What is the most widely followed statistic in business?
   a. Earnings per share
   b. Dividends
   c. Gross profit
   d. Retained earnings
10. Earnings per share is *not* computed for
   a. Extraordinary items.
   b. Comprehensive income.
   c. Discontinued operations.
   d. Net income.

Answers are given after Apply Your Knowledge (p. 708).

Assess Your Progress

■ Short Exercises

S12-1 *(L.OBJ. 1)* **Recording a small stock dividend [5–10 min]**
Waveside Pool Supply has 16,000 shares of $3 par common stock outstanding. Waveside distributes a 10% stock dividend when the market value of its stock is $15 per share.

Requirements

1. Journalize Waveside's distribution of the stock dividend on July 31. An explanation is not required.
2. What is the overall effect of the stock dividend on Waveside's total assets?
3. What is the overall effect on total stockholders' equity?

S12-2 *(L.OBJ. 1)* **Comparing and contrasting cash and stock dividends [5–10 min]**
Compare and contrast the accounting for cash dividends and stock dividends.

Requirement

1. In the space provided, insert either "Cash dividends," "Stock dividends," or "Both cash dividends and stock dividends" to complete each of the following statements:
   a. ______________ decrease Retained earnings.
   b. ______________ has(have) no effect on a liability.
   c. ______________ increase paid-in capital by the same amount that they decrease Retained earnings.
   d. ______________ decrease both total assets and total stockholders' equity, resulting in a decrease in the size of the company.

S12-3 *(L.OBJ. 2)* **Accounting for a stock split [5–10 min]**
Décor City Imports recently reported the following stockholders' equity (adapted and in millions except par value per share):

Paid in capital:	
Common stock, $1 par, 450 shares authorized, 104 shares issued	$ 104
Paid–in capital in excess of par	153
Total paid–in capital	257
Retained earnings	653
Other equity	(227)
Total stockholders' equity	$ 683

Suppose Décor City split its common stock 2 for 1 in order to decrease the market price of its stock. The company's stock was trading at $17 immediately before the split.

Requirements

1. Prepare the stockholders' equity section of Décor City Imports' balance sheet after the stock split.
2. Were the account balances changed or unchanged after the stock split?

S12-4 *(L.OBJ. 3)* **Accounting for the purchase and sale of treasury stock [10 min]**
Bargain Central Furniture, Inc., completed the following treasury stock transactions:

a. Purchased 1,300 shares of the company's $1 par common stock as treasury stock, paying cash of $6 per share
b. Sold 700 shares of the treasury stock for cash of $9 per share

Requirements

1. Journalize these transactions. Explanations are not required.
2. Show how Bargain Central will report treasury stock on its December 31, 2010 balance sheet after completing the two transactions. In reporting the treasury stock, report only on the Treasury Stock account. You may ignore all other accounts.

S12-5 *(L.OBJ. 4)* **Interpreting a restriction on retained earnings [5 min]**
AD Corporation reported the following stockholders' equity:

Paid–in capital:	
Preferred stock, $1.50, no par, 13,000 shares authorized; none issued, 0	
Common stock, $1 par, 486,000 shares authorized, 146,000 shares issued	$146,000
Paid–in capital in excess of par—common	346,000
Total paid–in capital	492,000
Retained earnings	505,000
Less: Treasury stock, 5,000 shares at cost	(40,000)
Total stockholders' equity	$957,000

Requirements

1. AD Corporation's agreement with its bank lender restricts AD's dividend payments for the cost of treasury stock the company holds. How much in dividends can AD declare?
2. Why would a bank lender restrict a corporation's dividend payments and treasury stock purchases?

S12-6 *(L.OBJ. 5)* **Preparing a corporate income statement [5–10 min]**
Consider the simple income statement learned in Chapter 1 and the more complex income statement discussed in this chapter.

Requirement

1. List the major parts of a complex corporate income statement for WRS Athletic Clubs, Inc., for the year ended December 31, 2011. Include all the major parts of the income statement, starting with net sales revenue and ending with net income (net loss). You may ignore dollar amounts and earnings per share.

S12-7 *(L.OBJ. 5)* **Explaining the items on a corporate income statement [10 min]**
Consider a corporate income statement.

Requirements

1. How do you measure gross profit?
2. What is the title of those items that are both unusual and infrequent?
3. Which income number is the best predictor of future net income?
4. What is the "bottom line"?
5. What does *EPS* abbreviate?

S12-8 *(L.OBJ. 5)* **Preparing a corporate income statement [10–15 min]**
OLP Corporation's accounting records include the following items, listed in no particular order, at December 31, 2012:

Other gains (losses)	$ (15,000)	Extraordinary loss	$ 5,000
Net sales revenue	176,000	Cost of goods sold	74,000
Gain on discontinued operations	10,000	Operating expenses	58,000
Accounts receivable	20,000		

Income tax of 40% applies to all items.

Requirement

1. Prepare OLP 's income statement for the year ended December 31, 2012. Omit earnings per share.

Note: Short Exercise 12-9 should be used only after completing Short Exercise 12-8.

S12-9 *(L.OBJ. 5)* **Reporting earnings per share [10–15 min]**
Return to the OLP data in Short Exercise 12-8. OLP had 10,000 shares of common stock outstanding during 2012. OLP declared and paid preferred dividends of $1,000 during 2012.

Requirement

1. Show how OLP reported EPS data on its 2012 income statement.

S12-10 *(L.OBJ. 5)* **Interpreting earnings per share data [10 min]**
Wells-Carolina, Inc., has preferred stock outstanding.

Requirements

1. Give the basic equation to compute earnings per share of common stock for net income.
2. List all the income items for which Wells-Carolina must report EPS data.

Note: Short Exercise 12-11 should be used only after completing Short Exercise 12-8.

S12-11 *(L.OBJ. 5)* **Reporting comprehensive income [5–10 min]**
Use the OLP data in Short Exercise 12-8. In addition, OLP had unrealized gains of $4,500 on investments during 2012.

Requirements

1. Start with OLP's net income from Short Exercise 12-8 and show how the company could report other comprehensive income on its 2012 income statement.
2. Should OLP report earnings per share for other comprehensive income?

S12-12 *(L.OBJ. 5)* **Reporting a prior-period adjustment [10 min]**
Real Statistical Research, Inc., (RSRI) ended 2010 with retained earnings of $72,000. During 2011 RSRI earned net income of $85,000 and declared dividends of $25,000. Also during 2011, RSRI got a $22,000 tax refund from the Internal Revenue Service. A tax audit revealed that RSRI paid too much income tax back in 2009.

Requirement

1. Prepare Real Statistical Research's statement of retained earnings for the year ended December 31, 2011, to report the prior-period adjustment.

Exercises

E12-13 *(L.OBJ. 1)* **Journalizing a stock dividend and reporting stockholders equity [10–15 min]**
The stockholders' equity of Seabury Occupational Therapy, Inc., on December 31, 2009, follows:

STOCKHOLDERS' EQUITY	
Paid–in capital:	
Common stock, $1 par, 1,000 shares authorized,	
450 issued	$ 450
Paid–in capital in excess of par—common	1,800
Total paid in capital	2,250
Retained earnings	128,000
Total stockholders' equity	$ 130,250

On April 30, 2010, the market price of Seabury's common stock was $17 per share and the company distributed a 10% stock dividend.

Requirements

1. Journalize the distribution of the stock dividend.
2. Prepare the stockholders' equity section of the balance sheet after the stock dividend.

E12-14 *(L.OBJ. 1)* **Journalizing cash and stock dividends [10–15 min]**
Pottery Schools, Inc., is authorized to issue 100,000 shares of $1 par common stock. The company issued 71,000 shares at $5 per share. When the market price of common stock was $7 per share, Pottery distributed a 10% stock dividend. Later, Pottery declared and paid a $0.20 per share cash dividend.

Requirements

1. Journalize the distribution of the stock dividend.
2. Journalize both the declaration and the payment of the cash dividend.

E12-15 *(L.OBJ. 1, 2, 3)* **Effect of stock dividends, stock splits, and treasury stock transactions [10–15 min]**
Many types of transactions may affect stockholders' equity.

Requirement

1. Identify the effects of the following transactions on total stockholders' equity. Each transaction is independent.

   a. A 10% stock dividend. Before the dividend, 560,000 shares of $1 par common stock were outstanding; market value was $8 at the time of the dividend.
   b. A 2-for-1 stock split. Prior to the split, 64,000 shares of $1 par common stock were outstanding.
   c. Purchase of 1,300 shares of treasury stock (par value at $0.50) at $4 per share.
   d. Sale of 300 shares of $.50 par treasury stock for $9 per share. Cost of the treasury stock was $4 per share.

E12-16 *(L.OBJ. 2)* **Reporting stockholders' equity after a stock split [10–15 min]**
Rattler Golf Club, Corp., had the following stockholders' equity at December 31, 2011:

STOCKHOLDERS' EQUITY	
Paid–in capital:	
Common stock, $2.00 par, 450 shares authorized, 270 issued	$ 540
Paid–in capital in excess of par—common	1,080
Total paid in capital	1,620
Retained earnings	2,300
Total stockholders' equity	$ 3,920

On June 30, 2012, Rattler split its common stock 2 for 1.

Requirements

1. Make the memorandum entry to record the stock split.
2. Prepare the stockholders' equity section of the balance sheet immediately after the split.

E12-17 *(L.OBJ. 3)* **Journalizing treasury stock transactions [10–15 min]**
Treasury stock transactions for Mr. Magoo Driving School, Inc., follow:

Feb 4	Issued 27,000 shares of $1 par common stock at $12 per share
Apr 22	Purchased 800 shares of treasury stock at $16 per share
Aug 22	Sold 200 shares of treasury stock at $18 per share

Requirement

1. Journalize the transactions.

E12-18 *(L.OBJ. 3)* **Journalizing treasury stock transactions and reporting stockholders' equity [10–15 min]**

Frontier Amusements Corporation had the following stockholders' equity on November 30:

STOCKHOLDERS' EQUITY	
Paid–in capital:	
Common stock, $5 par, 1,000 shares authorized,	
875 shares issued	$ 4,375
Paid–in capital in excess of par—common	13,125
Total paid in capital	17,500
Retained earnings	54,000
Total stockholders' equity	$ 71,500

On December 30, Frontier purchased 125 shares of treasury stock at $12 per share.

Requirements

1. Journalize the purchase of the treasury stock.
2. Prepare the stockholders' equity section of the balance sheet at December 31.
3. How many shares of common stock are outstanding after the purchase of treasury stock?

E12-19 *(L.OBJ. 4)* **Reporting a retained earnings restriction [10–15 min]**

The agreement under which Perfecto Printers issued its long-term debt requires the restriction of $200,000 of the company's retained earnings balance. Total retained earnings is $570,000, and common stock, no-par, has a balance of $30,000.

Requirement

1. Report stockholders' equity on Perfecto's balance sheet, assuming the following:
   a. Perfecto discloses the restriction in a note. Write the note.
   b. Perfecto appropriates retained earnings in the amount of the restriction and includes no note in its statements.

E12-20 *(L.OBJ. 5)* **Preparing a multi-step income statement [10–15 min]**

Zoom Photographic Supplies, Inc., accounting records include the following for 2012:

Income tax saving – extraordinary loss	$ 4,400	Sales revenue	$ 430,000
Income tax saving – loss		Operating expenses	
on discontinued operations	16,000	(including income taxes)	120,000
Extraordinary loss	11,000	Cost of goods sold	220,000
		Loss on discontinued operations	40,000

Requirement

1. Prepare Zoom's multistep income statement for 2012. Omit earnings per share.

E12-21 *(L.OBJ. 5)* **Computing EPS [5–10 min]**

Submarine, Corp., earned net income of $110,000 for 2011. Submarine's books include the following figures:

Preferred stock, 2%, $30 par, 1,000 shares issued	
and outstanding	$ 30,000
Common stock, $1 par, 52,000 issued	52,000
Paid–in capital in excess of par—common	450,000
Treasury stock, common, 2,000 at cost	40,000

Requirement

1. Compute Submarine's EPS for the year.

E12-22 *(L.OBJ. 5)* **Computing EPS [10–15 min]**
Prep Academy Surplus had 50,000 shares of common stock and 9,000 shares of 4%, $5 par preferred stock outstanding through December 31, 2010. Income from continuing operations of 2010 was $120,000, and loss on discontinued operations (net of income tax saving) was $8,000. Prep also had an extraordinary gain (net of tax) of $19,000.

Requirement

1. Compute Prep's EPS amounts for 2010, starting with income from continuing operations.

E12-23 *(L.OBJ. 5)* **Preparing a combined statement of income and retained earnings [10 min]**
Golden Times Express Company had retained earnings of $160 million at December 31, 2010. The company reported these figures for 2011:

		($ Millions)
Net income	$	130
Cash dividends – preferred		1
common		91

Requirement

1. Beginning with net income, prepare a combined income statement and retained earnings for Golden Times Express Company for the year ended December 31, 2011.

E12-24 *(L.OBJ. 5)* **Preparing a statement of retained earnings [10 min]**
Rachel Lou Bakery, Inc., reported a prior-period adjustment in 2010. An accounting error caused net income of prior years to be overstated by $2,000. Retained earnings at December 31, 2009, as previously reported, stood at $46,000. Net income for 2010 was $76,000, and dividends were $25,000.

Requirement

1. Prepare the company's statement of retained earnings for the year ended December 31, 2010.

E12-25 *(L.OBJ. 5)* **Preparing a combined statement of income and retained earnings [10 min]**
During 2011, Newfoundland, Corp., earned income from continuing operations of $136,000. The company also sold a segment of the business (discontinued operations) at a loss of $36,000 and had an extraordinary gain of $14,000. At year-end, Newfoundland had an unrealized loss on investments of $8,000.

Requirements

1. Compute Newfoundland's net income and comprehensive income for 2011. All amounts are net of income taxes.
2. What final EPS figure should Newfoundland report for 2011? Name the item and show its amount. Newfoundland had 50,000 shares of common stock (and no preferred stock) outstanding.

Problems (Group A)

P12-26A *(L.OBJ. 1, 2, 3)* **Journalizing stockholders' equity transactions [20–25 min]**
Airborne Manufacturing, Co., completed the following transactions during 2009:

Jan 16	Declared a cash dividend on the 4%, $102 par preferred stock (1,050 shares outstanding). Declared a $0.55 per share dividend on the 95,000 shares of common stock outstanding. The date of record is January 31, and the payment due date is February 15.
Feb 15	Paid the cash dividends
Jun 10	Split common stock 2 for 1. Before the split, Airborne had 95,000 shares of $10 par common stock outstanding.
Jul 30	Distributed a 25% stock dividend on the common stock. The market value of the common stock was $10 per share.
Oct 26	Purchased 3,000 shares of treasury stock at $15 per share
Nov 8	Sold 1,500 shares of treasury stock for $20 per share
Nov 30	Sold 1,500 shares of treasury stock for $9 per share

Requirement

1. Record the transactions in Airborne's general journal.

P12-27A *(L.OBJ. 1, 3)* **Journalizing dividend and treasury stock transactions, and preparing stockholders' equity [10–30 min]**
The balance sheet of World Foods, at December 31, 2011, reported 100,000 shares of no-par common stock authorized, with 15,000 shares issued and a Common stock balance of $170,000. Retained earnings had a balance of $125,000. During 2012, the company completed the following selected transactions:

Mar 15	Purchased 13,000 shares of treasury stock at $5 per share
Apr 30	Distributed a 20% stock dividend on the *outstanding* shares of common stock. The market value of common stock was $7 per share.
Dec 31	Earned net income of $109,000 during the year. Closed net income to Retained earnings.

Requirements

1. Record the transactions in the general journal. Explanations are not required.
2. Prepare the stockholders' equity section of World Foods' balance sheet at December 31, 2012.

P12-28A *(L.OBJ. 1,3)* **Journalizing dividend and treasury stock transactions, preparing a statement of retained earnings, and preparing stockholders' equity [30–45 min]**
The balance sheet of Patrick Management Consulting, Inc., at December 31, 2011, reported the following stockholders' equity:

Paid–in capital:	
Common stock, $15 par, 300,000 shares authorized, 20,000 shares issued	$ 300,000
Paid–in capital in excess of par—common	310,000
Total paid–in capital	610,000
Retained earnings	158,000
Total stockholders' equity	$ 768,000

During 2012, Patrick completed the following selected transactions:

Feb 6	Distributed a 10% stock dividend on the common stock. The market value of Patrick's stock was $26 per share.
Jul 29	Purchased 2,000 shares of treasury stock at $26 per share
Nov 27	Declared a $0.30 per share cash dividend on the 20,000 shares of common stock outstanding. The date of record is December 17, and the payment date is January 7, 2013.
Dec 31	Closed the $86,000 net income to Retained earnings

Requirements

1. Record the transactions in the general journal.
2. Prepare a retained earnings statement for the year ended December 31, 2012.
3. Prepare the stockholders' equity section of the balance sheet at December 31, 2012.

P12-29A *(L.OBJ. 4, 5)* **Computing EPS and reporting a retained earnings restriction [20–25 min]**

The capital structure of Rodeswell, Inc., at December 31, 2010, included 30,000 shares of $2.00 preferred stock and 40,000 shares of common stock. Common stock outstanding during 2011 totaled 40,000 shares. Income from continuing operations during 2011 was $104,000. The company discontinued a segment of the business at a gain of $20,000, and also had an extraordinary gain of $10,000. The Rodeswell board of directors restricts $98,000 of retained earnings for contingencies. Retained earnings at December 31, 2010, was $98,000 and the company declared preferred dividends of $60,000 during 2011.

Requirements

1. Compute Rodeswell's earnings per share for 2011. Start with income from continuing operations. All income and loss amounts are net of income tax.
2. Show two ways of reporting Rodeswell's retained earnings restriction.

P12-30A *(L.OBJ. 5)* **Preparing a detailed income statement [25–35 min]**

The following information was taken from the records of Underwood Motorsports, Inc., at September 30, 2010.

Selling expenses	$ 124,000	Common stock, $10 par, 21,100	
General expenses	131,000	shares authorized and issued	$ 211,000
Income from discontinued operations	8,000	Preferred stock, $5, no–par	
Retained earnings, beginning	87,000	3,000 shares issued	150,000
Cost of goods sold	437,000	Income tax expense:	
Treasury stock, common		Continuing operations	72,000
(1,100 shares)	12,100	Income from discontinued	
Net sales revenue	832,000	operations	3,200

Requirement

1. Prepare a multi-step income statement for Underwood Motorsports for the fiscal year ended September 30, 2010. Include earnings per share.

P12-31A *(L.OBJ. 5)* **Preparing a corrected combined statement of income and retained earnings [25–35 min]**

Jack Hodges, accountant for Home Mortgage Finance, was injured in a boating accident. Another employee prepared the accompanying income statement for the year ended December 31, 2010.

HOME MORTGAGE FINANCE **Income Statement** Year ended December 31, 2010		
Revenue and gains:		
Sales		$ 366,000
Paid–in capital in excess of par–common		92,000
Total revenues and gains		458,000
Expenses and losses:		
Cost of goods sold	100,000	
Selling expenses	67,000	
General expenses	61,500	
Sales returns	8,000	
Sales discounts	6,500	
Dividends	15,000	
Income tax expense	36,000	
Total expenses and losses		294,000
Income from operations		$ 164,000
Other gains and losses		
Gain on discontinued operations		4,000
Net income		$ 168,000
Earnings per share		$ 3.36

The individual *amounts* listed on the income statement are correct. However, some accounts are reported incorrectly, and two items do not belong on the income statement at all. Also, income tax has *not* been applied to all appropriate figures. The income tax rate on discontinued operations was 30%. Home Mortgage Finance issued 56,000 shares of common stock in 2010 and held 6,000 shares as treasury stock during 2010. Retained earnings at December 31, 2009, was $163,000.

Requirement

1. Prepare a corrected combined statement of income and retained earnings for 2010, including earnings per share. Prepare the income statement in single-step format.

Problems (Group B)

P12-32B *(L.OBJ. 1, 2, 3)* **Journalizing stockholders' equity transactions [20–25 min]**
Windborne Manufacturing, Co., completed the following selected transactions during 2009:

Jan 16	Declared a cash dividend on the 6%, $101 par preferred stock (950 shares outstanding). Declared a $0.40 per share dividend on the 85,000 shares of common stock outstanding. The date of record is January 31, and the payment due date is February 15.
Feb 15	Paid the cash dividends
Jun 10	Split common stock 2 for 1. Before the split, Windborne had 85,000 shares of $4 par common stock outstanding.
Jul 30	Distributed a 20% stock dividend on the common stock. The market value of the common stock was $9 per share.
Oct 26	Purchased 6,000 shares of treasury stock at $16 per share
Nov 8	Sold 3,000 shares of treasury stock for $18 per share
Nov 30	Sold 2,000 shares of treasury stock for $8 per share

Requirement

1. Record the transactions in the general journal.

P12-33B *(L.OBJ. 1, 3)* **Journalizing dividend and treasury stock transactions, and preparing stockholders' equity [10–30 min]**

The balance sheet of Mundo Health Foods, at December 31, 2011, reported 90,000 shares of no-par common stock authorized with 50,000 shares issued and a Common stock balance of $170,000. Retained Earnings had a balance of $140,000. During 2012 the company completed the following selected transactions:

Mar 15	Purchased 9,000 shares of treasury stock at $7 per share
Apr 30	Distributed a 10% stock dividend on the *outstanding* shares of common stock. The market value of common stock was $10 per share.
Dec 31	Earned net income of $105,000 during the year. Closed net income to Retained earnings.

Requirements

1. Record the transactions in the general journal. Explanations are not required.
2. Prepare the stockholders' equity section of Mundo Health Food's balance sheet at December 31, 2012.

P12-34B *(L.OBJ. 1,3)* **Journalizing dividend and treasury stock transactions, preparing a statement of retained earnings, and preparing stockholders' equity [30–45 min]**

The balance sheet of Collin Management Consulting, Inc., at December 31, 2011, reported the following stockholders' equity:

Paid–in capital:	
Common stock, $10 par, 200,000 shares authorized, 25,000 shares issued	$ 250,000
Paid–in capital in excess of par—common	320,000
Total paid–in capital	570,000
Retained earnings	163,000
Total stockholders' equity	$ 733,000

During 2012, Collin Management Consulting completed the following selected transactions:

Feb 6	Distributed a 10% stock dividend on the common stock. The market value of Collin's stock was $28 per share.
Jul 29	Purchased 2,100 shares of treasury stock at $28 per share
Nov 27	Declared a $0.20 per share cash dividend on the 25,400 shares of common stock outstanding. The date of record is December 17, and the payment date is January 7, 2013.
Dec 31	Closed the $88,000 net income to Retained earnings

Requirements

1. Record the transactions in the general journal.
2. Prepare the retained earnings statement for the year ended December 31, 2012.
3. Prepare the stockholders' equity section of the balance sheet at December 31, 2012.

P12-35B *(L.OBJ. 4, 5)* **Computing EPS and reporting a retained earnings restriction [20–25 min]**

The capital structure of Galyinscape, Inc., at December 31, 2010, included 18,000 shares of $1.50 preferred stock and 40,000 shares of common stock. Common shares outstanding during 2011 were 40,000. Income from continuing operations during 2011 was $104,000. The company discontinued a segment of the business at a gain of $20,000 and also had an extraordinary gain of $10,000. Galyinscape board of directors restricts $100,000 of retained earnings for contingencies. Retained earnings at December 31, 2010, was $100,000, and the company declared cash dividends of $27,000 during 2011.

Requirements

1. Compute Galyinscape's earnings per share for 2011. Start with income from continuing operations. Income and loss amounts are net of income tax.
2. Show two ways of reporting Galyinscape's retained earnings restriction.

P12-36B *(L.OBJ. 5)* **Preparing a detailed income statement [25–35 min]**
The following information was taken from the records of Clarkson Motorsports, Inc., at September 30, 2010:

Selling expenses	$ 121,000	Common stock, $10 par, 21,200	
General expenses	132,000	shares authorized and issued	$ 212,000
Income from discontinued operations	8,000	Preferred stock, $5, no–par	
Retained earnings, beginning	85,000	6,000 shares issued	300,000
Cost of goods sold	438,000	Income tax expense:	
Treasury stock, common		Continuing operations	70,000
(1,200 shares)	13,200	Income from discontinued	
Net sales revenue	836,000	operations	3,200

Requirement

1. Prepare a multi-step income statement for Clarkson Motorsports for the fiscal year ended September 30, 2010. Include earnings per share.

P12-37B *(L.OBJ. 5)* **Preparing a corrected combined statement of income and retained earnings [25–35 min]**
Joseph Hill, accountant for Complete Home Finance, was injured in a boating accident. Another employee prepared the following income statement for the year ended December 31, 2010:

COMPLETE HOME FINANCE **Income Statement** Year ended December 31, 2010		
Revenue and gains:		
Sales		$ 365,000
Paid–in capital in excess of par–common		94,000
Total revenues and gains		459,000
Expenses and losses:		
Cost of goods sold	103,000	
Selling expenses	66,000	
General expenses	59,500	
Sales returns	8,000	
Sales discounts	7,500	
Dividends	15,000	
Income tax expense	34,000	
Total expenses and losses		293,000
Income from operations		$ 166,000
Other gains and losses		
Gain on discontinued operations		4,500
Net income		$ 170,500
Earnings per share		$ 3.41

The individual *amounts* listed on the income statement are correct. However, some accounts are reported incorrectly, and two items do not belong on the income statement at all. Also, income tax has *not* been applied to all appropriate figures. The income tax rate on discontinued operations is 40%. Complete Home issued 55,000 shares of common stock in 2010 and held 5,000 shares as treasury stock during 2010. Retained earnings at December 31, 2009 was $168,000.

Requirement

1. Prepare a corrected combined statement of income and retained earnings for the fiscal year ended December 31, 2010. Prepare the income statement in single-step format.

■ Continuing Exercise

E12-38 This exercise continues the Sherman Lawn Service, Inc., situation from Exercise 11-45 of Chapter 11. On July 15, Sherman Lawn Service declares and distributes a 5% stock dividend to all common shareholders of record on July 15 when the market price per common share is $4.

Requirements

1. Is this a small or large stock dividend?
2. Journalize the entries related to the dividend.

■ Continuing Problem

P12-39 This problem continues the Haupt Consulting, Inc., situation from Problem 11-46 of Chapter 11. In July, Haupt has the following transactions related to its common shares:

Jul 1	Haupt repurchased 100 of its common shares for $10 per share
Jul 10	Haupt reissued 20 of its treasury common shares for $13 per share
Jul 20	Haupt reissued 30 of its treasury common shares for $12 per share

Requirements

1. Journalize the entry related to the transactions.
2. Calculate the balance in the T-accounts affected by the transactions.

Apply Your Knowledge

■ Decision Cases

Case 1. Valley Mills Construction, Inc., had the following stockholders' equity on June 30, 2010:

Common stock, no-par, 100,000 shares issued	$250,000
Retained earnings	190,000
Total stockholders' equity	$440,000

In the past, Valley Mills has paid an annual cash dividend of $1 per share. Despite the large retained earnings balance, the board of directors wished to conserve cash for expansion. The board delayed the payment of cash dividends and in July distributed a 5% stock dividend. During August, the company's cash position improved. The board then declared and paid a cash dividend of $0.9524 per share in September.

Suppose you owned 1,000 shares of Valley Mills common stock, acquired three years ago, prior to the 5% stock dividend. The market price of the stock was $30 per share before any of these dividends.

Requirements

1. What amount of cash dividends did you receive last year—before the stock dividend? What amount of cash dividends will you receive after the stock dividend?
2. How does the stock dividend affect your proportionate ownership in Valley Mills Construction? Explain.
3. Immediately after the stock dividend was distributed, the market value of Valley Mills stock decreased from $30 per share to $28.571 per share. Does this decrease represent a loss to you? Explain.

Case 2. The following accounting issues have arisen at T-Shirts Plus, Inc.:

Requirements

1. Corporations sometimes purchase their own stock. When asked why they do so, T-Shirts Plus management responds that the stock is undervalued. What advantage would T-Shirts Plus gain by buying and selling its own undervalued stock?
2. T-Shirts Plus earned a significant profit in the year ended December 31, 2008, because land that it held was purchased by the State of Nebraska for a new highway. The company proposes to treat the sale of land as operating revenue. Why do you think the company is proposing this plan? Is this disclosure appropriate?
3. The treasurer of T-Shirts Plus wants to report a large loss as an extraordinary item because the company produced too much product and cannot sell it. Why do you think the treasurer wants to report the loss as extraordinary? Would that be acceptable?

Ethical Issue

Bobby's Bagels just landed a contract to open 100 new stores in shopping malls across the country. The new business should triple the company's profits. Prior to disclosing the new contract to the public, top managers of the company quietly bought most of Bobby's Bagels stock for themselves. After the discovery was announced, Bobby's Bagels stock price shot up from $7 to $52.

Requirements

1. Did Bobby's Bagels managers behave ethically? Explain your answer.
2. Identify the accounting principle relevant to this situation. Review Chapter 1 if necessary.
3. Who was helped and who was harmed by management's action?

Financial Statement Case

Use the **Amazon.com** financial statements in Appendix A at the end of this book to answer the following questions.

Requirements

1. Show how **Amazon.com** computed basic earnings per share of $1.15 for 2007. (Ignore diluted earnings per share of $1.12.)
2. Prepare a T-account to show the beginning and ending balances and all activity in Retained earnings (Accumulated Deficit) for 2007.
3. How much in cash dividends did **Amazon** declare during 2007? Explain your answer.
4. How much treasury stock did **Amazon** have at December 31, 2007? Explain.

■ Team Project

Obtain the annual reports (or annual report data) of five well-known companies. You can get the reports either from the companies' Web sites, your college library, or by mailing a request directly to the company (allow two weeks for delivery). Or you can visit the Web site for this book (http://www.prenhall.com/horngren) or the SEC EDGAR database, which includes the financial reports of most well-known companies.

Requirements

1. After selecting five companies, examine their income statements to search for the following items:
   a. Income from continuing operations
   b. Discontinued operations
   c. Extraordinary gains and losses
   d. Net income or net loss
   e. Earnings-per-share data
2. Study the companies' balance sheets to see
   a. what classes of stock each company has issued.
   b. which item carries a larger balance—the Common stock account or Paid-in capital in excess of par (also labeled Additional paid-in capital).
   c. What percentage of each company's total stockholders' equity is made up of retained earnings?
   d. Whether the company has Treasury stock. If so, how many shares and how much is the cost?
3. Examine each company's statement of stockholders' equity for evidence of
   a. Cash dividends.
   b. Stock dividends. (Some companies use the term *stock split* to refer to a large stock dividend.)
   c. Treasury stock purchases and sales.
4. As directed by your instructor, either write a report or present your findings to your class. You may not be unable to understand *everything* you find, but neither can the Wall Street analysts! You will be amazed at how much you have learned.

Quick Check Answers

1. *c* 2. *a* 3. *c* . 4. *c* 5. *c* 6. *b* 7. *d* 8. *b* 9. *a* 10. *b*

For online homework, exercises, and problems that provide you immediate feedback, please visit www.myaccountinglab.com.

13 The Statement of Cash Flows

Learning Objectives/Success Keys

1. Identify the purposes of the Statement of Cash Flows
2. Distinguish among operating, investing, and financing cash flows
3. Prepare the Statement of Cash Flows by the indirect method
4. Prepare the Statement of Cash Flows by the direct method (Appendix 13A)

Why is cash so important? You can probably answer that question from your own experience: It takes cash to pay the bills. You have some income and you have expenses; and these events create cash receipts and payments.

Businesses, including Smart Touch Learning, Inc., and Greg's Groovy Tunes, Inc., work the same way. Net income is a good thing, but Smart Touch and Greg's both need enough cash to pay the bills and run their operations.

This chapter covers cash flows—cash receipts and cash payments. We will see how to prepare the Statement of Cash Flows, starting with the format used by the vast majority of non-public companies; it is called the *indirect method*. Chapter Appendix 13A covers the alternate format of the Statement of Cash Flows, the *direct method*.

The chapter has four distinct sections:

- Introduction: The Statement of Cash Flows
- Preparing the Statement of Cash Flows by the Indirect Method
- Chapter Appendix 13A: Preparing the Statement of Cash Flows by the Direct Method
- Chapter Appendix 13B: Preparing the Statement of Cash Flows Using a Spreadsheet

The focus company throughout the chapter once again is Smart Touch Learning.

Chapter Appendix 13B shows how to use a spreadsheet to prepare the Statement of Cash Flows. This appendix presents the indirect-method spreadsheet first, and the direct-method spreadsheet last—to maintain consistency with the order in which these topics are covered in the chapter.

Introduction: The Statement of Cash Flows

1 Identify the purposes of the Statement of Cash Flows

The Balance Sheet reports financial position. When a comparative Balance Sheet for two periods is presented, it shows whether cash increased or decreased. For example, Smart Touch Learning's comparative Balance Sheet reported the following:

	2011	2010	Increase (Decrease)
Cash..........	$22,000	$42,000	$(20,000)

Smart Touch's cash decreased by $20,000 during 2011. But the Balance Sheet does not show *why* cash decreased. We need the cash-flow statement for that.

The Statement of Cash Flows reports **cash flows**—cash receipts and cash payments. It

- shows where cash came from (receipts) and how cash was spent (payments).
- reports why cash increased or decreased during the period.
- covers a span of time and is dated the same as the Income Statement—"Year Ended December 31, 2011," for example.

The Statement of Cash Flows explains why net income as reported on the Income Statement does not equal the change in the cash balance. In essence the cash flow statement is the communicating link between the accrual based Income Statement and the cash reported on the Balance Sheet.

Exhibit 13-1 illustrates the relationships among the Balance Sheet, the Income Statement, and the Statement of Cash Flows.

How do people use cash-flow information? The Statement of Cash Flows helps

1. **predict future cash flows.** Past cash receipts and payments help predict future cash flows.
2. **evaluate management decisions.** Wise investment decisions help the business prosper, while unwise decisions cause problems. Investors and creditors use cash-flow information to evaluate managers' decisions.
3. **predict ability to pay debts and dividends.** Lenders want to know whether they will collect on their loans. Stockholders want dividends on their investments. The Statement of Cash Flows helps make these predictions.

Cash Equivalents

On a Statement of Cash Flows, *Cash* means more than cash on hand and cash in the bank. *Cash* includes **cash equivalents**, which are highly liquid investments that can be converted into cash quickly. As the name implies, cash equivalents are so close to cash that they are treated as "equals." Examples of cash equivalents are money-market accounts and investments in U.S. government securities. Throughout this chapter, the term *cash* refers to both cash and cash equivalents.

EXHIBIT 13-8 Comparative Balance Sheet

SMART TOUCH LEARNING, INC.
Comparative Balance Sheet
December 31, 2011 and 2010

(In thousands)	2011	2010	Increase (Decrease)	
Assets				
Current:				
Cash	$ 22	$ 42	$ (20)	
Accounts receivable	90	73	17	D
Inventory	143	145	(2)	
Plant assets, net	460	210	250	E/F
Total assets	$715	$470	$245	
Liabilities				
Current:			—	
Accounts payable	$ 90	$ 50	$ 40	D
Accrued liabilities	5	10	–5	
Long-term notes payable	160	80	80	G/H
Stockholders' Equity				
Common stock	370	250	120	I
Retained earnings	110	80	30	A/K
Less: Treasury stock	(20)	0	(20)	J
	$715	$470	$245	

EXHIBIT 13-9 Income Statement

SMART TOUCH LEARNING, INC.
Income Statement
Year Ended December 31, 2011

		(In thousands)	
	Revenues and gains:		
	Sales revenue	$286	
	Interest revenue	12	
	Dividend revenue	9	
C	Gain on sale of plant assets	10	
	Total revenues and gains		$317
	Expenses:		
	Cost of goods sold	$156	
	Salary and wage expense	56	
B	Depreciation expense	20	
	Other operating expense	16	
	Interest expense	15	
	Income tax expense	14	
	Total expenses		277
A	Net income		$ 40

B Depreciation, Depletion, and Amortization Expenses

These expenses are added back to net income to reconcile from net income to cash flow from operations. Let us see why this occurs. Depreciation is recorded as follows:

	Depreciation expense (E+)	20,000	
	Accumulated depreciation (CA+)		20,000

You can see that depreciation does not affect cash because there is no Cash account in the journal entry. However, depreciation, like all the other expenses, decreases net income. Therefore, to go from net income to cash flows, we must remove depreciation by adding it back to net income.

Example: Suppose you had only two transactions during the period:

- $40,000 cash sale
- Depreciation expense of $20,000

Accrual basis net income is $20,000 ($40,000 – $20,000). But cash flow from operations is $40,000. To reconcile from net income, $20,000, to cash flow from operations, $40,000, add back depreciation, $20,000. Also add back depletion and amortization expenses because they are similar to depreciation.

C Gains and Losses on the Sale of Assets

Sales of long-term assets such as land and buildings are investing activities, and these sales usually create a gain or a loss. The gain or loss is included in net income, which is already in the operating section of the cash flow statement. Gains and losses require an adjustment to cash flow from operating activities: The gain or loss must be removed from net income on the Statement of Cash Flows so the total cash from the transaction can be shown in the investing section.

Exhibit 13-4 includes an adjustment for a gain. During 2011 Smart Touch sold equipment and there was a gain of $10,000 on the sale. The gain was included in the calculation of net income on the Income Statement, so the gain must be removed from operating cash flows. The gain made net income bigger, so it is deducted from the operating section. On the other hand, a loss on the sale of plant assets would make net income smaller, so it would be added back to net income.

D Changes in the Current Assets and the Current Liabilities

Most current assets and current liabilities result from operating activities. For example,

- accounts receivable result from sales,
- inventory relates to cost of goods sold, and so on.

Changes in the current accounts create adjustments to net income on the cash-flow statement, as follows:

↑ Current assets ↓ Cash

1. **An increase in a current asset other than cash causes a decrease in cash.** It takes cash to acquire assets. If Accounts receivable, Inventory, or Prepaid expenses increased, then cash decreased. Therefore, subtract the increase in the current asset from net income to get cash flow from operations. For example, Smart Touch's Accounts Receivable went up by $17,000. That increase in the current asset shows as a decrease in cash on the cash flow statement (Exhibit 13-4).

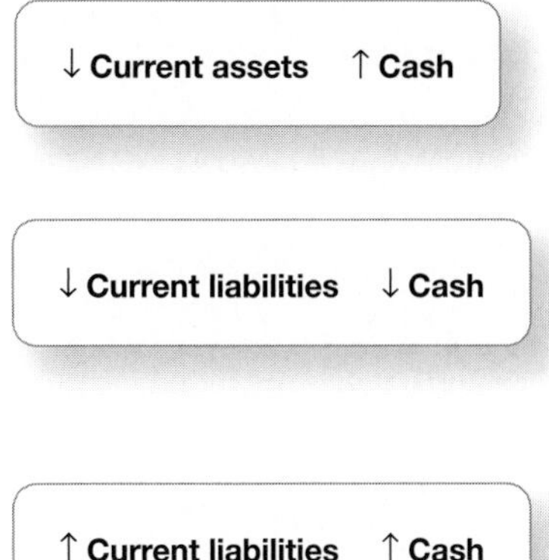

2. **A decrease in a current asset other than cash causes an increase in cash.** Smart Touch's Inventory decreased by $2,000. What caused the decrease? Smart Touch must have sold some inventory, and collected cash. Therefore, we add the decrease in Inventory of $2,000 in the cash flow statement (Exhibit 13-4).
3. **A decrease in a current liability causes a decrease in cash.** The payment of a current liability decreases cash. Therefore, we subtract decreases in current liabilities from net income to get cash flow from operations. Smart Touch's Accrued liabilities went down $5,000. That change shows up as a $5,000 decrease in cash flows in Exhibit 13-4.
4. **An increase in a current liability causes an increase in cash.** Smart Touch's Accounts payable increased by $40,000. This means that cash was not spent at the time the expense was incurred, but rather it will be paid at a later time—resulting in a liability. Accordingly, even though net income was reduced by the expense, cash was not reduced. However, cash will be reduced later when Smart Touch pays off its liability. Therefore, an increase in a current liability is *added* to net income in the Statement of Cash Flows (Exhibit 13-4).

Evaluating Cash Flows from Operating Activities

During 2011, Smart Touch Learning's operations provided net cash flow of $70,000. This amount exceeds net income (due to the various adjustments discussed in sections B, C, and D). However, to fully evaluate a company's cash flows, we must also examine its investing and financing activities. Exhibit 13-4 shows the completed operating activities section.

Stop & Think...

The operating activities represent the core of the day to day results of any business. Remember when we learned the difference between accrual and cash basis accounting? All the operating activities section represents is a cash basis income statement. With the indirect method, we indirectly back into cash basis—that is, we start with accrual basis net income and adjust it back to cash basis "operating" cash flows (cash basis net income).

Cash Flows from Investing Activities

Investing activities affect long-term assets, such as Plant assets and Investments. These are shown for Smart Touch in Exhibit 13-5. Let us see how to compute the investing cash flows.

Computing Acquisitions and Sales of Plant Assets

Companies keep a separate account for each asset. But for computing investing cash flows, it is helpful to combine all the plant assets into a single Plant assets account. We subtract Accumulated depreciation from the assets' cost in order to work with a single net figure for plant assets, such as Plant assets, net—$460,000. This simplifies the computations.

To illustrate, observe that Smart Touch Learning's

- Balance Sheet reports plant assets, net of depreciation, of $460,000 at the end of 2011 and $210,000 at the end of 2010 (Exhibit 13-8).
- Income Statement shows depreciation expense of $20,000 and a $10,000 gain on sale of plant assets (Exhibit 13-9).

Also, assume that Smart Touch's acquisitions of plant assets during 2011 totaled $310,000. E

This gives us an incomplete T-account as follows:

Plant assets, net			
12/31/10 Bal	210,000		
		Depreciation (from Inc Stmt)	20,000
Acquisitions	310,000	Sales	?
12/31/11 Bal	460,000		

We also know that Smart Touch sold some older plant assets because there was a gain on sale of assets reported on the Income Statement. We don't care about the gain itself, we need to know the cash amount of the sale. Remember, we are looking for cash movement. How much cash did the business receive from the sale of plant assets? First, let us look at the cost of the sold assets. This will be the missing value in our Plant assets, net T-account.

12/31/10 Bal + Acquisitions – Depreciation – Sales? = 12/31/11 Bal
210,000 + 310,000 – 20,000 – Sales? = 460,000
500,000 – Sales? = 460,000
Sales = 40,000

So our completed T-account is as follows:

Plant assets, net			
12/31/10 Bal	210,000		
		Depreciation (from Inc Stmt)	20,000
Acquisitions	310,000	Sales	40,000
12/31/11 Bal	460,000		

Cash received from selling plant assets can be computed by using the journal entry approach:

	Account	Debit	Credit
	Cash	?????	
	Gain on sale of plant assets (from the Income Statement)		10,000
	Plant assets (from the T-account)		40,000

The book-value information comes from the Plant assets (Net) account on the Balance Sheet. The gain or loss comes from the Income Statement. The missing amount must be the cash received from the sale.

So, we compute the cash receipt from the sale as follows:

Cash = $10,000 Gain + $40,000 Plant assets, net
Cash = $50,000

The cash receipt from the sale of plant assets of $50,000 is shown as item F in the investing activities section of the Statement of Cash Flows (see Exhibit 13-7).

Exhibit 13-10 summarizes the computation of the investing cash flows. Items to be computed are shown in color.

EXHIBIT 13-10 | Computing Cash Flows from Investing Activities

Cash Receipts

From sale of plant assets	Beginning plant assets (net)	+	Acquisition	−	Depreciation Expense	−	Book value of assets sold	=	Ending plant assets (net)
	Cash receipt	=	Book value of assets sold	+ or −	Gain on sale or Loss on sale				

Cash Payments

For acquisition of plant assets	Beginning plant assets (net)	+	Acquisition	−	Depreciation Expense	−	Book value of assets sold	=	Ending plant assets (net)

Cash Flows from Financing Activities

Financing activities affect the liability and owners' equity accounts, such as Long-Term notes payable, Bonds payable, Common stock, and Retained earnings. These are shown for Smart Touch in Exhibit 13-8.

Computing Issuances and Payments of Long-Term Notes Payable

The beginning and ending balances of Notes payable or Bonds payable are taken from the Balance Sheet. If either the amount of new issuances or payments is known, the other amount can be computed. For Smart Touch Learning, new issuances of notes payable total $90,000 (Shown as item **G** in Exhibit 13-6). The computation of note payments uses the Long-Term notes payable account, with amounts from Smart Touch Learning's Balance Sheet in Exhibit 13-8 to create the following incomplete T-account:

Long-Term notes payable

		12/31/10 Bal	80,000
Notes payments	?	New notes issued	90,000
		12/31/11 Bal	160,000

Then, solve for the missing payments value:

12/31/10 Bal	+	New Notes Issued	– Payments?	=	12/31/11 Bal
80,000	+	90,000	– Payments?	=	160,000
		170,000	– Payments?	=	160,000
			Payments	=	10,000

Complete the T-Account:

Long-Term notes payable

		12/31/10 Bal	80,000
Notes payments	10,000	New notes issued	90,000
		12/31/11 Bal	160,000

The payment of $10,000 as an outflow of cash is shown on the Statement of Cash Flows. (See item **H** in Exhibit 13-6).

Computing Issuances of Stock and Purchases of Treasury Stock

Cash flows for these financing activities can be determined by analyzing the stock accounts. For example, the amount of a new issuance of common stock is determined from Common stock. Using data from Exhibit 13-8, the incomplete Common stock T-account is as follows:

Common stock

		12/31/10 Bal	250,000
Retirements	?	Issuance	?
		12/31/11 Bal	370,000

We would have to be told if there were any stock retirements. Since there were not, we know the balance change must be represented by new stock issuances.

Solving for the missing value is completed as follows:

12/31/10 Bal + Issuance of Stock? − Retirements? = 12/31/11 Bal
250,000 + Issuance of Stock? − 0 = 370,000
Issuance of Stock = 120,000

The completed T-Account for Common stock is as follows:

Common stock

		12/31/10 Bal	250,000
Retirements	0	Issuance	120,000
		12/31/11 Bal	370,000

Therefore, the new stock issuance shows as $120,000 positive cash flows in the financing section of the statement (item **I** in Exhibit 13-6).

The last item that changed on Smart Touch Learning's Balance Sheet was Treasury stock. The T-account balances from the Treasury stock account on the Balance sheet show the following:

Treasury stock

12/31/10 Bal	0		
Purchases	?	Sales	?
12/31/11 Bal	20,000		

Since we were not told that any Treasury stock was sold, we must assume that 100% of the account change represents new acquisitions of Treasury stock. Solving for the amount, the equation follows:

12/31/10 Bal + Purchases? − Sales? = 12/31/11 Bal
0 + Purchases? − 0 = 20,000
Purchases = 20,000

Completing the T-account, we have the following:

Treasury stock

12/31/10 Bal	0		
Purchases	20,000	Sales	0
12/31/11 Bal	20,000		

So, $20,000 is shown as a cash outflow in the financing section of the cash flow statement for purchase of treasury stock (item **J** in Exhibit 13-6).

Computing Dividend Payments

The amount of dividend payments can be computed by analyzing the Retained earnings account. First we input the balances from the Balance Sheet:

Retained earnings

		12/31/10 Bal	80,000
Net loss	?	Net income	?
Dividend declarations	?		
		12/31/11 Bal	110,000

Retained earnings increases when companies earn net income. Retained earnings decreases when companies have a net loss and when they declare dividends. We know that Smart Touch earned net income of $40,000 from the Income Statement in Exhibit 13-9.

Retained earnings

		12/31/10 Bal	80,000
Net loss	?	Net income	40,000
Dividend declarations	?		
		12/31/11 Bal	110,000

Therefore, the missing value must be the amount of dividends Smart Touch declared. Solving for the value is as follows:

12/31/10 Bal + Net Income – Dividends Declared = 12/31/11 Bal
80,000 + 40,000 – Dividends Declared = 110,000
120,000 – Dividends Declared = 110,000
Dividends Declared = 10,000

So our final Retained earnings T-account shows the following:

Retained earnings

		12/31/10 Bal	80,000
		Net income	40,000
Dividend declarations	10,000		
		12/31/11 Bal	110,000

A stock dividend has *no* effect on Cash and is *not* reported on the cash-flow statement. Smart Touch had no stock dividends—only cash dividends. Exhibit 13-11 on page 722 summarizes the computation of cash flows from financing activities, highlighted in color.

Net Change in Cash and Cash Balances

The next line of the cash flow statement (underneath Net cash provided by financing activities in Exhibit 13-7) represents the total change in cash for the period. In the case of Smart Touch Learning, it is the net decrease in cash balances of $20,000 for the year. The decrease in cash of $20,000 is also represented by the following:

(amounts in thousands)

Net cash provided by Operating activities	–	Net cash used by Investing activities	+	Net cash provided by Financing activities		Net decrease in Cash
70	–	260	+	170	=	–20

EXHIBIT 13-11 | Computing Cash Flows from Financing Activities

Cash Receipts							
From issuance of notes payable	Beginning notes payable	+	Cash receipt from issuance of notes payable	−	Payment of notes payable	=	Ending notes payable
From issuance of stock	Beginning stock	+	Cash receipt from issuance of new stock	=	Ending stock		
Cash Payments							
Of notes payable	Beginning notes payable	+	Cash receipt from issuance of notes payable	−	Payment of notes payable	=	Ending notes payable
To purchase treasury stock	Beginning treasury stock	+	Cost of treasury stock purchased	=	Ending treasury stock		
Of dividends	Beginning retained earnings	+	Net income	−	Dividends Declared	=	Ending retained earnings

Next, the beginning cash from December 31, 2010, is listed at $42,000. The net decrease of $20,000 from beginning cash of $42,000 equals the ending cash balance on December 31, 2011, of $22,000. This is the key to the Statement of Cash Flows—it explains why the cash balance for Smart Touch decreased by $20,000, even though the company reported net income for the year.

Stop & Think...

Most of you probably have a checking or savings account. Think about how the balance changes from month to month. It does not always change because you have earned revenues or incurred expenses (operating). Sometimes it changes because you buy a long-lasting asset, such as a TV (investing). Sometimes it changes because you make a payment on your car note (financing). It is the same with business; business bank accounts do not change only because they earn revenue or incur expenses (operating). The cash flow statement explains all the reasons that cash changed (operating, investing, and financing).

Noncash Investing and Financing Activities

Companies make investments that do not require cash. They also obtain financing other than cash. Such transactions are called noncash investing and financing activities, and appear in a separate part of the cash flow statement. Our Smart Touch example did not include transactions of this type because the company did not have any noncash transactions during the year. So, to illustrate them, let us consider the three noncash transactions for Greg's Groovy Tunes. How would they be reported? First, we gather the noncash activity for the company:

1	Acquired $300,000 building by issuing stock
2	Acquired $70,000 land by issuing notes payable
3	Paid $100,000 note payable by issuing common stock

Now, we consider each transaction individually.

1. Greg's Groovy Tunes issued common stock of $300,000 to acquire a building. The journal entry to record the purchase would be as follows:

	Building (A+)	300,000	
	Common stock (Q+)		300,000

This transaction would not be reported on the cash-flow statement because no cash was paid. But the building and the common stock are important.

The purchase of the building is an investing activity. The issuance of common stock is a financing activity. Taken together, this transaction is a *noncash investing and financing activity*.

2. The second transaction listed indicates that Greg's Groovy Tunes acquired $70,000 of land by issuing a note. The journal entry to record the purchase would be as follows:

	Land (A+)	70,000	
	Notes payable (L+)		70,000

This transaction would not be reported on the cash-flow statement because no cash was paid. But the land and the notes payable are important.

The purchase of the land is an investing activity. The issuance of the note is a financing activity. Taken together, this transaction is a *noncash investing and financing activity*.

3. The third transaction listed indicates that Greg's Groovy Tunes exchanged $100,000 of debt by issuing common stock. The journal entry to record the purchase would be as follows:

	Notes payable (L–)	100,000	
	Common stock (Q+)		100,000

This transaction would not be reported on the cash-flow statement because no cash was paid. But the notes payable and the stock issuance are important.

The payment on the note and the issuance of the common stock are both financing activities. Taken together, this transaction, even though it is two financing transactions, is reported in the *noncash investing and financing activities*.

Noncash investing and financing activities can be reported in a separate schedule that accompanies the Statement of Cash Flows. Exhibit 13-12 on page 724 illustrates noncash investing and financing activities for Greg's Groovy Tunes (all amounts are assumed). This information either follows the cash-flow statement or can be disclosed in a note.

EXHIBIT 13-12 | **Noncash Investing & Financing Activities**

GREG'S GROOVY TUNES Statement of Cash Flows—partial Year Ended December 31, 2011		
		(In thousands)
Noncash investing and financing activities:		
Acquisition of building by issuing common stock		$300
Acquisition of land by issuing note payable		70
Payment of note payable by issuing common stock		100
Total noncash investing and financing activities		$470

Measuring Cash Adequacy: Free Cash Flow

Throughout this chapter we have focused on cash flows from operating, investing, and financing activities. Some investors want to know how much cash a company can "free up" for new opportunities. **Free cash flow** is the amount of cash available from operations after paying for planned investments in long-term assets. Free cash flow can be computed as follows:

Free cash flow = Net cash provided by operating activities − Cash payments planned for investments in plant, equipment, and other long-term assets

Many companies use free cash flow to manage their operations. Suppose Greg's Groovy Tunes expects net cash provided by operations of $200,000. Assume Greg's Groovy Tunes plans to spend $160,000 to modernize its production facilities. In this case, Greg's Groovy Tunes' free cash flow would be $40,000 ($200,000 – $160,000). If a good investment opportunity comes along, Greg's Groovy Tunes should have $40,000 to invest.

Now let us put into practice what you have learned about the Statement of Cash Flows prepared by the indirect method.

Decision Guidelines

USING CASH-FLOW AND RELATED INFORMATION TO EVALUATE INVESTMENTS

Ann Browning is a private investor. Through the years, she has devised some guidelines for evaluating investments. Here are some of her guidelines.

Question	Financial Statement	What to Look For
• Where is most of the company's cash coming from?	Statement of cash flows	Operating activities → Good sign Investing activities → Bad sign Financing activities → Okay sign
• Do high sales and profits translate into more cash?	Statement of cash flows	Usually, but cash flows from *operating* activities must be the main source of cash for long-term success.
• If sales and profits are low, how is the company generating cash?	Statement of cash flows	If *investing* activities are generating the cash, the business may be in trouble because it is selling off its long-term assets. If *financing* activities are generating the cash, that cannot go on forever. Sooner or later, investors will demand cash flow from operating activities.
• Is the cash balance large enough to provide for expansion?	Balance sheet	The cash balance should be growing over time. If not, the company may be in trouble.
• Can the business pay its debts?	Income statement	Does the trend indicate increasing net income.
	Statement of cash flows	Cash flows from operating activities should be the main source of cash.
	Balance sheet	Are the current ratio and debt ratio adequate?

Summary Problem

The Adams Corporation reported the following Income Statement and comparative Balance Sheet for 2011 and 2010, along with transaction data for 2011:

ADAMS CORPORATION
Income Statement
Year Ended December 31, 2011

Sales revenue		$662,000
Cost of goods sold		560,000
Gross profit		102,000
Operating expenses:		
Salary expense	$46,000	
Depreciation expense	10,000	
Rent expense	2,000	
Total operating expenses		58,000
Income from operations		44,000
Other items:		
Loss on sale of equipment		(2,000)
Income before income tax		42,000
Income tax expense		16,000
Net income		$ 26,000

ADAMS CORPORATION
Balance Sheet
December 31, 2011 and 2010

Assets	2011	2010	Liabilities	2011	2010
Current:			Current:		
Cash and equivalents	$ 22,000	$ 3,000	Accounts payable	$ 35,000	$ 26,000
Accounts receivable	22,000	23,000	Accrued liabilities	7,000	9,000
Inventories	35,000	34,000	Income tax payable	10,000	10,000
Total current assets	79,000	60,000	Total current liabilities	52,000	45,000
Equipment, net	126,000	72,000	Bonds payable	84,000	53,000
			Stockholders' Equity		
			Common stock	52,000	20,000
			Retained earnings	27,000	19,000
			Less: Treasury stock	(10,000)	(5,000)
Total assets	$205,000	$132,000	Total liabilities and equity	$205,000	$132,000

Transaction Data for 2011:	
Purchase of equipment	$140,000
Payment of dividends	18,000
Issuance of common stock to retire bonds payable	13,000
Issuance of bonds payable to borrow cash	44,000
Cash receipt from issuance of common stock	19,000
Cash receipt from sale of equipment (book value, $76,000)	74,000
Purchase of treasury stock	5,000

Requirement

1. Prepare Adams Corporation's Statement of Cash Flows for the year ended December 31, 2011. Format operating cash flows by the indirect method. Follow the four steps outlined below.

   STEP 1. Lay out the format of the Statement of Cash Flows.

   STEP 2. From the comparative Balance Sheet, compute the increase in cash during the year.

   STEP 3. From the Income Statement, take net income, depreciation, and the loss on sale of equipment to the Statement of Cash Flows.

   STEP 4. Complete the Statement of Cash Flows. Account for the year-to-year change in each Balance Sheet account. Prepare a T-account to show the transaction activity in each long-term balance-sheet account.

Solution

ADAMS CORPORATION Statement of Cash Flows Year Ended December 31, 2011		
Cash flows from operating activities:		
Net income		$26,000
Adjustments to reconcile net income to net cash provided by operating activities:		
Depreciation	$ 10,000	
Loss on sale of equipment	2,000	
Decrease in accounts receivable	1,000	
Increase in inventories	(1,000)	
Increase in accounts payable	9,000	
Decrease in accrued liabilities	(2,000)	19,000
Net cash provided by operating activities		45,000
Cash flows from investing activities:		
Purchase of equipment	(140,000)	
Sale of equipment	74,000	
Net cash used for investing activities		(66,000)
Cash flows from financing activities:		
Issuance of common stock	19,000	
Payment of dividends	(18,000)	
Issuance of bonds payable	44,000	
Purchase of treasury stock	(5,000)	
Net cash provided by financing activities		40,000
Net increase in cash		19,000
Cash balance, December 31, 2010		3,000
Cash balance, December 31, 2011		$22,000
Noncash investing and financing activities:		
Issuance of common stock to retire bonds payable		$13,000
Total noncash investing and financing activities		$13,000

Relevant T-Accounts:

Equipment, net

	Debit	Credit
Bal	72,000	
	140,000	10,000
		76,000
Bal	126,000	

Bonds payable

Debit		Credit
	Bal	53,000
13,000		44,000
	Bal	84,000

Common stock

Debit		Credit
	Bal	20,000
		13,000
		19,000
	Bal	52,000

Retained earnings

Debit		Credit
	Bal	19,000
18,000		26,000
	Bal	27,000

Treasury stock

	Debit	Credit
Bal	5,000	
	5,000	
Bal	10,000	

Review The Statement of Cash Flows

Accounting Vocabulary

Cash Equivalents (p. 710)
Highly liquid short-term investments that can be readily converted into cash.

Cash Flows (p. 710)
Cash receipts and cash payments.

Direct Method (p. 712)
Format of the operating activities section of the Statement of Cash Flows; lists the major categories of operating cash receipts and cash payments.

Financing Activities (p. 711)
Activities that obtain the cash needed to launch and sustain the business; a section of the Statement of Cash Flows.

Free Cash Flow (p. 724)
The amount of cash available from operations after paying for planned investments in plant, equipment, and other long-term assets.

Indirect Method (p. 712)
Format of the operating activities section of the Statement of Cash Flows; starts with net income and reconciles to net cash provided by operating activities.

Investing Activities (p. 711)
Activities that increase or decrease long-term assets; a section of the Statement of Cash Flows.

Operating Activities (p. 711)
Activities that create revenue or expense in the entity's major line of business; a section of the Statement of Cash Flows. Operating activities affect the Income Statement.

Quick Check

1. The purposes of the cash-flow statement are to
   a. evaluate management decisions.
   b. determine ability to pay liabilities and dividends.
   c. predict future cash flows.
   d. All of the above
2. The main categories of cash-flow activities are
   a. direct and indirect.
   b. operating, investing, and financing.
   c. current and long-term.
   d. noncash investing and financing.
3. Operating activities are most closely related to
   a. long-term assets.
   b. long-term liabilities and owners' equity.
   c. current assets and current liabilities.
   d. dividends and treasury stock.
4. Which item does *not* appear on a Statement of Cash Flows prepared by the indirect method?
   a. Collections from customers
   b. Depreciation
   c. Net income
   d. Gain on sale of land
5. Hobby Gas Station earned net income of $73,000 after deducting depreciation of $7,000 and all other expenses. Current assets decreased by $6,000, and current liabilities increased by $9,000. How much was Hobby Gas Station's cash provided by operating activities (indirect method)?
   a. $95,000
   b. $51,000
   c. $83,000
   d. $63,000

6. The Plant assets account of Vacation Club shows the following:

Plant assets, net

Beg	99,000	Depr	27,000
Purchase	437,000	Sale	54,000
End	455,000		

Vacation Club sold plant assets at a $16,000 loss. Where on the Statement of Cash Flows should Vacation Club report the sale of plant assets? How much should the business report for the sale?

a. Investing cash flows—cash receipt of $54,000
b. Investing cash flows—cash receipt of $38,000
c. Financing cash flows—cash receipt of $70,000
d. Investing cash flows—cash receipt of $70,000

7. Rock Music, Corp., borrowed $36,000, issued common stock of $15,000, and paid dividends of $21,000. What was Rock Music's net cash provided (used) by financing activities?

a. $0
b. ($21,000)
c. $30,000
d. $72,000

8. Which item appears on a Statement of Cash Flows prepared by the indirect method?

a. Payments to suppliers
b. Payments of income tax
c. Depreciation
d. Collections from customers

9. **(Appendix 13A: Direct Method)** Sun Copy Center had accounts receivable of $23,000 at the beginning of the year and $51,000 at year-end. Revenue for the year totaled $103,000. How much cash did the business collect from customers?

a. $75,000
b. $131,000
c. $177,000
d. $126,000

10. **(Appendix 13A: Direct Method)** Cell Call Company had operating expense of $44,000. At the beginning of the year, Cell Call owed $7,000 on accrued liabilities. At year-end, accrued liabilities were $3,500. How much cash did Cell Call pay for operating expenses?

a. $37,000
b. $47,500
c. $48,500
d. $40,500

Answers are given after Apply Your Knowledge (p. 748).

Assess Your Progress

■ Short Exercises

S13-1 *(L.OBJ. 1)* **Purposes of the Statement of Cash Flows [10 min]**
Financial statements all have a goal. The cash flow statement does as well.

Requirement

1. Describe how the Statement of Cash Flows helps investors and creditors perform each of the following functions:
   a. Predict future cash flows
   b. Evaluate management decisions
   c. Predict the ability to make debt payments to lenders and pay dividends to stockholders

S13-2 *(L.OBJ. 2)* **Classifying cash-flow items [10 min]**
Cash-flow items must be categorized into one of four categories.

Requirement

1. Answer the following questions about the Statement of Cash Flows:
   a. List the categories of cash flows in order of presentation.
   b. What is the "key reconciling figure" for the Statement of Cash Flows? Where do you get this figure?
   c. What is the first dollar amount to report for the indirect method?

S13-3 *(L.OBJ. 3)* **Classifying items on the indirect Statement of Cash Flows [10 min]**
Triumph Corporation is preparing its Statement of Cash Flows by the *indirect* method. Triumph has the following items for you to consider in preparing the statement:

_____	a. Increase in accounts payable	_____	g. Depreciation expense
_____	b. Payment of dividends	_____	h. Increase in inventory
_____	c. Decrease in accrued liabilities	_____	i. Decrease in accounts receivable
_____	d. Issuance of common stock	_____	j. Purchase of equipment
_____	e. Gain on sale of building		
_____	f. Loss on sale of land		

Requirement

1. Identify each item as an
   - Operating activity—addition to net income (O+), or subtraction from net income (O–)
   - Investing activity—addition to cash flow (I+), or subtraction from cash flow (I–)
   - Financing activity—addition to cash flow (F+), or subtraction from cash flow (F–)
   - Activity that is not used to prepare the indirect cash-flow statement (N)

S13-4 *(L.OBJ. 3)* **Computing cash flows from operating activities—indirect method [10 min]**
DVR Equipment, Inc., reported the following data for 2011:

Income Statement	
Net income	$ 40,000
Depreciation	10,000
Balance sheet	
Increase in Accounts receivable	9,000
Decrease in Accounts payable	6,000

Requirement

1. Compute DVR's net cash provided by operating activities—indirect method.

S13-5 *(L.OBJ. 3)* **Computing cash flows from operating activities—indirect method [10 min]**

Street Cellular accountants have assembled the following data for the year ended June 30, 2012:

Cash receipt from sale of land	$ 29,000	Net income	$ 64,000
Depreciation expense	19,000	Purchase of equipment	44,000
Payment of dividends	5,700	Decrease in current liabilities	7,000
Cash receipt from issuance of common stock	16,000	Increase in current assets other than cash	13,000

Requirement

1. Prepare the *operating* activities section using the indirect method for Street Cellular's Statement of Cash Flows for the year ended June 30, 2012.

Note: Short Exercise 13-5 data is used to complete Short Exercise 13-6.

S13-6 *(L.OBJ. 3)* **Computing cash flows—indirect method [15 min]**

Use the data in Short Exercise 13-5 to complete this exercise.

Requirement

1. Prepare Street Cellular's Statement of Cash Flows using the indirect method for the year ended June 30, 2012. Stop after determining the net increase (or decrease) in cash.

S13-7 *(L.OBJ. 3)* **Computing investing and financing cash flows [10 min]**

White Media Corporation had the following Income Statement and Balance Sheet for 2011:

WHITE MEDIA CORPORATION Income Statement Year Ended December 31, 2011	
Service revenue	$ 79,000
Depreciation expense	6,000
Other expenses	54,000
Net income	$ 19,000

WHITE MEDIA CORPORATION Comparative Balance Sheet December 31, 2011 and 2010					
Assets	**2011**	**2010**	**Liabilities**	**2011**	**2010**
Current:			Current:		
Cash	$ 5,100	$ 4,200	Accounts payable	$ 6,500	$ 4,500
Accounts receivable	10,100	8,100	Long-term notes payable	7,000	10,000
Equipment, net	76,000	68,000	**Stockholders' Equity**		
			Common stock	27,000	18,000
			Retained earnings	50,700	47,800
Total assets	$ 91,200	$ 80,300	Total liabilities and stockholders' equity	$ 91,200	$ 80,300

Requirement

1. Compute for White Media Corporation during 2011 the
   a. Acquisition of equipment. The business sold no equipment during the year.
   b. Payment of a long-term note payable. During the year the business issued a $5,100 note payable.

Note: Short Exercise 13-8 should be used only after completing Short Exercise 13-7.

S13-8 *(L.OBJ. 3)* **Preparing the Statement of Cash Flows—indirect method [15-20 min]**
Use the White Media Corporation data in Short Exercise 13-7 and the results you calculated from the requirements.

Requirement

1. Prepare White Media's Statement of Cash Flows—indirect method—for the year ended December 31, 2011.

S13-9 *(L.OBJ. 3)* **Computing the change in cash [5 min]**
Brianna's Wedding Shops earned net income of $76,000, which included depreciation of $17,000. Brianna's paid $122,000 for a building and borrowed $63,000 on a long-term note payable.

Requirement

1. How much did Brianna's cash balance increase or decrease during the year?

S13-10 *(L.OBJ. 3)* **Computing the change in cash [5 min]**
Roberta McLeary Company expects the following for 2011:

- Net cash provided by operating activities of $156,000
- Net cash provided by financing activities of $63,000
- Net cash used for investing activities of $78,000 (no sales of long-term assets)

Requirement

1. How much free cash flow does McLeary expect for 2011?

Exercises

E13-11 *(L.OBJ. 1)* **Predicting future cash flows [10 min]**
Magnuson's Magnets reported net loss for the year of $10,000; however, they reported an increase in cash balance of $20,000. The CFO states "Magnuson's Magnets would have shown a profit were it not for the depreciation expense recorded this year."

Requirements

1. Can the CFO be right? Why?
2. Based on the information provided, what would you predict future cash flows to be?

E13-12 *(L.OBJ. 2)* **Classifying cash-flow items [10 min]**
Consider the following transactions:

a. Purchased Building for $200,000 cash
b. Issued $10 par preferred stock for cash
c. Cash received from sales to customers of $20,000
d. Cash paid to vendors, $10,000
e. Sold Building for $5,000 gain for cash
f. Purchased common treasury shares for $15,000
g. Paid a notes payable with 1,000 of the company's common shares

Requirement

1. Identify the category of the Statement of Cash Flows in which each transaction would be reported.

E13-13 *(L.OBJ. 3)* **Classifying items on the indirect Statement of Cash Flows [5-10 min]**
The cash flow statement categorizes like transactions for optimal reporting.

Requirement

1. Identify each of the following transactions as an (a)
   - Operating activity (O),
   - Investing activity (I),
   - Financing activity (F),
   - Noncash investing and financing activity (NIF), or
   - transaction that is not reported on the Statement of Cash Flows (N).

   For each cash flow, indicate whether the item increases (+) or decreases (–) cash. The *indirect* method is used to report cash flows from operating activities.

_____	a. Loss on sale of land	_____	i. Cash sale of land
_____	b. Acquisition of equipment by issuance of note payable	_____	j. Issuance of long-term note payable to borrow cash
_____	c. Payment of long-term debt	_____	k. Depreciation
_____	d. Acquisition of building by issuance of common stock	_____	l. Purchase of treasury stock
_____	e. Accrual of salary expense	_____	m. Issuance of common stock
_____	f. Decrease in inventory	_____	n. Increase in accounts payable
_____	g. Increase in prepaid expenses	_____	o. Net income
_____	h. Decrease in accrued liabilities	_____	p. Payment of cash dividend

E13-14 *(L.OBJ. 3)* **Classifying transactions on the Statement of Cash Flows—indirect method [5–10 min]**
Consider the following transactions:

a. Cash	81,000		g. Land	18,000	
Common stock		81,000	Cash		18,000
b. Treasury stock	13,000		h. Cash	7,200	
Cash		13,000	Equipment		7,200
c. Cash	60,000		i. Bonds payable	45,000	
Sales revenue		60,000	Cash		45,000
d. Land	87,700		j. Building	164,000	
Cash		87,700	Note payable, long-term		164,000
e. Depreciation expense	9,000		k. Loss on disposal of equipment	1,400	
Accumulated depreciation		9,000	Equipment, net		1,400
f. Dividends payable	16,500				
Cash		16,500			

Requirement

1. Indicate whether each transaction would result in an operating activity, an investing activity, or a financing activity for an indirect method Statement of Cash Flows and the accompanying schedule of noncash investing and financing activities.

E13-15 *(L.OBJ. 3)* **Computing operating acitivites cash flow—indirect method [10–15 min]**

The records of Paramount Color Engraving reveal the following:

Net income	$ 42,000	Depreciation	$ 11,000
Sales revenue	12,000	Decrease in current liabilities	20,000
Loss on sale of land	7,000	Increase in current assets	
Acquisition of land	36,000	other than cash	8,000

Requirements

1. Compute cash flows from operating activities by the indirect method.
2. Evaluate the operating cash flow of Paramount Color Engraving. Give the reason for your evaluation.

E13-16 *(L.OBJ. 3)* **Computing operating activities cash flow—indirect method [15–20 min]**

The accounting records of CD Sales, Inc., include the following accounts:

Cash

Mar 1	7,000	
	????	
Mar 31	5,000	

Accounts receivable

Mar 1	19,000	
	????	
Mar 31	14,000	

Inventory

Mar 1	21,000	
	????	
Mar 31	24,000	

Accounts payable

	Mar 1	13,000
		????
	Mar 31	17,500

Accumulated depr.—equipment

	Mar 1	50,000
	Depr	4,000
	Mar 31	54,000

Retained earnings

		Mar 1	66,000
Dividend	16,000	Net Inc	81,000
		Mar 31	131,000

Requirement

1. Compute CD's net cash provided by (used for) operating activities during March. Use the indirect method.

E13-17 *(L.OBJ. 3)* **Preparing the Statement of Cash Flows—indirect method [20–30 min]**

The Income Statement and additional data of Minerals Plus, Inc., follow:

MINERALS PLUS, INC. Income Statement Year Ended June 30, 2010		
Revenues:		
Service revenue		$ 236,000
Expenses:		
Cost of goods sold	$ 96,000	
Salary expense	54,000	
Depreciation expense	27,000	
Income tax expense	9,000	186,000
Net income		$ 50,000

Additional data follow:

a. Acquisition of plant assets is $120,000. Of this amount, $103,000 is paid in cash and $17,000 by signing a note payable.
b. Cash receipt from sale of land totals $24,000. There was no gain or loss.
c. Cash receipts from issuance of common stock total $32,000.
d. Payment of note payable is $17,000.
e. Payment of dividends is $11,000.
f. From the balance sheet:

	June 30,	
	2010	2009
Current Assets:		
Cash	$ 32,000	$ 15,000
Accounts receivable	38,000	55,000
Inventory	92,000	86,000
Current Liabilities:		
Accounts payable	$ 36,000	$ 22,000
Accrued liabilities	15,000	25,000

Requirement

1. Prepare Minerals Plus' Statement of Cash Flows for the year ended June 30, 2010, using the indirect method. Include a separate section for noncash investing and financing activities.

E13-18 *(L.OBJ. 3)* **Computing operating activities cash flow—indirect method [10–15 min]**
Consider the following facts for Java Jolt:

a. Beginning and ending Retained earnings are $48,000 and $69,000, respectively. Net income for the period is $64,000.
b. Beginning and ending Plant assets, net, are $102,000 and $106,000, respectively. Depreciation for the period is $19,000, and acquisitions of new plant assets total $26,000. Plant assets were sold at a $4,000 gain.

Requirements

1. How much are cash dividends?
2. What was the amount of the cash receipt from the sale of plant assets?

E13-19 *(L.OBJ. 3)* **Computing the cash effect of acquiring assets [10 min]**
Cole Gymnastics Equipment, Inc., reported the following financial statements for 2011:

COLE GYMNASTICS EQUIPMENT, INC. Income Statement Year Ended December 31, 2011		
		(In thousands)
Sales revenue		$ 711
Cost of goods sold	$ 343	
Depreciation expense	49	
Other expenses	210	
Total expenses		602
Net income		$ 109

COLE GYMNASTICS EQUIPMENT, INC. Comparative Balance Sheet December 31, 2011 and 2010					
(In thousands)					
Assets	2011	2010	**Liabilities**	2011	2010
Current:			Current:		
Cash	$ 20	$ 16	Accounts payable	$ 75	$ 73
Accounts receivable	56	50	Salary payable	3	4
Inventory	80	87	Long–term notes payable	58	69
Long–term investments	91	74	**Stockholders' Equity**		
Plant assets, net	225	185	Common stock	45	32
			Retained earnings	291	234
Total	$ 472	$ 412	Total	$ 472	$ 412

Requirement

1. Compute the amount of Cole Gymnastics' acquisition of plant assets. Cole Gymnastics sold no plant assets.

E13-20 *(L.OBJ. 3)* **Computing the cash effect of transactions [15 min]**
Use the Cole Gymnastics data in Exercise 13-19.

Requirement

1. Compute the following:

   a. New borrowing or payment of long-term notes payable, with Cole Gymnastics having only one long-term note payable transaction during the year
   b. Issuance of common stock, with Cole Gymnastics having only one common stock transaction during the year
   c. Payment of cash dividends

Note: Exercise 13-21 should be used only after completing Exercises 13-19 and 13-20.

E13-21 *(L.OBJ. 3)* **Computing the cash effect of transactions [15 min]**
Use the Cole Gymnastics data in Exercises 13-19 and 13-20.

Requirement

1. Prepare the company's Statement of Cash Flows—indirect method—for the year ended December 31, 2011. Show all amounts in thousands.

■ Problems (Group A)

P13-22A *(L.OBJ. 1, 2, 3)* **Purpose of the statement and preparing the Statement of Cash Flows—indirect method [40–50 min]**

North American Reserve Rare Coins (NARRC) was formed on January 1, 2010, when NARRC issued its common stock for $475,000. Additional data for the year follows:

a. On January 1, 2010, NARRC issued common stock for $475,000.
b. Early in January, NARRC made the following cash payments:
   1. For store fixtures, $46,000
   2. For inventory, $330,000
   3. For rent expense on a store building, $11,000
c. Later in the year, NARRC purchased inventory on account for $235,000. Before year-end, NARRC paid $135,000 of this account payable.
d. During 2010, NARRC sold 2,900 units of inventory for $300 each. Before year-end, the company collected 85% of this amount. Cost of goods sold for the year was $310,000, and ending inventory totaled $255,000.
e. The store employs three people. The combined annual payroll is $96,000, of which NARRC still owes $5,000 at year-end.
f. At the end of the year, NARRC paid income tax of $16,000.
g. Late in 2010, NARRC paid cash dividends of $43,000.
h. For equipment, NARRC uses the straight-line depreciation method, over five years, with zero residual value.

Requirements

1. What is the purpose of the cash flow statement?
2. Prepare NARRC's Income Statement for the year ended December 31, 2010. Use the single-step format, with all revenues listed together and all expenses together.
3. Prepare NARRC's Balance Sheet at December 31, 2010.
4. Prepare NARRC's Statement of Cash Flows using the indirect method for the year ended December 31, 2010.

P13-23A *(L.OBJ. 3)* **Preparing the Statement of Cash Flows—indirect method [35–45 min]**

Accountants for Smithson, Inc., have assembled the following data for the year ended December 31, 2011:

	December 31,	
	2011	2010
Current Accounts:		
Current assets:		
Cash and cash equivalents	$105,600	$ 26,000
Accounts receivable	64,200	69,300
Inventories	85,000	83,000
Current liabilities:		
Accounts payable	57,800	56,000
Income tax payable	15,000	16,700

Transaction Data for 2011:			
Issuance of common stock for cash	$ 37,000	Payment of note payable	$45,100
Depreciation expense	18,000	Payment of cash dividends	51,000
Purchase of equipment	71,000	Issuance of note payable to borrow cash	60,000
Acquisition of land by issuing long-term note payable	118,000	Gain on sale of building	4,500
Cost basis of building sold	56,000	Net income	72,500

Requirement

1. Prepare Smithson's Statement of Cash Flows using the *indirect* method. Include an accompanying schedule of noncash investing and financing activities.

P13-24A *(L.OBJ. 3)* **Preparing the Statement of Cash Flows—indirect method—and evaluating cash flows [35–45 min]**

The comparative Balance Sheet of Morston Medical Supply at December 31, 2012, reported the following:

	December 31,	
	2012	2011
Current assets:		
Cash and cash equivalents	$ 87,800	$ 23,500
Accounts receivable	14,800	21,300
Inventories	63,200	60,000
Current Liabilities:		
Accounts payable	30,100	30,100
Accrued liabilities	10,500	11,100

Morston's transactions during 2012 included the following:

Payment of cash dividend	$ 14,200	Depreciation expense	$ 16,800
Purchase of equipment	54,600	Purchase of building	105,000
Issuance of long-term note payable to borrow cash	49,000	Net income	60,600
		Issuance of common stock for cash	109,000

Requirements

1. Prepare the Statement of Cash Flows of Morston Medical Supply for the year ended December 31, 2012. Use the *indirect* method to report cash flows from operating activities.
2. Evaluate Morston's cash flows for the year. Mention all three categories of cash flows and give the reason for your evaluation.

P13-25A *(L.OBJ. 3)* **Preparing the Statement of Cash Flows—indirect method [35-45 min]**
The 2012 comparative Balance Sheet and Income Statement of Cobbs Hill, Inc., follow:

COBBS HILL, INC. Comparative Balance Sheet December 31, 2012 and 2011			
	2012	2011	Increase (Decrease)
Current assets:			
Cash and cash equivalents	$ 26,000	$ 15,300	$ 10,700
Accounts receivable	26,700	25,000	1,700
Inventories	79,000	91,800	(12,800)
Plant assets:			
Land	34,700	10,000	24,700
Equipment, net	100,900	92,700	8,200
Total assets	$ 267,300	$ 234,800	$ 32,500
Current liabilities:			
Accounts payable	$ 35,600	$ 30,700	$ 4,900
Accrued liabilities	28,200	30,000	(1,800)
Long–term liabilities:			
Notes payable	77,000	104,000	(27,000)
Stockholders' equity:			
Common stock	88,200	64,400	23,800
Retained earnings	38,300	5,700	32,600
Total liabilities and stockholders' equity	$ 267,300	$ 234,800	$ 32,500

COBBS HILL, INC. Income Statement Year Ended December 31, 2012		
Revenues:		
Sales revenue		$ 443,000
Interest revenue		8,700
Total revenues		451,700
Expenses:		
Cost of goods sold	$ 200,200	
Salary expense	73,400	
Depreciation expense	14,200	
Other operating expense	10,000	
Interest expense	21,800	
Income tax expense	19,700	
Total expenses		339,300
Net income		$ 112,400

Cobbs Hill had no noncash investing and financing transactions during 2012. During the year, there were no sales of land or equipment, no issuances of notes payable, no retirements of stock, and no treasury stock transactions.

Requirements

1. Prepare the 2012 Statement of Cash Flows, formatting operating activities by the *indirect* method.
2. How will what you learned in this problem help you evaluate an investment?

Problems (Group B)

P13-26B *(L.OBJ. 1, 2, 3)* **Purpose of the statement and preparing the Statement of Cash Flows—indirect method [40–50 min]**

Official Reserve Rare Coins (ORRC) was formed on January 1, 2010, when ORRC issued its common stock for $475,000. Additional data for the year follows:

a. On January 1, 2010, ORRC issued common stock for $475,000.
b. Early in January, ORRC made the following cash payments:
   1. For store fixtures, $46,000
   2. For inventory, $310,000
   3. For rent expense on a store building, $10,000
c. Later in the year, ORRC purchased inventory on account for $237,000. Before year-end, ORRC paid $137,000 of this account payable.
d. During 2010, ORRC sold 2,800 units of inventory for $225 each. Before year end, the company collected 80% of this amount. Cost of goods sold for the year was $340,000, and ending inventory totaled $207,000.
e. The store employs three people. The combined annual payroll is $94,000, of which ORRC still owes $2,000 at year-end.
f. At the end of the year, ORRC paid income tax of $22,000.
g. Late in 2010, ORRC paid cash dividends of $44,000.
h. For equipment, ORRC uses the straight-line depreciation method, over 5 years, with zero residual value.

Requirements

1. What is the purpose of the cash flow statement?
2. Prepare ORRC's Income Statement for the year ended December 31, 2010. Use the single-step format, with all revenues listed together and all expenses together.
3. Prepare ORRC's Balance Sheet at December 31, 2010.
4. Prepare ORRC's Statement of Cash Flows using the *indirect* method for the year ended December 31, 2010.

P13-27B *(L.OBJ. 3)* **Preparing the Statement of Cash Flows—indirect method [35-45 min]**

Accountants for Carlson, Inc., have assembled the following data for the year ended December 31, 2011:

	December 31, 2011	December 31, 2010
Current Accounts:		
Current assets:		
Cash and cash equivalents	$ 60,100	$ 19,000
Accounts receivable	64,500	69,000
Inventories	86,000	84,000
Current liabilities:		
Accounts payable	57,600	56,200
Income tax payable	14,700	16,400

Transaction Data for 2011:

Issuance of common stock for cash	$ 42,000	Payment of note payable	$44,100
Depreciation expense	21,000	Payment of cash dividends	48,000
Purchase of equipment	66,000	Issuance of note payable to borrow cash	59,000
Acquisition of land by issuing long-term note payable	118,000	Gain on sale of building	4,500
		Net income	69,500
		Cost basis of building sold	$ 5,500

Requirement

1. Prepare Carlson's Statement of Cash Flows using the *indirect* method. Include an accompanying schedule of noncash investing and financing activities.

P13-28B *(L.OBJ. 3)* **Preparing the Statement of Cash Flows—indirect method—and evaluating cash flows [35–45 min]**

The comparative Balance Sheet of Smithson Medical Supply at December 31, 2012, reported the following:

	December 31,	
	2012	2011
Current assets:		
Cash and cash equivalents	$ 78,600	$ 19,500
Accounts receivable	14,700	21,400
Inventories	62,600	60,400
Current liabilities:		
Accounts payable	28,100	27,100
Accrued liabilities	10,300	11,300

Smithson's transactions during 2012 included the following:

Payment of cash dividend	$ 22,200	Depreciation expense	$ 16,800
Purchase of equipment	54,600	Purchase of building	109,000
Issuance of long-term note payable		Net income	61,600
to borrow cash	50,000	Issuance of common stock for cash	112,000

Requirements

1. Prepare the Statement of Cash Flows of Smithson Medical Supply for the year ended December 31, 2012. Use the *indirect* method to report cash flows from operating activities.
2. Evaluate Smithson's cash flows for the year. Mention all three categories of cash flows and give the reason for your evaluation.

P13-29B *(L.OBJ. 3)* **Preparing the statement of cash flow—indirect method [35–45 min]**
The 2012 comparative Balance Sheet and Income Statement of Digital Subscriptions, Inc., follow:

DIGITAL SUBSCRIPTIONS, INC. Comparative Balance Sheet December 31, 2012 and 2011			
	2012	2011	Increase (Decrease)
Current assets:			
Cash and cash equivalents	$ 26,800	$ 15,800	$ 11,000
Accounts receivable	26,500	25,000	1,500
Inventories	79,500	91,100	(11,600)
Plant assets:			
Land	34,700	10,000	24,700
Equipment, net	96,900	88,700	8,200
Total assets	$ 264,400	$ 230,600	$ 33,800
Current liabilities:			
Accounts payable	$ 35,500	$ 30,000	$ 5,500
Accrued liabilities	28,500	30,100	(1,600)
Long–term liabilities:			
Notes payable	73,000	102,000	(29,000)
Stockholders' equity:			
Common stock	88,700	64,300	24,400
Retained earnings	38,700	4,200	34,500
Total liabilities and stockholders' equity	$ 264,400	$ 230,600	$ 33,800

DIGITAL SUBSCRIPTIONS, INC. Income Statement Year Ended December 31, 2012		
Revenues:		
Sales revenue		$ 441,000
Interest revenue		8,100
Total revenues		449,100
Expenses:		
Cost of goods sold	$ 205,200	
Salary expense	79,400	
Depreciation expense	14,800	
Other operating expense	10,300	
Interest expense	21,900	
Income tax expense	19,900	
Total expenses		351,500
Net income		$ 97,600

Digital Subscriptions had no noncash investing and financing transactions during 2012. During the year, there were no sales of land or equipment, no issuances of notes payable, no retirements of stock, and no treasury stock transactions.

Requirements

1. Prepare the 2012 Statement of Cash Flows, formatting operating activities by the *indirect* method.
2. How will what you learned in this problem help you evaluate an investment?

Continuing Exercise

E13-30 This exercise continues the Sherman Lawn Service, Inc., situation from Exercise 12-38 of Chapter 12. Refer to the Comparative Balance Sheet for Sherman Lawn Service.

SHERMAN LAWN SERVICE, INC. Comparative Balance Sheet As of December 31, 2009 and 2010		
Assets	2010	2009
Cash	$ 5,000	$ 1,480
Accounts receivable	2,200	150
Lawn supplies	150	70
Equipment	1,400	1,400
(Less Accumulated depreciation)	(495)	(146)
Total Assets	$ 8,255	$ 2,954
Liabilities		
Accounts payable	$ 350	$ 1,400
Stockholders' Equity		
Common stock	2,000	1,000
Retained earnings	5,905	554
Total liabilities and stockholders' equity	$ 8,255	$ 2,954

Requirement

1. Prepare the Statement of Cash Flows using the *indirect* method. Assume no dividends were declared or paid during the year.

Continuing Problem

P13-31 This problem continues the Haupt Consulting, Inc., situation from Problem 12-39 of Chapter 12. Refer to the balance sheet and income statement for Haupt Consulting.

HAUPT CONSULTING, INC. Comparative Balance Sheet As of December 31, 2009 and 2010		
Assets	2010	2009
Cash	$ 5,000	$ 8,100
Accounts receivable	2,200	1,700
Supplies	420	300
Equipment	10,000	2,000
Furniture	3,600	3,600
Building	75,000	—
(Less Accumulated depreciation)	(2,753)	(93)
Total Assets	$ 93,467	$ 15,607
Liabilities		
Accounts payable	$ 350	$ 3,900
Salary payable	2,500	0
Notes payable	40,000	0
Stockholders' Equity		
Common stock	20,000	10,000
Retained earnings	30,617	1,707
Total liabilities and stockholders' equity	$ 93,467	$ 15,607

Additional Information: Haupt declared and paid $10,000 in dividends to stockholders.

Requirement

1. Prepare the Statement of Cash Flows using the indirect method.

Apply Your Knowledge

■ Decision Cases

Case 1. The 2010 comparative Income Statement and the 2010 comparative Balance Sheet of Golf America, Inc., have just been distributed at a meeting of the company's board of directors. The members of the board of directors raise a fundamental question: Why is the cash balance so low? This question is especially hard to understand because 2010 showed record profits. As the controller of the company, you must answer the question.

GOLF AMERICA, INC. Comparative Income Statement Years Ended December 31, 2010 and 2009		
(In thousands)	**2010**	**2009**
Revenues and gains:		
Sales revenue	$444	$310
Gain on sale of equipment (sale price, $33)	—	18
Total revenues and gains	$444	$328
Expenses and losses:		
Cost of goods sold	$221	$162
Salary expense	48	28
Depreciation expense	46	22
Interest expense	13	20
Amortization expense on patent	11	11
Loss on sale of land (sale price, $61)	—	35
Total expenses and losses	339	278
Net income	$105	$ 50

GOLF AMERICA, INC. Comparative Balance Sheet December 31, 2010 and 2009		
(In thousands)	**2010**	**2009**
Assets		
Cash	$ 25	$ 63
Accounts receivable, net	72	61
Inventories	194	181
Long-term investments	31	0
Property, plant, and equipment, net	125	61
Patents	177	188
Totals	$624	$554
Liabilities and Owners' Equity		
Accounts payable	$ 63	$ 56
Accrued liabilities	12	17
Notes payable, long-term	179	264
Common stock	149	61
Retained earnings	221	156
Totals	$624	$554

Requirements

1. Prepare a Statement of Cash Flows for 2010 in the format that best shows the relationship between net income and operating cash flow. The company sold no plant assets or long-term investments and issued no notes payable during 2010. There were *no* noncash investing and financing transactions during the year. Show all amounts in thousands.
2. Considering net income and the company's cash flows during 2010, was it a good year or a bad year? Give your reasons.

Case 2. Showcase Cinemas and Theater by Design are asking you to recommend their stock to your clients. Because Showcase and Theater by Design earn about the same net income and have similar financial positions, your decision depends on their cash-flow statements, summarized as follows:

	Theater by Design		Showcase Cinemas	
Net cash provided by operating activities		$ 30,000		$ 70,000
Cash provided by (used for) investing activities:				
Purchase of plant assets	$(20,000)		$(100,000)	
Sale of plant assets	40,000	20,000	10,000	(90,000)
Cash provided by (used for) financing activities:				
Issuance of common stock		—		30,000
Paying off long-term debt		(40,000)		—
Net increase in cash		$ 10,000		$ 10,000

Requirement

1. Based on their cash flows, which company looks better? Give your reasons.

Ethical Issue

Moss Exports is having a bad year. Net income is only $60,000. Also, two important overseas customers are falling behind in their payments to Moss, and Moss's accounts receivable are ballooning. The company desperately needs a loan. The Moss Exports board of directors is considering ways to put the best face on the company's financial statements. Moss's bank closely examines cash flow from operations. Daniel Peavey, Moss's controller, suggests reclassifying as long-term the receivables from the slow-paying clients. He explains to the board that removing the $80,000 rise in accounts receivable from current assets will increase net cash provided by operations. This approach may help Moss get the loan.

Requirements

1. Using only the amounts given, compute net cash provided by operations, both without and with the reclassification of the receivables. Which reporting makes Moss look better?
2. Under what condition would the reclassification of the receivables be ethical? Unethical?

Financial Statement Case

Use the **Amazon.com** Statement of Cash Flows, along with the company's other financial statements at the end of this book, to answer the following questions.

Requirements

1. Which method does **Amazon** use to report net cash flows from *operating* activities? How can you tell?
2. **Amazon** earned net income during 2007. Did operations *provide* cash or *use* cash during 2007? Give the amount. How did operating cash during 2007 compare with 2006? Be specific, and state the reason for your answer.

3. Suppose **Amazon** reported net cash flows from operating activities by the direct method. Compute these amounts for the year ended December 31, 2007:
   a. Collections from customers (Other current assets were $20 million at December 31, 2007, and $16 million at December 31, 2006.)
   b. Payments for inventory
4. Evaluate 2007 in terms of net income, cash flows, Balance Sheet position, and overall results. Be specific.

Team Projects

Project 1. Each member of the team should obtain the annual report of a different company. Select companies in different industries. Evaluate each company's trend of cash flows for the most recent two years. In your evaluation of the companies' cash flows, you may use any other information that is publicly available: for example, the other financial statements (Income Statement, Balance Sheet, statement of stockholders' equity, and the related notes) and news stories from magazines and newspapers. Rank the companies' cash flows from best to worst and write a two-page report on your findings.

Project 2. Select a company and obtain its annual report, including all the financial statements. Focus on the Statement of Cash Flows and, in particular, the cash flows from operating activities. Specify whether the company uses the *direct* method or the *indirect* method to report operating cash flows. As necessary, use the other financial statements (Income Statement, Balance Sheet, and Statement of Retained Earnings) and the notes to prepare the company's cash flows from operating activities by the *other* method.

Quick Check Answers

1. *d* 2. *b* 3. *c* 4. *a* 5. *a* 6. *b* 7. *c* 8. *c* 9. *a* 10. *b*

For online homework, exercises, and problems that provide you immediate feedback, please visit www.myaccountinglab.com.

Preparing The Statement Of Cash Flows By The Direct Method

4 Prepare the Statement of Cash Flows by the direct method

The Financial Accounting Standards Board (FASB) prefers the direct method of reporting cash flows from operating activities. The direct method provides clearer information about the sources and uses of cash than does the indirect method. However, very few non-public companies use the direct method because it takes more computations than the indirect method. Investing and financing cash flows are exactly the same presentation under both direct and indirect methods. Since only the preparation of the operating section differs, it is all we discuss in this Appendix.

To illustrate how the operating section of the Statement of Cash Flows differs for the direct method , we will be using the Smart Touch Learning data we used within the main chapter. The steps to prepare the Statement of Cash Flows by the direct method are as follows:

STEP 1: Lay out the operating section format of the Statement of Cash Flows by the direct method, as shown in Exhibit 13A-1.

EXHIBIT 13A-1 **Format of the Statement of Cash Flows: Direct Method**

SMART TOUCH LEARNING, INC. **Statement of Cash Flows** Year Ended December 31, 2011	
Cash flows from operating activities:	
Receipts:	
Collections from customers	
Interest received	
Dividends received on investments	
Total cash receipts	
Payments:	
To suppliers	
To employees	
For interest and income tax	
Total cash payments	
Net cash provided by operating activities	
± Cash flows from investing activities:	
+ Cash receipts from sales of long-term assets (investments, land, building, equipment, and so on)	
– Purchases of long-term assets	
Net cash provided by (used for) investing activities	
± Cash flows from financing activities:	
+ Cash receipts from issuance of stock	
+ Sale of treasury stock	
– Purchase of treasury stock	
+ Cash receipts from issuance of notes or bonds payable (borrowing)	
– Payment of notes or bonds payable	
– Payment of dividends	
Net cash provided by (used for) financing activities	
= Net increase (decrease) in cash during the year	
+ Cash at December 31, 2010	
= Cash at December 31, 2011	

STEP 2: Use the comparative Balance Sheet to determine the increase or decrease in cash during the period. The change in cash is the "reconciling key figure" for the Statement of Cash Flows. Smart Touch's comparative Balance Sheet shows that cash decreased by $20,000 during 2011. (See Exhibit 13A-2.)

EXHIBIT 13A-2 | Comparative Balance Sheet

SMART TOUCH LEARNING, INC.
Comparative Balance Sheet
December 31, 2011 and 2010

	(In thousands)	2011	2010	Increase (Decrease)
	Assets			
	Current:			
	Cash	$ 22	$ 42	$ (20)
Operating	Accounts receivable	90	73	17
Operating	Inventory	143	145	(2)
Investing	Plant assets, net	460	210	250
	Total assets	$715	$470	$245
	Liabilities			
	Current:			
Operating	Accounts payable	$ 90	$ 50	$ 40
Operating	Accrued liabilities	5	10	(5)
Financing	Long-term notes payable	160	80	80
	Stockholders' Equity			
Financing	Common stock	370	250	120
Net income—Operating Dividends Financing	Retained earnings	110	80	30
	Less: Treasury stock	(20)	0	(20)
	Total	$715	$470	$245

EXHIBIT 13A-3 | Income Statement

SMART TOUCH LEARNING, INC.
Income Statement
Year Ended December 31, 2011

	(In thousands)	
Revenues and gains:		
Sales revenue	$286	
Interest revenue	12	
Dividend revenue	9	
Gain on sale of plant assets	10	
Total revenues and gains		$317
Expenses:		
Cost of goods sold	$156	
Salary and wage expense	56	
Depreciation expense	20	
Other operating expense	16	
Interest expense	15	
Income tax expense	14	
Total expenses		277
Net income		$ 40

Step 3: Use the available data to prepare the Statement of Cash Flows. In the case of Smart Touch Learning, there was no additional data outside of the Balance Sheet and Income Statement data in Exhibit 13A-3 that affected the operating activities section.

The Statement of Cash Flows reports only transactions with cash effects. Exhibit 13A-4 shows Smart Touch Learning's completed direct method Statement of Cash Flows for 2011.

EXHIBIT 13A-4 Statement of Cash Flows—Direct Method

SMART TOUCH LEARNING, INC.
Statement of Cash Flows
Year Ended December 31, 2011

	(In thousands)	
Cash flows from operating activities:		
Receipts:		
Collections from customers	$ 269	
Interest received	12	
Dividends received	9	
Total cash receipts		$ 290
Payments:		
To suppliers	$(135)	
To employees	(56)	
For interest	(15)	
For income tax	(14)	
Total cash payments		(220)
Net cash provided by operating activities		70
Cash flows from investing activities:		
Acquisition of plant assets	$(310)	
Cash receipts from sale of plant assets	50	
Net cash used for investing activities		(260)
Cash flows from financing activities:		
Cash receipts from issuance of common stock	$ 120	
Cash receipts from issuance of notes payable	90	
Payment of notes payable	(10)	
Purchase of treasury stock	(20)	
Payment of dividends	(10)	
Net cash provided by financing activities		170
Net decrease in cash		$ (20)
Cash balance, December 31, 2010		42
Cash balance, December 31, 2011		$ 22

Next, we will explain how we calculated each number.

Cash Flows from Operating Activities

In the indirect method, we start with net income and then adjust it to "cash-basis" through a series of adjusting items. We take each line item of the Income Statement and convert it from accrual to cash basis. So, in essence, the operating activities section of the direct-method cash flows statement is really just a cash-basis Income Statement. We can do this using the T-account method (review the Demo Doc for this chapter in myaccountinglab.com) or we can modify the account change chart used earlier in the chapter as seen in Exhibit 13A-5 on the following page.

EXHIBIT 13A-5 **Direct Method: How Changes in Account Balances Affect Cash Receipts and Cash Payments**

Asset ↑ Cash Flow ↓ Cash Receipts ↓ or Cash Payments ↑
Asset ↓ Cash Flow ↑ Cash Receipts ↑ or Cash Payments ↓
Liability ↑ Cash Flow ↑ Cash Receipts ↑ or Cash Payments ↓
Liability ↓ Cash Flow ↓ Cash Receipts ↓ or Cash Payments ↑
Equity ↑ Cash Flow ↑ Cash Receipts ↑ or Cash Payments ↓
Equity ↓ Cash Flow ↓ Cash Receipts ↓ or Cash Payments ↑

Notice that we have added the Cash Receipts and Payments to the existing chart. An increase in Cash is either going to arise from increasing cash receipts or decreasing cash payments. Now let us apply this information to Smart Touch Learning.

Cash Collections from Customers

The first item on the Income Statement is Sales revenue. Sales revenue represents the total of all sales, whether for cash or on account. The Balance Sheet account related to Sales revenue is Accounts receivable. Accounts receivable went from $73,000 at 12/31/10 to $90,000 at 12/31/11, an increase of $17,000. Applying our chart appears as follows:

Sales Revenue	–	Increase in Accounts receivable	=	Cash Collections from Customers
$286,000	–	$17,000	=	$269,000

Asset ↑ Cash Flow ↓ Cash Receipts ↓ or Cash Payments ↑

So, the cash Smart Touch received from customers is $269,000. This is the first item in the operating activities section of the direct-method cash flow statement. You can verify this by looking at Exhibit 13A-4 on page 751.

Cash Receipts of Interest

The second item on the Income Statement is interest revenue. The Balance Sheet account related to Interest revenue is Interest receivable. Since there is no Interest receivable account on the Balance Sheet, the interest revenue must have all been received in cash. So, the cash flow statement shows Interest received of $12,000 (Exhibit 13A-4 on page 751).

Cash Receipts of Dividends

Dividend revenue is the third item reported on the Income Statement. The Balance Sheet account related to Dividend revenue is Dividends receivable. As with the interest, there is no Dividends receivable account on the Balance Sheet. Therefore, the dividend revenue must have all been received in cash. So, the cash flow statement shows cash received from dividends of $9,000 in Exhibit 13A-4 on page 751.

Gain on Sale of Plant Assets

The next item on the Income Statement is the gain on sale of plant assets. However, the cash received from the sale of the assets is reported in the investing section, not the operating section. As noted earlier, there is no difference in the investing section between the indirect method and direct method of the Statement of Cash Flows.

Payments to Suppliers

Payments to suppliers include all payments for

- inventory and
- operating expenses except employee compensation, interest, and income taxes.

Suppliers are those entities that provide the business with its inventory and essential services. The accounts related to supplier payments for inventory are Cost of goods sold, Inventory, and Accounts payable. Cost of goods sold on the Income statement was $156,000. Inventory decreased from $145,000 at 12/31/10 to $143,000 at 12/31/11. Accounts payable increased from $50,000 at 12/31/10 to $90,000 at 12/31/11. Applying our formula, we can calculate cash paid for inventory as follows:

Cost of goods sold	–	Decrease in Inventory	–	Increase in Accounts payable	=	Cash paid for Inventory
$156,000	–	$2,000	–	40,000	=	$114,000
Asset ↓ Cash Flow ↑ Cash Receipts ↑ or Cash Payments ↓				Liability ↑ Cash Flow ↑ Cash Receipts ↑ or Cash Payments ↓		

The accounts related to supplier payments for operating expenses are Operating expenses and Accrued liabilities. Operating expenses on the Income statement were $16,000. Accrued liabilities decreased from $10,000 at 12/31/10 to $5,000 at 12/31/11. Applying our formula, we can calculate cash paid for operating expenses as follows:

Operating expenses	+	Decrease in Accrued liabilities	=	Cash paid for operating
$16,000	+	5,000	=	$21,000
	+	Liability ↓ Cash Flow ↓ Cash Receipts ↓ or Cash Payments ↑		

Adding them together, we get total cash paid to suppliers of $135,000. (Confirm in Exhibit 13A-4 on page 751).

Cash paid for Inventory	+	Cash paid for operating	=	Cash paid to suppliers
$114,000	+	21,000	=	$135,000

Payments to Employees

This category includes payments for salaries, wages, and other forms of employee compensation. Accrued amounts are not cash flows because they have not yet been paid. The accounts related to employee payments are Salary and wage expense from the Income Statement and Salary and wage payable from the Balance Sheet. Since there is not a Salary payable account on the Balance Sheet, the salary and wage expense account must represent all amounts paid in cash to employees. So, the cash flow statement shows cash payments to employees of $56,000 (Exhibit 13A-4 on page 751).

Depreciation, Depletion, and Amortization Expense

These expenses are *not* reported on the direct method Statement of Cash Flows because they do not affect cash.

Payments for Interest Expense

These cash payments are reported separately from the other expenses. The accounts related to interest payments are Interest expense from the Income Statement and Interest payable from the Balance Sheet. Since there is no Interest payable account on the Balance Sheet, the interest expense account from the Income Statement must represent all amounts paid in cash for interest. So, the cash flow statement shows cash payments for interest of $15,000 (Exhibit 13A-4 on page 751).

Payments for Income Tax Expense

Like interest expense, these cash payments are reported separately from the other expenses. The accounts related to income tax payments are Income tax expense from the Income Statement and Income tax payable from the Balance Sheet. Since there is no Income tax payable account on the Balance Sheet, the income tax expense account from the Income Statement must represent all amounts paid in cash for income tax. So, the cash flow statement shows cash payments for income tax of $14,000 (Exhibit 13A-4 on page 751).

Net Cash Provided by Operating Activities

To calculate net cash provided by operating activities using the direct method, we add all the cash receipts and cash payments described previously and find the difference. For Smart Touch Learning, total Cash receipts were $290,000. Total Cash payments were $220,000. So, net cash provided by operating activities is $70,000. If you refer back to the indirect-method cash flow statement shown in Exhibit 13-7 on page 714, you will find that it showed the same $70,000 for net cash provided by operating activities—only the method by which it was calculated was different.

The remainder of Smart Touch's cash flow statement is exactly the same as what we calculated using the indirect method. (See Exhibit 13-7 on page 714).

Summary Problem

Assume that Berkshire Hathaway is considering buying Granite Shoals Corporation. Granite Shoals reported the following comparative Balance Sheet and Income Statement for 2011:

GRANITE SHOALS CORPORATION
Balance Sheet
December 31, 2011 and 2010

	2011	2010	Increase (Decrease)
Cash	$ 19,000	$ 3,000	$16,000
Accounts receivable	22,000	23,000	(1,000)
Inventory	34,000	31,000	3,000
Prepaid expenses	1,000	3,000	(2,000)
Equipment (net)	90,000	79,000	11,000
Intangible assets	9,000	9,000	—
Total assets	$175,000	$148,000	$27,000
Accounts payable	$ 14,000	$ 9,000	$ 5,000
Accrued liabilities	16,000	19,000	(3,000)
Income tax payable	14,000	12,000	2,000
Long-term note payable	45,000	50,000	(5,000)
Common stock	31,000	20,000	11,000
Retained earnings	64,000	40,000	24,000
Treasury stock	(9,000)	(2,000)	(7,000)
Total liabilities and stockholders' equity	$175,000	$148,000	$27,000

GRANITE SHOALS CORPORATION
Income Statement
Year Ended December 31, 2011

Sales revenue	$190,000
Gain on sale of equipment	6,000
Total revenue and gains	196,000
Cost of goods sold	$ 85,000
Depreciation expense	19,000
Other operating expenses	36,000
Total expenses	140,000
Income before income tax	56,000
Income tax expense	18,000
Net income	$ 38,000

Requirements

1. Compute the following cash-flow amounts for 2011.
   a. Collections from customers
   b. Payments for inventory
   c. Payments for other operating expenses
   d. Payment of income tax
   e. Acquisition of equipment. Granite Shoals sold equipment that had book value of $15,000.
   f. Cash receipt from sale of plant assets
   g. Issuance of long-term note payable. Granite Shoals paid off $10,000 of long-term notes payable.
   h. Issuance of common stock
   i. Payment of dividends
   j. Purchase of treasury stock
2. Prepare Granite Shoals Corporation's Statement of Cash Flows (*direct* method) for the year ended December 31, 2011. There were no noncash investing and financing activities.

Solution

1. Cash-flow amounts:

1. Cash-flow amounts:

a. Collections from customers = Sales revenue + Decrease in accounts receivables

$191,000 = $190,000 + $1,000

b. Payments for inventory = Cost of goods sold + Increase in inventory − Increase in accounts payable

$83,000 = $85,000 + $3,000 − $5,000

c. Payments for other operating expenses = Other Operating expenses − Decrease in prepaid expenses + Decrease in accrued liabilities

$37,000 = $36,000 − $2,000 + $3,000

d. Payment of income tax = Income tax expense − Increase in income tax payable

$16,000 = $18,000 − $2,000

e. Equipment, Net (let X = Acquisitions)

Beginning	+	Acquisitions	−	Depreciation expense	−	Book value sold	=	Ending
$79,000	+	X	−	$19,000	−	$15,000	=	$90,000
		X	=	$45,000				

f. Sale of plant assets

Cash received = Book value of assets sold + Gain on sale

$21,000 = $15,000 + $6,000

g. Long-term Note payable (let X = Issuance)

Beginning	+	Issuance	−	Payment	=	Ending
$50,000	+	X	−	$10,000	=	$45,000
		X	=	$ 5,000		

h. Common stock (let X = Issuance)

Beginning	+	Issuance	=	Ending
$20,000	+	X	=	$31,000
		X	=	$11,000

i. Retained earnings (let X = Dividends)

Beginning	+	Net income	−	Dividends	=	Ending
$40,000	+	$38,000	−	X	=	$64,000
				X	=	$14,000

j. Treasury stock (let X = Purchases)

Beginning	+	Purchases	=	Ending
$2,000	+	X	=	$9,000
		X	=	$7,000

2.

GRANITE SHOALS CORPORATION Statement of Cash Flows Year Ended December 31, 2011		
Cash flows from operating activities:		
Receipts:		
Collections from customers	$ 191,000	
Payments:		
To suppliers ($83,000 + $37,000)	(120,000)	
For income tax	(16,000)	
Net cash provided by operating activities		$ 55,000
Cash flows from investing activities:		
Acquisition of plant assets	$ (45,000)	
Sale of plant assets ($15,000 + $6,000)	21,000	
Net cash used for investing activities		(24,000)
Cash flows from financing activities:		
Payment of dividends	$ (14,000)	
Issuance of common stock	11,000	
Payment of note payable	(10,000)	
Purchase of treasury stock	(7,000)	
Issuance of note payable	5,000	
Net cash used for financing activities		(15,000)
Net increase in cash		$ 16,000
Cash balance, December 31, 2010		3,000
Cash balance, December 31, 2011		$ 19,000

Appendix 13A Assignments

■ Short Exercises

S13A-1 *(L.OBJ. 4)* **Preparing the direct method Statement of Cash Flows [15 min]**
White Chocolate, Inc., began 2011 with cash of $52,000. During the year White Chocolate earned revenue of $591,000 and collected $624,000 from customers. Expenses for the year totaled $423,000, of which White Chocolate paid $413,000 in cash to suppliers and employees. White Chocolate also paid $143,000 to purchase equipment and a cash dividend of $49,000 to its stockholders during 2011.

Requirement

1. Prepare the company's Statement of Cash Flows for the year ended December 31, 2011. Format operating activities by the direct method.

S13A-2 *(L.OBJ. 4)* **Preparing operating activities using the direct method [5 min]**
Stella's Learning Center has assembled the following data for the year ended June 30, 2011:

Payments to suppliers	$ 110,000
Purchase of equipment	37,000
Payments to employees	68,000
Payment of note payable	34,000
Payment of dividends	4,000
Cash receipt from issuance of stock	20,000
Collections from customers	196,000
Cash receipt from sale of land	61,000

Requirement

1. Prepare the *operating* activities section of the business' Statement of Cash Flows for the year ended June 30, 2011, using the direct method for operating cash flows.

Note: Short Exercise 13A-3 should be used only after completing Short Exercise 13A-2.

S13A-3 *(L.OBJ. 4)* **Preparing the direct method Statement of Cash Flows [15 min]**
Use the data in Short Exercise 13A-2 and your results.

Requirement

1. Prepare the business's complete Statement of Cash Flows for the year ended June 30, 2011, using the *direct* method for operating activities. Stop after determining the net increase (or decrease) in cash.

S13A-4 *(L.OBJ. 4)* **Preparing the direct method Statement of Cash Flows [15 min]**
White Toy Company reported the following comparative Balance Sheet:

WHITE TOY COMPANY Comparative Balance Sheet December 31, 2011 and 2010					
Assets	**2011**	**2010**	**Liabilities**	**2011**	**2010**
Current:			Current:		
Cash	$ 20,000	$ 16,000	Accounts payable	$ 46,000	$ 42,000
Accounts receivable	50,000	44,000	Salary payable	21,000	18,000
Inventory	75,000	82,000	Accrued liabilities	4,000	13,000
Prepaid expenses	2,500	1,500	Long-term notes payable	61,000	69,000
Long-term investments	72,000	88,000	**Stockholders' Equity**		
Plant assets, net	228,000	187,000	Common stock	36,000	30,000
			Retained earnings	279,500	246,500
Total assets	$447,500	$418,500	Total liabilities and stockholders' equity	$447,500	$418,500

Requirement

1. Compute the following for White Toy Company:
   a. Collections from customers during 2011. Sales totaled $142,000.
   b. Payments for inventory during 2011. Cost of goods sold was $79,000.

Exercises

E13A-5 *(L.OBJ. 4)* **Identifying activity categories—direct method [10–15 min]**
Consider the following transactions:

______	a. Collection of account receivable	______	i. Purchase of treasury stock
______	b. Issuance of note payable to borrow cash	______	j. Issuance of common stock for cash
______	c. Depreciation	______	k. Payment of account payable
______	d. Issuance of preferred stock for cash	______	l. Acquisition of building by issuance of common stock
______	e. Payment of cash dividend	______	m. Purchase of equipment
______	f. Sale of land	______	n. Payment of wages to employees
______	g. Acquisition of equipment by issuance of note payable	______	o. Collection of cash interest
______	h. Payment of note payable	______	p. Sale of building

Requirement

1. Identify each of the transactions as a(n)
   - Operating activity (O),
   - Investing activity (I),
   - Financing activity (F),
   - Noncash investing and financing activity (NIF), or
   - transaction that is not reported on the Statement of Cash Flows (N).

For each cash flow, indicate whether the item increases (+) or decreases (–) cash. The *direct* method is used for cash flows from operating activities.

E13A-6 *(L. OBJ. 4)* **Identifying activity categories of transactions—direct method [5–10 min]**

Consider the following transactions:

a. Land	18,000		g. Salary expense	4,300	
Cash		18,000	Cash		4,300
b. Cash	7,200		h. Cash	81,000	
Equipment		7,200	Common stock		81,000
c. Bonds payable	45,000		i. Treasury stock	13,000	
Cash		45,000	Cash		13,000
d. Building	164,000		j. Cash	2,000	
Note payable		164,000	Interest revenue		2,000
e. Cash	1,400		k. Land	87,700	
Accounts receivable		1,400	Cash		87,700
f. Dividends payable	16,500		l. Accounts payable	8,300	
Cash		16,500	Cash		8,300

Requirement

1. Indicate where, if at all, each of the transactions would be reported on a Statement of Cash Flows prepared by the *direct* method and the accompanying schedule of noncash investing and financing activities.

E13A-7 *(L. OBJ. 4)* **Preparing operating activities cash flow—direct method [10–15 min]**

The accounting records of Value Auto Parts reveal the following:

Payment of salaries and wages	$ 36,000	Net income	$ 23,000
Depreciation	12,000	Payment of income tax	13,000
Payment of interest	15,000	Collection of dividend revenue	5,000
Payment of dividends	5,000	Payment to suppliers	56,000
Collections from customers	118,000		

Requirement

1. Compute cash flows from operating activities by the *direct* method.

E13A-8 *(L. OBJ. 4)* **Identifying activity categories of transactions—direct method [5–10 min]**

Selected accounts of Routing Networks, Inc., show the following:

Accounts receivable

Beginning balance	9,300		
Service revenue	38,000	Cash collections	36,000
Ending balance	11,300		

Land

Beginning balance	93,000		
Acquisition	16,000		
Ending balance	109,000		

Long-term notes payable

		Beginning balance	277,000
Payments	69,000	Issuance for cash	85,000
		Ending balance	293,000

Requirement

1. For each account, identify the item or items that should appear on a Statement of Cash Flows prepared by the *direct* method. Also state each item's amount and where to report the item.

E13A-9 *(L. OBJ. 4)* **Preparing the Statement of Cash Flows—direct method [20–30 min]**

The Income Statement and additional data of Rolling Hills Corporation follow:

ROLLING HILLS CORPORATION Income Statement Year Ended June 30, 2010		
Revenues:		
Sales revenue	$ 228,000	
Dividend revenue	7,000	$ 235,000
Expenses:		
Cost of goods sold	$ 105,000	
Salary expense	42,000	
Depreciation expense	22,000	
Advertising expense	13,500	
Income tax expense	9,500	
Interest expense	2,500	194,500
Net income		$ 40,500

Additional data follow:

a. Collections from customers are $14,500 more than sales.
b. Dividend revenue, interest expense, and income tax expense equal their cash amounts.
c. Payments to suppliers are the sum of cost of goods sold plus advertising expense.
d. Payments to employees are $1,500 more than salary expense.
e. Acquisition of plant assets is $100,000.
f. Cash receipts from sale of land total $21,000.
g. Cash receipts from issuance of common stock total $38,000.
h. Payment of long-term note payable is $11,000.
i. Payment of dividends is $10,500.
j. Cash balance, June 30, 2009, was $20,000; June 30, 2010 was $33,000.

Requirement

1. Prepare Rolling Hills Corporation's Statement of Cash Flows for the year ended June 30, 2010. Use the *direct* method.

E13A-10 *(L. OBJ. 4)* **Computing cash flow items—direct method [10–15 min]**
Consider the following facts:

a. Beginning and ending Accounts receivable are $22,000 and $18,000, respectively. Credit sales for the period total $60,000.
b. Cost of goods sold is $75,000. Beginning Inventory balance is $25,000, and ending Inventory balance is $21,000. Beginning and ending Accounts payable are $11,000 and $8,000, respectively.

Requirements

1. Compute cash collections from customers.
2. Compute cash payments for inventory.

E13A-11 *(L. OBJ. 4)* **Computing cash flow items—direct method [20–30 min]**
TipTop Mobile Homes reported the following in its financial statements for the year ended December 31, 2011 (adapted, in millions):

	2011	2010
Income Statement		
Net sales	$ 24,859	$ 21,674
Cost of sales	18,121	15,497
Depreciation	270	234
Other operating expenses	4,432	4,221
Income tax expense	532	486
Net income	$ 1,504	$ 1,236
Balance Sheet		
Cash and cash equivalents	$ 17	$ 16
Accounts receivable	798	621
Inventories	3,483	2,830
Property and equipment, net	4,342	3,428
Accounts payable	1,546	1,362
Accrued liabilities	938	848
Long-term liabilities	477	467
Common stock	678	446
Retained earnings	5,001	3,772

Requirement

1. Determine the following for TipTop Mobile Homes during 2011:

   a. Collections from customers
   b. Payments for inventory
   c. Payments of operating expenses
   d. Acquisitions of property and equipment (no sales of property during 2011)
   e. Borrowing, with TipTop paying no long-term liabilities
   f. Cash receipt from issuance of common stock
   g. Payment of cash dividends

Problem (Group A)

P13A-12A *(L. OBJ. 4)* **Preparing the Statement of Cash Flows—direct method [35–45 min]** KTG, Inc., accountants have developed the following data from the company's accounting records for the year ended November 30, 2011:

a. Purchase of plant assets, $58,400
b. Cash receipt from issuance of notes payable, $48,100
c. Payments of notes payable, $49,000
d. Cash receipt from sale of plant assets, $22,500
e. Cash receipt of dividends, $4,200
f. Payments to suppliers, $371,300
g. Interest expense and payments, $13,500
h. Payments of salaries, $94,000
i. Income tax expense and payments, $39,000
j. Depreciation expense, $57,000
k. Collections from customers, $605,300
l. Payment of cash dividends, $50,400
m. Cash receipt from issuance of common stock, $68,900
n. Cash balance: November 30, 2010, $39,700; November 30, 2011, $113,100

Requirement

1. Prepare KTG's Statement of Cash Flows for the year ended November 30, 2011. Use the *direct* method for cash flows from operating activities.

P13A-13A *(L.OBJ. 4)* **Preparing the Statement of Cash Flows—direct method [40 min]** Use the North American Reserve Rare Coins data from Problem 13-22A.

Requirements

1. Prepare North American Reserve Rare Coins' Income Statement for the year ended December 31, 2010. Use the single-step format, with all revenues listed together and all expenses together.
2. Prepare North American Reserve's Balance Sheet at December 31, 2010.
3. Prepare North American Reserve's Statement of Cash Flows for the year ended December 31, 2010. Format cash flows from operating activities by the *direct* method.

P13A-14A *(L. OBJ. 4)* **Preparing the Statement of Cash Flows—direct method [30–40 min]** Use the Cobbs Hill data from Problem 13-25A.

Requirements

1. Prepare the 2012 Statement of Cash Flows by the *direct* method.
2. How will what you learned in this problem help you evaluate an investment?

P13A-15A *(L. OBJ. 4)* **Preparing the Statement of Cash Flows—direct method [45–60 min]**
To prepare the Statement of Cash Flows, accountants for I-M-Mobile, Inc., have summarized 2010 activity in the Cash account as follows:

Cash			
Beginning balance	87,300	Payments of operating expenses	46,200
Issuance of common stock	60,700	Payments of salaries and wages	65,500
Receipts of interest revenue	17,100	Payment of note payable	82,000
Collections from customers	308,600	Payment of income tax	6,000
		Payments on accounts payable	101,100
		Payments of dividends	1,500
		Payments of interest	21,100
		Purchase of equipment	54,500
Ending balance	95,800		

Requirement

1. Prepare I-M-Mobile's Statement of Cash Flows for the year ended December 31, 2010, using the *direct* method to report operating activities.

■ Problem (Group B)

P13A-16B *(L. OBJ. 4)* **Preparing the Statement of Cash Flows—direct method [35–45 min]**
SKG, Inc., accountants have developed the following data from the company's accounting records for the year ended November 30, 2011:

a. Purchase of plant assets, $55,400
b. Cash receipt from issuance of notes payable, $43,100
c. Payments of notes payable, $48,000
d. Cash receipt from sale of plant assets, $25,500
e. Cash receipt of dividends, $4,400
f. Payments to suppliers, $374,800
g. Interest expense and payments, $12,500
h. Payments of salaries, $95,000
i. Income tax expense and payments, $40,000
j. Depreciation expense, $56,500
k. Collections from customers, $605,500
l. Payment of cash dividends, $50,400
m. Cash receipt from issuance of common stock, $60,900
n. Cash balance: November 30, 2010, $40,000; November 30, 2011, $103,300

Requirement

1. Prepare SKG's Statement of Cash Flows for the year ended November 30, 2011. Use the *direct* method for cash flows from operating activities.

P13A-17B *(L. OBJ. 4)* **Preparing the Statement of Cash Flows—direct method [40 min]**
Use the Official Reserve Rare Coins data from Problem 13-26B.

Requirements

1. Prepare Official Reserve Rare Coins' Income Statement for the year ended December 31, 2010. Use the single-step format, with all revenues listed together and all expenses together.
2. Prepare Official Reserve's Balance Sheet at December 31, 2010.
3. Prepare Official Reserve's Statement of Cash Flows for the year ended December 31, 2010. Format cash flows from operating activities by the *direct* method.

P13A-18B *(L. OBJ. 4)* **Preparing the Statement of Cash Flows—direct method [30–40 min]**
Use the Digital Subscriptions data from Problem 13-29B.

Requirements

1. Prepare the 2012 Statement of Cash Flows by the *direct* method.
2. How will what you learned in this problem help you evaluate an investment?

P13A-19B *(L. OBJ.4)* **Preparing the Statement of Cash Flows—direct method [45–60 min]**
To prepare the Statement of Cash Flows, accountants for B-Mobile, Inc., have summarized 2010 activity in the Cash account as follows:

Cash

Beginning balance	87,400	Payments of operating expenses	46,700
Issuance of common stock	60,100	Payments of salaries and wages	69,500
Receipts of interest revenue	14,600	Payment of note payable	75,000
Collections from customers	308,900	Payment of income tax	9,500
		Payments on accounts payable	101,100
		Payments of dividends	1,300
		Payments of interest	21,100
		Purchase of equipment	49,500
Ending balance	97,300		

Requirement

1. Prepare B-Mobile's Statement of Cash Flows for the year ended December 31, 2010, using the *direct* method to report operating activities.

Preparing the Indirect Statement of Cash Flows Using a Spreadsheet

The body of this chapter discusses the uses of the Statement of Cash Flows in decision making and shows how to prepare the statement using T-accounts. The T-account approach works well as a learning device. In practice, however, most companies face complex situations. In these cases, a spreadsheet can help in preparing the Statement of Cash Flows.

The spreadsheet starts with the beginning Balance Sheet and concludes with the ending Balance Sheet. Two middle columns—one for debit amounts and the other for credit amounts—complete the spreadsheet. These columns, labeled "Transaction Analysis," hold the data for the Statement of Cash Flows. Accountants can prepare the statement directly from the lower part of the spreadsheet. This appendix is based on the Smart Touch Learning data used in the chapter. We illustrate this approach only with the indirect method for operating activities. This method could be used for the direct method as well.

The *indirect* method reconciles net income to net cash provided by operating activities. Exhibit 13B-1 on the following page is the spreadsheet for preparing the Statement of Cash Flows by the *indirect* method. Panel A shows the transaction analysis, and Panel B gives the Statement of Cash Flows.

Transaction Analysis on the Spreadsheet—Indirect Method

a. Net income of $40,000 is the first operating cash inflow. Net income is entered on the spreadsheet (Panel B) as a debit to Net Income under Cash flows from operating activities and as a credit to Retained earnings on the Balance Sheet (Panel A).

b. Next come the adjustments to net income, starting with depreciation of $20,000—transaction (b)—which is debited to Depreciation and credited to Plant assets, net.

c. This transaction is the sale of plant assets. The $10,000 gain on the sale is entered as a credit to Gain on sale of plant assets—a subtraction from net income—under operating cash flows. This credit removes the $10,000 gain from operations because the cash proceeds from the sale were $50,000, not $10,000. The $50,000 sale amount is then entered on the spreadsheet under investing activities. Entry (c) is completed by crediting the plant assets' book value of $40,000 to the Plant assets, net account.

d. Entry (d) debits Accounts receivable for its $17,000 increase during the year. This amount is credited to Increase in accounts receivable under operating cash flows.

e. This entry credits Inventory for its $2,000 decrease during the year. This amount is debited to Decrease in inventory under operating cash flows.

f. This entry credits Accounts payable for its $40,000 increase during the year. Then, it is debited to show as Increase in accounts payable under operating cash flows.

g. This entry debits Accrued liabilities for its $5,000 decrease during the year. Then, it is credited to show as Decrease in accrued liabilities under operating cash flows.

h. This entry debits Plant assets, net for their purchase ($310,000) and credits Acquisition of plant assets under investing cash flows.

i. This entry debits Cash receipts from issuance of common stock ($120,000) under financing cash flows. The offsetting credit is to Common stock.

j. This entry is represented by a credit to Long-term notes payable and a debit under cash flows from financing activities of $90,000 (Cash receipt from issuance of notes payable).

EXHIBIT 13B-1 | **Spreadsheet for Statement of Cash Flows—Indirect Method**

1	**SMART TOUCH LEARNING, INC.**				
2	**Spreadsheet for Statement of Cash Flows**				
3	Year Ended December 31, 2011				
4	*(In thousands)*	**Balance**	**Transaction**		**Balance**
5	**Panel A—Balance Sheet**	**12/31/2010**	**Analysis**		**12/31/2011**
6	Cash	42		20 (n)	22
7	Accounts receivable	73	(d) 17		90
8	Inventory	145		2 (e)	143
9	Plant assets, net	210	(h) 310	20 (b)	
10				40 (c)	460
11	Total Assets	470			715
12					
13	Accounts payable	50		40 (f)	90
14	Accrued liabilities	10	(g) 5		5
15	Long-term notes payable	80	(k) 10	90 (j)	160
16	Common stock	250		120 (i)	370
17	Retained earnings	80	(m) 10	40 (a)	110
18	Less: Treasury stock	0	(l) 20		–20
19	Total liabilities & stockholders' equity	470	372	372	715
20					
21					
22	**Panel B—Statement of Cash Flows**				
23	Cash flows from operating activities:				
24	Net income		(a) 40		
25	Adjustments to reconcile net income to net cash provided by operating activities:				
26	Depreciation		(b) 20		
27	Gain on sale of plant assets			10 (c)	
28	Increase in accounts receivable			17 (d)	
29	Decrease in inventory		(e) 2		
30	Increase in accounts payable		(f) 40		
31	Decrease in accrued liabilities			5 (g)	
32	Net cash provided by operating activities				
33	Cash flows from investing activities:				
34	Acquisition of plant assets			310 (h)	
35	Cash receipt from sale of plant asset		(c) 50		
36	Net cash used for investing activities				
37	Cash flows from financing activities:				
38	Cash receipt from issuance of common stock		(i) 120		
39	Cash receipt from issuance of notes payable		(j) 90		
40	Payment of notes payable			10 (k)	
41	Purchase of treasury stock			20 (l)	
42	Payment of dividends			10 (m)	
43	Net cash provided by financing activities				
44			362	382	
45			(n) 20		
46	Net decrease in cash		382	382	

k. This entry is the opposite of (j). It is represented by a debit (reduction) of $10,000 to Long-term notes payable and a credit under cash flows from financial activities for Payment of notes payable.

l. The purchase of treasury stock debited the Treasury stock account on the Balance Sheet $20,000. The corresponding cash flow entry "Purchase of treasury stock" credits $20,000 to reduce cash flow.

m. The $10,000 reduction (debit) to the Retained earnings account is the result of dividends declared and paid by the company. So, we show "Payment of dividends" as a credit in the financing section.

n. The final item in Exhibit 13B-1 on page 768 is the Net decrease in cash. It is shown as a credit to Cash and a debit to Net decrease in cash of $20,000.

Appendix 13B Assignments

Problem (Group A)

P13B-1A *(L. OBJ. 3)* **Preparing the Statement of Cash Flows—indirect method [45–60 min]**
The 2012 comparative Balance Sheet and Income Statement of Alden Group, Inc., follow. Alden had no noncash investing and financing transactions during 2012.

ALDEN GROUP, INC.
Comparative Balance Sheet
December 31, 2012 and 2011

	2012	2011	Increase (Decrease)
Current assets:			
Cash and cash equivalents	$ 13,700	$ 15,600	$ (1,900)
Accounts receivable	41,500	43,100	(1,600)
Inventories	96,600	93,000	3,600
Plant assets:			
Land	35,100	10,000	25,100
Equipment, net	100,900	93,700	7,200
Total assets	$ 287,800	$ 255,400	$ 32,400
Current liabilities:			
Accounts payable	$ 24,800	$ 26,000	$ (1,200)
Accrued liabilities	24,400	22,500	1,900
Long-term liabilities:			
Notes payable	55,000	65,000	(10,000)
Stockholders' equity:			
Common stock	131,100	122,300	8,800
Retained earnings	52,500	19,600	32,900
Total liabilities and stockholders' equity	$ 287,800	$ 255,400	$ 32,400

ALDEN GROUP, INC.		
Income Statement		
Year Ended December 31, 2012		
Revenues:		
Sales revenue		$ 438,000
Interest revenue		11,700
Total revenues		449,700
Expenses:		
Cost of goods sold	$ 205,200	
Salary expense	76,400	
Depreciation expense	15,300	
Other operating expense	49,700	
Interest expense	24,600	
Income tax expense	16,900	
Total expenses		388,100
Net income		$ 61,600

Requirement

1. Prepare the spreadsheet for the 2012 Statement of Cash Flows. Format cash flows from operating activities by the *indirect* method.

P13B-2A *(L. OBJ. 3)* **Preparing the Statement of Cash Flows—indirect method [45–60 min]** Review the data from P13-25A.

Requirement

1. Prepare the spreadsheet for Cobbs Hill's 2012 Statement of Cash Flows. Format cash flows from operating activities by the *indirect* method.

■ Problem (Group B)

P13B-3B *(L. OBJ. 3)* **Preparing the Statement of Cash Flows—indirect method [45–60 min]** The 2012 comparative Balance Sheet and Income Statement of Alden Group follow. Alden had no noncash investing and financing transactions during 2012.

ALDEN GROUP, INC. Comparative Balance Sheet December 31, 2012 and 2011			
	2012	2011	Increase (Decrease)
Current assets:			
Cash and cash equivalents	$ 10,700	$ 15,800	$ (5,100)
Accounts receivable	41,800	43,400	(1,600)
Inventories	96,600	93,200	3,400
Plant assets:			
Land	41,400	16,000	25,400
Equipment, net	100,500	93,800	6,700
Total assets	$ 291,000	$ 262,200	$ 28,800
Current liabilities:			
Accounts payable	$ 25,400	$ 26,500	$ (1,100)
Accrued liabilities	24,000	22,700	1,300
Long-term liabilities:			
Notes payable	54,000	66,000	(12,000)
Stockholders' equity:			
Common stock	136,200	127,900	8,300
Retained earnings	51,400	19,100	32,300
Total liabilities and stockholders' equity	$ 291,000	$ 262,200	$ 28,800

ALDEN GROUP, INC. Income Statement Year Ended December 31, 2012		
Revenues:		
Sales revenue		$ 438,000
Interest revenue		11,900
Total revenues		449,900
Expenses:		
Cost of goods sold	$ 205,800	
Salary expense	76,700	
Depreciation expense	15,600	
Other operating expense	49,600	
Interest expense	24,800	
Income tax expense	16,700	
Total expenses		389,200
Net income		$ 60,700

Requirement

1. Prepare the spreadsheet for the 2012 Statement of Cash Flows. Format cash flows from operating activities by the *indirect* method.

P13B-4B *(L. OBJ. 3)* **Preparing the Statement of Cash Flows—indirect method [45–60 min]**
Review the data from P13-29B.

Requirement

1. Prepare the spreadsheet for Digital Subscription's 2012 Statement of Cash Flows. Format cash flows from operating activities by the *indirect* method.

14 Financial Statement Analysis

Learning Objectives/Success Keys

1. Perform a horizontal analysis of financial statements
2. Perform a vertical analysis of financial statements
3. Prepare and use common-size financial statements
4. Compute the standard financial ratios

Now that you have learned some of the "how-to's" of financial statement preparation, we are going to show you how to analyze financial statements. We will be using our Smart Touch Learning, Inc., company for the first half of this chapter. Then in the second part of the chapter we will shift over to Greg's Groovy Tunes, Inc., to round out your introduction to financial statement analysis.

To get started, take a look at Smart Touch Learning's comparative income statement, as shown in Exhibit 14-1 on the following page.

You can see that 2014 was an incredible year for the company. Net income was over three times the net income of 2013, and investors were very happy.

Investors and creditors cannot evaluate a company by examining only one year's data. This is why most financial statements cover at least two periods, like the Smart Touch Learning income statement. In fact, most financial analysis covers trends of three to five years. This chapter shows you how to use some of the analytical tools for charting a company's progress through time.

To do that, we need some way to compare a company's performance

a. from year to year.
b. with a competing company, like **Learning Tree**.
c. with the education and training industry.

EXHIBIT 14-1 **Comparative Income Statement, Smart Touch Learning, Inc.**

SMART TOUCH LEARNING, INC.*
Income Statement (Adapted)
Year Ended December 31, 2014 and 2013

(In millions)	2014	2013
Revenues (same as Net sales)	$3,189	$1,466
Expenses:		
Cost of revenues (same as Cost of goods sold)	1,458	626
Sales and marketing expense	246	120
General and administrative expense	140	57
Research and development expense	225	91
Other expense	470	225
Income before income tax	650	347
Income tax expense	251	241
Net income	$ 399	$ 106

*All values are assumed.

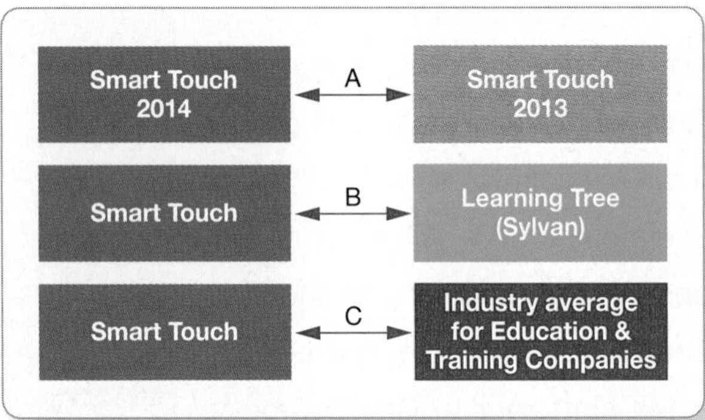

Then we will have a better idea of how to judge Smart Touch Learning's present situation and predict what might happen in the near future.

There are two main ways to analyze financial statements:

- Horizontal analysis provides a year-to-year comparison of a company's performance in different periods.
- Another technique, vertical analysis, is the standard way to compare different companies. Let us begin with horizontal analysis.

Horizontal Analysis

1 Perform a horizontal analysis of financial statements

Many decisions hinge on whether the numbers—in sales, expenses, and net income—are increasing or decreasing. Have sales and other revenues risen from last year? By how much? Sales may have increased by $20,000, but considered alone, this fact is not very helpful. The *percentage change* in sales over time is more relative and, therefore, more helpful. It is better to know that sales increased by 20% than to know that sales increased by $20,000.

The study of percentage changes in comparative statements is called **horizontal analysis.** Computing a percentage change in comparative statements requires two steps:

1. Compute the dollar amount of the change from the earlier period to the later period.

2. Divide the dollar amount of change by the earlier period amount. We call the earlier period the base period.

Illustration: Smart Touch Learning, Inc.

Horizontal analysis is illustrated for Smart Touch Learning as follows (dollar amounts in millions):

			Increase (Decrease)	
	2014	2013	Amount	Percentage
Revenues (same as net sales)..........	$3,189	$1,466	$1,723	117.5%

Sales increased by an incredible 117.5% during 2014, computed as follows:

STEP 1: Compute the dollar amount of change in sales from 2014 to 2013:

2014	2013	Increase
$3,189 –	$1,466 =	$1,723

STEP 2: Divide the dollar amount of change by the base-period amount. This computes the percentage change for the period:

$$\text{Percentage change} = \frac{\text{Dollar amount of change}}{\text{Base-year amount}}$$

$$= \frac{\$1,723}{\$1,466} = 1.175 = 117.5\%$$

Completed horizontal analyses for Smart Touch's financial statements are shown in the following exhibits:

- Exhibit 14-2 Income Statement
- Exhibit 14-3 Balance Sheet

EXHIBIT 14-2 **Comparative Income Statement—Horizontal Analysis**

SMART TOUCH LEARNING, INC.*
Income Statement (Adapted)
Year Ended December 31, 2014 and 2013

			Increase (Decrease)	
(Dollar amounts in millions)	2014	2013	Amount	Percentage
Revenues	$3,189	$1,466	$1,723	117.5%
Cost of revenues	1,458	626	832	132.9
Gross profit	1,731	840	891	106.1
Operating expenses:				
Sales and marketing expense	246	120	126	105.0
General and administrative expense	140	57	83	145.6
Research and development expense	225	91	134	147.3
Other expense	470	225	245	108.9
Income before income tax	650	347	303	87.3
Income tax expense	251	241	10	4.1
Net income	$ 399	$ 106	$ 293	276.4

*All values are assumed.

EXHIBIT 14-3 Comparative Balance Sheet—Horizontal Analysis

SMART TOUCH LEARNING, INC.*
Balance Sheet (Adapted)
December 31, 2014 and 2013

			Increase (Decrease)	
(Dollar amounts in millions)	2014	2013	Amount	Percentage
Assets				
Current Assets:				
Cash and cash equivalents	$ 427	$149	$ 278	186.6%
Other current assets	2,266	411	1,855	451.3
Total current assets	2,693	560	2,133	380.9
Property, plant, and equipment, net	379	188	191	101.6
Intangible assets, net	194	106	88	83.0
Other assets	47	17	30	176.5
Total assets	$3,313	$871	$2,442	280.4
Liabilities				
Current Liabilities:				
Accounts payable	$ 33	$ 46	$ (13)	(28.3)%
Other current liabilities	307	189	118	62.4
Total current liabilities	340	235	105	44.7
Long-term liabilities	44	47	(3)	(6.4)
Total liabilities	384	282	102	36.2
Stockholders' Equity				
Capital stock	1	45	(44)	(97.8)
Retained earnings and other equity	2,928	544	2,384	438.2
Total stockholders' equity	2,929	589	2,340	397.3
Total liabilities and equity	$3,313	$871	$2,442	280.4

*All values are assumed.

Horizontal Analysis of the Income Statement

Smart Touch's comparative income statement reveals exceptional growth during 2014. An increase of 100% occurs when an item doubles, so Smart Touch's 117.5% increase in revenues means that revenues more than doubled.

The item on Smart Touch's income statement with the slowest growth rate is income tax expense. Income taxes increased by only 4.1%. On the bottom line, net income grew by an incredible 276.4%. That is real progress!

Horizontal Analysis of the Balance Sheet

Smart Touch's comparative balance sheet also shows rapid growth in assets, with total assets increasing by 280.4%. That means total assets almost tripled in one year. Very few companies grow that fast.

Smart Touch's liabilities grew more slowly. Total liabilities increased by 36.2%, and Accounts payable actually decreased, as indicated by the liability figures in parentheses. This is another indicator of positive growth for Smart Touch.

Trend Percentages

Trend percentages are a form of horizontal analysis. Trends indicate the direction a business is taking. How have sales changed over a five-year period? What trend does net income show? These questions can be answered by trend percentages over a period, such as three to five years.

Trend percentages are computed by selecting a base year. The base-year amounts are set equal to 100%. The amounts for each subsequent year are expressed as a percentage of the base amount. To compute trend percentages, divide each item for the following years by the base-year amount.

$$\text{Trend \%} = \frac{\text{Any year \$}}{\text{Base year \$}} \times 100$$

Let us assume Smart Touch's total revenues were $1,000 million in 2010 and rose to $3,189 million in 2014. To illustrate trend analysis, let us review the trend of net sales during 2010–2014, with dollars in millions. The base year is 2010, so that year's percentage is set equal to 100.

(In millions)	2014	2013	2012	2011	2010
Net sales....................	$3,189	1,466	1,280	976	1,000
Trend percentages.....	318.9%	146.6%	128%	97.6%	100%

We want trend percentages for the five-year period 2010–2014. We compute these by dividing each year's amount by the 2010 net sales amount.

Net sales decreased a little in 2011 and then the rate of growth increased from 2012–2014.

You can perform a trend analysis on any one or multiple item(s) you consider important. Trend analysis is widely used to predict the future.

Vertical Analysis

2 Perform a vertical analysis of financial statements

As we have seen, horizontal analysis and trend percentages highlight changes in an item from year to year, or over *time*. But no single technique gives a complete picture of a business, so we also need vertical analysis.

Vertical analysis of a financial statement shows the relationship of each item to its base amount, which is the 100% figure. Every other item on the statement is then reported as a percentage of that base. For the income statement, net sales is the base.

$$\text{Vertical analysis \%} = \frac{\text{Each income-statement item}}{\text{Revenues (net sales)}} \times 100$$

Exhibit 14-4 on the following page shows the completed vertical analysis of Smart Touch Learning's 2014 income statement.

In this case, the vertical-analysis percentage for Smart Touch's cost of revenues is 45.7% of net sales ($1,458/$3,189 = 0.457). This means that for every $1 in net sales, almost 46 cents is spent on cost of revenue.

On the bottom line, Smart Touch's net income is 12.5% of revenues. That is extremely good. Suppose under normal conditions a company's net income is 10% of revenues. A drop to 4% may cause the investors to be alarmed and sell their stock.

Exhibit 14-5 on the following page the vertical analysis of Smart Touch's balance sheet.

The base amount (100%) is total assets. The base amount is also total liabilities and equity, because they are exactly the same number, $3,313. (Recall that they should always be the same number because of the accounting equation.)

EXHIBIT 14-4 Comparative Income Statement—Vertical Analysis

SMART TOUCH LEARNING, INC.*
Income Statement (Adapted)
Year Ended December 31, 2014

(Dollar amounts in millions)	Amount	Percent of Total
Revenues	$3,189	100.0%
Cost of revenues	1,458	45.7
Gross profit	1,731	54.3
Operating expenses:		
Sales and marketing expense	246	7.7
General and administrative expense	140	4.4
Research and development expense	225	7.1
Other expense	470	14.7
Income before income tax	650	20.4
Income tax expense	251	7.9
Net income	$ 399	12.5%

*All values are assumed.

EXHIBIT 14-5 Comparative Balance Sheet—Vertical Analysis

SMART TOUCH LEARNING, INC.*
Balance Sheet (Adapted)
December 31, 2014

(Dollar amount in millions)	Amount	Percent of Total
Assets		
Current Assets:		
Cash and cash equivalents	$ 427	12.9%
Other current assets	2,266	68.4
Total current assets	2,693	81.3
Property, plant, and equipment, net	379	11.4
Intangible assets, net	194	5.9
Other assets	47	1.4
Total assets	$3,313	100.0%
Liabilities		
Current Liabilities:		
Accounts payable	$ 33	1.0%
Other current liabilities	307	9.3
Total current liabilities	340	10.3
Long-term liabilities	44	1.3
Total liabilities	384	11.6
Stockholders' Equity		
Common stock	1	0.0
Retained earnings and other equity	2,928	88.4
Total stockholders' equity	2,929	88.4
Total liabilities and equity	$3,313	100.0%

*All values are assumed.

The vertical analysis of Smart Touch's balance sheet reveals several interesting things:

- Current assets make up 81.3% of total assets. For most companies this percentage is closer to 30%. The 81.3% of current assets represent a great deal of liquidity.

- Property, plant, and equipment make up only 11.4% of total assets. This percentage is low because of the nature of Smart Touch's business. Smart Touch's Web-based operations do not require lots of buildings and equipment.
- Total liabilities are only 11.6% of total assets, and stockholders' equity makes up 88.4% of total assets. Most of Smart Touch's equity is retained earnings and other equity—signs of a strong company because most of the equity is internally generated rather than externally generated (through stock share sales).

How Do We Compare One Company with Another?

3 Prepare and use common-size financial statements

Horizontal analysis and vertical analysis provide lots of useful data about a company. As we have seen, Smart Touch's percentages depict a very successful company. But the data apply only to one business.

To compare Smart Touch Learning to another company we can use a common-size statement. A **common-size statement** reports only percentages—the same percentages that appear in a vertical analysis. By only reporting percentages, it removes dollar value bias when comparing the companies. **Dollar value bias** is the bias one sees from comparing numbers in absolute (dollars) rather than relative (percentage) terms. For us, $1 million seems like a lot. For some large companies, it is immaterial. For example, Smart Touch's common-size income statement comes directly from the percentages in Exhibit 14-4.

We can use a common-size income statement to compare Smart Touch Learning and Learning Tree on profitability. The companies compete in the service-learning industry. Which company earns a higher percentage of revenues as profits for its shareholders? Exhibit 14-6 gives both companies' common-size income statements for 2014 so that we may compare them on a relative, not absolute basis.

EXHIBIT 14-6 Common-Size Income Statement Smart Touch vs. Learning Tree

SMART TOUCH vs. LEARNING TREE*
Common-Size Income Statement
Year ended Dec. 31, 2014

	Smart Touch	Learning Tree
Revenues	100.0%	100.0%
Cost of revenues	45.7	36.3
Gross profit	54.3	63.7
Sales and marketing expense	7.7	21.8
General and administrative expense	4.4	7.3
Research and development expense	7.1	10.3
Other expense (income)	14.7	(11.5)
Income before income tax	20.4	35.8
Income tax expense	7.9	12.3
Net income	12.5%	23.5%

*All values are assumed.

Exhibit 14-6 shows that Learning Tree was more profitable than Smart Touch in 2014. Learning Tree's gross profit percentage is 63.7%, compared to Smart Touch's 54.3%. This means that Learning Tree is getting more profit from every dollar than Smart Touch. And, most importantly, Learning Tree's percentage of net income to revenues is 23.5%. That means almost one-fourth of Learning Tree's revenues end up as profits for the company's stockholders. Smart Touch's percentage of net income to revenues, on the other hand, is 12.5%. Both are excellent percentages; however, the common-size statement highlights Learning Tree's advantages over Smart Touch.

Benchmarking

Benchmarking is the practice of comparing a company with other leading companies. There are two main types of benchmarks in financial statement analysis.

Benchmarking Against a Key Competitor

Exhibit 14-6 uses a key competitor, Learning Tree, to compare Smart Touch's profitability. The two companies compete in the same industry, so Learning Tree serves as an ideal benchmark for Smart Touch. The graphs in Exhibit 14-7 highlight the profitability difference between the companies. Focus on the segment of the graphs showing net income. Learning Tree is clearly more profitable than Smart Touch.

EXHIBIT 14-7 | **Graphical Analysis of Common-Size Income Statement Smart Touch Learning vs. Learning Tree**

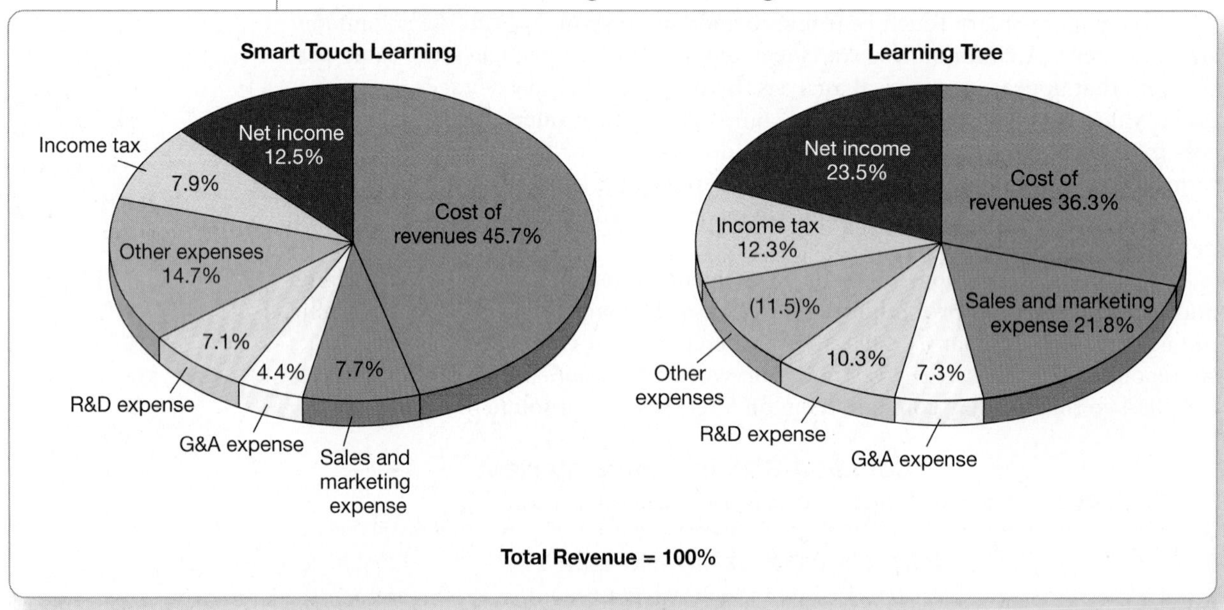

Benchmarking Against the Industry Average

The industry average can also serve as a very useful benchmark for evaluating a company. An industry comparison would show how Smart Touch is performing alongside the average for the e-learning industry. *Annual Statement Studies*, published by The Risk Management Association, provides common-size statements for most industries. To compare Smart Touch to the industry average, simply insert the industry-average common-size income statement in place of Learning Tree in Exhibit 14-6.

Stop & Think...

When you are driving down any road, how do you know how fast you can travel? The speed limit sign. You compare the speed at which you are traveling in your car to that speed limit sign. That is the same concept as benchmarking. The industry averages, for example, are the "sign" and your company results are the "speed at which you are traveling." Sometimes your company is going faster than other companies. Sometimes it is going slower.

Now let us put your learning to practice. Work the summary problem, which reviews the concepts from the first half of this chapter.

Summary Problem 1

Requirements

Perform a horizontal analysis and a vertical analysis of the comparative income statement of Kimball Corporation, which makes iPod labels. State whether 2011 was a good year or a bad year, and give your reasons.

KIMBALL CORPORATION Comparative Income Statement Years Ended December 31, 2011 and 2010		
	2011	**2010**
Net sales	$275,000	$225,000
Expenses:		
Cost of goods sold	$194,000	$165,000
Engineering, selling, and administrative expenses	54,000	48,000
Interest expense	5,000	5,000
Income tax expense	9,000	3,000
Other expense (income)	1,000	(1,000)
Total expenses	263,000	220,000
Net income	$ 12,000	$ 5,000

Solution

KIMBALL CORPORATION Horizontal Analysis of Comparative Income Statement Years Ended December 31, 2011 and 2010				
			Increase (Decrease)	
	2011	2010	Amount	Percent
Net sales	$275,000	$225,000	$50,000	22.2%
Expenses:				
Cost of goods sold	$194,000	$165,000	$29,000	17.6
Engineering, selling, and administrative expenses	54,000	48,000	6,000	12.5
Interest expense	5,000	5,000	—	—
Income tax expense	9,000	3,000	6,000	200.0
Other expense (income)	1,000	(1,000)	2,000	—*
Total expenses	263,000	220,000	43,000	19.5
Net income	$ 12,000	$ 5,000	$ 7,000	140.0%

*Percentage changes are typically not computed for shifts from a negative to a positive amount, and vice versa.

The horizontal analysis shows that total revenues increased 22.2%. Total expenses increased by 19.5%, and net income rose by 140%.

KIMBALL CORPORATION Vertical Analysis of Comparative Income Statement Years Ended December 31, 2011 and 2010	2011		2010	
	Amount	Percent	Amount	Percent
Net sales	$275,000	100.0%	$225,000	100.0%
Expenses:				
Cost of goods sold	$194,000	70.5	$165,000	73.3
Engineering, selling, and administrative expenses	54,000	19.6	48,000	21.3
Interest expense	5,000	1.8	5,000	2.2
Income tax expense	9,000	3.3	3,000	1.4**
Other expense (income)	1,000	0.4	(1,000)	(0.4)
Total expenses	263,000	95.6	220,000	97.8
Net income	$ 12,000	4.4%	$ 5,000	2.2%

**Number is rounded up.

The vertical analysis shows decreases in the percentages of net sales consumed by

- cost of goods sold (from 73.3% to 70.5%);
- engineering, selling, and administrative expenses (from 21.3% to 19.6%).

These two items are Kimball's largest dollar expenses, so their percentage decreases are important.

The 2011 net income rose to 4.4% of sales, compared with 2.2% the preceding year. The analysis shows that 2011 was significantly better than 2010.

Using Ratios to Make Decisions

4 Compute the standard financial ratios

Online financial databases, such as **Lexis/Nexis** and the **Dow Jones News Retrieval Service**, provide data on thousands of companies. Suppose you want to compare some companies' recent earnings histories. You might want to compare companies' returns on stockholders' equity. The computer could then search the databases and give you the names of the 20 companies with the highest return on equity. You can use any ratio for searching that is relevant to a particular decision.

Remember, however, that no single ratio tells the whole picture of any company's performance. Different ratios explain different aspects of a company. The ratios we discuss in this chapter may be classified as follows:

1. Measuring ability to pay current liabilities
2. Measuring ability to sell inventory and collect receivables
3. Measuring ability to pay long-term debt
4. Measuring profitability
5. Analyzing stock as an investment

Measuring Ability to Pay Current Liabilities

Working capital is defined as follows:

Working capital = Current assets − Current liabilities

Working capital measures the ability to meet short-term obligations with current assets. Two decision tools based on working-capital data are the *current ratio* and the *acid-test ratio*.

Current Ratio

The most widely used ratio is the *current ratio*, which is current assets divided by current liabilities. The current ratio measures ability to pay current liabilities with current assets.

Exhibit 14-8 on the following page gives the comparative income statement and balance sheet of Greg's Groovy Tunes, which we will be using in the remainder of this chapter.

The current ratios of Greg's Groovy Tunes, at December 31, 2012 and 2011, follow, along with the average for the entertainment industry:

Formula	Greg's Groovy Tunes' Current Ratio 2012	Greg's Groovy Tunes' Current Ratio 2011	Industry Average
Current ratio = $\frac{\text{Current assets}}{\text{Current liabilities}}$	$\frac{\$262{,}000}{\$142{,}000} = 1.85$	$\frac{\$236{,}000}{\$126{,}000} = 1.87$	.60

A high current ratio indicates that the business has sufficient current assets to maintain normal business operations. Compare Greg's Groovy Tunes' current ratio of 1.85 for 2012 with the industry average of .60.

What is an acceptable current ratio? The answer depends on the industry. The norm for companies in most industries is around 1.50, as reported by The Risk Management Association. Greg's Groovy Tunes' current ratio of 1.85 is strong. Keep in mind that we would not want to see a current ratio that is too high, say 25.0. This would indicate that the company is too liquid and, therefore, is not using its assets effectively.

EXHIBIT 14-8 | Comparative Financial Statements

GREG'S GROOVY TUNES, INC.
Comparative Income Statement
Years Ended December 31, 2012 and 2011

	2012	2011
Net sales	$858,000	$803,000
Cost of goods sold	513,000	509,000
Gross profit	345,000	294,000
Operating expenses:		
Selling expenses	126,000	114,000
General expenses	118,000	123,000
Total operating expenses	244,000	237,000
Income from operations	101,000	57,000
Interest revenue	4,000	—
Interest (expense)	(24,000)	(14,000)
Income before income taxes	81,000	43,000
Income tax expense	33,000	17,000
Net income	$ 48,000	$ 26,000

GREG'S GROOVY TUNES, INC.
Comparative Balance Sheet
December 31, 2012 and 2011

	2012	2011
Assets		
Current Assets:		
Cash	$ 29,000	$ 32,000
Accounts receivable, net	114,000	85,000
Inventories	113,000	111,000
Prepaid expenses	6,000	8,000
Total current assets	262,000	236,000
Long-term investments	18,000	9,000
Property, plant, and equipment, net	507,000	399,000
Total assets	$787,000	$644,000
Liabilities		
Current Liabilities:		
Notes payable	$ 42,000	$ 27,000
Accounts payable	73,000	68,000
Accrued liabilities	27,000	31,000
Total current liabilities	142,000	126,000
Long-term notes payable	289,000	198,000
Total liabilities	431,000	324,000
Stockholders' Equity		
Common stock, no par	186,000	186,000
Retained earnings	170,000	134,000
Total stockholders' equity	356,000	320,000
Total liabilities and equity	$787,000	$644,000

Acid-Test Ratio

The *acid-test* (or *quick*) *ratio* tells us whether the entity could pay all its current liabilities if they came due immediately. That is, could the company pass this *acid test?*

To compute the acid-test ratio, we add cash, short-term investments, and net current receivables (accounts and notes receivable, net of allowances) and divide this sum by current liabilities. Inventory and prepaid expenses are *not* included in the acid test because they are the least-liquid current assets. Greg's Groovy Tunes' acid-test ratios for 2012 and 2011 follow:

Formula	Greg's Groovy Tunes' Acid-Test Ratio 2012	2011	Industry Average
Acid-test ratio = (Cash + Short-term investments + Net current receivables) / Current liabilities	($29,000 + $0 + $114,000) / $142,000 = 1.01	($32,000 + $0 + $85,000) / $126,000 = 0.93	.46

The company's acid-test ratio improved during 2012 and is significantly better than the industry average. The norm for the acid-test ratio ranges from 0.20 for shoe retailers to 1.00 for manufacturers of equipment, as reported by The Risk Management Association. An acid-test ratio of 0.90 to 1.00 is acceptable in most industries.

Measuring Ability to Sell Inventory and Collect Receivables

The ability to sell inventory and collect receivables is fundamental to business. In this section, we discuss three ratios that measure the company's ability to sell inventory and collect receivables.

Inventory Turnover

The inventory turnover ratio measures the number of times a company sells its average level of inventory during a year. A high rate of turnover indicates ease in selling inventory; a low rate indicates difficulty. A value of 4 means that the company sold its average level of inventory four times—once every three months—during the year. If the company were a seasonal company, this would be a good ratio because it would mean it turned its inventory over each season, on average.

To compute inventory turnover, we divide cost of goods sold by the average inventory for the period. We use the cost of goods sold—not sales—because both cost of goods sold and inventory are stated *at cost*. Sales at *retail* are not comparable with inventory at *cost*.

Greg's Groovy Tunes' inventory turnover for 2012 is as follows:

Formula	Greg's Groovy Tunes' Inventory Turnover	Industry Average
Inventory turnover = Cost of goods sold / Average inventory	$513,000 / $112,000 = 4.6	27.65

Cost of goods sold comes from the income statement (Exhibit 14-8). Average inventory is figured by adding the beginning inventory ($111,000) to the ending inventory ($113,000) and dividing by two. (See the balance sheet, Exhibit 14-8.)

Inventory turnover varies widely with the nature of the business. For example, most manufacturers of farm machinery have an inventory turnover close to three times a year. In contrast, companies that remove natural gas from the ground hold their inventory for a very short period of time and have an average turnover of 30.

Greg's Groovy Tunes' turnover of 4.6 times a year is very low for its industry, which has an average turnover of 27.65 times per year. This ratio has identified an area that Greg's Groovy Tunes needs to improve.

Accounts Receivable Turnover

The **accounts receivable turnover ratio** measures the ability to collect cash from credit customers. The higher the ratio, the faster the cash collections. But a receivable turnover that is too high may indicate that credit is too tight, causing the loss of sales to good customers.

To compute accounts receivable turnover, divide net credit sales by average net accounts receivable. Average net accounts receivable is figured by adding the beginning accounts receivable balance ($85,000) and the ending balance ($114,000), then dividing by 2:

($85,000 + $114,000)/2 = $99,500

Greg's Groovy Tunes' accounts receivable turnover ratio for 2012 is computed as follows:

Formula	Greg's Groovy Tunes' Accounts Receivable Turnover	Industry Average
Accounts receivable turnover = Net credit sales / Average net accounts receivable	$858,000 / $99,500 = 8.6	29.10

Greg's receivable turnover of 8.6 times per year is much slower than the industry average of 29.1. Why the difference? Greg's is a fairly new business that sells to established people who pay their accounts over time. Further, this turnover coincides with the lower than average inventory turnover. So, Greg's may achieve a higher receivable turnover by increasing its inventory turnover ratio.

Days' Sales in Receivables

The *days'-sales-in-receivables* ratio also measures the ability to collect receivables. Days' sales in receivables tell us how many days' sales remain in Accounts receivable. To compute the ratio, we can follow a logical two-step process:

1. Divide net sales by 365 days to figure average sales for one day.
2. Divide this average day's sales amount into average net accounts receivable.

The data to compute this ratio for Greg's Groovy Tunes for 2012 are taken from the income statement and the balance sheet (Exhibit 14-8):

Formula	Greg's Groovy Tunes' Days' Sales in Accounts Receivable	Industry Average
Days' sales in *average* Accounts receivable:		
1. One day's sales = Net sales / 365 days	$858,000 / 365 days = $2,351	
2. Days' sales in average accounts receivable = Average net accounts receivable / One day's sales	$99,500 / $2,351 = 42 days	25

Average accounts receivable was calculated in the previous ratio example at $99,500.

Greg's Groovy Tunes' ratio tells us that 42 average days' sales remain in Accounts receivable and need to be collected. The company's days'-sales-in-receivables ratio is much higher (worse) than the industry average of 25 days. This is probably because Greg's collects its own receivables rather than paying a collection agency to collect for the company. Without the customers' good paying habits, the company's cash flow would suffer.

Measuring Ability to Pay Long-Term Debt

The ratios discussed so far yield insight into current assets and current liabilities. They help us measure ability to sell inventory, collect receivables, and pay current liabilities. Most businesses also have long-term debt. Two key indicators of a business's ability to pay long-term liabilities are the *debt ratio* and the *times-interest-earned ratio*.

Debt Ratio

A loan officer at Metro Bank is evaluating loan applications from two companies. Both companies have asked to borrow $500,000 and have agreed to repay the loan over a five-year period. The first firm already owes $600,000 to another bank. The second owes only $100,000. If all else is equal, the bank is more likely to lend money to Company 2 because that company owes less than Company 1.

This relationship between total liabilities and total assets—called the *debt ratio*—shows the proportion of assets financed with debt. If the debt ratio is 1, then all the assets are financed with debt. A debt ratio of 0.50 means that half the assets are financed with debt and the other half is financed by the owners of the business. The higher the debt ratio, the higher the company's financial risk.

The debt ratios for Greg's Groovy Tunes at the ends of 2012 and 2011 follow:

	Greg's Groovy Tunes' Debt Ratio		Industry
Formula	**2012**	**2011**	**Average**
$\text{Debt ratio} = \dfrac{\text{Total liabilities}}{\text{Total assets}}$	$\dfrac{\$431,000}{\$787,000} = 0.55$	$\dfrac{\$324,000}{\$644,000} = 0.50$	0.69

Greg's debt ratio in 2012 of 0.55 is not very high. The Risk Management Association reports that the average debt ratio for most companies ranges from 0.57 to 0.67, with relatively little variation from company to company. Greg's debt ratio indicates a fairly low-risk position compared with the industry average debt ratio of 0.69.

Times-Interest-Earned Ratio

The debt ratio says nothing about the ability to pay interest expense. Analysts use the **times-interest-earned ratio** to relate income to interest expense. This ratio is also called the **interest-coverage ratio.** It measures the number of times operating income can cover (pay) interest expense. A high interest-coverage ratio indicates ease in paying interest expense; a low ratio suggests difficulty.

To compute this ratio, we divide income from operations (operating income) by interest expense. Calculation of Greg's times-interest-earned ratio follows:

	Greg's Groovy Tunes' Times-Interest-Earned Ratio		Industry
Formula	**2012**	**2011**	**Average**
$\text{Times-interest-earned ratio} = \dfrac{\text{Income from operations}}{\text{Interest expense}}$	$\dfrac{\$101,000}{\$24,000} = 4.21$	$\dfrac{\$57,000}{\$14,000} = 4.07$	7.80

The company's times-interest-earned ratio of around 4.00 is significantly lower than the average for the industry of 7.80 times but is slightly better than the average U.S. business. The norm for U.S. business, as reported by The Risk Management Association, falls in the range of 2.0 to 3.0. When you consider Greg's debt ratio and its times-interest-earned ratio, Greg's Groovy Tunes appears to have little difficulty *servicing its debt*, that is, paying liabilities.

Measuring Profitability

The fundamental goal of business is to earn a profit. Ratios that measure profitability are reported in the business press. We will examine four profitability measures.

Rate of Return on Net Sales

In business, the term *return* is used broadly as a measure of profitability. Consider a ratio called the **rate of return on net sales,** or simply **return on sales.** (The word *net* is usually omitted for convenience, even though net sales is used to compute the ratio.) This ratio shows the percentage of each sales dollar earned as net income. Greg's Groovy Tunes' rate of return on sales follows:

Formula	Greg's Groovy Tunes' Rate of Return on Sales 2012	Greg's Groovy Tunes' Rate of Return on Sales 2011	Industry Average
$\text{Rate of return on sales} = \dfrac{\text{Net income}}{\text{Net sales}}$	$\dfrac{\$48{,}000}{\$858{,}000} = 0.056$	$\dfrac{\$26{,}000}{\$803{,}000} = 0.032$	.017

Companies strive for a high rate of return on sales. The higher the rate of return, the more sales dollars end up as profit. The increase in Greg's return on sales from 2011 to 2012 is significant and identifies the company as more successful than the average education service provider whose rate of return is .017.

Rate of Return on Total Assets

The *rate of return on total assets*, or simply *return on assets*, measures a company's success in using assets to earn a profit. Two groups finance a company's assets.

- Creditors have loaned money to the company, and they earn interest.
- Shareholders have invested in stock, and their return is net income.

The sum of interest expense and net income divided by total assets is the return to the two groups that have financed the company's assets. Average total assets is the average of beginning and ending total assets from the comparative balance sheet:

$$(\$644{,}000 + \$787{,}000)/2 = \$715{,}500$$

Computation of the return-on-assets ratio for Greg's Groovy Tunes follows:

Formula	Greg's Groovy Tunes' 2012 Rate of Return on Total Assets	Industry Average
$\text{Rate of return on assets} = \dfrac{\text{Net income} + \text{Interest expense}}{\text{Average total assets}}$	$\dfrac{\$48{,}000 + \$24{,}000}{\$715{,}500} = 0.101$	.0599

Greg's Groovy Tunes' return-on-assets ratio of .101 is much better than the industry average of .0599.

Rate of Return on Common Stockholders' Equity

A popular measure of profitability is *rate of return on common stockholders' equity*, often shortened to *return on equity*. This ratio shows the relationship between net income and common stockholders' equity—how much income is earned for each $1 invested by the common shareholders.

To compute this ratio, we first subtract preferred dividends from net income to get net income available to the common stockholders. (Greg's does not have any preferred stocks issued, so preferred dividends are zero.) Then divide net income available to common stockholders by average common equity during the year. Common equity is total stockholders' equity minus preferred equity. Average equity is the average of the beginning and ending balances.

($356,000 + $320,000)/2 = $338,000

The 2012 rate of return on common stockholders' equity for Greg's Groovy Tunes follows:

Formula	Greg's Groovy Tunes' 2012 Rate of Return on Common Stockholders' Equity	Industry Average
Rate of return on common stockholders' equity $= \dfrac{\text{Net income} - \text{Preferred dividends}}{\text{Average common stockholders' equity}}$	$\dfrac{\$48{,}000 - \$0}{\$338{,}000} = 0.142$	.105

Greg's return on equity of 0.142 is higher than its return on assets of 0.101. This difference results from borrowing at one rate—say, 8%—and investing the money to earn a higher rate, such as the firm's 14.2% return on equity. This practice is called **trading on the equity**, or using *leverage*. It is directly related to the debt ratio. The higher the debt ratio, the higher the leverage. Companies that finance operations with debt are said to *leverage* their positions.

During good times, leverage increases profitability. But leverage can have a negative impact on profitability as well. Therefore, leverage is a double-edged sword, increasing profits during good times but compounding losses during bad times. Compare Greg's Groovy Tunes' return on equity with the industry average of 0.105. Once again, Greg's Groovy Tunes is performing much better than the average company in its industry. A return on equity of 15% to 20% year after year is considered good in most industries. At 14.2%, Greg's is doing well.

Earnings per Share of Common Stock

Earnings per share of common stock, or simply *earnings per share (EPS)*, is perhaps the most widely quoted of all financial statistics. EPS is the only ratio that must appear on the face of the income statement. EPS is the amount of net income earned for each share of the company's outstanding *common* stock. Recall that

Outstanding stock = Issued stock – Treasury stock

Earnings per share is computed by dividing net income available to common stockholders by the number of common shares outstanding during the year. Preferred dividends are subtracted from net income because the preferred stockholders have the first claim to dividends. Greg's Groovy Tunes has no preferred stock outstanding and, therefore, paid no preferred dividends.

The firm's EPS for 2012 and 2011 follow. (Note that Greg's had 10,000 shares of common stock outstanding throughout both years.)

Formula	Earnings per Share 2012	Earnings per Share 2011	Industry Average
Earnings per share of common stock = (Net income − Preferred dividends) / Number of shares of common stock outstanding	$\frac{\$48{,}000 - \$0}{10{,}000} = \$4.80$	$\frac{\$26{,}000 - \$0}{10{,}000} = \$2.60$	\$9.76

Greg's Groovy Tunes' EPS increased significantly in 2012 (by almost 85%). Its stockholders should not expect this big a boost in EPS every year. Most companies strive to increase EPS by 10%–15% annually, and leading companies do so. But even the most successful companies have an occasional bad year. EPS for the industry at \$9.76 is a little over twice Greg's Groovy Tunes' 2012 EPS. Therefore, Greg's Groovy Tunes needs to work on continuing to increase EPS so that it is more competitive with other companies in its industry.

Analyzing Stock Investments

Investors purchase stock to earn a return on their investment. This return consists of two parts: (1) gains (or losses) from selling the stock at a price above or below purchase price and (2) dividends. The ratios we examine in this section help analysts evaluate stock investments.

Price/Earnings Ratio

The **price/earnings ratio** is the ratio of the market price of a share of common stock to the company's earnings per share. It shows the market price of \$1 of earnings. This ratio, abbreviated P/E, appears in *The Wall Street Journal* stock listings.

Calculations for the P/E ratios of Greg's Groovy Tunes follow. The market price of its common stock was \$60 at the end of 2012 and \$35 at the end of 2011. These prices for real companies can be obtained from a financial publication, a stockbroker, or the company's Web site.

Formula	Greg's Groovy Tunes' Price/Earnings Ratio 2012	Greg's Groovy Tunes' Price/Earnings Ratio 2011	Industry Average
P/E ratio = Market price per share of common stock / Earnings per share	$\frac{\$60.00}{\$4.80} = 12.5$	$\frac{\$35.00}{\$2.60} = 13.5$	17.79

Greg's P/E ratio of 12.5 means that the company's stock is selling at 12.5 times one year's earnings. The decline from the 2011 P/E ratio of 13.5 is no cause for alarm because the market price of the stock is not under Greg's Groovy Tunes' control. Net income is more controllable, and net income increased during 2012.

Greg's would like to see this ratio increase in future years in order to be more in line with the industry average P/E of 17.79.

Dividend Yield

Dividend yield is the ratio of dividends per share to the stock's market price per share. This ratio measures the percentage of a stock's market value that is returned annually as dividends. *Preferred* stockholders, who invest primarily to receive dividends, pay special attention to dividend yield.

Greg's paid annual cash dividends of $1.20 per share of common stock in 2012 and $1.00 in 2011. As noted previously, market prices of the company's common stock were $60 in 2012 and $35 in 2011. The firm's dividend yields on common stock follow:

Formula	Dividend Yield on Greg's Groovy Tunes' Common Stock 2012	2011	Industry Average
Dividend yield on common stock* $= \dfrac{\text{Dividend per share of common stock}}{\text{Market price per share of common stock}}$	$\dfrac{\$1.20}{\$60.00} = .020$	$\dfrac{\$1.00}{\$35.00} = .029$	.0356

*Dividend yields may also be calculated for preferred stock.

An investor who buys Greg's Groovy Tunes' common stock for $60 can expect to receive 2% of the investment annually in the form of cash dividends. The industry, however, is paying out 3.56% annually.

Book Value per Share of Common Stock

Book value per share of common stock is common equity divided by the number of common shares outstanding. Common equity equals total stockholders' equity less preferred equity. Greg's has no preferred stock outstanding. Its book-value-per-share-of-common-stock ratios follow. (Note that 10,000 shares of common stock were outstanding.)

Formula	Book Value per Share of Greg's Groovy Tunes' Common Stock 2012	2011
Book value per share of common stock $= \dfrac{\text{Total stockholders' equity} - \text{Preferred equity}}{\text{Number of shares of common stock outstanding}}$	$\dfrac{\$356{,}000 - \$0}{10{,}000} = \$35.60$	$\dfrac{\$320{,}000 - \$0}{10{,}000} = \$32.00$

Many experts argue that book value is not useful for investment analysis. It bears no relationship to market value and provides little information beyond stockholders' equity reported on the balance sheet. But some investors base their investment decisions on book value. For example, some investors rank stocks on the basis of the ratio of market price to book value. To these investors, the lower the ratio, the more attractive the stock.

Stop & Think...

If you have ever baked cookies from scratch, you know that you have to measure the ingredients properly to make the cookies taste "right." So say you are making peanut butter cookies and the recipe calls for 2/3 cup of peanut butter. If you only have 1/2 cup, it will not be enough to make the cookies taste like they should. If you put in 3/4; cup, it would be too much and again, the cookies will not taste as they should. Ratio analysis is like this. It measures performance of certain key figures that give you either a result you wanted (good peanut butter cookies) or a result you did not want (peanut butter cookies that do not taste like peanut butter).

Red Flags in Financial Statement Analysis

Analysts look for *red flags* that may signal financial trouble. Recent accounting scandals highlight the importance of these red flags. The following conditions may reveal that the company is too risky.

- **Movement of Sales, Inventory, and Receivables.** Sales, receivables, and inventory generally move together. Increased sales lead to higher receivables and require more inventory to meet demand. Unexpected or inconsistent movements among sales, inventory, and receivables make the financial statements look suspect.
- **Earnings Problems.** Has net income decreased significantly for several years in a row? Has income turned into a loss? Most companies cannot survive consecutive losses year after year.
- **Decreased Cash Flow.** Cash flow validates net income. Is cash flow from operations consistently lower than net income? If so, the company is in trouble. Are the sales of plant assets a major source of cash? If so, the company may face a cash shortage.
- **Too Much Debt.** How does the company's debt ratio compare to that of major competitors? If the debt ratio is too high, the company may be unable to pay its debts.
- **Inability to Collect Receivables.** Are days' sales in receivables growing faster than for competitors? A cash shortage may be looming.
- **Buildup of Inventories.** Is inventory turnover too slow? If so, the company may be unable to sell goods, or it may be overstating inventory.

Do any of these red flags apply to either Smart Touch Learning or Greg's Groovy Tunes from the analysis we did in the chapter? No, the financial statements of both companies depict strong and growing companies. Will both Smart Touch Learning and Greg's Groovy Tunes continue to grow? Time will tell.

The Decision Guidelines summarize the most widely used ratios.

Decision Guidelines

USING RATIOS IN FINANCIAL STATEMENT ANALYSIS

Mike and Roberta Robinson operate a financial-services firm. They manage other people's money and do most of their own financial-statement analysis. How do they measure companies' ability to pay bills, sell inventory, collect receivables, and so on? They use the standard ratios discussed in this chapter.

Ratio	Computation	Information Provided
Measuring ability to pay current liabilities:		
1. Current ratio	$\frac{\text{Current assets}}{\text{Current liabilities}}$	Measures ability to pay current liabilities with current assets
2. Acid-test (quick) ratio	$\frac{\text{Cash} + \text{Short-term investments} + \text{Net current receivables}}{\text{Current liabilities}}$	Shows ability to pay all current liabilities if they came due immediately
Measuring ability to sell inventory and collect receivables:		
3. Inventory turnover	$\frac{\text{Cost of goods sold}}{\text{Average inventory}}$	Indicates salability of inventory—the number of times a company sells its average inventory during a year
4. Accounts receivable turnover	$\frac{\text{Net credit sales}}{\text{Average net accounts receivable}}$	Measures ability to collect cash from customers
5. Days' sales in receivables	$\frac{\text{Average net accounts receivable}}{\text{One day's sales}}$	Shows how many days' sales remain in Accounts receivable—how many days it takes to collect the average level of receivables
Measuring ability to pay long-term debt:		
6. Debt ratio	$\frac{\text{Total liabilities}}{\text{Total assets}}$	Indicates percentage of assets financed with debt
7. Times-interest-earned ratio	$\frac{\text{Income from operations}}{\text{Interest expense}}$	Measures the number of times operating income can cover interest expense
Measuring profitability:		
8. Rate of return on net sales	$\frac{\text{Net income}}{\text{Net sales}}$	Shows the percentage of each sales dollar earned as net income
9. Rate of return on total assets	$\frac{\text{Net income} + \text{Interest expense}}{\text{Average total assets}}$	Measures how profitably a company uses its assets

Ratio	Computation	Information Provided
10. Rate of return on common stockholders' equity	$\dfrac{\text{Net income} - \text{Preferred dividends}}{\text{Average common stockholders' equity}}$	Gauges how much income is earned for each dollar invested by the common shareholders
11. Earnings per share of common stock	$\dfrac{\text{Net income} - \text{Preferred dividends}}{\text{Number of shares of common stock outstanding}}$	Gives the amount of net income earned for each share of the company's common stock
Analyzing stock as an investment:		
12. Price/earnings ratio	$\dfrac{\text{Market price per share of common stock}}{\text{Earnings per share}}$	Indicates the market price of $1 of earnings
13. Dividend yield	$\dfrac{\text{Annual dividend per share of common (or preferred) stock}}{\text{Market price per share of common (or preferred) stock}}$	Shows the percentage of a stock's market value returned as dividends to stockholders each year
14. Book value per share of common stock	$\dfrac{\text{Total stockholders' equity} - \text{Preferred equity}}{\text{Number of shares of common stock outstanding}}$	Indicates the recorded accounting amount for each share of common stock outstanding

Summary Problem 2

JAVA, INC.
Four-Year Selected Financial Data (adapted)
Years Ended January 31, 2013–2010

Operating Results*	2013	2012	2011	2010
Net sales	$13,848	$13,673	$11,635	$ 9,054
Cost of goods sold	9,704	8,599	6,775	5,318
Interest expense	109	75	45	46
Income from operations	338	1,455	1,817	1,333
Net income (net loss)	(8)	877	1,127	824
Cash dividends	76	75	76	77
Financial Position				
Merchandise inventory	1,677	1,904	1,462	1,056
Total assets	7,591	7,012	5,189	3,963
Current ratio	1.48:1	0.95:1	1.25:1	1.20:1
Stockholders' equity	3,010	2,928	2,630	1,574
Average number of shares of common stock outstanding (in thousands)	860	879	895	576

*Dollar amounts are in thousands.

Requirements

Compute the following ratios for 2011–2013, and evaluate Java's operating results. Are operating results strong or weak? Did they improve or deteriorate during this period? Your analysis should include the following:

1. Net income as a percentage of sales
2. Earnings per share
3. Inventory turnover
4. Times-interest-earned ratio
5. Rate of return on stockholders' equity

Solution

	2013	2012	2011
1. Net income as a percentage of sales	$\frac{\$(8)}{\$13{,}848} = (.06\%)$	$\frac{\$877}{\$13{,}673} = 6.4\%$	$\frac{\$1{,}127}{\$11{,}635} = 9.7\%$
2. Earnings per share	$\frac{\$(8)}{860} = \$(0.01)$	$\frac{\$877}{879} = \$1.00$	$\frac{\$1{,}127}{895} = \$1.26$
3. Inventory turnover	$\frac{\$9{,}704}{(\$1{,}677 + \$1{,}904)/2} = 5.4$ times	$\frac{\$8{,}599}{(\$1{,}904 + \$1{,}462)/2} = 5.1$ times	$\frac{\$6{,}775}{(\$1{,}462 + \$1{,}056)/2} = 5.4$ times
4. Times-interest-earned ratio	$\frac{\$338}{\$109} = 3.1$ times	$\frac{\$1{,}455}{\$75} = 19.4$ times	$\frac{\$1{,}817}{\$45} = 40.4$ times
5. Rate of return on stockholders' equity	$\frac{\$(8)}{(\$3{,}010 + \$2{,}928)/2} = (0.3\%)$	$\frac{\$877}{(\$2{,}928 + \$2{,}630)/2} = 31.6\%$	$\frac{\$1{,}127}{(\$2{,}630 + \$1{,}574)/2} = 53.6\%$

Evaluation: During this period, Java's operating results deteriorated on all these measures except inventory turnover. The times-interest-earned ratio and return on equity percentages are down sharply. From these data it is clear that Java could sell its coffee, but not at the markups the company enjoyed in the past. The final result, in 2013, was a net loss for the year.

Review *Financial Statement Analysis*

Accounting Vocabulary

Accounts Receivable Turnover Ratio (p. 786)
Measures a company's ability to collect cash from credit customers. To compute accounts receivable turnover, divide net credit sales by average net accounts receivable.

Benchmarking (p. 780)
The practice of comparing a company with other companies that are leaders.

Common-Size Statement (p. 779)
A financial statement that reports only percentages (no dollar amounts).

Dividend Yield (p. 791)
Ratio of dividends per share of stock to the stock's market price per share. Tells the percentage of a stock's market value that the company returns to stockholders annually as dividends.

Dollar Value Bias (p. 779)
The bias one sees from comparing numbers in absolute (dollars) rather than relative (percentages) terms.

Horizontal Analysis (p. 774)
Study of percentage changes in comparative financial statements.

Interest-Coverage Ratio (p. 787)
Ratio of income from operations to interest expense. Measures the number of times that operating income can cover interest expense. Also called the **times-interest-earned ratio**.

Price/Earnings Ratio (p. 790)
Ratio of the market price of a share of common stock to the company's earnings per share. Measures the value that the stock market places on $1 of a company's earnings.

Rate of Return on Net Sales (p. 788)
Ratio of net income to net sales. A measure of profitability. Also called **return on sales**.

Return on Sales (p. 788)
Ratio of net income to net sales. A measure of profitability. Also called **rate of return on net sales**.

Times-Interest-Earned Ratio (p. 787)
Ratio of income from operations to interest expense. Measures the number of times that operating income can cover interest expense. Also called the **interest-coverage ratio**.

Trading on the Equity (p. 789)
Earning more income on borrowed money than the related interest expense, thereby increasing the earnings for the owners of the business. Also called **leverage**.

Trend Percentages (p. 776)
A form of horizontal analysis in which percentages are computed by selecting a base year as 100% and expressing amounts for following years as a percentage of the base amount.

Vertical Analysis (p. 777)
Analysis of a financial statement that reveals the relationship of each statement item to a specified base, which is the 100% figure.

Working Capital (p. 783)
Current assets minus current liabilities. Measures a business's ability to meet its short-term obligations with its current assets.

Quick Check

Atlantic Corporation reported the following figures:

Account	2011	2010
Cash and cash equivalents	$ 2,106	$ 1,706
Receivables	1,872	1,708
Inventory	1,299	1,042
Prepaid expenses	1,616	2,300
Total current assets	6,893	6,756
Other assets	17,149	15,246
Total assets	24,042	22,002
Total current liabilities	7,120	8,284
Long–term liabilities	5,360	2,622
Common equity	11,562	11,096
Total liabilities and equity	$ 24,042	$ 22,002
Sales	$ 20,015	
Cost of sales	6,875	
Operating expenses	7,001	
Operating income	6,139	
Interest expense	202	
Other expenses	2,209	
Net income	$ 3,728	

1. Horizontal analysis of Atlantic's balance sheet for 2011 would report
   a. Cash as 8.76% of total assets.
   b. 23% increase in Cash.
   c. Current ratio of 0.97.
   d. Inventory turnover of 6 times.
2. Vertical analysis of Atlantic's balance sheet for 2011 would report
   a. Cash as 8.76% of total assets.
   b. Current ratio of 1.04.
   c. Inventory turnover of 6 times.
   d. 22% increase in Cash.
3. A common-size income statement for Atlantic would report (amounts rounded)
   a. Cost of sales at 34%.
   b. Net income of 19%.
   c. Sales of 100%.
   d. All of the above
4. Which statement best describes Atlantic's acid-test ratio?
   a. Greater than 1
   b. Equal to 1
   c. Less than 1
   d. None of the above

5. Atlantic's inventory turnover during 2011 was
   a. 7 times.
   b. 6 times.
   c. 8 times.
   d. Not determinable from the data given
6. During 2011, Atlantic's days' sales in receivables ratio was
   a. 37 days.
   b. 33 days.
   c. 43 days.
   d. 41 days.
7. Which measure expresses Atlantic's times-interest-earned ratio?
   a. 30 times
   b. 16 times
   c. 52.6%
   d. 35 times
8. Atlantic's return on common stockholders' equity can be described as
   a. weak.
   b. strong.
   c. average.
   d. normal.
9. The company has 2,300 shares of common stock outstanding. What is Atlantic's earnings per share?
   a. $4.89
   b. 5.16 times
   c. $1.62
   d. $2.39
10. Atlantic's stock has traded recently around $41 per share. Use your answer to question 9 to measure the company's price/earnings ratio.
    a. 0.94
    b. 25
    c. 41
    d. 86

Answers are given after Apply Your Knowledge (p. 817).

Assess Your Progress

Short Exercises

S14-1 *(L. OBJ. 1)* **Horizontal Analysis [5–10 min]**
Hooser, Corp., reported the following on its comparative income statement:

(In millions)	2012	2011	2010
Revenue	$9,610	$9,355	$9,050
Cost of sales........................	5,800	5,600	5,500

Requirement

1. Perform a horizontal analysis of revenues and gross profit—both in dollar amounts and in percentages—for 2012 and 2011.

S14-2 *(L. OBJ. 1)* **Trend Analysis [5–10 min]**
Muscateer, Corp., reported the following revenues and net income amounts:

(In millions)	2013	2012	2011	2010
Revenue	$9,610	$9,355	$9,050	$8,950
Net Income	7,290	6,790	5,020	4,300

Requirements

1. Show Muscateer's trend percentages for revenues and net income. Use 2010 as the base year, and round to the nearest percent.
2. Which measure increased faster during 2011–2013?

S14-3 *(L. OBJ. 2)* **Vertical Analysis [10–15 min]**
Milatin Optical Company reported the following amounts on its balance sheet at December 31, 2010:

		2010
Cash and receivables	$	48,285
Inventory		39,220
Property, plant, and equipment, net		97,495
Total assets	$	185,000

Requirement

1. Perform a vertical analysis of Milatin assets at the end of 2010.

S14-4 *(L. OBJ. 3)* **Common-size income statement [10 min]**
Data for Sanchez, Inc., and Bajo, Corp., follow:

	Sanchez		Bajo	
Net sales	$	10,900	$	17,650
Cost of goods sold		6,769		12,708
Other expenses		3,466		4,007
Net income	$	665	$	935

Requirements

1. Prepare common size income statements.
2. Which company earns a higher percentage net income?
3. Which company's cost of goods sold is a higher percentage of its net sales?

S14-5 *(L. OBJ. 4)* **Evaluating current ratio [5–10 min]**
Low's Companies, a home-improvement-store chain, reported the following summarized figures (in billions):

LOW'S COMPANIES Income Statement Year Ended January 31, 2011		
Net sales	$	40.6
Cost of goods sold		22.5
Interest expense		0.4
All other expenses		6.9
Net income	$	10.8

LOW'S COMPANIES Balance Sheet January 31, 2011 and 2010					
Assets	**2011**	**2010**	**Liabilities**	**2011**	**2010**
Cash	$ 2.2	$ 1.2	Total current liabilities	$ 24.0	$ 13.2
Short term investments	24.0	13.0	Long term liabilities	13.7	11.6
Accounts receivable	7.5	5.4	Total liabilities	37.7	24.8
Inventory	7.3	7.2	**Stockholder's Equity**		
Other current assets	9.0	1.5	Common stock	10.0	10.0
Total current assets	50.0	28.3	Retained earnings	35.3	21.5
All other assets	33.0	28.0	Total equity	45.3	31.5
Total assets	$ 83.0	$ 56.3	Total liabilities and equity	$ 83.0	$ 56.3

Requirements

1. Compute Low's Companies' current ratio at January 31, 2011 and 2010.
2. Did Low's Companies' current ratio improve, deteriorate, or hold steady during 2011?

S14-6 *(L. OBJ. 4)* **Computing inventory turnover and days sales in receivables [10–15 min]**
Use the Low's Companies data in Short Exercise 14-5 to complete the following requirements (amounts in billions).

Requirements

1. Compute the rate of inventory turnover for 2011.
2. Compute days' sales in average receivables during 2011. Round dollar amounts to three decimal places.

S14-7 *(L. OBJ. 4)* **Measuring ability to pay liabilities [5 min]**
Use the financial statements of Low's Companies in Short Exercise 14-5.

Requirements

1. Compute the debt ratio at December 31, 2011.
2. Is Low's ability to pay its liabilities strong or weak? Explain your reasoning.

S14-8 *(L. OBJ. 4)* **Measuring profitability [10 min]**
Use the financial statements of Low's Companies in Short Exercise 14-5 to complete the following profitability measures for 2011.

Requirements

1. Compute the rate of return on net sales.
2. Compute the rate of return on total assets. Interest expense for 2011 was $0.4 billion.
3. Compute the rate of return on common stockholders' equity.
4. Are these rates of return strong or weak? Explain your reasoning.

S14-9 *(L. OBJ. 4)* **Computing EPS and P/E ratio [5–10 min]**
Use the financial statements of Low's Companies in Short Exercise 14-5. Additionally, Low's has issued 0.8 billion common shares.

Requirements

1. Compute earnings per share (EPS) for Low's. Round to the nearest cent.
2. Compute Low's Companies' price/earnings ratio. The price of a share of Low's stock is $67.50.

S14-10 *(L. OBJ. 4)* **Using ratios to reconstruct an income statement [10 min]**
A skeleton of Heirloom Mills' income statement appears as follows (amounts in thousands):

Income Statement

Net sales	$ 7,000
Cost of goods sold	(a)
Selling and admin expenses	1,700
Interest expense	(b)
Other expenses	135
Income before taxes	1,200
Income tax expense	(c)
Net income	(d)

Requirement

1. Use the following ratio data to complete Heirloom Mills' income statement:
   a. Inventory turnover was 4.50 (beginning inventory was $790; ending inventory was $750).
   b. Rate of return on sales is 0.09.

S14-11 *(L. OBJ. 4)* **Using ratios to reconstruct a balance sheet [15–20 min]**
A skeleton of Heirloom Mills' balance sheet appears as follows (amounts in thousands):

Balance Sheet

Cash	$ 100	Total current liabilities	$ 2,250
Receivables	(a)	Long–term note payable	(e)
Inventories	600	Other long term liabilities	920
Prepaid expenses	(b)	Stockholder's equity	2,700
Total current assets	(c)		
Plant assets, net	(d)		
Other assets	2,100		
Total assets	$ 7,300	Total liabilities and equity	$ (f)

Requirement

1. Use the following ratio data to complete Heirloom Mills' balance sheet:
   a. Current ratio is 0.70
   b. Acid-test ratio is 0.20

Exercises

E14-12 *(L. OBJ. 1)* **Computing working capital changes [5–15 min]**
Data for Media Enterprises follows:

	2009	2008	2007
Total current assets	$370,000	$310,000	$280,000
Total current liabilities	175,000	155,000	140,000

Requirement

1. Compute the dollar amount of change and the percentage of change in Media Enterprises' working capital each year during 2008 and 2009. Is this trend favorable or unfavorable?

E14-13 *(L. OBJ. 1)* **Horizontal analysis-income statement [10–15 min]**
Data for Verifine Designs, Inc., follow:

VERIFINE DESIGNS, INC. Comparative Income Statement Years Ended December 31, 2011 and 2010		
	2011	2010
Net sales revenue	$ 428,950	$ 371,000
Expenses:		
Cost of goods sold	$ 203,850	$ 189,350
Selling and general expenses	99,350	93,000
Other expense	6,750	5,000
Total expenses	309,950	287,350
Cash and cash equivalents	$ 119,000	$ 83,650

Requirements

1. Prepare a horizontal analysis of the comparative income statement of Verifine Designs, Inc. Round percentage changes to the nearest one-tenth percent (three decimal places).
2. Why did 2011 net income increase by a higher percentage than net sales revenue?

E14-14 *(L. OBJ. 1)* **Computing trend percentages [5–10 min]**
Thousand Oaks Realty's net revenue and net income for the following five-year period, using 2010 as the base year, follow:

(In thousands)	2014	2013	2012	2011	2010
Net revenue	$1,314	$1,183	$1,006	$1,007	$1,043
Net income	120	115	81	71	85

Requirements

1. Compute trend percentages for net revenue and net income. Round to the nearest full percent.
2. Which grew faster during the period, net revenue or net income?

E14-15 *(L. OBJ. 2)* **Vertical analysis of a balance sheet [10–15 min]**
Eta Graphics, Inc., has the following data:

ETA GRAPHICS, INC. Balance Sheet December 31, 2010	
Assets	
Total current assets	$ 41,870
Property, plant, and equipment, net	206,870
Other assets	34,870
Total assets	$ 283,610
Liabilities	
Total current liabilities	$ 47,870
Long–term debt	107,870
Total liabilities	155,740
Stockholders' Equity	
Total stockholders' equity	127,870
Total liabilities and stockholders' equity	$ 283,610

Requirement

1. Perform a vertical analysis of Eta's balance sheet.

E14-16 *(L. OBJ. 3)* **Preparing common-size income statements [10–15 min]**
Consider the data presented in Exercise 14-13.

Requirements

1. Prepare a comparative common-size income statement for Verifine Designs, Inc., using the 2011 and 2010 data. Round percentages to one-tenth percent (three decimal places).
2. To an investor, how does 2011 compare with 2010? Explain your reasoning.

E14-17 *(L. OBJ. 4)* **Computing 4 key ratios [10–15 min]**
The financial statements of Jim's Health Foods include the following items:

	Current Year	Preceding Year
Balance sheet:		
Cash	$ 18,000	$ 22,000
Short–term investments	10,000	24,000
Net receivables	53,000	75,000
Inventory	75,000	73,000
Prepaid expenses	17,000	10,000
Total current assets	$ 173,000	$ 204,000
Total current liabilities	$ 129,000	$ 91,000
Income statement:		
Net credit sales	$ 463,000	
Cost of goods sold	319,000	

Requirement

1. Compute the following ratios for the current year:

   a. Current ratio
   b. Acid-test ratio
   c. Inventory turnover
   d. Days' sales in average receivables

E14-18 *(L. OBJ. 4)* **Analyzing the ability to pay liabilities [15–20 min]**
Big Bend Picture Frames has asked you to determine whether the company's ability to pay current liabilities and total liabilities improved or deteriorated during 2009. To answer this question, you gather the following data:

	2009	2008
Cash	$ 50,000	$ 47,000
Short–term investments	27,000	—
Net receivables	128,000	124,000
Inventory	237,000	272,000
Total assets	480,000	490,000
Total current liabilities	295,000	202,000
Long–term note payable	44,000	56,000
Income from operations	170,000	168,000
Interest expense	46,000	33,000

Requirement

1. Compute the following ratios for 2009 and 2008:

   a. Current ratio
   b. Acid-test ratio
   c. Debt ratio
   d. Times-interest-earned ratio

E14-19 *(L. OBJ. 4)* **Analyzing profitability [10–15 min]**
The Micatin, Inc., comparative income statement follows. The 2010 data are given as needed.

MICATIN, INC.
Comparative Income Statement
Years Ended December 31, 2012 and 2011

(Dollars in thousands)	2012	2011	2010
Net sales	$177,000	$159,000	
Cost of goods sold	93,200	86,100	
Selling and general expenses	46,500	41,600	
Interest expense	9,700	10,400	
Income tax expense	10,800	9,300	
Net income	$ 16,800	$ 11,600	
Additional data:			
Total assets	$202,000	$192,000	$174,000
Common stockholders' equity	$ 96,700	$ 89,600	$ 79,700
Preferred dividends	$ 3,900	$ 3,900	$ 0
Common shares outstanding during the year	19,000	19,000	17,500

Requirements

1. Calculate the rate of return on net sales.
2. Calculate the rate of return on total assets.
3. Calculate the rate of return on common stockholders' equity.
4. Calculate the EPS.
5. Did the company's operating performance improve or deteriorate during 2012?

E14-20 *(L. OBJ. 4)* **Evaluating a stock as an investment [10–15 min]**
Data for McNight State Bank follows:

	2011	2010
Net income	$ 62,000	$ 54,000
Dividends–common	22,000	22,000
Dividends–preferred	11,400	11,400
Total stockholders' equity at year–end		
(includes 80,000 shares of common stock)	780,000	620,000
Preferred stock, 6%	190,000	190,000
Market price per share of common stock	$ 17.50	$ 12

Requirement

1. Evaluate the common stock of McNight State Bank as an investment. Specifically, use the three stock ratios to determine whether the common stock has increased or decreased in attractiveness during the past year.

E14-21 *(L. OBJ. 4)* **Using ratios to reconstruct a balance sheet [20–30 min]**
The following data (dollar amounts in millions) are adapted from the financial statements of Virginia's Stores, Inc.:

Total current assets	$ 10,800
Accumulated depreciation	$ 1,700
Total liabilities	$ 15,200
Preferred stock	$ 0
Debt ratio	65%
Current ratio	1.60

Requirement

1. Complete Virginia's condensed balance sheet.

Current assets		
Property, plant, and equipment		
Less Accumulated depreciation		
Total assets		
Current liabilities		
Long–term liabilities		
Stockholders' equity		
Total liabilities and stockholders' equity		

Problems (Group A)

P14-22A *(L. OBJ. 1, 4)* **Trend percentages, return on common equity, and comparison with the industry [20–30 min]**
Net sales revenue, net income, and common stockholders' equity for Accurate Mission Corporation, a manufacturer of contact lenses, follow for a four-year period.

(In thousands)	2013	2012	2011	2010
Net sales revenue	$ 766	$ 700	$ 639	$ 661
Net income	63	39	33	47
Ending common stockholders' equity	360	348	328	302

Requirements

1. Compute trend percentages for each item for 2011–2013. Use 2010 as the base year, and round to the nearest whole percent.

2. Compute the rate of return on common stockholders' equity for 2011–2013, rounding to three decimal places.

P14-23A *(L. OBJ. 2, 3)* **Common-size statements, analysis of profitability and financial position, and comparison with the industry [20–30 min]**

The Russell Department Stores, Inc., chief executive officer (CEO) has asked you to compare the company's profit performance and financial position with the average for the industry. The CEO has given you the company's income statement and balance sheet, as well as the industry average data for retailers.

RUSSELL DEPARTMENT STORES, INC.
Income Statement Compared with Industry Average
Year Ended December 31, 2010

	Russell	Industry Average
Net sales	$ 777,000	100.0%
Cost of goods sold	523,698	65.8
Gross profit	253,302	34.2
Operating expenses	162,393	19.7
Operating income	90,909	14.5
Other expenses	7,770	0.4
Net income	$ 83,139	14.1%

RUSSELL DEPARTMENT STORES, INC.
Balance Sheet Compared with Industry Average
December 31, 2010

	Russell	Industry Average
Current assets	$ 330,750	70.9%
Fixed assets, net	123,480	23.6
Intangible assets, net	9,800	0.8
Other assets	25,970	4.7
Total assets	$ 490,000	100.0%
Current liabilities	$ 227,360	48.1%
Long–term liabilities	111,720	16.6
Stockholders' equity	150,920	35.3
Total liabilities and stockholders' equity	$ 490,000	100.0%

Requirements

1. Prepare a common-size income statement and balance sheet for Russell. The first column of each statement should present Russell's common-size statement, and the second column, the industry averages.
2. For the profitability analysis, compute Russell's (a) ratio of gross profit to net sales, (b) ratio of operating income to net sales, and (c) ratio of net income to net sales. Compare these figures with the industry averages. Is Russell's profit performance better or worse than the industry average?
3. For the analysis of financial position, compute Russell's (a) ratio of current assets to total assets and (b) ratio of stockholders' equity to total assets. Compare these ratios with the industry averages. Is Russell's financial position better or worse than the industry averages?

P14-24A *(L. OBJ. 4)* **Effects of business transactions on selected ratios [30–40 min]**
Financial statement data of Off Road Traveler Magazine include the following items (dollars in thousands):

Cash	$ 18,000
Accounts receivable, net	82,000
Inventories	183,000
Total assets	635,000
Short–term notes payable	48,000
Accounts payable	100,000
Accrued liabilities	41,000
Long–term liabilities	227,000
Net income	71,000
Common shares outstanding	40,000

Requirements

1. Compute Off Road Traveler's current ratio, debt ratio, and earnings per share. Round all ratios to two decimal places, and use the following format for your answer:

Current Ratio	Debt Ratio	Earnings Per Share

2. Compute the three ratios after evaluating the effect of each transaction that follows. Consider each transaction *separately*.

   a. Purchased inventory of $43,000 on account
   b. Borrowed $123,000 on a long-term note payable
   c. Issued 4,000 shares of common stock, receiving cash of $106,000
   d. Received cash on account, $6,000

P14-25A *(L. OBJ. 4)* **Using ratios to evaluate a stock investment [40–50 min]**
Comparative financial statement data of Sanfield, Inc., follow:

SANFIELD, INC. Comparative Income Statement Years Ended December 31, 2011 and 2010		
	2011	2010
Net sales	$ 458,000	$ 427,000
Cost of goods sold	240,000	216,000
Gross profit	218,000	211,000
Operating expenses	134,000	132,000
Income from operations	84,000	79,000
Interest expense	13,000	14,000
Income before income tax	71,000	65,000
Income tax expense	19,000	23,000
Net income	$ 52,000	$ 42,000

SANFIELD, INC. Comparative Balance Sheet December 31, 2011 and 2010	2011	2010	2009*
Current assets:			
Cash	$ 98,000	$ 95,000	
Current receivables, net	107,000	118,000	$ 100,000
Inventories	149,000	165,000	207,000
Prepaid expenses	15,000	8,000	
Total current assets	369,000	386,000	
Property, plant, and equipment, net	213,000	180,000	
Total assets	$ 582,000	$ 566,000	602,000
Total current liabilities	$ 229,000	$ 243,000	
Long–term liabilities	117,000	98,000	
Total liabilities	346,000	341,000	
Preferred stock, 4%	106,000	106,000	
Common stockholders' equity, no par	130,000	119,000	93,000
Total liabilities and stockholders' equity	$ 582,000	$ 566,000	

* Selected 2009 amounts

1. Market price of Sanfield's common stock: $81.26 at December 31, 2011, and $67.20 at December 31, 2010.
2. Common shares outstanding: 10,000 during 2011 and 9,000 during 2010.
3. All sales on credit.

Requirements

1. Compute the following ratios for 2011 and 2010:

   a. Current ratio
   b. Times-interest-earned ratio
   c. Inventory turnover
   d. Return on common stockholders' equity
   e. Earnings per share of common stock
   f. Price/earnings ratio

2. Decide (a) whether Sanfield's ability to pay debts and to sell inventory improved or deteriorated during 2011 and (b) whether the investment attractiveness of its common stock appears to have increased or decreased.

P14-26A *(L. OBJ. 4)* **Using ratios to decide between two stock investments [45–60 min]**
Assume that you are purchasing an investment and have decided to invest in a company in the digital phone business. You have narrowed the choice to Best Digital, Corp., and Every Zone, Inc., and have assembled the following data:

Selected income-statement data for the current year

	Best Digital	Every Zone
Net sales (all on credit)	$ 419,000	$ 494,000
Cost of goods sold	210,000	256,000
Interest expense	—	14,000
Net income	46,000	74,000

Selected balance-sheet and market-price data at the *end* of the current year

	Best Digital	Every Zone
Current assets:		
Cash	$ 26,000	$ 16,000
Short–term investments	41,000	17,000
Current receivables, net	35,000	47,000
Inventories	66,000	100,000
Prepaid expenses	18,000	17,000
Total current assets	$ 186,000	$ 197,000
Total assets	$ 263,000	$ 328,000
Total current liabilities	101,000	97,000
Total liabilities	101,000	134,000
Common stock, $1 par (10,000 shares)	10,000	
$2 par (15,000 shares)		30,000
Total stockholders' equity	162,000	194,000
Market price per share of common stock	$ 69.00	$ 118.32

Selected balance-sheet data at the *beginning* of the current year

	Best Digital	Every Zone
Balance sheet:		
Current receivables, net	$ 40,000	$ 52,000
Inventories	82,000	89,000
Total assets	257,000	270,000
Common stock, $1 par (10,000 shares)	10,000	
$2 par (15,000 shares)		30,000

Your strategy is to invest in companies that have low price/earnings ratios but appear to be in good shape financially. Assume that you have analyzed all other factors and that your decision depends on the results of ratio analysis.

Requirement

1. Compute the following ratios for both companies for the current year, and decide which company's stock better fits your investment strategy.

   a. Acid-test ratio
   b. Inventory turnover
   c. Days' sales in average receivables
   d. Debt ratio
   e. Earnings per share of common stock
   f. Price/earnings ratio

Problems (Group B)

P14-27B *(L. OBJ. 1, 4)* **Trend percentages, return on common equity, and comparison with the industry [20–30 min]**

Net sales revenue, net income, and common stockholders' equity for Azbel Mission Corporation, a manufacturer of contact lenses, follow for a four-year period.

(In thousands)	2013	2012	2011	2010
Net sales revenue	$ 766	$ 706	$ 640	$ 663
Net income	58	42	33	46
Ending common stockholders' equity ..	368	350	338	298

Requirements

1. Compute trend percentages for each item for 2011–2013. Use 2010 as the base year, and round to the nearest whole percent.
2. Compute the rate of return on common stockholders' equity for 2011–2013, rounding to three decimal places.

P14-28B *(L. OBJ. 2, 3)* **Common-size statements, analysis of profitability and financial position, and comparison with the industry [20–30 min]**

The Klein Department Stores, Inc., chief executive officer (CEO) has asked you to compare the company's profit performance and financial position with the average for the industry. The CEO has given you the company's income statement and balance sheet, as well as the industry average data for retailers.

KLEIN DEPARTMENT STORES, INC.
Income Statement Compared with Industry Average
Year Ended December 31, 2010

	Klein	Industry Average
Net sales	$ 780,000	100.0%
Cost of goods sold	525,720	65.8
Gross profit	254,280	34.2
Operating expenses	161,460	19.7
Operating income	92,820	14.5
Other expenses	6,240	0.4
Net income	$ 86,580	14.1%

KLEIN DEPARTMENT STORES, INC.
Balance Sheet Compared with Industry Average
December 31, 2010

	Klein	Industry Average
Current assets	$ 291,540	70.9%
Fixed assets, net	110,940	23.6
Intangible assets, net	6,880	0.8
Other assets	20,640	4.7
Total assets	$ 430,000	100.0%
Current liabilities	$ 200,380	48.1%
Long-term liabilities	96,320	16.6
Stockholders' equity	133,300	35.3
Total liabilities and stockholders' equity	$ 430,000	100.0%

Requirements

1. Prepare a common-size income statement and balance sheet for Klein. The first column of each statement should present Klein's common-size statement, and the second column, the industry averages.
2. For the profitability analysis, compute Klein's (a) ratio of gross profit to net sales, (b) ratio of operating income to net sales, and (c) ratio of net income to net sales. Compare these figures with the industry averages. Is Klein Department Stores' profit performance better or worse than the industry average?
3. For the analysis of financial position, compute Klein's (a) ratio of current assets to total assets and (b) ratio of stockholders' equity to total assets. Compare these ratios with the industry averages. Is Klein Department Stores' financial position better or worse than the industry averages?

P14-29B *(L.OBJ. 4)* **Effects of business transactions on selected ratios [30–40 min]**

Financial statement data of Yankee Traveler Magazine include the following items (dollars in thousands):

Cash	$ 25,000
Accounts receivable, net	81,000
Inventories	183,000
Total assets	636,000
Short-term notes payable	46,000
Accounts payable	98,000
Accrued liabilities	40,000
Long-term liabilities	227,000
Net income	74,000
Common shares outstanding	70,000

Requirements

1. Compute Yankee Traveler's current ratio, debt ratio, and earnings per share. Round all ratios to two decimal places, and use the following format for your answer:

Current Ratio	Debt Ratio	Earnings Per Share

2. Compute the three ratios after evaluating the effect of each transaction that follows. Consider each transaction, a–d, *separately*.

   a. Purchased inventory of $48,000 on account
   b. Borrowed $121,000 on a long-term note payable
   c. Issued 7,000 shares of common stock, receiving cash of $107,000
   d. Received cash on account, $2,000

P14-30B *(L. OBJ. 4)* **Using ratios to evaluate a stock investment [40–50 min]**
Comparative financial statement data of Canfield, Inc., follow:

CANFIELD, INC. Comparative Income Statement Years Ended December 31, 2011 and 2010		
	2011	2010
Net sales	$ 459,000	$ 427,000
Cost of goods sold	240,000	215,000
Gross profit	219,000	212,000
Operating expenses	132,000	130,000
Income from operations	87,000	82,000
Interest expense	10,000	11,000
Income before income tax	77,000	71,000
Income tax expense	22,000	25,000
Net income	$ 55,000	$ 46,000

CANFIELD, INC. Comparative Balance Sheet December 31, 2011 and 2010			
	2011	2010	2009*
Current assets:			
Cash	$ 93,000	$ 92,000	
Current receivables, net	108,000	117,000	$ 101,000
Inventories	144,000	162,000	205,000
Prepaid expenses	14,000	9,000	
Total current assets	359,000	380,000	
Property, plant, and equipment, net	211,000	173,000	
Total assets	$ 570,000	$ 553,000	595,000
Total current liabilities	$ 229,000	$ 246,000	
Long-term liabilities	119,000	95,000	
Total liabilities	348,000	341,000	
Preferred stock, 4%	106,000	106,000	
Common stockholders' equity, no par	116,000	106,000	86,000
Total liabilities and stockholders' equity	$ 570,000	$ 553,000	

* Selected 2009 amounts

1. Market price of Canfield's common stock: $54.99 at December 31, 2011, and $50.16 at December 31, 2010.
2. Common shares outstanding: 12,000 during 2011 and 10,000 during 2010.
3. All sales on credit.

Requirements

1. Compute the following ratios for 2011 and 2010:

    a. Current ratio
    b. Times-interest-earned ratio
    c. Inventory turnover
    d. Return on common stockholders' equity
    e. Earnings per share of common stock
    f. Price/earnings ratio

2. Decide (a) whether Canfield's ability to pay debts and to sell inventory improved or deteriorated during 2011 and (b) whether the investment attractiveness of its common stock appears to have increased or decreased.

P14-31B *(L. OBJ. 4)* **Using ratios to decide between two stock investments [45–60 min]** Assume that you are purchasing an investment and have decided to invest in a company in the digital phone business. You have narrowed the choice to Digital Plus, Corp., and Very Network, Inc., and have assembled the following data:

Selected income-statement data for the current year

	Digital Plus	Very Network
Net sales (all on credit)	$ 422,000	$ 495,000
Cost of goods sold	209,000	255,000
Interest expense	—	15,000
Net income	52,000	74,000

Selected balance-sheet and market-price data at the *end* of the current year

	Digital Plus	Very Network
Current assets:		
Cash	$ 28,000	$ 22,000
Short–term investments	41,000	19,000
Current receivables, net	40,000	49,000
Inventories	67,000	102,000
Prepaid expenses	20,000	15,000
Total current assets	$ 196,000	$ 207,000
Total assets	$ 262,000	$ 324,000
Total current liabilities	100,000	95,000
Total liabilities	100,000	134,000
Common stock, $1 par (10,000 shares)	10,000	
$1 par (15,000 shares)		15,000
Total stockholders' equity	162,000	190,000
Market price per share of common stock	$ 83.20	$ 108.46

Selected balance-sheet data at the *beginning* of the current year

	Digital Plus	Very Network
Balance sheet:		
Current receivables, net	$ 43,000	$ 51,000
Inventories	84,000	85,000
Total assets	257,000	279,000
Common stock, $1 par (10,000 shares)	10,000	
$1 par (15,000 shares)		15,000

Your strategy is to invest in companies that have low price/earnings ratios but appear to be in good shape financially. Assume that you have analyzed all other factors and that your decision depends on the results of ratio analysis.

Requirement

1. Compute the following ratios for both companies for the current year, and decide which company's stock better fits your investment strategy.

    a. Acid-test ratio
    b. Inventory turnover
    c. Days' sales in average receivables
    d. Debt ratio
    e. Earnings per share of common stock
    f. Price/earnings ratio

■ Continuing Exercise

E14-32 This exercise continues the Sherman Lawn Service, Inc., situation from Exercise 13-30 of Chapter 13.

Requirement

1. Prepare a vertical analysis from the income statement you prepared in Chapter 4.

■ Continuing Problem

P14-33 This problem continues the Haupt Consulting, Inc., situation from Problem 13-31 of Chapter 13.

Requirement

1. Using the results from Chapter 4, and knowing that the current market price of Haupt's stock is $50 per share, calculate the following ratios for the company:

    a. Current ratio
    b. Debt ratio
    c. Earnings per share
    d. P/E ratio
    e. Return on assets
    f. Return on common stockholders' equity

Apply Your Knowledge

■ Decision Cases

Case 1. General Motors, Inc., and **Ford Motor Company** both had a bad year in 2007; the companies' auto units suffered net losses. The loss pushed some return measures into the negative column, and the companies' ratios deteriorated. Assume top management of **GM** and **Ford** are pondering ways to improve their ratios. In particular, management is considering the following transactions:

1. **Borrow $100 million on long-term debt.**
2. **Purchase treasury stock for $500 million cash.**
3. **Expense one-fourth of the goodwill carried on the books.**
4. **Create a new auto-design division at a cash cost of $300 million.**
5. **Purchase patents from Daimler Chrysler, paying $20 million cash.**

Requirement

1. Top management wants to know the effects of these transactions (increase, decrease, or no effect) on the following ratios:
   a. Current ratio
   b. Debt ratio
   c. Return on equity

Case 2. Lance Berkman is the controller of Saturn, a dance club whose year-end is December 31. Berkman prepares checks for suppliers in December and posts them to the appropriate accounts in that month. However, he holds on to the checks and mails them to the suppliers in January.

Requirements

1. What financial ratio(s) is(are) most affected by the action?
2. What is Berkman's purpose in undertaking this activity? (Challenge)

■ Ethical Issue

Betsy Ross Flag Company's long-term debt agreements make certain demands on the business. For example, Ross may not purchase treasury stock in excess of the balance of retained earnings. Also, long-term debt may not exceed stockholders' equity, and the current ratio may not fall below 1.50. If Ross fails to meet any of these requirements, the company's lenders have the authority to take over management of the company.

Changes in consumer demand have made it hard for Ross to attract customers. Current liabilities have mounted faster than current assets, causing the current ratio to fall to 1.47. Before releasing financial statements, Ross management is scrambling to improve the current ratio. The controller points out that an investment can be classified as either long-term or short-term, depending on management's intention. By deciding to convert an investment to cash within one year, Ross can classify the investment as short-term—a current asset. On the controller's recommendation, Ross's board of directors votes to reclassify long-term investments as short-term.

Requirements

1. What effect will reclassifying the investments have on the current ratio? Is Ross's true financial position stronger as a result of reclassifying the investments?

2. Shortly after the financial statements are released, sales improve; so, too, does the current ratio. As a result, Ross management decides not to sell the investments it had reclassified as short-term. Accordingly, the company reclassifies the investments as long-term. Has management behaved unethically? Give the reasoning underlying your answer.

Financial Statement Case

Amazon.com's financial statements in Appendix A at the end of this book reveal some interesting relationships. Answer these questions about **Amazon.com**:

Requirements

1. What is most unusual about the balance sheet?
2. Compute trend percentages for net sales and net income. Use 2005 as the base year. Which trend percentage looks strange? Explain your answer.
3. Compute inventory turnover for 2007 and 2006. The inventory balance at December 31, 2005, was $566 million. Do the trend of net income from 2006 to 2007 and the change in the rate of inventory turnover tell the same story or a different story? Explain your answer.

Team Projects

Project 1. Select an industry you are interested in, and use the leading company in that industry as the benchmark. Then select two other companies in the same industry. For each category of ratios in the Decision Guidelines in the chapter, compute all the ratios for the three companies. Write a two-page report that compares the two companies with the benchmark company.

Project 2. Select a company and obtain its financial statements. Convert the income statement and the balance sheet to common size, and compare the company you selected to the industry average. The Risk Management Association's *Annual Statement Studies*, Dun & Bradstreet's *Industry Norms & Key Business Ratios*, and Prentice Hall's *Almanac of Business and Industrial Financial Ratios*, by Leo Troy, publish common-size statements for most industries.

Quick Check Answers

1. *b* 2. *a* 3. *d* 4. *c* 5. *b* 6. *b* 7. *a* 8. *b* 9. *c* 10. *b*

For online homework, exercises, and problems that provide you immediate feedback, please visit www.myaccountinglab.com.

Comprehensive Problem for Chapters 13 and 14

Analyzing a Company for its Investment Potential

In its annual report, WRS Athletic Supply, Inc., includes the following five-year financial summary.

WRS ATHLETIC SUPPLY, INC.
5-Year Financial Summary (Partial; adapted)

(Dollar amounts in thousands except per share data)	2015	2014	2013	2012	2011	2010
Net sales	$244,524	$217,799	$191,329	$165,013	$137,634	
Net sales increase	12%	14%	16%	20%	17%	
Domestic comparative store sales increase	5%	6%	5%	8%	9%	
Other income—net	2,001	1,873	1,787	1,615	1,391	
Cost of sales	191,838	171,562	150,255	129,664	108,725	
Operating, selling, and general and administrative expenses	41,043	36,173	31,550	27,040	22,363	
Interest costs:						
Debt	1,063	1,357	1,383	1,045	803	
Interest income	(138)	(171)	(188)	(204)	(189)	
Income tax expense	4,487	3,897	3,692	3,338	2,740	
Net income	8,039	6,671	6,295	5,377	4,430	
Per share of common stock:						
Net income	1.81	1.49	1.41	1.21	0.99	
Dividends	0.30	0.28	0.24	0.20	0.16	
Financial Position						
Current assets	$ 30,483	$ 27,878	$ 26,555	$ 24,356	$ 21,132	
Inventories at LIFO cost	24,891	22,614	21,442	19,793	17,076	$16,497
Net property, plant, and equipment	51,904	45,750	40,934	35,969	25,973	
Total assets	94,685	83,527	78,130	70,349	49,996	
Current liabilities	32,617	27,282	28,949	25,803	16,762	
Long-term debt	19,608	18,732	15,655	16,674	9,607	
Shareholders' equity	39,337	35,102	31,343	25,834	21,112	
Financial Ratios						
Current ratio	0.9	1.0	0.9	0.9	1.3	
Return on assets	9.2%	8.5%	8.7%	9.5%	9.6%	
Return on shareholders' equity	21.6%	20.1%	22.0%	22.9%	22.4%	

Requirements

Analyze the company's financial summary for the fiscal years 2011–2015 to decide whether to invest in the common stock of WRS. Include the following sections in your analysis, and fully explain your final decision.

1. Trend analysis for net sales and net income (use 2011 as the base year)
2. Profitability analysis
3. Measuring ability to sell inventory (WRS uses the LIFO method)
4. Measuring ability to pay debts
5. Measuring dividends

15 Introduction to Management Accounting

Learning Objectives/Success Keys

1. Distinguish management accounting from financial accounting
2. Identify trends in the business environment and the role of management accountability
3. Classify costs and prepare an income statement for a service company
4. Classify costs and prepare an income statement for a merchandising company
5. Classify costs and prepare an income statement and statement of cost of goods manufactured for a manufacturing company
6. Use reasonable standards to make ethical judgments

You got a 40% discount on your new mp3 player, and you are relaxing after a day of listening to good tunes. As you sit there, you wonder how Greg's Groovy Tunes, Inc., was able to sell the mp3 player at such a low price. Management accounting information helped Greg's Groovy Tunes design the player to maximize performance while holding down costs. Managing costs helps a company sell the right product for the right price.

Chapters 1–14 of this book laid your foundation in the building blocks of accounting:

- Accounts in the ledger for accumulating information
- Journals for recording transactions
- Financial statements for reporting operating results, financial position, and cash flows

What you have learned so far is called *financial accounting* because its main products are the financial statements.

This chapter shifts the focus to the accounting tools that managers use to run a business. As you can imagine, it is called *management (or managerial) accounting*. If you have ever dreamed of having your own business, you will find management accounting fascinating.

Before launching into how managers use accounting, let us see some of the groups to whom managers must answer. We call these groups the **stakeholders** of the company because each group has an interest of some sort in the business.

Management Accountability

1 Distinguish management accounting from financial accounting

Accountability is responsibility for one's actions. **Management accountability** is the manager's responsibility to the various stakeholders of the company. Many different stakeholders have an interest in an organization, as shown in Exhibit 15-1. Keep in mind that managers are the employees of the owners.

EXHIBIT 15-1 **Management Accountability and the Stakeholders of a Company**

Exhibit 15-2 shows the links between management and the various stakeholders of a company. The exhibit is organized by the three main categories of cash-flow activities: operating, investing, and financing. For each activity we list the stakeholders and what they provide to the organization. The far-right column then shows how managers are accountable to the stakeholders.

To earn the stakeholders' trust, managers provide information about their decisions and the results of those decisions. Thus, management accountability requires two forms of accounting:

- Financial accounting for *external* reporting
- Management (or managerial) accounting for *internal* planning and control

This chapter launches your study of management accounting.

Financial accounting provides financial statements that report results of operations, financial position, and cash flows both to managers and to external stakeholders: owners, creditors, suppliers, customers, the government, and society. Financial accounting satisfies management's accountability to

- Owners and creditors for their investment decisions
- Regulatory agencies, such as the Securities Exchange Commission, the Federal Trade Commission, and the Internal Revenue Service
- Customers and society to ensure that the company acts responsibly

EXHIBIT 15-2 | Management Accountability to Stakeholders

Stakeholders	Provide	and Management is accountable for
Operating activities		
Suppliers	Products and services	Using the goods and services to earn a profit
Employees	Time and expertise	Providing a safe and productive work environment
Customers	Cash	Providing products and services for a reasonable price
Investing activities		
Suppliers	Long-term assets	Purchasing the most productive assets
Financing activities		
Owners	Cash or other assets	Providing a return on the owners' investment
Creditors	Cash	Repaying principal and interest
Actions that affect society		
Governments	Permission to operate	Obeying laws and paying taxes
Communities	Human and physical resources	Providing jobs and operating in an ethical manner to support the community

The financial statements that you studied in Chapters 1–14 focused on financial accounting and reporting on the company as a whole.

Management accounting, on the other hand, provides information to help managers plan and control operations as they lead the business. This includes managing the company's plant, equipment, and human resources. Management accounting often requires forward-looking information because of the futuristic nature of business decisions.

Stop & Think...

You speak differently when you are speaking to your friends than when you are speaking to your boss or parents. This is the gist of managerial and financial accounting—the accounting data is formatted differently so that it "speaks" to the correct audience (stakeholders).

Managers are responsible to external stakeholders, so they must plan and control operations carefully.

- **Planning** means choosing goals and deciding how to achieve them. For example, a common goal is to increase operating income (profits). To achieve this goal, managers may raise selling prices or advertise more in the hope of increasing sales. The **budget** is a mathematical expression of the plan that managers use to coordinate the business's activities. The budget shows the expected financial impact of decisions and helps identify the resources needed to achieve goals.
- **Controlling** means implementing the plans and evaluating operations by comparing actual results to the budget. For example, managers can compare actual costs to budgeted costs to evaluate their performance. If actual costs fall below budgeted costs, that is usually good news. But if actual costs exceed the budget, managers may need to make changes. Cost data help managers make these types of decisions.

Exhibit 15-3 on the following page highlights the differences between management accounting and financial accounting. Both management accounting and financial accounting use the accrual basis of accounting. But management accounting is not required to meet external reporting requirements, such as generally accepted accounting principles. Therefore, managers have more leeway in preparing management accounting reports, as you can see in points 1–4 of the exhibit.

EXHIBIT 15-3 | Management Accounting Versus Financial Accounting

	Management Accounting	Financial Accounting
1. Primary users	Internal—the company's managers	External—investors, creditors, and government authorities
2. Purpose of information	Help managers plan and control operations	Help investors and creditors make investment and credit decisions
3. Focus and time dimension of the information	Relevance of the information and focus on the future—example: 2011 budget prepared in 2010	Relevance and reliability of the information and focus on the past—example: 2010 actual performance reported in 2011
4. Type of report	Internal reports are restricted only by cost/benefit analysis; no audit required	Financial statements are restricted by GAAP and audited by independent CPAs
5. Scope of information	Detailed reports on parts of the company (products, departments, territories), often on a daily or weekly basis	Summary reports primarily on the company as a whole, usually on a quarterly or annual basis
6. Behavioral	Concern about how reports will affect employee behavior	Concern about adequacy of disclosures; behavioral implications are secondary

Managers tailor their management accounting system to help them make wise decisions. Managers weigh the *benefits* of the system (better information leads to higher profits) against the *costs* to develop and run the system. Weighing the costs against the benefits is called **cost/benefit analysis.** To remain in service, a management accounting system's benefits must exceed its costs.

Point 5 of Exhibit 15-3 indicates that management accounting provides more detailed and timely information than does financial accounting. On a day-to-day basis, managers identify ways to cut costs, set prices, and evaluate employee performance. Company intranets and handheld computers provide this information with the click of a mouse. While detailed information is important to managers, summary information is more valuable to external users of financial data.

Point 6 of Exhibit 15-3 reminds us that management accounting reports affect people's behavior. Accountability is created through measuring results. Therefore, employees try to perform well on the parts of their jobs that the accounting system measures. For example, if a manufacturing company evaluates a plant manager based only on costs, the manager may use cheaper materials or hire less experienced workers. These actions will cut costs, but they can hurt profits if product quality drops and sales fall as a result. Therefore, managers must consider how their decisions will motivate company employees and if that motivation will achieve the overall results the company desires.

Today's Business Environment

Identify trends in the business environment and the role of management accountability

In order to be successful, managers of both large corporations and mom-and-pop businesses must consider recent business trends, such as the following:

- **Shift Toward a Service Economy. Service companies** provide health-care, communication, banking, and other important benefits to society. **FedEx**, **Google**, and **Citibank** do not sell products; they sell their services. In the last century, many developed economies shifted their focus from manufacturing to service, and now service companies employ more than 55% of the workforce. The U.S. Census Bureau expects services, such as technology and health care, to grow especially fast.

- **Global Competition.** To be competitive, many companies are moving operations to other countries to be closer to new markets. Other companies are partnering with foreign companies to meet local needs. For example, **Ford**, **General Motors**, and **DaimlerChrysler** all built plants in Brazil to feed Brazil's car-hungry middle class.
- **Time-Based Competition.** The Internet, electronic commerce (e-commerce), and express delivery speed the pace of business. Customers who instant message around the world will not wait two weeks to receive DVDs purchased online. Time is the new competitive turf for world-class business. To compete, companies have developed the following three time-saving responses:
  1. **Advanced Information Systems.** Many companies use **enterprise resource planning (ERP)** systems to integrate all their worldwide functions, departments, and data. ERP systems help to streamline operations, and that enables companies to respond quickly to changes in the marketplace.
  2. **E-Commerce.** Companies use the Internet in everyday operations of selling and customer service. The internet allows the "online sales clerk" to sell to thousands of customers around the world by providing every product the company offers 24/7.
  3. **Just-in-time Management.** Inventory held too long becomes obsolete. Storing goods takes space and must be insured—that costs money. The just-in-time philosophy helps managers cut costs by speeding the transformation of raw materials into finished products. **Just-in-time (JIT)** means producing *just in time* to satisfy needs. Ideally, suppliers deliver materials for today's production in exactly the right quantities *just in time* to begin production, and finished units are completed *just in time* for delivery to customers.
- **Total Quality Management.** Companies must deliver high-quality goods and services in order to be successful. **Total quality management (TQM)** is a philosophy designed to provide customers with superior products and services. Companies achieve this goal by continuously improving quality and reducing or eliminating defects and waste. In TQM, each business function sets higher and higher goals. With TQM, **General Motors** was able to cut warranty cost from $1,600 to $1,000 per vehicle.

Now let us see how different types of companies use management accounting.

Service Companies

3 Classify costs and prepare an income statement for a service company

Service companies, such as **eBay** (online auction), **Verizon** (cell phone service), and your local bank (financial services), sell services. As with other types of businesses, service companies seek to provide services with the following three characteristics:

- High quality
- Reasonable prices
- Timely delivery

We focused on financial statements for service companies in Chapters 1–14 using Smart Touch Learning, Inc.

Service companies have the simplest accounting, since they carry no inventories of products for sale. All of their costs are **period costs**, those costs that are incurred and expensed in the same accounting *period*.

Let us look first at Smart Touch Learning as it originally started out in early 2010 as a service company. Recall that this business sold e-learning. Smart Touch's income statement for the month ended May 31, 2010, reproduced from Chapter 3, follows:

EXHIBIT 15-4 **Income Statement—Service Company**

SMART TOUCH LEARNING, INC. Income Statement Month Ended May 31, 2010			
Revenue:			
Service revenue		$7,600	100%
Expenses:			
Salary expense	$1,800		24%
Rent expense	1,000		13%
Utilities expense	400		5%
Depreciation expense—furniture	300		4%
Depreciation expense—building	200		3%
Interest expense	100		1%
Supplies expense	100		1%
Total expenses		3,900	51%
Net income		$3,700	49%

Smart Touch had no inventory in May, so the company's income statement has no Cost of goods sold. The largest expense is for the salaries of personnel who work for the company. Salary expense was 24% of Smart Touch's revenue in May. However, the company still had a 49% profit margin.

Service companies need to know which services are most profitable, and that means evaluating both revenues and costs. Knowing the cost per service helps managers to set the price of each and then to calculate operating income. In May, 2010, Smart Touch Learning provided 1,950 e-learning services. What is the cost per service? Use the following formula to calculate the unit cost:

Unit cost per service = Total service costs ÷ Total number of services provided
= $3,900 ÷ 1,950
= $2 per e-learning service

Merchandising Companies

4 Classify costs and prepare an income statement for a merchandising company

Merchandising companies, such as **Amazon.com**, **Wal-Mart**, and **Footlocker**, resell products they buy from suppliers. Merchandisers keep an inventory of products, and managers are accountable for the purchasing, storage, and sale of the products. You learned about merchandising companies in Chapters 5 and 6 of this textbook, using the company Greg's Groovy Tunes.

In contrast with service companies, merchandisers' income statements report Cost of goods sold as the major expense. The cost-of-goods-sold section of the income statement shows the flow of the product costs through the inventory. These product costs are **inventoriable product costs** because the products are held in inventory until sold. For *external reporting*, Generally Accepted Accounting Principles (GAAP) require companies to treat inventoriable product costs as an asset until the product is sold, at which time the costs are expensed.

Merchandising companies' inventoriable product costs include *only* the cost to purchase the goods plus freight in—the cost to get the goods *in* the warehouse. The activity in the Inventory account provides the information for the cost-of-goods-sold section of the income statement as shown in the following formula:

Beginning Inventory + Purchases + Freight In – Ending Inventory = Cost of Goods Sold

To highlight the roles of beginning inventory, purchases, and ending inventory, we use the periodic inventory system. However, the concepts in this chapter apply equally to companies that use perpetual inventory systems.

In management accounting we distinguish inventoriable product costs from period costs. As noted previously, *period costs* are those operating costs that are expensed in the period in which they are incurred. Therefore, period costs are the expenses that are not part of inventoriable product cost.

Let us recall Greg's Groovy Tunes' December 31, 2011, results as presented in Chapter 5 as our merchandising example. Remember that Greg's Groovy Tunes first started as a service company selling musical services. Then, the company began selling music CDs and DVDs produced by other companies. At that point the company became a merchandiser. Exhibit 15-5 shows the income statement of Greg's Groovy Tunes for the year ended December 31, 2011.

EXHIBIT 15-5 **Income Statement—Merchandising Company**

GREG'S GROOVY TUNES
Income Statement
Year Ended December 31, 2011

Sales revenue		$169,300	102.0%
Less: Sales returns and allowances	$ (2,000)		–1.2%
Sales discounts	(1,400)		–0.8%
		(3,400)	–2.0%
Net sales revenue		165,900	100.0%
Cost of goods sold:			
Beginning inventory	$ 0		
Purchases and freight in	131,000		
Cost of goods available for sale	131,000		
Ending inventory	(40,200)		
Cost of goods sold		90,800	54.7%
Gross profit		75,100	45.3%
Operating expenses			0.0%
Wage expense	$ 10,200		6.1%
Rent expense	8,400		5.1%
Insurance expense	1,000		0.6%
Depreciation expense	600		0.4%
Supplies expense	500		0.0%
Total operating expenses		20,700	12.5%
Operating income		54,400	32.8%
Other income and (expense):			
Interest expense		(1,300)	–0.8%
Net income		$ 53,100	32.0%

Greg's was not selling DVDs and CDs in 2010, so the beginning inventory at December 31, 2010, was $0. During 2011, Greg's purchased DVDs and CDs at a total cost of $131,000. At the end of 2011, Greg's ending inventory was $40,200. (You can confirm this by reviewing the Balance Sheet in Exhibit 5-8.) Of the

$131,000 available for sale, the cost of DVDs and CDs sold in 2011 was $90,800. Notice that cost of goods sold is 54.7% of sales (cost of goods sold divided by net sales revenue of $165,900). Managers watch the gross profit percentage (45.3% for Greg's) to make sure it does not change too much. A large decrease in the gross profit percentage may indicate that the company has a problem with inventory theft or shrinkage (waste). It may also indicate a problem with retail pricing of the products. The company's profit margin (net income divided by net sales revenue) is 32% for the year ended December 31, 2011.

Merchandising companies need to know which products are most profitable. Knowing the unit cost per product helps managers to set appropriate selling prices. During the year Greg's sold 10,000 CDs and DVDs. What is the cost of each item sold? Use the following formula to calculate the unit cost per item:

Unit cost per item	= Total cost of goods sold	÷	Total number of items sold
	= $90,800	÷	10,000
	= $9.08 per item		

Now practice what you have learned by solving Summary Problem 1.

Summary Problem 1

Jackson, Inc., a retail distributor of futons, provided the following information for 2011:

Merchandise inventory, January 1	$ 20,000
Merchandise inventory, December 31	30,000
Selling expense	50,000
Delivery expense	18,000
Purchases of futons	265,000
Rent expense	15,000
Utilities expense	3,000
Freight in	15,000
Administrative expense	64,000
Sales revenue	500,000
Units sold during the year	2,500 futons

Requirements

1. Calculate the cost of goods sold. What is the cost per futon sold?
2. Calculate the total period costs.
3. Prepare Jackson's income statement for the year ended December 31, 2011. What is the gross profit percentage? What is the profit margin percentage?

Solution

1.

Cost of goods sold	=	Beginning inventory	+ Purchases	+ Freight in	– Ending inventory
$270,000	=	$20,000	+ $265,000	+ $15,000	– $30,000

The cost per futon sold	=	Cost of goods sold	÷	number of futons sold
$108	=	$270,000	÷	2,500 futons

2. Total period costs include all expenses not included in inventory:

Selling expense	$ 50,000
Delivery expense	18,000
Rent expense	15,000
Utilities expense	3,000
Administrative expense	64,000
Total period costs	$150,000

3. The Income Statement follows:

JACKSON, INC. **Income Statement** Year Ended December 31, 2011			
Sales revenue		$500,000	100%
Cost of goods sold:			
Merchandise inventory, January 1	$ 20,000		
Purchases and freight in ($265,000 + $15,000)	280,000		
Cost of goods available for sale	300,000		
Merchandise inventory, December 31	30,000		
Cost of goods sold		270,000	54%
Gross profit		230,000	46%
Operating expenses:			
Administrative expense	$ 64,000		
Selling expense	50,000		
Delivery expense	18,000		
Rent expense	15,000		
Utilities expense	3,000	150,000	30%
Operating income		$ 80,000	16%

Gross profit % = $230,000 / $500,000 × 100 = 46%
Profit margin % = $80,000 / $500,000 × 100 = 16%

Manufacturing Companies

5 Classify costs and prepare an income statement and statement of cost of goods manufactured for a manufacturing company

Manufacturing companies use labor, equipment, supplies, and facilities to convert raw materials into finished products. Managers in manufacturing companies must use these resources to create a product that customers want. They are responsible for generating profits and maintaining positive cash flows.

In contrast with service and merchandising companies, manufacturing companies have a broad range of production activities. This requires tracking costs on three kinds of inventory:

1. **Materials inventory** includes raw materials used in making a product. For example, a baker's raw materials include flour, sugar, and eggs. Materials to manufacture a DVD include casings, colored insert label, blank DVD, and software program.
2. **Work in process inventory** includes goods that are in the manufacturing process but not yet complete. Some production activities have transformed the raw materials, but the product is not yet finished or ready for sale. A baker's work in process inventory includes dough ready for cooking. A DVD manufacturer's work in process could include the DVD and software program, but not the casing and labeling.
3. **Finished goods inventory** includes completed goods that have not yet been sold. Finished goods are the products that the manufacturer sells to a merchandiser (or to other customers), such as a finished cake or boxed DVD.

Types of Costs

A **direct cost** is a cost that can be directly traced to a cost object, such as a product. Direct materials and direct labor are examples of direct costs. A **cost object** is anything for which managers want a separate measurement of cost. Managers may want to know the cost of a product, a department, a sales territory, or an activity. Costs that cannot be traced directly to a cost object, such as manufacturing overhead, are **indirect costs.** In manufacturing companies, product costs include both direct and indirect costs.

Inventoriable Product Costs

The completed product in finished goods inventory is an *inventoriable product cost.* The inventoriable product cost includes three components of manufacturing costs:

- **Direct materials** become a physical part of the finished product. The cost of direct materials (purchase cost plus freight in) can be traced directly to the finished product.
- **Direct labor** is the labor of employees who convert materials into the company's products. The cost of direct labor can be traced *directly* to the finished products.
- **Manufacturing overhead** includes all manufacturing costs other than direct materials and direct labor. These costs are created by all of the supporting production activities, including storing materials, setting up machines, and cleaning the work areas. These activities incur costs of indirect materials, indirect labor, repair and maintenance, utilities, rent, insurance, property taxes, and depreciation on manufacturing plant buildings and equipment. Manufacturing overhead is also called **factory overhead** or **indirect manufacturing cost.**

Exhibit 15-6 summarizes a manufacturer's inventoriable product costs.

EXHIBIT 15-6 | Manufacturer's Inventoriable Product Costs

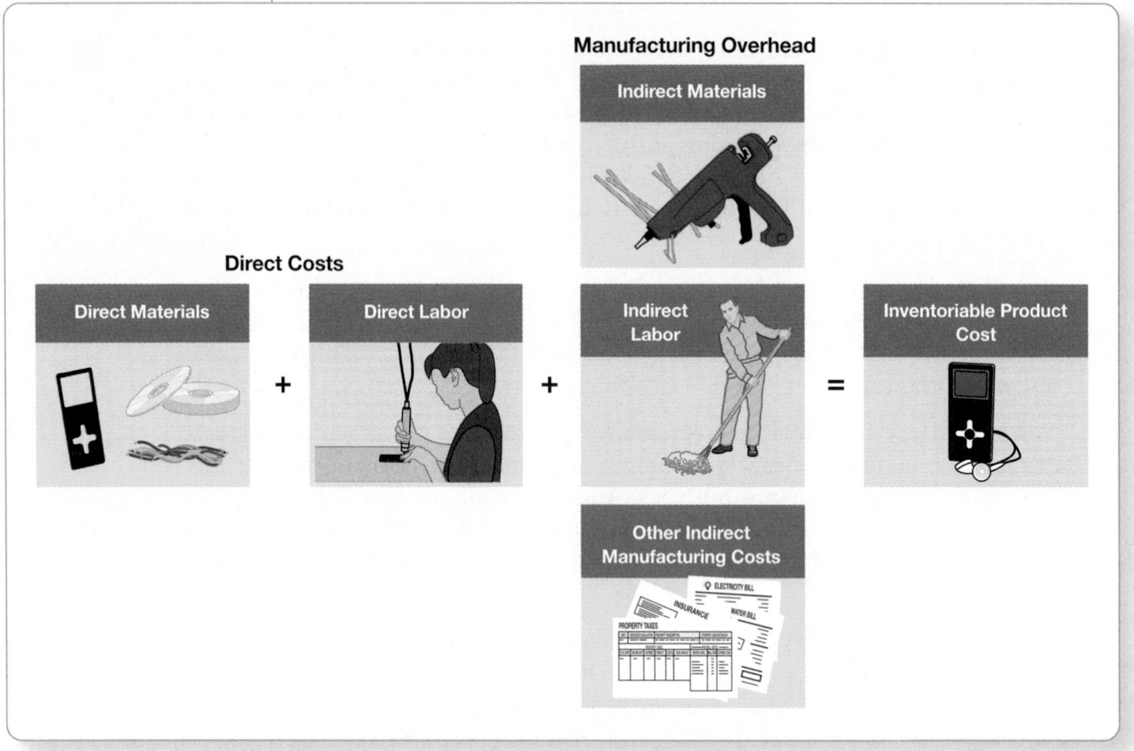

A Closer Look at Manufacturing Overhead

- Manufacturing overhead includes only those indirect costs that are related to the manufacturing operation. Insurance and depreciation on the *manufacturing plant's* building and equipment are indirect manufacturing costs, so they are part of manufacturing overhead. In contrast, depreciation on *delivery trucks* is not part of manufacturing overhead. Instead, depreciation on delivery trucks is a cost of moving the product to the customer. Its cost is delivery expense (a period cost), not an inventoriable product cost. Similarly, the cost of auto insurance for the sales force vehicles is a marketing expense (a period cost), not manufacturing overhead.
- *Manufacturing overhead includes indirect materials and indirect labor*. The spices used in cakes become physical parts of the finished product. But these costs are minor compared with the flour and sugar for the cake. Similarly, the label is necessary but minor in relation to the DVD, case, and software. Since those low-priced materials' costs cannot conveniently be traced to a particular cake or DVD, these costs are called **indirect materials** and become part of manufacturing overhead.

Like indirect materials, **indirect labor** is difficult to trace to specific products so it is part of manufacturing overhead. Examples include the pay of forklift operators, janitors, and plant managers.

Now let us assume that Smart Touch Learning has decided in 2012 to manufacture its own brand of learning DVDs. The company's first year of operations as a manufacturer of learning DVDs is presented in the income statement in Exhibit 15-7 for the year ended December 31, 2012.

Smart Touch's cost of goods sold represents 60% of the net sales revenue. This is the inventoriable product cost of the DVDs that Smart Touch sold in 2012. Smart Touch's balance sheet at December 31, 2012, reports the inventoriable product costs of the finished DVDs that are still on hand at the end of that year. The cost of the ending inventory, $50,000, will become the beginning inventory of next year and will then be included as part of the Cost of goods sold on next year's income statement as the DVDs are sold. The operating expenses that represent 24.1% of net sales revenue are period costs.

EXHIBIT 15-7 Income Statement—Manufacturing Company

SMART TOUCH LEARNING, INC. Income Statement Year Ended December 31, 2012			
Sales revenue		$1,200,000	120.0%
Less: Sales returns and allowances	(120,000)		–12.0%
Sales discounts	(80,000)		–8.0%
		(200,000)	–20.0%
Net sales revenue		1,000,000	100.0%
Cost of goods sold:			
Beginning finished goods inventory	$ 0		
Cost of goods manufactured*	650,000		
Cost of goods available for sale	650,000		
Ending finished goods inventory	(50,000)		
Cost of goods sold		600,000	60.0%
Gross profit		400,000	40.0%
Operating expenses			0.0%
Wage expense	$ 120,000		12.0%
Rent expense	100,000		10.0%
Insurance expense	10,000		1.0%
Depreciation expense	6,000		0.6%
Supplies expense	5,000		0.0%
Total operating expenses		241,000	24.1%
Operating income		159,000	15.9%
Other income and (expense):			
Interest expense		(7,500)	–0.8%
Net income		$ 151,500	15.2%

Exhibit 15-8 summarizes the differences between inventoriable product costs and period costs for service, merchandising, and manufacturing companies. This is a reference tool that will help you determine how to categorize costs.

EXHIBIT 15-8 Inventoriable Product Costs and Period Costs for Service, Merchandising, and Manufacturing Companies

Type of Company	Inventoriable Product Costs—Initially an asset (Inventory), and expensed (Cost of Goods Sold) when the inventory is sold	Period Costs—Expensed in the period incurred; never considered an asset
Service company	None	Salaries, depreciation, utilities, insurance, property taxes, advertising expenses
Merchandising company	Purchases plus freight in	Salaries, depreciation, utilities, insurance, property taxes, advertising, delivery expenses
Manufacturing company	Direct materials, direct labor, and manufacturing overhead (including indirect materials; indirect labor; depreciation on the manufacturing plant and equipment; plant insurance, utilities, and property taxes)	Delivery expense; depreciation expense, utilities, insurance, and property taxes on executive headquarters (separate from the manufacturing plant); advertising; CEO's salary

Let us compare Smart Touch's manufacturing income statement in Exhibit 15-7 with Greg's Groovy Tunes' merchandising income statement in Exhibit 15-5. The only difference is that the merchandiser (Greg's) uses *purchases* in computing cost of goods sold, while the manufacturer (Smart Touch) uses the *cost of goods manufactured*. Notice that the term **cost of goods manufactured** is in the past tense. It is the manufacturing cost of the goods that Smart Touch *completed during 2012*. The following is the difference between a manufacturer and a merchandiser:

- The manufacturer *made* the product that it later sold.
- The merchandiser *purchased* a pre-manufactured product that was complete and ready for sale.

Calculating the Cost of Goods Manufactured The cost of goods manufactured summarizes the activities and the costs that take place in a manufacturing plant over the period. Let us begin by reviewing these activities. Exhibit 15-9 reminds us that the manufacturer starts by buying materials. Then the manufacturer uses direct labor and manufacturing plant and equipment (overhead) to transform these materials into work in process inventory. When inventory is completed, it becomes finished goods inventory. These are all inventoriable product costs because they are related to the inventory production process.

EXHIBIT 15-9 **Manufacturing Company: Inventoriable Product Costs and Period Costs**

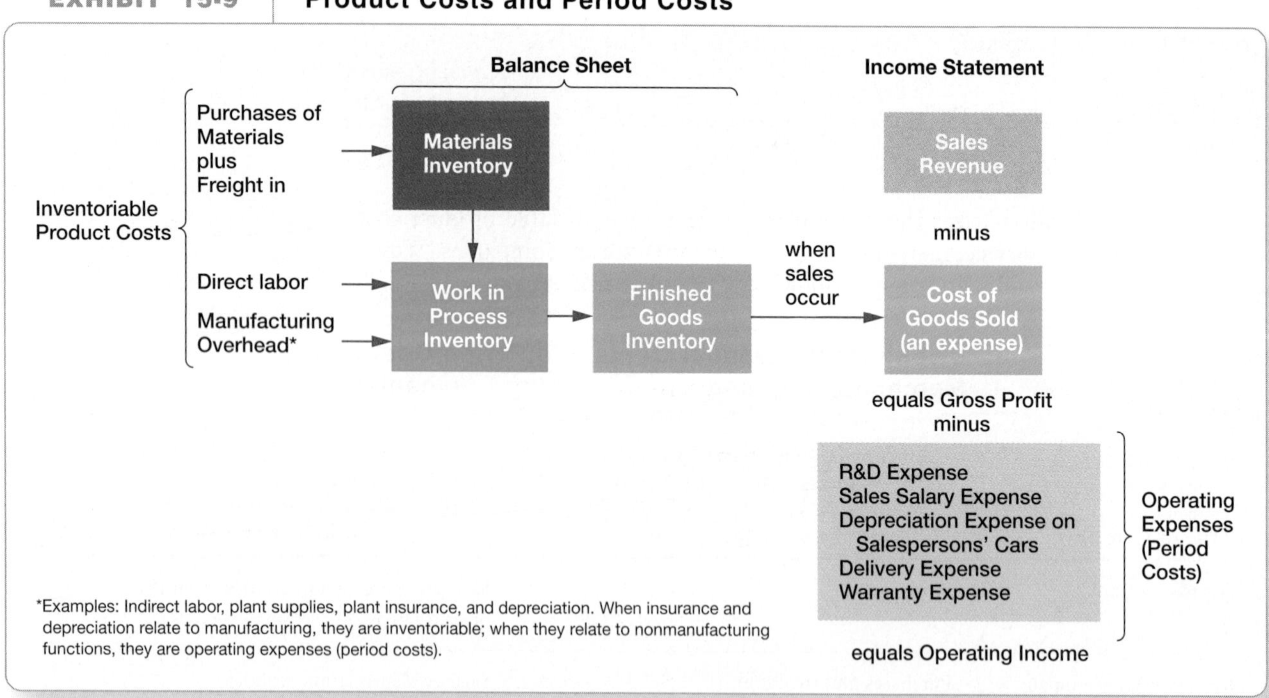

*Examples: Indirect labor, plant supplies, plant insurance, and depreciation. When insurance and depreciation relate to manufacturing, they are inventoriable; when they relate to nonmanufacturing functions, they are operating expenses (period costs).

Finished goods are the only category of inventory that is ready to sell. The cost of the finished goods that the manufacturer sells becomes its cost of goods sold on the income statement. Costs the manufacturer incurs in nonmanufacturing activities, such as sales salaries, are operating expenses—period costs—that are expensed in the period incurred. Exhibit 15-9 shows that these operating costs are deducted from gross profit to compute operating income.

You now have a clear understanding of the flow of activities and costs in the plant, and you are ready to figure the cost of goods manufactured. Exhibit 15-10 shows how Smart Touch computed its cost of goods manufactured for 2012 of $650,000. This is the cost of making 15,000 custom DVDs that Smart Touch *finished* during 2012.

EXHIBIT 15-10 | Schedule of Cost of Goods Manufactured

SMART TOUCH LEARNING, INC.
Schedule of Cost of Goods Manufactured
Year Ended December 31, 2012

A	Beginning work in process inventory			$ 80,000
	Add: Direct materials used:			
B	Beginning direct materials	$ 70,000		
C	Purchases of direct materials (including freight in)	350,000		
D	Available for use	420,000		
E	Ending materials inventory	(65,000)		
F	Direct materials used		$355,000	
G	Direct labor		169,000	
	Manufacturing overhead:			
H	Indirect materials	$ 17,000		
I	Indirect labor	28,000		
J	Depreciation—plant and equipment	10,000		
K	Plant utilities, insurance, and property taxes	18,000		
L			73,000	
M	Total manufacturing costs incurred during the year			597,000
N	Total manufacturing costs to account for			$677,000
O	Less: Ending work in process inventory			(27,000)
P	Cost of goods manufactured			$650,000

B + C = D
D − E = F
H + I + J + K = L
F + G + L = M
A + M = N
N − O = P

Cost of goods manufactured summarizes the activities and related costs incurred to produce inventory during the year. As of December 31, 2011, Smart Touch had just started up manufacturing and had not completed the first custom learning DVD yet. However, the company had started several in production and had spent a total of $80,000 to partially complete them. This 2011 ending work in process inventory became the beginning work in process inventory for 2012.

Exhibit 15-10 shows that during the year, Smart Touch Learning used $355,000 of direct materials, $169,000 of direct labor, and $73,000 of manufacturing overhead.

Total manufacturing costs incurred during the year are the sum of the following three amounts:

Total Manufacturing Costs	
Direct materials used	$355,000
Direct labor	169,000
Manufacturing overhead	73,000
Total manufacturing costs incurred during the year	$597,000

Adding total manufacturing cost for the year, $597,000 to the beginning Work in Process Inventory of $80,000 gives the total manufacturing cost to account for, $677,000. At December 31, 2012, unfinished DVDs costing only $27,000 remained in Work in Process (WIP) Inventory. The company finished 130,000 DVDs and sent them to Finished Goods (FG) Inventory. Cost of goods manufactured for the year was $650,000. The following is the computation of the cost of goods manufactured:

Beginning WIP	+	Direct materials used	+	Direct labor	+	Manufacturing overhead	–	Ending WIP	=	Cost of goods manufactured
$80,000	+	355,000	+	169,000	+	73,000	–	27,000	=	$650,000

If you refer back to Smart Touch's December, 2012, income statement in Exhibit 15-7, you will find the $650,000 listed as the cost of goods manufactured.

Flow Of Costs Through the Inventory Accounts Exhibit 15-11 diagrams the flow of costs through Smart Touch's inventory accounts. The format is the same for all three stages:

- Direct materials
- Work in process
- Finished goods

EXHIBIT 15-11 Flow of Costs Through a Manufacturer's Inventory Accounts

Direct Materials Inventory		Work in Process Inventory			Finished Goods Inventory	
Beginning inventory	$ 70,000	Beginning inventory		$ 80,000	Beginning inventory	$ 0
+ Purchases and freight in	350,000	+ Direct materials used	$355,000		+ Cost of goods manufactured	650,000
		+ Direct labor	169,000			
		+ Manufacturing overhead	73,000			
		Total manufacturing costs incurred during the year		597,000		
= Direct materials available for use	420,000	= Total manufacturing costs to account for		677,000	= Cost of goods available for sale	650,000
– Ending inventory	(65,000)	– Ending inventory		(27,000)	– Ending inventory	(50,000)
= Direct materials used	$355,000	= Cost of goods manufactured		$650,000	= Cost of goods sold	$600,000

Source: The authors are indebted to Judith Cassidy for this presentation.

The final amount at each stage flows into the beginning of the next stage. Take time to see how the schedule of cost of goods manufactured in Exhibit 15-11 uses the flows of the direct materials and work in process stages for Smart Touch's year ended December 31, 2012. Then examine the income statement for Greg's Groovy Tunes in Exhibit 15-5 on page 825. Because Greg's is a merchandising company, it uses only a single Inventory account.

Calculating Unit Product Cost

Manufacturing companies need to know which products are most profitable. Knowing the unit product cost helps managers decide on the prices to charge for each product. They can then measure operating income and determine the cost of finished goods inventory. Smart Touch produced 130,000 DVDs during 2012. What did it cost to make each DVD?

Cost of goods manufactured	÷	Total units produced	=	Unit product cost
$650,000	÷	130,000	=	$5

During 2012, Smart Touch sold 120,000 DVDs, and the company knows each DVD cost $5 to produce. With this information Smart Touch can compute its cost of goods sold as a manager would, as follows:

Number of units sold	×	Unit product cost	=	Cost of goods sold
120,000	×	$5		$600,000

Stop & Think...

It seems lately that every time we go to the gas pump to fill up our cars, the price per gallon has changed. This change causes us to rethink our expected fuel expense each month. Similarly, the unit cost to make a product will change over time because the cost of the inputs to the production process changes over time. This is why the cost of goods manufactured statement is prepared more than once—to update management's cost data about the products the company is producing and selling.

Ethical Standards

6 Use reasonable standards to make ethical judgments

The **WorldCom** and **Enron** scandals underscore that ethical behavior is a critical component of quality. Unfortunately, the ethical path is not always clear. You may want to act ethically and do the right thing, but the consequences can make it difficult to decide what to do. Consider the following examples:

- Sarah Baker is examining the expense reports of her staff, who counted inventory at Top-Flight's warehouses in Arizona. She discovers that Mike Flinders has claimed travel expenses of $1,000 for hotel bills. Flinders could not show the paid receipts. Another staff member, who also claimed $1,000, did attach hotel receipts. When asked about the receipt, Mike admits that he stayed with an old friend, not in the hotel, but he believes he deserves the money he saved. After all, the company would have paid his hotel bill.
- As the accountant of Casey Computer, Co., you are aware of Casey's weak financial condition. Casey is close to signing a lucrative contract that should ensure its future. To do so, the controller states that the company *must* report a profit this year. He suggests: "Two customers have placed orders that are to be shipped in early January. Ask production to fill and ship those orders on December 31, so we can record them in this year's sales."

These situations pose ethical challenges for a manager. The Institute of Management Accountants (IMA) has developed standards to help management accountants meet the ethical challenge. The IMA standards remind us that society expects professional accountants to exhibit the highest level of ethical behavior. An excerpt from the *Standards of Ethical Conduct for Management Accountants* appears in Exhibit 15-12. These standards require management accountants to

- Maintain their professional competence
- Preserve the confidentiality of the information they handle
- Act with integrity and objectivity

EXHIBIT 15-12 | IMA Statement of Ethical Professional Practice (excerpt)

Management accountants have a commitment to ethical professional practice which includes principles of Honesty, Fairness, Objectivity, and Responsibility. The standards of ethical practice include the following:

I. COMPETENCE

1. Maintain an appropriate level of professional expertise by continually developing knowledge and skills.
2. Perform professional duties in accordance with relevant laws, regulations, and technical standards.
3. Provide decision support information and recommendations that are accurate, clear, concise, and timely.
4. Recognize and communicate professional limitations or other constraints that would preclude responsible judgment or successful performance of an activity.

II. CONFIDENTIALITY

1. Keep information confidential except when disclosure is authorized or legally required.
2. Inform all relevant parties regarding appropriate use of confidential information. Monitor subordinates' activities to ensure compliance.
3. Refrain from using confidential information for unethical or illegal advantage.

III. INTEGRITY

1. Mitigate actual conflicts of interest, regularly communicate with business associates to avoid apparent conflicts of interest. Advise all parties of any potential conflicts.
2. Refrain from engaging in any conduct that would prejudice carrying out duties ethically.
3. Abstain from engaging in or supporting any activity that might discredit the profession.

IV. CREDIBILITY

1. Communicate information fairly and objectively.
2. Disclose all relevant information that could reasonably be expected to influence an intended user's understanding of the reports, analyses, or recommendations.
3. Disclose delays or deficiencies in information, timeliness, processing, or internal controls in conformance with organization policy and/or applicable law.

Source: © Courtesy of the Institute of Management Accountants, www.imanet.org.

To resolve ethical dilemmas, the IMA also suggests discussing ethical situations with your immediate supervisor, or with an objective adviser.

Let us return to the two ethical dilemmas. By asking to be reimbursed for hotel expenses he did not incur, Mike Flinders violated the IMA's integrity standards (conflict of interest in which he tried to enrich himself at the company's expense). Because Sarah Baker discovered the inflated expense report, she would not be fulfilling her ethical responsibilities (integrity and objectivity) if she allowed the reimbursement and did not take disciplinary action.

The second dilemma, in which the controller asked you to accelerate the shipments, is less clear-cut. You should discuss the available alternatives and their consequences with others. Many people believe that following the controller's suggestion to manipulate the company's income would violate the standards of competence, integrity, and objectivity. Others would argue that because Casey Computer already has the customer order, shipping the goods and recording the sale in December is still ethical behavior. If you refuse to ship the goods in December and you simply resign without attempting to find an alternative solution, you might only hurt yourself and your family.

Decision Guidelines

BUILDING BLOCKS OF MANAGEMENT ACCOUNTING

Hewlett-Packard (HP) engages in *manufacturing* when it assembles its computers, *merchandising* when it sells them on its Web site, and support *services* such as start-up and implementation services. **HP** had to make the following decisions in designing its management accounting system to provide managers with the information they need to run the manufacturing, merchandising, and service operations efficiently and effectively.

Decision	Guidelines
• What information should management accountants provide? What is the primary focus of management accounting?	Management accounting provides information that helps managers make better decisions; it has a • focus on *relevance* to business decisions • *future* orientation
• How do you decide on a company's management accounting system, which is not regulated by GAAP?	Use cost/benefit analysis: Design the management accounting system so that benefits (from helping managers make wise decisions) outweigh the costs of the system.

• How do you distinguish among service, merchandising, and manufacturing companies? How do their balance sheets differ?	*Service companies:*
	• Provide customers with intangible services
	• Have no inventories on the balance sheet
	Merchandising companies:
	• Resell tangible products purchased ready-made from suppliers
	• Have only one category of inventory
	Manufacturing companies:
	• Use labor, plant, and equipment to transform raw materials into new finished products
	• Have three categories of inventory:
	  • Materials inventory
	  • Work in process inventory
	  • Finished goods inventory

• How do you compute the cost of goods sold?	• *Service companies:* No cost of goods sold, because they do not sell tangible goods • *Merchandising companies:* Beginning *merchandise* inventory + Purchases and freight in – Ending *merchandise* inventory = Cost of goods sold • *Manufacturing companies:* Beginning *finished goods* inventory + Cost of goods manufactured – Ending *finished goods* inventory = Cost of goods sold

Decision	Guidelines
• How do you compute the cost of goods manufactured for a manufacturer?	Beginning *work in process* inventory + Current period manufacturing costs (direct materials used + direct labor + manufacturing overhead) – Ending *work in process* inventory = Cost of goods manufactured
• Which costs are initially treated as assets for external reporting? When are these costs expensed?	*Inventoriable product costs* are initially treated as assets (Inventory); these costs are expensed (as Cost of goods sold) when the products are sold.
• What costs are inventoriable under GAAP?	• *Service companies:* No inventoriable product costs • *Merchandising companies:* Purchases and freight in • *Manufacturing companies:* Direct materials used, direct labor, and manufacturing overhead
• Which costs are never inventoriable product costs?	Period costs. These are never assets. They are always expenses.

Summary Problem 2

Requirements

1. For a manufacturing company, identify the following as either an inventoriable product cost or a period cost:
   a. Depreciation on plant equipment
   b. Depreciation on salespersons' automobiles
   c. Insurance on plant building
   d. Marketing manager's salary
   e. Raw materials
   f. Manufacturing overhead
   g. Electricity bill for home office
   h. Production employee wages
2. Show how to compute cost of goods manufactured. Use the following amounts: direct materials used ($24,000); direct labor ($9,000); manufacturing overhead ($17,000); beginning work in process inventory ($5,000); and ending work in process inventory ($4,000).

Solution

Requirement 1

Inventoriable product cost: a, c, e, f, h
Period cost: b, d, g

Requirement 2

Cost of goods manufactured:

Beginning work in process inventory		$ 5,000
Add: Direct materials used	$24,000	
Direct labor	9,000	
Manufacturing overhead	17,000	
Total manufacturing costs incurred during the period		50,000
Total manufacturing costs to account for		55,000
Less: Ending work in process inventory		(4,000)
Cost of goods manufactured		$51,000

Review *Introduction to Management Accounting*

Accounting Vocabulary

Budget (p. 821)
A mathematical expression of the plan that managers use to coordinate the business's activities.

Controlling (p. 821)
Implementing plans and evaluating the results of business operations by comparing the actual results to the budget.

Cost/Benefit Analysis (p. 822)
Weighing costs against benefits to help make decisions.

Cost Object (p. 829)
Anything for which managers want a separate measurement of cost.

Cost of Goods Manufactured (p. 832)
The manufacturing or plant-related costs of the goods that finished the production process in a given period.

Direct Cost (p. 829)
A cost that can be traced to a cost object.

Direct Labor (p. 829)
The compensation of employees who physically convert materials into finished products.

Direct Materials (p. 829)
Materials that become a physical part of a finished product and whose costs are traceable to the finished product.

Enterprise Resource Planning (ERP) (p. 823)
Software systems that can integrate all of a company's worldwide functions, departments, and data into a single system.

Factory Overhead (p. 829)
All manufacturing costs other than direct materials and direct labor. Also called **manufacturing overhead** or **indirect manufacturing costs**.

Finished Goods Inventory (p. 829)
Completed goods that have not yet been sold.

Indirect Costs (p. 829)
Costs that cannot be traced to a cost object.

Indirect Labor (p. 830)
Labor costs that are difficult to trace to specific products.

Indirect Manufacturing Cost (p. 829)
All manufacturing costs other than direct materials and direct labor. Also called **factory overhead** or **manufacturing overhead**.

Indirect Materials (p. 830)
Materials whose costs cannot conveniently be directly traced to particular finished products.

Inventoriable Product Costs (p. 824)
All costs of a product that the GAAP require companies to treat as an asset for external financial reporting. These costs are not expensed until the product is sold.

Just-in-Time (JIT) (p. 823)
A system in which a company produces just in time to satisfy needs. Suppliers deliver materials just in time to begin production and finished units are completed just in time for delivery to the customer.

Management Accountability (p. 820)
The manager's fiduciary responsibility to manage the resources of an organization.

Manufacturing Company (p. 829)
A company that uses labor, plant, and equipment to convert raw materials into new finished products.

Manufacturing Overhead (p. 829)
All manufacturing costs other than direct materials and direct labor. Also called **factory overhead** or **indirect manufacturing costs**.

Materials Inventory (p. 829)
Raw materials for use in manufacturing.

Merchandising Company (p. 824)
A company that resells products previously bought from suppliers.

Period Costs (p. 823)
Operating costs that are expensed in the period in which they are incurred.

Planning (p. 821)
Choosing goals and deciding how to achieve them.

Service Companies (p. 822)
Companies that sell intangible services, rather than tangible products.

Stakeholders (p. 820)
Groups that have a stake in a business.

Total Quality Management (TQM) (p. 823)
A philosophy of delighting customers by providing them with superior products and services. Requires improving quality and eliminating defects and waste throughout the value chain.

Work in Process Inventory (p. 829)
Goods that are partway through the manufacturing process but not yet complete.

Quick Check

1. Which is *not* a characteristic of management accounting information?
   a. Focuses on the future
   b. Emphasizes the external financial statements
   c. Emphasizes relevance
   d. Provides detailed information about individual parts of the company

2. World-class businesses must compete based on time. To compete effectively many companies have developed
   a. enterprise resource planning.
   b. cost standards.
   c. just-in-time management.
   d. All of the above

3. Today's business environment is characterized by
   a. a shift toward a service economy.
   b. time-based competition.
   c. global competition.
   d. All of the above

4. Which account does a manufacturing company, but not a service company, have?
   a. Retained earnings
   b. Advertising expense
   c. Cost of goods sold
   d. Salary payable

5. In computing cost of goods sold, which of the following is the manufacturer's counterpart to the merchandiser's purchases?
   a. Total manufacturing costs to account for
   b. Cost of goods manufactured
   c. Total manufacturing costs incurred during the period
   d. Direct materials used

6. Which is a direct cost of manufacturing a sportboat?
   a. Cost of customer hotline
   b. Cost of boat engine
   c. Salary of engineer who rearranges plant layout
   d. Depreciation on plant and equipment

7. Which of the following is *not* part of manufacturing overhead for producing a computer?
   a. Manufacturing plant property taxes
   b. Manufacturing plant utilities
   c. Depreciation on delivery trucks
   d. Insurance on plant and equipment

Questions 8 and 9 use the data that follow. Suppose a bakery reports this information (in thousands of dollars):

Beginning materials inventory	$ 4
Ending materials inventory	3
Beginning work in process inventory ...	3
Ending work in process inventory	2
Beginning finished goods inventory ...	2
Ending finished goods inventory	4
Direct labor	31
Purchases of direct materials	105
Manufacturing overhead	22

8. If the cost of direct materials used is $106, what is cost of goods manufactured?
   a. $159
   b. $157
   c. $160
   d. $158
9. If the cost of goods manufactured were $156, what is cost of goods sold?
   a. $159
   b. $151
   c. $156
   d. $154
10. A management accountant who avoids conflicts of interest meets the ethical standard of
    a. integrity.
    b. confidentiality.
    c. objectivity.
    d. competence.

Answers are given after Apply Your Knowledge (p. 858).

Assess Your Progress

Short Exercises

S15-1 *(L. OBJ. 1)* **Management accounting vs. financial accounting [5–10 min]**
Managerial and financial accounting differ in many aspects.

Requirement

1. For each of the following, indicate whether the statement relates to management accounting (MA) or financial accounting (FA):

_____ a. Helps investors make investment decisions

_____ b. Provides detailed reports on parts of the company

_____ c. Helps in planning and controlling operations

_____ d. Reports can influence employee behavior

_____ e. Reports must follow Generally Accepted Accounting Principles (GAAP)

_____ f. Reports audited annually by independent certified public accountants

S15-2 *(L. OBJ. 1)* **Management accountability and the stakeholders [10 min]**
Management has the responsibility to manage the resources of an organization in a responsible manner.

Requirement

1. For each of the following management responsibilities, indicate the primary stakeholder group to whom management is responsible. In the space provided, write the letter corresponding to the appropriate stakeholder group.

_____ 1. Providing high-quality, reliable products/services for a reasonable price in a timely manner

_____ 2. Paying taxes in a timely manner

_____ 3. Providing a safe, productive work environment

_____ 4. Generating a profit

_____ 5. Repaying principal plus interest in a timely manner

a. Owners
b. Creditors
c. Suppliers
d. Employees
e. Customers
f. Government
g. Community

S15-3 *(L. OBJ. 2)* **Business trends terminology [10 min]**
Consider the terms and definitions that follow:

_____ 1. A philosophy of delighting customers by providing them with superior products and services. Requires improving quality and eliminating defects and waste.

_____ 2. Use of the Internet for such business functions as sales and customer service. Enables companies to reach thousands of customers around the world.

_____ 3. Software systems that integrate all of a company's worldwide functions, departments, and data into a single system.

_____ 4. A system in which a company produces just in time to satisfy needs. Suppliers deliver materials just in time to begin production, and finished units are completed just in time for delivery to customers.

a. ERP
b. Just-in-time (JIT)
c. E-commerce
d. Total quality management

Requirement

1. Match the term with the correct definition.

S15-4 *(L. OBJ. 3)* **Calculating income and cost per unit for a service organization [5–10 min]**
Martin and Reynolds provides hair cutting services in the local community. In January, the business incurred the following operating costs to cut the hair of 220 clients:

Hair supplies expense	$ 700
Building rent expense	1,400
Utilities	100
Depreciation on equipment	60

Martin and Reynolds earned $4,900 in revenues from haircuts for the month of January.

Requirements

1. What is the net operating income for the month?
2. What is the cost of one haircut?

S15-5 *(L. OBJ. 4)* **Computing cost of goods sold [5 min]**
The Glass Pro, a retail merchandiser of auto windshields, has the following information:

Web site maintenance	$ 6,900
Delivery expense	800
Freight in	2,800
Purchases	41,000
Ending inventory	5,000
Revenues	60,000
Marketing expenses	10,200
Beginning inventory	8,200

Requirement

1. Compute The Glass Pro's cost of goods sold.

S15-6 *(L. OBJ. 4)* **Computing cost of goods sold [5–10 min]**
Consider the following partially completed Income Statements:

	Rustic Gear		Fit Apparel	
Sales	$	102,000		(d)
Cost of goods sold				
Beginning inventory		(a)	$	31,000
Purchases and freight in		51,000		(e)
Cost of goods available for sale		(b)		91,000
Ending inventory		1,800		1,800
Cost of goods sold		61,000		(f)
Gross margin	$	41,000	$	114,000
Selling and administrative expenses		(c)		83,000
Operating income	$	11,000		(g)

Requirement

1. Compute the missing amounts.

S15-7 *(L. OBJ. 5)* **Match type of company with product and period costs [5 min]**
Consider the following costs:

S, Mer, Man Example: Advertising costs
______ 1. Cost of goods manufactured
______ 2. The CEO's salary
______ 3. Cost of goods sold
______ 4. Building rent expense
______ 5. Customer service expense

Requirement

1. For each of the costs, indicate if the cost would be found on the income statement of a service company (S), a merchandising company (Mer), and/or a manufacturing company (Man). Some costs can be found on the income statements of more than one type of company.

S15-8 *(L. OBJ. 5)* **Computing direct materials used [5 min]**
You are a new accounting intern at 101 Cookies. Your boss gives you the following information:

Purchases of direct materials	$ 6,700
Freight in	100
Property taxes	800
Ending inventory of direct materials	1,600
Beginning inventory of direct materials	4,200

Requirement

1. Compute direct materials used.

S15-9 *(L. OBJ. 5)* **Distinguishing between direct and indirect costs [5–10 min]**
Consider Maher Cards' manufacturing plant.

Requirement

1. Match one of the following terms with each example of a manufacturing cost given below:

1. Direct materials	_____ a. Artists' wages
2. Direct labor	_____ b. Wages of warehouse workers
3. Indirect materials	_____ c. Paper
4. Indirect labor	_____ d. Depreciation on equipment
5. Other manufacturing overhead	_____ e. Manufacturing plant manager's salary
	_____ f. Property taxes on manufacturing plant
	_____ g. Glue for envelopes

S15-10 *(L. OBJ. 5)* **Computing manufacturing overhead [5–10 min]**
Sun Pro Company manufactures sunglasses. Suppose the company's October records include the following items:

Glue for frames	$ 400	Company president's salary	$ 26,000
Depreciation expense on company cars used by sales force	2,000	Plant foreman's salary	3,000
		Plant janitor's wages	1,100
Plant depreciation expense	6,500	Oil for manufacturing equipment	150
Interest expense	2,500	Lenses	48,000

Requirements

1. List the items and amounts that are manufacturing overhead costs.
2. Calculate Sun Pro's total manufacturing overhead cost in October.

S15-11 *(L. OBJ. 5)* **Compute cost of goods manufactured [5 min]**
Max-Fli Golf Company had the following inventory data for the year ended December 31, 2010:

Direct materials used	$ 15,000
Manufacturing overhead	18,000
Work in process inventory:	
Beginning	6,000
Ending	3,000
Direct labor	7,000
Finished goods inventory	11,000

Requirement

1. Compute Max-Fli's cost of goods manufactured for 2010.

S15-12 *(L. OBJ. 5)* **Inventoriable product costs vs. period costs [5–10 min]**
Manufacturer's costs are either inventoriable product costs or period costs.

Requirement

1. Classify each of a paper manufacturer's costs as either an inventoriable product cost or a period cost:

a. Salaries of scientists studying ways to speed forest growth
b. Cost of computer software to track inventory
c. Cost of electricity at a paper mill
d. Salaries of the company's top executives
e. Cost of chemicals to treat paper
f. Cost of TV ads
g. Depreciation on the gypsum board plant
h. Cost of lumber to be cut into boards
i. Life insurance on CEO

S15-13 *(L. OBJ. 6)* **Ethical decisions [5 min]**
The Institute of Management Accountants' *Standards of Ethical Conduct for Management Accountants* (Exhibit 15-12) require management accountants to meet standards regarding the following:

- Competence
- Confidentiality
- Integrity
- Credibility

Requirement

1. Consider the following situations. Which guidelines are violated in each situation?

a. You tell your brother that your company will report earnings significantly above financial analysts' estimates.
b. You see that others take home office supplies for personal use. As an intern, you do the same thing, assuming that this is a "perk."
c. At a conference on e-commerce, you skip the afternoon session and go sightseeing.
d. You failed to read the detailed specifications of a new general ledger package that you asked your company to purchase. After it is installed, you are surprised that it is incompatible with some of your company's older accounting software.
e. You do not provide top management with the detailed job descriptions they requested because you fear they may use this information to cut a position from your department.

Exercises

E15-14 *(L. OBJ. 1)* **Management vs. financial accounting and managers' use of information [5 min]**
The following statements consider how managers use information.

a. Companies must follow GAAP in their ____ systems.
b. Financial accounting develops reports for external parties, such as ____ and ____.
c. When managers compare the company's actual results to the plan, they are performing the ____ role of management.
d. ____ are decision makers inside a company.
e. ____ provides information on a company's past performance.
f. ____ systems are not restricted by GAAP but are chosen by comparing the costs versus the benefits of the system.
g. Choosing goals and the means to achieve them is the ____ function of management.

Requirement

1. Complete the statements with one of the terms listed here. You may use a term more than once, and some terms may not be used at all.

Budget	Creditors	Managers	Planning
Controlling	Financial accounting	Management accounting	Shareholders

E15-15 *(L. OBJ. 2)* **Understanding today's business environment [5 min]**
The following statements relate to understanding today's business environment.

a. ____ is a management philosophy that focuses on producing products as needed by the customer.
b. The goal of ____ is to please customers by providing them with superior products and services by eliminating defects and waste.
c. ____ can integrate all of a company's worldwide functions, departments, and data.
d. Firms adopt ____ to conduct business on the Internet.

Requirement

1. Complete the statements with one of the terms listed here. You may use a term more than once, and some terms may not be used at all.

E-commerce	Just-in-time (JIT) manufacturing
Enterprise Resource Planning (ERP)	Total quality management (TQM)

E15-16 *(L. OBJ. 3)* **Calculating income and cost per unit for a service company [5–10 min]**
Buddy Grooming provides grooming services in the local community. In November, Isaac Smith, the owner, incurred the following operating costs to groom 690 dogs:

Wages	$ 4,300
Grooming supplies expense	1,700
Building rent expense	1,400
Utilities	260
Depreciation on equipment	150

Buddy Grooming earned $15,600 in revenues from grooming for the month of November.

Requirements

1. What is Buddy's net operating income for November?
2. What is the cost to groom one dog?

E15-17 *(L. OBJ. 3)* **Preparing an income statement and computing the unit cost for a service company [5–10 min]**
Georgie's Grooming is a competitor of Buddy Grooming. Georgie Oliver, owner, incurred the following operating costs to groom 2,700 dogs for the first quarter of 2011 (January, February, and March):

Wages	$ 16,700
Grooming supplies expense	4,000
Building rent expense	2,500
Utilities	1,100
Depreciation on furniture and equipment	300

Georgie's Grooming earned $46,300 in revenues for the first quarter of 2011.

Requirements

1. Prepare an income statement for the first quarter of 2011. Compute the ratio of operating expense to total revenue and operating income to total revenue.
2. Compute Georgie's unit cost to groom one dog.

E15-18 *(L. OBJ. 4)* **Preparing an income statement and computing the unit cost for a merchandising company [15 min]**

Gonzales Brush Company sells standard hair brushes. The following information summarizes Gonzales's operating activities for 2011:

Selling and administrative expenses	$ 45,400
Purchases	62,800
Sales revenue	128,500
Merchandise inventory, January 1, 2011	7,400
Merchandise inventory, December 31, 2011	6,000

Requirements

1. Prepare an income statement for 2011. Compute the ratio of operating expense to total revenue and operating income to total revenue.
2. Gonzales sold 5,700 brushes in 2011. Compute the unit cost for one brush.

E15-19 *(L. OBJ. 5)* **Computing cost of goods manufactured [15–20 min]**

Consider the following partially completed cost of goods manufactured statements.

	Flynt Corp.	White Corp.	Fit Apparel
Beginning work in process inventory	(a)	$ 40,000	$ 2,100
Direct materials used	$ 14,900	$ 35,000	(g)
Direct labor	10,100	20,100	1,100
Manufacturing overhead	(b)	10,700	900
Total manufacturing costs incurred during year	45,700	(d)	(h)
Total manufacturing costs to account for	$ 56,400	(e)	$ 7,700
Less: Ending work in process inventory	(c)	(25,700)	(2,800)
Cost of goods manufactured	$ 51,900	(f)	(i)

Requirement

1. Complete the missing amounts.

E15-20 *(L.OBJ. 5)* **Preparing a statement of cost of goods manufactured [15–20 min]**

Clarkson, Corp., a lamp manufacturer, provided the following information for the year ended December 31, 2012:

Inventories:	Beginning	Ending
Materials	$ 55,000	$ 25,000
Work in process	105,000	61,000
Finished goods	43,000	44,000

Other information:			
Depreciation: plant building and equipment	$ 18,000	Repairs and maintenance–plant	$ 7,000
Materials purchases	150,000	Indirect labor	33,000
Insurance on plant	28,000	Direct labor	127,000
Sales salaries expense	49,000	Administrative expenses	51,000

Requirements

1. Prepare a schedule of cost of goods manufactured.
2. What is the unit product cost if Clarkson manufactured 3,200 lamps for the year?

E15-21 *(L. OBJ. 5)* **Flow of costs through a manufacturer's inventory accounts [15–20 min]**
Consider the following data for a manufacturer:

	Beginning of Year	End of Year
Direct materials inventory	$ 21,000	$ 31,000
Work in process inventory	43,000	29,000
Finished goods inventory	15,000	26,000
Purchases of direct materials ...		72,000
Direct labor		89,000
Manufacturing overhead		46,000

Requirement

1. Compute cost of goods manufactured and cost of goods sold.

E15-22 *(L. OBJ. 6)* **Ethical decisions [15 min]**
Mary Gonzales is the controller at Automax, a car dealership. Cory Loftus recently has been hired as bookkeeper. Cory wanted to attend a class on Excel spreadsheets, so Mary temporarily took over Cory's duties, including overseeing a fund for topping-off a car's gas before a test drive. Mary found a shortage in this fund and confronted Cory when he returned to work. Cory admitted that he occasionally uses this fund to pay for his own gas. Mary estimated that the amount involved is close to $300.

Requirements

1. What should Mary Gonzales do?
2. Would you change your answer to the previous question if Mary Gonzales was the one recently hired as controller and Cory Loftus was a well-liked longtime employee who indicated that he always eventually repaid the fund?

Problems (Group A)

P15-23A *(L. OBJ. 1, 2, 3)* **Calculating income and cost per unit for a service company [15–20 min]**
The Tree Doctors provide tree-spraying services in the company's home county. Ivan Peters, the owner, incurred the following operating costs for the month of January 2012:

Salaries and wages	$ 8,000
Chemicals	4,400
Depreciation on truck	400
Depreciation on building and equipment	1,200
Supplies expense	400
Gasoline and utilities	1,400

The Tree Doctors earned $28,000 in revenues for the month of January by spraying trees totaling 35,000 feet in height.

Requirements

1. Prepare an income statement for the month of January. Compute the ratio of total operating expense to total revenue and operating income to total revenue.
2. Compute the unit operating cost of spraying one foot of tree height.
3. The manager of The Tree Doctors must keep unit operating cost below $.60 per foot in order to get his bonus. Did he meet the goal?
4. What kind of system could The Tree Doctors use to integrate all its data?

P15-24A *(L. OBJ. 4)* **Preparing an income statement for a merchandising company [45–55 min]**

In 2011 Clyde Conway opened Clyde's Pets, a small retail shop selling pet supplies. On December 31, 2011, Clyde's accounting records showed the following:

Inventory on December 31, 2011	$	10,700
Inventory on January 1, 2011		15,300
Sales revenue		55,000
Utilities for shop		3,200
Rent for shop		4,300
Sales commissions		2,850
Purchases of merchandise		25,000

Requirement

1. Prepare an income statement for Clyde's Pets, a merchandiser, for the year ended December 31, 2011.

P15-25A *(L. OBJ. 5)* **Preparing cost of goods manufactured schedule and income statement for a manufacturing company [30–45 min]**

Clyde's Pets succeeded so well that Clyde decided to manufacture his own brand of chewing bone—Denim Bones. At the end of December 2011, his accounting records showed the following:

Inventories:	Beginning		Ending
Materials	$ 13,900		$ 10,500
Work in process	0		3,500
Finished goods	0		5,200
Other information:			
Direct material purchases	$ 39,000	Utilities for plant	$ 1,500
Plant janitorial services	200	Rent of plant	14,000
Sales salaries expense	5,800	Customer service hotline expense	1,000
Delivery expense	1,300	Direct labor	24,000
Sales revenue	108,000		

Requirements

1. Prepare a schedule of cost of goods manufactured for Denim Bones for the year ended December 31, 2011.
2. Prepare an income statement for Denim Bones for the year ended December 31, 2011.

3. How does the format of the income statement for Denim Bones differ from the income statement of a merchandiser?
4. Denim Bones manufactured 17,400 units of its product in 2011. Compute the company's unit product cost for the year.

P15-26A *(L. OBJ. 5)* **Preparing financial statements for a manufacturer [25–35 min]**
Certain item descriptions and amounts are missing from the monthly schedule of cost of goods manufactured and the income statement of Webber Manufacturing Company.

______ MANUFACTURING COMPANY ____________________ ______ June 30, 2012			
Beginning __________			$ 20,000
Direct ________:			
Beginning materials inventory	$ X		
Purchase of materials	56,000		
____	77,000		
Ending materials inventory	(27,000)		
Direct ________		$ X	
Direct ________		X	
Manufacturing overhead:		44,000	
Total _____ costs ______			$ 171,000
Total _____ costs ______			X
Ending ________			(22,000)
______			X
Sales revenue		$ X	
Cost of goods sold:			
Beginning ________	$ 114,000		
____	X		
Cost of goods ______	X		
Ending ______	X		
Cost of goods sold		222,000	
Gross profit		238,000	
______ expenses:			
Marketing expenses	96,000		
Administrative expenses	X	156,000	
_____ income		$ X	

Requirement

1. Fill in the missing items.

P15-27A *(L. OBJ. 5)* **Flow of costs through a manufacturer's inventory accounts [20–25 min]**
West Shoe Company makes loafers. During the most recent year, West incurred total manufacturing costs of $25.8 M. Of this amount, $2.3 M was direct materials used

and $18.8 M was direct labor. Beginning balances for the year were Direct Materials Inventory, $.9 M; Work in Process Inventory, $1.2 M; and Finished Goods Inventory, $.4 M. At the end of the year, inventory accounts showed these amounts:

	Materials	Direct Labor	Manufacturing Overhead
Direct Materials Inventory	$ 0.60 M	$ 0	$ 0
Work in Process Inventory	0.60 M	0.65 M	0.45 M
Finished Goods Inventory	0.10 M	0.35 M	0.05 M

Requirements

1. Compute West Shoe Company's cost of goods manufactured for the year.
2. Compute West's cost of goods sold for the year.
3. Compute the cost of materials purchased during the year.

P15-28A *(L. OBJ. 6)* **Making ethical decisions [20–25 min]**

Lee Reinhardt is the new controller for Night Software, Inc., which develops and sells education software. Shortly before the December 31 fiscal year-end, Robert Tau, the company president, asks Reinhardt how things look for the year-end numbers. He is not happy to learn that earnings growth may be below 15% for the first time in the company's five-year history. Tau explains that financial analysts have again predicted a 15% earnings growth for the company and that he does not intend to disappoint them. He suggests that Reinhardt talk to the assistant controller, who can explain how the previous controller dealt with such situations. The assistant controller suggests the following strategies:

a. Persuade suppliers to postpone billing $15,000 in invoices until January 1.
b. Record as sales $100,000 in certain software awaiting sale that is held in a public warehouse.
c. Delay the year-end closing a few days into January of the next year, so that some of next year's sales are included as this year's sales.
d. Reduce the allowance for bad debts from 2% to 1% (and bad debts expense), given the company's continued strong performance.
e. Postpone routine monthly maintenance expenditures from December to January.

Requirements

1. Which of these suggested strategies are inconsistent with IMA standards?
2. What should Reinhardt do if Tau insists that she follow all of these suggestions?

Problems (Group B)

P15-29B *(L. OBJ. 1, 2, 3)* **Calculating income and cost per unit for a service company [15–20 min]**

The Tree People provide tree-spraying services in the company's home county. George Renkas, owner, incurred the following operating costs for the month of March 2012:

Salaries and wages	$ 7,000
Chemicals	4,900
Depreciation on truck	250
Depreciation on building and equipment	1,100
Supplies expense	600
Gasoline and utilities	1,000

The Tree People earned $22,000 in revenues for the month of March by spraying trees totaling 20,000 feet in height.

Requirements

1. Prepare an income statement for the month of March. Compute the ratio of total operating expense to total revenue and operating income to total revenue.
2. Compute the unit operating cost of spraying one foot of tree height.
3. The manager of The Tree People must keep unit operating cost below $.60 per foot in order to get his bonus. Did he meet the goal?
4. What kind of system could The Tree People use to integrate all its data?

P15-30B *(L. OBJ. 4)* **Preparing an income statement for a merchandising company [45–55 min]**

In 2011 Cam Snyder opened Cam's Pets, a small retail shop selling pet supplies. On December 31, 2011, Cam's accounting records showed the following:

Inventory on December 31, 2011	$	10,400
Inventory on January 1, 2011		15,900
Sales revenue		55,000
Utilities for shop		3,800
Rent for shop		4,100
Sales commissions		2,550
Purchases of merchandise		24,000

Requirement

1. Prepare an income statement for Cam's Pets, a merchandiser, for the year ended December 31, 2011.

P15-31B *(L. OBJ. 5)* **Preparing cost of goods manufactured scheduled and income statement for a manufacturing company [30–45 min]**

Cam's Pets succeeded so well that Cam decided to manufacture his own brand of chewing bone—Chewy Bones. At the end of December 2011, his accounting records showed the following:

Inventories:	Beginning		Ending
Materials	$ 13,300		$ 9,500
Work in process	0		3,500
Finished goods	0		5,700
Other information:			
Direct material purchases	$ 33,000	Utilities for plant	$ 1,100
Plant janitorial services	300	Rent on plant	8,000
Sales salaries expense	5,200	Customer service hotline expense	1,600
Delivery expense	1,300	Direct labor	25,000
Sales revenue	106,000		

Requirements

1. Prepare a schedule of cost of goods manufactured for Chewy Bones for the year ended December 31, 2011.
2. Prepare an income statement for Chewy Bones for the year ended December 31, 2011.
3. How does the format of the income statement for Chewy Bones differ from the income statement of a merchandiser?
4. Chewy Bones manufactured 17,300 units of its product in 2011. Compute the company's unit product cost for the year.

P15-32B *(L. OBJ. 5)* **Preparing financial statements for a manufacturer [25–35 min]**
Certain item descriptions and amounts are missing from the monthly schedule of cost of goods manufactured and the income statement of Nelly Manufacturing Company.

______ MANUFACTURING COMPANY ______________ ______ June 30, 2012			
Beginning ______			$ 28,000
Direct ______:			
Beginning materials inventory	$ X		
Purchase of materials	51,000		
______	78,000		
Ending materials inventory	(28,000)		
Direct ______		$ X	
Direct ______		X	
Manufacturing overhead:		44,000	
Total ______ costs ______			$ 173,000
Total ______ costs ______			X
Ending ______			(22,000)
______			$ X
Sales revenue		$ X	
Cost of goods sold:			
Beginning ______	$ 115,000		
______	X		
Cost of goods ______	X		
Ending ______	X		
Cost of goods sold		232,000	
Gross profit		238,000	
______ expenses:			
Marketing expenses	92,000		
Administrative expenses	X	159,000	
______ income		$ X	

Requirement

1. Fill in the missing items.

P15-33B *(L. OBJ. 5)* **Flow of costs through a manufacturer's inventory accounts [20–25 min]**
Happy Feet Shoe Company makes loafers. During the most recent year, Happy Feet incurred total manufacturing costs of $25.8 M. Of this amount, $2.7 M was direct materials used and $11.8 M was direct labor. Beginning balances for the year were Direct Materials Inventory, $.5 M; Work in Process Inventory, $1.8 M; and Finished Goods Inventory, $1.1 M. At the end of the year, inventory accounts showed these amounts:

	Materials	Direct Labor	Manufacturing Overhead
Direct Materials Inventory	$ 0.60 M	$ 0	$ 0
Work in Process Inventory	0.90 M	0.65 M	0.45 M
Finished Goods Inventory	0.50 M	0.15 M	0.05 M

Requirements

1. Compute Happy Feet Shoe Company's cost of goods manufactured for the year.
2. Compute Happy Feet's cost of goods sold for the year.
3. Compute the cost of materials purchased during the year.

P15-34B *(L. OBJ. 6)* **Making ethical decisions [20–25 min]**
Mary Hajjar is the new controller for Sun Software, Inc., which develops and sells education software. Shortly before the December 31 fiscal year-end, William Cauvet, the company president, asks Hajjar how things look for the year-end numbers. He is not happy to learn that earnings growth may be below 15% for the first time in the company's five-year history. Cauvet explains that financial analysts have again predicted a 15% earnings growth for the company and that he does not intend to disappoint them. He suggests that Hajjar talk to the assistant controller, who can explain how the previous controller dealt with such situations. The assistant controller suggests the following strategies:

a. Persuade suppliers to postpone billing $10,000 in invoices until January 1.
b. Record as sales $140,000 in certain software awaiting sale that is held in a public warehouse.
c. Delay the year-end closing a few days into January of the next year so that some of next year's sales are included as this year's sales.
d. Reduce the allowance for bad debts from 9% to 8% (and bad debts expense), given the company's continued strong performance.
e. Postpone routine monthly maintenance expenditures from December to January.

Requirements

1. Which of these suggested strategies are inconsistent with IMA standards?
2. What should Hajjar do if Cauvet insists that she follow all of these suggestions?

Continuing Exercise

E15-35 This exercise continues the Sherman Lawn Service, Inc., situation from Exercise 14-32 of Chapter 14. Sherman is considering manufacturing a weed eater. Sherman expects to incur the following manufacturing costs:

Shaft and handle of weed eater

Motor of weed eater

Factory labor for workers assembling weed eaters

Nylon thread in weed eater

Glue to hold housing together

Plant janitorial wages

Depreciation on factory equipment

Rent on plant

Sales commission expense

Administrative salaries

Plant utilities

Shipping costs to deliver finished weed eaters to customers

Requirement

1. Classify each cost as either direct materials, direct labor, factory overhead, or period costs.

Continuing Problem

P15-36 This problem continues the Haupt Consulting, Inc., situation from Problem 14-33 of Chapter 14. Haupt is going to manufacture billing software. During its first month of manufacturing, Haupt incurred the following manufacturing costs:

Inventories:	Beginning		Ending
Materials	$ 10,000		$ 9,000
Work in process	0		22,000
Finished goods	0		30,000

Other information:			
Direct material purchases	$ 15,000	Utilities for plant	$ 12,000
Plant janitorial services	300	Rent of plant	8,000
Sales salaries expense	7,000	Customer service hotline expense	15,000
Delivery expense	2,000	Direct labor	300,000
Sales revenue	1,000,000		

Requirement

1. Prepare a Schedule of Cost of Goods Manufactured for Haupt for the month ended January 31, 2010.

Apply Your Knowledge

Decision Cases

Case 1. PowerSwitch, Inc., designs and manufactures switches used in telecommunications. Serious flooding throughout North Carolina affected PowerSwitch's facilities. Inventory was completely ruined, and the company's computer system, including all accounting records, was destroyed.

Before the disaster recovery specialists clean the buildings, Stephen Plum, the company controller, is anxious to salvage whatever records he can to support an insurance claim for the destroyed inventory. He is standing in what is left of the accounting department with Paul Lopez, the cost accountant.

"I didn't know mud could smell so bad," Paul says. "What should I be looking for?"

"Don't worry about beginning inventory numbers," responds Stephen, "we'll get them from last year's annual report. We need first-quarter cost data."

"I was working on the first-quarter results just before the storm hit," Paul says. "Look, my report's still in my desk drawer. All I can make out is that for the first quarter, material purchases were $476,000 and direct labor, manufacturing overhead, and total manufacturing costs to account for were $505,000, $245,000, and $1,425,000, respectively. Wait! Cost of goods available for sale was $1,340,000."

"Great," says Stephen. "I remember that sales for the period were approximately $1.7 million. Given our gross profit of 30%, that's all you should need."

Paul is not sure about that, but decides to see what he can do with this information. The beginning inventory numbers are

- Direct materials, $113,000
- Work in process, $229,000
- Finished goods, $154,000

He remembers a schedule he learned in college that may help him get started.

Requirements

1. Exhibit 15-11 resembles the schedule Paul has in mind. Use it to determine the ending inventories of direct materials, work in process, and finished goods.
2. Draft an insurance claim letter for the controller, seeking reimbursement for the flood damage to inventory. PowerSwitch's insurance representative is Gary Ogleby, at Industrial Insurance, Co., 1122 Main Street, Hartford, CT 06268. The policy number is #3454340-23. PowerSwitch's address is 5 Research Triangle Way, Raleigh, NC 27698.

Case 2. The IMA's *Standards of Ethical Conduct for Management Accountants* can be applied to more than just management accounting. They are also relevant to college students.

Requirement

1. Explain at least one situation that shows how each IMA standard in Exhibit 15-12 is relevant to your experiences as a student. For example, the ethical standard of competence would suggest not cutting classes!

Ethical Issue

Becky Knauer recently resigned from her position as controller for Shamalay Automotive, a small, struggling foreign car dealer in Upper Saddle River, New Jersey. Becky has just started a new job as controller for Mueller Imports, a much larger dealer for the same car manufacturer. Demand for this particular make of car is exploding, and the manufacturer cannot produce enough to satisfy demand. The manufacturer's regional sales managers are each given a certain number of cars. Each sales manager then decides how to divide the cars among the independently owned dealerships in the region. Because most dealerships can sell every car they receive, the key is getting a large number of cars from the manufacturer's regional sales manager.

Becky's former employer, Shamalay Automotive, receives only about 25 cars a month. Consequently, the dealership was not very profitable.

Becky is surprised to learn that her new employer, Mueller Imports, receives over 200 cars a month. Becky soon gets another surprise. Every couple of months, a local jeweler bills the dealer $5,000 for "miscellaneous services." Franz Mueller, the owner of the dealership, personally approves payment of these invoices, noting that each invoice is a "selling expense." From casual conversations with a salesperson, Becky learns that Mueller frequently gives Rolex watches to the manufacturer's regional sales manager and other sales executives. Before talking to anyone about this, Becky decides to work through his ethical dilemma using the framework from Chapter 15.

Requirement

1. Put yourself in Becky's place and complete the framework.
   a. What is the ethical issue?
   b. What are my options?
   c. What are the possible consequences?
   d. What shall I do?

Team Project

Search the Internet for a nearby company that also has a Web page. Arrange an interview with a management accountant, a controller, or other accounting/ finance officer of the company.

Requirements

Before you conduct the interview, answer the following questions:

1. Is this a service, merchandising, or manufacturing company? What is its primary product or service?
2. Is the primary purpose of the company's Web site to provide information about the company and its products, to sell online, or to provide financial information for investors?

3. Are parts of the company's Web site restricted so that you need password authorization to enter? What appears to be the purpose of limiting access?
4. Does the Web site provide an e-mail link for contacting the company?

At the interview, begin by clarifying your answers to questions 1 through 4, and ask the following additional questions:

5. If the company sells over the Web, what benefits has the company derived? Did the company perform a cost-benefit analysis before deciding to begin Web sales?

   Or

   If the company does not sell over the Web, why not? Has the company performed a cost-benefit analysis and decided not to sell over the Web?
6. What is the biggest cost of operating the Web site?
7. Does the company make any purchases over the Internet? What percentage?
8. How has e-commerce affected the company's management accounting system? Have the management accountant's responsibilities become more or less complex? More or less interesting?
9. Does the company use Web-based accounting applications, such as accounts receivable or accounts payable?
10. Does the company use an ERP system? If so, do managers view the system as a success? What have been the benefits? The costs?

Quick Check Answers

1. *b* 2. *c* 3. *d* 4. *c* 5. *b* 6. *b* 7. *c* 8. *c* 9. *d* 10. *a*

For online homework, exercises, and problems that provide you immediate feedback, please visit www.myaccountinglab.com.

16 Job Order and Process Costing

Learning Objectives/Success Keys

1. Distinguish between job order costing and process costing
2. Record materials and labor in a job order costing system
3. Record overhead in a job order costing system
4. Record completion and sales of finished goods and the adjustment for under- or overallocated overhead
5. Calculate unit costs for a service company

Many schools use fundraising events to finance extracurricular activities. Let us say that you are responsible for organizing a spaghetti dinner to finance new equipment for the school playground. You have to decide how many dinners you expect to sell, what price to charge, and the ingredients needed. Knowing the cost to prepare one spaghetti dinner is important. You want to set a price low enough to draw a crowd and high enough to generate a profit so that the needed equipment can be purchased.

This chapter shows how to measure cost in situations similar to the spaghetti dinner. This type of cost accounting system is called job order costing because production is arranged by the job. The appendix to this chapter then covers the other main type of costing system—called process costing.

Businesses face the same situation. They must draw a crowd—sell enough goods and services to earn a profit. So, regardless of the type of business you own or manage, you need to know how much it costs to produce your product or service. This applies regardless of the type of career you plan to have.

For example, marketing managers must consider their unit product cost in order to set the selling price high enough to cover costs. Engineers study the materials, labor, and overhead that go into a product to pinpoint ways to cut costs. Production managers then decide whether it is more profitable to make the product or to *outsource* it (buy from an outside supplier). The Finance Department arranges financing for the venture. The Accounting Department provides all the cost data for making these decisions.

You can see that it is important for managers in all areas to know how much it costs to make a product. This chapter shows you how to figure these costs for Smart Touch Learning.

How Much Does it Cost to Make a Product? Two Approaches

1 Distinguish between job order costing and process costing

Cost accounting systems accumulate cost information so that managers can measure how much it costs to produce each unit of merchandise. For example, **Intel** must know how much each processor costs to produce. **FedEx** knows its cost of flying each pound of freight one mile. These unit costs help managers

- set selling prices that will lead to profits.
- compute cost of goods sold for the income statement.
- compute the cost of inventory for the balance sheet.

If a manager knows the cost to produce each product, then the manager can plan and control the cost of resources needed to create the product and deliver it to the customer. A cost accounting system assigns these costs to the company's product or service.

Job Order Costing

Some companies manufacture batches of unique products or specialized services. A **job order costing** system accumulates costs for each batch, or job. Accounting firms, music studios, health-care providers, building contractors, and furniture manufacturers are examples of companies that use job order costing systems. For example, **Dell** makes personal computers based on customer orders (see the "Customize" button on **Dell's** Web site). As we move to a more service-based economy and with the advent of ERP systems, job order costing has become more prevalent.

Process Costing

Other companies, such as **Procter & Gamble** and **Coca-Cola** produce identical units through a series of production steps or processes. A **process costing** system accumulates the costs of each *process* needed to complete the product. **Chevron, General Motors,** and **Kraft Foods** are additional examples of companies that use process costing systems. This method is used primarily by large producers of similar goods.

Both job order and process costing systems

- accumulate the costs incurred to make the product.
- assign costs to the products.

Accountants use **cost tracing** to assign directly traceable costs, such as direct materials and direct labor, to the product. They use a less precise technique—**cost allocation**—to assign manufacturing overhead and other indirect costs to the product. Let us see how a job order costing system works for a manufacturing company.

How Job Costs Flow Through the Accounts: An Overview

2 Record materials and labor in a job order costing system

The job order costing system tracks costs as raw materials move from the storeroom, to the production floor, to finished products. Exhibit 16-1 diagrams the flow of costs through a job order costing system. Let us consider how a manufacturer, Smart Touch Learning, uses job order costing. For Smart Touch, each customer order is a separate job. Smart Touch uses a job cost record to accumulate the costs of each job's

- Direct materials.
- Direct labor.
- Manufacturing overhead.

The company starts the job cost record when work begins on the job. As Smart Touch incurs costs, the company adds costs to the job cost record. For jobs started but not yet finished, the job cost records show the Work in process inventory. When Smart Touch finishes a job, the company totals the costs and transfers costs from Work in process inventory to Finished goods inventory.

When the job's units are sold, the costing system moves the costs from Finished goods inventory, an asset, to Cost of goods sold, an expense. Exhibit 16-1 summarizes this sequence.

EXHIBIT 16-1 **Flow of Costs Through the Accounts in a Job Order Costing System**

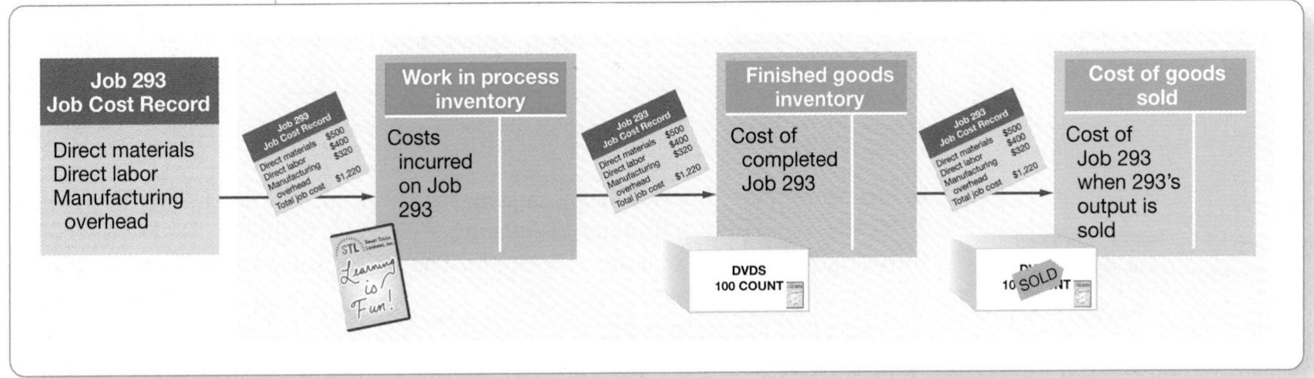

Purchasing Materials On December 31, 2011, Smart Touch had the following inventory balances:

Materials inventory		Work in process inventory		Finished goods inventory	
12/31/11 70,000		12/31/11 80,000		12/31/11 0	

During the year, Smart Touch purchased direct materials of $350,000 and indirect materials of $17,000 on account. We record the purchase of materials as follows:

(1)	Materials inventory (direct) (A+)	350,000	
	Materials inventory (indirect) (A+)	17,000	
	Accounts payable (L+)		367,000

Materials inventory		
12/31/11	70,000	
(1) Purchased	350,000	
(1) Purchased	17,000	

Materials inventory is a general ledger account. Smart Touch Learning also uses a subsidiary ledger for materials. The subsidiary materials ledger includes a separate record for each type of material, so there is a subsidiary ledger for the software, the blank DVDs, the paper inserts, and the casings. Exhibit 16-2 shows the subsidiary ledger of one type of casing that Smart Touch uses. The balance of the Materials inventory account in the general ledger should always equal the sum of the balances in the subsidiary materials ledger.

EXHIBIT 16-2 Example Subsidiary Materials Ledger Record

SUBSIDIARY MATERIALS LEDGER RECORD

STL SMART TOUCH LEARNING, INC.

Item No. C–101 **Description** 5 × 6 Casings

	Received			Used				Balance		
Date	Units	Cost	Total Cost	Mat. Req. No.	Units	Cost	Total Cost	Units	Cost	Total Cost
2012										
1–20								20	$14	$280
1–23	**20**	**$14**	**$280**					40	14	560
7–24				334	10	$14	$140	30	14	420

Using Materials Smart Touch Learning works on many jobs during the year. In 2012 the company used materials costing $355,000, including DVDs, $80,000, software, $200,000, and casings, $75,000. The DVDs, software, and casings can be traced to a specific job(s), so these are all *direct materials*. Direct material costs go directly into the Work in process inventory account.

By contrast, the cost of paper inserts, $17,000, is difficult to trace to a specific job, so paper inserts are an *indirect material*. The cost of indirect material is recorded first as Manufacturing overhead. The following journal entry then records the use of materials in production:

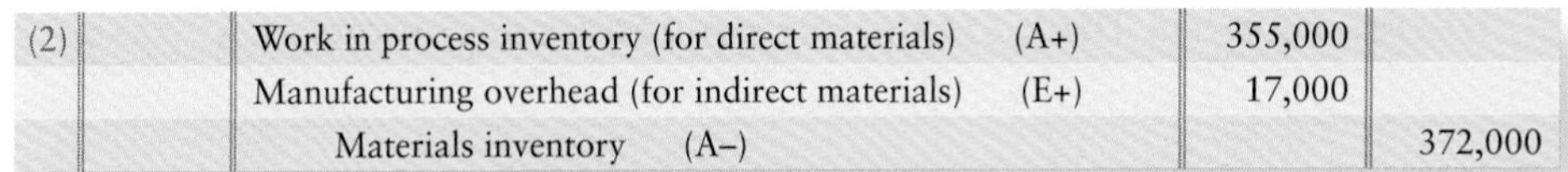

(2)		Work in process inventory (for direct materials) (A+)	355,000	
		Manufacturing overhead (for indirect materials) (E+)	17,000	
		Materials inventory (A–)		372,000

We can summarize the flow of materials costs through the T-accounts as follows:

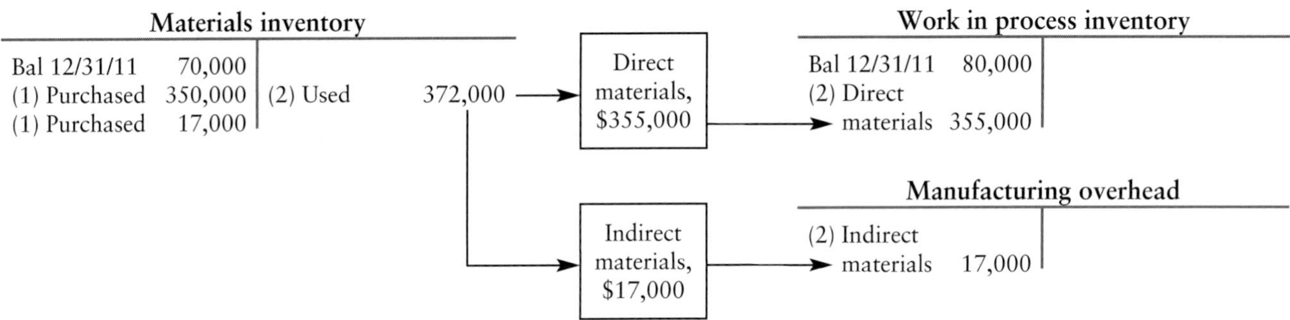

For both direct materials and indirect materials, the production team completes a document called a **materials requisition** to request the transfer of materials to the production floor. Exhibit 16-3 shows Smart Touch Learning's materials requisition for the 10 units of casings needed to make 10 Excel DVDs for Job 16.

EXHIBIT 16-3 Materials Requisition

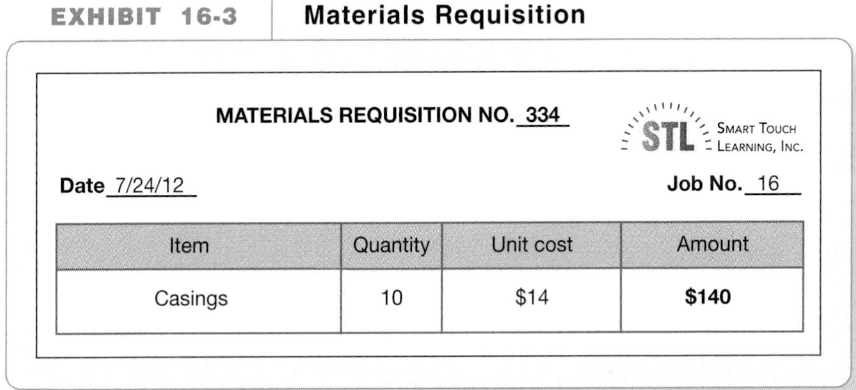

MATERIALS REQUISITION NO. 334

STL SMART TOUCH LEARNING, INC.

Date 7/24/12

Job No. 16

Item	Quantity	Unit cost	Amount
Casings	10	$14	**$140**

Exhibit 16-4 is a **job cost record.** It assigns the cost of the direct material (casings) to Job 16. Follow the $140 cost of the casings from the materials inventory record (Exhibit 16-2), to the materials requisition (Exhibit 16-3), and to the job cost record in Exhibit 16-4. Notice that all the dollar amounts in these exhibits show Smart Touch's *costs*—not the prices at which Smart Touch sells its products.

EXHIBIT 16-4 Direct Materials on Job Cost Record

JOB COST RECORD

STL SMART TOUCH LEARNING, INC.

Job No. 16

Customer Name and Address Macy's New York City

Job Description 10 Excel DVDs

Date Promised 7–31			Date Started 7–24		Date Completed		
Date	Direct Materials		Direct Labor		Manufacturing Overhead Allocated		
	Requisition Numbers	Amount	Labor Time Record Numbers	Amount	Date	Rate	Amount
7–24	334	$140					
					Overall Cost Summary Direct Materials.......$ Direct Labor............ Manufacturing Overhead Allocated		
Totals					Total Job Cost.......$		

Let us see how to account for labor costs.

Accounting for Labor

Smart Touch incurred labor costs of $197,000 during 2011. We record manufacturing wages as follows:

(3)			
	Manufacturing wages (E+)	197,000	
	Wages payable (L+)		197,000

This entry includes the costs of both direct labor and indirect labor.

Each employee completes a labor time record for each job he or she works on. The **labor time record** in Exhibit 16-5 identifies the employee (Ryan Oliver), the amount of time he spent on Job 16 (5 hours), and the labor cost charged to the job ($60 = 5 hours × $12 per hour).

Smart Touch Learning totals the labor time records for each job. Exhibit 16-6 shows how Smart Touch adds the direct labor cost to the job cost record. The "Labor Time Record Numbers" show that on July 24, three employees worked on Job 16. Labor time record 251 is Ryan Oliver's, from Exhibit 16-5. Labor time

EXHIBIT 16-5 | **Labor Time Record**

LABOR TIME RECORD

No. 251
Employee Ryan Oliver **Date** 7–24
Job 16

TIME:

Started	1:00	Rate	$12.00
Stopped	6:00	Cost of Labor	
Elapsed	5:00	Charged to Job	**$60.00**

Employee RO Supervisor GDC

records 236 and 258 (not shown) indicate that two other employees also worked on Job 16. The job cost record shows that Smart Touch assigned Job 16 a total of $200 of direct labor costs for the three employees' work.

During 2011 Smart Touch incurred $169,000 for direct labor and $28,000 for indirect labor (overhead). These amounts include the labor costs for Job 16 that we have been working with plus all the company's other jobs worked on during the year.

Smart Touch Learning's accounting for labor cost requires the company to:

- Assign labor cost to individual jobs, as we saw for Ryan Oliver's work on Job 16
- Transfer labor cost out of the Manufacturing wages account and into Work in process inventory (for direct labor) and into Manufacturing overhead (for indirect labor)

EXHIBIT 16-6 | **Direct Labor on Job Cost Record**

JOB COST RECORD

STL Smart Touch Learning, Inc.

Job No. 16
Customer Name and Address Macy's New York City
Job Description 10 Excel DVDs

Date Promised 7–31			Date Started 7–24		Date Completed		
Date	Direct Materials		Direct Labor		Manufacturing Overhead Allocated		
	Requisition Numbers	Amount	Labor Time Record Numbers	Amount	Date	Rate	Amount
7–24	**334**	**$140**	236, 251, 258	$200			
					Overall Cost Summary Direct Materials..........$ Direct Labor................ Manufacturing Over-head Allocated............		
Totals					Total Job Cost..........$		

The following journal entry zeroes out the Manufacturing wages account and shifts the labor cost to Work in process and the overhead account.

(4)		Work in process inventory (for direct labor) (A+)	169,000	
		Manufacturing overhead (for indirect labor) (E+)	28,000	
		Manufacturing wages (E–)		197,000

This entry brings the balance in Manufacturing wages to zero. Its transferred balance is now divided between Work in process inventory ($169,000 of direct labor) and Manufacturing overhead ($28,000 of indirect labor), as shown in the following T-accounts:

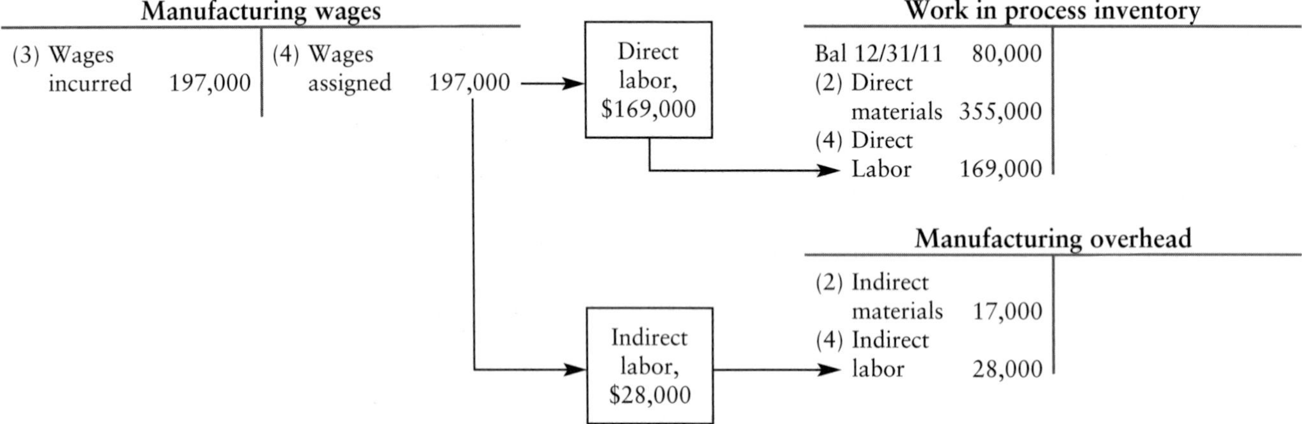

Many companies have automated these accounting procedures. The addition of labor and manufacturing overhead to materials is called **conversion costs** because the labor and overhead costs *convert* materials into a finished product.

Study the Decision Guidelines to summarize the first half of the chapter. Then work the summary problem that follows.

Decision Guidelines

JOB ORDER COSTING: TRACING DIRECT MATERIALS AND DIRECT LABOR

Smart Touch Learning uses a job order costing system that assigns manufacturing costs to each individual job for DVDs. These guidelines explain some of the decisions Smart Touch made in designing its system.

Decision	Guidelines
• Should we use job costing or process costing?	Use *job order costing* when the company produces unique products (DVDs) in small batches (usually a "batch" contains a specific learning program). Use *process costing* when the company produces identical products in large batches, often in a continuous flow.
• How to record:	
• Purchase and use of materials?	*Purchase of materials:*

	Materials inventory	XX	
	Accounts payable (or Cash)		XX

Use of materials:

	Work in process inventory (direct materials)	XX	
	Manufacturing overhead (indirect materials)	XX	
	Materials inventory		XX

Decision	Guidelines
• Incurrence and assignment of labor to jobs?	*Incurrence of labor cost:*

	Manufacturing wages	XX	
	Wages payable (or Cash)		XX

Assignment of labor cost to jobs:

	Work in process inventory (direct labor)	XX	
	Manufacturing overhead (indirect labor)	XX	
	Manufacturing wages		XX

Summary Problem 1

Tom Baker manufactures custom teakwood patio furniture. Suppose Baker has the following transactions:

a. Purchased raw materials on account, $135,000.
b. Materials costing $130,000 were requisitioned (used) for production. Of this total, $30,000 were indirect materials.
c. Labor time records show that direct labor of $22,000 and indirect labor of $5,000 were incurred (but not yet paid).
d. Assigned labor cost to work in process and manufacturing overhead.

Requirement

1. Prepare journal entries for each transaction. Then explain each journal entry in terms of what got increased and what got decreased.

Solution

a.

	Materials inventory (A+)	135,000	
	Accounts payable (L+)		135,000

When materials are purchased on account

- Debit (increase) Materials inventory for the *cost* of the materials purchased.
- Credit (increase) Accounts payable to record the liability for the materials.

b.

	Work in process inventory (A+)	100,000	
	Manufacturing overhead (E+)	30,000	
	Materials inventory (A–)		130,000

When materials are requisitioned (used) in production, we record the movement of materials out of materials inventory and into production, as follows:

- Debit (increase) Work in process inventory for the cost of the *direct* materials (in this case, $100,000—the $130,000 total materials requisitioned less the $30,000 indirect materials).
- Debit (increase) Manufacturing overhead for the *indirect* materials cost.
- Credit (decrease) Materials inventory for the cost of both direct materials and indirect materials moved into production from the materials storage area.

c.

	Manufacturing wages ($22,000 + $5,000) (E+)	27,000	
	Wages payable (L+)		27,000

To record total labor costs actually incurred,

- Debit (increase) Manufacturing wages.
- Credit (increase) Wages payable to record the liability for wages not paid.

d.

	Work in process inventory (A+)	22,000	
	Manufacturing overhead (E+)	5,000	
	Manufacturing wages (E–)		27,000

To assign the labor costs,

- Debit (increase) Work in process inventory for the cost of the *direct* labor.
- Debit (increase) Manufacturing overhead for the cost of the *indirect* labor.
- Credit (decrease) Manufacturing wages to zero out its balance.

Job Order Costing: Allocating Manufacturing Overhead

3 Record overhead in a job order costing system

All manufacturing overhead costs are *accumulated* as debits to a single general ledger account—Manufacturing overhead. We have already assigned the costs of indirect materials (entry 2, $17,000) and indirect labor (entry 4, $28,000) to Manufacturing overhead. In addition to indirect materials and indirect labor, Smart Touch incurred the following overhead costs:

- Depreciation on plant and equipment, $10,000
- Plant utilities, $7,000
- Plant insurance, $6,000
- Property taxes on the plant, $5,000

Entries 5 through 8 record these manufacturing overhead costs. The account titles in parentheses indicate the specific records that were debited in the overhead subsidiary ledger.

(5)		Manufacturing overhead (Depreciation—plant and equipment) (E+)	10,000	
		Accumulated depreciation—plant and equipment (CA+)		10,000
(6)		Manufacturing overhead (Plant utilities) (E+)	7,000	
		Cash (A–)		7,000
(7)		Manufacturing overhead (Plant insurance) (E+)	6,000	
		Prepaid insurance—plant (A–)		6,000
(8)		Manufacturing overhead (Property taxes—plant) (E+)	5,000	
		Property taxes payable (L+)		5,000

The actual manufacturing overhead costs (such as indirect materials, indirect labor, plus depreciation, utilities, insurance, and property taxes on the plant) are debited to Manufacturing overhead as they occur throughout the year. By the end of the year, the Manufacturing overhead account has accumulated all the actual overhead costs as debits:

Manufacturing overhead		
(2) Indirect materials	17,000	
(4) Indirect labor	28,000	
(5) Depreciation—plant and equipment	10,000	
(6) Plant utilities	7,000	
(7) Plant insurance	6,000	
(8) Property taxes—plant	5,000	
Total overhead cost	73,000	

Now you have seen how Smart Touch *accumulates* actual overhead costs in the accounting records. But how does Smart Touch *assign* overhead costs to individual jobs? As you can see, overhead includes a variety of costs that the company cannot trace to individual jobs. For example, it is impossible to say how much of the cost of plant utilities is related to Job 16. Yet manufacturing overhead costs are as essential as direct materials and direct labor, so Smart Touch must find some way to assign overhead costs to specific jobs. Otherwise, each job would not bear its fair share of the total cost. Smart Touch may then set unrealistic prices for some of its DVDs and wind up losing money on some of its hard-earned sales.

1. **Compute the predetermined overhead rate.** The **predetermined manufacturing overhead rate** is computed as follows:

$$\text{Predetermined manufacturing overhead rate} = \frac{\text{Total estimated manufacturing overhead costs}}{\text{Total estimated quantity of the manufacturing overhead allocation base}}$$

The most accurate allocation can be made only when total overhead cost is known—and that is not until the end of the year. But managers cannot wait that long for product cost information. So the predetermined overhead rate is calculated before the year begins. Then throughout the year, companies use this predetermined rate to allocate estimated overhead cost to individual jobs. The predetermined overhead rate is based on two factors:

- Total *estimated* manufacturing overhead costs for the year
- Total *estimated* quantity of the manufacturing overhead allocation base

The key to assigning indirect manufacturing costs to jobs is to identify a workable manufacturing overhead allocation base. The **allocation base** is a common denominator that links overhead costs to the products. Ideally, the allocation base is the primary cost driver of manufacturing overhead—that is the more "allocation base," the more overhead costs and vice-versa. As the phrase implies, a **cost driver** is the primary factor that causes (drives) a cost. Traditionally, manufacturing companies have used the following:

- Direct labor hours (for labor-intensive production environments)
- Direct labor cost (for labor-intensive production environments)
- Machine hours (for machine-intensive production environments)

Smart Touch uses only one allocation base, direct labor cost, to assign manufacturing overhead to jobs. Later in the textbook, we will look at other ways to assign overhead to jobs.

2. **Allocate manufacturing overhead costs to jobs as the company makes its products.** Allocate manufacturing overhead cost to jobs as follows:

$$\text{Allocated manufacturing overhead cost} = \textit{Predetermined}\text{ manufacturing overhead rate (from Step 1)} \times \textit{Actual}\text{ quantity of the allocation base used by each job}$$

As we have seen, Smart Touch traces direct costs directly to each job. Now let us see how it allocates overhead cost to jobs. Recall that indirect manufacturing costs include plant depreciation, utilities, insurance, and property taxes, plus indirect materials and indirect labor.

1. Smart Touch uses direct labor cost as the allocation base. In 2011, Smart Touch estimated that total overhead costs for 2012 would be $68,000 and direct labor cost would total $170,000. Using this information, we can compute the predetermined manufacturing overhead rate as follows:

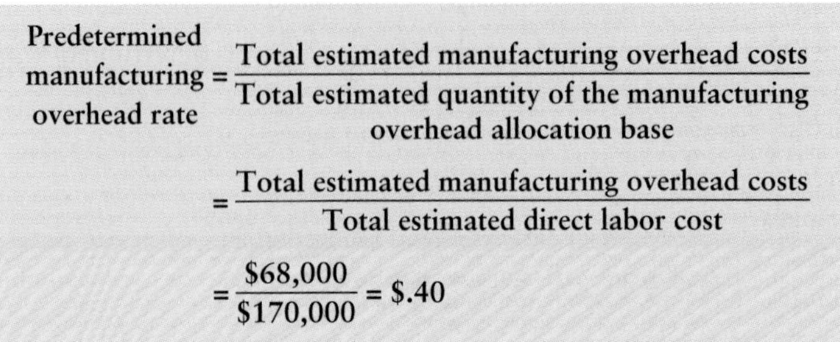

$$\text{Predetermined manufacturing overhead rate} = \frac{\text{Total estimated manufacturing overhead costs}}{\text{Total estimated quantity of the manufacturing overhead allocation base}}$$

$$= \frac{\text{Total estimated manufacturing overhead costs}}{\text{Total estimated direct labor cost}}$$

$$= \frac{\$68,000}{\$170,000} = \$.40$$

As jobs are completed in 2012, Smart Touch will allocate $0.40 of overhead cost for each $1 of labor cost incurred for the job ($0.40 = 40% × $1). Smart Touch uses the same predetermined overhead rate (40% of direct labor cost) to allocate manufacturing overhead to all jobs worked on throughout the year. Now back to Job 16.

2. The total direct labor cost for Job 16 is $200 and the predetermined overhead allocation rate is 40% of direct labor cost. Therefore, Smart Touch allocates $80 ($200 × 0.40) of manufacturing overhead to Job 16.

The completed job cost record for the Macy's order (Exhibit 16-7) shows that Job 16 cost Smart Touch a total of $420: $140 for direct materials, $200 for direct labor, and $80 of allocated manufacturing overhead. Job 16 produced 10 DVDs, so Smart Touch's cost per DVD is $42 ($420 ÷ 10).

EXHIBIT 16-7 Manufacturing Overhead on Job Cost Record

JOB COST RECORD

STL Smart Touch Learning, Inc.

Job No. 16

Customer Name and Address Macy's New York City

Job Description 10 Excel DVDs

Date Promised 7–31			Date Started 7–24		Date Completed 7–29		
Date	Direct Materials		Direct Labor		Manufacturing Overhead Allocated		
	Requisition Numbers	Amount	Labor Time Record Numbers	Amount	Date	Rate	Amount
7–24	**334**	**$140**	**236, 251, 258**	**$200**	7–29	40% of Direct Labor Cost	$80
					Overall Cost Summary Direct Materials ....$140 Direct Labor....................200 Manufacturing Overhead Allocated 80		
Totals		**$140**		**$200**	Total Job Cost.............$420		

Smart Touch worked on many jobs, including Job 16, during 2012. The company allocated manufacturing overhead to each of these jobs. Smart Touch's direct labor cost for 2012 was $169,000, so total overhead allocated to all jobs is 40% of the $169,000 direct labor cost, or $67,600. The journal entry to allocate manufacturing overhead cost to Work in process inventory is as follows:

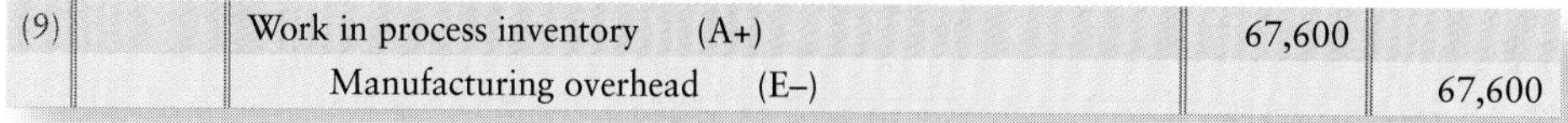

(9)		Work in process inventory (A+)	67,600	
		Manufacturing overhead (E–)		67,600

The flow of manufacturing overhead through the T-accounts follows:

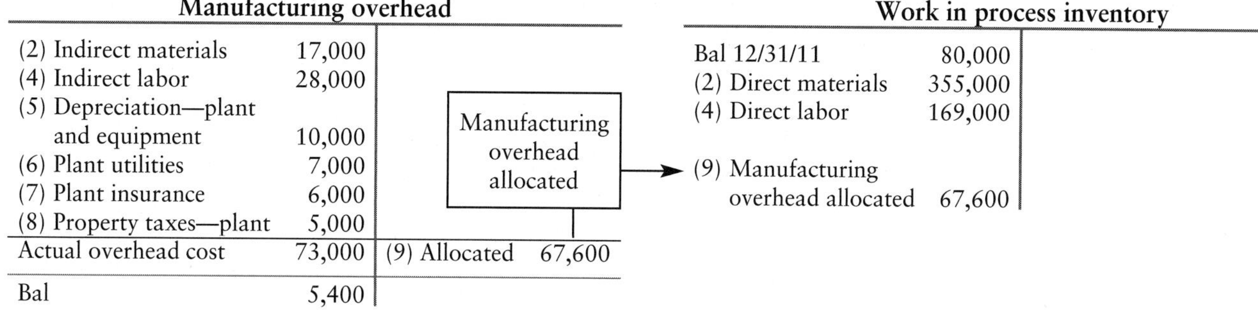

Manufacturing overhead

(2) Indirect materials	17,000		
(4) Indirect labor	28,000		
(5) Depreciation—plant and equipment	10,000		
(6) Plant utilities	7,000		
(7) Plant insurance	6,000		
(8) Property taxes—plant	5,000		
Actual overhead cost	73,000	(9) Allocated	67,600
Bal	5,400		

Work in process inventory

Bal 12/31/11	80,000	
(2) Direct materials	355,000	
(4) Direct labor	169,000	
(9) Manufacturing overhead allocated	67,600	

After allocation, a $5,400 debit balance remains in the Manufacturing overhead account. This means that Smart Touch's actual overhead costs ($73,000) exceeded the overhead allocated to Work in process inventory ($67,600). We say that Smart Touch's Manufacturing overhead is *underallocated* because the company allocated only $67,600 to jobs but actually incurred $73,000 of manufacturing overhead. We will show how to correct this problem later in the chapter.

Stop & Think...

Have you ever set up a special savings account to save for something you wanted to purchase in the future, or maybe saved for spring vacation? Maybe you set aside 10% of each of your paychecks into this special account. Allocating overhead to jobs is very similar. We estimate how much total overhead will be and divide that number by the estimated cost driver (such as labor) and allocate overhead to jobs based on this rate. Special savings accounts work the same way. You decide how much you need in the future and then allocate a percentage of your paychecks to reach your goal.

Accounting for Completion and Sale of Finished Goods and Adjusting Manufacturing Overhead

Now you know how to accumulate and assign the cost of direct materials, direct labor, and overhead to jobs. To complete the process, we must do the following:

- Account for the completion and sale of finished goods
- Adjust manufacturing overhead at the end of the period

4 Record completion and sales of finished goods and the adjustment for under- or overallocated overhead

Accounting for the Completion and Sale of Finished Goods

Study Exhibit 16-1 to review the flow of costs as a job goes from work in process to finished goods to cost of goods sold. Smart Touch Learning reported the following inventory balances one year ago, back on December 31, 2011:

Materials inventory	$70,000
Work in process inventory	80,000
Finished goods inventory	0

The following transactions occurred in 2012:

Cost of goods manufactured	$ 644,600
Sales on account	1,200,000
Cost of goods sold	594,600

The $644,600 cost of goods manufactured is the cost of the jobs Smart Touch completed during 2012. The cost of goods manufactured goes from Work in process inventory to Finished goods inventory as completed products move into the finished goods storage area. Smart Touch records goods completed in 2012 as follows:

(10)	Finished goods inventory (A+)	644,600	
	Work in process inventory (A–)		644,600

As the DVDs are sold, Smart Touch records sales revenue and accounts receivable, as follows:

(11)	Accounts receivable (A+)	1,200,000	
	Sales revenue (R+)		1,200,000

The goods have been shipped to customers, so Smart Touch must also decrease the Finished goods inventory account and increase Cost of goods sold (perpetual inventory) with the following journal entry:

(11)	Cost of goods sold (E+)	594,600	
	Finished goods inventory (A–)		594,600

The key T-accounts for Smart Touch Learning's manufacturing costs now show:

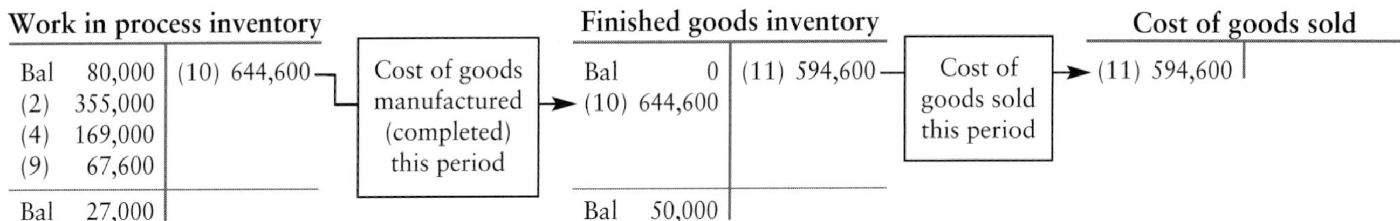

Some jobs are completed, and their costs are transferred out to Finished goods inventory, $644,600. We end the period with other jobs started but not finished ($27,000 ending balance of Work in process inventory) and jobs completed and not sold ($50,000 ending balance of Finished goods inventory).

During the year, Smart Touch Learning

- debits Manufacturing overhead for actual overhead costs.
- credits Manufacturing overhead for amounts allocated to Work in process inventory.

The total debits to the Manufacturing overhead account rarely equal the total credits. Why? Because Smart Touch allocates overhead to jobs using a *predetermined* allocation rate that is based on *estimates*. The predetermined allocation rate represents the *expected* relationship between overhead costs and the allocation base. In our example, the $5,400 debit balance of Manufacturing overhead is called **underallocated overhead** because the manufacturing overhead allocated to Work in process inventory is *less* than actual overhead cost. (If it had been **overallocated** instead, **Manufacturing overhead** would have a credit balance.)

Accountants adjust underallocated and overallocated overhead at year-end when closing the Manufacturing overhead account. Closing the account means zeroing it out, so when overhead is underallocated, as in our example, a credit to Manufacturing overhead of $5,400 is needed to bring the account balance to zero. What account should we debit?

Because Smart Touch *undercosted* jobs during the year, the correction should increase (debit) the Cost of goods sold:

(12)		Cost of goods sold (E+)	5,400	
		Manufacturing overhead (E–)		5,400

The Manufacturing overhead balance is now zero and the Cost of goods sold is up to date.

Manufacturing overhead

	Debit		Credit
Actual	73,000	Allocated (9)	67,600
		Closed (12)	5,400
	0		

Cost of goods sold

	Debit	Credit
(11)	594,600	
(12)	5,400	
	600,000	

Exhibit 16-8 summarizes the accounting for manufacturing overhead:

EXHIBIT 16-8 **Summary of Accounting for Manufacturing Overhead**

Before the Period

$$\text{Compute predetermined manufacturing overhead rate} = \frac{\text{Total estimated manufacturing overhead cost}}{\text{Total estimated quantity of allocation base}}$$

During the Period

$$\text{Allocate the overhead} = \text{Actual quantity of the manufacturing overhead allocation base} \times \text{Predetermined manufacturing overhead rate}$$

At the End of the Period

Close the Manufacturing Overhead account:

Jobs are *undercosted*

If actual > allocated → ***Underallocated*** manufacturing overhead
Need to ***increase*** Cost of Goods Sold, as follows:

		Cost of goods sold	XXX	
		Manufacturing overhead		XXX

Jobs are *overcosted*

If allocated > actual → ***Overallocated*** manufacturing overhead
Need to ***reduce*** Cost of Goods Sold, as follows:

		Manufacturing overhead	XXX	
		Cost of goods sold		XXX

Job Order Costing in a Service Company

5 Calculate unit costs for a service company

As we have seen, service firms have no inventory. These firms incur only noninventoriable costs. But their managers still need to know the costs of different jobs in order to set prices for their services as follows (amounts assumed):

Cost of Job 19	$6,000
Add standard markup of 50% ($6,000 × .50)	3,000
Sale price of Job 19	$9,000

A merchandising company can set the selling price of its products this same way.

We now illustrate how service firms assign costs to jobs. The law firm of Walsh Associates considers each client a separate job. Walsh's most significant cost is direct labor—attorney time spent on clients' cases. How do service firms trace direct labor to individual jobs?

Suppose Walsh's accounting system is not automated. Walsh employees can fill out a weekly **time record**. Software totals the amount of time spent on each job. For example, attorney Lois Fox's time record in Exhibit 16-9 shows that she devoted 14 hours to client 367 during the week of June 10, 2009.

EXHIBIT 16-9 | **Employee Time Record**

Walsh Associates
Name Lois Fox

Employee Time Record
Week of 6/10/09

Weekly Summary

Client #	Total hours
367	14
415	13
520	13

	M	T	W	Th	F
8:00 – 8:30	367	520	415	367	415
8:30 – 9:00					
9:00 – 9:30					
9:30 – 10:00					
10:00 – 10:30			367		
10:30 – 11:00					
11:00 – 11:30	520				
11:30 – 12:00	520				
12:00 – 1:00					
1:00 – 1:30	520	367	415	520	415
1:30 – 2:00					
2:00 – 2:30					
2:30 – 3:00					
3:00 – 3:30					
3:30 – 4:00					
4:00 – 4:30			367		
4:30 – 5:00					

Fox's salary and benefits total \$100,000 per year. Assuming a 40-hour workweek and 50 workweeks in each year, Fox has 2,000 available work hours per year (50 weeks × 40 hours per week). Fox's hourly pay rate is as follows:

$$\text{Hourly rate to the employer} = \frac{\$100{,}000 \text{ per year}}{2{,}000 \text{ hours per year}} = \$50 \text{ per hour}$$

Fox worked 14 hours for client 367, so the direct labor cost traced to client 367 is 14 hours × \$50 per hour = \$700.

For automated services like Web site design, employees enter the client number when they start on the client's job. Software records the time elapsed until the employee signs off on that job.

Founding partner John Walsh wants to know the total cost of serving each client, not just the direct labor cost. Walsh Associates also allocates indirect costs to individual jobs (clients). The law firm develops a predetermined indirect cost allocation rate, following the same approach that Smart Touch used. In December 2008, Walsh estimates that the following indirect costs will be incurred in 2009:

Office rent	\$200,000
Office support staff	70,000
Maintaining and updating law library for case research	25,000
Advertisements in the yellow pages	3,000
Sponsorship of the symphony	2,000
Total indirect costs	\$300,000

Walsh uses direct labor hours as the allocation base, because direct labor hours are the main driver of indirect costs. He estimates that Walsh attorneys will work 10,000 direct labor hours in 2009.

STEP 1: Compute the predetermined indirect cost allocation rate.

$$\text{Predetermined indirect cost allocation rate} = \frac{\$300{,}000 \text{ expected indirect costs}}{10{,}000 \text{ expected direct labor hours}}$$
$$= \$30 \text{ per direct labor hour}$$

STEP 2: Allocate indirect costs to jobs by multiplying the predetermined indirect cost rate (Step 1) by the actual quantity of the allocation base used by each job. Client 367, for example, required 14 direct labor hours, so the indirect costs are allocated as follows:

$$14 \text{ direct labor hours} \times \$30/\text{hour} = \$420$$

To summarize, the total costs assigned to client 367 are as follows:

Direct labor: 14 hours × \$50/hour...........	\$ 700
Indirect costs: 14 hours × \$30/hour.........	420
Total costs...	\$1,120

You have now learned how to use a job order cost system and assign costs to jobs.

Stop & Think...

When you have a toothache, you probably go to your dentist and ask him or her to give you an estimate of what it will cost to fix it. That estimated cost is based on the time the dentist thinks it will take to fix your tooth. The dentist has overhead, such as the dental chairs, equipment, and building. When you receive the final bill for fixing your tooth, that bill will be based on both the time it actually took the dentist to fix your tooth and an hourly rate that includes the dentist's overhead. This is an example of service job costing. Your tooth is the job for the dentist.

Review the Decision Guidelines to solidify your understanding.

Decision Guidelines

JOB ORDER COSTING

Companies using a job order costing system treat each job separately. The following are some of the decisions that a company makes when designing its job order costing system.

Decision	Guidelines
• Are utilities, insurance, property taxes, and depreciation • manufacturing over head or • operating expenses?	These costs are part of manufacturing overhead *only* if they are incurred in the manufacturing plant. If unrelated to manufacturing, they are operating expenses. For example, if related to the research lab, they are R&D expenses. If related to executive headquarters, they are administrative expenses. If related to distribution centers, they are selling expenses. These are all operating expenses, not manufacturing overhead.

• How to record *actual* manufacturing overhead costs?	Manufacturing overhead XX
	  Accumulated depreciation—plant and equipment XX
	  Prepaid insurance—Plant & Equip. XX
	  Utilities payable (or Cash) and so on XX

• How to compute a predetermined manufacturing overhead rate?	$\frac{\textbf{Total estimated manufacturing overhead cost}}{\textbf{Total estimated quantity of allocation base}}$
• How to record allocation of manufacturing overhead?	Work in process inventory XX Manufacturing overhead XX
• What is the *amount* of the allocated manufacturing overhead?	**Actual quantity of the manufacturing overhead allocation base** × **Predetermined manufacturing overhead rate**

• How to close Manufacturing overhead at the end of the period?	Close directly to Cost of goods sold, as follows:
	For *underallocated* overhead:
	Cost of goods sold XX
	  Manufacturing overhead XX
	For *overallocated* overhead:
	Manufacturing overhead XX
	  Cost of goods sold XX

• When providing services, how to trace employees' direct labor to individual jobs?	Either using automated software that directly captures the amount of time employees spend on a client's job, or having employees fill out a time record.
• Why allocate non-inventoriable costs to jobs?	Managers need total product costs for internal decisions (such as setting selling prices).

Summary Problem 2

Skippy Scooters manufactures motor scooters. The company has automated production, so it allocates manufacturing overhead based on machine hours. Skippy expects to incur $240,000 of manufacturing overhead costs and to use 4,000 machine hours during 2011.

At the end of 2010, Skippy reported the following inventories:

Materials inventory	$20,000
Work in process inventory	17,000
Finished goods inventory	11,000

During January 2011, Skippy actually used 300 machine hours and recorded the following transactions:

a. Purchased materials on account, $31,000
b. Used direct materials, $39,000
c. Manufacturing wages incurred totaled $40,000
d. Manufacturing labor was 90% direct labor and 10% indirect labor
e. Used indirect materials, $3,000
f. Incurred other manufacturing overhead, $13,000 (credit Accounts payable)
g. Allocated manufacturing overhead for January 2011
h. Cost of completed motor scooters, $100,000
i. Sold motor scooters on account, $175,000; cost of motor scooters sold, $95,000

Requirements

1. Compute Skippy's predetermined manufacturing overhead rate for 2011.
2. Record the transactions in the general journal.
3. Enter the beginning balances and then post the transactions to the following accounts:

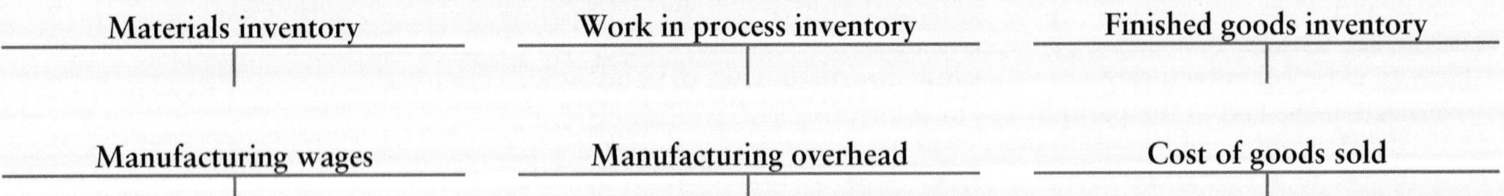

4. Close the ending balance of Manufacturing overhead. Post your entry to the T-accounts.
5. What are the ending balances in the three inventory accounts and in Cost of goods sold?

Solution

Requirement 1

$$\text{Predetermined manufacturing overhead rate} = \frac{\text{Total estimated manufacturing overhead cost}}{\text{Total estimated quantity of allocation base}}$$

$$= \frac{\$240,000}{4,000 \text{ machine hours}}$$

$$= \$60/\text{machine hour}$$

Requirement 2

Journal entries:

a.

	Materials inventory (A+)	31,000	
	Accounts payable (L+)		31,000

b.

	Work in process inventory (A+)	39,000	
	Materials inventory (A–)		39,000

c.

	Manufacturing wages (E+)	40,000	
	Wages payable (L+)		40,000

d.

	Work in process inventory ($40,000 × 0.90) (A+)	36,000	
	Manufacturing overhead ($40,000 × 0.10) (E+)	4,000	
	Manufacturing wages (E–)		40,000

e.

	Manufacturing overhead (E+)	3,000	
	Materials inventory (A–)		3,000

f.

	Manufacturing overhead (E+)	13,000	
	Accounts payable (L+)		13,000

g.

	Work in process inventory (300 × $60) (A+)	18,000	
	Manufacturing overhead (E–)		18,000

h.

	Finished goods inventory (A+)	100,000	
	Work in process inventory (A–)		100,000

i.

	Accounts receivable (A+)	175,000	
	Sales revenue (R+)		175,000

j.

	Cost of goods sold (E+)	95,000	
	Finished goods inventory (A–)		95,000

Requirement 3

Post the transcriptions:

Materials inventory

	Debit		Credit
Bal	20,000	(b)	39,000
(a)	31,000	(e)	3,000
Bal	9,000		

Work in process inventory

	Debit		Credit
Bal	17,000	(h)	100,000
(b)	39,000		
(d)	36,000		
(g)	18,000		
Bal	10,000		

Finished goods inventory

	Debit		Credit
Bal	11,000	(j)	95,000
(h)	100,000		
Bal	16,000		

Manufacturing wages

	Debit		Credit
(c)	40,000	(d)	40,000

Manufacturing overhead

	Debit		Credit
(d)	4,000	(g)	18,000
(e)	3,000		
(f)	13,000		
Bal	2,000		

Cost of goods sold

	Debit		Credit
(j)	95,000		

Requirement 4

Close Manufacturing overhead:

		Debit	Credit
k.	Cost of goods sold (E+)	2,000	
	Manufacturing overhead (E–)		2,000

Manufacturing overhead

	Debit		Credit
(d)	4,000	(g)	18,000
(e)	3,000	(k)	2,000
(f)	13,000		

Cost of goods sold

	Debit		Credit
(j)	95,000		
(k)	2,000		
Bal	97,000		

Requirement 5

Ending Balances:

Materials inventory (from requirement 3)	$ 9,000
Work in process inventory (from requirement 3)	10,000
Finished goods inventory (from requirement 3)	16,000
Cost of goods sold (from requirement 4)	97,000

Review *Job Order and Process Costing*

Accounting Vocabulary

Allocation Base (p. 871)
A common denominator that links indirect costs to cost objects. Ideally, the allocation base is the primary cost driver of the indirect costs.

Conversion Costs (p. 866)
Direct labor plus manufacturing overhead.

Cost Allocation (p. 861)
Assigning indirect costs (such as manufacturing overhead) to cost objects (such as jobs or production processes).

Cost Driver (p. 871)
The primary factor that causes a cost.

Cost Tracing (p. 861)
Assigning direct costs (such as direct materials and direct labor) to cost objects (such as jobs or production processes) that used those costs.

Equivalent Units (p. 908)
Allows us to measure the amount of work done on a partially finished group of units during a period and to express it in terms of fully complete units of output.

Job Cost Record (p. 864)
Document that accumulates the direct materials, direct labor, and manufacturing overhead costs assigned to an individual job.

Job Order Costing (p. 860)
A system that accumulates costs for each job. Law firms, music studios, health-care providers, mail-order catalog companies, building contractors, and custom furniture manufacturers are examples of companies that use job order costing systems.

Labor Time Record (p. 864)
Identifies the employee, the amount of time spent on a particular job, and the labor cost charged to the job; a record used to assign direct labor cost to specific jobs.

Materials Requisition (p. 863)
Request for the transfer of materials to the production floor, prepared by the production team.

Overallocated (Manufacturing) Overhead (p. 875)
Occurs when the manufacturing overhead allocated to Work in process inventory is more than the amount of manufacturing overhead costs actually incurred.

Predetermined Manufacturing Overhead Rate (p. 871)
Estimated manufacturing overhead cost per unit of the allocation base, computed at the beginning of the year.

Process Costing (p. 860)
System for assigning costs to large numbers of identical units that usually proceed in a continuous fashion through a series of uniform production steps or processes.

Production Cost Report (p. 919)
Summarizes operations for one department for a month. Combines the costs to account for and the cost per equivalent unit and shows how those costs were assigned to the goods completed and transferred out.

Time Record (p. 876)
Source document used to trace direct labor to specific jobs.

Transferred-In Costs (p. 917)
Costs that were incurred in a previous process and brought into a later process as part of the product s cost.

Underallocated (Manufacturing) Overhead (p. 875)
Occurs when the manufacturing overhead allocated to Work in process inventory is less than the amount of manufacturing overhead costs actually incurred.

Weighted-Average Process Costing Method (p. 915)
Determines the average cost of all of a specific department's equivalent units of work.

Quick Check

1. Would an advertising agency use job or process costing? What about a paper mill?
   a. Advertising agency—job order costing; Paper mill—process costing
   b. Advertising agency—process costing; Paper mill—process costing
   c. Advertising agency—job order costing; Paper mill—job order costing
   d. Advertising agency—process costing; Paper mill—job order costing
2. When a manufacturing company *uses* direct materials, it *traces* the cost by debiting
   a. Manufacturing overhead.
   b. Direct materials.
   c. Work in process inventory.
   d. Materials inventory.

3. When a manufacturing company *uses* indirect materials, it *assigns* the cost by debiting
   a. Indirect materials.
   b. Materials inventory.
   c. Manufacturing overhead.
   d. Work in process inventory.
4. When a manufacturing company *uses* direct labor, it *traces* the cost by debiting
   a. Work in process inventory.
   b. Manufacturing overhead.
   c. Manufacturing wages.
   d. Direct labor.

Questions 5, 6, 7, and 8 are based on the following information about Well Corporation's manufacturing of computers. Assume that Well

- Allocates manufacturing overhead based on machine hours.
- Budgeted 11 million machine hours and $91 million of manufacturing overhead costs.
- Actually used 14 million machine hours and incurred the following actual costs (in millions):

Indirect labor	$ 10
Depreciation on plant	44
Machinery repair	15
Direct labor	76
Plant supplies	3
Plant utilities	9
Advertising	33
Sales commissions	25

5. What is Well's predetermined manufacturing overhead rate?
   a. $8.27/machine hour
   b. $5.79/machine hour
   c. $7.36/machine hour
   d. $6.50/machine hour
6. What is Well's actual manufacturing overhead cost?
   a. $157
   b. $81
   c. $215
   d. $114
7. How much manufacturing overhead would Well allocate?
   a. $91
   b. $220
   c. $84
   d. $116

8. What entry would Well make to close the manufacturing overhead account?

a.

Cost of goods sold	10	
Manufacturing overhead		10

b.

Manufacturing overhead	10	
Cost of goods sold		10

c.

Cost of goods sold	35	
Manufacturing overhead		35

d.

Manufacturing overhead	35	
Cost of goods sold		35

9. A manufacturing company's management can use product cost information to
   a. Set prices of its products.
   b. Identify ways to cut production costs.
   c. Decide which products to emphasize.
   d. All of the above

10. For which of the following reasons would John Walsh, owner of the Walsh Associates law firm, want to know the total costs of a job (serving a particular client)?
    a. To determine the fees to charge clients
    b. For inventory valuation
    c. For external reporting
    d. All of the above

Answers are given after Apply Your Knowledge (p. 904).

Assess Your Progress

Short Exercises

S16-1 *(L. OBJ. 1)* **Distinguishing between job costing and process costing [5 min]**
Job costing and process costing track costs differently.

Requirement

1. Would the following companies use job order costing or process costing?

   a. A manufacturer of plywood
   b. A manufacturer of wakeboards
   c. A manufacturer of luxury yachts
   d. A professional services firm
   e. A landscape contractor

S16-2 *(L. OBJ. 2)* **Flow of costs in job order costing [10 min]**
For a manufacturer that uses job order costing, there is a correct order that the costs flow through the accounts.

Requirement

1. Order the following from 1–4. Item 1 has been completed for you.

   __1__ a. Materials inventory
   _____ b. Finished goods inventory
   _____ c. Cost of goods sold
   _____ d. Work in process inventory

S16-3 *(L. OBJ. 2)* **Accounting for materials [5–10 min]**
Gear Packs manufactures backpacks. Its plant records include the following materials-related transactions:

Purchases of canvas (on account)	$ 75,000
Purchases of thread (on account)	1,400
Materials requisitions:	
Canvas	63,000
Thread	450

Requirements

1. What journal entries record these transactions?
2. Post these transactions to the Materials inventory account.
3. If the company had $35,000 of Materials inventory at the beginning of the period, what is the ending balance of Materials inventory?

S16-4 *(L. OBJ. 2)* **Accounting for materials [10 min]**
Consider the following T-accounts:

Materials inventory

Bal	30		
Purchases	210	Used	[ ]
Bal	70		

Work in process inventory

Bal	40		
Direct materials	[ ]	Cost of goods manufactured	630
Direct labor	320		
Manufacturing overhead	140		
Bal	20		

Requirement

1. Use the T-accounts to determine direct materials used and indirect materials used.

S16-5 *(L. OBJ. 2)* **Accounting for labor [5 min]**
Seattle Creations reports the following labor-related transactions at its plant in Seattle, Washington.

Plant janitor's wages	$ 550
Furnace operator's wages	940
Glass blower's wages	77,000

Requirement

1. Journalize the entries for the incurrence and assignment of these wages.

S16-6 *(L. OBJ. 2)* **Accounting for materials and labor [5 min]**
Boston Enterprises produces LCD touch screen products. The company reports the following information at December 31, 2010:

Materials inventory

51,000	32,000

Work in process inventory

29,500	126,000
60,000	
52,500	

Finished goods inventory

126,000	115,000

Manufacturing wages

71,000	71,000

Manufacturing overhead

2,500	52,500
11,000	
37,000	

Boston began operations on January 30, 2010.

Requirements

1. What is the cost of direct materials used? The cost of indirect materials used?
2. What is the cost of direct labor? The cost of indirect labor?

S16-7 *(L. OBJ. 3)* **Accounting for overhead [5 min]**
Evergreen Furniture manufactures wood patio furniture. The company reports the following costs for June 2011:

Wood	$ 260,000
Nails, glue, and stain	21,000
Depreciation on saws	4,500
Indirect manufacturing labor	41,000
Depreciation on delivery truck	2,100
Assembly–line workers' wages	59,000

Requirement

1. What is the balance in the Manufacturing overhead account?

S16-8 *(L. OBJ. 3)* **Allocating overhead [5 min]**
Job 303 includes a direct materials cost of $470 and direct labor costs of $350.

Requirement

1. If the manufacturing overhead allocation rate is 60% of direct labor cost, what is the total cost assigned to Job 303?

Note: Short Exercise S16-6 must be completed before attempting Short Exercise S16-9.

S16-9 *(L. OBJ. 4)* **Comparing actual to allocated overhead [10 min]**
Refer to the data in S16-6.

Requirements

1. What is the actual manufacturing overhead of Boston Enterprises?
2. What is the allocated manufacturing overhead?
3. Is manufacturing overhead underallocated or overallocated? By how much?

S16-10 *(L. OBJ. 4)* **Under/overallocated overhead [10 min]**
The T-account showing the manufacturing overhead activity for Edith, Corp., for 2011 is as follows:

Manufacturing overhead	
199,000	215,000

Requirements

1. What is the actual manufacturing overhead?
2. What is the allocated manufacturing overhead?
3. What is the predetermined manufacturing overhead rate as a percentage of direct labor cost, if actual direct labor costs were $170,000?
4. Is manufacturing overhead underallocated or overallocated? By how much?
5. Is Cost of goods sold too high or too low?

Note: Short Exercise S16-10 must be completed before attempting Short Exercise S16-11.

S16-11 *(L. OBJ. 4)* **Closing out under/overallocated overhead [5 min]**
Refer to the data in S16-10.

Requirement

1. Journalize the entry to close out the company's Manufacturing overhead account.

S16-12 *(L. OBJ. 5)* **Job order costing in a service company [5 min]**
Blake Advertising pays Amanda Hilton $108,000 per year. Hilton works 2,000 hours per year.

Requirements

1. What is the hourly cost to Blake Advertising of employing Hilton?
2. What direct labor cost would be traced to client 507 if Hilton works 18 hours to prepare client 507's magazine ad?

Note: Short Exercise S16-12 must be completed before attempting Short Exercise S16-13.

S16-13 *(L. OBJ. 5)* **Job order costing in a service company [5 min]**
Refer to the data in S16-12. Assume that Blake's Advertising agents are expected to work a total of 12,000 direct labor hours in 2011. Blake's estimated total indirect costs are $360,000.

Requirements

1. What is Blake's indirect cost allocation rate?
2. What indirect costs will be allocated to client 507 if Hilton works 18 hours to prepare the magazine ad?

Exercises

E16-14 *(L. OBJ. 1)* **Distinguishing between job order costing and process costing [5–10 min]**
Consider the following incomplete statements.

a. _____ is used by companies that produce small quantities of many different products.
b. Georgia-Pacific pulverizes wood into pulp to manufacture cardboard. The company uses a _____ system.
c. To record costs of maintaining thousands of identical mortgage files, financial institutions like Money Tree use a _____ system.
d. Companies that produce large numbers of identical products use _____ systems for product costing.
e. The computer repair service that visits your home and repairs your computer uses a _____ system.

Requirement

1. Complete each of the statements with the term job order costing or the term process costing.

E16-15 *(L. OBJ. 2, 3, 4)* **Accounting for job costs [15 min]**
Great Quality Trailers' job cost records yielded the following information:

Job	Date			Total Cost of Job
No.	Started	Finished	Sold	at May 31
1	April 21	May 16	May 17	$ 3,800
2	April 29	May 21	May 26	13,700
3	May 3	June 11	June 13	6,500
4	May 7	May 29	June 1	4,200

Requirement

1. Using the dates above to identify the status of each job, compute Great Quality 's cost of (a) Work in process inventory at May 31, (b) Finished goods inventory at May 31, and (c) Cost of goods sold for May.

E16-16 *(L. OBJ. 2, 3, 4)* **Job order costing journal entries [20–25 min]**
Consider the following transactions for Sleek's Furniture:

a. Incurred and paid Web site expenses, $2,100
b. Incurred and paid manufacturing wages, $17,000
c. Purchased materials on account, $15,000
d. Used in production: direct materials, $9,000; indirect materials, $1,500
e. Assigned $17,000 of manufacturing labor to jobs, 55% of which was direct labor and 45% of which was indirect labor
f. Recorded manufacturing overhead: depreciation on plant, $11,000; plant insurance, $1,000; plant property tax, $4,100 (credit Property Tax Payable)
g. Allocated manufacturing overhead to jobs, 160% of direct labor costs
h. Completed production, $32,000
i. Sold inventory on account, $24,000; cost of goods sold, $16,000

Requirement

1. Journalize the transactions in Sleek's general journal.

E16-17 *(L. OBJ. 2, 3, 4)* **Identifying job order costing journal entries [15 min]**
Consider the following:

Materials inventory	
(a)	(b)

Work in process inventory	
(b)	(g)
(d)	
(f)	

Finished goods inventory	
(g)	(h)

Manufacturing wages	
(c)	(d)

Manufacturing overhead	
(b)	(f)
(d)	(i)
(e)	

Cost of goods sold	
(h)	
(i)	

Requirement

1. Describe the letter transactions in the above accounts.

E16-18 *(L. OBJ. 2, 3, 4)* **Using the Work in process inventory account [15–20 min]**
April production generated the following activity in Premier Chassis Company's Work in process inventory account:

Work in process inventory		
Apr 1 Bal	18,000	
Direct materials used	29,000	
Direct labor assigned to jobs	31,000	
Manufacturing overhead allocated to jobs	9,000	

Additionally, Premier completed production, but has not recorded Jobs 142 and 143, with total costs of $37,000 and $35,000, respectively.

Requirements

1. Compute the cost of work in process at April 30.
2. Prepare the journal entry for production completed in April.
3. Prepare the journal entry to record the sale (on credit) of Job 143 for $45,000. Also, make the Cost of goods sold entry.
4. What is the gross profit on Job 143? What other costs must gross profit cover?

E16-19 *(L. OBJ. 3, 4)* **Allocating manufacturing overhead [15–20 min]**
Selected cost data for European Print, Co., are as follows:

Estimated manufacturing overhead cost for the year	$ 93,000
Estimated direct labor cost for the year	75,000
Actual manufacturing overhead cost for the year	84,000
Actual direct labor cost for the year	64,000

Requirements

1. Compute the predetermined manufacturing overhead rate per direct labor dollar.
2. Prepare the journal entry to allocate overhead cost for the year.
3. Use a T-account to determine the amount of underallocated or overallocated manufacturing overhead.
4. Prepare the journal entry to close the balance of the Manufacturing overhead account.

E16-20 *(L. OBJ. 3, 4)* **Allocating manufacturing overhead [15–20 min]**
Patel Foundry uses a predetermined manufacturing overhead rate to allocate overhead to individual jobs, based on the machine hours required. At the beginning of 2011, the company expected to incur the following:

Manufacturing overhead costs	$ 730,000
Direct labor costs	1,450,000
Machine hours	66,000

At the end of 2011, the company had actually incurred:

Direct labor cost	$	1,250,000
Depreciation on manufacturing property, plant, and equipment		440,000
Property taxes on plant		18,000
Sales salaries		30,000
Delivery drivers' wages		22,500
Plant janitor's wages		9,000
Machine hours		58,000 hours

Requirements

1. Compute Patel's predetermined manufacturing overhead rate.
2. Record the summary journal entry for allocating manufacturing overhead.
3. Post the manufacturing overhead transactions to the Manufacturing overhead T-account. Is manufacturing overhead underallocated or overallocated? By how much?
4. Close the Manufacturing overhead account to Cost of goods sold. Does your entry increase or decrease cost of goods sold?

E16-21 *(L. OBJ. 3, 4)* **Allocating manufacturing overhead [10–15 min]**
Refer to the data in E16-20. Patel's accountant found an error in her 2011 cost records. Depreciation on manufacturing property, plant, and equipment was actually $570,000, not the $440,000 she originally reported. Unadjusted balances at the end of 2011 include:

Finished goods inventory	$ 127,000
Cost of goods sold	610,000

Requirements

1. Use a T-account to determine whether manufacturing overhead is underallocated or overallocated, and by how much.
2. Record the entry to close out the underallocated or overallocated manufacturing overhead.
3. What is the adjusted ending balance of Cost of goods sold?

E16-22 *(L. OBJ. 3, 4)* **Allocating manufacturing overhead [15–20 min]**
The manufacturing records for Smooth Canoes at the end of the 2010 fiscal year show the following information about manufacturing overhead:

Overhead allocated to production	$ 402,000
Actual manufacturing overhead costs	$ 432,000
Overhead allocation rate for the year	$ 43 per machine hour

Requirements

1. How many machine hours did Smooth Canoes use in 2010?
2. Was manufacturing overhead over- or underallocated for the year and by how much?
3. Record the entry to close out the over- or underallocated overhead.

E16-23 *(L. OBJ. 5)* **Job order costing in a service company [15–20 min]**
Simms Realtors, a real estate consulting firm, specializes in advising companies on potential new plant sites. The company uses a job order costing system with a predetermined indirect cost allocation rate, computed as a percentage of direct labor costs. At the beginning of 2011, managing partner Debra Simms prepared the following budget for the year:

Direct labor hours (professionals)	14,000 hours
Direct labor costs (professionals)	$ 2,150,000
Office rent	260,000
Support staff salaries	850,000
Utilities	350,000

Maynard Manufacturing, Inc., is inviting several consultants to bid for work. Debra Simms estimates that this job will require about 260 direct labor hours.

Requirements

1. Compute Simms Realtors' (a) hourly direct labor cost rate and (b) indirect cost allocation rate.
2. Compute the predicted cost of the Maynard Manufacturing job.
3. If Simms wants to earn a profit that equals 55% of the job's cost, how much should she bid for the Maynard Manufacturing job?

■ Problems (Group A)

P16-24A *(L. OBJ. 1, 2, 3, 4)* **Analyzing cost data [25–35 min]**
Huntley Manufacturing makes carrying cases for portable electronic devices. Its costing records yield the following information:

Job	Date			Total Cost of Job	Total Manufacturing Costs Added
No.	Started	Finished	Sold	at November 30	in December
1	11/3	11/12	11/13	$ 1,300	
2	11/3	11/30	12/1	1,200	
3	11/17	12/24	12/27	600	$ 700
4	11/29	12/29	1/3	1,100	1,400
5	12/8	12/12	12/14		650
6	12/23	1/6	1/9		900

Requirements

1. Which type of costing system is Huntley using? What piece of data did you base your answer on?
2. Using the dates above to identify the status of each job, compute Huntley's account balances at November 30 for Work in process inventory, Finished goods inventory, and Cost of goods sold. Compute account balances at December 31 for Work in process inventory, Finished goods inventory, and Cost of goods sold.
3. Record summary journal entries for the transfer of completed units from work in process to finished goods for November and December.
4. Record the sale of Job 3 for $2,400.
5. What is the gross profit for Job 3? What other costs must this gross profit cover?

P16-25A *(L. OBJ. 2, 3, 4)* **Accounting for construction transactions [30–45 min]**

Sherborn Construction, Inc., is a home builder in New Mexico. Sherborn uses a job order costing system in which each house is a job. Because it constructs houses, the company uses accounts titled Construction wages and Construction overhead. The following events occurred during August:

a. Purchased materials on account, $470,000
b. Incurred construction wages of $230,000
c. Requisitioned direct materials and used direct labor in construction as follows:

	Direct Materials	Direct Labor
House 402	$ 58,000	$ 40,000
House 403	63,000	34,000
House 404	60,000	52,000
House 405	89,000	51,000

d. Depreciation of construction equipment, $6,800
e. Other overhead costs incurred on houses 402 through 405:

Indirect labor	$ 53,000
Equipment rentals paid in cash	33,000
Worker liability insurance expired ..	7,000

f. Allocated overhead to jobs at the predetermined rate of 40% of direct labor cost
g. Houses completed: 402, 404
h. House sold: 404 for $220,000

Requirements

1. Record the events in the general journal.
2. Open T-accounts for Work in process inventory and Finished goods inventory. Post the appropriate entries to these accounts, identifying each entry by letter. Determine the ending account balances, assuming that the beginning balances were zero.
3. Add the costs of the unfinished houses, and show that this total amount equals the ending balance in the Work in process inventory account.
4. Add the cost of the completed house that has not yet been sold, and show that this equals the ending balance in Finished goods inventory.
5. Compute gross profit on the house that was sold. What costs must gross profit cover for Sherborn Construction?

P16-26A *(L. OBJ. 2, 3, 4)* **Preparing and using a job cost record [30–35 min]**

Classic Technology, Co., manufactures CDs and DVDs for computer software and entertainment companies. Classic uses job order costing and has a perpetual inventory system.

On November 2, Classic began production of 5,100 DVDs, Job 423, for Cheetah Pictures for $1.30 each. Classic promised to deliver the DVDs to Cheetah by November 5. Classic incurred the following costs:

Date	Labor Time Record No.	Description	Amount
11/2	655	10 hours @ $20	$ 200
11/3	656	20 hours @ $12	240

Date	Materials Requisition No.	Description	Amount
11/2	63	31 lbs. polycarbonate plastic @ $10	$ 310
11/2	64	25 lbs. acrylic plastic @ $26	650
11/3	74	3 lbs. refined aluminum @ $40	120

Classic Technology allocates manufacturing overhead to jobs based on the relation between estimated overhead ($520,000) and estimated direct labor costs ($450,000). Job 423 was completed and shipped on November 3.

Requirements

1. Prepare a job cost record similar to Exhibit 16-7 for Job 423. Calculate the predetermined overhead rate; then apply manufacturing overhead to the job.
2. Journalize in summary form the requisition of direct materials and the assignment of direct labor and manufacturing overhead to Job 423.
3. Journalize completion of the job and the sale of the 5,100 DVDs.

P16-27A *(L. OBJ. 2, 3, 4)* **Comprehensive accounting for manufacturing transactions [90–120 min]**

Sneeches' Stars produces stars for elementary teachers to reward their students. Sneeches' Stars' trial balance on April 1 follows:

SNEECHES' STARS
Trial Balance
April 1, 2010

Account Title	Balance Debit	Balance Credit
Cash	$ 18,000	
Accounts receivable	170,000	
Inventories:		
Materials	5,300	
Work in process	41,300	
Finished goods	21,300	
Plant assets	250,000	
Accumulated depreciation		$ 68,000
Accounts payable		129,000
Wages payable		2,800
Common stock		140,000
Retained earnings		166,100
Sales revenue		—
Cost of goods sold	—	
Manufacturing wages	—	
Manufacturing overhead	—	
Marketing and general expenses	—	
	$505,900	$505,900

April 1 balances in the subsidiary ledgers were as follows:

- Materials subledger: Paper, $4,800; indirect materials, $500
- Work in progress subledger: Job 120, $41,300
- Finished goods subledger: Large Stars, $9,300; Small Stars, $12,000

April transactions are summarized as follows:

a. Collections on account, $149,000
b. Marketing and general expenses incurred and paid, $25,000
c. Payments on account, $38,000
d. Materials purchases on credit: Paper, $24,500; indirect materials, $4,600
e. Materials used in production (requisitioned):
   - Job 120: paper, $750
   - Job 121: paper, $7,800
   - Indirect materials, $2,000
f. Manufacturing wages incurred during April, $38,000, of which $36,000 was paid. Wages payable at March 31 were paid during April, $2,800
g. Labor time records for the month: Job 120, $4,000; Job 121, $18,000; indirect labor, $16,000
h. Depreciation on plant and equipment, $2,400
i. Manufacturing overhead was allocated at the predetermined rate of 70% of direct labor cost
j. Jobs completed during the month: Job 120, 400,000 Large Stars at total cost of $48,850
k. Credit sales on account: all of Job 120 for $110,000
l. Closed the Manufacturing overhead account to Cost of goods sold

Requirements

1. Open T-accounts for the general ledger, the Materials ledger, the Work in process ledger, and the Finished goods ledger. Insert each account balance as given, and use the reference *Bal.*
2. Record the April transactions directly in the accounts, using the letters as references. Sneeches uses a perpetual inventory system.
3. Prepare a trial balance at April 30.
4. Use the Work in process T-account to prepare a schedule of cost of goods manufactured for the month of April. (You may want to review Exhibit 15-10.)
5. Prepare an income statement for the month of April. To calculate cost of goods sold, you may want to review Exhibit 15-7. (*Hint*: In transaction l you closed any under/overallocated manufacturing overhead to Cost of goods sold. In the income statement, show this correction as an adjustment to Cost of goods sold. If manufacturing overhead is underallocated, the adjustment will increase Cost of goods sold. If overhead is overallocated, the adjustment will decrease Cost of goods sold.)

P16-28A *(L. OBJ. 3, 4)* **Accounting manufacturing overhead [25–35 min]**
Weiters Woods manufactures jewelry boxes. The primary materials (wood, brass, and glass) and direct labor are traced directly to the products. Manufacturing overhead costs are allocated based on machine hours. Data for 2010 follow:

	Budget	Actual
Machine hours	24,000 hours	32,000 hours
Maintenance labor (repairs to equipment)	11,000	24,500
Plant supervisor's salary	42,000	45,000
Screws, nails, and glue	29,000	44,000
Plant utilities	48,000	92,850
Freight out	34,000	49,500
Depreciation on plant and equipment	82,000	81,000
Advertising expense	42,000	58,000

Requirements

1. Compute the predetermined manufacturing overhead rate.
2. Post actual and allocated manufacturing overhead to the Manufacturing overhead T-account.
3. Close the under- or overallocated overhead to Cost of goods sold.
4. The predetermined manufacturing overhead rate usually turns out to be inaccurate. Why don't accountants just use the actual manufacturing overhead rate?

P16-29A *(L. OBJ. 5)* **Job order costing in a service company [20–25 min]**
Robin Design, Inc., is a Web site design and consulting firm. The firm uses a job order costing system, in which each client is a different job. Robin Design traces direct labor, licensing costs, and travel costs directly to each job. It allocates indirect costs to jobs based on a predetermined indirect cost allocation rate, computed as a percentage of direct labor costs.

At the beginning of 2011, managing partner Judi Jacquin prepared the following budget:

Direct labor hours (professional)	10,000	hours
Direct labor costs (professional)	$1,400,000	
Support staff salaries	170,000	
Computer leases	49,000	
Office supplies	29,000	
Office rent	60,000	

In November 2011, Robin Design served several clients. Records for two clients appear here:

	Dining Coop		Root Chocolates	
Direct labor hours	740	hours	65	hours
Software licensing costs	$ 2,100		$ 300	
Travel costs	9,000		—	

Requirements

1. Compute Robin Design's predetermined indirect cost allocation rate for 2011.
2. Compute the total cost of each job.
3. If Jacquin wants to earn profits equal to 20% of service revenue, how much (what fee) should she charge each of these two clients?
4. Why does Robin Design assign costs to jobs?

Problems (Group B)

P16-30B *(L. OBJ. 1, 2, 3, 4)* **Analyzing cost data [25–35 min]**

Hartley Manufacturing makes carrying cases for portable electronic devices. Its costing records yield the following information:

Job No.	Date Started	Date Finished	Date Sold	Total Cost of Job at October 31	Total Manufacturing Costs Added in November
1	10/3	10/12	10/13	$ 1,400	
2	10/3	10/30	11/1	1,500	
3	10/17	11/24	11/27	1,000	$ 1,200
4	10/29	11/29	12/3	1,100	1,000
5	11/8	11/12	11/14		550
6	11/23	12/6	12/9		200

Requirements

1. Which type of costing system is Hartley using? What piece of data did you base your answer on?
2. Using the dates above to identify the status of each job, compute Hartley's account balances at October 31 for Work in process inventory, Finished goods inventory, and Cost of goods sold. Compute account balances at November 30 for Work in process inventory, Finished goods inventory, and Cost of goods sold.
3. Record summary journal entries for the transfer of completed units from work in process to finished goods for October and November.
4. Record the sale of Job 3 for $3,000.
5. What is the gross profit for Job 3? What other costs must this gross profit cover?

P16-31B *(L. OBJ. 2, 3, 4)* **Accounting for construction transactions [30–45 min]**

Superior Construction, Inc., is a home builder in New Mexico. Superior uses a job order costing system in which each house is a job. Because it constructs houses, the company uses accounts titled Construction wages and Construction overhead. The following events occurred during August:

a. Purchased materials on account, $470,000

b. Incurred construction wages of $260,000

c. Requisitioned direct materials and used direct labor in construction as follows:

	Direct materials	Direct labor
House 402	$ 59,000	$ 40,000
House 403	68,000	32,000
House 404	61,000	58,000
House 405	83,000	57,000

d. Depreciation of construction equipment, $6,200

e. Other overhead costs incurred on houses 402 through 405:

Indirect labor	$ 73,000
Equipment rentals paid in cash	30,000
Worker liability insurance expired ..	9,000

f. Allocated overhead to jobs at the predetermined rate of 40% of direct labor costs

g. Houses completed: 402, 404

h. House sold: 404 for $260,000

Requirements

1. Record the events in the general journal.
2. Open T-accounts for Work in process inventory and Finished goods inventory. Post the appropriate entries to these accounts, identifying each entry by letter. Determine the ending account balances, assuming that the beginning balances were zero.
3. Add the costs of the unfinished houses, and show that this total amount equals the ending balance in the Work in process inventory account.
4. Add the cost of the completed house that has not yet been sold, and show that this equals the ending balance in Finished goods inventory.
5. Compute gross profit on the house that was sold. What costs must gross profit cover for Superior Construction?

P16-32B *(L. OBJ. 2, 3, 4)* **Preparing and using a job cost record [30–35 min]**
True Technology, Co., manufactures CDs and DVDs for computer software and entertainment companies. True uses job order costing and has a perpetual inventory system.

On April 2, True began production of 5,400 DVDs, Job 423, for Stick People Pictures for $1.10 each. True promised to deliver the DVDs to Stick People by April 5. True incurred the following costs:

Date	Labor Time Record No.	Description	Amount
4/2	655	10 hours @ $16	$ 160
4/3	656	20 hours @ $15	300

Date	Materials Requisition No.	Description	Amount
4/2	63	31 lbs. polycarbonate plastic @ $13	$ 403
4/2	64	25 lbs. acrylic plastic @ $26	650
4/3	74	3 lbs. refined aluminum @ $40	120

True Technology allocates manufacturing overhead to jobs based on the relation between estimated overhead ($560,000) and estimated direct labor costs ($450,000). Job 423 was completed and shipped on April 3.

Requirements

1. Prepare a job cost record similar to Exhibit 16-7 for Job 423. Calculate the predetermined overhead rate, then apply manufacturing overhead to the job.
2. Journalize in summary form the requisition of direct materials and the assignment of direct labor and manufacturing overhead to Job 423.
3. Journalize completion of the job and the sale of the 5,400 DVDs.

P16-33B *(L. OBJ. 2, 3, 4)* **Comprehensive accounting for manufacturing transactions [90–120 min]**
Mighties' Stars produces stars for elementary teachers to reward their students.

Mighties' Stars' trial balance on September 1 follows:

MIGHTIES' STARS Trial Balance September 1, 2010		
	Balance	
Account Title	Debit	Credit
Cash	$ 15,000	
Accounts receivable	185,000	
Inventories:		
Materials	6,000	
Work in process	39,500	
Finished goods	20,200	
Plant assets	270,000	
Accumulated depreciation		$ 76,000
Accounts payable		129,000
Wages payable		2,900
Common stock		145,000
Retained earnings		182,800
Sales revenue		—
Cost of goods sold	—	
Manufacturing wages	—	
Manufacturing overhead	—	
Marketing and general expenses	—	
	$535,700	$535,700

September 1 balances in the subsidiary ledgers were:

- Materials subledger: $4,600 paper and $1,400 indirect
- WIP subledger - job 120 $39,500; $0 for job 121
- Finished goods subledger - $7,900 large stars and $12,300 small stars

September transactions are summarized as follows:

a. Collections on account, $153,000
b. Marketing and general expenses incurred and paid, $28,000
c. Payments on account, $41,000
d. Materials purchases on credit: paper, $4,600; indirect materials, $4,600
e. Materials used in production (requisitioned):
   - Job 120: paper, $800
   - Job 121: paper, $7,650
   - Indirect materials, $1,800
f. Manufacturing wages incurred during September, $37,000, of which $34,300 was paid. Wages payable at August 31 were paid during September, $2,900
g. Labor time records for the month: Job 120, $3,700; Job 121, $18,800; indirect labor, $14,500
h. Depreciation on plant and equipment, $3,300
i. Manufacturing overhead was allocated at the predetermined rate of 80% of direct labor cost
j. Jobs completed during the month: Job 120, 800,000 Large Stars at total cost of $46,960
k. Credit sales on account: all of Job 120 for $105,000
l. Closed the Manufacturing overhead account to Cost of goods sold

Requirements

1. Open T-accounts for the general ledger, the Materials ledger, the Work in process ledger, and the Finished goods ledger. Insert each account balance as given, and use the reference *Bal.*

2. Record the September transactions directly in the accounts, using the letters as references. Mighties' uses a perpetual inventory system.
3. Prepare a trial balance at September 30.
4. Use the Work in process T-account to prepare a schedule of cost of goods manufactured for the month of September. (You may want to review Exhibit 15-10.)
5. Prepare an income statement for the month of September. To calculate cost of goods sold, you may want to review Exhibit 15-7. (*Hint*: In transaction l you closed any under/overallocated manufacturing overhead to Cost of goods sold. In the income statement, show this correction as an adjustment to Cost of goods sold. If manufacturing overhead is underallocated, the adjustment will increase Cost of goods sold. If overhead is overallocated, the adjustment will decrease Cost of goods sold.)

P16-34B *(L. OBJ. 3, 4)* **Accounting manufacturing overhead [25–35 min]**
Regal Woods manufactures jewelry boxes. The primary materials (wood, brass, and glass) and direct labor are traced directly to the products. Manufacturing overhead costs are allocated based on machine hours. Data for 2010 follow:

	Budget	Actual
Machine hours	26,000 hours	32,500 hours
Maintenance labor (repairs to equipment)	14,000	28,500
Plant supervisor's salary	43,000	49,000
Screws, nails, and glue	25,000	45,000
Plant utilities	47,000	97,850
Freight out	37,000	44,500
Depreciation on plant and equipment	85,000	83,000
Advertising expense	43,000	55,000

Requirements

1. Compute the predetermined manufacturing overhead rate.
2. Post actual and allocated manufacturing overhead to the Manufacturing overhead T-account.
3. Close the under- or overallocated overhead to Cost of goods sold.
4. The predetermined manufacturing overhead rate usually turns out to be inaccurate. Why don't accountants just use the actual manufacturing overhead rate?

P16-35B *(L. OBJ. 5)* **Job order costing in a service company [20–25 min]**
Crow Design, Inc., is a Web site design and consulting firm. The firm uses a job order costing system, in which each client is a different job. Crow Design traces direct labor, licensing costs, and travel costs directly to each job. It allocates indirect costs to jobs based on a predetermined indirect cost allocation rate, computed as a percentage of direct labor costs.

At the beginning of 2011, managing partner Sheila Biggs prepared the following budget:

Direct labor hours (professional)	6,250 hours
Direct labor costs (professional)	$1,000,000
Support staff salaries	120,000
Computer leases	45,000
Office supplies	25,000
Office rent	60,000

In October 2011, Crow Design served several clients. Records for two clients appear here:

	Dining Coop	Mesilla Chocolates
Direct labor hours	770 hours	40 hours
Software licensing costs	$ 2,000	$ 300
Travel costs	10,000	—

Requirements

1. Compute Crow Design's predetermined indirect cost allocation rate for 2011.
2. Compute the total cost of each job.
3. If Biggs wants to earn profits equal to 20% of sales revenue, how much (what fee) should she charge each of these two clients?
4. Why does Crow Design assign costs to jobs?

Continuing Exercise

E16-36 This exercise continues the Sherman Lawn Service, Inc., situation from Exercise 15-35 of Chapter 15. Sherman completed a special landscaping job for Feimer's Fancy Fonts. Sherman collected the following data about the job:

Feimer job details:	
Direct materials	$400
Direct labor	$900

Requirements

1. Sherman allocates overhead costs based on 40% of Direct Labor cost. What is the total cost of the Feimer job?
2. If the price Feimer paid for the job is $2,500, what is the profit or loss on the job?

Continuing Problem

P16-37 This problem continues the Haupt Consulting, Inc., situation from Problem 15-36 of Chapter 15. Haupt Consulting uses a job order costing system, in which each client is a different job. Haupt traces direct labor, daily per diem, and travel costs directly to each job. It allocates indirect costs to jobs based on a predetermined indirect cost allocation rate, computed as a percentage of direct labor costs.

At the beginning of 2010, the controller prepared the following budget:

Direct labor hours (professional)	5,000 hours
Direct labor costs (professional)	$1,000,000
Support staff salaries	100,000
Computer leases	80,000
Office supplies	20,000
Office rent	60,000

In November, 2010, Haupt served several clients. Records for two clients appear here:

	Owen's Trains	Caleigh's Cookies
Direct labor hours	700 hours	100 hours
Meal—per diem	$ 2,200	$ 500
Travel costs	9,000	0

Requirements

1. Compute Haupt's predetermined indirect cost allocation rate for 2010.
2. Compute the total cost of each job.
3. If Haupt wants to earn profits equal to 25% of sales revenue, how much (what fee) should it charge each of these two clients?
4. Why does Haupt assign costs to jobs?

Apply Your Knowledge

■ Decision Cases

Case 1. Hiebert Chocolate, Ltd., is located in Memphis. The company prepares gift boxes of chocolates for private parties and corporate promotions. Each order contains a selection of chocolates determined by the customer, and the box is designed to the customer's specifications. Accordingly, Hiebert uses a job order costing system and allocates manufacturing overhead based on direct labor cost.

One of Hiebert's largest customers is the Goforth and Leos law firm. This organization sends chocolates to its clients each Christmas and also provides them to employees at the firm's gatherings. The law firm's managing partner, Bob Goforth, placed the client gift order in September for 500 boxes of cream-filled dark chocolates. But Goforth and Leos did not place its December staff-party order until the last week of November. This order was for an additional 100 boxes of chocolates identical to the ones to be distributed to clients.

Hiebert budgeted the cost per box for the original 500-box order as follows:

Chocolate, filling, wrappers, box	$14.00
Employee time to fill and wrap the box (10 min.)	2.00
Manufacturing overhead	1.00
Total manufacturing cost	$17.00

Ben Hiebert, president of Hiebert Chocolate, Ltd., priced the order at $20 per box.

In the past few months, Hiebert has experienced price increases for both dark chocolate and direct labor. All other costs have remained the same. Hiebert budgeted the cost per box for the second order as:

Chocolate, filling, wrappers, box	$15.00
Employee time to fill and wrap the box (10 min.)	2.20
Manufacturing overhead	1.10
Total manufacturing cost	$18.30

Requirements

1. Do you agree with the cost analysis for the second order? Explain your answer.

2. Should the two orders be accounted for as one job or two in Hiebert's system?
3. What sale price per box should Ben Hiebert set for the second order? What are the advantages and disadvantages of this price?

Case 2. Nature's Own manufactures organic fruit preserves sold primarily through health food stores and on the Web. The company closes for two weeks each December to enable employees to spend time with their families over the holiday season. Nature's Own's manufacturing overhead is mostly straight-line depreciation on its plant and air-conditioning costs for keeping the berries cool during the summer months. The company uses direct labor hours as the manufacturing overhead allocation base. President Cynthia Ortega has just approved new accounting software and is telling Controller Jack Strong about her decision.

"I think this new software will be great," Ortega says. "It will save you time in preparing all those reports."

"Yes, and having so much more information just a click away will help us make better decisions and help control costs," replies Strong. "We need to consider how we can use the new system to improve our business practices."

"And I know just where to start," says Ortega. "You complain each year about having to predict the weather months in advance for estimating air-conditioning costs and direct labor hours for the denominator of the predetermined manufacturing overhead rate, when professional meteorologists can't even get tomorrow's forecast right! I think we should calculate the predetermined overhead rate on a monthly basis."

Controller Strong is not so sure this is a good idea.

Requirements

1. What are the advantages and disadvantages of Ortega's proposal?
2. Should Nature's Own compute its predetermined manufacturing overhead rate on an annual basis or monthly basis? Explain.

Ethical Issue

Farley, Inc., is a contract manufacturer that produces customized computer components for several well-known computer-assembly companies. Farley's latest contract with CompWest.com calls for Farley to deliver sound cards that simulate surround sound from two speakers. Farley spent several hundred thousand dollars to design the sound card to meet CompWest.com's specifications.

Farley's president, Bryon Wilson, has stipulated a pricing policy that requires the bid price for a new job to be based on Farley's estimated costs to design, manufacture, distribute, and provide customer service for the job, plus a profit margin. Upon reviewing the contract figures, Farley's controller, Paul York, was startled to find that the cost estimates developed by Farley's cost accountant, Tony Hayes, for the CompWest.com bid were based on only the manufacturing costs. York is upset with Hayes. He is not sure what to do next.

Requirements

1. How did using manufacturing cost only rather than all costs associated with the CompWest.com job affect the amount of Farley's bid for the job?
2. Identify the parties involved in Paul York's ethical dilemma. What are his alternatives? How would each party be affected by each alternative? What should York do next?

Team Project

Major airlines like **American, Delta,** and **Continental** are struggling to meet the challenges of budget carriers such as **Southwest** and **JetBlue**. Suppose the **Delta** CFO has just returned from a meeting on strategies for responding to competition from budget carriers. The vice president of operations suggested doing nothing: "We just need to wait until these new airlines run out of money. They cannot be making money with their low fares." In contrast, the vice president of marketing, not wanting to lose market share, suggests cutting **Delta's** fares to match the competition. "If **JetBlue** charges only $75 for that flight from New York, so must we!" Others, including the CFO, emphasized the potential for cutting costs. Another possibility is starting a new budget airline within **Delta.** The CEO cut the meeting short, and directed the CFO to "get some hard data."

As a start, the CFO decides to collect cost and revenue data for a typical **Delta** flight, and then compare it to the data for a competitor. Assume she prepares the following schedule:

	Delta	JetBlue
Route: New York to Tampa..................	Flight 1247	Flight 53
Distance..	1,000 miles	1,000 miles
Seats per plane	142	162
One-way ticket price	$80–$621*	$75
Food and beverage	Meal	Snack

*The highest price is first class airfare.

Excluding food and beverage, the CFO estimates that the cost per available seat mile is 8.4 cents for **Delta**, compared to 5.3 cents for **JetBlue.** (That is, the cost of flying a seat for one mile—whether or not the seat is occupied—is 8.4 cents for **Delta**, and 5.3 cents for **JetBlue.**) Assume the average cost of food and beverage is $5 per passenger for snacks and $10 for a meal.

Split your team into two groups. Group 1 should prepare its response to Requirement 1 and group 2 should prepare its response to Requirement 2 before the entire team meets to consider Requirements 3 and 4.

Requirements

1. Use the data to determine for **Delta:**
   a. the total cost of Flight 1247, assuming a full plane (100% load factor)
   b. the revenue generated by Flight 1247, assuming a 100% load factor and average revenue per one-way ticket of $102
   c. the profit per Flight 1247, given the responses to a. and b.
2. Use the data to determine for **JetBlue:**
   a. the total cost of Flight 53, assuming a full plane (100% load factor)
   b. the revenue generated by Flight 53, assuming a 100% load factor
   c. the profit per Flight 53, given the responses to a. and b.
3. Based on the responses to Requirements 1 and 2, carefully evaluate each of the four alternative strategies discussed in **Delta's** executive meeting.
4. The analysis in this project is based on several simplifying assumptions. As a team, brainstorm factors that your quantitative evaluation does not include, but that may affect a comparison of **Delta's** operations to budget carriers.

Quick Check Answers

1. *a* 2. *c* 3. *c* 4. *a* 5. *a* 6. *b* 7. *d* 8. *d* 9. *d* 10. *a*

For online homework, exercises, and problems that provide you immediate feedback, please visit www.myaccountinglab.com.

Process Costing—Weighted-Average Method

Process Costing: An Overview

We saw in the chapter that companies like **Dell Computer**, **Boeing**, and Smart Touch Learning use job order costing to determine the cost of their custom goods and services. In contrast, **Shell Oil**, **Crayola**, and **Sony** use a series of steps (called *processes*) to make large quantities of similar products, called *process costing* systems. There are two methods for handling process costing: weighted-average and FIFO. We focus on the weighted-average method in this appendix.

To introduce process costing, we will look at the crayon manufacturing process. Let us combine **Crayola's** manufacturing into three processes: Mixing, Molding, and Packaging. **Crayola** accumulates the costs of each process. The company then assigns these costs to the crayons passing through that process.

Suppose **Crayola's** production costs incurred to make 10,000 crayons and the costs per crayon are as follows:

	Total Costs	Cost per Crayon
Mixing	$200	$0.02
Molding	100	0.01
Packaging	300	0.03
Total cost	$600	$0.06

The total cost to produce 10,000 crayons is the sum of the costs incurred for the three processes. The cost per crayon is the total cost divided by the number of crayons, or

$600/10,000 = $.06 per crayon

Crayola Company uses the cost per unit of each process to

- control costs. The company can find ways to cut the costs where actual process costs are more than planned process costs.
- set selling prices. The company wants the selling price to cover the costs of making the crayons and it also wants to earn a profit.
- calculate the ending inventory of crayons for the balance sheet and the cost of goods sold for the income statement.

At any moment, some crayons are in the Mixing process, some are in the Molding process, and others are in the Packaging Department. Computing the crayons' cost becomes more complicated when some of the units are still in process. In this appendix, you will learn how to use process costing to calculate the cost of homogeneous products, using crayons as an example.

Exhibit 16A-1 on the following page compares cost flows in

- A job order costing system for **Dell Computer**, and
- A process costing system for **Crayola**.

EXHIBIT 16A-1 Comparison of Job Order Costing and Process Costing

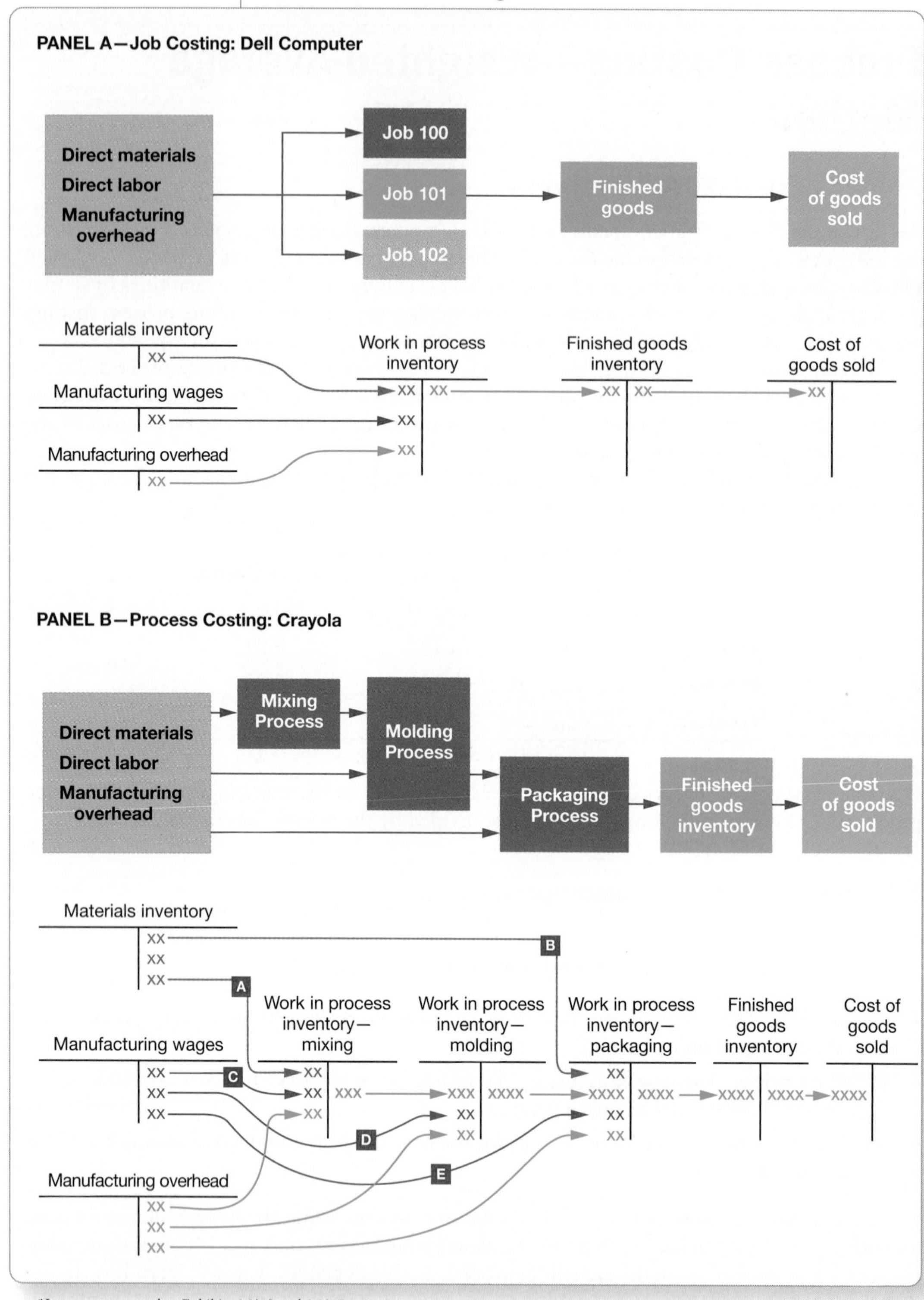

*Letters correspond to Exhibits 16A-2 and 16A-7

Panel A shows that **Dell's** job order costing system has a single Work in process inventory control account. The Work in process inventory account in **Dell's** general ledger is supported by an individual subsidiary cost record for each job (for example, each custom-built computer). Panel B summarizes the flow of costs for **Crayola**. Notice that

1. Each process (Mixing, Molding, and Packaging) is a separate department and each department has its own Work in process inventory account.
2. Direct materials, direct labor, and manufacturing overhead are assigned to Work in process inventory for each process that uses them.
3. When the Mixing Department's process is complete, the wax moves out of mixing and into the Molding Department. The Mixing Department's cost is also transferred out of Work in process inventory—Mixing into Work in process inventory—Molding.
4. When the Molding Department's process is complete, the finished crayons move from molding into the Packaging Department. The cost of the crayons flows out of Work in process inventory—Molding into Work in process inventory—Packaging.
5. When production is complete, the boxes of crayons go into finished goods storage. The combined costs from all departments then flow into Finished goods inventory, but only from the Work in process inventory account of the *last manufacturing process* (For **Crayola**, Packaging is the last department).
6. Note that the letters in the charts correspond to the letters in Exhibit 16A-7.

Exhibit 16A-2 illustrates this cost flow for **Crayola**.

EXHIBIT 16A-2 | Flow of Costs in Production of Crayons

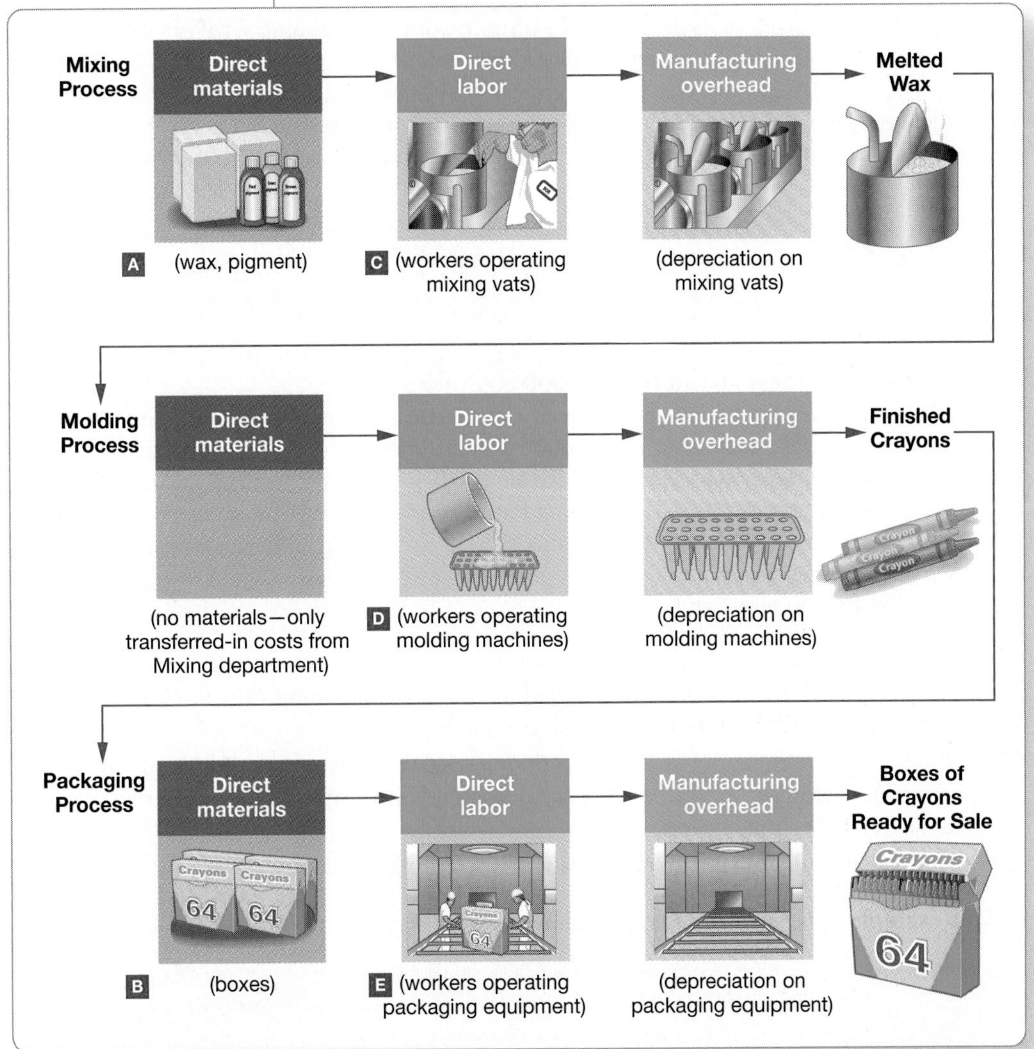

*Note letters correspond to Exhibit 16A-7

Building Blocks of Process Costing

We use two building blocks for process costing:

- Conversion costs
- Equivalent units of production

Chapter 15 introduced three kinds of manufacturing costs: direct materials, direct labor, and manufacturing overhead. Many companies are highly automated, so direct labor is a small part of total manufacturing costs. Such companies often use only two categories:

- Direct materials
- Conversion costs (direct labor plus manufacturing overhead)

Combining direct labor and manufacturing overhead in a single category simplifies the accounting. We call this category *conversion costs* because it is the cost (direct labor plus manufacturing overhead) to *convert* raw materials into finished products.

Completing most products takes time, so the **Crayola** Company may have Work in process inventories for crayons that are only partially completed. The concept of **equivalent units** allows us to measure the amount of work done on a partially finished group of units during a period and to express it in terms of fully complete units of output. Assume **Crayola's** production plant has 10,000 crayons in ending Work in process inventory—Packaging. Each of the 10,000 crayons is 80% complete. If conversion costs are incurred evenly throughout the process, then getting 10,000 crayons 80% of the way through production is the same amount of work as getting 8,000 crayons 100% of the way through the process (10,000 × 80%).

Number of partially complete units	×	Percentage of process completed	=	Number of equivalent units
10,000	×	80%	=	8,000

So, ending Work in process inventory has 8,000 equivalent units.

Use this formula when costs are incurred evenly throughout production. This is usually true for conversion costs. However, direct materials are often added at a specific point in the process. For example, Crayola's wax is added at the beginning of production in the Mixing Department, and packaging materials are added at the end in the Packaging Department. How many equivalent units of wax, conversion costs, and packaging materials are in the ending inventory of 10,000 crayons?

Look at the time line in Exhibit 16A-3.

The 10,000 crayons in Ending work in process inventory have

- 100% of their wax because wax was added at the very beginning. So, they have 10,000 equivalent units of wax. (10,000 × 100% have the wax material.)
- They have none of their boxes because that is the very last thing that happens in the Packaging Department. So, they have 0 equivalent units of packaging materials. (The crayons have not been packaged yet.)
- 8,000 equivalent units of conversion costs that we completed earlier.

This example illustrates an important point:

> We must compute separate equivalent units for the following:
> - Materials
> - Conversion costs

EXHIBIT 16A-3 | Crayola Production Plant Time Line

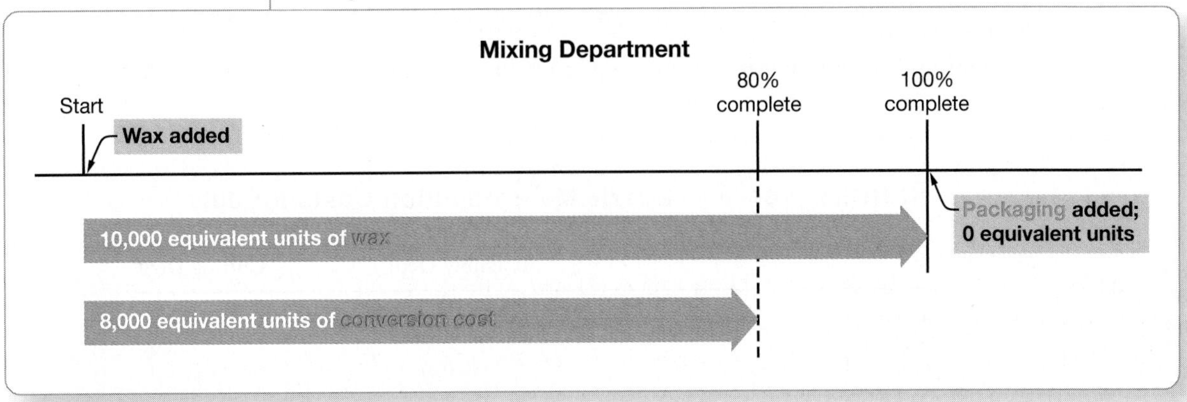

Process Costing in the First Department with No Beginning Inventory

To illustrate process costing, we will use Puzzle Me, a company that recycles calendars into jigsaw puzzles. Exhibit 16A-4 illustrates the two major production processes:

- The Assembly Department applies the glue to cardboard and then presses a calendar page onto the cardboard.
- The Cutting Department cuts the calendar board into puzzle pieces and packages the puzzles in a box. The box is then moved to finished goods storage.

EXHIBIT 16A-4 | Flow of Costs in Producing Puzzles

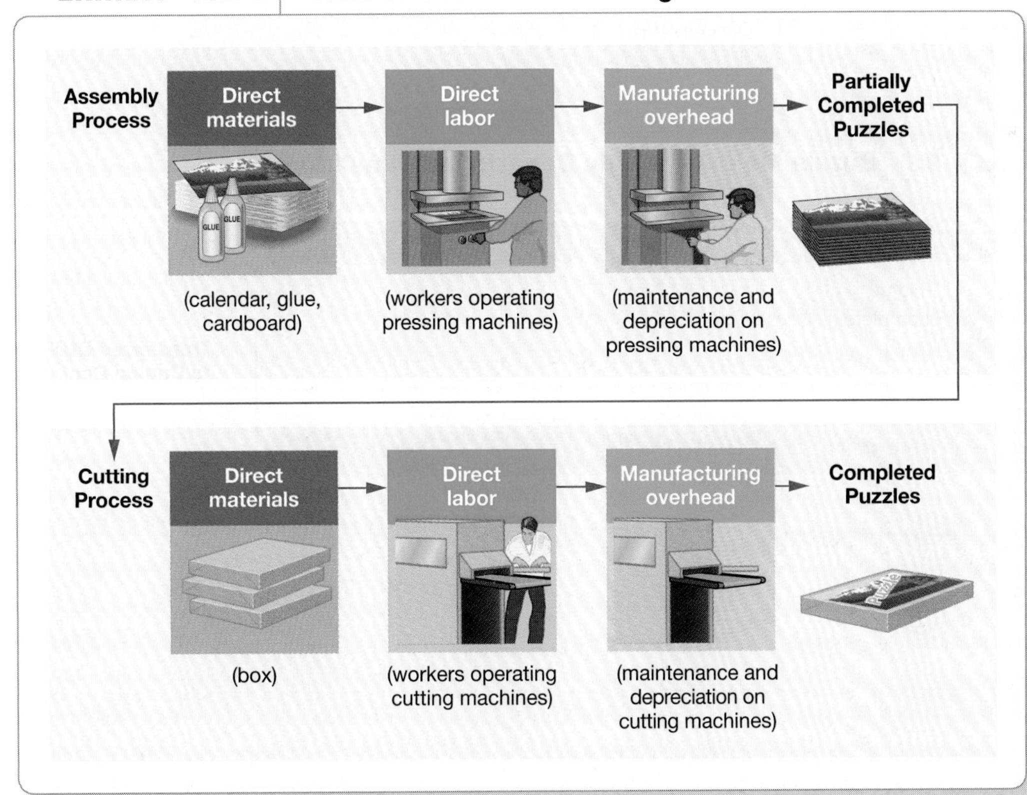

The production process uses materials, machines, and labor in both departments, and there are two Work in process inventory accounts: one for the Assembly Department and one for the Cutting Department.

During July, Puzzle Me incurred the following costs as shown in Exhibit 16A-5:

EXHIBIT 16A-5 | Puzzle Me Production Costs for July

	Assembly Dept	Cutting Dept
Units:		
Beginning WIP-units	0	5,000
Started in production	50,000	must calculate
Transferred out in July	40,000	38,000
Beginning WIP-% complete	N/A	60%
Ending WIP-% complete	25%	30%
Costs:		
Beginning WIP-Transferred in costs	$ 0	$22,000
Beginning WIP-Materials costs	$ 0	$ 0
Beginning WIP-Conversion costs	$ 0	$ 1,200
Direct materials	$140,000	$19,000
Conversion costs:		
Direct labor	$ 20,000	$ 3,840
Manufacturing overhead	$ 48,000	$11,000
Total conversion costs	$ 68,000	$14,840

The accounting period ends before all of the puzzle boards are made. Exhibit 16A-6 shows a time line for the Assembly Department.

EXHIBIT 16A-6 | Puzzle Me's Assembly Department Time Line

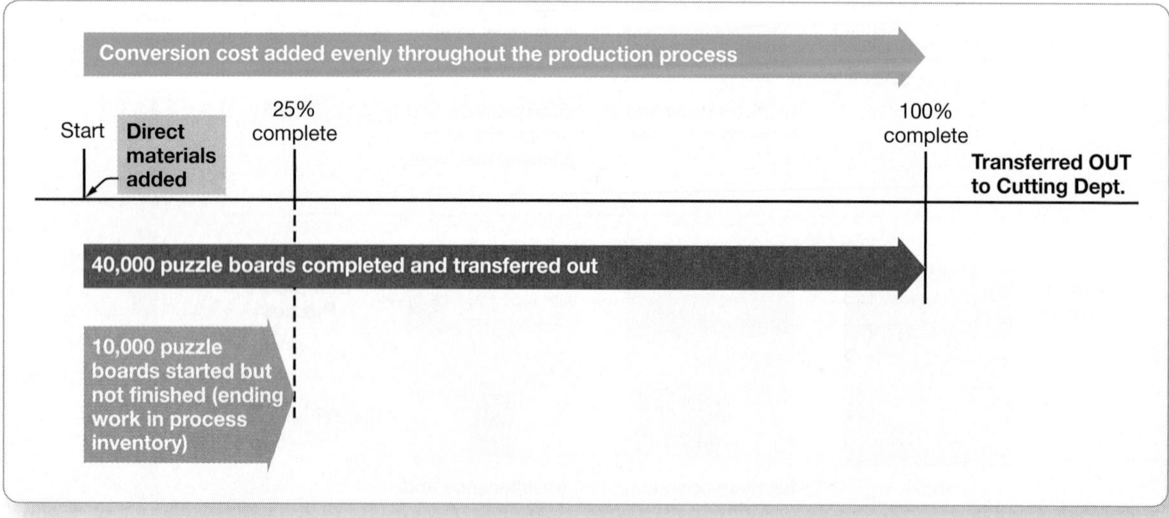

The four steps to process costing are as follows:

- Step 1: Summarize the flow of physical units.
- Step 2: Compute output in terms of equivalent units.
- Step 3: Compute the cost per equivalent unit.
- Step 4: Assign costs to units completed and to units still in ending Work in process inventory.

- "Units to account for" include the number of puzzle boards still in process at the beginning of July plus the number of puzzle boards started during July.
- "Units accounted for" shows what happened to the puzzle boards in process during July. We want to take the July costs incurred in each department and allocate them to the puzzle boards completed and to the puzzle boards still in process at the end of July.

Of the 50,000 puzzle boards started by the Assembly Department in July, 40,000 were completed and transferred out to the Cutting Department. The remaining 10,000 are only partially completed. These partially complete units are the Assembly Department's Ending work in process inventory on July 31.

The Assembly Department time line in Exhibit 16A-6 shows that all direct materials are added at the beginning of the process. In contrast, conversion costs are incurred evenly throughout the process. This is because labor and overhead production activities occur daily. Thus, we must compute equivalent units separately for the following:

- Direct materials
- Conversion costs

The Assembly Department worked on 50,000 puzzle boards during July, as shown in Exhibit 16A-7. As Exhibit 16A-8 shows, 40,000 puzzle boards are now complete for both materials and conversion costs. Another 10,000 puzzle boards are only 25% complete. How many equivalent units did Assembly produce during July?

Equivalent Units for Materials

Equivalent units for materials total 50,000 because all the direct materials have been added to all 50,000 units worked on during July.

Equivalent Units for Conversion Costs

Equivalent units for conversion costs total 42,500. Conversion costs are complete for the 40,000 puzzle boards completed and transferred out. But only 25% of the conversion work has been done on the 10,000 puzzle boards in Ending work in process inventory. Therefore, ending inventory represents only 2,500 equivalent units for conversion costs.

Exhibit 16A-8 summarizes steps 1 and 2.

The cost per equivalent unit requires information about total costs and equivalent units. The computations are as follows:

$$\text{Cost per equivalent unit for direct materials} = \frac{\text{Total direct materials cost}}{\text{Equivalent units of materials}}$$

$$\text{Cost per equivalent unit for conversion costs} = \frac{\text{Total conversion cost}}{\text{Equivalent units for conversion}}$$

EXHIBIT 16A-7 **Step 1: Summarize Physical Flow of Goods**

PUZZLE ME
Cost of Production—ASSEMBLY DEPT.
Month Ended July 31, 2010

	Flow of Production		
1	Step 1: PHYSICAL FLOW	Whole Units	
	Units to account for:		
	Beginning work in process, June 30	0	
	Started in production during July	50,000	
	Total physical units to account for	50,000 A	

Exhibit 16A-5, presented earlier, summarizes the total costs to account for in the Assembly Department. The Assembly Department has 50,000 physical units and $208,000 of costs to account for. Our next task is to split these costs between the following:

- 40,000 puzzle boards transferred out to the Cutting Department
- 10,000 partially complete puzzle boards that remain in the Assembly Department's Ending work in process inventory

In step 2, we computed equivalent units for direct materials (50,000) and conversion costs (42,500). Because the equivalent units differ, we must compute a separate cost per unit for direct materials and for conversion costs. Exhibit 16A-5 shows that the direct materials costs are $140,000. Conversion costs are $68,000, which is the sum of direct labor ($20,000) and manufacturing overhead ($48,000).

The cost per equivalent unit of material is $2.80, and the cost per equivalent unit of conversion cost is $1.60, as shown in Exhibit 16A-9.

We must determine how much of the $208,000 total costs to be accounted for by the Assembly Department should be assigned to

- the 40,000 completed puzzle boards that have been transferred out to the Cutting Department.
- the 10,000 partially completed puzzle boards remaining in the Assembly Department's Ending work in process inventory.

Exhibit 16A-10 shows how to assign costs.

The total cost of completed puzzle boards for the Assembly Department is $176,000, as shown in Exhibit 16A-10. The cost of the 10,000 partially completed puzzle boards in Ending work in process inventory is $32,000, which is the sum of direct material costs ($28,000) and conversion costs ($4,000) allocated in Exhibit 16A-10.

Exhibit 16A-10 has accomplished our goal of splitting the $208,000 total cost between the following:

The 40,000 puzzles completed and transferred out to the Cutting Department	$176,000
The 10,000 puzzles remaining in the Assembly Department's ending work in process inventory on July 31 ($28,000 + $4,000)	32,000
Total costs of the Assembly Department	$208,000

Journal entries to record July costs placed into production in the Assembly Department follow (data from Exhibit 16A-5):

	(1) Work in process inventory—Assembly	208,000	
	Materials inventory		140,000
	Manufacturing wages		20,000
	Manufacturing overhead		48,000
	To assign materials, labor, and overhead cost to Assembly.		

The entry to transfer the cost of the 40,000 completed puzzles out of the Assembly Department and into the Cutting Department follows (Item P from Exhibit 16A-10):

	P Work in process inventory—Cutting	176,000	
	Work in process inventory—Assembly		176,000
	To transfer costs from Assembly to Cutting.		

After these entries are posted, the Work in process inventory—Assembly account appears as follows:

Work in process inventory—Assembly			
Balance, June 30	—	Transferred to Cutting	176,000 P
Direct materials	140,000		
Direct labor	20,000		
Manufacturing overhead	48,000		
Q Balance, July 31	32,000		

Note that the ending balance is the same $32,000 as item Q on Exhibit 16A-10's cost of production report.

Process Costing in a Second Department

Most products require a series of processing steps. In this section, we consider a second department—Puzzle Me's Cutting Department for July—to complete the picture of process costing.

EXHIBIT 16A-11 | Puzzle Me's Cutting Department Time Line

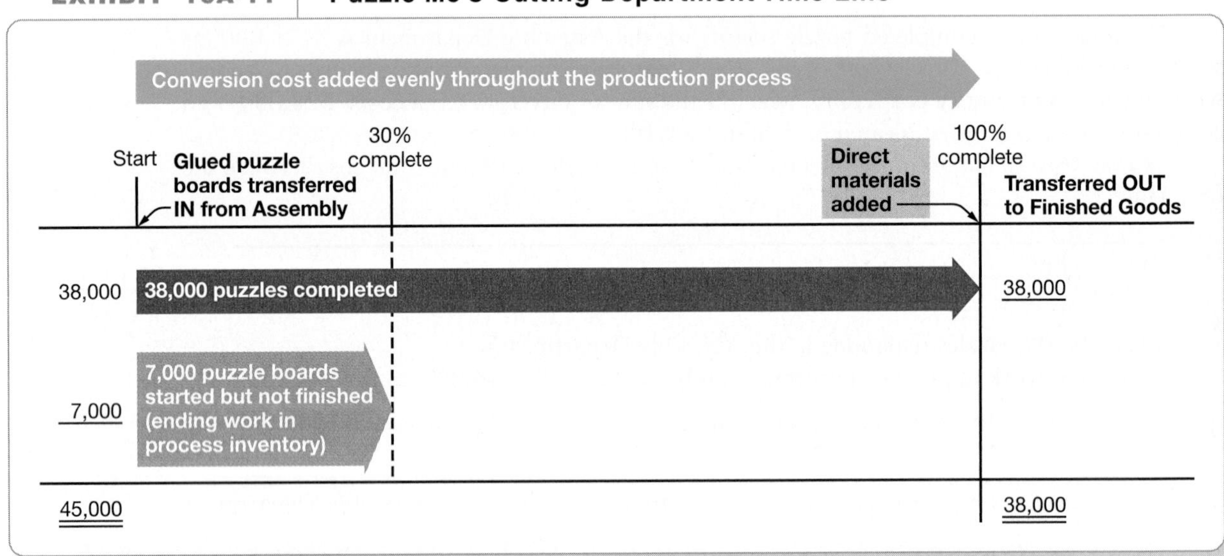

The Cutting Department receives the puzzle boards and cuts the board into puzzle pieces before inserting the pieces into the box at the end of the process. Exhibit 16A-11 shows the following:

- Glued puzzle boards are transferred in from the Assembly Department at the beginning of the Cutting Department's process.
- The Cutting Department's conversion costs are added evenly throughout the process.
- The Cutting Department's direct materials (box) are added at the end of the process.

Keep in mind that *direct materials* in the Cutting Department refers to the boxes added *in that department* and not to the materials (cardboard and glue) added in the Assembly Department. The materials from Assembly that are *transferred into* the Cutting Department are called *transferred in costs*. Likewise, *conversion costs* in the Cutting Department refers to the direct labor and manufacturing overhead costs incurred only in the Cutting Department.

Exhibit 16A-5, presented earlier in the chapter, lists July information for both of Puzzle Me's departments. We will be referring to this data as we complete our Cutting Department allocation for July. Remember that Work in process inventory at the close of business on June 30 is both of the following:

- Ending inventory for June
- Beginning inventory for July

Exhibit 16A-5 shows that Puzzle Me's Cutting Department started the July period with 5,000 puzzle boards partially completed through work done in the Cutting Department in June. During July, the Cutting Department started work on 40,000 additional puzzle boards that were received from the Assembly Department (which we calculated earlier in Exhibits 16A-7 thru 16A-10).

The weighted-average method combines the Cutting Department's

- work done last month—Beginning work in process—to start the Cutting process on the 5,000 puzzle boards that were in Beginning work in process inventory.
- work done in July to complete the 5,000 puzzle boards in Beginning inventory and to work on the 40,000 additional puzzle boards that were transferred in from the Assembly Department during July.

Thus, the **weighted-average process costing method** determines the average cost of all the Cutting Department's equivalent units of work on these 45,000 puzzle boards (5,000 Beginning work in process inventory + 40,000 transferred in from the previous department).

Just as we did for the Assembly Department, our goal is to split the total cost in the Cutting Department between the following:

- 38,000 puzzles that the Cutting Department completed and transferred out to Finished goods inventory
- 7,000 partially completed puzzles remaining in the Cutting Department's ending Work in process inventory at the end of July

We use the same four-step costing procedure that we used for the Assembly Department.

STEP 1: **Summarize the Flow of Physical Units** Let us account for July production, using the data about Physical units given in Exhibit 16A-5 and the results from Exhibit 16A-10 for the Assembly Department.

We must account for these 45,000 units (beginning inventory of 5,000 plus 40,000 started). Exhibit 16A-12 on the following page shows this.

Exhibit 16A-13 shows that, of the 45,000 units to account for, Puzzle Me completed and transferred out 38,000 units. That left 7,000 units as Ending work in process in the Cutting Department on July 31. Steps 2 and 3 will help us determine the costs of these units.

STEP 2: **Compute Equivalent Units** Exhibit 16A-13 computes the Cutting Department's equivalent units of work. Under the weighted-average method, Puzzle Me computes the equivalent units for the total work done to date. This includes all the work done in the current period (July), plus the work done last period (June) on the Beginning work in process inventory.

We can see in Exhibit 16A-13 that the total equivalent units with respect to

- Transferred-in costs include all 45,000 units because they are complete with respect to work done in the Assembly Department. The equivalent units for transferred-in costs will always be 100% of the units to account for, because these units must be 100% complete on previous work before coming to the Cutting Department.
- Direct materials include only the 38,000 finished puzzles because Cutting Department materials (boxes) are added at the end.
- Conversion costs include the 38,000 finished puzzles plus the 2,100 puzzles (7,000 puzzle boards × 30%) that are still in process at the end of the month. Conversion work occurs evenly throughout the cutting process.

EXHIBIT 16A-12 | Step 1: Summarize Physical Flow of Goods

PUZZLE ME
Cost of Production—CUTTING DEPT.
Month Ended July 31, 2010

	Flow of Production		
1	Step 1: PHYSICAL FLOW	Whole Units	
	Units to account for:		
	Beginning work in process,		
	June 30 (from Exhibit 16A-5)	5,000	
	Started in production during		
	July (from Exhibit 16A-10)	40,000	
	Total physical units to account for	45,000	A

Exhibit 16A-14 accumulates the Cutting Department's total costs to account for. In addition to direct material and conversion costs, the Cutting Department must account for transferred-in costs. **Transferred-in costs** are those costs that were incurred in a previous process (the Assembly Department, in this case) and brought into a later process (the Cutting Department) as part of the product's cost.

Exhibit 16A-14 shows that the Cutting Department's total cost to account for ($233,040) is the sum of the following:

- The cost incurred in June to start the Cutting process on the 5,000 puzzles in Cutting's Beginning work in process inventory ($22,000 + $1,200)
- The costs added to Work in process inventory—Cutting during July ($209,840 = $176,000 transferred in from the Assembly Department + $19,000 direct materials added in the Cutting Department + $14,840 conversion costs added in the Cutting Department)

Exhibit 16A-14 also shows the cost per equivalent unit. For each cost category, we divide total cost by the number of equivalent units. Perform this computation for all cost categories: transferred-in costs, direct materials, and conversion costs. In this illustration the total cost per equivalent unit is $5.30 ($4.40 + $0.50 + $0.40).

Exhibit 16A-15 on the previous page shows how Puzzle Me assigns the total Cutting Department costs ($233,040, from Exhibit 16A-5) to

- Units completed and transferred out to Finished goods inventory ($201,400).
- Units remaining in the Cutting Department's Ending work in process inventory ($31,640).

We use the same approach as we used for the Assembly Department in Exhibit 16A-10. Multiply the number of equivalent units from step 2 by the cost per equivalent unit from step 3.

Exhibit 16A-16 shows how Exhibit 16A-15 divided the Cutting Department's costs.

EXHIBIT 16A-16 Assigning Cutting Department Costs to Units Completed and Transferred Out, and to Ending Work in Process Inventory

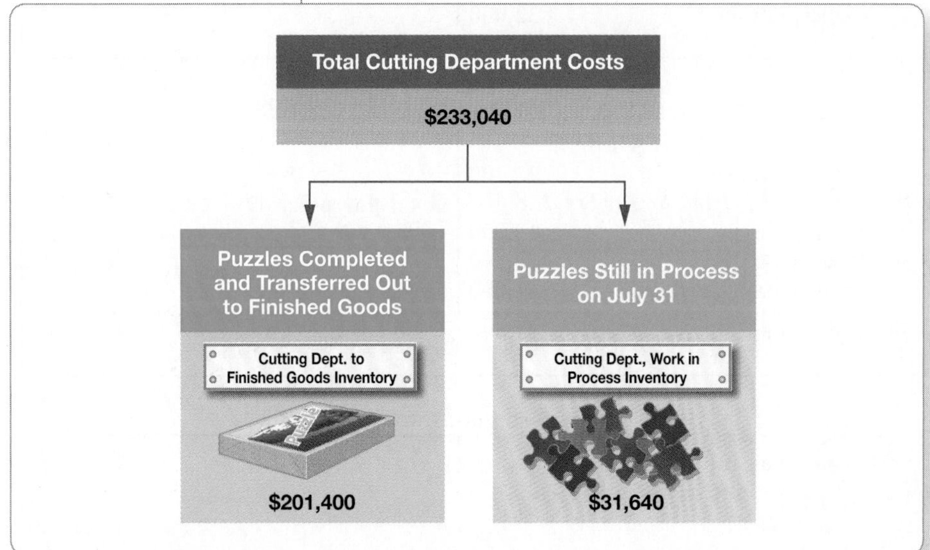

The Cutting Department's journal entries previously recorded the $176,000 in transferred in costs of puzzle boards from the Assembly Department into the Cutting Department on page 913.

The following entry records the Cutting Department's other costs during July (data from Exhibit 16A-15):

	Account	Debit	Credit
	Work in process inventory—Cutting	33,840	
	Materials inventory		19,000
	Manufacturing wages		3,840
	Manufacturing overhead		11,000
	To assign materials and conversion costs to the Cutting Department.		

The entry to transfer the cost of completed puzzles out of the Cutting Department and into Finished goods inventory is based on the dollar amount in Exhibit 16A-15:

	Account	Debit	Credit
	Finished goods inventory	201,400	
	Work in process inventory—Cutting		201,400
	To transfer costs from Finished Goods.		

After posting, the key accounts appear as follows:

Work in process inventory—Assembly

	(Exhibit 16A-10)			
	Balance, June 30	—	Transferred to Cutting	176,000 P
	Direct materials	140,000		
	Direct labor	20,000		
	Manufacturing overhead	48,000		
Q	Balance, July 31	32,000		

Work in process inventory—Cutting

	(Exhibit 16A-15)			
	Balance, June 30	23,200	Transferred to Finished	
P	Transferred in from Assembly	176,000	Goods Inventory	201,400 X
	Direct materials	19,000		
	Direct labor	3,840		
	Manufacturing overhead	11,000		
Y	Balance, July 31	31,640		

Finished goods inventory

	Balance, June 30	0	
X	Transferred in from Cutting	201,400	

As we saw earlier in this chapter, accountants prepare cost reports to help production managers evaluate the efficiency of their manufacturing operations. Both job order and process costing are similar in that they

- *accumulate* costs as the product moves through production.
- *assign* costs to the units (such as gallons of gasoline or number of crayons) passing through that process.

The difference between job order costing and process costing lies in the way costs are accumulated. Job order costing uses a *job cost sheet* and process costing uses a *production cost report.* (See Exhibits 16A-10 and 16A-15 that we completed for the Assembly and Cutting Departments.)

The **production cost report** in Exhibit 16A-15 summarizes Puzzle Me's Cutting Department operations during July. The report combines the costs to account for and the cost per equivalent unit. It shows how those costs were assigned to the puzzles completed and transferred out of the Cutting Department ($201,400) and to Ending work in process inventory remaining in the department ($31,640).

How do managers use the production cost report?

- Controlling cost: Puzzle Me uses product cost data to reduce costs. A manager may decide that the company needs to change either suppliers or a certain component to reduce the cost of its materials. To reduce labor costs, it may need either different employee job requirements or new production equipment.
- Evaluating performance: Managers are often rewarded based on how well they meet the budget. Puzzle Me compares the actual direct materials and conversion costs with expected amounts. If actual unit costs are too high, managers look for ways to cut. If actual costs are less than expected, the Cutting Department's managers may receive a pay raise.
- Pricing products: Puzzle Me must set its selling price high enough to cover the manufacturing cost of each puzzle ($5.30 = $4.40 + $0.50 + $0.40 in Exhibit 16A-15) plus marketing and distribution costs.
- Identifying the most profitable products: Selling price and cost data help managers figure out which products are most profitable. They can then promote these products.
- Preparing the financial statements: Finally, the production cost report aids financial reporting. It provides inventory data for the balance sheet and cost of goods sold for the income statement.

Appendix 16A Assignments

■ Short Exercises

S16A-1 Calculating conversion costs and unit cost [5–10 min]

Cold Spring produces premium bottled water. Cold Spring purchases artesian water, stores the water in large tanks, and then runs the water through two processes: filtration and bottling.

During February, the filtration process incurred the following costs in processing 190,000 liters:

Wages of workers operating the filtration equipment	$ 21,950
Manufacturing overhead allocated to filtration	25,050
Water	150,000

Cold Spring had no beginning inventory in the Filtration Department in February.

Requirements

1. Compute the February conversion costs in the Filtration Department.
2. The Filtration Department completely processed 190,000 liters in February. What was the filtration cost per liter?

Note: Short Exercise 16A-1 must be completed before attempting Short Exercise 16A-2.

S16A-2 Drawing a time line, and computing equivalent units [10 min]

Refer to S16A-1. At Cold Spring, water is added at the beginning of the filtration process. Conversion costs are added evenly throughout the process. Now assume that in February, 125,000 liters were completed and transferred out of the Filtration Department into the Bottling Department. The 65,000 units remaining in Filtration's Ending work in process inventory were 80% of the way through the filtration process. Recall that Cold Spring has no beginning inventories.

Requirements

1. Draw a time line for the filtration process.
2. Compute the equivalent units of direct materials and conversion costs for the Filtration Department.

S16A-3 Computing equivalent units [5 min]

The Mixing Department of Best Foods had 52,000 units to account for in October. Of the 52,000 units, 26,000 units were completed and transferred to the next department, and 26,000 units were 25% complete. All of the materials are added at the beginning of the process. Conversion costs are added equally throughout the filtration process.

Requirement

1. Compute the total equivalent units of direct materials and conversion costs for October.

Note: Short Exercise 16A-3 must be completed before attempting Short Exercise 16A-4.

S16A-4 Computing the cost per equivalent unit [5 min]

Refer to the data in S16A-3 and your results for equivalent units. The Mixing Department of Best Foods has direct materials costs of $44,000 and conversion costs of $18,100 for October.

Requirement

1. Compute the cost per equivalent unit for direct materials and for conversion costs.

Note: Short Exercises 16A-3 and 16A-4 must be completed before attempting Short Exercise 16A-5.

S16A-5 Computing cost of units transferred out and units in ending work in process [5 min]

Refer to S16A-3 and S16A-4. Use Best Foods' costs per equivalent unit for direct materials and conversion costs that you calculated in S16A-4.

Requirement

1. Calculate the cost of the 26,000 units completed and transferred out and the 26,000 units, 25% complete, in the Ending work in process inventory.

S16A-6 Compute the physical flow [15–20 min]

Consider the following incomplete data:

Units to account for:	Dept. A	Dept. 33	Dept. Z17
Beginning work in progress	97	(c)	45
Started in production during month	253	113	(g)
Total physical units to account for	350	172	(f)
Units accounted for:			
Completed and transferred out during month	(b)	117	121
Ending work in progress	119	(d)	26
Total physical units accounted for	(a)	172	(e)

Requirement

1. Calculate the missing items.

■ Exercises

E16A-7 Drawing a time line, computing equivalent units, and assigning cost to completed units and ending work in process; no beginning inventory or cost transferred in [20 min]

Paint My World prepares and packages paint products. Paint My World has two departments: (1) Blending and (2) Packaging. Direct materials are added at the beginning of the blending process (dyes) and at the end of the packaging process (cans). Conversion costs are added evenly throughout each process. Data from the month of May for the Blending Department are as follows:

Gallons:	
Beginning work in process inventory	0
Started production	9,200 gallons
Completed and transferred out to Packaging in May	6,300 gallons
Ending work in process inventory (30% of the way through blending process)	2,900 gallons
Costs:	
Beginning work in process inventory	$ 0
Costs added during May:	
Direct materials	4,500
Direct labor	1,050
Manufacturing overhead	2,400
Total costs added during May	$ 7,950

Requirements

1. Fill in the time line for the Blending Department.
2. Use the time line to help you compute the Blending Department's equivalent units for direct materials and for conversion costs.
3. Compute the total costs of the units (gallons)
   a. Completed and transferred out to the Packaging Department.
   b. In the Blending Department Ending work in process inventory.

Note: Exercise 16A-7 must be completed before attempting Exercise 16A-8.

E16A-8 Preparing journal entries and posting to work in process T-accounts [15 min]

Refer to your answers from E16A-7.

Requirements

1. Present the journal entries to record the assignment of direct materials and direct labor, and the allocation of manufacturing overhead to the Blending Department. Also, give the journal entry to record the costs of the gallons completed and transferred out to the Packaging Department.
2. Post the journal entries to the Work in process inventory—Blending T-account. What is the ending balance?
3. What is the average cost per gallon transferred out of Blending into Packaging? Why would the company managers want to know this cost?

E16A-9 Drawing a time line, computing equivalent units, and assigning cost to completed units and ending work in process; no beginning inventory or cost transferred in [20 min]

Paulson Winery in Napa Valley, California, has two departments: Fermenting and Packaging. Direct materials are added at the beginning of the fermenting process (grapes) and at the end of the packaging process (bottles). Conversion costs are added evenly throughout each process. Data from the month of March for the Fermenting Department are as follows:

Gallons:	
Beginning work in process inventory	0
Started production	7,800 gallons
Completed and transferred out to Packaging in March	6,400 gallons
Ending work in process inventory (80% of the way through fermenting process)	1,400 gallons
Costs:	
Beginning work in process inventory	$ 0
Costs added during March:	
Direct materials	9,360
Direct labor	3,662
Manufacturing overhead	4,610
Total costs added during March	$17,632

Requirements

1. Draw a time line for the Fermenting Department.
2. Use the time line to help you compute the equivalent units for direct materials and for conversion costs.
3. Compute the total costs of the units (gallons)
   a. Completed and transferred out to the Packaging Department.
   b. In the Fermenting Department Ending work in process inventory.

Note: Exercise 16A-9 must be completed before attempting Exercise 16A-10.

E16A-10 Preparing journal entries and posting to work in process T-accounts [15 min]

Refer to the data and your answers from E16A-9.

Requirements

1. Present the journal entries to record the assignment of Direct materials and Direct labor and the allocation of Manufacturing overhead to the Fermenting Department. Also give the journal entry to record the cost of the gallons completed and transferred out to the Packaging Department.
2. Post the journal entries to the Work in process inventory—Fermenting T-account. What is the ending balance?
3. What is the average cost per gallon transferred out of Fermenting into Packaging? Why would Paulson Winery's managers want to know this cost?

E16A-11 Drawing a time line, computing equivalent units, computing cost per equivalent unit; assigning costs; journalizing; second department, weighted-average method [25–30 min]

Clear Water Company produces premium bottled water. In the second department, the Bottling Department, conversion costs are incurred evenly throughout the bottling process, but packaging materials are not added until the end of the process. Costs in Beginning work in process inventory include transferred in costs of $1,400, direct labor of $500, and manufacturing overhead of $430. February data for the Bottling Department follow:

CLEAR WATER COMPANY Work in Process Inventory—Bottling Month Ended February 28, 2011					
	Physical Units	Dollars		Physical Units	Dollars
Beginning inventory, January 31 (40% complete)	8,000	$ 2,330	Transferred out	150,000	$?
Production started:					
Transferred in	162,000	132,900			
Direct materials		33,000			
Conversion costs:					
Direct labor		33,500			
Manufacturing overhead		22,970			
Total to account for	170,000	224,700			
Ending inventory, February 28 (70% complete)	20,000	$?			

Requirements

1. Draw a time line.
2. Compute the Bottling Department equivalent units for the month of February. Use the weighted-average method.
3. Compute the cost per equivalent unit for February.
4. Assign the costs to units completed and transferred out and to Ending inventory.
5. Prepare the journal entry to record the cost of units completed and transferred out.
6. Post all transactions to the Work in process inventory—Bottling Department T-account. What is the ending balance?

■ Problems (Group A)

P16A-12A Computing equivalent units and assigning costs to completed units and ending work in process; no beginning inventory or cost transferred in [30–45 min]

Beth Electronics makes CD players in three processes: assembly, programming, and packaging. Direct materials are added at the beginning of the assembly process. Conversion costs are incurred evenly throughout the process. The Assembly Department had no Work in process on May 31. In mid-June, Beth Electronics started production on 101,000 CD players. Of this number, 76,900 CD players were assembled during June and transferred out to the Programming Department. The June 30 Work in process in the Assembly Department was 35% of the way through the assembly process. Direct materials costing $376,000 were placed in production in Assembly during June, and Direct labor of $157,500 and Manufacturing overhead of $100,900 were assigned to that department.

Requirements

1. Draw a time line for the Assembly Department.
2. Use the time line to help you compute the number of equivalent units and the cost per equivalent unit in the Assembly Department for June.
3. Assign total costs in the Assembly Department to (a) units completed and transferred to Programming during June and (b) units still in process at June 30.
4. Prepare a T-account for Work in process inventory—Assembly to show its activity during June, including the June 30 balance.

P16A-13A Computing equivalent units and assigning costs to completed units and ending work in process; no beginning inventory or cost transferred in [30–45 min]

Smith Paper, Co., produces the paper used by wallpaper manufacturers. Smith's four-stage process includes mixing, cooking, rolling, and cutting. During August, the Mixing Department started and completed mixing for 4,405 rolls of paper. The department started but did not finish the mixing for an additional 600 rolls, which were 20% complete with respect to both direct materials and conversion work at the end of August. Direct materials and conversion costs are incurred evenly throughout the mixing process. The Mixing Department incurred the following costs during August:

Work in process inventory—mixing		
Bal, Aug 1	0	
Direct materials	5,430	
Direct labor	550	
Manufacturing overhead	5,785	

Requirements

1. Draw a time line for the Mixing Department.
2. Use the time line to help you compute the number of equivalent units and the cost per equivalent unit in the Mixing Department for August.
3. Show that the sum of (a) cost of goods transferred out of the Mixing Department and (b) ending Work in process inventory—Mixing equals the total cost accumulated in the department during August.
4. Journalize all transactions affecting the company's mixing process during August, including those already posted.

P16A-14A Computing equivalent units and assigning costs to completed units and ending WIP inventory; two materials, added at different points; no beginning inventory or cost transferred in [30–45 min]

Hall's Exteriors produces exterior siding for homes. The Preparation Department begins with wood, which is chopped into small bits. At the end of the process, an adhesive is added. Then the wood/adhesive mixture goes on to the Compression Department, where the wood is compressed into sheets. Conversion costs are added evenly throughout the preparation process. January data for the Preparation Department are as follows (in millions):

Sheets		Costs	
Beginning work in process inventory	0 sheets	Beginning work in process inventory	$ 0
Started production	3,600 sheets	Costs adding during January:	
Completed and transferred out to		Wood	2,664
Compression in January	1,910 sheets	Adhesives	1,337
		Direct labor	650
Ending work in process inventory (40%		Manufacturing overhead	1,936
of the way through preparation process)	1,690 sheets	Total costs	$ 6,587

Requirements

1. Draw a time line for the Preparation Department.
2. Use the time line to help you compute the equivalent. (*Hint*: Each direct material added at a different point in the production process requires its own equivalent-unit computation.)
3. Compute the total costs of the units (sheets)
   a. Completed and transferred out to the Compression Department.
   b. In the Preparation Department's Ending work in process inventory.

4. Prepare the journal entry to record the cost of the sheets completed and transferred out to the Compression Department.
5. Post the journal entries to the Work in process inventory—Preparation T-account. What is the ending balance?

P16A-15A Computing equivalent units for a second department with beginning inventory; preparing a production cost report and recording transactions on the basis of the report's information; weighted-average method [45–60 min]

Casey Carpet manufactures broadloom carpet in seven processes: spinning, dyeing, plying, spooling, tufting, latexing, and shearing. In the Dyeing Department, direct materials (dye) are added at the beginning of the process. Conversion costs are incurred evenly throughout the process. Casey uses weighted-average process costing. Information for March 2011 follows:

Units:	
Beginning work in process inventory	75 rolls
Transferred in from Spinning Department during March	560 rolls
Completed during March	500 rolls
Ending work in process (80% complete as to conversion work)	135 rolls
Costs:	
Beginning work in process (transferred–in cost, $4,500; materials cost, $1,755; conversion costs, $5,199)	$ 11,454
Transferred in from Spinning Department during March	21,535
Materials cost added during March	12,850
Conversion costs added during March (manufacturing wages, $8,445; manufacturing overhead, $43,508)	51,953

Requirements

1. Prepare a time line for Casey's Dyeing Department.
2. Use the time line to help you compute the equivalent units, cost per equivalent unit, and total costs to account for in Casey's Dyeing Department for March.
3. Prepare the March production cost report for Casey's Dyeing Department.
4. Journalize all transactions affecting Casey's Dyeing Department during March, including the entries that have already been posted.

P16A-16A Computing equivalent units for a second department with beginning inventory; assigning costs to completed units and ending work in process; weighted-average method [50–60 min]

SeaWorthy uses three processes to manufacture lifts for personal watercraft: forming a lift's parts from galvanized steel, assembling the lift, and testing the completed lifts. The lifts are transferred to finished goods before shipment to marinas across the country.

SeaWorthy's Testing Department requires no direct materials. Conversion costs are incurred evenly throughout the testing process. Other information follows:

Units:	
Beginning work in process	2,100 units
Transferred in from the Assembling Dept. during the period	7,300 units
Completed during the period	4,300 units
Ending work in process (40% complete as to conversion work)	5,100 units
Costs:	
Beginning work in process (transferred–in cost, $93,200; conversion costs, $18,300)	$ 111,500
Transferred in from the Assembling Dept. during the period	687,000
Conversion costs added during the period	76,800

The cost transferred into Finished Goods Inventory is the cost of the lifts transferred out of the Testing Department. SeaWorthy uses weighted-average process costing.

Requirements

1. Draw a time line for the Testing Department.
2. Use the time line to compute the number of equivalent units of work performed by the Testing Department during the period.
3. Compute SeaWorthy's transferred-in and conversion costs per equivalent unit. Use the unit costs to assign total costs to (a) units completed and transferred out of Testing and (b) units in Testing's Ending work in process inventory.
4. Compute the cost per unit for lifts completed and transferred out to Finished goods inventory. Why would management be interested in this cost?

■ Problems (Group B)

P16A-17B Computing equivalent units and assigning costs to completed units and ending work in process; no beginning inventory or cost transferred in [30–45 min]

Sue Electronics makes CD players in three processes: assembly, programming, and packaging. Direct materials are added at the beginning of the assembly process. Conversion costs are incurred evenly throughout the process. The Assembly Department had no work in process on March 31. In mid-June, Sue Electronics started production on 100,000 CD players. Of this number, 76,100 CD players were assembled during June and transferred out to the Programming Department. The April 30 work in process in the Assembly Department was 40% of the way through the assembly process. Direct materials costing $373,000 were placed in production in Assembly during April, and direct labor of $157,700 and manufacturing overhead of $100,100 were assigned to that department.

Requirements

1. Draw a time line for the Assembly Department.
2. Use the time line to help you compute the number of equivalent units and the cost per equivalent unit in the Assembly Department for April.
3. Assign total costs in the Assembly Department to (a) units completed and transferred to Programming during April and (b) units still in process at April 30.
4. Prepare a T-account for Work in Process Inventory—Assembly to show its activity during April, including the April 30 balance.

P16A-18B Computing equivalent units and assigning costs to completed units and ending work in process; no beginning inventory or cost transferred in [30–45 min]

Reed Paper, Co., produces the paper used by wallpaper manufacturers. Reed's four-stage process includes mixing, cooking, rolling, and cutting. During October, the Mixing Department started and completed mixing for 4,420 rolls of paper. The department started but did not finish the mixing for an additional 650 rolls, which were 25% complete with respect to both direct materials and conversion work at the end of October. Direct materials and conversion costs are incurred evenly throughout the mixing process. The Mixing Department incurred the following costs during October:

Work in process inventory–mixing

Bal, Aug 1	0	
Direct materials	5,675	
Direct labor	570	
Manufacturing overhead	6,240	

Requirements

1. Draw a time line for the Mixing Department.
2. Use the time line to help you compute the number of equivalent units and the cost per equivalent unit in the Mixing Department for October.
3. Show that the sum of (a) cost of goods transferred out of the Mixing Department and (b) Ending work in process inventory—Mixing equals the total cost accumulated in the department during October.
4. Journalize all transactions affecting the company's mixing process during October, including those already posted.

P16A-19B Computing equivalent units and assigning costs to completed units and ending WIP inventory; two materials, added at different points; no beginning inventory or cost transferred in [30–45 min]

Root's Exteriors produces exterior siding for homes. The Preparation Department begins with wood, which is chopped into small bits. At the end of the process, an adhesive is added. Then the wood/adhesive mixture goes on to the Compression Department, where the wood is compressed into sheets. Conversion costs are added evenly throughout the preparation process. March data for the Preparation Department are as follows (in millions):

Sheets		Costs	
Beginning work in process inventory	0 sheets	Beginning work in process inventory	$ 0
Started production	3,300 sheets	Costs adding during March:	
Completed and transferred out to		Wood	2,600
Compression in March	1,900 sheets	Adhesives	1,365
		Direct labor	640
Ending work in process inventory (45%		Manufacturing overhead	2,445
of the way through the preparation process)	1,400 sheets	Total costs	$ 7,050

Requirements

1. Draw a time line for the Preparation Department.
2. Use the time line to help you compute the equivalent. (*Hint*: Each direct material added at a different point in the production process requires its own equivalent-unit computation.)
3. Compute the total costs of the units (sheets)
   a. Completed and transferred out to the Compression Department.
   b. In the Preparation Department's Ending work in process inventory.
4. Prepare the journal entry to record the cost of the sheets completed and transferred out to the Compression Department.
5. Post the journal entries to the Work in process inventory—Preparation T-account. What is the ending balance?

P16A-20B Computing equivalent units for a second department with beginning inventory; preparing a production cost report and recording transactions on the basis of the report's information; weighted-average method [45–60 min]

Claudia Carpet manufactures broadloom carpet in seven processes: spinning, dyeing, plying, spooling, tufting, latexing, and shearing. In the Dyeing Department, direct materials (dye) are added at the beginning of the process. Conversion costs are incurred evenly throughout the process. Claudia uses weighted-average process costing. Information for July 2011 follows:

Units:	
Beginning work in process inventory	75 rolls
Transferred in from Spinning Department during July	560 rolls
Completed during July	500 rolls
Ending work in process (75% complete as to conversion work)	135 rolls
Costs:	
Beginning work in process (transferred–in cost, $4,600; materials cost, $1,650; conversion costs, $5,199)	$ 11,449
Transferred in from Spinning Department during July	22,070
Materials cost added during July	12,320
Conversion costs added during July (manufacturing wages, $8,445; manufacturing overhead, $43,508)	51,953

Requirements

1. Prepare a time line for Claudia's Dyeing Department.
2. Use the time line to help you compute the equivalent units, cost per equivalent unit, and total costs to account for in Claudia's Dyeing Department for July.
3. Prepare the July production cost report for Claudia's Dyeing Department.
4. Journalize all transactions affecting Claudia's Dyeing Department during July, including the entries that have already been posted.

P16A-21B Computing equivalent units for a second department with beginning inventory; assigning costs to completed units and ending work in process; weighted average method [50–60 min]

WaterBound uses three processes to manufacture lifts for personal watercrafts: forming a lift's parts from galvanized steel, assembling the lift, and testing the completed lifts. The lifts are transferred to finished goods before shipment to marinas across the country.

WaterBound's Testing Department requires no direct materials. Conversion costs are incurred evenly throughout the testing process. Other information follows:

Units:	
Beginning work in process	2,300 units
Transferred in from the Assembling Dept. during the period	6,800 units
Completed during the period	4,100 units
Ending work in process (15% complete as to conversion work)	5,000 units
Costs:	
Beginning work in process (transferred–in cost, $93,400; conversion costs, $18,100)	$ 111,500
Transferred in from the Assembling Dept. during the period	671,000
Conversion costs added during the period	49,000

The cost transferred into Finished goods inventory is the cost of the lifts transferred out of the Testing Department. WaterBound uses weighted-average process costing.

Requirements

1. Draw a time line for the Testing Department.
2. Use the time line to compute the number of equivalent units of work performed by the Testing Department during the period.
3. Compute WaterBound's transferred-in and conversion costs per equivalent unit. Use the unit costs to assign total costs to (a) units completed and transferred out of Testing and (b) units in Testing's ending work in process inventory.
4. Compute the cost per unit for lifts completed and transferred out to Finished goods inventory. Why would management be interested in this cost?

17 Activity-Based Costing and Other Cost Management Tools

Learning Objectives/ Success Keys

1. Develop activity-based costs (ABC)
2. Use activity-based management (ABM) to achieve target costs
3. Describe a just-in-time (JIT) production system, and record its transactions
4. Use the four types of quality costs to make decisions

David Larimer, Matt Sewell, and Brian Jobe are college friends who share an apartment. They split the monthly costs equally as shown below:

Rent and utilities	$570
Cable TV	50
High-speed Internet access	40
Groceries	240
Total monthly costs	$900

Each roommate's share is $300 ($900/3).

Things go smoothly the first few months. But then David calls a meeting. "Since I started having dinner at Amy's, I shouldn't have to pay a full share for the groceries." Matt then pipes in: "I'm so busy surfing the Net that I never have time to watch TV. I don't want to pay for the cable TV any more. And Brian, since your friend Jennifer eats here most evenings, you should pay a double share of the grocery bill." Brian retorts, "Matt, then you should pay for the Internet access, since you're the only one around here who uses it!"

What happened? The friends originally shared the costs equally. But they are not participating equally in eating, watching TV, and surfing the Net. Splitting these costs equally is not the best arrangement.

The roommates could better match their costs with the people who participate in each activity. This means splitting cable TV between David and Brian, letting Matt pay for Internet access, and allocating the grocery bill 1/3 to Matt and 2/3 to Brian. Exhibit 17-1 compares the results of this refined system with the original system.

EXHIBIT 17-1 **More-Refined Versus Original Cost Allocation System**

	David	Matt	Brian
More-refined cost allocation system:			
Rent and utilities	$190	$190	$190
Cable TV	25	—	25
High-speed Internet access	—	40	—
Groceries	—	80	160
Total costs allocated	$215	$310	$375
Original cost allocation system	$300	$300	$300
Difference	$ (85)	$ 10	$ 75

No wonder David called the meeting! The original system cost him $300 a month, but under the refined system David pays only $215.

Large companies such as **Microsoft** or **Sony**, as well as smaller companies like Smart Touch Learning, face situations like this every day. What is the best way to allocate our costs to the things we do? Fair allocations have high stakes: friendships for David, Matt, and Brian and profits and losses for companies.

Refining Cost Systems

1 Develop activity-based costs (ABC)

Sharpening the Focus: Assigning Costs Based on the Activities That Caused the Costs

Let us illustrate cost refinement by looking at Smart Touch Learning. In today's competitive market, Smart Touch needs to know what it costs to make a DVD. The cost information helps Smart Touch set a selling price to cover costs and provide a profit. To remain competitive with other learning DVD manufacturers, Smart Touch must hold costs down.

We have seen that direct costs (materials and labor) are easy to assign to products. But indirect costs (utilities, supervisor salaries, and plant depreciation) are another story. It is the indirect costs—and they are significant—that must be allocated somehow. One way to manage costs is to refine the way indirect costs are allocated. Exhibit 17-2 provides an example. The first column of Exhibit 17-2 starts with Smart Touch's production function—making the DVDs. Production is where most companies begin refining their cost systems.

Before business got so competitive, managers could limit their focus to a broad business function such as production, and use a single plant-wide rate to allocate manufacturing overhead cost to their inventory, as we demonstrated in Chapter 16. But today's environment calls for more refined cost accounting. Managers need better data to set prices and identify the most profitable products. They drill down to focus on the costs incurred by each activity within the production function, as shown in the lower right of Exhibit 17-2. This has led to a better way to allocate indirect cost to production, and it is called activity-based costing.

EXHIBIT 17-2 **Focus on the Activities That Cause the Costs—Smart Touch Learning**

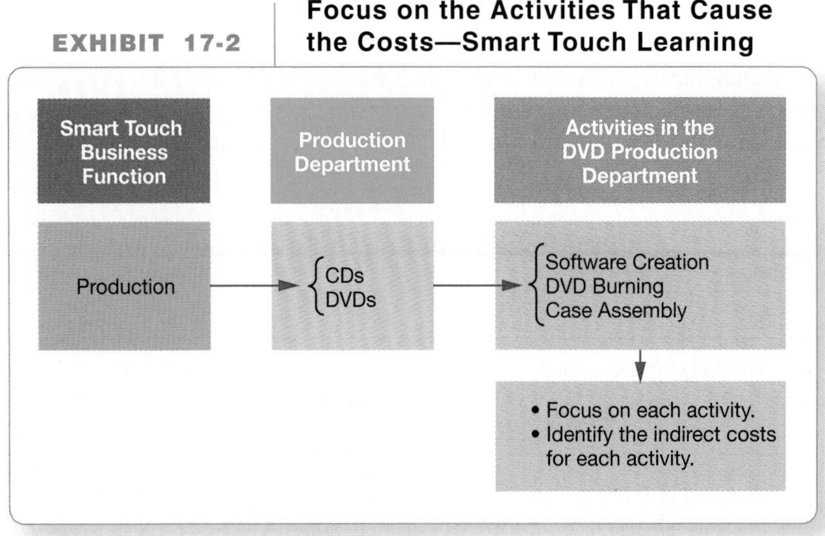

Activity-based costing (**ABC**) focuses on *activities*. The costs of those activities become the building blocks for measuring (allocating) the costs of products and services. Companies like **Dell**, **Coca-Cola**, and **American Express** use ABC.

Each activity has its own (usually unique) cost driver. For example, Smart Touch allocates indirect assembly costs to DVDs based on the number of inserts a worker must put in the DVD case. DVDs that require more inserts cost more to manufacture. Exhibit 17-3 shows some representative activities and cost drivers for manufacturing companies.

EXHIBIT 17-3 **Examples of Activities and Cost Drivers**

Stop & Think...

You go to a restaurant with three of your friends and the waiter brings one bill for \$100. How do you split it up? The meal you ordered only cost \$20 of the total bill. Do you pay ¼; of the bill, or \$25, or do you pay based on the cost of what you ordered, \$20? Paying based on what you ordered is the gist of activity-based costing. Production costs get allocated based on the amount of each activity of production that the products use.

Developing an Activity-Based Costing System

The main difference between ABC and traditional systems is that ABC uses a separate allocation rate for each activity. Traditional systems, as demonstrated in Chapter 16, usually use one rate. ABC requires four steps, as outlined in Exhibit 17-4, using Smart Touch's data.

EXHIBIT 17-4 Activity-Based Costing in Four Easy Steps

ABC Step	Application
1. Identify each activity and estimate its total indirect cost.	Activity: Case Assembly Estimated total indirect cost per year: \$10,000
2. Identify the cost driver for each activity and estimate the total quantity of each driver's allocation base.	Cost driver for case assembly: number of inserts Estimated total number of inserts each year: 100,000
3. Compute the cost allocation rate for each activity. $\text{Cost allocation rate} = \dfrac{\text{Estimated total indirect cost}}{\text{Estimated total quantity of the allocation base}}$	$\text{Cost allocation rate} = \dfrac{\$10{,}000}{100{,}000 \text{ inserts}} = \$.10 \text{ per insert}$
4. Allocate indirect costs to the cost object—in this case, all the inserts put in DVD cases during January. $\text{Allocated activity cost} = \text{Cost allocation rate} \times \text{Actual quantity of the allocation base}$	$\text{Cost of DVD Assembly for January} = \$.10 \times 8{,}000 \text{ inserts during January} = \underline{\underline{\$800}}$

The first step in developing an activity-based costing system is to identify the activities. Analyzing all the activities required for a product or service forces managers to think about how each activity might be improved—or whether it is necessary at all.

Traditional Versus Activity-Based Costing Systems: Smart Touch Learning

To illustrate an ABC system, we use Smart Touch Learning. Smart Touch produces hundreds of different learning DVDs, including mass quantities of large audience DVDs and small quantities of "specialty" learning DVDs for specific companies.

We begin with a traditional cost system to show its weakness. You will see shortly that the ABC system that follows is clearly superior.

A Traditional Cost System

Smart Touch Learning's cost system allocates all manufacturing overhead the traditional way—based on a single allocation rate: 40% of direct labor cost. Smart Touch's controller, James Kolen, gathered data for two of the company's products:

- Microsoft Excel Training DVD (Multiple customers use this DVD)
- Specialty DVD created for a company's custom software application (A single customer uses this DVD)

Based on Smart Touch's traditional cost system, Kolen computed each product's gross profit as shown in Exhibit 17-5.

EXHIBIT 17-5 Smart Touch's Manufacturing Cost and Gross Profit Using Traditional Overhead Allocation

	Excel DVD	Specialty DVD
Sale price per DVD	$12.00	$70.00
Less: Manufacturing cost per DVD:		
Direct materials	2.40	2.40
Direct labor	4.00	34.00
Manufacturing overhead (40% of Direct Labor Cost)	1.60	13.60
Total manufacturing cost per DVD	8.00	50.00
Gross profit per DVD	$ 4.00	$20.00

The gross profit for the specialty DVD is $20 per DVD—five times as high as the gross profit for the Excel DVD ($4). Smart Touch CEO Sheena Bright is surprised that the specialty DVD appears so much more profitable. She asks Kolen to check this out. Kolen confirms that the gross profit per DVD is five times as high for the specialty DVD. Bright wonders whether Smart Touch should produce more specialty DVDs.

Key Point: Because direct labor cost is the single allocation base for all products, Smart Touch allocates far more total overhead cost to the Excel DVDs than to the specialty DVDs. This costing is accurate only if direct labor really is the overhead cost driver, and only if the Excel DVD really does cause more overhead than the specialty DVD.

CEO Sheena Bright calls a meeting with production foreman Ryan Oliver and controller Kolen. Sheena is perplexed: The accounting numbers show that the specialty DVD is much more profitable than the Excel DVD. She expected the Excel DVD to be more efficiently produced and, therefore, more profitable because it is produced in a few large batches. By contrast, the specialty DVD is produced in many small batches.

Kolen fears that the problem could be Smart Touch's cost accounting system. Kolen suggests that foreman Oliver work with him to develop a pilot ABC system. Exhibit 17-6 compares the traditional single-allocation-base system (Panel A) to the new ABC system that Kolen's team developed (Panel B).

EXHIBIT 17-6 | Overview of Smart Touch's Traditional and ABC Systems

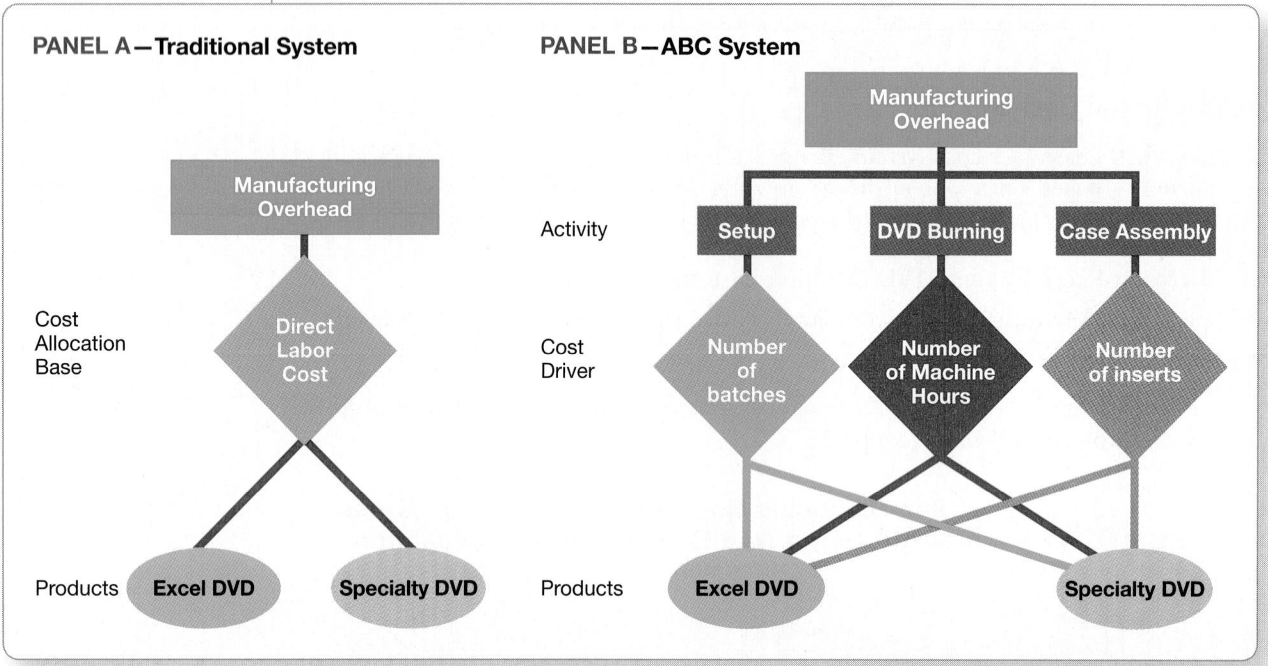

Activity-Based Cost System

Panel B of Exhibit 17-6 shows that Smart Touch's ABC team identifies three activities: setup, DVD burning, and case assembly. Each activity has its own cost driver. But exactly how does ABC work? The ABC team develops the new system by following the four steps described in Exhibit 17-4.

Let us see how an ABC system works, with a focus on the setup activity. Exhibit 17-7 develops Smart Touch's ABC system. Follow the details of each step. Make sure you understand exactly how each ABC step applies to Smart Touch's setup process.

Controller Kolen then uses the ABC costs allocated from Exhibit 17-7 to recompute manufacturing overhead costs, as shown in Exhibit 17-8. For each product, Kolen adds the total costs of setup, DVD burning, and assembly. He then divides each product's total manufacturing overhead cost by the number of DVDs produced to get the overhead cost per DVD.

Activity-based costs are more accurate because ABC considers the resources each product actually uses. Focus on the bottom line of Exhibit 17-8. Manufacturing overhead costs of

- Excel DVDs are $.60 per DVD, which is less than the $1.60 cost allocated under the old system (shown in color in Exhibit 17-5).
- specialty DVDs are $33.70 per DVD, which far exceeds the $13.60 cost under the old system (shown in color in Exhibit 17-5).

Now that we know the indirect costs of Excel and specialty DVDs under ABC, let us see how Smart Touch's managers *use* the ABC cost information to make better decisions.

EXHIBIT 17-7 | **Smart Touch's ABC System**

Step 1: Identify activities and estimate their total indirect costs.

Controller Kolen's team identifies all the manufacturing activities. Focus on setup.

Foreman Oliver estimates total setup costs for all production at $600,000. This cost is for all products that Smart Touch produces.

Step 2: Identify the cost driver for each activity.
Then estimate the total quantity of each driver's allocation base.

The allocation base for each activity should be its cost driver. The number of batches drive setup costs.

Kolen and Oliver estimate the setup department will have 40 batches.

Step 3: Compute the allocation rate for each activity.

Kolen computes the allocation rate for setup as follows:

$$\text{Cost allocation rate} = \frac{\$600{,}000}{40 \text{ batches}} = \$15{,}000 \text{ per batch}$$

Step 4: Allocate indirect costs to the cost object—batches of DVDs in this case.*

Kolen allocates setup costs as follows:

Excel DVD: 3 batches × $15,000 per batch = $45,000
Specialty DVD: 1 batch × $15,000 per batch = $15,000

*Other Smart Touch products represent the remaining 36 batches.

EXHIBIT 17-8 | **Smart Touch's Manufacturing Overhead Costs Under ABC**

Manufacturing Overhead Costs	Excel DVD	Specialty DVD
Setup (from Exhibit 17-7)	$45,000	$15,000
DVD Burning (amounts assumed)	5,000	1,500
Case Assembly (from Exhibit 17-4, based on .10 per insert) Each Excel DVD has 1 insert. Each specialty DVD has 7 inserts.	10,000	350
Total manufacturing overhead cost	60,000	16,850
Divide by number of DVDs produced	100,000	500
Manufacturing overhead cost per DVD under ABC	$ 0.60	$ 33.70

Activity-Based Management: Using ABC for Decision Making

Activity-based management (ABM) uses activity-based costs to make decisions that increase profits while meeting customer needs. In this section, we show how Smart Touch can use ABC in two kinds of decisions:

2 Use activity-based management (ABM) to achieve target costs

1. Pricing and product mix
2. Cost cutting

Pricing and Product Mix Decisions

Controller Kolen now knows the ABC manufacturing overhead cost per DVD (Exhibit 17-8). To determine which products are the most profitable, he recomputes each product's total manufacturing cost and gross profit. Panel A of Exhibit 17-9 shows that the total manufacturing cost per DVD for the Excel DVDs is $7.00 under the ABC system. Contrast this with the $8.00 cost per DVD under Smart Touch's traditional cost system, as shown in Panel B. More important, the ABC data in Panel A show that the specialty DVDs cost $70.10 per DVD, rather than the $50 per DVD indicated by the old system (Panel B). Smart Touch has been losing $.10 on each specialty DVD—and this is *before* R&D, marketing, and distribution expenses! It seems that specialty DVDs are not currently profitable for Smart Touch.

EXHIBIT 17-9 **Smart Touch's Cost Comparison—ABC vs. Traditional Allocation**

PANEL A—Total Manufacturing Cost and Gross Profit Under ABC

	Excel DVD	Specialty DVD
Sale price per DVD	$12.00	$70.00
Less: Manufacturing cost per DVD:		
Direct materials	2.40	2.40
Direct labor	4.00	34.00
Manufacturing overhead (from Exhibit 17-8)	0.60	33.70
Total manufacturing cost per DVD	7.00	70.10
Gross profit per DVD	$ 5.00	$ (0.10)

PANEL B—Total Manufacturing Cost and Gross Profit Under Traditional Allocation of Costs

	Excel DVD	Specialty DVD
Sale price per DVD	$12.00	$70.00
Less: Manufacturing cost per DVD:		
Direct materials	2.40	2.40
Direct labor	4.00	34.00
Manufacturing overhead (40% of Direct Labor Cost)	1.60	13.60
Total manufacturing cost per DVD	8.00	50.00
Gross profit per DVD	$ 4.00	$20.00

This illustration shows that ABC is often the best way to measure the cost of manufacturing a product. As a result, ABC helps businesses set the selling prices of their products. The selling price must cover *all* costs—both manufacturing costs and operating expenses—plus provide a profit.

As you will see in the next section, Smart Touch may be able to use ABC to cut costs. If Smart Touch cannot cut costs enough to earn a profit on the specialty DVDs, then the company may have to raise the sale price. If customers will not pay more, Smart Touch may have to drop the specialty DVDs. *This is the exact opposite of the strategy suggested by cost data from the traditional system. That system favored specialty DVDs.*

Cutting Costs

Most companies adopt ABC to get better product costs for pricing and product-mix decisions. However, they often benefit more by cutting costs. ABC and value engineering can work together. **Value engineering** means reevaluating activities to reduce costs. It requires the following cross-functional teams:

- Marketers to identify customer needs
- Engineers to design more efficient products
- Accountants to estimate costs

Why are managers turning to value engineering? Because it gets results! Companies like **General Motors** and **Carrier Corporation** are following Japanese automakers **Toyota** and **Nissan** and setting sale prices based on **target prices**—what customers are willing to pay for the product or service. Exhibit 17-10 provides an example. Study each column separately.

EXHIBIT 17-10 | Target Pricing Versus Traditional Cost-Based Pricing

Target Pricing	Traditional Cost-Based Pricing
Target Sale Price	Full Product Cost (all elements of value chain)
How much are you willing to pay for specialty DVDs?	
Minus	Plus
Desired Profit	Desired Profit
Target Profit	Target Profit
Equals	Equals
Target Cost	Sale Price
Target Cost	We'll sell you the specialty DVDs for $70 each.

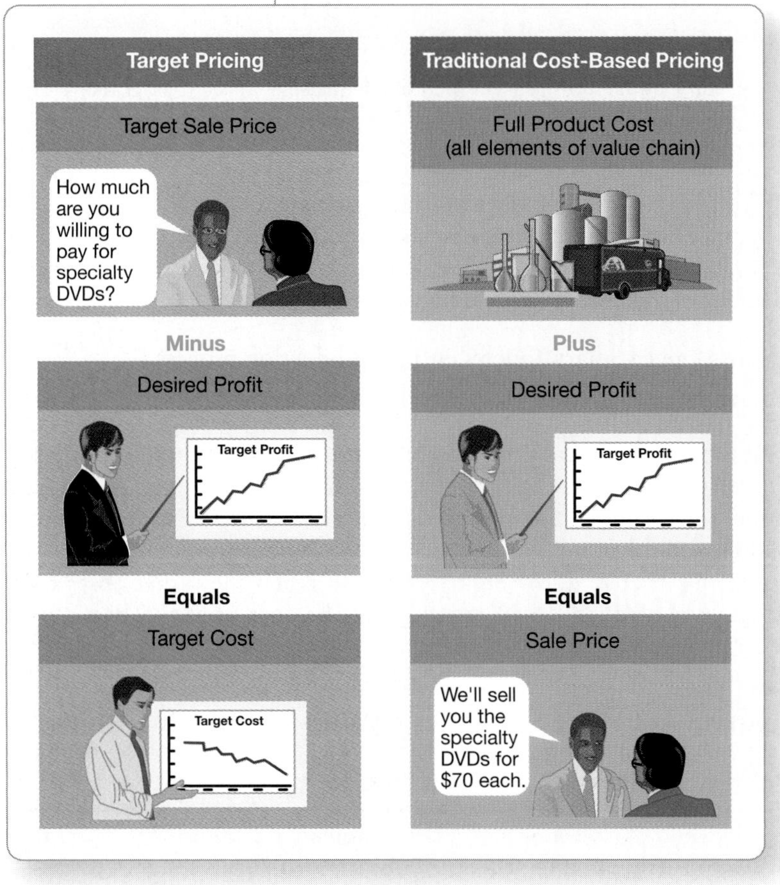

Instead of starting with product cost and then adding a profit to determine the sale price (right column of the exhibit), target pricing (left column) does just the opposite. Target pricing starts with the price that customers are willing to pay and then subtracts the company's desired profit to determine the **target cost**. Then the company works backward to develop the product at the target cost. The target cost is a goal for which the company must aim.

Let us return to our Smart Touch illustration. The ABC analysis in Exhibit 17-9, Panel A, prompts CEO Sheena Bright to push Excel DVDs because it appears that the specialty DVD is losing money. The marketing department says the selling price of the Excel DVDs is likely to fall to $10.00 per DVD. Bright wants to earn a profit equal to 20% of the sale price.

Full-product costs consider *all* costs, including nonmanufacturing costs, when determining target costs and target profits. What is Smart Touch's target full-product cost per Excel DVD? The following is the computation:

Target sale price per Excel DVD	$10.00
– Desired profit ($10.00 × 20%)	(2.00)
= Target cost per Excel DVD	$ 8.00

Does Smart Touch's current full-product cost meet this target? Let us see.

Current total manufacturing cost per Excel DVD	$7.00
+ Nonmanufacturing costs (operating expenses—amount assumed)	1.10
= Current full-product cost per Excel DVD	$8.10

Smart Touch's current cost does not meet the target cost.

Because Smart Touch's current full-product cost, $8.10, exceeds the target cost of $8.00, Bright assembles a value-engineering team to identify ways to cut costs. The team analyzes each production activity. For each activity, the team considers how to

- cut costs, given Smart Touch's current production process.
- redesign the production process to further cut costs.

Of the team's several proposals, Bright decides to *Redesign Setup to reduce the setup cost per batch*. Group raw materials that are used together to reduce the time required to assemble the materials for each setup. Estimated cost saving is $160,000, and the number of batches remains unchanged at 40.

Will this change allow Smart Touch to reach the target cost? Exhibit 17-11 shows how controller Kolen recomputes the cost of Setup based on the value-engineering study.

EXHIBIT 17-11 Recomputing Activity Costs After a Value-Engineering Study

		Manufacturing Overhead						
		Setup		DVD burning		Assembly		Total Cost
Estimated total indirect costs of activity:								
Setup ($600,000 – $160,000)		$440,000						
Estimated total quantity of each allocation base		40 batches						
Compute the cost allocation rate for each activity:								
(Divide estimated indirect cost by estimated		$440,000		Amounts		Amounts		
quantity of the allocation base)	÷	40 batches		From		From		
Cost allocation rate for each activity	=	$ 11,000		Exhibit		Exhibit		
Actual quantity of each allocation base used by Excel DVDs:				17-8		17-8		
Setup	×	3 batches						
Allocated Costs	=	$ 33,000	+	$5,000	+	$10,000	=	$48,000

Exhibit 17-12 shows that value engineering cuts total manufacturing overhead cost of the Excel DVDs to $48,000 from $60,000 (in Exhibit 17-8). Now Kolen totals the revised cost estimates for Excel DVDs.

EXHIBIT 17-12 **ABC Costs After Value–Engineering Study**

PANEL A—Manufacturing Cost under ABC After Value–Engineering Study

	Excel DVD
Manufacturing Overhead Costs	
Setup (from Exhibit 17-11)	$33,000
DVD Burning (amounts assumed)	5,000
Case Assembly (from Exhibit 17-4, based on .10 per insert) Each Excel DVD has 1 insert. Each specialty DVD has 7 inserts.	10,000
Total manufacturing overhead cost	48,000
Divide by number of DVDs produced	100,000
Manufacturing overhead cost per DVD under ABC after Value-Engineering Study	$ 0.48

PANEL B—Total Manufacturing Cost and Full Product Cost Under ABC After Value–Engineering Study

	Excel DVD
Manufacturing cost per DVD:	
Direct materials	2.40
Direct labor	4.00
Manufacturing overhead (from Panel A)	0.48
Total manufacturing cost per DVD-after Value-Engineering Study	6.88
Non manufacturing costs (assumed)	$1.10
Full product cost-after Value-Engineering Study	$7.98

Cost of $6.88 is quite an improvement from the prior manufacturing cost of $7.00 per DVD (Exhibit 17-9, Panel A). Now Smart Touch's full cost of $7.98 is less than its target full product cost of $8.00. Value engineering worked.

Decision Guidelines

ACTIVITY-BASED COSTING

Several years ago **Dell** refined its cost system. Starting with an Excel spreadsheet, **Dell** developed a simple ABC system to focus on its 10 most critical activities. Here are some of the decisions **Dell** faced as it began refining its cost system.

Decision	Guidelines
• How to develop an ABC system?	1. Identify each activity and estimate its total indirect costs. 2. Identify the cost driver for each activity. Then estimate the total quantity of each driver's allocation base. 3. Compute the cost allocation rate for each activity. 4. Allocate indirect costs to the cost object.
• How to compute a cost allocation rate for an activity?	$\dfrac{\text{Estimated total indirect cost of the activity}}{\text{Estimated total quantity of the allocation base}}$
• How to allocate an activity's cost to the cost object?	**Cost allocation rate for the activity × Actual quantity of the allocation base used by the cost object**
• For what kinds of decisions do managers use ABC?	Managers use ABC data to decide on the following: • Pricing and product mix • Cost cutting
• How to set target costs?	**Target sale price (based on market research) – Desired profit = Target cost**
• How to achieve target costs?	Use value engineering to cut costs by improving product design and production processes.
• What are the main benefits of ABC?	• More accurate product cost information • More detailed information on the costs of activities and their cost drivers helps managers control costs.

Summary Problem 1

Indianapolis Auto Parts (IAP) has a Seat Manufacturing Department that uses activity-based costing. IAP's system has the following features:

Activity	Allocation Base	Cost Allocation Rate
Purchasing	Number of purchase orders	$50.00 per purchase order
Assembling	Number of parts	$0.50 per part
Packaging	Number of finished seats	$1.00 per finished seat

Each auto seat has 20 parts. Direct materials cost per seat is $11. Suppose **Ford** has asked IAP for a bid on 50,000 built-in baby seats that would be installed as an option on some **Ford** SUVs. IAP will use a total of 200 purchase orders if **Ford** accepts IAP's bid.

Requirements

1. Compute the total cost IAP will incur to (a) purchase the needed materials and then (b) assemble and (c) package 50,000 baby seats. Also compute the average cost per seat.
2. For bidding, IAP adds a 30% markup to total cost. What total price will IAP bid for the entire **Ford** order?
3. Suppose that instead of an ABC system, IAP has a traditional product costing system that allocates all costs other than direct materials at the rate of $65 per direct labor hour. The baby-seat order will require 10,000 direct labor hours. What price will IAP bid using this system's total cost?
4. Use your answers to requirements 2 and 3 to explain how ABC can help IAP make a better decision about the bid price to offer **Ford**.

Solution

Requirement 1

Total Cost of Order and Average Cost per Seat:

Direct materials, 50,000 × $11.00	$ 550,000
Activity costs:	
Purchasing, 200 × $50.00	10,000
Assembling, 50,000 × 20 × $0.50	500,000
Packaging, 50,000 × $1.00	50,000
Total cost of order	$1,110,000
Divide by number of seats	÷ 50,000
Average cost per seat	$ 22.20

Requirement 2

Bid Price (ABC System):

Bid price ($1,110,000 × 130%)	**$1,443,000**

Requirement 3

Bid Price (Traditional System):

Direct materials, 50,000 × $11.00	$ 550,000
Other product costs, 10,000 × $65	650,000
Total cost of order	$1,200,000
Bid price ($1,200,000 × 130%)	$1,560,000

Requirement 4

IAP's bid would be $117,000 higher using the traditional system than using ABC ($1,560,000 – $1,443,000). Assuming the ABC system more accurately captures the costs caused by the order, the traditional system over costs the order. This leads to a higher bid price and reduces IAP's chance of winning the bid. The ABC system can increase IAP's chance of getting the order by bidding a lower price.

Just-In-Time (JIT) Systems

3 Describe a just-in-time (JIT) production system, and record its transactions

Competition is fierce, especially in manufacturing and technology-related services. Chinese and Indian companies are producing high-quality goods at very low costs. As we saw in the discussion of activity-based costing, there is a never-ending quest to cut costs.

The cost of buying, storing, and moving inventory can be significant for **Home Depot**, **Toyota**, and **Dell**. To lower inventory costs, many companies use a just-in-time (JIT) system.

Companies with JIT systems buy materials and complete finished goods *just in time* for delivery to customers. Production is completed in self-contained work cells as shown in Exhibit 17-13 on the following page. Each cell includes the machinery and labor resources to manufacture a product. Employees work in a team and are empowered to complete the work without supervision. Workers complete a small batch of units and are responsible for inspecting for quality throughout the process. As the completed product moves out of the work cell, the suppliers deliver more materials just in time to keep production moving along.

By contrast, traditional production systems separate manufacturing into various processing departments that focus on a single activity. Work in process moves from one department to another. That wastes time, and wasted time is wasted money.

Under JIT, a customer's order—customer demand—triggers manufacturing. The sales order "pulls" materials, labor, and overhead into production. This "demand–pull" system extends back to the suppliers of materials. Suppliers make frequent deliveries of defect-free materials *just in time* for production. Purchasing only what customers demand reduces inventory. Less inventory frees floor space for more productive use. Thus, JIT systems help to reduce waste. Exhibit 17-13 shows a traditional production system in Panel B. The traditional system requires more inventory, more workers, and usually costs more to operate than a JIT system.

Companies like **Toyota**, **Carrier**, and **Dell** credit JIT for saving the companies millions. But JIT systems are not without problems. With no inventory buffers, JIT users lose sales when they cannot get materials on time, or when poor-quality materials arrive just in time. There is no way to make up for lost time. As a result, strong relationships with quality raw materials vendors are very important to JIT. Additionally, many JIT companies still maintain small inventories of critical materials.

EXHIBIT 17-13 Production Flow Comparison: Just-in-Time versus Traditional Production

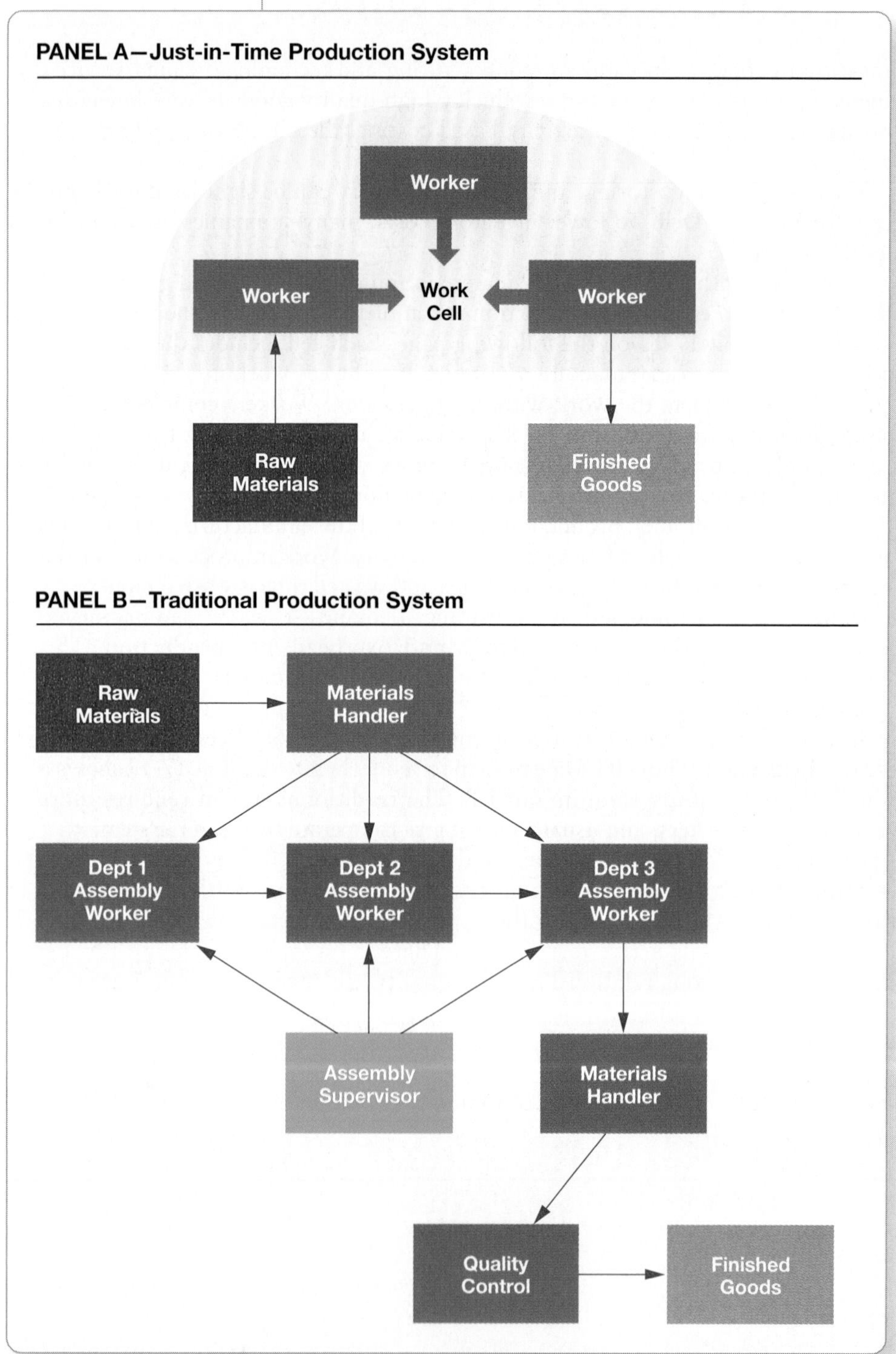

Just-in-Time Costing

JIT costing leads many companies to simplify their accounting. **Just-in-time costing,** sometimes called **backflush costing,** seems to work backwards. JIT costing starts with output that has been completed and then assigns manufacturing costs to units sold and to inventories. There are three major differences between JIT costing and traditional standard costing as shown in Exhibit 17-14:

1. JIT systems do not track the cost of products from Raw materials inventory to Work in process inventory to Finished goods inventory. Instead, JIT costing waits until the units are completed to record the cost of production.
2. JIT systems combine raw materials and work in process inventories into a single account called **Raw and in-process inventory**.
3. Under the JIT philosophy, workers perform many tasks. Most companies using JIT combine labor and manufacturing overhead costs into a single account called Conversion costs. *Conversion costs* is a temporary account that works just like the Manufacturing overhead account. Actual conversion costs accumulate as debits in the Conversion costs account. This account is credited when conversion costs are allocated to completed units. Accountants close any under- or overallocated conversion costs to Cost of goods sold at the end of the year, just like they do for under- or overallocated manufacturing overhead.

EXHIBIT 17-14 | Comparison of Traditional and Just-in-Time Costing

	Traditional	Just-in-Time
Recording production activity	Build the costs of products as they move from raw materials into work in process and on to finished goods inventory	Record the costs of products when units are completed
Inventory accounts	Materials inventory Work in process inventory Finished goods inventory	Raw and in-process inventory Finished goods inventory
Manufacturing costs	Direct materials Direct labor Manufacturing overhead	Direct materials Conversion costs

JIT Costing Illustrated: Smart Touch Learning

To illustrate JIT costing, let us continue with our Smart Touch Learning example. Smart Touch has only one direct material cost: blank DVDs. This cost is recorded in the Raw and in-process inventory account. All other manufacturing costs—including labor, various materials, and overhead—are indirect costs of converting the "raw" DVDs into finished goods (DVD learning systems). All these indirect costs are collected in the Conversion costs account.

JIT does not use a separate Work in process inventory account. Instead, it uses only two inventory accounts:

- Raw and in-process inventory, which combines direct materials with work in process
- Finished goods inventory

Assume that on January 31, Smart Touch had $100,000 of beginning Raw and in-process inventory, and $200,000 of beginning Finished goods inventory. During February, Smart Touch uses JIT costing to record the following transactions:

1. Smart Touch purchased $240,000 of direct materials (blank DVDs) on account.

1.		Raw and in-process inventory (A+)	240,000	
		Accounts payable (L+)		240,000
		Purchased direct materials on account.		

2. Smart Touch spent $590,000 on labor and overhead.

2.		Conversion costs (E+)	590,000	
		Wages payable, Accumulated depreciation, etc.		590,000
		Incurred conversion costs.		

3. Smart Touch completed 115,000 Excel DVDs that it moved to Finished goods. Recall that the standard cost of each Excel DVD in Exhibit 17-9 is $7 ($2.40 direct materials + $4.60 conversion costs). The debit (increase) to Finished goods inventory is a standard cost of $805,000 (115,000 completed Excel DVDs × $7). There is no work in process inventory in JIT costing, so Smart Touch credits the following:

3.		Finished goods inventory (115,000 × $7) (A+)	805,000	
		Raw and in-process inventory (115,000 × $2.40) (A–)		276,000
		Conversion costs (115,000 × $4.60) (E–)		529,000
		Completed production.		

- Raw and in-process inventory for the blank DVDs, $276,000 (115,000 completed Excel DVDs × $2.40 standard raw material cost per DVD)
- Conversion costs for the labor and other indirect costs allocated to the finished circuits, $529,000 (115,000 completed Excel DVDs × $4.60 standard conversion cost per DVD)

This is the essence of JIT costing. The system does not track costs as the DVDs move through manufacturing. Instead, *completion* of the DVDs triggers the accounting system to go back and pull costs from Raw and in-process inventory and to allocate conversion costs to the finished products.

4. Smart Touch sold 110,000 Excel DVDs (110,000 DVDs × cost of $7 per DVD = $770,000). The cost of goods sold entry is as follows:

4.		Cost of goods sold (E+)	770,000	
		Finished goods inventory (A–)		770,000
		Cost of sales.		

Exhibit 17-15 shows Smart Touch's relevant accounts. Combining raw materials with work in process to form the single Raw and in-process inventory account eliminates detail.

EXHIBIT 17-15 | Smart Touch Learning's JIT Costing Accounts

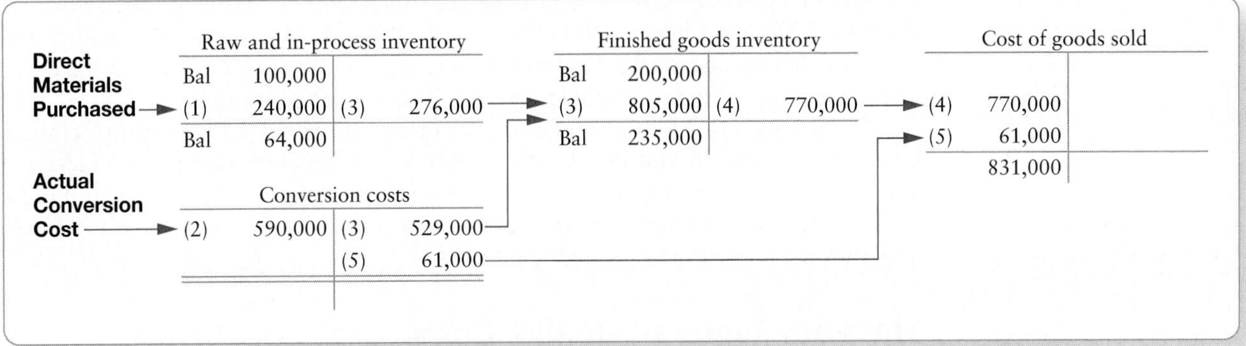

5. You can see from Exhibit 17-15 that conversion costs are underallocated by $61,000 (actual cost of $590,000 – applied cost of $529,000). Under- and overallocated conversion costs are treated just like under- and overallocated manufacturing overhead and closed to Cost of goods sold, as follows:

5.		Cost of goods sold (E+)	61,000	
		Conversion costs (E–)		61,000
		Closed conversion costs on account.		

In the final analysis, cost of goods sold for February is $831,000, as shown in the T-account in Exhibit 17-15.

Stop & Think...

If you were to go to the grocery store today, you could either buy just the ingredients you need to make dinner tonight or you could purchase enough groceries to last you two weeks. If you purchase for two weeks, can you be sure you'll use all the groceries you buy or will some of it "go bad" before you eat it? Choosing to purchase just enough to get you through a short period (today) is like Just-In-Time costing. Companies purchase just enough raw materials for the production needs of the next day or two, rather than purchasing large amounts of raw materials that have to be stored.

Continuous Improvement and the Management of Quality

Companies using just-in-time production systems strive for high-quality production. Poor-quality materials or defective products shut down production, and that runs counter to the JIT philosophy.

4 Use the four types of quality costs to make decisions

To meet this challenge, many companies adopt *total quality management (TQM)*. The goal of TQM is to provide customers with superior products and services. In TQM, each business function monitors its activities to improve quality and eliminate defects and waste. Continuous improvement is the goal. Take a break, or miss a beat, and another manufacturer will put you out of business.

Well-designed products reduce inspections, rework, and warranty claims. Investing in research and development (R&D) can generate savings in marketing and customer service. World-class companies like **Toyota** and **Dell** *design* and *build* quality into their products rather than having to *inspect* and *repair* later. Let us see how they achieve the goal of high quality.

The Four Types of Quality Costs

The four types of quality-related costs are as follows:

1. **Prevention costs** are costs spent to *avoid* poor-quality goods or services.
2. **Appraisal costs** are costs spent to *detect* poor-quality goods or services.
3. **Internal failure costs** are costs spent to avoid poor-quality goods or services *before* delivery to customers.
4. **External failure costs** are costs spent after the company *delivers poor-quality goods or services* to customers and then has to make things right with the customer.

Exhibit 17-16 gives examples of the four types of quality costs. Most prevention costs occur in the R&D stage of the value chain. In contrast, most appraisal and internal failure costs occur in production. External failure occurs in customer service or, worse, it results from lost sales due to an unhappy customer. Prevention is much cheaper than external failure.

EXHIBIT 17-16 Four Types of Quality Costs

Prevention Costs	Appraisal Costs
Training personnel	Inspection at various stages of production
Improved materials	Inspection of final products or services
Preventive maintenance	Product testing
Internal Failure Costs	**External Failure Costs**
Production loss caused by downtime	Lost profits due to unhappy customers
Rework	Warranty costs
Rejected product units	Service costs at customer sites
	Sales returns due to product defects

Stop & Think...

Do you go to the dentist every six months to have your teeth cleaned? The cost of the cleaning is a prevention cost. By investing in the care of your teeth, not only do your teeth look nice, but you hope to *prevent* decay in your teeth. Preventing that decay helps you to avoid a bigger dentist bill for repairing your teeth in the future. The same is true for producing products. Monies spent on improving quality are much cheaper than monies spent to repair defective products in the future.

Deciding Whether to Adopt a New Quality Program

Let us revisit Smart Touch Learning. CEO Sheena Bright is considering spending the following on a new quality program:

Inspect raw materials	$100,000
Reengineer to improve product quality	750,000
Inspect finished goods	150,000
Preventive maintenance of equipment	100,000

Smart Touch expects this quality program to reduce costs by the following amounts:

Avoid lost profits due to unhappy customers	$800,000
Fewer sales returns	50,000
Decrease the cost of rework	250,000
Lower warranty costs	100,000

Bright asks controller Kolen to

1. classify each cost into one of the four categories (prevention, appraisal, internal failure, external failure). Total the estimated cost for each category.
2. recommend whether Smart Touch should undertake the quality program. Kolen uses Exhibit 17-17 to compare the costs to
   - undertake the quality program, or
   - not undertake the quality program.

EXHIBIT 17-17 Analysis of Smart Touch's Proposed Quality Program

Undertake the Quality Program		Do Not Undertake the Quality Program	
Prevention		**Internal Failure**	
Reengineer to improve product quality	$ 750,000	Cost of rework	$ 250,000
Preventive maintenance of equipment	100,000	Total internal failure costs	$ 250,000
Total prevention costs	$ 850,000		
		External Failure	
		Lost profits due to unhappy customers	$ 800,000
Appraisal		Sales returns	50,000
Inspect raw materials	$ 100,000	Warranty costs	100,000
Inspect finished goods	150,000	Total external failure costs	$ 950,000
Total appraisal costs	$ 250,000	**Total costs of not undertaking the quality program**	$1,200,000
Total costs of the quality program	$1,100,000		

Decision: Undertake the Quality Program and Save $100,000.

These estimates suggest that Smart Touch would save $100,000 ($1,200,000 – $1,100,000) by undertaking the quality program.

Quality costs can be hard to measure. For example, it is very hard to measure external failure costs. Lost profits due to unhappy customers do not appear in the accounting records! Therefore, TQM uses lots of nonfinancial measures such as the number of customer complaints and the volume of incoming customer-service phone calls as a means to measure success or failure.

Decision Guidelines

JUST-IN-TIME AND QUALITY COSTS

Dell is famous for using just-in-time production and total quality management. **Dell's** managers made the following decisions.

Decision	Guidelines	
• How to change from traditional production to JIT?	*Traditional*	*JIT*
	Similar machines grouped together	Production cells
	Larger batches	Smaller batches
	Higher inventories	Lower inventories
	Each worker does a few tasks	Each worker does a wide range of tasks
	Many suppliers	Fewer, but well-coordinated suppliers
• How does costing work under JIT?	Under JIT costing, 1. raw materials and work in process are combined into a single Raw and in-process inventory account. 2. labor and overhead are combined into a Conversion costs account. 3. summary journal entries are recorded *after* units are completed.	
• What are the four types of quality costs?	Prevention Appraisal Internal failure External failure	
• How to manage the four types of quality costs?	Invest up front in prevention and appraisal to reduce internal and external failure costs.	

Summary Problem 2

Flores Company manufactures cell phones and uses JIT costing. The standard unit cost is $30: $20 direct materials and $10 conversion costs. Direct materials purchased on account during June totaled $2,500,000. Actual conversion costs totaled $1,100,000. Flores completed 100,000 cell phones in June and sold 98,000.

Requirements

1. Journalize these transactions.
2. Were conversion costs under- or overallocated? Explain your answer and then make the entry to close the Conversion costs account.
3. How much Cost of goods sold did Flores have in June?

Solution

Requirement 1

	Raw and in-process inventory (A+)	2,500,000	
	Accounts payable (L+)		2,500,000
	Conversion costs (E+)	1,100,000	
	Wages payable, Accumulated depreciation, etc.		1,100,000
	Finished goods inventory (A+)	3,000,000	
	Raw and in-process inventory (100,000 × $20) (A–)		2,000,000
	Conversion costs (100,000 × $10) (E–)		1,000,000
	Cost of goods sold (98,000 × $30) (E+)	2,940,000	
	Finished goods inventory (A–)		2,940,000

Requirement 2

	Conversion costs were underallocated. Actual costs ($1,100,000) exceeded the cost allocated to inventory ($1,000,000).		
	Cost of goods sold (E+)	100,000	
	Conversion costs (E–)		100,000

Requirement 3

COGS = $3,040,000 ($2,940,000 + $100,000)

Review Activity-Based Costing and Other Cost Management Tools

Accounting Vocabulary

Activity-Based Costing (ABC) (p. 931)
Focuses on activities as the fundamental cost objects. The costs of those activities become building blocks for compiling the indirect costs of products, services, and customers.

Activity-Based Management (ABM) (p. 935)
Using activity-based cost information to make decisions that increase profits while satisfying customers need s.

Appraisal Costs (p. 948)
Costs incurred to detect poor-quality goods or services.

Backflush Costing (p. 944)
A standard costing system that starts with output completed and then assigns manufacturing costs to units sold and to inventories. Also called **just-in-time costing**.

External Failure Costs (p. 948)
Costs incurred when the company does not detect poor-quality goods or services until after delivery to customers.

Internal Failure Costs (p. 948)
Costs incurred when the company detects and corrects poor-quality goods or services before delivery to customers.

Just-in-Time (JIT) Costing (p. 944)
A standard costing system that starts with output completed and then assigns manufacturing costs to units sold and to inventories. Also called **backflush costing**.

Prevention Costs (p. 948)
Costs incurred to avoid poor-quality goods or services.

Raw and In-Process Inventory (p. 945)
Combined account for raw materials and work in process inventories under JIT systems.

Target Cost (p. 937)
Allowable cost to develop, produce, and deliver the product or service. Equals target price minus desired profit.

Target Price (p. 937)
What customers are willing to pay for the product or service.

Value Engineering (p. 937)
Reevaluating activities to reduce costs while satisfying customer needs.

Quick Check

1. Which statement is *false*?
   a. Information technology makes it feasible for most companies to adopt ABC.
   b. An ABC system is more refined than one that uses a company-wide overhead rate.
   c. ABC focuses on indirect costs.
   d. ABC is primarily for manufacturing companies.

Use the following information for questions 2–4. Two of Keyboard's production activities are *kitting* (assembling the raw materials needed for each computer in one kit) and *boxing* the completed products for shipment to customers. Assume that Keyboard spends $8 million a month on kitting and $16 million a month on boxing. Keyboard allocates the following:

- Kitting costs based on the number of parts used in the computer
- Boxing costs based on the cubic feet of space the computer requires

Suppose Keyboard estimates it will use 700 million parts a month and ship products with a total volume of 25 million cubic feet.

Assume that each desktop computer requires 100 parts and has a volume of 5 cubic feet.

2. What is the activity cost allocation rate?

	Kitting	Boxing
a.	$0.01/part	$0.02/cubic foot
b.	$0.01/part	$0.64/cubic foot
c.	$0.32/part	$0. 02/cubic foot
d.	$87.50/part	$1.56/cubic foot

3. What are the kitting and boxing costs assigned to one desktop computer?

	Kitting	Boxing
a.	$1.92	$0.26
b.	$3.20	$4.00
c.	$0.50	$0.16
d.	$1.00	$3.20

4. Keyboard contracts with its suppliers to pre-kit certain component parts before delivering them to Keyboard. Assume this saves $1.0 million of the kitting cost and reduces the total number of parts by 300 million (because Keyboard considers each pre-kit as one part). If a desktop now uses 80 parts, what is the new kitting cost assigned to one desktop?
   a. $1.00
   b. $1.60
   c. $0.80
   d. $4.00

5. Keyboard can use ABC information for what decisions?
   a. Product mix
   b. Cost cutting
   c. Pricing
   d. All of the above

6. Which of the following is true for **Dell**, the computer company?
   a. Most of **Dell's** costs are for direct materials and direct labor. Indirect costs are a small proportion of total costs.
   b. ABC helps **Dell** keep costs low and remain competitive.
   c. **Dell** uses only a few activities, so a companywide overhead allocation rate would serve **Dell** quite well.
   d. All the above are true.

7. Companies enjoy many benefits from using JIT. Which is *not* a benefit of adopting JIT?
   a. More space available for production
   b. Ability to continue production despite disruptions in deliveries of raw materials
   c. Ability to respond quickly to changes in customer demand
   d. Lower inventory carrying costs

8. Which account is *not* used in JIT costing?
   a. Finished goods inventory
   b. Raw and in-process inventory
   c. Work in process inventory
   d. Conversion costs

9. The cost of lost future sales after a customer finds a defect in a product is which type of quality cost?
   a. Internal failure cost
   b. Prevention cost
   c. External failure cost
   d. Appraisal cost

10. Spending on testing a product before shipment to customers is which type of quality cost?
   a. Appraisal cost
   b. External failure cost
   c. Prevention cost
   d. None of the above

Answers are given after Apply Your Knowledge (p. 974).

Assess Your Progress

■ Short Exercises

S17-1 *(L. OBJ. 1)* **Activity-based costing [5–10 min]**
Activity-based costing requires four steps.

Requirement

1. Rank the following steps in the order in which they would be completed. Number the first step as "1" until you have ranked all four steps.
   a. Compute the cost allocation rate for each activity.
   b. Identify the cost driver for each activity and estimate the total quantity of each driver's allocation base.
   c. Allocate indirect costs to the cost object.
   d. Identify each activity and estimate its total indirect cost.

S17-2 *(L. OBJ. 1)* **Calculating costs using Traditional and ABC [10 min]**
Blake and Roscoe are college friends planning a skiing trip to Aspen before the New Year. They estimated the following costs for the trip:

	Estimated Costs	Cost Driver	Activity Allocation	
			Blake	Roscoe
Food	$ 600	Pounds of food eaten	20	30
Skiing	210	# of lift tickets	3	0
Lodging	400	# of nights	2	2
	$ 1,210			

Requirements

1. Blake suggests that the costs be shared equally. Calculate the amount each person would pay.
2. Roscoe does not like the idea because he plans to stay in the room rather than ski. Roscoe suggests that each type of cost be allocated to each person based on the above listed cost driver. Using the activity allocation for each person, calculate the amount that each person would pay based on his own consumption of the activity.

S17-3 *(L.OBJ. 1)* **Computing indirect manufacturing costs per unit [15 min]**
Durkin, Corp., is considering the use of activity-based costing. The following information is provided for the production of two product lines:

Activity		Cost	Cost Driver
Setup	$	107,000	Number of setups
Machine maintenance		50,000	Machine hours
Total indirect manufacturing costs	$	157,000	

	Product A	Product B	Total
Direct labor hours	7,000	3,000	10,000
Number of setups	30	70	100
Number of machine hours	1,200	3,800	5,000

Durkin plans to produce 350 units of Product A and 225 units of Product B.

Requirement

1. Compute the ABC indirect manufacturing cost per unit for each product.

S17-4 *(L.OBJ. 1)* **Computing indirect manufacturing costs per unit [15 min]**
The following information is provided for the Asteroid Antenna, Corp., which manufactures two products: Lo-Gain antennas, and Hi-Gain antennas for use in remote areas.

Activity		Cost	Cost Driver
Setup	$	55,000	Number of setups
Machine maintenance		39,000	Machine hours
Total indirect manufacturing costs	$	94,000	

	Lo-Gain	Hi-Gain	Total
Direct labor hours	1,700	5,800	7,500
Number of setups	25	25	50
Number of machine hours	2,100	1,400	3,500

Asteroid plans to produce 200 Lo-Gain antennas and 325 Hi-Gain antennas.

Requirements

1. Compute the ABC indirect manufacturing cost per unit for each product.
2. Compute the indirect manufacturing cost per unit using direct labor hours from the single-allocation-base system.

S17-5 *(L.OBJ. 1)* **Using ABC to compute product costs per unit [15 min]**
Daily, Corp., makes two products: C and D. The following data have been summarized:

		Product C		Product D
Direct materials cost per unit	$	900	$	2,100
Direct labor cost per unit		400		200
Indirect manufacturing cost per unit		?		?

Indirect manufacturing cost information includes the following:

Activity	Allocation Rate		Allocation Base Units	
			Product C	Product D
Setup	$	1,000	37	77
Machine maintenance	$	11	1,350	3,850

The company plans to manufacture 225 units of each product.

Requirement

1. Calculate the product cost per unit for Products C and D using activity-based costing.

S17-6 *(L.OBJ. 1)* **Using ABC to compute product costs per unit [15 min]**
Johnstone, Corp., manufactures mid-fi and hi-fi stereo receivers. The following data have been summarized:

	Mid–Fi		Hi–Fi	
Direct materials cost per unit	$	500	$	1,200
Direct labor cost per unit		300		200
Indirect manufacturing cost per unit		?		?

Indirect manufacturing cost information includes:

Activity	Allocation Rate		Allocation Base Units	
			Mid–Fi	Hi–Fi
Setup	$	1,000	36	36
Inspections	$	600	35	20
Machine maintenance	$	14	1,650	1,450

The company plans to manufacture 75 units of the mid-fi receivers and 325 units of the hi-fi receivers.

Requirement

1. Calculate the product cost per unit for both products using activity-based costing.

S17-7 *(L.OBJ. 1)* **Allocating indirect costs and computing income [10 min]**
Antics, Inc., is a technology consulting firm focused on Web site development and integration of Internet business applications. The president of the company expects to incur $719,600 of indirect costs this year, and she expects her firm to work 8,000 direct labor hours. Antics' systems consultants earn $350 per hour. Clients are billed at 150% of direct labor cost. Last month Antics' consultants spent 100 hours on Crickett's engagement.

Requirements

1. Compute Antics' indirect cost allocation rate per direct labor hour.
2. Compute the total cost assigned to the Crickett engagement.
3. Compute the operating income from the Crickett engagement.

Note: Short Exercise 17-7 must be completed before attempting Short Exercise 17-8.

S17-8 *(L.OBJ. 1)* **Computing ABC allocation rates [5 min]**

Refer to Short Exercise 17-7. The president of Antics suspects that her allocation of indirect costs could be giving misleading results, so she decides to develop an ABC system. She identifies three activities: documentation preparation, information technology support, and training. She figures that documentation costs are driven by the number of pages, information technology support costs are driven by the number of software applications used, and training costs are driven by the number of direct labor hours worked. Estimates of the costs and quantities of the allocation bases follow:

Activity	Estimated Cost	Allocation Base	Estimated Quantity of Allocation Base
Documentation preparation	$ 100,000	Pages	3,125 pages
Information technology support	159,600	Applications used	760 applications
Training	460,000	Direct labor hours	4,600 hours
Total indirect costs	$ 719,600		

Requirement

1. Compute the cost allocation rate for each activity.

Note: Short Exercises 17-7 and 17-8 must be completed before attempting Short Exercise 17-9.

S17-9 *(L.OBJ. 1)* **Using ABC to allocate costs and compute profit [10–15 min]**

Refer to Short Exercises 17-7 and 17-8. Suppose Antics' direct labor rate was $350 per hour, the documentation cost was $32 per page, the information technology support cost was $210 per application, and training costs were $100 per direct labor hour. The Crickett engagement used the following resources last month:

Cost Driver	Crickett
Direct labor hours	100
Pages	300
Applications used	74

Requirements

1. Compute the cost assigned to the Crickett engagement, using the ABC system.
2. Compute the operating income from the Crickett engagement, using the ABC system.

Note: Short Exercise 17-9 must be completed before attempting Short Exercise 17-10.

S17-10 *(L.OBJ. 2)* **Using ABC to achieve target profit [10–15 min]**

Refer to Short Exercise 17-9. Antics desires a 20% target profit after covering all costs.

Requirement

1. Considering the total costs assigned to the Crickett engagement in 17-9, what would Antics have to charge the customer to achieve that profit?

S17-11 *(L.OBJ. 3)* **Just-in-time characteristics [5–10 min]**
Consider the following characteristics of either a JIT production system or a traditional production system.

a. Products produced in large batches.
b. Large stocks of finished goods protect against lost sales if customer demand is higher than expected.
c. Suppliers make frequent deliveries of small quantities of raw materials.
d. Long setup times.
e. Employees do a variety of jobs, including maintenance and setups as well as operating machines.
f. Machines are grouped into self-contained production cells or production lines.
g. Machines are grouped according to function. For example, all cutting machines are located in one area.
h. Suppliers can access the company's intranet.
i. The final operation in the production sequence "pulls" parts from the preceding operation.
j. Each employee is responsible for inspecting his or her own work.
k. Management works with suppliers to ensure defect-free raw materials.

Requirement

1. Indicate whether each is characteristic of a JIT production system or a traditional production system.

S17-12 *(L.OBJ. 3)* **Recording JIT costing journal entries [10 min]**
Prized Products uses a JIT system to manufacture trading pins for the **Hard Rock Café**. The standard cost per pin is $1 for raw materials and $2 for conversion costs. Last month Prized recorded the following data:

Number of pins completed	4,100 pins	Raw material purchases	$	7,500
Number of pins sold	3,700 pins	Conversion costs	$	12,000

Requirement

1. Use JIT costing to prepare journal entries for the month, including the entry to close the Conversion costs account.

S17-13 *(L.OBJ. 4)* **Matching cost-of-quality examples to categories [5–10 min]**
Harry, Inc., manufactures motor scooters. Consider each of the following examples of quality costs.

_____ 1. Preventive maintenance on machinery
_____ 2. Direct materials, direct labor, and manufacturing overhead costs incurred to rework a defective scooter that is detected in-house through inspection
_____ 3. Lost profits from lost sales if company's reputation was hurt because customers previously purchased a poor-quality scooter
_____ 4. Costs of inspecting raw materials, such as chassis and wheels
_____ 5. Working with suppliers to achieve on-time delivery of defect-free raw materials
_____ 6. Cost of warranty repairs on a scooter that malfunctions at customer's location
_____ 7. Costs of testing durability of vinyl
_____ 8. Cost to re-inspect reworked scooters

Requirement

1. Indicate which of the following quality cost categories each example represents.
   - P Prevention costs
   - A Appraisal costs
   - IF Internal failure costs
   - EF External failure costs

■ Exercises

E17-14 *(L.OBJ. 1)* **Product costing in an activity-based costing system [15–20 min]**
Farragut, Inc., uses activity-based costing to account for its chrome bumper manufacturing process. Company managers have identified four manufacturing activities: materials handling, machine setup, insertion of parts, and finishing. The budgeted activity costs for 2010 and their allocation bases are as follows:

Activity	Total Budgeted Cost		Allocation Base
Materials handling	$	6,000	Number of parts
Machine setup		3,300	Number of setups
Insertion of parts		54,000	Number of parts
Finishing		80,000	Finishing direct labor hours
Total	$	143,300	

Farragut expects to produce 1,000 chrome bumpers during the year. The bumpers are expected to use 3,000 parts, require 20 setups, and consume 2,000 hours of finishing time.

Requirements

1. Compute the cost allocation rate for each activity.
2. Compute the indirect manufacturing cost of each bumper.

E17-15 *(L.OBJ. 1)* **Product costing in an activity-based costing system [15–20 min]**
Tyler Champs Corp. uses activity-based costing to account for its motorcycle manufacturing process. Company managers have identified three supporting manufacturing activities: inspection, machine setup, and machine maintenance. The budgeted activity costs for 2011 and their allocation bases are as follows:

Activity	Total Budgeted Cost		Allocation Base
Inspection	$	6,600	Number of inspections
Machine setup		26,000	Number of setups
Machine maintenance		8,000	Maintenance hours
Total	$	40,600	

Tyler Champs expects to produce 10 custom-built motorcycles for the year. The motorcycles are expected to require 30 inspections, 10 setups, and 200 maintenance hours.

Requirements

1. Compute the cost allocation rate for each activity.
2. Compute the indirect manufacturing cost of each motorcycle.

E17-16 *(L.OBJ. 1)* **Product costing in an activity-based costing system [20–30 min]**
Erickson Company manufactures wheel rims. The controller budgeted the following ABC allocation rates for 2010:

Activity	Allocation Base	Cost Allocation Rate	
Materials handling	Number of parts	$ 6.00	per part
Machine setup	Number of setups	600.00	per setup
Insertion of parts	Number of parts	24.00	per part
Finishing	Finishing direct labor hours	30.00	per hour

The number of parts is now a feasible allocation base because Erickson recently purchased bar coding technology. Erickson produces two wheel rim models: standard and deluxe. Budgeted data for 2010 are as follows:

	Standard	Deluxe
Parts per rim	5.0	7.0
Setups per 1,000 rims	15.0	15.0
Finishing direct labor hours per rim	3.0	4.5
Total direct labor hours per rim	5.0	8.0

The company expects to produce 1,000 units of each model during the year.

Requirements

1. Compute the total budgeted indirect manufacturing cost for 2010.
2. Compute the ABC indirect manufacturing cost per unit of each model. Carry each cost to the nearest cent.
3. Prior to 2010, Erickson used a direct labor hour single-allocation-base system. Compute the (single) allocation rate based on direct labor hours for 2010. Use this rate to determine the indirect manufacturing cost per wheel rim for each model, to the nearest cent.

E17-17 *(L.OBJ. 1, 2)* **Using activity-based costing to make decisions [10 min]**
Fetch Dog Collars uses activity-based costing. Fetch's system has the following features:

Activity	Allocation Base	Cost Allocation Rate
Purchasing	Number of purchase orders	$57 per purchase order
Assembling	Number of parts	0.50 per part
Packaging	Number of finished collars	0.15 per collar

Each collar has 2 parts; direct materials cost per collar is $10. Suppose PetStart has asked for a bid on 20,000 dog collars. Fetch will issue a total of 175 purchase orders if PetStart accepts Fetch's bid.

Requirements

1. Compute the total cost Fetch will incur to purchase the needed materials and then assemble and package 20,000 dog collars. Also compute the cost per collar.
2. For bidding, Fetch adds a 35% markup to total cost. What total price will the company bid for the entire PetStart order?
3. Suppose that instead of an ABC system, Fetch has a traditional product costing system that allocates all costs other than direct materials at the rate of $9.20 per direct labor hour. The dog collar order will require 10,000 direct labor hours. What total price will Fetch bid using this system's total cost?
4. Use your answers to requirements 2 and 3 to explain how ABC can help Fetch make a better decision about the bid price it will offer PetSmart.

Note: Exercise 17-16 must be completed before attempting Exercise 17-18.

E17-18 *(L.OBJ. 2)* **Using activity-based costing to make decisions [15–20 min]**

Refer to Exercise 17-16. For 2011, Erickson's managers have decided to use the same indirect manufacturing costs per wheel rim that they computed in 2010. In addition to the unit indirect manufacturing costs, the following data are budgeted for the company's standard and deluxe models for 2011:

	Standard	Deluxe
Sales price	900.00	1,040.00
Direct materials	34.00	51.00
Direct labor	48.00	54.00

Because of limited machine-hour capacity, Erickson can produce *either* 2,000 standard rims *or* 2,000 deluxe rims.

Requirements

1. If Erickson's managers rely on the ABC unit cost data computed in 17-16, which model will they produce? Carry each cost to the nearest cent. (All nonmanufacturing costs are the same for both models.)
2. If the managers rely on the single-allocation-base cost data, which model will they produce?
3. Which course of action will yield more income for Erickson?

Note: Exercises 17-16 and 17-18 must be completed before attempting Exercise 17-19.

E17-19 *(L.OBJ. 2)* **Activity-based management and target cost [10 min]**

Refer to Exercises 17-16 and 17-18. Controller Michael Bender is surprised by the increase in cost of the deluxe model under ABC. Market research shows that for the deluxe rim to provide a reasonable profit, Erickson will have to meet a target manufacturing cost of $454 per rim. A value engineering study by Erickson's employees suggests that modifications to the finishing process could cut finishing cost from $30 to $20 per hour and reduce the finishing direct labor hours per deluxe rim from 4.5 hours to 4 hours. Direct materials would remain unchanged at $51 per rim, as would direct labor at $54 per rim. The materials handling, machine setup, and insertion of parts activity costs also would remain the same.

Requirement

1. Would implementing the value engineering recommendation enable Erickson to achieve its target cost for the deluxe rim?

E17-20 *(L.OBJ. 3)* **Recording manufacturing costs in a JIT costing system [15–20 min]**

Lally, Inc., produces universal remote controls. Lally uses a JIT costing system. One of the company's products has a standard direct materials cost of $7 per unit and a standard conversion cost of $26 per unit.

During January 2011, Lally produced 575 units and sold 570. It purchased $6,800 of direct materials and incurred actual conversion costs totaling $14,000.

Requirements

1. Prepare summary journal entries for January.
2. The January 1, 2011, balance of the Raw and in-process inventory account was $40. Use a T-account to find the January 31 balance.
3. Use a T-account to determine whether Conversion costs are over- or underallocated for the month. By how much? Give the journal entry to close the Conversion costs account.

E17-21 *(L.OBJ. 3)* **Recording manufacturing costs in a JIT costing system [10–15 min]**
Smith produces electronic calculators. Suppose Smith's standard cost per calculator is $26 for materials and $65 for conversion costs. The following data apply to July production:

Materials purchased	$ 7,200	
Conversion costs incurred	18,500	
Number of calculators produced		250 calculators
Number of calculators sold		245 calculators

Requirements

1. Prepare summary journal entries for July using JIT costing, including the entry to close the Conversion costs account.
2. The beginning balance of Finished goods inventory was $1,400. Use a T-account to find the ending balance of Finished goods inventory.

E17-22 *(L.OBJ. 4)* **Classifying quality costs [5–10 min]**
Millan & Co. makes electronic components. Mike Millan, the president, recently instructed vice president Steve Bensen to develop a total quality control program. "If we don't at least match the quality improvements our competitors are making," he told Bensen, "we'll soon be out of business." Bensen began by listing various "costs of quality" that Millan incurs. The first six items that came to mind were:

a. Costs incurred by Millan customer representatives traveling to customer sites to repair defective products
b. Lost profits from lost sales due to reputation for less-than-perfect products
c. Costs of inspecting components in one of Millan's production processes
d. Salaries of engineers who are designing components to withstand electrical overloads
e. Costs of reworking defective components after discovery by company inspectors
f. Costs of electronic components returned by customers

Requirement

1. Classify each item as a prevention cost, an appraisal cost, an internal failure cost, or an external failure cost.

E17-23 *(L.OBJ. 4)* **Classifying quality costs and using these costs to make decisions [15–20 min]**
Cleary, Inc., manufactures door panels. Suppose Cleary is considering spending the following amounts on a new total quality management (TQM) program:

Strength–testing one item from each batch of panels	$ 70,000
Training employees in TQM	27,000
Training suppliers in TQM	32,000
Identifying suppliers who commit to on–time delivery of perfect–quality materials	55,000

Cleary expects the new program would save costs through the following:

Avoid lost profits from lost sales due to disappointed customers	$ 92,000
Avoid rework and spoilage	66,000
Avoid inspection of raw materials	56,000
Avoid warranty costs	25,000

Requirements

1. Classify each cost as a prevention cost, an appraisal cost, an internal failure cost, or an external failure cost.
2. Should Cleary implement the new quality program? Give your reason.

E17-24 *(L.OBJ. 4)* **Classifying quality costs and using these costs to make decisions [10–15 min]**

Kelley manufactures high-quality speakers. Suppose Kelley is considering spending the following amounts on a new quality program:

Additional 20 minutes of testing for each speaker	$ 675,000
Negotiating with and training suppliers to obtain higher–quality materials and on–time delivery	430,000
Redesigning the speakers to make them easier to manufacture	1,100,000

Kelley expects this quality program to save costs, as follows:

Reduce warranty repair costs	$ 310,000
Avoid inspection of raw materials	510,000
Avoid rework because of fewer defective units	780,000

It also expects this program to avoid lost profits from the following:

Lost sales due to disappointed customers	$ 850,000
Lost production time due to rework	279,000

Requirements

1. Classify each of these costs into one of the four categories of quality costs (prevention, appraisal, internal failure, external failure).
2. Should Kelley implement the quality program? Give your reasons.

Problems (Group A)

P17-25A *(L.OBJ. 1)* **Product costing in an ABC system [15–20 min]**

The Alright Manufacturing Company in Hondo, Texas, assembles and tests electronic components used in handheld video phones. Consider the following data regarding component T24:

Direct materials cost	$ 84.00
Activity costs allocated	?
Manufacturing product cost	$?

The activities required to build the component follow:

Activity	Allocation Base	Cost Allocated to Each Unit
Start station	Number of raw component chasis	2 × $ 1.40 = $ 2.80
Dip insertion	Number of dip insertions	? × $ 0.40 = 12.00
Manual insertion	Number of manual insertions	12 × $ 0.60 = ?
Wave solder	Number of components soldered	2 × $ 1.40 = 2.80
Backload	Number of backload insertions	6 × $? = 5.40
Test	Testing hours	0.38 × $ 80.00 = ?
Defect analysis	Defect analysis hours	0.12 × $? = $ 3.60
Total		$?

Requirements

1. Fill in the blanks in both the opening schedule and the list of activities.
2. How is labor cost assigned to products under this ABC product costing system?
3. Why might managers favor this ABC system instead of Alright's older system, which allocated all conversion costs on the basis of direct labor?

P17-26A *(L.OBJ. 1, 2)* **Product costing in an ABC system [20–30 min]**
Allen, Inc., manufactures bookcases and uses an activity-based costing system. Allen's activity areas and related data follow:

Activity	Budgeted Cost of Activity	Allocation Base	Cost Allocation Rate
Materials handling	$ 22,000	Number of parts	$ 0.90
Assembly	3,000,000	Direct labor hours	12.00
Finishing	170,000	Number of finished units	3.90

Allen produced two styles of bookcases in April: the standard bookcase and an unfinished bookcase, which has fewer parts and requires no finishing. The totals for quantities, direct materials costs, and other data follow:

Product	Total Units Produced	Total Direct Materials Costs	Total Number of Parts	Total Assembling Direct Labor Hours
Standard bookcase	2,000	$ 29,600	82,000	3,300
Unfinished bookcase	2,600	28,600	86,000	2,000

Requirements

1. Compute the manufacturing product cost per unit of each type of bookcase.
2. Suppose that premanufacturing activities, such as product design, were assigned to the standard bookcases at $5 each, and to the unfinished bookcases at $4 each. Similar analyses were conducted of postmanufacturing activities such as distribution, marketing, and customer service. The postmanufacturing costs were $21 per standard bookcase and $18 per unfinished bookcase. Compute the full product costs per unit.
3. Which product costs are reported in the external financial statements? Which costs are used for management decision making? Explain the difference.
4. What price should Allen's managers set for unfinished bookcases to earn a unit profit of $19?

P17-27A *(L.OBJ. 1, 2)* **Comparing costs from ABC and single-rate systems [30–40 min]**
Willitte Pharmaceuticals manufactures an over-the-counter allergy medication. The company sells both large commercial containers of 1,000 capsules to health-care facilities and travel packs of 20 capsules to shops in airports, train stations, and hotels. The following information has been developed to determine if an activity-based costing system would be beneficial:

Activity	Estimated Indirect Activity Costs	Allocation Base	Estimated Quantity of Allocation Base
Materials handling	$ 115,000	Kilos	23,000 kilos
Packaging	204,000	Machine hours	2,125 hours
Quality assurance	118,000	Samples	2,000 samples
Total indirect costs	$ 437,000		

Other production information includes the following:

	Commerical Containers		Travel Packs	
Units produced	2,400	containers	41,000	packs
Weight in kilos	8,000		6,000	
Machine hours	1,500		500	
Number of samples	200		300	

Requirements

1. Compute the cost allocation rate for each activity.
2. Use the activity-based cost allocation rates to compute the activity costs per unit of the commercial containers and the travel packs. (*Hint*: First compute the total activity costs allocated to each product line, and then compute the cost per unit.)
3. Willitte's original single-allocation-base costing system allocated indirect costs to products at $158 per machine hour. Compute the total indirect costs allocated to the commercial containers and to the travel packs under the original system. Then compute the indirect cost per unit for each product.
4. Compare the activity-based costs per unit to the costs from the single-allocation-base system. How have the unit costs changed? Explain why the costs changed.

P17-28A *(L. OBJ. 3)* **Recording manufacturing costs for a JIT costing system [15–25 min]**

Low Range produces fleece jackets. The company uses JIT costing for its JIT production system.

Low Range has two inventory accounts: Raw and in-process inventory and Finished goods inventory. On February 1, 2010, the account balances were Raw and in-process inventory, $13,000; Finished goods inventory, $2,000.

The standard cost of a jacket is $45: $18 direct materials plus $27 conversion costs. Data for February's activities follow:

Number of jackets completed	16,000	Direct materials purchased	$ 283,000
Number of jackets sold	15,600	Conversion costs incurred	$ 533,000

Requirements

1. What are the major features of a JIT production system such as that of Low Range?
2. Prepare summary journal entries for February. Under- or overallocated conversion costs are closed to Cost of goods sold monthly.
3. Use a T-account to determine the February 28, 2010, balance of Raw and in-process inventory.

P17-29A *(L.OBJ. 4)* **Analyzing costs of quality [20–30 min]**

Lori, Inc., is using a costs-of-quality approach to evaluate design engineering efforts for a new skateboard. Lori's senior managers expect the engineering work to reduce appraisal, internal failure, and external failure activities. The predicted reductions in activities over the 2-year life of the skateboards follow. Also shown are the cost allocation rates for each activity.

Activity	Predicted Reduction in Activity Units	Activity Cost Allocation Rate Per Unit
Inspection of incoming materials	380	$ 46
Inspection of finished goods	380	25
Number of defective units discovered in-house	1,200	50
Number of defective units discovered by customers	275	74
Lost sales to dissatisfied customers	175	101

Requirements

1. Calculate the predicted quality cost savings from the design engineering work.
2. Lori spent $102,000 on design engineering for the new skateboard. What is the net benefit of this "preventive" quality activity?
3. What major difficulty would Lori's managers have in implementing this costs-of-quality approach? What alternative approach could they use to measure quality improvement?

Problems (Group B)

P17-30B *(L.OBJ. 1)* **Product costing in an ABC system [15–20 min]**

The Arial Manufacturing Company in Hondo, Texas, assembles and tests electronic components used in handheld video phones. Consider the following data regarding component T24:

Direct materials cost	$ 82.00
Activity costs allocated	?
Manufacturing product cost	$?

The activities required to build the component follow:

Activity	Allocation Base	Cost Allocated to Each Unit
Start station	Number of raw component chasis	3 × $ 1.30 = $ 3.90
Dip insertion	Number of dip insertions	? × $ 0.25 = 6.75
Manual insertion	Number of manual insertions	13 × $ 0.70 = ?
Wave solder	Number of components soldered	3 × $ 1.30 = 3.90
Backload	Number of backload insertions	6 × ? = 2.40
Test	Testing hours	0.40 × $ 60.00 = ?
Defect analysis	Defect analysis hours	0.15 × ? = $ 7.50
Total		$?

Requirements

1. Fill in the blanks in both the opening schedule and the list of activities.
2. How is labor cost assigned to products under this ABC product costing system?
3. Why might managers favor this ABC system instead of Arial's older system, which allocated all conversion costs on the basis of direct labor?

P17-31B *(L.OBJ. 1, 2)* **Product costing in an ABC system [20–30 min]**
Johnston, Inc., manufactures bookcases and uses an activity-based costing system. Johnston's activity areas and related data follow:

Activity	Budgeted Cost of Activity	Allocation Base	Cost Allocation Rate
Materials handling	$ 210,000	Number of parts	$ 0.90
Assembly	3,200,000	Direct labor hours	13.00
Finishing	180,000	Number of finished units	4.00

Johnston produced two styles of bookcases in May: the standard bookcase and an unfinished bookcase, which has fewer parts and requires no finishing. The totals for quantities, direct materials costs, and other data follow:

Product	Total Units Produced	Total Direct Materials Costs	Total Number of Parts	Total Assembling Direct Labor Hours
Standard bookcase	7,000	$ 29,500	80,500	3,200
Unfinished bookcase	7,600	28,700	84,500	2,100

Requirements

1. Compute the manufacturing product cost per unit of each type of bookcase.
2. Suppose that premanufacturing activities, such as product design, were assigned to the standard bookcases at $6 each, and to the unfinished bookcases at $2 each. Similar analyses were conducted of postmanufacturing activities such as distribution, marketing, and customer service. The postmanufacturing costs were $23 per standard bookcase and $14 per unfinished bookcase. Compute the full product costs per unit.
3. Which product costs are reported in the external financial statements? Which costs are used for management decision making? Explain the difference.
4. What price should Johnston's managers set for unfinished bookcases to earn a unit profit of $15?

P17-32B *(L.OBJ. 1, 2)* **Comparing costs from ABC and single-rate systems [30–40 min]**
Corbertt Pharmaceuticals manufactures an over-the-counter allergy medication. The company sells both large commercial containers of 1,000 capsules to health-care facilities and travel packs of 20 capsules to shops in airports, train stations, and hotels. The following information has been developed to determine if an activity-based costing system would be beneficial:

Activity	Estimated Indirect Activity Costs	Allocation Base	Estimated Quantity of Allocation Base
Materials handling	$ 98,000	Kilos	24,500 kilos
Packaging	200,000	Machine hours . .	2,000 hours
Quality assurance	118,000	Samples	2,000 samples
Total indirect costs	$ 416,000		

Other production information includes the following:

	Commerical Containers		Travel Packs	
Units produced	2,800	containers	43,000	packs
Weight in kilos	8,000		6,000	
Machine hours	1,800		600	
Number of samples	100		200	

Requirements

1. Compute the cost allocation rate for each activity.
2. Use the activity-based cost allocation rates to compute the activity costs per unit of the commercial containers and the travel packs. (*Hint*: First compute the total activity costs allocated to each product line, and then compute the cost per unit.)
3. Corbertt's original single-allocation-base costing system allocated indirect costs to products at $152 per machine hour. Compute the total indirect costs allocated to the commercial containers and to the travel packs under the original system. Then compute the indirect cost per unit for each product.
4. Compare the activity-based costs per unit to the costs from the single-allocation-base system. How have the unit costs changed? Explain why the costs changed as they did.

P17-33B *(L.OBJ. 3)* **Recording manufacturing costs for a JIT costing system [15–25 min]**
High Range produces fleece jackets. The company uses JIT costing for its JIT production system.

High Range has two inventory accounts: Raw and in-process inventory and Finished goods inventory. On March 1, 2010, the account balances were Raw and in-process inventory, $13,000; Finished goods inventory, $2,100.

The standard cost of a jacket is $34: $12 direct materials plus $22 conversion costs. Data for March's activities follow:

Number of jackets completed	17,000	Direct materials purchased	$ 196,500
Number of jackets sold	16,600	Conversion costs incurred	$ 469,000

Requirements

1. What are the major features of a JIT production system such as that of High Range?
2. Prepare summary journal entries for March. Under- or overallocated conversion costs are closed to Cost of goods sold monthly.
3. Use a T-account to determine the March 31, 2010, balance of Raw and in-process inventory.

P17-34B *(L.OBJ. 4)* **Analyzing costs of quality [20–30 min]**
Rachael, Inc., is using a costs-of-quality approach to evaluate design engineering efforts for a new wakeboard. Rachael's senior managers expect the engineering work to reduce appraisal, internal failure, and external failure activities. The predicted reductions in activities over the 2-year life of the wakeboards follow. Also shown are the cost allocation rates for each activity.

	Predicted Reduction in Activity Units	Activity Cost Allocation Rate Per Unit
Inspection of incoming materials	400	$ 43
Inspection of finished goods	400	25
Number of defective units discovered in–house	1,000	53
Number of defective units discovered by customers	325	74
Lost sales to dissatisfied customers	175	99

Requirements

1. Calculate the predicted quality cost savings from the design engineering work.
2. Rachael spent $101,000 on design engineering for the new wakeboard. What is the net benefit of this "preventive" quality activity?
3. What major difficulty would Rachael's managers have in implementing this costs-of-quality approach? What alternative approach could they use to measure quality improvement?

■ Continuing Exercise

E17-35 This exercise continues the Sherman Lawn Service, Inc., situation from Exercise 16-36 of Chapter 16. Recall that Sherman completed a special landscaping job for Feimer's Fancy Fonts. If Sherman had used activity-based costing, Sherman's data about the job, including ABC information, would be as follows:

Feimer Job details:	
Direct Materials	$400
Direct Labor	$900

ABC Costing Rates:
$350 per setup
$10 per plant

Requirements

1. Sherman uses one setup for the Feimer job and installs 20 plants. What is the total cost of the Feimer job?
2. If Feimer paid $2500 for the job, what is the profit or loss under ABC?

■ Continuing Problem

P17-36 This problem continues the Haupt Consulting, Inc., situation from Problem 16-37 of Chapter 16. Recall that Haupt allocated indirect costs to jobs based on a predetermined indirect cost allocation rate, computed as a percentage of direct labor costs. Haupt is now considering using an ABC system. Information about ABC costs follows:

Activity	Budgeted Cost of Activity	Allocation Base	Cost Allocation Rate
Design	$ 300,000	Number of designs	$ 10,000
Programming	760,000	Direct labor hours	200
Testing	200,000	Number of tests	5,000

Records for two clients appear here:

Job	Total Direct Costs	Total Number of Designs	Total Programming Direct Labor Hours	Number of Tests
Owen's Trains	$ 11,200	1	700	4
Caleigh's Cookies	500	2	100	5

Requirements

1. Compute the total cost of each job.
2. Is the job cost greater or less than that computed in Problem 16-37 for each job? Why?
3. If Haupt wants to earn profits equal to 25% of sales revenue, how much (what fee) should it charge each of these two clients?

Apply Your Knowledge

Decision Cases

Case 1. Harris Systems specializes in servers for workgroup, e-commerce, and ERP applications. The company's original job costing system has two direct cost categories: direct materials and direct labor. Overhead is allocated to jobs at the single rate of $22 per direct labor hour.

A task force headed by Harris's CFO recently designed an ABC system with four activities. The ABC system retains the current system's two direct cost categories. Thus, it budgets only overhead costs for each activity. Pertinent data follow:

Activity	Allocation Base	Cost Allocation Rate
Materials handling	Number of parts	$ 0.85
Machine setup	Number of setups	500.00
Assembling	Assembling hours	80.00
Shipping	Number of shipments	1,500.00

Harris Systems has been awarded two new contracts, which will be produced as Job A and Job B. Budget data relating to the contracts follow:

	Job A	Job B
Number of parts	15,000	2,000
Number of setups	6	4
Number of assembling hours	1,500	200
Number of shipments	1	1
Total direct labor hours	8,000	600
Number of output units	100	10
Direct materials cost	$220,000	$30,000
Direct labor cost	$160,000	$12,000

Requirements

1. Compute the product cost per unit for each job, using the original costing system (with two direct cost categories and a single overhead allocation rate).
2. Suppose Harris Systems adopts the ABC system. Compute the product cost per unit for each job using ABC.
3. Which costing system more accurately assigns to jobs the costs of the resources consumed to produce them? Explain.
4. A dependable company has offered to produce both jobs for Harris for $5,400 per output unit. Harris may outsource (buy from the outside company) either Job A only, Job B only, or both jobs. Which course of action will Harris's managers take if they base their decision on (a) the original system? (b) ABC system costs? Which course of action will yield more income? Explain.

Case 2. To remain competitive, Harris Systems' management believes the company must produce Job B-type servers (from Decision Case 1) at a target cost of $5,400. Harris Systems has just joined a B2B e-market site that management believes will enable the firm to cut direct materials costs by 10%. Harris's management also believes that a value-engineering team can reduce assembly time.

Requirement

1. Compute the assembling cost savings per Job B-type server required to meet the $5,400 target cost. (*Hint*: Begin by calculating the direct materials, direct labor, and allocated activity costs per server.)

■ Ethical Issue

Cassidy Manning is assistant controller at LeMar Packaging, Inc., a manufacturer of cardboard boxes and other packaging materials. Manning has just returned from a packaging industry conference on activity-based costing. She realizes that ABC may help LeMar meet its goal of reducing costs by 5% over each of the next three years.

LeMar Packaging's Order Department is a likely candidate for ABC. While orders are entered into a computer that updates the accounting records, clerks manually check customers' credit history and hand-deliver orders to shipping. This process occurs whether the sales order is for a dozen specialty boxes worth $80, or 10,000 basic boxes worth $8,000.

Manning believes that identifying the cost of processing a sales order would justify (1) further computerization of the order process and (2) changing the way the company processes small orders. However, the significant cost savings would arise from elimination of two positions in the Order Department. The company's sales order clerks have been with the company many years. Manning is uncomfortable with the prospect of proposing a change that will likely result in terminating these employees.

Requirement

1. Use the IMA's ethical standards to consider Manning's responsibility when cost savings come at the expense of employees' jobs.

Team Project

Bronson Shrimp Farms, in Brewton, Alabama, has a Processing Department that processes raw shrimp into two products:

- Headless shrimp
- Peeled and deveined shrimp

Bronson recently submitted bids for two orders: (1) headless shrimp for a cruise line and (2) peeled and deveined shrimp for a restaurant chain. Bronson won the first bid, but lost the second. The production and sales managers are upset. They believe that Bronson's state-of-the-art equipment should have given the company an edge in the peeled and deveined market. Consequently, production managers are starting to keep their own sets of product cost records.

Bronson is reexamining both its production process and its costing system. The existing costing system has been in place since 1991. It allocates all indirect costs based on direct labor hours. Bronson is considering adopting activity-based costing. Controller Heather Barefield and a team of production managers performed a preliminary study. The team identified six activities, with the following (department-wide) estimated indirect costs and cost drivers for 2010:

Activity	Estimated Total Cost of Activity	Allocation Base
Redesign of production process (costs of changing process and equipment)	$ 5,000	Number of design changes
Production scheduling (production scheduler's salary)	6,000	Number of batches
Chilling (depreciation on refrigerators)	1,500	Weight (in pounds)
Processing (utilities and depreciation on equipment)	20,675	Number of cuts
Packaging (indirect labor and depreciation on equipment)	1,425	Cubic feet of surface exposed
Order filling (order-takers' and shipping clerks' wages)	7,000	Number of orders
Total indirect costs for the entire department	$41,600	

The raw shrimp are chilled and then cut. For headless shrimp, employees remove the heads, then rinse the shrimp. For peeled and deveined shrimp, the headless shrimp are further processed—the shells are removed and the backs are slit for deveining. Both headless shrimp and peeled and deveined shrimp are packaged in foam trays and covered with shrink wrap. Order-filling personnel assemble orders of headless shrimp as well as peeled and deveined shrimp.

Barefield estimates that Bronson will produce 10,000 packages of headless shrimp and 50,000 packages of peeled and deveined shrimp in 2010. The two products incur the following costs per package:

	Costs per Package	
	Headless Shrimp	Peeled and Deveined Shrimp
Shrimp	$3.50	$4.50
Foam trays	$0.05	$0.05
Shrink wrap	$0.05	$0.02
Number of cuts	12 cuts	48 cuts
Cubic feet of exposed surface	1 cubic foot	0.75 cubic foot
Weight (in pounds)	2.5 pounds	1 pound
Direct labor hours	0.01 hour	0.05 hour

Bronson pays direct laborers $20 per hour. Barefield estimates that each product line also will require the following *total* resources:

	Headless Shrimp		Peeled and Deveined Shrimp	
Design changes	1 change	for all 10,000 packages	4 changes	for all 50,000 packages
Batches	40 batches		20 batches	
Sales orders	90 orders		110 orders	

Requirements

Form groups of four students. All group members should work together to develop the group's answers to the three requirements.

(Carry all computations to at least four decimal places.)

1. Using the original costing system with the single indirect cost allocation base (direct labor hours), compute the total budgeted cost per package for the headless shrimp and then for the peeled and deveined shrimp. (*Hint*: First, compute the indirect cost allocation rate—that is, the predetermined overhead rate. Then, compute the total budgeted cost per package for each product.)
2. Use activity-based costing to recompute the total budgeted cost per package for the headless shrimp and then for the peeled and deveined shrimp. (*Hint*: First, calculate the budgeted cost allocation rate for each activity. Then, calculate the total indirect costs of (a) the entire headless shrimp product line and (b) the entire peeled and deveined shrimp product line. Next, compute the indirect cost per package of each product. Finally, calculate the total cost per package of each product.)
3. Write a memo to Bronson CEO Gary Pololu explaining the results of the ABC study. Compare the costs reported by the ABC system with the costs reported by the original system. Point out whether the ABC system shifted costs toward headless shrimp or toward peeled and deveined shrimp, and explain why. Finally, explain whether Pololu should feel more comfortable making decisions using cost data from the original system or from the new ABC system.

Quick Check Answers

1. *d* 2. *b* 3. *d* 4. *b* 5. *d* 6. *b* 7. *b* 8. *c* 9. *c* 10. *a*

For online homework, exercises, and problems that provide you immediate feedback, please visit www.myaccountinglab.com.

18 Cost-Volume-Profit Analysis

Learning Objectives/Success Keys

1. Identify how changes in volume affect costs
2. Use CVP analysis to compute breakeven points
3. Use CVP analysis for profit planning, and graph the CVP relations
4. Use CVP methods to perform sensitivity analyses
5. Calculate the breakeven point for multiple product lines or services

As Smart Touch Learning and Greg's Groovy Tunes consider different growth and marketing strategies, they also have to consider what effect these changes will have on profitability.

This chapter will look at cost behavior and you will learn how cost-volume-profit (CVP) analysis is used to manage a business. **Cost-volume-profit (CVP) analysis** expresses the relationships among costs, volume, and profit or loss. It is a wonderful management tool and easy to understand.

Cost Behavior

1 Identify how changes in volume affect costs

Some costs increase as the volume of activity increases. Other costs are not affected by volume changes. Managers need to know how a business's costs are affected by changes in its volume of activity. Let us look at the three different types of costs:

- Variable costs
- Fixed costs
- Mixed costs

Variable Costs

Total variable costs change in direct proportion to changes in the volume of activity. For our purposes, an activity is a business action that affects costs. Those activities include selling, producing, driving, and calling. The activities can be measured by units sold, units produced, miles driven, and the number of phone calls placed. So **variable costs** are those costs that increase or decrease in total as the volume of activity increases or decreases.

As you may recall, Greg's Groovy Tunes offers DJ services for parties, weddings, and other events. For each event, Greg's spends $15 for equipment rental. Greg's can perform for 15 to 30 events per month. To calculate total variable costs Natalie Blanding, the office manager, would show the following:

Number of Events per Month	Equipment Rental Cost per Event	Total Equipment Rental Cost per Month
15	$15	$225
20	$15	$300
30	$15	$450

As you can see, the total variable cost of equipment rental increases as the number of events increases. But the equipment rental cost per event does not change. Exhibit 18-1 graphs total variable costs for equipment rental as the number of events increases from 0 to 30.

EXHIBIT 18-1 | Variable Costs

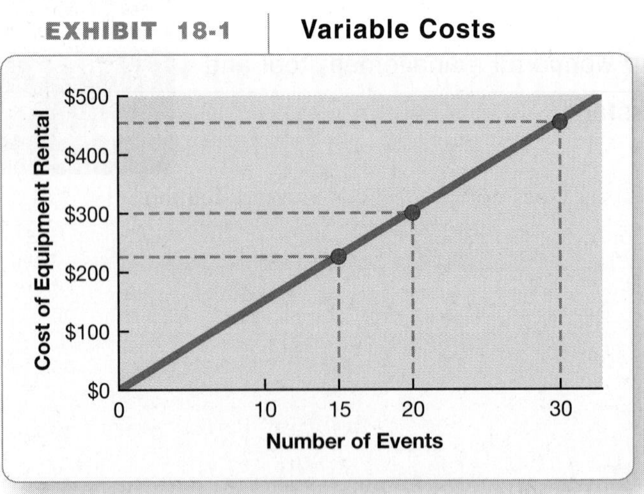

If there are no events, Greg's incurs no equipment rental costs, so the total variable cost line begins at the bottom left corner. This point is called the *origin*, and it represents zero volume and zero cost. The *slope* of the variable cost line is the change in equipment rental cost (on the vertical axis) divided by the change in the number of events (on the horizontal axis). The slope of the graph equals the variable cost per unit. In Exhibit 18-1, the slope of the variable cost line is 15 because Greg's spends $15 on equipment rental for each event.

If Greg's Groovy Tunes performs at 15 events during the month, it will spend a total of $225 (15 events × $15 each) for equipment rental. Follow this total variable cost line to the right to see that doubling the number of events to 30 likewise doubles the total variable cost to $450 (30 × $15 = $450). Exhibit 18-1 shows how the *total variable cost* of equipment rental varies with the number of events. But note that *the per-event cost remains constant* at $15.

Remember this important fact about *variable costs*:

> Total variable costs fluctuate with changes in volume, but the variable cost per unit remains constant.

Fixed Costs

In contrast, **total fixed costs** are costs that do not change over wide ranges of volume. Greg's fixed costs include depreciation on the cars, as well as the DJs' salaries. Greg's has these fixed costs regardless of the number of events—15, 20, or 30.

Suppose Greg's incurs $12,000 of fixed costs each month, and the number of monthly events is between 15 and 30. Exhibit 18-2 graphs total fixed costs as a flat line that intersects the cost axis at $12,000, because Greg's will incur the same $12,000 of fixed costs regardless of the number of events.

EXHIBIT 18-2 | Fixed Costs

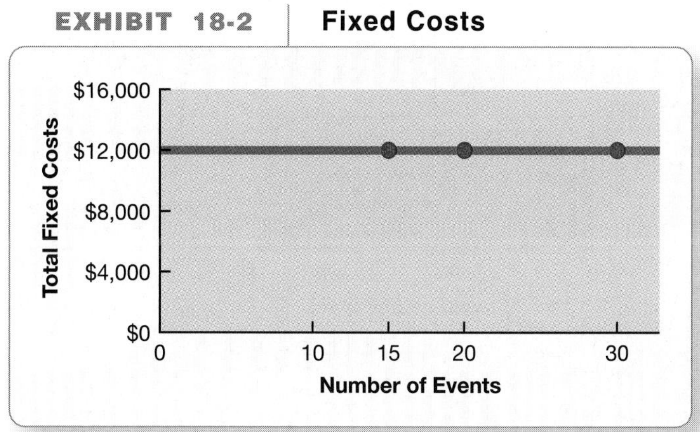

Total fixed cost does not change, as shown in Exhibit 18-2. But the *fixed cost per event* depends on the number of events. If Greg's Groovy Tunes performs at 15 events, the fixed cost per event is $800 ($12,000 ÷ 15 events). If the number of events doubles to 30, the fixed cost per event is cut in half to $400 ($12,000 ÷ 30 events). Therefore, the fixed cost per event is *inversely* proportional to the number of events, as follows:

Total Fixed Costs	Number of Events	Fixed Cost per Event
$12,000	15	$800
$12,000	20	$600
$12,000	30	$400

Remember the following important fact about *fixed costs*:

Total fixed costs remain constant, but the fixed cost per unit is inversely proportional to volume.

Mixed Costs

Costs that have both variable and fixed components are called **mixed costs.** For example, Greg's Groovy Tunes' cell-phone company charges $10 a month to provide the service and $0.15 for each minute of use. If the cell phone is used for 100 minutes, the company will bill Greg's $25 [$10 + (100 minutes × $0.15)].

Exhibit 18-3 shows how Greg's can separate its cell-phone bill into fixed and variable components. The $10 monthly charge is a fixed cost because it is the same no matter how many minutes the company uses the cell phone. The $0.15-per-minute charge is a variable cost that increases in direct proportion to the number of minutes of use. If Greg's uses the phone for 100 minutes, its total variable cost is $15 (100 minutes × $0.15). If it doubles the use to 200 minutes, total variable cost also doubles to $30 (200 minutes × $0.15), and the total bill rises to $40 ($10 + $30).

EXHIBIT 18-3 | Mixed Costs

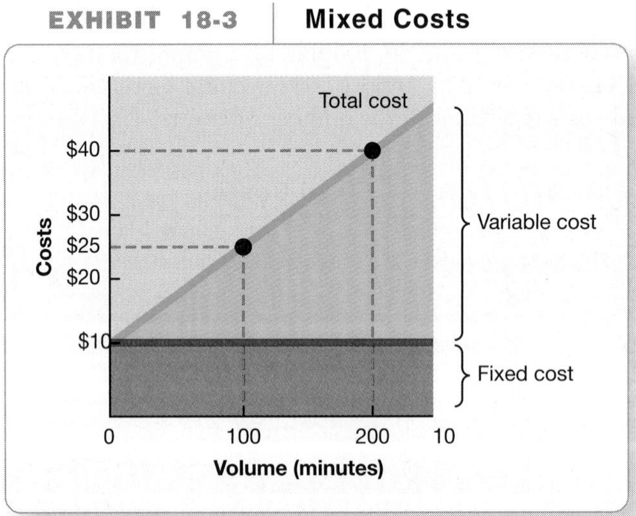

Stop & Think...

Think about your costs related to taking this class. Which ones are fixed? Which ones are variable? The cost of your tuition and books are fixed costs, because you pay one price for the class and your books, no matter how many days you come to class. If you drive to class, the cost of gas put in your car is variable, because you only incur gas costs when you come to class. Are there any mixed costs associated with your class? Maybe your internet service provider charges you a flat fee each month plus a rate for every hour you are online. Your time using myaccountinglab would be a mixed cost associated with this class.

High-Low Method to Separate Fixed Cost from Variable Cost

An easy method to separate mixed costs into variable and fixed components is the **high-low method.** This method requires you to identify the highest and lowest levels of activity over a period of time. Using this information, complete the following three steps:

STEP 1: Calculate the variable cost per unit.

Variable cost per unit = Change in total cost ÷ Change in volume of activity

STEP 2: Calculate the total fixed costs.

Total fixed cost = Total mixed cost – Total variable cost

STEP 3: Create and use an equation to show the behavior of a mixed cost.

Total mixed cost = (Variable cost per unit × number of units) + Total fixed costs

Let us revisit the Greg's Groovy Tunes illustration. A summary of Greg's Groovy Tunes' music equipment maintenance costs for the past year shows the following costs for each quarter:

	Event-Playing Hours	Total Maintenance Cost	
1st Quarter	360	$1,720	
2nd Quarter	415	1,830	
3rd Quarter	480	1,960	← Highest Volume and Cost
4th Quarter	240	1,480	← Lowest Volume and Cost

The highest volume is 480 event-playing hours in the 3rd quarter of the year, and the lowest volume is 240 event-playing hours. We can use the high-low method to identify Greg's Groovy Tunes' fixed and variable costs of music equipment maintenance.

STEP 1: Calculate the variable cost per unit.

Variable cost per unit = Change in total cost ÷ Change in volume of activity
= ($1,960 – $1,480) ÷ (480 hours – 240 hours)
= $480 ÷ 240 hours
= $2 per event-playing hour

Step 2: Calculate the total fixed costs.

Total fixed cost	= Total mixed cost	– Total variable cost
	= \$1,960	– (\$2 × 480)
	= \$1,960	– \$960
	= \$1,000	

This example uses the highest cost and volume to calculate the total fixed costs, but you can use any volume and calculate the same \$1,000 total fixed cost.

Step 3: Create and use an equation to show the behavior of a mixed cost.

Total mixed cost	= (Variable cost per unit × number of units)	+	Total fixed costs
Total equipment maintenance cost	= \$2 per event-playing hour × No. of hours	+	\$1,000

Using this equation, the estimated music equipment maintenance cost for 400 event-playing hours would be as follows:

(\$2 × 400 event-playing hours) + \$1,000 = \$1,800

This method provides a rough estimate of fixed and variable costs for cost-volume-profit analysis. The high and low volumes become the relevant range, which we discuss in the next section. Managers find the high-low method to be quick and easy, but regression analysis provides the most accurate estimates and is discussed in cost accounting textbooks.

Relevant Range

The **relevant range** is the band of volume where total fixed costs remain constant and the variable cost *per unit* remains constant. To estimate costs, managers need to know the relevant range. Why? Because,

- total "fixed" costs can differ from one relevant range to another.
- the variable cost *per unit* can differ in various relevant ranges.

Exhibit 18-4 shows fixed costs for Greg's Groovy Tunes over three different relevant ranges. If the company expects to offer 15,000 event-playing hours next year, the relevant range is between 10,000 and 20,000 event-playing hours, and managers budget fixed costs of \$80,000.

To offer 22,000 event-playing hours, Greg's will have to expand the company. This will increase total fixed costs for added rent and equipment costs. Exhibit 18-4 shows that total fixed costs increase to \$120,000 as the relevant range shifts to this higher band of volume. Conversely, if Greg's expects to offer only 8,000 event-playing hours, the company will budget only \$40,000 of fixed costs. Managers will have to lay off employees or take other actions to cut fixed costs.

Variable cost per unit can also change outside the relevant range. For example, Greg's Groovy Tunes may get a quantity discount for equipment maintenance if it can provide more than 20,000 event-playing hours.

EXHIBIT 18-4 | **Relevant Range**

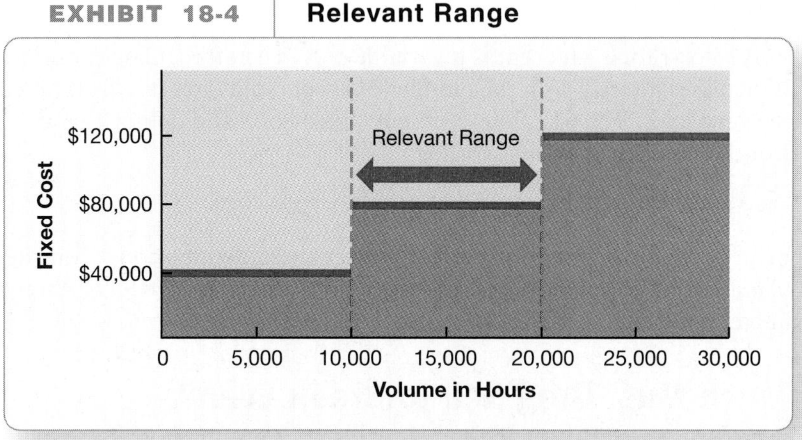

We have now covered the basics of CVP analysis. Let us apply CVP analysis to answer some interesting management questions.

Basic CVP Analysis: What Must We Sell To Break Even?

Greg's Groovy Tunes is considering expanding its events coverage to include weddings. Greg's first analyzes its existing costs, partially covered in the previous section. (For simplicity, we ignore the mixed costs.) Variable costs are $15 for gas per event plus $100 in contracted labor per event. All the other business expenses are fixed costs, $12,000. Average sales price per event is $235.

2 Use CVP analysis to compute breakeven points

Selling price per event.................	$ 235
Variable cost per event...............	$ 115
Fixed costs	$12,000

Greg's Groovy Tunes faces several important questions:

- How many DJ services (hereinafter, events) must the company sell to break even?
- What will profits be if sales double?
- How will changes in selling price, variable costs, or fixed costs affect profits?

Before getting started, let us review the assumptions required for CVP analysis to be accurate.

Assumptions

CVP analysis assumes that

1. managers can classify each cost as either variable or fixed.
2. the only factor that affects costs is change in volume. Fixed costs do not change.

Greg's Groovy Tunes' business meets these assumptions:

1. The $115 cost for each event is a variable cost. Therefore, Greg's *total variable cost* increases directly with the number of events sold (an extra $115 in cost for each event sold). The $12,000 represents fixed costs and do not change regardless of the number of events worked.
2. Sales volume is the only factor that affects Greg's costs.

Most business conditions do not perfectly meet these assumptions (consider that most businesses have some mixed costs), so managers regard CVP analysis as approximate, not exact.

How Much Must Greg Sell to Break Even? Three Approaches

Virtually all businesses want to know their breakeven point. The **breakeven point** is the sales level at which operating income is zero: Total revenues equal total costs. Sales below the breakeven point result in a loss. Sales above break even provide a profit. Greg's Groovy Tunes needs to know how many DJ events must be held to break even.

There are several ways to figure the breakeven point, including the

- income statement approach.
- contribution margin approach.

We start with the income statement approach because it is the easiest method to remember. You are already familiar with the income statement.

The Income Statement Approach

Start by expressing income in equation form:

Sales revenue –	Total costs	= Operating income
Sales revenue –	Variable costs – Fixed costs	= Operating income

Sales revenue equals the unit sale price ($235 per event in this case) multiplied by the number of units (events) sold. Variable costs equal variable cost per unit ($115 in this case) times the number of units sold. Greg's fixed costs total $12,000. At the breakeven point, operating income is zero. We use this information to solve the income statement equation for the number of DJ events Greg's must sell to break even.

Sales revenue		–	Variable costs		– Fixed costs	=	Operating income
(Sale price per unit	× Units sold)	–	(Variable cost per unit	× Units sold)	– Fixed costs	=	Operating income
($235	× Units sold)	–	($115	× Units sold)	– $12,000	=	$0
($235		–	$115)	× Units sold	– $12,000	=	$0
			$120	× Units sold		=	$12,000
				Units sold		=	$12,000/120
			Breakeven sales in units			=	100 events

Greg's Groovy Tunes must sell 100 events to break even. The breakeven sales level in dollars is $23,500 (100 events × $235).

Be sure to check your calculations. "Prove" the breakeven point by substituting the breakeven number of units into the income statement. Then check to ensure that this level of sales results in zero profit.

Proof	Sales revenue	–	Variable cost	–	Fixed costs	=	Operating income
	($235 × 100)	–	($115 × 100)	–	$12,000	=	$0
	$23,500	–	$11,500	–	$12,000	=	$0

The Contribution Margin Approach: A Shortcut

This shortcut method of computing the breakeven point uses Greg's contribution margin. The **contribution margin** is sales revenue minus variable costs. It is called the *contribution margin* because the excess of sales revenue over variable costs contributes to covering fixed costs and then to providing operating income.

The **contribution margin income statement** shows costs by cost behavior—variable costs and fixed costs—and highlights the contribution margin. The format shows the following:

Sales revenue
– Variable costs
= Contribution margin
– Fixed costs
= Operating income

Now let us rearrange the income statement formula and use the contribution margin to develop a shortcut method for finding the number of DJ events Greg's must hold to break even.

$$\text{Sales revenue} - \text{Variable costs} - \text{Fixed costs} = \text{Operating income}$$

$$\left(\frac{\text{Sale price}}{\text{per unit}} \times \text{Units sold}\right) - \left(\frac{\text{Variable cost}}{\text{per unit}} \times \text{Units sold}\right) - \text{Fixed costs} = \text{Operating income}$$

$$\left(\frac{\text{Sale price}}{\text{per unit}} - \frac{\text{Variable cost}}{\text{per unit}}\right) \times \text{Units sold} = \text{Fixed costs} + \text{Operating income}$$

$$\text{Contribution margin per unit} \times \text{Units sold} = \text{Fixed costs} + \text{Operating income}$$

Dividing both sides of the equation by the contribution margin per unit yields the cost-volume-profit equation:

$$\text{Units sold} = \frac{\text{Fixed costs} + \text{Operating income}}{\text{Contribution margin per unit}}$$

Greg's Groovy Tunes can use this contribution margin approach to find its breakeven point. Fixed costs total $12,000. Operating income is zero at break even. The contribution margin per event is $120 ($235 sale price – $115 variable cost). Greg's breakeven computation is as follows:

$$\text{Breakeven sales in units} = \frac{\$12{,}000}{\$120}$$
$$= 100 \text{ events}$$

Why does this shortcut method work? Each event Greg's Groovy Tunes sells provides $120 of contribution margin. To break even, Greg's must generate enough contribution margin to cover $12,000 of fixed costs. At the rate of $120 per event, Greg's must sell 100 events ($12,000/$120) to cover fixed costs. You can see that the contribution margin approach just rearranges the income statement equation, so the breakeven point is the same under both methods.

To "prove" the breakeven point, you can also use the contribution margin income statement format:

GREG'S GROOVY TUNES, INC. **Income Statement** For one month	
Sales revenue ($235 × 100 events)	$ 23,500
Less: Variable costs ($115 × 100 events)	(11,500)
Contribution margin ($120 × 100 events)	12,000
Less: Fixed costs	(12,000)
Operating income	$ 0

Using the Contribution Margin Ratio to Compute the Breakeven Point in Sales Dollars

Companies can use the contribution margin ratio to compute their breakeven point in terms of *sales dollars*. The **contribution margin ratio** is the ratio of contribution margin to sales revenue. For Greg's Groovy Tunes, we have the following:

$$\text{Contribution margin ratio} = \frac{\text{Contribution margin}}{\text{Sales revenue}} = \frac{\$120}{\$235} = 51.06\%$$

The 51% contribution margin ratio means that each dollar of sales revenue contributes $0.51 toward fixed costs and profit.

The contribution margin *ratio* approach differs from the shortcut contribution margin approach we have just seen in only one way: Here we use the contribution margin *ratio* rather than the dollar amount of the contribution margin.

$$\text{Breakeven sales in dollars} = \frac{\text{Fixed costs}}{\text{Contribution margin ratio}}$$

Using this ratio formula, Greg's breakeven point in sales dollars is as follows:

$$\text{Breakeven sales in dollars} = \frac{\$12,000}{.5106} = \$23,502$$

This is $2 larger than the breakeven sales revenue we calculated in the contribution margin approach, due to rounding. Therefore, it is basically the same.

Why does the contribution margin ratio formula work? Each dollar of Greg's sales contributes 51.06% to fixed costs and profit. To break even, Greg's must generate enough contribution margin at the rate of 51.06% of sales to cover the $12,000 fixed costs ($12,000 ÷ 0.5106 = $23,502).

Now, we have seen how companies use *contribution margin* to estimate breakeven points in CVP analysis. But managers use the contribution margin for other purposes too, such as motivating the sales force. Salespeople who know the contribution margin of each product can generate more profit by emphasizing high-margin products over low-margin products. This is why many companies base sales commissions on the contribution margins produced by sales rather than on sales revenue alone.

Using CVP To Plan Profits

3 Use CVP analysis for profit planning, and graph the CVP relations

For established products and services, managers are more interested in the sales level needed to earn a target profit than in the breakeven point. Managers of new business ventures are also interested in the profits they can expect to earn. For example, now that Greg's Groovy Tunes knows it must sell 100 events to break even, Natalie Blanding, the controller for Greg's, wants to know how many more events must be sold to earn a monthly operating profit of $6,000.

How Much Must Greg's Sell to Earn a Profit?

What is the only difference from our prior analysis? Here, Greg's wants to know how many events must be sold to earn a $6,000 profit. We can use the income statement approach or the shortcut contribution margin approach to find the answer. Let us start with the income statement approach.

	Sales revenue	–	Variable cost	– Fixed costs	=	Operating income
	($235 × units sold)	–	($115 × units sold)	– $12,000	=	$ 6,000
	[($235 – 115) × units sold]			– $12,000	=	$ 6,000
	$120 × units sold				=	$18,000
				units sold	=	$18,000/$120
				units sold	=	150 events
Proof	($235 × 150)	–	($115 × 150)	– $12,000	=	**Operating income**
	$35,250	–	$17,250	– $12,000	=	$6,000

This analysis shows that Greg's must sell 150 posters each month to earn an operating profit of $6,000. This is 150 – 100 = 50 more events than the breakeven sales level (100 events).

The proof shows that Greg's needs sales revenues of $35,250 to earn a profit of $6,000. Alternatively, we can compute the dollar sales necessary to earn a $6,000 profit directly, using the contribution margin ratio form of the CVP formula:

$$\text{Target sales in dollars} = \frac{\text{Fixed costs + Operating income}}{\text{Contribution margin ratio}}$$

$$= \frac{\$12{,}000 + \$6{,}000}{0.5106}$$

$$= \frac{\$18{,}000}{0.5106}$$

$$= \$35{,}253$$

This shows that Greg's needs $35,253 in sales revenue, which is $3 off due to rounding. Essentially, this is the same result.

Graphing Cost-Volume-Profit Relations

Controller Natalie Blanding can graph the CVP relations for Greg's Groovy Tunes. A graph provides a picture that shows how changes in the levels of sales will affect profits. As in the variable-, fixed-, and mixed-cost graphs of Exhibits 18-1, 18-2, and 18-3, Blanding shows the volume of units (events) on the horizontal axis and dollars on the vertical axis. Then she follows four steps to graph the CVP relations for Greg's Groovy Tunes, as illustrated in Exhibit 18-5.

EXHIBIT 18-5 **Cost-Volume-Profit Graph**

Events	Sales Revenue	Total Expenses	Income
0	0	12,000	(12,000)
100	23,500	23,500	0
150	35,250	29,250	6,000
200	47,000	35,000	12,000

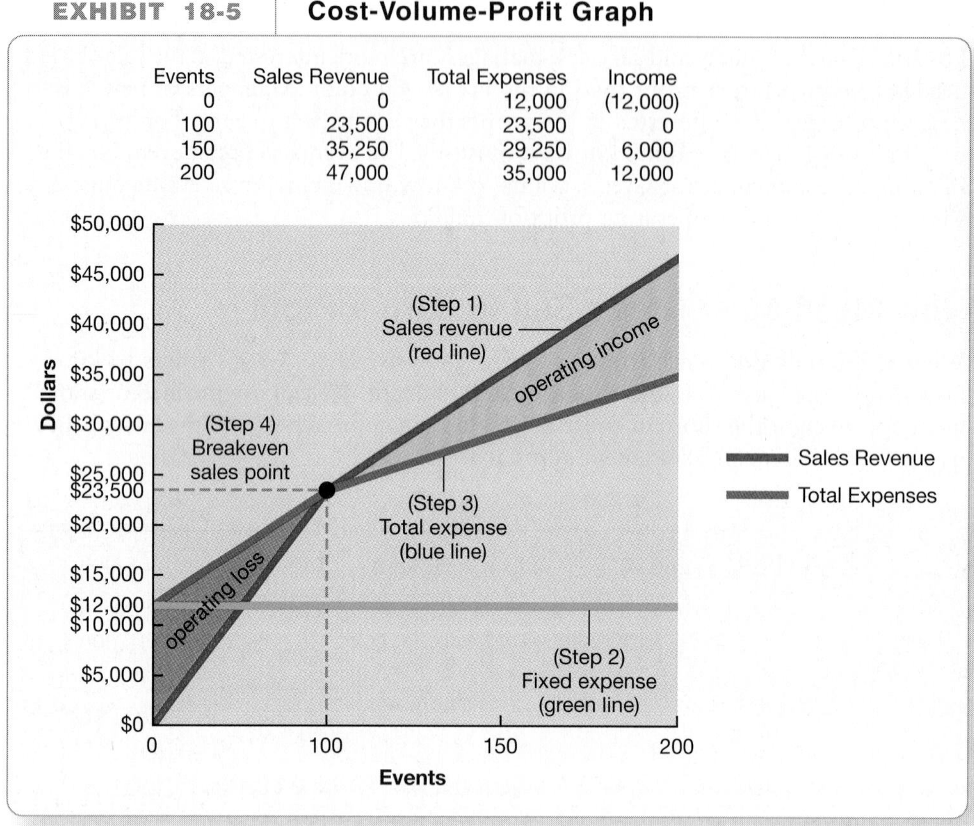

STEP 1: Choose a sales volume, such as 200 events. Plot the point for total sales revenue at that volume: 200 events × $235 per event = sales of $47,000. Draw the *sales revenue line* from the origin (0) through the $47,000 point. Why start at the origin? If Greg's sells no events, there is no revenue.

STEP 2: Draw the *fixed cost line*, a horizontal line that intersects the dollars axis at $12,000. The fixed cost line is flat because fixed costs are the same, $12,000, no matter how many events are sold.

STEP 3: Draw the *total cost line.* Total cost is the sum of variable cost plus fixed cost. Thus, total cost is *mixed.* So the total cost line follows the form of the mixed cost line in Exhibit 18-3. Begin by computing variable cost at the chosen sales volume: 200 events× $115 per event = variable cost of $23,000. Add variable cost to fixed cost: $23,000 + $12,000 = $35,000. Plot the total cost point ($35,000) for 200 events. Then draw a line through this point from the $12,000 fixed cost intercept on the dollars vertical axis. This is the *total cost line.* The total cost line starts at the fixed cost line because even if Greg's Groovy Tunes sells no events, the company still incurs the $12,000 fixed cost.

STEP 4: Identify the *breakeven point* and the areas of operating income and loss. The breakeven point is where the sales revenue line intersects the total cost line. This is where revenue exactly equals total costs—at 100 events, or $23,500 in sales.

Mark the *operating loss* area on the graph. To the left of the breakeven point, total costs exceed sales revenue—leading to an operating loss, indicated by the orange zone.

Mark the *operating income* area on the graph. To the right of the breakeven point, the business earns a profit because sales revenue exceeds total cost, as shown by the green zone.

Why bother with a graph? Why not just use the income statement approach or the shortcut contribution margin approach? Graphs like Exhibit 18-5 help managers quickly estimate the profit or loss earned at different levels of sales. The income statement and contribution margin approaches indicate income or loss for only a single sales amount.

Summary Problem 1

Happy Feet buys hiking socks for $6 a pair and sells them for $10. Management budgets monthly fixed costs of $10,000 for sales volumes between 0 and 12,000 pairs.

Requirements

1. Use both the income statement approach and the shortcut contribution margin approach to compute the company's monthly breakeven sales in units.
2. Use the contribution margin ratio approach to compute the breakeven point in sales dollars.
3. Compute the monthly sales level (in units) required to earn a target operating income of $6,000. Use either the income statement approach or the shortcut contribution margin approach.
4. Prepare a graph of Happy Feet's CVP relationships, similar to Exhibit 18-5. Draw the sales revenue line, the fixed cost line, and the total cost line. Label the axes, the breakeven point, the operating income area, and the operating loss area.

Solution

Requirement 1

Income statement approach:

Sales revenue	–	Variable costs	– Fixed costs	= Operating income
(Sale price per unit × Units sold)	–	(Variable cost per unit × Units sold)	– Fixed costs	= Operating income
($10 × Units sold)	–	($6 × Units sold)	– $10,000	= $0
($10	–	$6) × Units sold		= $10,000
		$4 × Units sold		= $10,000
		Units sold		= $10,000 ÷ $4
		Breakeven sales in units		= 2,500 units

Shortcut contribution margin approach:

$$\text{Units sold} = \frac{\text{Fixed costs + Operating income}}{\text{Contribution margin per unit}}$$

$$\text{Breakeven sales in units} = \frac{\$10{,}000 + \$0}{\$10 - \$6}$$

$$= \frac{\$10{,}000}{\$4}$$

$$= 2{,}500 \text{ units}$$

Requirement 2

$$\text{Breakeven sales in dollars} = \frac{\text{Fixed costs + Operating income}}{\text{Contribution margin ratio}}$$

$$= \frac{\$10{,}000 + \$0}{0.40^{*}}$$

$$= \$25{,}000$$

$$^{*}\text{Contribution margin ratio} = \frac{\text{Contribution margin per unit}}{\text{Sale price per unit}} = \frac{\$4}{\$10} = 0.40$$

Requirement 3

Income statement equation approach:

$$\text{Sales revenue} - \text{Variable costs} - \text{Fixed costs} = \text{Operating income}$$

$$\left(\begin{array}{c}\text{Sale price}\\ \text{per unit}\end{array} \times \text{Units sold}\right) - \left(\begin{array}{c}\text{Variable cost}\\ \text{per unit}\end{array} \times \text{Units sold}\right) - \text{Fixed costs} = \text{Operating income}$$

$$(\$10 \times \text{Units sold}) - (\$6 \times \text{Units sold}) - \$10{,}000 = \$6{,}000$$

$$(\$10 - \$6) \times \text{Units sold} = \$10{,}000 + \$6{,}000$$

$$\$4 \times \text{Units sold} = \$16{,}000$$

$$\text{Units sold} = \$16{,}000 \div \$4$$

$$\text{Units sold} = 4{,}000 \text{ units}$$

Shortcut contribution margin approach:

$$\text{Units sold} = \frac{\text{Fixed costs} + \text{Operating income}}{\text{Contribution margin per unit}}$$

$$= \frac{\$10{,}000 + \$6{,}000}{(\$10 - \$6)}$$

$$= \frac{\$16{,}000}{\$4}$$

$$= 4{,}000 \text{ units}$$

Requirement 4

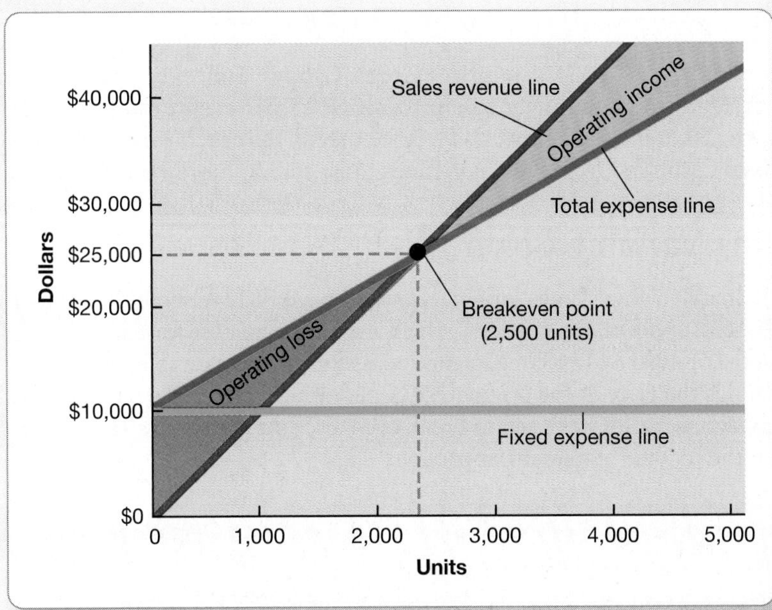

Using CVP For Sensitivity Analysis

4 Use CVP methods to perform sensitivity analyses

Managers often want to predict how changes in sale price, costs, or volume affect their profits. Managers can use CVP relationships to conduct sensitivity analysis. **Sensitivity analysis** is a "what if" technique that asks what results are likely if selling price or costs change, or if an underlying assumption changes. Let us see how Greg's Groovy Tunes can use CVP analysis to estimate the effects of some changes in its business environment.

Changing the Selling Price

Competition in the DJ event services business is so fierce that Greg's Groovy Tunes believes it must cut the selling price to $215 per event to maintain market share. Suppose Greg's Groovy Tunes' variable costs remain $115 per event and fixed costs stay at $12,000. How will the lower sale price affect the breakeven point?

Using the income statement approach, the results are as follows:

Sales revenue – Variable cost	– Fixed costs	= Operating income
($215 × units sold) – ($115 × units sold)	– $12,000	= $0
[($215 – 115) × units sold]	– $12,000	= $0
$100 × units sold		= $12,000
	units sold	= $12,000/$100
	units sold	= 120 events

Proof							
	($215 × 120)	–	($115 × 120)	–	$12,000	=	**Operating income**
	$25,800	–	$13,800	–	$12,000	=	$0

With the original $235 sale price, Greg's Groovy Tunes' breakeven point was 100 events. With the new lower sale price of $215 per event, the breakeven point increases to 120 events. The lower sale price means that each event contributes less toward fixed costs, so Greg's Groovy Tunes must sell 20 more events to break even.

Changing Variable Costs

Return to Greg's Groovy Tunes' original data on page 981. Assume that one of Greg's Groovy Tunes' suppliers raises prices, which increases the cost for each event to $155 (instead of the original $115). Greg's cannot pass this increase on to its customers, so the company holds the price at the original $235 per event. Fixed costs remain at $12,000. How many events must Greg's sell to break even after the supplier raises prices?

Using the income statement approach:

Sales revenue – Variable cost	– Fixed costs	= Operating income
($235 × units sold) – ($155 × units sold)	– $12,000	= $0
[($235 – 155) × units sold]	– $12,000	= $0
$80 × units sold		= $12,000
	units sold	= $12,000/$80
	units sold	= 150 events

Proof							
	($235 × 150)	–	($155 × 150)	–	$12,000	=	**Operating income**
	$35,250	–	$23,250	–	$12,000	=	$0

Higher variable costs per event reduce Greg's Groovy Tunes' per-unit contribution margin from $120 per event to $80 per event. As a result, Greg's must sell more events to break even—150 rather than the original 100. This analysis shows why managers are particularly concerned with controlling costs during an economic downturn. Increases in cost raise the breakeven point, and a higher breakeven point can lead to problems if demand falls due to a recession.

Of course, a decrease in variable costs would have the opposite effect. Lower variable costs increase the contribution margin on each event and, therefore, lower the breakeven point.

Changing Fixed Costs

Return to Greg's original data on page 981. Controller Natalie Blanding is considering spending an additional $3,000 on Web site banner ads. This would increase fixed costs from $12,000 to $15,000. If the events are sold at the original price of $235 each and variable costs remain at $115 per event, what is the new breakeven point?

Using the income statement approach:

Sales revenue – Variable cost	–	Fixed costs	=	Operating income
($235 × units sold) – ($115 × units sold)	–	$15,000	=	$0
[($235 – 115) × units sold]	–	$15,000	=	$0
$120 × units sold			=	$15,000
		units sold	=	$15,000/$120
		units sold	=	125 events

Proof	($235 × 125)	–	($115 × 125)	–	$15,000	= Operating income
	$29,375	–	$14,375	–	$15,000	= $0

Higher fixed costs increase the total contribution margin required to break even. In this case, increasing the fixed costs from $12,000 to $15,000 increases the breakeven point to 125 events (from the original 100 events).

Managers usually prefer a lower breakeven point to a higher one. But do not overemphasize this one aspect of CVP analysis. Even though investing in the Web banner ads increases Greg's Groovy Tunes' breakeven point, the company should pay the extra $3,000 if that would increase both sales and profits.

Exhibit 18-6 shows how all of these changes affect the contribution margin and break even.

EXHIBIT 18-6 **How Changes in Selling Price, Variable Costs, and Fixed Costs Affect the Contribution Margin per Unit and the Breakeven Point**

Cause	Effect	Result
Change	Contribution Margin per Unit	Breakeven Point
Selling Price per Unit Increases	Increases	Decreases
Selling Price per Unit Decreases	Decreases	Increases
Variable Cost per Unit Increases	Decreases	Increases
Variable Cost per Unit Decreases	Increases	Decreases
Total Fixed Cost Increases	Is not affected	Increases
Total Fixed Cost Decreases	Is not affected	Decreases

Stop & Think...

The sensitivity analysis can be applied to many types of situations. For example, consider that you are deciding between purchasing a hybrid SUV and a subcompact car. In your decision, you consider the gas mileage, maintenance costs, insurance, and the price of the cars. You compare these factors and purchase the car that is most economical to use (least costly).

Margin of Safety

The **margin of safety** is the excess of expected sales over breakeven sales. The margin of safety is therefore the "cushion" or drop in sales that the company can absorb without incurring a loss.

Managers use the margin of safety to evaluate the risk of both their current operations and their plans for the future. Let us apply the margin of safety to Greg's Groovy Tunes.

Greg's Groovy Tunes' original breakeven point was 100 events. Suppose the company expects to sell 170 events. The margin of safety is as follows:

Expected sales	–	Breakeven sales	=	Margin of safety in units
170 events	–	100 events	=	70 events

Margin of safety in units	×	Sales price	=	Margin of safety in dollars
70 events	×	$235	=	$16,450

Sales can drop by 70 events, or $16,450, before Greg's incurs a loss. This margin of safety (70 events) is 41.2% of total expected sales (170 events). That is a comfortable margin of safety.

Stop & Think...

If you have done really well on all your assignments in a particular course for the semester, you have created a sort of "margin of safety" for your grade. That is, by performing above the minimum (break even), you have a cushion to help you maintain a good grade even if you happen to perform poorly on a future assignment.

Information Technology and Sensitivity Analysis

Information technology allows managers to perform lots of sensitivity analyses before launching a new product or shutting down a plant. Excel spreadsheets are useful for sensitivity analyses like those we just did for Greg's Groovy Tunes. Spreadsheets can show how one change (or several changes simultaneously) affects operations. Managers can plot basic CVP data to show profit-planning graphs similar to the one shown in Exhibit 18-5.

Large companies use enterprise resource planning software—**SAP**, **Oracle**, and **Peoplesoft**—for their CVP analysis. For example, after **Sears** stores lock their doors at 9:00 P.M., records for each individual transaction flow into a massive database. From a Diehard battery sold in California to a Trader Bay polo shirt sold in New Hampshire, the system compiles an average of 1.5 million transactions a day. With the click of a mouse, managers can conduct break even or profit planning analysis on any product they choose.

Effect of Sales Mix on CVP Analysis

5 Calculate the breakeven point for multiple product lines or services

Most companies sell more than one product. Selling price and variable costs differ for each product, so each product line makes a different contribution to profits. The same CVP formulas we used earlier apply to a company with multiple products.

To calculate break even for each product line, we must compute the *weighted-average contribution margin* of all the company's products. The sales mix provides the weights. **Sales mix** is the combination of products that make up total sales. For example, Fat Cat Furniture sold 6,000 cat beds and 4,000 scratching posts during the past year. The sales mix of 6,000 beds and 4,000 posts creates a ratio of 3:2 or a percentage of 60% for the beds and 40% for the posts. For every 3 cat beds, Fat Cat expects to sell 2 scratching posts, so Fat Cat expects 3/5 of the sales to be cat beds and 2/5 to be scratching posts.

Fat Cat's total fixed costs are $40,000. The cat bed's unit selling price is $44 and variable costs per bed are $24. The scratching post's unit selling price is $100 and variable cost per post is $30. To compute breakeven sales in units for both product lines, Fat Cat completes the following three steps.

STEP 1: Calculate the weighted-average contribution margin per unit, as follows:

	Cat Beds	Scratching Posts	Total
Sale price per unit	$ 44	$100	
Deduct: Variable cost per unit	(24)	(30)	
Contribution margin per unit	$ 20	$ 70	
Sales mix in units	× 3	× 2	5
Contribution margin	$ 60	$140	$200
Weighted-average contribution margin per unit ($200/5)			$ 40

STEP 2: Calculate the breakeven point in units for the "package" of products:

$$\text{Breakeven sales in total units} = \frac{\text{Fixed costs + Operating income}}{\text{Weighted-average contribution margin per unit}}$$

$$= \frac{\$40{,}000 + \$0}{\$40}$$

$$= 1{,}000 \text{ items}$$

STEP 3: Calculate the breakeven point in units for each product line. Multiply the "package" breakeven point in units by each product line's proportion of the sales mix.

Breakeven sales of cat beds (1,000 × 3/5)	600 cat beds
Breakeven sales of scratching posts (1,000 × 2/5)	400 scratching posts

In this example the calculations yield round numbers. When the calculations do not yield round numbers, round your answer up to the next whole number.

The overall breakeven point in sales dollars is $66,400:

600 cat beds at $44 selling price each.............................	$26,400
400 scratching posts at $100 selling price each	40,000
Total revenues..	$66,400

We can prove this breakeven point by preparing a contribution margin income statement:

	Cat Beds	Scratching Posts	Total
Sales revenue:			
Cat beds (600 × $44)	$26,400		
Scratching posts (400 × $100)		$40,000	$ 66,400
Variable costs:			
Cat beds (600 × $24)	14,400		
Scratching posts (400 × $30)		12,000	26,400
Contribution margin	$12,000	$28,000	$ 40,000
Fixed costs			(40,000)
Operating income			$ 0

If the sales mix changes, then Fat Cat can repeat this analysis using new sales mix information to find the breakeven points for each product line.

In addition to finding the breakeven point, Fat Cat can also estimate the sales needed to generate a certain level of operating profit. Suppose Fat Cat would like to earn operating income of $20,000. How many units of each product must Fat Cat now sell?

$$\text{Breakeven sales in total units} = \frac{\text{Fixed costs} + \text{Operating income}}{\text{Weighted-average contribution margin per unit}}$$
$$= \frac{\$40{,}000 + \$20{,}000}{\$40}$$
$$= 1{,}500 \text{ items}$$

Breakeven sales of cat beds (1,500 × 3/5)	900 cat beds
Breakeven sales of scratching posts (1,500 × 2/5)	600 scratching posts

We can prove this planned profit level by preparing a contribution margin income statement:

	Cat Beds	Scratching Posts	Total
Sales revenue:			
Cat beds (900 × $44)	$39,600		
Scratching posts (600 × $100)		$60,000	$ 99,600
Variable costs:			
Cat beds (900 × $24)	21,600		
Scratching posts (600 × $30)		18,000	39,600
Contribution margin	$18,000	$42,000	$ 60,000
Fixed costs			(40,000)
Operating income			$ 20,000

You have learned how to use CVP analysis as a managerial tool. Review the CVP Analysis Decision Guidelines to make sure you understand these basic concepts.

Decision Guidelines

COST-VOLUME-PROFIT ANALYSIS

As a manager, you will find CVP very useful. Here are some questions you will ask, and guidelines for answering them.

Decision	Guidelines
• How do changes in volume of activity affect	
• total costs?	Total *variable* costs → Change in proportion to changes in volume (number of products or services sold) Total *fixed* costs → No change
• cost per unit?	Variable cost per unit → No change
• Fixed cost per unit:	• Decreases when volume rises (Fixed costs are spread over *more* units) • Increases when volume drops (Fixed costs are spread over *fewer* units)
• How do I calculate the sales needed to break even or earn a target operating income	
• in units?	*Income Statement Method:*

$$\text{Sales revenue} - \text{Variable costs} - \text{Fixed costs} = \text{Operating income}$$

$$\left(\begin{array}{c}\text{Sale price}\\\text{per unit}\end{array} \times \text{Units sold}\right) - \left(\begin{array}{c}\text{Variable cost}\\\text{per unit}\end{array} \times \text{Units sold}\right) - \text{Fixed costs} = \text{Operating income}$$

$$\underbrace{\left(\begin{array}{c}\text{Sale price}\\\text{per unit}\end{array} - \begin{array}{c}\text{Variable cost}\\\text{per unit}\end{array}\right)}_{} \times \text{Units sold} = \text{Fixed costs} + \text{Operating income}$$

$$\text{Contribution margin per unit} \times \text{Units sold} = \text{Fixed costs} + \text{Operating income}$$

$$\text{Units sold} = \frac{\text{Fixed Costs} + \text{Operating income}}{\text{Contribution margin per unit}}$$

Shortcut Contribution Margin Method:

$$\frac{\text{Fixed costs} + \text{Operating income}}{\text{Contribution margin per unit}}$$

• in dollars? — *Shortcut Contribution Margin Ratio Method:*

$$\frac{\text{Fixed costs} + \text{Operating income}}{\text{Contribution margin ratio}}$$

Decision	Guidelines		
• How will changes in sale price, or variable, or fixed costs affect the breakeven point?	**Cause**	**Effect**	**Result**
	Change	**Contribution Margin per Unit**	**Breakeven Point**
	Selling Price per Unit Increases	Increases	Decreases
	Selling Price per Unit Decreases	Decreases	Increases
	Variable Cost per Unit Increases	Decreases	Increases
	Variable Cost per Unit Decreases	Increases	Decreases
	Total Fixed Cost Increases	Is not affected	Increases
	Total Fixed Cost Decreases	Is not affected	Decreases
• How do I use CVP analysis to measure risk?	**Margin of safety = Expected sales – Breakeven sales**		
• How do I calculate my breakeven point when I sell more than one product or service?	STEP 1: Compute the weighted-average contribution margin per unit. STEP 2: Calculate the breakeven point in units for the "package" of products. STEP 3: Calculate breakeven point in units for each product line. Multiply the "package" breakeven point in units by each product line's proportion of the sales mix.		

Summary Problem 2

Happy Feet buys hiking socks for $6 a pair and sells them for $10. Management budgets monthly fixed costs of $12,000 for sales volumes between 0 and 12,000 pairs.

Requirements

Consider each of the following questions separately by using the foregoing information each time.

1. Calculate the breakeven point in units.
2. Happy Feet reduces its selling price from $10 a pair to $8 a pair. Calculate the new breakeven point in units.
3. Happy Feet finds a new supplier for the socks. Variable costs will decrease by $1 a pair. Calculate the new breakeven point in units.
4. Happy Feet plans to advertise in hiking magazines. The advertising campaign will increase total fixed costs by $2,000 per month. Calculate the new breakeven point in units.
5. In addition to selling hiking socks, Happy Feet would like to start selling sports socks. Happy Feet expects to sell 1 pair of hiking socks for every 3 pairs of sports socks. Happy Feet will buy the sports socks for $4 a pair and sell them for $8 a pair. Total fixed costs will stay at $12,000 per month. Calculate the breakeven point in units for both hiking socks and sports socks.

Solution

Requirement 1

$$\text{Units sold} = \frac{\text{Fixed costs}}{\text{Contribution margin per unit}}$$

$$\text{Breakeven sales in units} = \frac{\$12{,}000}{\$10 - \$6}$$

$$= \frac{\$12{,}000}{\$4}$$

$$= 3{,}000 \text{ units}$$

Requirement 2

$$\text{Units sold} = \frac{\text{Fixed costs}}{\text{Contribution margin per unit}}$$

$$\text{Breakeven sales in units} = \frac{\$12{,}000}{\$8 - \$6}$$

$$= \frac{\$12{,}000}{\$2}$$

$$= 6{,}000 \text{ units}$$

Requirement 3

$$\text{Units sold} = \frac{\text{Fixed costs}}{\text{Contribution margin per unit}}$$

$$\text{Breakeven sales in units} = \frac{\$12{,}000}{\$10 - \$5}$$

$$= \frac{\$12{,}000}{\$5}$$

$$= 2{,}400 \text{ units}$$

Requirement 4

$$\text{Units sold} = \frac{\text{Fixed costs}}{\text{Contribution margin per unit}}$$

$$\text{Breakeven sales in units} = \frac{\$14{,}000}{\$10 - \$6}$$

$$= \frac{\$14{,}000}{\$4}$$

$$= 3{,}500 \text{ units}$$

Requirement 5

STEP 1: Calculate the weighted-average contribution margin:

	Hiking	Sports	
Sale price per unit	$10.00	$ 8.00	
Variable expenses per unit	6.00	4.00	
Contribution margin per unit	$ 4.00	$ 4.00	
Sales mix in units	× 1	× 3	4
Contribution margin per unit	$ 4.00	$12.00	$16.00
Weighted-average CM ($16/4)			$ 4.00

STEP 2: Calculate breakeven point for "package" of products:

$$\text{Breakeven sales in units} = \frac{\text{Fixed costs}}{\text{Contribution margin per unit}}$$

$$= \frac{\$12{,}000}{\$4}$$

$$= 3{,}000 \text{ units}$$

STEP 3: Calculate breakeven point for each product line:

Number of hiking socks (3,000 × (1/4))	750
Number of sport socks (3,000 × (3/4))	2,250

Review Cost-Volume-Profit Analysis

Accounting Vocabulary

Absorption Costing (p. 1014)
The costing method that assigns both variable and fixed manufacturing costs to products.

Breakeven Point (p. 982)
The sales level at which operating income is zero: Total revenues equal total expenses.

Contribution Margin (p. 983)
Sales revenue minus variable expenses.

Contribution Margin Income Statement (p. 983)
Income statement that groups costs by behavior—variable costs or fixed costs—and highlights the contribution margin.

Contribution Margin Ratio (p. 984)
Ratio of contribution margin to sales revenue.

Cost-Volume-Profit (CVP) Analysis (p. 975)
Expresses the relationships among costs, volume, and profit or loss.

Fixed Costs (p. 977)
Costs that tend to remain the same in amount, regardless of variations in level of activity.

High-Low Method (p. 979)
A method used to separate mixed costs into variable and fixed components, using the highest and lowest total cost.

Margin of Safety (p. 992)
Excess of expected sales over breakeven sales. A drop in sales that a company can absorb without incurring an operating loss.

Mixed Costs (p. 978)
Costs that have both variable and fixed components.

Relevant Range (p. 980)
The band of volume where total fixed costs remain constant and the variable cost per unit remains constant.

Sales Mix (p. 993)
Combination of products that make up total sales.

Sensitivity Analysis (p. 990)
A "what if" technique that asks what results will be if actual prices or costs change, or if an underlying assumption changes.

Total Fixed Costs (p. 977)
Costs that do not change in total despite wide changes in volume.

Total Variable Costs (p. 976)
Costs that change in total in direct proportion to changes in volume.

Variable Costing (p. 976)
The costing method that assigns only variable manufacturing costs to products.

Quick Check

1. For Greg's Groovy Tunes, straight-line depreciation on the trucks is
   a. fixed cost.
   b. mixed cost.
   c. variable cost.
   d. None of the above
2. Assume Cape Cod Railway is considering hiring a reservations agency to handle passenger reservations. The agency would charge a flat fee of $7,000 per month, plus $2 per passenger reservation. What is the total reservation cost if 100,000 passengers take the trip next month?
   a. $200,000
   b. $207,000
   c. $2.07
   d. $7,000
3. If Cape Cod's fixed costs total $40,000 per month, the variable cost per passenger is $10, and tickets sell for $50, what is the breakeven point in units?
   a. 1,000 passengers
   b. 686 passengers
   c. 100 passengers
   d. 8,100 passengers

4. Suppose Cape Cod Railway's total revenues are $4,900,000, its variable costs are $2,900,000, and its fixed costs are $1,300,000. Compute the breakeven point in dollars.

   a. $410,000
   b. $4,200,000
   c. $3,170,732
   d. $4,900,000

5. If Cape Cod Railway's fixed costs total $40,000 per month, the variable cost per passenger is $10, and tickets sell for $59, how much revenue must the Railway have to generate to earn $150,000 in operating income per month? (*Hint:* Begin by calculating contribution margin in whole units.)

   a. $268,802
   b. $228,802
   c. $188,802
   d. $190,022

6. On a CVP graph, the total cost line intersects the vertical (dollars) axis at

   a. the level of the variable costs.
   b. the breakeven point.
   c. the level of the fixed costs.
   d. the origin.

7. If a company increases its selling price per unit for Product A, then the new breakeven point will

   a. increase.
   b. decrease.
   c. remain the same.

8. If a company increases its fixed costs for Product B, then the contribution margin per unit will

   a. increase.
   b. decrease.
   c. remain the same.

9. Telluride Railway had the following revenue over the past five years:

2005	$ 400,000
2006	500,000
2007	700,000
2008	600,000
2009	800,000

   To predict revenues for 2010, Telluride uses the average for the past five years. The company's breakeven revenue is $600,000 per year. What is Telluride's margin of safety?

   a. $100,000
   b. $50,000
   c. $0
   d. $110,000

10. Intervale Railway sells half of its tickets for the regular price of $65. The other half go to senior citizens and children for the discounted price of $45. Variable cost per passenger is $10 for both groups, and fixed costs total $45,000 per month. What is Intervale's breakeven point in total passengers? Regular passengers? Discount passengers?

   a. 1,000/500/500

   b. 600/300/300

   c. 1,500/750/750

   d. 1,250/625/625

Answers are given after Apply Your Knowledge (p. 1013).

Assess Your Progress

■ Short Exercises

S18-1 *(L. OBJ. 1)* **Variable and fixed costs [5–10 min]**
Chicago Acoustics builds innovative loudspeakers for music and home theater systems. Consider the following costs:

☐	1. Depreciation on routers used to cut wood enclosures
☐	2. Wood for speaker enclosures
☐	3. Patents on crossover relays
☐	4. Crossover relays
☐	5. Grill cloth
☐	6. Glue
☐	7. Quality inspector's salary

Requirement

1. Identify the costs as variable or fixed. Indicate V for variable costs and F for fixed costs.

S18-2 *(L. OBJ. 1)* **Variable and fixed costs [5–10 min]**
Sally's DayCare has been in operation for several years. Consider the following costs:

☐	1. Building rent
☐	2. Toys
☐	3. Playground equipment
☐	4. Afternoon snacks
☐	5. Sally's salary
☐	6. Wages of afterschool employees
☐	7. Drawing paper
☐	8. Tables and chairs

Requirement

1. Identify the costs as variable or fixed. Indicate V for variable costs and F for fixed costs.

S18-3 *(L. OBJ. 1)* **Mixed costs [5–10 min]**
Suppose Worldwide-Link offers an international calling plan that charges $10.00 per month plus $0.30 per minute for calls outside the United States.

Requirements

1. Under this plan, what is your monthly international long-distance cost if you call Europe for
   a. 20 minutes?
   b. 50 minutes?
   c. 95 minutes?
2. Draw a graph illustrating your total cost under this plan. Label the axes, and show your costs at 20, 50, and 95 minutes.

S18-4 *(L. OBJ. 1)* **Mixed costs [5–10 min]**
Mel owns a machine shop. In reviewing his utility bill for the last 12 months he found that his highest bill of $2,400 occurred in August when his machines worked 1,000 machine hours. His lowest utility bill of $2,200 occurred in December when his machines worked 500 machine hours.

Requirement

1. Calculate (a) the variable rate per machine hour and (b) Mel's total fixed utility cost.

S18-5 *(L. OBJ. 2)* **Computing breakeven point in sales units [5–10 min]**
Storytime Park competes with Daisy World by providing a variety of rides. Storytime sells tickets at $70 per person as a one-day entrance fee. Variable costs are $15 per person, and fixed costs are $371,250 per month.

Requirement

1. Compute the number of tickets Storytime must sell to break even. Perform a numerical proof to show that your answer is correct.

Note: Short Exercise 18-5 must be completed before attempting Short Exercise 18-6.

S18-6 *(L. OBJ. 2)* **Computing breakeven point in sales dollars [5 min]**
Refer to Short Exercise 18-5.

Requirements

1. Compute Storytime Park's contribution margin ratio. Carry your computation to five decimal places.
2. Use the contribution margin ratio CVP formula to determine the sales revenue Storytime Park needs to break even.

S18-7 *(L. OBJ. 3)* **Computing contribution margin, breakeven point, and units to achieve operating income [10–15 min]**

Consider the following facts:

	A	B	C
Number of units	1,100	3,000	8,000
Sale price per unit	$ 12	$ 16	$ 30
Variable costs per unit	6	8	21
Total fixed costs	50,000	21,000	180,000
Target operating income	50,000	70,000	90,000
Calculate:			
Contribution margin per unit	______	______	______
Contribution margin ratio	______	______	______
Breakeven points in units	______	______	______
Breakeven point in sales dollars	______	______	______
Units to achieve target operating income	______	______	______

Requirement

1. Compute the missing information.

Note: Short Exercise 18-5 must be completed before attempting Short Exercise 18-8.

S18-8 *(L. OBJ. 4)* **Sensitivity analysis of changing sale price and variable costs on breakeven point [10 min]**

Refer to Short Exercise 18-5.

Requirements

1. Suppose Storytime Park cuts its ticket price from $70 to $60 to increase the number of tickets sold. Compute the new breakeven point in tickets and in sales dollars. Carry your computations to five decimal places.
2. Ignore the information in requirement 1. Instead, assume that Storytime Park reduces the variable cost from $15 to $10 per ticket. Compute the new breakeven point in tickets and in dollars. Carry your computations to five decimal places.

Note: Short Exercise 18-5 must be completed before attempting Short Exercise 18-9.

S18-9 *(L. OBJ. 4)* **Sensitivity analysis of changing fixed cost on breakeven point [5–10 min]**

Refer to Short Exercise S18-5. Suppose Storytime Park reduces fixed costs from $371,250 per month to $343,750 per month.

Requirement

1. Compute the new breakeven point in tickets and in sales dollars.

Note: Short Exercise 18-5 must be completed before attempting Short Exercise 18-10.

S18-10 *(L. OBJ. 4)* **Computing margin of safety [5–10 min]**

Refer to Short Exercise 18-5.

Requirement

1. If Storytime Park expects to sell 6,900 tickets, compute the margin of safety in tickets and in sales dollars.

S18-11 *(L. OBJ. 5)* **Calculating weighted average contribution margin [5–10 min]**
SoakNSun Swim Park sells individual and family tickets, which include a meal, 3 beverages, and unlimited use of the swimming pools. SoakNSun has the following ticket prices and variable costs for 2010:

	Individual	Family
Sale price per ticket	$ 35	$ 105
Variable cost per ticket ...	25	100

SoakNSun expects to sell 1 individual ticket for every 3 family tickets.

Requirement

1. Compute the weighted-average contribution margin per ticket.

Note: Short Exercise 18-11 must be completed before attempting Short Exercise 18-12.

S18-12 *(L. OBJ. 5)* **Calculating breakeven point for two product lines [5–10 min]**
Refer to Short Exercise 18-11. For 2011, SoakNSun expects a sales mix of 2 individual tickets for every 3 family tickets. In this mix, the weighted-average contribution margin per ticket is $7. SoakNSun's total fixed costs are $21,000.

Requirements

1. Calculate the total number of tickets SoakNSun must sell to break even.
2. Calculate the number of individual tickets and the number of family tickets the company must sell to break even.

Exercises

E18-13 *(L. OBJ. 1)* **CVP definitions [15 min]**
Consider the following terms and definitions.

_____ 1. Costs that do not change in total despite wide changes in volume
_____ 2. The sales level at which operating income is zero: Total revenues equal total costs
_____ 3. Drop in sales a company can absorb without incurring an operating loss
_____ 4. Combination of products that make up total sales
_____ 5. Sales revenue minus variable costs
_____ 6. Describes how costs change as volume changes
_____ 7. Costs that change in total in direct proportion to changes in volume
_____ 8. The band of volume where total fixed costs remain constant and the variable cost *per unit* remains constant

a. Breakeven
b. Contribution margin
c. Cost behavior
d. Margin of safety
e. Relevant range
f. Sales mix
g. Fixed costs
h. Variable costs

Requirement

1. Match the terms with the correct definitions.

E18-14 *(L. OBJ. 1)* **Mixed costs; the high-low method [10–15 min]**
The manager of Swift Car Inspection reviewed his monthly operating costs for the past year. His costs ranged from $4,400 for 1,400 inspections to $4,000 for 900 inspections.

Requirements

1. Calculate the variable cost per inspection.
2. Calculate the total fixed costs.
3. Write the equation and calculate the operating costs for 1,000 inspections.

E18-15 *(L. OBJ. 2)* **Preparing contribution margin income statements and calculating breakeven sales [15 min]**
For its top managers, Countrywide Travel formats its income statement as follows:

COUNTRYWIDE TRAVEL Contribution Margin Income Statement Three Months Ended March 31, 2011	
Sales revenue	$ 316,500
Variable costs	127,000
Contribution margin	189,500
Fixed costs	174,000
Operating income	$ 15,500

Countrywide's relevant range is between sales of $251,000 and $365,000.

Requirements

1. Calculate the contribution margin ratio.
2. Prepare two contribution margin income statements: one at the $251,000 level and one at the $365,000 level. (*Hint*: The proportion of each sales dollar that goes toward variable costs is constant within the relevant range. The proportion of each sales dollar that goes toward contribution margin also is constant within the relevant range.)
3. Compute breakeven sales in dollars.

E18-16 *(L. OBJ. 2)* **Computing breakeven sales by the contribution margin approach [15 min]**
Hang Ten, Co., produces sports socks. The company has fixed costs of $90,000 and variable costs of $0.90 per package. Each package sells for $1.80.

Requirements

1. Compute the contribution margin per package and the contribution margin ratio.
2. Find the breakeven point in units and in dollars, using the contribution margin approach.

E18-17 *(L. OBJ. 3)* **Computing a change in breakeven sales [10–15 min]**
Owner Shan Lo is considering franchising her Noodles restaurant concept. She believes people will pay $8 for a large bowl of noodles. Variable costs are $1.60 per bowl. Lo estimates monthly fixed costs for a franchise at $8,600.

Requirements

1. Use the contribution margin ratio approach to find a franchise's breakeven sales in dollars.
2. Lo believes most locations could generate $22,313 in monthly sales. Is franchising a good idea for Lo if franchisees want a minimum monthly operating income of $8,850?

E18-18 *(L. OBJ. 3)* **Computing breakeven sales and operating income or loss under different conditions [10–15 min]**

Gary's Steel Parts produces parts for the automobile industry. The company has monthly fixed costs of $630,000 and a contribution margin of 95% of revenues.

Requirements

1. Compute Gary's monthly breakeven sales in dollars. Use the contribution margin ratio approach.
2. Use contribution margin income statements to compute Gary's monthly operating income or operating loss if revenues are $510,000 and if they are $1,000,000.
3. Do the results in requirement 2 make sense given the breakeven sales you computed in requirement 1? Explain.

E18-19 *(L. OBJ. 3)* **Analyzing a cost-volume profit graph [15–20 min]**

Zac Hill is considering starting a Web-based educational business, e-Prep MBA. He plans to offer a short-course review of accounting for students entering MBA programs. The materials would be available on a password-protected Web site; students would complete the course through self-study. Hill would have to grade the course assignments, but most of the work is in developing the course materials, setting up the site, and marketing. Unfortunately, Hill's hard drive crashed before he finished his financial analysis. However, he did recover the following partial CVP chart:

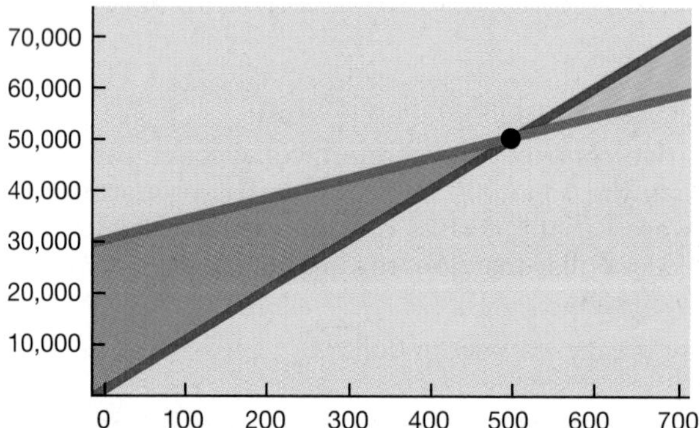

Requirements

1. Label each axis, the sales revenue line, the total costs line, the fixed costs, the operating income area, and the breakeven point.
2. If Hill attracts 400 students to take the course, will the venture be profitable?
3. What are the breakeven sales in students and dollars?

E18-20 *(L. OBJ. 4)* **Impact on breakeven point if sale price, variable costs, and fixed costs change [15 min]**

Country Road Driving School charges $230 per student to prepare and administer written and driving tests. Variable costs of $70 per student include trainers' wages, study materials, and gasoline. Annual fixed costs of $112,000 include the training facility and fleet of cars.

Requirements

1. For each of the following independent situations, calculate the contribution margin per unit and the breakeven point in units:
   a. Breakeven point with no change in information
   b. Decrease sales price to $200 per student
   c. Decrease variable costs to $50 per student
   d. Decrease fixed costs to $102,000
2. Compare the impact of changes in the sales price, variable costs, and fixed costs on the contribution margin per unit and the breakeven point in units.

E18-21 *(L. OBJ. 4)* **Computing margin of safety [15 min]**
Ronnie's Repair Shop has a monthly target operating income of $17,000. Variable costs are 80% of sales, and monthly fixed costs are $12,000.

Requirements

1. Compute the monthly margin of safety in dollars if the shop achieves its income goal.
2. Express Ronnie's margin of safety as a percentage of target sales.

E18-22 *(L. OBJ. 5)* **Calculating breakeven point for two product lines [15–20 min]**
Scotty's Scooters plans to sell a standard scooter for $40 and a chrome scooter for $50. Scotty's purchases the standard scooter for $25 and the chrome scooter for $30. Scotty expects to sell two standard scooters for every three chrome scooters. His monthly fixed costs are $18,900.

Requirements

1. How many of each type of scooter must Scotty's Scooters sell each month to break even?
2. To earn $14,400?

Problem (Group A)

P18-23A *(L .OBJ. 1, 2, 3)* **Calculating cost-volume profit elements [45–60 min]**
The budgets of four companies yield the following information:

	Company			
	North	South	East	West
Sales revenue	$ 710,000	$ (4)	$ 600,000	$ (10)
Variable costs	(1)	150,000	288,000	160,160
Fixed costs	(2)	121,000	139,000	(11)
Operating income (loss)	$ 13,800	$ (5)	$ (7)	$ 42,840
Units sold	190,000	10,000	(8)	(12)
Contribution margin per unit	$ 1.42	$ (6)	$ 97.50	$ 14.72
Contribution margin ratio	(3)	0.20	(9)	0.23

Requirements

1. Fill in the blanks for each missing value.
2. Which company has the lowest breakeven point in sales dollars? What causes the low breakeven point?

P18-24A *(L. OBJ. 2, 3)* **Break even sales; sales to earn a target operating income; contribution margin income statement [30–45 min]**
British Productions performs London shows. The average show sells 1,200 tickets at $50 per ticket. There are 120 shows a year. The average show has a cast of 70, each earning an average of $300 per show. The cast is paid after each show. The other variable cost is a program-printing cost of $7 per guest. Annual fixed costs total $459,000.

Requirements

1. Compute revenue and variable costs for each show.
2. Use the income statement equation approach to compute the number of shows British Productions must perform each year to break even.
3. Use the contribution margin approach to compute the number of shows needed each year to earn a profit of $3,825,000. Is this profit goal realistic? Give your reasoning.
4. Prepare British Productions' contribution margin income statement for 120 shows for 2011. Report only two categories of costs: variable and fixed.

P18-25A *(L. OBJ. 2, 3, 4)* **Analyzing CVP relationships [30–45 min]**
Allen Company sells flags with team logos. Allen has fixed costs of $588,000 per year plus variable costs of $5.50 per flag. Each flag sells for $12.50.

Requirements

1. Use the income statement equation approach to compute the number of flags Allen must sell each year to break even.
2. Use the contribution margin ratio CVP formula to compute the dollar sales Allen needs to earn $32,200 in operating income for 2011.
3. Prepare Allen's contribution margin income statement for the year ended December 31, 2011, for sales of 73,000 flags. Cost of goods sold is 60% of variable costs. Operating costs make up the rest of variable costs and all of fixed costs.
4. The company is considering an expansion that will increase fixed costs by 20% and variable costs by $0.60 cents per flag. Compute the new breakeven point in units and in dollars. Should Allen Company undertake the expansion? Give your reasoning.

P18-26A *(L. OBJ. 2, 3, 4)* **Computing breakeven sales and sales needed to earn a target operating income; graphing CVP relationships; sensitivity analysis [30–45 min]**
Big Time Investor Group is opening an office in Dallas. Fixed monthly costs are office rent ($8,200), depreciation on office furniture ($1,500), utilities ($2,300), special telephone lines ($1,300), a connection with an online brokerage service ($2,900), and the salary of a financial planner ($11,800). Variable costs include payments to the financial planner (9% of revenue), advertising (12% of revenue), supplies and postage (4% of revenue), and usage fees for the telephone lines and computerized brokerage service (5% of revenue).

Requirements

1. Use the contribution margin ratio CVP formula to compute Big Time's breakeven revenue in dollars. If the average trade leads to $800 in revenue for Big Time, how many trades must be made to break even?
2. Use the income statement equation approach to compute the dollar revenues needed to earn a target monthly operating income of $11,200.
3. Graph Big Time's CVP relationships. Assume that an average trade leads to $800 in revenue for Big Time. Show the breakeven point, the sales revenue line, the fixed cost line, the total cost line, the operating loss area, the operating income area, and the sales in units (trades) and dollars when monthly operating income of $11,200 is earned. The graph should range from 0 to 80 units.
4. Suppose that the average revenue Big Time earns increases to $900 per trade. Compute the new breakeven point in trades. How does this affect the breakeven point?

P18-27A *(L. OBJ. 4, 5)* **Calculating breakeven point for two product lines; margin of safety [20 min]**

The contribution margin income statement of Cosmic Donuts for March 2012 follows:

COSMIC DONUTS Contribution Margin Income Statement For the Month of March 2012		
Sales revenue		$ 127,000
Variable costs:		
Cost of goods sold	$ 32,400	
Marketing costs	17,300	
General and administrative cost	10,625	60,325
Contribution margin		66,675
Fixed costs:		
Marketing costs	56,700	
General and administrative cost	6,300	63,000
Operating income		$ 3,675

Cosmic sells 2 dozen plain donuts for every dozen custard-filled donuts. A dozen plain donuts sells for $6, with total variable cost of $2 per dozen. A dozen custard-filled donuts sells for $8, with total variable cost of $5.50 per dozen.

Requirements

1. Determine Cosmic's monthly breakeven point in dozens of plain donuts and custard-filled donuts. Prove your answer by preparing a summary contribution margin income statement at the breakeven level of sales. Show only two categories of costs: variable and fixed.
2. Compute Cosmic's margin of safety in dollars for March 2012.
3. If Cosmic can increase monthly sales volume by 10%, what will operating income be? (The sales mix remains unchanged.)

Problem (Group B)

P18-28B *(L. OBJ. 1, 2, 3)* **Calculating cost-volume profit elements [45–60 min]**

The budgets of four companies yield the following information:

	Company			
	Blue	Red	Green	Yellow
Sales revenue	$ 705,000	$ (4)	$ 616,000	$ (10)
Variable costs	(1)	152,100	295,680	164,320
Fixed costs	(2)	122,000	136,000	(11)
Operating income (loss)	$ 12,900	$ (5)	$ (7)	$ 35,680
Units sold	190,000	10,000	(8)	(12)
Contribution margin per unit	$ 1.41	$ (6)	$ 100.10	$ 13.44
Contribution margin ratio	(3)	0.22	(9)	0.21

Requirements

1. Fill in the blanks for each missing value.
2. Which company has the lowest breakeven point in sales dollars? What causes the low breakeven point?

P18-29B *(L. OBJ. 2, 3)* **Breakeven sales; sales to earn a target operating income; contribution margin income statement [30–45 min]**
England Productions performs London shows. The average show sells 1,100 tickets at $55 per ticket. There are 110 shows a year. The average show has a cast of 65, each earning an average of $310 per show. The cast is paid after each show. The other variable cost is program-printing cost of $7 per guest. Annual fixed costs total $522,400.

Requirements

1. Compute revenue and variable costs for each show.
2. Use the income statement equation approach to compute the number of shows England Productions must perform each year to break even.
3. Use the contribution margin approach to compute the number of shows needed each year to earn a profit of $4,113,900. Is this profit goal realistic? Give your reasoning.
4. Prepare England Productions' contribution margin income statement for 110 shows for 2011. Report only two categories of costs: variable and fixed.

P18-30B *(L. OBJ. 2, 3, 4)* **Analyzing CVP relationships [30–45 min]**
Webb company sells flags with team logos. Webb has fixed costs of $639,600 per year plus variable costs of $4.20 per flag. Each flag sells for $12.00.

Requirements

1. Use the income statement equation approach to compute the number of flags Webb must sell each year to break even.
2. Use the contribution margin ratio CVP formula to compute the dollar sales. Webb needs to earn $32,500 in operating income for 2011.
3. Prepare Webb's contribution margin income statement for the year ended December 31, 2011, for sales of 76,000 flags. Cost of goods sold is 65% of variable costs. Operating costs make up the rest of variable costs and all of fixed costs.
4. The company is considering an expansion that will increase fixed costs by 20% and variable costs by $0.30 per flag. Compute the new breakeven point in units and in dollars. Should Webb undertake the expansion? Give your reasoning.

P18-31B *(L. OBJ. 2, 3, 4)* **Computing breakeven sales and sales needed to earn a target operating income; graphing CVP relationships; sensitivity analysis [30–45 min]**
Big Time Advisor Group is opening an office in Dallas. Fixed monthly costs are office rent ($8,000), depreciation on office furniture ($1,400), utilities ($2,000), special telephone lines ($1,300), a connection with an online brokerage service ($2,600), and the salary of a financial planner ($12,700). Variable costs include payments to the financial planner (9% of revenue), advertising (12% of revenue), supplies and postage (4% of revenue), and usage fees for the telephone lines and computerized brokerage service (5% of revenue).

Requirements

1. Use the contribution margin ratio CVP formula to compute Big Time's breakeven revenue in dollars. If the average trade leads to $800 in revenue for Big Time, how many trades must be made to break even?

2. Use the income statement equation approach to compute the dollar revenues needed to earn a target monthly operating income of $10,000.
3. Graph Big Time's CVP relationships. Assume that an average trade leads to $800 in revenue for Big Time. Show the breakeven point, the sales revenue line, the fixed cost line, the total cost line, the operating loss area, the operating income area, and the sales in units (trades) and dollars when monthly operating income of $10,000 is earned. The graph should range from 0 to 80 units.
4. Suppose that the average revenue Big Time earns increases to $900 per trade. Compute the new breakeven point in trades. How does this affect the breakeven point?

P18-32B *(L. OBJ. 4, 5)* **Calculating breakeven point for two product lines; margin of safety [20 min]**

The contribution margin income statement of Krazy Kustard Donuts for October 2012 follows:

KRAZY KUSTARD DONUTS Contribution Margin Income Statement For the Month of October 2012		
Sales revenue		$ 125,020
Variable costs:		
Cost of goods sold	$ 32,000	
Marketing costs	16,556	
General and administrative cost	5,400	53,956
Contribution margin		71,064
Fixed costs:		
Marketing costs	33,880	
General and administrative cost	4,320	43,200
Operating income		$ 27,864

Krazy Kustard sells 2 dozen plain donuts for every dozen custard-filled donuts. A dozen plain donuts sells for $6, with a variable cost of $2 per dozen. A dozen custard-filled donuts sells for $7, with a variable cost of $4.20 per dozen.

Requirements

1. Determine Krazy Kustard's monthly breakeven point in dozens of plain donuts and custard-filled donuts. Prove your answer by preparing a summary contribution margin income statement at the breakeven level of sales. Show only two categories of costs: variable and fixed.
2. Compute Krazy Kustard's margin of safety in dollars for October 2012.
3. If Krazy Kustard can increase the monthly sales volume by 10%, what will operating income be? (The sales mix remains unchanged.)

Continuing Exercise

E18-33 This exercise continues the Sherman Lawn Service, Inc., situation from Exercise 17-35 of Chapter 17. Sherman Lawn Service currently charges $50 for a standard lawn service and incurs $20 in variable cost. Assume fixed costs are $1,200 per month.

Requirements

1. What is the number of lawns that must be serviced to reach break even?
2. If Sherman desires to make a profit of $1,500, how many lawns must be serviced?

■ Continuing Problem

P18-34 This problem continues the Haupt Consulting, Inc., situation from Problem 17-36 of Chapter 17. Haupt Consulting provides consulting service at an average price of $100 per hour and incurs variable cost of $40 per hour. Assume average fixed costs are $4,000 a month.

Requirements

1. What is the number of hours that must be billed to reach break even?
2. If Haupt desires to make a profit of $5,000, how many lawns must be serviced?
3. Haupt thinks it can reduce fixed cost to $3,000 per month, but variable cost will increase to $42 per hour. What is the new break even in hours?

Apply Your Knowledge

■ Decision Cases

Case 1. Steve and Linda Hom live in Bartlesville, Oklahoma. Two years ago, they visited Thailand. Linda, a professional chef, was impressed with the cooking methods and the spices used in the Thai food. Bartlesville does not have a Thai restaurant, and the Homs are contemplating opening one. Linda would supervise the cooking, and Steve would leave his current job to be the maitre d'. The restaurant would serve dinner Tuesday—Saturday.

Steve has noticed a restaurant for lease. The restaurant has seven tables, each of which can seat four. Tables can be moved together for a large party. Linda is planning two seatings per evening, and the restaurant will be open 50 weeks per year.

The Homs have drawn up the following estimates:

Average revenue, including beverages and dessert	$ 45 per meal
Average cost of food	$ 15 per meal
Chef's and dishwasher's salaries	$61,200 per *year*
Rent (premises, equipment)	$ 4,000 per month
Cleaning (linen and premises)	$ 800 per month
Replacement of dishes, cutlery, glasses	$ 300 per month
Utilities, advertising, telephone	$ 2,300 per month

Requirements

1. Compute the *annual* breakeven number of meals and sales revenue for the restaurant.
2. Also compute the number of meals and the amount of sales revenue needed to earn operating income of $75,600 for the year.

3. How many meals must the Homs serve each night to earn their target income of $75,600?
4. Should the couple open the restaurant?

■ Ethical Issue

You have just begun your summer internship at Omni Instruments. The company supplies sterilized surgical instruments for physicians. To expand sales, Omni is considering paying a commission to its sales force. The controller, Matthew Barnhill, asks you to compute: (1) the new breakeven sales figure, and (2) the operating profit if sales increase 15% under the new sales commission plan. He thinks you can handle this task because you learned CVP analysis in your accounting class.

You spend the next day collecting information from the accounting records, performing the analysis, and writing a memo to explain the results. The company president is pleased with your memo. You report that the new sales commission plan will lead to a significant increase in operating income and only a small increase in breakeven sales.

The following week, you realize that you made an error in the CVP analysis. You overlooked the sales personnel's $2,800 monthly salaries and you did not include this fixed marketing cost in your computations. You are not sure what to do. If you tell Matthew Barnhill of your mistake, he will have to tell the president. In this case, you are afraid Omni might not offer you permanent employment after your internship.

Requirements

1. How would your error affect breakeven sales and operating income under the proposed sales commission plan? Could this cause the president to reject the sales commission proposal?
2. Consider your ethical responsibilities. Is there a difference between: (a) initially making an error, and (b) subsequently failing to inform the controller?
3. Suppose you tell Matthew Barnhill of the error in your analysis. Why might the consequences not be as bad as you fear? Should Barnhill take any responsibility for your error? What could Barnhill have done differently?
4. After considering all the factors, should you inform Barnhill or simply keep quiet?

Quick Check Answers

1. *a* 2. *b* 3. *a* 4. *c* 5. *b* 6. *c* 7. *b* 8. *c* 9. *c* 10. *a*

For online homework, exercises, and problems that provide you immediate feedback, please visit www.myaccountinglab.com.

Appendix 18A

Variable Costing and Absorption Costing

Up to this point, we have focused on the income statements that companies report to the public under the generally accepted accounting principles (GAAP). GAAP requires that we assign both variable and fixed manufacturing costs to products. This approach is called **absorption costing** because products absorb both fixed and variable manufacturing costs. Supporters of absorption costing argue that companies cannot produce products without incurring fixed costs, so these costs are an important part of product costs. Financial accountants usually prefer absorption costing.

The alternate method is called variable costing. **Variable costing** assigns only variable manufacturing costs to products. Fixed costs are considered *period costs* and are *expensed immediately* because the company incurs these fixed costs whether or not it produces any products or services. In variable costing, fixed costs are not product costs. Management accountants often prefer variable costing for their planning and control decisions.

The key difference between absorption costing and variable costing is that:

- Absorption costing considers fixed manufacturing costs as inventoriable product costs.
- Variable costing considers fixed manufacturing costs as period costs (expenses).

All other costs are treated the same way under both absorption and variable costing:

- Variable manufacturing costs are inventoriable products costs.
- All nonmanufacturing costs—both fixed and variable—are period costs and are expensed immediately when incurred.

Exhibit 18A-1 summarizes the difference between variable and absorption costing, with the differences shown in color.

EXHIBIT 18A-1 | Differences Between Absorption Costing and Variable Costing

Type of Cost	Absorption Costing	Variable Costing
Product Costs (Capitalized as Inventory until expensed as Cost of Goods Sold)	Direct materials Direct labor Variable manufacturing overhead Fixed manufacturing overhead	Direct materials Direct labor Variable manufacturing overhead
Period Costs (Expensed in period incurred)	Variable nonmanufacturing costs Fixed nonmanufacturing costs	Fixed manufacturing overhead Variable nonmanufacturing costs Fixed nonmanufacturing costs
Income Statement Format	Conventional income statement, as in Chapters 1–16	Contribution margin income statement

Applying Variable Costing Versus Absorption Costing: Limonade

To see how absorption costing and variable costing differ, let us consider the following example. Limonade incurs the following costs for its powdered sports beverage mix in March 2010:

Direct materials cost per case	$ 8.00
Direct labor cost per case	$ 3.00
Variable manufacturing overhead cost per case	$ 2.00
Total fixed manufacturing overhead costs	$50,000
Total fixed selling and administrative costs	$25,000
Cases of powdered mix produced	10,000
Cases of powdered mix sold	8,000
Sale price per case of powdered mix	$ 25

There were no beginning inventories, so Limonade has 2,000 cases of powdered mix in ending inventory (10,000 cases produced – 8,000 cases sold).

What is Limonade's inventoriable product cost per case under absorption costing and variable costing?

	Absorption Costing	Variable Costing
Direct materials	$ 8.00	$ 8.00
Direct labor	3.00	3.00
Variable manufacturing overhead	2.00	2.00
Fixed manufacturing overhead ($50,000/10,000 cases)	5.00	
Total cost per case	$18.00	$13.00

The only difference between absorption and variable costing is that fixed manufacturing overhead is a product cost under absorption costing, but a period cost under variable costing. This is why the cost per case is $5 higher under absorption (total cost of $18) than under variable costing ($13).

Exhibit 18A-2 on the following page shows the income statements using absorption costing and variable costing. The exhibit also shows the calculation for ending inventory at March 31, 2010.

Absorption costing income is higher because of the differing treatments of fixed manufacturing cost. Look at the two ending inventory amounts:

- $36,000 under absorption costing
- $26,000 under variable costing

This $10,000 difference results because ending inventory under absorption costing holds $10,000 of fixed manufacturing cost that got expensed under variable costing, as follows:

Units of ending finished goods inventory		Fixed manufacturing cost per unit		Difference in ending inventory
2,000	×	$5	=	$10,000

EXHIBIT 18A-2 **Absorption Costing and Variable Costing Income Statements and Ending Inventory Amount**

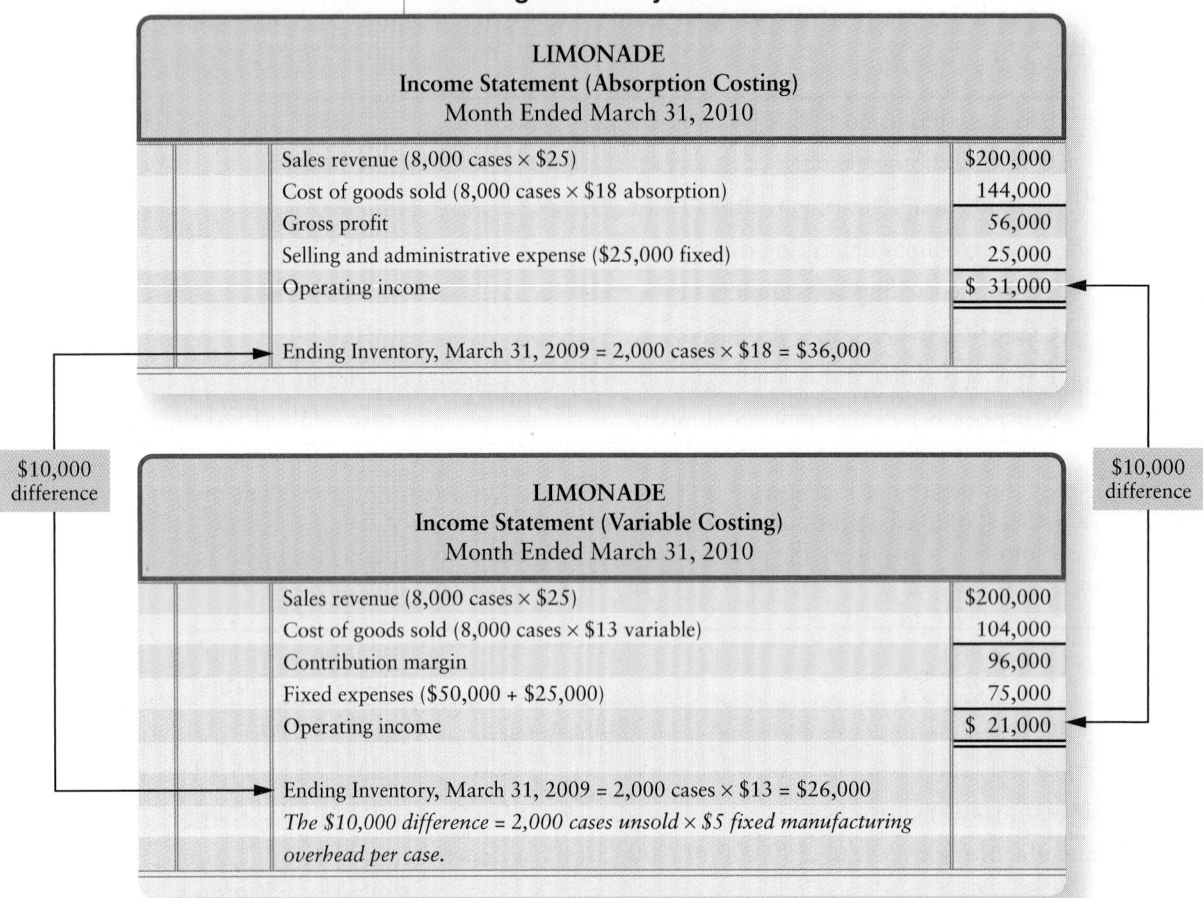

LIMONADE Income Statement (Absorption Costing) Month Ended March 31, 2010	
Sales revenue (8,000 cases × $25)	$200,000
Cost of goods sold (8,000 cases × $18 absorption)	144,000
Gross profit	56,000
Selling and administrative expense ($25,000 fixed)	25,000
Operating income	$ 31,000
Ending Inventory, March 31, 2009 = 2,000 cases × $18 = $36,000	

LIMONADE Income Statement (Variable Costing) Month Ended March 31, 2010	
Sales revenue (8,000 cases × $25)	$200,000
Cost of goods sold (8,000 cases × $13 variable)	104,000
Contribution margin	96,000
Fixed expenses ($50,000 + $25,000)	75,000
Operating income	$ 21,000
Ending Inventory, March 31, 2009 = 2,000 cases × $13 = $26,000 *The $10,000 difference = 2,000 cases unsold × $5 fixed manufacturing overhead per case.*	

Production Exceeds Sales Limonade produced 10,000 units and sold only 8,000 units, leaving 2,000 units in ending inventory. Whenever production exceeds sales, as for Limonade, absorption costing will produce more reported income.

Sales Exceed Production Companies sometimes sell more units of inventory than they produced that period. How can they do that? By drawing down inventories built up in prior periods. In these situations, inventory quantities decrease, and fixed costs in the earlier inventory get expensed under variable costing. That leads to the opposite result: Variable costing will produce more reported income whenever sales exceed production.

Absorption Costing and Manager Incentives

Suppose the Limonade manager receives a bonus based on absorption costing income. Will the manager increase or decrease production? The manager knows that absorption costing assigns each case of Limonade $5 of fixed manufacturing overhead.

- For every case that is produced but not sold, absorption costing "hides" $5 of fixed overhead in ending inventory (an asset).
- The more cases added to inventory, the more fixed overhead is "hidden" in ending inventory at the end of the month.
- The more fixed overhead in ending inventory, the smaller the cost of goods sold and the higher the operating income.

To maximize the bonus under absorption costing, the manager may increase production to build up inventory.

This incentive directly conflicts with the just-in-time philosophy, which emphasizes minimal inventory levels. Companies that have adopted just-in-time should either: (1) evaluate their managers based on variable costing income, or (2) use strict controls to prevent inventory buildup.

Appendix 18A Assignments

■ Short Exercises

S18A-1 Variable costing income statements [15–25 minutes]
RefreshAde produced 12,000 cases of powdered drink mix and sold 10,000 cases in April 2009. The sale price was $27, variable costs were $10 per case ($8 manufacturing and $2 selling and administrative), and total fixed costs were $45,000 ($35,000 manufacturing and $10,000 selling and administrative). The company had no beginning inventory.

Requirement

1. Prepare the April income statement using variable costing.

Note: Short Exercise 18A-1 must be completed before attempting Short Exercise 18A-2.

S18A-2 Absorption costing income statements [15–25 minutes]
Refer to Short Exercise 18A-1.

Requirements

1. Prepare the April income statement under absorption costing.
2. Is absorption costing income higher or lower than variable costing income? Explain why.

■ Exercise

E18A-3 Variable and absorption costing income statements [25–30 minutes]
The 2010 data that follow pertain to Swim Clearly, a manufacturer of swimming goggles. (Swim Clearly had no beginning inventories in January 2010.)

Sale price	$ 41	Fixed manufacturing overhead. . . .	$ 2,000,000
Variable manufacturing expense per unit.	22	Fixed operating expense.	250,000
		Number of goggles produced	200,000
Sales commission expense per unit . . .	6	Number of goggles sold	185,000

Requirements

1. Prepare both conventional (absorption costing) and contribution margin (variable costing) income statements for Swim Clearly for the year ended December 31, 2010.
2. Which statement shows the higher operating income? Why?
3. Swim Clearly's marketing vice president believes a new sales promotion that costs $150,000 would increase sales to 200,000 goggles. Should the company go ahead with the promotion? Give your reasoning.

Problem (Group A)

P18A-4A Variable and absorption costing income statements [25–30 minutes]
Clarita's Foods produces frozen meals that it sells for $12 each. The company computes a new monthly fixed manufacturing overhead rate based on the planned number of meals to be produced that month. All costs and production levels are exactly as planned. The following data are from Clarita's Foods' first month in business:

	January 2011
Sales	850 meals
Production	1,050 meals
Variable manufacturing cost per meal	$ 5
Sales commission cost per meal	$ 2
Total fixed manufacturing overhead	$ 315
Total fixed marketing and administrative costs	$ 750

Requirements

1. Compute the product cost per meal produced under absorption costing and under variable costing.
2. Prepare income statements for January 2011 using
   a. absorption costing
   b. variable costing
3. Is operating income higher under absorption costing or variable costing in January?

P18A-5A Variable and absorption costing income statements [25–30 minutes]
Game King manufactures video games that it sells for $36 each. The company uses a fixed manufacturing overhead rate of $3 per game. All costs and production levels are exactly as planned. The following data are from Game King's first two months in business during 2010:

	October	November
Sales	1,600 units	3,000 units
Production	2,800 units	2,800 units
Variable manufacturing cost per game	$ 13	$ 13
Sales commission per game	$ 6	$ 6
Total fixed manufacturing overhead	$ 8,400	$ 8,400
Total fixed marketing and administrative costs	$ 7,500	$ 7,500

Requirements

1. Compute the product cost per game produced under absorption costing and under variable costing.
2. Prepare monthly income statements for November, using
   a. absorption costing.
   b. variable costing.
3. Is operating income higher under absorption costing or variable costing in November? Explain the pattern of differences in operating income based on absorption costing versus variable costing.

■ Problem (Group B)

P18A-6B Variable and absorption costing income statements [25–30 minutes]

Stella's Foods produces frozen meals that it sells for $13 each. The company computes a new monthly fixed manufacturing overhead rate based on the planned number of meals to be produced that month. All costs and production levels are exactly as planned. The following data are from Stella's Foods' first month in business.

	January 2011
Sales	1,200 meals
Production	1,500 meals
Variable manufacturing cost per meal	$ 6
Sales commission cost per meal	$ 2
Total fixed manufacturing overhead	$ 1,050
Total fixed marketing and administrative costs	$ 300

Requirements

1. Compute the product cost per meal produced under absorption costing and under variable costing.
2. Prepare income statements for January 2011 using
   a. absorption costing.
   b. variable costing.
3. Is operating income higher under absorption costing or variable costing in January?

P18A-7B Variable and absorption costing income statements [25–30 minutes]

Arcade Away manufactures video games that it sells for $45 each. The company uses a fixed manufacturing overhead rate of $6 per game. All costs and production levels are exactly as planned. The following data are from Arcade Away's first two months in business during 2010:

	October	November
Sales	1,700 units	3,000 units
Production	2,700 units	2,700 units
Variable manufacturing cost per game	$ 17	$ 17
Sales commission per game	$ 6	$ 6
Total fixed manufacturing overhead	$ 16,200	$ 16,200
Total fixed marketing and administrative costs	$ 8,500	$ 8,500

Requirements

1. Compute the product cost per game produced under absorption costing and under variable costing.
2. Prepare monthly income statements for November, using
   a. absorption costing.
   b. variable costing.
3. Is operating income higher under absorption costing or variable costing in November? Explain the pattern of differences in operating income based on absorption costing versus variable costing.

■ Team Project

FASTPACK Manufacturing produces filament packaging tape. In 2009, FASTPACK produced and sold 15 million rolls of tape. The company has recently expanded its capacity, so it now can produce up to 30 million rolls per year. FASTPACK's accounting records show the following results from 2009:

Sale price per roll	$ 3.00
Variable manufacturing costs per roll	$ 2.00
Variable marketing and administrative costs per roll	$ 0.50
Total fixed manufacturing overhead costs	$8,400,000
Total fixed marketing and administrative costs	$1,100,000
Sales	15 million rolls
Production	15 million rolls

There were no beginning or ending inventories in 2009.

In January 2010, FASTPACK hired a new president, Kevin McDaniel. McDaniel has a one-year contract that specifies he will be paid 10% of FASTPACK's 2010 absorption costing operating income, instead of a salary. In 2010, McDaniel must make two major decisions:

- Should FASTPACK undertake a major advertising campaign? This campaign would raise sales to 24 million rolls. This is the maximum level of sales FASTPACK can expect to make in the near future. The ad campaign would add an additional $2.3 million in fixed marketing and administrative costs. Without the campaign, sales will be 15 million rolls.
- How many rolls of tape will FASTPACK produce?

At the end of the year, FASTPACK Manufacturing's Board of Directors will evaluate McDaniel's performance and decide whether to offer him a contract for the following year.

Requirements

Within your group, form two subgroups. The first subgroup assumes the role of Kevin McDaniel, FASTPACK Manufacturing's new president. The second subgroup assumes the role of FASTPACK Manufacturing's Board of Directors. McDaniel will meet with the Board of Directors shortly after the end of 2010 to decide whether he will remain at FASTPACK. Most of your effort should be devoted to advance preparation for this meeting. Each subgroup should meet separately to prepare for the meeting between the Board and McDaniel. (*Hint:* Keep computations other than per-unit amounts in millions.)

Kevin McDaniel should:

1. compute FASTPACK Manufacturing's 2009 operating income.
2. decide whether to adopt the advertising campaign. Prepare a memo to the Board of Directors explaining this decision. Give this memo to the Board of Directors as soon as possible (before the joint meeting).
3. assume FASTPACK adopts the advertising campaign. Decide how many rolls of tape to produce in 2010.
4. (given the response to requirement 3) prepare an absorption costing income statement for the year ended December 31, 2010, ending with operating income before bonus. Then compute the bonus separately. The variable cost per unit and the total fixed costs (with the exception of the advertising campaign) remain the same as in 2009. Give this income statement and bonus computation to the Board of Directors as soon as possible (before the meeting with the Board).

5. decide whether he wishes to remain at FASTPACK for another year. He currently has an offer from another company. The contract with the other company is identical to the one he currently has with FASTPACK—he will be paid 10% of absorption costing operating income instead of a salary.

The Board of Directors should:

1. compute FASTPACK's 2009 operating income.
2. determine whether FASTPACK should adopt the advertising campaign.
3. determine how many rolls of tape FASTPACK should produce in 2010.
4. evaluate McDaniel's performance, based on his decisions and the information he provided the Board. (*Hint*: You may want to prepare a variable costing income statement.)
5. evaluate the contract's bonus provision. Is the Board satisfied with this provision? If so, explain why. If not, recommend how it should be changed.

After McDaniel has given the Board his memo and income statement, and after the Board has had a chance to evaluate McDaniel's performance, McDaniel and the Board should meet. The purpose of the meeting is to decide whether it is in their mutual interest for McDaniel to remain with FASTPACK, and if so, the terms of the contract FASTPACK will offer McDaniel.

19 Short-Term Business Decisions

Learning Objectives/ Success Keys

1. Describe and identify information relevant to business decisions
2. Make special order and pricing decisions
3. Make dropping a product and product-mix decisions
4. Make outsourcing and sell as is or process further decisions

Most major companies outsource work as they grow. As Smart Touch Learning, Inc., expands, it is considering subcontracting its call center operations. But why would Smart Touch consider hiring other people to handle such an important function? Primarily it would do so to save money. Most companies are experiencing financial difficulties due to rising fuel costs and tight competition so they need to find ways to reduce their costs. One way to reduce costs is through outsourcing. Companies can save 20% or more by outsourcing call center work to English-speaking workers in developing countries.

Outsourcing also enables companies to concentrate on their core competencies—the operating activities in which they are experts. When companies focus on just their core competencies, they often outsource the activities that do not give them a competitive advantage. For example, call center operations require expertise that can be purchased through outsourcing, leaving Smart Touch to focus on its core competency—developing learning solutions.

In Chapter 18, we saw how managers use cost behavior to determine the company's breakeven point and to estimate the sales volume needed to achieve target profits. In this chapter, we will see how managers use their knowledge of cost behavior to make six special business decisions, such as whether or not to outsource operating activities. The decisions we will discuss in this chapter pertain to short periods of time so managers do not need to worry about the time value of money. In other words, they do not need to compute the present value of the revenues and expenses relating to the decision. In Chapter 20 we will discuss longer-term decisions (such as plant expansions) in which the time value of money becomes important. Before we look at the six business decisions in detail, let us consider a manager's decision-making process and the information managers need to evaluate their options.

How Managers Make Decisions

Exhibit 19-1 illustrates how managers make decisions among alternative courses of action. Management accountants help with the third step: gathering and analyzing *relevant information* to compare alternatives.

1 Describe and identify information relevant to business decisions

EXHIBIT 19-1 | **How Managers Make Decisions**

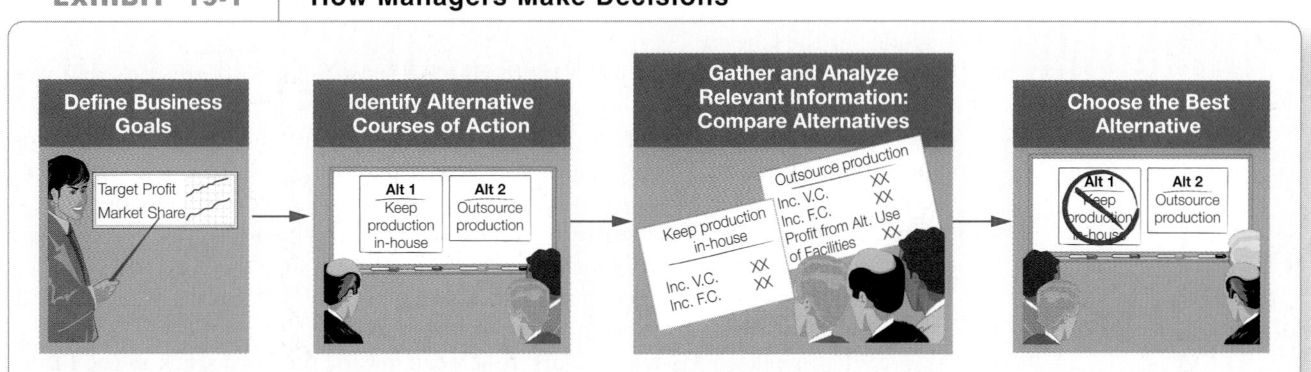

Relevant Information

When managers make decisions, they focus on costs and revenues that are relevant to the decisions. Exhibit 19-2 on the following page shows that **relevant information** is

1. expected *future* data that
2. *differs* among alternatives.

Relevant costs are those costs that are relevant to a particular decision. To illustrate, if Smart Touch were considering purchasing a Dodge or a Chevy delivery truck, the cost of the truck, the sales tax, and the insurance premium costs would all be relevant because these costs

- are incurred in the *future* (after Smart Touch decides which truck to buy), and
- *differ between alternatives* (each truck has a different invoice price, sales tax, and insurance premium).

These costs are *relevant* because they can affect the decision of which truck to purchase.

EXHIBIT 19-2 | **Relevant Information**

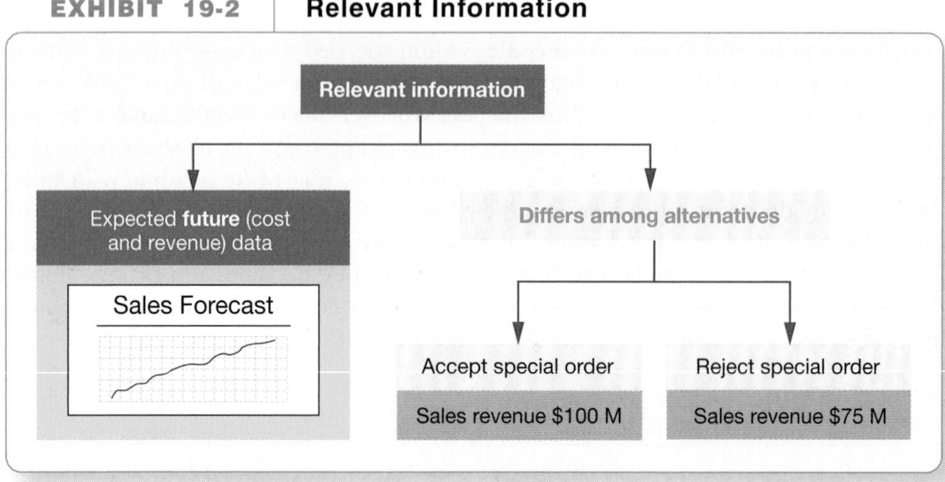

Irrelevant costs are costs that *do not* affect the decision. For example, because the Dodge and Chevy both have similar fuel efficiency and maintenance ratings, we do not expect the truck operating costs to differ between those two alternatives. Because these costs do not differ, they do not affect Smart Touch's decision. In other words, they are *irrelevant* to the decision. Similarly, the cost of an annual license tag is also irrelevant because the tag costs the same whether Smart Touch buys the Dodge or the Chevy.

Sunk costs are always irrelevant to your decision. Sunk costs are costs that were incurred in the *past* and cannot be changed regardless of which future action is taken. Perhaps Smart Touch wants to trade in its current Ford truck when the company buys the new truck. The amount Smart Touch paid for the Ford truck—which the company bought for $15,000 a year ago—is a sunk cost. No decision made *now* can alter the past. Smart Touch already bought the Ford truck so *the price the company paid for it is a sunk cost.* All Smart Touch can do *now* is keep the Ford truck, trade it in, or sell it for the best price the company can get, even if that price is substantially less than what Smart Touch originally paid for the truck.

What *is* relevant is what Smart Touch can get for the Ford truck in the future. Suppose that the Dodge dealership offers $8,000 for the Ford truck, but the Chevy dealership offers $10,000. Because the amounts differ and the transaction will take place in the future, the trade-in cost *is* relevant to Smart Touch's decision. Why? Because the trade-in value alternatives are different.

The same principle applies to all situations—*only relevant data affect decisions.* Let us consider another application of this general principle.

Suppose Smart Touch is deciding whether to use non-recycled DVDs or DVDs made from recycled materials for their Excel Learning DVDs. Assume Smart Touch predicts the following costs under the two alternatives:

	New Materials	Recycled Materials	Cost Difference
Manufacturing cost per DVD:			
Direct materials	$2.40	$2.60	$0.20
Direct labor	$4.00	$4.00	$0.00

The cost of direct materials is relevant because this cost differs between alternatives (the Recycled DVDs cost $0.20 more per DVD than the non-recycled DVDs). The labor cost is irrelevant because that cost is the same for both.

Stop & Think...

You are considering replacing your Pentium IV computer with the latest model. Is the $1,200 you spent in 2005 on the Pentium relevant to your decision about buying the new model?

Answer: The $1,200 cost of your Pentium is irrelevant. It is a *sunk* cost that you incurred in the past so it is the same whether or not you buy the new computer.

Relevant Nonfinancial Information

Nonfinancial, or qualitative factors, also play a role in managers' decisions. For example, closing manufacturing plants and laying off employees can seriously hurt employee morale. **Outsourcing**, the decision to buy or subcontract a product or service rather than produce it in-house, can reduce control over delivery time or product quality. Offering discounted prices to select customers can upset regular customers and tempt them to take their business elsewhere. Managers must always fully consider the likely quantitative *and* qualitative effects of their decisions.

Managers who ignore qualitative factors can make serious mistakes. For example, the City of Nottingham, England, spent $1.6 million on 215 solar-powered parking meters after seeing how well the parking meters worked in countries along the Mediterranean Sea. However, they did not consider that British skies are typically overcast. The result was that the meters did not always work because of the lack of sunlight. The city *lost* money because people ended up parking for free! Relevant qualitative information has the same characteristics as relevant financial information: The qualitative factor occurs in the *future* and it *differs* between alternatives. In the example, the amount of *future* sunshine required *differed* between alternatives. The mechanical meters did not require any sunshine, but the solar-powered meters needed a lot of sunshine.

Keys to Making Short-Term Special Decisions

Our approach to making short-term special decisions is called the **relevant information approach**, or the **incremental analysis approach**. Instead of looking at the company's *entire* income statement under each decision alternative, we will just look at how operating income would *change or differ* under each alternative. Using this approach, we will leave out irrelevant information—the costs and revenues that will not differ between alternatives. We will consider six kinds of decisions in this chapter:

1. Special sales orders
2. Pricing
3. Dropping products, departments, and territories
4. Product mix
5. Outsourcing (make or buy)
6. Selling as is or processing further

As you study these decisions, keep in mind the two keys in analyzing short-term special business decisions shown in Exhibit 19-3:

1. **Focus on relevant revenues, costs, and profits.** Irrelevant information only clouds the picture and creates information overload.
2. **Use a contribution margin approach that separates variable costs from fixed costs.** Because fixed costs and variable costs behave differently, they must be analyzed separately. Traditional (absorption costing) income statements, which

blend fixed and variable costs together, can mislead managers. Contribution margin income statements, which isolate costs by behavior (variable or fixed), help managers gather the cost-behavior information they need. Keep in mind that unit manufacturing costs are mixed costs, too, so they can also mislead managers. If you use unit manufacturing costs in your analysis, be sure to first separate the cost's fixed and variable components.

We will use these two keys in each decision.

EXHIBIT 19-3 | Two Keys to Making Short-Term Special Decisions

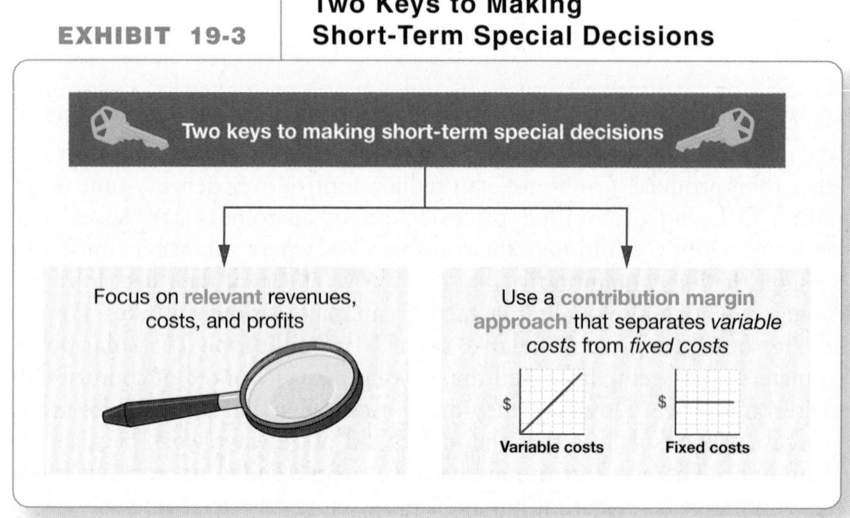

Special Sales Order and Regular Pricing Decisions

2 Make special order and pricing decisions

We will start our discussion by looking at special sales order decisions and regular pricing decisions. In the past, managers did not consider pricing to be a short-term decision. However, product life cycles are shrinking in most industries. Companies often sell products for only a few months before replacing them with an updated model, even if the updating is barely noticeable. The clothing and technology industries have always had short life cycles. Even auto and housing styles change frequently. Pricing has become a shorter-term decision than it was in the past.

Let us examine a special sales order in detail, and then we will discuss regular pricing decisions.

When to Accept a Special Sales Order

A special order occurs when a customer requests a one-time order at a *reduced* sale price. Before agreeing to the special deal, management must consider the questions shown in Exhibit 19-4.

EXHIBIT 19-4 | Special Order Considerations

- Does the company have excess capacity available to fill this order?
- Will the reduced sales price be high enough to cover the *incremental* costs of filling the order (the variable costs and any additional fixed costs)?
- Will the special order affect regular sales in the long run?

First, managers must consider available capacity. If the company is already making as many units as possible with its existing manufacturing capacity and selling them all at its *regular* sales price, it would not make sense to fill a special order at a *reduced* sales price. Therefore, available excess capacity that is not being used is almost a necessity for accepting a special order. This is true for service firms (law firms, hair salons, and so forth) as well as manufacturers.

Second, managers need to consider whether the special reduced sales price is high enough to cover the incremental costs of filling the order. The special price *must* exceed the variable costs of filling the order or the company will lose money on the deal. In other words, the special order must provide a *positive* contribution margin.

Next, the company must consider fixed costs. If the company has excess capacity, fixed costs probably will not be affected by producing more units (or delivering more service). However, in some cases, management may have to incur some other fixed cost to fill the special order, for example, additional insurance premiums. If so, they will need to consider whether the special sales price is high enough to generate a positive contribution margin *and* cover the additional fixed costs.

Finally, managers need to consider whether the special order will affect regular sales in the long run. Will regular customers find out about the special order and demand a lower price or take their business elsewhere? Will the special order customer come back *again and again*, asking for the same reduced price? Will the special order price start a price war with competitors? Managers should determine the answers to these questions and/or consider how customers will respond. Managers may decide that any profit from the special sales order is not worth these risks.

Let us consider a special sales order example. We learned in Chapter 17 that Smart Touch normally sells its Excel DVDs for $12.00 each. Assume that a company has offered Smart Touch $67,500 for 10,000 DVDs, or $6.75 per DVD. This sale

- will use manufacturing capacity that would otherwise be idle (excess capacity).
- will not change fixed costs.
- will not require any variable *nonmanufacturing* expenses (because no extra marketing costs are incurred with this special order).
- will not affect regular sales.

We have addressed every consideration except one: Is the special sales price high enough to cover the variable *manufacturing* costs associated with the order? Let us first take a look at the *wrong* way and then the *right* way to figure out the answer to this question.

Suppose Smart Touch made and sold 100,000 DVDs before considering the special order. Using the traditional (absorption costing) income statement on the left-hand side of Exhibit 19-5, the ABC manufacturing cost per unit is $7.00 (as calculated in Exhibit 17-9). A manager who does not examine these numbers carefully may believe that Smart Touch should *not* accept the special order at a sale price of $6.75 because each DVD costs $7.00 to manufacture. But appearances can be deceiving! Remember that the unit manufacturing cost of a product, $7.00, is a *mixed* cost, containing both fixed and variable cost components. To correctly answer our question, we need to find only the *variable* portion of the manufacturing unit cost.

The right-hand side of Exhibit 19-5 shows the contribution margin income statement that separates variable expenses from fixed expenses. The contribution margin income statement allows us to see that the *variable* manufacturing cost per unit is only $6.50 ($650,000 ÷ 100,000). The special sales price of $6.75 per DVD is *higher* than the variable manufacturing cost of $6.50. Therefore, the special order will provide a positive contribution margin of $0.25 per unit ($6.75 – $6.50). Since the special order is for 10,000 units, Smart Touch's total contribution margin should increase by $2,500 (10,000 units × $0.25 per unit) if it accepts this order.

EXHIBIT 19-5 **Traditional (Absorption Costing) Format and Contribution Margin Format Income Statements**

SMART TOUCH LEARNING, INC. Income Statement (at a production and sales level of 100,000 Excel DVDs) Year Ended December 31, 2011				
Traditional (Absorption Costing) Format		**Contribution Margin Format**		
Sales revenue	$1,200,000	Sales revenue		$1,200,000
Less cost of goods sold	(700,000)	Less variable expenses:		
Gross profit	$ 500,000	Manufacturing	$(640,000)	
Less marketing and administrative expenses	(110,000)	Marketing and administrative	(10,000)	(650,000)
		Contribution margin		$ 550,000
		Less fixed expenses:		
		Manufacturing	$ (60,000)	
		Marketing and administrative	(100,000)	(160,000)
Operating income	$ 390,000	Operating income		$ 390,000

Using an incremental analysis approach, Smart Touch compares the additional revenues from the special order with the incremental expenses to see if the special order will contribute to profits. Exhibit 19-6 shows that the special sales order will increase revenue by $67,500 (10,000 × $6.75), but will also increase variable manufacturing cost by $65,000 (10,000 × $6.50). As a result, Smart Touch's contribution margin will increase by $2,500, as previously anticipated. The other costs seen in Exhibit 19-5 are irrelevant. Variable marketing and administrative expenses will be the same whether or not Smart Touch accepts the special order, because Smart Touch made no special efforts to get this sale. Fixed manufacturing expenses will not change because Smart Touch has enough idle capacity to produce 10,000 extra Excel DVDs without requiring additional facilities. Fixed marketing and administrative expenses will not be affected by this special order either. Because there are no additional fixed costs, the total increase in contribution margin flows directly to operating income. As a result, the special sales order will increase operating income by $2,500.

EXHIBIT 19-6 **Incremental Analysis of Special Sales Order of 10,000 Excel DVDs**

Expected increase in revenues (10,000 DVDs × $6.50)	$ 67,500
Expected increase in variable manufacturing costs (10,000 DVDs × $6.50)	(65,000)
Expected increase in operating income	$ 2,500

Notice that the analysis follows the two keys to making short-term special business decisions discussed earlier: (1) Focus on relevant data (revenues and costs that *will change* if Smart Touch accepts the special order) and (2) use of a contribution margin approach that separates variable costs from fixed costs.

To summarize, for special sales orders, the decision rule is as follows:

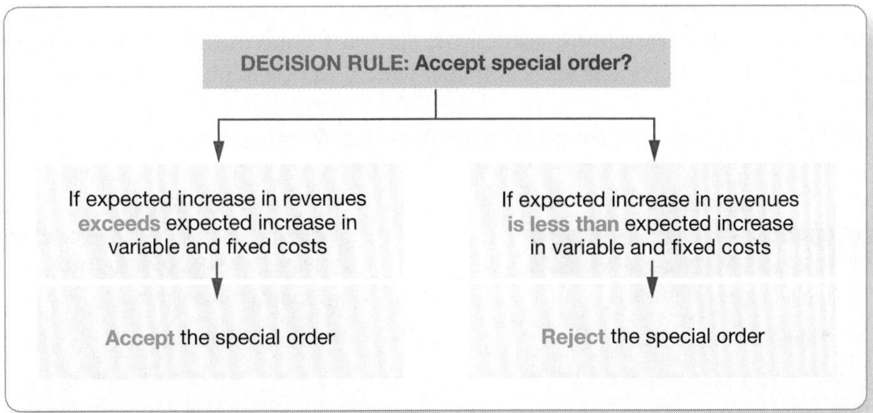

How to Set Regular Prices

In the special order decision, Smart Touch decided to sell a limited quantity of DVDs for $6.75 each, even though the normal price was $12.00 per unit. But how did Smart Touch decide to set its regular price at $12.00 per DVD? Exhibit 19-7 shows that managers start with three basic questions when setting regular prices for their products or services.

EXHIBIT 19-7 Regular Pricing Considerations

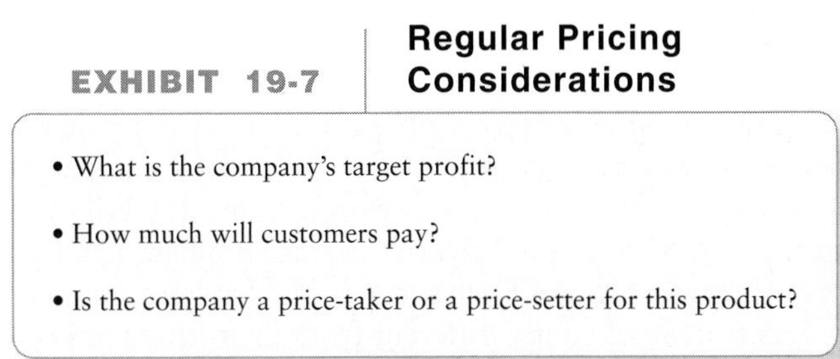

The answers to these questions are often complex and ever-changing. Stockholders expect the company to achieve certain profits. Economic conditions, historical company earnings, industry risk, competition, and new business developments all affect the level of profit that stockholders expect. Stockholders usually tie their profit expectations to the amount of assets invested in the company. For example, stockholders may expect a 10% annual return on their investment. A company's stock price tends to decline if it does not meet target profits, so managers must keep costs low while generating enough revenue to meet target profits.

This leads to the second question: How much will customers pay? Managers cannot set prices above what customers are willing to pay or sales will decline. The amount customers will pay depends on the competition, the product's uniqueness, the effectiveness of marketing campaigns, general economic conditions, and so forth.

To address the third pricing question, imagine a horizontal line with price-takers at one end and price-setters at the other end. A company's products and services fall somewhere along this line, shown in Exhibit 19-8. Companies are price-takers when they have little or no control over the prices of their products or services. This occurs when their products and services are *not* unique or when competition is intense. Examples include food commodities (milk and corn), natural resources (oil and lumber), and generic consumer products and services (paper towels, dry cleaning, and banking).

EXHIBIT 19-8 | Price-Takers Versus Price-Setters

Price-takers ◄——————► **Price-setters**

Characteristics of price-takers	Characteristics of price-setters
• Product lacks uniqueness	• Product is more unique
• Intense competition	• Less competition
• Pricing approach emphasizes target pricing	• Pricing approach emphasizes cost-plus pricing

Companies are price-setters when they have more control over pricing—in other words, they can "set" the price to some extent. Companies are price-setters when their products are unique, which results in less competition. Unique products, such as original art and jewelry, specially manufactured machinery, patented perfume scents, and custom-made furniture, can command higher prices.

Obviously, managers would rather be price-setters than price-takers. To gain more control over pricing, companies try to differentiate their products. They want to make their products unique, in terms of features, service, or quality, or at least make you *think* their product is unique or somehow better—companies achieve this differentiation through their advertising efforts. Consider **Nike's** tennis shoes, **Starbucks'** coffee, **Kleenex's** tissues, **Tylenol's** acetaminophen, **Capital One's** credit cards, **Shell's** gas, **Abercrombie and Fitch's** jeans—the list goes on and on. Are these products really better or significantly different from their lower-priced competitors? It is possible. If these companies can make customers *believe* that this is true, they have gained more control over their pricing because customers are willing to pay *more* for their product or service. What is the downside? These companies must charge higher prices or sell more just to cover their advertising costs.

A company's approach to pricing depends on whether its product or service is on the price-taking or price-setting side of the spectrum. Price-takers emphasize a target-pricing approach. Price-setters emphasize a cost-plus pricing approach. Keep in mind that many products fall somewhere along the horizontal line in Exhibit 19-8. Therefore, managers tend to use both approaches to some extent. We will now discuss each approach in turn.

Stop & Think...

It is lunchtime....you are hungry for a hamburger. Where do you go—**Wendy's**, **McDonald's**, or your college's cafeteria? Why? A hamburger is the same wherever you go, right? The answer to that question is the key to changing a product (a hamburger) from a commodity to a unique product (a **Wendy's** hamburger). The advertising, conditioning of your family, etc. have possibly made you think that the three companies' hamburgers are different. The perceived uniqueness of the hamburger helps the company (say **Wendy's**) be a price-setter instead of a price-taker.

Target Pricing

When a company is a price-taker, it emphasizes a target pricing approach to pricing. Target pricing starts with the market price of the product (the price customers are willing to pay) and then subtracts the company's desired profit to determine the product's **target full cost**—the *full* cost to develop, produce, and deliver the product or service.

Revenue at market price
Less: Desired profit
Equals Target full cost

In this relationship, the market price is "taken." Recall from Chapter 15 that a product's *full* cost contains all elements from the value chain—both inventoriable costs and period costs. It also includes both fixed and variable costs. If the product's current cost is higher than the target cost, the company must find ways to reduce costs or it will not meet its profit goals. Managers often use ABC costing along with value engineering (as discussed in Chapter 17) to find ways to cut costs. Let us look at an example of target pricing.

Let us assume that Excel Learning DVDs are a commodity, and that the current market price is $11.00 per DVD (not the $12.00 sales price assumed in the earlier Smart Touch example). Because the DVDs are a commodity, Smart Touch will emphasize a target-pricing approach. Let us assume Smart Touch's stockholders expect a 10% annual return on the company's assets. If the company has $3,000,000 of assets, the desired profit is $300,000 ($3,000,000 × 10%). Exhibit 19-9 calculates the target full cost at the current sales volume (100,000 units). Once we know the target full cost, we can analyze the fixed and variable cost components separately.

EXHIBIT 19-9 Calculating Target Full Cost

	Calculations	
Revenue at market price	100,000 DVDs × $11.00 price	$1,100,000
Less: Desired profit	10% × $3,000,000 average assets	(300,000)
Target full cost		$ 800,000

Can Smart Touch make and sell 100,000 Excel Learning DVDs at a full cost of $800,000? We know from Smart Touch's contribution margin income statement (Exhibit 19-5) that the company's variable costs are $6.50 per unit ($650,000 ÷ 100,000 units). This variable cost per unit includes both manufacturing costs ($6.40 per unit) and marketing and administrative costs ($0.10 per unit). We also know the company incurs $160,000 in fixed costs in its current relevant range. Again, some fixed costs stem from manufacturing and some from marketing and administrative activities. *In setting regular sales prices, companies must cover* ***all*** *of their costs—whether inventoriable or period, fixed or variable.*

Making and selling 100,000 DVDs currently costs the company $810,000 [(100,000 units × $6.50 variable cost per unit) + $160,000 of fixed costs], which is more than the target full cost ($800,000). So, what are Smart Touch's options?

1. Accept a lower profit (an operating income of $290,000, which is a 9.67% return, not the 10% target return required by stockholders).
2. Reduce fixed costs by $10,000 or more.
3. Reduce variable costs by $10,000 or more.

4. Use other strategies. For example, Smart Touch could attempt to increase sales volume. Recall that the company has excess capacity so making and selling more units would only affect variable costs; however, it would mean that current fixed costs are spread over more units. The company could also consider changing or adding to its product mix. Finally, it could attempt to differentiate its Excel Learning DVDs from the competition to gain more control over sales prices (be a price-setter).

Let us look at some of these options. Smart Touch may first try to cut fixed costs. As shown in Exhibit 19-10, the company would have to reduce fixed costs to $150,000 to meet its target profit level.

EXHIBIT 19-10 | Calculating Target Fixed Cost

	Calculations	
Target full cost	(From Exhibit 19-9)	$ 800,000
Less: Current variable costs	100,000 DVDs × $6.50	(650,000)
Target fixed cost		$ 150,000

If the company cannot reduce its fixed costs by $10,000 ($160,000 current fixed costs – $150,000 target fixed costs), it would have to lower its variable cost to $ 6.40 per unit, as shown in Exhibit 19-11.

EXHIBIT 19-11 | Calculating Target DVD Variable Cost

	Calculations	
Target full cost	(From Exhibit 19-9)	$ 800,000
Less: Current fixed costs	(From Exhibit 19-5)	(160,000)
Target total variable costs		$ 640,000
Divided by the number of DVDs		÷ 100,000
Target variable cost per unit		$ 6.40

If Smart Touch cannot reduce variable costs to that level either, could it meet its target profit through a combination of lowering both fixed costs and variable costs?

Another strategy would be to increase sales. Smart Touch's managers can use CVP analysis, as you learned in Chapter 18, to figure out how many Excel Learning DVDs the company would have to sell to achieve its target profit. How could the company increase demand for the Excel Learning DVDs? Perhaps it could reach new markets or advertise. How much would advertising cost—and how many extra Excel Learning DVDs would the company have to sell to cover the cost of advertising? These are only some of the questions managers must ask. As you can see, managers do not have an easy task when the current cost exceeds the target full cost. Sometimes companies just cannot compete given the current market price. If that is the case, they may have no other choice than to exit the market for that product.

Cost-Plus Pricing

When a company is a price-setter, it emphasizes a cost-plus approach to pricing. This pricing approach is essentially the *opposite* of the target-pricing approach. Cost-plus pricing starts with the company's full costs (as a given) and *adds* its desired profit to determine a cost-plus price.

Full cost
Plus: Desired profit
Equals Cost-plus price

When the product is unique, the company has more control over pricing. The company still needs to make sure that the cost-plus price is not higher than what customers are willing to pay. Let us go back to our original Smart Touch example. This time, let us say the Excel Learning DVDs benefit from brand recognition so the company has some control over the price it charges for its DVDs. Exhibit 19-12 takes a cost-plus pricing approach, assuming the current level of sales:

EXHIBIT 19-12 | Calculating Cost-Plus Price

	Calculations	
Current variable costs	100,000 DVDs × $6.50	$ 650,000
Plus: Current fixed costs	(From Exhibit 19-5)	160,000
Full product cost		$ 810,000
Plus: Desired profit	10% of $3,000,000 average assets	300,000
Target revenue		$1,110,000
Divided by the number of DVDs		÷ 100,000
Cost-plus price per DVD		$ 11.10

If the current market price for generic Excel Learning DVDs is $11.00, as we assumed earlier, can Smart Touch sell its brand-name filters for $11.10, or more, apiece? The answer depends on how well the company has been able to differentiate its product or brand name. The company may use focus groups or marketing surveys to find out how customers would respond to its cost-plus price. The company may find out that its cost-plus price is too high, or it may find that it could set the price even higher without jeopardizing sales.

Notice how pricing decisions used our two keys to decision making: (1) focus on relevant information and (2) use a contribution margin approach that separates variable costs from fixed costs. In pricing decisions, all cost information is relevant because the company must cover *all* costs along the value chain before it can generate a profit. However, we still need to consider variable costs and fixed costs separately because they behave differently at different volumes.

Our pricing decision rule is as follows:

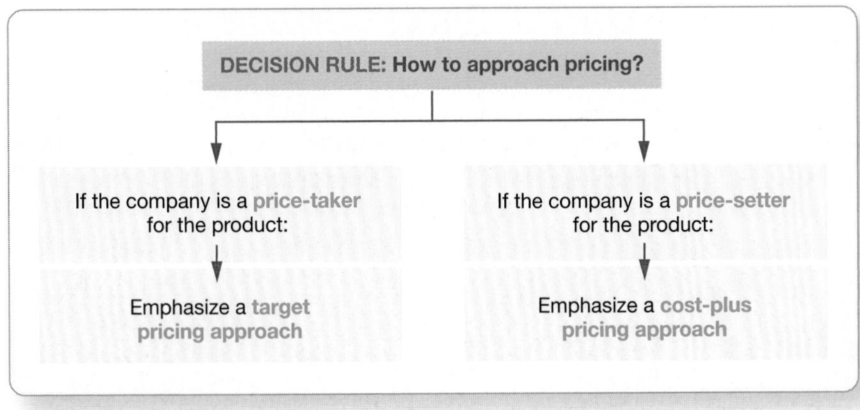

Decision Guidelines

RELEVANT INFORMATION FOR BUSINESS DECISIONS

Nike makes special order and regular pricing decisions. Even though it sells mass-produced tennis shoes and sport clothing, **Nike** has differentiated its products with advertising and with athlete endorsements. **Nike's** managers consider both quantitative and qualitative factors as they make pricing decisions. Here are key guidelines **Nike's** managers follow in making their decisions.

Decision	**Guidelines**
• What information is relevant to a short-term special business decision?	Relevant data 1. are expected *future* data. 2. *differ* between alternatives.
• What are two key guidelines in making short-term special business decisions?	1. Focus on *relevant* data 2. Use a *contribution margin* approach that separates variable costs from fixed costs
• Should **Nike** accept a lower sale price than the regular price for a large order from a customer in Roatan Bay, Honduras?	If the revenue from the order exceeds the extra variable and fixed costs incurred to fill the order, then accepting the order will increase operating income.
• What should **Nike** consider in setting its regular product prices?	**Nike** considers 1. the profit stockholders expect it to make. 2. the price customers will pay. 3. whether it is a price-setter or a price-taker.
• What approach should **Nike** take to pricing?	**Nike** has differentiated its products by advertising. Thus, **Nike** tends to be a price-setter. **Nike's** managers can emphasize a cost-plus approach to pricing.
• What approach should discount shoe stores, such as **Payless Shoes**, take to pricing?	**Payless Shoes** sells generic shoes (no-name brands) at low prices. **Payless** is a price-taker so managers use a target-pricing approach to pricing.

Summary Problem 1

MC Alexander Industries makes tennis balls. Its only plant can produce up to 2.5 million cans of balls per year. Current production is 2 million cans. Annual manufacturing, selling, and administrative fixed costs total $700,000. The variable cost of making and selling each can of balls is $1.00. Stockholders expect a 12% annual return on the company's $3 million of assets.

Requirements

1. What is MC Alexander's current full cost of making and selling 2 million cans of tennis balls? What is the current full *unit* cost of each can of tennis balls?
2. Assume MC Alexander is a price-taker, and the current market price is $1.45 per can of balls (this is the price at which manufacturers sell to retailers). What is the *target* full cost of producing and selling 2 million cans of balls? Given MC Alexander Industries' current costs, will the company reach stockholders' profit goals?
3. If MC Alexander cannot change its fixed costs, what is the target variable cost per can of balls?
4. Suppose MC Alexander could spend an extra $100,000 on advertising to differentiate its product so that it could be a price-setter. Assuming the original volume and costs, plus the $100,000 of new advertising costs, what cost-plus price will MC Alexander want to charge for a can of balls?
5. **Nike** has just asked MC Alexander to supply the company with 400,000 cans of balls at a special order price of $1.20 per can. **Nike** wants MC Alexander to package the balls under the **Nike** label (MC Alexander will imprint the **Nike** logo on each ball and can). MC Alexander will have to spend $10,000 to change the packaging machinery. Assuming the original volume and costs, should MC Alexander Industries accept this special order? (Unlike the chapter problem, assume MC Alexander will incur variable selling costs as well as variable manufacturing costs related to this order.)

Solutions

Requirement 1

The full unit cost is as follows:

Fixed costs	$ 700,000
Plus: Total variable costs (2 million cans × $1.00 per unit)	+ 2,000,000
Total full costs	$2,700,000
Divided by the number of cans	÷ 2,000,000
Full cost per can	$ 1.35

Requirement 2

The target full cost is as follows:

	Calculations	Total
Revenue at market price	2,000,000 units × $1.45 price =	$2,900,000
Less: Desired profit	12% × $3,000,000 of assets	(360,000)
Target *full* cost		$2,540,000

MC Alexander's current total full costs ($2,700,000 from requirement 1) are $160,000 higher than the target full cost ($2,540,000). If MC Alexander cannot reduce costs, it will not be able to meet stockholders' profit expectations.

Requirement 3

Assuming MC Alexander cannot reduce its fixed costs, the target variable cost per can is as follows:

	Total
Target *full* cost (from requirement 2)	$2,540,000
Less: Fixed costs	(700,000)
Target total variable cost	$1,840,000
Divided by the number of units	÷2,000,000
Target variable cost per unit	$ 0.92

Since MC Alexander cannot reduce its fixed costs, it needs to reduce variable costs by $0.08 per can ($1.00 – $0.92) to meet its profit goals. This would require an 8% cost reduction, which may not be possible.

Requirement 4

If MC Alexander can differentiate its tennis balls, it will gain more control over pricing. The company's new cost-plus price would be as follows:

Current total costs (from requirement 1)	$2,700,000
Plus: Additional cost of advertising	+ 100,000
Plus: Desired profit (from requirement 2)	+ 360,000
Target revenue	$3,160,000
Divided by the number of units	÷ 2,000,000
Cost-plus price per unit	$ 1.58

MC Alexander must study the market to determine whether retailers would pay $1.58 per can of balls.

Requirement 5

Nike's special order price ($1.20) is less than the current full cost of each can of balls ($1.35 from requirement 1). However, this should not influence management's decision. MC Alexander could fill **Nike's** special order using existing excess capacity. MC Alexander takes an incremental analysis approach to its decision: comparing the extra revenue with the incremental costs of accepting the order. Variable costs will increase if MC Alexander accepts the order, so the variable costs are relevant. Only the *additional* fixed costs of changing the packaging machine ($10,000) are relevant since all other fixed costs will remain unchanged.

Revenue from special order (400,000 × $1.20 per unit)	$ 480,000
Less: Variable cost of special order (400,000 × $1.00)	(400,000)
Contribution margin from special order	$ 80,000
Less: Additional fixed costs of special order	(10,000)
Operating income provided by special order	$ 70,000

MC Alexander should accept the special order because it will increase operating income by $70,000. However, MC Alexander also needs to consider whether its regular customers will find out about the special price and demand lower prices too.

When to Drop Products, Departments, or Territories

3 Make dropping a product and product-mix decisions

Managers must often decide whether to drop products, departments, or territories that are not as profitable as desired. How do managers make these decisions? Exhibit 19-13 lists some of the questions managers must consider when deciding whether to drop a product line, department, or territory.

EXHIBIT 19-13 **Considerations for Dropping Products, Departments, or Territories**

- Does the product provide a positive contribution margin?
- Will fixed costs continue to exist, even if the company drops the product?
- Are there any direct fixed costs that can be avoided if the company drops the product?
- Will dropping the product affect sales of the company's other products?
- What could the company do with the freed capacity?

Once again, we follow the two key guidelines for special business decisions: (1) focus on relevant data and (2) use a contribution margin approach. The relevant financial data are still the changes in revenues and expenses, but now we are considering a *decrease* in volume rather than an *increase*, as we did in the special sales order decision. In the following example, we will consider how managers decide to drop a product. Managers would use the same process in deciding whether to drop a department or territory.

Earlier, we focused on only one of Smart Touch's products—Excel Learning DVDs. Now let us focus on both of its products—the Excel Learning DVDs and the specialty DVDs we covered in Chapter 17. Exhibit 19-14 shows the company's

EXHIBIT 19-14 **Contribution Margin Income Statements by Product Line**

SMART TOUCH LEARNING, INC.
Income Statement
For the month ended January 31, 2012

		Product Line	
	Total	Excel DVDs (100,000 DVDs) (From Exhibit 19-5)	Specialty DVDs (350 DVDs)
Sales revenue	$1,224,500	$1,200,000	$ 24,500
Less: Variable expenses			
Manufacturing	(652,740)	(640,000)	(12,740)
Marketing and administrative	(10,035)	(10,000)	(35)
Total variable expenses	(662,775)	(650,000)	(12,775)
Contribution margin	561,725	550,000	11,725
Less: Fixed expenses:			
Manufacturing	(71,795)	(60,000)	(11,795)
Marketing and administrative	(100,350)	(100,000)	(350)
Total fixed expenses	(172,145)	(160,000)	(12,145)
Operating income (loss)	$ 389,580	$ 390,000	$ (420)

contribution margin income statement by product line, assuming fixed costs are shared by both products. Because the specialty DVD line has an operating *loss* of $420, management is considering dropping the line.

The first question management should ask is "Does the product provide a positive contribution margin?" If the product line has a negative contribution margin, then the product is not even covering its variable costs. Therefore, the company should drop the product line. However, if the product line has a positive contribution margin, then it is *helping* to cover at least some of the company's fixed costs. In Smart Touch's case, the specialty DVDs provide a positive contribution margin of $11,725. Smart Touch's managers now need to consider fixed costs.

Suppose Smart Touch allocates fixed costs using the ABC costs per unit calculated in Chapter 17, Exhibit 17-9 ($7.00 per unit). Smart Touch could allocate fixed costs in many different ways, and each way would have allocated a different amount of fixed costs to each product line. Therefore, allocated fixed costs are *irrelevant* because they are arbitrary in amount. What is relevant, however, are the following:

1. Will the fixed costs continue to exist *even if* the product line is dropped?
2. Are there any *direct* fixed costs of the specialty DVDs that can be avoided if the product line is dropped?

Dropping Products Under Various Assumptions

Fixed Costs Continue to Exist and Will Not Change

Fixed costs that will continue to exist even after a product is dropped are often called unavoidable fixed costs. Unavoidable fixed costs are *irrelevant* to the decision because they *will not change* if the company drops the product line—they will be incurred either way. Let us assume that all of Smart Touch's fixed costs ($172,145) will continue to exist even if the company drops the specialty DVDs. Assume that Smart Touch makes the specialty DVDs in the same plant using the same machinery as the Excel Learning DVDs. Since this is the case, only the contribution margin the specialty DVDs provide is relevant. If Smart Touch drops the specialty DVDs, it will lose the $11,725 contribution margin.

The incremental analysis shown in Exhibit 19-15 verifies the loss. If Smart Touch drops the specialty DVDs, revenue will decrease by $24,500, but variable expenses will decrease by only $12,775, resulting in a net $11,725 decrease in operating income. Because fixed costs are unaffected, they are not included in the analysis. This analysis suggests that management should *not* drop specialty DVDs. It is actually more beneficial for Smart Touch to lose $475 than to drop the specialty DVDs and lose $11,725 in operating income.

EXHIBIT 19-15 **Incremental Analysis for Dropping a Product When Fixed Costs Will *Not* Change**

Expected decrease in revenues (350 specialty DVDs × $70.00)	$(24,500)
Expected decrease in variable costs (From Exhibit 19-14)	12,775
Expected *decrease* in operating income	$(11,725)

Direct Fixed Costs That Can Be Avoided

Since Smart Touch allocates its fixed costs using ABC costing, some of the fixed costs *belong* only to the specialty DVD product line. These would be direct fixed costs of the specialty DVDs only.[1] Assume that $12,000 of the fixed costs will be avoidable if Smart Touch drops the specialty DVD line. The $12,000 are then avoidable fixed costs and *are relevant* to the decision because they would change (go away) if the product line is dropped.

Exhibit 19-16 shows that, in this situation, operating income will *increase* by $275 if Smart Touch drops the specialty DVDs. Why? Because revenues will decline by $24,500 but expenses will decline even more—by $24,775. The result is a net increase to operating income of $275. This analysis suggests that management should drop specialty DVDs.

EXHIBIT 19-16 Incremental Analysis for Dropping a Product When Fixed Costs *Will* Change

Expected decrease in revenues (350 specialty DVDs × $70.00)		$(24,500)
Expected decrease in variable costs (From Exhibit 19-14)	12,775	
Expected decrease in fixed costs	12,000	
Expected decrease in total expenses		24,775
Expected increase in operating income		$ 275

Other Considerations

Management must also consider whether dropping the product line, department, or territory would hurt other sales. In the examples given so far, we assumed that dropping the specialty DVDs would not affect Smart Touch's other product sales. However, think about a grocery store. Even if the produce department is not profitable, would managers drop it? Probably not, because if they did, they would lose customers who want one-stop shopping. In such situations, managers must also include the loss of contribution margin from *other* departments affected by the change when deciding whether or not to drop a department.

Management should also consider what it could do with freed capacity. In the Smart Touch example, we assumed that the company produces both Excel Learning DVDs and specialty DVDs using the same manufacturing equipment. If Smart Touch drops the specialty DVDs, could it make and sell another product using the freed machine hours? Managers should consider whether using the machinery to produce a different product would be more profitable than using the machinery to produce specialty DVDs.

Special decisions should take into account all costs affected by the choice of action. Managers must ask: What total costs—variable and fixed—will change? As Exhibits 19-15 and 19-16 show, the key to deciding whether to drop products, departments, or territories is to compare the lost revenue against the costs that can

[1]To aid in decision-making, companies should separate direct fixed costs from indirect fixed costs on their contribution margin income statements. Companies should *trace direct fixed costs* to the appropriate product line and only *allocate indirect fixed costs* among product lines.

be saved and to consider what would be done with the freed capacity. The decision rule is as follows:

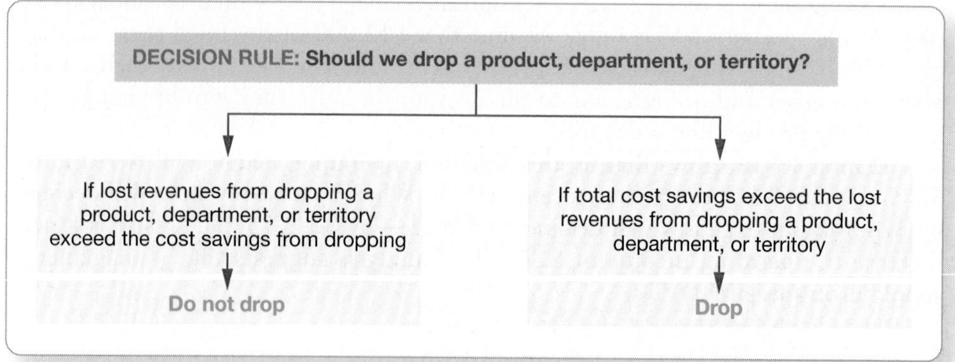

Product Mix: Which Product to Emphasize?

Companies do not have unlimited resources. **Constraints** that restrict production or sale of a product vary from company to company. For a manufacturer like Smart Touch Learning, the production constraint may be labor hours, machine hours, or available materials. For a merchandiser like **Wal-Mart**, the primary constraint is cubic feet of display space. Other companies are constrained by sales demand. Competition may be stiff, and so the company may be able to sell only a limited number of units. In such cases, the company produces only as much as it can sell. However, if a company can sell all the units it can produce, which products should it emphasize? For which items should production be increased? Companies facing constraints consider the questions shown in Exhibit 19-17.

EXHIBIT 19-17 Product Mix Considerations

- What constraint(s) stops the company from making (or displaying) all the units the company can sell?
- Which products offer the highest contribution margin per unit of the constraint?
- Would emphasizing one product over another affect fixed costs?

Let us return to our Smart Touch example. Assume the company can sell all the Excel DVDs and all the specialty DVDs it produces, but it only has 2,000 machine hours of capacity. The company uses the same machines to produce both types of DVDs. In this case, machine hours is the constraint. Note that this is a short-term decision because in the long run, Smart Touch could expand its production facilities to meet sales demand, if it made financial sense to do so. The following data in Exhibit 19-18 suggest that specialty DVDs are more profitable than Excel DVDs:

EXHIBIT 19-18 Smart Touch's Contribution Margin per Unit

	Excel DVD	Specialty DVD
Sale price per DVD	$12.00	$70.00
Less: Variable cost per DVD:	(6.50)	(36.50)
Contribution margin	5.50	33.50
Contribution margin ratio:		
Excel DVDs $5.50/$12.00	46%	
Specialty DVDs $33.50/$70.00		48%

However, an important piece of information is missing—the time it takes to make each product. Let us assume that Smart Touch can produce either 80 Excel DVDs *or* 10 specialty DVDs per machine hour. *The company will incur the same fixed costs either way so fixed costs are irrelevant.* Which product should it emphasize?

To maximize profits when fixed costs are irrelevant, follow the decision rule:

DECISION RULE: Which product to emphasize?

↓

Emphasize the product with the **highest contribution margin per unit of the constraint.**

Because *machine hours* is the constraint, Smart Touch needs to figure out which product has the *highest contribution margin per machine hour*. Exhibit 19-19 determines the contribution margin per machine hour for each product.

EXHIBIT 19-19 Smart Touch's Contribution Margin per Machine Hour

	Excel DVD	Specialty DVD
(1) DVDs that can be produced each machine hour	80	10
(2) Contribution margin per DVD from Exhibit 19-18	$ 5.50	$ 33.50
Contribution margin per machine hour (1) × (2)	$ 440	$ 335
Available capacity—number of machine hours	2,000	2,000
Total contribution margin at full capacity	$880,000	$670,000

Excel DVDs have a higher contribution margin per machine hour, $440, than specialty DVDs, $335. Smart Touch will earn more profit by producing Excel DVDs. Why? Because even though Excel DVDs have a lower contribution margin *per unit*, Smart Touch can make eight times as many Excel DVDs as specialty DVDs in the 2,000 available machine hours. Exhibit 19-19 also proves that Smart Touch earns more total profit by making Excel DVDs. Multiplying the contribution margin per machine hour by the available number of machine hours shows that Smart Touch can earn $880,000 of contribution margin by producing Excel DVDs, but only $670,000 by producing specialty DVDs.

To maximize profit, Smart Touch should make 160,000 Excel DVDs (2,000 machine hours × 80 Excel DVDs per hour) and zero specialty DVDs. Why should Smart Touch make zero specialty DVDs? Because for every machine hour spent making specialty DVDs, Smart Touch would *give up* $105 of contribution margin ($440 per hour for Excel DVDs versus $335 per hour for specialty DVDs).

We made two assumptions here: (1) Smart Touch's sales of other products, if any, will not be hurt by this decision and (2) Smart Touch can sell as many Excel DVDs as it can produce. Let us challenge these assumptions. First, how could making only Excel DVDs hurt sales of other products? By producing the specialty DVDs, Smart Touch also sells many of its standard offerings like the Excel DVDs that coordinate with the specialty DVDs. Other DVD sales might fall if Smart Touch no longer offers specialty DVDs.

Let us challenge our second assumption. Suppose that a new competitor has decreased the demand for Smart Touch's Excel DVDs. Now the company can only sell 120,000 Excel DVDs. Smart Touch should only make as many Excel DVDs as it can sell, and use the remaining machine hours to produce specialty DVDs. Let us see how this constraint in sales demand changes profitability.

Recall from Exhibit 19-19 that Smart Touch will make $880,000 of contribution margin from using all 2,000 machine hours to produce Excel DVDs. However, if Smart Touch only makes 120,000 Excel DVDs, it will only use 1,500 machine hours (120,000 Excel DVDs ÷ 80 Excel DVDs per machine hour). That leaves 500 machine hours available for making specialty DVDs. Smart Touch's new contribution margin will be as shown in Exhibit 19-20.

EXHIBIT 19-20 **Smart Touch's Contribution Margin per Machine Hour—Limited Market for Product**

	Excel DVD	Specialty DVD	Total
(1) DVDs that can be produced each machine hour	80	10	
(2) Contribution margin per DVD from Exhibit 19-18	$ 5.50	$ 33.50	
Contribution margin per machine hour (1) × (2)	$ 440	$ 335	
Machine hours devoted to product	1,500	500	
Total contribution margin at full capacity	$660,000	$167,500	$827,500

Because of the change in product mix, Smart Touch's total contribution margin will fall from $880,000 to $827,500, a $52,500 decline. Smart Touch had to give up $105 of contribution margin per machine hour ($440 – $335) on the 500 hours it spent producing specialty DVDs rather than Excel DVDs. However, Smart Touch had no choice—the company would have incurred an *actual loss* from producing Excel DVDs that it could not sell. If Smart Touch had produced 160,000 Excel DVDs but only sold 120,000, the company would have spent $220,000 to make the unsold DVDs (40,000 Excel DVDs × $5.50 variable cost per Excel DVD), yet received no sales revenue from them.

What about fixed costs? In most cases, changing the product mix emphasis in the short run will not affect fixed costs, so fixed costs are irrelevant. However, it is possible that fixed costs could differ by emphasizing a different product mix. What if Smart Touch had a month-to-month lease on a production camera used only for making specialty DVDs? If Smart Touch only made Excel DVDs, it could *avoid* the lease cost. However, if Smart Touch makes any specialty DVDs, it needs the camera. In this case, the fixed costs become relevant because they differ between alternative product mixes (specialty DVDs only *versus* Excel DVDs only, or Excel DVDs and specialty DVDs).

Notice that the analysis again follows the two guidelines for special business decisions: (1) focus on relevant data (only those revenues and costs that differ) and (2) use a contribution margin approach, which separates variable from fixed costs.

Outsourcing and Sell as is or Process Further Decisions

4 Make outsourcing and sell as is or process further decisions

When to Outsource

Delta outsources much of its reservation work and airplane maintenance. **IBM** outsources most of its desktop production of personal computers. Make-or-buy decisions are often called outsourcing decisions because managers must decide whether to buy a component product or service, or produce it in-house. The heart of these decisions is *how best to use available resources*.

Let us see how managers make outsourcing decisions. Greg's Groovy Tunes, a manufacturer of music CDs, is deciding whether to make the paper liners for the CD cases in-house or whether to outsource them to Becky's Box Designs, a company that specializes in producing paper liners. Greg's Groovy Tunes' cost to produce 250,000 liners is as follows:

	Total Cost (250,000 liners)
Direct materials	$ 40,000
Direct labor	20,000
Variable manufacturing overhead	15,000
Fixed manufacturing overhead	50,000
Total manufacturing cost	$125,000
Number of liners	÷ 250,000
Cost per liner	$ 0.50

Becky's Box Designs offers to sell Greg's Groovy Tunes the liners for $0.37 each. Should Greg's Groovy Tunes make the liners or buy them from Becky's Box Designs? Greg's Groovy Tunes' $0.50 cost per unit to make the liner is $0.13 higher than the cost of buying it from Becky's Box Designs. It appears that Greg's Groovy Tunes should outsource the liners. But the correct answer is not so simple. Why? Because manufacturing unit costs contain both fixed and variable components. In deciding whether or not to outsource, managers must assess fixed and variable costs separately. Exhibit 19-21 shows some of the questions managers must consider when deciding whether or not to outsource.

EXHIBIT 19-21 | Outsourcing Considerations

- How do the company's variable costs compare to the outsourcing cost?
- Are any fixed costs avoidable if the company outsources?
- What could the company do with the freed capacity?

Let us see how these considerations apply to Greg's Groovy Tunes. By purchasing the liners, Greg's Groovy Tunes can avoid all variable manufacturing costs—$40,000 of direct materials, $20,000 of direct labor, and $15,000 of variable manufacturing overhead. In total, the company will save $75,000 in variable manufacturing costs, or $0.30 per liner ($75,000 ÷ 250,000 liners). However, Greg's Groovy Tunes will have to pay the variable outsourcing price of $0.37 per unit, or $92,500 for the 250,000 liners. Based only on variable costs, the lower cost alternative is to manufacture the liners in-house. However, managers must still consider fixed costs.

Assume first, that Greg's Groovy Tunes cannot avoid any of the fixed costs by outsourcing. In this case, the company's fixed costs are irrelevant to the decision because Greg's Groovy Tunes would continue to incur $50,000 of fixed costs either way (the fixed costs do not differ between alternatives). Greg's Groovy Tunes should continue to make its own liners because the variable cost of outsourcing the liners, $92,500, exceeds the variable cost of making the liners, $75,000.

However, what if Greg's Groovy Tunes can avoid some fixed costs by outsourcing the liners? Let us assume that management can reduce fixed overhead cost by $10,000 by outsourcing the liners. Greg's Groovy Tunes will still incur $40,000 of fixed overhead ($50,000 – $10,000) even if it outsources the liners. In this case, fixed costs become relevant to the decision because they differ between alternatives.

Exhibit 19-22 shows the differences in costs between the make and buy alternatives under this scenario.

EXHIBIT 19-22 | Incremental Analysis for Outsourcing Decision

Liner Costs	Make Liners	Buy Liners	Difference
Variable costs:			
Direct materials	$ 40,000	—	$40,000
Direct labor	20,000	—	20,000
Variable overhead	15,000	—	15,000
Purchase cost from Becky's (250,000 × $0.37)	—	$ 92,500	(92,500)
Fixed overhead	50,000	40,000	10,000
Total cost of liners	$125,000	$132,500	$ (7,500)

Exhibit 19-22 shows that it would still cost Greg's Groovy Tunes less to make the liners than to buy them from Becky's Box Designs, even with the $10,000 reduction in fixed costs. The net savings from making 250,000 liners is $7,500. Exhibit 19-22 also shows that outsourcing decisions follow our two key guidelines for special business decisions: (1) Focus on relevant data (differences in costs in this case) and (2) use a contribution margin approach that separates variable costs from fixed costs.

Note how the unit cost—which does *not* separate costs according to behavior—can be deceiving. If Greg's Groovy Tunes' managers made their decision by comparing the total manufacturing cost per liner ($0.50) to the outsourcing unit cost per liner ($0.37), they would have incorrectly decided to outsource. Recall that the manufacturing unit cost ($0.50) contains both fixed and variable components, whereas the outsourcing cost ($0.37) is strictly variable. To make the correct decision, Greg's Groovy Tunes had to separate the two cost components and analyze them separately.

Our decision rule for outsourcing is as follows:

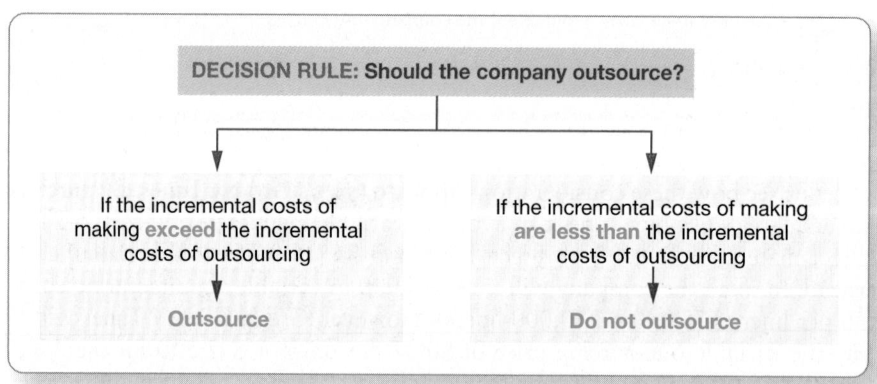

We have not considered what Greg's Groovy Tunes could do with the freed capacity it would have if it outsourced the liners. The analysis in Exhibit 19-22 assumes there is no other use for the production facilities if Greg's Groovy Tunes buys the liners from Becky's Box Designs. But suppose Greg's Groovy Tunes has an opportunity to use its freed-up facilities to make more CDs, which have an expected profit of $18,000. Now, Greg's Groovy Tunes must consider its **opportunity cost**—the benefit forgone by not choosing an alternative course of action. In this case, Greg's Groovy Tunes' opportunity cost of making the liners is the $18,000 profit it forgoes if it does not free its production facilities to make the additional CDs.

Let us see how Greg's Groovy Tunes' managers decide among three alternatives:

1. Use the facilities to make the liners.
2. Buy the liners and leave facilities idle (continue to assume $10,000 of avoidable fixed costs from outsourcing liners).
3. Buy the liners and use facilities to make more CDs (continue to assume $10,000 of avoidable fixed costs from outsourcing liners).

The alternative with the lowest *net* cost is the best use of Greg's Groovy Tunes' facilities. Exhibit 19-23 compares the three alternatives.

EXHIBIT 19-23 | Best Use of Facilities, Given Opportunity Costs

		Buy Liners	
	Make Liners	Facilities Idle	Make Additional CDs
Expected cost of 250,000 liners (from Exhibit 19-22)	$125,000	$132,500	$132,500
Expected *profit* from additional CDs	—	—	(18,000)
Expected net cost of obtaining 250,000 liners	$125,000	$132,500	$114,500

Greg's Groovy Tunes should buy the liners from Becky's Box Designs and use the vacated facilities to make more CDs. If Greg's Groovy Tunes makes the liners, or if it buys the liners from Becky's Box Designs but leaves its production facilities idle, it will forgo the opportunity to earn $18,000.

Greg's Groovy Tunes' managers should consider qualitative factors as well as revenue and cost differences in making their final decision. For example, Greg's Groovy Tunes' managers may believe they can better control quality by making the liners themselves. This is an argument for Greg's to continue making the liners.

Stop & Think...

Assume you and two of your friends are working on a team project for a class. The project has three equal portions to it. The visual portion requires the team to develop a **PowerPoint** presentation. The written portion requires the team to write a group report of the results of the team's research. The auditory portion requires the team to present its findings. You all contribute equally to the research, but you will divide the other three portions. Which part will you do—the visual, written, or auditory portion? Because you are the best at **PowerPoint**, the team would want you to prepare the visual portion. This is similar to the outsourcing decision—focus on doing what jobs you do best.

Outsourcing decisions are increasingly important in today's globally wired economy. In the past, make-or-buy decisions often ended up as "make" because coordination, information exchange, and paperwork problems made buying from suppliers too inconvenient. Now, companies can use the Internet to tap into information systems of suppliers and customers located around the world. Paperwork vanishes, and information required to satisfy the strictest JIT delivery schedule is available in real time. As a result, companies are focusing on their core competencies and are outsourcing more functions.

Sell As Is or Process Further?

At what point in processing should a company sell its product? Many companies, especially in the food processing and natural resource industries, face this business decision. Companies in these industries process a raw material (milk, corn, livestock, crude oil, lumber, to name a few) to a point before it is saleable. For example, **Kraft** pasteurizes raw milk before it is saleable. **Kraft** must then decide whether it should sell the pasteurized milk "as is," or process it further into other dairy products (reduced-fat milk, butter, sour cream, cottage cheese, yogurt, blocks of cheese, shredded cheese, and other dairy products). Managers consider the questions shown in Exhibit 19-24 when deciding whether to sell as is or process further.

EXHIBIT 19-24 | Sell As Is or Process Further Considerations

- How much revenue will the company receive if we sell the product as is?
- How much revenue will the company receive if the company sells the product after processing it further?
- How much will it cost to process the product further?

Let us look at one of **Chevron's** sell as is or process further decisions. Suppose **Chevron** spent $125,000 to process crude oil into 50,000 gallons of regular gasoline, as shown in Exhibit 19-25. After processing crude oil into regular gasoline, should **Chevron** sell the regular gas as is or should it spend more to process the gasoline into premium grade? In making the decision, **Chevron's** managers consider the following relevant information:

EXHIBIT 19-25 | Sell As Is or Process Further Decision

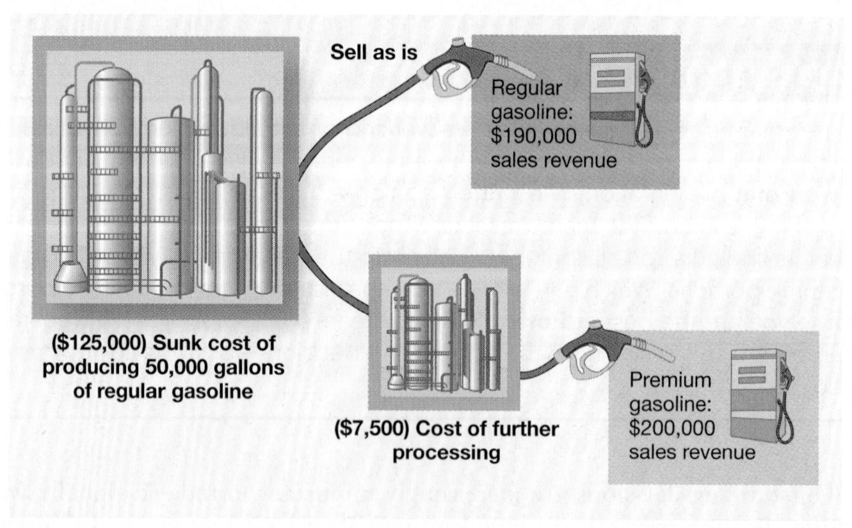

- **Chevron** could sell premium gasoline for $4.00 per gallon, for a total of $200,000 (50,000 × $4.00).
- **Chevron** could sell regular gasoline for $3.80 per gallon, for a total of $190,000 (50,000 × $3.80).
- **Chevron** would have to spend $0.15 per gallon, or $7,500 (50,000 gallons × $0.15) to further process regular gasoline into premium-grade gas.

Notice that **Chevron's** managers do *not* consider the $125,000 spent on processing crude oil into regular gasoline. Why? It is a *sunk* cost. Recall from our previous discussion that a sunk cost is a past cost that cannot be changed regardless of which future action the company takes. **Chevron** has incurred $125,000—regardless of whether it sells the regular gasoline as is or processes it further into premium gasoline. Therefore, the cost is *not* relevant to the decision.

By analyzing only the relevant costs in Exhibit 19-26, managers see that they can increase profit by $2,500 if they convert the regular gasoline into premium gasoline. The $10,000 extra revenue ($200,000 – $190,000) outweighs the incremental $7,500 cost of the extra processing.

EXHIBIT 19-26 | Incremental Analysis for Sell As Is or Process Further Decision

	Sell As Is	Process Further	Difference
Expected revenue from selling 50,000 gallons of regular gasoline at $3.80 per gallon	$190,000		
Expected revenue from selling 50,000 gallons of premium gasoline at $4.00 per gallon		$200,000	$10,000
Additional costs of $0.15 per gallon to convert 50,000 gallons of regular gasoline into premium gasoline		(7,500)	(7,500)
Total net revenue	$190,000	$192,500	$ 2,500

Thus, the decision rule is as follows:

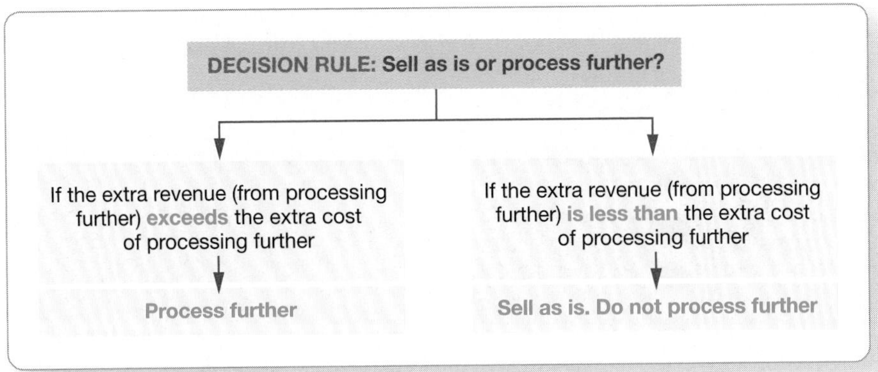

Recall that our keys to decision making include (1) focusing on relevant information and (2) using a contribution margin approach that separates variable costs from fixed costs. The analysis in Exhibit 19-26 includes only those *future* costs and revenues that *differ* between alternatives. We assumed **Chevron** already has the equipment and labor necessary to convert regular gasoline into premium grade gasoline. Because fixed costs would not differ between alternatives, they were irrelevant. However, if **Chevron** has to acquire equipment, or hire employees to convert the gasoline into premium grade gasoline, the extra fixed costs would be relevant. Once again, we see that fixed costs are only relevant if they *differ* between alternatives.

Decision Guidelines

SHORT-TERM SPECIAL BUSINESS DECISIONS

Amazon.com has confronted most of the special business decisions we have covered. Here are the key guidelines **Amazon.com's** managers follow in making their decisions.

Decision	Guidelines
• Should **Amazon.com** drop its electronics product line?	If the cost savings exceed the lost revenues from dropping the electronics product line, then dropping will increase operating income.
• Given limited warehouse space, which products should **Amazon.com** focus on selling?	**Amazon.com** should focus on selling the products with the highest contribution margin per unit of the constraint, which is cubic feet of warehouse space.
• Should **Amazon.com** outsource its warehousing operations?	If the incremental costs of operating its own warehouses exceed the costs of outsourcing, then outsourcing will increase operating income.
• How should **Amazon** decide whether to sell a product as is or process further?	It should process further only if the extra sales revenue (from processing further) exceeds the extra costs of additional processing.

Summary Problem 2

Shelly's Shades produces standard and deluxe sunglasses:

	Per Pair	
	Standard	**Deluxe**
Sale price	$20	$30
Variable expenses	16	21

The company has 15,000 machine hours available. In one machine hour, Shelly's Shades can produce either 70 pairs of the standard model or 30 pairs of the deluxe model.

Requirements

1. Which model should Shelly's Shades emphasize?
2. Shelly's Shades incurs the following costs for 20,000 of its high-tech hiking shades:

Direct materials	$ 20,000
Direct labor	80,000
Variable manufacturing overhead	40,000
Fixed manufacturing overhead	80,000
Total manufacturing cost	$220,000
Cost per pair ($220,000 ÷ 20,000)	$ 11

Another manufacturer has offered to sell Shelly's Shades similar shades for $10, a total purchase cost of $200,000. If Shelly's Shades outsources *and* leaves its plant idle, it can save $50,000 of fixed overhead cost. Or, the company can use the released facilities to make other products that will contribute $70,000 to profits. In this case, the company will not be able to avoid any fixed costs. Identify and analyze the alternatives. What is the best course of action?

Solutions

Requirement 1

	Style of Sunglasses	
	Standard	**Deluxe**
Sale price per pair	$ 20	$ 30
Variable expense per pair	(16)	(21)
Contribution margin per pair	$ 4	$ 9
Units produced each machine hour	× 70	× 30
Contribution margin per machine hour	$ 280	$ 270
Capacity—number of machine hours	× 15,000	× 15,000
Total contribution margin at full capacity	$4,200,000	$4,050,000

Decision: Emphasize the standard model because it has the higher contribution margin per unit of the constraint—machine hours—resulting in a higher contribution margin for the company.

Requirement 2

	Make Shades	Buy Shades: Facilities Idle	Buy Shades: Make Other Products
Relevant costs:			
Direct materials	$ 20,000	—	—
Direct labor	80,000	—	—
Variable overhead	40,000	—	—
Fixed overhead	80,000	$ 30,000	$ 80,000
Purchase cost from outsider (20,000 × $10)	—	200,000	200,000
Total cost of obtaining shades	220,000	230,000	280,000
Profit from other products	—	—	(70,000)
Net cost of obtaining 20,000 shades	$220,000	$230,000	$210,000

Decision: Shelly's Shades should buy the shades from the outside supplier and use the released facilities to make other products.

Review Short-Term Business Decisions

Accounting Vocabulary

Constraint (p. 1040)
A factor that restricts production or sale of a product.

Incremental Analysis Approach (p. 1025)
A method that looks at how operating income would *change or differ* under each decision alternative. Leaves out irrelevant information—the costs and revenues that will not differ between alternatives. Also called the **relevant information approach**.

Irrelevant costs (p. 1024)
Costs that *do not* affect a decision.

Opportunity Cost (p. 1044)
The benefit forgone by not choosing an alternative course of action.

Outsourcing (p. 1025)
The decision to buy or subcontract a component product or service rather than produce it in-house.

Relevant costs (p. 1023)
Costs that *do* affect a decision.

Relevant Information (p. 1023)
Expected *future* data that *differs* among alternatives.

Relevant Information Approach (p. 1025)
A method that looks at how operating income would *change or differ* under each decision alternative. Leaves out irrelevant information—the costs and revenues that will not differ between alternatives. Also called the **incremental analysis approach**.

Sunk Cost (p. 1024)
A past cost that cannot be changed regardless of which future action is taken.

Target Full Cost (p. 1031)
The total cost in developing, producing, and delivering a product or service.

Quick Check

1. In making short-term special decisions, you should
   a. separate variable from fixed costs.
   b. use a traditional absorption costing approach.
   c. only focus on quantitative factors.
   d. focus on total costs.
2. Which of the following is relevant to Bookworm.com's decision to accept a special order at a lower sale price from a large customer in China?
   a. The cost of Bookworm.com's warehouses in the United States
   b. The cost of shipping the order to the customer
   c. Founder Leon Lyons's salary
   d. Bookworm.com's investment in its Web site
3. Which of the following costs are irrelevant to business decisions?
   a. Variable costs
   b. Sunk costs
   c. Avoidable costs
   d. Costs that differ between alternatives
4. When making decisions, managers should
   a. consider revenues that differ between alternatives.
   b. consider costs that do not differ between alternatives.
   c. consider sunk costs in their decisions.
   d. consider only variable costs.

5. When pricing a product or service, managers must consider which of the following?
   a. Only variable costs
   b. Only manufacturing costs
   c. Only period costs
   d. All costs
6. When companies are price-setters, their products and services
   a. are priced by managers using a target-pricing emphasis.
   b. tend to be unique.
   c. tend to be commodities.
   d. tend to have a lot of competitors.
7. In deciding whether to drop its electronics product line, Bookworm.com would consider
   a. how dropping the electronics product line would affect sales of its other products like CDs.
   b. the revenues it would lose from dropping the product line.
   c. the costs it could save by dropping the product line.
   d. All of the above
8. In deciding which product lines to emphasize, Bookworm.com should focus on the product line that has the highest
   a. contribution margin per unit of the constraining factor.
   b. contribution margin per unit of product.
   c. profit per unit of product.
   d. contribution margin ratio.
9. When making outsourcing decisions
   a. avoidable fixed costs are irrelevant.
   b. expected use of the freed capacity is irrelevant.
   c. the variable cost of producing the product in-house is relevant.
   d. the manufacturing unit cost of making the product in-house is relevant.
10. When deciding whether to sell as is or process a product further, managers should ignore which of the following?
   a. The revenue if the product is processed further
   b. The costs of processing the product thus far
   c. The cost of processing further
   d. The revenue if the product is sold as is

Answers are given after Apply Your Knowledge (p. 1069).

Assess Your Progress

■ Short Exercises

S19-1 *(L.OBJ. 1)* **Describing and identifying information relevant to business decisions [5 min]**
You are trying to decide whether to trade in your inkjet printer for a more recent model. Your usage pattern will remain unchanged, but the old and new printers use different ink cartridges.

Requirement

1. Indicate if the following items are relevant or irrelevant to your decision:

   a. The price of the new printer
   b. The price you paid for the old printer
   c. The trade-in value of the old printer
   d. Paper costs
   e. The difference between ink cartridges' costs

S19-2 *(L.OBJ. 2)* **Making special order and pricing decisions [10 min]**
SnowDelight operates a Rocky Mountain ski resort. The company is planning its lift ticket pricing for the coming ski season. Investors would like to earn a 13% return on the company's $105 million of assets. The company primarily incurs fixed costs to groom the runs and operate the lifts. SnowDelight projects fixed costs to be $34,250,000 for the ski season. The resort serves about 650,000 skiers and snowboarders each season. Variable costs are about $11 per guest. Currently, the resort has such a favorable reputation among skiers and snowboarders that it has some control over the lift ticket prices.

Requirements

1. Would SnowDelight emphasize target pricing or cost-plus pricing. Why?
2. If other resorts in the area charge $82 per day, what price should SnowDelight charge?

Note: Short Exercise 19-2 must be completed before attempting Short Exercise 19-3.

S19-3 *(L.OBJ. 2)* **Making special order and pricing decisions [10 min]**
Consider SnowDelight from Short Exercise 19-2. Assume that SnowDelight's reputation has diminished and other resorts in the vicinity are only charging $75 per lift ticket. SnowDelight has become a price-taker and will not be able to charge more than its competitors. At the market price, SnowDelight managers believe they will still serve 650,000 skiers and snowboarders each season.

Requirements

1. If SnowDelight cannot reduce its costs, what profit will it earn? State your answer in dollars and as a percent of assets. Will investors be happy with the profit level?
2. Assume SnowDelight has found ways to cut its fixed costs to $28 million. What is its new target variable cost per skier/snowboarder?

S19-4 *(L.OBJ. 3)* **Making dropping a product and product-mix decisions [5–10 min]**
Linda Fashions operates three departments: Men's, Women's, and Accessories. Departmental operating income data for the third quarter of 2011 are as follows:

LINDA FASHIONS
Income Statement
For the quarter ended September 30, 2011

	Department			
	Men's	Women's	Accessories	Total
Sales revenue	$ 109,000	$ 53,000	$ 102,000	$ 264,000
Variable expenses	61,000	32,000	89,000	182,000
Fixed expenses	24,000	20,000	24,000	68,000
Total expenses	85,000	52,000	113,000	250,000
Operating income (loss)	$ 24,000	$ 1,000	$ (11,000)	$ 14,000

Assume that the fixed expenses assigned to each department include only direct fixed costs of the department:

- Salary of the department's manager
- Cost of advertising directly related to that department

If Linda Fashions drops a department, it will not incur these fixed expenses.

Requirement

1. Under these circumstances, should Linda Fashions drop any of the departments? Give your reasoning.

Note: Short Exercise 19-4 must be completed before attempting Short Exercise 19-5.

S19-5 *(L.OBJ. 3)* **Making dropping a product and product-mix decisions [10 min]**
Consider Linda Fashions from Short Exercise 19-4. Assume that Linda Fashions allocates all fixed costs based on square footage. If Linda Fashions drops one of the current departments, it plans to replace the dropped department with a shoe department. The company expects the shoe department to produce $76,000 in sales and have $54,000 of variable costs. Because the shoe business would be new to Linda Fashions, the company would have to incur an additional $7,100 of fixed costs (advertising, depreciation on new shoe display racks, and so forth) per period related to the department.

Requirements

1. What is the potential profit from the new shoe department?
2. Should Linda Fashions consider replacing one of its existing departments with a new shoe department?

S19-6 *(L.OBJ. 3)* **Making dropping a product and product-mix decisions [15 min]**
Store-It produces plastic storage bins for household storage needs. The company makes two sizes of bins: large (50 gallon) and regular (35 gallon). Demand for the product is so high that Store-It can sell as many of each size as it can produce. The company uses the same machinery to produce both sizes. The machinery can only be run for 3,400 hours per period. Store-It can produce 10 large bins every hour, whereas it can produce 17 regular bins in the same amount of time. Fixed costs amount to $105,000 per period. Sales prices and variable costs are as follows:

	Regular	Large
Sales price per unit	$8.50	$10.50
Variable cost per unit	$3.50	$ 4.30

Requirements

1. Which product should Store-It emphasize? Why?
2. To maximize profits, how many of each size bin should Store-It produce?
3. Given this product mix, what will the company's operating income be?

Note: Short Exercise 19-6 must be completed before attempting Short Exercise 19-7.

S19-7 *(L.OBJ. 3)* **Making dropping a product and product-mix decisions [15 min]**
Consider Store-It in Short Exercise 19-6. Assume demand for regular bins is limited to 32,000 units and demand for large bins is limited to 27,000 units.

Requirements

1. How many of each size bin should Store-It make now?
2. Given this product mix, what will the company's operating income be?
3. Explain why the operating income is less than it was when Store-It was producing its optimal product mix in 19-6.

S19-8 *(L.OBJ. 4)* **Making outsourcing and sell as is or process further decisions [10 min]**
Suppose an Olive Tree restaurant is considering whether to (1) bake bread for its restaurant in-house or (2) buy the bread from a local bakery. The chef estimates that variable costs of making each loaf include $0.56 of ingredients, $0.22 of variable overhead (electricity to run the oven), and $0.76 of direct labor for kneading and forming the loaves. Allocating fixed overhead (depreciation on the kitchen equipment and building) based on direct labor assigns $1.00 of fixed overhead per loaf. None of the fixed costs are avoidable. The local bakery would charge $1.74 per loaf.

Requirements

1. What is the unit cost of making the bread in-house (use absorption costing)?
2. Should Olive Tree bake the bread in-house or buy from the local bakery? Why?
3. In addition to the financial analysis, what else should Olive Tree consider when making this decision?

S19-9 *(L.OBJ. 4)* **Making outsourcing decisions [10–15 min]**
Rita Riley manages a fleet of 200 delivery trucks for Greely Corp. Riley must decide if the company should outsource the fleet management function. If she outsources to Fleet Management Services (FMS), FMS will be responsible for maintenance and scheduling activities. This alternative would require Riley to lay off her five employees. However, her own job would be secure; she would be Greely's liaison with FMS. If she continues to manage the fleet she will need fleet-management software that costs $8,000 a year to lease. FMS offers to manage this fleet for an annual fee of $280,000. Rita performed the following analysis:

GREELY CORPORATION
Outsourcing Decision Analysis

	Retain In–House	Outsource to FMS	Difference
Annual leasing fee for software	$ 8,000	$ —	$ 8,000
Annual maintenance of trucks	145,000	—	145,000
Total annual salaries of five other fleet management employees	150,000	—	150,000
Fleet Management Services' annual fee	—	280,000	(280,000)
Total cost / cost savings	$ 303,000	$ 280,000	$ 23,000

Requirements

1. Which alternative will maximize Greely's short-term operating income?
2. What qualitative factors should Riley consider before making a final decision?

S19-10 *(L.OBJ. 4)* **Sell as is or process further decisions [10 min]**
Chocolicious processes cocoa beans into cocoa powder at a processing cost of $9,800 per batch. Chocolicious can sell the cocoa powder as is or it can process the cocoa powder further into either chocolate syrup or boxed assorted chocolates. Once processed, each batch of cocoa beans would result in the following sales revenue:

Cocoa powder	$ 14,500
Chocolate syrup	$100,000
Boxed assorted chocolates	$200,000

The cost of transforming the cocoa powder into chocolate syrup would be $72,000. Likewise, the company would incur a cost of $178,000 to transform the cocoa powder into boxed assorted chocolates. The company president has decided to make boxed assorted chocolates owing to its high sales value and to the fact that the cocoa bean processing cost of $9,800 eats up most of the cocoa powder profits.

Requirement

1. Has the president made the right or wrong decision? Explain your answer. Be sure to include the correct financial analysis in your response.

Exercises

E19-11 *(L.OBJ. 1)* **Describing and identifying information relevant to business decisions [5–10 min]**

Joe Roberts, production manager for Fabricut, invested in computer-controlled production machinery last year. He purchased the machinery from Advanced Design at a cost of $2 million. A representative from Advanced Design has recently contacted Joe because the company has designed an even more efficient piece of machinery. The new design would double the production output of the year-old machinery but cost Fabricut another $3 million. Roberts is afraid to bring this new equipment to the company president's attention because he convinced the president to invest $2 million in the machinery last year.

Requirement

1. Explain what is relevant and irrelevant to Roberts's dilemma. What should he do?

E19-12 *(L.OBJ. 2)* **Making special order and pricing decisions [10–15 min]**

Suppose the Baseball Hall of Fame in Cooperstown, New York, has approached Active-Cardz with a special order. The Hall of Fame wishes to purchase 50,000 baseball card packs for a special promotional campaign and offers $0.37 per pack, a total of $18,500. Active-Cardz's total production cost is $0.57 per pack, as follows:

Variable costs:	
Direct materials	$ 0.14
Direct labor	0.07
Variable overhead	0.11
Fixed overhead	0.25
Total cost	$ 0.57

Active-Cardz has enough excess capacity to handle the special order.

Requirements

1. Prepare an incremental analysis to determine whether Active-Cardz should accept the special sales order.
2. Now assume that the Hall of Fame wants special hologram baseball cards. Active-Cardz will spend $5,800 to develop this hologram, which will be useless after the special order is completed. Should Active-Cardz accept the special order under these circumstances?

E19-13 *(L.OBJ. 2)* **Making special order and pricing decisions [20–25 min]**
Maui Smith Sunglasses sell for about $150 per pair. Suppose that the company incurs the following average costs per pair:

Direct materials	$ 42
Direct labor	10
Variable manufacturing overhead	6
Variable marketing expenses	4
Fixed manufacturing overhead	16*
Total cost	$ 78

* $2,100,000 total fixed manufacturing overhead ÷ 131,250 pairs of sunglasses

Maui Smith has enough idle capacity to accept a one-time-only special order from Montana Glasses for 18,000 pairs of sunglasses at $70 per pair. Maui Smith will not incur any variable marketing expenses for the order.

Requirements

1. How would accepting the order affect Maui Smith's operating income? In addition to the special order's effect on profits, what other (longer-term qualitative) factors should Maui Smith's managers consider in deciding whether to accept the order?
2. Maui Smith's marketing manager, Jim Revo, argues against accepting the special order because the offer price of $70 is less than Maui Smith's $78 cost to make the sunglasses. Revo asks you, as one of Maui Smith's staff accountants, to explain whether his analysis is correct.

E19-14 *(L.OBJ. 2)* **Making special order and pricing decisions [10–15 min]**
White Builders builds 1,500 square-foot starter tract homes in the fast-growing suburbs of Atlanta. Land and labor are cheap, and competition among developers is fierce. The homes are "cookie-cutter," with any upgrades added by the buyer after the sale. White Builders' costs per developed sub-lot are as follows:

Land	$ 54,000
Construction	$ 122,000
Landscaping	$ 5,000
Variable marketing costs	$ 3,000

White Builders would like to earn a profit of 15% of the variable cost of each home sale. Similar homes offered by competing builders sell for $206,000 each.

Requirements

1. Which approach to pricing should White Builders emphasize? Why?
2. Will White Builders be able to achieve its target profit levels?
3. Bathrooms and kitchens are typically the most important selling features of a home. White Builders could differentiate the homes by upgrading the bathrooms and kitchens. The upgrades would cost $20,000 per home, but would enable White Builders to increase the selling prices by $35,000 per home. (Kitchen and bathroom upgrades typically add about 150% of their cost to the value of any home.) If White Builders makes the upgrades, what will the new cost-plus price per home be? Should the company differentiate its product in this manner?

E19-15 *(L.OBJ. 3)* **Making dropping a product and product-mix decisions [10 min]**
Top managers of Movie Plus are alarmed by their operating losses. They are considering dropping the VCR-tape product line. Company accountants have prepared the following analysis to help make this decision:

MOVIE PLUS Income Statement For the year ended December 31, 2010			
	Total	DVD Discs	VCR Tapes
Sales revenue	$ 438,000	$ 309,000	$ 129,000
Variable expenses	250,000	157,000	93,000
Contribution margin	188,000	152,000	36,000
Fixed expenses:			
Manufacturing	134,000	76,000	58,000
Marketing and administrative	70,000	59,000	11,000
Total fixed expenses	204,000	135,000	69,000
Operating income (loss)	$ (16,000)	$ 17,000	$ (33,000)

Total fixed costs will not change if the company stops selling VCR tapes.

Requirement

1. Prepare an incremental analysis to show whether Movie Plus should drop the VCR-tape product line. Will dropping VCR tapes add $33,000 to operating income? Explain.

Note: Exercise 19-15 must be completed before attempting Exercise 19-16.

E19-16 *(L.OBJ. 3)* **Making dropping a product and product-mix decisions [10 min]**
Refer to Exercise 19-15. Assume that Movie Plus can avoid $26,000 of fixed expenses by dropping the VCR-tape product line (these costs are direct fixed costs of the VCR product line).

Requirement

1. Prepare an incremental analysis to show whether Movie Plus should stop selling VCR tapes.

E19-17 *(L.OBJ. 3)* **Product mix under production constraints [15 min]**
ExerLight produces two types of exercise treadmills: regular and deluxe. The exercise craze is such that ExerLight could use all its available machine hours to produce either model. The two models are processed through the same production departments. Data for both models is as follows:

	Per Unit	
	Deluxe	Regular
Sale price	$ 1,000	$ 580
Costs:		
Direct materials	310	110
Direct labor	80	184
Variable manufacturing overhead	252	84
Fixed manufacturing overhead*	108	36
Variable operating expenses	113	69
Total cost	863	483
Operating income	$ 137	$ 97

*Allocated on the basis of machine hours.

Requirements

1. What is the constraint?
2. Which model should ExerLight produce? (*Hint:* Use the allocation of fixed manufacturing overhead to determine the proportion of machine hours used by each product.)
3. If ExerLight should produce both models, compute the mix that will maximize operating income.

E19-18 *(L.OBJ. 3)* **Making dropping a product and product-mix decisions [10–15 min]**
Cole sells both designer and moderately priced fashion accessories. Top management is deciding which product line to emphasize. Accountants have provided the following data:

	Per Item	
	Designer	Moderately Priced
Average sale price	$ 195	$ 83
Average variable expenses	95	22
Average contribution margin	100	61
Average fixed expenses (allocated)	20	15
Average operating income	$ 80	$ 46

The Cole store in Reno, Nevada, has 8,000 square feet of floor space. If Cole emphasizes moderately priced goods, it can display 560 items in the store. If Cole emphasizes designer wear, it can only display 240 designer items. These numbers are also the average monthly sales in units.

Requirement

1. Prepare an analysis to show which product the company should emphasize.

E19-19 *(L.OBJ. 3)* **Making dropping a product and product-mix decisions [15–20 min]**
Each morning, Mike Smith stocks the drink case at Mike's Beach Hut in Myrtle Beach, South Carolina. Mike's Beach Hut has 100 linear feet of refrigerated display space for cold drinks. Each linear foot can hold either five 12-ounce cans or four 20-ounce plastic or glass bottles.

Mike's Beach Hut sells three types of cold drinks:

1. Grand – Cola in 12-oz. cans, for $1.55 per can
2. Grand – Cola in 20-oz. plastic bottles, for $1.65 per bottle
3. Right – Cola in 20-oz. glass bottles, for $2.25 per bottle

Mike's Beach Hut pays its suppliers:

1. $0.25 per 12-oz. can of Grand – Cola
2. $0.30 per 20-oz. bottle of Grand – Cola
3. $0.70 per 20-oz. bottle of Right – Cola

Mike's Beach Hut's monthly fixed expenses include:

Hut rental	$ 375
Refrigerator rental	60
Mike's salary	1,600
Total fixed expenses	$ 2,035

Mike's Beach Hut can sell all the drinks stocked in the display case each morning.

Requirements

1. What is Mike's Beach Hut's constraining factor? What should Mike stock to maximize profits?
2. Suppose Mike's Beach Hut refuses to devote more than 65 linear feet to any individual product. Under this condition, how many linear feet of each drink should Mike's stock? How many units of each product will be available for sale each day?

E19-20 *(L.OBJ. 4)* **Making outsourcing decisions [10–15 min]**
Opti Systems manufactures an optical switch that it uses in its final product. The switch has the following manufacturing costs per unit:

Direct materials	$ 11.00
Direct labor	2.00
Variable overhead	3.00
Fixed overhead	7.00
Manufacturing product cost	$ 23.00

Another company has offered to sell Opti Systems the switch for $17.50 per unit. If Opti Systems buys the switch from the outside supplier, the manufacturing facilities that will be idled cannot be used for any other purpose, yet none of the fixed costs are avoidable.

Requirement

1. Prepare an outsourcing analysis to determine if Opti Systems should make or buy the switch.

Note: Exercise 19-20 must be completed before attempting Exercise 19-21.

E19-21 *(L.OBJ. 4)* **Making outsourcing decisions [10–15 min]**
Refer to Exercise 19-20. Opti Systems needs 82,000 optical switches. By outsourcing them, Opti Systems can use its idle facilities to manufacture another product that will contribute $223,000 to operating income.

Requirements

1. Identify the *incremental* costs that Opti Systems will incur to acquire 82,000 switches under three alternative plans.
2. Which plan makes the best use of Opti System's facilities? Support your answer.

E19-22 *(L.OBJ. 4)* **Making sell as is or process further decisions [10 min]**
Organicmaid processes organic milk into plain yogurt. Organicmaid sells plain yogurt to hospitals, nursing homes, and restaurants in bulk, one-gallon containers. Each batch, processed at a cost of $820, yields 540 gallons of plain yogurt. Organicmaid sells the one-gallon tubs for $6 each, and spends $0.12 for each plastic tub. Organicmaid has recently begun to reconsider its strategy. Organicmaid wonders if it would be more profitable to sell individual-size portions of fruited organic yogurt at local food stores. Organicmaid could further process each batch of plain yogurt into 11,520 individual portions (3/4 cup each) of fruited yogurt. A recent market analysis indicates that demand for the product exists. Organicmaid would sell each individual portion for $0.56. Packaging would cost $0.06 per portion, and fruit would cost $0.10 per portion. Fixed costs would not change.

Requirement

1. Should Organicmaid continue to sell only the gallon-size plain yogurt (sell as is), or convert the plain yogurt into individual-size portions of fruited yogurt (process further)? Why?

Problems (Group A)

P19-23A *(L.OBJ. 1, 2)* **Identifying which information is relevant and making special order and pricing decisions [15–20 min]**

Maritime manufactures flotation vests in Tampa, Florida. Maritime's contribution-margin income statement for the month ended December 31, 2010, contains the following data:

MARITIME Income Statement For the month ended December 31, 2010	
Sales in units	30,000
Sales revenue	$ 480,000
Variable expenses:	
Manufacturing	90,000
Marketing and administrative	105,000
Total variable expenses	195,000
Contribution margin	285,000
Fixed expenses:	
Manufacturing	126,000
Marketing and administrative	89,000
Total fixed expenses	215,000
Operating income	$ 70,000

Suppose Overton wishes to buy 4,500 vests from Maritime. Acceptance of the order will not increase Maritime's variable marketing and administrative expenses. The Maritime plant has enough unused capacity to manufacture the additional vests. Overton has offered $11.00 per vest, which is below the normal sale price of $16.

Requirements

1. Identify each cost in the income statement as either relevant or irrelevant to Maritime's decision.
2. Prepare an incremental analysis to determine whether Maritime should accept this special sales order.
3. Identify long-term factors Maritime should consider in deciding whether to accept the special sales order.

P19-24A *(L.OBJ. 2)* **Making special order and pricing decisions [15–20 min]**

Garden House operates a commercial plant nursery where it propagates plants for garden centers throughout the region. Garden House has $5,000,000 in assets. Its yearly fixed costs are $625,000 and the variable costs for the potting soil, container, label, seedling, and labor for each gallon-size plant total $1.70. Garden House's volume is currently 500,000 units. Competitors offer the same plants, at the same quality, to garden centers for $4.00 each. Garden centers then mark them up to sell to the public for $8 to $10, depending on the type of plant.

Requirements

1. Garden House's owners want to earn a 12% return on the company's assets. What is Garden House's target full cost?
2. Given Garden House's current costs, will its owners be able to achieve their target profit?

3. Assume Garden House has identified ways to cut its variable costs to $1.55 per unit. What is its new target fixed cost? Will this decrease in variable costs allow the company to achieve its target profit?

4. Garden House started an aggressive advertising campaign strategy to differentiate its plants from those grown by other nurseries. Monrovia Plants made this strategy work so Garden House has decided to try it, too. Garden House does not expect volume to be affected, but it hopes to gain more control over pricing. If Garden House has to spend $120,000 this year to advertise, and its variable costs continue to be $1.55 per unit, what will its cost-plus price be? Do you think Garden House will be able to sell its plants to garden centers at the cost-plus price? Why or why not?

P19-25A *(L.OBJ. 3)* **Making dropping a product and product-mix decisions [20–25 min]**
Members of the board of directors of Security Force have received the following operating income data for the year ended December 31, 2010:

SECURITY FORCE Income Statement For the year ended December 31, 2010			
	Product Line		
	Industrial Systems	Household Systems	Total
Sales revenue	$ 320,000	$ 340,000	$ 660,000
Cost of goods sold:			
Variable	38,000	45,000	83,000
Fixed	250,000	67,000	317,000
Total cost of goods sold	288,000	112,000	400,000
Gross profit	32,000	228,000	260,000
Marketing and administrative expenses:			
Variable	67,000	70,000	137,000
Fixed	42,000	23,000	65,000
Total marketing and administrative exp.	109,000	93,000	202,000
Operating income (loss)	$ (77,000)	$ 135,000	$ 58,000

Members of the board are surprised that the industrial systems product line is losing money. They commission a study to determine whether the company should drop the line. Company accountants estimate that dropping industrial systems will decrease fixed cost of goods sold by $85,000 and decrease fixed marketing and administrative expenses by $13,000.

Requirements

1. Prepare an incremental analysis to show whether Security Force should drop the industrial systems product line.
2. Prepare contribution margin income statements to show Security Force's total operating income under the two alternatives: (a) with the industrial systems line and (b) without the line. Compare the *difference* between the two alternatives' income numbers to your answer to requirement 1.
3. What have you learned from the comparison in requirement 2?

P19-26A *(L.OBJ. 3)* **Making dropping a product and product-mix decisions [10–15 min]**
Britt, located in St. Cloud, Minnesota, produces two lines of electric toothbrushes: deluxe and standard. Because Britt can sell all the toothbrushes it can produce, the

owners are expanding the plant. They are deciding which product line to emphasize. To make this decision, they assemble the following data:

	Per Unit	
	Deluxe Toothbrush	Standard Toothbrush
Sale price	$ 80	$ 58
Variable expenses	21	19
Contribution margin	$ 59	$ 39
Contribution margin ratio	73.8%	67.2%

After expansion, the factory will have a production capacity of 4,300 machine hours per month. The plant can manufacture either 65 standard electric toothbrushes or 23 deluxe electric toothbrushes per machine hour.

Requirements

1. Identify the constraining factor for Britt.
2. Prepare an analysis to show which product line to emphasize.

P19-27A *(L.OBJ. 4)* **Making outsourcing decisions [20–30 min]**
Wild Ride manufactures snowboards. Its cost of making 1,800 bindings is as follows:

Direct materials	$ 17,530
Direct labor	2,700
Variable overhead	2,120
Fixed overhead	7,100
Total manufacturing costs for 1,800 bindings	$ 29,450

Suppose Lewis will sell bindings to Wild Ride for $15 each. Wild Ride would pay $1 per unit to transport the bindings to its manufacturing plant, where it would add its own logo at a cost of $0.60 per binding.

Requirements

1. Wild Ride's accountants predict that purchasing the bindings from Lewis will enable the company to avoid $2,600 of fixed overhead. Prepare an analysis to show whether Wild Ride should make or buy the bindings.
2. The facilities freed by purchasing bindings from Lewis can be used to manufacture another product that will contribute $2,600 to profit. Total fixed costs will be the same as if Wild Ride had produced the bindings. Show which alternative makes the best use of Wild Ride's facilities: (a) make bindings, (b) buy bindings and leave facilities idle, or (c) buy bindings and make another product.

P19-28A *(L.OBJ. 4)* **Making sell as is or process further decisions [20–25 min]**
Rouse Petroleum has spent $201,000 to refine 64,000 gallons of petroleum distillate, which can be sold for $6.00 a gallon. Alternatively, Rouse can process the distillate further and produce 57,000 gallons of cleaner fluid. The additional processing will cost $1.70 per gallon of distillate. The cleaner fluid can be sold for $9.20 a gallon. To sell the cleaner fluid, Rouse must pay a sales commission of $0.12 a gallon and transportation charge of $0.17 a gallon.

Requirements

1. Diagram Rouse's decision alternatives, using Exhibit 19-25 as a guide.
2. Identify the sunk cost. Is the sunk cost relevant to Rouse's decision?
3. Should Rouse sell the petroleum distillate or process it into cleaner fluid? Show the expected net revenue difference between the two alternatives.

Problems (Group B)

P19-29B *(L.OBJ. 1, 2)* **Identifying which information is relevant and making special order and pricing decisions [15–20 min]**

Buoy manufactures flotation vests in Tampa, Florida. Buoy's contribution-margin income statement for the month ended January 31, 2010, contains the following data:

BUOY Income Statement For the month ended January 31, 2010	
Sales in units	32,000
Sales revenue	$ 448,000
Variable expenses:	
Manufacturing	96,000
Marketing and administrative	112,000
Total variable expenses	208,000
Contribution margin	240,000
Fixed expenses:	
Manufacturing	125,000
Marketing and administrative	94,000
Total fixed expenses	219,000
Operating income	$ 21,000

Suppose Overton wishes to buy 5,300 vests from Buoy. Acceptance of the order will not increase Buoy's variable marketing and administrative expenses. The Buoy plant has enough unused capacity to manufacture the additional vests. Overton has offered $9.00 per vest, which is below the normal sale price of $14.

Requirements

1. Identify each cost in the income statement as either relevant or irrelevant to Buoy's decision.
2. Prepare an incremental analysis to determine whether Buoy should accept this special sales order.
3. Identify long-term factors Buoy should consider in deciding whether to accept the special sales order.

P19-30B *(L.OBJ. 2)* **Making special order and pricing decisions [15–20 min]**

Green Thumb operates a commercial plant nursery, where it propagates plants for garden centers throughout the region. Green Thumb has $5,000,000 in assets. Its yearly fixed costs are $600,000 and the variable costs for the potting soil, container, label, seedling, and labor for each gallon-size plant total $1.35. Green Thumb's volume is currently 500,000 units. Competitors offer the same plants, at the same quality, to garden centers for $3.60 each. Garden centers then mark them up to sell to the public for $8 to $10, depending on the type of plant.

Requirements

1. Green Thumb's owners want to earn a 12% return on the company's assets. What is Green Thumb's target full cost?
2. Given Green Thumb's current costs, will its owners be able to achieve their target profit?

3. Assume Green Thumb has identified ways to cut its variable costs to $1.20 per unit. What is its new target fixed cost? Will this decrease in variable costs allow the company to achieve its target profit?
4. Green Thumb started an aggressive advertising campaign strategy to differentiate its plants from those grown by other nurseries. Monrovia Plants made this strategy work so Green Thumb has decided to try it, too. Green Thumb does not expect volume to be affected, but it hopes to gain more control over pricing. If Green Thumb has to spend $120,000 this year to advertise, and its variable costs continue to be $1.20 per unit, what will its cost-plus price be? Do you think Green Thumb will be able to sell its plants to garden centers at the cost-plus price? Why or why not?

P19-31B *(L.OBJ. 3)* **Making dropping a product and product-mix decisions [20–25 min]**
Members of the board of directors of Security First have received the following operating income data for the year ended August 31, 2010:

SECURITY FIRST Income Statement For the year ended August 31, 2010			
	Product Line		
	Industrial Systems	Household Systems	Total
Sales revenue	$ 340,000	$ 360,000	$ 700,000
Cost of goods sold:			
Variable	33,000	45,000	78,000
Fixed	250,000	63,000	313,000
Total cost of goods sold	283,000	108,000	391,000
Gross profit	57,000	252,000	309,000
Marketing and administrative expenses:			
Variable	68,000	75,000	143,000
Fixed	42,000	24,000	66,000
Total marketing and administrative exp.	110,000	99,000	209,000
Operating income (loss)	$ (53,000)	$ 153,000	$ 100,000

Members of the board are surprised that the industrial systems product line is losing money. They commission a study to determine whether the company should drop the line. Company accountants estimate that dropping industrial systems will decrease fixed cost of goods sold by $84,000 and decrease fixed marketing and administrative expenses by $12,000.

Requirements

1. Prepare an incremental analysis to show whether Security First should drop the industrial systems product line.
2. Prepare contribution margin income statements to show Security First's total operating income under the two alternatives: (a) with the industrial systems line and (b) without the line. Compare the *difference* between the two alternatives' income numbers to your answer to requirement 1.
3. What have you learned from this comparison?

P19-32B *(L.OBJ. 3)* **Making dropping a product and product-mix decisions [10–15 min]**
Brett, located in Rochester, New York, produces two lines of electric toothbrushes: deluxe and standard. Because Brett can sell all the toothbrushes it can produce, the owners are expanding the plant. They are deciding which product line to emphasize. To make this decision, they assemble the following data:

	Per Unit	
	Deluxe Toothbrush	Standard Toothbrush
Sale price	$ 80	$ 52
Variable expenses	24	16
Contribution margin	$ 56	$ 36
Contribution margin ratio	70.0%	69.2%

After expansion, the factory will have a production capacity of 4,100 machine hours per month. The plant can manufacture either 55 standard electric toothbrushes or 23 deluxe electric toothbrushes per machine hour.

Requirements

1. Identify the constraining factor for Brett.
2. Prepare an analysis to show which product line the company should emphasize.

P19-33B *(L.OBJ. 4)* **Making outsourcing decisions [20–30 min]**
X-Perience manufactures snowboards. Its cost of making 1,700 bindings is as follows:

Direct materials	$ 17,600
Direct labor	3,100
Variable overhead	2,080
Fixed overhead	6,600
Total manufacturing costs for 1,700 bindings	$ 29,380

Suppose Livingston will sell bindings to X-Perience for $14 each. X-Perience would pay $2 per unit to transport the bindings to its manufacturing plant, where it would add its own logo at a cost of $0.60 per binding.

Requirements

1. X-Perience's accountants predict that purchasing the bindings from Livingston will enable the company to avoid $1,800 of fixed overhead. Prepare an analysis to show whether X-Perience should make or buy the bindings.
2. The facilities freed by purchasing bindings from Livingston can be used to manufacture another product that will contribute $2,800 to profit. Total fixed costs will be the same as if X-Perience had produced the bindings. Show which alternative makes the best use of X-Perience's facilities: (a) make bindings, (b) buy bindings and leave facilities idle, or (c) buy bindings and make another product.

P19-34B *(L.OBJ. 4)* **Make sell as is or process further decisions [20–25 min]**
Castillo Petroleum has spent $205,000 to refine 64,000 gallons of petroleum distillate, which can be sold for $6.10 a gallon. Alternatively, Castillo can process the distillate further and produce 56,000 gallons of cleaner fluid. The additional processing will cost $1.70 per gallon of distillate. The cleaner fluid can be sold for $9.30 a gallon. To sell the cleaner fluid, Castillo must pay a sales commission of $0.11 a gallon and transportation charge of $0.18 a gallon.

Requirements

1. Diagram Castillo's decision alternatives, using Exhibit 19-25 as a guide.
2. Identify the sunk cost. Is the sunk cost relevant to Castillo's decision?
3. Should Castillo sell the petroleum distillate or process it into cleaner fluid? Show the expected net revenue difference between the two alternatives.

■ Continuing Exercise

E19-35 This exercise continues the Sherman Lawn Service, Inc., situation from Exercise 18-33 of Chapter 18. Sherman Lawn Service currently charges $50 for a standard lawn service and incurs $20 in variable cost. Assume fixed costs are $1,200 per month. Sherman has been offered a special contract for $35 each for 10 lawns in one subdivision. This special contract will not affect Sherman's other business.

Requirements

1. Should Sherman take the special contract?
2. What will Sherman's incremental profit be on the special contract?

■ Continuing Problem

P19-36 This problem continues the Haupt Consulting, Inc., situation from Problem 18-34 of Chapter 18. Haupt Consulting provides consulting service at an average price of $100 per hour and incurs variable costs of $40 per hour. Assume average fixed costs are $4,000 a month.

Haupt has developed new software that will revolutionize billing for companies. Haupt has already invested $300,000 in the software. It can market the software as is at $50,000 a client and expects to sell to eight clients. Haupt can develop the software further, adding integration to Microsoft products at an additional development cost of $150,000. The additional development will allow Haupt to sell the software for $60,000 each, but to ten clients.

Requirement

1. Should Haupt sell the software as is or develop it further?

Apply Your Knowledge

■ Decision Cases

Case 1. BKFin.com provides banks access to sophisticated financial information and analysis systems over the Web. The company combines these tools with benchmarking data access, including e-mail and wireless communications, so that banks can instantly evaluate individual loan applications and entire loan portfolios.

BKFin.com's CEO Jon Wise is happy with the company's growth. To better focus on client service, Wise is considering outsourcing some functions. CFO Jenny Lee suggests that the company's e-mail may be the place to start. She recently attended a conference and learned that companies like **Continental Airlines, DellNet, GTE,** and **NBC** were outsourcing their e-mail function. Wise asks Lee to identify costs related to BKFin.com's in-house Microsoft Exchange mail application, which has 2,300 mailboxes. This information follows:

Variable costs:	
E-mail license	$7 per mailbox per month
Virus protection license	$1 per mailbox per month
Other variable costs	$8 per mailbox per month
Fixed costs:	
Computer hardware costs	$94,300 per month
$8,050 monthly salary for two information technology staff members who work only on e-mail	$16,100 per month

Requirements

1. Compute the *total cost* per mailbox per month of BKFin.com's current e-mail function.
2. Suppose Mail.com, a leading provider of Internet messaging outsourcing services, offers to host BKFin.com's e-mail function for $9 per mailbox per month. If BKFin.com outsources its e-mail to Mail.com, BKFin.com will still need the virus protection software, its computer hardware, and one information technology staff member, who would be responsible for maintaining virus protection, quarantining suspicious e-mail, and managing content (e.g., screening e-mail for objectionable content). Should CEO Wise accept Mail.com's offer?
3. Suppose for an additional $5 per mailbox per month, Mail.com will also provide virus protection, quarantine, and content-management services. Outsourcing these additional functions would mean that BKFin.com would not need either an e-mail information technology staff member or the separate virus protection license. Should CEO Wise outsource these extra services to Mail.com?

Ethical Issue

Mary Tan is the controller for Duck Associates, a property management company in Portland, Oregon. Each year Tan and payroll clerk Toby Stock meet with the external auditors about payroll accounting. This year, the auditors suggest that Tan consider outsourcing Duck Associates' payroll accounting to a company specializing in payroll processing services. This would allow Tan and her staff to focus on their primary responsibility: accounting for the properties under management. At present, payroll requires 1.5 employee positions—payroll clerk Toby Stock and a bookkeeper who spends half her time entering payroll data in the system.

Tan considers this suggestion, and she lists the following items relating to outsourcing payroll accounting:

a. The current payroll software that was purchased for $4,000 three years ago would not be needed if payroll processing were outsourced.
b. Duck Associates' bookkeeper would spend half her time preparing the weekly payroll input form that is given to the payroll processing service. She is paid $450 a week.
c. Duck Associates would no longer need payroll clerk Toby Stock, whose annual salary is $42,000.
d. The payroll processing service would charge $2,000 a month.

Requirements

1. Would outsourcing the payroll function increase or decrease Duck Associates' operating income?
2. Tan believes that outsourcing payroll would simplify her job, but she does not like the prospect of having to lay off Stock, who has become a close personal friend. She does not believe there is another position available for Stock at his current salary. Can you think of other factors that might support keeping Stock, rather than outsourcing payroll processing? How should each of the factors affect Tan's decision if she wants to do what is best for Duck Associates and act ethically?

■ Team Project

John Menard is the founder and sole owner of **Menards**. Analysts have estimated that his chain of home improvement stores scattered around nine midwestern states generate about $3 billion in annual sales. But how can **Menards** compete with giant **Home Depot**?

Suppose Menard is trying to decide whether to invest $45 million in a state-of-the-art manufacturing plant in Eau Claire, Wisconsin. Menard expects the plant would operate for 15 years, after which it would have no residual value. The plant would produce **Menards'** own line of Formica countertops, cabinets, and picnic tables.

Suppose **Menards** would incur the following unit costs in producing its own product lines:

	Per Unit		
	Countertops	Cabinets	Picnic Tables
Direct materials	$15	$10	$25
Direct labor	10	5	15
Variable manufacturing overhead	5	2	6

Rather than making these products, assume that **Menards** could buy them from outside suppliers. Suppliers would charge **Menards** $40 per countertop, $25 per cabinet, and $65 per picnic table.

Whether Menard makes or buys these products, assume that he expects the following annual sales:

- Countertops—487,200 at $130 each
- Picnic tables—100,000 at $225 each
- Cabinets—150,000 at $75 each

If "making" is sufficiently more profitable than outsourcing, Menard will build the new plant. John Menard has asked your consulting group for a recommendation. Menard uses the straight-line depreciation method.

Requirements

1. Are the following items relevant or irrelevant in Menard's decision to build a new plant that will manufacture his own products?
   a. The unit sale prices of the countertops, cabinets, and picnic tables (the sale prices that **Menards** charges its customers)
   b. The prices outside suppliers would charge **Menards** for the three products, if **Menards** decides to outsource the products rather than make them
   c. The $45 million to build the new plant
   d. The direct materials, direct labor, and variable overhead **Menards** would incur to manufacture the three product lines
   e. John Menard's salary
2. Determine whether **Menards** should make or outsource the countertops, cabinets, and picnic tables, *assuming that the company has already built the plant and, therefore, has the manufacturing capacity to produce these products*. In other words, what is the annual difference in cash flows if **Menards** decides to make rather than outsource each of these three products?
3. Write a memo giving your recommendation to John Menard. The memo should clearly state your recommendation, along with a brief summary of the reasons for your recommendation.

Quick Check Answers

1. *a* 2. *b* 3. *b* 4. *a* 5. *d* 6. *b* 7. *d* 8. *a* 9. *c* 10. *b*

For online homework, exercises, and problems that provide you immediate feedback, please visit www.myaccountinglab.com.

20 Capital Investment Decisions and the Time Value of Money

Learning Objectives/ Success Keys

1. Describe the importance of capital investments and the capital budgeting process
2. Use the payback and accounting rate of return methods to make capital investment decisions
3. Use the time value of money to compute the present and future values of single lump sums and annuities
4. Use discounted cash flow models to make capital investment decisions

Music DVDs and learning DVDs seem to have little or nothing to do with accounting. But every part of the growth and expansion of Smart Touch Learning and Greg's Groovy Tunes began first with the decision—do we spend the money to expand the business?

In this chapter, we will see how companies like Smart Touch and Greg's Groovy Tunes use capital investment analysis techniques to decide which long-term capital investments to make.

Capital Budgeting

1 Describe the importance of capital investments and the capital budgeting process

The process of making capital investment decisions is often referred to as **capital budgeting**. Companies make capital investments when they acquire *capital assets*—assets used for a long period of time. Capital investments include buying new equipment, building new plants, automating production, and developing major commercial Web sites. In addition to affecting operations for many years, capital investments usually require large sums of money.

Capital investment decisions affect all businesses as they try to become more efficient by automating production and implementing new technologies. Grocers and retailers, such as **Wal-Mart**, have invested in expensive self-scan check-out machines, while airlines, such as **Delta** and **Continental**, have invested in self check-in kiosks. These new technologies cost money. How do managers decide whether these expansions in plant and equipment will be good investments? They use capital budgeting analysis. Some companies, such as **Georgia Pacific**, employ staff solely dedicated to capital budgeting analysis. They spend thousands of hours a year determining which capital investments to pursue.

Four Popular Methods of Capital Budgeting Analysis

In this chapter, we discuss four popular methods of analyzing potential capital investments:

1. Payback period
2. Accounting rate of return (ARR)
3. Net present value (NPV)
4. Internal rate of return (IRR)

The first two methods, payback period and accounting rate of return, are fairly quick and easy and work well for capital investments that have a relatively short life span, such as computer equipment and software that may have a useful life of only three to five years. Payback period and accounting rate of return are also used to screen potential investments from those that are less desirable. The payback period provides management with valuable information on how fast the cash invested will be recouped. The accounting rate of return shows the effect of the investment on the company's accrual-based income. However, these two methods are inadequate if the capital investments have a longer life span. Why? Because these methods do not consider the time value of money. The last two methods, net present value and internal rate of return, factor in the time value of money so they are more appropriate for longer-term capital investments, such as Smart Touch's expansion to manufacturing DVDs. Management often uses a combination of methods to make final capital investment decisions.

Capital budgeting is not an exact science. Although the calculations these methods require may appear precise, remember that they are based on predictions about an uncertain future—estimates. These estimates must consider many unknown factors, such as changing consumer preferences, competition, the state of the economy, and government regulations. The further into the future the decision extends, the more likely that actual results will differ from predictions. Long-term decisions are riskier than short-term decisions.

Focus on Cash Flows

Generally accepted accounting principles (GAAP) are based on accrual accounting, but capital budgeting focuses on cash flows. The desirability of a capital asset depends on its ability to generate net cash inflows—that is, inflows in excess of outflows—over the asset's useful life. Recall that operating income based on accrual accounting contains noncash expenses, such as depreciation expense and bad-debt expense. The capital investment's *net cash inflows,* therefore, will differ from its operating income. Of the four capital budgeting methods covered in this chapter, only the accounting rate of return method uses accrual-based accounting income. The other three methods use the investment's projected *net cash inflows.*

What do the projected *net cash inflows* include? Cash *inflows* include future cash revenue generated from the investment, any future savings in ongoing cash operating costs resulting from the investment, and any future residual value of the asset. To determine the investment's *net* cash inflows, the inflows are *netted* against the investment's *future cash outflows*, such as the investment's ongoing cash operating costs and refurbishment, repairs, and maintenance costs. The initial investment itself is also a significant cash outflow. However, in our calculations, *we will always consider the amount of the investment separately from all other cash flows related to the investment.* The projected net cash inflows are "given" in our examples and in the assignment material. In reality, much of capital investment analysis revolves around projecting these figures as accurately as possible using input from employees throughout the organization (production, marketing, and so forth, depending on the type of capital investment).

Capital Budgeting Process

The first step in the capital budgeting process is to identify potential investments—for example, new technology and equipment that may make the company more efficient, competitive, and/or profitable. Employees, consultants, and outside sales vendors often offer capital investment proposals to management. After identifying potential capital investments, managers project the investments' net cash inflows and then analyze the investments using one or more of the four capital budgeting methods previously described. Sometimes the analysis involves a two-stage process. In the first stage, managers screen the investments using one or both of the methods that do *not* incorporate the time value of money: payback period or accounting rate of return. These simple methods quickly weed out undesirable investments. Potential investments that "pass stage one" go on to a second stage of analysis. In the second stage, managers further analyze the potential investments using the net present value and/or internal rate of return methods. Because these methods consider the time value of money, they provide more accurate information about the potential investment's profitability.

Some companies can pursue all of the potential investments that meet or exceed their decision criteria. However, because of limited resources, other companies must engage in **capital rationing**, and choose among alternative capital investments. Based on the availability of funds, managers determine if and when to make specific capital investments. For example, management may decide to wait three years to buy a certain piece of equipment because it considers other investments more important. In the intervening three years, the company will reassess whether it should still invest in the equipment. Perhaps technology has changed, and even better equipment is available. Perhaps consumer tastes have changed so the company no longer needs the equipment. Because of changing factors, long-term capital budgets are rarely set in stone.

Most companies perform **post-audits** of their capital investments. After investing in the assets, they compare the actual net cash inflows generated from the investment to the projected net cash inflows. Post-audits help companies determine whether the investments are going as planned and deserve continued support, or whether they should abandon the project and sell the assets. Managers also use feedback from post-audits to better estimate net cash flow projections for future projects. If managers expect routine post-audits, they will more likely submit realistic net cash flow estimates with their capital investment proposals.

Using Payback and Accounting Rate of Return to Make Capital Investment Decisions

Payback Period

2 Use the payback and accounting rate of return methods to make capital investment decisions

Payback is the length of time it takes to recover, in net cash inflows, the cost of the capital outlay. The payback model measures how quickly managers expect to recover their investment dollars. All else being equal, the shorter the payback period the more attractive the asset. Computing the payback period depends on whether net cash inflows are equal each year, or whether they differ over time. We consider each in turn.

Payback with Equal Annual Net Cash Inflows

Smart Touch Learning is considering investing $240,000 in hardware and software to upgrade its website to provide a business-to-business (B2B) portal. Employees throughout the company will use the B2B portal to access company-approved suppliers. Smart Touch expects the portal to save $60,000 a year for each of the six years of its useful life. The savings will arise from reducing the number of purchasing personnel the company employs and from lower prices on the goods and services purchased. Net cash inflows arise from an increase in revenues, a decrease in expenses, or both. In Smart Touch's case, the net cash inflows result from lower expenses.

When net cash inflows are equal each year, managers compute the payback period as shown in Exhibit 20-1.

EXHIBIT 20-1 Calculating Payback Period—Equal Cash Flows

$$\text{Payback period} = \frac{\text{Amount invested}}{\text{Expected annual net cash inflow}}$$

Smart Touch computes the investment's payback as follows:

$$\text{Payback period for B2B portal} = \frac{\$240{,}000}{\$60{,}000} = 4 \text{ years}$$

Exhibit 20-2 verifies that Smart Touch expects to recoup the $240,000 investment in the B2B portal by the end of year 4, when the accumulated net cash inflows total $240,000.

Smart Touch is also considering investing $240,000 to upgrade its Web site. The company expects the upgraded Web site to generate $80,000 in net cash inflows each year of its three-year life. The payback period is computed as follows:

$$\text{Payback period for Web site development} = \frac{\$240{,}000}{\$80{,}000} = 3 \text{ years}$$

Exhibit 20-2 verifies that Smart Touch will recoup the $240,000 investment for the Web site upgrade by the end of year 3, when the accumulated net cash inflows total $240,000.

EXHIBIT 20-2 | **Payback—Equal Annual Net Cash Inflows**

		Net Cash Inflows			
		B2B Portal		Web Site Upgrade	
Year	Amount Invested	Annual	Accumulated	Annual	Accumulated
0	240,000	—	—	—	—
1	—	$60,000	$ 60,000	$80,000	$ 80,000
2	—	60,000	120,000	80,000	160,000
3	—	60,000	180,000	80,000	240,000
4	—	60,000	240,000		
5	—	60,000	300,000		
6	—	60,000	360,000		

Useful Life

Payback with Unequal Net Cash Inflows

The payback equation in Exhibit 20-1 only works when net cash inflows are the same each period. When periodic cash flows are unequal, you must total net cash inflows until the amount invested is recovered. Assume that Smart Touch is considering an alternate investment, the Z80 portal. The Z80 portal differs from the B2B portal and the Web site in two respects: (1) It has *unequal* net cash inflows during its life and (2) it has a $30,000 residual value at the end of its life. The Z80 portal will generate net cash inflows of $100,000 in year 1, $80,000 in year 2, $50,000 each year in years 3 through 5, $30,000 in year 6, and $30,000 when it is sold at the end of its life. Exhibit 20-3 shows the payback schedule for these unequal annual net cash inflows.

EXHIBIT 20-3 | **Payback: Unequal Annual Net Cash Inflows**

		Net Cash Inflows Z80 Portal	
Year	Amount Invested	Annual	Accumulated
0	$240,000	—	—
1	—	100,000	$100,000
2	—	80,000	180,000
3	—	50,000	230,000
4	—	50,000	280,000
5	—	50,000	330,000
6	—	30,000	360,000
6–Residual Value		30,000	390,000

Useful Life

By the end of year 3, the company has recovered $230,000 of the $240,000 initially invested, so it is only $10,000 short of payback. Because the expected net cash inflow in year 4 is $50,000, by the end of year 4 the company will have recovered *more* than the initial investment. Therefore, the payback period is somewhere between three and four years. Assuming that the cash flow occurs evenly throughout the fourth year, the payback period is calculated as follows:

$$\text{Payback} = 3 \text{ years} + \frac{\$10{,}000 \text{ (amount needed to complete recovery in year 4)}}{\$50{,}000 \text{ (net cash inflow in year 4)}}$$

$$= 3.2 \text{ years}$$

Criticism of the Payback Period Method

A major criticism of the payback method is that it focuses only on time, not on profitability. The payback period considers only those cash flows that occur *during* the payback period. This method ignores any cash flows that occur *after* that period. For example, Exhibit 20-2 shows that the B2B portal will continue to generate net cash inflows for two years after its payback period. These additional net cash inflows amount to \$120,000 (\$60,000 × 2 years), yet the payback method ignores this extra cash. A similar situation occurs with the Z80 portal. As shown in Exhibit 20-3, the Z80 portal will provide an additional \$150,000 of net cash inflows, including residual value, after its payback period of 3.2 years (\$390,000 total accumulated cash inflows – \$240,000 amount invested). However, the Web site's useful life, as shown in Exhibit 20-2, is the *same* as its payback period (three years). No cash flows are ignored, yet the Web site will merely cover its cost and provide no profit. Because this is the case, the company has no financial reason to invest in the Web site.

Exhibit 20-4 compares the payback period of the three investments. As the exhibit illustrates, the payback method does not consider the asset's profitability. The method only tells management how quickly it will recover the cash. Even though the Web site has the shortest payback period, both the B2B portal and the Z80 portal are better investments because they provide profit. The key point is that the investment with the shortest payback period is best *only if all other factors are the same*. Therefore, managers usually use the payback method as a screening device to "weed out" investments that will take too long to recoup. They rarely use payback period as the sole method for deciding whether to invest in the asset. When using the payback period method, managers are guided by following decision rule:

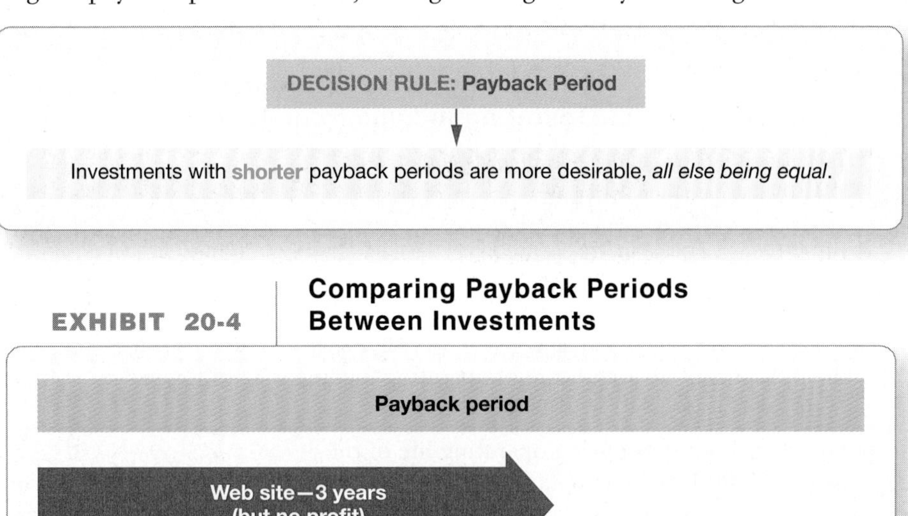

EXHIBIT 20-4 | **Comparing Payback Periods Between Investments**

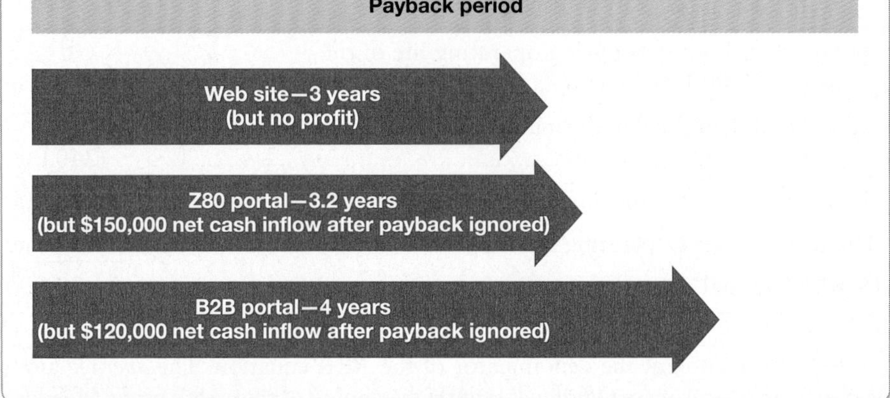

Stop & Think...

Let us say you loan \$50 to a friend today (a Friday). The friend says he will pay you \$25 next Friday when he gets paid and another \$25 the following Friday. What is your payback period? The friend will pay you back in 2 weeks.

Accounting Rate of Return (ARR)

Companies are in business to earn profits. One measure of profitability is the **accounting rate of return (ARR)** on an asset. The formula for calculating ARR is shown in Exhibit 20-5.

EXHIBIT 20-5 | Calculating Accounting Rate of Return

$$\text{Accounting rate of return} = \frac{\text{Average annual operating income from an asset}}{\text{Average amount invested in an asset}}$$

The ARR focuses on the *operating income, not the net cash inflow,* an asset generates. The ARR measures the *average* rate of return over the asset's entire life. Let us first consider investments with no residual value.

Recall the B2B portal, which costs $240,000, has equal annual net cash inflows of $60,000, a six-year useful life, and no (zero) residual value.

Let us look at the average annual operating income in the numerator first. The average annual operating income of an asset is simply the asset's total operating income over the course of its operating life divided by its lifespan (number of years). Operating income is based on *accrual accounting*. Therefore, any noncash expenses, such as depreciation expense, must be subtracted from the asset's net cash inflows to arrive at its operating income. Exhibit 20-6 displays the formula for calculating average annual operating income.

EXHIBIT 20-6 | Calculating Average Annual Operating Income from Asset

Total net cash inflows during operating life of the asset	A
Less: Total depreciation during operating life of the asset (Cost – Residual Value)	B
Total operating income during operating life	(A – B)
Divide by: Asset's operating life in years	C
Average annual operating income from asset	[(A – B)/C]

The B2B portal's average annual operating income is as follows:

Total net cash inflows during operating life of the asset ($60,000 × 6 years)	$ 360,000
Less: Total depreciation during operating life of asset (cost – any salvage value)	(240,000)
Total operating income during operating life	$ 120,000
Divide by: Asset's operating life (in years)	÷ 6 years
Average annual operating income from asset	$ 20,000

Now let us look at the denominator of the ARR equation. The *average* amount invested in an asset is its *net book value* at the beginning of the asset's useful life plus the net book value at the end of the asset's useful life divided by two. Another way to say that is the asset's cost plus the asset's residual value divided by two. The net book value of the asset decreases each year because of depreciation, as shown in Exhibit 20-6.

Because the B2B portal does not have a residual value, the *average* amount invested is \$120,000 [(\$240,000 cost + 0 residual value) ÷ 2].

We calculate the B2B's ARR as:

$$\text{Accounting rate of return} = \frac{\$20{,}000}{(\$240{,}000 - \$0)/2} = \frac{\$20{,}000}{\$120{,}000} = 0.167 = 16.70\%$$

Now consider the Z80 portal (data from Exhibit 20-3). Recall that the Z80 portal differed from the B2B portal only in that it had unequal net cash inflows during its life and a \$30,000 residual value at the end of its life. Its average annual operating income is calculated as follows:

Total net cash inflows *during* operating life of asset (does not include the residual value at end of life) (Year 1 + Year 2, etc.)	\$ 360,000
Less: Total depreciation during operating life of asset (cost – any salvage value) (\$240,000 cost – \$30,000 residual value)	(210,000)
Total operating income during operating life of asset	\$ 150,000
Divide by: Asset's operating life (in years)	÷ 6 years
Average annual operating income from asset	\$ 25,000

Notice that the Z80 portal's average annual operating income of \$25,000 is higher than the B2B portal's operating income of \$20,000. Since the Z80 asset has a residual value at the end of its life, less depreciation is expensed each year, leading to a higher average annual operating income.

Now let us calculate the denominator of the ARR equation, the average amount invested in the asset. For the Z80, the average asset investment is as follows:

Average amount invested	=	(Amount invested in asset	+	Residual value)/2
\$135,000	=	(\$240,000	+	\$30,000) /2

We calculate the Z80's ARR as follows:

$$\text{Accounting rate of return} = \frac{\$25{,}000}{(\$240{,}000 + \$30{,}000)/2} = \frac{\$25{,}000}{\$135{,}000} = 0.185 = 18.5\%$$

Companies that use the ARR model set a minimum required accounting rate of return. If Smart Touch requires an ARR of at least 20%, then its managers would not approve an investment in the B2B portal or the Z80 portal because the ARR for both investments is less than 20%.

The decision rule is as follows:

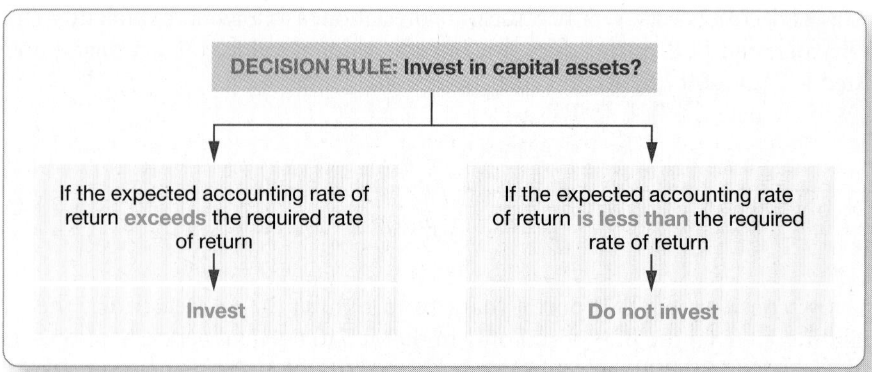

In summary, the payback period focuses on the time it takes for the company to recoup its cash investment but ignores all cash flows occurring after the payback period. Because it ignores any additional cash flows (including any residual value), the method does not consider the profitability of the project.

The ARR, however, measures the profitability of the asset over its entire life using accrual accounting figures. It is the only method that uses accrual accounting rather than net cash inflows in its computations. The payback period and ARR methods are simple and quick to compute so managers often use them to screen out undesirable investments. However, both methods ignore the time value of money.

Decision Guidelines

CAPITAL BUDGETING

Amazon.com started as a virtual retailer. It held no inventory. Instead, it bought books and CDs only as needed to fill customer orders. As the company grew, its managers decided to invest in their own warehouse facilities. Why? Owning warehouse facilities allows **Amazon.com** to save money by buying in bulk. Also, shipping all items in the customer's order in one package, from one location, saves shipping costs. Here are some of the guidelines **Amazon.com's** managers used as they made the major capital budgeting decision to invest in building warehouses.

Decision	Guidelines
• Why is this decision important?	Capital budgeting decisions typically require large investments and affect operations for years to come.
• What method shows us how soon we will recoup our cash investment?	The payback method shows managers how quickly they will recoup their investment. This method highlights investments that are too risky due to long payback periods. However, it does not reveal any information about the investment's profitability.
• Does any method consider the impact of the investment on accrual accounting income?	The accounting rate of return is the only capital budgeting method that shows how the investment will affect accrual accounting income, which is important to financial statement users. All other methods of capital investment analysis focus on the investment's net cash inflows.
• How do we compute the payback period if cash flows are *equal*?	$\text{Payback period} = \dfrac{\text{Amount invested}}{\text{Expected annual net cash inflow}}$
• How do we compute the payback period if cash flows are *unequal*?	Accumulate net cash inflows until the amount invested is recovered.
• How do we compute the ARR?	$\text{Accounting rate of return} = \dfrac{\text{Average annual operating income from asset}}{\text{Average amount invested in asset}}$

Summary Problem 1

Reality-max is considering buying a new bar-coding machine for its Austin, Texas, plant. The company screens its potential capital investments using the payback period and accounting rate of return methods. If a potential investment has a payback period of less than four years and a minimum 12% accounting rate of return, it will be considered further. The data for the machine follow:

Cost of machine	$48,000
Estimated residual value	$ 0
Estimated annual net cash inflow (each year for 5 years)	$13,000
Estimated useful life	5 years

Requirements

1. Compute the bar-coding machine's payback period.
2. Compute the bar-coding machine's ARR.
3. Should Reality-max turn down this investment proposal or consider it further?

Solution

Requirement 1

$$\text{Payback period} = \frac{\text{Amount invested}}{\text{Expected annual net cash inflow}} = \frac{\$48{,}000}{\$13{,}000} = 3.7 \text{ years (rounded)}$$

Requirement 2

$$\text{Accounting rate of return} = \frac{\text{Average annual operating income from asset}}{\text{Average amount invested in asset}}$$

$$= \frac{\$3{,}400^*}{(\$48{,}000 + \$0)/2}$$

$$= \frac{\$3{,}400}{\$24{,}000}$$

$$= 0.142 \text{ (rounded)}$$

$$= 14.2\%$$

**Total net cash inflows during life ($13,000 × 5 years)*	$ 65,000
Less: total depreciation during life	(48,000)
Total operating income during life	$ 17,000
Divided by: life of the asset	*÷ 5 years*
Average annual operating income	$ 3,400

Requirement 3

The bar-coding machine proposal passes both initial screening tests. The payback period is slightly less than four years, and the accounting rate of return is higher than 12%. Reality-max should further analyze the proposal using a method that incorporates the time value of money.

A Review of the Time Value of Money

3 Use the time value of money to compute the present and future values of single lump sums and annuities

A dollar received today is worth more than a dollar to be received in the future. Why? Because you can invest today's dollar and earn extra income. The fact that invested money earns income over time is called the *time value of money*, and this explains why we would prefer to receive cash sooner rather than later. The time value of money means that the timing of capital investments' net cash inflows is important. Two methods of capital investment analysis incorporate the time value of money: the NPV and IRR. This section reviews time value of money to make sure you have a firm foundation for discussing these two methods.

Factors Affecting the Time Value of Money

The time value of money depends on several key factors:

1. the principal amount (p)
2. the number of periods (n)
3. the interest rate (i)

The principal (p) refers to the amount of the investment or borrowing. Because this chapter deals with capital investments, we will primarily discuss the principal in terms of investments. However, the same concepts apply to borrowings (which we covered in Chapter 7). We state the principal as either a single lump sum or an annuity. For example, if you win the lottery, you have the choice of receiving all the winnings now (a single lump sum) or receiving a series of equal payments for a period of time in the future (an annuity). An **annuity** is a stream of *equal installments* made at *equal time intervals under the same interest rate.*[1]

The number of periods (n) is the length of time from the beginning of the investment until termination. All else being equal the shorter the investment period the lower the total amount of interest earned. If you withdraw your savings after four years, rather than five years, you will earn less interest. In this chapter, the number of periods is stated in years.[2]

The interest rate (i) is the annual percentage earned on the investment. **Simple interest** means that interest is calculated *only* on the principal amount. **Compound interest** means that interest is calculated on the principal *and* on all interest earned to date. *Compound interest assumes that all interest earned will remain invested and earn additional interest at the same interest rate.* Exhibit 20-7 compares simple interest

EXHIBIT 20-7 **Simple Versus Compound Interest for a Principal Amount of $10,000, at 6%, over 5 Years**

Year	Simple Interest Calculation	Simple Interest	Compound Interest Calculation	Compound Interest
1	$10,000 × 6% =	$ 600	$10,000 × 6% =	$ 600
2	$10,000 × 6% =	600	($10,000 + 600) × 6% =	636
3	$10,000 × 6% =	600	($10,000 + 600 + 636) × 6% =	674
4	$10,000 × 6% =	600	($10,000 + 600 + 636 + 674) × 6% =	715
5	$10,000 × 6% =	600	($10,000 + 600 + 636 + 674 + 715) × 6% =	758
	Total interest	$3,000	Total interest	$3,383

[1] An *ordinary annuity* is an annuity in which the installments occur at the *end* of each period. An *annuity due* is an annuity in which the installments occur at the beginning of each period. Throughout this chapter we use ordinary annuities since they are better suited to capital budgeting cash flow assumptions.

[2] The number of periods can also be stated in days, months, or quarters. If so, the interest rate needs to be adjusted to reflect the number of time periods in the year.

(6%) on a five-year, $10,000 CD with interest compounded yearly (rounded to the nearest dollar). As you can see, the amount of compound interest earned yearly grows as the base on which it is calculated (principal plus cumulative interest to date) grows. Over the life of this investment, the total amount of compound interest is about 10% more than the total amount of simple interest. Most investments yield compound interest so we assume compound interest, rather than simple interest, for the rest of this chapter.

Fortunately, time value calculations involving compound interest do not have to be as tedious as those shown in Exhibit 20-7. Formulas and tables (or proper use of business calculators programmed with these formulas, or spreadsheet software such as Microsoft Excel) simplify the calculations. In the next sections, we will discuss how to use these tools to perform time value calculations.

Future Values and Present Values: Points Along the Time Line

Consider the time line in Exhibit 20-8. The future value or present value of an investment simply refers to the value of an investment at different points in time.

EXHIBIT 20-8 **Present Value and Future Value Along the Time Continuum**

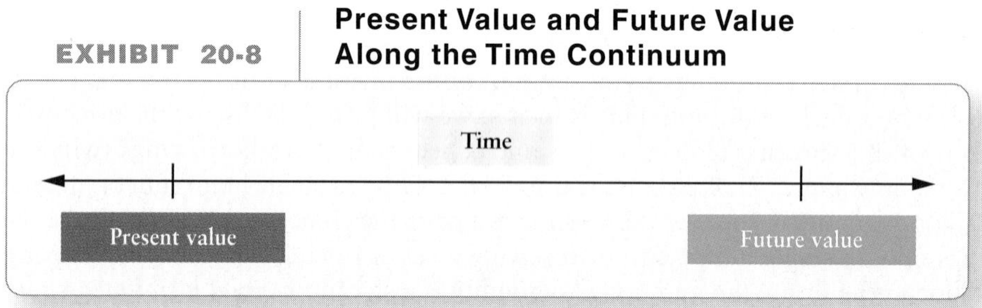

We can calculate the future value or the present value of any investment by knowing (or assuming) information about the three factors we listed earlier: (1) the principal amount, (2) the period of time, and (3) the interest rate. For example, in Exhibit 20-7, we calculated the interest that would be earned on (1) a $10,000 principal, (2) invested for five years, (3) at 6% interest. The future value of the investment is simply its worth at the end of the five-year time frame—the original principal *plus* the interest earned. In our example, the future value of the investment is as follows:

Future value	= Principal	+ Interest earned
	= $10,000	+ $3,383
	= $13,383	

If we invest $10,000 *today*, its *present value* is simply $10,000. So another way of stating the future value is as follows:

Future value = Present value + Interest earned

We can rearrange the equation as follows:

Present value	= Future value	– Interest earned
$10,000	= $13,383	– $3,383

The only difference between present value and future value is the amount of interest that is earned in the intervening time span.

Future Value and Present Value Factors

Calculating each period's compound interest, as we did in Exhibit 20-7, and then adding it to the present value to figure the future value (or subtracting it from the future value to figure the present value) is tedious. Fortunately, mathematical formulas have been developed that specify future values and present values for unlimited combinations of interest rates (i) and time periods (n). Separate formulas exist for single lump-sum investments and annuities.

These formulas are programmed into most business calculators so that the user only needs to correctly enter the principal amount, interest rate, and number of time periods to find present or future values. These formulas are also programmed into spreadsheets functions in Microsoft Excel. Because the specific steps to operate business calculators differ between brands, we will use tables instead. These tables contain the results of the formulas for various interest rate and time period combinations.

The formulas and resulting tables are shown in Appendix B at the end of this book:

1. Present Value of \$1 (Appendix B, Table A, p. B-1)—*used for lump-sum amounts*
2. Present Value of Annuity of \$1 (Appendix B, Table B, p. B-3)—*used for annuities*
3. Future Value of \$1 (Appendix B, Table C, p. B-5)—*used for lump-sum amounts*
4. Future Value of Annuity of \$1 (Appendix B, Table D, p. B-6)—*used for annuities*

Take a moment to look at these tables because we are going to use them throughout the rest of the chapter. Note that the columns are interest rates (i) and the rows are periods (n).

The data in each table, known as future value factors (FV factors) and present value factors (PV factors), are for an investment (or loan) of \$1. To find the future value of an amount other than \$1, you simply multiply the FV factor by the present amount. To find the present value of an amount other than \$1, you multiply the PV factor by the future amount.

The annuity tables are derived from the lump-sum tables. For example, the Annuity PV factors (in the Present Value of Annuity of \$1 table) are the *sums* of the PV factors found in the Present Value of \$1 tables for a given number of time periods. The annuity tables allow us to perform "one-step" calculations rather than separately computing the present value of each annual cash installment and then summing the individual present values.

Calculating Future Values of Single Sums and Annuities Using FV Factors

Let us go back to our \$10,000 lump-sum investment. If we want to know the future value of the investment five years from now at an interest rate of 6%, we determine the FV factor from the table labeled Future Value of \$1 (Appendix B, Table C). We use this table for lump-sum amounts. We look down the 6% column, and across the 5 periods row, and find the future value factor is 1.338. We finish our calculations as follows:

$$\begin{aligned} \text{Future value} &= \text{Principal amount} \times (\text{FV factor for } i = 6\%, n = 5) \\ &= \$10{,}000 \times (1.338) \\ &= \$13{,}380 \end{aligned}$$

This figure materially agrees with our earlier calculation of the investment's future value of \$13,383 in Exhibit 20-7. (The difference of \$3 is due to two facts:

(1) The tables round the FV and PV factors to three decimal places and (2) we rounded our earlier yearly interest calculations in Exhibit 20-7 to the nearest dollar.)

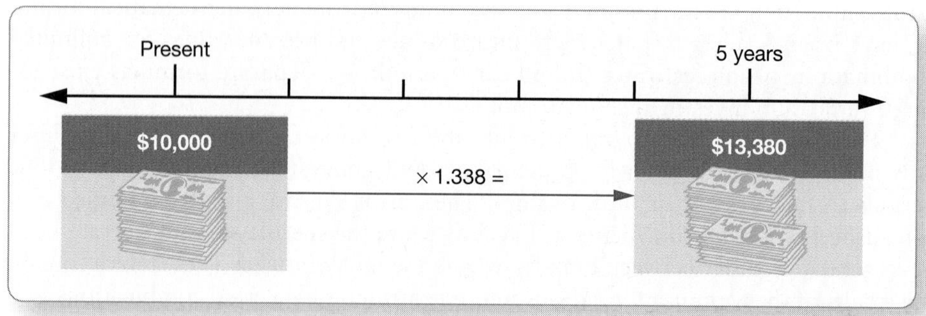

Let us also consider our alternative investment strategy, investing $2,000 at the end of each year for five years. The procedure for calculating the future value of an *annuity* is quite similar to calculating the future value of a lump-sum amount. This time, we use the Future Value of Annuity of $1 table (Appendix B, Table D). Assuming 6% interest, we once again look down the 6% column. Because we will be making five annual installments, we look across the row marked 5 periods. The Annuity FV factor is 5.637. We finish the calculation as follows:

Future value = Amount of each cash installment × (Annuity FV factor for i = 6%, n = 5)
= $2,000 × (5.637)
= $11,274

This is considerably less than the future value of $13,380 of the lump sum of $10,000, even though we have invested $10,000 out-of-pocket either way.

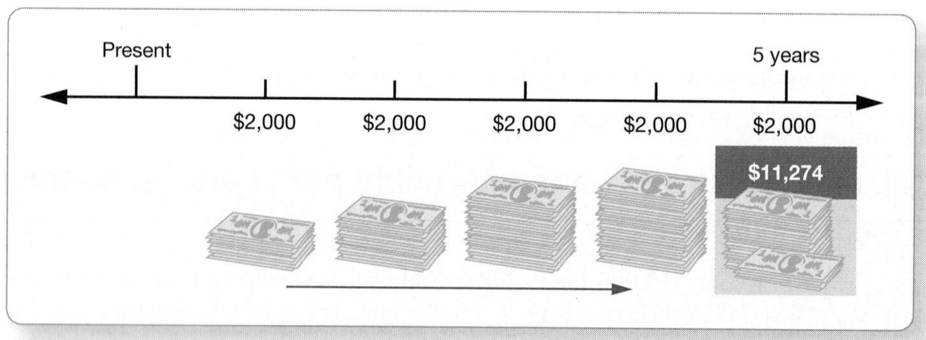

Calculating Present Values of Single Sums and Annuities Using PV Factors

The process for calculating present values—often called discounting cash flows—is similar to the process for calculating future values. The difference is the point in time at which you are assessing the investment's worth. Rather than determining its value at a future date, you are determining its value at an earlier point in time (today). For our example, let us assume you have just won the lottery after purchasing one $5 lottery ticket. The state offers you the following three payout options for your after-tax prize money:

Option #1: $1,000,000 now
Option #2: $150,000 at the end of each year for the next 10 years
Option #3: $2,000,000 10 years from now

Which alternative should you take? You might be tempted to wait 10 years to "double" your winnings. You may be tempted to take the money now and spend it. However, let us assume you plan to prudently invest all money received—no matter when you receive it—so that you have financial flexibility in the future (for example, for buying a house, retiring early, or taking exotic vacations). How can you choose among the three payment alternatives, when the total amount of each option varies ($1,000,000 versus $1,500,000 versus $2,000,000) and the timing of the cash flows varies (now versus some each year versus later)? Comparing these three options is like comparing apples to oranges—we just cannot do it—unless we find some common basis for comparison. Our common basis for comparison will be the prize-money's worth at a certain point in time—namely, today. In other words, if we convert each payment option to its *present value*, we can compare apples to apples.

We already know the principal amount and timing of each payment option, so the only assumption we will have to make is the interest rate. The interest rate will vary, depending on the amount of risk you are willing to take with your investment. Riskier investments (such as stock investments) command higher interest rates; safer investments (such as FDIC-insured bank deposits) yield lower interest rates. Let us say that after investigating possible investment alternatives, you choose an investment contract with an 8% annual return. We already know that the present value of Option #1 is $1,000,000. Let us convert the other two payment options to their present values so that we can compare them. We will need to use the Present Value of Annuity of $1 table (Appendix B, Table B) to convert payment Option #2 (since it is an annuity) and the Present Value of $1 table (Appendix B, Table A) to convert payment Option #3 (since it is a single-lump-sum). To obtain the PV factors, we will look down the 8% column and across the 10 period row. Then, we finish the calculations as follows:

Option #2

Present value = Amount of each cash installment × (Annuity PV factor for i = 8%, n = 10)
Present value = $150,000 × (6.710)
Present value = $1,006,500

Option #3

Present value = Principal amount × (PV factor for i = 8%, n = 10)
Present value = $2,000,000 × (0.463)
Present value = $926,000

Exhibit 20-9 shows that we have converted each payout option to a common basis—its worth *today*—so we can make a valid comparison among the options. Based on this comparison, we should choose Option #2 because its worth, in today's dollars, is the highest of the three options.

Now that you have reviewed time value of money concepts, we will discuss the two capital budgeting methods that incorporate the time value of money: net present value (NPV) and internal rate of return (IRR).

EXHIBIT 20-9 | Present Value of Lottery Payout Options

Payment Options	Present Value of Lottery Payout ($i = 8\%, n = 10$)
Option #1	$1,000,000
Option #2	$1,006,500
Option #3	$ 926,000

Using Discounted Cash Flow Models to Make Capital Budgeting Decisions

4 Use discounted cash flow models to make capital investment decisions

Neither the payback period nor the ARR recognizes the time value of money. That is, these models fail to consider the *timing* of the net cash inflows an asset generates. *Discounted cash flow models*—the NPV and the IRR—overcome this weakness. These models incorporate compound interest by assuming that companies will reinvest future cash flows when they are received. Over 85% of large industrial firms in the United States use discounted cash-flow methods to make capital investment decisions. Companies that provide services also use these models.

The NPV and IRR methods rely on present value calculations to *compare* the amount of the investment (the investment's initial cost) with its expected net cash inflows. Recall that an investment's *net cash inflows* includes all *future* cash flows related to the investment, such as future increased sales or cost savings netted against the investment's cash operating costs. Because the cash outflow for the investment occurs *now*, but the net cash inflows from the investment occur in the *future*, companies can only make valid "apple-to-apple" comparisons if they convert the cash flows to the *same point in time*—namely the present value. Companies use the present value to make the comparison (rather than the future value) because the investment's initial cost is already stated at its present value.[3]

As shown in Exhibit 20-10, in a favorable investment, the present value of the investment's net cash inflows exceeds the initial cost of the investment. In terms of our earlier lottery example, the lottery ticket turned out to be a "good investment" because the present value of its net cash inflows (the present value of the lottery payout under *any* of the three payout options) exceeded the cost of the investment (the lottery ticket cost $5 to purchase). Let us begin our discussion by taking a closer look at the NPV method.

Net Present Value (NPV)

Greg's Groovy Tunes is considering producing CD players and digital video recorders (DVRs). The products require different specialized machines that each cost $1 million. Each machine has a five-year life and zero residual value. The two products have different patterns of predicted net cash inflows, as shown in Exhibit 20-11.

The CD-player project generates more net cash inflows, but the DVR project brings in cash sooner. To decide how attractive each investment is, we find its **net present value (NPV)**. The NPV is the *net difference* between the present value of the

[3] If the investment is to be purchased through lease payments, rather than a current cash outlay, we would still use the current cash price of the investment as its initial cost. If no current cash price is available, we would discount the future lease payments back to their present value to estimate the investment's current cash price.

EXHIBIT 20-10 | **Comparing the Present Value of an Investment's Net Cash Inflows Against the Investment's Initial Cost**

Investment's initial cost

Present value of investment's net cash inflows

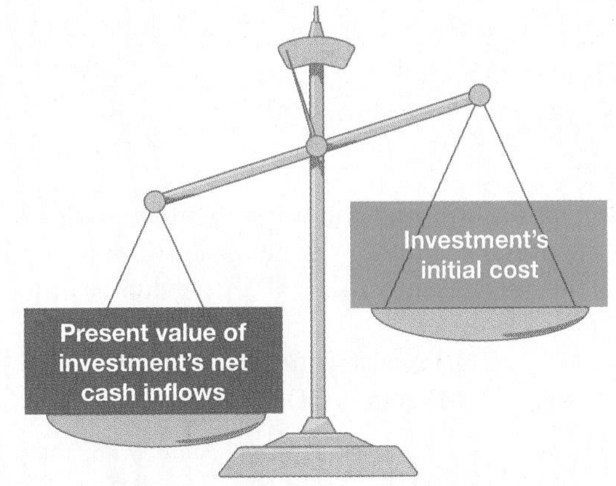

EXHIBIT 20-11 | **Expected Cash Flows for Two Projects**

Year	*Annual Net Cash Inflows* CD Players	DVRs
1	$ 305,450	$ 500,000
2	$ 305,450	350,000
3	$ 305,450	300,000
4	$ 305,450	250,000
5	$ 305,450	40,000
Total	$1,527,250	$1,440,000

investment's net cash inflows and the investment's cost (cash outflows). We *discount* the net cash inflows—just as we did in the lottery example—using Greg's minimum desired rate of return. This rate is called the **discount rate** because it is the interest rate used for the present value calculations. It is also called the **required rate of return** because the investment must meet or exceed this rate to be acceptable. The discount rate depends on the riskiness of investments. The higher the risk, the higher the discount (interest) rate. Greg's discount rate for these investments is 14%.

We then compare the present value of the net cash inflows to the investment's initial cost to decide which projects meet or exceed management's minimum desired rate of return. In other words, management is deciding whether the $1 million option is worth more (because the company would give it up now to invest in the project) or whether the project's future net cash inflows are worth more. Management can only make a valid comparison between the two sums of money by comparing them at the *same* point in time—namely, at their present value.

NPV with Equal Periodic Net Cash Inflows (Annuity)

Greg's expects the CD-player project to generate $305,450 of net cash inflows each year for five years. Because these cash flows are equal in amount, and occur every year, they are an annuity. Therefore, we use the Present Value of Annuity of $1 table (Appendix B, Table B) to find the appropriate Annuity PV factor for $i = 14\%$, $n = 5$.

The present value of the net cash inflows from Greg's CD-player project is as follows:

Present value = Amount of each cash net cash inflow × (Annuity PV factor for i = 14%, n = 5)
= $305,450 × (3.433)
= $1,048,610

Next, we simply subtract the investment's initial cost of $1 million (cash outflows) from the present value of the net cash inflows of $1,048,610. The difference of $48,610 is the *net* present value (NPV), as shown in Exhibit 20-12.

EXHIBIT 20-12 **NPV of Equal Net Cash Inflows—CD-Player Project**

Time		Annuity PV Factor (i = 14%, n = 5)		Net Cash Inflow	Present Value
1–5 yrs	Present value of annuity of equal annual net cash inflows for 5 years at 14%	3.433*	×	$305,450 =	$ 1,048,610
0	Investment				(1,000,000)
	Net present value of the CD-player project				$ 48,610

*Annuity PV Factor is found in Appendix B, Table B.

A *positive* NPV means that the project earns *more* than the required rate of return. A negative NPV means that the project earns less than the required rate of return. This leads to the following decision rule:

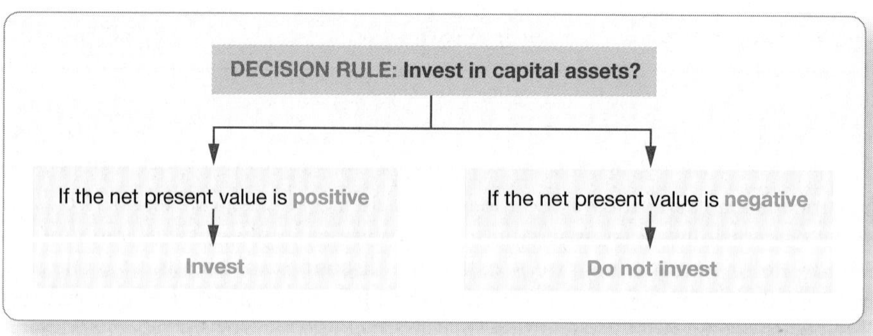

In Greg's Groovy Tunes' case, the CD-player project is an attractive investment. The $48,610 positive NPV means that the CD-player project earns *more than* Greg's Groovy Tunes' 14% target rate of return.

Another way managers can use present value analysis is to start the capital budgeting process by computing the total present value of the net cash inflows from the project to determine the *maximum* the company can invest in the project and still earn the target rate of return. For Greg's, the present value of the net cash inflows is $1,048,610. This means that Greg's Groovy Tunes can invest a maximum of $1,048,610 and still earn the 14% target rate of return (i.e., if Greg's invests $1,048,610, NPV will be 0 and return will be exactly 14%). Because Greg's Groovy Tunes' managers believe they can undertake the project for $1 million, the project is an attractive investment.

NPV with Unequal Periodic Net Cash Inflows

In contrast to the CD-player project, the net cash inflows of the DVR project are unequal—$500,000 in year 1, $350,000 in year 2, and so on. Because these amounts vary by year, Greg's Groovy Tunes' managers *cannot* use the annuity table to compute the present value of the DVR project. They must compute the present value of each individual year's net cash inflows *separately (as separate lump sums received in different years)*, using the Present Value of $1 table (Appendix B, Table A). Exhibit 20-13 shows that the $500,000 net cash inflow received in year 1 is discounted using a PV factor of $i = 14\%, n = 1$, while the $350,000 net cash inflow received in year 2 is discounted using a PV factor of $i = 14\%, n = 2$, and so forth. After separately discounting each of the five year's net cash inflows, we add each result to find that the *total* present value of the DVR project's net cash inflows is $1,078,910. Finally, we subtract the investment's cost of $1 million (cash outflows) to arrive at the DVR project's NPV: $78,910.

EXHIBIT 20-13 **NPV with Unequal Net Cash Inflows—DVR Project**

Year		PV Factor (i = 14%)		Net Cash Inflow		Present Value
	Present value of each year's net cash inflows discounted at 14%					
1	Year 1 (n = 1)	0.877†	×	$500,000	=	$ 438,500
2	Year 2 (n = 2)	0.769	×	350,000	=	269,150
3	Year 3 (n = 3)	0.675	×	300,000	=	202,500
4	Year 4 (n = 4)	0.592	×	250,000	=	148,000
5	Year 5 (n = 5)	0.519	×	40,000	=	20,760
	Total present value of net cash inflows					1,078,910
0	Investment					(1,000,000)
	Net present value of the DVR project					$ 78,910

†PV Factors are found in Appendix B, Table A.

Because the NPV is positive, Greg's Groovy Tunes expects the DVR project to earn more than the 14% target rate of return, making this an attractive investment.

Stop & Think...

Assume you win the lottery today and you have the choice of taking $1,000,000 today or $120,000 a year for the next 10 years. If you think that you can earn 6%, which option should you take? That is the key to NPV. We must find the NPV of the $120,000 annuity at 6% (PV factor is 7.360) to compare. The value of the $120,000 annuity today is $883,200, which is less than the $1,000,000. So, you should take the $1,000,000 payout today rather than the $120,000 annuity.

Capital Rationing and the Profitability Index

Exhibits 20-12 and 20-13 show that both the CD player and DVR projects have positive NPVs. Therefore, both are attractive investments. Because resources are limited, companies are not always able to invest in all capital assets that meet their investment criteria. This is called *capital rationing*. For example, Greg's may not have the funds to invest in both the DVR and CD-player projects at this time. In this case, Greg's should choose the DVR project because it yields a higher NPV. The DVR project should earn an additional $78,910 beyond the 14% required rate of return, while the CD-player project returns an additional $48,610.

This example illustrates an important point. The CD-player project promises more *total* net cash inflows. But the *timing* of the DVR cash flows—loaded near the beginning of the project—gives the DVR investment a higher NPV. The DVR project is more attractive because of the time value of money. Its dollars, which are received sooner, are worth more now than the more-distant dollars of the CD-player project.

If Greg's had to choose between the CD and DVR project, the company would choose the DVR project because it yields a higher NPV ($78,910). However, comparing the NPV of the two projects is *only* valid because both projects require the same initial cost—$1 million. In contrast, Exhibit 20-14 summarizes three capital investment options faced by Smart Touch. Each capital project requires a different initial investment. All three projects are attractive because each yields a positive NPV. Assuming Smart Touch can only invest in one project at this time, which one should it choose? Project B yields the highest NPV, but it also requires a larger initial investment than the alternatives.

EXHIBIT 20-14 Smart Touch Capital Investment Options

Year	Project A	Project B	Project C
Present value of net cash inflows	$ 150,000	$ 238,000	$ 182,000
Investment	(125,000)	(200,000)	(150,000)
Net present value (NPV)	$ 25,000	$ 38,000	$ 32,000

To choose among the projects, Smart Touch computes the **profitability index** (also known as the **present value index**). The profitability index is computed as follows:

Profitability index = Present value of net cash inflows ÷ Investment

The profitability index computes the number of dollars returned for every dollar invested, *with all calculations performed in present value dollars*. It allows us to compare alternative investments in present value terms (like the NPV method), but it also considers differences in the investments' initial cost. Let us compute the profitability index for all three alternatives.

	Present value of net cash inflows	÷ Investment	= Profitability index
Project A:	$150,000	÷ $125,000 =	1.20
Project B:	$238,000	÷ $200,000 =	1.19
Project C:	$182,000	÷ $150,000 =	1.21

The profitability index shows that Project C is the best of the three alternatives because it returns $1.21 (in present value dollars) for every $1.00 invested. Projects A and B return slightly less.

Let us also compute the profitability index for Greg's Groovy Tunes' CD-player and DVR projects:

CD-player: $1,048,610 ÷ $1,000,000 = 1.048
DVR: $1,078,910 ÷ $1,000,000 = 1.078

The profitability index confirms our prior conclusion that the DVR project is more profitable than the CD-player project. The DVR project returns $1.078 (in present value dollars) for every $1.00 invested (beyond the 14% return already used to discount the cash flows). We did not need the profitability index to determine that the DVR project was preferable because both projects required the same investment ($1 million).

NPV of a Project with Residual Value

Many assets yield cash inflows at the end of their useful lives because they have residual value. Companies discount an investment's residual value to its present value when determining the *total* present value of the project's net cash inflows. The residual value is discounted as a single lump sum—not an annuity—because it will be received only once, when the asset is sold. In short, it is just another type of cash inflow of the project.

Suppose Greg's expects that the CD project equipment will be worth $100,000 at the end of its five-year life. To determine the CD-player project's NPV, we discount the residual value of $100,000 using the Present Value of $1 table ($i$ = 14%, n = 5). (See Appendix B, Table A, page B-1.) We then *add* its present value of $51,900 to the present value of the CD project's other net cash inflows we calculated in Exhibit 20-13 ($1,048,610). This gives the new net present value calculation as shown in Exhibit 20-15 below:

EXHIBIT 20-15 | NPV of a Project with Residual Value

Year		PV Factor (i = 14%, n = 5)		Net Cash Inflow	Present Value
1–5	Present value of annuity	3.433	×	$305,450 =	$ 1,048,610
5	Present value of residual value (single lump sum)	0.519	×	$100,000 =	51,900
	Total present value of net cash inflows				$ 1,100,510
0	Investment				$(1,000,000)
	Net present value (NPV)				$ 100,510

Because of the expected residual value, the CD-player project is now more attractive than the DVR project. If Greg's could pursue only the CD or DVR project, it would now choose the CD project, because its NPV of $100,510 is higher than the DVR project's NPV of $78,910, and both projects require the same investment of $1 million.

Sensitivity Analysis

Capital budgeting decisions affect cash flows far into the future. Greg's managers might want to know whether their decision would be affected by any of their major assumptions, for example,

- changing the discount rate from 14% to 12% or to 16%.
- changing the net cash flows by 10%.

After reviewing the basic information for NPV analysis, managers perform sensitivity analyses to recalculate and review the results.

Internal Rate of Return (IRR)

Another discounted cash flow model for capital budgeting is the internal rate of return. The **internal rate of return (IRR)** is the rate of return (based on discounted cash flows) a company can expect to earn by investing in the project. *It is the interest rate that makes the NPV of the investment equal to zero.*

Let us look at this concept in another light by substituting in the definition of NPV:

Present value of the investment's net cash inflows – Investment's cost (Present value of cash outflows) = 0

In other words, the IRR is the *interest rate* that makes the cost of the investment equal to the present value of the investment's net cash inflows. The higher the IRR, the more desirable the project.

IRR with Equal Periodic Net Cash Inflows (Annuity)

Let us first consider Greg's CD-player project, which would cost $1 million and result in five equal yearly cash inflows of $305,450. We compute the IRR of an investment with equal periodic cash flows (annuity) by taking the following steps:

1. The IRR is the interest rate that makes the cost of the investment *equal to* the present value of the investment's net cash inflows, so we set up the following equation:

Investment's cost = Present value of investment's net cash inflows
Investment's cost = Amount of each equal net cash inflow × Annuity PV factor (i = ?, n = given)

2. Next, we plug in the information we do know—the investment cost, $1,000,000, the equal annual net cash inflows, $305,450, no residual value, and the number of periods (five years):

$1,000,000 = $305,450 × Annuity PV factor (i = ?, n = 5)

3. We then rearrange the equation and solve for the Annuity PV factor (i = ?, n = 5):

$1,000,000 ÷ $305,450 = Annuity PV factor (i = ?, n = 5)
3.274 = Annuity PV factor (i = ?, n = 5)

4. Finally, we find the interest rate that corresponds to this Annuity PV factor. Turn to the Present Value of Annuity of $1 table (Appendix B, Table B). Scan the row corresponding to the project's expected life—five years, in our example. Choose the column(s) with the number closest to the Annuity PV factor you calculated in step 3. The 3.274 annuity factor is in the 16% column. Therefore, the IRR of the CD-player project is 16%. Greg's expects the project to earn an internal rate of return of 16% over its life. Exhibit 20-16 confirms this result: Using a 16% discount rate, the project's NPV is zero. In other words, 16% is the discount rate that makes the investment cost equal to the present value of the investment's net cash inflows.

EXHIBIT 20-16 | IRR—CD-Player Project

Years		Annuity PV Factor (i = 16%, n = 5)		Net Cash Inflow		Total Present Value
1–5	Present value of annuity of equal annual net cash inflows for 5 years at 16%	3.274	×	$305,450	=	$1,000,000†
0	Investment					(1,000,000)
	Net present value of the CD-player project					$ 0‡

†Slight rounding error.
‡The zero difference proves that the IRR is 16%.

To decide whether the project is acceptable, compare the IRR with the minimum desired rate of return. The decision rule is as follows:

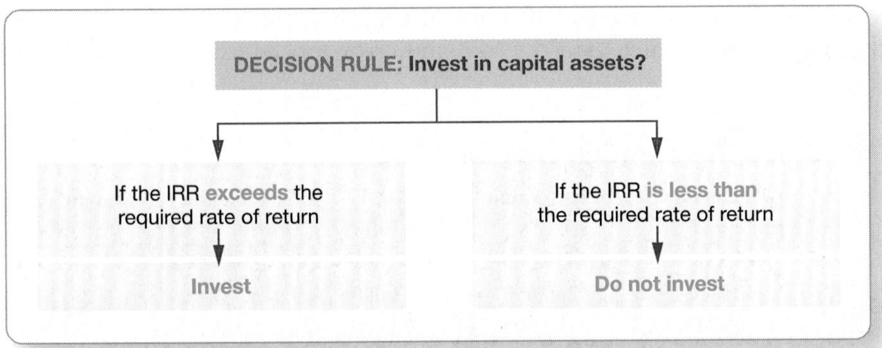

Recall that Greg's Groovy Tunes' required rate of return is 14%. Because the CD project's IRR (16%) is higher than the hurdle rate (14%), Greg's would invest in the project.

In the CD-player project, the exact Annuity PV factor (3.274) appears in the Present Value of an Annuity of $1 table (Appendix B, Table B). Many times, the exact factor will not appear in the table. For example, let us find the IRR of Smart Touch's B2B Web portal. Recall the B2B portal had a six-year life with annual net cash inflows of $60,000. The investment costs $240,000. We find its Annuity PV factor using the same steps:

Investment's cost	= Present value of investment's net cash inflows
Investment's cost	= Amount of each equal net cash inflow × Annuity PV factor (i = ?, n = given)
$240,000	= $60,000 × Annuity PV factor (i = ?, n = 6)
$240,000 ÷ $60,000	= Annuity PV factor (i = ?, n = 6)
4.00	= Annuity PV factor (i = ?, n = 6)

Now look in the Present Value of Annuity of $1 table in the row marked 6 periods (Appendix B, Table B). You will not see 4.00 under any column. The closest two factors are 3.889 (at 14%) and 4.111 (at 12%). Thus, the B2B portal's IRR must be somewhere between 12% and 14%. If we need a more precise figure, we could interpolate, or use a business calculator or Microsoft Excel to find the portal's exact IRR of 12.978%. If Smart Touch had a 14% required rate of return, it would *not* invest in the B2B portal because the portal's IRR is less than 14%.

IRR with Unequal Periodic Cash Flows

Because the DVR project has unequal cash inflows, Greg's cannot use the Present Value of Annuity of $1 table to find the asset's IRR. Rather, Greg's must use a trial-and-error procedure to determine the discount rate making the project's NPV equal to zero. For example, because the company's minimum required rate of return is 14%, Greg's might start by calculating whether the DVR project earns at least 14%. Recall from Exhibit 20-13 that the DVR's NPV using a 14% discount rate is $78,910. Since the NPV is *positive*, the IRR must be *higher* than 14%. Greg's continues the trial-and-error process using *higher* discount rates until the company finds the rate that brings the net present value of the DVR project to *zero*. Exhibit 20-17 shows that at 16%, the DVR has an NPV of $40,390. Therefore, the IRR must be higher than 16%. At 18%, the NPV is $3,980, which is very close to zero. Thus, the IRR must be slightly higher than 18%. If we use a business calculator, rather than the trial-and-error procedure, we would find the IRR is 18.23%.

EXHIBIT 20-17 | Finding the DVR's IRR Through Trial-and-Error

Years		Net Cash Inflow		PV Factor (for i = 16%)		Present Value at 16%	Net Cash Inflow		PV Factor (for i = 18%)		Present Value at 18%
1	Inflows	$500,000	×	0.862*	=	$ 431,000	$500,000	×	0.847*	=	$ 423,500
2	Inflows	350,000	×	0.743	=	260,050	350,000	×	0.718	=	251,300
3	Inflows	300,000	×	0.641	=	192,300	300,000	×	0.609	=	182,700
4	Inflows	250,000	×	0.552	=	138,000	250,000	×	0.516	=	129,000
5	Inflows	40,000	×	0.476	=	19,040	40,000	×	0.437	=	17,480
	Total present value of net cash inflows					$ 1,040,390					$ 1,003,980
0	Investment					(1,000,000)					(1,000,000)
	Net present value (NPV)					$ 40,390					$ 3,980

*PV Factors are found in Appendix B, Table A.

The DVR's internal rate of return is higher than Greg's 14% required rate of return so the DVR project is attractive.

Comparing Capital Budgeting Methods

We have discussed four capital budgeting methods commonly used by companies to make capital investment decisions. Two of these methods do not incorporate the time value of money: payback period and ARR. Exhibit 20-18 summarizes the similarities and differences between these two methods.

EXHIBIT 20-18 | Capital Budgeting Methods That *Ignore* the Time Value of Money

Payback period	Accounting rate of return
• Simple to compute • Focuses on the time it takes to recover the company's cash investment • Ignores any cash flows occurring after the payback period, including any residual value • Highlights risks of investments with longer cash recovery periods • Ignores the time value of money	• The only method that uses accrual accounting figures • Shows how the investment will affect operating income, which is important to financial statement users • Measures the profitability of the asset over its entire life • Ignores the time value of money

The discounted cash-flow methods are superior because they consider both the time value of money and profitability. These methods compare an investment's initial cost (cash outflow) with its future net cash inflows—all converted to the *same point in time*—the present value. Profitability is built into the discounted cash-flow methods because they consider *all* cash inflows and outflows over the project's life. Exhibit 20-19 considers the similarities and differences between the two discounted cash-flow methods.

EXHIBIT 20-19 **Capital Budgeting Methods That *Incorporate* the Time Value of Money**

Net present value	Internal rate of return
• Incorporates the time value of money and the asset's net cash flows over its entire life	• Incorporates the time value of money and the asset's net cash flows over its entire life
• Indicates whether or not the asset will earn the company's minimum required rate of return	• Computes the project's unique rate of return
• Shows the excess or deficiency of the asset's present value of net cash inflows over its initial investment cost	• No additional steps needed for capital rationing decisions
• The profitability index should be computed for capital rationing decisions when the assets require different initial investments	

Managers often use more than one method to gain different perspectives on risks and returns. For example, Smart Touch Learning could decide to pursue capital projects with positive NPVs, provided that those projects have a payback of four years or fewer.

Decision Guidelines

CAPITAL BUDGETING

Here are more of the guidelines **Amazon.com's** managers used as they made the major capital budgeting decision to invest in building warehouses.

Decision	Guideline
• Which capital budgeting methods are best?	Discounted cash-flow methods (NPV and IRR) are best because they incorporate both profitability and the time value of money.
• Why do the NPV and IRR models use the present value?	Because an investment's cash inflows and cash outflows occur at different points in time, they must be converted to a common point in time to make a valid comparison (that is, to determine whether inflows exceed cash outflows). These methods use the *present* value as the common point in time.
• How do we know if investing in warehouse facilities will be worthwhile?	An investment in warehouse facilities may be worthwhile if the NPV is positive or the IRR exceeds the required rate of return.
• How do we compute the net present value with	
• equal annual cash flows?	Compute the present value of the investment's net cash inflows using the Present Value of an Annuity of $1 table and then subtract the investment's cost.
• unequal annual cash flows?	Compute the present value of each year's net cash inflows using the Present Value of $1 (lump sum) table, sum the present values of the inflows, and then subtract the investment's cost.
• How do we compute the internal rate of return with	
• equal annual cash flows?	Find the interest rate that yields the following PV factor: $$\text{Annuity PV factor} = \frac{\text{Investment cost}}{\text{Expected annual net cash inflow}}$$
• unequal annual cash flows?	Trial and error, spreadsheet software, or business calculator

Summary Problem 2

Recall from Summary Problem 1 that Reality-max is considering buying a new bar-coding machine. The investment proposal passed the initial screening tests (payback period and accounting rate of return) so the company now wants to analyze the proposal using the discounted cash flow methods. Recall that the bar-coding machine costs $48,000, has a five-year life, and no residual value. The estimated net cash inflows are $13,000 per year over its life. The company's required rate of return is 16%.

Requirements

1. Compute the bar-coding machine's NPV.
2. Find the bar-coding machine's IRR (exact percentage is not required).
3. Should Reality-max buy the bar-coding machine? Why?

Solution

Requirement 1

Present value of annuity of equal annual net cash inflows at 16% ($13,000 × 3.274*).................................	$ 42,562
Investment...	(48,000)
Net present value	$ (5,438)

*Annuity PV factor (i = 16%, n = 5)

Requirement 2

$$\text{Investment's cost} = \text{Amount of each equal net cash inflow} \times \text{Annuity PV factor } (i = ?, n = 5)$$

$$\$48{,}000 = \$13{,}000 \times \text{Annuity PV factor } (i = ?, n = 5)$$

$$\$48{,}000 \div \$13{,}000 = \text{Annuity PV factor } (i = ?, n = 5)$$

$$3.692 = \text{Annuity PV factor } (i = ?, n = 5)$$

Because the cash flows occur for five years, we look for the PV factor 3.692 in the row marked n = 5 on the Present Value of Annuity of $1 table (Appendix B, Table B). The PV factor is 3.605 at 12% and 3.791 at 10%. Therefore, the bar-coding machine has an IRR that falls between 10% and 12%. (*Optional:* Using a business calculator, we find an 11.038% internal rate of return.)

Requirement 3

Decision: Do not buy the bar-coding machine. It has a negative NPV and its IRR falls below the company's required rate of return. Both methods consider profitability and the time value of money.

Review *Capital Investment Decisions and the Time Value of Money*

Accounting Vocabulary

Accounting Rate of Return (p. 1076)
A measure of profitability computed by dividing the average annual operating income from an asset by the average amount invested in the asset.

Annuity (p. 1081)
A stream of equal installments made at equal time intervals.

Capital Budgeting (p. 1071)
The process of making capital investment decisions. Companies make capital investments when they acquire *capital assets*—assets used for a long period of time.

Capital Rationing (p. 1072)
Choosing among alternative capital investments due to limited funds.

Compound Interest (p. 1081)
Interest computed on the principal *and* all interest earned to date.

Discount Rate (p. 1087)
Management's minimum desired rate of return on an investment. Also called the required rate of return.

Internal Rate of Return (IRR) (p. 1091)
The rate of return (based on discounted cash flows) that a company can expect to earn by investing in a capital asset. The interest rate that makes the NPV of the investment equal to zero.

Net Present Value (NPV) (p. 1086)
The *difference* between the present value of the investment's net cash inflows and the investment's cost.

Payback (p. 1073)
The length of time it takes to recover, in net cash inflows, the cost of a capital outlay.

Post-Audits (p. 1072)
Comparing a capital investment's actual net cash inflows to its projected net cash inflows.

Present Value Index (p. 1090)
An index that computes the number of dollars returned for every dollar invested, *with all calculations performed in present value dollars*. Computed as present value of net cash inflows divided by investment. Also called **profitability index**.

Profitability Index (p. 1090)
An index that computes the number of dollars returned for every dollar invested, *with all calculations performed in present value dollars*. Computed as present value of net cash inflows divided by investment. Also called **present value index**.

Required Rate of Return (p. 1087)
The rate an investment must meet or exceed in order to be acceptable.

Simple Interest (p. 1081)
Interest computed *only* on the principal amount.

Quick Check

1. What is the first step of capital budgeting?
   a. Gathering the money for the investment
   b. Getting the accountant involved
   c. Identifying potential projects
   d. All of the above
2. Which of the following methods uses accrual accounting, rather than net cash flows, as a basis for calculations?
   a. Payback
   b. ARR
   c. NPV
   d. IRR
3. Which of the following methods does not consider the investment's profitability?
   a. ARR
   b. NPV
   c. Payback
   d. IRR

4. Suppose Stephanie Feigenbaum's Sweets is considering investing in warehouse-management software that costs \$450,000, has \$35,000 residual value, and should lead to cost savings of \$120,000 per year for its five-year life. In calculating the ARR, which of the following figures should be used as the equation's denominator (average amount invested in the asset)?
   a. \$242,500
   b. \$257,500
   c. \$272,500
   d. \$277,000
5. Your rich aunt has promised to give you \$3,000 a year at the end of each of the next four years to help you pay for college. Using a discount rate of 10%, the present value of the gift can be stated as
   a. PV = \$3,000 (Annuity PV factor, i = 10%, n = 4).
   b. PV = \$3,000 (PV factor, i = 4%, n = 10).
   c. PV = \$3,000 × 10% × 5.
   d. PV = \$3,000 (Annuity FV factor, i = 10%, n = 4).
6. Which of the following affects the present value of an investment?
   a. The type of investment (annuity versus single lump sum)
   b. The interest rate
   c. The number of time periods (length of the investment)
   d. All of the above
7. Which of the following is true regarding capital rationing decisions?
   a. Companies should always choose the investment with the shortest payback period.
   b. Companies should always choose the investment with the highest ARR.
   c. Companies should always choose the investment with the highest NPV.
   d. None of the above
8. In computing the IRR on an expansion at Snow Park Lodge, Deer Valley would consider all of the following *except?*
   a. The cost of the expansion
   b. Predicted cash inflows over the life of the expansion
   c. Present value factors
   d. Depreciation on the assets built in the expansion
9. The IRR is
   a. the interest rate at which the NPV of the investment is zero.
   b. the same as the ARR.
   c. the firm's hurdle rate.
   d. None of the above
10. Which of the following is the most reliable method for making capital budgeting decisions?
   a. Post-audit method
   b. NPV method
   c. ARR method
   d. Payback method

Answers are given after Apply Your Knowledge (p. 1110).

Assess Your Progress

■ Short Exercises

S20-1 *(L. OBJ. 1)* **The importance of capital investments and the capital budgeting process [10 min]**
Review the following activities of the capital budgeting process:

a. Budget capital investments
b. Project investments' cash flows
c. Perform post-audits
d. Make investments
e. Use feedback to reassess investments already made
f. Identify potential capital investments
g. Screen/analyze investments using one or more of the methods discussed

Requirement

1. Place the activities in sequential order as they occur in the capital budgeting process.

S20-2 *(L. OBJ. 2)* **Using the payback and accounting rate of return methods to make capital investment decisions [10 min]**
Consider how White Valley Snow Park Lodge could use capital budgeting to decide whether the $12,500,000 Brook Park Lodge expansion would be a good investment.

Assume White Valley's managers developed the following estimates concerning the expansion:

Number of additional skiers per day	120
Average number of days per year that weather conditions allow skiing at White Valley	149
Useful life of expansion (in years)	12
Average cash spent by each skier per day	$ 159
Average variable cost of serving each skier per day	$ 85
Cost of expansion	$12,500,000
Discount rate	12%

Assume that White Valley uses the straight-line depreciation method and expects the lodge expansion to have a residual value of $600,000 at the end of its 12-year life.

Requirements

1. Compute the average annual net cash inflow from the expansion.
2. Compute the average annual operating income from the expansion.

Note: Short Exercise 20-2 must be completed before attempting Short Exercise 20-3.

S20-3 *(L. OBJ. 2)* **Using the payback method to make capital investment decisions [5 min]**
Refer to the White Valley Snow Park Lodge expansion project in S20-2.

Requirement

1. Compute the payback period for the expansion project.

Note: Short Exercise 20-2 must be completed before attempting Short Exercise 20-4.

S20-4 *(L. OBJ. 2)* **Using the accounting rate of return method to make capital investment decisions [5–10 min]**
Refer to the White Valley Snow Park Lodge expansion project in S20-2.

Requirement

1. Calculate the ARR.

Note: Short Exercise 20-2 must be completed before attempting Short Exercise 20-5.

S20-5 *(L. OBJ. 2)* **Using the payback and accounting rate of return methods to make capital investment decisions [5–10 min]**
Refer to the White Valley Snow Park Lodge expansion project in S20-2. *Assume the expansion has zero residual value.*

Requirements

1. Will the payback period change? Explain your answer and recalculate if necessary.
2. Will the project's ARR change? Explain your answer and recalculate if necessary.
3. Assume White Valley screens its potential capital investments using the following decision criteria:

Maximum payback period	5.4 years
Minimum accounting rate of return	12.0%

Will White Valley consider this project further, or reject it?

S20-6 *(L.OBJ. 2)* **Using the payback and accounting rate of return methods to make capital investment decisions [5–10 min]**
Suppose White Valley is deciding whether to purchase new accounting software. The payback period for the $27,375 software package is five years, and the software's expected life is three years. White Valley's required rate of return is 12.0%.

Requirement

1. Assuming equal yearly cash flows, what are the expected annual cash savings from the new software?

S20-7 *(L.OBJ. 3)* **Using the time value of money to compute the present and future values of single lump sums and annuities [10–15 min]**
Your grandfather would like to share some of his fortune with you. He offers to give you money under one of the following scenarios (you get to choose):

1. $7,550 a year at the end of each of the next eight years
2. $48,350 (lump sum) now
3. $100,050 (lump sum) eight years from now

Requirement

1. Calculate the present value of each scenario using an 8% discount rate. Which scenario yields the highest present value? Would your preference change if you used a 10% discount rate?

S20-8 *(L.OBJ. 3)* **Using the time value of money to compute the present and future values of single lump sums and annuities [5–10 min]**
Assume you make the following investments:

a. You invest $7,250 for three years at 12% interest.
b. In a different account earning 12% interest, you invest $2,500 at the end of each year for three years.

Requirement

1. Calculate the value of each investment at the end of three years.

S20-9 *(L. OBJ. 3)* **Using the time value of money to compute the present and future values of single lump sums and annuities [10–15 min]**
Refer to the lottery payout options summarized in Exhibit 20-9.

Requirement

1. Rather than comparing the payout options at their present values (as done in the chapter), compare the payout options at their future value, 10 years from now.
   a. Using a 8% interest rate, what is the future value of each payout option?
   b. Rank your preference among payout options.
   c. Does computing the future value, rather than the present value of the options, change your preference between payout options? Explain your reasoning.

S20-10 *(L.OBJ. 3)* **Using the time value of money to compute the present and future values of single lump sums and annuities [10–15 min]**
Use the Present Value of $1 table (Appendix B, Table A) to determine the present value of $1 received one year from now. Assume a 14% interest rate. Use the same table to find the present value of $1 received two years from now. Continue this process for a total of five years.

Requirements

1. What is the *total* present value of the cash flows received over the five-year period?
2. Could you characterize this stream of cash flows as an annuity? Why, or why not?
3. Use the Present Value of Annuity of $1 table (Appendix B, Table B) to determine the present value of the same stream of cash flows. Compare your results to your answer to part 1.
4. Explain your findings.

Note: Short Exercise 20-2 must be completed before attempting Short Exercise 20-11.

S20-11 *(L. OBJ. 4)* **Using discounted cash flow models to make capital investment decisions [10–15 min]**
Refer to the White Valley Snow Park Lodge expansion project in S20-2.

Requirement

1. What is the project's NPV? Is the investment attractive? Why?

Note: Short Exercise 20-2 must be completed before attempting Short Exercise 20-12.

S20-12 *(L. OBJ. 4)* **Using discounted cash flow models to make capital investment decisions [10–15 min]**
Refer to S20-2. *Assume the expansion has no residual value.*

Requirement

1. What is the project's NPV? Is the investment still attractive? Why?

Note: Short Exercise 20-12 must be completed before attempting Short Exercise 20-13.

S20-13 *(L. OBJ. 4)* **Using discounted cash flow models to make capital investment decisions [10–15 min]**
Refer to S20-12. *Continue to assume that the expansion has no residual value.*

Requirement

1. What is the project's IRR? Is the investment attractive? Why?

Exercises

E20-14 *(L. OBJ. 1)* **The importance of capital investments and the capital budgeting process [15–20 min]**

You have just started a business and want your new employees to be well informed about capital budgeting.

Requirement

1. Match each definition with its capital budgeting method.

METHODS

1. Accounting rate of return
2. Internal rate of return
3. Net present value
4. Payback period

DEFINITIONS

A. Is only concerned with the time it takes to get cash outflows returned
B. Considers operating income but not the time value of money in its analyses
C. Compares the present value of cash out to the cash in to determine investment worthiness
D. The true rate of return an investment earns

E20-15 *(L. OBJ. 2)* **Using the payback and accounting rate of return methods to make capital investment decisions [5–10 min]**

Stenback, Co., is considering acquiring a manufacturing plant. The purchase price is $1,300,000. The owners believe the plant will generate net cash inflows of $314,000 annually. It will have to be replaced in seven years.

Requirement

1. Use the payback method to determine whether Stenback should purchase this plant.

E20-16 *(L. OBJ. 2)* **Using the payback and accounting rate of return methods to make capital investment decisions [5–10 min]**

Pace Hardware is adding a new product line that will require an investment of $1,512,000. Managers estimate that this investment will have a 10-year life and generate net cash inflows of $320,000 the first year, $280,000 the second year, and $240,000 each year thereafter for eight years.

Requirement

1. Compute the payback period.

E20-17 *(L. OBJ. 2)* **Using the payback and accounting rate of return methods to make capital investment decisions [10–15 min]**

Transport Design is shopping for new equipment. Managers are considering two investments. Equipment manufactured by Rouse, Inc., costs $1,020,000 and will last for five years, with no residual value. The Rouse equipment will generate annual operating income of $265,000. Equipment manufactured by Vargas Co. costs $1,240,000 and will remain useful for six years. It estimates annual operating income of $230,000, and its expected residual value is $100,000.

Requirement

1. Which equipment offers the higher ARR?

Note: Exercise 20-16 must be completed before attempting Exercise 20-18.

E20-18 *(L. OBJ. 2)* **Using the payback and accounting rate of return methods to make capital investment decisions [10–15 min]**

Refer to the Pace Hardware information in E20-16. Assume the project has no residual value.

Requirement

1. Compute the ARR for the investment.

E20-19 *(L. OBJ. 3)* **Using the time value of money to compute the present and future values of single lump sums and annuities [15–20 min]**

Assume you want to retire early at age 52. You plan to save using one of the following two strategies: (1) save $2,700 a year in an IRA beginning when you are 27 and ending when you are 52 (25 years), or (2) wait until you are 42 to start saving and then save $6,750 per year for the next 10 years. Assume you will earn the historic stock market average of 12% per year.

Requirements

1. How much "out-of-pocket" cash will you invest under the two options?
2. How much savings will you have accumulated at age 52 under the two options?
3. Explain the results.
4. If you were to let the savings continue to grow for 10 more years (with no further out-of-pocket investments), what would the investments be worth when you are age 62?

E20-20 *(L. OBJ. 3)* **Using the time value of money to compute the present and future values of single lump sums and annuities [15–20 min]**

Your best friend just received a gift of $6,000 from his favorite aunt. He wants to save the money to use as "starter" money after college. He can invest it (1) risk-free at 4%, (2) taking on moderate risk at 10%, or (3) taking on high risk at 16%.

Requirement

1. Help your friend project the investment's worth at the end of four years under each investment strategy and explain the results to him.

E20-21 *(L.OBJ. 3)* **Using the time value of money to compute the present and future values of single lump sums and annuities [5–10 min]**

Janet wants to take the next six years off work to travel around the world. She estimates her annual cash needs at $35,000 (if she needs more, she will work odd jobs). Janet believes she can invest her savings at 12% until she depletes her funds.

Requirements

1. How much money does Janet need now to fund her travels?
2. After speaking with a number of banks, Janet learns she will only be able to invest her funds at 6%. How much does she need now to fund her travels?

E20-22 *(L. OBJ. 3)* **Using the time value of money to compute the present and future values of single lump sums and annuities [10–15 min]**

Congratulations! You have won a state lotto. The state lottery offers you the following (after-tax) payout options:

Option #1: $13,000,000 after five years
Option #2: $2,300,000 per year for the next five years
Option #3: $12,000,000 after three years

Requirement

1. Assuming you can earn 6% on your funds, which option would you prefer?

E20-23 *(L. OBJ. 4)* **Using discounted cash flow models to make capital investment decisions [15–20 min]**
Use the NPV method to determine whether Stenback Products should invest in the following projects:

- *Project A*: Costs $290,000 and offers eight annual net cash inflows of $57,000. Stenback Products requires an annual return of 14% on projects like A.
- *Project B*: Costs $380,000 and offers nine annual net cash inflows of $77,000. Stenback Products demands an annual return of 12% on investments of this nature.

Requirements

1. What is the NPV of each project?
2. What is the maximum acceptable price to pay for each project?

E20-24 *(L.OBJ. 4)* **Using discounted cash flow models to make capital investment decisions [15–20 min]**
Bevil Industries is deciding whether to automate one phase of its production process. The manufacturing equipment has a six-year life and will cost $900,000. Projected net cash inflows are as follows:

Year 1	$264,000
Year 2	$251,000
Year 3	$228,000
Year 4	$213,000
Year 5	$202,000
Year 6	$176,000

Requirements

1. Compute this project's NPV using Bevil Industries's 14% hurdle rate. Should Bevil Industries invest in the equipment?
2. Bevil Industries could refurbish the equipment at the end of six years for $106,000. The refurbished equipment could be used one more year, providing $78,000 of net cash inflows in year 7. Additionally, the refurbished equipment would have a $52,000 residual value at the end of year 7. Should Bevil Industries invest in the equipment and refurbishing it after six years? (*Hint:* In addition to your answer to requirement 1, discount the additional cash outflow and inflows back to the present value.)

Note: Exercise 20-23 must be completed before attempting Exercise 20-25.

E20-25 *(L.OBJ. 4)* **Using discounted cash flow models to make capital investment decisions [15 min]**
Refer to Stenback Products in E20-23.

Requirement

1. Compute the IRR of each project, and use this information to identify the better investment.

E20-26 *(L.OBJ. 4)* **Using discounted cash flow models to make capital investment decisions [10–15 min]**
Sheffield Manufacturing is considering three capital investment proposals. At this time, Sheffield Manufacturing only has funds available to pursue one of the three investments.

	Equipment A	Equipment B	Equipment C
Present value of net cash inflows	$ 1,775,424	$ 2,004,215	$ 2,242,989
Investment	$ (1,467,293)	$ (1,629,443)	$ (1,808,862)
NPV	$ 308,131	$ 374,772	$ 434,127

Requirement

1. Which investment should Sheffield Manufacturing pursue at this time? Why?

Problems (Group A)

P20-27A *(L. OBJ. 1)* **Describing the importance of capital investments and the capital budgeting process [10–15 min]**

Consider the following statements about capital budgeting.

a. ______ and ______ incorporate the time value of money.

b. ______ focuses on time, not profitability.

c. ______ uses accrual accounting income.

d. ______ finds the discount rate which brings the investment's NPV to zero.

e. In capital rationing decisions, the profitability index must be computed to compare investments requiring different initial investments when the ______ method is used.

f. ______ ignores salvage value.

g. ______ uses discounted cash flows to determine the asset's unique rate of return.

h. ______ highlights risky investments.

i. ______ measures profitability, but ignores the time value of money.

Requirement

1. Fill in each statement with the appropriate capital budgeting method: Payback period, ARR, NPV, or IRR.

P20-28A *(L. OBJ. 2, 4)* **Using the payback and accounting rate of return methods to make capital investment decisions, and using discounted cash flow models to make capital investment decisions [20–30 min]**

Water Nation is considering purchasing a water park in San Antonio, Texas, for \$1,850,000. The new facility will generate annual net cash inflows of \$440,000 for nine years. Engineers estimate that the facility will remain useful for nine years and have no residual value. The company uses straight-line depreciation, and its stockholders demand an annual return of 12% on investments of this nature.

Requirements

1. Compute the payback period, the ARR, the NPV of this investment, and its IRR.
2. Recommend whether the company should invest in this project.

P20-29A *(L. OBJ. 2, 4)* **Using the payback and accounting rate of return methods to make capital investment decisions, and using discounted cash flow models to make capital investment decisions [30–45 min]**

Locos operates a chain of sandwich shops. The company is considering two possible expansion plans. Plan A would open eight smaller shops at a cost of \$8,410,000. Expected annual net cash inflows are \$1,650,000, with zero residual value at the end of nine years. Under Plan B, Locos would open three larger shops at a cost of \$8,340,000. This plan is expected to generate net cash inflows of \$1,120,000 per year for nine years, the estimated useful life of the properties. Estimated residual value for Plan B is \$1,300,000. Locos uses straight-line depreciation and requires an annual return of 8%.

Requirements

1. Compute the payback period, the ARR, and the NPV of these two plans. What are the strengths and weaknesses of these capital budgeting models?
2. Which expansion plan should Locos choose? Why?
3. Estimate Plan A's IRR. How does the IRR compare with the company's required rate of return?

P20-30A *(L. OBJ. 3)* **Using the time value of money to compute the present and future values of single lump sums and annuities [15–20 min]**

You are planning for a very early retirement. You would like to retire at age 40 and have enough money saved to be able to draw $225,000 per year for the next 35 years (based on family history, you think you will live to age 75). You plan to save by making 10 equal annual installments (from age 30 to age 40) into a fairly risky investment fund that you expect will earn 14% per year. You will leave the money in this fund until it is completely depleted when you are 75 years old.

Requirements

1. How much money must you accumulate by retirement to make your plan work? (*Hint:* Find the present value of the $225,000 withdrawals.)
2. How does this amount compare to the total amount you will draw out of the investment during retirement? How can these numbers be so different?
3. How much must you pay into the investment each year for the first 10 years? (*Hint:* Your answer from requirement 1 becomes the future value of this annuity.)
4. How does the total "out-of-pocket" savings compare to the investment's value at the end of the 10-year savings period and the withdrawals you will make during retirement?

Problems (Group B)

P20-31B *(L. OBJ. 1)* **Describing the importance of capital investments and the capital budgeting process [10–15 min]**

Consider the following statements about capital budgeting.

a. _______ and _______ work well for capital investments with a relatively short life span.

b. _______ highlights risky investments.

c. _______ uses accrual accounting income rather than net cash flows in its computation.

d. _______ uses discounted cash flows to determine the asset's unique rate of return.

e. In capital rationing decisions, management must identify the required rate of return when the _______ method is used.

f. _______ provides management with information on how fast the cash invested will be recouped.

g. _______ finds the discount rate which brings the investment's NPV to zero.

h. _______ does not consider the asset's profitability.

i. _______ is calculated by dividing the average amount invested by the asset's average annual operating income.

Requirement

1. Fill in each statement with the appropriate capital budgeting method: Payback period, ARR, NPV, or IRR.

P20-32B *(L. OBJ. 2, 4)* **Using the payback and accounting rate of return methods to make capital investment decisions, and using discounted cash flow models to make capital investment decisions [20–30 min]**

Water World is considering purchasing a water park in San Antonio, Texas, for $1,910,000. The new facility will generate annual net cash inflows of $481,000 for eight years. Engineers estimate that the facility will remain useful for eight years and have no residual value. The company uses straight-line depreciation, and its stockholders demand an annual return of 12% on investments of this nature.

Requirements

1. Compute the payback period, the ARR, the NPV of this investment, and its IRR.
2. Recommend whether the company should invest in this project.

P20-33B *(L. OBJ. 2, 4)* **Using the payback and accounting rate of return methods to make capital investment decisions, and using discounted cash flow models to make capital investment decisions [30–45 min]**

Lolas operates a chain of sandwich shops. The company is considering two possible expansion plans. Plan A would open eight smaller shops at a cost of $8,500,000. Expected annual net cash inflows are $1,600,000, with zero residual value at the end of ten years. Under Plan B, Lolas would open three larger shops at a cost of $8,100,000. This plan is expected to generate net cash inflows of $1,090,000 per year for ten years, which is the estimated useful life of the properties. Estimated residual value for Plan B is $1,300,000. Lolas uses straight-line depreciation and requires an annual return of 8%

Requirements

1. Compute the payback period, the ARR, and the NPV of these two plans. What are the strengths and weaknesses of these capital budgeting models?
2. Which expansion plan should Lolas choose? Why?
3. Estimate Plan A's IRR. How does the IRR compare with the company's required rate of return?

P20-34B *(L. OBJ. 3)* **Using the time value of money to compute the present and future values of single lump sums and annuities [15–20 min]**

You are planning for an early retirement. You would like to retire at age 40 and have enough money saved to be able to draw $220,000 per year for the next 45 years (based on family history, you think you will live to age 85). You plan to save by making 20 equal annual installments (from age 20 to age 40) into a fairly risky investment fund that you expect will earn 14% per year. You will leave the money in this fund until it is completely depleted when you are 85 years old.

Requirements

1. How much money must you accumulate by retirement to make your plan work? (*Hint:* Find the present value of the $220,000 withdrawals.)
2. How does this amount compare to the total amount you will draw out of the investment during retirement? How can these numbers be so different?
3. How much must you pay into the investment each year for the first 20 years? (*Hint:* Your answer from requirement 1 becomes the future value of this annuity.)
4. How does the total "out-of-pocket" savings compare to the investment's value at the end of the 20-year savings period and the withdrawals you will make during retirement?

Continuing Exercise

E20-35 This exercise continues the Sherman Lawn Service, Inc., situation from Exercise 19-35 of Chapter 19. Sherman Lawn Service is considering purchasing a mower that will generate cash inflows of $5,000 per year. The mower has a zero residual value and an estimated useful life of three years. The mower costs $10,000. Sherman's required rate of return is 10%.

Requirements

1. Calculate payback period, accounting rate of return, and net present value for the mower investment.
2. Should Sherman invest in the new mower?

Continuing Problem

P20-36 This problem continues the Haupt Consulting, Inc., situation from Problem 19-36 of Chapter 19. Haupt Consulting is considering purchasing two different types of servers. Server A will generate cash inflows of $20,000 per year and has a zero residual value. Server A's estimated useful life is three years and it costs $50,000.

Server B will generate cash inflows of $30,000 in year 1, $15,000 in year 2, and $5,000 in year 3. Server B has a $1,000 residual value and an estimate life of three years. Server B also costs $50,000. Haupt's required rate of return is 8%.

Requirements

1. Calculate payback period, accounting rate of return, and net present value for both server investments.
2. Assuming capital rationing applies, which server should Haupt invest in?

Apply Your Knowledge

Decision Case

Case 1. Dominic Hunter, a second-year business student at the University of Utah, will graduate in two years with an accounting major and a Spanish minor. Hunter is trying to decide where to work this summer. He has two choices: work full-time for a bottling plant or work part-time in the accounting department of a meat-packing plant. He probably will work at the same place next summer as well. He is able to work 12 weeks during the summer.

The bottling plant will pay Hunter $380 per week this year and 7% more next summer. At the meat-packing plant, he could work 20 hours per week at $8.75 per hour. By working only part-time, he could take two accounting courses this summer. Tuition is $225 per hour for each of the four-hour courses. Hunter believes that the experience he gains this summer will qualify him for a full-time accounting position with the meat-packing plant next summer. That position will pay $550 per week.

Hunter sees two additional benefits of working part-time this summer. First, he could reduce his studying workload during the fall and spring semesters by one course each term. Second, he would have the time to work as a grader in the university's accounting department during the 15-week fall term. Grading pays $50 per week.

Requirements

1. Suppose that Hunter ignores the time value of money in decisions that cover this short time period. Suppose also that his sole goal is to make as much money as possible between now and the end of next summer. What should he do? What nonquantitative factors might Dominic consider? What would *you* do if you were faced with these alternatives?
2. Now suppose that Hunter considers the time value of money for all cash flows that he expects to receive one year or more in the future. Which alternative does this consideration favor? Why?

Quick Check Answers

1. *c* 2. *b* 3. *c* 4. *a* 5. *a* 6. *d* 7. *d* 8. *d* 9. *a* 10. *b*

For online homework, exercises, and problems that provide you immediate feedback, please visit www.myaccountinglab.com.

21 The Master Budget and Responsibility Accounting

Learning Objectives/Success Keys

1. Learn why managers use budgets
2. Understand the components of the master budget
3. Prepare an operating budget
4. Prepare a financial budget
5. Use sensitivity analysis in budgeting
6. Prepare performance reports for responsibility centers

If you are one of the millions of customers worldwide who point and click to buy your books and CDs (or other items) on **Amazon.com**, then you are part of **Amazon.com's** strategy to "get big fast." This strategy increased **Amazon.com's** sales, but at a cost. Spending was out of control. There was no budget, and managers spared no expense to help the company grow. As a result, **Amazon.com** lost more than $860 *million* dollars in 2000.

Founder and CEO Jeff Bezos had to turn this sea of red ink into income. Bezos set up a *budget* for **Amazon.com's** plan of action. Now, each division budgets both sales and expenses. In weekly meetings, managers compare actual results to the budget, which helps them correct problems quickly.

So what happened? Between 2000 and 2002, **Amazon.com's** sales increased 42%. With such an increase in sales, you would expect expenses to also increase. But **Amazon.com's** new budget helped managers *cut* operating expenses. How did they decrease expenses when sales were increasing so dramatically? The budget helped **Amazon.com** reduce order-filling and distribution costs by 5%. Switching to lower-cost computer systems reduced "technical and content" operating costs by 20%. The result? **Amazon.com** reported its first-ever income from operations in 2002. By 2004, income from operations had risen to over $588 million.[1]

Perhaps, like **Amazon.com**, you have prepared a budget to ensure that you have enough cash to pay your expenses. The budget is just a tool that forces you to plan. If your budgeted cash inflow falls short of expenses, you can

- increase your cash inflow (by taking on a job or a student loan), or
- cut your expenses.

In addition to planning, your personal budget can help you control expenses. To stay within your grocery budget, you may buy macaroni and cheese instead of steak. At the end of the month, if your bank balance is less than expected, you can compare your actual cash inflows and expenses to your budget to see why. You need to know whether cash inflows are lower than expected or expenses are higher than expected to know what corrective action to take.

As **Amazon.com** learned, it is easy for spending to get out of control if you do not have a budget. That is why everyone, from individuals like you, to complex international organizations like **Amazon.com**, to mid-size companies like Greg's Groovy Tunes use budgets. Careful budgeting helps both individuals and businesses stay out of trouble by reducing the risk that they will spend more than they earn.

As you will see throughout this chapter, knowing how costs behave continues to be important when forming budgets. Total fixed costs will not change as volume changes within the relevant range. However, total variable costs must be adjusted when sales volume is expected to fluctuate.

Why Managers Use Budgets

1 Learn why managers use budgets

Let us continue our study of budgets by moving from your personal budget to see how a small service business develops a simple budget. When Smart Touch Learning, Inc., first began, it was a small online service company that provided e-learning services to customers. Assume Smart Touch wanted to earn $550 a month and expected to sell 20 e-learning courses per month at a price of $30 each. Over the past six months, it paid Internet service providers an average of $18 a month, and spent an additional $20 per month on reference materials. Smart Touch expected these monthly costs to remain about the same, so these were the monthly fixed costs. Finally, Smart Touch spent 5% of its sales revenues for banner ads on other Web sites. Because advertising costs fluctuate with sales revenue, these costs are variable.

Exhibit 21-1 shows how to compute budgeted revenues and then subtract budgeted expenses to arrive at budgeted operating income.

As you can see from the figure, if business goes according to plan, Smart Touch will not meet its $550 per month operating income goal. It will have to increase revenue (perhaps through word-of-mouth advertising) or cut expenses (perhaps by finding a less-expensive Internet-access provider).

---

[1]*Sources:* Katrina Brooker, "Beautiful Dreamer," *Fortune*, December 18, 2000, pp. 234–239; Fred Vogelstein, "Bezos," *Fortune*, September 2, 2002, pp. 186–187; Fred Vogelstein, "What Went Right 2002," *Fortune*, December 30, 2002, p. 166; Nick Wingfield, "Survival Strategy: Amazon Takes Page from Wal-Mart to Prosper on Web," *Wall Street Journal*, November 22, 2002, A1; Fred Vogelstein, "Mighty Amazon," *Fortune*, May 26, 2003, pp. 60–74.

EXHIBIT 21-1 | **Service Company Budget**

SMART TOUCH LEARNING, INC. Sales Budget For the month ended May 31, 2010		
	in thousands	
Budgeted sales revenue (20 × $30)		$600
Less budgeted expenses:		
Internet-access expense	$18	
Reference-materials expense	20	
Advertising expense (5% × $600)	30	68
Budgeted operating income		$532

Using Budgets to Plan and Control

Large international for-profit companies, such as **Amazon.com**, and nonprofit organizations, such as **Habitat for Humanity**, use budgets for the same reasons as you do in your personal life or in your small business—to plan and control actions and the related revenues and expenses. Exhibit 21-2 shows how managers use budgets in fulfilling their major responsibilities. First, they develop strategies—overall business goals like **Amazon.com's** goal to expand its international operations, or **Gateway's** goal to be a value leader in the personal computer market, while diversifying into other markets. Companies then plan and budget for specific actions to achieve those goals. The next step is to act. For example, **Amazon.com** recently planned for and then added a grocery feature to its Web sites. And **Gateway** is leaning on its suppliers to cut costs, while at the same time it is pumping out new products like plasma TVs and audio and video gear.

EXHIBIT 21-2 | **Managers Use Budgets to Plan and Control Business Activities**

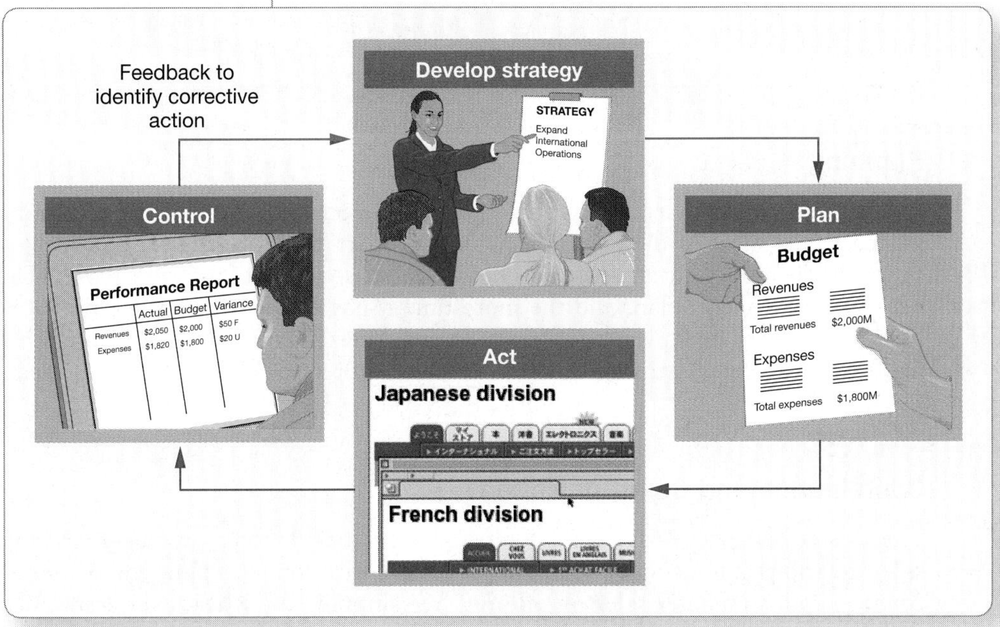

After acting, managers compare actual results with the budget. This feedback allows them to determine what, if any, corrective action to take. If, for example, **Amazon.com** spent more than expected to add the grocery feature to its Web sites, managers must cut other costs or increase revenues. These decisions affect the company's future strategies and plans.

Amazon.com has a number of budgets, as its managers develop budgets for their own divisions. Software then "rolls up" the division budgets to create an organization-wide budget for the whole company. Managers also prepare both long-term and short-term budgets. Some of the budgets are long-term forecasts that project demand for various business segments for the next 20 years.

However, most companies budget their cash flows monthly, weekly, and even daily to ensure that they have enough cash. They also budget revenues and expenses—and operating income—for months, quarters, and years. This chapter focuses on short-term budgets of one year or less. Chapter 20 explained how companies budget for major capital expenditures on property, plant, and equipment.

Benefits of Budgeting

Exhibit 21-3 summarizes three key benefits of budgeting. Budgeting forces managers to plan, promotes coordination and communication, and provides a benchmark for evaluating actual performance.

EXHIBIT 21-3 | **Benefits of Budgeting**

Budgets force managers to plan.

Budgets promote coordination and communication.

Budgets provide a benchmark that motivates employees and helps managers evaluate performance.

Planning

Exhibit 21-1 shows that the expected income from Smart Touch's online e-learning business falls short of the target. The sooner Smart Touch learns of the expected shortfall, the more time it has to plan how to increase revenues or cut expenses. The better Smart Touch's plan, and the more time it has to act on the plan, the more likely it will be to find a way to meet the target. **Amazon.com's** budget required that managers plan the expansion of the Web sites tailored for customers in Germany, France, and Japan.

Coordination and Communication

The master budget coordinates a company's activities. It forces managers to consider relations among operations across the entire value chain. For example, **Amazon.com** stimulates sales by offering free shipping on orders over a specified dollar amount. The budget encourages managers to ensure that the extra profits from increased sales outweigh the revenue lost from not charging for shipping.

Budgets also communicate a consistent set of plans throughout the company. For example, the initial **Amazon.com** budget communicated the message that all employees should help control costs.

Benchmarking

Budgets provide a benchmark that motivates employees and helps managers evaluate performance. In most companies, part of the manager's performance evaluation depends on how actual results compare to the budget. So, for example, the budgeted expenses for international expansion encourage **Amazon.com's** employees to increase the efficiency of international warehousing operations and to find less-expensive technology to support the Web sites.

Let us return to Smart Touch's e-learning business. Suppose that comparing actual results to the budget in Exhibit 21-1 leads to the performance report in Exhibit 21-4.

EXHIBIT 21-4 | Summary Performance Report

SMART TOUCH LEARNING, INC.
Partial Income Statement (in thousands)

	Actual	Budget	Variance (Actual–Budget)
Sales revenue	$550	$600	$(50)
Less: Total expenses	90	68	(22)
Net income	$460	$532	$(72)

This report should prompt you to investigate why actual sales are $50 less than budgeted ($550 – $600). There are three possibilities:

1. The budget was unrealistic.
2. You did a poor selling job.
3. Uncontrollable factors (such as a sluggish economy) reduced sales.

All three may have contributed to the poor results.

You will also want to know why expenses are $22 higher than expected ($90 – $68). Did the Internet service provider increase rates? Did Smart Touch have to buy more reference materials than planned? Did Smart Touch spend more than 5% of its revenue on Web banner ads? Smart Touch needs to know the answers to these kinds of questions to decide how to get its business back on track.

Understanding the Components of the Master Budget

Now that you know *why* managers go to the trouble of developing budgets, let us consider the steps they take to prepare a budget.

2 Understand the components of the master budget

Components of the Master Budget

The **master budget** is the set of budgeted financial statements and supporting schedules for the entire organization. Exhibit 21-5 shows the order in which managers prepare the components of the master budget for a merchandiser such as **Amazon.com** or Greg's Groovy Tunes.

EXHIBIT 21-5 | **Master Budget for a Merchandising Company**

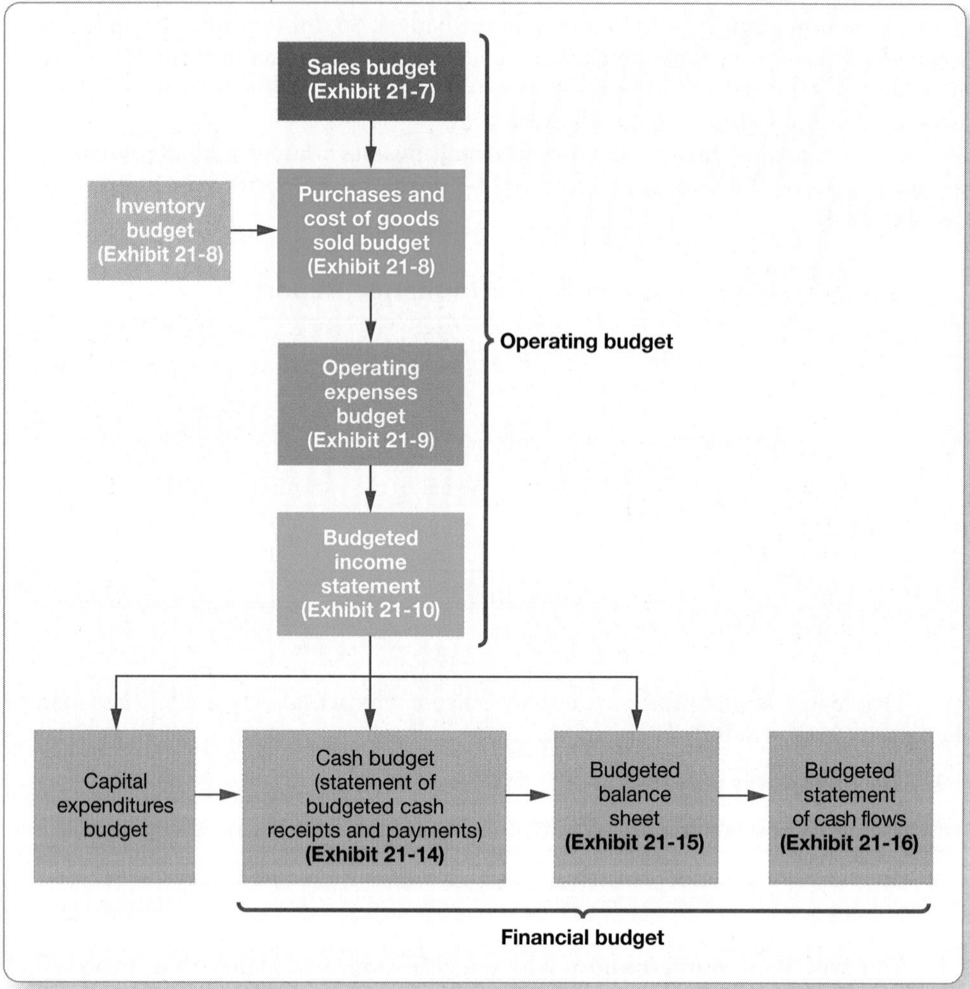

Sales budget (Exhibit 21-7)

Inventory budget (Exhibit 21-8)

Purchases and cost of goods sold budget (Exhibit 21-8)

Operating expenses budget (Exhibit 21-9)

Budgeted income statement (Exhibit 21-10)

Operating budget

Capital expenditures budget

Cash budget (statement of budgeted cash receipts and payments) **(Exhibit 21-14)**

Budgeted balance sheet **(Exhibit 21-15)**

Budgeted statement of cash flows **(Exhibit 21-16)**

Financial budget

The exhibit shows that the master budget includes three types of budgets:

1. The operating budget
2. The capital expenditures budget
3. The financial budget

Let us consider each, in turn.

The first component of the **operating budget** is the sales budget, the cornerstone of the master budget. Why? Because sales affect most other components of the master budget. After projecting sales revenue, cost of goods sold, and operating expenses, management prepares the end result of the operating budget: the **budgeted income statement** that projects operating income for the period.

The second type of budget is the **capital expenditures budget**. This budget presents the company's plan for purchasing property, plant, equipment, and other long-term assets.

The third type is the **financial budget**. Prior components of the master budget, including the budgeted income statement and the capital expenditures budget, along with plans for raising cash and paying debts, provide information for the first element of the financial budget: the cash budget. The cash budget, which projects cash inflows and outflows, feeds into the budgeted period-end balance sheet, which, in turn, feeds into the budgeted statement of cash flows. These budgeted financial statements look exactly like ordinary statements. The only difference is that they list budgeted (projected) rather than actual amounts.

Data for Greg's Groovy Tunes

We will use Greg's Groovy Tunes to see how managers prepare operating and financial budgets. Chapter 20 explained the capital budgeting process. Here is the information you have. We will refer back to this information as we create the operating and financial budgets.

1. **You manage Greg's Groovy Tunes, Inc., which carries a complete line of music CDs and DVDs.** You are to prepare the store's master budget for April, May, June, and July, the main selling season. The division manager and the head of the accounting department will arrive from headquarters next week to review the budget with you.
2. **Cash collections follow sales because the company sells on account.**
3. **Your store's balance sheet at March 31, 2010, the beginning of the budget period, appears in Exhibit 21-6.**

EXHIBIT 21-6 **Balance Sheet**

GREG'S GROOVY TUNES, INC.
Balance Sheet
March 31, 2010

Assets		Liabilities	
Current assets:		Current liabilities:	
Cash	$ 15,000	Accounts payable	$ 16,800
Accounts receivable	16,000	Salary and commissions	
Inventory	48,000	payable	4,250
Prepaid insurance	1,800	Total liabilities	21,050
Total current assets	80,800		
Plant assets:		**Stockholders' Equity**	
Equipment and fixtures	32,000	Stockholders' equity	78,950
Accumulated depreciation	(12,800)		
Total plant assets	19,200	Total liabilities and stockholders'	
Total assets	$100,000	equity	$100,000

4. **Sales in March were $40,000.** The sales force predicts the following future monthly sales:

April	$50,000
May	80,000
June	60,000
July	50,000

Sales are 60% cash and 40% on credit. Greg's Groovy Tunes collects all credit sales the month after the sale. The $16,000 of accounts receivable at March 31 arose from credit sales in March (40% of $40,000). Uncollectible accounts are immaterial.

5. **Greg's Groovy Tunes maintains inventory equal to $20,000 plus 80% of the budgeted cost of goods sold for the following month.** Target ending inventory on July 31 is $42,400. Cost of goods sold averages 70% of sales. This is a variable cost. Inventory on March 31 is $48,000:

March 31 inventory = $20,000 + 0.80 × (0.70 × April sales of $50,000)
= $20,000 + (0.80 × $35,000)
= $20,000 + $28,000
= $48,000

Greg's pays for inventory as follows: 50% during the month of purchase and 50% during the next month. Accounts payable consists of inventory purchases only. March purchases were $33,600 so accounts payable at the end of March totals $16,800 ($33,600 × 0.50).

6. **Monthly payroll has two parts: a salary of $2,500 plus sales commissions equal to 15% of sales.** This is a mixed cost, with both a fixed and variable component. The company pays half this amount during the month and half early in the following month. Therefore, at the end of each month, Greg's reports salary and commissions payable equal to half the month's payroll. The $4,250 liability on the March 31 balance sheet is half the March payroll of $8,500:

March payroll = Salary of $2,500 + Sales commissions of $6,000 (0.15 × $40,000)
= $8,500

March 31 salary and commissions payable = 0.50 × $8,500 = $4,250

7. **Other monthly expenses are as follows:**

Rent expense (fixed cost)........................	$2,000, paid as incurred
Depreciation expense, including truck (fixed cost)	500
Insurance expense (fixed cost)................	200 expiration of prepaid amount
Miscellaneous expenses (variable cost)....	5% of sales, paid as incurred

8. **Greg's plans to purchase a used delivery truck in April for $3,000 cash.**

9. **Greg's requires each store to maintain a minimum cash balance of $10,000 at the end of each month.** The store can borrow money on six-month notes payable of $1,000 each at an annual interest rate of 12%. Management borrows no more than the amount needed to maintain the $10,000 minimum. Total interest expense will vary as the amount of borrowing varies from month to month. Notes payable require six equal monthly payments of principal, plus monthly interest on the entire unpaid principal. Borrowing and all principal and interest payments occur at the end of the month.

10. **Income taxes are the responsibility of corporate headquarters, so you can ignore tax.**

As you prepare the master budget, remember that you are developing the store's operating and financial plan for the next four months. The steps in this process may seem mechanical, but you must think carefully about pricing, product lines, job assignments, needs for additional equipment, and negotiations with banks. Successful managers use this opportunity to make decisions that affect the future course of business.

Preparing the Operating Budget

3 Prepare an operating budget

The first three components of the operating budget as shown in Exhibit 21-5 are as follows:

1. Sales budget (Exhibit 21-7)
2. Inventory, purchases, and cost of goods sold budget (Exhibit 21-8)
3. Operating expenses budget (Exhibit 21-9)

The results of these three budgets feed into the fourth element of the operating budget: the budgeted income statement (Exhibit 21-10). We consider each, in turn.

The Sales Budget

The forecast of sales revenue is the cornerstone of the master budget because the level of sales affects expenses and almost all other elements of the master budget. Budgeted total sales for each product are the sales price multiplied by the expected number of units sold. The overall sales budget in Exhibit 21-7 is the sum of the budgets for the individual products. Trace the April through July total sales of $240,000 to the budgeted income statement in Exhibit 21-10.

EXHIBIT 21-7 | **Sales Budget**

GREG'S GROOVY TUNES, INC.
Sales Budget
April–July, 2010

	April	May	June	July	April–July Total
Cash sales, 60%	$30,000	$48,000	$36,000	$30,000	
Credit sales, 40%	20,000	32,000	24,000	20,000	
Total sales, 100%	$50,000	$80,000	$60,000	$50,000	$240,000

The Inventory, Purchases, and Cost of Goods Sold Budget

This budget determines cost of goods sold for the budgeted income statement, ending inventory for the budgeted balance sheet, and purchases for the cash budget. The familiar cost-of-goods-sold computation specifies the relations among these items:

Beginning inventory + Purchase – Ending inventory = Cost of goods sold

Beginning inventory is known from last month's balance sheet, budgeted cost of goods sold is 70% of sales, and budgeted ending inventory is a computed amount. You must solve for the budgeted purchases figure. To do this, rearrange the previous equation to isolate purchases on the left side:

Purchases = Cost of goods sold + Ending inventory – Beginning inventory

This equation makes sense. How much does Greg's Groovy Tunes have to purchase? Enough to cover sales and desired ending inventory, less the amount of beginning inventory already on hand at the start of the period. Exhibit 21-8 shows Greg's inventory, purchases, and cost of goods sold budget.

EXHIBIT 21-8 **Inventory, Purchases, and Cost of Goods Sold Budget**

GREG'S GROOVY TUNES, INC.
Inventory, Purchases, and Cost of Goods Sold Budget
April–July, 2010

	April	May	June	July	April–July Total
Cost of goods sold (0.70 × sales, from sales budget in Exhibit 21-7)	$ 35,000	$ 56,000	$ 42,000	$ 35,000	$168,000
+ Desired ending inventory					
($20,000 + 0.80 × Cost of goods sold for the next month)	64,800*	53,600	48,000	42,400‡	
= Total inventory required	99,800	109,600	90,000	77,400	
– Beginning inventory	(48,000)†	(64,800)	(53,600)	(48,000)	
= Purchases	$ 51,800	$ 44,800	$ 36,400	$ 29,400	

*$20,000 + (0.80 × $56,000) = $64,800
†Balance at March 31 (Exhibit 21-6)
‡Given in item 5 on page 1118

Trace the total budgeted cost of goods sold from Exhibit 21-8 ($168,000) to the budgeted income statement in Exhibit 21-10. We will use the budgeted inventory and purchases amounts later.

The Operating Expenses Budget

Exhibit 21-9 shows the operating expense budget. Study each expense to make sure you know how it is computed. For example, sales commissions fluctuate with sales. Other expenses, such as rent and insurance, are the same each month (fixed).

Trace the April through July totals from the operating expenses budget in Exhibit 21-9 (salary and commissions of $46,000, rent expense of $8,000, and so on) to the budgeted income statement in Exhibit 21-10.

EXHIBIT 21-9 | **Operating Expenses Budget**

GREG'S GROOVY TUNES, INC. Operating Expenses Budget April–July, 2010					
	April	May	June	July	April–July Total
Salary, fixed amount	$ 2,500	$ 2,500	$ 2,500	$ 2,500	
Commission, 15% of sales from sales budget (Exhibit 21-7)	7,500	12,000	9,000	7,500	
Total salary and commissions	10,000	14,500	11,500	10,000	$46,000
Rent expense, fixed amount	2,000	2,000	2,000	2,000	8,000
Depreciation expense, fixed amount	500	500	500	500	2,000
Insurance expense, fixed amount	200	200	200	200	800
Miscellaneous expenses, 5% of sales from sales budget (Exhibit 21-7)	2,500	4,000	3,000	2,500	12,000
Total operating expenses	$15,200	$21,200	$17,200	$15,200	$68,800

The Budgeted Income Statement

Use the sales budget (Exhibit 21-7), the inventory, purchases, and cost of goods sold budget (Exhibit 21-8), and the operating expenses budget (Exhibit 21-9) to prepare the budgeted income statement in Exhibit 21-10. (We explain the computation of interest expense as part of the cash budget in the next section.)

EXHIBIT 21-10 | **Budgeted Income Statement**

GREG'S GROOVY TUNES, INC. Budgeted Income Statement Four Months Ending July 31, 2010			
		Amount	Source
Sales revenue		$240,000	Sales budget (Exhibit 21-7)
Cost of goods sold		168,000	Inventory, Purchases, and Cost of Goods
Gross profit		72,000	Sold budget (Exhibit 21-8)
Operating expenses:			
Salary and commissions	$46,000		Operating expenses budget (Exhibit 21-9)
Rent expense	8,000		Operating expenses budget (Exhibit 21-9)
Depreciation expense	2,000		Operating expenses budget (Exhibit 21-9)
Insurance expense	800		Operating expenses budget (Exhibit 21-9)
Miscellaneous expenses	12,000	68,800	Operating expenses budget (Exhibit 21-9)
Operating income		3,200	
Interest expense		225*	Cash budget (Exhibit 21-14)
Net income		$ 2,975	

*$90 + $75 + $60

Take this opportunity to solidify your understanding of operating budgets by carefully working out Summary Problem 1.

Summary Problem 1

Review the Greg's Groovy Tunes example. You now think July sales might be $40,000 instead of the projected $50,000 in Exhibit 21-7. You want to see how this change in sales affects the budget.

Requirement

1. Revise the sales budget (Exhibit 21-7), the inventory, purchases, and cost of goods sold budget (Exhibit 21-8), and the operating expenses budget (Exhibit 21-9). Prepare a revised budgeted income statement for the four months ended July 31, 2010.

Note: You need not repeat the parts of the revised schedules that do not change. Assume that interest does not change.

Solution

Requirement

1. Although not required, this solution repeats the budgeted amounts for April, May, and June. Revised figures appear in color for emphasis.

GREG'S GROOVY TUNES, INC.
Revised—Sales Budget
April–July, 2010

	April	May	June	July	Total
Cash sales, 60%	$30,000	$48,000	$36,000	$24,000	
Credit sales, 40%	20,000	32,000	24,000	16,000	
Total sales, 100%	$50,000	$80,000	$60,000	$40,000	$230,000

GREG'S GROOVY TUNES, INC.
Revised—Inventory, Purchases, and Cost of Goods Sold Budget
April–July, 2010

	April	May	June	July	Total
Cost of goods sold (0.70 × sales, from revised sales budget)	$ 35,000	$ 56,000	$ 42,000	$ 28,000	$161,000
+ Desired ending inventory					
($20,000 + 0.80 × Cost of goods sold for next month)	64,800	53,600	42,400	42,400	
= Total inventory required	99,800	109,600	84,400	70,400	
– Beginning inventory	(48,000)*	(64,800)	(53,600)	(42,400)	
= Purchases	$ 51,800	$ 44,800	$ 30,800	$ 28,000	

*Balance at March 31 (Exhibit 21-6)

GREG'S GROOVY TUNES, INC.
Revised—Operating Expenses Budget

	April	May	June	July	Total
Salary, fixed amount	$ 2,500	$ 2,500	$ 2,500	$ 2,500	
Commission, 15% of sales from revised sales budget	7,500	12,000	9,000	6,000	
Total salary and commissions	10,000	14,500	11,500	8,500	$44,500
Rent expense, fixed amount	2,000	2,000	2,000	2,000	8,000
Depreciation expense, fixed amount	500	500	500	500	2,000
Insurance expense, fixed amount	200	200	200	200	800
Miscellaneous expenses, 5% of sales from revised sales budget	2,500	4,000	3,000	2,000	11,500
Total operating expenses	$15,200	$21,200	$17,200	$13,200	$66,800

GREG'S GROOVY TUNES, INC.
Revised Budgeted Income Statement
Four Months Ending July 31, 2010

		Amount	Source
Sales revenue		$230,000	Revised sales budget
Cost of goods sold		161,000	Revised inventory, purchases, and cost of goods sold budget
Gross profit		69,000	
Operating expenses:			
Salary and commissions	$44,500		Revised operating expenses budget
Rent expense	8,000		Revised operating expenses budget
Depreciation expense	2,000		Revised operating expenses budget
Insurance expense	800		Revised operating expenses budget
Miscellaneous expenses	11,500	66,800	Revised operating expenses budget
Operating income		2,200	
Interest expense		225	Given, Exhibit 21-10
Net income		$ 1,975	

Preparing the Financial Budget

4 Prepare a financial budget

Armed with a clear understanding of Greg's Groovy Tunes' operating budget, you are now ready to prepare the financial budget. Exhibit 21-5 shows that the financial budget includes the cash budget, the budgeted balance sheet, and the budgeted statement of cash flows. We start with the cash budget.

Preparing the Cash Budget

The **cash budget**, or statement of budgeted cash receipts and payments, details how the business expects to go from the beginning cash balance to the desired ending balance. The cash budget has four major parts:

- Cash collections from customers (Exhibit 21-11)
- Cash payments for purchases (Exhibit 21-12)
- Cash payments for operating expenses (Exhibit 21-13)
- Cash payments for capital expenditures (for example, the $3,000 capital expenditure to acquire the delivery truck)

Cash collections and payments depend on revenues and expenses, which appear in the operating budget. This is why you cannot prepare the cash budget until you have finished the operating budget.

Budgeted Cash Collections from Customers

Exhibit 21-11 shows that April's budgeted cash collections consist of two parts: (1) April's cash sales from the sales budget in Exhibit 21-7 ($30,000) plus (2) collections of March's credit sales ($16,000 from the March 31 balance sheet, Exhibit 21-6). Trace April's $46,000 ($30,000 + $16,000) total cash collections to the cash budget in Exhibit 21-14 on page 1126.

EXHIBIT 21-11 | **Budgeted Cash Collections**

GREG'S GROOVY TUNES, INC.
Budgeted Cash Collections from Customers
April–July, 2010

	April	May	June	July	April–July Total
Cash sales from sales budget (Exhibit 21-7)	$30,000	$48,000	$36,000	$30,000	
Collections of last month's credit sales, from sales budget (Exhibit 21-7)	16,000*	20,000	32,000	24,000	
Total collections	$46,000	$68,000	$68,000	$54,000	$236,000

*March 31 accounts receivable (Exhibit 21-6)

Budgeted Cash Payments for Purchases

Exhibit 21-12 uses the inventory, purchases, and cost of goods sold budget from Exhibit 21-8 and payment information from item 5 of the original information list to compute budgeted cash payments for purchases of inventory. April's cash payments for purchases consist of two parts: (1) payment of 50% of March's purchases ($16,800 accounts payable balance from the March 31 balance sheet, Exhibit 21-6) plus (2) payment for 50% of April's purchases ($25,900 = 50% × $51,800 from Exhibit 21-8). Trace April's $42,700 ($16,800 + $25,900) cash outlay for purchases to the cash budget in Exhibit 21-14.

EXHIBIT 21-12 | Budgeted Cash Payments for Purchases

GREG'S GROOVY TUNES, INC.
Budgeted Cash Payments for Purchases
April–July, 2010

	April	May	June	July	April–July Total
50% of last month's purchases from inventory, purchases, and cost of goods sold budget (Exhibit 21-8)	$16,800*	$25,900	$22,400	$18,200	
50% of this month's purchases from inventory, purchases, and cost of goods sold budget (Exhibit 21-8)	25,900	22,400	18,200	14,700	
Total payments for purchases	$42,700	$48,300	$40,600	$32,900	$164,500

*March 31 accounts payable (Exhibit 21-6)

Budgeted Cash Payments for Operating Expenses

Exhibit 21-13 uses items 6 and 7 of the original information list and the operating expenses budget (Exhibit 21-9) to compute cash payments for operating expenses. April's cash payments for operating expenses consist of four items:

Payment of 50% of March's salary and commissions (from March 31 balance sheet, Exhibit 21-6)	$ 4,250
Payment of 50% of April's salary and commissions (50% × $10,000, Exhibit 21-9)	5,000
Payment of rent expense (Exhibit 21-9)	2,000
Payment of miscellaneous expenses (Exhibit 21-9)	2,500
Total April cash payments for operating expenses	$13,750

Follow April's $13,750 cash payments for operating expenses from Exhibit 21-13 to the cash budget in Exhibit 21-14 on the following page.

EXHIBIT 21-13 | Budgeted Cash Payments for Operating Expenses

GREG'S GROOVY TUNES, INC.
Budgeted Cash Payments for Operating Expenses
April–July, 2010

	April	May	June	July	April–July Total
Salary and commissions:					
50% of last month's expenses, from operating expenses budget (Exhibit 21-9)	$ 4,250*	$ 5,000	$ 7,250	$ 5,750	
50% of this month's expenses, from operating expenses budget (Exhibit 21-9)	5,000	7,250	5,750	5,000	
Total salary and commissions	9,250	12,250	13,000	10,750	
Rent expense, from operating expenses budget (Exhibit 21-9)	2,000	2,000	2,000	2,000	
Miscellaneous expenses, from operating expenses budget (Exhibit 21-9)	2,500	4,000	3,000	2,500	
Total payments for operating expenses	$13,750	$18,250	$18,000	$15,250	$65,250

*March 31 salary and commissions payable (Exhibit 21-6)

Stop & Think...

Why are depreciation expense and insurance expense from the operating expenses budget (Exhibit 21-9) *excluded* from the budgeted cash payments for operating expenses in Exhibit 21-13?

Answer: These expenses do not require cash outlays in the current period. Depreciation is the periodic write-off of the cost of the equipment and fixtures that Greg's Groovy Tunes acquired previously. Insurance expense is the expiration of prepaid insurance paid for in a previous period; thus, no cash was required this period.

The Cash Budget

To prepare the cash budget in Exhibit 21-14, start with the beginning cash balance and add the budgeted cash collections from Exhibit 21-11 to determine the cash available. Then, subtract cash payments for purchases (Exhibit 21-12), operating expenses (Exhibit 21-13), and any capital expenditures. This yields the ending cash balance before financing.

Item 9 on page 1118 states that Greg's Groovy Tunes requires a minimum cash balance of $10,000. April's $1,550 budgeted cash balance before financing falls $8,450 short of the minimum required ($10,000 – $1,550). Because Greg's borrows in $1,000 notes, the company will have to borrow $9,000 to cover April's expected shortfall. The budgeted ending cash balance equals the "ending cash balance before financing," adjusted for the total effects of the financing (a $9,000 inflow in April). Exhibit 21-14 shows that Greg's expects to end April with $10,550 of cash ($1,550 + $9,000). The exhibit also shows the cash balance at the end of May, June, and July.

EXHIBIT 21-14 Cash Budget

GREG'S GROOVY TUNES, INC.
Cash Budget
Four Months Ending July 31, 2010

	April	May	June	July
Beginning cash balance	$ 15,000*	$ 10,550	$ 10,410	$ 18,235
Cash collections (Exhibit 21-11)	46,000	68,000	68,000	54,000
Cash available	$ 61,000	$ 78,550	$ 78,410	$ 72,235
Cash payments:				
Purchases of inventory (Exhibit 21-12)	$ 42,700	$ 48,300	$ 40,600	$ 32,900
Operating expenses (Exhibit 21-13)	13,750	18,250	18,000	15,250
Purchase of delivery truck	3,000	—	—	—
Total cash payments	59,450	66,550	58,600	48,150
(1) Ending cash balance before financing	1,550	12,000	19,810	24,085
Less: Minimum cash balance desired	(10,000)	(10,000)	(10,000)	(10,000)
Cash excess (deficiency)	$ (8,450)	$ 2,000	$ 9,810	$ 14,085
Financing of cash deficiency (see notes *a–c*):				
Borrowing (at end of month)	$ 9,000			
Principal payments (at end of month)		$ (1,500)	$ (1,500)	$ (1,500)
Interest expense (at 12% annually)		(90)	(75)	(60)
(2) Total effects of financing	9,000	(1,590)	(1,575)	(1,560)
Ending cash balance (1) + (2)	$ 10,550	$ 10,410	$ 18,235	$ 22,525

*March 31 cash balance (Exhibit 21-6)

Notes

[a]Borrowing occurs in multiples of $1,000 and only for the amount needed to maintain a minimum cash balance of $10,000.

[b]Monthly principal payments: $9,000 ÷ 6 = $1,500

[c]Interest expense:

May: $9,000 × (0.12 × 1/12) = $90

June: ($9,000 – $1,500) × (0.12 × 1/12) = $75

July: ($9,000 – $1,500 – $1,500) × (0.12 × 1/12) = $60

Item 9 states that Greg's must repay the notes in six equal installments. Thus, May through July show principal repayments of $1,500 ($9,000 ÷ 6) per month. Greg's also pays interest expense on the outstanding notes payable, at 12% per year. The June interest expense is $75 [($9,000 principal – $1,500 repayment at the end of May) × 12% × 1/12]. Interest expense for the four months totals $225 ($90 + $75 + $60). This interest expense appears on the budgeted income statement in Exhibit 21-10.

The cash balance at the end of July ($22,525) is the cash balance in the July 31 budgeted balance sheet in Exhibit 21-15.

EXHIBIT 21-15 | Budgeted Balance Sheet

GREG'S GROOVY TUNES, INC. Budgeted Balance Sheet July 31, 2010		
Assets		
Current assets:		
Cash (Exhibit 21-14)	$ 22,525	
Accounts receivable (sales budget, Exhibit 21-7)	20,000	
Inventory (inventory, purchases, and cost of goods sold budget, Exhibit 21-8)	42,400	
Prepaid insurance (beginning balance of $1,800 – $800* for four months' expiration; operating expenses budget, Exhibit 21-9)	1,000	
Total current assets		$ 85,925
Plant assets:		
Equipment and fixtures (beginning balance of $32,000* + $3,000 truck acquisition	$ 35,000	
Accumulated depreciation (beginning balance of $12,800* + $2,000 for four months' depreciation; operating expenses budget, Exhibit 21-9)	(14,800)	
Total plant assets		20,200
Total assets		$106,125
Liabilities		
Current liabilities:		
Account payable (0.50 × July purchases of $29,400; inventory, purchases, and cost of goods sold budget, Exhibit 21-8)	$ 14,700	
Short-term note payable ($9,000 – $4,500 paid back; Exhibit 21-14)	4,500	
Salary and commissions payable (0.50 × July expenses of $10,000; operating expenses budget, Exhibit 21-9)	5,000	
Total liabilities		$ 24,200
Stockholders' Equity		
Stockholders' equity (beginning balance of $78,950* + $2,975 net income; Exhibit 21-10)		81,925
Total liabilities and stockholders' equity		$106,125

*March 31, 2010, Balance Sheet (Exhibit 21-6)

The Budgeted Balance Sheet

To prepare the budgeted balance sheet, project each asset, liability, and stockholders' equity account based on the plans outlined in the previous exhibits.

Study the budgeted balance sheet in Exhibit 21-15 to make certain you understand the computation of each figure. For example, on the budgeted balance sheet as of July 31, 2010, budgeted cash equals the ending cash balance from the cash budget in Exhibit 21-14. Accounts receivable as of July 31 equal July's credit sales of $20,000, shown in the sales budget (Exhibit 21-7). July 31 inventory of $42,400 is July's desired ending inventory in the inventory, purchases, and cost of goods sold budget in Exhibit 21-8. Detailed computations for each of the other accounts appear in Exhibit 21-15.

The Budgeted Statement of Cash Flows

The final step is preparing the budgeted statement of cash flows. Use the information from the schedules of cash collections and payments, the cash budget, and the beginning balance of cash to project cash flows from operating, investing, and financing activities. Take time to study Exhibit 21-16 and make sure you understand the origin of each figure.

EXHIBIT 21-16 Budgeted Statement of Cash Flows

GREG'S GROOVY TUNES, INC.
Budgeted Statement of Cash Flows
Four Months Ending July 31, 2010

Cash flows from operating activities:		
Receipts:		
Collections from customers (Exhibit 21-11)	$ 236,000	
Total cash receipts		$ 236,000
Payments:		
Purchases of inventory (Exhibit 21-12)	$(164,500)	
Operating expenses (Exhibit 21-13)	(65,250)	
Payment of interest expense (Exhibits 21-14 and 21-10)	(225)	
Total cash payments		(229,975)
Net cash inflow from operating activities		6,025
Cash flows from investing activities:		
Acquisition of delivery truck	$ (3,000)	
Net cash outflow from investing activities		(3,000)
Cash flows from financing activities:		
Proceeds from issuance of notes payable (Exhibit 21-14)	$ 9,000	
Payment of notes payable (Exhibit 21-14)	(4,500)	
Net cash inflow from financing activities		4,500
Net increase in cash		$ 7,525
Cash balance, April 1, 2010 (Exhibit 21-6 and 21-14)		15,000
Cash balance, July 31, 2010 (Exhibits 21-14 and 21-15)		$ 22,525

Getting Employees to Accept the Budget

What is the most important part of Greg's Groovy Tunes' budgeting system? Despite all the numbers we have crunched, it is not the mechanics. It is getting managers and employees to accept the budget so Greg's can reap the planning, coordination, and control benefits illustrated in Exhibit 21-3.

Few people enjoy having their work monitored and evaluated. So if managers use the budget as a benchmark to evaluate employees' performance, managers must first motivate employees to accept the budget's goals. Here is how they can do it:

- Managers must support the budget themselves, or no one else will.
- Managers must show employees how budgets can help them achieve better results.
- Managers must have employees participate in developing the budget.

But these principles alone are not enough. As the manager of Greg's, your performance is evaluated by comparing actual results to the budget. When you develop the company's budget, you may be tempted to build in *slack*. For example, you might want to budget fewer sales and higher purchases than you expect. This increases the chance that actual performance will be better than the budget and that you will receive a good evaluation. But adding slack into the budget makes it less accurate—and less useful for planning and control. When the division manager and the head of the accounting department arrive from headquarters next week, they will scour your budget to find any slack you may have inserted.

Using Information Technology for Sensitivity Analysis and Rolling Up Unit Budgets

Exhibits 21-7 through 21-16 show that the manager must prepare many calculations to develop the master budget for just one of the retail stores in the Greg's Groovy Tunes merchandising chain. No wonder managers embrace information technology to help prepare budgets! Let us see how advances in information technology make it more cost-effective for managers to

5 Use sensitivity analysis in budgeting

- conduct sensitivity analysis on their own unit's budget, and
- roll up individual unit budgets to create the companywide budget.

Sensitivity Analysis

The master budget models the company's *planned* activities. Top management pays special attention to ensure that the results of the budgeted income statement (Exhibit 21-10), the cash budget (Exhibit 21-14), and the budgeted balance sheet (Exhibit 21-15) support key strategies.

But actual results often differ from plans so management wants to know how budgeted income and cash flows would change if key assumptions turned out to be incorrect. In Chapter 18, we defined *sensitivity analysis* as a *what-if* technique that asks *what* a result will be *if* a predicted amount is not achieved or *if* an underlying assumption changes. *What if* the stock market crashes? How will this affect **Amazon.com's** sales? Will it have to postpone the planned expansion in Asia and Europe? *What* will be Greg's Groovy Tunes' cash balance on July 31 *if* the period's sales are 45% cash, not 60% cash? Will Greg's have to borrow more cash?

Most companies use computer spreadsheet programs to prepare master budget schedules and statements. One of the earliest spreadsheet programs was developed by graduate business students who realized that computers could take the drudgery out of hand-computed master budget sensitivity analyses. Today, managers answer what-if questions simply by changing a number. At the press of a key, the computer screen flashes a revised budget that includes all the effects of the change.

Technology makes it cost-effective to perform more comprehensive sensitivity analyses. Armed with a better understanding of how changes in sales and costs are likely to affect the company's bottom line, today's managers can react quickly if key assumptions underlying the master budget (such as sales price or quantity) turn out to be wrong.

Rolling Up Individual Unit Budgets into the Companywide Budget

Greg's Groovy Tunes is just one of the company's many retail stores. As Exhibit 21-17 shows, Greg's Groovy Tunes' headquarters must roll up the budget data from each of the stores to prepare the companywide master budget. This roll-up can be difficult for companies whose units use different spreadsheets to prepare the budgets.

EXHIBIT 21-17 **Rolling Up Individual Unit Budgets into the Companywide Budget**

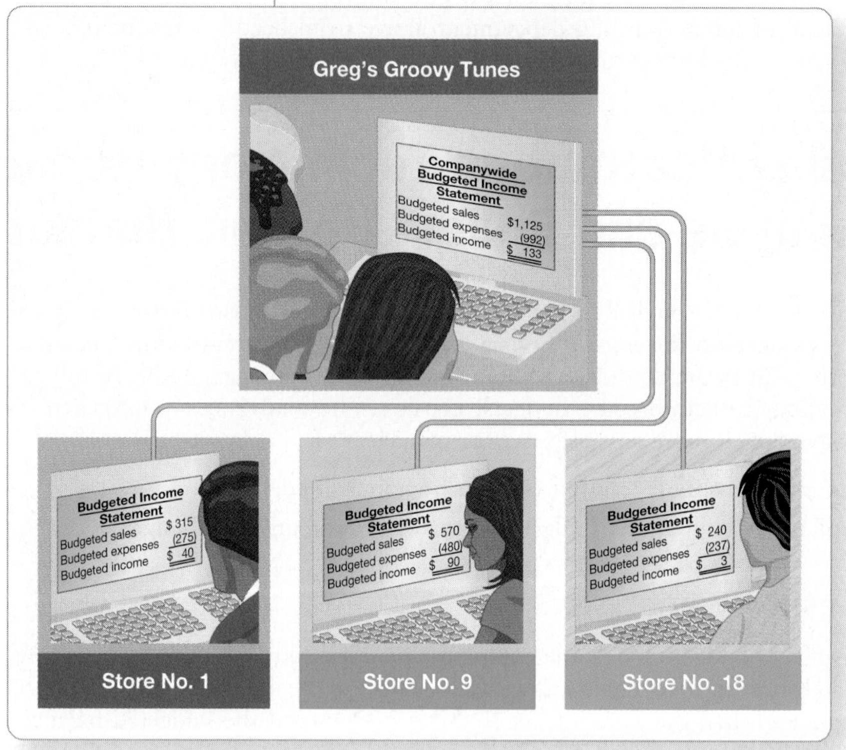

Companies like **Sunoco** turn to budget-management software to solve this problem. Often designed as a component of the company's Enterprise Resource Planning (ERP) system (or data warehouse), this software helps managers develop and analyze budgets.

Across the globe, managers sit at their desks, log into the company's budget system, and enter their numbers. The software allows them to conduct sensitivity analyses on their own unit's data. When the manager is satisfied with his or her budget, he or she can enter it in the companywide budget with the click of a mouse. His or her unit's budget automatically rolls up with budgets from all other units around the world.

Whether at headquarters or on the road, top executives can log into the budget system and conduct their own sensitivity analyses on individual units' budgets or on the companywide budget. Managers can spend less time compiling and summarizing data and more time analyzing it to ensure that the budget leads the company to achieve its key strategic goals.

Stop & Think...

Consider two budget situations: (1) Greg's Groovy Tunes' marketing analysts produce a near-certain forecast for four-month sales of $4,500,000 for the company's 20 stores. (2) Much uncertainty exists about the period's sales. The most likely amount is $4,500,000, but marketing considers any amount between $3,900,000 and $5,100,000 to be possible. How will the budgeting process differ in these two circumstances?

Answer: Greg's will prepare a master budget for the expected sales level of $4,500,000 in either case. Because of the uncertainty in the second situation, executives will want a set of budgets covering the entire range of volume rather than a single level. Greg's Groovy Tunes' managers may prepare budgets based on sales of, for example, $3,900,000, $4,200,000, $4,500,000, $4,800,000, and $5,100,000. These budgets will help managers plan for sales levels throughout the forecasted range.

Responsibility Accounting

6 Prepare performance reports for responsibility centers

You have now seen how managers set strategic goals and then develop plans and budget resources for activities that will help reach those goals. Let us look more closely at how managers *use* budgets to control operations.

Each manager is responsible for planning and controlling some part of the firm's activities. A **responsibility center** is a part or subunit of an organization whose manager is accountable for specific activities. Lower-level managers are often responsible for budgeting and controlling costs of a single value-chain function. For example, one manager is responsible for planning and controlling the *production* of Greg's Groovy Tunes CDs and DVDs at the plant, while another is responsible for planning and controlling the *distribution* of the product to customers. Lower-level managers report to higher-level managers, who have broader responsibilities. Managers in charge of production and distribution report to senior managers responsible for profits (revenues minus costs) earned by an entire product line.

Four Types of Responsibility Centers

Responsibility accounting is a system for evaluating the performance of each responsibility center and its manager. Responsibility accounting performance reports compare plans (budgets) with actions (actual results) for each center. Superiors then evaluate how well each manager: (1) used the budgeted resources to achieve the responsibility center's goals, and thereby (2) controlled the operations for which he or she was responsible.

Exhibit 21-18 on the following page illustrates four types of responsibility centers.

1. **In a cost center, managers are accountable for costs (expenses) only.** Manufacturing operations, such as the CD production lines, are cost centers. The line foreman controls costs by ensuring that employees work efficiently. The foreman is *not* responsible for generating revenues because he or she is not involved in selling the product. The plant manager evaluates the foreman on his or her ability to control *costs* by comparing actual costs to budgeted costs. All else being equal (for example, holding quality constant), the foreman is likely to receive a more favorable evaluation if actual costs are less than budgeted costs.

EXHIBIT 21-18 | **Four Types of Responsibility Centers**

In a **cost center**, such as a production line for CDs, managers are responsible for costs.

In a **revenue center**, such as the Midwest sales region, managers are responsible for generating sales revenue.

In a **profit center**, such as a line of products, managers are responsible for generating income.

In an **investment center**, such as the CD & DVD division, managers are responsible for income and invested capital.

2. **In a revenue center, managers are primarily accountable for revenues.** Examples include the Midwest and Southeast sales regions of businesses that carry Greg's Groovy Tunes products, such as CDs and DVDs. These managers of revenue centers may also be responsible for the costs of their own sales operations. Revenue center performance reports compare actual with budgeted revenues and may include the costs incurred by the revenue center itself. All else being equal, the manager is likely to receive a more favorable evaluation if actual revenues exceed the budget.
3. **In a profit center, managers are accountable for both revenues and costs (expenses) and, therefore, profits.** The (higher-level) manager responsible for the entire CD product line would be accountable for increasing sales revenue *and* controlling costs to achieve the profit goals. Profit center reports include both revenues and expenses to show the profit center's income. Superiors evaluate the manager's performance by comparing actual revenues, expenses, and profits to the budget. All else being equal, the manager is likely to receive a more favorable evaluation if actual profits exceed the budget.
4. **In an investment center, managers are accountable for investments, revenues, and costs (expenses).** Examples include the **Saturn** division of **General Motors** and the North American CD and DVD Division (which includes CDs) of Greg's Groovy Tunes. Managers of investment centers are responsible for: (1) generating sales, (2) controlling expenses, and (3) managing the amount of investment required to earn the income (revenues minus expenses).

Top management often evaluates investment center managers based on return on investment (ROI), residual income, or economic value added (EVA). Chapter 23 explains how these measures are calculated and used. All else being equal, the manager will receive a more favorable evaluation if the division's actual ROI, residual income, or EVA exceeds the amount budgeted.

Responsibility Accounting Performance Reports

Exhibit 21-19 shows how an organization like Greg's Groovy Tunes may assign responsibility.

At the top level, the CEO oversees each of the four divisions. Division managers generally have broad responsibility, including deciding how to use assets to maximize ROI. Most companies consider divisions as *investment centers*.

EXHIBIT 21-19 | **Partial Organization Chart**

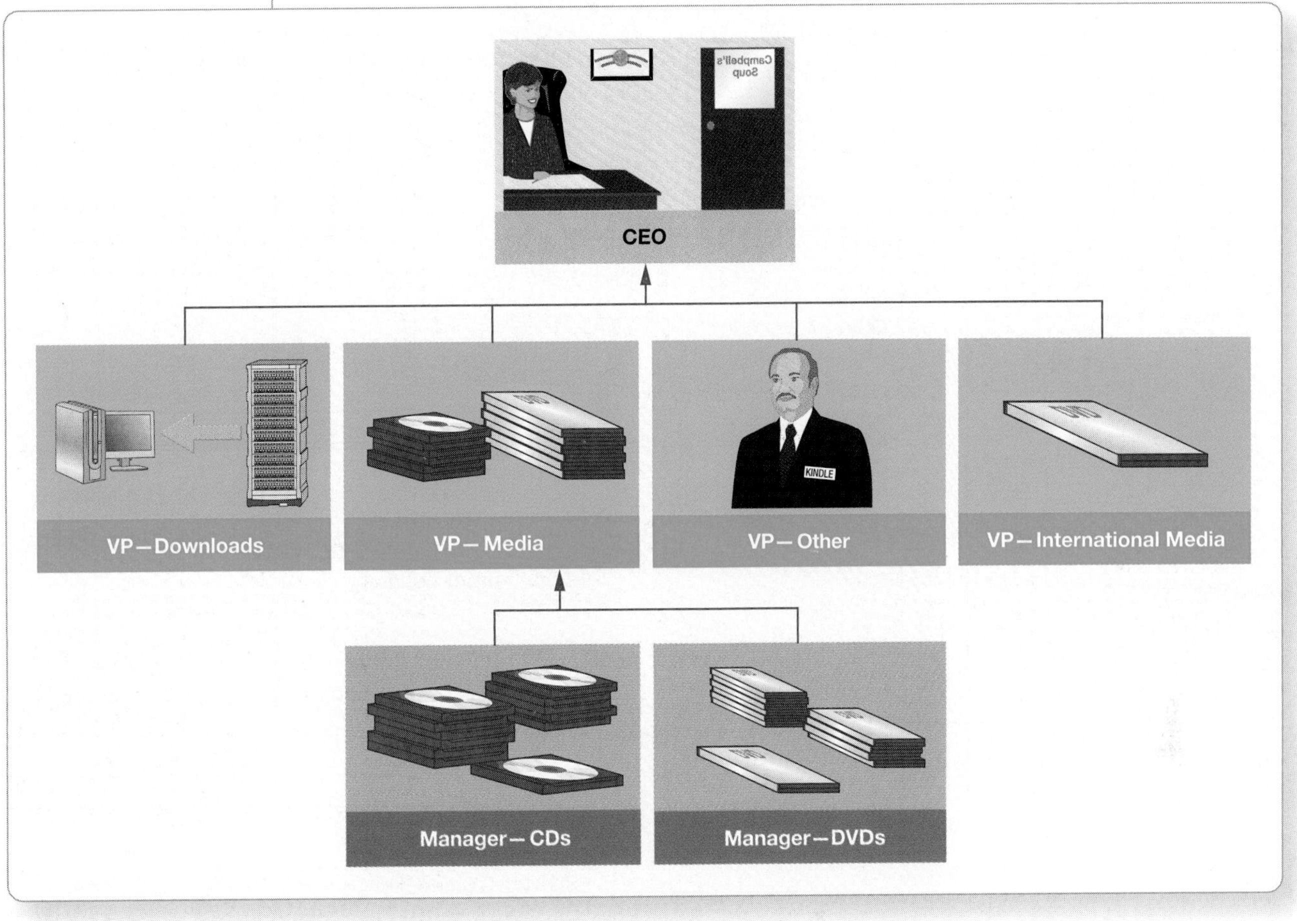

CEO

VP—Downloads | VP—Media | VP—Other | VP—International Media

Manager—CDs | Manager—DVDs

Each division manager supervises all the product lines in that division. Exhibit 21-19 shows that the VP of Media oversees the CD and DVD lines. Product lines are generally considered *profit centers*. Thus, the manager of the CD product line is responsible for evaluating lower-level managers of both

- *cost centers* (such as plants that make CD products) and
- *revenue centers* (such as managers responsible for selling CD products).

Exhibit 21-20 on the next page illustrates responsibility accounting performance reports for each level of management shown in Exhibit 21-19. Exhibit 21-20 uses assumed numbers to illustrate reports like those

- the CEO may use to evaluate divisions.
- the divisional VPs may use to evaluate individual product lines.
- the product-line managers may use to evaluate the development, production, marketing, and distribution of their products.

At each level, the reports compare actual results with the budget.

Start with the lowest level and move to the top. Follow the $25 million budgeted operating income from the CDs product-line report to the report of the VP–Media. The VP's report summarizes the budgeted and actual operating incomes for each of the two product lines he or she supervises.

Now, trace the $70 million budgeted operating income from the VP's report to the CEO's report. The CEO's report includes a summary of each division's budgeted and actual profits, as well as the costs incurred by corporate headquarters, which are not assigned to any of the divisions.

EXHIBIT 21-20 Responsibility Accounting Performance Reports at Various Levels

CEO'S QUARTERLY RESPONSIBILITY REPORT
(in millions of dollars)

Operating Income of Divisions and Corporate Headquarters Expense	Budget	Actual	Variance Favorable/ (Unfavorable)
Downloads	$218	$209	$ (9)
Media	70	84	14
Other	79	87	8
International Media	35	34	(1)
Corporate Headquarters Expense	(33)	(29)	4
Operating Income	$369	$385	$16

VP—MEDIA
QUARTERLY RESPONSIBILITY REPORT
(in millions of dollars)

Operating Income of Product Lines	Budget	Actual	Variance Favorable/ (Unfavorable)
CDs	25	38	13
DVDs	45	46	1
Operating Income	$70	$84	$14

MANAGER—CDs
QUARTERLY RESPONSIBILITY REPORT
(in millions of dollars)

Revenue and Expenses	Budget	Actual	Variance Favorable/ (Unfavorable)
Sales revenue	$ 80	$ 84	$ 4
Cost of goods sold	(36)	(30)	6
Gross profit	44	54	10
Marketing expenses	(12)	(9)	3
Research and development expenses	(2)	(3)	(1)
Other expenses	(5)	(4)	1
Operating income	$ 25	$ 38	$13

Management by Exception

The variances reported in Exhibit 21-20 aid **management by exception**, which directs executives' attention to important differences between actual and budgeted amounts. Look at the CEO's report. The International Media Division's actual operating income of $34 million is very close to the budgeted $35 million. Unless there are other signs of trouble, the CEO will not waste time investigating such a small variance.

In contrast, the Media earned much more profit than budgeted. The CEO will want to know why. Suppose the VP of the division believes a national sales promotion was especially effective. That promotion may be repeated or adapted by other divisions. To identify the reason for exceptional results, so that other parts of the organization may benefit, is one reason why managers investigate large favorable variances (not just large unfavorable ones). Another reason is to ensure that employees are not skimping on ingredients, marketing, or R&D, which could hurt the company's long-term success.

A CEO who received the report at the top of Exhibit 21-20 would likely concentrate on improving the Downloads Division because its actual income fell $9 million below budget. The CEO will want to see which product lines caused the shortfall so that he or she and the VP of the division can work together to correct any problems.

Exhibit 21-20 also shows how summarized data may hide problems. Although the Media Division as a whole performed well, the DVD lines did not perform as well as the CD lines. If the CEO received only the condensed report at the top of the exhibit, he or she would rely on division managers to spot and correct problems in individual product lines.

Not a Question of Blame

Responsibility accounting assigns managers responsibility for their unit's actions and provides a way to evaluate both their individual and their unit's performance. But superiors should not misuse responsibility accounting to find fault or place blame. The question is not "Who is to blame for an unfavorable variance?" Instead, the question is "Who can best explain why a specific variance occurred?" Consider the Downloads Division in Exhibit 21-20. Suppose a tornado devastated the primary production plant. It may be that the remaining plants operated very efficiently, and this efficiency kept the income variance down to $9 million. If so, the Downloads Division and its VP may actually have done a good job.

Other Performance Measures

Top management uses responsibility accounting performance reports to assess each responsibility center's *financial* performance. Top management also often assesses each responsibility center's nonfinancial *operating* performance. Typical nonfinancial performance measures include customer satisfaction ratings, delivery time, product quality, employee expertise, and so forth. Chapter 23 discusses the broader view of performance evaluation, known as the "balanced scorecard." In that chapter, we will look at how managers use both financial and nonfinancial performance measures to form a "balanced view" of each responsibility center's performance.

The "Decision Guidelines" review budgets and how managers use them in responsibility accounting. Study these guidelines before working on Summary Problem 2.

Decision Guidelines

THE MASTER BUDGET AND RESPONSIBILITY ACCOUNTING

Amazon.com's initial strategy was to "get big fast." But without a budget, spending got out of control. So founder and CEO Jeff Bezos added a second strategic goal—to become the world's most cost-efficient, high-quality e-tailer. Today, **Amazon.com's** managers use budgets to help reach both the growth and cost-efficiency goals. Let us consider some of the decisions **Amazon.com** made as it set up its budgeting process.

Decision	Guidelines
• What benefits should **Amazon.com** expect to obtain from developing a budget?	• Requires managers to *plan* how to increase sales and how to cut costs • Promotes *coordination and communication*, such as communicating the importance of the cost-efficiency goal • Provides a *benchmark* that motivates employees and helps managers evaluate how well employees contributed to the sales growth and cost-efficiency goals
• In what order should **Amazon.com's** managers prepare the components of the master budget?	Begin with the *operating budget.* • Start with the *sales budget*, which feeds into all other budgets. • The sales and *ending inventory budgets* determine the *purchases and cost of goods sold budget.* • The sales, cost of goods sold, and *operating expense budgets* determine the *budgeted income statement.* Next, prepare the *capital expenditures budget*. Finally, prepare the *financial budget.* • Start with the *cash budget.* • The cash budget provides the ending cash balance for the *budgeted balance sheet* and the details for the *budgeted statement of cash flows.*
• What extra steps should **Amazon.com** take given the uncertainty of Internet-based sales forecasts?	Prepare a *sensitivity analysis* and project budgeted results at different sales levels.
• How does **Amazon.com** compute budgeted purchases?	$\text{Beginning inventory} + \text{Purchases} - \text{Ending inventory} = \text{Cost of goods sold}$ so, $\text{Purchases} = \text{Cost of goods sold} + \text{Ending inventory} - \text{Beginning inventory}$
• What kind of a responsibility center does each manager supervise?	• *Cost center*: The manager is responsible for costs. • *Revenue center*: The manager is responsible for revenues. • *Profit center*: The manager is responsible for both revenues and costs, and, therefore, profits. • *Investment center*: The manager is responsible for revenues, costs, and the amount of the investment required to earn the income.
• How should **Amazon.com** evaluate managers?	Compare actual performance with the budget for the manager's responsibility center. *Management by exception* focuses on large differences between budgeted and actual results.

Summary Problem 2

Continue the revised Greg's Groovy Tunes illustration from Summary Problem 1. Now that you think July sales will be $40,000 instead of $50,000, as projected in Exhibit 21-7, how will this affect the financial budget?

Requirement

1. Revise the schedule of budgeted cash collections (Exhibit 21-11), the schedule of budgeted cash payments for purchases (Exhibit 21-12), and the schedule of budgeted cash payments for operating expenses (Exhibit 21-13).
2. Prepare a revised cash budget (Exhibit 21-14), a revised budgeted balance sheet at July 31, 2010 (Exhibit 21-15), and a revised budgeted statement of cash flows for the four months ended July 31, 2010 (Exhibit 21-16). *Note*: You need not repeat the parts of the revised schedule that do not change.

Solution

Requirement 1

1. Although not required, this solution repeats the budgeted amounts for April, May, and June. Revised figures appear in color for emphasis.

GREG'S GROOVY TUNES, INC.
Revised—Budgeted Cash Collections from Customers

	April	May	June	July	Total
Cash sales, from revised sales budget	$30,000	$48,000	$36,000	$24,000	
Collections of last month's credit sales, from revised sales budget	16,000*	20,000	32,000	24,000	
Total collections	$46,000	$68,000	$68,000	$48,000	$230,000

*March 31 accounts receivable (Exhibit 21-6)

GREG'S GROOVY TUNES, INC.
Revised—Budgeted Cash Payments for Purchases

	April	May	June	July	Total
50% of last month's purchases, from revised inventory, purchases, and cost of goods sold budget	$16,800*	$25,900	$22,400	$15,400	
50% of this month's purchases, from revised inventory, purchases, and cost of goods sold budget	25,900	22,400	15,400	14,000	
Total payments for purchases	$42,700	$48,300	$37,800	$29,400	$158,200

*March 31 accounts payable (Exhibit 21-6)

GREG'S GROOVY TUNES, INC. Revised—Budgeted Cash Payments for Operating Expenses					
	April	May	June	July	Total
Salary and commissions:					
50% of last month's expenses, from revised operating expenses budget	$ 4,250*	$ 5,000	$ 7,250	$ 5,750	
50% of this month's expenses, from revised operating expenses budget	5,000	7,250	5,750	4,250	
Total salary and commissions	9,250	12,250	13,000	10,000	
Rent expense, from revised operating expenses budget	2,000	2,000	2,000	2,000	
Miscellaneous expenses, from revised operating expenses budget	2,500	4,000	3,000	2,000	
Total payments for operating expenses	$13,750	$18,250	$18,000	$14,000	$64,000

*March 31 salary and commissions payable (Exhibit 21-6)

Requirement 2

GREG'S GROOVY TUNES, INC. Revised Cash Budget Four Months Ending July 31, 2010				
	April	May	June	July
Beginning cash balance	$ 15,000*	$ 10,550	$ 10,410	$ 21,035
Cash collections (revised budgeted cash collections)	46,000	68,000	68,000	48,000
Cash available	$ 61,000	78,550	78,410	69,035
Cash payments:				
Purchases of inventory (revised budgeted cash payments for purchases)	$ 42,700	$ 48,300	$ 37,800	$ 29,400
Operating expenses (revised budgeted cash payments for operating expenses)	13,750	18,250	18,000	14,000
Purchase of delivery truck	3,000	—	—	—
Total cash payments	59,450	66,550	55,800	43,400
(1) Ending cash balance before financing	1,550	12,000	22,610	25,635
Less: Minimum cash balance desired	(10,000)	(10,000)	(10,000)	(10,000)
Cash excess (deficiency)	$ (8,450)	$ 2,000	$ 12,610	$ 15,635
Financing of cash deficiency (see notes *a–c*):				
Borrowing (at end of month)	$ 9,000			
Principal payments (at end of month)		$ (1,500)	$ (1,500)	$ (1,500)
Interest expense (at 12% annually)		(90)	(75)	(60)
(2) Total effects of financing	9,000	(1,590)	(1,575)	(1,560)
Ending cash balance (1) + (2)	$ 10,550	$ 10,410	$ 21,035	$ 24,075

*March 31 cash balance (Exhibit 21-6)

Notes

[a]Borrowing occurs in multiples of $1,000 and only for the amount needed to maintain a minimum cash balance of $10,000.

[b]Monthly principal payments: $9,000 ÷ 6 = $1,500

[c]Interest expense: May: $9,000 × (0.12 × 1/12) = $90; June: ($9,000 – $1,500) × (0.12 × 1/12) = $75; July: ($9,000 – $1,500 – $1,500) × (0.12 × 1/12) = $60

GREG'S GROOVY TUNES, INC.
Revised Budgeted Balance Sheet
July 31, 2010

Assets		
Current assets:		
Cash (revised cash budget)	$ 24,075	
Accounts receivable (revised sales budget)	16,000	
Inventory	42,400	
Prepaid insurance	1,000	
Total current assets		$ 83,475
Plant assets:		
Equipment and fixtures	$ 35,000	
Accumulated depreciation	(14,800)	
Total plant assets		20,200
Total assets		$103,675
Liabilities		
Current liabilities:		
Accounts payable (0.50 × July purchases of $28,000; revised inventory, purchases, and cost of goods sold budget)	$ 14,000	
Short-term note payable	4,500	
Salary and commissions payable (0.50 × July expenses of $8,500; revised operating expenses budget)	4,250	
Total liabilities		$ 22,750
Stockholders' Equity		
Stockholders' equity (beginning balance of $78,950* + $1,975 net income, revised budgeted income statement)		80,925
Total liabilities and stockholders' equity		$103,675

*March 31, 2010, balance sheet (Exhibit 21-6)

GREG'S GROOVY TUNES, INC. **Revised Budgeted Statement of Cash Flows** Four Months Ending July 31, 2010		
Cash flows from operating activities:		
Receipts:		
Collections (revised budgeted cash collections)	$ 230,000	
Total cash receipts		$ 230,000
Payments:		
Purchases of inventory (revised budgeted cash payments for purchases)	(158,200)	
Operating expenses (revised budgeted cash payments for operating expenses)	(64,000)	
Payment of interest expense	(225)	
Total cash payments		(222,425)
Net cash inflow from operating activities		7,575
Cash flows from investing activities:		
Acquisition of delivery truck	$ (3,000)	
Net cash outflow from investing activities		(3,000)
Cash flows from financing activities:		
Proceeds from issuance of notes payable	$ 9,000	
Payment of notes payable	(4,500)	
Net cash inflow from financing activities		4,500
Net increase in cash		$ 9,075
Cash balance, April 1, 2010 (Exhibit 21-6)		15,000
Cash balance, July 31, 2010 (revised cash budget)		$ 24,075

Review The Master Budget and Responsibility Accounting

Accounting Vocabulary

Budgeted Income Statement (p. 1116)
Projects operating income for a period.

Capital Expenditures Budget (p. 1116)
A company s plan for purchases of property, plant, equipment, and other long-term assets.

Cash Budget (p. 1124)
Details how the business expects to go from the beginning cash balance to the desired ending balance. Also called the statement of budgeted cash receipts and payments.

Financial Budget (p. 1117)
The cash budget (cash inflows and outflows), the budgeted period-end balance sheet, and the budgeted statement of cash flows.

Management by Exception (p. 1134)
Directs management's attention to important differences between actual and budgeted amounts.

Master Budget (p. 1116)
The set of budgeted financial statements and supporting schedules for the entire organization. Includes the operating budget, the capital expenditures budget, and the financial budget.

Operating Budget (p. 1116)
Projects sales revenue, cost of goods sold, and operating expenses, leading to the budgeted income statement that projects operating income for the period.

Responsibility Accounting (p. 1131)
A system for evaluating the performance of each responsibility center and its manager.

Responsibility Center (p. 1131)
A part or subunit of an organization whose manager is accountable for specific activities.

Quick Check

1. **Amazon.com** expected to receive which of the following benefits when it started its budgeting process?
   a. The budget provides **Amazon.com's** managers with a benchmark against which to compare actual results for performance evaluation.
   b. The planning required to develop the budget helps managers foresee and avoid potential problems before they occur.
   c. The budget helps motivate employees to achieve **Amazon.com's** sales growth and cost-reduction goals.
   d. All of the above
2. Which of the following is the cornerstone (or most critical element) of the master budget?
   a. The sales budget
   b. The purchases and cost of goods sold budget
   c. The operating expenses budget
   d. The inventory budget
3. The income statement is part of which element of **Amazon.com's** master budget?
   a. The operating budget
   b. The capital expenditures budget
   c. The financial budget
   d. None of the above

   Use the following information to answer Questions 4 through 6. Suppose **Amazon.com** sells one million hardcover books a day at an average price of $37. Assume that **Amazon.com's** purchase price for the books is 60% of the selling price it charges retail customers. **Amazon.com** has no beginning inventory, but it wants to have a three-day supply of ending inventory. Assume that operating expenses are $2 million per day.

4. Compute **Amazon.com's** budgeted sales for the next (seven-day) week.
   a. $273 million
   b. $259 million
   c. $481 million
   d. $155 million
5. Determine **Amazon.com's** budgeted purchases for the next (seven-day) week.
   a. $222 million
   b. $68 million
   c. $160 million
   d. $266 million
6. What is **Amazon.com's** budgeted operating income for a (seven-day) week?
   a. $85 million
   b. $31 million
   c. $90 million
   d. $191 million
7. Which of the following expenses would *not* appear in **Amazon.com's** cash budget?
   a. Wages expense
   b. Depreciation expense
   c. Marketing expense
   d. Interest expense
8. Information Technology has made it easier for **Amazon.com's** managers to perform all of the following tasks *except*
   a. preparing responsibility center performance reports that identify variances between actual and budgeted revenues and costs.
   b. sensitivity analyses.
   c. rolling up individual units' budgets into the companywide budget.
   d. removing slack from the budget.
9. Which of the following managers is at the highest level of the organization?
   a. Revenue center manager
   b. Investment center manager
   c. Profit center manager
   d. Cost center manager
10. Suppose **Amazon.com** budgets $5 million for customer service costs but actually spends $4 million. Which of the following is true?
    a. Management will investigate this $1 million favorable variance to ensure that the cost savings do not reflect skimping on customer service.
    b. Management should investigate every variance, especially unfavorable ones.
    c. Because this $1 million variance is favorable, management does not need to investigate further.
    d. Management will investigate this $1 million unfavorable variance to try to identify and then correct the problem that led to the unfavorable variance.

Answers are given after Apply Your Knowledge (p. 1158).

Assess Your Progress

■ Short Exercises

S21-1 *(L.OBJ. 1)* **Why managers use budgets [5 min]**
Consider the budget for any business.

Requirement

1. Explain how you benefit from preparing the budget.

S21-2 *(L.OBJ. 2)* **Understanding the components of the master budget [5–10 min]**
The following components are included in the reports of the master budget.

a. Budgeted balance sheet
b. Sales budget
c. Capital expenditure budget
d. Budgeted income statement
e. Cash budget
f. Inventory, purchases, and cost of goods sold budget

Requirement

1. List in order of preparation the items of the master budget.

S21-3 *(L.OBJ. 3)* **Preparing an operating budget [5 min]**
Mountaineers sells its rock-climbing shoes worldwide. Mountaineers expects to sell 4,000 pairs of shoes for $165 each in January, and 2,000 pairs of shoes for $220 each in February. All sales are cash only.

Requirement

1. Prepare the sales budget for January and February.

Note: Short Exercise 21-3 must be completed before attempting Short Exercise 21-4.

S21-4 *(L.OBJ. 3)* **Preparing an operating budget [10 min]**
Review your results from S21-3. Mountaineers expects cost of goods sold to average 75% of sales revenue, and the company expects to sell 4,600 pairs of shoes in March for $240 each. Mountaineers' target ending inventory is $18,000 plus 45% of the next month's cost of goods sold.

Requirement

1. Use this information and the sales budget prepared in S21-3 to prepare Mountaineers' inventory, purchases, and cost of goods sold budget for January and February.

Note: Short Exercise 21-3 must be completed before attempting Short Exercise 21-5.

S21-5 *(L.OBJ. 4)* **Preparing a financial budget [15–20 min]**
Refer to the Mountaineers' sales budget that you prepared in S21-3. Now assume that Mountaineers' sales are 20% cash and 80% on credit. Mountaineers' collection history indicates that credit sales are collected as follows:

30% in the month of the sale
60% in the month after the sale
7% two months after the sale
3% never collected

November sales totaled $386,000 and December sales were $399,500.

Requirement

1. Prepare a schedule for the budgeted cash collections for January and February.

S21-6 *(L.OBJ. 4)* **Preparing a financial budget [5–10 min]**
Mountaineers has $8,600 cash on hand on December 1. The company requires a minimum cash balance of $7,400. December cash collections are $548,600. Total cash payments for December are $563,230.

Requirement

1. Prepare a cash budget for December. Will Mountaineers need to borrow cash by the end of December?

S21-7 *(L.OBJ. 5)* **Using sensitivity analysis in budgeting [10–15 min]**
Riverbed Sporting Goods has the following sales budget:

RIVERBED SPORTING GOODS STORE Sales Budget					
	April	May	June	July	April–July Total
Cash sales, 60%	$ 32,400	$ 51,600	$ 36,000	$ 32,400	
Credit sales, 40%	21,600	34,400	24,000	21,600	
Total sales, 100%	$ 54,000	$ 86,000	$ 60,000	$ 54,000	$ 254,000

Suppose June sales are expected to be $40,000 rather than $60,000.

Requirement

1. Revise Riverbed Sporting Goods' sales budget.

S21-8 *(L.OBJ. 6)* **Preparing performance reports for responsibility centers [5 min]**
Consider the following list of responsibility centers and phrases.

A cost center	A revenue center
An investment center	Lower
A profit center	Higher
A responsibility center	

Requirement

1. Fill in the blanks with the phrase that best completes the sentence.

a. The maintenance department at the San Diego Zoo is ________.
b. The concession stand at the San Diego Zoo is ________.
c. The menswear department at Bloomingdale's, which is responsible for buying and selling merchandise, is ________.
d. A production line at a Palm Pilot plant is ________.
e. ________ is any segment of the business whose manager is accountable for specific activities.
f. Gatorade, a division of Quaker Oats, is ________.
g. The sales manager in charge of Nike's northwest sales territory oversees ________.
h. Managers of cost and revenue centers are at ________ levels of the organization than are managers of profit and investment centers.

S21-9 *(L.OBJ. 6)* **Preparing performance reports for responsibility centers [5–10 min]**
Look at the following performance report:

MANAGER – MEXICAN SAUCES Quarterly Responsibility Report (in millions of dollars)			
Revenues and Expenses	**Budget**	**Actual**	**Variance Favorable/ (Unfavorable)**
Sales revenue	$ 79	$ 84	$ 5
Cost of goods sold	(36)	(29)	7
Gross profit	43	55	12
Marketing expenses	(12)	(10)	2
Research and development expenses	(3)	(4)	(1)
Other expenses	(4)	(2)	2
Operating income	$ 24	$ 39	$ 15

Requirement

1. On which variances should the manager of the Mexican sauces product line focus his or her efforts, according to the management by exception principle? For these variances, compute the variance as a percent of the budgeted amount, and suggest some questions the manager may want to investigate.

■ Exercises

E21-10 *(L.OBJ.1)* **Why managers use budgets [15 min]**
Diego Garcia owns a chain of travel goods stores. Last year, his sales staff sold 10,000 suitcases at an average sale price of $150. Variable expenses were 80% of sales revenue, and the total fixed expense was $110,000. This year, the chain sold more expensive product lines. Sales were 8,000 suitcases at an average price of $200. The variable expense percentage and the total fixed expense were the same both years. Garcia evaluates the chain manager by comparing this year's income with last year's income.

Requirement

1. Prepare a performance report for this year, similar to Exhibit 21-4. How would you improve Garcia's performance evaluation system to better analyze this year's results?

E21-11 *(L.OBJ. 2)* **Understanding the components of the master budget [15–20 min]**
Chloe Allred, division manager for Tires Plus, is speaking to the controller, Crystal Thayer, about the budgeting process. Chloe states, "I'm not an accountant, so can you explain the three main parts of the master budget to me and tell me their purpose?"

Requirement

1. Answer Chloe's question.

E21-12 *(L.OBJ. 3)* **Preparing an operating budget [15–20 min]**
Swenson Inc. sells tire rims. Its sales budget for the nine months ended September 30 follows:

	Quarter Ended			Nine–Month
	March 31	June 30	September 30	Total
Cash sales, 30%	$ 30,000	$ 45,000	$ 37,500	$ 112,500
Credits sales, 70% ...	70,000	105,000	87,500	262,500
Total sales, 100%	$ 100,000	$ 150,000	$ 125,000	$ 375,000

In the past, cost of goods sold has been 60% of total sales. The director of marketing and the financial vice president agree that each quarter's ending inventory should not be below $25,000 plus 10% of cost of goods sold for the following quarter. The marketing director expects sales of $200,000 during the fourth quarter. The January 1 inventory was $11,000.

Requirement

1. Prepare an inventory, purchases, and cost of goods sold budget for each of the first three quarters of the year. Compute cost of goods sold for the entire nine-month period.

E21-13 *(L.OBJ. 3)* **Preparing an operating budget [15–20 min]**
Posh International, Inc., is an exotic car dealership. Suppose that its Los Angeles office projects that 2011 quarterly sales will increase by 3% in Quarter 1, by 4% in Quarter 2, by 6% in Quarter 3, and by 5% in Quarter 4. Management expects operating expenses to be 80% of revenues during each of the first two quarters, 79% of revenues during the third quarter, and 81% during the fourth. The office manager expects to borrow $500,000 on July 1, with quarterly principal payments of $10,000 beginning on September 30 and interest paid at an annual rate of 14%. Assume that fourth-quarter 2010 sales were $7,000,000.

Requirement

1. Prepare a budgeted income statement for each of the four quarters of 2011 and for the entire year. Present the 2011 budget as follows:

Quarter 1	Quarter 2	Quarter 3	Quarter 4	Full Year

E21-14 *(L.OBJ. 4)* **Preparing a financial budget [20–30 min]**
Aqua Ole is a distributor of bottled water.

Requirement

1. For each of the Items a. through c., compute the amount of cash receipts or payments Aqua Ole will budget for September. The solution to one item may depend on the answer to an earlier item.

   a. Management expects to sell equipment that cost $22,000 at a gain of $4,000. Accumulated depreciation on this equipment is $7,000.
   b. Management expects to sell 7,800 cases of water in August and 9,100 in September. Each case sells for $13. Cash sales average 30% of total sales, and credit sales make up the rest. Three-fourths of credit sales are collected in the month of sale, with the balance collected the following month.
   c. The company pays rent and property taxes of $4,000 each month. Commissions and other selling expenses average 25% of sales. Agua Ole pays two-thirds of commissions and other selling expenses in the month incurred, with the balance paid in the following month.

E21-15 *(L.OBJ. 4, 5)* **Preparing a financial budget, and using sensitivity analysis in budgeting [15–20 min]**

Lipman Auto Parts, a family-owned auto parts store, began January with $10,300 cash. Management forecasts that collections from credit customers will be $11,400 in January and $14,800 in February. The store is scheduled to receive $5,000 cash on a business note receivable in January. Projected cash payments include inventory purchases ($13,000 in January and $13,600 in February) and operating expenses ($2,700 each month).

Lipman Auto Parts' bank requires a $10,000 minimum balance in the store's checking account. At the end of any month when the account balance dips below $10,000, the bank automatically extends credit to the store in multiples of $1,000. Lipman Auto Parts borrows as little as possible and pays back loans in quarterly installments of $2,000, plus 4% interest on the entire unpaid principal. The first payment occurs three months after the loan.

Requirements

1. Prepare Lipman Auto Parts' cash budget for January and February.
2. How much cash will Lipman Auto Parts borrow in February if collections from customers that month total $13,800 instead of $14,800?

E21-16 *(L.OBJ. 4)* **Preparing a financial budget [20 min]**

You recently began a job as an accounting intern at Ralph Golf Park. Your first task was to help prepare the cash budget for April and May. Unfortunately, the computer with the budget file crashed, and you did not have a backup or even a hard copy. You ran a program to salvage bits of data from the budget file. After entering the following data in the budget, you may have just enough information to reconstruct the budget.

RALPH GOLF PARK Cash Budget April and May	April	May
Beginning cash balance	$ 16,200	$?
Cash collections	?	80,100
Cash from sale of plant assets	0	2,000
Cash available	106,300	?
Cash payments:		
Purchase of inventory	$?	$ 41,600
Operating expenses	47,400	?
Total payments	98,000	?
Ending cash balance before financing	?	27,500
Less: Minimum cash balance desired	(25,000)	(25,000)
Cash excess (deficiency)	$?	$?
Financing of cash deficiency:		
Borrowing (at end of month)	?	?
Principal repayments (at end of month)	?	?
Interest expense	?	?
Total effects of financing	?	?
Ending cash balance	$?	$?

Ralph Golf Park eliminates any cash deficiency by borrowing the exact amount needed from State Street Bank, where the current interest rate is 8%. Ralph Golf Park pays interest on its outstanding debt at the end of each month. The company also repays all borrowed amounts at the end of the month, as cash becomes available.

Requirement

1. Complete the cash budget.

E21-17 *(L.OBJ. 4)* **Preparing a financial budget [25–30 min]**
Consider the following information for Omas.com at March 31, 2011.

a. February 28 inventory balance, $17,780
b. March payments for inventory, $4,400
c. March payments of accounts payable and accrued liabilities, $8,400
d. February 28 accounts payable balance, $10,100
e. February 28 furniture and fixtures balance, $34,600; accumulated depreciation balance $29,870
f. February 28 equity, $29,040
g. March depreciation expense, $600
h. Cost of goods sold, 40% of sales
i. Other March expenses, including income tax, total $7,000, paid in cash
j. February 28 cash balance, $11,500
k. March budgeted credit sales, $12,400
l. February 28 accounts receivable balance, $5,130
m. March cash receipts, $14,600

Requirement

1. Prepare a budgeted balance sheet.

E21-18 *(L.OBJ. 6)* **Preparing performance reports for responsibility centers [5 min]**
Consider the following:

a. The bakery department of a **Publix** supermarket reports income for the current year.
b. **Pace Foods** is a subsidiary of **Campbell Soup Company**.
c. The personnel department of **State Farm Insurance Companies** prepares its budget and subsequent performance report on the basis of its expected expenses for the year.
d. The shopping section of **Burpee.com** reports both revenues and expenses.
e. **Burpee.com**'s investor relations Web site provides operating and financial information to investors and other interested parties.
f. The manager of a **BP** service station is evaluated based on the station's revenues and expenses.
g. A charter airline records revenues and expenses for each airplane each month. Each airplane's performance report shows its ratio of operating income to average book value.
h. The manager of the southwest sales territory is evaluated based on a comparison of current period sales against budgeted sales.

Requirement

1. Identify each responsibility center as a cost center, a revenue center, a profit center, or an investment center.

E21-19 *(L.OBJ. 6)* **Preparing performance reports for responsibility centers [15–20 min]**
Web Touch is a Fresno company that sells cell phones and PDAs on the Web. Web Touch has assistant managers for its digital and video cell phone operations. These assistant managers report to the manager of the total cell phone product line, who,

with the manager of PDAs, reports to the manager for all sales of handheld devices, Mary Burton. Burton received the following data for September 2011 operations:

	Cell Phones		
	Digital	Video	PDAs
Revenues, budget	$ 202,000	$ 800,000	$ 400,000
Expenses, budget	143,000	420,000	275,000
Revenues, actual	213,000	890,000	350,000
Expenses, actual	130,000	440,000	260,000

Requirement

1. Arrange the data in a performance report similar to Exhibit 21-20. Show September results, in thousands of dollars, for digital cell phones, for the total cell phone product line, and for all devices. Should Burton investigate the performance of digital cell phone operations?

Problems (Group A)

P21-20A *(L.OBJ. 1, 2, 6)* **Why managers use budgets, understanding the components of the master budget, and preparing performance reports for responsibility centers [50–60 min]**

Doggy World operates a chain of pet stores in the Midwest. The manager of each store reports to the regional manager, who, in turn, reports to the headquarters in Milwaukee, Wisconsin. The *actual* income statements for the Dayton store, the Ohio region (including the Dayton store), and the company as a whole (including the Ohio region) for July 2011 are as follows:

DOGGY WORLD
Income Statement
For the month ended July 31, 2011

	Dayton	Ohio	Companywide
Revenue	$ 158,400	$ 1,760,000	$ 4,400,000
Expenses:			
Regional manager/headquarters office	$ –	$ 58,000	$ 122,000
Cost of materials	85,536	880,000	1,760,000
Salary expense	41,184	440,000	1,100,000
Depreciation expense	7,800	91,000	439,000
Utilities expense	4,000	46,600	264,000
Rent expense	2,500	34,500	178,000
Total expenses	141,020	1,550,100	3,863,000
Operating income	$ 17,380	$ 209,900	$ 537,000

Budgeted amounts for July were as follows:

DOGGY WORLD **Budgeted Income Statement** For the month ended July 31, 2011			
	Dayton	Ohio	Companywide
Revenue	$ 173,400	$ 1,883,000	$ 4,650,000
Expenses:			
Regional manager/headquarters office	$ –	$ 64,600	$ 124,000
Cost of materials	91,902	1,035,650	2,092,500
Salary expense	41,616	470,750	1,162,500
Depreciation expense	7,800	87,500	446,000
Utilities expense	4,900	54,600	274,000
Rent expense	3,400	32,700	169,000
Total expenses	149,618	1,745,800	4,268,000
Operating income	$ 23,782	$ 137,200	$ 382,000

Requirements

1. Prepare a report for July 2011 that shows the performance of the Dayton store, the Ohio region, and the company as a whole. Follow the format of Exhibit 21-20.
2. As the Ohio regional manager, would you investigate the Dayton store on the basis of this report? Why or why not?
3. Should Doggy World prepare the master budget? Briefly discuss the benefits of budgeting. Base your discussion on Doggy World's performance report.

P21-21A *(L.OBJ. 2)* **Preparing an operating budget [30 min]**
The budget committee of Clipboard Office Supply has assembled the following data. As the business manager, you must prepare the budgeted income statements for May and June 2011.

Requirement

a. Sales in April were $50,000. You forecast that monthly sales will increase 2.0% in May and 2.4% in June.

b. Clipboard maintains inventory of $9,000 plus 25% of the sales revenue budgeted for the following month. Monthly purchases average 50% of sales revenue in that same month. Actual inventory on April 30 is $13,000. Sales budgeted for July are $65,000.

c. Monthly salaries amount to $3,000. Sales commissions equal 4% of sales for that month. Combine salaries and commissions into a single figure.

d. Other monthly expenses are as follows:

Rent expense	$2,600, paid as incurred
Depreciation expense	$300
Insurance expense	$200, expiration of prepaid amount
Income tax	20% of operating income

1. Prepare Clipboard Office Supply's budgeted income statements for May and June. Show cost of goods sold computations. Round *all* amounts to the nearest $100. (Round amounts ending in $50 or more upward, and amounts ending in less than $50 downward.) For example, budgeted May sales are $51,000 ($50,000 × 1.02), and June sales are $52,200 ($51,000 × 1.024).

Note: Problem 21-21A must be completed before attempting Problem 21-22A.

P21-22A *(L.OBJ. 4)* **Preparing a financial budget [30 min]**

Refer to P21-21A. Clipboard Office Supply's sales are 75% cash and 25% credit. (Use the rounded sales values.) Credit sales are collected in the month after sale. Inventory purchases are paid 25% in the month of purchase and 75% the following month. Salaries and sales commissions are also paid half in the month earned and half the next month. Income tax is paid at the end of the year.

The April 30, 2011, balance sheet showed the following balances:

Cash	$ 25,000
Accounts payable	53,000
Salaries and commissions payable	2,500

Requirements

1. Prepare schedules of (a) budgeted cash collections, (b) budgeted cash payments for purchases, and (c) budgeted cash payments for operating expenses. Show amounts for each month and totals for May and June. *Round* your computations to the nearest dollar.
2. Prepare a cash budget similar to Exhibit 21-14. If no financing activity took place, what is the budgeted cash balance on June 30, 2011?

P21-23A *(L.OBJ. 4)* **Preparing a financial budget [50–60 min]**

Box Printing of Baltimore has applied for a loan. **Bank of America** has requested a budgeted balance sheet at April 30, 2011, and a budgeted statement of cash flows for April. As Box Printing's controller, you have assembled the following information:

a. March 31 equipment balance, $80,900; accumulated depreciation, $12,900
b. April capital expenditures of $16,900 budgeted for cash purchase of equipment
c. April depreciation expense, $600
d. Cost of goods sold, 45% of sales
e. Other April operating expenses, including income tax, total $33,000, 40% of which will be paid in cash and the remainder accrued at the end of April
f. March 31 stockholders' equity, $136,700
g. March 31 cash balance, $50,200
h. April budgeted sales, $84,000, 60% of which is for cash; of the remaining 40%, half will be collected in April and half in May
i. April cash collections on March sales, $15,300
j. April cash payments of March 31 liabilities incurred for March purchases of inventory, $8,600
k. March 31 inventory balance, $11,800
l. April purchases of inventory, $10,800 for cash and $37,200 on credit. Half the credit purchases will be paid in April and half in May.

Requirements

1. Prepare the budgeted balance sheet for Box Printing at April 30, 2011. Show separate computations for cash, inventory, and stockholders' equity balances.
2. Prepare the budgeted statement of cash flows for April.
3. Suppose that Box Printing has become aware of more efficient (and more expensive) equipment than it budgeted for purchase in April. What is the total amount of cash available for equipment purchases in April, before financing, if the minimum desired ending cash balance is $21,000? (For this requirement, disregard the $16,900 initially budgeted for equipment purchases.)

Note: Problem 21-23A must be completed before attempting Problem 21-24A.

P21-24A *(L.OBJ. 4, 5)* **Preparing a financial budget, and using sensitivity analysis in budgeting [30–40 min]**

Refer to P21-23A. Before granting a loan to Box Printing, **Bank of America** asks for a sensitivity analysis assuming April sales are only $56,000 rather than the $84,000 originally budgeted. (While the cost of goods sold will change, assume that purchases, depreciation, and the other operating expenses will remain the same as in P21-23A.)

Requirements

1. Prepare a revised budgeted balance sheet for Box Printing, showing separate computations for cash, inventory, and owners' equity balances.
2. Suppose Box Printing has a minimum desired cash balance of $21,000. Will the company need to borrow cash in April?
3. In this sensitivity analysis, sales declined by 33 1/3% ($28,000 ÷ $84,000). Is the decline in expenses and income more or less than 33 1/3%? Explain why.

Problems (Group B)

P21-25B *(L.OBJ. 1, 2, 6)* **Why managers use budgets, understanding the components of the master budget, and preparing performance reports for responsibility centers [50–60 min]**

Cat World operates a chain of pet stores in the Midwest. The manager of each store reports to the regional manager, who, in turn, reports to the headquarters in Milwaukee, Wisconsin. The *actual* income statements for the Dayton store, the Ohio region (including the Dayton store), and the company as a whole (including the Ohio region) for July 2011 are as follows:

CAT WORLD
Income Statements
Month Ended July 31, 2011

	Dayton	Ohio	Companywide
Revenue	$ 162,000	$ 1,800,000	$ 4,500,000
Expenses:			
Regional manager/headquarters office	$ –	$ 56,000	$ 110,000
Cost of materials	87,480	900,000	1,800,000
Salary expense	42,120	450,000	1,125,000
Depreciation expense	7,300	95,000	438,000
Utilities expense	4,200	46,300	264,000
Rent expense	2,500	34,900	175,000
Total expenses	143,600	1,582,200	3,912,000
Operating income	$ 18,400	$ 217,800	$ 588,000

Budgeted amounts for July were as follows:

CAT WORLD
Budgeted Income Statements
Month Ended July 31, 2011

	Dayton	Ohio	Companywide
Revenue	$ 176,000	$ 1,923,000	$ 4,750,000
Expenses:			
Regional manager/headquarters office	$ –	$ 62,600	$ 112,000
Cost of materials	93,280	1,057,650	2,137,500
Salary expense	42,240	480,750	1,187,500
Depreciation expense	7,300	87,500	449,000
Utilities expense	4,700	54,800	271,000
Rent expense	3,800	32,700	173,000
Total expenses	151,320	1,776,000	4,330,000
Operating income	$ 24,680	$ 147,000	$ 420,000

Requirements

1. Prepare a report for July 2011 that shows the performance of the Dayton store, the Ohio region, and the company as a whole. Follow the format of Exhibit 21-20.
2. As the Ohio regional manager, would you investigate the Dayton store on the basis of this report? Why or why not?
3. Should Cat World prepare the master budget? Briefly discuss the benefits of budgeting. Base your discussion on Cat World's performance report.

P21-26B *(L.OBJ. 3)* **Preparing an operating budget [30 min]**
The budget committee of Omaha Office Supply has assembled the following data. As the business manager, you must prepare the budgeted income statements for May and June 2011.

a. Sales in April were $42,000. You forecast that monthly sales will increase 2.0% in May and 2.4% in June.
b. Omaha maintains inventory of $10,000 plus 25% of the sales revenue budgeted for the following month. Monthly purchases average 50% of sales revenue in that same month. Actual inventory on April 30 is $13,000. Sales budgeted for July are $70,000.
c. Monthly salaries amount to $4,000. Sales commissions equal 4% of sales for that month. Combine salaries and commissions into a single figure.
d. Other monthly expenses are as follows:

Rent expense	$2,800, paid as incurred
Depreciation expense	$600
Insurance expense	$300, expiration of prepaid amount
Income tax	20% of operating income

Requirement

1. Prepare Omaha Office Supply's budgeted income statements for May and June. Show cost of goods sold computations. Round *all* amounts to the nearest $100. (Round amounts ending in $50 or more upward, and amounts ending in less than $50 downward.) For example, budgeted May sales are $42,800 ($42,000 × 1.02), and June sales are $43,800 ($42,800 × 1.024).

Note: Problem 21-26B must be completed before attempting Problem 21-27B.

P21-27B *(L.OBJ. 4)* **Preparing a financial budget [30 min]**
Refer to P21-26B. Omaha Office Supply's sales are 75% cash and 25% credit. (Use the rounded sales values.) Credit sales are collected in the month after the sale. Inventory purchases are paid 25% in the month of purchase and 75% the following month. Salaries and sales commissions are also paid half in the month earned and half the next month. Income tax is paid at the end of the year.

The April 30, 2011, balance sheet showed the following balances:

Cash	$ 25,000
Accounts payable	50,000
Salaries and commissions payable	2,850

Requirements

1. Prepare schedules of: (a) budgeted cash collections, (b) budgeted cash payments for purchases, and (c) budgeted cash payments for operating expenses. Show amounts for each month and totals for May and June. *Round* your computations to the nearest dollar. Sales in April were $42,000.
2. Prepare a cash budget similar to Exhibit 21-14. If no financing activity took place, what is the budgeted cash balance on June 30, 2011?

P21-28B *(L.OBJ. 4)* **Preparing a financial budget [50–60 min]**

Note Printing of Baltimore has applied for a loan. **Bank of America** has requested a budgeted balance sheet at April 30, 2011, and a budgeted statement of cash flows for April. As Note Printing's controller, you have assembled the following information:

a. March 31 equipment balance, $80,500; accumulated depreciation, $12,100
b. April capital expenditures of $16,500, budgeted for cash purchase of equipment
c. April depreciation expense, $600
d. Cost of goods sold, 55% of sales
e. Other April operating expenses, including income tax, total $35,000, 40% of which will be paid in cash and the remainder accrued at the end of April
f. March 31 stockholders' equity, $138,600
g. March 31 cash balance, $50,900
h. April budgeted sales, $89,000, 60% of which is for cash; of the remaining 40%, half will be collected in April and half in May
i. April cash collections on March sales, $15,300
j. April cash payments of March 31 liabilities incurred for March purchases of inventory, $7,900
k. March 31 inventory balance, $11,900
l. April purchases of inventory, $10,700 for cash and $37,000 on credit. Half the credit purchases will be paid in April and half in May.

Requirements

1. Prepare the budgeted balance sheet for Note Printing at April 30, 2011. Show separate computations for cash, inventory, and stockholders' equity balances.
2. Prepare the budgeted statement of cash flows for April.
3. Suppose that Note Printing has become aware of more efficient (and more expensive) equipment than it budgeted for purchase in April. What is the total amount of cash available for equipment purchases in April, before financing, if the minimum desired ending cash balance is $12,000? (For this requirement, disregard the $16,500 initially budgeted for equipment purchases.)

Note: Problem 21-28B must be completed before attempting Problem 21-29B.

P21-29B *(L.OBJ. 4, 5)* **Preparing a financial budget, and using sensitivity analysis in budgeting [30–40 min]**

Refer to P21-28B. Before granting a loan to Note Printing, **Bank of America** asks for a sensitivity analysis assuming that April sales are only $59,350 rather than the $89,000 originally budgeted. (While the cost of goods sold will change, assume that purchases, depreciation, and the other operating expenses will remain the same as in P21-28B.)

Requirements

1. Prepare a revised budgeted balance sheet for Note Printing, showing separate computations for cash, inventory, and stockholders' equity balances.
2. Suppose Note Printing has a minimum desired cash balance of $19,000. Will the company need to borrow cash in April?
3. In this sensitivity analysis, sales declined by 33 1/3% (29,650 ÷ $89,000). Is the decline in expenses and income more or less than 33 1/3%? Explain why.

Continuing Exercise

E21-30 This exercise continues the Sherman Lawn Service, Inc., situation from Exercise 20-35 of Chapter 20. Sherman Lawn Service is projecting sales for April of $20,000. May's sales will be 5% higher than April's. June's sales are expected to be 6% higher than May's.

Requirement

1. Prepare a sales budget for the quarter ended June 30.

Continuing Problem

P21-31 This problem continues the Haupt Consulting, Inc., situation from P20-36 of Chapter 20. Assume Haupt Consulting began January with $10,000 cash. Management forecasts that collections from credit customers will be $50,000 in January and $53,500 in February. Projected cash payments include equipment purchases ($18,000 in January and $40,400 in February) and operating expenses ($5,000 each month).

Haupt's bank requires a $25,000 minimum balance in the store's checking account. At the end of any month when the account balance dips below $25,000, the bank automatically extends credit to the store in multiples of $5,000. Haupt borrows as little as possible and pays back loans in each month in $1,000 increments, plus 8% interest on the entire unpaid principal. The first payment occurs one month after the loan.

Requirements

1. Prepare Haupt Consulting's cash budget for January and February.
2. How much cash will Haupt borrow in February if collections from customers that month total $30,000 instead of $53,500?

Apply Your Knowledge

Decision Cases

Case 1. Donna Tse has recently accepted the position of assistant manager at Cycle World, a bicycle store in St. Louis. She has just finished her accounting courses. Cycle World's manager and owner, Jeff Towry, asks Tse to prepare a budgeted income statement for 2011 based on the information he has collected. Tse's budget follows:

CYCLE WORLD Budgeted Income Statement For the Year Ending July 31, 2011		
Sales revenue		$244,000
Cost of goods sold		177,000
Gross profit		67,000
Operating expenses:		
Salary and commission expense	$ 46,000	
Rent expense	8,000	
Depreciation expense	2,000	
Insurance expense	800	
Miscellaneous expenses	12,000	68,800
Operating loss		(1,800)
Interest expense		(225)
Net loss		$ (2,025)

Requirement

1. Tse does not want to give Towry this budget without making constructive suggestions for steps Towry could take to improve expected performance. Write a memo to Towry outlining your suggestions.

Case 2. Each autumn, as a hobby, Anne Magnuson weaves cotton place mats to sell through a local craft shop. The mats sell for $20 per set of four. The shop charges a 10% commission and remits the net proceeds to Magnuson at the end of December. Magnuson has woven and sold 25 sets each of the last two years. She has enough cotton in inventory to make another 25 sets. She paid $7 per set for the cotton. Magnuson uses a four-harness loom that she purchased for cash exactly two years ago. It is depreciated at the rate of $10 per month. The accounts payable relate to the cotton inventory and are payable by September 30.

Magnuson is considering buying an eight-harness loom so that she can weave more intricate patterns in linen. The new loom costs $1,000; it would be depreciated at $20 per month. Her bank has agreed to lend her $1,000 at 18% interest, with $200 principal plus accrued interest payable each December 31. Magnuson believes she can weave 15 linen place mat sets in time for the Christmas rush if she does not weave any cotton mats. She predicts that each linen set will sell for $50. Linen costs $18 per set. Magnuson's supplier will sell her linen on credit, payable December 31.

Magnuson plans to keep her old loom whether or not she buys the new loom. The balance sheet for her weaving business at August 31, 2011, is as follows:

ANNE MAGNUSON, WEAVER Balance Sheet August 31, 2011			
Current assets:		Current liabilities:	
Cash	$ 25	Accounts payable	$ 74
Inventory of cotton	175		
	200		
Fixed assets:			
Loom	500	Stockholders' equity	386
Accumulated depreciation	(240)		
	260		
Total assets	$ 460	Total liabilities and owner's equity	$460

Requirements

1. Prepare a cash budget for the four months ending December 31, 2011, for two alternatives: weaving the place mats in cotton using the existing loom, and weaving the place mats in linen using the new loom. For each alternative, prepare a budgeted income statement for the four months ending December 31, 2011, and a budgeted balance sheet at December 31, 2011.
2. On the basis of financial considerations only, what should Magnuson do? Give your reason.
3. What nonfinancial factors might Magnuson consider in her decision?

Ethical Issue

Residence Suites operates a regional hotel chain. Each hotel is operated by a manager and an assistant manager/controller. Many of the staff who run the front desk, clean the rooms, and prepare the breakfast buffet work part-time or have a second job so turnover is high.

Assistant manager/controller Terry Dunn asked the new bookkeeper to help prepare the hotel's master budget. The master budget is prepared once a year and is submitted to company headquarters for approval. Once approved, the master budget is used to evaluate the hotel's performance. These performance evaluations affect hotel managers' bonuses and they also affect company decisions on which hotels deserve extra funds for capital improvements.

When the budget was almost complete, Dunn asked the bookkeeper to increase amounts budgeted for labor and supplies by 15%. When asked why, Dunn responded that hotel manager

Clay Murry told her to do this when she began working at the hotel. Murry explained that this budgetary cushion gave him flexibility in running the hotel. For example, because company headquarters tightly controls capital improvement funds, Murry can use the extra money budgeted for labor and supplies to replace broken televisions or pay "bonuses" to keep valued employees. Dunn initially accepted this explanation because she had observed similar behavior at the hotel where she worked previously.

Requirements

Put yourself in Dunn's position. In deciding how to deal with the situation, answer the following questions:

1. What is the ethical issue?
2. What are my options?
3. What are the possible consequences?
4. What should I do?

■ Team Project

Xellnet provides e-commerce software for the pharmaceuticals industry. Xellnet is organized into several divisions. A companywide planning committee sets general strategy and goals for the company and its divisions, but each division develops its own budget.

Lonnie Draper is the new division manager of wireless communications software. His division has two departments: Development and Sales. Chad Sanchez manages the 20 or so programmers and systems specialists typically employed in the development department to create and update the division's software applications. Liz Smith manages the sales department.

Xellnet considers the divisions to be investment centers. To earn his bonus next year, Draper must achieve a 30% return on the $3 million invested in his division. Within the wireless division, development is a cost center, while sales is a revenue center.

Budgeting is in progress. Sanchez met with his staff and is now struggling with two sets of numbers. Alternative A is his best estimate of next year's costs. However, unexpected problems can arise when writing software, and finding competent programmers is an ongoing challenge. He knows that Draper was a programmer before he earned an MBA so he should be sensitive to this uncertainty. Consequently, he is thinking of increasing his budgeted costs (Alternative B). His department's bonuses largely depend on whether the department meets its budgeted costs.

XELLNET
Wireless Division
Development Budget 2011

	Alternative A	Alternative B
Salaries expense (including overtime and part time)	$2,400,000	$2,640,000
Software expense	120,000	132,000
Travel expense	65,000	71,500
Depreciation expense	255,000	255,000
Miscellaneous expense	100,000	110,000
Total expense	$2,940,000	$3,208,500

Liz Smith is also struggling with her sales budget. Companies have made their initial investments in communications software so it is harder to win new customers. If things go well, she believes her sales team can maintain the level of growth achieved over the last few years. This is Alternative A in the sales budget. However, if Smith is too optimistic, sales may fall short of the budget. If this happens, her team will not receive bonuses. Therefore, Smith is considering reducing the sales numbers and submitting Alternative B.

XELLNET Wireless Division Sales Budget 2011		
	Alternative A	Alternative B
Sales revenue	$5,000,000	$4,500,000
Salaries expense	360,000	360,000
Travel expense	240,000	210,500

Split your team into three groups. Each group should meet separately before the entire team meets.

Requirements

1. The first group plays the role of development manager Chad Sanchez. Before meeting with the entire team, determine which set of budget numbers you are going to present to Lonnie Draper. Write a memo supporting your decision. Use the format shown in Decision Case 1. Give this memo to the third group before the team meeting.
2. The second group plays the role of sales manager Liz Smith. Before meeting with the entire team, determine which set of budget numbers you are going to present to Lonnie Draper. Write a memo supporting your decision. Use the format shown in Decision Case 1. Give this memo to the third group before the team meeting.
3. The third group plays the role of division manager Lonnie Draper. Before meeting with the entire team, use the memos that Sanchez and Smith provided you to prepare a division budget based on the sales and development budgets. Your divisional overhead costs (additional costs beyond those incurred by the development and sales departments) are approximately $390,000. Determine whether the wireless division can meet its targeted 30% return on assets given the budgeted alternatives submitted by your department managers.

During the meeting of the entire team, the group playing Draper presents the division budget and considers its implications. Each group should take turns discussing its concerns with the proposed budget. The team as a whole should consider whether the division budget must be revised. The team should prepare a report that includes the division budget and a summary of the issues covered in the team meeting.

Quick Check Answers

1. *d* 2. *a* 3. *a* 4. *b* 5. *a* 6. *c* 7. *b* 8. *d* 9. *b* 10. *a*

For online homework, exercises, and problems that provide you immediate feedback, please visit www.myaccountinglab.com.

22 Flexible Budgets and Standard Costs

Learning Objectives/Success Keys

1. Prepare a flexible budget for the income statement
2. Prepare an income statement performance report
3. Identify the benefits of standard costs and learn how to set standards
4. Compute standard cost variances for direct materials and direct labor
5. Analyze manufacturing overhead in a standard cost system
6. Record transactions at standard cost and prepare a standard cost income statement

Suppose you bought soft drinks for a party. Your budget was $30, but you actually spent $35. You need to stay within your budget in the future. It would be helpful to know *why* you spent more than the $30 budget. Here are some possibilities:

1. If each case of drinks costs more than the budget, then you might
   - find a cheaper price at a place like **Wal-mart**, or wait for the drinks to go on sale.
   - buy less-expensive store-brand drinks.

2. If you bought a larger quantity of soft drinks than you budgeted, why did you need this larger quantity?
    - If too many folks came to the party, next time you can restrict the invitation list.
    - If each guest drank more than you budgeted, perhaps you can cut per-guest consumption, start the party later, end it earlier, or reduce the salty snacks.
3. If the budget for soft drinks was too low, you may need to increase the budget.

This chapter builds on your knowledge of budgeting. A budget variance is just the difference between an actual amount and a budgeted figure. This chapter shows how managers use variances to operate a business. It is important to know *why* actual costs differ from the budget. That will enable you to identify problems and decide what action to take.

In this chapter, you will learn how to figure out *why* actual results differ from your budget. This is the first step in correcting problems. You will also learn to use another management tool—standard costing.

How Managers Use Flexible Budgets

1 Prepare a flexible budget for the income statement

Let us revisit Smart Touch Learning, Inc. At the beginning of the year, Smart Touch's managers prepared a master budget. The master budget is a **static budget,** which means that it is prepared for only *one* level of sales volume. The static budget does not change after it is developed.

Exhibit 22-1 shows that Smart Touch's actual operating income for the month of June is $16,000. This is $4,000 higher than expected from the static budget. This is a $4,000 favorable variance for June operating income. A **variance** is the difference between an actual amount and the budget. The variances in the third column of Exhibit 22-1 are as follows:

- Favorable (F) if an actual amount increases operating income
- Unfavorable (U) if an actual amount decreases operating income

EXHIBIT 22-1 | **Actual Results Versus Static Budget**

SMART TOUCH LEARNING, INC.
Comparison of Actual Results with Static Budget
Month Ended June 30, 2010

	Actual Results	Static Budget	Variance
Output units	10,000	8,000	2,000 F
Sales revenue	$ 121,000	$ 96,000	$ 25,000 F
Cost	(105,000)	(84,000)	(21,000) U
Operating income	$ 16,000	$ 12,000	$ 4,000 F

Smart Touch Learning's variance for operating income is favorable because Smart Touch sold 10,000 learning DVDs rather than the 8,000 DVDs it budgeted to sell during June. But there is more to this story. Smart Touch needs a flexible budget to show *why* operating income was favorable during June. Let us see how to prepare and use a flexible budget.

What Is a Flexible Budget?

The report in Exhibit 22-1 is hard to analyze because the static budget is based on 8,000 DVDs, but the actual results are for 10,000 DVDs. This report raises more questions than it answers—for example,

- why did the $21,000 unfavorable cost variance occur?
- did workers waste materials?
- did the cost of materials suddenly increase?
- how much of the additional cost arose because Smart Touch sold 10,000 rather than 8,000 DVDs?

We need a flexible budget to help answer these questions.

A **flexible budget** summarizes costs and revenues for several different volume levels within a relevant range. Flexible budgets separate variable costs from fixed costs; it is the variable costs that put the "*flex*" in the flexible budget. To create a flexible budget, you need to know the following:

- Budgeted selling price per unit
- Variable cost per unit
- Total fixed costs
- Different volume levels within the relevant range

Exhibit 22-2 is a flexible budget for Smart Touch's revenues and costs that shows what will happen if sales reach 5,000, 8,000, or 10,000 DVDs during June. The budgeted sale price per DVD is $12. Budgeted variable costs (such as direct materials and direct labor) are $8 per DVD, and budgeted fixed costs total $20,000. The formula for total cost is as follows:

$$\text{Total cost} = \left(\begin{matrix}\text{Number of}\\ \text{output units}\end{matrix} \times \begin{matrix}\text{Variable cost}\\ \text{per output unit}\end{matrix}\right) + \text{Total fixed cost}$$

EXHIBIT 22-2 | **Flexible Budget**

SMART TOUCH LEARNING, INC.
Flexible Budget
Month Ended June 30, 2010

	Flexible Budget per Output Units	Output Units (DVDs sold) 5,000	8,000	10,000
Sales revenue	$12	$60,000	$96,000	$120,000
Variable costs	$ 8	40,000	64,000	80,000
Fixed costs*		20,000	20,000	20,000
Total costs		60,000	84,000	100,000
Operating income		$ 0	$12,000	$ 20,000

*Fixed costs are usually given as a total amount rather than as a cost per unit.

Notice in Exhibit 22-2 that sales revenue and variable costs increase as more DVDs are sold. But fixed costs remain constant regardless of the number of DVDs sold within the relevant range of 5,000–10,000 DVDs. Remember: *The cost formula applies only to a specific relevant range.* Why? Because fixed costs and the variable cost per DVD may change outside this range. In our example, Smart Touch's relevant range is 5,000–10,000 DVDs. If the company sells 12,000 DVDs it will have to rent additional equipment, so fixed costs will exceed $20,000. Smart Touch will also have to pay workers for overtime pay, so the variable cost per DVD will be more than $8.

Stop & Think...

Assume you are a waiter or waitress. Each night, you cannot be sure how much you will receive in tips from your customers. The more tips you receive, the more income you have to spend on gas, CDs, or possibly saving for a vacation. Informally, you probably figure in your head each night how much you receive in average tips and of that amount, how much you want to save or spend. The flexible budget is just a formalization of that same process for a business.

Using The Flexible Budget: Why Do Actual Results Differ From The Static Budget?

2 Prepare an income statement performance report

It is not enough to know that a variance occurred. That is like knowing you have a fever. The doctor needs to know *why* your temperature is above normal.

Managers must know *why* a variance occurred in order to pinpoint problems and take corrective action. As you can see in Exhibit 22-1, the static budget underestimated both sales and total costs. The variance in Exhibit 22-1 is called a static budget variance because actual activity differed from what was expected in the static budget. To develop more useful information, managers divide the static budget variance into two broad categories:

- **Sales volume variance**—arises because the number of units actually sold differed from the number of units on which the static budget was based.
- **Flexible budget variance**—arises because the company had more or less revenue, or more or less cost, than expected for the *actual* level of output.

Exhibit 22-3 diagrams these variances.

EXHIBIT 22-3 The Static Budget Variance: The Sales Volume Variance and the Flexible Budget Variance

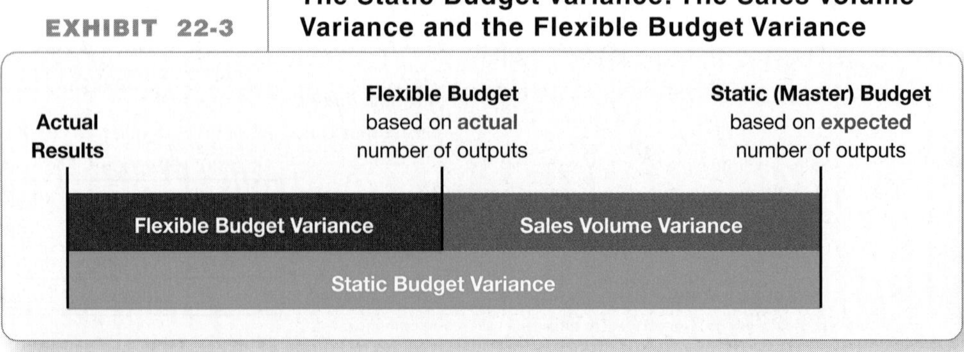

Following are the formulas for computing the two variances:

$$\text{Sales Volume Variance} = \begin{array}{c}\text{Static (Master) Budget}\\\text{(for the number of units}\\\text{expected to be sold}\\\text{8,000 DVDs)}\end{array} - \begin{array}{c}\text{Flexible Budget}\\\text{(for the number of units}\\\text{actually sold}\\\text{10,000 DVDs)}\end{array}$$

$$\text{Flexible Budget Variance} = \begin{array}{c}\text{Flexible Budget}\\\text{(for the number of units}\\\text{actually sold}\\\text{10,000 DVDs)}\end{array} - \begin{array}{c}\text{Actual Results}\\\text{(for the number of units}\\\text{actually sold}\\\text{10,000 DVDs)}\end{array}$$

We have seen that Smart Touch budgeted for 8,000 DVDs during June. Actual production was 10,000 DVDs. We will need to compute a sales volume variance for Smart Touch, and there may also be a flexible budget variance. Exhibit 22-4 is Smart Touch's income statement performance report for June.

EXHIBIT 22-4 | **Income Statement Performance Report**

SMART TOUCH LEARNING, INC.
Income Statement Performance Report
Month Ended June 30, 2010

	1 Actual Results at Actual Prices	2 (1) – (3) Flexible Budget Variance	3 Flexible Budget for Actual Number of Output Units*	4 (3) – (5) Sales Volume Variance	5 Static (Master) Budget*
Output Units	10,000	0	10,000	2,000 F	8,000
Sales revenue	$121,000	$1,000 F	$120,000	$24,000 F	$96,000
Variable costs	83,000	3,000 U	80,000	16,000 U	64,000
Fixed costs	22,000	2,000 U	20,000	0	20,000
Total costs	105,000	5,000 U	100,000	16,000 U	84,000
Operating income	$ 16,000	$4,000 U	$ 20,000	$ 8,000 F	$12,000

Flexible budget variance, $4,000 U (columns 1–3) | *Sales volume variance, $8,000 F* (columns 3–5)

Static budget variance, $4,000 F

*Budgeted sale price is $12 per DVD, budgeted variable cost is $8 per DVD, and budgeted total monthly fixed costs are $20,000.

Column 1 of the performance report shows the actual results—based on the 10,000 DVDs actually sold. Operating income was $16,000 for June.

Column 3 is Smart Touch's flexible budget for the 10,000 DVDs actually sold. Operating income should have been $20,000.

Column 5 gives the static budget for the 8,000 DVDs expected to be sold for June. Smart Touch budgeted to earn $12,000.

The budget variances appear in columns 2 and 4 of the exhibit. Let us begin with the static budget in column 5. These data come from Exhibit 22-2.

The flexible budget for 10,000 units is in column 3. The differences between the static budget and the flexible budget—column 4—arise only because Smart Touch sold 10,000 DVDs rather than 8,000 during June. Column 4 shows the sales volume variances. Operating income is favorable by $8,000 because Smart Touch sold more DVDs than it planned to sell (10,000 sold rather than the 8,000 budgeted).

Column 1 of Exhibit 22-4 gives the actual results for June—10,000 DVDs and operating income of $16,000. Operating income is $4,000 less than Smart Touch would have expected for 10,000 DVDs. Why did operating income not measure up to the flexible budget?

- It was not because the selling price of DVDs took a dive. Sales revenue was $1,000 more than expected for 10,000 DVDs.
- Variable costs were $3,000 too high for 10,000 DVDs.
- Fixed costs were $2,000 too high for 10,000 DVDs.

Overall, expenses rose by $5,000 above the flexible budget, while sales revenue only increased by $1,000.

The static budget is developed *before* the period. The performance report in Exhibit 22-4 is developed after the *end* of the period. Why? Because *flexible budgets used in performance reports are based on the actual number of outputs, and the actual outputs are not known until the end of the period.*

Decision Guidelines

FLEXIBLE BUDGETS

You and your roommate have started a business that prints T-shirts (for example, for school and student organizations). How can you use flexible budgets to plan and control your costs?

Decision	Guidelines
• How do you estimate sales revenue, costs, and profits over your relevant range?	Prepare a set of flexible budgets for different sales levels.
• How do you prepare a flexible budget for total costs?	$\text{Total cost} = \left(\begin{matrix}\text{Number}\\ \text{of T-shirts}\end{matrix} \times \begin{matrix}\text{Variable cost}\\ \text{per T-shirt}\end{matrix}\right) + \begin{matrix}\text{Fixed}\\ \text{cost}\end{matrix}$
• How do you use budgets to help control costs?	Prepare an income statement performance report, as in Exhibit 22-4.
• On which output level is the budget based?	Static (master) budget—*expected* number of T-shirts, estimated before the period Flexible budget—*actual* number of T-shirts, not known until the end of the period
• Why does your actual income differ from budgeted income?	Prepare an income statement performance report comparing actual results, flexible budget for the actual number of T-shirts sold, and static (master) budget, as in Exhibit 22-4.
• How much of the difference arises because the actual number of T-shirts sold does not equal budgeted sales?	Compute the sales volume variance (SVV) by comparing the flexible budget with the static budget. • Favorable SVV—Actual number of T-shirts sold > Expected number of T-shirts sold • Unfavorable SVV—Actual number of T-shirts sold < Expected number of T-shirts sold
• How much of the difference occurs because revenues and costs are not what they should have been for the actual number of T-shirts sold?	Compute the flexible budget variance (FBV) by comparing actual results with the flexible budget. • Favorable FBV—Actual sales revenue > Flexible budget sales revenue • Actual costs < Flexible budget costs • Unfavorable FBV—Actual sales revenue < Flexible budget sales revenue • Actual costs > Flexible budget costs
• What actions can you take to avoid an unfavorable sales volume variance?	• Design more attractive T-shirts to increase demand. • Provide marketing incentives to increase number of T-shirts sold.
• What actions can you take to avoid an unfavorable flexible budget variance?	• Avoid an unfavorable flexible budget variance for *sales revenue* by maintaining (not discounting) your selling price. • Avoid an unfavorable flexible budget variance for *costs* by controlling variable costs, such as the cost of the T-shirts, dye, and labor, and by controlling fixed costs.

Summary Problem 1

Exhibit 22-4 shows that Smart Touch sold 10,000 DVDs during June. Now assume that Smart Touch sold 7,000 DVDs (instead of 10,000) and that the actual sale price averaged $12.50 per DVD. Actual variable costs were $57,400, and actual fixed costs were $19,000.

Requirements

1. Prepare a revised income statement performance report using Exhibit 22-4 as a guide.
2. As the company owner, which employees would you praise or criticize after you analyze this performance report?

Solution

Requirement 1

SMART TOUCH LEARNING, INC.
Income Statement Performance Report—Revised
Month Ended June 30, 2010

	1 Actual Results at Actual Prices	2 (1) – (3) Flexible Budget Variance	3 Flexible Budget for Actual Number of Output Units	4 (3) – (5) Sales Volume Variance	5 Static (Master) Budget
Output Units (DVDs sold)	7,000	0	7,000	1,000 U	8,000
Sales revenue	$87,500	$3,500 F	$84,000	$12,000 U	$96,000
Variable costs	57,400	1,400 U	56,000	8,000 F	64,000
Fixed costs	19,000	1,000 F	20,000	—	20,000
Total costs	76,400	400 U	76,000	8,000 F	84,000
Operating income	$11,100	$3,100 F	$ 8,000	$ 4,000 U	$12,000

Flexible budget variance, $3,100 F — *Sales volume variance, $4,000 U*

Static budget variance, $900 U

Requirement 2

As the company owner, you should determine the *causes* of the variances before praising or criticizing employees. It is especially important to determine whether the variance is due to factors the manager can control. For example,

- the unfavorable sales volume variance could be due to an ineffective sales staff. Or it could be due to a long period of snow that made it difficult for employees to get to work and brought work to a standstill.
- the $1,000 favorable flexible budget variance for fixed costs could be due to an employee finding less expensive equipment. Or the savings might have come from delaying a needed overhaul of equipment that could decrease the company's costs in the long run.

Smart managers use variances to raise questions and direct attention, not to fix blame.

Standard Costing

3 Identify the benefits of standard costs and learn how to set standards

Most companies use **standard costs** to develop their flexible budgets. Think of a standard cost as a budget for a single unit. For example, Smart Touch Learning's standard variable cost is $8 per DVD (Exhibit 22-2). This $8 variable cost includes the standard cost of inputs like the direct materials, direct labor, and variable overhead needed for one DVD.

In a standard cost system, each input has both a quantity standard and a price standard. Smart Touch has a standard for the following:

- Amount of vinyl for making the DVDs
- Price it pays per square foot of vinyl (this determines the price standard)

Let us see how managers set these price and quantity standards.

Price Standards

The price standard for direct materials starts with the base purchase cost of each unit of inventory. Accountants help managers set a price standard for materials after considering early-pay discounts, freight in, and receiving costs.

World-class businesses demand continuous reductions in costs. This can be achieved several ways. You can work with suppliers to cut their costs. You can use the Internet to solicit price quotes from suppliers around the world, and you can share information.

For direct labor, accountants work with human resource managers to determine standard labor rates. They must consider basic pay rates, payroll taxes, and fringe benefits. Job descriptions reveal the level of experience needed for each task.

Accountants work with production managers to estimate manufacturing overhead costs. Production managers identify an appropriate allocation base such as direct labor hours or direct labor cost, as you learned in Chapter 16. Accountants then compute the standard overhead rates. Exhibit 22-5 summarizes the setting of standard costs.

EXHIBIT 22-5 Summary of Standard Setting Issues

	Price Standard	Quantity Standard
Direct Materials	Responsibility: Purchasing manager Factors: Purchase price, discounts, delivery requirements, credit policy	Responsibility: Production manager and engineers Factors: Product specifications, spoilage, production scheduling
Direct Labor	Responsibility: Human resource managers Factors: Wage rate based on experience requirements, payroll taxes, fringe benefits	Responsibility: Production manager and engineers Factors: Time requirements for the production level of experience needed
Manufacturing Overhead	Responsibility: Production managers Factors: Nature and amount of resources needed for support activities (e.g., moving materials, maintaining equipment, and inspecting output)	

Application

Let us see how Smart Touch might determine its cost standards for materials, labor, and overhead.

The manager in charge of purchasing for Smart Touch indicates that the purchase price, net of discounts, is $1.90 per square foot of vinyl. Delivery, receiving, and inspection add an average of $0.10 per square foot. Smart Touch's hourly wage for workers is $8 and payroll taxes and fringe benefits total $2.50 per direct labor hour. Variable and fixed overhead will total $6,400 and $9,600, respectively, and overhead is allocated based on 3,200 estimated direct-labor hours.

Requirement

Compute Smart Touch Learning's cost standards for direct materials, direct labor, and overhead.

Answer

Direct materials price standard for vinyl:

Purchase price, net of discounts	$1.90 per square foot
Delivery, receiving, and inspection	0.10 per square foot
Total standard cost per square foot of vinyl	$2.00 per square foot

Direct labor price (or rate) standard:

Hourly wage	$ 8.00 per direct labor hour
Payroll taxes and fringe benefits	2.50 per direct labor hour
Total standard cost per direct labor hour	$10.50 per direct labor hour

Variable overhead price (or rate) standard:

$$\frac{\text{Estimated variable overhead cost}}{\text{Estimated quantity of allocation base}} = \frac{\$6{,}400}{3{,}200 \text{ direct labor hours}} = \$2.00 \text{ per direct labor hour}$$

Fixed overhead price (or rate) standard:

$$\frac{\text{Estimated fixed overhead cost}}{\text{Estimated quantity of allocation base}} = \frac{\$9{,}600}{3{,}200 \text{ direct labor hours}} = \$3.00 \text{ per direct labor hour}$$

Quantity Standards

Production managers and engineers set direct material and direct labor *quantity standards*. To set its labor standards, **Westinghouse Air Brake's** Chicago plant analyzed every moment in the production of the brakes.

To eliminate unnecessary work, **Westinghouse** rearranged machines in tight U-shaped cells so that work could flow better. Workers no longer had to move parts all over the plant floor, as illustrated in the following diagram.

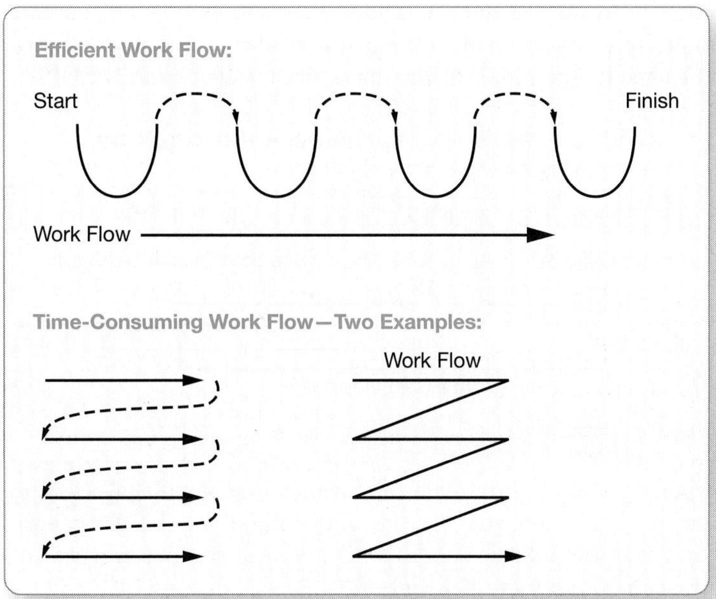

Westinghouse conducted time-and-motion studies to streamline various tasks. For example, the plant installed a conveyer at waist height to minimize bending and lifting. The result? Workers slashed one element of standard time by 90%.

Companies from the **Ritz-Carlton** to **Federal Express** develop quantity standards based on "best practices." This is often called *benchmarking*. The *best practice* may be an internal benchmark from other plants or divisions within the company or it may be an external benchmark from other companies. Internal benchmarks are easy to obtain, but managers can also purchase external benchmark data. For example, **Riverside Hospital** in Columbus, Ohio, can compare its cost of performing an appendectomy with the "best practice" cost developed by a consulting firm that compares many different hospitals' costs for the same procedure.

Why Do Companies Use Standard Costs?

U.S. surveys show that more than 80% of responding companies use standard costing. Over half of responding companies in the United Kingdom, Ireland, Sweden, and Japan use standard costing. Why? Standard costing helps managers:

- Prepare the budget
- Set target levels of performance
- Identify performance standards
- Set sales prices of products and services
- Decrease accounting costs

Standard cost systems might appear to be expensive. Indeed, the company must invest up front to develop the standards. But standards can save accounting costs. It is cheaper to value inventories at standard rather than actual costs. With standard costs, accountants avoid the LIFO, FIFO, or average-cost computations.

Variance Analysis

Once we establish standard costs, we can use the standards to assign costs to production. At least once a year, we will compare our actual production costs to the standard costs to locate variances. Exhibit 22-6 shows how to separate total variances for materials and labor into price and efficiency (quantity) variances. Study this exhibit carefully. It is used for the materials variances and the labor variances.

EXHIBIT 22-6 Variance Relationships

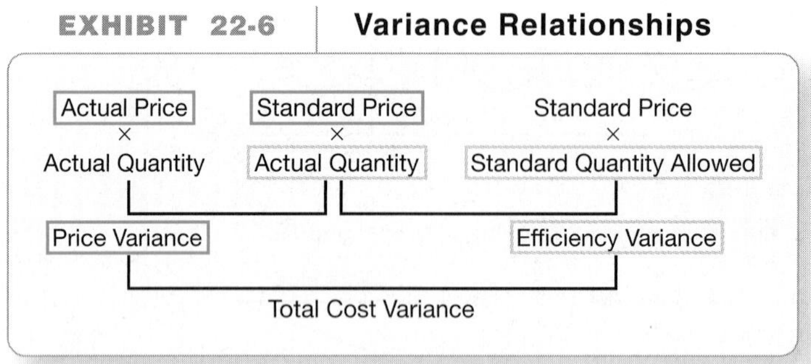

A **price variance** measures how well the business keeps unit prices of material and labor inputs within standards. As the name suggests, the price variance is the *difference in prices* (actual price per unit – standard price per unit) of an input, multiplied by the *actual quantity* of the input:

Price Variance = (Actual Price × Actual Quantity) – (Standard Price × Actual Quantity)
Or, Price Variance = (Actual Price – Standard Price) × Actual Quantity
= (AP – SP) × AQ

An **efficiency or quantity variance** measures how well the business uses its materials or human resources. The efficiency variance is the difference in quantities (actual quantity of input used – standard quantity of input allowed for the actual number of outputs) multiplied by the standard price per unit of the input:

Efficiency Variance = (Standard Price × Actual Quantity) – (Standard Price × Standard Quantity)
Or, Efficiency Variance = (Actual Quantity – Standard Quantity) × Standard Price
= (AQ – SQ) × SP

Exhibit 22-7 illustrates these variances and emphasizes two points.

EXHIBIT 22-7 The Relationships Among Price, Efficiency, Flexible Budget, Sales Volume, and Static Budget Variances

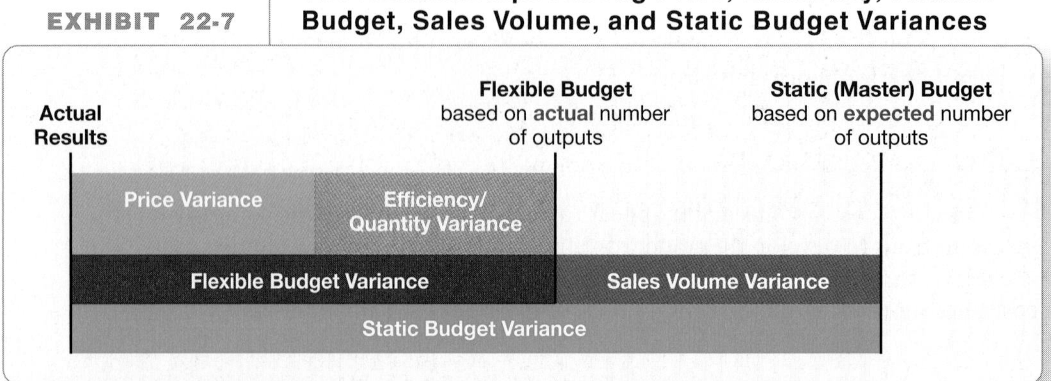

- First, the price and efficiency variances add up to the flexible budget variance.
- Second, static budgets like column 5 of Exhibit 22-4 play no role in the price and efficiency variances.

The static budget is used only to compute the sales volume variance—never to compute the flexible budget variance or the price and efficiency cost variances for materials and labor.

Stop & Think...

When you go to the gas station, do you fill up your car? How many miles per gallon does your car normally get? What is the usual price per gallon that you pay for gas? Let us assume you normally pay $4.00 per gallon and buy 10 gallons of gas. That is your standard cost for gas for your car. But what if the next time you need to fill up, you have to pay $4.25 per gallon, but you only have to buy 9.8 gallons of gas? The price variance is unfavorable because it is $0.25 more per gallon, but your car is using the gas more efficiently because you used .2 gallons less than normal.

How Smart Touch Uses Standard Costing: Analyzing The Flexible Budget Variance

4 Compute standard cost variances for direct materials and direct labor

Let us return to our Smart Touch Learning example. Exhibit 22-4 showed that the main cause for concern at Smart Touch is the $4,000 unfavorable flexible budget variance for total costs. The first step in identifying the causes of the cost variance is to identify the variable and fixed costs, as shown in Panel A of Exhibit 22-8.

Carefully study Exhibit 22-8 shown on the next page. Panel B shows how to compute the flexible budget amounts. Panel C shows how to compute actual materials and labor costs. Trace the following:

- Flexible budget amounts from Panel B to column (2) of Panel A
- Actual costs from Panel C to column (1) of Panel A

Column 3 of Panel A gives the flexible budget variances for direct materials and direct labor. For now, focus on materials and labor. We will cover overhead later.

Direct Material Variances

Direct Materials Price Variance

Let us investigate the $2,800 unfavorable variance for direct materials. Recall that the direct materials standard price was $2.00 per square foot, and 10,000 square feet are needed for 10,000 DVDs (1 square foot per DVD × 10,000 DVDs). The actual price of materials was $1.90 per square foot, and 12,000 square feet were actually used to make 10,000 DVDs. Using the formula, the materials price variance is $1,200 favorable. The calculation follows:

Materials Price Variance = (AP – SP) × AQ
= ($1.90 per square foot – $2.00 per square foot) × 12,000 square feet
= –$0.10 per square foot × 12,000 square feet
= $1,200 F

EXHIBIT 22-8 | **Data for Standard Costing Example**

PANEL A—Comparison of Actual Results with Flexible Budget for 10,000 DVDs

SMART TOUCH LEARNING, INC.
Data for Standard Costing Example
Month Ended June 30, 2010

	Actual Results at Actual Prices	Flexible Budget for 10,000 DVDs	Flexible Budget Variance
Variable costs:			
Direct materials	$ 22,800*	$ 20,000†	$2,800 U
Direct labor	41,800*	42,000†	200 F
Variable overhead	9,000	8,000†	1,000 U
Marketing and administrative costs	9,400	10,000	600 F
Total variable costs	83,000	80,000	3,000 U
Fixed costs:			
Fixed overhead	12,300	9,600‡	2,700 U
Marketing and administrative expense	9,700	10,400	700 F
Total fixed costs	22,000	20,000	2,000 U
Total costs	$105,000	$100,000	$5,000 U

*See Panel C.
†See Panel B.
‡Fixed overhead was budgeted at $9,600 per month (Application Answer on page 1168).

PANEL B—Computation of Flexible Budget for Direct Materials, Direct Labor, and Variable Overhead for 7,000 DVDs—Based on Standard Costs

	(1) Standard Quantity of Inputs Allowed for 10,000 DVDs	(2) Standard Price per Unit of Input	(3) (1) × (2) Flexible Budget for 10,000 DVDs
Direct materials	1 square foot per DVD × 10,000 DVDs = 10,000 square feet	$ 2.00	$20,000
Direct labor	.40 hours per DVD × 10,000 DVDs = 4,000 hours	$10.50	42,000
Variable overhead	.40 hours per DVD × 10,000 DVDs = 4,000 hours	$ 2.00	8,000

PANEL C—Computation of Actual Costs for Direct Materials and Direct Labor for 10,000 DVDs

	(1) Actual Quantity of Inputs Used for 10,000 DVDs	(2) Actual Price per Unit of Input	(3) (1) × (2) Actual Cost for 10,000 DVDs
Direct materials	12,000 square feet actually used	$1.90 actual cost/square foot	$22,800
Direct labor	3,800 hours actually used	$11.00 actual cost/hour	41,800

The $1,200 direct materials price variance (from page 1171) is *favorable,* because the purchasing manager spent $0.10 *less* per square foot of vinyl than budgeted ($1.90 actual price – $2.00 standard price).

Direct Materials Efficiency Variance

Now let us see what portion of the unfavorable materials variance was due to the quantity used.

The standard quantity of inputs is the *quantity that should have been used* for the actual output. For Smart Touch, the *standard quantity of inputs (vinyl) that workers should have used for the actual number of outputs* (10,000 DVDs) is 1 square foot of vinyl per DVD, or a total of 10,000 square feet.

Thus, the direct materials efficiency variance is as follows:

Direct Materials Efficiency Variance = (AQ – SQ) × SP
= (12,000 square feet – 10,000 square feet) × $2.00 per square foot
= + 2,000 square feet × $2.00 per square foot
= $4,000 U

The $4,000 direct materials efficiency variance is *unfavorable,* because workers used 2,000 *more* square feet of vinyl than they planned (budgeted) to use for 10,000 DVDs.

Summary of Direct Material Variances Exhibit 22-9 summarizes how Smart Touch splits the $2,800 unfavorable direct materials flexible budget variance into price and efficiency effects.

EXHIBIT 22-9 **Smart Touch Learning—Direct Materials Variance**

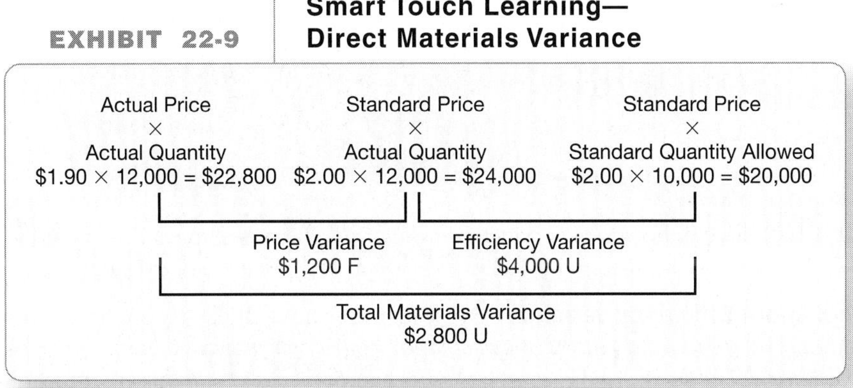

In summary, Smart Touch spent $2,800 more than it should have for vinyl because

- a good price for the vinyl increased profits by $1,200, but
- inefficient use of the vinyl reduced profits by $4,000.

Let us review who is responsible for each of these variances and consider why each variance may have occurred.

1. The purchasing manager is in the best position to explain the favorable price variance. Smart Touch's purchasing manager may have negotiated a good price for vinyl.

2. The manager in charge of making DVDs can explain why workers used so much vinyl to make the 10,000 DVDs. Was the vinyl of lower quality? Did workers waste materials? Did their equipment malfunction? Smart Touch's top management needs this information to decide what corrective action to take.

These variances raise questions that can help pinpoint problems. But be careful! A favorable variance does not always mean that a manager did a good job, nor does an unfavorable variance mean that a manager did a bad job. Perhaps Smart Touch's purchasing manager got a lower price by purchasing inferior-quality materials. This would lead to waste and spoilage. If so, the purchasing manager's decision hurt the company. This illustrates why good managers

- use variances as a guide for investigation rather than merely to assign blame.
- investigate favorable as well as unfavorable variances.

Direct Labor Variances

Smart Touch uses a similar approach to analyze the direct labor flexible budget variance.

Why did Smart Touch spend $200 less on labor than it should have used for 10,000 DVDs? To answer this question, Smart Touch computes the labor price and efficiency variances, in exactly the same way as it did for direct materials. Recall that the standard price for direct labor is $10.50 per hour, and 4,000 hours were budgeted for 10,000 DVDs (.40 hours per DVD × 10,000 DVDs). But actual direct labor cost was $11.00 per hour, and it took 3,800 hours to make 10,000 DVDs.

Direct Labor Price Variance

Using the formula, the direct labor price variance was $1,900 unfavorable. The calculation follows:

Direct Labor Price Variance = (AP – SP) × AH
= ($11.00 – $10.50) × $3,800 hours
= $1,900 U

The $1,900 direct labor price variance is *unfavorable* because Smart Touch paid workers $0.50 *more* per hour than budgeted ($11.00 actual price – $10.50 standard price).

Direct Labor Efficiency Variance Now let us see how efficiently Smart Touch used its labor. The *standard quantity of direct labor hours that workers should have used to make 10,000 DVDs* is .40 direct labor hours each or 4,000 total direct labor hours. Thus, the direct labor efficiency variance is as follows:

Direct Labor Efficiency Variance = (AH – SH) × SP
= (3,800 hours – 4,000 hours) × $10.50 per hour
= – 200 hours × $10.50
= $2,100 F

The $2,100 direct labor efficiency variance is *favorable* because laborers actually worked 200 *fewer* hours than the budget called for.

Summary of Direct Labor Variances Exhibit 22-10 summarizes how Smart Touch computes the labor price and efficiency variances.

EXHIBIT 22-10 Smart Touch Learning—Direct Labor Variance

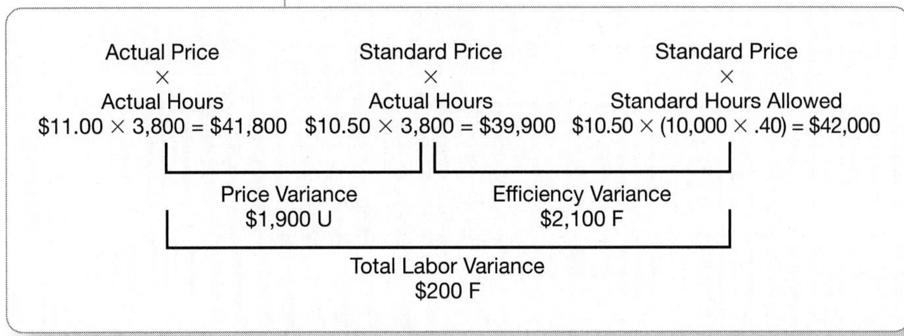

The $200 favorable direct labor variance suggests that labor costs were close to expectations. But to manage Smart Touch's labor costs, we need to gain more insight:

- Smart Touch paid its employees an average of $11.00 per hour in June instead of the standard rate of $10.50—for an unfavorable price variance.
- Workers made 10,000 DVDs in 3,800 hours instead of the budgeted 4,000 hours—for a favorable efficiency variance.

This situation reveals a trade-off. Smart Touch hired more experienced (and thus more expensive) workers and had an unfavorable price variance. But the workers turned out more work than expected, and the strategy was successful. The overall effect on profits was favorable. This possibility reminds us that managers should take care in using variances to evaluate performance. Go slow, analyze the data, and then take action.

Manufacturing Overhead Variances

5 Analyze manufacturing overhead in a standard cost system

In this section of the chapter we use the terms *manufacturing overhead* and *overhead* interchangeably. The total overhead variance is the difference between

Actual overhead cost and **Standard overhead allocated to production**

Exhibit 22-8 shows that Smart Touch actually incurred $21,300 of overhead: $9,000 variable and $12,300 fixed. The next step is to see how Smart Touch allocates overhead in a standard cost system.

Allocating Overhead in a Standard Cost System

In a standard costing system, the manufacturing overhead allocated to production is as follows:

Overhead allocated to production = Standard (predetermined) overhead rate × Standard quantity of the allocation base allowed for *actual* output

Let us begin by computing Smart Touch's standard overhead rate, as follows (data from page 1168):

$$\text{Standard overhead rate} = \frac{\text{Budgeted manufacturing overhead cost}}{\text{Budgeted direct labor hours}}$$
$$= \frac{\text{Variable overhead + Fixed overhead}}{\text{Budgeted direct labor hours}}$$
$$= \frac{\$6{,}400 + \$9{,}600}{3{,}200 \text{ direct labor hours}}$$
$$= \frac{\$6{,}400}{3{,}200} + \frac{\$9{,}600}{3{,}200}$$
$$= \$2.00 \text{ variable} + \$3.00 \text{ fixed}$$
$$= \$5.00 \text{ per direct labor hour}$$

Now let us determine the standard quantity of direct labor hours that Smart Touch allowed for actual output (10,000 DVDs), as follows (data from Exhibit 22-8, Panel B):

$$\text{Standard quantity of direct labor hours for actual output} = .4 \text{ hours per DVD} \times 10{,}000 \text{ DVDs}$$
$$= 4{,}000 \text{ direct labor hours}$$

Thus, Smart Touch allocates the cost of overhead to production based on standard costs as follows:

Standard overhead allocated to production	= *Standard* overhead rate	×	*Standard* quantity of the allocation base allowed for *actual* output
	= $5.00 per hour		× 4,000 hours
	= $20,000		

Smart Touch computes its total overhead cost variance as follows:

Total overhead variance	=	Actual overhead cost (Exhibit 22-8, Panel A)	–	Standard overhead allocated to production ($4,000 hours × $5.00 per hour)
	=	$21,300*	–	$20,000
	=	$1,300 U		

*Variable ($9,000) + fixed ($12,300) = $21,300.

Smart Touch actually spent $1,300 more on overhead than it allocated to production. To see why this unfavorable variance occurred, Smart Touch "drills down" by splitting the total overhead variance into two components:

- The overhead flexible budget variance
- The production volume variance

Exhibit 22-11 shows the computation of the overhead variances, and the discussion that follows explains them.

EXHIBIT 22-11 | **Manufacturing Overhead Variances**

SMART TOUCH LEARNING, INC. **Manufacturing Overhead Variances** Month Ended June 30, 2010			
	(1) Actual Overhead Cost (Exhibit 22-8)	(2) Flexible Budget Overhead for Actual Output (Exhibit 22-8)	(3) Standard Overhead Allocated to Production for Actual Output (Rates from page 1176)
Variable overhead	$ 9,000	$ 8,000	$2.00 × 4,000 direct labor hours = $ 8,000
Fixed overhead	12,300	9,600	$3.00 × 4,000 direct labor hours = $12,000
Total overhead	$21,300	$17,600	$5.00 × 4,000 direct labor hours = $20,000
	Flexible budget variance, $3,700 U		*Production volume variance, $2,400 F*
	Total manufacturing overhead variance, $1,300 U		

Overhead Flexible Budget Variance

The **overhead flexible budget variance** tells how well managers controlled overhead costs. Smart Touch actually spent $21,300 on overhead ($9,000 variable + $12,300 fixed from Exhibit 22-8, panel A, Actual Column) to sell the 10,000 DVDs. The flexible budget for 10,000 DVDs called for overhead of only $17,600 ($8,000 variable + $9,600 fixed from Exhibit 22-8, Panel A, Flexible Budget Column). So Smart Touch's overhead flexible budget variance is computed as follows:

Overhead Flexible Budget Variance	=	Actual overhead cost	–	Flexible budget overhead for actual output
	=	$21,300	–	$17,600
	=	$ 3,700 U		

Why did Smart Touch spend $3,700 more on overhead than it should have spent to sell the 10,000 DVDs in June? You can see from Exhibit 22-11 that $1,000 ($9,000 – $8,000) of the variance is due to higher-than-expected spending on *variable* overhead. The remaining $2,700 ($12,300 – $9,600) is due to higher spending on *fixed* overhead. Smart Touch will investigate the reason for each of these variances.

Overhead Production Volume Variance

The second component of the total overhead variance is the overhead **production volume variance.** This variance arises when actual production differs from expected production. Smart Touch expected to sell 8,000 DVDs during June, but actually sold 10,000. The overhead production volume variance is computed as follows:

Overhead Production Volume Variance	=	Flexible budget overhead for actual output (10,000 DVDs)	–	Standard overhead allocated to (actual) production
	=	$17,600 (Exhibit 22-11, column 2)	–	$20,000 (Exhibit 22-11, column 3)
	=	$ 2,400 F		

The production volume variance is favorable because Smart Touch's actual output (10,000 DVDs) exceeded expected output (8,000 DVDs). By selling 10,000 DVDs Smart Touch used its production capacity more fully than originally planned. If Smart Touch had sold 7,000 or fewer DVDs, the production volume variance would have been unfavorable because the company would have had unused production capacity.

Summary of Overhead Variances

Most companies compile cost information for the individual items of overhead, such as indirect materials, indirect labor, and utilities. Managers drill down by comparing actual to budgeted costs for each item. For example, Smart Touch's analysis might reveal that variable overhead costs were higher than expected because utility rates increased or because workers used more power than expected. Perhaps spending on fixed overhead increased because Smart Touch purchased new equipment and its depreciation increased.

Standard Cost Accounting Systems

6 Record transactions at standard cost and prepare a standard cost income statement

Journal Entries

We use Smart Touch Learning's June transactions to demonstrate standard costing in a job costing context. Management needs to know about variances to address each problem. Therefore, Smart Touch records variances from standards as soon as possible. This means that Smart Touch records direct materials price variances when materials are purchased. It also means that Work in process inventory is debited (DVDs are costed) at standard input quantities and standard prices. The entries for the month of June follow:

1.		Materials inventory (12,000 square feet × \$2.00) (A+)	24,000	
		Direct materials price variance (CE+)		1,200
		Accounts payable (12,000 × \$1.90) (L+)		22,800
		To record purchase of direct materials.		

The credit to Accounts payable is for the *actual quantity* of vinyl purchased (12,000 square feet) at the *actual price* (\$1.90 per square foot). In contrast, the debit to Materials inventory is recorded at the *standard price* (\$2 per square foot). Maintaining Materials inventory at the *standard price* (\$2.00) allows Smart Touch to record the direct materials price variance at time of purchase. Recall that Smart Touch's direct materials price variance was \$1,200 favorable. A favorable variance has a credit balance and is a contra expense. An unfavorable variance means more expense and has a debit balance.

2.		Work in process inventory (10,000 square feet × \$2.00) (A+)	20,000	
		Direct materials efficiency variance (E+)	4,000	
		Materials inventory (12,000 × \$2.00) (A–)		24,000
		To record use of direct materials.		

Smart Touch debits Work in process inventory for the *standard cost* of the 10,000 square feet of direct materials that should have been used to make 10,000 DVDs. This maintains Work in process inventory at standard cost. Materials inventory is credited for the *actual quantity* of materials put into production (12,000 square feet) costed at the *standard price*.

Smart Touch's direct materials efficiency variance was $4,000 unfavorable. An unfavorable variance has a debit balance, which increases expense and decreases profits.

3.		Manufacturing wages (3,800 hours × $10.50) (E+)	39,900	
		Direct labor price variance (E+)	1,900	
		Wages payable (3,800 × $11.00) (L+)		41,800
		To record direct labor costs incurred.		

Manufacturing wages is debited for the *standard price* ($10.50) of direct labor hours actually used (3,800). Wages payable is credited for the *actual cost* (the *actual* hours worked at the *actual* wage rate) because this is the amount Smart Touch must pay the workers. The direct labor price variance is $1,900 unfavorable, a debit amount.

4.		Work in process inventory (4,000 hours × $10.50) (A+)	42,000	
		Direct labor efficiency variance (CE+)		2,100
		Manufacturing wages (3,800 × $10.50) (E–)		39,900
		To allocate direct labor cost to production.		

Smart Touch debits Work in process inventory for the standard cost per direct labor hour ($10.50) that should have been used for 10,000 DVDs (4,000 hours), like direct materials entry 2. Manufacturing wages is credited to close its prior debit balance. The Direct labor efficiency variance is credited for the $2,100 favorable variance. This maintains Work in process inventory at standard cost.

5.		Manufacturing overhead (actual cost) (E+)	21,300	
		Accounts payable, Accumulated depreciation, etc.		21,300
		To record actual overhead costs incurred (Exhibit 22-11).		

This entry records Smart Touch's actual overhead cost for June.

6.		Work in process inventory (4,000 hours × $5.00) (A+)	20,000	
		Manufacturing overhead (E–)		20,000
		To allocate overhead to production (See Exhibit 22-11).		

In standard costing, the overhead allocated to Work in process inventory is computed as the standard overhead rate ($5.00 per hour) × standard quantity of the allocation base allowed for actual output (4,000 hours for 10,000 DVDs).

7.		Finished goods inventory (A+)	82,000	
		Work in process inventory (A–)		82,000
		To record completion of 10,000 DVDs ($20,000 of materials + $42,000 of labor + $20,000 of manufacturing overhead), all at standard cost.		

This entry transfers the standard cost of the 10,000 DVDs completed during June from Work in process inventory to Finished goods.

8.		Cost of goods sold (E+)	82,000	
		Finished goods inventory (A–)		82,000
		To record the cost of sales of 10,000 DVDs at standard cost.		

Entry 9 closes the Manufacturing overhead account and records the overhead variances.

9.	Overhead flexible budget variance (E+)	3,700	
	Overhead production volume variance (CE+)		2,400
	Manufacturing overhead (E−)		1,300
	To record overhead variances and close the Manufacturing Overhead account. (Exhibit 22-11)		

Exhibit 22-12 shows the relevant Smart Touch accounts after posting these entries.

EXHIBIT 22-12 Smart Touch's Flow of Costs in a Standard Costing System

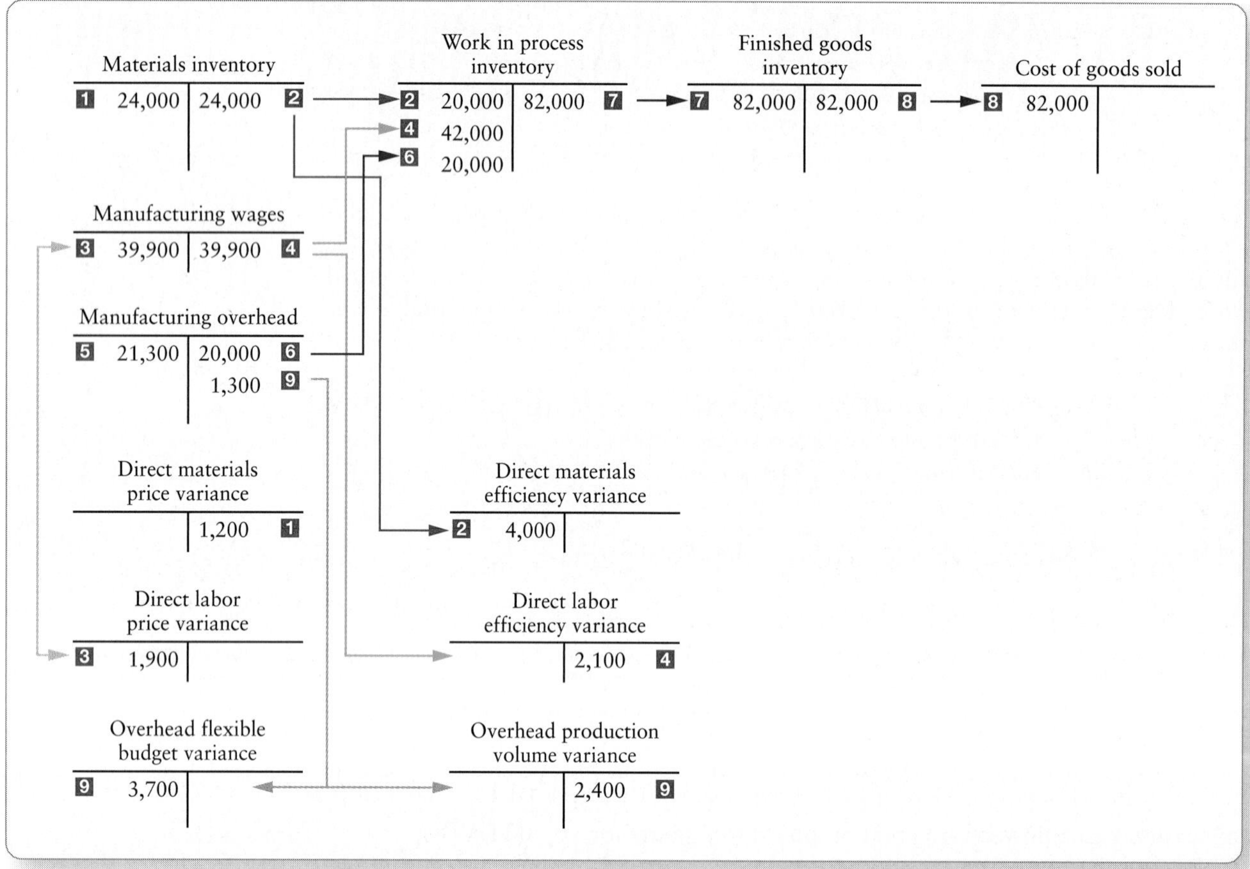

Standard Cost Income Statement for Management

Smart Touch's top management needs to know about the company's cost variances. Exhibit 22-13 shows a standard cost income statement that highlights the variances for management.

The statement starts with sales revenue at standard and adds the favorable sales revenue variance of $1,000 (Exhibit 22-4) to yield actual sales revenue. Next, the statement shows the cost of goods sold at standard cost. Then the statement separately lists each manufacturing cost variance, followed by cost of goods sold at actual cost. At the end of the period, all the variance accounts are closed to zero out their balances. Operating income is thus closed to Income summary.

The income statement shows that the net effect of all the manufacturing cost variances is $3,900 unfavorable. Therefore, June's operating income is $3,900 lower than it would have been if all the actual manufacturing costs had been equal to their standard costs.

EXHIBIT 22-13 | Standard Cost Income Statement

SMART TOUCH LEARNING, INC.
Standard Cost Income Statement
Month Ended June 30, 2010

Sales revenue at standard (10,000 × $12)			$120,000
Sales revenue variance			1,000
Sales revenue at actual			121,000
Cost of goods sold at standard cost		$82,000	
Manufacturing cost variances (parentheses denote a credit balance):			
Direct materials price variance	$(1,200)		
Direct materials efficiency variance	4,000		
Direct labor rate variance	1,900		
Direct labor efficiency variance	(2,100)		
Overhead flexible budget variance	3,700		
Overhead production volume variance	(2,400)		
Total manufacturing variance		3,900	
Cost of goods sold at actual cost			85,900
Gross profit			35,100
Marketing and administrative expense*			(19,100)
Operating income			$ 16,000

*$9,400 + $9,700 from Exhibit 22-8, Panel A.

The Decision Guidelines summarize standard costing and variance analysis.

Decision Guidelines

STANDARD COSTS AND VARIANCE ANALYSIS

Now you have seen how managers use standard costs and variances to identify potential problems. Variances help managers see *why* actual costs differ from the budget. This is the first step in determining how to correct problems. Let us review how Smart Touch Learning made some key decisions in setting up and using its standard cost system.

Decision	Guidelines
• How to set standards?	• Historical performance data • Engineering analysis/time-and-motion studies • Continuous improvement standards • Benchmarking
• How to compute a price variance for materials or labor?	Price variance = (Actual price per input unit − Standard price per input unit) × Actual quantity of input
• How to compute an efficiency variance for materials or labor?	Efficiency variance = (Actual quantity of input − Standard quantity of input for actual output) × Standard price per input unit
• Who is best able to explain a	
• sales volume variance?	The Marketing Department
• sales revenue variance?	The Marketing Department
• direct material price variance?	The Purchasing Department
• direct material efficiency variance?	The Production Department
• direct labor price variance?	The Human Resources Department
• direct labor efficiency variance?	The Production Department
• How do you allocate manufacturing overhead in a standard costing system?	Manufacturing overhead allocated = (Standard overhead rate) × (Standard quantity of allocation base allowed for actual output)
• How do you analyze over- or underallocated overhead?	Split over- or underallocated overhead into Flexible budget variance = Actual overhead − Flexible budget overhead for actual output Production volume variance = Flexible budget overhead for actual output − Standard overhead allocated to actual output
• How do you record standard costs in the accounts?	• Materials Inventory: Actual quantity at standard price • Work in process inventory (and Finished goods inventory and Cost of goods sold): Standard quantity of inputs allowed for actual outputs, at standard price of inputs
• How do you analyze cost variances?	• Debit balance → more expense • Credit balance → less expense

Summary Problem 2

Exhibit 22-8 indicates that Smart Touch Learning sold 10,000 DVDs in June. Suppose Smart Touch had sold 7,000 DVDs instead of 10,000 and that *actual costs* were as follows:

Direct materials (vinyl)	7,400 square feet @ $2.00 per square foot
Direct labor	2,740 hours @ $10.00 per hour
Variable overhead	$5,400
Fixed overhead	$11,900

Requirements

1. Given these new data, prepare an exhibit similar to Exhibit 22-8. Ignore marketing and administrative expense.
2. Compute price and efficiency variances for direct materials and direct labor.
3. Compute the total variance, the flexible budget variance, and the production volume variance for manufacturing overhead. Standard total overhead allocated to production is $5.00 per direct labor hour.

Solution

Requirement 1

PANEL A—Comparison of Actual Results with Flexible Budget for 7,000 DVDs

SMART TOUCH LEARNING, INC.
Revised Data for Standard Costing Example
Month Ended June 30, 2010

	Actual Results at Actual Prices	Flexible Budget for 7,000 DVDs	Flexible Budget Variance
Variable costs:			
Direct materials	$14,800*	$14,000†	$ 800 U
Direct labor	27,400*	29,400†	2,000 F
Variable overhead	5,400	5,600†	200 F
Total variable costs	47,600	49,000	1,400 F
Fixed costs:			
Fixed overhead	11,900	9,600‡	2,300 U
Total costs	$59,500	$58,600	$ 900 U

*See Panel C.
†See Panel B.
‡Fixed overhead was budgeted at $9,600 per month.

PANEL B—Computation of Flexible Budget for Direct Materials, Direct Labor, and Variable Overhead for 7,000 DVDs—Based on Standard Costs

	(1) Standard Quantity of Inputs Allowed for 7,000 DVDs	(2) Standard Price per Unit of Input	(3) (1) × (2) Flexible Budget for 7,000 DVDs
Direct materials	1 square foot per DVD × 7,000 DVDs = 7,000 square feet	$ 2.00	$14,000
Direct labor	.40 hours per DVD × 7,000 DVDs = 2,800 hours	$10.50	29,400
Variable overhead	.40 hours per DVD × 7,000 DVDs = 2,800 hours	$ 2.00	5,600

PANEL C—Computation of Actual Costs for Direct Materials and Direct Labor for 7,000 DVDs

	(1) Actual Quantity of Inputs Used for 7,000 DVDs	(2) Actual Price per Unit of Input	(3) (1) × (2) Actual Cost for 7,000 DVDs
Direct materials	7,400 square feet actually used	$2.00 actual cost/square foot	$14,800
Direct labor	2,740 hours actually used	$10.00 actual cost/hour	27,400

Requirement 2

$$\text{Price variance} = \left(\begin{array}{c}\text{Actual price}\\ \text{per input unit}\end{array} - \begin{array}{c}\text{Standard price}\\ \text{per input unit}\end{array}\right) \times \text{Actual quantity of input}$$

Direct materials:

Price variance = ($2.00 – $2.00) × 7,400 square feet = $0

Direct labor:

Rate variance = ($10.00 – $10.50) × 2,740 hours = $1,370 F

$$\text{Efficiency variance} = \left(\begin{array}{c}\text{Actual quantity}\\ \text{of input}\end{array} - \begin{array}{c}\text{Standard quantity}\\ \text{of input}\end{array}\right) \times \text{Standard price per input unit}$$

Direct materials:

Efficiency variance = (7,400 square feet – 7,000 square feet) × $2.00 per square foot = $800 U

Direct labor:

Efficiency variance = (2,740 hours – 2,800 hours) × $10.50 per hours = $630 F

Requirement 3

Total overhead variance:	
Actual overhead cost ($5,400 variable + $11,900 fixed)	$17,300
Standard overhead allocated to actual output (2,800 standard direct labor hours × $5.00)	14,000
Total overhead variance	$ 3,300 U
Overhead flexible budget variance:	
Actual overhead cost ($5,400 + $11,900)	$17,300
Flexible budget overhead for actual output ($5,600 + $9,600)	15,200
Overhead flexible budget variance	$2,100 U
Overhead production volume variance:	
Flexible budget overhead for actual output ($5,600 + $9,600)	$15,200
Standard overhead allocated to actual output (2,800 standard direct labor hours × $5.00)	14,000
Overhead production volume variance	$ 1,200 U

Review *Flexible Budgets and Standard Costs*

Accounting Vocabulary

Efficiency (Quantity) Variance (p. 1170)
Measure whether the quantity of materials or labor used to make the actual number of outputs is within the standard allowed for that number of outputs. Computed as the difference in quantities (actual quantity of input used minus standard quantity of input allowed for the actual number of outputs) multiplied by the standard price per unit of the input.

Flexible Budget (p. 1161)
A summarized budget that managers can easily compute for several different volume levels; separates variable costs from fixed costs.

Flexible Budget Variance (p. 1162)
The difference arising because the company actually earned more or less revenue, or incurred more or less cost, than expected for the actual level of output. Equals the difference between the actual amount and a flexible budget amount.

Overhead Flexible Budget Variance (p. 1177)
Shows how well management has controlled overhead costs. The difference between the actual overhead cost and the flexible budget overhead for the actual number of outputs.

Price (Rate) Variance (p. 1170)
Measures how well the business keeps unit prices of material and labor inputs within standards. Computed as the difference in prices (actual price per unit minus standard price per unit) of an input multiplied by the actual quantity of the input.

Production Volume Variance (p. 1177)
Arises when actual production differs from expected production. The difference between: (1) the manufacturing overhead cost in the flexible budget or actual outputs, and (2) the standard overhead allocated to production.

Sales Volume Variance (p. 1162)
The difference arising only because the number of units actually sold differs from the static budget units. Equals the difference between a static budget amount and a flexible budget amount.

Standard Cost (p. 1167)
A budget for a single unit.

Static Budget (p. 1160)
The budget prepared for only one level of sales volume. Also called the **master budget**.

Variance (p. 1160)
The difference between an actual amount and the budget. Labeled as favorable if it increases operating income and unfavorable if it decreases operating income.

Quick Check

Questions 1–4 rely on the following data. FastNet Systems is a start-up company that makes connectors for high-speed Internet connections. The company has budgeted variable costs of $120 for each connector and fixed costs of $7,000 per month.

FastNet's static budget predicted production and sales of 100 connectors in August, but the company actually produced and sold only 76 connectors at a total cost of $25,000.

1. FastNet's total flexible budget cost for 76 connectors per month is
   a. $16,120.
   b. $7,120.
   c. $12,000.
   d. $9,120.

2. FastNet's sales volume variance for total costs is
   a. $2,880 U.
   b. $2,880 F.
   c. $8,880 F.
   d. $8,880 U.

3. FastNet's flexible budget variance for total costs is
   a. $2,880 U.
   b. $2,880 F.
   c. $8,880 F.
   d. $8,880 U.

4. FastNet Systems' managers could set direct labor standards based on
   a. continuous improvement.
   b. time-and-motion studies.
   c. benchmarking.
   d. past actual performance.
   e. Any of the above

Questions 5–7 rely on the following data. ProNet Systems has budgeted 3 hours of direct labor per connector, at a standard cost of $15 per hour. During January, technicians actually worked 198 hours completing 76 connectors. ProNet paid the technicians $15.50 per hour.

5. What is ProNet's direct labor price variance for January?
   a. $99.00 U
   b. $114.00 U
   c. $106.50 U
   d. $38.00 U

6. What is ProNet's direct labor efficiency variance for January?
   a. $605.00 F
   b. $77.50 F
   c. $1,386.00 F
   d. $450.00 F

7. The journal entry to record ProNet's *use* of direct labor in January is which of the following?

a.

Work in process inventory
Direct labor efficiency variance
Manufacturing wages

b.

Work in process inventory
Direct labor efficiency variance
Manufacturing wages

c.

Manufacturing wages
Direct labor efficiency variance
Work in process inventory

d.

Manufacturing wages
Direct labor efficiency variance
Work in process inventory

8. BackFill Systems allocates manufacturing overhead based on machine hours. Each connector should require 11 machine hours. According to the static budget, BackFill expected to incur:

   1,045 machine hours per month (95 connectors × 11 machine hours per connector)

   $5,650 in variable manufacturing overhead costs

   $7,900 in fixed manufacturing overhead costs

   During August, BackFill actually used 865 machine hours to make the 78 connectors. BackFill's predetermined standard *total* manufacturing overhead rate is
   a. $12.97 per machine hour.
   b. $15.66 per machine hour.
   c. $7.56 per machine hour.
   d. $5.41 per machine hour.

9. The total manufacturing overhead variance is composed of
   a. price variance and production volume variance.
   b. flexible budget variance and production volume variance.
   c. efficiency variance and production volume variance.
   d. price variance and efficiency variance.
10. When a company *uses* direct materials, the amount of the debit to Work in process inventory is based on which of the following:
   a. Standard quantity of the materials allowed for actual production × Standard price per unit of the materials
   b. Actual quantity of the materials used × Actual price per unit of the materials
   c. Actual quantity of the materials used × Standard price per unit of the materials
   d. Standard quantity of the materials allowed for actual production × Actual price per unit of the materials

Answers are given after Apply Your Knowledge (p. 1203).

Assess Your Progress

■ Short Exercises

S22-1 *(L. OBJ. 1)* **Matching terms [10 min]**
Consider the following terms:

a. Flexible Budget
b. Flexible Budget Variance
c. Sales Volume Variance
d. Static Budget
e. Variance

Consider the following definitions:

______ 1. The budget prepared for only one level of sales volume.
______ 2. The difference between an actual amount and the budget.
______ 3. A summarized budget for several levels of volume that separates variable costs from fixed costs.
______ 4. The difference arising only because the number of units actually sold differs from the static budget units.
______ 5. The difference arising because the company actually earned more or less revenue, or incurred more or less cost, than expected for the actual level of output.

Requirement

1. Match each term to the correct definition.

S22-2 *(L. OBJ. 1)* **Matching terms [10 min]**
Consider the following terms:

a. Benchmarking
b. Efficiency Variance
c. Overhead Flexible Budget Variance
d. Price Variance
e. Production Volume Variance
f. Standard Cost

Consider the following definitions:

______ 1. A budget for a single unit.

______ 2. Using standards based on "best practice."

______ 3. Measures how well the business keeps unit prices of material and labor inputs within standards.

______ 4. Measures whether the quantity of materials or labor used to make the actual number of outputs is within the standard allowed for that number of outputs.

______ 5. Shows how well management has controlled overhead costs.

______ 6. Arises when actual production differs from expected production.

Requirement

1. Match each term to the correct definition.

S22-3 *(L. OBJ. 1)* **Flexible budget preparation [10 min]**
Tik-a-Lock, Inc., manufactures travel locks. The budgeted selling price is $18 per lock, the variable cost is $12 per lock, and budgeted fixed costs are $12,000.

Requirement

1. Prepare a flexible budget for output levels of 6,000 locks and 9,000 locks for the month ended April 30, 2011.

S22-4 *(L. OBJ. 2)* **Flexible budget variance [10–15 min]**
Consider the following partially completed income statement performance report for Woje, Inc.

WOJE, INC. Income Statement Performance Report (partial) Month Ended April 30, 2011				
	Actual Results at Actual Prices	Flexible Budget Variance		Flexible Budget for Actual Number of Output Units
Output units	10,000			10,000
Sales revenue	$ 170,000			$ 150,000
Variable costs	52,100			49,700
Fixed costs	15,700			14,600
Total costs	67,800			64,300
Operating income	$ 102,200			$ 85,700

Requirement

1. Complete the flexible budget variance analysis by filling in the blanks in the partial Income Statement Performance Report for 10,000 travel locks.

S22-5 *(L. OBJ. 3)* **Identifying the benefits of standard costs [5 min]**
Setting standards for a product may involve many employees of the company.

Requirement

1. Identify some of the employees who may be involved in setting the standard costs and describe what their role might be in setting those standards.

S22-6 *(L. OBJ. 4)* **Calculate materials variances [10–15 min]**
Smithson, Inc., is a manufacturer of lead crystal glasses. The standard materials quantity is .9 pound per glass at a price of $0.45 per pound. The actual results for the production of 7,100 glasses was 1.3 pounds per glass, at a price of $0.55 per pound.

Requirement

1. Calculate the materials price variance and the materials efficiency variance.

S22-7 *(L. OBJ. 4)* **Calculate labor variances [10–15 min]**
Smithson, Inc., manufactures lead crystal glasses. The standard direct labor time is 1/4 hour per glass, at a price of $15 per hour. The actual results for the production of 6,800 glasses were 1/3 hour per glass, at a price of $14 per hour.

Requirement

1. Calculate the labor price variance and the labor efficiency variance.

Note: Short Exercises 22-6 and 22-7 should be completed before attempting Short Exercise 22-8.

S22-8 *(L. OBJ. 4)* **Interpreting material and labor variances [5–10 min]**
Refer to your results from S22-6 and S22-7.

Requirements

1. For each variance, who in Smithson's organization is most likely responsible?
2. Interpret the direct materials and direct labor variances for Smithson's management.

S22-9 *(L. OBJ. 5)* **Standard overhead rates [5 min]**
Smithson, Inc., manufactures lead crystal glasses. The following information relates to the company's overhead costs:

Static budget variable overhead	$ 7,500
Static budget fixed overhead	$ 3,000
Static budget direct labor hours	1,500 hours
Static budget number of glasses	4,800

Smithson allocates manufacturing overhead to production based on standard direct labor hours. Last month, Smithson reported the following actual results for the production of 7,500 glasses: actual variable overhead, $10,500; actual fixed overhead, $2,760.

Requirement

1. Compute the standard variable overhead rate and the standard fixed overhead rate.

Note: Short Exercise 22-9 should be completed before attempted Short Exercise 22-10.

S22-10 *(L. OBJ. 6)* **Computing overhead variances [10 min]**
Refer to the Smithson data in S22-9.

Requirement

1. Compute the overhead variances.

S22-11 *(L. OBJ. 6)* **Materials journal entries [5–10 min]**
The following materials variance analysis was performed for Goldman.

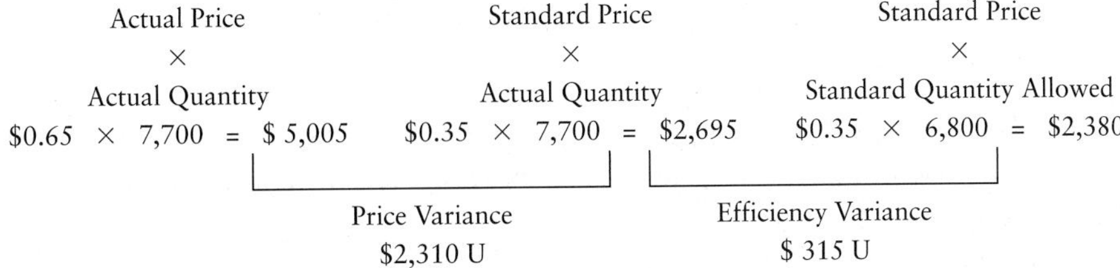

Requirement

1. Record Goldman's direct materials journal entries.

S22-12 *(L. OBJ. 6)* **Labor journal entries [5–10 min]**
The following labor variance analysis was performed for Goldman.

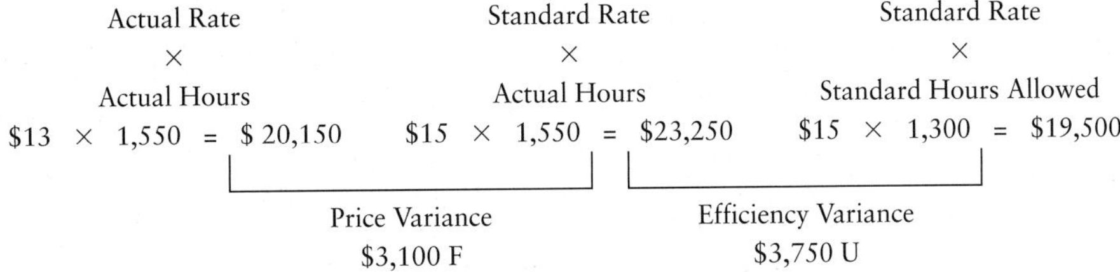

Requirement

1. Record Goldman's direct labor journal entries.

S22-13 *(L. OBJ. 6)* **Journal entries for goods completed and sold [5–10 min]**
Goldman completed 70,000 glasses in 2011, at a standard cost of $360,000. The company sold all of them on account at a sale price of $8.00 each. There were no beginning or ending inventories of any kind.

Requirement

1. Record the journal entries for the completion and sale of the 70,000 glasses.

S22-14 *(L. OBJ. 6)* **Standard cost income statement [10–15 min]**
Consider the following information:

Cost of goods sold	$362,000	Direct labor efficiency variance	$16,500 F
Sales revenue	$530,000	Overhead flexible budget variance	$3,300 U
Direct materials price variance	$7,200 U	Production volume variance	$11,700 F
Direct materials efficiency variance	$2,200 U	Marketing and administrative costs were	$71,000
Direct labor price variance	$45,000 U		

Requirement

1. Use the previous information to prepare a standard cost income statement for Goldman, using Exhibit 22-13 as a guide. Remember that unfavorable variances are added to cost of goods sold.

■ Exercises

E22-15 *(L. OBJ. 1)* **Preparing a flexible budget [10–15 min]**
ErgoNow sells its main product, ergonomic mouse pads, for $13 each. Its variable cost is $5.60 per pad. Fixed costs are $200,000 per month for volumes up to 60,000 pads. Above 60,000 pads, monthly fixed costs are $255,000.

Requirement

1. Prepare a monthly flexible budget for the product, showing sales revenue, variable costs, fixed costs, and operating income for volume levels of 30,000, 45,000, and 80,000 pads.

E22-16 *(L. OBJ.2)* **Preparing an income statement performance report [15–20 min]**
White Pro Company managers received the following incomplete performance report:

WHITE PRO COMPANY Income Statement Performance Report Year Ended July 31, 2011					
	Actual Results at Actual Prices	Flexible Budget Variance	Flexible Budget for Actual Number of Output Units	Sales Volume Variance	Static (Master) Budget
Output units	41,000	—	41,000	7,000 F	—
Sales revenue	$ 215,000	—	$ 215,000	$ 19,000 F	—
Variable costs	85,000	—	79,000	9,000 U	—
Fixed costs	107,000	—	101,000	0	—
Total costs	192,000	—	180,000	9,000 U	—
Operating income	$ 23,000	—	$ 35,000	$ 10,000 F	—

Requirement

1. Complete the performance report. Identify the employee group that may deserve praise and the group that may be subject to criticism. Give your reasoning.

E22-17 *(L. OBJ. 2)* **Preparing an income statement performance report [20–25 min]**
Top managers of Root Industries predicted 2010 sales of 15,000 units of its product at a unit price of $7.50 Actual sales for the year were 14,100 units at $9.00 each. Variable costs were budgeted at $2.60 per unit, and actual variable costs were $2.70 per unit. Actual fixed costs of $46,000 exceeded budgeted fixed costs by $2,000.

Requirement

1. Prepare Root's income statement performance report. What variance contributed most to the year's favorable results? What caused this variance?

E22-18 *(L. OBJ. 3, 4)* **Defining the benefits of setting cost standards, and calculating materials and labor variances [10–15 min]**
Quality, Inc., produced 1,000 units of the company's product in 2011. The standard quantity of materials was three yards of cloth per unit at a standard price of $1.10 per yard. The accounting records showed that 2,900 yards of cloth were used and the company paid $1.15 per yard. Standard time was one direct labor hour per unit at a standard rate of $10 per direct labor hour. Employees worked 650 hours and were paid $9.50 per hour.

Requirements

1. What are the benefits of setting cost standards?
2. Calculate the materials price variance and the materials efficiency variance, as well as the labor price and efficiency variances.

E22-19 *(L. OBJ. 4)* **Calculating materials variances [10–15 min]**
The following direct materials variance computations are incomplete:

1. Price variance =	($? − $2) × 9,800 pounds = $4,900 U
2. Efficiency variance =	(? − 15,800 pounds) × $2 = ? F
3. Flexible budget variance =	$?

Requirement

1. Fill in the missing values, and identify the flexible budget variance as favorable or unfavorable.

E22-20 *(L. OBJ. 4)* **Calculating materials and labor variances [20–30 min]**
All-Star Fender, which uses a standard cost accounting system, manufactured 20,000 boat fenders during the year, using 146,000 feet of extruded vinyl purchased at $1.15 per square foot. Production required 480 direct labor hours that cost $15.00 per hour. The materials standard was 7 feet of vinyl per fender, at a standard cost of $1.20 per square foot. The labor standard was 0.026 direct labor hour per fender, at a standard price of $14.00 per hour.

Requirement

1. Compute the price and efficiency variances for direct materials and direct labor. Does the pattern of variances suggest All-Star Fender's managers have been making trade-offs? Explain.

E22-21 *(L. OBJ. 5)* **Computing overhead variances [20–30 min]**
Houston Paint Company's budgeted production volume for the month was 30,000 gallons of paint. The standard overhead cost included a $0.55 variable overhead per gallon and fixed overhead costs of $30,000.

Houston Paint actually produced 33,000 gallons of paint. Actual variable overhead was $16,400, and fixed overhead was $32,000.

Requirement

1. Compute the total overhead variance, the overhead flexible budget variance, and the production volume variance.

E22-22 *(L. OBJ. 5)* **Preparing a standard cost income statement [15 min]**
The May 2010 revenue and cost information for Boise Outfitters, Inc., follows:

Sales revenue	$ 580,000	
Cost of goods sold (standard)	344,000	
Direct materials price variance	900	F
Direct materials efficiency variance	6,500	F
Direct labor price variance	4,500	U
Direct labor efficiency variance	2,200	F
Overhead flexible budget variance	3,100	U
Production volume variance	8,400	F

Requirement

1. Prepare a standard cost income statement for management through gross profit. Report all standard cost variances for management's use. Has management done a good or poor job of controlling costs? Explain.

Note: Exercise 22-20 should be completed before attempting Exercise 22-23.

E22-23 *(L. OBJ. 6)* **Preparing journal entries [20–30 min]**
Review the results from E22-20.

Requirement

1. Make the journal entries to record the purchase and use of direct materials and direct labor from E22-20.

E22-24 *(L. OBJ. 6)* **Preparing a standard cost income statement [15–20 min]**
The managers of Johnson DVD, Co., a contract manufacturer of DVD drives, are seeking explanations for the variances in the following report.

JOHNSON DVD CO. Standard Cost Income Statement Year Ended December 31, 2011		
Sales revenue		$1,200,000
Cost of goods sold at standard cost		$700,000
Manufacturing cost variances:		
Direct materials price variance	$ 10,000 F	
Direct materials efficiency variance	32,000 U	
Direct labor price variance	24,000 F	
Direct labor efficiency variance	10,000 U	
Overhead flexible budget variance	28,000 U	
Production volume variance	8,000 F	
Total manufacturing variances		28,000
Cost of goods sold at actual cost		728,000
Gross profit		472,000
Marketing and administrative costs		418,000
Operating income		$ 54,000

Requirement

1. Explain the meaning of each of Johnson's materials, labor, and overhead variances.

■ Problems (Group A)

P22-25A *(L. OBJ. 1, 3, 4, 5)* **Preparing a flexible budget and computing standard cost variances [60–75 min]**
Root Recliners manufactures leather recliners and uses flexible budgeting and a standard cost system. Root allocates overhead based on yards of direct materials. The company's performance report includes the following selected data:

	Static Budget (1,025 recliners)	Actual Results (1,005 recliners)
Sales (1,025 recliners × $ 505)	$ 517,625	
(1,005 recliners × $ 485)		$ 487,425
Variable manufacturing costs:		
Direct materials (6,150 yds @ $8.90)	54,735	
(6,300 yds @ $8.70)		54,810
Direct labor (10,250 hrs @ $9.40)	96,350	
(9,850 hrs @ $9.55)		94,068
Variable overhead (6,150 yds @ $5.10)	31,365	
(6,300 yds @ $6.50)		40,950
Fixed manufacturing costs:		
Fixed overhead	62,730	64,730
Total cost of goods sold	245,180	254,558
Gross profit	$ 272,445	$ 232,867

Requirements

1. Prepare a flexible budget based on the actual number of recliners sold.
2. Compute the price variance and the efficiency variance for direct materials and for direct labor. For manufacturing overhead, compute the total variance, the flexible budget variance, and the production volume variance.
3. Have Root's managers done a good job or a poor job controlling materials and labor costs? Why?
4. Describe how Root's managers can benefit from the standard costing system.

P22-26A *(L. OBJ. 2)* **Preparing an income statement performance report [30 min]**
CellBase Technologies manufactures capacitors for cellular base stations and other communications applications. The company's December 2011 flexible budget income statement shows output levels of 7,500, 9,000, and 11,000 units. The static budget was based on expected sales of 9,000 units.

CELLBASE TECHNOLOGIES Flexible Budget Income Statement Month Ended December 31, 2011				
	Flexible Budget per Output Unit	Output Units (Capacitors)		
		7,500	9,000	11,000
Sales revenue	23	$ 172,500	$ 207,000	$ 253,000
Variable costs	11	82,500	99,000	121,000
Fixed costs		57,000	57,000	57,000
Total costs		139,500	156,000	178,000
Operating income		$ 33,000	$ 51,000	$ 75,000

The company sold 11,000 units during December, and its actual operating income was as follows:

CELLBASE TECHNOLOGIES Income Statement Month Ended December 31, 2011	
Sales revenue	$ 260,000
Variable costs	$ 126,000
Fixed costs	58,500
Total costs	184,500
Operating income	$ 75,500

Requirements

1. Prepare an income statement performance report for December.
2. What was the effect on CellBase Technologies' operating income of selling 2,000 units more than the static budget level of sales?
3. What is CellBase Technologies' static budget variance? Explain why the income statement performance report provides more useful information to CellBase Technologies' managers than the simple static budget variance. What insights can CellBase Technologies' managers draw from this performance report?

P22-27A *(L. OBJ. 4)* **Using incomplete cost and variance information to determine the number of direct labor hours worked [30–35 min]**

Abby's Shades manufactures lamp shades. Abby Sanders, the manager, uses standard costs to judge performance. Recently, a clerk mistakenly threw away some of the records, and Sanders has only partial data for October. She knows that the direct labor flexible budget variance for the month was $1,385 U, the standard labor rate was $10 per hour, and the actual labor rate was $10.50 per hour. The standard direct labor hours for the actual October output were 4,450.

Requirements

1. Find the actual number of direct labor hours worked during October. First, calculate the standard labor cost. Next, calculate the actual labor cost by adding the unfavorable flexible budget variance of $1,385 to the standard labor cost. Finally, divide the actual labor cost by the actual labor rate per hour.
2. Compute the direct labor price and efficiency variances. Do these variances suggest the manager may have made a trade-off? Explain.

P22-28A *(L. OBJ. 4, 5, 6)* **Computing and journalizing standard cost variances [45 min]**

Stenback manufactures coffee mugs that it sells to other companies for customizing with their own logos. Stenback prepares flexible budgets and uses a standard cost system to control manufacturing costs. The standard unit cost of a coffee mug is based on static budget volume of 59,900 coffee mugs per month:

Direct materials (0.2 lbs @ $0.25 per lb)		$ 0.05
Direct labor (3 minutes @ $0.10 per minute)		0.30
Manufacturing overhead:		
Variable (3 minutes @ $0.05 per minute)	$ 0.15	
Fixed (3 minutes @ $0.13 per minute)	0.39	0.54
Total cost per coffee mug		$ 0.89

Actual cost and production information for July follow:

a. Actual production and sales were 62,600 coffee mugs.
b. Actual direct materials usage was 12,000 lbs., at an actual price of $0.18 per lb.
c. Actual direct labor usage of 199,000 minutes at a total cost of $25,870.
d. Actual overhead cost was $40,500.

Requirements

1. Compute the price and efficiency variances for direct materials and direct labor.
2. Journalize the usage of direct materials and the assignment of direct labor, including the related variances.
3. For manufacturing overhead, compute the total variance, the flexible budget variance, and the production volume variance. (*Hint:* Remember that the fixed overhead in the flexible budget equals the fixed overhead in the static budget.)
4. Stenback intentionally hired more-skilled workers during July. How did this decision affect the cost variances? Overall, was the decision wise?

P22-29A *(L. OBJ. 4, 5, 6)* **Computing standard cost variances and reporting to management [45–60 min]**

SmartSound manufactures headphone cases. During September 2011, the company produced and sold 105,000 cases and recorded the following cost data:

Standard Cost Information:

	Quantity	Price
Direct materials	2 parts	$ 0.15 per part
Direct labor	0.02 hours	$ 9.00 per hour
Variable manufacturing overhead	0.02 hours	$ 9.00 per hour
Fixed manufacturing overhead ($28,500 for static budget volume of 95,000 units and 1,900 hours, or $ 15 per hour)		

Actual Information:

Direct materials (235,000 parts @ $0.20 per part = $47,000)
Direct labor (1,700 hours @ $9.15 per hour = $15,555)
Manufacturing overhead $61,000

Requirements

1. Compute the price and efficiency variances for direct materials and direct labor.
2. For manufacturing overhead, compute the total variance, the flexible budget variance, and the production volume variance.
3. Prepare a standard cost income statement through gross profit to report all variances to management. The sale price of the headset cases was $1.50 each.
4. SmartSound's management used more-experienced workers during September. Discuss the trade-off between the two direct labor variances.

■ Problems (Group B)

P22-30B *(L. OBJ. 1, 3, 4, 5)* **Preparing a flexible budget and computing standard cost variances [60–75 min]**

McKnight Recliners manufactures leather recliners and uses flexible budgeting and a standard cost system. McKnight allocates overhead based on yards of direct materials. The company's performance report includes the following selected data:

	Static Budget (1,000 recliners)	Actual Results (980 recliners)
Sales (1,000 recliners × $ 505)	$ 505,000	
(980 recliners × $ 485)		$ 475,300
Variable manufacturing costs:		
Direct materials (6,000 yds @ $8.90)	53,400	
(6,150 yds @ $8.65)		53,198
Direct labor (10,000 hrs @ $9.40)	94,000	
(9,600 hrs @ $9.60)		92,160
Variable overhead (6,000 yds @ $5.20)	31,200	
(6,150 yds @ $6.60)		40,590
Fixed manufacturing costs:		
Fixed overhead	60,600	62,600
Total cost of goods sold	239,200	248,548
Gross profit	$ 265,800	$ 226,752

Requirements

1. Prepare a flexible budget based on the actual number of recliners sold.
2. Compute the price variance and the efficiency variance for direct materials and for direct labor. For manufacturing overhead, compute the total variance, the flexible budget variance, and the production volume variance.
3. Have McKnight's managers done a good job or a poor job controlling materials and labor costs? Why?
4. Describe how McKnight's managers can benefit from the standard costing system.

P22-31B *(L. OBJ. 2)* **Preparing an income statement performance report [30 min]**

AllTalk Technologies manufactures capacitors for cellular base stations and other communication applications. The company's January 2011 flexible budget income statement shows output levels of 6,500, 8,000, and 10,000 units. The static budget was based on expected sales of 8,000 units.

ALLTALK TECHNOLOGIES Flexible Budget Income Statement Month Ended January 31, 2011				
	Flexible Budget per Output Unit	Output Units (Capacitors)		
		6,500	8,000	10,000
Sales revenue	21	$ 136,500	$ 168,000	$ 210,000
Variable costs	11	71,500	88,000	110,000
Fixed costs		57,000	57,000	57,000
Total costs		128,500	145,000	167,000
Operating income		$ 8,000	$ 23,000	$ 43,000

The company sold 10,000 units during January, and its actual operating income was as follows:

ALLTALK TECHNOLOGIES Income Statement Month Ended January 31, 2011		
Sales revenue		$ 217,000
Variable costs		$ 115,100
Fixed costs		58,500
Total costs		173,600
Operating income		$ 43,400

Requirements

1. Prepare an income statement performance report for January 2011.
2. What was the effect on AllTalk Technologies' operating income of selling 2,000 units more than the static budget level of sales?
3. What is AllTalk Technologies' static budget variance? Explain why the income statement performance report provides more useful information to AllTalk Technologies' managers than the simple static budget variance. What insights can AllTalk Technologies' managers draw from this performance report?

P22-32B *(L. OBJ. 4)* **Using incomplete cost and variance information to determine the number of direct labor hours worked [30–35 min]**
Lilly's Shades manufactures lamp shades. Lilly Sanders, the manager, uses standard costs to judge performance. Recently, a clerk mistakenly threw away some of the records, and Sanders has only partial data for October. She knows that the direct labor flexible budget variance for the month was $1,585 U, the standard labor rate was $9 per hour, and the actual labor rate was $9.50 per hour. The standard direct labor hours for the actual October output were 4,500.

Requirements

1. Find the actual number of direct labor hours worked during October. First, calculate the standard labor cost. Next, calculate the actual labor cost by adding the unfavorable flexible budget variance of $1,585 to the standard labor cost. Finally, divide the actual labor cost by the actual labor rate per hour.
2. Compute the direct labor price and efficiency variances. Do these variances suggest the manager may have made a trade-off? Explain.

P22-33B *(L. OBJ. 4, 5, 6)* **Computing and journalizing standard cost variances [45 min]**
Smith manufactures coffee mugs that it sells to other companies for customizing with their own logos. Smith prepares flexible budgets and uses a standard cost system to control manufacturing costs. The standard unit cost of a coffee mug is based on static budget volume of 59,700 coffee mugs per month:

Direct materials (0.2 lbs @ $0.25 per lb)		$ 0.05
Direct labor (3 minutes @ $0.12 per minute)		0.36
Manufacturing overhead:		
Variable (3 minutes @ $0.05 per minute)	$ 0.15	
Fixed (3 minutes @ $0.14 per minute)	0.42	0.57
Total cost per coffee mug		$ 0.98

Actual cost and production information for July:

a. Actual production and sales were 62,400 coffee mugs.
b. Actual direct materials usage was 12,000 lbs., at an actual price of $0.18 per lb.
c. Actual direct labor usage of 203,000 minutes at a total cost of $28,420.
d. Actual overhead cost was $40,900.

Requirements

1. Compute the price variance and efficiency variance for direct materials and direct labor.
2. Journalize the usage of direct materials and the assignment of direct labor, including the related variances.
3. For manufacturing overhead, compute the total variance, the flexible budget variance, and the production volume variance. (*Hint:* Remember that the fixed overhead in the flexible budget equals the fixed overhead in the static budget.)
4. Smith intentionally hired more-skilled workers during July. How did this decision affect the cost variances? Overall, was the decision wise?

P22-34B *(L. OBJ. 4, 5, 6)* **Computing standard cost variances and reporting to management [45–60 min]**

HeadSmart manufactures headphone cases. During September 2011, the company produced 106,000 cases and recorded the following cost data:

Standard Cost Information:

	Quantity	Price
Direct materials	2 parts	$ 0.17 per part
Direct labor	0.02 hours	$ 9.00 per hour
Variable manufacturing overhead	0.02 hours	$10.00 per hour
Fixed manufacturing overhead ($32,640 for static budget volume of 96,000 units and 1,920 hours, or $ 17 per hour)		

Actual Information:

Direct materials (215,000 parts @ $0.22 per part = $47,300)
Direct labor (1,720 hours @ $9.10 per hour = $15,652)
Manufacturing overhead $60,500

Requirements

1. Compute the price variance and efficiency variance for direct materials and direct labor.
2. For manufacturing overhead, compute the total variance, the flexible budget variance, and the production volume variance.
3. Prepare a standard cost income statement through gross profit to report all variances to management. The sale price of the headset cases was $1.60 each.
4. HeadSmart's management used more-experienced workers during September. Discuss the trade-off between the two direct labor variances.

■ Continuing Exercise

E22-35 This exercise continues the Sherman Lawn Service, Inc., situation from Exercise 21-30 of Chapter 21. Sherman Lawn Service budgeted production volume for the month was 500 lawns. The standard overhead cost included $20.00 variable cost per lawn and fixed overhead costs of $5,000.

Sherman actually mowed 550 lawns in October. Actual variable overhead was $12,400, and fixed overhead was $5,600.

Requirement

1. Compute the total overhead variance, the overhead flexible budget variance, and the production volume variance.

■ Continuing Problem

P22-36 This problem continues the Haupt Consulting, Inc., situation from Problem 21-31 of Chapter 21. Assume Haupt Consulting has created a standard cost card for each job. Standard direct materials include 10 software packages at a cost of $1,000 per package. Standard direct labor costs per job include 100 hours at $100 per hour. Haupt plans on completing 10 jobs during October.

Actual direct materials costs for October included 95 software packages at a total cost of $97,000. Actual direct labor costs included 110 hours at an average rate of $105 per hour. Haupt completed all 10 jobs in October.

Requirements

1. Calculate direct materials price and efficiency variances.
2. Calculate direct labor rate and efficiency variances.
3. Prepare journal entries to record the use of both materials and labor for October for the company.

Apply Your Knowledge

■ Decision Cases

Case 1. Movies Galore distributes DVDs to movie retailers, including dot.coms. Movies Galore's top management meets monthly to evaluate the company's performance. Controller Allen Walsh prepared the following performance report for the meeting:

MOVIES GALORE
Income Statement Performance Report
Month Ended July 31, 2010

	Actual Results	Static Budget	Variance
Sales revenue	$1,640,000	$1,960,000	$320,000 U
Variable costs:			
Cost of goods sold	775,000	980,000	205,000 F
Sales commisions	77,000	107,800	30,800 F
Shipping cost	43,000	53,900	10,900 F
Fixed costs:			
Salary cost	311,000	300,500	10,500 U
Depreciation cost	209,000	214,000	5,000 F
Rent cost	129,000	108,250	20,750 U
Advertising cost	81,000	68,500	12,500 U
Total costs	1,625,000	1,832,950	207,950 F
Operating income	$ 15,000	$ 127,050	$112,050 U

Walsh also revealed that the actual sale price of $20 per movie was equal to the budgeted sale price and that there were no changes in inventories for the month.

Management is disappointed by the operating income results. CEO Jilinda Robinson exclaims, "How can actual operating income be roughly 12% of the static budget amount when there are so many favorable variances?"

Requirements

1. Prepare a more informative performance report. Be sure to include a flexible budget for the actual number of DVDs bought and sold.
2. As a member of Movies Galore's management team, which variances would you want investigated? Why?
3. Robinson believes that many consumers are postponing purchases of new movies until after the introduction of a new format for recordable DVD players. In light of this information, how would you rate the company's performance?

Case 2. Suppose you manage the local Scoopy's ice cream parlor. In addition to selling ice-cream cones, you make large batches of a few flavors of milk shakes to sell throughout the day. Your parlor is chosen to test the company's "Made-for-You" system. This new system enables patrons to customize their milk shakes by choosing different flavors.

Customers like the new system and your staff appears to be adapting, but you wonder whether this new made-to-order system is as efficient as the old system in which you just made a few large batches. Efficiency is a special concern because your performance is evaluated in part on the restaurant's efficient use of materials and labor. Your superiors consider efficiency variances greater than 5% to be unacceptable.

You decide to look at your sales for a typical day. You find that the parlor used 390 lbs. of ice cream and 72 hours of direct labor to produce and sell 2,000 shakes. The standard quantity allowed for a shake is 0.2 pound of ice cream and 0.03 hour (1.8 minutes) of direct labor. The standard prices are $1.50 per pound for ice cream and $8 an hour for labor.

Requirements

1. Compute the efficiency variances for direct labor and direct materials.
2. Provide likely explanations for the variances. Do you have reason to be concerned about your performance evaluation? Explain.
3. Write a memo to Scoopy's national office explaining your concern and suggesting a remedy.

Ethical Issues

Rita Lane is the accountant for Outdoor Living, a manufacturer of outdoor furniture that is sold through specialty stores and Internet companies. Lane is responsible for reviewing the standard costs. While reviewing the standards for the coming year, two ethical issues arise. Use the IMA's ethical guidelines (https://www.imanet.org/about_ethics_statement.asp) to identify the ethical dilemma in each situation. Identify the relevant factors in each situation and suggest what Lane should recommend to the controller.

Requirements

Issue 1. Lane has been approached by Casey Henderson, a former colleague who worked with Lane when they were both employed by a public accounting firm. Henderson has recently started his own firm, Henderson Benchmarking Associates, which collects and sells data on industry benchmarks. He offers to provide Lane with benchmarks for the outdoor furniture industry free of charge if she will provide him with the last three years of Outdoor Living's standard and actual costs. Henderson explains that this is how he obtains most of his firm's benchmarking data. Lane always has a difficult time with the standard-setting process and believes that the benchmark data would be very useful.

Issue 2. Outdoor Living's management is starting a continuous improvement policy that requires a 10% reduction in standard costs each year for the next three years. Dan Jacobs, manufacturing foreman of the Teak furniture line, asks Lane to set loose standard costs this year before the continuous improvement policy is implemented. Jacobs argues that there is no other way to meet the tightening standards while maintaining the high quality of the Teak line.

Team Project

Lynx, Corp., manufactures wood windows and doors. Lynx has been using a standard cost system that bases price and quantity standards on Lynx's historical long-run average performance. Suppose Lynx's controller has engaged your team of management consultants to advise him or her whether Lynx should use some basis other than historical performance for setting standards.

Requirements

1. List the types of variances you recommend that Lynx compute (for example, direct materials price variance for glass). For each variance, what specific standards would Lynx need to develop? In addition to cost standards, do you recommend that Lynx develop any nonfinancial standards?
2. There are many approaches to setting standards other than simply using long-run average historical prices and quantities.
   a. List three alternative approaches that Lynx could use to set standards, and explain how Lynx could implement each alternative.
   b. Evaluate each alternative method of setting standards, including the pros and cons of each method.
   c. Write a memo to Lynx's controller detailing your recommendations. First, should Lynx retain its historical data-based standard cost approach? If not, which of the alternative approaches should it adopt?

Quick Check Answers

1. *a* 2. *b* 3. *d* 4. *e* 5. *a* 6. *d* 7. *b* 8. *a* 9. *b* 10. *a*

For online homework, exercises, and problems that provide you immediate feedback, please visit www.myaccountinglab.com.

23 Performance Evaluation and the Balanced Scorecard

Learning Objectives/ Success Keys

1. Explain why and how companies decentralize
2. Explain why companies use performance evaluation systems
3. Describe the balanced scorecard and identify key performance indicators for each perspective
4. Use performance reports to evaluate cost, revenue, and profit centers
5. Use ROI, RI, and EVA to evaluate investment centers

To deliver over 3.6 billion packages a year in over 200 countries, **United Parcel Service (UPS)** employs over 370,000 people. But how does management successfully guide the actions of all of these employees? First, it divides—or decentralizes—the company into three segments: domestic packaging, international packaging, and non-packaging services (such as supply chain and logistics). It further breaks each packaging segment into geographic regions and each region into districts. Management gives each district manager authority to make decisions for his or her own district. Because top management wants *every* employee to know how his or her day-to-day job contributes to the company's goals, it implemented a system, called the balanced scorecard, for communicating strategy to all district managers and employees. Management can also use the balanced scorecard to measure whether each district is meeting its goals and to assess where it should make changes. According to one **UPS** executive, "The balanced scorecard provided a road map—the shared vision of our future goals—with action elements that let *everyone* contribute to our success." After reading this article, Smart Touch's CEO, Sheena Bright, wants to learn more about this managerial tool.

In 2000, *Forbes* named **UPS** the "Company of the Year" and in 2004, *Fortune* rated **UPS** as the "World's Most Admired Company in its Industry" for the sixth consecutive year.[1]

Many companies, like **UPS**, decentralize their operations into subunits. Decentralization provides large companies with many advantages. Because top management is not directly involved in running the day-to-day operations of each subunit, it needs a system—such as the balanced scorecard—for communicating the company's strategy to subunit managers and for measuring how well the subunits are achieving their goals. Let us first take a look at the advantages and disadvantages of decentralization.

Decentralized Operations

1 Explain why and how companies decentralize

In a small company, the owner or top manager often makes all planning and operating decisions. Small companies are most often considered to be **Centralized companies** because centralizing decision making is easier due to the smaller scope of their operations. However, when a company grows, it is impossible for a single person to manage the entire organization's daily operations. Therefore, most companies decentralize as they grow. These are called **decentralized companies.**

Companies decentralize by splitting their operations into different divisions or operating units. Top management delegates decision-making responsibility to the unit managers. Top management determines the type of decentralization that best suits the company's strategy. For example, decentralization may be based on geographic area, product line, customer base, business function, or some other business characteristic. **Citizen's Bank** segments its operations by state (different geographic areas). **Sherwin-Williams** segments by customer base (commercial and consumer paint divisions). **PepsiCo** segments by brands (**Pepsi, Frito-Lay, Quaker, Gatorade, and Tropicana**). And **UPS** segmented first by function (domestic packaging, international packaging, and nonpackaging services), then by geographic area. Smart Touch Learning thinks it will segment by product line (DVDs and Web-based learning).

[1]*Sources*: Robert Kaplan and David Norton, *The Strategy-Focused Organization: How Balanced Scorecard Companies Thrive in the New Business Environment*, Harvard Business School Press, Boston, 2001, pp. 21–22, 239–241; UPS Web site.

Advantages of Decentralization

What advantages does decentralization offer large companies? Let us take a look.

Frees Top Management Time

By delegating responsibility for daily operations to unit managers, top management can concentrate on long-term strategic planning and higher-level decisions that affect the entire company. It also naturally places the decision makers (top management) closer to the source of the decisions.

Supports Use of Expert Knowledge

Decentralization allows top management to hire the expertise each business unit needs to excel in its own specific operations. For example, decentralizing by state allows **Citizens Bank** to hire managers with specialized knowledge of the banking laws in each state. Such specialized knowledge can help unit managers make better decisions, than could the company's top managers, about product and business improvements within the business unit (state).

Improves Customer Relations

Unit managers focus on just one segment of the company. Therefore, they can maintain closer contact with important customers than can upper management. Thus, decentralization often leads to improved customer relations and quicker customer response time.

Provides Training

Decentralization also provides unit managers with training and experience necessary to become effective top managers. For example, in politics, presidential candidates often have experience as senators or state governors. Likewise, companies often choose CEOs based on their past performance as division managers.

Improves Motivation and Retention

Empowering unit managers to make decisions increases managers' motivation and retention. This improves job performance and satisfaction.

Disadvantages of Decentralization

Despite its advantages, decentralization can also cause potential problems, including those outlined in this section.

Duplication of Costs

Decentralization may cause the company to duplicate certain costs or assets. For example, each business unit may hire its own payroll department and purchase its own payroll software. Companies can often avoid such duplications by providing centralized services. For example, **Doubletree Hotels** segments its business by property, yet each property shares one centralized reservations office and one centralized Web site.

Problems Achieving Goal Congruence

Goal congruence occurs when unit managers' goals align with top management's goals. Decentralized companies often struggle to achieve goal congruence. Unit managers may not fully understand the "big picture" of the company. They may make decisions that are good for their division but could harm another division or the rest of the company. For example, the purchasing department may buy cheaper components to decrease product cost. However, cheaper components may hurt the product line's quality, and the company's brand, *as a whole*, may suffer. Later in this chapter, we will see how managerial accountants can design performance evaluation systems that encourage goal congruence.

As Exhibit 23-1 illustrates, the many advantages of decentralization usually outweigh the disadvantages.

EXHIBIT 23-1 | **Advantages Outweigh Disadvantages**

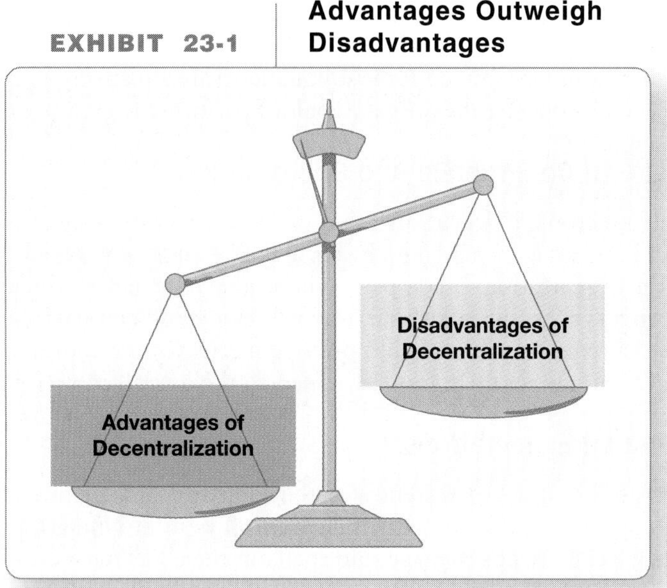

Responsibility Centers

Decentralized companies delegate responsibility for specific decisions to each subunit, creating responsibility centers. Recall from Chapter 21 that a *responsibility center* is a part or subunit of an organization whose manager is accountable for specific activities. Exhibit 23-2 reviews the four most common types of responsibility centers.

EXHIBIT 23-2 | **The Four Most Common Types of Responsibility Centers**

Responsibility Center	Manager is responsible for...	Examples
Cost center	Controlling costs	Production line at Dell Computer; legal department and accounting departments at Nike
Revenue center	Generating sales revenue	Midwest sales region at Pace Foods; central reservation office at Delta
Profit center	Producing profit through generating sales and controlling costs	Product line at Anheuser-Busch; individual Home Depot stores
Investment center	Producing profit and managing the division's invested capital	Company divisions, such as Walt Disney World Resorts and Toon Disney

Performance Measurement

2 Explain why companies use performance evaluation systems

Once a company decentralizes operations, top management is no longer involved in running the subunits' day-to-day operations. Performance evaluation systems provide top management with a framework for maintaining control over the entire organization.

Goals of Performance Evaluation Systems

When companies decentralize, top management needs a system to communicate its goals to subunit managers. Additionally, top management needs to determine whether the decisions being made at the subunit level are effectively meeting company goals. We will now consider the primary goals of performance evaluation systems.

Promoting Goal Congruence and Coordination

As previously mentioned, decentralization increases the difficulty of achieving goal congruence. Unit managers may not always make decisions consistent with the overall goals of the organization. A company will be able to achieve its goals only if each unit moves, in a synchronized fashion, toward the overall company goals. The performance measurement system should provide incentives for coordinating the subunits' activities and direct them toward achieving the overall company goals.

Communicating Expectations

To make decisions that are consistent with the company's goals, unit managers must know the goals and the specific part their unit plays in attaining those goals. The performance measurement system should spell out the unit's most critical objectives. Without a clear picture of what management expects, unit managers have little to guide their daily operating decisions.

Motivating Unit Managers

Unit managers are usually motivated to make decisions that will help to achieve top management's expectations. For additional motivation, upper management may offer bonuses to unit managers who meet or exceed performance targets. Top management must exercise extreme care in setting performance targets. For example, a manager measured solely by his ability to control costs may take whatever actions are necessary to achieve that goal, including sacrificing quality or customer service. But such actions would *not* be in the best interests of the firm as a whole. Therefore, upper management must consider the ramifications of the performance targets it sets for unit managers.

Providing Feedback

In decentralized companies, top management is no longer involved in the day-to-day operations of each subunit. Performance evaluation systems provide upper management with the feedback it needs to maintain control over the entire organization, even though it has delegated responsibility and decision-making authority to unit managers. If targets are not met at the unit level, upper management will take corrective actions, ranging from modifying unit goals (if the targets were unrealistic) to replacing the unit manager (if the targets were achievable, but the manager failed to reach them).

Benchmarking

Performance evaluation results are often used for benchmarking, which is the practice of comparing the company's achievements against the best practices in the industry. Comparing results against industry benchmarks is often more revealing than comparing results against budgets. To survive, a company must keep up with its competitors. Benchmarking helps the company determine whether or not it is performing at least as well as its competitors.

Stop & Think...

Do companies, such as **UPS**, only benchmark subunit performance against competitors and industry standards?

Answer: No. Companies also benchmark performance against the subunit's past performance. Historical trend data (measuring performance over time) helps managers assess whether their decisions are improving, having no effect, or adversely affecting subunit performance. Some companies also benchmark performance against other subunits with similar characteristics.

Limitations of Financial Performance Measurement

In the past, performance measurement revolved almost entirely around *financial* performance. Until 1995, 95% of **UPS's** performance measures were financial. On the one hand, this focus makes sense because the ultimate goal of a company is to generate profit. On the other hand, *current* financial performance tends to reveal the results of *past* actions rather than indicate *future* performance. For this reason, financial measures tend to be **lag indicators** (after the fact), rather than **lead indicators** (future predictors). Management needs to know the results of past decisions, but it also needs to know how current decisions may affect the future. To adequately assess the company, managers need both lead indicators and lag indicators.

Another limitation of financial performance measures is that they tend to focus on the company's short-term achievements, rather than on long-term performance. Why is this the case? Because financial statements are prepared on a monthly, quarterly, or annual basis. To remain competitive, top management needs clear signals that assess and predict the company's performance over longer periods of time.

The Balanced Scorecard

3 Describe the balanced scorecard and identify key performance indicators for each perspective

In the early 1990s, Robert Kaplan and David Norton introduced the **balanced scorecard.**[2] The balanced scorecard recognizes that management must consider *both* financial performance measures (which tend to measure the results of actions already taken—lag indicators) and operational performance measures (which tend to drive future performance—lead indicators) when judging the performance of a company and its subunits. These measures should be linked with the company's goals and its strategy for achieving those goals. The balanced scorecard represents a major shift in corporate performance measurement. Rather than treating financial indicators as the sole measure of performance, companies recognize that they are only one measure among a broader set. Keeping score of operating measures *and* traditional financial measures gives management a "balanced" view of the organization.

[2]Robert Kaplan and David Norton, "The Balanced Scorecard—Measures That Drive Performance," *Harvard Business Review on Measuring Corporate Performance*, Boston, 1991, pp. 123–145; Robert Kaplan and David Norton, *Translating Strategy into Action: The Balanced Scorecard*, Boston, Harvard Business School Press, 1996.

Kaplan and Norton use the analogy of an airplane pilot to illustrate the necessity for a balanced scorecard approach to performance evaluation. The pilot of an airplane cannot rely on only one factor, such as wind speed, to fly a plane. Rather, the pilot must consider other critical factors, such as altitude, direction, and fuel level. Likewise, management cannot rely on only financial measures to guide the company. Management needs to consider other critical factors, such as customer satisfaction, operational efficiency, and employee excellence. Similar to the way a pilot uses cockpit instruments to measure critical factors, management uses *key performance indicators*—such as customer satisfaction ratings and revenue growth—to measure critical factors that affect the success of the company. As shown in Exhibit 23-3, **key performance indicators (KPIs)** are summary performance measures that help managers assess whether the company is achieving its goals.

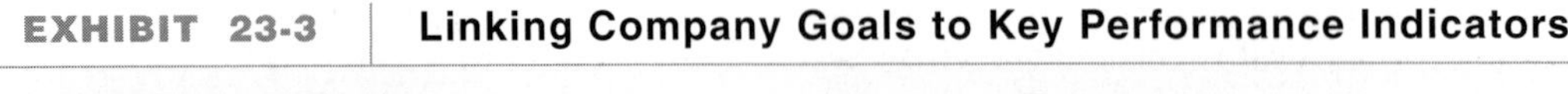
EXHIBIT 23-3 | **Linking Company Goals to Key Performance Indicators**

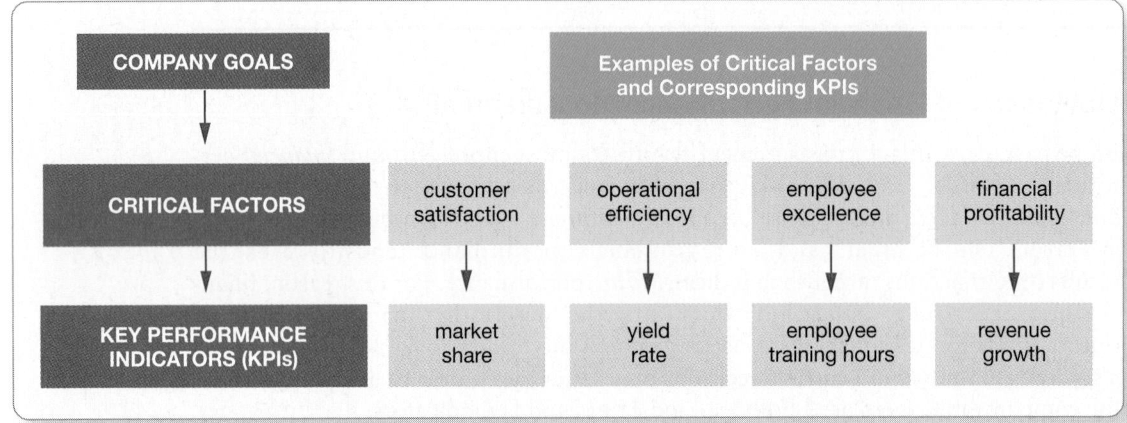

The Four Perspectives of the Balanced Scorecard

The balanced scorecard views the company from four different perspectives, each of which evaluates a specific aspect of organizational performance:

1. Financial perspective
2. Customer perspective
3. Internal business perspective
4. Learning and growth perspective

Exhibit 23-4 on the following page illustrates how the company's strategy affects, and, in turn, is affected by all four perspectives. Additionally, it shows the cause-and-effect relationship linking the four perspectives.

Companies that adopt the balanced scorecard usually have specific objectives they wish to achieve within each of the four perspectives. Once management clearly identifies the objectives, it develops KPIs that will assess how well the objectives are being achieved. To focus attention on the most critical elements and prevent information overload, management should use only a few KPIs for each perspective. Let us now look at each of the perspectives and discuss the links between them.

Financial Perspective

This perspective helps managers answer the question, "How do we look to shareholders?" The ultimate goal of companies is to generate income for their owners. Therefore, company strategy revolves around increasing the company's profits through increasing revenue growth and increasing productivity. Companies grow revenue through introducing new products, gaining new customers, and increasing

EXHIBIT 23-4 **The Four Perspectives of the Balanced Scorecard**

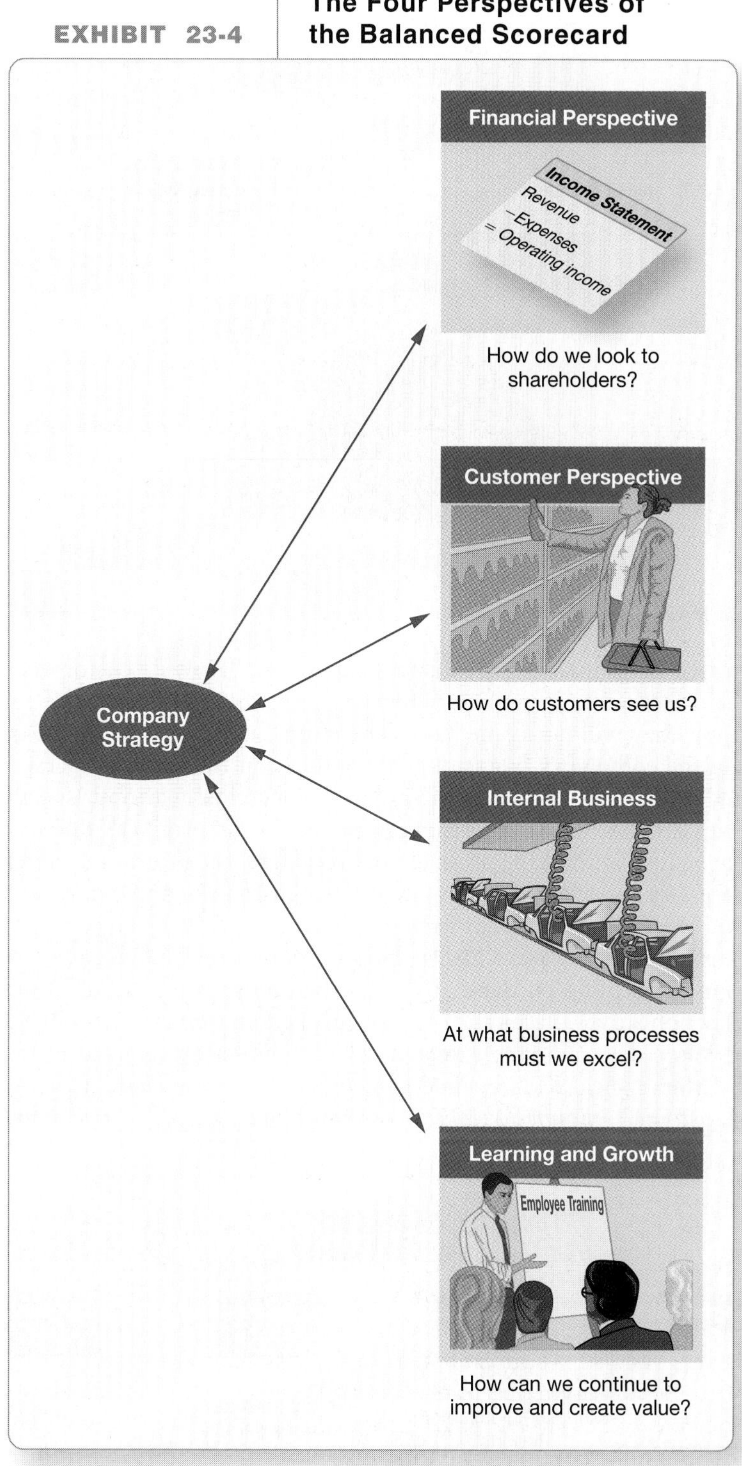

sales to existing customers. Companies increase productivity through reducing costs and using the company's assets more efficiently. Managers may implement seemingly sensible strategies and initiatives, but the test of their judgment is whether these decisions increase company profits. The financial perspective focuses management's attention on KPIs that assess financial objectives, such as revenue growth and cost cutting. Some commonly used KPIs include: *sales revenue growth, gross margin growth,* and *return on investment.* The latter portion of this chapter discusses in detail the most commonly used financial perspective KPIs.

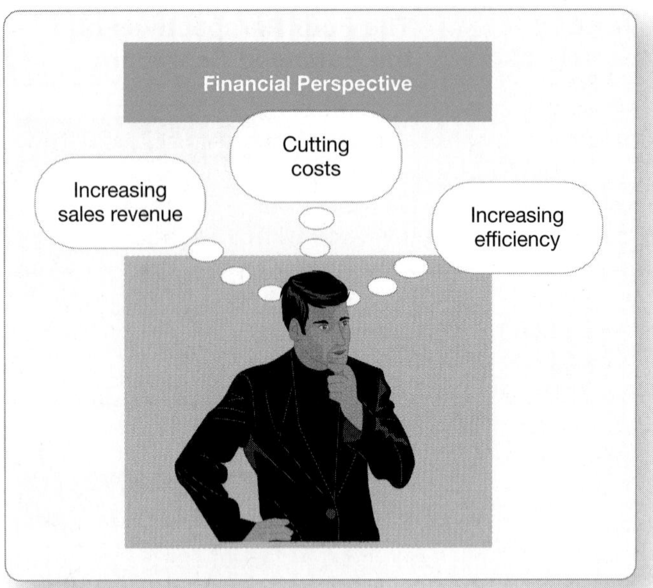

Customer Perspective

This perspective helps managers evaluate the question, "How do customers see us?" Customer satisfaction is a top priority for long-term company success. If customers are not happy, they will not come back. Therefore, customer satisfaction is critical to achieving the company's financial goals outlined in the financial perspective of the balanced scorecard. Customers are typically concerned with four specific product or service attributes: (1) the product's price, (2) the product's quality, (3) the sales service quality, and (4) the product's delivery time (the shorter the better). Since each of these attributes is critical to making the customer happy, most companies have specific objectives for each of these attributes.

Businesses commonly use KPIs, such as *customer satisfaction ratings*, to assess how they are performing on these attributes. No doubt you have filled out a customer satisfaction survey. Because customer satisfaction is crucial, customer satisfaction ratings often determine the extent to which bonuses are granted to restaurant managers. Other typical KPIs include *percentage of market share, increase in the number of customers, number of repeat customers*, and *rate of on-time deliveries*.

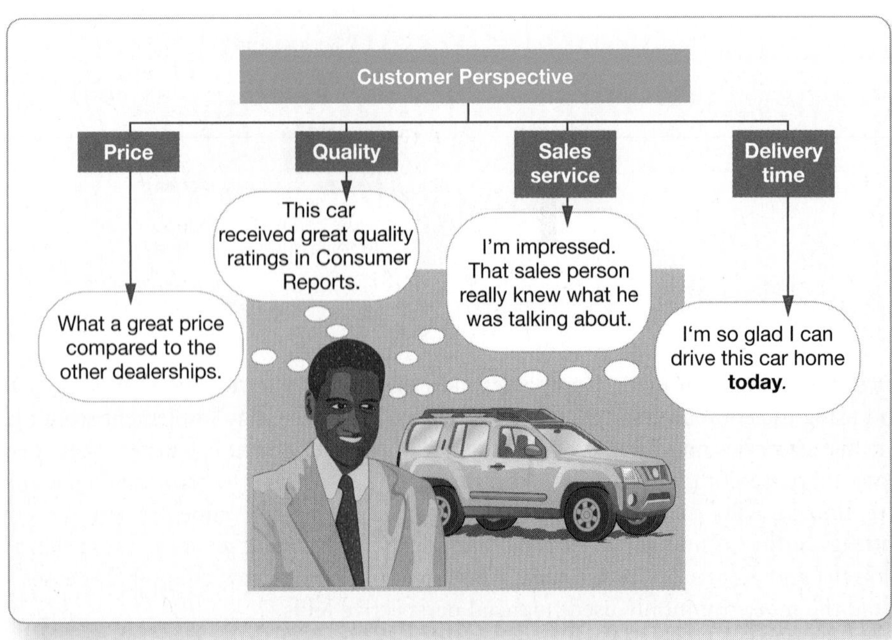

Internal Business Perspective

This perspective helps managers address the question, "At what business processes must we excel to satisfy customer and financial objectives?" The answer to this question incorporates three factors: innovation, operations, and post-sales service. All three factors critically affect customer satisfaction, which will affect the company's financial success.

Satisfying customers once does not guarantee future success, which is why the first important factor of the internal business perspective is innovation. Customers' needs and wants change as the world around them changes. Just a couple of years ago, digital cameras, flat-panel computer monitors, plasma screen televisions, and digital video recorders (DVRs) did not exist. Companies must continually improve existing products (such as adding cameras to cell phones) and develop new products (such as iPods and portable DVD players) to succeed in the future. Companies commonly assess innovation using KPIs, such as the *number of new products developed* or *new-product development time*.

The second important factor of the internal business perspective is operations. Efficient and effective internal operations allow the company to meet customers' needs and expectations. For example, the time it takes to manufacture a product (*manufacturing cycle time*) affects the company's ability to deliver quickly to meet a customer's demand. Production efficiency (*number of units produced per hour*) and product quality (*defect rate*) also affect the price charged to the customer. To remain competitive, companies must be at least as good as the industry leader at those internal operations that are essential to their business.

The third factor of the internal business perspective is post-sales service. How well does the company service customers after the sale? Claims of excellent post-sales service help to generate more sales. Management assesses post-sales service through the following typical KPIs: *number of warranty claims received, average repair time*, and *average wait time on the phone for a customer service representative*.

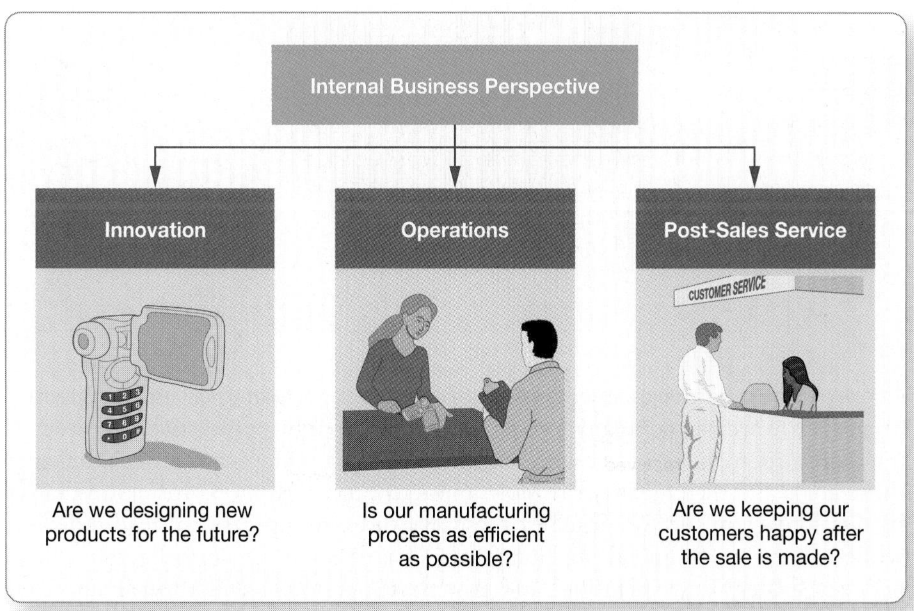

Learning and Growth Perspective

This perspective helps managers assess the question, "How can we continue to improve and create value?" The learning and growth perspective focuses on three factors: (1) employee capabilities, (2) information system capabilities, and (3) the company's "climate for action." The learning and growth perspective lays the foundation needed to improve internal business operations, sustain customer satisfaction, and generate financial success. Without skilled employees, updated technology, and a positive corporate culture, the company will not be able to meet the objectives of the other perspectives.

Let us consider each of these factors. First, because most routine work is automated, employees are freed up to be critical and creative thinkers who, therefore, can help achieve the company's goals. The learning and growth perspective measures employees' skills, knowledge, motivation, and empowerment. KPIs typically include *hours of employee training*, *employee satisfaction*, *employee turnover*, and *number of employee suggestions implemented*. Second, employees need timely and accurate information on customers, internal processes, and finances; therefore, other KPIs measure the maintenance and improvement of the company's information system. For example, KPIs might include the *percentage of employees having online access to information about customers*, and the *percentage of processes with real-time feedback on quality, cycle time, and cost*. Finally, management must create a corporate culture that supports communication, change, and growth. For example, **UPS** used the balanced scorecard to communicate strategy to every employee and to show each employee how his or her daily work contributed to company success.

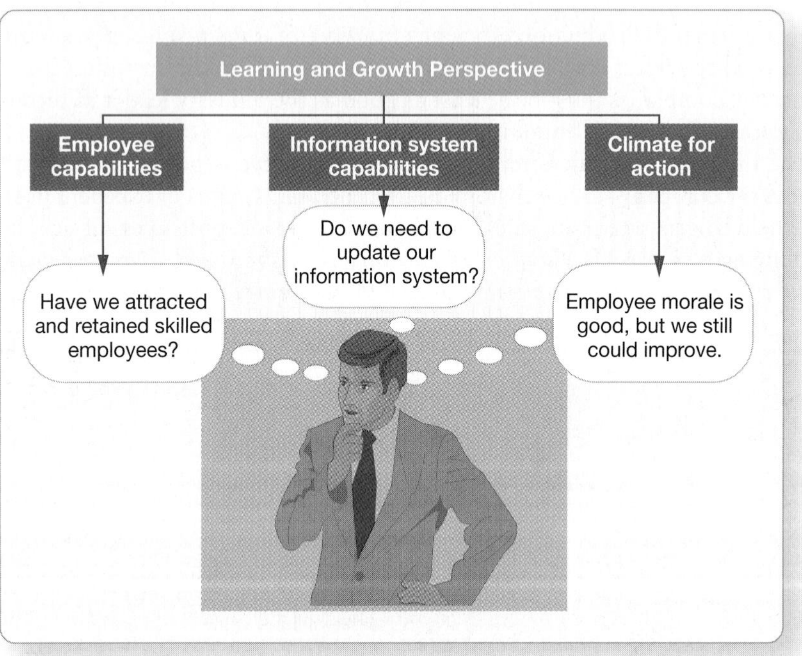

In summary, the balanced scorecard focuses performance measurement on progress toward the company's goals in each of the four perspectives. In designing the scorecard, managers start with the company's goals and its strategy for achieving those goals and then identify the *most* important measures of performance that will predict long-term success. Some of these measures are operational lead indicators, while others are financial lag indicators. Managers must consider the linkages between strategy and operations and how those operations will affect finances now and in the future.

So far, we have looked at why companies decentralize, why they need to measure subunit performance, and how the balanced scorecard can help. In the second half of the chapter, we will focus on how companies measure the financial perspective of the balanced scorecard.

Decision Guidelines

UPS had to make the following types of decisions when it decentralized and developed its balanced scorecard for performance evaluation.

Decision	Guidelines
• On what basis should the company be decentralized?	The manner of decentralization should fit the company's strategy. Many companies decentralize based on geographic region, product line, business function, or customer type.
• Will decentralization have any negative impact on the company?	Decentralization usually provides many benefits; however, decentralization also has potential drawbacks: • Subunits may duplicate costs or assets. • Subunit managers may not make decisions that are favorable to the entire company.
• How can responsibility accounting be incorporated at decentralized companies?	Subunit managers are given responsibility for specific activities and are only held accountable for the results of those activities. Subunits generally fall into one of the following four categories according to their responsibilities: 1. Cost centers—responsible for controlling costs 2. Revenue centers—responsible for generating revenue 3. Profit centers—responsible for controlling costs and generating revenue 4. Investment centers—responsible for controlling costs, generating revenue, and efficiently managing the division's invested capital (assets)
• Is a performance evaluation system necessary?	While not mandatory, most companies will reap many benefits from implementing a well-designed performance evaluation system. Such systems will promote goal congruence, communicate expectations, motivate managers, provide feedback, and enable benchmarking.
• Should the performance evaluation system include lag or lead measures?	Better performance evaluation systems include *both* lag and lead measures. Lag measures indicate the results of past actions, while lead measures a project's future performance.
• What are the four balanced scorecard perspectives?	1. Financial perspective 2. Customer perspective 3. Internal Business perspective 4. Learning and Growth perspective
• Must all four perspectives be included in the company's balanced scorecard?	Every company's balanced scorecard will be unique to its business and strategy. Because each of the four perspectives is causally linked, most companies will benefit from developing performance measures for each of the four perspectives.

Summary Problem 1

The balanced scorecard gives performance perspective from 4 different viewpoints.

Requirements

1. Each of the following describes a key performance indicator. Determine which of the following balanced scorecard perspectives is being addressed (financial, customer, internal business, or learning and growth):
   a. Employee turnover
   b. Earnings per share
   c. Percentage of on-time deliveries
   d. Revenue growth rate
   e. Percentage of defects discovered during manufacturing
   f. Number of warranties claimed
   g. New product development time
   h. Number of repeat customers
   i. Number of employee suggestions implemented
2. Read the following company initiatives and determine which of the balanced scorecard perspectives is being addressed (financial, customer, internal business, learning and growth):
   a. Purchasing efficient production equipment
   b. Providing employee training
   c. Updating retail store lighting
   d. Paying quarterly dividends
   e. Updating the company's information system

Solution

Requirement 1

a. Learning and growth
b. Financial
c. Customer
d. Financial
e. Internal business
f. Internal business
g. Internal business
h. Customer
i. Learning and growth

Requirement 2

a. Internal business
b. Learning and growth
c. Customer
d. Financial
e. Learning and growth

Measuring the Financial Performance of Cost, Revenue, and Profit Centers

4 Use performance reports to evaluate cost, revenue, and profit centers

In this half of the chapter we will take a more detailed look at how companies measure the financial perspective of the balanced scorecard for different subunits of the company. We will focus now on the financial performance measurement of each type of responsibility center.

Responsibility accounting performance reports capture the financial performance of cost, revenue, and profit centers. Recall from Chapter 21 that responsibility accounting performance reports compare *actual* results with *budgeted* amounts and display a variance, or difference, between the two amounts. Because *cost centers* are only responsible for controlling costs, their performance reports only include information on actual versus budgeted *costs*. Likewise, performance reports for *revenue centers* only contain actual versus budgeted *revenue*. However, *profit centers* are responsible for both controlling costs and generating revenue. Therefore, their performance reports contain actual and budgeted information on both their *revenues and costs*.

Cost center performance reports typically focus on the *flexible budget variance*—the difference between actual results and the flexible budget (as described in Chapter 22). Exhibit 23-5 shows an example of a cost center performance report for a regional payroll processing department of Smart Touch Learning. Because the payroll processing department only incurs expenses and does not generate revenue, it is classified as a cost center.

EXHIBIT 23-5 Example of Cost Center Performance Report

SMART TOUCH LEARNING, INC.
Payroll Processing Department Performance Report
July 2011

	Actual	Flexible Budget	Flexible Budget Variance (U or F)	% Variance* (U of F)
Salary and wages	$18,500	$18,000	$ 500 U	2.8% U
Payroll benefits	6,100	5,000	1,100 U	22.0% U
Equipment depreciation	3,000	3,000	0	0%
Supplies	1,850	2,000	150 F	7.5% F
Other expenses	1,900	2,000	100 F	5.0% F
Total expenses	$31,350	$30,000	$1,350 U	4.5% U

*Flexible budget variance/flexible budget

Managers use management by exception to determine which variances in the performance report are worth investigating. For example, management may only investigate variances that exceed a certain dollar amount (for example, over $1,000) or a certain percentage of the budgeted figure (for example, over 10%). Smaller variances signal that operations are close to target and do not require management's immediate attention. For example, in the cost center performance report illustrated in Exhibit 23-5, management might only investigate "payroll benefits" because the variance exceeds both $1,000 and 10%. Companies that use standard costs can compute price and efficiency variances, as described in Chapter 22, to better understand why significant flexible budget variances occurred.

Revenue center performance reports often highlight both the flexible budget variance and the sales volume variance. The performance report for the specialty DVD department of Smart Touch Learning might look similar to Exhibit 23-6, with detailed sales volume and revenue shown for each brand and type of DVD sold. (For simplicity, the exhibit shows volume and revenue for only one item.) The cash register bar-coding system provides management with the sales volume and sales revenue generated by individual products.

EXHIBIT 23-6 **Example of a Revenue Center Performance Report**

SMART TOUCH LEARNING, INC.
Specialty DVD Department Performance Report
July 2011

Sales revenue	Actual Sales	Flexible Budget Variance	Flexible Budget	Sales Volume Variance	Static (Master) Budget
Number of DVDs	2,480	-0-	2,480	155 (F)	2,325
Specialty DVDs	$40,920	$3,720 (U)	$44,640	$2,790 (F)	$41,850

Recall from Chapter 22 that the sales volume variance is due strictly to volume differences—selling more or fewer units (DVDs) than originally planned. The flexible budget variance, however, is due strictly to differences in the sales price—selling units for a higher or lower price than originally planned. Both the sales volume variance and the flexible budget variance help revenue center managers understand why they have exceeded or fallen short of budgeted revenue.

Managers of profit centers are responsible for both generating revenue and controlling costs so their performance reports include both revenues and expenses. Exhibit 23-7 shows an example of a profit center performance report for the DVD department.

EXHIBIT 23-7 **Example of a Profit Center Performance Report**

SMART TOUCH LEARNING, INC.
DVD—Performance Report
July 2011

	Actual	Flexible Budget	Flexible Budget Variance	% Variance
Sales revenue	$5,243,600	$5,000,000	$243,600F	4.9%F
Operating expenses	4,183,500	4,000,000	183,500U	4.6%U
Income from operations before service department charges	1,060,100	1,000,000	60,100F	6.0%F
Service department charges (allocated)	84,300	75,000	9,300U	12.4%U
Income from operations	$ 975,800	$ 925,000	$ 50,800F	5.5%F

Notice how this profit center performance report contains a line called "Service department charges." Recall that one drawback of decentralization is that subunits may duplicate costs or assets. Many companies avoid this problem by providing centralized service departments where several subunits, such as profit centers, share assets or costs. For example, the payroll processing cost center shown in Exhibit 23-5 serves all of Smart Touch Learning. In addition to centralized payroll departments, companies often provide centralized human resource departments, legal departments, and information systems.

When subunits share centralized services, should those services be "free" to the subunits? If they are free, the subunit's performance report will *not* include any charge for using those services. However, if they are not free, the performance report will show a charge, as you see in Exhibit 23-7. Most companies charge subunits for their use of centralized services because the subunit would incur a cost to buy those services on its own. For example, if Smart Touch Learning did not operate a centralized payroll department, the DVD Department would have to hire its own payroll department personnel and purchase computers, payroll software, and supplies necessary to process the department's payroll. As an alternative, it could outsource payroll to a company, such as **Paychex** or **ADP**. In either event, the department would incur a cost for processing payroll. It only seems fair that the department is charged for using the centralized payroll processing department. Appendix 23A at the end of this chapter describes how companies allocate service department costs between subunits. Because the charges are the result of allocation, rather than a direct cost of the profit center, they are usually shown on a separate line rather than "buried" in the subunit's other operating expenses.

Regardless of the type of responsibility center, performance reports should focus on information, not blame. Analyzing budget variances helps managers understand the underlying *reasons* for the unit's performance. Once management understands these reasons, it may be able to take corrective actions. But some variances are uncontrollable. For example, the 2005 hurricanes in the Gulf Coast increased prices of gasoline (due to damaged oil refineries) and building materials (as people repaired hurricane-damaged homes). These price increases resulted in unfavorable cost variances for many companies. Managers should not be held accountable for conditions they cannot control. Responsibility accounting can help management identify the causes of variances, thereby allowing them to determine what was controllable, and what was not.

We have just looked at the detailed financial information presented in responsibility accounting performance reports. In addition to these *detailed* reports, upper management often uses *summary* measures—financial KPIs—to assess the financial performance of cost, revenue, and profit centers. Examples include the *cost per unit of output* (for cost centers), *revenue growth* (for revenue centers), and *gross margin growth* (for profit centers). KPIs, such as these, are used to address the financial perspective of the balanced scorecard for cost, revenue, and profit centers. In the next section we will look at the most commonly used KPIs for investment centers.

Stop & Think...

We have just seen that companies like Smart Touch Learning use responsibility accounting performance reports to evaluate the financial performance of cost, revenue, and profit centers. Are these types of responsibility reports sufficient for evaluating the financial performance of investment centers? Why or why not?

Answer: Investment centers are responsible not only for generating revenue and controlling costs, but also for efficiently managing the subunit's invested capital. The performance reports we have just seen address how well the subunits control costs and generate revenue, but they do not address how well the subunits manage their assets. Therefore, these performance reports will be helpful but not sufficient for evaluating investment center performance.

Measuring the Financial Performance of Investment Centers

5 Use ROI, RI, and EVA to evaluate investment centers

Investment centers are typically large divisions of a company, such as the media division of **Amazon.com** or of Smart Touch Learning. The duties of an investment center manager are similar to those of a CEO. The CEO is responsible for maximizing income, in relation to the company's invested capital, by using company assets efficiently. Likewise, investment center managers are responsible not only for generating profit but also for making the best use of the investment center's assets.

How does an investment center manager influence the use of the division's assets? An investment center manager has the authority to open new stores or close old stores. The manager may also decide how much inventory to hold, what types of investments to make, how aggressively to collect accounts receivable, and whether to invest in new equipment. In other words, the manager has decision-making responsibility over all of the division's assets.

Companies cannot evaluate investment centers the way they evaluate profit centers, based only on operating income. Why? Because income does not indicate how *efficiently* the division is using its assets. The financial evaluation of investment centers must measure two factors: (1) how much income the division is generating and (2) how efficiently the division is using its assets.

Consider Smart Touch Learning. In addition to its DVD Division, it also has an online e-learning Division. Operating income, total assets, and sales for the two divisions follow (in thousands of dollars):

Smart Touch Learning	e-learning	DVD
Operating income	$ 450,000	$ 975,800
Total assets	2,500,000	6,500,000
Sales	7,500,000	5,243,600

Based on operating income alone, the DVD Division (with operating income of $975,800) appears to be more profitable than the e-learning Division (with operating income of $450,000). However, this comparison is misleading because it does not consider the assets invested in each division. The DVD Division has more assets to use for generating income than does the e-learning Division.

To adequately evaluate an investment center's financial performance, companies need summary performance measures—or KPIs—that include *both* the division's operating income *and* its assets. (See Exhibit 23-8.) In the next sections, we discuss three commonly used performance measures: return on investment (ROI), residual income (RI), and economic value added (EVA). All three measures incorporate both the division's assets and its operating income. For simplicity, we will leave the word *divisional* out of the equations. However, keep in mind that all of the equations use divisional data when evaluating a division's performance.

EXHIBIT 23-8 **Summary Performance Measures (KPIs) for Investment Centers**

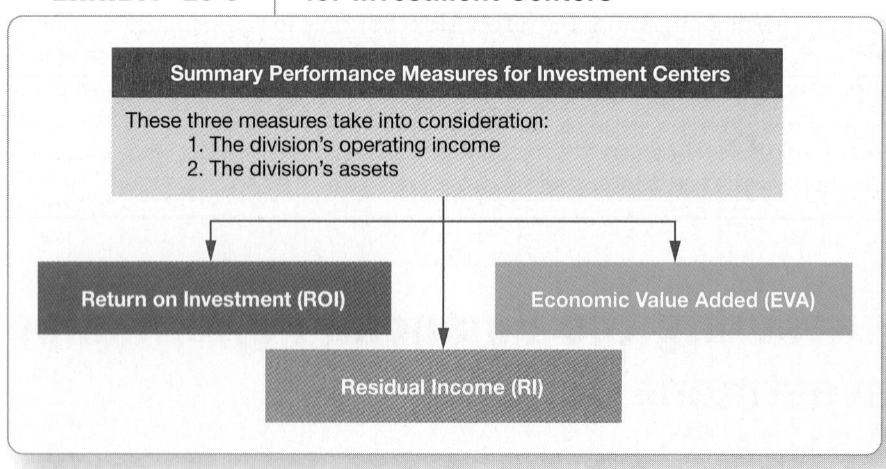

Return on Investment (ROI)

Return on Investment (ROI) is one of the most commonly used KPIs for evaluating an investment center's financial performance. Companies typically define ROI as follows:

$$\text{ROI} = \frac{\text{Operating income}}{\text{Total assets}}$$

ROI measures the amount of income an investment center earns relative to the amount of its assets. Let us calculate each division's ROI:

$$\text{e-learning Division ROI} = \frac{\$450{,}000}{\$2{,}500{,}000} = 18\%$$

$$\text{DVD Division ROI} = \frac{975{,}800}{\$6{,}500{,}000} = 15\%$$

Although the DVD Division has a higher operating income than the e-learning Division, the DVD Division is actually *less* profitable than the e-learning Division when we consider that the DVD Division has more assets from which to generate its profit.

If you had $1,000 to invest, would you rather invest it in the DVD Division or the e-learning Division? The DVD Division earns a profit of $0.15 on every $1.00 of assets, but the e-learning Division earns $0.18 on every $1.00 of assets. When top management decides how to invest excess funds, it often considers each division's ROI. A division with a higher ROI is more likely to receive extra funds because it has a history of providing a higher return.

In addition to comparing ROI across divisions, management also compares a division's ROI across time to determine whether the division is becoming more or less profitable in relation to its assets. Additionally, management often benchmarks divisional ROI with other companies in the same industry to determine how each division is performing compared to its competitors.

To determine what is driving a division's ROI, management often restates the ROI equation in its expanded form. Notice that Sales is incorporated in the denominator of the first term, and in the numerator of the second term. When the two terms are multiplied together, Sales cancels out, leaving the original ROI formula.

$$\text{ROI} = \frac{\text{Operating income}}{\text{Sales}} \times \frac{\text{Sales}}{\text{Total assets}} = \frac{\text{Operating income}}{\text{Total assets}}$$

Why do managers rewrite the ROI formula this way? Because it helps them better understand how they can improve their ROI. The first term in the expanded equation is called the **profit margin:**

$$\text{Profit margin} = \frac{\text{Operating income}}{\text{Sales}}$$

The profit margin shows how much operating income the division earns on every $1.00 of sales, so this term focuses on profitability. Let us calculate each division's sales margin:

$$\text{e-learning Division's profit margin} = \frac{\$450{,}000}{\$7{,}500{,}000} = 6\%$$

$$\text{DVD Division's profit margin} = \frac{\$975{,}800}{\$5{,}243{,}600} = 19\%$$

The e-learning Division has a profit margin of 6%, meaning that it earns a profit of $0.06 on every $1.00 of sales. The DVD Division, however, is much more profitable with a profit margin of 19%, earning $0.19 on every $1.00 of sales.

Capital turnover is the second term of the expanded ROI equation:

$$\text{Capital turnover} = \frac{\text{Sales}}{\text{Total assets}}$$

Capital turnover shows how efficiently a division uses its assets to generate sales. Rather than focusing on profitability, capital turnover focuses on efficiency. Let us calculate each division's capital turnover:

$$\text{e-learning Division's capital turnover} = \frac{\$7{,}500{,}000}{\$2{,}500{,}000} = 3$$

$$\text{DVD Division's capital turnover} = \frac{\$5{,}243{,}600}{\$6{,}500{,}000} = 0.80$$

The e-learning Division has a capital turnover of 3. This means that the e-learning Division generates $3.00 of sales with every $1.00 of assets. The DVD Division's capital turnover is only 0.80. The DVD Division generates only $0.80 of sales with every $1.00 of assets. The e-learning Division uses its assets much more efficiently in generating sales than the DVD Division.

Let us put the two terms back together in the expanded ROI equation:

	Profit margin	×	Capital turnover	= ROI
e-learning Division:	6%	×	3	= 18%
DVD Division:	19%	×	0.80	= 15%

As you can see, the expanded ROI equation gives management more insight into the division's ROI. Management can now see that the DVD is more profitable on its sales (19%) than the e-learning Division, but the e-learning Division is doing a better job of generating sales with its assets (capital turnover of 3) than the DVD Division (capital turnover of 0.80). Consequently, the e-learning Division has a higher ROI of 18%.

If a manager is not satisfied with his division's capital turnover rate, how can he improve it? He might try to eliminate nonproductive assets, for example, by being more aggressive in collecting accounts receivables or decreasing inventory levels. He might decide to change retail-store layout to generate sales.

What if management is not satisfied with the current profit margin? To increase the profit margin, management must increase the operating income earned on every dollar of sales. Management may cut product costs or selling and administrative costs, but it needs to be careful when trimming costs. Cutting costs in the short term can hurt long-term ROI. For example, sacrificing quality or cutting back on research and development could decrease costs in the short run, but may hurt long-term sales. The balanced scorecard helps management carefully consider the consequences of cost-cutting measures before acting on them.

ROI has one major drawback. Evaluating division managers based solely on ROI gives them an incentive to adopt *only* projects that will maintain or increase their current ROI. Let us say that top management has set a company-wide target ROI of 16%. Both divisions are considering investing in in-store video display equipment that shows customers how to use featured products. This equipment will increase sales because customers are more likely to buy the products when they see these infomercials. The equipment would cost each division $100,000 and is expected to provide each division with $17,000 of annual income. The *equipment's* ROI is as follows:

$$\text{Equipment ROI} = \frac{\$17{,}000}{\$100{,}000} = 17\%$$

Upper management would want the divisions to invest in this equipment since the equipment will provide a 17% ROI, which is higher than the 16% target rate. But what will the managers of the divisions do? Because the DVD Division currently has an ROI of 15%, the new equipment (with its 17% ROI) will *increase* the division's *overall* ROI. Therefore, the DVD Division manager will buy the equipment. However, the e-learning Division currently has an ROI of 18%. If the e-learning Division invests in the equipment, its *overall* ROI will *decrease*. Therefore, the manager of the e-learning Division will probably turn down the investment. In this case, goal congruence is *not* achieved—only one division will invest in equipment. Yet top management wants both divisions to invest in the equipment because the equipment return exceeds the 16% target ROI. Next, we discuss a performance measure that overcomes this problem with ROI.

Residual Income (RI)

Residual income (RI) is another commonly used KPI for evaluating an investment center's financial performance. Similar to ROI, RI considers both the division's operating income and its total assets. RI measures the division's profitability and the efficiency with which the division uses its assets. RI also incorporates another piece of information: top management's target rate of return (such as the 16% target return in the previous example). The target rate of return is the minimum acceptable rate of return that top management expects a division to earn with its assets.

RI compares the division's operating income with the minimum operating income expected by top management *given the size of the division's assets*. A positive RI means that the division's operating income exceeds top management's target rate of return. A negative RI means the division is not meeting the target rate of return. Let us look at the RI equation and then calculate the RI for both divisions using the 16% target rate of return from the previous example.

$$\text{RI} = \text{Operating income} - \text{Minimum acceptable income}$$

In this equation, the minimum acceptable income is defined as top management's target rate of return multiplied by the division's total assets. Therefore,

RI = Operating income – (Target rate of return × Total assets)

e-learning Division RI = \$450,000 – (16% × \$2,500,000)
= \$450,000 – \$400,000
= \$50,000

The positive RI indicates that the e-learning Division exceeded top management's 16% target return expectations. The RI calculation also confirms what we learned about the e-learning Division's ROI. Recall that the e-learning Division's ROI was 18%, which is higher than the targeted 16%.

Let us also calculate the RI for the DVD Division:

DVD Division RI = \$975,800 – (16% × \$6,500,000)
= \$975,800 – \$1,040,000
= \$(64,200)

The DVD Division's RI is negative. This means that the DVD Division did not use its assets as effectively as top management expected. Recall that the DVD Division's ROI of 15% fell short of the target rate of 16%.

Why would a company prefer to use RI over ROI for performance evaluation? The answer is that RI is more likely to lead to goal congruence than ROI. Let us once again consider the video display equipment that both divisions could buy. In both divisions, the equipment is expected to generate a 17% return. If the divisions are evaluated based on ROI, we learned that the DVD Division will buy the equipment because it will increase the division's ROI. The e-learning Division, on the other hand, will probably not buy the equipment because it will lower the division's ROI.

However, if management evaluates divisions based on RI rather than ROI, what will the divisions do? The answer depends on whether the project yields a positive or negative RI. Recall that the equipment would cost each division \$100,000, but will provide \$17,000 of operating income each year. The RI provided by *just* the equipment would be as follows:

Equipment RI = \$17,000 – (\$100,000 × 16%)
= \$17,000 – \$16,000
= \$1,000

If purchased, this equipment will *improve* each division's current RI by \$1,000. As a result, both divisions will be motivated to invest in the equipment. Goal congruence is achieved because both divisions will take the action that top management desires. That is, both divisions will invest in the equipment.

Another benefit of RI is that management may set different target returns for different divisions. For example, management might require a higher target rate of return from a division operating in a riskier business environment. If the DVD industry were riskier than the e-learning industry, top management might decide to set a higher target return—perhaps 17%—for the DVD Division.

Economic Value Added (EVA)

Economic Value Added (EVA) is a special type of RI calculation. Unlike the RI calculation we have just discussed, EVA looks at a division's RI through the eyes of the company's primary stakeholders: its investors and long-term creditors (such as bondholders). Since these stakeholders provide the company's capital, management often wishes to evaluate how efficiently a division is using its assets from these two stakeholders' viewpoints. EVA calculates RI for these stakeholders by specifically considering the following:

1. The income available to these stakeholders
2. The assets used to generate income for these stakeholders
3. The minimum rate of return required by these stakeholders (referred to as the **weighted average cost of capital**, or WACC)

Let us compare the EVA equation with the RI equation and then explain the differences in more detail:

RI = Operating income – (Total assets × Target rate of return)
EVA = After-tax operating income – [(Total assets – Current liabilities) × WACC%]

Both equations calculate whether any income was created by the division above and beyond expectations. They do this by comparing actual income with the minimum acceptable income. But note the differences in the EVA calculation:

1. The EVA calculation uses *after-tax operating income*, which is the income left over after subtracting income taxes. Why? Because the portion of income paid to the government is not available to investors and long-term creditors.
2. *Total assets is reduced by current liabilities.* Why? Because funds owed to short-term creditors, such as suppliers (accounts payable) and employees (wages payable), will be paid in the immediate future and will not be available for generating income in the long run. The division is not expected to earn a return for investors and long-term creditors on those funds that will soon be paid out to short-term creditors.
3. The *WACC* replaces management's target rate of return. Since EVA focuses on investors and creditors, it is *their* expected rate of return that should be used, not management's expected rate of return. The WACC, which represents the minimum rate of return expected by *investors and long-term creditors*, is based on the company's cost of raising capital from both groups of stakeholders. The riskier the business, the higher the expected return. Detailed WACC computations are discussed in advanced accounting and finance courses.

In summary, EVA incorporates all the elements of RI from the perspective of investors and long-term creditors. Now that we have walked through the equation's components, let us calculate EVA for the e-learning and DVD Divisions discussed earlier. We will need the following additional information:

Effective income tax rate	30%
WACC	13%
e-learning Division's current liabilities	$150,000
DVD Division's current liabilities	$250,000

The 30% effective income tax rate means that the government takes 30% of the company's income, leaving only 70% to the company's stakeholders. Therefore, we calculate *after-tax operating income* by multiplying the division's operating income by 70% (100% – effective tax rate of 30%).

$$\text{EVA} = \text{After-tax operating income} - [(\text{Total assets} - \text{Current liabilities}) \times \text{WACC\%}]$$

$$\begin{aligned}\text{e-learning Division EVA} &= (\$450{,}000 \times 70\%) - [(\$2{,}500{,}000 - \$150{,}000) \times 13\%] \\ &= \$315{,}000 - (\$2{,}350{,}000 \times 13\%) \\ &= \$315{,}000 - \$305{,}500 \\ &= \$9{,}500\end{aligned}$$

$$\begin{aligned}\text{DVD Division EVA} &= (\$975{,}800 \times 70\%) - [(\$6{,}500{,}000 - 250{,}000) \times 13\%] \\ &= \$683{,}060 - (\$6{,}250{,}000 \times 13\%) \\ &= \$683{,}060 - \$812{,}500 \\ &= \$(129{,}440)\end{aligned}$$

These EVA calculations show that the e-learning Division has generated income in excess of expectations for its investors and long-term debt-holders, whereas the DVD Division has not.

Many firms, such as **Coca-Cola, Amazon.com,** and **J.C. Penney,** measure the financial performance of their investment centers using EVA. EVA promotes goal congruence, just as RI does. Additionally, EVA looks at the income generated by the division in excess of expectations, solely from the perspective of investors and long-term creditors. Therefore, EVA specifically addresses the financial perspective of the balanced scorecard that asks, "How do we look to shareholders?"

Exhibit 23-9 summarizes the three performance measures and some of their advantages.

EXHIBIT 23-9 Three Investment Center Performance Measures: A Summary

ROI:

Equation	$\text{ROI} = \dfrac{\text{Operating income}}{\text{Sales}} \times \dfrac{\text{Sales}}{\text{Total assets}} = \dfrac{\text{Operating income}}{\text{Total assets}}$
Advantages	• The expanded equation provides management with additional information on profitability and efficiency • Management can compare ROI across divisions and with other companies • ROI is useful for resource allocation

RI:

Equation	RI = Operating income − (Total assets × Target rate of return)
Advantages	• Promotes goal congruence better than ROI • Incorporates management's minimum required rate of return • Management can use different target rates of return for divisions with different levels of risk

EVA:

Equation	EVA = (After-tax operating income) − [(Total assets − Current liabilities) × WACC%]
Advantages	• Considers income generated for investors and long-term creditors in excess of their expectations • Promotes goal congruence

Limitations of Financial Performance Measures

We have just finished looking at three KPIs (ROI, RI, and EVA) commonly used to evaluate the financial performance of investment centers. As discussed in the following sections, all of these measures have drawbacks that management should keep in mind when evaluating the financial performance of investment centers.

Measurement Issues

The ROI, RI, and EVA calculations appear to be very straightforward; however, management must make some decisions before these calculations can be made. For example, all three equations use the term *total assets*. Recall that total assets is a balance sheet figure, which means that it is a snapshot at any given point in time. Because the total assets figure will be *different* at the beginning of the period and at the end of the period, most companies choose to use a simple average of the two figures in their ROI, RI, and EVA calculations.

Management must also decide if it really wants to include *all* assets in the total asset figure. Many firms, such as **Wal-mart**, are continually buying land on which to build future retail outlets. Until those stores are built and opened, the land (including any construction in progress) is a nonproductive asset, which is not adding to the company's operating income. Including nonproductive assets in the total asset figure will naturally drive down the ROI, RI, and EVA figures. Therefore, some firms will not include nonproductive assets in these calculations.

Another asset measurement issue is whether to use the gross book value of assets (the historical cost of the assets), or the net book value of assets (historical cost less accumulated depreciation). Many firms will use the net book value of assets because the figure is consistent with and easily pulled from the balance sheet. Because depreciation expense factors into the firm's operating income, the net book value concept is also consistent with the measurement of operating income. However, using the net book value of assets has a definite drawback. Over time, the net book value of assets decreases because accumulated depreciation continues to grow until the assets are fully depreciated. Therefore, ROI, RI, and EVA get *larger* over time *simply because of depreciation* rather than from actual improvements in operations. In addition, the rate of this depreciation effect will depend on the depreciation method used.

In general, calculating ROI based on the net book value of assets gives managers incentive to continue using old, outdated equipment because its low net book value results in a higher ROI. However, top management may want the division to invest in new technology to create operational efficiency (internal business perspective of the balanced scorecard) or to enhance its information systems (learning and growth perspective). The long-term effects of using outdated equipment may be devastating, as competitors use new technology to produce and sell at lower cost. Therefore, to create *goal congruence*, some firms prefer calculating ROI based on the gross book value of assets. The same general rule holds true for RI and EVA calculations: All else being equal, using net book value will increase RI and EVA over time.

Short-Term Focus

One serious drawback of financial performance measures is their short-term focus. Companies usually prepare performance reports and calculate ROI, RI, and EVA figures over a one-year time frame or less. If upper management uses a short time frame, division managers have an incentive to take actions that will lead to an immediate increase in these measures, even if such actions may not be in the company's long-term interest (such as cutting back on R&D or advertising). On the other hand, some potentially positive actions considered by subunit managers may take longer than one year to generate income at the targeted level. Many product life cycles start slow, even incurring losses in the early stages, before generating profit. If managers are measured on short-term financial performance only, they may not introduce new products because they are not willing to wait several years for the positive effect to show up in their financial performance measures.

As a potential remedy, management can measure financial performance using a longer time horizon, such as three to five years. Extending the time frame gives subunit managers the incentive to think long term rather than short term and make decisions that will positively impact the company over the next several years.

The limitations of financial performance measures confirm the importance of the balanced scorecard. The deficiencies of financial measures can be overcome by taking a broader view of performance—including KPIs from all four balanced scorecard perspectives rather than concentrating on only the financial measures.

Decision Guidelines

When managers at **UPS** developed the financial perspective of their balanced scorecard, they had to make decisions such as the examples that follow.

Decision	**Guidelines**
• How should the financial section of the balanced scorecard be measured for cost, revenue, and profit centers?	Responsibility accounting performance reports measure the financial performance of cost, revenue, and profit centers. These reports typically highlight the variances between budgeted and actual performance.
• How should the financial section of the balanced scorecard be measured for investment centers?	Investment centers require measures that take into account the division's operating income *and* the division's assets. Typical measures include the following: • Return on investment (ROI) • Residual income (RI) • Economic value added (EVA)
• How is ROI computed and interpreted?	**ROI = Operating income ÷ Total assets** ROI measures the amount of income earned by a division relative to the size of its assets—the higher, the better.
• Can managers learn more by writing the ROI formula in its expanded form?	In its expanded form, ROI is written as follows: **ROI = Profit margin × Capital turnover** where, **Profit margin = Operating income ÷ Sales** **Capital turnover = Sales ÷ Total assets** Profit margin focuses on profitability (the amount of income earned on every dollar of sales), while capital turnover focuses on efficiency (the amount of sales generated with every dollar of assets).
• How is RI computed and interpreted?	$\text{RI} = \text{Operating income} - \left(\text{Target rate of return} \times \text{Total assets}\right)$ If RI is positive, the division is earning income at a rate that exceeds management's minimum expectations.
• How does EVA differ from RI?	EVA is a special type of RI calculation that focuses on the income (in excess of expectations) created by the division for two specific stakeholders: investors and long-term creditors.
• When calculating ROI, RI, or VA, are there any measurement issues of concern?	If the net book value of assets is used to measure total assets, ROI, RI, and EVA will "artificially" rise over time due to the depreciation of the assets. Using gross book value to measure total assets eliminates this measurement issue. Many firms use the average balance of total assets, rather than the beginning or ending balance of assets, when they calculate ROI, RI, and EVA.

Summary Problem 2

Assume Smart Touch Learning expects each division to earn a 16% target rate of return. Smart Touch Learning's weighted average cost of capital (WACC) is 13%, and its effective tax rate is 30%. Assume the company's original CD Division had the following results last year (in millions of dollars):

Operating income	$ 1,450
Total assets	16,100
Current liabilities	3,600
Sales	26,500

Requirements

1. Compute the CD Division's profit margin, capital turnover, and ROI. Round your results to three decimal places. Interpret the results in relation to the e-learning and DVD Divisions discussed in the chapter.
2. Compute and interpret the CD Division's RI.
3. Compute the CD Division's EVA. What does this tell you?
4. What can you conclude based on all three financial performance KPIs?

Solution

Requirement 1

ROI =	Profit margin	×	Capital turnover
	= (Operating income ÷ Sales)	×	(Sales ÷ Total assets)
=	($1,450 ÷ $26,500)	×	($26,500 ÷ $16,100)
=	0.055	×	1.646
=	0.091		

The original CD Division is far from meeting top management's expectations. Its ROI is only 9.1%. The profit margin of 5.5% is slightly lower than the e-learning Division and significantly lower than both Divisions (6% for e-learning and 19% for the DVD division). The capital turnover (1.646) is much lower than the e-learning Division (3.0 capital turnover) but much higher than the DVD capital turnover of 0.80. This means that the original CD Division is not generating sales from its assets as efficiently as the e-learning Division, but is more efficient than the DVD Division. Division management needs to consider ways to increase the efficiency with which it uses divisional assets.

Requirement 2

RI =	Operating income	–	(Target rate of return × Total assets)
=	$1,450	–	(16% × $16,100)
=	$1,450	–	$2,576
=	$(1,126)		

The negative RI confirms the ROI results: The division is not meeting management's target rate of return.

Requirement 3

EVA =	After-tax operating income	–	[(Total assets – Current liabilities) × WACC%]
=	(\$1,450 × 70%)	–	[(\$16,100 – \$3,600) × 13%]
=	\$1,015	–	(\$12,500) × 13%)
=	\$1,015	–	\$1,625
=	\$(610)		

The negative EVA means that the division is not generating income for investors and long-term creditors at the rate desired by these stakeholders.

Requirement 4

All three investment center performance measures (ROI, RI, and EVA) point to the same conclusion: The original CD Division is not meeting financial expectations. Either top management and stakeholders' expectations are unrealistic or the division is not *currently* performing up to par. Recall, however, that financial performance measures tend to be lag indicators—measuring the results of decisions made in the past. The division's managers may currently be implementing new initiatives to improve the division's future profitability. Lead indicators should be used to project whether such initiatives are pointing the company in the right direction.

Review Performance Evaluation and the Balanced Scorecard

Accounting Vocabulary

Balanced Scorecard (p. 1209)
Recognition that management must consider both financial performance measures and operational performance measures when judging the performance of a company and its subunits.

Capital Turnover (p. 1222)
The amount of sales revenue generated for every dollar of invested assets; a component of the ROI calculation, computed as sales divided by total assets.

Centralized Companies (p. 1205)
Companies in which all major planning and operating decisions are made by top management.

Cost Center (p. 1207)
A subunit responsible only for controlling costs.

Decentralized Companies (p. 1205)
Companies that are segmented into smaller operating units; unit managers make planning and operating decisions for their unit.

Economic Value Added (EVA) (p. 1224)
A residual income measure calculating the amount of income generated by the company or its divisions in excess of stockholders and long-term creditors expectations.

Goal Congruence (p. 1206)
Aligning the goals of subunit managers with the goals of top management.

Investment Center (p. 1207)
A subunit responsible for generating profits and efficiently managing the division's invested capital (assets).

Key Performance Indicator(s) (KPIs) (p. 1210)
Summary performance measures that help managers assess whether the company is achieving its long-term and short-term goals.

Lag Indicators (p. 1209)
Performance measures that indicate past performance.

Lead Indicators (p. 1209)
Performance measures that forecast future performance.

Profit Center (p. 1207)
A subunit responsible for generating revenue and controlling costs.

Profit Margin (p. 1221)
The amount of income earned on every dollar of sales; a component of the ROI calculation, computed as operating income divided by sales.

Residual Income (RI) (p. 1223)
A measure of profitability and efficiency, computed as the excess of actual income over a specified minimum acceptable income.

Return on Investment (ROI) (p. 1221)
A measure of profitability and efficiency, computed as operating income divided by total assets.

Revenue Center (p. 1207)
A subunit responsible only for generating revenue.

Weighted Average Cost of Capital (WACC) (p. 1225)
The company's cost of capital; the target return used in EVA calculations to denote the return expected by stockholders and long-term creditors.

Quick Check

1. Which is *not* one of the potential advantages of decentralization?
   a. Improves motivation and retention
   b. Increases goal congruence
   c. Supports use of expert knowledge
   d. Improves customer relations
2. The **Quaker Foods** division of **PepsiCo** is most likely treated as a
   a. revenue center.
   b. cost center.
   c. profit center.
   d. investment center.

3. Decentralization is often based on all the following except
   a. geographic region.
   b. product line.
   c. business function.
   d. revenue size.
4. Manufacturing yield rate (number of units produced per unit of time) would be a typical measure for which of the following balanced scorecard perspectives:
   a. Learning and growth
   b. Internal business
   c. Financial
   d. Customer
5. Which of the following balanced scorecard perspectives essentially asks, "Can we continue to improve and create value?"
   a. Financial
   b. Learning and growth
   c. Customer
   d. Internal business

The following data applies to Questions 6 through 9. Assume the Residential Division of Krandell Faucets had the following results last year (in thousands of dollars):

Sales	$ 4,648,000	Management's Target Rate of return	17%
Operating income	1,208,480	WACC	10%
Total assets	5,600,000		
Current liabilities	250,000		

6. What is the division's profit margin?
   a. 26%
   b. 83%
   c. 4%
   d. 22%
7. What is the division's capital turnover?
   a. 117%
   b. 17%
   c. 83%
   d. 21%
8. What is the division's ROI?
   a. 18%
   b. 5.83%
   c. 22%
   d. 81%
9. What is the division's RI?
   a. ($407,080)
   b. $407,080
   c. ($256,480)
   d. $256,480

10. The performance evaluation of a cost center is typically based on its
    a. static budget variance.
    b. ROI.
    c. sales volume variance.
    d. flexible budget variance.

Answers are given after Apply Your Knowledge (p. 1243).

Assess Your Progress

■ Short Exercises

S23-1 *(L. OBJ. 1)* **Explaining why and how companies decentralize [5 min]**
Decentralization divides company operations into various reporting units.

Requirement

1. Explain why companies decentralize. Describe some typical methods of decentralization.

S23-2 *(L. OBJ. 1)* **Explaining why and how companies decentralize [5 min]**
Most decentralized subunits can be described as one of four different types of responsibility centers.

Requirement

1. List the four most common types of responsibility centers and describe their responsibilities.

S23-3 *(L. OBJ. 1)* **Explaining why and how companies decentralize [5 min]**
Each of the following managers has been given certain decision-making authority:

1. Manager of Holiday Inn's Central Reservation Office
2. Managers of various corporate-owned Holiday Inn locations
3. Manager of the Holiday Inn Corporate Division
4. Manager of the Housekeeping Department at a Holiday Inn
5. Manager of the Holiday Inn Express Corporate Division
6. Manager of the complimentary breakfast buffet at a Holiday Inn Express

Requirement

1. Classify each of the managers according to the type of responsibility center they manage.

S23-4 *(L. OBJ. 2)* **Explaining why companies use performance evaluation systems [5 min]**
Well-designed performance evaluation systems accomplish many goals. Consider the following actions:

a. Comparing targets to actual results
b. Providing subunit managers with performance targets
c. Comparing actual results with industry standards
d. Providing bonuses to subunit managers who achieve performance targets
e. Aligning subunit performance targets with company strategy
f. Comparing actual results to the results of competitors
g. Taking corrective actions
h. Using the adage, "you get what you measure," when designing the performance evaluation system

Requirement

1. State which goal is being achieved by the action.

S23-5 *(L. OBJ. 3)* **Describing the balanced scorecard and identifying key performance indicators for each perspective [5–10 min]**

Consider the following key performance indicators:

a. Number of employee suggestions implemented
b. Revenue growth
c. Number of on-time deliveries
d. Percentage of sales force with access to real-time inventory levels
e. Customer satisfaction ratings
f. Number of defects found during manufacturing
g. Number of warranty claims
h. ROI
i. Variable cost per unit
j. Percentage of market share
k. Number of hours of employee training
l. Number of new products developed
m. Yield rate (number of units produced per hour)
n. Average repair time
o. Employee satisfaction
p. Number of repeat customers

Requirement

1. Classify each of the preceding key performance indicators according to the balanced scorecard perspective it addresses. Choose from financial perspective, customer perspective, internal business perspective, or learning and growth perspective.

S23-6 *(L. OBJ. 4)* **Using performance reports to evaluate cost, revenue, and profit centers [5 min]**

Management by exception is a term often used in performance evaluation.

Requirement

1. Describe management by exception and how it is used in the evaluation of cost, revenue, and profit centers.

S23-7 *(L. OBJ. 5)* **Using ROI, RI, and EVA to evaluate investment centers [5–10 min]**

Consider the following data:

	Domestic	International
Operating income	$ 9 million	$ 11 million
Total assets	$ 24 million	$ 36 million

Requirement

1. Which of the corporate divisions is more profitable? Explain.

S23-8 *(L. OBJ. 5)* **Using ROI, RI, and EVA to evaluate investment centers [5–10 min]**

Speedy Sports Company makes snowboards, downhill skis, cross-country skis, skateboards, surfboards, and in-line skates. The company has found it beneficial to split operations into two divisions based on the climate required for the sport: Snow sports and Non-snow sports. The following divisional information is available for the past year:

	Sales	Operating Income	Total Assets	Current Liabilities	ROI
Snow sports	$ 5,700,000	$ 1,083,000	$ 4,700,000	$ 410,000	23.0%
Non-snow sports	8,900,000	1,691,000	6,800,000	660,000	24.9%

Speedy's management has specified a 13% target rate of return. The company's weighted average cost of capital (WACC) is 11% and its effective tax rate is 33%.

Requirement

1. Calculate each division's profit margin. Interpret your results.

Note: Short Exercise 23-8 should be completed before attempting Short Exercise 23-9.

S23-9 *(L. OBJ. 5)* **Using ROI, RI, and EVA to evaluate investment centers [10 min]**
Refer to the information in S23-8.

Requirements

1. Compute each division's capital turnover (round to two decimal places). Interpret your results.
2. Use your answers to question 1, along with the profit margin, to recalculate ROI using the expanded formula. Do your answers agree with the basic ROI in S23-8?

Note: Short Exercise 23-8 should be completed before attempting Short Exercise 23-10.

S23-10 *(L. OBJ. 5)* **Using ROI, RI, and EVA to evaluate investment centers [5–10 min]**
Refer to the information in S23-8.

Requirement

1. Compute each division's RI. Interpret your results. Are your results consistent with each division's ROI?

Note: Short Exercise 23-8 should be completed before attempting Short Exercise 23-11.

S23-11 *(L. OBJ. 5)* **Using ROI, RI, and EVA to evaluate investment centers [10–15 min]**
Refer to the information in S23-8.

Requirement

1. Compute each division's EVA. Interpret your results.

Exercises

E23-12 *(L. OBJ. 1)* **Explaining why and how companies decentralize [10–15 min]**
Grandma Jones Cookie Company sells homemade cookies made with organic ingredients. Her sales are strictly Web-based. The business is taking off more than Grandma Jones ever expected, with orders coming from across the country from both consumers and corporate event planners. Even by employing a full-time baker and a Web designer, Grandma Jones can no longer handle the business on her own. She wants your advice on whether she should decentralize and, if so, how she should do it.

Requirement

1. Explain some of the advantages and disadvantages of decentralization and offer her three ways she might decentralize her company.

E23-13 *(L. OBJ. 2)* **Explaining why companies use performance evaluation systems [5–10 min]**
Financial performance is measured in many ways.

Requirement

1. Explain the difference between lag and lead indicators. Are financial performance measures typically referred to as lag or lead indicators? Are operational measures (such as customer satisfaction ratings, defect rates, number of on-time deliveries, and so forth) typically referred to as lag or lead indicators? Explain why, using **L.L.Bean** (a catalog clothing merchandiser) as an example.

E23-14 *(L. OBJ. 2)* **Explaining why companies use performance evaluation systems [10 min]**

Well-designed performance evaluation systems accomplish many goals.

Requirement

1. Describe the potential benefits performance evaluation systems offer.

E23-15 *(L. OBJ. 3)* **Describing the balanced scorecard and identifying key performance indicators for each perspective [10–15 min]**

Consider the following key performance indicators:

a. Number of customer complaints
b. Number of information system upgrades completed
c. EVA
d. New product development time
e. Employee turnover rate
f. Percentage of products with online help manuals
g. Customer retention
h. Percentage of compensation based on performance
i. Percentage of orders filled each week
j. Gross margin growth
k. Number of new patents
l. Employee satisfaction ratings
m. Manufacturing cycle time (average length of production process)
n. Earnings growth
o. Average machine setup time
p. Number of new customers
q. Employee promotion rate
r. Cash flow from operations
s. Customer satisfaction ratings
t. Machine downtime
u. Finished products per day per employee
v. Percentage of employees with access to upgraded system
w. Wait time per order prior to start of production

Requirement

1. Classify each indicator according to the balanced scorecard perspective it addresses. Choose from the financial perspective, customer perspective, internal business perspective, or the learning and growth perspective.

E25-16 *(L. OBJ. 4)* **Using performance reports to evaluate cost, revenue, and profit centers [10–15 min]**

One subunit of Racer Sports Company had the following financial results last month:

Racer – Subunit X	Actual	Flexible Budget	Flexible Budget Variance (U or F)	% Variance (U or F)
Direct materials	$ 28,600	$ 26,800		
Direct labor	13,100	13,900		
Indirect labor	26,300	23,000		
Utilities	12,300	11,200		
Depreciation	30,000	30,000		
Repairs and maintenance	4,500	5,600		
Total	$ 114,800	$ 110,500		

Requirements

1. Complete the performance evaluation report for this subunit. Enter the variance percent as a percentage rounded to two decimal places.
2. Based on the data presented, what type of responsibility center is this subunit?
3. Which items should be investigated if part of management's decision criteria is to investigate all variances exceeding $3,000 or 10%?
4. Should only unfavorable variances be investigated? Explain.

E23-17 *(L. OBJ. 4)* **Using performance reports to evaluate cost, revenue, and profit centers [15–20 min]**

The accountant for a subunit of Racer Sports Company went on vacation before completing the subunit's monthly performance report. This is as far as she got:

Racer – Subunit X Revenue by Product	Actual	Flexible Budget Variance	Flexible Budget	Sales Volume Variance	Static (Master) Budget
Downhill Model RI	$ 330,000			$ 16,000 F	$ 305,000
Downhill Model RII	150,000		$ 163,000		144,000
Cross-Country Model EXI	285,000	$ 2,000 U	287,000		302,000
Cross-Country Model EXII	256,000		251,000	15,500 U	266,500
Snowboard Model LXI	429,000	7,000 F			406,000
Total	$ 1,450,000				$ 1,423,500

Requirements

1. Complete the performance evaluation report for this subunit.
2. Based on the data presented, what type of responsibility center is this subunit?
3. Which items should be investigated if part of management's decision criteria is to investigate all variances exceeding $15,000?

E23-18 *(L. OBJ. 5)* **Using ROI, RI, and EVA to evaluate investment centers [10–15 min]**

Zuds, a national manufacturer of lawn-mowing and snow-blowing equipment, segments its business according to customer type: professional and residential. The following divisional information was available for the past year (in thousands of dollars):

	Sales	Operating Income	Total Assets	Current Liabilities
Residential	$ 580,000	$ 63,700	$ 196,000	$ 66,000
Professional	1,100,000	162,400	406,000	147,000

Management has a 27% target rate of return for each division. Zuds' weighted average cost of capital is 15% and its effective tax rate is 30%.

Requirements

1. Calculate each division's ROI. Round all of your answers to four decimal places.
2. Calculate each division's profit margin. Interpret your results.
3. Calculate each division's capital turnover. Interpret your results.
4. Use the expanded ROI formula to confirm your results from requirement 1. What can you conclude?

Note: Exercise 23-18 should be completed before attempting Exercise 23-19.

E23-19 *(L. OBJ. 5)* **Using ROI, RI, and EVA to evaluate investment centers [10–15 min]**
Refer to the data in E23-18.

Requirements

1. Calculate each division's RI. Interpret your results.
2. Calculate each division's EVA. Interpret your results.
3. Describe the conceptual and computational similarities and differences between RI and EVA.

Problems (Group A)

P23-20A *(L. OBJ. 1, 2, 3, 4)* **Explaining why and how companies decentralize and why they use performance evaluation systems [30–45 min]**
One subunit of Field Sports Company had the following financial results last month:

Subunit X	Flexible Budget	Actual	Flexible Budget Variance (U or F)	Percentage Variance
Sales	$ 451,000	$ 480,000		
Cost of goods sold	256,000	266,000		
Gross margin	$ 195,000	$ 214,000		
Operating expenses	48,000	55,000		
Operating income before service department charges	$ 147,000	$ 159,000		
Service department charges (allocated)	31,000	41,000		
Operating income	$ 116,000	$ 118,000		

Requirements

1. Complete the performance evaluation report for this subunit (round to two decimal places).
2. Based on the data presented and your knowledge of the company, what type of responsibility center is this subunit?
3. Which items should be investigated if part of management's decision criteria is to investigate all variances equal to or exceeding $10,000 *and* exceeding 10% (both criteria must be met)?
4. Should only unfavorable variances be investigated? Explain.
5. Is it possible that the variances are due to a higher-than-expected sales volume? Explain.
6. Will management place equal weight on each of the $10,000 variances? Explain.
7. Which balanced scorecard perspective is being addressed through this performance report? In your opinion, is this performance report a lead or lag indicator? Explain.
8. List one key performance indicator for the three other balanced scorecard perspectives. Make sure to indicate which perspective is being addressed by the indicators you list. Are they lead or lag indicators? Explain.

P23-21A *(L. OBJ. 5)* **Using ROI, RI, and EVA to evaluate investment centers [30–45 min]**
Benjamin Doore is a national paint manufacturer and retailer. The company is segmented into five divisions: Paint stores (branded retail locations), Consumer (paint sold through stores like **Sears, Home Depot,** and **Lowe's**), Automotive (sales to auto manufacturers), International, and Administration. The following is selected divisional information for its two largest divisions: Paint stores and Consumer (in thousands of dollars).

	Sales	Operating Income	Total Assets	Current Liabilities
Paint stores	$ 4,020,000	$ 478,000	$ 1,385,000	$ 335,000
Consumer	1,310,000	193,000	1,585,000	607,000

Management has specified a 22% target rate of return. The company's weighted average cost of capital is 17%. The company's effective tax rate is 33%.

Requirements

1. Calculate each division's ROI.
2. Calculate each division's profit margin. Interpret your results.
3. Calculate each division's capital turnover. Interpret your results.
4. Use the expanded ROI formula to confirm your results from requirement 1. Interpret your results.
5. Calculate each division's RI. Interpret your results and offer a recommendation for any division with negative RI.
6. Calculate each division's EVA. Interpret your results.
7. Describe the conceptual and computational similarities and differences between RI and EVA.
8. Total asset data was provided in this problem. If you were to gather this information from an annual report, how would you measure total assets? Describe your measurement choices and some of the pros and cons of those choices.
9. Describe some of the factors that management considers when setting its minimum target rate of return.
10. Explain why some firms prefer to use RI rather than ROI for performance measurement.
11. Explain why budget versus actual performance reports are insufficient for evaluating the performance of investment centers.

■ Problems (Group B)

P23-22B *(L. OBJ. 1, 2, 3, 4)* **Explaining why and how companies decentralize and why they use performance evaluation systems [30–45 min]**

One subunit of Athlete Sports Company had the following financial results last month:

Subunit X	Flexible Budget	Actual	Flexible Budget Variance (U or F)	Percentage Variance
Sales	$ 454,000	$ 479,000		
Cost of goods sold	252,000	262,000		
Gross margin	$ 202,000	$ 217,000		
Operating expenses	51,000	54,000		
Operating income before service department charges	$ 151,000	$ 163,000		
Service department charges (allocated)	27,000	37,000		
Operating income	$ 124,000	$ 126,000		

Requirements

1. Complete the performance evaluation report for this subunit (round to two decimal places).
2. Based on the data presented and your knowledge of the company, what type of responsibility center is this subunit?
3. Which items should be investigated if part of management's decision criteria is to investigate all variances equal to or exceeding $10,000 *and* exceeding 10% (both criteria must be met)?
4. Should only unfavorable variances be investigated? Explain.
5. Is it possible that the variances are due to a higher-than-expected sales volume? Explain.
6. Will management place equal weight on each of the $10,000 variances? Explain.
7. Which balanced scorecard perspective is being addressed through this performance report? In your opinion, is this performance report a lead or lag indicator? Explain.
8. List one key performance indicator for the three other balanced scorecard perspectives. Make sure to indicate which perspective is being addressed by the indicators you list. Are they lead or lag indicators? Explain.

P23-23B *(L. OBJ. 5)* **Using ROI, RI, and EVA to evaluate investment centers [30–45 min]**

Ralph Laurel is a national paint manufacturer and retailer. The company is segmented into five divisions: Paint stores (branded retail locations), Consumer (paint sold through stores like **Sears, Home Depot,** and **Lowe's**), Automotive (sales to auto manufacturers), International, and Administration. The following is selected divisional information for its two largest divisions: Paint stores and Consumer (in thousands of dollars):

	Sales	Operating Income	Total Assets	Current Liabilities
Paint stores	$ 3,970,000	$ 478,000	$ 1,390,000	$ 355,000
Consumer	1,275,000	184,000	1,585,000	610,000

Management has specified a 20% target rate of return. The company's weighted average cost of capital is 17%. The company's effective tax rate is 36%.

Requirements

1. Calculate each division's ROI.
2. Calculate each division's profit margin. Interpret your results.
3. Calculate each division's capital turnover. Interpret your results.
4. Use the expanded ROI formula to confirm your results from requirement 1. Interpret your results.
5. Calculate each division's RI. Interpret your results and offer a recommendation for any division with negative RI.
6. Calculate each division's EVA. Interpret your results.
7. Describe the conceptual and computational similarities and differences between RI and EVA.
8. Total asset data was provided for this problem. If you were to gather this information from an annual report, how would you measure total assets? Describe your measurement choices and some of the pros and cons of those choices.
9. Describe some of the factors that management considers when setting its minimum target rate of return.
10. Explain why some firms prefer to use RI rather than ROI for performance measurement.
11. Explain why budget versus actual performance reports are insufficient for evaluating the performance of investment centers.

■ Continuing Exercise

E23-24 This exercise continues the Sherman Lawn Service, Inc., situation from Exercise 22-35 of Chapter 22. Sherman Lawn Service experienced Sales of $400,000 and Operating income of $75,000 for 2011. Total assets were $200,000 and total liabilities were $20,000 at the end of 2011. Sherman's target rate of return is 14% and WACC is 10%. Its 2011 tax rate was 30%.

Requirement

1. Calculate Sherman's profit margin for 2011.

■ Continuing Problem

P23-25 This problem continues the Haupt Consulting, Inc., situation from Problem 22-36 of Chapter 22. Haupt Consulting reported 2011 Sales of $2,500,000 and Operating income of $250,000. Total assets were $700,000 and total liabilities were $200,000 at the end of 2011. Haupt's target rate of return is 16% and WACC is 8%. Its 2011 tax rate was 35%.

Requirement

1. Calculate Haupt's profit margin, capital turnover, and EVA for 2011.

Apply Your Knowledge

Decision Case

Case 1. Colgate-Palmolive operates two product segments. Using the company Web site, locate segment information for 2007 in the company's 2007 annual report. (*Hint*: Look under investor relations on the company Web site.)

Requirements

1. What are the two segments? Gather data about each segment's net sales, operating income, and identifiable assets.
2. Calculate ROI for each segment.
3. Which segment has the highest ROI? Explain why.
4. If you were on the top management team and could allocate extra funds to only one division, which division would you choose? Why?

Ethical Issue

Dixie Irwin is the department manager for Religious Books, a manufacturer of religious books that are sold through Internet companies. Irwin's bonus is based on reducing production costs.

Requirement

Issue 1. Irwin has identified a supplier, Cheap Paper, that can provide paper products at a 10% cost reduction. The paper quality is not the same as that of the current paper used in production. If Irwin uses the supplier, he will certainly achieve his personal bonus goals; however, other company goals may be in jeopardy. Identify the key performance issues at risk and recommend a plan of action for Irwin.

Team Project

Each group should identify one public company's product that it wishes to evaluate. The team should gather all the information it can about the product.

Requirement

1. Develop a list of key performance indicators for the product.

Quick Check Answers

1. *b* 2. *d* 3. *d* 4. *b* 5. *b* 6. *a* 7. *c* 8. *c* 9. *d* 10. *d*

For online homework, exercises, and problems that provide you immediate feedback, please visit www.myaccountinglab.com.

Allocating Service Department Costs

How do companies charge subunits for their use of service departments? For example, suppose Smart Touch Learning incurs $30,000 per month to operate the centralized payroll department. To simplify the illustration, let us assume the region only has three division allocations: CDs, DVDs, and e-learning. How should the company split, or allocate, the $30,000 cost among the three divisions? Splitting the cost equally—charging each division $10,000—may not be fair, especially if the three units do not use the services equally.

Ideally, the company should allocate the $30,000 based on each subunit's use of centralized payroll services. The company should use the primary activity that drives the cost of central payroll services as the allocation base. As you may recall from Chapter 17, companies identify cost drivers when they implement ABC. Therefore, a company that has already implemented ABC should know what cost drivers would be suitable for allocating service department charges. For example, payroll processing cost may be driven by the number of employee payroll checks or direct deposits processed. The cost driver chosen for allocating the $30,000 might be the "number of employees" employed by each store, as shown in the following table.

Subunits Sharing Central Payroll Services	Number of Employees (allocation base)	Percentage of Total Employees	Service Department Charge ($30,000 × %)
CD	100	25%	$ 7,500
DVD	140	35%	10,500
e-learning	160	40%	12,000
Total	400	100%	$30,000

Most companies will use some type of usage-related cost driver to allocate service department costs. The following table lists additional centralized services and common allocation bases.

Centralized Service Departments	Typical Allocation Base
Human resources	Number of employees
Legal	Number of hours spent on legal matters
Travel	Number of business trips booked

However, when usage data are not available or are too costly to collect, companies will resort to allocating service department costs based on each subunit's "ability to bear" the cost. In such cases, companies allocate the service department cost based on the relative amount of revenue or operating income each subunit generates. The following table illustrates this type of allocation.

Subunits Sharing Centralized Payroll Services	Unit Operating Income Before Service Department Charges	Percentage of Total Operating Income	Service Department Charge ($30,000 × %)
CD	$ 320,000	20%	$ 6,000
DVD	480,000	30%	9,000
e-learning	800,000	50%	15,000
Total	$1,600,000	100%	$30,000

This type of allocation is like a tax: the higher the subunit's income, the higher the charge.

Even usage-related allocation systems have limitations. What if the cost of running the service department is fixed rather than variable? Then, much of the cost cannot be attributed to a specific cost driver. In our payroll example, suppose $20,000 of the total $30,000 is straight-line depreciation on the equipment and software. Should the company still use the number of employees to allocate the entire $30,000 of cost? As another example, suppose the CD Division downsizes and its relative percentage of employees drops from 25% to 10%, while the number of employees in each of the other two divisions stays constant. If that happens, the DVD and E-learning Divisions will be charged higher costs even though they did nothing to cause an increase. These are just two examples of how the best allocation systems are still subject to inherent flaws. More complex service department allocation systems, such as the step-down and reciprocal methods, are discussed in more advanced accounting texts.

Appendix 23A Assignment

■ Exercise

E23A-1 Allocating shared costs among divisions (10–15 min)

Integrity Company has 3 departments using the services of the payroll department. The following data are available:

Subunits Sharing Central Payroll Services	Number of Employees	Number of Employee Requests
Division A	100	200
Division B	140	400
Division C	160	400
Total	400	1,000

Requirements

1. Allocate the cost to each division using total number of employees as the allocation cost base.
2. Allocate the cost to each division using total number of employee requests as the allocation cost base.
3. Evaluate the results. Which allocation cost base would you recommend?

Appendix A

2 0 0 7

PARTIAL
ANNUAL REPORT

http://media.corporate-ir.net/media_files/irol/97/97664/2007AR.pdf

Report of Independent Registered Public Accounting Firm

The Board of Directors and Stockholders
Amazon.com, Inc.

We have audited the accompanying consolidated balance sheets of Amazon.com, Inc. as of December 31, 2007 and 2006, and the related consolidated statements of operations, stockholders' equity, and cash flows for each of the three years in the period ended December 31, 2007. Our audits also included the financial statement schedule listed in the Index at Item 15(a)(2). These financial statements and schedule are the responsibility of the Company's management. Our responsibility is to express an opinion on these financial statements and schedule based on our audits.

We conducted our audits in accordance with the standards of the Public Company Accounting Oversight Board (United States). Those standards require that we plan and perform the audit to obtain reasonable assurance about whether the financial statements are free of material misstatement. An audit includes examining, on a test basis, evidence supporting the amounts and disclosures in the financial statements. An audit also includes assessing the accounting principles used and significant estimates made by management, as well as evaluating the overall financial statement presentation. We believe that our audits provide a reasonable basis for our opinion.

In our opinion, the financial statements referred to above present fairly, in all material respects, the consolidated financial position of Amazon.com, Inc. at December 31, 2007 and 2006, and the consolidated results of its operations and its cash flows for each of the three years in the period ended December 31, 2007, in conformity with U.S. generally accepted accounting principles. Also, in our opinion, the related financial statement schedule, when considered in relation to the basic financial statements taken as a whole, presents fairly in all material respects the information set forth therein.

As discussed in Note 1 to the consolidated financial statements, the Company adopted FASB Interpretation No. 48 *Accounting for Uncertainty in Income Taxes*, effective January 1, 2007.

We also have audited, in accordance with the standards of the Public Company Accounting Oversight Board (United States), the effectiveness of Amazon.com, Inc.'s internal control over financial reporting as of December 31, 2007, based on criteria established in Internal Control—Integrated Framework issued by the Committee of Sponsoring Organizations of the Treadway Commission and our report dated February 8, 2008 expressed an unqualified opinion thereon.

/s/ ERNST & YOUNG LLP

Seattle, Washington
February 8, 2008

AMAZON.COM, INC.

CONSOLIDATED STATEMENTS OF CASH FLOWS
(in millions)

	Year Ended December 31,		
	2007	2006	2005
CASH AND CASH EQUIVALENTS, BEGINNING OF PERIOD	$1,022	$ 1,013	$ 1,303
OPERATING ACTIVITIES:			
Net income	476	190	359
Adjustments to reconcile net income to net cash from operating activities:			
Depreciation of fixed assets, including internal-use software and website development, and other amortization	246	205	121
Stock-based compensation	185	101	87
Other operating expense, net	9	10	7
Losses (gains) on sales of marketable securities, net	1	(2)	(1)
Remeasurements and other	12	(6)	(37)
Deferred income taxes	(99)	22	70
Excess tax benefits from stock-based compensation	(257)	(102)	(7)
Cumulative effect of change in accounting principle	—	—	(26)
Changes in operating assets and liabilities:			
Inventories	(303)	(282)	(104)
Accounts receivable, net and other	(255)	(103)	(84)
Accounts payable	928	402	274
Accrued expenses and other	429	241	67
Additions to unearned revenue	244	206	156
Amortization of previously unearned revenue	(211)	(180)	(149)
Net cash provided by operating activities	1,405	702	733
INVESTING ACTIVITIES:			
Purchases of fixed assets, including internal-use software and website development	(224)	(216)	(204)
Acquisitions, net of cash acquired, and other	(75)	(32)	(24)
Sales and maturities of marketable securities and other investments	1,271	1,845	836
Purchases of marketable securities and other investments	(930)	(1,930)	(1,386)
Net cash provided by (used in) investing activities	42	(333)	(778)
FINANCING ACTIVITIES:			
Proceeds from exercises of stock options	91	35	59
Excess tax benefits from stock-based compensation	257	102	7
Common stock repurchased	(248)	(252)	—
Proceeds from long-term debt and other	24	98	11
Repayments of long-term debt and capital lease obligations	(74)	(383)	(270)
Net cash provided by (used in) financing activities	50	(400)	(193)
Foreign-currency effect on cash and cash equivalents	20	40	(52)
Net increase (decrease) in cash and cash equivalents	1,517	9	(290)
CASH AND CASH EQUIVALENTS, END OF PERIOD	$2,539	$ 1,022	$ 1,013
SUPPLEMENTAL CASH FLOW INFORMATION:			
Cash paid for interest	$ 67	$ 86	$ 105
Cash paid for income taxes	24	15	12
Fixed assets acquired under capital leases and other financing arrangements	74	69	6
Fixed assets acquired under build-to-suit leases	15	—	—

See accompanying notes to consolidated financial statements.

AMAZON.COM, INC.

CONSOLIDATED STATEMENTS OF OPERATIONS
(in millions, except per share data)

	Year Ended December 31,		
	2007	2006	2005
Net sales	$14,835	$10,711	$8,490
Cost of sales	11,482	8,255	6,451
Gross profit	3,353	2,456	2,039
Operating expenses (1):			
Fulfillment	1,292	937	745
Marketing	344	263	198
Technology and content	818	662	451
General and administrative	235	195	166
Other operating expense, net	9	10	47
Total operating expenses	2,698	2,067	1,607
Income from operations	655	389	432
Interest income	90	59	44
Interest expense	(77)	(78)	(92)
Other income (expense), net	(1)	(4)	2
Remeasurements and other	(7)	11	42
Total non-operating income (expense)	5	(12)	(4)
Income before income taxes	660	377	428
Provision for income taxes	184	187	95
Income before cumulative effect of change in accounting principle	476	190	333
Cumulative effect of change in accounting principle	—	—	26
Net income	$ 476	$ 190	$ 359
Basic earnings per share:			
Prior to cumulative effect of change in accounting principle	$ 1.15	$ 0.46	$ 0.81
Cumulative effect of change in accounting principle	—	—	0.06
	$ 1.15	$ 0.46	$ 0.87
Diluted earnings per share:			
Prior to cumulative effect of change in accounting principle	$ 1.12	$ 0.45	$ 0.78
Cumulative effect of change in accounting principle	—	—	0.06
	$ 1.12	$ 0.45	$ 0.84
Weighted average shares used in computation of earnings per share:			
Basic	413	416	412
Diluted	424	424	426

(1) Includes stock-based compensation as follows:

	2007	2006	2005
Fulfillment	$ 39	$ 24	$ 16
Marketing	8	4	6
Technology and content	103	54	45
General and administrative	35	19	20

See accompanying notes to consolidated financial statements.

46

AMAZON.COM, INC.

CONSOLIDATED BALANCE SHEETS
(in millions, except per share data)

	December 31,	
	2007	2006
ASSETS		
Current assets:		
Cash and cash equivalents	$ 2,539	$ 1,022
Marketable securities	573	997
Inventories	1,200	877
Accounts receivable, net and other	705	399
Deferred tax assets	147	78
Total current assets	5,164	3,373
Fixed assets, net	543	457
Deferred tax assets	260	199
Goodwill	222	195
Other assets	296	139
Total assets	$ 6,485	$ 4,363
LIABILITIES AND STOCKHOLDERS' EQUITY		
Current liabilities:		
Accounts payable	$ 2,795	$ 1,816
Accrued expenses and other	919	716
Total current liabilities	3,714	2,532
Long-term debt	1,282	1,247
Other long-term liabilities	292	153
Commitments and contingencies		
Stockholders' equity:		
Preferred stock, $0.01 par value:		
Authorized shares—500		
Issued and outstanding shares—none	—	—
Common stock, $0.01 par value:		
Authorized shares—5,000		
Issued shares—431 and 422		
Outstanding shares—416 and 414	4	4
Treasury stock, at cost	(500)	(252)
Additional paid-in capital	3,063	2,517
Accumulated other comprehensive income (loss)	5	(1)
Accumulated deficit	(1,375)	(1,837)
Total stockholders' equity	1,197	431
Total liabilities and stockholders' equity	$ 6,485	$ 4,363

See accompanying notes to consolidated financial statements.

47

AMAZON.COM, INC.

CONSOLIDATED STATEMENTS OF STOCKHOLDERS' EQUITY
(in millions)

	Common Stock		Treasury Stock	Additional Paid-In Capital	Accumulated Other Comprehensive Income (Loss)	Accumulated Deficit	Total Stockholders' Equity
	Shares	Amount					
Balance at January 1, 2005	410	4	$ —	$2,123	$ 32	$(2,386)	$ (227)
Net income	—	—	—	—	—	359	359
Foreign currency translation losses, net	—	—	—	—	(15)	—	(15)
Change in unrealized gains on available-for-sale securities, net of tax	—	—	—	—	(14)	—	(14)
Amortization of unrealized loss on terminated Euro Currency Swap, net of tax	—	—	—	—	3	—	3
Comprehensive income							333
Exercise of common stock options, net and vesting of restricted stock	6	—	—	58	—	—	58
Change in accounting principle	—	—	—	(26)	—	—	(26)
Excess tax benefits from stock-based compensation	—	—	—	10	—	—	10
Stock-based compensation and issuance of employee benefit plan stock	—	—	—	98	—	—	98
Balance at December 31, 2005	416	4	—	2,263	6	(2,027)	246
Net income	—	—	—	—	—	190	190
Foreign currency translation losses, net of tax	—	—	—	—	(13)	—	(13)
Change in unrealized losses on available-for-sale securities, net of tax	—	—	—	—	4	—	4
Amortization of unrealized loss on terminated Euro Currency Swap, net of tax	—	—	—	—	2	—	2
Comprehensive income							183
Exercise of common stock options	6	—	—	35	—	—	35
Repurchase of common stock	(8)	—	(252)	—	—	—	(252)
Excess tax benefits from stock-based compensation	—	—	—	102	—	—	102
Stock-based compensation and issuance of employee benefit plan stock	—	—	—	117	—	—	117
Balance at December 31, 2006	414	4	(252)	2,517	(1)	(1,837)	431
Net income	—	—	—	—	—	476	476
Foreign currency translation losses, net of tax	—	—	—	—	(3)	—	(3)
Change in unrealized losses on available-for-sale securities, net of tax	—	—	—	—	8	—	8
Amortization of unrealized loss on terminated Euro Currency Swap, net of tax	—	—	—	—	1	—	1
Comprehensive income							482
Change in accounting principle	—	—	—	2	—	(14)	(12)
Unrecognized excess tax benefits from stock-based compensation	—	—	—	4	—	—	4
Exercise of common stock options and conversion of debt	8	—	—	92	—	—	92
Repurchase of common stock	(6)	—	(248)	—	—	—	(248)
Excess tax benefits from stock-based compensation	—	—	—	257	—	—	257
Stock-based compensation and issuance of employee benefit plan stock	—	—	—	191	—	—	191
Balance at December 31, 2007	416	4	$(500)	$3,063	$ 5	$(1,375)	$1,197

See accompanying notes to consolidated financial statements.

AMAZON.COM, INC.

NOTES TO CONSOLIDATED FINANCIAL STATEMENTS

Note 1—DESCRIPTION OF BUSINESS AND ACCOUNTING POLICIES

Description of Business

Amazon.com, a Fortune 500 company, opened its virtual doors on the World Wide Web in July 1995 and today offers Earth's Biggest Selection. We seek to be Earth's most customer-centric company. Amazon.com serves three primary customer sets: consumer customers, seller customers and developer customers. We serve consumer customers through our retail websites, which include *www.amazon.com, www.amazon.ca, www.amazon.de, www.amazon.fr, www.amazon.co.jp, www.amazon.co.uk, www.shopbop.com, www.endless.com,* and the Joyo Amazon websites at *www.joyo.cn* and *www.amazon.cn.* We serve seller customers by offering programs and services that enable them to sell products on our websites and operate their e-commerce businesses under their own brand name and website address. We serve developers by offering a suite of web services that provide developer customers with direct access to Amazon.com's robust technology platform in order to enable them to build innovative applications on their own. In addition, we generate revenue through co-branded credit card agreements and other marketing and promotional services, such as online advertising.

We have organized our operations into two principal segments: North America and International. See "Note 13—Segment Information."

Principles of Consolidation

The consolidated financial statements include the accounts of the Company, its wholly-owned subsidiaries, and those entities (relating primarily to the Joyo Amazon websites) in which we have a variable interest. Intercompany balances and transactions have been eliminated.

Use of Estimates

The preparation of financial statements in conformity with GAAP requires estimates and assumptions that affect the reported amounts of assets and liabilities, revenues and expenses, and related disclosures of contingent liabilities in the consolidated financial statements and accompanying notes. Estimates are used for, but not limited to, valuation of investments, receivables valuation, sales returns, incentive discount offers, inventory valuation, depreciable lives of fixed assets, internally-developed software, valuation of acquired intangibles, income taxes, stock-based compensation, and contingencies. Actual results could differ materially from those estimates.

Earnings per Share

Basic earnings per share is calculated using our weighted-average outstanding common shares. Diluted earnings per share is calculated using our weighted-average outstanding common shares including the dilutive effect of stock awards as determined under the treasury stock method.

Our convertible debt instruments are excluded from the calculation of diluted earnings per share as their effect under the if-converted method is antidilutive. See "Note 4—Long-Term Debt."

The following table shows the calculation of diluted shares (in millions):

	Year Ended December 31,		
	2007	2006	2005
Shares used in computation of basic earnings per share	413	416	412
Total dilutive effect of outstanding stock awards (1)	11	8	14
Shares used in computation of diluted earnings per share	424	424	426

(1) Calculated using the treasury stock method that assumes proceeds available to reduce the dilutive affect of outstanding stock awards, which include the exercise price of stock options, the unrecognized deferred compensation of stock awards, and assumed tax proceeds from excess stock-based compensation deductions.

Treasury Stock

We account for treasury stock under the cost method and include treasury stock as a component of stockholders' equity.

Business Acquisitions

We acquired certain companies during 2007 for an aggregate cash purchase price of $33 million, including cash payments of $24 million and future cash payments of $9 million. We also made principal payments of $13 million on acquired debt in connection with one of these acquisitions. Additional cash consideration for these acquisitions is contingent upon continued employment. This amount is expensed as compensation over the employment period and not included in the purchase price. Acquired intangibles totaled $18 million and have estimated useful lives of between two and ten years. The excess of purchase price over the fair value of the net assets acquired was $21 million and is classified as "Goodwill" on our consolidated balance sheets.

We acquired certain companies during 2006 for an aggregate cash purchase price of $50 million, including cash paid of $30 million and $19 million in 2006 and 2007, and additional cash payments of $1 million due in 2008. Acquired intangibles totaled $17 million and have estimated useful lives of between one and ten years. The excess of purchase price over the fair value of the net assets acquired was $33 million and is classified as "Goodwill" on our consolidated balance sheets.

In 2005, we acquired certain companies for an aggregate cash purchase price of $29 million. Acquired intangibles totaled $10 million and have estimated useful lives of between one and three years. The excess of purchase price over the fair value of the net assets acquired was $19 million and is classified as "Goodwill" on our consolidated balance sheets.

The results of operations of each of the businesses acquired in 2007, 2006, and 2005 have been included in our consolidated results from each transaction closing date forward. The effect of these acquisitions on consolidated net sales and operating income during 2007, 2006, and 2005 was not significant.

Cash and Cash Equivalents

We classify all highly liquid instruments, including money market funds that comply with Rule 2a-7 of the Investment Company Act of 1940, with a remaining maturity of three months or less at the time of purchase as cash equivalents.

Inventories

Inventories, consisting of products available for sale, are accounted for using the FIFO method, and are valued at the lower of cost or market value. This valuation requires us to make judgments, based on currently-available information, about the likely method of disposition, such as through sales to individual customers, returns to product vendors, or liquidations, and expected recoverable values of each disposition category. Based on this evaluation, we adjust the carrying amount of our inventories to lower of cost or market value.

We provide fulfillment-related services in connection with certain of our marketplace sellers and Amazon Enterprise Solutions programs. In those arrangements, as well as all other product sales by other sellers, the marketplace seller maintains ownership of the related products.

Accounts Receivable, Net and Other Current Assets

Included in "Accounts receivable, net and other current assets" are customer and vendor receivables, as well as prepaid expenses of $23 million and $17 million at December 31, 2007 and 2006, representing advance payments for insurance, licenses, and other miscellaneous expenses.

Allowance for Doubtful Accounts

We estimate losses on receivables based on known troubled accounts, if any, and historical experience of losses incurred. The allowance for doubtful accounts receivable was $64 million and $40 million at December 31, 2007 and 2006.

Internal-use Software and Website Development

Costs incurred to develop software for internal use are required to be capitalized and amortized over the estimated useful life of the software in accordance with Statement of Position (SOP) 98-1, *Accounting for the Costs of Computer Software Developed or Obtained for Internal Use.* Costs related to design or maintenance of internal-use software are expensed as incurred. For the years ended 2007, 2006, and 2005, we capitalized $129 million (including $21 million of stock-based compensation), $123 million (including $16 million of stock-based compensation), and $90 million (including $11 million of stock-based compensation) of costs associated with internal-use software and website development. Amortization of previously capitalized amounts was $116 million, $86 million, and $50 million for 2007, 2006, and 2005.

Depreciation of Fixed Assets

Fixed assets include assets such as furniture and fixtures, heavy equipment, technology infrastructure, internal-use software and website development. Depreciation is recorded on a straight-line basis over the estimated useful lives of the assets (generally two years or less for assets such as internal-use software, two or three years for our technology infrastructure, five years for furniture and fixtures, and ten years for heavy equipment). Depreciation expense is generally classified within the corresponding operating expense categories on our consolidated statements of operations, and certain assets are amortized as "Cost of sales."

Leases and Asset Retirement Obligations

We account for our lease agreements pursuant to Statement of Financial Accounting Standards (SFAS) No. 13, *Accounting for Leases*, which categorizes leases at their inception as either operating or capital leases depending on certain defined criteria. On certain of our lease agreements, we may receive rent holidays and other incentives. We recognize lease costs on a straight-line basis without regard to deferred payment terms, such as rent holidays that defer the commencement date of required payments. Additionally, incentives we receive are treated as a reduction of our costs over the term of the agreement. Leasehold improvements are capitalized at cost and amortized over the lesser of their expected useful life or the life of the lease, without assuming renewal features, if any, are exercised. We account for build-to-suit lease arrangements in accordance with Emerging Issues Task Force (EITF) 97-10, *The Effect of Lessee Involvement in Asset Construction,* to the extent we are involved in the construction of structural improvements prior to commencement of a lease.

In accordance with SFAS No. 143, *Accounting for Asset Retirement Obligations,* we establish assets and liabilities for the present value of estimated future costs to return certain of our leased facilities to their original condition. Such assets are depreciated over the lease period into operating expense, and the recorded liabilities are accreted to the future value of the estimated restoration costs.

Goodwill

We evaluate goodwill for impairment, at a minimum, on an annual basis and whenever events and changes in circumstances suggest that the carrying amount may not be recoverable. Impairment of goodwill is tested at the reporting unit level by comparing the reporting unit's carrying amount, including goodwill, to the fair value of the reporting unit. The fair values of the reporting units are estimated using discounted projected cash flows. If the carrying amount of the reporting unit exceeds its fair value, goodwill is considered impaired and a second step is performed to measure the amount of impairment loss, if any. We conduct our annual impairment test as of October 1 of each year, and have determined there to be no impairment in 2007 or 2006. There were no events or circumstances from the date of our assessment through December 31, 2007 that would impact this assessment.

At December 31, 2007 and December 31, 2006, approximately 55% and 60% of our acquired goodwill was assigned to our International segment, the majority of which relates to our acquisition of Joyo.com Limited.

Other Assets

Included in "Other assets" on our consolidated balance sheets are amounts primarily related to marketable securities restricted for longer than one year; intellectual property rights; certain equity investments; and intangible assets, net of amortization. At December 31, 2007 and 2006, the cost basis and fair value of marketable securities restricted for longer than one year was $197 million and $86 million, primarily attributable to collateralization of bank guarantees and debt related to our international operations. At December 31, 2007, intellectual property rights were $28 million; at December 31, 2006, these amounts were not significant. At December 31, 2007, and 2006, equity investments were $17 million and $19 million.

Other intangibles, net, included within "Other assets," were $26 million and $21 million at December 31, 2007 and 2006. Accumulated amortization was $29 million and $16 million at December 31, 2007 and 2006, which excludes the accumulated amortization of fully-amortized intangibles. Amortization expense was $13 million, $10 million, and $5 million in 2007, 2006, and 2005. Amortization expense of intangible assets over the next five years is as follows: $8 million in 2008; $4 million in 2009; $3 million in 2010; $2 million in 2011; $2 million in 2012. The weighted-average amortization period is five years based on useful life assumptions between one and ten years.

Investments

The initial carrying cost of our investments is the price we paid. Investments are accounted for using the equity method of accounting if the investment gives us the ability to exercise significant influence, but not control, over an investee. We classify our investments in equity-method investees on our consolidated balance sheets as "Other assets" and our share of the investees' earnings or losses as "Remeasurements and other" on our consolidated statements of operations. Losses from equity-method investees were not significant for any period presented.

All other equity investments consist of investments for which we do not have the ability to exercise significant influence. Under the cost method of accounting, investments in private companies are carried at cost and are adjusted only for other-than-temporary declines in fair value, distributions of earnings, and additional investments. For public companies that have readily determinable fair values, we classify our equity investments as available-for-sale and, accordingly, record these investments at their fair values with unrealized gains and losses, net of tax, included in "Accumulated other comprehensive income (loss)," a separate component of stockholders' equity.

We generally invest our excess cash in investment grade short to intermediate term fixed income securities and AAA-rated money market mutual funds. Such investments are included in "Cash and cash equivalents," or "Marketable securities" on the accompanying consolidated balance sheets and are reported at fair value with unrealized gains and losses included in "Accumulated other comprehensive income (loss)." The weighted average method is used to determine the cost of Euro-denominated securities sold, and the specific identification method is used to determine the cost of all other securities.

We periodically evaluate whether declines in fair values of our investments below their cost are other-than-temporary. This evaluation consists of several qualitative and quantitative factors regarding the severity and duration of the unrealized loss as well as our ability and intent to hold the investment until a forecasted recovery occurs. Factors considered include quoted market prices, if available; recent financial results and operating trends; other publicly available information; implied values from any recent purchase/sales offers of investee securities; or other conditions that may affect the value of our investments. At December 31, 2007, gross unrealized losses on our marketable securities were $3 million and were determined to be temporary based on our assessment of the qualitative and quantitative factors discussed above.

Long-Lived Assets

Long-lived assets, other than goodwill, are reviewed for impairment whenever events or changes in circumstances indicate that the carrying amount of the assets might not be recoverable. Conditions that would necessitate an impairment assessment include a significant decline in the observable market value of an asset, a significant change in the extent or manner in which an asset is used, or any other significant adverse change that would indicate that the carrying amount of an asset or group of assets may not be recoverable.

For long-lived assets used in operations, impairment losses are only recorded if the asset's carrying amount is not recoverable through its undiscounted, probability-weighted future cash flows. We measure the impairment loss based on the difference between the carrying amount and estimated fair value.

Long-lived assets are considered held for sale when certain criteria are met, including: management has committed to a plan to sell the asset, the asset is available for sale in its immediate condition, and the sale is probable within one year of the reporting date. Assets held for sale are reported at the lower of cost or fair value less costs to sell. Assets held for sale were not significant at December 31, 2007 or 2006.

Accrued Expenses and Other

Included in "Accrued expenses and other" at December 31, 2007 and 2006 were liabilities of $240 million and $183 million for unredeemed gift certificates. We recognize revenue from a gift certificate when a customer redeems it. If a gift certificate is not redeemed, we recognize revenue when it expires or, for a certificate without an expiration date, when the likelihood of its redemption becomes remote, generally two years from date of issuance.

Unearned Revenue

Unearned revenue is recorded when payments are received in advance of performing our service obligations and is recognized over the service period. Current unearned revenue is included in "Accrued expenses and other" and non-current unearned revenue is included in "Other long-term liabilities" on our consolidated balance sheets. Current unearned revenue was $91 million and $78 million at December 31, 2007 and 2006.

Income Taxes

Income tax expense includes U.S. and international income taxes. We do not provide for U.S. taxes on our undistributed earnings of foreign subsidiaries, totaling $126 million at December 31, 2007, since we intend to invest such undistributed earnings indefinitely outside of the U.S. If such amounts were repatriated, determination of the amount of U.S. income taxes that would be incurred is not practicable due to the complexities associated with this calculation.

Deferred income tax balances reflect the effects of temporary differences between the carrying amounts of assets and liabilities and their tax bases and are stated at enacted tax rates expected to be in effect when taxes are actually paid or recovered. At December 31, 2007, our deferred tax assets, net of deferred tax liabilities and valuation allowance, were $385 million, which includes $148 million relating to net operating loss carryforwards ("NOLs") that were primarily attributed to stock-based compensation. The majority of our NOLs begin to expire in 2019 and thereafter.

SFAS No. 109, *Accounting for Income Taxes,* requires that deferred tax assets be evaluated for future realization and reduced by a valuation allowance to the extent we believe a portion will not be realized. We consider many factors when assessing the likelihood of future realization of our deferred tax assets, including our recent cumulative earnings experience and expectations of future taxable income by taxing jurisdiction, the carry-forward periods available to us for tax reporting purposes, and other relevant factors. In accordance with SFAS No. 109, we allocate our valuation allowance to current and long-term deferred tax assets on a pro-rata basis.

Effective January 1, 2007, we adopted the provisions of FASB Interpretation (FIN) No. 48, *Accounting for Uncertainty in Income Taxes—an Interpretation of FASB Statement No. 109.* FIN 48 contains a two-step approach to recognizing and measuring uncertain tax positions (tax contingencies) accounted for in accordance with SFAS No. 109. The first step is to evaluate the tax position for recognition by determining if the weight of available evidence indicates it is more likely than not that the position will be sustained on audit, including resolution of related appeals or litigation processes, if any. The second step is to measure the tax benefit as the largest amount which is more than 50% likely of being realized upon ultimate settlement. We consider many factors when evaluating and estimating our tax positions and tax benefits, which may require periodic adjustments and which may not accurately forecast actual outcomes.

Adopting FIN 48 increased long-term assets by $10 million, long-term liabilities by $21 million, accumulated deficit by $14 million and additional paid-in capital by $2 million. These amounts include the associated federal benefit related to unrecognized tax benefits, and interest and penalties which collectively are not material. As of January 1, 2007, we had $110 million of tax contingencies.

Revenue

We recognize revenue from product sales or services rendered when the following four revenue recognition criteria are met: persuasive evidence of an arrangement exists, delivery has occurred or services have been rendered, the selling price is fixed or determinable, and collectibility is reasonably assured. Additionally, revenue arrangements with multiple deliverables are divided into separate units of accounting if the deliverables in the arrangement meet the following criteria: the delivered item has value to the customer on a standalone basis; there is objective and reliable evidence of the fair value of undelivered items; and delivery of any undelivered item is probable.

We evaluate the criteria outlined in EITF Issue No. 99-19, *Reporting Revenue Gross as a Principal Versus Net as an Agent*, in determining whether it is appropriate to record the gross amount of product sales and related costs or the net amount earned as commissions. Generally, when we are primarily obligated in a transaction, are subject to inventory risk, have latitude in establishing prices and selecting suppliers, or have several but not all of these indicators, revenue is recorded gross. If we are not primarily obligated and amounts earned are determined using a fixed percentage, a fixed-payment schedule, or a combination of the two, we generally record the net amounts as commissions earned.

Product sales and shipping revenues, net of promotional discounts, rebates, and return allowances, are recorded when the products are shipped and title passes to customers. Retail sales to customers are made pursuant to a sales contract that provides for transfer of both title and risk of loss upon our delivery to the carrier. Return allowances, which reduce product revenue, are estimated using historical experience. Revenue from product sales and services rendered is recorded net of sales taxes. Amounts received in advance for subscription services, including amounts received for Amazon Prime and other membership programs, are deferred and recognized as revenue over the subscription term. For our products with multiple elements, where a standalone value for each element cannot be established, we recognize the revenue and related cost over the estimated economic life of the product.

We periodically provide incentive offers to our customers to encourage purchases. Such offers include current discount offers, such as percentage discounts off current purchases, inducement offers, such as offers for future discounts subject to a minimum current purchase, and other similar offers. Current discount offers, when accepted by our customers, are treated as a reduction to the purchase price of the related transaction, while inducement offers, when accepted by our customers, are treated as a reduction to purchase price based on estimated future redemption rates. Redemption rates are estimated using our historical experience for similar inducement offers. Current discount offers and inducement offers are presented as a net amount in "Net sales."

Commissions and per-unit fees received from sellers and similar amounts earned through Amazon Enterprise Solutions are recognized when the item is sold by seller and our collectibility is reasonably assured. We record an allowance for estimated refunds on such commissions using historical experience.

Shipping Activities

Outbound shipping charges to customers are included in "Net sales" and were $740 million, $567 million, and $511 million for 2007, 2006, and 2005. Outbound shipping-related costs are included in "Cost of sales" and totaled $1.2 billion, $884 million, and $750 million for 2007, 2006, and 2005. The net cost to us of shipping activities was $434 million, $317 million, and $239 million for 2007, 2006 and 2005.

Cost of Sales

Cost of sales consists of the purchase price of consumer products and content sold by us, inbound and outbound shipping charges, packaging supplies, and costs incurred in operating and staffing our fulfillment and customer service centers on behalf of other businesses. Shipping charges to receive products from our suppliers are included in our inventory, and recognized as "Cost of sales" upon sale of products to our customers. Payment processing and related transaction costs, including those associated with seller transactions, are classified in "Fulfillment" on our consolidated statements of operations.

Vendor Agreements

We have agreements to receive cash consideration from certain of our vendors, including rebates and cooperative marketing reimbursements. We generally presume amounts received from our vendors are a reduction of the prices we pay for their products and, therefore, we reflect such amounts as either a reduction of "Cost of sales" on our consolidated statements of operations, or, if the product inventory is still on hand, as a reduction of the carrying value of inventory. Vendor rebates are typically dependent upon reaching minimum purchase thresholds. We evaluate the likelihood of reaching purchase thresholds using past experience and current year forecasts. When volume rebates can be reasonably estimated, we record a portion of the rebate as we make progress towards the purchase threshold.

When we receive direct reimbursements for costs incurred by us in advertising the vendor's product or service, the amount we receive is recorded as an offset to "Marketing" on our consolidated statements of operations.

Fulfillment

Fulfillment costs represent those costs incurred in operating and staffing our fulfillment and customer service centers, including costs attributable to buying, receiving, inspecting, and warehousing inventories; picking, packaging, and preparing customer orders for shipment; payment processing and related transaction costs, including costs associated with our guarantee for certain seller transactions; and responding to inquiries from customers. Fulfillment costs also include amounts paid to third parties that assist us in fulfillment and customer service operations. Certain of our fulfillment-related costs that are incurred on behalf of other businesses, such as Target Corporation, are classified as cost of sales rather than fulfillment.

Marketing

Marketing costs consist primarily of online advertising, including through our Associates program, sponsored search, portal advertising, e-mail campaigns, and other initiatives. We pay commissions to participants in our Associates program when their customer referrals result in product sales and classify such costs as "Marketing" on our consolidated statements of operations.

We also participate in cooperative advertising arrangements with certain of our vendors, and other third parties. To the extent co-operative marketing reimbursements decline in future periods, we may incur additional expenses to continue certain promotions or elect to reduce or discontinue them.

Marketing expenses also consist of public relations expenditures; payroll and related expenses for personnel engaged in marketing, business development, and selling activities; and to a lesser extent, traditional advertising such as newspaper inserts.

Advertising and other promotional costs, which consist primarily of online advertising, are expensed as incurred, and were \$306 million, \$226 million, and \$168 million in 2007, 2006, and 2005. Prepaid advertising costs were not significant at December 31, 2007 and 2006.

Technology and Content

Technology and content expenses consist principally of payroll and related expenses for employees involved in, application development, category expansion, editorial content, buying, merchandising selection, and systems support, as well as costs associated with the compute, storage and telecommunications infrastructure.

Technology and content costs are expensed as incurred, except for certain costs relating to the development of internal-use software and website development, including software used to upgrade and enhance our websites and processes supporting our business, which are capitalized and amortized over two years.

General and Administrative

General and administrative expenses consist of payroll and related expenses for employees involved in general corporate functions, including accounting, finance, tax, legal, and human relations, among others; costs associated with use by these functions of facilities and equipment, such as depreciation expense and rent; professional fees and litigation costs; and other general corporate costs.

Stock-Based Compensation

As of January 1, 2005, we adopted SFAS No. 123(R), which requires measurement of compensation cost for all stock-based awards at fair value on date of grant and recognition of compensation over the service period for awards expected to vest. The fair value of restricted stock and restricted stock units is determined based on the number of shares granted and the quoted price of our common stock. Such value is recognized as expense over the service period, net of estimated forfeitures, using the accelerated method. The estimation of stock awards that will ultimately vest requires judgment, and to the extent actual results or updated estimates differ from our current estimates, such amounts will be recorded as a cumulative adjustment in the period estimates are revised. We consider many factors when estimating expected forfeitures, including types of awards, employee class, and historical experience. Actual results and future estimates may differ substantially from our current estimates.

Foreign Currency

We have the following internationally-focused websites: *www.amazon.co.uk, www.amazon.de, www.amazon.fr, www.amazon.co.jp, www.amazon.ca*, and services for the Joyo Amazon websites at *www.joyo.cn* and *www.amazon.cn*. Net sales generated from internationally-focused websites, as well as most of the related expenses directly incurred from those operations, are denominated in the functional currencies of the resident countries. Additionally, the functional currency of our subsidiaries that either operate or support these international websites is the same as the local currency of the United Kingdom, Germany, France, Japan, Canada, and China. Assets and liabilities of these subsidiaries are translated into U.S. Dollars at period-end exchange rates, and revenues and expenses are translated at average rates prevailing throughout the period. Translation adjustments are included in "Accumulated other comprehensive income (loss)," a separate component of stockholders' equity, and in the "Foreign currency effect on cash and cash equivalents," on our consolidated statements of cash flows. Transaction gains and losses arising from transactions denominated in a currency other than the functional currency of the entity involved are included in "Other income (expense), net" on our consolidated statements of operations. See "Note 10—Other Income (Expense), Net."

Gains and losses arising from intercompany foreign currency transactions are included in net income. In connection with the remeasurement of intercompany balances, we recorded gains of $32 million and $50 million in 2007 and 2006, and a loss of $47 million in 2005.

Recent Accounting Pronouncements

In September 2006, the Financial Accounting Standards Board (FASB) issued SFAS No. 157, *Fair Value Measurements*, which defines fair value, establishes a framework for measuring fair value in generally accepted accounting principles and expands disclosures about fair value measurements. SFAS No. 157 is effective for fiscal years beginning after November 15, 2007, and interim periods within those fiscal years. We do not expect the adoption of SFAS No. 157 to have a material impact on our consolidated financial statements. The FASB may delay a portion of this standard.

In February 2007, the FASB issued SFAS No. 159, *The Fair Value Option for Financial Assets and Financial Liabilities*. SFAS No. 159 permits companies to choose to measure many financial instruments and certain other items at fair value. SFAS No. 159 is effective for financial statements issued for fiscal years beginning after November 15, 2007. We do not expect the adoption of SFAS No. 159 to have a material impact on our consolidated financial statements.

In December 2007, the FASB issued SFAS No. 141 (R), *Business Combinations*, and SFAS No. 160, *Noncontrolling Interests in Consolidated Financial Statements.* SFAS No. 141 (R) requires an acquirer to measure the identifiable assets acquired, the liabilities assumed and any noncontrolling interest in the acquiree at their fair values on the acquisition date, with goodwill being the excess value over the net identifiable assets acquired. SFAS No. 160 clarifies that a noncontrolling interest in a subsidiary should be reported as equity in the consolidated financial statements. The calculation of earnings per share will continue to be based on income amounts attributable to the parent. SFAS No. 141 (R) and SFAS No. 160 are effective for financial statements issued for fiscal years beginning after December 15, 2008. Early adoption is prohibited. We have not yet determined the effect on our consolidated financial statements, if any, upon adoption of SFAS No. 141 (R) or SFAS No. 160.

Note 2—CASH, CASH EQUIVALENTS, AND MARKETABLE SECURITIES

We measure our cash, cash equivalents and marketable securities at fair value based on the quoted prices in active markets. The following tables summarize, by major security type, our cash, cash equivalents and marketable securities (in millions):

	December 31, 2007			
	Cost or Amortized Cost	Gross Unrealized Gains	Gross Unrealized Losses (1)	Estimated Fair Value
Cash	$ 813	$—	$—	$ 813
Money market funds	1,408	—	—	1,408
Corporate debt securities	116	1	(1)	116
U.S. government and agency securities	298	4	(1)	301
Asset-backed securities	101	1	(1)	101
Foreign government and agency securities	358	—	(1)	357
Equity securities	5	7	—	12
Other securities	4	—	—	4
Total cash, cash equivalents, and marketable securities (2)	$3,103	$ 13	$ (4)	$3,112

(1) The fair value of investments with loss positions was $515 million. We evaluated the nature of these investments, which are primarily U.S. Treasury Notes, the duration of the impairments (substantially all less than twelve months), and concluded that such amounts were not "other-than-temporary."

(2) Includes investments in foreign currencies of $1.2 billion, principally Euros, British Pounds, and Japanese Yen.

AMAZON.COM, INC.

NOTES TO CONSOLIDATED FINANCIAL STATEMENTS—(Continued)

	December 31, 2006			
	Cost or Amortized Cost	Gross Unrealized Gains	Gross Unrealized Losses (1)	Estimated Fair Value
Cash	$ 118	$—	$—	$ 118
Money market funds	763	—	—	763
Bank of certificates of deposits	50	—	—	50
Corporate debt securities	420	—	(1)	419
U.S. government and agency securities	208	1	(2)	207
Asset-backed securities	348	—	(1)	347
Foreign government and agency securities	105	—	(1)	104
Equity securities	4	3	—	7
Other securities	4	—	—	4
Total cash, cash equivalents, and marketable securities (2)	$2,020	$ 4	$ (5)	$2,019

(1) The fair value of investments with loss positions was $978 million. We evaluated the nature of these investments, which are primarily U.S. Treasury Notes, the duration of the impairments (all less than twelve months), and the amount of the impairments relative to the underlying portfolio and concluded that such amounts were not "other-than-temporary."

(2) Includes investments in foreign currencies of $623 million, principally Euros, British Pounds, and Japanese Yen.

The following table summarizes contractual maturities of our cash equivalent and marketable fixed-income securities as of December 31, 2007 (in millions):

	Amortized Cost	Estimated Fair Value
Due within one year	$1,818	$1,818
Due after one year through five years	466	469
	$2,284	$2,287

Gross gains of $2 million, $18 million, and $7 million and gross losses of $3 million, $16 million and $12 million were realized on sales of available-for-sale marketable securities, including Euro-denominated securities, for 2007, 2006, and 2005.

We are required to pledge a portion of our cash equivalents or marketable securities as collateral for standby letters of credit that guarantee certain of our contractual obligations, a line of credit, and real estate lease agreements. See "Note 6—Commitments and Contingencies."

Note 3—FIXED ASSETS

Fixed assets, at cost, consisted of the following (in millions):

	December 31,	
	2007	2006
Gross Fixed Assets:		
Fulfillment and customer service	$ 464	$379
Technology infrastructure	196	153
Internal-use software, content, and website development	285	230
Construction in progress (1)	15	—
Other corporate assets	63	62
Gross fixed assets	1,023	824
Accumulated Depreciation:		
Fulfillment and customer service	216	171
Technology infrastructure	74	55
Internal-use software, content, and website development	146	108
Other corporate assets	44	33
Total accumulated depreciation	480	367
Total fixed assets, net	$ 543	$457

(1) We capitalize construction in progress and record a corresponding long-term liability for certain lease agreements related to our Seattle, Washington corporate office space subject to leases scheduled to begin in 2010 and 2011. See "Note 5—Other Long-Term Liabilities" and "Note 6—Commitments and Contingencies" for further discussion.

Depreciation expense on fixed assets was $258 million, $200 million, and $113 million, which includes amortization of fixed assets acquired under capital lease obligations of $40 million, $26 million and $4 million for 2007, 2006, and 2005. Gross assets remaining under capital leases were $150 million and $77 million at December 31, 2007 and 2006. Accumulated depreciation associated with capital leases was $64 million and $28 million at December 31, 2007 and 2006.

Note 4—LONG-TERM DEBT

Our long-term debt is summarized as follows:

	December 31,	
	2007	2006
	(in millions)	
4.75% Convertible Subordinated Notes due February 2009	$ 899	$ 900
6.875% PEACS due February 2010	350	317
Other long-term debt	50	46
	1,299	1,263
Less current portion of long-term debt	(17)	(16)
	$1,282	$1,247

4.75% Convertible Subordinated Notes

In February 1999, we completed an offering of $1.25 billion of 4.75% Convertible Subordinated Notes. The 4.75% Convertible Subordinated Notes are convertible into our common stock at the holders' option at a conversion price of $78.0275 per share. Total common stock issuable, as of December 31, 2007, upon conversion of our outstanding 4.75% Convertible Subordinated Notes was 11.5 million shares, which is excluded from our calculation of earnings per share as its effect is currently anti-dilutive. Interest on the 4.75% Convertible Subordinated Notes is payable semi-annually in arrears in February and August of each year. The 4.75% Convertible Subordinated Notes are unsecured and are subordinated to any existing and future senior indebtedness as defined in the indenture governing the 4.75% Convertible Subordinated Notes. We have the right to redeem the 4.75% Convertible Subordinated Notes, in whole or in part, by paying the principal plus a redemption premium, plus any accrued and unpaid interest. The redemption premium was 0.950% of the principal at December 31, 2007, and decreased to 0.475% on February 1, 2008 and will decrease to zero at maturity in February 2009.

Upon the occurrence of a "fundamental change" prior to the maturity of the 4.75% Convertible Subordinated Notes, each holder thereof has the right to require us to redeem all or any part of such holder's 4.75% Convertible Subordinated Notes at a price equal to 100% of the principal amount of the notes being redeemed, together with accrued interest. As defined in the indenture, a "fundamental change" is the occurrence of certain types of transactions in which our stockholders do not receive publicly-traded securities.

The indenture governing the 4.75% Convertible Subordinated Notes contains certain affirmative covenants for us, including making principal and interest payments when due, maintaining our corporate existence and properties, and paying taxes and other claims in a timely manner. We were in compliance with these covenants through December 31, 2007.

Based upon quoted market prices, the fair value of our 4.75% Convertible Subordinated Notes as of December 31, 2007 and 2006 was $1.1 billion and $883 million.

6.875% PEACS

In February 2000, we completed an offering of €690 million of our 6.875% PEACS. The 6.875% PEACS are convertible, at the holder's option, into our common stock at a conversion price of €84.883 per share ($123.84, based on the exchange rates as of December 31, 2007). Total common stock issuable, as of December 31, 2007, upon conversion of our outstanding 6.875% PEACS was 2.8 million shares, which is excluded from our calculation of earnings per share as its effect is currently anti-dilutive. The U.S. Dollar equivalent principal, interest, and conversion price fluctuate based on the Euro/U.S. Dollar exchange ratio. Interest on the 6.875% PEACS is payable annually in arrears in February of each year. The 6.875% PEACS are unsecured and are subordinated to any existing and future senior indebtedness. The 6.875% PEACS rank equally with our outstanding 4.75% Convertible Subordinated Notes. We have the right to redeem the 6.875% PEACS, in whole or in part, by paying the principal, plus any accrued and unpaid interest. No premium payment is required for early redemption.

Upon the occurrence of a "fundamental change" prior to the maturity of the 6.875% PEACS, each holder thereof has the right to require us to redeem all or any part of such holder's 6.875% PEACS at a price equal to 100% of the principal amount of the notes being redeemed, together with accrued interest. As defined in the indenture, a "fundamental change" is the occurrence of certain types of transactions in which our stockholders do not receive publicly-traded securities.

The indenture governing the 6.875% PEACS contains certain affirmative covenants for us, including making principal and interest payments when due, maintaining our corporate existence and properties, and paying taxes and other claims in a timely manner. We were in compliance with these covenants through December 31, 2007.

In 2006 and 2005, we redeemed principal amounts of €250 million and €200 million ($300 million and $265 million based on the Euro to U.S. Dollar exchange rate on the date of redemption) of our outstanding 6.875% PEACS. As a result of these redemptions, in 2006 and 2005 we recorded a charge classified in "Remeasurements and other," of approximately $6 million and $4 million related to the redemption, consisting of $3 million and $2 million in unamortized deferred issuance charges and $3 million and $2 million relating to unrealized losses on our terminated currency swap that previously hedged a portion of our 6.875% PEACS.

Based upon quoted market prices, the fair value of the 6.875% PEACS was $358 million and $320 million (outstanding principal of €240 million) as of December 31, 2007 and 2006.

Debt Repurchase Authorization

In February 2008 our Board of Directors authorized a debt repurchase program, replacing our previous debt repurchase authorization in its entirety, pursuant to which we may from time to time repurchase (through open market repurchases or private transactions), redeem, or otherwise retire up to an aggregate of all of our outstanding 4.75% Convertible Subordinated Notes and 6.875% PEACS. The outstanding principal of our 4.75% Convertible Subordinated Notes as of this authorization was $899 million, and the outstanding principal amount of our 6.875% PEACS was €240 million.

Note 5—OTHER LONG-TERM LIABILITIES

Our other long-term liabilities are summarized as follows:

	December 31,	
	2007	2006
	(in millions)	
Tax contingencies	$ 98	$ 75
Long-term capital lease obligations	62	20
Construction liability	15	—
Other	117	58
	$292	$153

Tax Contingencies

As of December 31, 2007 and 2006, we have provided tax reserves for tax contingencies of approximately $98 million and $75 million for U.S. and foreign income taxes, which primarily relate to restructuring of certain foreign operations and intercompany pricing between our subsidiaries. See "Note 12—Income Taxes" for discussion of tax contingencies.

Capital Leases

Certain of our equipment fixed assets, primarily related to technology, have been acquired under capital leases. Long-term capital lease obligations were as follows:

	December 31, 2007
	(in millions)
Gross capital lease obligations	$101
Less imputed interest	(13)
Present value of net minimum lease payments	88
Less current portion	(26)
Total long-term capital lease obligations	$ 62

Construction Liability Related to Seattle Campus

We capitalize construction in progress and record a corresponding long-term liability for certain lease agreements related to our Seattle, Washington corporate office space subject to leases scheduled to begin in 2010 and 2011.

In accordance with EITF No. 97-10, for build-to-suit lease arrangements where we are involved in the construction of structural improvements prior to the commencement of the lease or take some level of construction risk, we are considered the owner of the assets during the construction period under generally accepted accounting principles. Accordingly, as the landlord incurs the construction project costs, the assets and corresponding financial obligation are recorded in "Fixed assets, net" and "Other long-term liabilities" on our consolidated balance sheet. Once the construction is completed, if the lease meets certain "sale-leaseback" criteria in accordance with SFAS No. 98, *Accounting for Leases*, we will remove the asset and related financial obligation from the balance sheet and treat the building lease as an operating lease. If upon completion of construction, the project does not meet the "sale-leaseback" criteria, the leased property will be treated as a capital lease for financial reporting purposes.

The remainder of our other long-term liabilities primarily include deferred tax liabilities, unearned revenue, asset retirement obligations, and deferred rental liabilities.

Note 6—COMMITMENTS AND CONTINGENCIES

Commitments

We lease office and fulfillment center facilities and fixed assets under non-cancelable operating and capital leases. Rental expense under operating lease agreements was $141 million, $132 million, and $84 million for 2007, 2006, and 2005.

In December 2007, we entered into a series of leases and other agreements for the lease of corporate office space to be developed in Seattle, Washington with initial terms of up to 16 years commencing on completion of development in 2010 and 2011 and options to extend for two five year periods. Under the agreements we will occupy approximately 800,000 square feet of office space. We also have the right to occupy up to an additional approximately 800,000 square feet subject to a termination fee, estimated to be up to approximately $40 million, if the Company elects not to occupy the additional space. In addition, we have options to lease up to an additional approximately 500,000 square feet at rates based on fair market values at the time the options are exercised, subject to certain conditions. In addition, if interest rates exceed a certain threshold, we have the option to provide financing for some of the buildings.

The following summarizes our principal contractual commitments, excluding open orders for inventory purchases that support normal operations, as of December 31, 2007:

	Year Ended December 31,						
	2008	2009	2010	2011	2012	Thereafter	Total
				(in millions)			
Operating and capital commitments:							
Debt principal (1)	$ 17	$ 932	$350	$—	$—	$—	$1,299
Debt interest (1)	69	46	24	—	—	—	139
Capital leases, including interest	32	29	23	6	6	5	101
Operating leases	132	107	89	69	52	201	650
Other commitments (2)(3)	60	64	80	60	43	579	886
Total commitments	$310	$1,178	$566	$135	$101	$785	$3,075

---

(1) Under our 6.875% PEACS, the principal payment due in 2010 and the annual interest payments fluctuate based on the Euro/U.S. Dollar exchange ratio. At December 31, 2007, the Euro to U.S. Dollar exchange rate was 1.459. Due to changes in the Euro/U.S. Dollar exchange ratio, our remaining principal debt obligation under this instrument since issuance in February 2000 has increased by $114 million as of December 31, 2007. The principal and interest commitments at December 31, 2007 reflect the partial redemptions of the 6.875% PEACS and 4.75% Convertible Subordinated Notes.

(2) Includes the estimated timing and amounts of payments for rent, operating expenses, and tenant improvements associated with approximately 800,000 square feet of corporate office space in Seattle, Washington. We also have the right to occupy up to an additional approximately 800,000 square feet subject to a termination fee, estimated to be up to approximately $40 million, if we do not elect to occupy this additional space. The amount of space available and our financial and other obligations under the lease agreements are affected by various factors, including government approvals and permits, interest rates, development costs and other expenses and our exercise of certain rights under the lease agreements.

(3) Includes commitments to acquire intellectual property and unrecognized tax benefits under FIN 48, but excludes $105 million of such unrecognized tax benefits for which we cannot make a reasonably reliable estimate of the amount and period of payment. See Item 8 of Part II, "Financial Statements and Supplementary Data—Note 12—Income Taxes."

In January 2008 we closed or entered into agreements, subject to regulatory approvals and other conditions, to acquire or invest in certain companies. These acquisitions and investments result in aggregate cash payments of approximately $400 million, net of cash acquired.

Pledged Securities

We are required to pledge or otherwise restrict a portion of our cash and marketable securities as collateral for standby letters of credit, guarantees, debt, and real estate leases. We classify cash and marketable securities with use restrictions of twelve months or longer as non-current "Other assets" on our consolidated balance sheets. The balance of pledged securities at December 31, 2007 consisted of $14 million in "Cash and cash equivalents" and "Marketable securities," and $197 million in "Other assets." The amount required to be pledged for certain real estate lease agreements changes over the life of our leases based on our credit rating and changes in our market capitalization (common shares outstanding multiplied by the closing price of our common stock). Information about collateral required to be pledged under these agreements is as follows:

	Standby and Trade Letters of Credit and Guarantees	Debt (1)	Real Estate Leases (2)	Total
		(in millions)		
Balance at December 31, 2006	$ 60	$56	$20	$136
Net change in collateral pledged	78	4	(7)	75
Balance at December 31, 2007	$138	$60	$13	$211

---

(1) Represents collateral for certain debt related to our international operations.

(2) At December 31, 2007, our market capitalization was $38.6 billion. The required amount of collateral to be pledged will increase by $5 million if our market capitalization is equal to or below $18 billion and by an additional $6 million if our market capitalization is equal to or below $13 billion.

Legal Proceedings

The Company is involved from time to time in claims, proceedings and litigation, including the following:

In October 2002, Gary Gerlinger, individually and on behalf of all other similarly situated consumers in the United States who, during the period from August 1, 2001 to the present, purchased books online from either Amazon.com or Borders.com, instituted an action against us and Borders in the United States District Court for the Northern District of California. The complaint alleges that the agreement pursuant to which an affiliate of Amazon.com operates Borders.com as a co-branded site violates federal anti-trust laws, California statutory law, and the common law of unjust enrichment. The complaint seeks injunctive relief, damages, including treble damages or statutory damages where applicable, attorneys' fees, costs, and disbursements, disgorgement of all sums obtained by allegedly wrongful acts, interest, and declaratory relief. In November 2005, the Court dismissed all of the plaintiff's claims with prejudice. The plaintiff is appealing that dismissal. We dispute the allegations of wrongdoing in this complaint, and we will continue to defend ourselves vigorously in this matter.

Beginning in March 2003, we were served with complaints filed in several different states, including Illinois, by a private litigant, Beeler, Schad & Diamond, P.C., purportedly on behalf of the state governments under various state False Claims Acts. The complaints allege that we (along with other companies with which we have commercial agreements) wrongfully failed to collect and remit sales and use taxes for sales of personal property to customers in those states and knowingly created records and statements falsely stating we were not required to collect or remit such taxes. In December 2006, we learned that one additional complaint was filed in the state of Illinois by a different private litigant, Matthew T. Hurst, alleging similar violations of the Illinois state law. All of the complaints seek injunctive relief, unpaid taxes, interest, attorneys' fees, civil penalties of up to $10,000 per violation, and treble or punitive damages under the various state False Claims Acts. It is possible that we have been or will be named in similar cases in other states as well. We dispute the allegations of wrongdoing in these complaints and intend to vigorously defend ourselves in these matters.

In May 2004, Toysrus.com LLC filed a complaint against us for breach of contract in the Superior Court of New Jersey. The complaint alleged that we breached our commercial agreement with Toysrus.com LLC by selling, and by permitting other third parties to sell, products that Toysrus.com LLC alleged it has an exclusive right to sell on our website. We disputed the allegations in the complaint and brought counterclaims alleging breach of contract and seeking damages and declaratory relief. The trial of both parties' claims concluded in November 2005. In March 2006, the Court entered a judgment in favor of Toysrus.com LLC, terminating the contract but declining to award damages to either party. We are pursuing an appeal of the lower court's rulings terminating the contract, declining to award us damages, and denying our motion to compel Toysrus.com to pay certain fees incurred during the wind-down period.

In December 2005, Registrar Systems LLC filed a complaint against us and Target Corporation for patent infringement in the United States District Court for the District of Colorado. The complaint alleges that our website technology, including the method by which Amazon.com enables customers to use Amazon.com account information on websites that Amazon.com operates for third parties, such as Target.com, infringes two patents obtained by Registrar Systems purporting to cover methods and apparatuses for a "World Wide Web Registration Information Processing System" (U.S. Patent Nos. 5,790,785 and 6,823,327) and seeks injunctive relief, monetary damages in an amount no less than a reasonable royalty, prejudgment interest, costs, and attorneys' fees. We dispute the allegations of wrongdoing in this complaint and intend to vigorously defend ourselves in this matter. In September 2006, the Court entered an order staying the lawsuit pending the outcome of the Patent and Trademark Office's re-examination of the patents in suit.

In August 2006, Cordance Corporation filed a complaint against us for patent infringement in the United States District Court for the District of Delaware. The complaint alleges that our website technology, including our 1-Click ordering system, infringes a patent obtained by Cordance purporting to cover an "Object-Based Online Transaction Infrastructure" (U.S. Patent No. 6,757,710) and seeks injunctive relief, monetary damages in an amount no less than a reasonable royalty, treble damages for alleged willful infringement, prejudgment interest, costs, and attorneys' fees. In response, we asserted a declaratory judgment counterclaim in the same action alleging that a service that Cordance has advertised its intent to launch infringes a patent owned by us entitled "Networked Personal Contact Manager" (U.S. Patent No. 6,269,369). We dispute Cordance's allegations of wrongdoing and intend to vigorously defend ourselves in this matter.

In April 2007, SBJ Holdings 1, LLC filed a complaint against us in the United States District Court for the Eastern District of Texas. The complaint alleges that our website technology infringes a patent obtained by SBJ Holdings 1 purporting to cover a "Method, Memory, Product, and Code for Displaying Pre-Customized Content Associated with Visitor Data" (U.S. Patent No. 6,330,592) and seeks injunctive relief, monetary damages, treble damages for alleged willful infringement, prejudgment and post-judgment interest, costs and attorneys' fees. We dispute the allegations of wrongdoing and intend to vigorously defend ourselves in the matter.

In August 2007, Polaris IP, LLC filed a complaint against us and others in the United States District Court for the Eastern District of Texas. The complaint alleges that our website technology infringes a patent obtained by Polaris purporting to cover an "Automatic Message Interpretation and Routing System" (U.S. Patent No. 6,411,947) and seeks injunctive relief, monetary damages, prejudgment and post-judgment interest, costs and attorneys' fees. In November 2007, we entered into a settlement of the litigation that included, among other things, a non-exclusive license to the patent in suit.

Depending on the amount and the timing, an unfavorable resolution of some or all of these matters could materially affect our business, results of operations, financial position, or cash flows.

See also "Note 12—Income Taxes."

Inventory Suppliers

During 2007, no vendor accounted for 10% or more of our inventory purchases. We do not have long-term contracts or arrangements with most of our vendors to guarantee the availability of merchandise, particular payment terms, or the extension of credit limits.

Note 7—STOCKHOLDERS' EQUITY

Preferred Stock

We have authorized 500 million shares of $0.01 par value Preferred Stock. No preferred stock was outstanding for any period presented.

Stock Repurchase Activity

In August 2006, our Board of Directors authorized a 24-month program to repurchase up to $500 million of our common stock, pursuant to which we repurchased $252 million and $248 million of our common stock in 2006 and 2007, respectively. In April 2007, our Board authorized a new 24-month program to repurchase up to $500 million of our common stock, which was replaced in February 2008 by a 24-month program to repurchase up to $1 billion of our common stock.

Stock Award Plans

Employees vest in restricted stock unit awards and stock options over the corresponding service term, generally between two and five years. Outstanding stock options generally have a term of 10 years from the date of grant. Stock options outstanding have a weighted average exercise life of 3.5 years, with a weighted average exercise price of $17.46.

Stock Award Activity

We granted stock awards, which consist primarily of restricted stock units, representing 7.6 million, 9.1 million, and 6.0 million shares of common stock during 2007, 2006, and 2005 with a per share weighted average fair value of $47.04, $36.48, and $36.50.

Common shares underlying outstanding stock awards were as follows:

	Year Ended December 31,	
	2007	2006
	(in millions)	
Restricted stock units	16.3	14.5
Stock options	1.9	7.4
Total outstanding stock awards	18.2	21.9

Common shares outstanding (which includes restricted stock), plus shares underlying outstanding stock options and restricted stock units totaled 435 million, 436 million, and 438 million at December 31, 2007, 2006 and 2005. These totals include all stock-based awards outstanding, without regard for estimated forfeitures, consisting of vested and unvested awards and in-the-money and out-of-the-money stock options. Common shares outstanding decreased in both 2007 and 2006 due to repurchases of common stock, offset by exercises of stock options, vesting of restricted stock units, and matching contributions under our 401(k) savings plan.

The following summarizes our restricted stock unit activity (in millions):

	Number of Units
Outstanding at January 1, 2005	6.4
Units granted	6.0
Units vested	(1.2)
Units cancelled	(1.3)
Outstanding at December 31, 2005	9.9
Units granted	9.1
Units vested	(1.7)
Units cancelled	(2.8)
Outstanding at December 31, 2006	14.5
Units granted	7.6
Units vested	(3.3)
Units cancelled	(2.5)
Outstanding at December 31, 2007	16.3

Scheduled vesting for outstanding restricted stock units at December 31, 2007 is as follows (in millions):

	Year Ended December 31,						
	2008	2009	2010	2011	2012	Thereafter	Total
Scheduled vesting—restricted stock units	5.6	5.8	2.9	1.4	0.4	0.2	16.3

As matching contributions under our 401(k) savings plan, we granted 0.09 million and 0.15 million shares of common stock for years ended 2007 and 2006. Shares granted as matching contributions under our 401(k) plan are included in outstanding common stock when issued.

As of December 31, 2007, there was $252 million of net unrecognized compensation cost related to unvested stock-based compensation arrangements. This compensation is recognized on an accelerated basis resulting in approximately half of the compensation expected to be expensed in the next twelve months, and has a weighted average recognition period of 1.2 years.

During 2007 and 2006, the fair value of restricted stock units vested was $224 million and $68 million.

Common Stock Available for Future Issuance

At December 31, 2007, common stock available for future issuance is as follows (in millions):

	December 31, 2007
Stock awards	129.3
Shares issuable upon conversion of 4.75% Convertible Subordinated Notes	11.5
Shares issuable upon conversion of 6.875% PEACS	2.8
Total common stock reserved for future issuance	143.6

Note 8—OTHER COMPREHENSIVE INCOME (LOSS)

The changes in the components of other comprehensive income (loss) were as follows:

	Year Ended December 31,		
	2007	2006	2005
	(in millions)		
Net income	$476	$190	$359
Net activity on available-for-sale securities:			
Unrealized gains (losses) arising during the year, net of tax	8	4	(14)
Reclassification adjustment for net realized gains/losses included in net income, net of tax	—	—	—
Net change in unrealized gains/losses on available-for-sale securities	8	4	(14)
Foreign currency translation adjustment, net of tax	(3)	(13)	(15)
Amortization of net unrealized losses on terminated Euro Currency Swap, net of tax	1	2	3
Other comprehensive income (loss)	6	(7)	(26)
Comprehensive income	$482	$183	$333

Accumulated balances within other comprehensive income (loss) were as follows:

	December 31,	
	2007	2006
	(in millions)	
Net unrealized gains (losses) on foreign currency translation, net of tax	$(1)	$ 2
Net unrealized gains (losses) on available-for-sale securities, net of tax	7	(1)
Net unrealized losses on terminated Euro Currency Swap, net of tax	(1)	(2)
Total accumulated other comprehensive income (loss)	$ 5	$(1)

Note 9—OTHER OPERATING EXPENSE, NET

Other operating expense, net, was $9 million and $10 million in 2007 and 2006, primarily attributable to amortization of other intangibles. Other operating expense, net, was $47 million in 2005, primarily attributable to our settlement of a patent lawsuit for $40 million, as well as amortization of other intangibles of $5 million.

Note 10—OTHER INCOME (EXPENSE), NET

Other income (expense), net, was $(1) million, $(4) million, and $2 million, in 2007, 2006 and 2005, and consisted primarily of gains and losses on sales of marketable securities, foreign-currency transaction gains and losses, and other miscellaneous losses.

Foreign-currency transaction gains and losses primarily relate to the interest payable on our 6.875% PEACS, as well as foreign-currency gains and losses on cross-currency investments. Since interest payments on our 6.875% PEACS are settled in Euros, the balance of interest payable is subject to gains or losses resulting from changes in exchange rates between the U.S. Dollar and Euro between reporting dates and payment.

Note 11—REMEASUREMENTS AND OTHER

Remeasurements and other consisted of the following:

	Year Ended December 31,		
	2007	2006	2005
	(in millions)		
Foreign-currency gain (loss) on remeasurement of 6.875% PEACS	$(33)	$(37)	$ 90
Loss on redemption of long-term debt	—	(6)	(6)
Foreign-currency gain (loss) on intercompany balances	32	50	(47)
Other	(6)	4	5
Total remeasurements and other	$ (7)	$ 11	$ 42

Note 12—INCOME TAXES

In 2007, 2006 and 2005 we recorded net tax provisions of $184 million, $187 million, and $95 million. A majority of this provision is non-cash. We have current tax benefits and net operating losses relating to excess stock-based compensation that are being utilized to reduce our taxable income. As such, cash taxes paid were $24 million, $15 million, and $12 million for 2007, 2006, and 2005.

The components of the provision for income taxes, net were as follows:

	Year Ended December 31,		
	2007	2006	2005
		(in millions)	
Current taxes:			
U.S. and state	$275	$162	$16
International	8	3	9
Current taxes	283	165	25
Deferred taxes	(99)	22	70
Provision for income taxes, net	$184	$187	$95

U.S. and international components of income before income taxes were as follows:

	Year Ended December 31,		
	2007	2006	2005
		(in millions)	
U.S.	$360	$396	$ 601
International	300	(19)	(173)
Income before income taxes	$660	$377	$ 428

The items accounting for differences between income taxes computed at the federal statutory rate and the provision recorded for income taxes are as follows:

	Year Ended December 31,		
	2007	2006	2005
Federal statutory rate	35.0%	35.0%	35.0%
Effect of:			
Valuation allowance	(1.2)	(2.6)	(31.1)
Impact of international operations restructuring	(12.3)	16.0	15.1
Other, net	6.4	1.2	3.3
Total	27.9%	49.6%	22.3%

The effective tax rate in 2007 was lower than the 35% U.S. federal statutory rate primarily due to earnings of our subsidiaries outside of the U.S. in jurisdictions where our effective tax rate is lower than in the U.S. The effective tax rate in 2006 was higher than the 35% U.S. federal statutory rate resulting from establishment of our European headquarters in Luxembourg. Associated with the establishment of our European headquarters, we transferred certain of our operating assets in 2005 and 2006 from the U.S. to international locations. These transfers resulted in taxable income and exposure to additional taxable income assertions by taxing jurisdictions.

Included in the 2005 provision and reducing the impact of the international restructure was a tax benefit of $90 million, resulting from certain of our deferred tax assets becoming more likely than not realizable. This tax benefit represented $0.22 and $0.21 of basic and diluted earnings per share.

The significant components of deferred income tax expense attributable to income from operations for 2007, 2006, and 2005 were as follows:

	Year Ended December 31,		
	2007	2006	2005
		(in millions)	
Deferred tax expense (benefit) exclusive of the effect of the items listed below	$(91)	$ 32	$188
Decrease in valuation allowance	(8)	(10)	(90)
Tax benefit of net operating and capital loss carryforwards	—	—	(28)
Total deferred tax expense (benefit)	$(99)	$ 22	$ 70

Deferred income tax assets and liabilities were as follows:

	December 31,	
	2007	2006
	(in millions)	
Deferred tax assets:		
Net operating losses—stock-based compensation (1)	$ 120	$ 120
Net operating losses—other	28	23
Assets held for investment	167	174
Revenue items	58	20
Expense items, including stock-based compensation	210	149
Net tax credits (2)	2	7
Deferred tax assets under FIN 48	22	—
Total gross deferred tax assets	607	493
Less valuation allowance (3)	(195)	(216)
Deferred tax assets, net of valuation allowance	412	277
Deferred tax liabilities:		
Expense items	(24)	(13)
Deferred tax liabilities under FIN 48	(3)	—
Deferred tax assets, net of valuation allowance and deferred tax liabilities	$ 385	$ 264

(1) Presented net of fully reserved NOL deferred tax asset of $219 million and $381 million at December 31, 2007 and 2006. The total gross deferred tax assets relating to our excess stock-based compensation NOLs at December 31, 2007 and 2006 were $339 million and $501 million (relating to approximately $1.1 billion and $1.6 billion of NOLs).

(2) Presented net of fully reserved deferred tax assets associated with tax credits of $95 million and $67 million at December 31, 2007 and 2006. Total tax credits available to be claimed in future years are approximately $129 million and $101 million as of December 31, 2007 and 2006.

(3) Relates primarily to deferred tax assets that would only be realizable upon the generation of future capital gains and net income in certain taxing jurisdictions.

We have not fully utilized NOLs which were generated in the years 1996 through 2003, so that the statute of limitations for these years remains open for purposes of adjusting the amounts of the losses carried forward from those years. The majority of our NOLs begin to expire in 2019 and thereafter.

Tax Contingencies

We are subject to income taxes in the U.S. and numerous foreign jurisdictions. Significant judgment is required in evaluating our tax positions and determining our provision for income taxes. During the ordinary course of business, there are many transactions and calculations for which the ultimate tax determination is uncertain. We establish reserves for tax-related uncertainties based on estimates of whether, and the extent to which, additional taxes will be due. These reserves are established when we believe that certain positions might be challenged despite our belief that our tax return positions are fully supportable. We adjust these reserves in light of changing facts and circumstances, such as the outcome of tax audit. The provision for income taxes includes the impact of reserve provisions and changes to reserves that are considered appropriate. Accruals for tax contingencies are provided for in accordance with the requirements of FIN 48.

The reconciliation of our tax contingencies is as follows (in millions):

Gross tax contingencies—January 1, 2007	$110
Gross increases to tax positions in prior periods	6
Gross decreases to tax positions in prior periods	(3)
Gross increases to current period tax positions	4
Audit settlements paid during 2007	(5)
Gross tax contingencies—December 31, 2007 (1)	$112

(1) As of December 31, 2007, we had $112 million of tax contingencies of which $118 million, if fully recognized, would affect our effective tax rate and increase additional paid-in capital by $6 million to reflect the tax benefits of excess stock-based compensation deductions.

As of December 31, 2007, changes to our tax contingencies that are reasonably possible in the next 12 months are not material. Our policy is to include interest and penalties related to our tax contingencies in income tax expense. As of December 31, 2007, we had accrued interest and penalties related to tax contingencies of $9 million, net of federal income tax benefits, on our balance sheet. Interest and penalties recognized for the year ended December 31, 2007 was $1 million, net of federal income tax benefits.

We are under examination, or may be subject to examination, by the Internal Revenue Service ("IRS") for calendar years 2004 through 2006. Additionally, any net operating losses that were generated in prior years and utilized in these years may also be subject to examination by the IRS. We are under examination, or may be subject to examination, in the following major jurisdictions for the years specified: Kentucky for 2003 through 2006, France for 2005 through 2006, Germany for 2004 through 2006, Luxembourg for 2003 through 2006, and the United Kingdom for 1999 through 2006. In addition, in February 2007, Japanese tax authorities assessed income tax, including penalties and interest, of approximately $93 million against one of our U.S. subsidiaries for the years 2003 through 2005. We believe that these claims are without merit and are disputing the assessment. Further proceedings on the assessment will be stayed during negotiations between U.S. and Japanese authorities over the double taxation issues the assessment raises, and we have provided bank guarantees to suspend enforcement of the assessment. We also may be subject to income tax examination by Japanese tax authorities for 2006.

Note 13—SEGMENT INFORMATION

We have organized our operations into two principal segments: North America and International. We present our segment information along the same lines that our chief executive reviews our operating results in assessing performance and allocating resources.

We allocate to segment results the operating expenses "Fulfillment," "Marketing," "Technology and content," and "General and administrative," but exclude from our allocations the portions of these expense lines attributable to stock-based compensation. Additionally, we do not allocate the line item "Other operating expense, net" to our segment operating results. A significant majority of our costs for "Technology and content" are incurred in the United States and most of these costs are allocated to our North America segment. There are no internal revenue transactions between our reporting segments.

North America

The North America segment consists of amounts earned from retail sales of consumer products (including from sellers) and subscriptions through North America-focused websites such as *www.amazon.com, www.amazon.ca, www.shopbop.com,* and *www.endless.com*; from our Amazon Prime membership program; and from non-retail activities such as North America-focused Amazon Enterprise Solutions, Amazon Web Services and marketing, and promotional services. This segment includes export sales from *www.amazon.com* and *www.amazon.ca.*

International

The International segment consists of amounts earned from retail sales of consumer products (including from sellers) and subscriptions through internationally focused websites such as *www.amazon.co.uk, www.amazon.de, www.amazon.co.jp, www.amazon.fr,* and our Joyo Amazon websites at *www.joyo.cn* and *www.amazon.cn*; from our Amazon Prime membership program; and from non-retail activities such as internationally focused Amazon Enterprise Solutions, Amazon Web Services and marketing and promotional services. This segment includes export sales from these internationally based sites (including export sales from these sites to customers in the U.S. and Canada), but excludes export sales from *www.amazon.com* and *www.amazon.ca.*

AMAZON.COM, INC.

NOTES TO CONSOLIDATED FINANCIAL STATEMENTS—(Continued)

Information on reportable segments and reconciliation to consolidated net income was as follows:

	Year Ended December 31,		
	2007	2006	2005
		(in millions)	
North America			
Net sales	$ 8,095	$ 5,869	$4,711
Cost of sales	6,064	4,344	3,444
Gross profit	2,031	1,525	1,267
Direct segment operating expenses	1,631	1,295	971
Segment operating income	$ 400	$ 230	$ 296
International			
Net sales	$ 6,740	$ 4,842	$3,779
Cost of sales	5,418	3,911	3,007
Gross profit	1,322	931	772
Direct segment operating expenses	873	661	502
Segment operating income	$ 449	$ 270	$ 270
Consolidated			
Net sales	$14,835	$10,711	$8,490
Cost of sales	11,482	8,255	6,451
Gross profit	3,353	2,456	2,039
Direct segment operating expenses	2,504	1,956	1,473
Segment operating income	849	500	566
Stock-based compensation	(185)	(101)	(87)
Other operating expense, net	(9)	(10)	(47)
Income from operations	655	389	432
Total non-operating income (expense), net	5	(12)	(4)
Provision for income taxes	(184)	(187)	(95)
Cumulative effect of change in accounting principle	—	—	26
Net income	$ 476	$ 190	$ 359

Net sales shipped to customers outside of the U.S. represented approximately half of net sales for 2007, 2006, and 2005. Net sales from *www.amazon.co.uk*, *www.amazon.de*, and *www.amazon.co.jp* each represented 10% or more of consolidated net sales in 2007, 2006 and 2005. Net fixed assets held in locations outside the U.S. were $139 million, $108 million, and $68 million at December 31, 2007, 2006, and 2005.

Total assets, by segment, reconciled to consolidated amounts were (in millions):

	December 31,	
	2007	2006
North America	$4,227	$2,801
International	2,258	1,562
Consolidated	$6,485	$4,363

Depreciation expense, by segment, was as follows (in millions):

	Year Ended December 31,		
	2007	2006	2005
North America	$212	$166	$ 94
International	46	34	19
Consolidated	$258	$200	$113

Note 14—FAIR VALUES OF FINANCIAL INSTRUMENTS

The carrying amount and estimated fair values of our financial instruments were as follows (in millions):

	December 31,			
	2007		2006	
	Carrying Amount	Fair Value	Carrying Amount	Fair Value
Cash and cash equivalents	$2,539	$2,539	$1,022	$1,022
Marketable securities (1)	573	573	997	997
Other equity investments (2)	17	43	19	51
Long-term debt (3)	1,282	1,466	1,247	1,234

(1) The fair value of marketable securities is determined from publicly quoted prices. See "Note 2—Cash, Cash Equivalents, and Marketable Securities."

(2) The fair value of other equity investments is determined from publicly quoted prices, plus the carrying amount of privately-held investments for which market values are not readily determinable. We evaluate "Other equity investments" for impairment in accordance with our stated policy. See "Note 1—Description of Business and Accounting Policies."

(3) The fair value of our long-term debt is determined based on quoted prices. See "Note 4—Long-Term Debt."

Note 15—QUARTERLY RESULTS (UNAUDITED)

The following tables contain selected unaudited statement of operations information for each quarter of 2007 and 2006. The following information reflects all normal recurring adjustments necessary for a fair presentation of the information for the periods presented. The operating results for any quarter are not necessarily indicative of results for any future period. Our business is affected by seasonality, which historically has resulted in higher sales volume during our fourth quarter, which ends December 31.

Unaudited quarterly results were as follows (in millions, except per share data):

	Year Ended December 31, 2007 (1)			
	Fourth Quarter	Third Quarter	Second Quarter	First Quarter
Net sales	$5,673	$3,262	$2,886	$3,015
Gross profit	1,170	762	701	719
Income before income taxes	281	124	111	144
Provision for income taxes	74	44	33	33
Net income	207	80	78	111
Basic earnings per share	$ 0.50	$ 0.19	$ 0.19	$ 0.27
Diluted earnings per share	$ 0.48	$ 0.19	$ 0.19	$ 0.26
Shares used in computation of earnings per share:				
Basic	416	414	412	412
Diluted	427	425	423	420

	Year Ended December 31, 2006 (1)			
	Fourth Quarter	Third Quarter	Second Quarter	First Quarter
Net sales	$3,986	$2,307	$2,139	$2,279
Gross profit	850	549	509	547
Income before income taxes	189	38	54	96
Provision for income taxes	91	19	32	45
Net income	98	19	22	51
Basic earnings per share	$ 0.24	$ 0.05	$ 0.05	$ 0.12
Diluted earnings per share	$ 0.23	$ 0.05	$ 0.05	$ 0.12
Shares used in computation of earnings per share:				
Basic	413	417	418	417
Diluted	422	424	426	426

(1) The sum of quarterly amounts, including per share amounts, may not equal amounts reported for year-to-date periods. This is due to the effects of rounding and changes in the number of weighted-average shares outstanding for each period.

Appendix B

Present Value Tables

TABLE A | **Present Value of $1**

	Present Value										
Periods	1%	2%	3%	4%	5%	6%	7%	8%	9%	10%	12%
1	0.990	0.980	0.971	0.962	0.952	0.943	0.935	0.926	0.917	0.909	0.893
2	0.980	0.961	0.943	0.925	0.907	0.890	0.873	0.857	0.842	0.826	0.797
3	0.971	0.942	0.915	0.889	0.864	0.840	0.816	0.794	0.772	0.751	0.712
4	0.961	0.924	0.888	0.855	0.823	0.792	0.763	0.735	0.708	0.683	0.636
5	0.951	0.906	0.883	0.822	0.784	0.747	0.713	0.681	0.650	0.621	0.567
6	0.942	0.888	0.837	0.790	0.746	0.705	0.666	0.630	0.596	0.564	0.507
7	0.933	0.871	0.813	0.760	0.711	0.665	0.623	0.583	0.547	0.513	0.452
8	0.923	0.853	0.789	0.731	0.677	0.627	0.582	0.540	0.502	0.467	0.404
9	0.914	0.837	0.766	0.703	0.645	0.592	0.544	0.500	0.460	0.424	0.361
10	0.905	0.820	0.744	0.676	0.614	0.558	0.508	0.463	0.422	0.386	0.322
11	0.896	0.804	0.722	0.650	0.585	0.527	0.475	0.429	0.388	0.350	0.287
12	0.887	0.788	0.701	0.625	0.557	0.497	0.444	0.397	0.356	0.319	0.257
13	0.879	0.773	0.681	0.601	0.530	0.469	0.415	0.368	0.326	0.290	0.229
14	0.870	0.758	0.661	0.577	0.505	0.442	0.388	0.340	0.299	0.263	0.205
15	0.861	0.743	0.642	0.555	0.481	0.417	0.362	0.315	0.275	0.239	0.183
16	0.853	0.728	0.623	0.534	0.458	0.394	0.339	0.292	0.252	0.218	0.163
17	0.844	0.714	0.605	0.513	0.436	0.371	0.317	0.270	0.231	0.198	0.146
18	0.836	0.700	0.587	0.494	0.416	0.350	0.296	0.250	0.212	0.180	0.130
19	0.828	0.686	0.570	0.475	0.396	0.331	0.277	0.232	0.194	0.164	0.116
20	0.820	0.673	0.554	0.456	0.377	0.312	0.258	0.215	0.178	0.149	0.104
21	0.811	0.660	0.538	0.439	0.359	0.294	0.242	0.199	0.164	0.135	0.093
22	0.803	0.647	0.522	0.422	0.342	0.278	0.226	0.184	0.150	0.123	0.083
23	0.795	0.634	0.507	0.406	0.326	0.262	0.211	0.170	0.138	0.112	0.074
24	0.788	0.622	0.492	0.390	0.310	0.247	0.197	0.158	0.126	0.102	0.066
25	0.780	0.610	0.478	0.375	0.295	0.233	0.184	0.146	0.116	0.092	0.059
26	0.772	0.598	0.464	0.361	0.281	0.220	0.172	0.135	0.106	0.084	0.053
27	0.764	0.586	0.450	0.347	0.268	0.207	0.161	0.125	0.098	0.076	0.047
28	0.757	0.574	0.437	0.333	0.255	0.196	0.150	0.116	0.090	0.069	0.042
29	0.749	0.563	0.424	0.321	0.243	0.185	0.141	0.107	0.082	0.063	0.037
30	0.742	0.552	0.412	0.308	0.231	0.174	0.131	0.099	0.075	0.057	0.033
40	0.672	0.453	0.307	0.208	0.142	0.097	0.067	0.046	0.032	0.022	0.011
50	0.608	0.372	0.228	0.141	0.087	0.054	0.034	0.021	0.013	0.009	0.003

TABLE A | Present Value of $1 (con't)

Present Value											
14%	15%	16%	18%	20%	25%	30%	35%	40%	45%	50%	Periods
0.877	0.870	0.862	0.847	0.833	0.800	0.769	0.741	0.714	0.690	0.667	1
0.769	0.756	0.743	0.718	0.694	0.640	0.592	0.549	0.510	0.476	0.444	2
0.675	0.658	0.641	0.609	0.579	0.512	0.455	0.406	0.364	0.328	0.296	3
0.592	0.572	0.552	0.516	0.482	0.410	0.350	0.301	0.260	0.226	0.198	4
0.519	0.497	0.476	0.437	0.402	0.328	0.269	0.223	0.186	0.156	0.132	5
0.456	0.432	0.410	0.370	0.335	0.262	0.207	0.165	0.133	0.108	0.088	6
0.400	0.376	0.354	0.314	0.279	0.210	0.159	0.122	0.095	0.074	0.059	7
0.351	0.327	0.305	0.266	0.233	0.168	0.123	0.091	0.068	0.051	0.039	8
0.308	0.284	0.263	0.225	0.194	0.134	0.094	0.067	0.048	0.035	0.026	9
0.270	0.247	0.227	0.191	0.162	0.107	0.073	0.050	0.035	0.024	0.017	10
0.237	0.215	0.195	0.162	0.135	0.086	0.056	0.037	0.025	0.017	0.012	11
0.208	0.187	0.168	0.137	0.112	0.069	0.043	0.027	0.018	0.012	0.008	12
0.182	0.163	0.145	0.116	0.093	0.055	0.033	0.020	0.013	0.008	0.005	13
0.160	0.141	0.125	0.099	0.078	0.044	0.025	0.015	0.009	0.006	0.003	14
0.140	0.123	0.108	0.084	0.065	0.035	0.020	0.011	0.006	0.004	0.002	15
0.123	0.107	0.093	0.071	0.054	0.028	0.015	0.008	0.005	0.003	0.002	16
0.108	0.093	0.080	0.060	0.045	0.023	0.012	0.006	0.003	0.002	0.001	17
0.095	0.081	0.069	0.051	0.038	0.018	0.009	0.005	0.002	0.001	0.001	18
0.083	0.070	0.060	0.043	0.031	0.014	0.007	0.003	0.002	0.001		19
0.073	0.061	0.051	0.037	0.026	0.012	0.005	0.002	0.001	0.001		20
0.064	0.053	0.044	0.031	0.022	0.009	0.004	0.002	0.001			21
0.056	0.046	0.038	0.026	0.018	0.007	0.003	0.001	0.001			22
0.049	0.040	0.033	0.022	0.015	0.006	0.002	0.001				23
0.043	0.035	0.028	0.019	0.013	0.005	0.002	0.001				24
0.038	0.030	0.024	0.016	0.010	0.004	0.001	0.001				25
0.033	0.026	0.021	0.014	0.009	0.003	0.001					26
0.029	0.023	0.018	0.011	0.007	0.002	0.001					27
0.026	0.020	0.016	0.010	0.006	0.002	0.001					28
0.022	0.017	0.014	0.008	0.005	0.002						29
0.020	0.015	0.012	0.007	0.004	0.001						30
0.005	0.004	0.003	0.001	0.001							40
0.001	0.001	0.001									50

TABLE B Present Value of Annuity of $1

	Present Value										
Periods	1%	2%	3%	4%	5%	6%	7%	8%	9%	10%	12%
1	0.990	0.980	0.971	0.962	0.952	0.943	0.935	0.926	0.917	0.909	0.893
2	1.970	1.942	1.913	1.886	1.859	1.833	1.808	1.783	1.759	1.736	1.690
3	2.941	2.884	2.829	2.775	2.723	2.673	2.624	2.577	2.531	2.487	2.402
4	3.902	3.808	3.717	3.630	3.546	3.465	3.387	3.312	3.240	3.170	3.037
5	4.853	4.713	4.580	4.452	4.329	4.212	4.100	3.993	3.890	3.791	3.605
6	5.795	5.601	5.417	5.242	5.076	4.917	4.767	4.623	4.486	4.355	4.111
7	6.728	6.472	6.230	6.002	5.786	5.582	5.389	5.206	5.033	4.868	4.564
8	7.652	7.325	7.020	6.733	6.463	6.210	5.971	5.747	5.535	5.335	4.968
9	8.566	8.162	7.786	7.435	7.108	6.802	6.515	6.247	5.995	5.759	5.328
10	9.471	8.983	8.530	8.111	7.722	7.360	7.024	6.710	6.418	6.145	5.650
11	10.368	9.787	9.253	8.760	8.306	7.887	7.499	7.139	6.805	6.495	5.938
12	11.255	10.575	9.954	9.385	8.863	8.384	7.943	7.536	7.161	6.814	6.194
13	12.134	11.348	10.635	9.986	9.394	8.853	8.358	7.904	7.487	7.103	6.424
14	13.004	12.106	11.296	10.563	9.899	9.295	8.745	8.244	7.786	7.367	6.628
15	13.865	12.849	11.938	11.118	10.380	9.712	9.108	8.559	8.061	7.606	6.811
16	14.718	13.578	12.561	11.652	10.838	10.106	9.447	8.851	8.313	7.824	6.974
17	15.562	14.292	13.166	12.166	11.274	10.477	9.763	9.122	8.544	8.022	7.120
18	16.398	14.992	13.754	12.659	11.690	10.828	10.059	9.372	8.756	8.201	7.250
19	17.226	15.678	14.324	13.134	12.085	11.158	10.336	9.604	8.950	8.365	7.366
20	18.046	16.351	14.878	13.590	12.462	11.470	10.594	9.818	9.129	8.514	7.469
21	18.857	17.011	15.415	14.029	12.821	11.764	10.836	10.017	9.292	8.649	7.562
22	19.660	17.658	15.937	14.451	13.163	12.042	11.061	10.201	9.442	8.772	7.645
23	20.456	18.292	16.444	14.857	13.489	12.303	11.272	10.371	9.580	8.883	7.718
24	21.243	18.914	16.936	15.247	13.799	12.550	11.469	10.529	9.707	8.985	7.784
25	22.023	19.523	17.413	15.622	14.094	12.783	11.654	10.675	9.823	9.077	7.843
26	22.795	20.121	17.877	15.983	14.375	13.003	11.826	10.810	9.929	9.161	7.896
27	23.560	20.707	18.327	16.330	14.643	13.211	11.987	10.935	10.027	9.237	7.943
28	24.316	21.281	18.764	16.663	14.898	13.406	12.137	11.051	10.116	9.307	7.984
29	25.066	21.844	19.189	16.984	15.141	13.591	12.278	11.158	10.198	9.370	8.022
30	25.808	22.396	19.600	17.292	15.373	13.765	12.409	11.258	10.274	9.427	8.055
40	32.835	27.355	23.115	19.793	17.159	15.046	13.332	11.925	10.757	9.779	8.244
50	39.196	31.424	25.730	21.482	18.256	15.762	13.801	12.234	10.962	9.915	8.305

TABLE B | Present Value of Annuity of $1 (con't)

Present Value											
14%	15%	16%	18%	20%	25%	30%	35%	40%	45%	50%	Periods
0.877	0.870	0.862	0.847	0.833	0.800	0.769	0.741	0.714	0.690	0.667	1
1.647	1.626	1.605	1.566	1.528	1.440	1.361	1.289	1.224	1.165	1.111	2
2.322	2.283	2.246	2.174	2.106	1.952	1.816	1.696	1.589	1.493	1.407	3
2.914	2.855	2.798	2.690	2.589	2.362	2.166	1.997	1.849	1.720	1.605	4
3.433	3.352	3.274	3.127	2.991	2.689	2.436	2.220	2.035	1.876	1.737	5
3.889	3.784	3.685	3.498	3.326	2.951	2.643	2.385	2.168	1.983	1.824	6
4.288	4.160	4.039	3.812	3.605	3.161	2.802	2.508	2.263	2.057	1.883	7
4.639	4.487	4.344	4.078	3.837	3.329	2.925	2.598	2.331	2.109	1.922	8
4.946	4.772	4.607	4.303	4.031	3.463	3.019	2.665	2.379	2.144	1.948	9
5.216	5.019	4.833	4.494	4.192	3.571	3.092	2.715	2.414	2.168	1.965	10
5.553	5.234	5.029	4.656	4.327	3.656	3.147	2.752	2.438	2.185	1.977	11
5.660	5.421	5.197	4.793	4.439	3.725	3.190	2.779	2.456	2.197	1.985	12
5.842	5.583	5.342	4.910	4.533	3.780	3.223	2.799	2.469	2.204	1.990	13
6.002	5.724	5.468	5.008	4.611	3.824	3.249	2.814	2.478	2.210	1.993	14
6.142	5.847	5.575	5.092	4.675	3.859	3.268	2.825	2.484	2.214	1.995	15
6.265	5.954	5.669	5.162	4.730	3.887	3.283	2.834	2.489	2.216	1.997	16
6.373	6.047	5.749	5.222	4.775	3.910	3.295	2.840	2.492	2.218	1.998	17
6.467	6.128	5.818	5.273	4.812	3.928	3.304	2.844	2.494	2.219	1.999	18
6.550	6.198	5.877	5.316	4.844	3.942	3.311	2.848	2.496	2.220	1.999	19
6.623	6.259	5.929	5.353	4.870	3.954	3.316	2.850	2.497	2.221	1.999	20
6.687	6.312	5.973	5.384	4.891	3.963	3.320	2.852	2.498	2.221	2.000	21
6.743	6.359	6.011	5.410	4.909	3.970	3.323	2.853	2.498	2.222	2.000	22
6.792	6.399	6.044	5.432	4.925	3.976	3.325	2.854	2.499	2.222	2.000	23
6.835	6.434	6.073	5.451	4.937	3.981	3.327	2.855	2.499	2.222	2.000	24
6.873	6.464	6.097	5.467	4.948	3.985	3.329	2.856	2.499	2.222	2.000	25
6.906	6.491	6.118	5.480	4.956	3.988	3.330	2.856	2.500	2.222	2.000	26
6.935	6.514	6.136	5.492	4.964	3.990	3.331	2.856	2.500	2.222	2.000	27
6.961	6.534	6.152	5.502	4.970	3.992	3.331	2.857	2.500	2.222	2.000	28
6.983	6.551	6.166	5.510	4.975	3.994	3.332	2.857	2.500	2.222	2.000	29
7.003	6.566	6.177	5.517	4.979	3.995	3.332	2.857	2.500	2.222	2.000	30
7.105	6.642	6.234	5.548	4.997	3.999	3.333	2.857	2.500	2.222	2.000	40
7.133	6.661	6.246	5.554	4.999	4.000	3.333	2.857	2.500	2.222	2.000	50

TABLE C Future Value of $1

Periods	Future Value 1%	2%	3%	4%	5%	6%	7%	8%	9%	10%	12%	14%	15%
1	1.010	1.020	1.030	1.040	1.050	1.060	1.070	1.080	1.090	1.100	1.120	1.140	1.150
2	1.020	1.040	1.061	1.082	1.103	1.124	1.145	1.166	1.188	1.210	1.254	1.300	1.323
3	1.030	1.061	1.093	1.125	1.158	1.191	1.225	1.260	1.295	1.331	1.405	1.482	1.521
4	1.041	1.082	1.126	1.170	1.216	1.262	1.311	1.360	1.412	1.464	1.574	1.689	1.749
5	1.051	1.104	1.159	1.217	1.276	1.338	1.403	1.469	1.539	1.611	1.762	1.925	2.011
6	1.062	1.126	1.194	1.265	1.340	1.419	1.501	1.587	1.677	1.772	1.974	2.195	2.313
7	1.072	1.149	1.230	1.316	1.407	1.504	1.606	1.714	1.828	1.949	2.211	2.502	2.660
8	1.083	1.172	1.267	1.369	1.477	1.594	1.718	1.851	1.993	2.144	2.476	2.853	3.059
9	1.094	1.195	1.305	1.423	1.551	1.689	1.838	1.999	2.172	2.358	2.773	3.252	3.518
10	1.105	1.219	1.344	1.480	1.629	1.791	1.967	2.159	2.367	2.594	3.106	3.707	4.046
11	1.116	1.243	1.384	1.539	1.710	1.898	2.105	2.332	2.580	2.853	3.479	4.226	4.652
12	1.127	1.268	1.426	1.601	1.796	2.012	2.252	2.518	2.813	3.138	3.896	4.818	5.350
13	1.138	1.294	1.469	1.665	1.886	2.133	2.410	2.720	3.066	3.452	4.363	5.492	6.153
14	1.149	1.319	1.513	1.732	1.980	2.261	2.579	2.937	3.342	3.798	4.887	6.261	7.076
15	1.161	1.346	1.558	1.801	2.079	2.397	2.759	3.172	3.642	4.177	5.474	7.138	8.137
16	1.173	1.373	1.605	1.873	2.183	2.540	2.952	3.426	3.970	4.595	6.130	8.137	9.358
17	1.184	1.400	1.653	1.948	2.292	2.693	3.159	3.700	4.328	5.054	6.866	9.276	10.76
18	1.196	1.428	1.702	2.026	2.407	2.854	3.380	3.996	4.717	5.560	7.690	10.58	12.38
19	1.208	1.457	1.754	2.107	2.527	3.026	3.617	4.316	5.142	6.116	8.613	12.06	14.23
20	1.220	1.486	1.806	2.191	2.653	3.207	3.870	4.661	5.604	6.728	9.646	13.74	16.37
21	1.232	1.516	1.860	2.279	2.786	3.400	4.141	5.034	6.109	7.400	10.80	15.67	18.82
22	1.245	1.546	1.916	2.370	2.925	3.604	4.430	5.437	6.659	8.140	12.10	17.86	21.64
23	1.257	1.577	1.974	2.465	3.072	3.820	4.741	5.871	7.258	8.954	13.55	20.36	24.89
24	1.270	1.608	2.033	2.563	3.225	4.049	5.072	6.341	7.911	9.850	15.18	23.21	28.63
25	1.282	1.641	2.094	2.666	3.386	4.292	5.427	6.848	8.623	10.83	17.00	26.46	32.92
26	1.295	1.673	2.157	2.772	3.556	4.549	5.807	7.396	9.399	11.92	19.04	30.17	37.86
27	1.308	1.707	2.221	2.883	3.733	4.822	6.214	7.988	10.25	13.11	21.32	34.39	43.54
28	1.321	1.741	2.288	2.999	3.920	5.112	6.649	8.627	11.17	14.42	23.88	39.20	50.07
29	1.335	1.776	2.357	3.119	4.116	5.418	7.114	9.317	12.17	15.86	26.75	44.69	57.58
30	1.348	1.811	2.427	3.243	4.322	5.743	7.612	10.06	13.27	17.45	29.96	50.95	66.21
40	1.489	2.208	3.262	4.801	7.040	10.29	14.97	21.72	31.41	45.26	93.05	188.9	267.9
50	1.645	2.692	4.384	7.107	11.47	18.42	29.46	46.90	74.36	117.4	289.0	700.2	1,084

TABLE D Future Value of Annuity of $1

Periods	1%	2%	3%	4%	5%	6%	7%	8%	9%	10%	12%	14%	15%
							Future Value						
1	1.000	1.000	1.000	1.000	1.000	1.000	1.000	1.000	1.000	1.000	1.000	1.000	1.000
2	2.010	2.020	2.030	2.040	2.050	2.060	2.070	2.080	2.090	2.100	2.120	2.140	2.150
3	3.030	3.060	3.091	3.122	3.153	3.184	3.215	3.246	3.278	3.310	3.374	3.440	3.473
4	4.060	4.122	4.184	4.246	4.310	4.375	4.440	4.506	4.573	4.641	4.779	4.921	4.993
5	5.101	5.204	5.309	5.416	5.526	5.637	5.751	5.867	5.985	6.105	6.353	6.610	6.742
6	6.152	6.308	6.468	6.633	6.802	6.975	7.153	7.336	7.523	7.716	8.115	8.536	8.754
7	7.214	7.434	7.662	7.898	8.142	8.394	8.654	8.923	9.200	9.487	10.09	10.73	11.07
8	8.286	8.583	8.892	9.214	9.549	9.897	10.26	10.64	11.03	11.44	12.30	13.23	13.73
9	9.369	9.755	10.16	10.58	11.03	11.49	11.98	12.49	13.02	13.58	14.78	16.09	16.79
10	10.46	10.95	11.46	12.01	12.58	13.18	13.82	14.49	15.19	15.94	17.55	19.34	20.30
11	11.57	12.17	12.81	13.49	14.21	14.97	15.78	16.65	17.56	18.53	20.65	23.04	24.35
12	12.68	13.41	14.19	15.03	15.92	16.87	17.89	18.98	20.14	21.38	24.13	27.27	29.00
13	13.81	14.68	15.62	16.63	17.71	18.88	20.14	21.50	22.95	24.52	28.03	32.09	34.35
14	14.95	15.97	17.09	18.29	19.60	21.02	22.55	24.21	26.02	27.98	32.39	37.58	40.50
15	16.10	17.29	18.60	20.02	21.58	23.28	25.13	27.15	29.36	31.77	37.28	43.84	47.58
16	17.26	18.64	20.16	21.82	23.66	25.67	27.89	30.32	33.00	35.95	42.75	50.98	55.72
17	18.43	20.01	21.76	23.70	25.84	28.21	30.84	33.75	36.97	40.54	48.88	59.12	65.08
18	19.61	21.41	23.41	25.65	28.13	30.91	34.00	37.45	41.30	45.60	55.75	68.39	75.84
19	20.81	22.84	25.12	27.67	30.54	33.76	37.38	41.45	46.02	51.16	63.44	78.97	88.21
20	22.02	24.30	26.87	29.78	33.07	36.79	41.00	45.76	51.16	57.28	72.05	91.02	102.4
21	23.24	25.78	28.68	31.97	35.72	39.99	44.87	50.42	56.76	64.00	81.70	104.8	118.8
22	24.47	27.30	30.54	34.25	38.51	43.39	49.01	55.46	62.87	71.40	92.50	120.4	137.6
23	25.72	28.85	32.45	36.62	41.43	47.00	53.44	60.89	69.53	79.54	104.6	138.3	159.3
24	26.97	30.42	34.43	39.08	44.50	50.82	58.18	66.76	76.79	88.50	118.2	158.7	184.2
25	28.24	32.03	36.46	41.65	47.73	54.86	63.25	73.11	84.70	98.35	133.3	181.9	212.8
26	29.53	33.67	38.55	44.31	51.11	59.16	68.68	79.95	93.32	109.2	150.3	208.3	245.7
27	30.82	35.34	40.71	47.08	54.67	63.71	74.48	87.35	102.7	121.1	169.4	238.5	283.6
28	32.13	37.05	42.93	49.97	58.40	68.53	80.70	95.34	113.0	134.2	190.7	272.9	327.1
29	33.45	38.79	45.22	52.97	62.32	73.64	87.35	104.0	124.1	148.6	214.6	312.1	377.2
30	34.78	40.57	47.58	56.08	66.44	79.06	94.46	113.3	136.3	164.5	241.3	356.8	434.7
40	48.89	60.40	75.40	95.03	120.8	154.8	199.6	259.1	337.9	442.6	767.1	1,342	1,779
50	64.46	84.58	112.8	152.7	209.3	290.3	406.5	573.8	815.1	1,164	2,400	4,995	7,218

Appendix C

Check Figures (Provided for Quick Check through A problems only)
(NCF = No check figure)
(IO* = Intentionally Omitted)

Chapter 1

Quick Check 1. c; 2. a; 3. d; 4. c; 5. c; 6. b; 7. c; 8. b; 9. b; 10. c

S1-1	NCF
S1-2	NCF
S1-3	NCF
S1-4	NCF
S1-5	d, c, e, b, g, h, a, f
S1-6	Equity $13,000
S1-7	Equity: (a) $420 (b) ($135)
S1-8	NCF
S1-9	Total assets $2,400
S1-10	Equity: (a) $300 (b) 0
S1-11	Total assets $35,400
S1-12	Net income $47,100
S1-13	Net income $47,100
E1-14	NCF
E1-15	NCF
E1-16	Nice Cuts Assets = $68,000
E1-17	Net income: a. $6,000; b. $25,000; c. $24,000
E1-18	NCF
E1-19	NCF
E1-20	IO*
E1-21	2. Net income $2,200
E1-22	1. Equity increased $4,000
E1-23	1. Net income $7 billion 2. Equity, increased $7 billion
E1-24	1. Net income $21,000
E1-25	NCF
E1-26	1. Total assets $21,300
E1-27	1. Net income $61,800
P1-28A	NCF
P1-29A	2. Total assets $138,100
P1-30A	2a. Total assets $50,200
P1-31A	2a. Total assets $120,100 2d. Net income $13,400
P1-32A	NCF
P1-33A	2. Net income $4,100
P1-34A	1. Net income $81,300
P1-35A	1a. Net income $39,000
P1-36A	1. Total assets $50,200

Chapter 2

Quick Check 1. c; 2. b; 3. a; 4. d; 5. a; 6. c; 7. a; 8. b; 9. a; 10. d

S2-1	NCF
S2-2	NCF
S2-3	NCF
S2-4	NCF
S2-5	NCF
S2-6	NCF
S2-7	2. Accounts payable bal $600
S2-8	3. a. Earned $9,000 b. Total assets $9,000
S2-9	2. Trial bal total $50,000
S2-10	Trial bal total $75,000
S2-11	Incorrect Trial bal total debits $68,900
S2-12	Incorrect Trial bal total debits $36,900
E2-13	NCF
E2-14	NCF
E2-15	1. Owners' equity $80,000 2. Net income $80,000
E2-16	NCF
E2-17	2. Cash Balance $30,200
E2-18	NCF
E2-19	2. Trial bal total $50,800
E2-20	4. Trial bal total $99,600
E2-21	NCF
E2-22	2. Trial bal total $27,900
E2-23	NCF
E2-24	1. Cash bal $7,300
E2-25	Trial bal total $196,500
E2-26	Trial bal total $35,300
P2-27A	2. Cash bal $255,800
P2-28A	2. Cash bal $58,950
P2-29A	2. Cash bal $10,930
P2-30A	Cash bal, $16,290
P2-31A	3. Cash bal $4,400
P2-32A	3. Cash bal $4,400
P2-33A	3. Cash bal $28,300
P2-34A	3. Cash bal $3,800
P2-35A	Total trial bal $111,600
P2-36A	Total trial bal $82,700
P2-37A	3. Total assets $576,800
P2-38A	3. Total assets $88,750
P2-39A	3. Total assets $37,330
P2-40A	3. Total assets $45,490
P2-41A	3. Total assets $30,100
P2-42A	3. Total assets $31,500
P2-43A	3. Total assets $70,300
P2-44A	3. Total assets $67,500

Chapter 3

Quick Check 1. b; 2. c; 3. d; 4. d; 5. b; 6. b; 7. a; 8. b; 9. a; 10. d

S3-1	1. Service revenue: Cash basis $600; Accrual basis $2,000
S3-2	1a. Expense $5,000 b. Asset $5,000
S3-3	1b. Revenue is 3/12 of the annual subscription amount
S3-4	Prepaid rent $1,050
S3-5	NCF
S3-6	3. Rent expense bal $800
S3-7	2. Book value $50,231
S3-8	2. Interest payable, Nov 30 $888
S3-9	NCF
S3-10	Adjusted trial bal total $24,300
S3-11	Net income $5,700
S3-12	Total assets $14,800
E3-13	NCF
E3-14	3. Net income (loss), Cash Basis ($2,800); Accrual Basis $3,500
E3-15	NCF
E3-16	1. A Rent expense $1,300 C Total amount to account for $1,800
E3-17	NCF
E3-18	Service revenue bal $6,100
E3-19	Adjusted trial bal total $42,480
E3-20	NCF
E3-21	1. Adjustments total $3,700
E3-22	2. Net income overstated by $11,800
E3-23	Unearned service revenue end bal $12,000
E3-24	2. Total assets $29,500
E3-25	1. Net income $3,400
E3-26	1. Net income $71,100
E3-27	IO*
P3-28A	3. Net income (loss), Cash Basis ($4,300); Accrual Basis $2,200
P3-29A	NCF
P3-30A	NCF

P3-31A 3. Adjusted trial bal total $66,900
P3-32A 3. Adjusted trial bal total $461,500
P3-33A 1. Adjusted trial bal total $92,580
P3-34A 3. Total assets $37,100

Chapter Appendix 3A

E3A-1 Supplies bal $500
E3A-2 Unearned service revenue bal $3,800
P3A-3A 4. Prepaid rent bal $1,300; Unearned service revenue bal $3,300

Chapter 4

Quick Check 1. b; 2. a; 3. b; 4. c; 5. b; 6. b; 7. d; 8. d; 9. a; 10. b

S4-1 NCF
S4-2 NCF
S4-3 NCF
S4-4 1d. Net income closed to Capital is $10,800
S4-5 IO* $21,800
S4-6 NCF
S4-7 Income summary credit bal $2,500
S4-8 Postclosing trial bal total $7,300
S4-9 NCF
S4-10 a. $800
b. $700
c. $2,000
d. 0
S4-11 1. Current ratio 1.86
Debt ratio 0.78
S4-12 2. Net income $47,800
E4-13 2. Net income $4,000
E4-14 Closing Entry 3 Sep 30 Close net income of $4,000 to Capital
E4-15 IO*
E4-16 2. Rent expense bal $6,000; Service revenue bal $4,500
E4-17 1. Closing Entry 3 Sep 30 Close net income of $11,600 to Capital
E4-18 IO*
E4-19 2. Ending bal for Service revenue and Rent expense accounts is zero.
E4-20 IO*
E4-21 Postclosing trial bal total $44,500
E4-22 1. Total assets $64,600
P4-23A Net income $16,800
P4-24A 2. Net income $50,200
P4-25A 3. Net income $16,500
P4-26A 3. Net income $17,500
P4-27A 3. Net income $40,100
P4-28A 1. Net income overstated by $1,500
P4-29A 1. Total assets $85,600

Chapter Appendix 4A

P4A-1A Salary payable $0; Salary expense $500

Chapter 5

Quick Check 1. d; 2. a; 3. c; 4. c; 5. b; 6. b; 7. c; 8. d; 9. a; 10. c

S5-1 NCF
S5-2 Inventory without discount $95,360. With discount $93,453
S5-3 2. $93,453
S5-4 2. $58,800
S5-5 Jul 10 Debit Cash for $58,800
S5-6 Oct 22 Debit Cash for $35,378
S5-7 2. Gross profit $13,718
S5-8 Debit Cost of goods sold $1,300
S5-9 Third closing entry includes: Hart, Capital credit $268,000
S5-10 Net income $4,700
S5-11 Total assets $10,500
S5-12 Gross profit percentage 28% Inventory turnover 57.9 times
E5-13 NCF
E5-14 May 22 Credit Cash for $902.84
E5-15 May 14 Credit Cash for $4,365
E5-16 a. $31,490 b. $4,930, c. $60,200, d. $63,990, f. $114,100
E5-17 Feb 23 Debit Cash for $4,214
E5-18 May 14 Debit Cash for $4,365
E5-19 3. Gross profit $42,700
E5-20 IO*
E5-21 3. Net income $71,400
E5-22 Net sales $232,500
E5-23 1. 5.3 times
E5-24 2. Gross profit %—current year 50.2%
E5-25 Gross profit % 39.3%
Inventory turnover 6.17 times
P5-26A 3. Oct 13 Debit Cash for $784
P5-27A Feb 29 Debit Cash $1,050
P5-28A 1. Jan 27 Credit Cash for $1,750
P5-29A May 28 Debit Cash for $9,114
P5-30A 1. Net income $34,300
P5-31A 2. Net income $60,200
P5-32A 1. Net income $70,800
P5-33A 1. Net income $69,700
2. Gross profit percentage = 43.3%

Chapter Appendix 5A

E5A-1 Net income $71,400
P5A-2A Net income $45,200

Chapter Appendix 5B

S5B-1 Cost of goods sold $82,000
E5B-2 Oct 14 Debit cash $7,663
E5B-3 Oct 14 Credit cash $7,663
E5B-4 1c. $80,000
P5B-5A Sep 27 Credit cash for $1,850

Chapter 6

Quick Check 1. c; 2. a; 3. c; 4. d; 5. c; 6. d; 7. b; 8. a; 9. a; 10. b

S6-1 Consistency Principle
S6-2 1. Average Cost Method
2. LIFO
S6-3 End Inventory $350
S6-4 End Inventory $300
S6-5 End Inventory $333
S6-6 3. COGS $1,650
S6-7 3. COGS $1,700
S6-8 3. COGS $1,667
S6-9 1. FIFO, 2. LIFO, 3. FIFO
S6-10 End Inventory $460
S6-11 COGS $30,700
S6-12 COGS overstated by $2,200
E6-13 Estimated End Inventory $71,000
E6-14 NCF
E6-15 1. End Inventory $396

E6-16 1. End Inventory $386
E6-17 1. End Inventory $391
E6-18 2. End Inventory $16,000; Gross Profit $38,000
E6-19 1. FIFO End Inventory $120, 2. LIFO End Inventory $90
E6-20 1. COGS: FIFO $245; 2. LIFO $275
E6-21 Gross Profit: FIFO $884; LIFO $731; Avg. Cost $800
E6-22 1. COGS $1,500 2. Report inventory at $12,500
E6-23 1. Debit COGS $1,000; Credit Inventory $1,000 2. Gross profit $70,000
E6-24 Gross profit is $15,000 with inventory overstated; $21,000 with inventory understated
E6-25 1. Net income: 2012 $51,000; 2011 $32,500
E6-26 Estimated cost of inventory destroyed $392,000
E6-27 Estimated cost of End inventory $36,350
P6-28A 1. COGS $25,000; 2. End Inventory $80,000
P6-29A 1. FIFO 2. LIFO COGS $13,800; LIFO End Inventory $1,200
P6-30A Net income $9,100
P6-31A 1. FIFO COGS $4,922; FIFO End Inventory at $1,552
2. LIFO COGS $4,972; LIFO End Inventory at $1,502
3. Avg Cost COGS $4,933; Avg Cost End Inventory at $1,541
P6-32A 1. Credit Inventory $2,000
P6-33A Corrected Net income 2012 $18; 2011 $16; 2010 $48
P6-34A Estimated ending inventory $2,617

Chapter Appendix 6A

E6A-1 End Inventory: Avg $335; FIFO $385; LIFO $295
COGS: Avg $1,409; FIFO $1,359; LIFO $1,449
E6A-2 c.4. Credit COGS for $1,900
E6A-3 a. $65,000 b. $136,000 c. $23,000 d. $28,000 e. $30,000 f. $32,000 g. $34,000

P6A-4A 2. Gross profit: Avg $14,472; FIFO $14,921; LIFO $14,005

Chapter 7

Quick Check 1. d; 2. c; 3. d; 4. a; 5. a; 6. d; 7. c; 8. b; 9. b; 10. d

S7-1 NCF
S7-2 NCF
S7-3 NCF
S7-4 NCF
S7-5 NCF
S7-6 Adjusted bank balance $3,160
S7-7 First entry: Debit Cash $680; Credit Accounts receivable-Ryan Saar $680
S7-8 Cash in drawer will be $500 less than the amount in the register.
S7-9 NCF
S7-10 NCF
S7-11 Aug 1 Debit Petty cash $300
S7-12 NCF
E7-13 NCF
E7-14 NCF
E7-15 NCF
E7-16 3. $860
E7-17 NCF
E7-18 1. Adjusted bank balance $1,210
E7-19 1. Adjusted bank balance $2,180
E7-20 NCF
E7-21 NCF
E7-22 b. Credit Cash $185
E7-23 2b. Credit Cash $136
E7-24 NCF
P7-25A NCF
P7-26A NCF
P7-27A 1. Adjusted bank balance $17,380
P7-28A 1. Adjusted bank balance $4,460
P7-29A NCF
P7-30A 2. $240
P7-31A 1. 85
P7-32A NCF

Chapter 8

Quick Check 1. d; 2. d; 3. c; 4. d; 5. a; 6. d; 7. b; 8. b; 9. c; 10. c

S8-1 F
S8-2 NCF
S8-3 1. Debit Uncollectible-account expense $15,520; Credit Allowance for uncollectible accounts $15,520
S8-4 1c. Debit Allowance for uncollectible accounts $6,000; Credit Accounts receivable $6,000
S8-5 2. $1,910
S8-6 2. $20,560
S8-7 Jul 19, Debit Allowance for uncollectible accounts $900
S8-8 2. Accounts receivable, net $2,220
S8-9 First entry: Debit Credit-card discount expense $204. Second entry: Debit Bankcard discount expense $120
S8-10 1. $4,333 2. $100 3. $550 4. $3,375
S8-11 1b. Credit Interest revenue $825
S8-12 1a. Acid-test ratio = 1.19
E8-13 NCF
E8-14 NCF
E8-15 1. Adjusting entry amount = $2,520
E8-16 2. Eagle Mountain expects to collect $59,780
E8-17 2. $64,800
E8-18 2. nothing. Accounts receivable has a zero balance.
E8-19 Oct 1, 2012 Credit Cash $24,000
E8-20 3. $85,133
E8-21 Jun 30 Credit Interest revenue $523
E8-22 Dec 31 Debit Cash $24,480
E8-23 2. 31 days
E8-24 1. 28 days
P8-25A NCF
P8-26A 1. Uncollectible-account expense $10,600
2. Uncollectible-account expense $5,000
P8-27A 3. Accounts receivable, net $160,900
P8-28A 3. Accounts receivable, net $127,100
P8-29A Dec 31, 2010 Credit Interest revenue $225
P8-30A 1. Note 1, June 1, 2011 $19,800; Note 2, Dec 30, 2010 $15,413; Note 3, Dec 18, 2010 $7,105
P8-31A Dec 30 Cash collected from Pop Music is $15,600

P8-32A 1a. Current Ratio: 2012: 1.56 2011: 1.31

Chapter Appendix 8A

E8A-1 Dec 1 Debit Interest expense $300

E8A-2 Oct 15 Credit Interest revenue $184

Chapter 9

Quick Check 1. a; 2. c; 3. c; 4. c; 5. a; 6. c; 7. d; 8. d; 9. c; 10. d

S9-1 NCF

S9-2 Credit Note payable $140,000

S9-3 2. Book Value $50,000,000

S9-4 1. a. $10,800,000 b. $11,700,000 c. $14,160,000

S9-5 2. $17,500,000

S9-6 $6,000

S9-7 1. $10,000

S9-8 Debit Cash for $43,000

S9-9 Credit Cash $2,900

S9-10 2. Depletion expense $8.4 billion

S9-11 2. Debit Goodwill $200,000

S9-12 Net income overstated

E9-13 1. Building cost = $550,000

E9-14 Land 3 = $96,000

E9-15 NCF

E9-16 NCF

E9-17 1. 2010 Depreciaton Expense: Straight-line $3,000 UOP $1,200 DDB $7,500

E9-18 Year 2 DDB $19,200; Straight-line $8,000

E9-19 Depreciation expense, year 15 = $10,250

E9-20 Aug 31, Debit Cash $7,600

E9-21 1. Debit Office fixtures (new) $131,000 2. Debit Office fixtures (new) $123,000

E9-22 $296,400

E9-23 a. Debit Mineral asset $488,500 b. Debit Mineral asset $90,000 c. Debit Depletion expense $29,000

E9-24 b. Credit Patents $40,000

E9-25 1. Goodwill $4,000,000

E9-26 1. a. and b. Understated by $500,000

P9-27A 1. Land $100,300; Land Improvements $83,000; Buildings $470,400; Furniture $13,700

P9-28A 1. Straight-line depreciation expense $10,000 each year UOP: 2010-$11,250 UOP depreciation expense: 2010, $11,250

P9-29A Jan 1 Debit Office Equipment (new) $108,000; Sep 1 Credit Gain on sale of building $58,667

P9-30A Depletion expense, year 1 = $1,034,600

P9-31A 1. Debit Goodwill $510,000

P9-32A 1. Increase net income for 2010 by $2 billion.

Chapter 10

Quick Check 1. b; 2. c; 3. a; 4. b; 5. d; 6. b; 7. a; 8. d; 9. c; 10. b

S10-1 2. Credit Cash $7,840

S10-2 2. End Balance Estimated warranty payable $6,950

S10-3 NCF

S10-4 2. Net pay = $751.68

S10-5 Total expense to employer $1,263.01

S10-6 Net pay $4,038

S10-7 1. Credit Salary payable $751.68

S10-8 NCF

S10-9 1a. $227,250 b. $315,750 c. $283,500 d. $314,250

S10-10 NCF

S10-11 b. Debit Interest expense $2,800

S10-12 1. $2,955,000

S10-13 6%, discount

S10-14 1. Jan 1 Debit Cash $76,000 2. Jul 1 Credit to Discount on bonds payable $200

S10-15 1. Jan 1 Debit Cash $43,600 2. Jul 1 Debit to Premium on bonds payable $180

S10-16 2. Dec 31 Credit Interest payable $3,375; Feb 1 Credit to Cash $4,050

S10-17 1. May 1 Debit Cash $334,750 2. Jul 1 Debit Interest expense $4,875

S10-18 Total current liabilities $44,300

S10-19 EPS, Plan A $5.24 EPS, Plan B $3.10

E10-20 Aug 6 Debit Sales tax payable $16,800

E10-21 Dec 31, Credit Interest payable $1,200

E10-22 Dec 31 Debit Unearned subscription revenue $100

E10-23 4th entry Debit Salary expense $3,800

E10-24 2. $4,750

E10-25 1. Net pay = $838.26

E10-26 Debit Payroll tax expense $6,138

E10-27 NCF

E10-28 1. Jan 1 Debit Cash $67,900 2. July 1 Debit Interest expense $3,203

E10-29 1. Jul 1 Debit Interest expense $3,200

E10-30 3. Apr 30 Debit Interest expense $5,133

E10-31 Current portion of note payable-2011 thru 2013 $200,000

E10-32 Total current liabilities $99,000

E10-33 EPS-Plan A $2.46; EPS-Plan B $2.00

P10-34A Jan 29 Debit Cash $17,755; Jul 9 Credit Cash $10,400; Feb 28, 2011, first installment on long term note, Credit Cash $71,400

P10-35A 3. Total current liabilities $175,645

P10-36A 1. Net pay = $58,020 2. Total expense to employer = $86,763

P10-37A 3a. Debit Cash $873,000 b. Credit Cash $27,000 c. Credit Interest payable $18,000 d. Credit Cash $27,000

P10-38A 1.c. $12,000 d. $16,500

P10-39A 2. Interest payable $3,000 Bonds payable $450,000

P10-40A Total current liabilities $122,300

P10-41A EPS-Plan A $7.19; EPS-Plan B $2.85

Chapter Appendix 10A

P10A-1A 1. $170,595 2. $279,450

P10A-2A 1. $88,018 1. $78,640 3. $98,975

P10A-3A b. first interest payment-Debit Interest expense $5,505
c. first interest payment-Debit Interest expense $4,949
P10A-4A 1. $451,130
P10A-5A 1. $108,178
P10A-6A 2. Jul 2 Debit Interest expense $11,180
P10A-7A 12/31/2015 Bond Carrying Value = $100,000
P10A-8A 3. Dec 31, 2010, Debit Cash $162,548

Chapter Appendix 10B

S10B-1 1. $312,000 2. $285,000 3. $27,000
S10B-2 1. $1,938,000 2. Credit Common stock $400,000
E10B-3 Oct 1, 2015-bond retirement Credit Cash $594,000 and Credit Discount on bonds payable $13,500
E10B-4 2. $576,000
E10B-5 1. Debit Loss on retirement of bonds payable $13,500

Chapter 11

Quick Check 1. a; 2. b; 3. a; 4. a; 5. a; 6. c; 7. b; 8. a; 9. c; 10. a
S11-1 NCF
S11-2 NCF
S11-3 a. Credit Paid-in capital in excess of par $6,000
b. Credit Preferred stock $30,000
S11-4 NCF
S11-5 Credit Paid-in capital in excess of par $3,950
S11-6 Total stockholders' equity $113,800
S11-7 Third closing entry, Debit Retained earnings $2,300
S11-8 1b. Debit Dividends payable $67,200
S11-9 2. Preferred stock dividend, 2010 $3,900; Common stock dividend $11,100
S11-10 Book value per share-preferred stock $17.55;
Book value per share-common stock $0.71
S11-11 Rate of return on total assets = 17.2 %
S11-12 2. Net income = $55,250
E11-13 NCF
E11-14 $315,500
E11-15 2. $43,600
E11-16 1a. Credit Common stock $12,000
1b. Credit Common stock $2,000 and credit Paid-in capital in excess of stated value $10,000
E11-17 2. The account balances are the same for both case A & case B
E11-18 2. Total stockholders' equity $94,000
E11-19 1. Total stockholders' equity $130,940
E11-20 2. Retained earnings bal $140,000
E11-21 2. 2010: P/S: $7,600 2011: P/S: $11,600 C/S: $36,400
E11-22 P/S: $25,600; C/S: $124,400
E11-23 Book value per share of common stock $41.51
E11-24 Book value per share of preferred stock $49.60
Book value per share of common stock $37.26
E11-25 1. Rate of return on total assets 9.3%;
Rate of return on common stockholders' equity 9.9%
E11-26 1. Deferred tax liability = $39,590,000
P11-27A 3. 40,000 shares
P11-28A 2. $5 par
P11-29A 2. $289,000
3. $310,000
4. Book value per share of common stock $34.54
P11-30A 2. Total stockholders' equity $365,000
P11-31A 2. Total stockholders' equity $342,900
P11-32A Maryland Service, Inc: Retained earnings balance $152,000; Total stockholders' equity $752,000
P11-33A 1a. Common Dividend: 2010- $0; 2011- $11,250; 2012- $16,250
1b. Common Dividend: 2010- $0; 2011- $9,500 ; 2012- $16,250
P11-34A 1. Total assets $601,000
P11-35A 1. Taxable income = $185,000

Chapter 12

Quick Check 1. c; 2. a; 3. c; 4. c; 5. c; 6. b; 7. b; 8. b; 9. a; 10. b
S12-1 1. Debit Retained earnings for $24,000
S12-2 NCF
S12-3 1. Total stockholders' equity $683
S12-4 2. Less Treasury stock 600 shares at cost $(3,600)
S12-5 1. $465,000
S12-6 NCF
S12-7 NCF
S12-8 Net income $20,400
S12-9 EPS, Net income $1.94
S12-10 NCF
S12-11 1. Comprehensive income $24,900
S12-12 Retained earnings, December 31, 2011 $154,000
E12-13 2. Total stockholders' equity $130,250
E12-14 1. Credit Common stock for $7,100 and credit Paid-in capital in excess of par for $42,600
E12-15 b. No effect d. Increase $2,700
E12-16 2. Total stockholders' equity $3,920
E12-17 Aug 22 Debit Cash for $3,600
E12-18 2. Total stockholders' equity $70,000
3. 750
E12-19 1a. Total stockholders' equity $600,000. Note X indicates restriction to retained earnings of $200,000.
E12-20 1. Net income $59,400
E12-21 EPS $2.19
E12-22 EPS, Extraordinary gain is $0.38
E12-23 Retained earnings, December 31, 2011 $198 million
E12-24 Retained earnings, December 31, 2010 $95,000
E12-25 1. Net income is $114,000. Comprehensive income is $106,000 2. EPS $2.28
P12-26A Nov 30 Debits are as follows: Cash $13,500; Paid-in capital from treasury stock transactions $7,500; and Retained earnings $1,500
P12-27A 2. Total stockholders' equity $339,000
P12-28A 2. Retained earnings, December 31, 2012 $186,000
3. Total stockholders' equity $796,000

P12-29A 1. EPS, net income is $1.85

P12-30A Net income $72,800

P12-31A Net income $89,800. EPS, net income is $1.80

Chapter 13

Quick Check 1. d; 2. b; 3. c; 4. a; 5. a; 6. b; 7. c; 8. c; 9. a; 10. b

S13-1 NCF

S13-2 NCF

S13-3 NCF

S13-4 Net cash provided by operating activities $35,000

S13-5 Net cash provided by operating activities $63,000

S13-6 Net increase in cash $58,300

S13-7 a. $14,000
b. $8,100

S13-8 Net cash used in financing activities (10,100)

S13-9 Increase in cash $34,000

S13-10 $78,000

S13-11 NCF

S13-12 NCF

E13-13 NCF

E13-14 NCF

E13-15 1. $32,000

E13-16 1. $91,500

E13-17 Net cash provided by operating activities $92,000

E13-18 1. $43,000 2. $7,000

E13-19 $89 thousand

E13-20 a. Payment of LTNP $11 thousand
b. Issuance of common stock $13 thousand
c. Payment of cash dividends $52 thousand

E13-21 Net cash used for investing activities $(106)

P13-22A 4. Net cash provided by operating activities $156,500; investing activities $(46,000) and financing activities $432,000

P13-23A Noncash investing and financing activities $118,000

P13-24A 1. Net cash provided by operating activities $80,100; investing activities $(159,600) and financing activities $143,800

P13-25A Net cash used for financing activities $(83,000)

Chapter Appendix 13A

S13A-1 Net cash provided by operating activities $211,000; investing activities $(143,000) and financing activities $(49,000)

S13A-2 Net cash provided by operating activities $18,000

S13A-3 Net cash provided by operating activities $18,000; investing activities $24,000 and financing activities $(18,000)

S13A-4 1a. $136,000 1b. $68,000

E13A-5 NCF

E13A-6 NCF

E13A-7 Net cash provided by operating activities $3,000

E13A-8 Accounts receivable: Cash collections as an operating cash flow of $36,000

E13A-9 Net cash provided by operating activities $75,500; investing activities $(79,000) and financing activities $16,500

E13A-10 a. $64,000 b. $74,000

E13A-11 a. $24,682 b. $18,590
c. $4,342 d. $1,184
e. $10 f. $232 g. $275

P13A-12A Net cash provided by operating activities $91,700; investing activities $(35,900) and financing activities $17,600

P13A-13A 1. Net income $427,800

P13A-14A 1. Net cash provided by operating activities $140,800; investing activities $(47,100) and financing activities $(83,000)

P13A-15A Net cash provided by operating activities $85,800; investing activities $(54,500) and financing activities $(22,800)

Chapter Appendix 13B

P13B-1A Transaction analysis total columns $91,100

P13B-2A Transaction analysis total columns $168,100

Chapter 14

Quick Check 1. b; 2. a; 3. d; 4. c; 5. b; 6. b; 7. a; 8. b; 9. c; 10. b

S14-1 Gross profit Increase 2012 $55 or 1.46%

S14-2 1. Net income Trend 2013–2011 170% 158% 117%

S14-3 Inventory 21.2% of total

S14-4 1. COGS, Sanchez 62.1% COGS, Bajo 72.0%

S14-5 1. Current ratio: 2011 2.08, 2010 2.14

S14-6 1. 3.1 times 2. 58.108 days

S14-7 1. 0.45 debt ratio

S14-8 1. 26.6% 2. 16.1% 3. 28.1%

S14-9 1. $13.50 2. 5 times

S14-10 Net income $630

S14-11 Receivables $350

E14-12 The percentage change in working capital in 2008 is 10.7% and in 2009 is 25.8%

E14-13 1. Net income increased $35,350 or 42.3%

E14-14 Net revenue 2014–2010 126% 113% 96% 97% 100%

E14-15 Long-term debt is 38.0%

E14-16 1. COGS is 47.5% in 2011 and 51.0% in 2010

E14-17 a. 1.34 b. 0.63
c. 4.31 times d. 50 days

E14-18 2009 a. 1.50 b. 0.69 c. 0.71 d. 3.70 times

E14-19 2012 a. 0.095 b. 0.135 c. 0.138 d. $0.68

E14-20 2011 P/E ratio 27.8; Dividend Yield 0.016; Book value per common share $7.38

E14-21 Total assets $23,385

P14-22A 2. 2011 0.105 2012 0.115 2013 0.178

P14-23A Russell Net income 10.7%

P14-24A 1. Current ratio 1.50; debt ratio 0.66 EPS $1.78

P14-25A 1. 2011: a. 1.61
b. 6.46 times c. 1.53 times
d. 0.38 e. $4.78 f. 17

P14-26A Best Digital: a. 1.01 b. 2.84 c. 33 d. 0.38 e. $4.60 f. 15

Chapter 15

Quick Check 1. b; 2. c; 3. d; 4. c; 5. b; 6. b; 7. c; 8. c; 9. d; 10. a

S15-1 NCF

S15-2 NCF

S15-3 NCF

S15-4 1. Net operating income $2,640 2. $10.27

S15-5 COGS $47,000

S15-6 Fit Apparel Operating income $31,000

S15-7 NCF

S15-8 Direct materials used $9,400

S15-9 NCF
S15-10 2. Total manufacturing overhead $11,150
S15-11 Cost of goods manufactured $43,000
S15-12 NCF
S15-13 NCF
E15-14 NCF
E15-15 NCF
E15-16 1. Net operating income $7,790 2. $11.32
E15-17 1. Net operating income $21,700 2. $9.11
E15-18 1. Operating income $18,900 2. $11.26
E15-19 Fit Apparel Cost of goods manufactured $4,900
E15-20 1. Cost of goods manufactured $437,000
2. $136.56
E15-21 Cost of goods sold $200,000
E15-22 NCF
P15-23A 1. Net operating income $12,200 2. $0.45 per foot
P15-24A Operating income $15,050
P15-25A 1. Cost of goods manufactured $78,600 2. Operating income $26,500
P15-26A 1. Cost of goods manufactured $169,000 2. Operating income $82,000
P15-27A 2. COGS 25.2
P15-28A NCF

Chapter 16

Quick Check 1. a; 2. c; 3. c; 4. a; 5. a; 6. b; 7. d; 8. d; 9. d; 10. a
S16-1 NCF
S16-2 NCF
S16-3 3. $47,950
S16-4 Indirect materials used $20
S16-5 Debit WIP $77,000 and Debit MOH $1,490
S16-6 2. Direct labor $60,000; Indirect labor $11,000
S16-7 MOH bal $66,500
S16-8 $1,030
S16-9 3. Overallocated $2,000
S16-10 4. Overallocated $16,000
S16-11 Debit MOH $16,000
S16-12 1. $54 2. $972
S16-13 1. $30 2. $540
E16-14 NCF
E16-15 1c. COGS, Jobs 1 & 2 = $17,500
E16-16 f. Debit to MOH for $16,100
E16-17 NCF
E16-18 1. WIP Balance $15,000
E16-19 3. MOH underallocated by $4,640
E16-20 1. $11 per machine hour
E16-21 1. Overallocated by $41,000
E16-22 2. Underallocated by $30,000
E16-23 1a. DL $154/hour
b. Indirect cost 68%
P16-24A 5. Gross Profit Job 3 $1,100
P16-25A 2. WIP ending bal $271,000; Finished goods ending bal $114,000
P16-26A 1. Job 423 total cost is $2,030
P16-27A 3. Cost of goods manufactured $48,850
P16-28A 1. $8.83 per machine hour
P16-29A 2. Total Direct Costs, Dining Coop: $114,700; Root Chocolates $9,400

Chapter Appendix 16A

S16A-1 1. $47,000
S16A-2 2. EU: Direct Materials: 190,000; Conversion Costs 177,000
S16A-3 1. EU: Direct Materials: 52,000; Conversion Costs 32,500
S16A-4 1. Direct Materials: $0.90; Conversion Costs $0.85
S16A-5 1. $45,500
S16A-6 231 units completed and transferred out
E16A-7 2. EU: Direct Materials: 9,200; Conversion Costs 7,170
3. Total cost accounted for $7,950
E16A-8 3. $0.92 per unit
E16A-9 2. EU: Direct Materials: 7,800; Conversion Costs 7,520
Cost per EU: Direct Materials: $1.29; Conversion Costs $0.90
E16A-10 2. Bal Mar 31 WIP-fermenting $2,884
E16A-11 2. EU: Trans In: 170,000 Direct Materials: 150,000; Conversion Costs 164,000
Cost per EU: Trans In: $0.79 Direct Materials: $0.22; Conversion Costs $0.35
P16A-12A 2. EU: Direct Materials: 101,000; Conversion Costs 85,335
Cost per EU: Direct Materials: $3.72; Conversion Costs $3.03
4. End WIP-Assembly Jun 30 $115,325
P16A-13A 2. EU: Direct Materials: 4,525; Conversion Costs 4,525
Cost per EU: Direct Materials: $1.20; Conversion Costs $1.40
P16A-14A 2. EU: Wood: 3,600 Adhesives: 1,910; Conversion Costs 2,586
Cost per EU: Wood: $0.74 Adhesives: $0.71; Conversion Costs $1.00
4. End WIP-Preparation Jan 31 $2,074
P16A-15A 2. EU: Trans In: 635; Direct Materials: 635; Conversion Costs 608
Cost per EU: Trans In: $41; Direct Materials: $23; Conversion Costs $94
P16A-16A 2. EU: Trans In: 9,400; Conversion Costs 6,340
Cost per EU: Trans In: $83; Conversion Costs $15

Chapter 17

Quick Check 1. d; 2. b; 3. d; 4. b; 5. d; 6. b; 7. b; 8. c; 9. c; 10. a
S17-1 NCF
S17-2 1. $605 2. Blake $650; Roscoe $560
S17-3 Product A $126.00; Product B $501.78
S17-4 1. Lo-Gain $254.47; Hi-Gain $132.60
2. Lo-Gain $106.51; Hi-Gain $223.61
S17-5 Product C $1,530.44; Product D $2,830.44
S17-6 Mid-Fi $1,868.00; Hi-Fi $1,610.15
S17-7 1. $89.95
2. $43,995
3. $8,505
S17-8 Document prep $32/page; Info Tech Support $210/app; Training $100/direct labor hour

S17-9 1. $70,140
2. $(17,640)

S17-10 $98,925

S17-11 NCF

S17-12 Purchase materials: Debit Raw and in process inventory for $7,500

E17-13 NCF

E17-14 2. Total $143.30

E17-15 2. Total $4,060

E17-16 1. $603,000
2. Standard $249.00; Deluxe $354.00
3. Standard $231.90; Deluxe $371.04

E17-17 4. $79,684 higher

E17-18 1. Gross Profit: Standard $569.00; Deluxe $581.00
2. Gross Profit: Standard $586.10; Deluxe $563.96

E17-19 1. $80.00 Finishing activity cost per rim

E17-20 2. Ending bal RIP $2,815
3. Conversion cost over-allocated $950

E17-21 2. Ending bal Finished Goods $1,855

E17-22 NCF

E17-23 2. Cost of implementing program is $55,000 less

E17-24 2. Cost of implementing program is $524,000 less

P17-25A 1. Total manufacturing product cost $148.20

P17-26A 1. Manufacturing cost per unit: Standard: $75; Unfinished $50
2. Full product cost per unit: Standard: $101; Unfinished $72

P17-27A 2. ABC: Commercial: $81.58; Travel: $2.33

P17-28A 3. Ending bal RIP $8,000

P17-29A 1. $125,005 2. $23,005

Chapter 18

Quick Check 1. a; 2. b; 3. a; 4. c; 5. b; 6. c; 7. b; 8. c; 9. c; 10. a

S18-1 NCF

S18-2 NCF

S18-3 1a. $16.00 b. $25.00 c. $38.50

S18-4 1a. $0.40 b. $2,000

S18-5 6,750 tickets

S18-6 1. 0.78571 2. 472,503

S18-7 Break even in units: A: 8,333 B: 2,625 C: 20,000

S18-8 1. BE tickets 8,250; BE $495,000 2. BE tickets 6,188; BE $433,160

S18-9 BE tickets 6,250; BE $437,500

S18-10 Margin of safety = 150 tickets or $10,500

S18-11 $6.25

S18-12 1. 3,000 tickets
2. 1,200 individual tickets and 1,800 family tickets

E18-13 NCF

E18-14 1. $0.80 2. $3,280

E18-15 1. 60% 2. Operating loss at $251,000 in sales is $(23,400) 3. $290,000

E18-16 1. $0.90 per package. CM ratio = 50% 2. BE units 100,000; BE $180,000

E18-17 1. CM ratio 80%; BE $10,750 2. Target sales $21,813

E18-18 1. BE $663,158 2. Operating loss at $510,000 in sales is $(145,500)

E18-19 1. D 2. Will not be profitable - loss $6,000
3. Students – 500 Dollars - $50,000

E18-20 1a. CM $160/unit; BE 700 units

E18-21 1. $85,000 2. 59%

E18-22 1. Sell 420 standard and 630 chrome scooters to Break Even.
2. Sell 740 standard and 1,110 chrome scooters to reach target operating income

P18-23A 2. BE sales: North $673,684; East $605,000; South $267,308; West $21,739

P18-24A 1. Per show: Revenue: $60,000; Variable Cost: $29,400 2. BE Shows = 15

P18-25A 1. 84,000 flags
2. $1,107,500
3. Operating loss $(77,000)
4. BE: 110,250 flags or $1,378,125

P18-26A 1. BE 50 trades 2. Sales of $56,000 needed to earn $11,200

P18-27A 1. BE 12,000 plain and 6,000 custard-filled
2. $7,000 3. Operating income $10,343

Chapter Appendix 18A

S18A-1 Operating income $125,000

S18A-2 1. Operating income $131,000

E18A-3 1. Operating income: Absorption costing $305,000; Variable costing $155,000

P18A-4A 1. Absorption costing $5.30; Variable costing $5.00
2a. Operating income: Absorption costing $3,245;
2b. Variable costing $3,185

P18A-5A 1. October-Absorption costing $16; Variable costing $13
November-Absorption costing $16; Variable costing $13
2a. Operating income: Absorption costing $34,500;
2b.Variable costing $35,100

Chapter 19

Quick Check 1. a; 2. b; 3. b; 4. a; 5. d; 6. b; 7. d; 8. a; 9. c; 10. b

S19-1 NCF

S19-2 NCF

S19-3 1. SnowDelight's expected profit shortfall $(6,300,000)

S19-4 Drop Accessories Dept because expenses > revenues

S19-5 1. 14,900 2. Contribution margin – men's dept $48,000 – women's dept $21,000 – accessories dept $13,000 Replace with shoe dept

S19-6 1. Should emphasize the production of regular bins
2. Should spend 3,400 machine hours making regular size bins, and 0 machine hours making large size bins
3. Operating income $184,000

S19-7 1. Store-It should produce 32,000 regular size bins and 15,180 large size bins.
2. Operating income – $149,116 3. C.

S19-8 Absorption cost per unit – $2.54 2. Bake bread in-house – variable cost < outsourcing 3. C.

S19-9 NCF

S19-10 President made wrong decision – highest profit by transforming cocoa powder into chocolate syrup

S19-11 NCF

S19-12 1. Accept special sales order 2. Reject special sales order

E19-13 1. D.

E19-14 1. Target-costing 2. 178,400 3. Cost-plus price $234,600

E19-15 Decrease in operating income – $(36,000) – do not drop VCR tapes

E19-16 Decrease in operating income – $(10,000) – do not drop VCR tapes

E19-17 2. Deluxe $245 CM per machine hour; Regular $399 CM per machine hour

E19-18 CM at capacity: Designer, $24,000; Moderately Priced, $34,160

E19-19 1. Constraining factor is linear feet of shelf space. Stock all 12 oz. cans of Grand-Cola. 2. 325 - 12 oz cans 140 - 20 oz bottles

E19-20 Incremental cost $16.00 to make < $17.50 to buy – Decision: make the optical switch

E19-21 1. Make $1,312,000; Buy and Leave Facilities Idle $1,435,000; Buy and Use Facilities for Other Product $1,212,000 2. Best use is to outsource the optical switches and use the facilities to manufacture the other product.

E19-22 It is more profitable to sell fruited yogurt as individual portions. Net benefit $4,608 > $3,175

P19-23A 1. Variable manufacturing expenses are relevant 2. Accept the special order – $36,000 increase in operating income 3. D.

P19-24A 1. Target full cost $1,400,000 3. Actual full costs $1,475,000 > target cost – will not meet stockholders' expectations 3. New target fixed cost $625,000 4. Cost plus price $4.24

P19-25A 1. Decrease in operating income $(117,000) 3. The operating income difference calculated on the total analysis of dropping a product line equals the expected decrease in operating income if Security Force drops the industrial systems product line.

P19-26A 1. Constraint is machine hours 2. Deluxe $1,357 Standard $2,535 – Emphasize standard electric toothbrushes

P19-27A 1. Make the bindings $29,450 < buy the bindings $34,380 2. Continue to make the bindings

P19-28A 1. $384,000 Petroleum distillate sales revenue - $201,000 cost of producing - $125,330 further processing - $524,400 cleaner sales revenue 2. $201,000 a sunk cost that is irrelevant 3. Net revenue difference $15,070

Chapter 20

Quick Check 1. c; 2. b; 3. c; 4. a; 5. a; 6. d; 7. d; 8. d; 9. a; 10. b

S20-1 NCF

S20-2 1. Net cash flow $2,753,520 2. Operating income $1,761,853

S20-3 1. 4.5 years payback period

S20-4 1. ARR 26.90%

S20-5 1. Payback period will not change – does not consider any cash flows after payback period. Residual value will not affect cash flows until end of asset's life – not considered in calculation. 2. ARR will change if asset now has no residual value. Operating income will be lower since more depreciation expense. Average investment is lower when asset doesn't have residual value. New ARR 28.19% 3. Payback period is shorter than 5.4-year max and ARR is higher than 18.25% min; investment meets both decision criteria – will want to consider investment.

S20-6 Expected annual cash savings $5,475

S20-7 Scenario 1 – 8% - $43,390 – 10% - $40,279 Scenario 2 – 8% - $48,350 – 10% - $48,350 Scenario 3 - 8% - $54,027 – 10% - $46,723 Scenario 3 best option based on 8%; Scenario 2 best option based on 10%

S20-8 1a. $10,186 b. $8,435

S20-9 1a. Option 1: $2,159,000 b. Option 2 is most preferable

S20-10 1. Total present value 3.432 2. This is an annuity 3. Present value of an annuity - 5 years at 14% per year is $3,433 4. Annuity PV factors are the sums of the PV factors found in Present Value of $1 tables.

S20-11 1. $4,709,503

S20-12 $4,555,303

S20-13 18–20%

E20-14 NCF

E20-15 Payback period for plant is 4.1 years.

E20-16 Payback period is 5.8 years.

E20-17 Rouse equipment offers higher rate of return – 52.0% > 34.3%

E20-18 ARR 13.33%

E20-19 1. Out-of-pocket costs option 1 – $67,500; option 2 – $67,500 2. Savings option 1 – $359,991; option 2 – $118,456 3. Strategy involving earlier savings grows substantially larger over time. 4. Total savings at age 62 option 1 – $1,118,132; option 2 – $367,924.

E20-20 Option 1 - $7,020 Option 2 – $8,784 Option 3 – $10,866 Interest rates rises – future value of investment rises, but riskier.

E20-21 1. $143,885 2. $172,095

E20-22 Present value of the payout: Option 1 – $9,711,000; Option 2 – $9,687,600; Option 3 – $10,080,000

E20-23 1. Net present value Project A $(25,577) Project B $30,256 2. Maximum acceptable price Project A $264,423 Project B $410,256

E20-24 1. Net present value $(10,363) 2. Additional NPV provided from refurbishment $3,664; refurbishment provides positive NPV

E20-25 Project A: 10–12%; Project B: 14–16% - better investment

E20-26 Profitability index Equip A 1.21 < Equip B 1.23 < Equip C 1.24 – invest here

P20-27A NCF

P20-28A 1. payback period is 4.2 yrs; ARR is 25.3%; net present value $494,320; IRR between 18–20% 2. Invest in new facility.

P20-29A 1. Payback period - Plan A 5.1 yrs; Plan B 7.4 yrs AAR – Plan A 17.0%; plan B 7.0% 2. Invest in Plan A – has higher net present value with shorter payback period. 3. IRR of Plan A is between 12–14% - it exceeds company's hurdle rate of 8%.

P20-30A 1. Present value $1,590,750 2. Withdrawing $7,875,000 over course of retirement; numbers are different – B. 3. Pay $82,265 4. Out of pocket savings $822,650 – less than the investment's worth at end of 10 years

Chapter 21

Quick Check 1. d; 2. a; 3. a; 4. b; 5. a; 6. c; 7. b; 8. d; 9. b; 10. a

S21-1 NCF

S21-2 NCF

S21-3 Total sales $1,100,000

S21-4 Purchases – Jan $420,750; Feb $554,100

S21-5 Total cash collections – Jan $503,776; Feb $532,772

S21-6 Cash deficiency $(13,430)

S21-7 April-July $234,000

S21-8 NCF

S21-9 Variance % sales revenue 6.33%; cost of goods sold 19.44%; gross profit 27.91%

E21-10 $20,000 Operating Income Variance

E21-11 NCF

E21-12 Purchases March 31 $83,000; June 30 $88,500; September 30 $79,500

E21-13 Net income: Qtr 1 $1,442,000; Qtr 2 $1,499,680; Qtr 3 $1,651,644; Qtr 4 $1,568,537

E21-14 1a. $19,000 b. $115,343 c. $32,167

E21-15 1. Jan $11,000; Feb $10,500 2. $2,000

E21-16 Apr $25,000 May $25,000

E21-17 Mar 31 bal stockholders' equity $28,880

E21-18 NCF

E21-19 Operating income for video and digital cell phones - Budget: $439 Actual: $533 Variance: $94 Operating income for PDAs and cell phones - Budget: $564 Actual: $623 Variance: $59 Yes, investigate performance of digital cell phones – favorable operations are significant.

P21-20A 1. Operating income – Budget: $382,000 Actual: $537,000 Variance: $155,000 2. Should investigate – income variance of $(6,042) – unfavorable – 26.92% of budgeted income – worth investigating.

P21-21A May COGS: $16,400 June COGS: $22,900 May Net Income $21,200 – June Net Income $16,900

P21-22A 1a. Budgeted Cash Collections – May: $50,750 June: $51,900 b. Budgeted Cash Payments for Purchases – May: $59,375 June: $25,650 c. Budgeted Cash Payments for Operating Expenses – May: $7,600 June: $7,650 2. Cash Budget – May: $8,775 June: $27,375

P21-23A 1. Cash – $64,600 Inventory – $22,000 Stockholders' Equity – $149,300 Balance Sheet: Total Assets $187,700 Total liabilities and stockholders' equity $187,700 2. Budgeted Statement of Cash Flows – $64,600 3. $60,500

P21-24A 1. Cash $42,200 Inventory $34,600 Stockholders' equity $133,900 Balance Sheet: $172,300 2. Company will not have to borrow cash. $21,200 > $21,000 3. Decline in expenses is less than 33 1/3%. Expenses are $71,400. Sales decline to $56,000; expenses decline to $58,800, a decline of 17.6%.

Chapter 22

Quick Check 1. a; 2. b; 3. d; 4. e; 5. a; 6. d; 7. b; 8. a; 9. b; 10. a

S22-1 NCF

S22-2 NCF

S22-3 Flexible Budget 6,000 units – $24,000; 9,000 units – $42,000

S22-4 Operating income – Actual – $102,200; Variance – $16,500; Output Units – $85,700

S22-5 NCF

S22-6 Materials price variance $923 - unfavorable. Efficiency variance $1,278 – unfavorable.

S22-7 Direct labor price variance $2,267 – favorable. Direct labor efficiency variance $8,505 – unfavorable.

S22-8 1. Materials price variance – purchasing; materials efficiency variance – production; labor price variance – human resources; labor efficiency variance – production 2. $923 unfavorable materials price variance means actual price exceeded standard budgeted price for materials. $1,278 unfavorable materials efficiency variance means employees used more materials than they should have. $2,267 favorable labor price variance means employees earned less per hour than budgeted – increased operating income. $8,505 unfavorable labor efficiency variance means it took more direct labor hours than it should – reduced operating income.

S22-9 Standard variable overhead rate – $5 per direct labor hour.

S22-10 Total manufacturing overhead variance $2,760 – unfavorable; overhead flexible budget variance is $2,760 – unfavorable; production volume variance is 0 – neither favorable nor unfavorable.

S22-11 Use of materials: Debit WIP $2,380; Debit Direct materials efficiency variance $315

S22-12 Use Direct labor: Debit WIP $19,500; Debit Direct labor efficiency variance $3,750

S22-13 Completion: Debit Finished goods inventory $360,000

S22-14 Operating income $67,500

E22-15 Operating Income – 30,000 – $22,000; 45,000 – $133,000; 80,000 – $337,000.

E22-16 Marketing personnel deserve praise for selling more than expected – reflected in favorable sales volume variance.

E22-17 The favorable flexible budget variance for sales revenue resulted from selling at a higher-than-expected price.

E22-18 1. Helps managers to prepare the budget; set target levels of performance; identify performance standards; set sales prices of products and services; decrease accounting costs 2. Price variances for direct materials $145 – unfavorable; direct labor $325 – favorable. Efficiency variances for direct materials $110 – favorable; direct labor $3,500 – favorable.

E22-19 3. $7,100 favorable

E22-20 Price variances for direct materials $7,300 – favorable; direct labor $480 – unfavorable. Efficiency variances for direct materials $7,200 – unfavorable; direct labor $560 – favorable. Net effect is favorable.

E22-21 Total overhead variance $2,750 – favorable; overhead flexible budget variance $250 – unfavorable; production volume variance $3,000 – favorable.

E22-22 Gross profit $246,400 – management appears to have done a good job at controlling costs – favorable.

E22-23 Use Direct materials: Debit WIP $168,000; Debit Direct materials efficiency variance $7,200

E22-24 NCF

P22-25A 1. Gross profit $265,905 2. Price variance – direct materials $1,260 – favorable; direct labor $1,478 – unfavorable. Efficiency variances – direct materials $2,403 – unfavorable; direct labor $1,880 – favorable. Total overhead variance $13,421 – Unfavorable; overhead flexible budget variance $12,197 – unfavorable; production volume variance $1,224 – unfavorable. 3. Managers have done a reasonable job controlling material and labor costs.

P22-26A 1. Operating income – actual – $75,500; flexible $500 – favorable; output units $75,000; sales volume $24,000 – favorable; static budget $51,000 2. Selling 2000 units more increased operating income 3. Static budget $24,500 – favorable. A favorable sales volume variance reveals whether profits increased due to more units being sold. A favorable sales revenue flexible budget variance means the sale price was higher.

P22-27A 1. Direct labor hours – 4,370 2. Direct labor price variance $2,185 – unfavorable; efficiency variance $800 – favorable. Used higher-paid, more efficient workers. Due to overall net effect – no tradeoff.

P22-28A 1. Price variance - direct materials $840 – favorable; direct labor $5,970 – unfavorable; efficiency variance – direct materials $130 – favorable; direct labor $1,120 – unfavorable. 2. Work in process inventory (debit) 3,130; direct materials efficiency variance (credit) 130; materials inventory (credit) 3,000. Work in process inventory (debit) 18,780; direct labor efficiency variance (debit) 1,120; manufacturing wages (credit) 19.900. 3. Total overhead variance $6,696 – unfavorable; overhead flexible budget variance $7,749 – unfavorable; production volume variance $1,053 – favorable.

P22-29A 1. Price variances - direct materials $11,750 – unfavorable; direct labor $255 – unfavorable. Efficiency variances – direct materials $3,750 – unfavorable; direct labor $3,600 – favorable. 2. Total overhead variance $10,600 – unfavorable; flexible budget variance $11,100 – unfavorable; production volume variance $500 – favorable. 3. Gross profit – $33,945.

Chapter 23

Quick Check 1. b; 2. d; 3. d; 4. b; 5. b; 6. a; 7. c; 8. c; 9. d; 10. d

S23-1 NCF

S23-2 NCF

S23-3 NCF

S23-4 NCF

S23-5 NCF

S23-6 NCF

S23-7 Domestic ROI 7% > International ROI

S23-8 Profit margins (both) 19%

S23-9 1. capital turnover 1.21; 1.31 times. 2. ROI's are 23%; 24.9%

S23-10 The RI $472,000 and $807,000 are positive residual income

S23-11 EVA $253,710; $457,570 - positive economic value added

S23-12 NCF

E23-13 NCF

E23-14 NCF

E23-15 NCF

E23-16 1. Actual $114,800; flexible budget $110,500; variance $4,300 – unfavorable; % variance 3.89% – unfavorable 2. Cost Center 3. Indirect labor, repairs and maintenance 4. No

E23-17 1. Actual $1,450,000; variance $6,000 – favorable; flexible budget $1,444,000; sales volume variance $20,500 – favorable; static budget $1,423,500 2. Revenue center

E23-18 1. ROI residential 32.50%; ROI professional 40.00%; both very high 2. Profit margin for residential 10.98% – earning $0.11 on the dollar; profit margin for professional 14.76% – earning $0.15 on the dollar 3. Capital turnover for residential 2.96 – generating $2.96 on the dollar; capital turnover for professional 2.71 – generating $2.71 on the dollar 4. ROI for residential 32.50%; ROI for professional 40.00%

E23-19 1. RI for residential $10,780; for professional $52,780 – both exceeding expectations 2. EVA for residential $25,090 for professional $74,830 – both exceeding stakeholders' expectations

P23-20A 1. operating income – flexible budget $116,000; actual $118, 000; variance $2,000 – favorable; percentage 1.72% 2. Both revenue and cost data are included in performance report – this is a profit center.

P23-21A 1. ROI paint store 34.51%; ROI consumer 12.18% 2. Profit margin paint store 11.89%; profit margin for consumer 14.73% 3. Capital turnover paint store 2.9025 times – more efficient in generating sales; capital turnover consumer 0.8265 times 4. ROI for the paint stores 34.51%; ROI for the consumer 12.17%; 5. RI for the paint stores $173,300; RI for consumer $(155,700) 6. EVA for paint store $141,760; EVA for consumer $(36,950)

Glindex *A Combined Glossary/Subject Index*

This text contains acetate inserts that were taken directly from the U.S. edition. As a result pages in parenthesis are out of page sequence.

C

D

G

H

I

J

N

Q

R

S

T

Company Index

This text contains acetate inserts that were taken directly from the U.S. edition. As a result pages in parenthesis are out of page sequence.

U

V

W

X

Y

Z

MyAccountingLab

MyAccountingLab is web-based, tutorial and assessment accounting software that not only gives students more "I Get It" moments, but gives instructors the flexibility to make technology an integral part of their course. It's also an excellent supplementary resource for students.

For Instructors

MyAccountingLab provides instructors with a rich and flexible set of course materials, along with course-management tools that make it easy to deliver all or a portion of your course online.

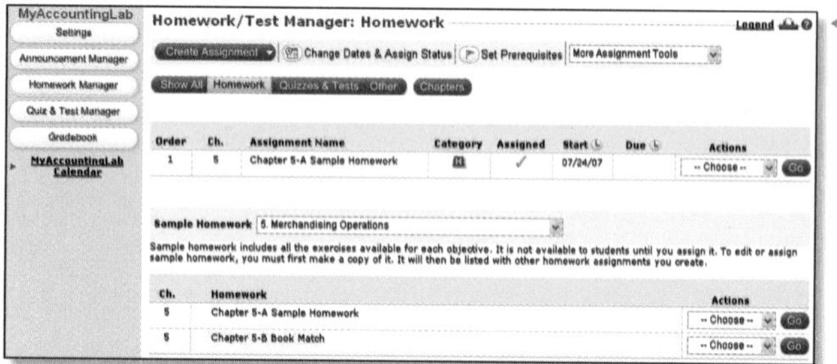

Powerful Homework and Test Manager

Create, import, and manage online homework assignments, quizzes, and tests. Create assignments from online exercises directly correlated to your textbook. Homework exercises include guided solutions and DemoDocs to help students understand and master concepts. You can choose from a wide range of assignment options, including time limits, proctoring, and maximum number of attempts allowed.

Comprehensive Gradebook Tracking

MyAccountingLab's online gradebook automatically tracks your students' results on tests, homework, and tutorials and gives you control over managing results and calculating grades. All MyAccountingLab grades can be exported to a spreadsheet program, such as Microsoft® Excel. The MyAccountingLab Gradebook provides a number of student data views and gives you the flexibility to weigh assignments, select which attempts to include when calculating scores, and omit or delete results for individual assignments.

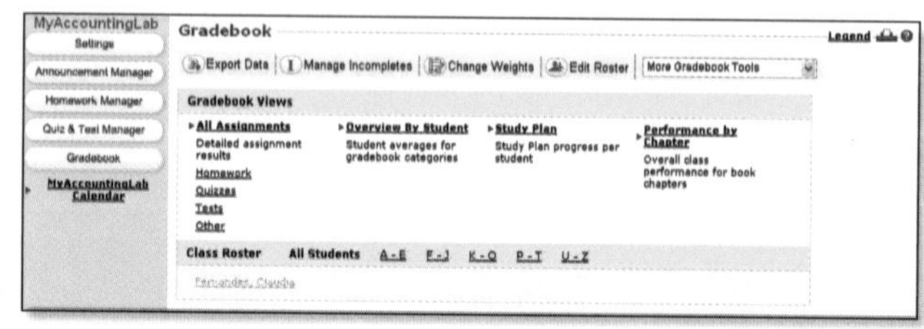

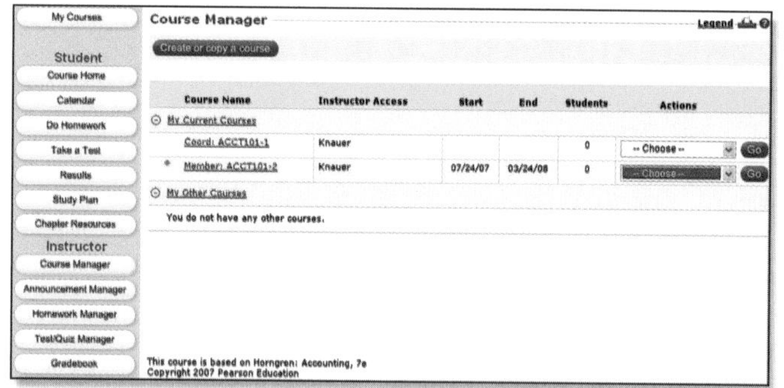

Department-Wide Solutions

Get help managing multiple sections and working with Teaching Assistants using MyAccountingLab Coordinator Courses. After your MyAccountingLab course is set up, it can be copied to create sections or "member courses." Changes to the Coordinator Course ripple down to all members, so changes only need to be made once.

For Students

MyAccountingLab provides students with a personalized interactive learning environment, where they can learn at their own pace and measure their progress.

Interactive Tutorial Exercises

MyAccountingLab's homework and practice questions are correlated to the textbook, and they regenerate algorithmically to give students unlimited opportunity for practice and mastery. Questions include guided solutions, DemoDoc examples, and learning aids for extra help at point-of-use, and they offer helpful feedback when students enter incorrect answers.

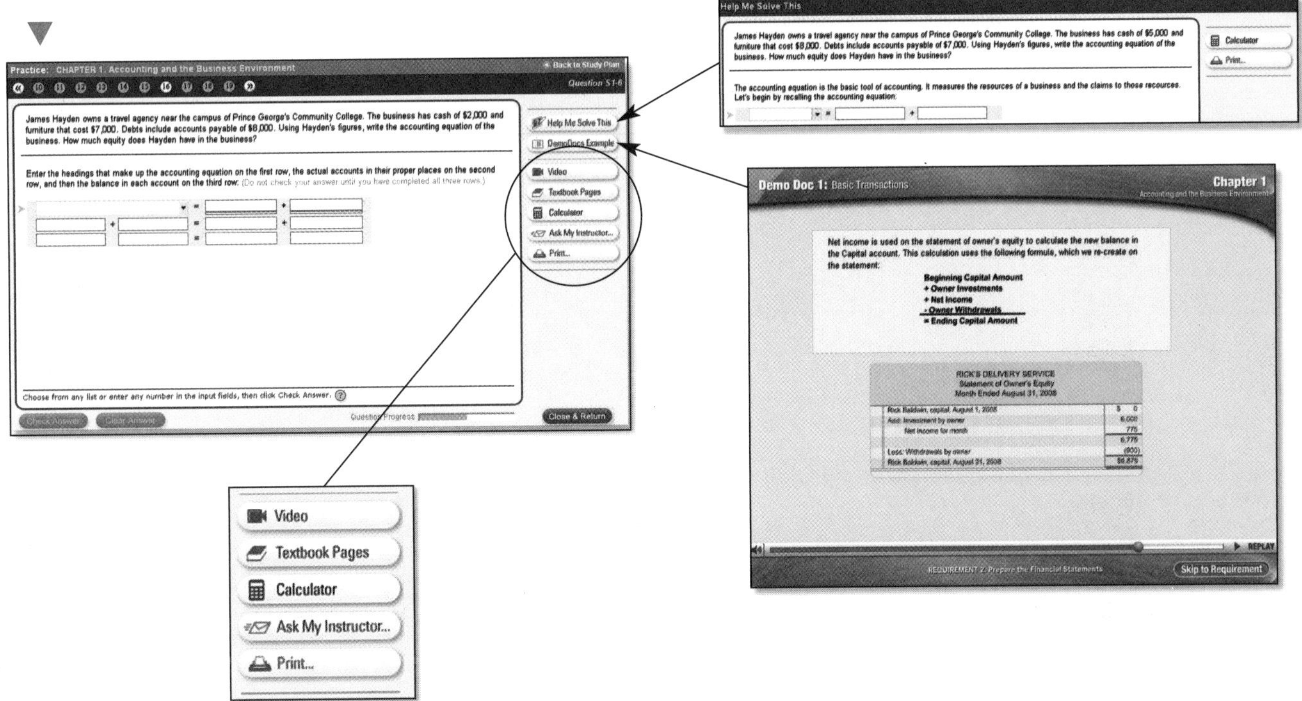

Study Plan for Self-Paced Learning

MyAccountingLab's study plan helps students monitor their own progress, letting them see at a glance exactly which topics they need to practice. MyAccountingLab generates a personalized study plan for each student based on his or her test results, and the study plan links directly to interactive, tutorial exercises for topics the student hasn't yet mastered. Students can regenerate these exercises with new values for unlimited practice, and the exercises include guided solutions and multimedia learning aids to give students the extra help they need.

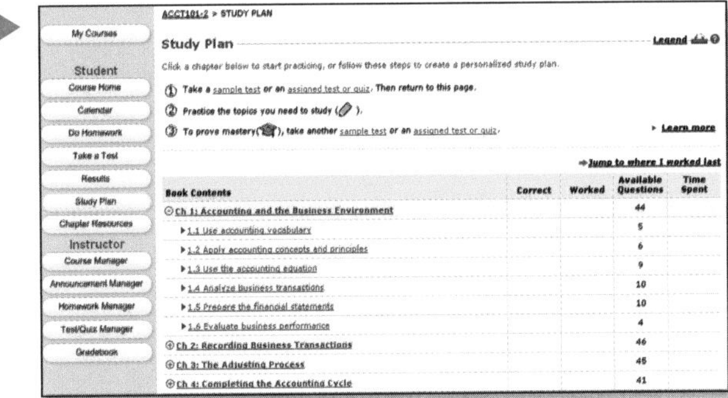

View a guided tour of MyAccountingLab at http://www.myaccountinglab.com/support/tours.